CONDITION OF THE INDIAN TRIBES.

REPORT

OF THE

JOINT SPECIAL COMMITTEE,

APPOINTED UNDER

JOINT RESOLUTION OF MARCH 3, 1865.

WITH

AN APPENDIX.

WASHINGTON:
GOVERNMENT PRINTING OFFICE.
1867.

IN THE SENATE OF THE UNITED STATES.

JANUARY 26, 1867.—Ordered to be printed.

Mr. DOOLITTLE submitted the following

REPORT.

The Joint Special Committee of the two Houses of Congress, appointed under the joint resolution of March 3, 1865, directing an inquiry into the condition of the Indian tribes and their treatment by the civil and military authorities of the United States, submit the following report, with an appendix accompanying the same:

At its meeting on the 9th of March the following subdivision of labor was made: To Messrs. Doolittle, Foster, and Ross was assigned the duty of inquiring into Indian affairs in the State of Kansas, the Indian Territory, Colorado, New Mexico, and Utah.

To Messrs. Nesmith and Higby the same duty was assigned in the States of California, Oregon, and Nevada, and in the Territories of Washington, Idaho, and Montana.

To Messrs. Windom and Hubbard the same duty was assigned in the State of Minnesota and in the Territories of Nebraska, Dakota, and upper Montana. The result of their inquiries is to be found in the appendix accompanying this report.

The work was immense, covering a continent. While they have gathered a vast amount of testimony and important information bearing upon our Indian affairs, they are still conscious that their explorations have been imperfect.

As it was found impossible for the members of the committee in person to take the testimony or from personal observations to learn all that they deemed necessary to form a correct judgment of the true condition of the Indian tribes, they deemed it wise, by a circular letter addressed to officers of the regular army, experienced Indian agents and superintendents, and to other persons of great knowledge in Indian affairs, to obtain from them a statement of the result of their experience and information; which, with the testimony taken by the various members of the sub-committees, is also to be found in the appendix.

The committee have arrived at the following conclusions:

First. The Indians everywhere, with the exception of the tribes within the Indian Territory, are rapidly decreasing in numbers from various causes: By disease; by intemperance; by wars, among themselves and with the whites; by the steady and resistless emigration of white men into the territories of the west, which, confining the Indians to still narrower limits, destroys that game which, in their normal state, constitutes their principal means of subsistence; and by the irrepressible conflict between a superior and an inferior race when brought in presence of each other. Upon this subject all the testimony agrees.

In answer to the question, whether the Indians "are increasing or decreasing in numbers, and from what causes," Major General Pope says:

"They are rapidly decreasing in numbers from various causes: By disease; by wars; by cruel treatment on the part of the whites—both by irresponsible persons and by government officials; by unwise policy of the government, by inhumane and dishonest administration of that policy; and by steady resistless encroachments of the white emigration toward the west, which every day confining the Indians to narrower limits, and driving off or killing the game, their only means of subsistence."—(See appendix, page 425.)

To the same question, General John T. Sprague gives the following answer:

"The Indians are decreasing in numbers, caused by their proximity to the white man. So soon as Indians adopt the habits of white men they begin to decrease, aggravated by imbibing all the vices and none of their virtues. Other causes exist, too numerous to be detailed in this paper."—(Appendix, 228.)

The following is the answer of General Carleton to the same question:

"As a general rule, the Indians alluded to are decreasing very rapidly in numbers, in my opinion. The causes for this have been many, and may be summed up as follows:

1st. Wars with our pioneers and our armed forces; change of climate and country among those who have been moved from east of the Mississippi to the far west.

2d. Intemperance, and the exposure consequent thereon.

3d. Veneral diseases, which they are unable, from the lack of medicines and skill, to eradicate from their systems, and which, among Indians who live nearest the whites, is generally diffused either in scrofula or some other form of its taint.

4th. Small-pox, measles, and cholera—diseases unknown to them in the early days of the country.

5th. The causes which the Almighty originates, when in their appointed time He wills that one race of men—as in races of lower animals—shall disappear off the face of the earth and give place to another race, and so on, in the great cycle traced out by Himself, which may be seen, but has reasons too deep to be fathomed by us. The races of the mammoths and mastodons, and the great sloths, came and passed away: the red man of America is passing away!" (Appendix, 432–3.)

General Wright gives his testimony to the same point as follows:

"The Indian tribes are rapidly decreasing in numbers, especially west of the Rocky mountains, caused in some measure by the wars waged against them and more particularly by the encroachments of the whites upon their hunting grounds and fisheries and other means of subsistence, and by the readiness with which they adopt the vices of the whites rather than their virtues; hence their numbers are rapidly diminished by disease and death."—(Appendix, 440.

These officers have had large experience in Indian affairs, and they are supported by the concurrent testimony of many other of the most experienced officers and civilians, to be found at length in the Appendix.

The tribes in the Indian Territory were most happily exempted from this constant tendency to decay up to the commencement of the late civil war. Until they became involved in that they were actually advancing in population, education, civilization, and agricultural wealth.

Their exceptional condition may be attributed to the fact that, from their earliest history these tribes had, to a considerable extent, cultivated the soil and kept herds of cattle and horses; that they were located in a most fertile territory and withdrawn from the neighborhood and influence of white settlements and to the legitimate influence of education and Christianity among them.

The war has made a terrible diminution of their number, and brought disease and demoralization in its train. A full account of the condition of the Cherokees will be found in the reply of the Hon. J. Harlan, agent of the Cherokees (See Appendix, pages 441–50.) The recent treaties with the tribes in the

Indian territory, and the reports of their improved condition since the pacification, give strong hopes that their former prosperity will return.

The committee determined, if possible, to ascertain the real cause of the destruction of the tribes, and proposed to the officers above named, and to many others, the following most important inquiry bearing upon that subject, viz:

"What diseases are most common and most fatal among them, and from what causes?"

To this General Sprague answers:

"The children die rapidly and suddenly from dysentery and measles, and from neglect and exposure to the weather. The adults die from fevers, small-pox, drunkenness, and diseases engendered from sexual intercourse. These diseases are among the men and women in the most malignant form, as the Indian doctors are unable to manage them. Indulgence in liquor, exposure, and the absence of remedies aggravate the disease. In this, striking at the very basis of procreation, is to be found the active cause of the destruction of the Indian race."

General Pope is of opinion that "venereal diseases, particularly secondary syphilis, is the most common and destructive. It is to be doubted whether one Indian, man or woman, in five, is free from this disease or its effects."

Without quoting from others, it will be found, by the united testimony of all, that this disease, more than all other diseases, and perhaps more than all other causes, is the active agent of the destruction of the Indian race. Add to this intemperance, exposure, the want of sufficient food and clothing, wars among themselves and wars with the whites, and we are at no loss to account for the utter extinction of many of the most powerful tribes, and the ultimate disappearance of nearly all upon this continent. It is a sad but faithful picture.

INDIAN WARS WITH THE WHITES.

Second. The committee are of opinion that in a large majority of cases Indian wars are to be traced to the aggressions of lawless white men, always to be found upon the frontier, or boundary line between savage and civilized life. Such is the statement of the most experienced officers of the army, and of all those who have been long conversant with Indian affairs.

Colonel Bent, who has lived upon the Upper Arkansas, near Bent's fort, for thirty-six years, states that in nearly every instance difficulties between Indians and the whites arose from aggressions on the Indians by the whites. The war with the Sioux, commencing in 1854, the war with the Arrapahoes and Cheyennes in 1865, are traced by him directly to those aggressions. (Appendix, page 93.

Colonel Kit Carson, who has lived upon the plains and in the mountains since 1826, and has been all that time well acquainted with the Indian tribes in peace and in war, confirms this statement. He says, "as a general thing the difficulties arise from aggressions on the part of the whites." "The whites are always cursing the Indians, and are not willing to do them justice." (Appendix, page 96.)

From whatever cause wars may be brought on, either between different Indian tribes or between the Indians and the whites, they are very destructive, not only of the lives of the warriors engaged in it, but of the women and children also, often becoming a war of extermination. Such is the rule of savage warfare, and it is difficult if not impossible to restrain white men, especially white men upon the frontiers, from adopting the same mode of warfare against the Indians. The indiscriminate slaughter of men, women, and children has frequently occurred in the history of Indian wars. But the fact which gives such terrible force to the condemnation of the wholesale massacre of Arrapahoes and

Cheyennes, by the Colorado troops under Colonel Chivington, near Fort Lyon, was, that those Indians were there encamped under the direction of our own officers, and believed themselves to be under the protection of our flag. A full account of this bloody affair will be found also in the appendix. To the honor of the government it may be said that a just atonement for this violation of its faith was sought to be made in the late treaty with these tribes.

Third. Another potent cause of their decay is to be found in the loss of their hunting grounds and in the destruction of that game upon which the Indian subsists. This cause, always powerful, has of late greatly increased. Until the white settlements crossed the Mississippi, the Indians could still find hunting grounds without limit and game, especially the buffalo, in great abundance upon the western plains.

But the discovery of gold and silver in California, and in all the mountain territories, poured a flood of hardy and adventurous miners across those plains, and into all the valleys and gorges of the mountains from the east.

Two lines of railroad are rapidly crossing the plains, one by the valley of the Platte, and the other by the Smoky Hill. They will soon reach the Rocky mountains, crossing the centre of the great buffalo range in two lines from east to west. It is to be doubted if the buffalo in his migrations will many times cross a railroad where trains are passing and repassing, and with the disappearance of the buffalo from this immense region, all the powerful tribes of the plains will inevitably disappear, and remain north of the Platte or south of the Arkansas. Another route futher north, from Minnesota by the Upper Missouri, and one fnrther south, from Arkansas by the Canadian, are projected, and will soon be pressed forward. These will drive the last vestige of the buffalo from all the region east of the Rocky mountains, and put an end to the wild man's means of life.

On the other hand, the emigration from California and Oregon into the Territories from the west is filling every valley and gorge of the mountains with the most energetic and fearless men in the world. In those wild regions, where no civil law has ever been administered, and where our military forces have scarcely penetrated, these adventurers are practically without any law, except such as they impose upon themselves, viz: the law of necessity and of self-defence.

Even after territorial governments are established over them in form by Congress, the population is so sparse and the administration of the civil law so feeble that the people are practically without any law but their own will. In their eager search for gold or fertile tracts of land, the boundaries of Indian reservations are wholly disregarded; conflicts ensue; exterminating wars follow, in which the Indian is, of course, at the last, overwhelmed if not destroyed.

THE INDIAN BUREAU.

Fourth. The question whether the Indian bureau should be placed under the War Department or retained in the Department of the Interior is one of considerable importance, and both sides have very warm advocates. Military men generally, unite in recommending that change to be made, while civilians, teachers, missionaries, agents and superintendents, and those not in the regular army generally oppose it. The arguments and objections urged by each are not without force.

The argument in favor of it is that in case of hostilities the military forces must assume control of our relations to the hostile tribes, and therefore it is better for the War Department to have the entire control, both in peace and in war; secondly, that the annuity goods and clothing, paid to Indians under treaty stipulations, will be more faithfully and honestly made by officers of the regular army, who hold their places for life, and are subject to military trials for up. A narrow strip has been cleared along the bay, where they have about fifty small board and frame houses erected. They also have a few potatoes planted and garden vegetables, which gave but small promise of producing much. I saw nothing being done worthy of being called farming. The little property possessed by these people consists of their canoes, nets, and other fishing gear, with which they are generally enabled to supply their daily wants of food, beyond which they seem to give themselves no especial trouble or care. Here was the only place upon the sound where I witnessed any attempts being made to educate Indian children. The Rev. C. C. Chirouse, a Catholic priest, having some time since established himself here as a teacher, has succeeded in collecting from thirty to forty Indian boys under his care, and by a system of manual labor is attempting to make them support themselves while obtaining an education. His efforts are not confined to the school-room, but he accompanies his pupils in their out-door labors and gives them all needful instruction. The boys under the reverend father's care, and by his aid, have succeeded in clearing up a sufficiently large piece of heavily timbered land for a garden, from which they draw a small supply of vegetables; the remainder of their living is obtained by catching fish in the neighboring waters. The boys are kept entirely separate from their parents, which is indispensable for their proper culture; they are mostly dependent upon the charity of the whites for their clothing. It is a matter of regret that the worthy father is compelled to pursue his benevolent and Christian labors under so many disadvantages, and some further provision should be made to aid him in feeding and clothing the pupils, who seem so anxious to avail themselves of his instructions. In visiting their school-room I was struck with their cleanliness and good manners, as well as with the progress they had made in reading, writing, and arithmetic. Herewith I submit two communications addressed to me by the pupils themselves, and written in a fair and legible hand; they are marked, respectively, C and D.

Lummi reservation is situated near the head of Bellingham bay. Owing to the brief period of my stay, and the stage of the tide, it was inconvenient to visit the village, but from what I saw of the people they appear much of the same character as those at Tulalip. Their agent informed me that the reservation is better adapted to the wants of the Indians than the latter-named point, and that they had made considerable progress in agriculture.

Other points were visited bordering on the sound where Indians occasionally congregate in great numbers for the purpose of taking fish, but as their general features are the same, and as there was but little improvement worthy of note at any of them, they will not require special mention.

Shokomish reservation is situated near the southern end of an arm of Puget sound, known as Hood's canal, which extends southward about one hundred miles from the straits of Juan de Fuca. The Indians who belong to this reservation are the Shokomish and Skallams, and two remnants of other tribes, parties to the treaty of Point No-Point. They are variously estimated at from twelve hundred to four thousand souls; indeed, I do not believe their actual number ever was or ever will be known. I saw but very few of them upon the reservation, but learned that they were absent gathering berries, catching fish, prostituting their women, gambling, and getting drunk, the latter of which appears to be their favorite occupation. Special Agent Knox, who is in charge of them, told me that there were twelve hundred of them came to receive their annuities in November, 1863. Superintendent Waterman estimates them at a much greater number. This reservation appears to be well enough adapted to their wants as a home. But little, however, has been done upon it in the way of improvement. The fish and game, both of which are abundant in the neighborhood, are nearly equally as abundant upon all other portions of the sound; and as these people manifest no disposition to labor, there appears to be no inducement for them to remain at the home to which they have been assigned, consequently they are scattered all along the western shore of Hood's canal and the straits of Juan de Fuca nearly to Cape Flattery, a distance of about one hundred and fifty miles. But little control is exercised over them, and with the means at present at the disposal of the superintendent I am unable to perceive how he is to exercise more, as he is without means to subsist them upon their reservation, and as they are mostly lazy, drunken, dissolute vagabonds, who can neither be persuaded nor compelled to labor. They are brought in contact with the white population at all of the villages and lumber camps along the western portion of the sound, and rapidly falling victims to venereal diseases and noxious whiskey which they can but too readily obtain. The few of them who reside upon the reservation, with a white farmer to assist them, have only about ten acres of ground in cultivation. The annuities and other appropriations are too limited to enable the superintendent to collect and subsist such a demoralized and drunken herd of savages while the experiment of their reformation is being attempted. It is not certain that any amount of means would enable the department to improve the condition of these people. Possibly a few of them may be reclaimed and induced to cultivate the soil. I look, however, upon the great majority of them as doomed to a speedy extinction as the result of indolence, loathsome diseases, and bad whiskey.

At all of the agencies which I visited upon Puget sound the Indians manifested a great desire that the government should furnish them with clothing and trinkets as the principal portion of their annuities. My own impression and advice is against such a course, as I believe that with the facilities which they have for laboring and obtaining good prices therefor, they should measurably be thrown upon their own resources to obtain their clothing, and that feeling the need of it would be an additional stimulus to their industry. When large quantities of clothing and blankets are distributed among them it usually is followed by a period of gambling and dissipation. It would evidently be better for them to have the greater portion of their annuities expended in procuring domestic animals, agricultural implements, and in opening farms. To obtain these articles they cannot be induced to labor, while on the other hand they have the stimulant of physical suffering to urge them to work for the clothes necessary for their personal comfort.

The Chehalis and Cowlitz are a couple of small tribes who reside upon the rivers of those names within the settled portion of Washington Territory. No treaties have been made with them, though their land has been surveyed and much of it disposed of by the government. They are a docile people, and more industrious than the majority of the Indians within that Territory, and it would seem but just that some permanent provision should be made for them.

The Yakama reservation is situated upon the river of that name, east of the Cascade mountains, and about seventy miles north of the Columbia river. The Indians located here by the provisions of the treaty of 1855 consist of fourteen tribes and bands, the principal of which are the Yakamas and Klikatats. The superintendent reports them to consist of five thousand persons: perhaps half that number reside upon the reservation, which is exceedingly well adapted to the purpose for which it was selected, the mountains furnishing good timber, while the upland or hills are covered with an abundance of good grass. Several fine streams of water pass through the reservation, along the margins of which is excellent land for agricultural purposes.

A great advantage enjoyed by the Indians here is their isolation from the white settlements, which prevents them being brought in contact with vicious persons and those disposed to sell them intoxicating drinks. They have two thousand five hundred acres under fence, and about twelve hundred acres in cultivation. Their crops last year consisted of two thousand bushels of wheat, two hundred bushels of peas, six hundred bushels of corn, and three thousand bushels of potatoes, in addition to large quantities of garden vegetables. The government has erected for them a good grist and saw mill, both of which are in good repair and successful operation. The abandoned military post of Fort Simcoe furnishes excellent buildings for residences, shops, storerooms, school-rooms, and all other purposes for which buildings are required at an agency. In visiting the Indian farms and houses many of them gave evidence of the habits of industry of the tribe. Agent Wilbur, who is in charge of the reservation, manifests a determination to test the practicability of reducing an Indian to a state of civilization. His example is certainly valuable to them, and he neglects no opportunity to give them instruction of a practical character. He is energetic and enthusiastic in his efforts to elevate the character and condition of the people under his charge. If he fails, the failure must be attributed to some other cause than a want of zeal on his part. So far they have greatly improved under his management.

I found the school in full and successful operation, and well attended by both boys and girls. Both are boarded and clothed at the agency, and kept separate from their parents. Both sexes are taught the elementary branches, and there is a farm connected with the boys' school, upon which they labor a certain portion of their time; the proceeds of their labor is applied towards their support. Some of the boys are taught to work at trades, under the direction of employés upon the reservation, and bid fair to make proficient workmen. The girls, in addition to their studies, are taught sewing and housework. The school here and at Puyallup were the only ones that I saw which seem to be resulting in much practical good.

IDAHO TERRITORY.

The Nez Percés are located upon an extensive reservation, embracing the Clearwater river and its tributaries in Idaho Territory, and extending westward across the Snake river includes small portions of the State of Oregon and of Washington Territory, and contains about ten thousand square miles. They were assigned to this location by the provisions of the treaty negotiated with them by Isaac I. Stevens, then governor, and superintendent of Indian affairs for Washington Territory, and General Joel Palmer, superintendent for Oregon, in the year 1855. By that treaty they relinquished to the United States their claims to a vast region of territory, embracing portions of what are now Oregon, Washington, and Idaho. In consideration of this cession of territory the United States stipulated among other things, that the reservation "tract shall be set apart, and, so far as necessary, to administer oaths; and said board shall be authorized to suspend for cause any officer or employé of the Indian department in their respective districts, and to remove them from office, subject to the approval of the President. And said board shall report annually, or as often as may be required, to the Commissioner of Indian Affairs; and in all cases of suspension or removal from office by said board of any officer or employé of the Indian department, said board shall make immediate report thereon in writing, stating the cause thereof, for the action of the President.

SEC. 4. *And be it further enacted,* That all superintendents of Indian affairs, all Indian agents, and the assistant commissioners to be appointed under this act, in addition to the powers now conferred by law, shall also possess all the powers and perform all the duties now conferred by law upon circuit court commissioners, or court commissioners in all cases or matters wherein any Indian tribe or any member of any Indian tribe shall be concerned or be a party; and that in all matters or proceedings wherein any Indian tribe or member of an Indian tribe shall be concerned or a party, the testimony of Indian witnesses shall be received in all courts and before all officers of the United States.

The purpose of the bill is to provide boards of high character, and to organize them in such a manner and to clothe them with such powers as to supervise and inspect the whole administration of Indian affairs in its three-fold character—civil, military, and educational.

To the position of chief of this board there should be appointed an assistant commissioner, with a salary sufficient to command the services of a man of character and great ability, whose whole time is to be devoted to this important work.

One of the board is to be an officer of the regular army, to be assigned by the Secretary of War; (it is believed that he would be an officer of high standing in the army;) and a third is to be selected from among those persons who may be named by the great religious conventions or bodies of the United States. It is impossible to believe that these great bodies could name any other than a man of high character and great ability. Such a board not organized upon political grounds at all, and possessing, as they will, the important powers conferred in the third section of this bill, will, in the judgment of the committee, do more to secure the faithful administration of Indian affairs than any other measure which has been suggested.

The assistant commissioner will report to the Secretary of the Interior; the officer of the army to the Secretary of War; and the third will report, not only to the government, but to that religious body which may have recommended his appointment. Thus the treatment of the Indians by the civil authorities, by the military authorities, and by their teachers and missionaries, will be subject to constant inspection and supervision.

It is urged that the expenses of these boards will be considerable; but in comparison with the greater economy and efficiency their supervision would secure, that expense will be comparatively trifling.

Such boards, charged with the duty, among other things, to preserve amity, will doubtless sometimes save the government from unnecessary and expensive Indian wars.

As an instance bearing upon this point, when that portion of the committee who were charged with the duty of inquiring into the condition of Indian affairs in Kansas, New Mexico, and Colorado, arrived at Fort Larned, they found that the officer there in command had just issued an order to his troops to cross the Arkansas, going south into an Indian territory where not a single white man lived, to make war upon the Comanches, a most powerful tribe which roams over all that region from the Arkansas to Mexico. Your committee felt that such an expedition would of necessity bring on a long war with that tribe; that it was wholly unnecessary, and they took the responsibilty of advising

General McCook, a member of the staff of General Pope, who accompanied them, to countermand that order until he could communicate with General Pope at St. Louis. The order was countermanded; the troops then in motion were recalled, and thus by the mere presence and advice of the committee a war was avoided with the Comanches, which, had it once begun, would not have been prosecuted to a successful termination without an expenditure of twenty millions of dollars.

Your committee took the testimony, among others, of Colonel Ford, then in command at Fort Larned, upon this subject. He says, speaking of the Comanches, (see appendix, page 64:) "From the best information I can get, there are about seven thousand warriors well mounted, some on fleet Texan horses. On horseback they are the finest skirmishers I ever saw. How large a force, mounted and infantry, would be required to defend the Santa Fé road and wage a successful war against the Indians south of the Arkansas? It would require at least ten thousand men—four thousand constantly in the field, well mounted; the line of defence to extend from Fort Lyon to Fort Riley, and south about three hundred miles. All supplies would have to come from the States. Contract price for corn delivered at this point was $5 26 per bushel." With corn at this enormous price, and hay, and wood, and all supplies in proportion, the expense of such an Indian war is beyond belief. By many it was estimated that such a war would have required at least ten thousand men, and a war of two or three years' duration, to make it successful, with an expenditure of more than thirty millions of dollars.

It is believed that such boards of inspection thus organized and composed of the men who should be appointed to fill them, would save the country from many useless wars with the Indians, and secure in all branches of the Indian service greater efficiency and fidelity. If such boards should cost the government a hundred and fifty thousand dollars annually, and should avert but one Indian war in ten years, still, upon the score of economy alone, the government would be repaid five hundred per cent.

Respectfully submitted.

J. R. DOOLITTLE,
Chairman Joint Special Committee.

January 26, 1867.

APPENDIX.

APPENDIX.

SUB-REPORT OF HON. J. W. NESMITH.

Hon. J. R. Doolittle,
Chairman of committee to inquire into the condition of the Indian tribes.

Sir: The committee at its meeting on the 9th of March last, under the authority of the joint resolution approved March 3, 1865, assigned me to the duty of inquiring into the condition of the tribes within the State of Oregon, Washington, Idaho, and southern Montana.

Leaving New York on the 13th of April, I reached Oregon on the 15th of May, and proceeded at once to the discharge of the duty to which I had been assigned.

THE COAST RESERVATION, SILETZ AGENCY.

This reservation is situated upon the coast, entirely within the State of Oregon, and embraces a distance of about one hundred and twenty miles from north to south, and varies from, probably, about fifteen to thirty miles in width. The greater portion of it is rugged mountains, covered with dense forests which abound in game. Along the margins of the streams is excellent productive land in sufficient quantity to supply the wants of the Indians for agricultural purposes. The bays along the coast as well as the streams passing through the reservation furnish an abundant supply of fish at certain seasons of the year. The Indians, located at and near what is known as the Siletz agency, consist of fourteen bands or remnants of tribes, each keeping up its distinct tribal organization. They amount in the aggregate to about two thousand souls. Treaties had been concluded with but two of those tribes, viz., the Chasta Scoton, who number but one hundred and twenty-three, and the Rogue Rivers, who number one hundred and twenty-one. By the aid of their annuities, those two tribes are enabled to make some progress in cultivating the soil and improving their homes, while the remaining seventeen hundred and fifty-six are dependent upon the limited amount of means which can be spared from the annual appropriations made by Congress for the Oregon superintendency, under the head of "removal and subsistence." The tendency of such a discrimination between bands of Indians upon the same reservation is, to make the tribes, who receive no annuities, dissatisfied, and it is a constant source of trouble and irritation among them. The reason why such apparent favoritism towards the Rogue River and Chasta Scotons to the prejudice of the other tribes and bands exists, is accounted for as follows:

On the 10th of September, 1853, a treaty was negotiated with the Rogue River tribe, by the terms of which they were assigned to a reservation within their own country, in the southern portion of Oregon, and were to receive from the United States certain annuities. On the 18th of November, 1854, a similar treaty was negotiated with the Chasta Scotons. Both treaties having been ratified by the Senate, the Indians, who were parties to them, were in receipt of their annuities until in the fall of 1855, when a general Indian war was inaugurated, in which all of the tribes in southern Oregon participated, including the treaty as well as the non-treaty Indians. After the southern portion of the then Territory of Oregon became nearly desolated, the policy was adopted by the government of removing all of the Indians from their old homes in the south and keeping them assembled upon the coast reservation, under military surveillance. The location was well adapted to the purposes for which it was intended, and all the Indians in southern Oregon were removed by military force. The Rogue River and Chasta Scotons, who were upon reservations by virtue of their treaties, were forced to abandon them and remove with the other tribes, with whom no treaties had ever been made. The experiment of removing them was a success, and resulted in the maintenance of a permanent peace. The twelve bands or remnants of tribes who were thus forcibly removed from their homes now complain that they are as much entitled to compensation for their country as the other tribes, who are annually in receipt of government annuities, notwithstanding the fact that the superintendent and agent have done much to remove the disparity of their condition by a judicious disbursement in their favor, from the limited appropriations for removal and subsistence; but the amount is too small to procure for them the teams, seed, and agricultural implements necessary to start them fairly in farming. If it is not deemed prudent to make a treaty with those bands, it would but seem just that some general provision should be made by Congress to enable them to engage in agricultural pursuits.

When those tribes were removed to their present location in 1856, they amounted in the aggregate to about five thousand persons. They were fierce, warlike, turbulent and intractable, and averse to the performance of any species of labor. For several years it was only possible to retain them upon that reservation by issuing them full rations of food and considerable quantities of clothing. Indeed, this course became a necessity, as they had been deprived of their arms by the military and congregated upon a reservation under the charge of the troops, without the requisite knowledge or means of gaining their own subsistence. Murders and other outrages were of frequent occurrence among them, and it was at times with great difficulty that the agent, assisted by the military, could restrain them from leaving the reservation *en masse*, for the purpose of depredating upon the neighboring white settlements. Within the last few years loathsome diseases have made sad inroads upon their numbers, and more than half of them have died, while a large majority of those still alive are infected with diseases, which will in a few years sweep them off.

On my visit to their reservation I found the condition of the Indians greatly improved in point of subordination and industry—results attributable to the firm and judicious management of Agent Simpson, under whose charge they have been for some time. His policy of encouraging the industrious and peaceable members of the tribes in their efforts to support themselves and families, and of punishing the vicious and indolent, has been productive of the most salutary results. The manner in which they had cultivated their lands gave evidence of their industry. Many of them had raised a surplus of provisions during the last year, and I saw large quantities of potatoes in their houses, of which they desired to dispose for the purpose of procuring clothing and other articles necessary to their comfort. In the talk which I had with them the influential men unanimously justified Agent Simpson in the course he had taken to enforce obedience and habits of industry upon the turbulent and lazy members of their tribes, and they earnestly implored that they might be furnished by government with teams and agricultural implements to enable them more generally to cultivate the soil.

Agent Simpson reports that during the last year, with the assistance of five white employés, these people have raised one thousand two hundred and sixty-two bushels of wheat, two hundred and twelve bushels of peas, four thousand two hundred and sixty-five bushels of oats, thirty-two thousand one hundred bushels of potatoes, and thirty-one tons of hay. At Acquinna bay, which is within the boundaries of the reservation, valuable beds of oysters have been discovered. Superintendent Huntingdon and Agent Simpson, impressed with the opinion, and, as I believe, correctly, regarded these oyster beds as appertaining to the reservation, have rented them to certain parties, the proceeds being applied by them for the benefit of the tribes. They have, however, been interfered with by persons in San Francisco, who could not resist the temptation to trespass upon the rights of the Indians; the consequence is that a suit is now pending in the State courts of Oregon for the purpose of determining the question. If the suit should be decided adverse to the claims of the Indian department, that the Indians have the exclusive right to take oysters from the bay included within the limits of their reservation, those people will suffer from being deprived of one of their largest sources for obtaining subsistence and clothing.

GRANDE RONDE AGENCY.

This agency is on the eastern side of the coast range of mountains, and is within the limits of what is known as the coast reservation. There are located here eight tribes or bands, who, like those at the Siletz agency, keep up their distinct tribal organization. They number in the aggregate one thousand and sixty-four souls. Five of those tribes originally inhabited different portions of the Willamette and Umpqua valleys. With those treaties have been made, and they are in receipt of government annuities. They were placed on this reservation in 1856, at the time the policy was inaugurated of assembling the Indians upon reservations to prevent their hostile contact with the whites. The other three tribes are known as Tillamooks, Nestuckas, and Salmon Rivers, and number in the aggregate three hundred souls. They have never been treated with, and, like the non-treaty tribes at the Siletz agency, are dependent upon such aid as the superintendent can spare them from the limited appropriations for removal and sustenance. They have always resided upon that portion of the reservation near the coast, and claim it still as their country. Some provision should be made to put them upon an equality with the other tribes who are assembled here. Upon visiting the Grande Ronde agency I found the Indians as a general thing less inclined to industrial pursuits than at the Siletz They have long been in close contact with the white settlers of the Willamette and Rogue River valleys. Being as a general thing docile in character, they have led a listless life, depending more upon their ability to beg than upon their disposition to labor for their subsistence. When first located here, like the Indians at the Siletz, and for the same reasons, they were subsisted by the government, until their long-established habit of depending upon charity has rendered them almost incapable of procuring a living in any other way. It is true that some of them work for the farmers in the neighboring settlements, and make good hands; some of them also cultivate small farms upon the reservation; but these are exceptions; the majority of the tribe have been spoiled by ill-advised charity, until they are now the most persistent and importunate of beggars. They will, however, within a few years cease to be a burden upon the government, as the universal prostitution of their women has entailed diseases upon them, which must soon cause their extermination. Two-thirds of those originally located here have already died, and the surgeon who was employed to attend them last year says in his report: "I am satisfied, from over a year's experience in doctoring them, that it is impracticable, not to say impossible, under the circumstances, to eradicate wholly from their systems the scrofulous and constitutional syphilitic diseases so deeply and thoroughly seated; and while such is the case, a greater fatality will attend acute inflammatory diseases, especially those of the lungs."

Their close proximity to the settlements offers them increased facilities for obtaining whiskey, which contributes to increase indolence, disease, and demoralization among them. Government has expended large sums of money in erecting buildings and opening farms for those people. The buildings seem to be in a dilapidated condition, and the fields growing up to weeds. These results arise from the fact that the appropriations are too limited to employ the necessary labor to keep the buildings in repair, and overcome the aversion of the Indians to the cultivation of the ground. This selection, in point of agricultural fitness, was never well adapted to the purposes for which it was selected, and I think that it would be better for both the government and the Indians to dispose of this portion of the reservation and remove them to the Siletz, where they could be more easily and better provided for, until such time as the diseases with which they are now so universally infected shall result in their total extinction.

At the Siletz there is ample room for these people; by their being incorporated with the tribes now there, the services of one agent and several employés might be dispensed with. The government would also be relieved of the expense of keeping up a military post and garrison, as is now done at their present location. Herewith I submit a communication from Captain L. S. Scott, marked A. The reports of the agent show that during the last year there was produced at this agency 3,060 bushels of wheat, 3,058 bushels of oats, 705 bushels of potatoes, and 46 tons of hay. The schools, provided for at both the Siletz and Grande Ronde, seem to result in but little, if any, practical benefit to the Indians, and this remark applies with equal force to all of the tribes, with two or three exceptions, that I have visited.

There is usually incorporated in Indian treaties a provision that a teacher shall be employed and paid by the government; then follows inadequate appropriations for his services, with, occasionally, some slight provision for school books, and here the government terminates its efforts at educating the Indians, without taking into consideration the fact that a poorly paid teacher and a small supply of books furnish but inadequate means for educational purposes. The consequence is, that there is an occasional spasmodic effort made, when some ill adapted and empty building can be obtained for the purpose, in which to teach a few young Indians the alphabet, and usually before that feat is accomplished the teacher leaves, disgusted with the inadequacy of his compensation, or the appropriations become exhausted, and the school is discontinued, to be resumed again at an interval sufficiently remote to give the pupils ample time to forget the lessons but imperfectly learned under the former teacher.

An institution conducted upon such a plan among white people would seldom become famous for its educational advantages. All experience has demonstrated the impossibility of educating Indian children while they are permitted to consort and associate with their ignorant, barbarous, and superstitious parents. It is admitted by all teachers who have ever made the experiment, that the vicious home influences of the Indian lodge or wigwam during the recess of school hours are more than sufficient to counterbalance and destroy all that is taught to the pupil during the period allotted to study.

The only Indian schools which have attained to any degree of success are those where the means have been supplied to feed, clothe, and lodge the children separate and apart from their parents and members of their tribes. Where the Indian youth is left to the alternate struggle between civilization and barbarism the contest is likely to culminate on the side of his savage instincts. To provide for a school for the education of savages in the usual manner which we have adopted is not only a waste of funds, but a mockery.

Where the government has entered into treaty stipulations for the support of Indian schools, it should redeem the pledge by procuring suitable buildings for the purposes of the schools remote from the tribe and its influences. It should board, lodge, and clothe the pupils, and employ suitable persons to instruct them in not only what is taught in books, but in other things pertaining to civilization. When this is done, the Indian who parts with his land under the impression that his offspring is to receive an instalment of civilization and intelligence in return, will not be defrauded by a humbug too transparent to deceive any one except a savage. If it is thought that it will require too great an outlay of money to comply in this manner with our treaty stipulations, it would be better to abolish the farce of our annual meagre appropriations for Indian schools, as, under the present system, the most of those appropriations are wasted without doing the Indians or any one else any good.

INDIANS OF SOUTHEASTERN AND MIDDLE OREGON.

The few facilities for travelling, together with the remoteness of those tribes, and the short space of time at my disposal, prevented my visiting them. Among them are the confederated tribes known as the Wascoes, the Des Chutes, and Tyghs, who are located upon what is known as the Warm Spring reservation, situated east of the Cascade range of mountains, and about one hundred miles south of the Columbia river. Those three tribes number 1,070 souls. They were located in their present reservation in pursuance of the treaty made with them June 25, 1855. Their isolated condition exempts them in a great measure from the deleterious influences of vicious whites, and it is believed that their condition has been greatly improved since their establishment in their present home. For the last four years they have been under the charge of late Agent William Logan, who lost his life in August last on board of the ill-fated steamer Brother Jonathan. Mr. Logan's reports of last year show that they raised 4,965 bushels of wheat, 275 bushels of corn, 170 bushels of peas, 450 bushels of oats, 1,600 bushels of potatoes, together with large quantities of other vegetables.

Those people have devoted considerable attention to stock-raising, and would now have been wealthy had they not suffered great losses from the severity of the winter of 1861 and the constant depredations of the Snake Indians, who inhabit the country south and east of theirs, and who are constantly engaged in making forays upon the peaceable tribes, committing murders, and driving off their stock. Frequent calls have been made upon the military for the purpose of protecting the reservation against the periodical raids of the Snakes, and detachments of troops have sometimes been stationed upon the reservation; but the wily savages have generally eluded the vigilance of the soldiers, and pursued their maraudings unmolested.

The Snakes, Klamaths, and Modocs comprise what are known as the untamed tribes, and are variously estimated at from two to three thousand souls. They claim and wander over the entire southeastern quarter of the State of Oregon, and in their marauding expeditions infest portions of northern California and Nevada and southwestern Idaho.

They have been—particularly that portion of them known as the Snakes—the natural thieves and murderers infesting the great interior region above referred to. They have taken many valuable lives and destroyed hundreds of thousands of dollars' worth of property, greatly retarding the settlement and development of a country rich in agricultural and mineral resources. It is, unfortunately, not their habit to assemble in sufficiently large force to enable the military to find or bring them to a general battle. If they would congregate in large numbers and assume a defiant attitude there would be some hopes of our being able either to conquer or exterminate them. By dividing into small and prowling bands they are enabled to pounce at any moment upon remote settlements, isolated mining camps, or passing pack trains. Their stealthy presence is never indicated except by a consummated murder or robbery, while their parties are so small and so perfectly on the alert that pursuit is useless. They infest all the routes of inland travel east of the Cascade mountains and south of the Columbia river, and pay their respects alike and simultaneously to the stage stations, the ranch men, the farmers, and the miners. They respect neither age, sex, nor condition, and seem to live solely for blood and plunder.

Superintendent Huntingdon succeeded, in October, 1864, in negotiating a treaty with the Klamaths and Modocs, by the terms of which they are to be assembled upon a reservation near Fort Klamath, in the southern portion of Oregon. This treaty has not yet been ratified by the Senate. The location selected for them is well adapted to their wants, and it is said that they are anxious to be located upon their reservation. Herewith I submit a communication relative to them from Lindsay Applegate, esq., marked B.

During the last summer Superintendent Huntingdon has been enabled to hold a council with some of the chiefs of the Snakes, at which a treaty was negotiated with them which stipulates that they shall remove to the vicinity of Fort Klamath and remain there in the future, being confederated with the Klamath and Modoc tribes.

If those two treaties should receive the sanction of the President and Senate, and the Indians adhere to their promises, Oregon, northern California, and southwestern Idaho will be happily rid forever of the curse of hostile Indians, their murders, robberies, and depredations. I think it probable that the Klamaths and Modocs will adhere to their treaties, but have less faith in any honest compliance on the part of the Snakes. One reason for this opinion is their constitutional and ingrained tendency to rob and murder, and another is based upon the fact that within one month, from the time Superintendent Huntingdon made his treaty with the Snakes I heard of parties of them murdering and robbing persons, destroying stage stations, and running off stock, on Burnt, Malheur, and Owyhee rivers; also upon the stage route leading from Chico, in California, to Ruby City, in Idaho. It is barely possible that those outrages were committed by some marauding bands who had not yet heard of the treaty. In any event no effort should be spared to carry out the provisions of the treaty, as the cost of its execution will bear no comparison to the expense of making a single campaign against them. However desirable it might be to rid the world of such thieves and murderers by exterminating them, I look upon it as impossible to do so in consequence of the difficulties of prosecuting a campaign in so vast a region, where all the peculiarities of the country are in favor of the savage. The sums already spent in fruitless endeavors to chastise them would be more than doubly ample to carry out the provisions of the treaty.

The Walla-Wallas, Cayuses, and Umatillas are, by virtue of the treaty of June, 1855, located upon the Umatilla reservation in the northeastern portion of Oregon. They number, by actual census taken in June last, as follows: Walla-Wallas, 160; Cayuses, 370; Umatillas, 229; making an aggregate of 759 souls.

Their reservation is large, consisting principally of rolling uplands covered with nutritious grasses, which furnish abundant pasture for their stock. Along the margin of the streams which traverse the reservation are some of the finest agricultural lands in the State, with a supply of timber ample for farming purposes. They pay much attention to raising horses and cattle, and are comparatively wealthy—the most so, perhaps, of any tribe upon the Pacific slope. When I visited them in August last in company with Agent Barnhardt we passed over many of their farms, and found that they were managed with a degree of intelligence and industry which would have done credit to a more civilized people. The treaty provides for the erection of a saw and grist mill upon their reservation, but owing in part to the mismanagement of a former agent that duty had been entirely neglected, which caused much complaint and dissatisfaction among them. The last Congress made an appropriation for the erection of these mills, and I found that the money was being judiciously expended for that purpose, thus removing the principal ground of their complaint.

Their crops last year were as follows: 3,000 bushels of wheat, 1,300 bushels of oats, 850 bushels of corn, 2,100 bushels of potatoes, 700 bushels of peas, together with large quantities of garden vegetables. The vice of prostitution, so common among other tribes, is almost unknown among the Cayuses, Walla-Wallas and Umatillas, and they are consequently free from the diseases which are so rapidly decimating the tribes west of them, along the coast. Many of them are members of the Catholic church, and it is admitted by all that the labors of the priests of that denomination have had a salutary effect upon those tribes. Their principal vices are gambling and drunkenness, but even these are not as common as among many other tribes, and would measurably disappear were it not for vicious white men, who inculcate bad habits for the purpose of profiting thereby. With the rich pastures and agricultural lands and fine herds possessed by these people, they ought to be happy and contented, if it were in the nature of an Indian to be so. In the talks which I had with their principal chiefs they had but few complaints to make, and they were principally confined to the delays in receiving their annuities, and the worthless character of the articles sent out from the east by the department. They manifested great apprehension and uneasiness lest the government should desire to remove them to some other reservation. In fact, that idea has long been inculcated among them by reckless white persons, who are anxious to stir up difficulties, and desire, upon some pretext, to obtain the rich farms now occupied by the Indians. As the white population becomes more dense, and as the value of the lands increases, the desire to intrude upon the reservations for purposes of settlement and trade also increases. I assured the chiefs that their apprehensions of having their homes taken from them were groundless, and that so long as they conducted themselves in a peaceable and proper manner, the government would protect them in their homes, which had been guaranteed to them by solemn treaty stipulations. They also made some complaint about the public thoroughfare crossing their reservation. In reply to which I pointed them to the provisions of the treaty authorizing it, and explained to them that while the government would protect them, in accordance with the stipulations of the treaty, in the quiet possession of their homes, it would also adhere to its right to make public roads over their land as provided for in the same treaty, and that they could not be permitted to obstruct the great thoroughfare of commerce between the navigable waters of the Columbia and the rich productive interior.

While this reservation is the best adapted to the wants of the Indians, I cannot but regard its location as unfavorable, from the fact that it lies in the way of the greatest thoroughfare leading from the Columbia to all of the rich mining region east of the Blue mountains, rendering a conflict between the Indians and reckless white persons imminent at any moment. As before stated, the Indians are averse to being removed, and the amount of money already expended in opening farms, building mills and houses, would seem to forbid any attempt in that direction at present.

WASHINGTON TERRITORY.

On the 11th of July I arrived at Olympia, and proceeded to visit such of the reservations bordering upon Puget sound as the time at my disposal would permit, and first visited, in company with Mr. Elder, the agent in charge, the Nisqually reservation, which is about fifteen miles from Olympia, and on the Nisqually river. The most of the reservation is high and dry gravelly ridges, covered with a growth of sorrel. The only lands fit for cultivation are the bottoms bordering upon the margins of the streams, and they are covered with a dense growth of timber too heavy to be cleared by Indian labor. The reservation is better adapted to grazing than farming, but I should not regard it as valuable for either. The agent informed me that there were five hundred and fifty Indians belonging to the reservation, but they were nearly all absent gathering berries and fishing, so that I had no opportunity to make a personal inspection of their condition. It would be advantageous to the Indians as well as the government to have this tribe concentrated with the Puyallups and removed to their reservation, which is about twenty miles distant, in a northeasterly direction.

PUYALLUPS.

This tribe is located upon a reservation upon and near the mouth of the Puyallup river. They number about six hundred souls, and obtain the principal part of their subsistence from the fish which abound in the neighboring waters; they also cultivate the land to some extent which borders along the river and is of excellent quality, but more labor is required to clear off the timber and brush than the Indians are disposed to devote to that purpose. When I visited this tribe they had about one hundred and forty acres planted in potatoes, wheat, barley, oats, peas, and other vegetables, the labor being nearly all done by themselves. The extensive salt marshes upon this reservation afford fine opportunities for cutting hay, which finds a ready market in the neighboring lumber camps. Upon the whole, I know of no reservation so well adapted to the wants of the Indians, or where their living could be more easily obtained; yet they manifest but little disposition to improve their condition by adopting habits of industry necessary to clearing and cultivating their fertile lands, cutting hay for market, or erecting comfortable houses. Here, as elsewhere, I observed that general tendency to idleness, vagrancy, dissipation, and indifference upon the subject of future wants, which seems to be an aboriginal characteristic. The mildness of their climate, together with the facilities for obtaining fish along the sound, prevents any great amount of suffering among them from want of food or clothing; yet with all the natural advantages by which they are surrounded, they have made comparatively no advances toward civilization. About twenty families have adopted the habits of the whites, to the extent of living in rude houses of their own construction; yet they are influenced by the prevailing superstition of all the tribes against residing in or in any way using a building in which one of their tribe has died; consequently, when a death occurs in one of their houses the family moves out and at once consigns their former residence to the flames. Their agent informs me that the tribe is decreasing, a result to be attributed to the presence of venereal diseases which prevail among them.

Squoxon reservation, like the Nisqually and Puyallup, is also under charge of Agent Elder. It is situated upon an island in Puget sound. The land is poor and heavily timbered, and the large sums of money heretofore spent in attempts to open farms and make improvements upon it have resulted in no corresponding benefit. It would be beneficial to the few Indians who reside here to remove them, as well as the Nisquallies, to the Puyallup reservation. The three tribes are parties to the treaty of Medicine creek, and should all be located at Puyallup, which is so well adapted to their wants. On the evening of the 14th of July I embarked, in company with Superintendent Waterman and three gentlemen who had been appointed by the department, to appraise certain improvements upon the reservation. Our only means of conveyance was an open boat. After being buffeted about by adverse winds and tides for two days and nights we reached Seattle, where we abandoned our open boat and took passage upon a small steamer chartered for the remainder of our trip.

On the 18th we reached the Tulalip reservation, situated upon the margin of the Tulalip bay, and near the mouth of Shokomish river. At the time of my visit the reservation was under charge of Agent Howe, who reports that there are eleven hundred Indians who make their homes there for a portion of the year. They rely for support upon fishing and hunting; indeed they can do little else, as the soil, in addition to being poor, is covered with a growth of timber sufficiently dense to deter even a white man from attempting to clear it up. A narrow strip has been cleared along the bay, where they have about fifty small board and frame houses erected. They also have a few potatoes planted and garden vegetables, which gave but small promise of producing much. I saw nothing being done worthy of being called farming. The little property possessed by these people consists of their canoes, nets, and other fishing gear, with which they are generally enabled to supply their daily wants of food, beyond which they seem to give themselves no especial trouble or care. Here was the only place upon the sound where I witnessed any attempts being made to educate Indian children. The Rev. C. C. Chirouse, a Catholic priest, having some time since established himself here as a teacher, has succeeded in collecting from thirty to forty Indian boys under his care, and by a system of manual labor is attempting to make them support themselves while obtaining an education. His efforts are not confined to the school-room, but he accompanies his pupils in their out-door labors and gives them all needful instruction. The boys under the reverend father's care, and by his aid, have succeeded in clearing up a sufficiently large piece of heavily timbered land for a garden, from which they draw a small supply of vegetables; the remainder of their living is obtained by catching fish in the neighboring waters. The boys are kept entirely separate from their parents, which is indispensable for their proper culture; they are mostly dependent upon the charity of the whites for their clothing. It is a matter of regret that the worthy father is compelled to pursue his benevolent and Christian labors under so many disadvantages, and some further provision should be made to aid him in feeding and clothing the pupils, who seem so anxious to avail themselves of his instructions. In visiting their school-room I was struck with their cleanliness and good manners, as well as with the progress they had made in reading, writing, and arithmetic. Herewith I submit two communications addressed to me by the pupils themselves, and written in a fair and legible hand; they are marked, respectively, C and D.

Lummi reservation is situated near the head of Bellingham bay. Owing to the brief period of my stay, and the stage of the tide, it was inconvenient to visit the village, but from what I saw of the people they appear much of the same character as those at Tulalip. Their agent informed me that the reservation is better adapted to the wants of the Indians than the latter-named point, and that they had made considerable progress in agriculture.

Other points were visited bordering on the sound where Indians occasionally congregate in great numbers for the purpose of taking fish, but as their general features are the same, and as there was but little improvement worthy of note at any of them, they will not require special mention.

Shokomish reservation is situated near the southern end of an arm of Puget sound, known as Hood's canal, which extends southward about one hundred miles from the straits of Juan de Fuca. The Indians who belong to this reservation are the Shokomish and Skallams, and two remnants of other tribes, parties to the treaty of Point No-Point. They are variously estimated at from twelve hundred to four thousand souls; indeed, I do not believe their actual number ever was or ever will be known. I saw but very few of them upon the reservation, but learned that they were absent gathering berries, catching fish, prostituting their women, gambling, and getting drunk, the latter of which appears to be their favorite occupation. Special Agent Knox, who is in charge of them, told me that there were twelve hundred of them came to receive their annuities in November, 1863. Superintendent Waterman estimates them at a much greater number. This reservation appears to be well enough adapted to their wants as a home. But little, however, has been done upon it in the way of improvement. The fish and game, both of which are abundant in the neighborhood, are nearly equally as abundant upon all other portions of the sound; and as these people manifest no disposition to labor, there appears to be no inducement for them to remain at the home to which they have been assigned, consequently they are scattered all along the western shore of Hood's canal and the straits of Juan de Fuca nearly to Cape Flattery, a distance of about one hundred and fifty miles. But little control is exercised over them, and with the means at present at the disposal of the superintendent I am unable to perceive how he is to exercise more, as he is without means to subsist them upon their reservation, and as they are mostly lazy, drunken, dissolute vagabonds, who can neither be persuaded nor compelled to labor. They are brought in contact with the white population at all of the villages and lumber camps along the western portion of the sound, and rapidly falling victims to venereal diseases and noxious whiskey which they can but too readily obtain. The few of them who reside upon the reservation, with a white farmer to assist them, have only about ten acres of ground in cultivation. The annuities and other appropriations are too limited to enable the superintendent to collect and subsist such a demoralized and drunken herd of savages while the experiment of their reformation is being attempted. It is not certain that any amount of means would enable the department to improve the condition of these people. Possibly a few of them may be reclaimed and induced to cultivate the soil. I look, however, upon the great majority of them as doomed to a speedy extinction as the result of indolence, loathsome diseases, and bad whiskey.

At all of the agencies which I visited upon Puget sound the Indians manifested a great desire that the government should furnish them with clothing and trinkets as the principal portion of their annuities. My own impression and advice is against such a course, as I believe that with the facilities which they have for laboring and obtaining good prices therefor, they should measurably be thrown upon their own resources to obtain their clothing, and that feeling the need of it would be an additional stimulus to their industry. When large quantities of clothing and blankets are distributed among them it usually is followed by a period of gambling and dissipation. It would evidently be better for them to have the greater portion of their annuities expended in procuring domestic animals, agricultural implements, and in opening farms. To obtain these articles they cannot be induced to labor, while on the other hand they have the stimulant of physical suffering to urge them to work for the clothes necessary for their personal comfort.

The Chehalis and Cowlitz are a couple of small tribes who reside upon the rivers of those names within the settled portion of Washington Territory. No treaties have been made with them, though their land has been surveyed and much of it disposed of by the government. They are a docile people, and more industrious than the majority of the Indians within that Territory, and it would seem but just that some permanent provision should be made for them.

The Yakama reservation is situated upon the river of that name, east of the Cascade mountains, and about seventy miles north of the Columbia river. The Indians located here by the provisions of the treaty of 1855 consist of fourteen tribes and bands, the principal of which are the Yakamas and Klikatats. The superintendent reports them to consist of five thousand persons: perhaps half that number reside upon the reservation, which is exceedingly well adapted to the purpose for which it was selected, the mountains furnishing good timber, while the upland or hills are covered with an abundance of good grass. Several fine streams of water pass through the reservation, along the margins of which is excellent land for agricultural purposes.

A great advantage enjoyed by the Indians here is their isolation from the white settlements, which prevents them being brought in contact with vicious persons and those disposed to sell them intoxicating drinks. They have two thousand five hundred acres under fence, and about twelve hundred acres in cultivation. Their crops last year consisted of two thousand bushels of wheat, two hundred bushels of peas, six hundred bushels of corn, and three thousand bushels of potatoes, in addition to large quantities of garden vegetables. The government has erected for them a good grist and saw mill, both of which are in good repair and successful operation. The abandoned military post of Fort Simcoe furnishes excellent buildings for residences, shops, storerooms, school-rooms, and all other purposes for which buildings are required at an agency. In visiting the Indian farms and houses many of them gave evidence of the habits of industry of the tribe. Agent Wilbur, who is in charge of the reservation, manifests a determination to test the practicability of reducing an Indian to a state of civilization. His example is certainly valuable to them, and he neglects no opportunity to give them instruction of a practical character. He is energetic and enthusiastic in his efforts to elevate the character and condition of the people under his charge. If he fails, the failure must be attributed to some other cause than a want of zeal on his part. So far they have greatly improved under his management.

I found the school in full and successful operation, and well attended by both boys and girls. Both are boarded and clothed at the agency, and kept separate from their parents. Both sexes are taught the elementary branches, and there is a farm connected with the boys' school, upon which they labor a certain portion of their time; the proceeds of their labor is applied towards their support. Some of the boys are taught to work at trades, under the direction of employés upon the reservation, and bid fair to make proficient workmen. The girls, in addition to their studies, are taught sewing and housework. The school here and at Puyallup were the only ones that I saw which seem to be resulting in much practical good.

IDAHO TERRITORY.

The Nez Percés are located upon an extensive reservation, embracing the Clearwater river and its tributaries in Idaho Territory, and extending westward across the Snake river includes small portions of the State of Oregon and of Washington Territory, and contains about ten thousand square miles. They were assigned to this location by the provisions of the treaty negotiated with them by Isaac I. Stevens, then governor, and superintendent of Indian affairs for Washington Territory, and General Joel Palmer, superintendent for Oregon, in the year 1855. By that treaty they relinquished to the United States their claims to a vast region of territory, embracing portions of what are now Oregon, Washington, and Idaho. In consideration of this cession of territory the United States stipulated among other things, that the reservation "tract shall be set apart, and, so far as necessary, surveyed and marked out for the exclusive use and benefit of said tribe as an Indian reservation, nor shall any white man, excepting those in the employment of the Indian department, be permitted to reside upon the said reservation without permission of the tribe and the superintendent and agent." In article 5 "The United States further agree to establish at suitable points within said reservation, within one year after the ratification hereof, two schools, erecting the necessary buildings, keeping the same in repair, and providing them with furniture, books, and stationery; one of which shall be an agricultural and industrial school, to be located at the agency and to be free to the children of said tribe; and to employ one superintendent of teaching and two teachers." Article 10 provides: "The Nez Perces desire to exclude from their reservation the use of ardent spirits, and to prevent their people from drinking the same; and therefore it is provided that any Indian belonging to said tribe who is guilty of bringing liquor into said reservation, or who shall drink liquor, may have his or her portion of the annuities withheld."

The fact that not one of these excellent provisions has been complied with, on the part of the government, presents a striking contrast between what has been promised and what has been performed. For the last three or four years the reservation has been overrun with white people, not only by those in search of gold, but by others who have made locations there for agricultural purposes, and who have erected buildings, enclosed lands, and exercised all the rights of ownership over it. A town has been located there, which was designated as the capital of the Territory, and a lively trade carried on not only with the whites, but with the Indians, supplying them with ardent spirits, upon their own reservation, in open violation of the intercourse law, and of the provisions of the treaty above quoted. The agent, in his report of last year, and which, for some reason, was not published, states that "It is difficult to say what remedy can be taken. Of course we know that the sale of all merchandise in Lewiston and the different mining camps upon the reservation is in direct violation of the intercourse laws, yet these merchants say they are paying the United States taxes for the sale of liquors and other goods. The capital of the Territory is located upon the reservation, counties and towns laid off, judges, sheriffs and constables appointed, county roads laid off, town and county licenses granted, &c. It is sincerely to be hoped that some way be found to check this growing evil. Take the sale and traffic of liquor to these Indians away from them, and no better, more friendly, or kind-hearted people can be found on the coast." The people who are now and have been upon this reservation located themselves there at a time when rich gold mines were being discovered and worked, and remained under the impression that a treaty would be made with the Indians, by which they would relinquish to the government that portion of their lands occupied by the town of Lewiston and neighboring settlements. Such a treaty was negotiated by the commissioners appointed by the government, in June, 1863; but never having been ratified by the Senate, the leading chiefs are now opposed to its ratification, and, as a reason, allege that the government has defrauded them by not complying with the provisions of the treaty of 1855, and that it would be useless to enter into a new treaty while the provisions of the old one remain unfulfilled.

There are two thousand eight hundred of these people. They are the finest specimens of the aboriginal race to be found on this continent. They are possessed of considerable herds of cattle and horses, are brave and warlike, and are of good habits. They have always been the friends of the white man, from the days when Lewis and Clarke visited them to the present time. They have just reason to complain of the many infractions of their treaty, and more particularly of that clause of it which guarantees that the whites shall be kept off their reservation. Under the leadership of "Big Thunder," a principal chief, a party is forming which is hostile to the government, and if something is not speedily done to remove the causes of complaint there is great danger to be apprehended of their resorting to open hostility. No one can go upon their reservation with the treaty in his hand without being convinced that their complaints are well founded. I am only surprised that they have exercised so much forbearance under the wrongs and injustice which they have suffered.

The fifth article of the treaty, providing for the erection of school-houses and the support of schools, like most of the other provisions, has been neglected, and nothing worthy of the name of school has ever existed upon the reservation. Agent James O'Neill, who is in charge of the Nez Perces, says, in his report of 1864, above referred to, "That no provision is made for the support or boarding of children. The different bands of these Indians are located from half a mile to sixty miles from the agency, and, therefore, only those living near can attend."

"Those living near will not attend unless hired to do so. A school-house was erected last summer, and school taught for a short time, but five or six attending, and at sometimes but one or two, there being no regular attendance. The building was afterward, by order of Superintendent Wallace, exchanged with Dr. Newell for a house belonging to him, which has since been occupied by one of the employés. This spring a room formerly used as an office was taken for a school-room, but still the children will not attend; and until such an appropriation is made for the support of the children from the distant bands, it seems as though an appropriation of thirty-two hundred dollars per annum for the support of two teachers was a useless expenditure." Upon investigation, I found that teachers had been appointed, but, for the reasons set forth by the agent, they had been unable to accomplish anything; and I concur in the opinion expressed by Agent O'Neill, that the present expenditure is a useless one. All the other stipulations of the treaty with the Nez Perces are fulfilled with the same sort of fidelity as are the provisions for excluding the whites and whiskey from the reservation, and for the establishment of schools. The annuities, which the treaty stipulates shall be paid annually, for some reasons have been withheld, and not a dollar has been paid to the tribe for more than two years.

I found Agent O'Neill a competent officer, and doing all in his power to pacify the Indians and protect the interests of the government, but he was entirely destitute of funds, and had been for the last year. The treaty employés upon the reservation have eighteen months' pay due them, and, in order to live, are forced to dispose of their vouchers for services at from fifty to sixty cents on the dollar in currency. The chiefs, who have a stated salary by the provisions of the treaty, have been forced to make similar sacrifices. The credit of the Indian department is utterly destroyed, and the tribe greatly disaffected towards the government, and I think it safe to assert that there is no portion of the United States in which Indian affairs are in so chaotic and disorganized à state as in Idaho Territory. Mr. O'Neill, who is the only Indian agent within the Territory, is utterly powerless to remedy the evils. The regulations of the department require him to conduct his correspondence through the superintendent of Indian affairs for his district. "Caleb Lyon, of Lyonsdale," who is governor and ex-officio superintendent of Indian affairs, has not been heard of in Idaho since early last spring.

His absence from his post, however, seems to entail no embarrassment upon the management of Indian affairs. When present, he conducted them with an ignorance unparalleled, and a disregard of the rights and wants of the Indians, and of the laws regulating intercourse with them, deserving the severest rebuke. In a council which I held with all of the principal chiefs of the Nez Percés tribe, they unanimously denounced his conduct, and accused him, among other things, of negotiating with one of the tribe for the private purchase of an eligible situation within the boundaries of the reservation for his own benefit, and upon which he proposed to locate "New Lyonsdale." The charge made by the Indians is corroborated by the statement of Rev. H. H. Spalding, herewith submitted, and marked E.

The most prominent feature of Governor Lyon of Lyonsdale's administration of Indian affairs is to be seen in his abortive attempts at erecting a stone church upon the Nez Percé reservation. The site chosen is at the eastern base of a steep hill, or mountain. The walls are constructed of large, rough basaltic stones, laid up in common earth, or mud. Its dimensions outside are thirty-six feet by fifty-six, and the walls are three feet thick and sixteen feet high, and without a roof, bearing a strong resemblance, in all but height, to a Mexican corral, or a New England cattle pound. The freezing and thawing of the mud mortar has caused it all to fall out, so daylight is visible in any direction through the walls, while the accumulated water from the rains passing down the mountain side has made the walls settle in such a manner as to be in constant danger of falling. The expenses already incurred in erecting this novel structure amount to $5,943 13; $1,185 50 of which is still due to the Indians for labor performed by them at one dollar per day in its erection, and for the neglect to pay which the Indians make very uncomplimentary remarks of the governor, who employed and promised to pay them therefor. Fortunately no roof has been placed upon it, and the period is not far distant when its fallen and dilapidated walls will constitute a costly ruin to commemorate the extravagant folly and want of common sense of his excellency Caleb Lyon of Lyonsdale.

It is not known what authority, if any, the governor had for this expenditure, nor is it known from what appropriation the money expended was taken. The treaty certainly provided for nothing of the kind; and if it did, no sane man would think of erecting it in its present form, upon its present site, or of the materials selected. The amount thus foolishly squandered should be disallowed in Governor Lyon's accounts, and he or his sureties compelled to refund the money. The attempted erection of this structure seems to be in perfect keeping with the rest of Governor Lyon's official acts connected with his administration of Indian affairs in Idaho. Hence his continual absence will cause no detriment to the service. For further particulars relative to Governor Lyon's conduct I refer you to the statements made by Agent O'Neill and Rev. H. H. Spalding.

I was unable to find any records in Idaho connected with or pertaining to the office of superintendent of Indian affairs. By an application to Mr. Gibson, who had been in charge of the office, he submitted the following under oath:

"I was engaged by Governor Lyon in New York, in June, 1864, as clerk in the Indian department, and assisted the Secretary. I expected to receive fifteen hundred dollars per annum as my compensation. The governor agreed to allow me one thousand dollars per annum. I made out a voucher for one year's services, at the rate of fifteen hundred dollars per annum, and sent it to Governor Lyon by mail. I forget how much I have been paid, and did not sign vouchers for the amount received. Governor Lyon paid my expenses from New York to Lewiston, Idaho, and I was in his employment up to the 25th of August, 1865.

"I conducted a portion of the correspondence of the office of superintendent of Indian affairs. I am not aware that Governor Lyon brought out any funds from Washington applicable to the Indian department since in Idaho.

"Governor Lyon only had one set of accounts made up for the superintendency during the period that I was in his employment, and they embraced the whole period. I made up those accounts.

"I do not know what amount of money Governor Lyon received or disbursed as superintendent of Indian affairs, nor what were the balances in the accounts. I know that he disbursed some money on account of the erection of a stone church at Lapwai, but have no recollection of the amount. I don't remember whether or no any funds were disbursed on account of annuities while Governor Lyon was in charge of the office. My business in the office was to examine the accounts of agents, and I only had the quarterly accounts of one agent to examine—they were Agent O'Neill's. Governor Lyon had no interpreter employed for the office; when one was wanted Whitman was sent for, or some one else temporarily employed. I remained in the office at Lewiston when Governor Lyon came to Boisé valley to make treaties with the Indians. I never saw the treaties he negotiated, and know nothing of their provisions.

"When Governor Lyon left the Territory he said nothing about turning over the office, but directed me to repair to Boisé City, and remain in charge of the office. I complied with his directions. All that I have done was to receive Agent O'Neill's returns and forward them to Washington. I have kept no letter-book, and made no communication in relation to O'Neill's accounts, but simply forwarded them to Washington without letter or comment.

"I have no accounts belonging to the office of superintendent, except the retained copies of O'Neill's accounts.

"WALTER W. GIBSON."

"Subscribed and sworn to before me this eighteenth day of September, 1865, at Boisé City, Idaho Territory.

"MILTON KELLEY,
"*Associate Justice.*"

It would appear from Gibson's statement that there were no records kept in the superintendent's office, and I imagine that it will be difficult to determine what Mr. Gibson was employed and paid for, unless it was, as he states, to remail at the end of each quarter one set of Agent O'Neill's accounts. It would seem hardly necessary to pay a clerk a thousand or fifteen hundred dollars a year for that service. A total change is required in the administration of Indian affairs in Idaho Territory; and the most salutary change that could be made would be the appointment of a suitable superintendent who would attend to the duties of his office. The sooner that is done the better it will be for the Indians and the government.

The department in Idaho requires the services of two additional agents, there now being but one.

I herewith submit a statement relative to Indians in Idaho, from Mr. A. L Downer, clerk of the supreme court of the Territory, and marked F.

ANNUITIES.

Among all the tribes that I visited, with whom we have negotiated and ratified treaties, I found a universal complaint in relation to both the quantity and quality of their annuities. There is no general circulation of paper money, as currency, within the States or Territories bordering upon the Pacific; consequently the Indians there, who have never seen or known any kind of money excepting gold and silver, are unable to comprehend the representative value of a bank or treasury note as being above that of any other piece of paper. At the time the treaties were negotiated with them, and the value and quantity of the articles they were to receive annually from the government was explained to them, all values had reference to a gold basis. The practical effect has been to reduce their annuities one-half in quantity. Their suspicious natures cause them to look upon such a diminution as an actual and intentional fraud on the part of the government, while their ignorance precludes the possibility of making them comprehend the abstract question involved in financial fluctuations. In their simplicity, they insist that paper is not money, and that they are annually and unjustly defrauded of one-half that was promised them. However erroneous their reasoning may be, it is not in the power of man to convince them of it, and it is hardly reasonable to expect that one party to a compact should be scrupulous in their compliance with its provisions under a conviction that the other party is unjustly evading it. Another great cause of complaint is the worthless quality of the goods which are bought in the Atlantic States and sent out for distribution among them. There is a great fault somewhere, either on the part of the agents who make the purchases in the eastern market, or on the part of the merchants or contractors who supply the goods. From the personal inspection which I have given those goods, and on comparing them with the invoices, I am thoroughly convinced that the contractors are guilty of the most outrageous and systematic *swindling* and *robbery*. Their acts can be properly characterized by no other terms. There is evidence also that the persons employed in the department to make the purchases are accomplices in these crimes. I have examined invoices of purchases made by the department or its agents in eastern cities, where the prices charged were from fifty to one hundred per cent. above the market value of good articles. Upon an examination of the goods I have found them, as a general thing, worthless and deficient in quantity. Among them were "steel spades," made of sheet iron; "chopping axes," which were purely cast iron; "best brogans," with paper soles; "blankets," made of shoddy and glue, which came to shreds the first time they were wet, &c., &c., &c.

Add to these villainous purchases, made with depreciated currency, the fact that the goods are generally sent by the most expensive means of transportation, and it can be easily imagined how small a proportion is received by the Indians. But the folly or wrong of these purchases, made by dishonest agents from dishonest contractors, does not cease here. Many articles are purchased which would be utterly useless to the Indians, if their quality was ever so good, such as iron spoons, mirrors, gimlets, jewsharps, hair oil, finger rings, and, in one case which came under my observation, forty dozen pairs of *elastic garters* were sent out to a tribe in which there was not a single pair of *stockings*. Agent Wilbur, in charge of the Yakama reservation, in a report upon this subject, says:

"The goods furnished from the Atlantic States have been of an inferior quality, *often damaged*, and sometimes *short in quantity*. Of the first invoice of annuity goods received here there was a large number of blankets short; of other goods which arrived here in 1862 there was a deficiency of fourteen pairs of blankets, twenty-one yards of checks and stripes, and six pairs of brogans, besides twenty-five pairs of blankets rat-eaten to that extent that they were considered worthless. Thirty-seven pairs of pants and twenty-two coats, on opening the case, were found to be wet and completely rotten. The woollen goods sent out have been almost universally worthless; clothes made up for the schools from annuity goods, many of them, were not worth the making. The same might be truthfully said in regard to the quality of hoes, axes, pitchforks, and shovels, many of which were not worth the transportation from Dalles, Oregon, to this place, a distance of seventy-five miles. The calico has been of a very inferior quality. One would suppose that the sentiment prevailed, where such goods were purchased, that they were for the Indians, and no matter about the quality or quantity. I think, in justice, that the government owes the Indians of this agency twenty thousand dollars for deficiencies in quality and quantity of goods purchased, and previously distributed to the Indians of the Yakama nation."

Independent of the frauds which have been perpetrated in these purchases, a great inconvenience has resulted from the ignorance of the parties perpetrating them in their not knowing what would be most useful to the Indians, and it often occurs that at some remote agency the tribe is destitute of some useful and indispensable article, while the storehouse is full of those for which they never had any use. I have seen hundreds of dollars' worth of paints, mirrors, jewsharps, finger rings, elastic garters, and other equally useless gewgaws stowed away upon a reservation, while the Indians were destitute of seeds, teams, and agricultural implements, which they would have used to some purpose.

Not a dollar's worth of goods intended for distribution among the Indians upon the Pacific coast should be purchased in the eastern markets. All the articles of woollen goods which the Indians require are manufactured in Oregon and California, and sold at reasonable prices, while the quality is admitted by all good judges to be superior to similar goods purchased in the Atlantic States. These States not only manufacture their own substantial woollen goods, but are large exporters of wool. The small quantities of cotton goods and hardware required by the Indians can be purchased in the Pacific markets cheaper than they ever have been furnished there by the Indian department from eastern cities, and as for the baubles and trinkets for ornaments, they should not be purchased, as they only tend to degrade the Indians by stimulating a barbarous fondness for useless display. What the Indian really requires for his comfort and elevation is domestic animals, agricultural implements and seeds, and, under any judicious management of their affairs, their annuities would be principally given in these articles.

The appropriation bills usually pass at or near the close of a session of Congress, so late in the season that the purchases of annuity goods cannot be made in eastern cities and sent around Cape Horn in time to reach the tribes during the current year in which the appropriations are made. Sometimes the alternative is adopted of sending the goods more expeditiously by express over the isthmus of Panama, on which route the charges for transportation usually amount to two or three times the value of such goods as are required by the Indians.

Persons who have witnessed the distribution of annuity goods to Indians without being aware of how, where, or by whom they were purchased, have come to the conclusion that the tribes were being defrauded by the agents who made the distribution. My experience, resulting from an investigation of the matter, forces the conclusion upon my mind, that, under the present system of purchasing annuity goods, the depredations upon the funds commence *sometimes before,* and *always soon after* it gets out of the Indian bureau in Washington, to such an extent, that by the time the goods reach the agent, who is to distribute them, there is nothing left either in quantity or quality to tempt his cupidity.

The evils resulting from improper and dishonest practices in the purchase of Indian goods by the department, and its agents selected for that purpose, and who know nothing of the Indians or their wants, have long been felt by all persons who had any knowledge of the system and the enormous frauds which have been perpetrated under it. An attempt was made to correct this evil by congressional legislation, and the following provision was, for that purpose, incorporated in the act approved July 5, 1862 :

"SEC 5. *And be it further enacted,* That hereafter no goods shall be purchased by the Indian department, or its agents, for any tribe, except upon the written requisition of the superintendent in charge of the tribe."

As pertinent to this subject, and to show how little regard was paid to the law by the Indian bureau, I quote the following from the replies made by Superintendent Huntingdon, of Oregon, to certain interrogatories propounded to him by myself ; and also append a copy of a letter from late Commissioner William P. Dole :

"Prior to my appointment as superintendent the practice appears to have been to make the purchases by the superintendent or the agent having charge of the tribe, and in the remittance of funds for the first half year of my incumbency, 1863, no change was made, the funds for annuities for all the tribes being remitted, and in due time turned over to the agent, and by them expended. On the 2d of May, 1863, however, Commissioner Dole advised me 'that it was his design to change the practice, and cause the goods to be purchased in the Atlantic cities,' and, in pursuance of this plan, I was directed to transmit my estimate of the articles required for the Indians in the entire superintendency in such time as to reach Washington '*not later than 1st October*, 1863,' and I was especially enjoined to '*a strict compliance with these instructions*' upon my part. This letter was received on the 2d day of June, 1863, and acknowledged on the following day. A copy of it, marked A, is hereto appended for your information.

"On the 18th day of June Commissioner Dole informed me that he had ordered certain goods to be purchased in New York without waiting for my estimate of what was required, and enclosed a list of the goods so ordered. On the 15th of July Mr. J. B. Gordon, special agent, wrote, enclosing invoice of goods purchased in New York and Baltimore, and advising me of their shipment. On the 24th September I forwarded to the Commissioner a carefully prepared estimate of the articles which it was deemed most expedient to purchase for the Indians, which, of course, did not arrive at Washington until after the purchases for that year had been made. No further communication has ever been received by me from the Commissioner's office upon this subject; but, on the 4th of July, 1864, I received a letter from Mr. J. B. Gordon, special agent, advising me of the purchase and shipment of annuity goods for all the tribes in Oregon. No allusion to this purchase has ever been made in any letter received from the Commissioner of Indian Affairs, and this omission cannot be chargeable to the failure of the mails, for my monthly statements of correspondence sent to Washington have been found to correspond with the records of the commission. The goods purchased in 1863 were shipped via Panama at enormous freights, and arrived at the several agencies in time for distribution the same year. The goods bought in 1864 were shipped via Cape Horn, did not arrive here until the present year, and could not be distributed to the Indians for whom they were designed until very recently. Indeed, a portion of those designed for the *Shasta*, *Scoton*, *Umpquas*, and *Rogue Rivers* are yet in this town. Thus the Indians have been one year without annuities, and much dissatisfaction exists among them in consequence.

"The time and manner in which the goods have been shipped have been most unfortunately chosen. The goods of 1863 were not only shipped by the costly isthmus route, but they were subject to exorbitant charge for packing, drayage, &c., (for detail of which see comparative schedule, marked G, and the bulky nature of some of the articles was such as to make the freight *a great deal more than the value of the goods delivered.* Handled axes, hatchets, pitchforks, garden hoes, &c., were cased in huge pine boxes, to be transported over the route from Baltimore and New York to Warm Springs and Umatilla. The transportation of the bulky wooden handles was *five times the value of the articles, handle and all, after delivery*, while the Indians would have thought it no hardship to have made the handles themselves out of the timber which grows upon their own reservation.

"The purchases of 1864 were all shipped via Cape Horn and San Francisco to Salem. Salem was the proper destination *of no part of the goods*. Your familiar acquaintance with the country enables you to see at once the absurdity of shipping goods bound for Warm Springs or Umatilla, up the Willamette river to Salem, thence down the river to Portland again, toward their final destination. The goods designed for Siletz agency afford a still more marked instance of mismanagement. They have been transported from San Francisco to Salem at a cost of about $75 per ton, and now the most economical way to get them to their destination will probably be to *ship them back to San Francisco again at like cost*, and thence *direct* to Siletz at a cost of about $16 per ton. The only other alternative is to transport them on pack-mules from Salem to Siletz, which probably will not cost less than $100 per ton. In regard to the quality and suitableness of the goods shipped, it has generally been such as could have been anticipated where the purchaser was entirely unacquainted with the country, or the Indians who inhabit it, and there has uniformly been an unfavorable discrepancy between the invoices and the articles actually shipped. I shall not swell this letter to the inordinate length necessary to point out all of these failures or swindles, but a few of the most glaring must suffice.

"Merrimac prints are named in the invoices of both years. This, as is well known, is the most costly sort of calico, and the prices paid have corresponded with the invoice quality, *but not a yard of Merrimac calico has ever been put in the package;* on the contrary, the article shipped has always been of a very inferior quality, such as can be bought for twenty-five or thirty per cent. less than the Merrimac, and is worth to the Indians, who are expected to consume it, less than half. The article shipped as cotton duck was a light and inferior article of common drilling. A considerable part of the thread sent out was rotten and utterly worthless. The needles, the buttons the fish-hooks and lines were of the most inferior description, and of very little value to the Indians. Spoons enough were brought to give nearly half a dozen to every one of the tribe, and they were so worthless that the Indians generally refused to carry them away after they were given out. Fancy mirrors, costing $5 per dozen, were sent; they proved to be little looking-glasses about two inches in diameter, and worth absolutely nothing to the Indians. A lot of steel weeding-hoes, handled, proved to be little affairs, intended for the use of some delicate lady, if indeed they were intended for use at all. Scissors and shears in inordinate quantity, and utterly worthless in quality, were sent. Tin ware, packed in roomy cases, until the freight was far in excess of the value. Frying-pans of thin sheet-iron, utterly worthless, and so esteemed by the Indians. In short, the entire purchases show either ignorance of the Indians' wants, or design to defraud them. If the purchases are made intelligently and honestly in New York, it may be that the government and Indians will be as well served; but if the invoices hitherto bought are to be taken as a sample of those to be bought in the future, it would be as well to spend half the amount here. No merchant of any interior town in Oregon or Washington ever thinks of buying his stock of goods in New York, and the same reasons which impel individuals to trade at the nearest wholesale mart, apply with two-fold force to all such purchases as are necessarily made by the government. The facts which I have detailed, in my judgment, make evident these propositions:

"1st. The purchase of goods should invariably be made by a person acquainted with the Indians and their wants, and with the character of the climate and country where they are to be consumed.

"2d. That purchases should be made at the wholesale mart nearest to the agency where they are required.

"3d. That purchases in Baltimore and New York necessarily involve enormous transportation charges, or else the withholding of the goods from the Indians for a year.

"For your further information, I take the liberty to transmit herewith a comparative schedule, marked B, showing the purchases made in Baltimore and New York in 1863, of the articles for which, in my judgment, the annuity funds should be expended. A careful examination of this schedule will give you a pretty thorough understanding of what has been purchased, and where; and it will also advise you of what, in my judgment, ought to have been purchased."

"DEPARTMENT OF THE INTERIOR,
"*Office of Indian Affairs, May* 2, 1863.

"SIR: On account of the appreciation of gold and the consequent increase in the prices of merchandise generally on the Pacific coast, it has been demonstrated that articles of general utility required for Indian purposes in the States of California and Oregon, and the Territory of Washington, can be procured in and shipped from the Atlantic States upon better terms, both for the government and the Indians, than can be done in the localities where they are required. I have, therefore, to direct, that you transmit to this office your estimate for the articles required for the Indians within your superintendency, so as to reach here not later than the first October next. You will be careful to state the amount of money you wish expended in each article required, and not the quantity of the article.

"A strict compliance with these instructions is expected on your part.

"Very respectfully,

"W. P. DOLE, *Commissioner.*"

Notwithstanding the restrictions imposed by the section of the law above quoted, it would seem, from Mr. Dole's letter, that he was determined to *buy something* And without waiting for Superintendent Huntingdon to make a requisition for goods of his own volition, as the law contemplated, he, the superior, addresses his subordinate a mandatory letter on the 2d of May, 1863, in which he orders him to send in his requisitions, but, apparently fearing that the subordinate officer might exercise the discretion which the law allowed him, the order is closed with the implied threat of official coercion, that "*a strict compliance with these instructions is expected on your part*"

It seems that Mr. Dole became impatient to make the purchase; therefore, on the 18th of June, and before he could possibly know what Mr. Huntingdon's requisitions would be, or whether he would make any, makes the purchases, and the goods are shipped, with the results detailed by Superintendent Huntingdon. It seems that again in 1864 the annuity goods were bought and shipped by Mr. Gordon without awaiting for any further requisition.

Huntingdon's requisitions of the 24th of September, 1863, were in the department at Washington when the purchases of 1864 were made, and by reference to Huntingdon's schedule, which I append, it will be seen that Messrs. Dole and Gordon had as little comprehension of the requisition as they had regard for the law of Congress, which they were palpably violating. Huntingdon asked for "small steel ploughs," and they sent him "fancy mirrors;" he asked for "harness for ponies," and they sent him "frying-pans" and "knitting-needles;" he asked for "axes and grain cradles," and they responded with "scissors and iron spoons."

In this sort of disregard of the laws of Congress and official malfeasance is to be found the true foundation of the complaints of the Indians about the quality and quantity of their annuities. Superintendents and agents among the Indians who are conscious of these wrongs are restrained from protesting against a practice which is so much in favor with the head of the Indian bureau. If the practice of disobeying so plain a law of Congress is adhered to, I know of no remedy but to make it a criminal offence, punishable by incarcerating the offenders in prison among the more honorable robbers of their own race.

The civilization of the Indians is a question which has attracted the attention of statesmen and philanthropists since the discovery of the continent. All schemes resorted to for that humane purpose seem to have resulted in failure and disappointment, until it is now very generally conceded, at least by all practical people, to be an impossibility. The humane and liberal efforts of the government in their behalf have sometimes had the zealous aid and co-operation of honest and devoted Christian missionaries, who have given their time and talents to their elevation without having accomplished any great apparent benefit. In some instances those efforts gave promise of being rewarded with beneficial results, but the barbarous instinct of the savage has generally reasserted its sway, and the missionaries and teachers have lived to witness the futility of their labors in seeing their pupils neglect and repudiate their teachings, and returning to their barbarous habits with the vices of the white men superadded. The Indians of Oregon, Washington, and Idaho are as susceptible of being instructed perhaps as any others of their race, yet they all have the same great characteristics and the same savage instincts which experience has taught us the impossibility of overcoming, and I do not believe that they will ever be very much elevated above their present condition. Their condition, however, can be ameliorated to some extent by honestly devoting the annuities which we have stipulated to pay them to the improvement of their homes and opening their farms, thus enabling them to gain a better and more reliable subsistence than they now have. The syphilitic disease, with which most of them are infected, is making terrible inroads upon their numbers, and seems to defy the efforts of our physicians; while the Indians' belief in demons, witchcraft, and magic, induces them to treat all diseases with a system of savage incantations administered by their own "medicine man," in whom they have great faith: if, however, the patient dies, the doctor is killed by the surviving relations as a punishment for his malpractice.

Another great obstacle to their advancement is their habit of leaving their homes when a death occurs in one of them. This superstition is so thoroughly implanted in all of the Pacific tribes that no efforts of their agents can eradicate it, and when a death occurs in a residence, hospital, or school-house, it is shunned by the survivors of the tribe and condemned to the flames So long as this superstition exists among them it will be difficult to improve their condition by inducing them to reside in permanent homes, and thus adopt even the first step necessary to their civilization. Occasionally a family evade what they consider the fatal consequence of a death by removing the sufferer before he expires to some outside, temporary hut erected for the purpose. Thus, by adopting an expedient which the agents have taught them, they sometimes save their residences at the cost of the less expensive building, which is always destroyed by fire. The arguments of the agents have no tendency to remove the prejudice and superstitions of the Indians, but simply furnish an expedient which is occasionally resorted to for the purpose of saving their homes from destruction.

In conclusion, I have to state that, after such an investigation of the Indian tribes in Oregon, Washington, and Idaho, as the limited time at my disposal would permit me to make, I am unable to perceive that the system there could be benefited by any general change of policy, excepting such as is incidentally suggested in the foregoing report, which is respectfully submitted.

J. W. NESMITH.

A.

FORT YAMHILL, OREGON, *June* 13, 1865.

SIR : In reply to your request of the 10th instant, I have the honor to inform you that the affairs of this agency, under the present agent, A. Harvey, esq., have, so far as my observation extends, been conducted with a view to the welfare of the Indians and the best interests of the government. The Indians are generally contented, peaceable, and are fast adopting the habits of the white man. They are compelled to sow or plant a small piece of ground, some of them having quite large fields of grain. I would recommend that in the future, if they are kept on this reserve, that they have less blankets, trinkets, and articles of that class issued to them, and they be furnished with farming implements in lieu thereof; in fact, the most of the annuities should be of something of a more substantial character than is usually issued to them. The most of them are supplied with good clothing, which they purchase outside of the reservation, working in the various little towns and on farms with the consent of the agent There are at this time from seven to eight hundred men, women, and children belonging to this reservation. Of this number there are less than three hundred on the reserve at this time.

I consider the selection of this site for an Indian reservation an unfortunate one owing to its proximity to the white settlements, they being less than two miles distant, while the capital of the State is only thirty miles distant. I desire also to state that the number of Indians on this reservation is diminishing very rapidly. This decrease is chiefly owing to the large number of deaths from syphilitic diseases. There are more deaths from this alone than from all other causes. I believe the condition of these Indians would be materially advanced by a removal from here to some place where they would be beyond the immediate influence of that class of white men whose association has a tendency to degrade to a lower depth this already degraded race. The Siletz reservation, distant eighty miles from this post, I believe to be the proper place for them There are now about fifteen hundred Indians on the Siletz reserve, many of whom belong to the same tribes but not under the same chiefs as those on this reserve. I am credibly informed that that reservation is amply large enough to contain five thousand. My own observation induces me to believe that it would support eight or ten thousand. If these Indians on this reserve are removed there, the whole number would be increased to twenty-five hundred. The soil is better adapted to esculents than cereals. The Indian trader there informs me that he purchased of the Indians and shipped to San Francisco over twelve hundred bushels of potatoes last year. By removing the Indians on this reserve to the Siletz it would do away with the whole expense of one agency. It would also reduce the military expense of this post, as the necessity for it would no longer exist. In my opinion the cost of removal would not exceed three thousand dollars. In view of these circumstances, I would recommend that a commission be appointed to treat with these Indians, having for its object their removal to the Siletz reservation

I desire also to state that the military post known as the Siletz block-house, on the Siletz reservation, is a dependency of this post, and is therefore embraced in this command. B. Simpson, esq., is the agent on this reserve. The Indians subsist chiefly on potatoes and fish—salmon—of which there is an endless quantity in the Yaquina and Siletz rivers. The reserve extends to the ocean, which is only a few miles distant. The sanitary condition of these Indians is much better than those at the Grande Ronde agency, there being but little disease of a syphilitic form among them as compared with the others. Before closing I desire to state that my intercourse with the agents of the Grande Ronde and Siletz agencies has been of a friendly character.

I am, sir, very respectfully, your obedient servant,

L. S. SCOTT,
Capt. 4th Cal. Infantry, com'dg post and dependencies.

Hon. J. W. NESMITH,
U. S. Senate, and member of Joint Committee, &c., &c.

B.

ASHLAND MILLS, OREGON, *June* 23, 1865.

DEAR SIR: Yours of June 7, inviting me to give you what information I could in regard to the Indians of southeastern Oregon, having been received, I will now give you what information in regard to them I am able.

The exact number of Indians present at the treaty at Fort Klamath, last autumn, I do not now remember, though I think it was something between eight hundred and one thousand. The superintendent doubtless can give you the exact number.

The Modocs, the country of which tribe lies surrounding Tule and Clear lakes, were not all present at the treaty, but their wishes were expressed by their chiefs who attended the treaty as representatives of the tribe.

Of late years the Lake Indians have been greatly reduced in numbers by their continued wars with the tribes east, so that now I think the aggregate number of Klamaths and Modocs about 1,200 souls, whilst the Indians immediately bordering on their country, viz., the Bonacks, Snakes, and Pitt Rivers, who would in all probability establish themselves on the Klamath reservation if the treaty were carried out, amount to more than twice that number.

Some individuals of the last named tribes have this spring expressed a desire to go on to the Klamath reservation and thus secure the benefits of the treaty, and all of them, I think, with proper management, in a very short time could be induced to leave their own country, to be received upon the reservation, if proper provision were made to care for them. This would clear the country of Indians from Klamath lake to Humboldt on the east, and Snake river on the north, and thus leave open thousands of acres of good country for settlement, and take from the government the expense of hunting those Indians with soldiers, and from travellers the almost certainty of being massacred or robbed in passing through the country not sufficiently prepared for defence.

The importance of carrying out the treaty is evident. Had that treaty been ratified last session, those Indians might have been collected last spring, thus preventing robberies and murders which they are every opportunity committing. You are aware that our 1st Oregon cavalry were all last summer pursuing the Snake Indians bordering on the lakes; but against the Indians acquainted with every mountain recess, and possessing superior means of traversing a rough, mountainous country, they could do but little, and spent the summer in pursuing them, with no success of note, but with the loss of Lieutenant Watson and other brave men.

From what knowledge I have gained by conversation with Klamath Indians and some of the chiefs of the Snakes, who are disposed to give up war and live peaceably with the Klamaths and the whites, I earnestly believe that through the influence of the Klamaths the whole of the Snake tribe could be induced to give up their country and come upon the reservation.

The Klamaths are exceedingly anxious to have the provisions of the treaty put in force, that they may till the soil and "live as the white people live," as they express it; but seeing the tardiness of complying with the promises made at the treaty, they are getting fearful that the authorities will be remiss enough to neglect it altogether.

The district of country decided upon at the treaty for the reservation I consider well adapted for such purpose.

Your obedient, humble servant,

LINDSAY APPLEGATE.

Hon. J. W. NESMITH, *Salem, Oregon.*

C.

TULALIP INDIAN RESERVATION.

SIR: We feel happy and glad to see you coming amongst us, because we all know that the motive which brings you here is for the welfare of all the Indians, and especially for our own good. We have been told that you should like to get all the information possible in order to help us at Washington. I thank God that I am able to express myself on paper, and with the permission of my father, Chirouse, I take the liberty, sir, to address you the following about the past and the present state of our school and the help that we should like to ask from our foster father, the government.

The government made fine promises to us; the whites always give us good advices, and we should like very much to follow them, to become civilized, to live as they want us to live, and do as they tell us to do, but most of these incitements have been mere words, with but very little effective help to us.

I am one of the boys who first came to this school, and I think that I can give a correct account of what has been done. In the beginning, the first three years, we had no other dwelling but the Indian lodges and the poor little cot built by our father, Chirouse. During the same period we had no help of any kind from the department; since that time till now we always had some assistance, but never proportionate to our wants. For instance, at present we have no other clothing but those given to us by the charitable people of the Sound. Let the department furnish us with sufficient implements of husbandry, as plough, wagon, oxen, some milking cows, pigs, &c. Let the provisions that we cannot raise yet be abundant enough to keep us strong and healthy; let us have a seine, so that we may catch enough fish without losing too much time. If not a doctor, at least let us have the medicines required to help our poor health; let a carpenter, blacksmith, and a farmer give us the first principles of these trades so necessary to an Indian to make his own living. Upon leaving the school, to fix our permanent home on the reservation, let the department assist us in building comfortable houses, and furnish us with some of the necessary implements of husbandry, and in that let the government fulfil its generous promises, and then complaints may be deservedly made against us if we do not make in industry the progress that can be expected. I am acquainted with some Klikatute Indians, and according to what they say they have been and are yet far better treated than we are by the American government A large plain has been cleared for them by the Almighty hand; on the contrary, we have to work in a very dense forest. Notwithstanding this, wagons, ploughs, oxen, cows, pigs, and many sheep, clothing, medicines, and everything to make the small number of pupils happy have always been furnished to them, and never to us, as every one in the country is well aware of. Our parents have been and will always be friends to the whites, and for that reason we think we have a right to be trusted and looked on with a kind eye by them. To what concerns our poor sisters, the Indian girls, we have to lament upon their piteous situation; four years ago the Sisters of Charity were promised them to take care of them; but they and we have waited in vain. Every Sunday many little girls come and play around the new house erected for them; they look through the windows, but their mourning eyes never can find those mothers of charity so long expected. Please, Mr. Nesmith, have pity on so many little orphans, and send to them those Sisters of Charity who shall be true mothers to them and save them from ruin. Tell Andrew Johnson, our father at Washington, that the children of the Indians of the Sound, boys and girls, have the feeling of children towards him; and we trust and believe that you will aid the kind efforts of Mr. Waterman in our behalf at Washington, to be looked upon accordingly by him.

Yours respectfully, the schoolboys of Tulalip Indian school,

GEORGE.	JOSEPH.	WILLIAM KERI.	ACHILLES.
MAURICE.	AUGUSTE.	THOMAS S.	THOMAS.
JAMEY.	HILAIRE, 3D.	DAMIENS.	ANDREW.
JUSTIN.	HYACINTHE.	WILLIAM.	WILLSON.
BILL.	VICTORIN.	TULLES.	TULLIUS.
PATRICE.	HILAIRE, 2D.	MARCK.	EDWARD.
PIERRE.	DAILEN.	PETTER.	LOUIS.
HILAIRE.	WILLIAMS.		

Hon. Mr. NESMITH, *United States Senator.*

D

TULALIP INDIAN RESERVATION,
Washington Territory, July —, 1865.

SIR: On my own behalf and that of my schoolmates I extend to you a cordial welcome. Some of us are orphans, and we are very happy to have this opportunity of making our wants known to you.

For the past five years we have been educated in the habits of the whites. We never have been discouraged from the hard work we had to perform on the land owned by the school. Now we can read and write, and we should each like to build a comfortable house and fix our permanent home on the reservation as honest farmers; but at school, notwithstanding our continual labor, we have not been able to make a single cent; we therefore apply to you, as to our father, for some help to get a start in a life of industry. Our kind teacher says that our conduct at school has always been satisfactory, and it makes us hope that you will have pity on us, and be our devoted advocate at Washington. We trust that the proper means may be placed at the disposal of our agent, Mr. Howe, to afford us the help and encouragement we ask.

Your obedient children,

HILAIRE S.	WILLIAM.	WILLIAM.	* PATRICE. ×
AUGUSTE.	DAMIENS.	TULLIUS.	* EDWARD. ×
TULLIS.	VICTORIN.	THOMAS.	* MAURICE. ×
WILLIAM.	ANDREW.	* HILAIRE, 3D. ×	* JUSTIN. ×
THOMAS.	PIERRE.	* HILAIRE, 2D. ×	* JAMEY. ×
ACHILLES.	LOUIS.	* BILL ×	* DAILEN. ×
PETTER.	ANDROW.	* GEORGE. ×	* ALFRED. ×
HYACINTHE.	MARCK.	* JOSEPH. ×	

Hon. Mr. NESMITH, *United States Senator.*

E.

LAPWAI INDIAN AGENCY, I. T., *September* 1, 1865.

SIR: In reply to your kind inquiry, "have any white children attended my school?" there have been altogether eleven (11) white children connected with the school, eight girls and three boys. The average attendance has been seven. The third term in which white children have been in attendance is now in progress, under the charge of Miss O'Neill. I open the school in the morning, and visit it once a day, at one o'clock, to hear the class in geography. Miss O'Neill teaches reading, writing, arithmetic, geography, and spelling.

Miss Spalding teaches the Indians, as we can collect individuals, in reading English, Nez Percés, writing, sewing, and history.

As to the stone church commenced by Governor Lyon, I have to say I know not by what authority he commenced the building, or by what funds he promised to build it. The Indians, to the number of some forty, whom he employed to assist, promising to pay them as soon as the walls were finished, have not been paid, as the governor started early one morning after, not "a wild goose," but wild ducks, and the poor Indians cannot find him. He said he was to build the church to get rid of a "nasty mission claim." He did not consult me as to the place, or the material. The church, which he also called a school-house, is not finished, and the walls are falling down.

As to the "New Lyonsdale," I have to say the whole thing is a disgrace to any man. What I know of it is as follows, to wit:

Some time in August, 1864, Governor Lyon, being at Lapwai, requested me to hire for him two Indians and a canoe to go to Lewiston, and wished me to accompany him. Although quite feeble, I consented. He showed much peevishness and want of sense, and seemed determined to run the canoe on dry land to Lewiston. On reaching Hortwai, six miles from C. agency, he stopped, and walked all over the little bottom, examining it, and stepped upon a little point and said, "This I name New Lyonsdale; this shall be my home; here I will build my dwelling of stone, and over the river I will build a house for you. I have more influence at Washington than any other man. I got my appointment from headquarters. Do not depend upon the Pacific senators. I will get the reservation line, which divides the little bottom, moved up so as to leave the whole bottom outside

---

* These are not able yet to sign.

the reservation; and I will get for you, as an old pioneer, a donation of a section of land, as has been donated to Mr. Craig and many others, a half section here to extend over the river, and a half section opposite Lewiston, and all I will ask for my services is this quarter. Let us see how much the Indians will ask?" The Indians, or rather Noah, agreed to take $150 for that side, and $100 for the opposite side, but wished to see his brother. He did so, and returned to see Governor Lyon next day, and for several times, but the governor was never ready to make the payment.

Respectfully submitted.

H. H. SPALDING.

Senator NESMITH,
Chairman of Committee of Investigation Indian Reservation.

F.

BOISÉ CITY, IDAHO TERRITORY, *September* 14, 1865.

SIR: The Spokane and Cœur d'Alene Indians, in all about 500 to 600, very much like the Nez Percés, cultivate land about the mission, and need a flour and saw mill, and an agent to protect them in their rights from encroachments, and they need farming tools. They reside north of the Nez Percès over 100 miles.

The Nez Percés Indians, numbering about 3,000, are located on their reserve near Lewiston, are peaceable, industrious and quiet, and would be contented if the stipulations of their treaty were carried out, and they were paid their annuities, which has not been done for three years, of which I am cognizant; and I have been requested by that excellent Indian lawyer, their head chief, to urge in their behalf that justice be done them.

In the part of the Territory south and east of Salmon river are about 1,000 Indians somewhat domesticated, straggling about near the settlements, and about 8,000 to 9,000 wandering around in the mountains, obtaining a precarious and scanty subsistence, and make excursions for plunder frequently among settlers. These are the Shoshonees or Snake Indians.

There is a valley about four miles from Boisé City containing about 8,000 acres of good agricultural land surrounded with mountain pasturage for many miles of extent, which would make a good reservation for these Indians, who are disposed generally to work for a living. It would cost, to carry out the design properly, about the same number of employés and amount of appropriation as is provided in the treaty with the Nez Percés, as per treaty of June 11, 1855. Yet it will undoubtedly be most proper to adopt the plan of congregating these Indians upon the reservation, same as at Round valley, in California, and the annuities necessary for their use to be distributed according to the best judgment of some practical and prudent man acting as agent.

The whole Territory is divided into counties by the legislature, all of which, except two at the extreme northern part, are organized and being settled quite fast, which makes it very necessary that prudent and efficient measures be adopted to conciliate these Indians, who are necessarily driven from their hunting-grounds and deprived of their accustomed means of making or getting a sustenance.

Respectfully submitted.

A. L. DOWNER, *Clerk Supreme Court.*

Hon. J. W. NESMITH,
U. S. Senator, en route for Washington, D. C.

G.—*Statement showing the annuity goods purchased in New York and Baltimore in* 1863 *and* 1864, *with prices, with my requisition of* 1863, *in columns in juxtaposition for comparison.*

Name of tribes.	Purchases made in 1863.			Superintendent's requisition dated September 24, 1863.	Amount to be expended.	Purchases made in 1864.		
	When and where purchased.	Articles purchased.	Amount.			When and where purchased.	Articles purchased.	Amo'nt.
Walla-Walla, Cayuse, and Umatillas.	New York, June 24, 1863.	6 pair 3-point scarlet Mackinac blankets, at $11	$66 00	For purchase of harness for ponies	$1,000	New York, May 31, 1864.	1,532 yards unbleached domestic sheeting, at 35 cents	$536 20
		5 pairs 2½-point scarlet Mackinac blankets, at $10	50 00	For small 2-horse steel ploughs	500		3,578 yards Merrimac, at 25 cents	894 50
		3 pairs 3-point indigo Mackinac blankets, at $10 50	31 50	For grain sickles	200		43 yards sand list scarlet cloth, at $2 90	124 70
		4 pairs 2½-point indigo Mackinac blankets, at $8 50	34 00	For assorted tin ware	200		79 yards sand list blue cloth, at $2 75	217 25
		400½ yards checks, stripes, and plaids, at 30 cents	120 15	For blankets	2,500		6½ dozen extra large wool shawls, at $48	312 00
		790½ yards hickory shirting, at 30 cents	237 15	For heavy cotton sheeting	1,000		930½ yards stripes, at 40 cents	372 20
		725 yards ticking, at 40 cents	290 00	For woollen linsey	800		400 yards ticking, at 50 cents	200 00
		1,859½ yards calico, Merrimac, at 22 cents	409 09	For Merrimac prints	800		40 pounds cotton thread, at $1 50	60 00
		1,098½ yards brown sheeting, at 25 cents	274 63	For scarlet cloth	200		9 pounds sewing thread, at $2	18 00
		27 pounds cotton thread, at 60 cents	16 20	For blue cloth	200		3 G. G. buttons, at $4 50	13 50
		332½ yards heavy twilled, mixed jeans, at 60 cents	199 50	For woollen shawls, small	500		Baling	26 65
		600 yards brown cotton duck, at 40 cents	240 00	For thread, buttons, needles, &c	100	Baltimore. No date.	5 thousand needles, assorted, at $3	15 00
		2 G. G. buttons, $9; 2 thousand needles, $4	13 00				48 dozen knitting pins, at 25 cents	12 00
		1 pair wrappers, $4; baling, $14 78	18 78				14 dozen 6-quart pans, at $6	84 00
	Baltimore, June, 1863.	25 dozen 4 quart pans, at $2	50 00				20 dozen 2-quart pans, at $1 75	35 00
		30 dozen tin cups, at 80 cents	24 00				60 tin kettles, at 83 cents	49 80
		250 dozen fish-hooks, at 5 cents	12 50				20 dozen tin cups, at 90 cents	18 00
		62 dozen fish-lines, at 20 cents	12 40				Packages, strapping, and cartage	11 20
		50 dozen scissors, at $1	50 00					
		33 dozen shears, at $1 50	49 50					
		8 dozen black handle butcher knives, extra, at $6	48 00					
		4 dozen fancy mirrors, extra, at $5	20 00					
		6 dozen steel weeding hoes, (handled,) extra, at $8	48 00					

G.—*Statement showing the annuity goods purchased in New York and Baltimore, &c.*—Continued.

Name of tribes.	Purchases made in 1863.			Superintendent's requisition dated September 24, 1863.	Amount to be expended.	Purchases made in 1864.		
	When and where purchased.	Articles purchased.	Amount.			When and where purchased.	Articles purchased.	Amo'nt.
Walla-Walla, Cayuse, and Umatillas—Continued.	Baltimore, June, 1863.	228 fry pans, at 22 cents	$50 10					
		168 dozen iron table spoons, at 25 cents	42 00					
		6 dozen light chopping axes, extra, with handles, at $12	72 00					
		Packing, strapping, cartage, &c	21 50					
			2,500 00		$8,000			$3,000 00
Confederated tribes and bands in middle Oregon.	New York, June 24, 1863.	6 pairs 3-point scarlet Mackinac blankets, at $11	66 00	For Salem blankets	2,000	New York, May 31, 1864.	3,591 yards Merrimac calico, at 25 cents	897 75
		5 pairs 2½-point scarlet Mackinac blankets, at $10 50	50 00	For Merrimac prints	800		1,575 yards unbleached domestic sheeting, at 35 cents	551 25
		3 pairs 3-point indigo Mackinac blankets, at $10 50	31 50	For brown sheeting	1,000		1,258 yards blue denims, at 36 cents	452 88
		2 pairs 2½-point indigo Mackinac blankets, at $8 50	17 00	For blue denims	500		50 pounds cotton thread, at $1 50	75 00
		427½ yards checks, stripes, and plaids, at 30 cents	128 25	For thread, linen, and cotton, assorted	100		9 pounds linen thread, at $2	18 00
		1,074 yards hickory shirting, at 30 cents	322 20	For assorted needles	50		693 yards stripes, at 40 cents	277 20
		769½ yards ticking, at 40 cents	307 80	For assorted buttons	50		395½ yards ticking, at 20 cts	197 75
		1,897 yards calico, Merrimac, at 22 cents	417 34	For knitting pins, assorted	25		10 G. gross buttons, at $4 50	45 00
		1,016 yards brown sheeting, at 25 cents	254 00	For shawls, assorted	200		2½ dozen extra large wool shawls, at $48	108 00
		333 yards heavy twilled, mixed jeans, at 60 cents	199 80	For tobacco	300		Baling	27 17
		400 yards brown cotton duck, at 40 cents	160 00	For matches	60	Baltimore, June 2, 1864.	17 thousand needles, assorted, at $3	51 00
		27 pounds cotton thread, at 60 cents	16 20	For teams, (oxen)	1,600		100 dozen knitting pins, at 25 cents	25 00
		2 G. G. buttons, $9; 2 thousand needles, $4	13 00	For chains	100		21 kegs nails, at $8	168 00
		1 pair wrappers	4 00	For nails, 6*d*, 8*d*, and 10*d*	200		3½ dozen polished cast steel spades, at $14 50	50 75
		Baling	12 91	For spades, Ames's med. sizes	50		4 dozen handled axes, extra, at $15	60 00
	Baltimore, June, 1863.	25 dozen 4 quart pans, at $2	50 00	For ploughs, small, strong, 2 horses, steel	400		5 dozen extra strong hoes, at $10	50 00
		30 dozen tin cups, at 80 cents	24 00	For harness, strong, plain, and cheap, suitable for small ponies	400		Packing, strapping, cartage, &c	20 25
		8 dozen black handle butcher knives, extra, at $6	48 00	For axes	50	New York, May 25, 1864.	4 boxes lump tobacco, 416 pounds, at 75 cents	312 00
				For grain cradles	65		Cartage	25
				For hoes, strong	50			

		500 dozen fish-hooks, at 5 cts.	25 00					
		125 dozen fish-lines, at 20 cts.	25 00					
		50 dozen scissors, at $1	50 00					
		33 dozen shears, at $1 50	49 50					
		3 dozen fancy mirrors, extra, at $5	15 00					
		6 dozen steel weeding hoes, (handled,) extra, at $8	48 00					
		228 fry pans, at 22 cents	50 10					
		168 dozen iron table spoons, at 25 cents	42 00					
		10 dozen half axes, at $5	50 00					
		Packing, strapping, cartage, &c	23 40					
			2,500 00		8,000			3,387 25
Callapooias, Molallas, and Clackamas.	New York, June 24, 1863.	2 pairs 3-point scarlet Mackinac blankets, at $11	22 00	For blankets	2,500	New York, May 31, 1864.	478 yards heavy red twilled flannel, at 65 cents	310 70
		5 pairs 2½-point scarlet Mackinac blankets, at $10	50 00	For woollen cloth (heavy) for coats and pants	600		2¼ dozen extra large shawls, at $48	108 00
		6 pairs 3-point indigo Mackinac blankets, at $10 50	63 00	For flannel, gray, coarse, and heavy	300		1,195 yards Merrimac calico, at 25 cents	298 75
		5 pairs 2½-point indigo Mackinac blankets, at $8 50	42 50	For linsey, $200; calico, Merrimac, $300	500		741 yards heavy brown sheeting, at 35 cents	259 35
		391½ yards checks, stripes, and plaids, at 30 cents	117 45	For shawls, small, woollen	200		259 yards stripes, at 40 cents	103 60
		1,097 yards hickory shirting, at 30 cents	329 10	For unbleached sheeting	300		50 yards ticking, at 50 cents	25 00
		719½ yards ticking, at 40 cents	287 80	For yarn	50		18 pounds linen thread, at $2	36 00
		1,959 yards calico, Merrimac, at 22 cents	430 98	For linen, thread, buttons, needles, and knitting pins, assorted	100		7 pounds cotton thread, at $1 50	10 50
		1,012 yards brown sheeting, at 25 cents	253 00	For shoes for men and women, coarse	200		6 G. gross buttons, at $4 50	27 00
		331½ yards heavy twilled mixed jeans, at 60 cents	198 90	For hats for men, coarse wool	100		70 pairs men's brogans, at $1 65	115 50
		400 yards brown cotton duck, at 40 cents	160 00	For harness, small, cheap, and suitable for ponies	500		60 pairs women's shoes, at $1 45	87 00
		28 pounds cotton thread, at 60 cents	16 80	For grain cradles	100		3 dozen hats, at $25	75 00
		2 G. gross buttons, $9; 2 thousand needles, $4	13 00	For cut nails, 6*d*, 8*d*. and 10*d*	100		Baling	18 60
		1 pair wrappers	4 00	For mowing scythes and sheaths	50	May 25, 1864	1 box lump tobacco, 105 lbs., at 75 cents	78 75
		Baling	11 47	For hoes, strong	50		Cartage	25
	Baltimore, June, 1863.	25 dozen 4-quart pans, at $2	50 00	For spades, Ames's cast steel	50	Baltimore, June 2, 1864.	5 thousand needles, at $3	15 00
		30 dozen tin cups, at 80 cents	24 00	For hay forks	25		48 dozen knitting pins, at 25 cents	12 00
		8 dozen black handle butcher knives, extra, at $6	48 00	For camp kettles, iron, tin pans, 4 and 6 quarts, and tin cups	100		8 kegs nails, at $8	64 00
		50 dozen scissors, at $1	50 00	For grain sickles, $50; axes, $75	125		5 dozen extra strong hoes, at $10	50 00
		33 dozen shears, at $1 50	49 50	For ploughs, small, strong, steel, 2-horse	250		3 dozen polished cast steel spades, at $14 50	43 50
		2 dozen fancy mirrors, extra, at $5	10 00	For cows and heifers	375		2 dozen cast steel pronged hay forks, at $12 50	25 00
				For ox teams	1,200		6 nests iron kettles, assorted, at $8 50	51 00
				For chains, $75; tobacco, $75	150		4 dozen 4-quart pans, at $2 25	9 00

G.—*Statement showing the annuity goods purchased in New York and Baltimore, &c.*—Continued.

Name of tribes.	Purchases made in 1863.			Superintendent's requisition dated September 24, 1863.	Amount to be expended.	Purchases made in 1864.		
	When and where purchased.	Articles purchased.	Amount.			When and where purchased.	Articles purchased.	Amo'nt.
Callapooias, Molallas, and Clackamas—Continued.	Baltimore, June, 1863.	10 dozen steel weeding hoes, (handled,) extra, at $8	$80 00	For butcher knives	$50	Baltimore, June 2, 1864.	7 dozen 6-quart pans, at $6	$42 00
		228 fry pans, at 22 cents	50 10	For matches	25		10 dozen tin cups, at 90 cents	9 00
		168 dozen iron table spoons, at 25 cents	42 00				5 dozen grain sickles, at $10	50 00
		6 dozen light chopping axes, (handled,) at $12	72 00				4 dozen handled axes, extra, at $15	60 00
		Packing, strapping, cartage, &c	24 40				20 dozen butcher knives, at $3 50	70 00
							Packing, strapping, cartage, &c	24 50
			2, 500 00		8, 000			2, 079 00

G.—*Statement showing the annuity goods purchased in New York and Baltimore, &c.*—Continued.

Name of tribes.	Superintendent's requisition dated September 24, 1863.	Amount to be expended.	Purchases made in 1864.		
			When and where purchased.	Articles purchased.	Amount.
Umpquas and Callapoolas of Umpqua Valley.	For blankets	$500 00	New York, May 31, 1864	365 yards Merrimac calico, at 25 cents	$91 25
	For woollen cloth, heavy, for pants and coats	300 00		168 yards unbleached domestic sheeting, at 35 cents	58 80
	For linsey	150 00		20 pounds linen thread, at $2	40 00
	For flannel, coarse gray	100 00		13 pounds cotton thread, at $1 50	19 50
	For calico, Merrimac	100 00		15 pairs men's brogans, at $1 65	24 75
	For brown sheeting	100 00		10 pairs women's shoes, at $1 45	14 50
	For shoes for men and women, coarse	50 00		2 dozen hats, at $25	50 00
	For hats for men, coarse	50 00		145½ yards stripes, at 40 cents	58 20
	For stocking yarn, linen thread, knitting needles, needles, &c	80 00		Baling	3 00
	For harness, small and cheap, suitable for ponies	150 00	Baltimore, June 2, 1864	3.000 needles, assorted, at $3	9 00
	For cut-nails, *6d*, *8d*, and *10d*	50 00		48 dozen knitting pins, at 25 cents	12 00
	For axes, $25; matches, $20; hoes, $25	70 00		5 kegs nails, at $8	40 00
	For ox teams	600 00		2 dozen handled axes, extra, at $15	30 00
				2½ dozen extra strong hoes, at $10	25 00
				Packing, strapping, cartage, &c	4 00
	Total	2, 300 00		Total	480 00

Umpquas, (Cow-Creek band.)	For blankets	250 00	New York, May 31, 1864	165 yards unbleached domestic sheeting, at 35 cents	57 75
	For brown sheeting	100 00		411 yards Merrimac calico, at 25 cents	102 75
	For calico, Merrimac	100 00		15 pairs men's brogans, at $1 65	24 75
	For shoes for men and women, heavy	50 00		10 pairs women's shoes, at $1 45	14 50
	For nails, 6*d*, 8*d*, and 10*d*	50 00		118 yards stripes, at 40 cents	47 20
				Baling	3 05
			Baltimore, June 2, 1864	6 kegs nails, at $8	48 00
				Cartage	2 00
	Total	550 00		Total	300 00
Shasta, Scotons, and Umpquas.	For blankets	500 00	New York, May 31, 1864	741 yards Merrimac calico, at 25 cents	185 25
	For heavy gray flannel for shirts	200 00		287 yards unbleached domestic sheeting, at 35 cents	100 45
	For woollen yarn	50 00		156 yards stripes, at 40 cents	62 40
	For calico, Merrimac	200 00		6 lbs. linen thread, $12; 10 lbs. cotton thread, $15	27 00
	For unbleached sheeting, heavy	100 00		3 G. gross buttons, at $4 50	13 50
	For linen thread, buttons, knitting needles, and needles	50 00		25 pairs men's brogans, at $1 65	41 25
				20 pairs women's shoes, at $1 45	29 00
	For shoes, men and women, heavy	75 00		Baling	6 15
	For nails, 6*d*, 8*d*, and 10*d*	75 00	New York, May 25, 1864	33 lbs. lump tobacco, 75 cts., $24 75; cartage, 25 cts	25 00
	For axes	50 00	Baltimore, June 2, 1864	7 kegs nails, $8, $56; 2,000 needles, assorted, $3, $6	62 00
	For ox teams	500 00		16 dozen knitting pins, at 25 cents	4 00
	For chains	50 00		4 dozen handled axes, extra, at $15	60 00
	For butcher knives	25 00		7 dozen butcher knives, at $3 50	24 50
	For watches	25 00		2¼ dozen extra strong hoes, at $10	25 00
	For tobacco	25 00		Packing, strapping, cartage, &c	9 50
	For hoes, strong	25 00			
	Total	2,000 00		Total	675 00
Rogue River Indians	For blankets	500 00	New York, May 31, 1864	742 yards Merrimac calico, at 25 cents	185 50
	For woollen cloth, heavy, for coats and pants	200 00		369 yards unbleached domestic sheeting, at 35 cents	129 15
	For gray flannel, heavy	200 00		45 yards ticking, at 50 cents, $22 50; 152½ yards stripes, at 40 cents, $61	83 50
	For calico, Merrimac	200 00			
	For sheeting, unbleached, heavy	200 00		8 lbs. linen thread, $16; 10 lbs. cotton thread, $15	31 00
	For woollen yarn, coarse	50 00		3 G. gross buttons, $13 50; 25 pairs men's brogans, at $1 65. $41 25	54 75
	For linen thread, buttons, needles, &c	50 00			
	For shoes, men and women, heavy	75 00		20 pairs women's shoes, at $1 45, $29; baling, $6 10	35 10
	For nails, 6*d*, 8*d*, 10*d*, $75; axes, $50	125 00	New York, May 25, 1864	33 lbs. lump tobacco, 75 cts., $24 75; cartage, 25 cts	25 00
	For ox teams, $500; chains, $50	550 00	Baltimore, June 2, 1864	7 kegs nails, at $8	56 00
	For butcher knives, $25; matches, $25	50 00		4 dozen handled axes, extra, at $15	60 00
	For tobacco, $25; hoes, strong, $25	50 00		7 dozen butcher knives, at $3 50	24 50
	For cows and heifers	250 00		2½ dozen extra strong hoes, at $10	25 00
				Packing, strapping, cartage, &c	9 50
	Total	2,500 00		Total	719 00

THE CHIVINGTON MASSACRE.

WASHINGTON, *Tuesday, March* 7, 1865.

Samuel G. Colley sworn and examined.

By Mr. DOOLITTLE:

Question. What is your age?
Answer. I was fifty-seven last December.
Question. Are you agent for the Cheyennes and Arapahoes?
Answer. I am.
Question. How long have you acted as such?
Answer. My commission dates from July, 1861. I filed my bonds October, 1861.
Question. When did you go upon the ground where they are located?
Answer. I went upon the ground in August, 1861.
Question. Have you been in charge of those Indians, as agent, ever since?
Answer. I have.
Question. State in brief terms about where they are located.
Answer. Their reservation commences at a point fifteen miles south of Fort Lyon; thence up the Arkansas river north to a point on the north bank of the Arkansas, some twenty-five miles above Fort Lyon; it then runs down till it strikes the old line of New Mexico, follows that line due north till it intersects a certain line described in the treaty, thence north till it strikes Sand creek, thence down Sand creek to the place of beginning, including the fort. The reservation is in the form of a triangle.
Question. Have the Arapahoes a reservation adjoining the Cheyennes?
Answer Yes; the tract which I have described is divided in two, half for the Cheyennes and half for the Arapahoes, the Cheyennes taking the west part of it.
Question. About how many of those Cheyennes are there, according to your best estimate?
Answer. I have enumerated them as well as I could. We have had, when I have given them some presents, between 200 and 300 lodges of Cheyennes there at a time, and something over 200 lodges of Arapahoes. There is another band that were not satisfied with the treaty who ran north of the Platte and have never come down there to mingle with these Indians much. Some of them may have been on the reservation, but they do not claim that as their reservation; they claim land north.
Question. Are those Cheyennes or Arapahoes?
Answer. A band of each.
Question. Do the Cheyennes and Arapahoes, any of them, live in houses?
Answer. No; they live wild.
Question. Do they have any kind of tents or skins, or anything of that sort, for shelter?
Answer. They build a tent of buffalo skins on lodge poles, very much like a Sibley tent.
Question. They move about from place to place?
Answer. Yes; they move about; wherever the game goes they go.
Question. They are nomadic?
Answer. Entirely so. They break up into parties of twenty or thirty.
Question. What was the occasion of the recent difficulty between our people and the Cheyennes and Arapahoes?
Answer. It commenced early last spring on the Platte. There was a collision there between the Indians and the soldiers. I am not able to say which party was the aggressor; the claim there is differently made, the Indians claiming one way and the soldiers the other.
Question. Was there much fighting then?
Answer. Not much fighting; they were small parties. I think Major Downing went out first and destroyed a few lodges, and killed one man and took some of their ponies. I heard immediately that there had been a fight there, and knowing that it is very difficult to keep one party of Indians from fighting when their brethren are at it, I went 240 miles to find the Arapahoes and Cheyennes. I found the former, and explained as well as I could that there had been trouble between some soldiers and Indians, and asked them if they knew anything about the cause of it. They said they did not; they had not heard of it. They told me at that time that they did not want any trouble with the whites; that if there had been trouble over there they were not to blame for it. They called those Indians that ran north their dog soldiers. They did not pretend to have much control over them. They pledged me solemnly that if the whites would not follow them up and fight them they would remain peaceable and quiet. Coming back I met a party of Cheyennes and told them the same. They said they would go over towards the Platte and get those Indians in, and get them away. I told them to go over on the Arkansas, their country, and if they behaved them-

selves they should be protected as far as I could protect them. The very day that I saw them there another party of soldiers came out from Denver, some of the first Colorado regiment, that were sent out by Colonel Chivington, I suppose, and they followed up these Indians some 200 miles, and came in collision with them over on Smoky Hill, in the buffalo country. They had quite a fight there, the Indians claiming that they were attacked, and the soldiers claiming that they were attacked. I do not know how that was. One of their main chiefs was killed at that time. After that there were depredations committed.

Question. By the Indians upon the whites?

Answer. Yes; they came up to work the reservation. Some parties came up, drove in the stock of the contractor, killed two of his men. We supposed at that time the Indians were united against us that the whole country was going to be at war, and they would unite. Previous to this, however, some Sioux Indians had been laboring with the Cheyennes and Arapahoes to get them to join them, but they disclaimed any idea of it. I got a circular from Governor Evans, in June, requesting me to send out runners and invite all friendly Indians of the Cheyennes and Arapahoes who belonged to the southern bands, as he called them, and to my band, into Fort Lyon, and there feed and protect them. I did so. I sent out one particular Indian who remained there all the while, only as I sent him out. I sent out my interpreter. I sent out Colonel William Bent, who has a wife, a Cheyenne squaw. He has been in that country thirty or forty years. He came back, and said that he had seen Black Kettle, the head chief of the Cheyennes, and that they had promised to come in; that they did not want any trouble; were willing to cease hostilities and get all the war parties in that were out and would come up. In the last of September the one-eyed Indian whom I had sent out came in. He said the Indians had three or four white prisoners with them whom they wanted to give up, and if we would go out we could get them. Major Wynkoop went out with a command of 100 men, had an interview with them, brought in their main chief, and brought in four prisoners whom they had, one young lady and three children. They expressed a desire to be friendly. Major Wynkoop went to Denver, took them up to Governor Evans, and had an interview; I was not present. They came back again; they went out to their lodges towards Smoky Hill; brought in about 100 lodges of Cheyennes, and about the same number of Arapahoes came into Fort Lyon; and Major Wynkoop issued them half rations for a time. Soon General Curtis relieved Major Wynkoop, ordered him to report to headquarters at Leavenworth or Fort Riley, I am not sure which, and placed Major Anthony in command, with orders to fight these Indians; that there could be no peace until they were chastised, as I understood the order. Major Anthony came up, looked the matter over, and said, "It is different from what I expected here; I supposed these Indians were riding in here making demands, and you were obliged to give in to them. I cannot fight them." He called a council of them. He told them what his orders were, and told them he wanted them to give up their arms and their stolen horses. They came in in about two hours, having seen their tribes, and gave up their bows and arrows and perhaps four or five field guns, and a dozen or fifteen government horses and mules; and he fed them for fifteen days, I think, on prisoners' rations. He considered them his prisoners and gave them prisoners' rations. This continued for some days. Not hearing from General Curtis he got a little afraid, and told them to go down to Sand creek until he heard from General Curtis. They were in frequently; Black Kettle was in three days before the attack, and Major Anthony and I made up a purse and bought tobacco for them, thinking it was better to keep them peaceable. We had them right there, and there was no use going to fight those Indians at that time, as they were friendly. There they remained till Colonel Chivington came down with his regiment.

Question. When was that?

Answer. It was the 28th of November, 1864, I think.

By Mr. Nesmith:

Question. How many of the Indians were there, and did the number embrace both Cheyennes and Arapahoes?

Answer. About one-half of each tribe were there.

Question. Where were the rest?

Answer. They were, I suppose, on Smoky Hill—I know some of them were—and scattered around through the country.

Question. Were any still up on the emigrant route on the Platte?

Answer. I suppose there might have been some on the Platte. We did not know that Colonel Chivington was coming there until the morning he came in. We had had no mail from Denver for over three weeks, I think. We did not know what trouble there was, and were afraid the Indians had gone off and cut off the settlements above. The evening before he came in some one came down and said he had seen some camp-fires above, and he thought they were the Kioway Indians. He knew they were not our Indians, for if they were they would have come to see him. He came down and reported to the major that camp-fires were there, and he was fearful the Kioway Indians had come in. The major sent out scouts and found that it was Colonel Chivington's command coming from Denver. He came in in the morning, and that evening marched for their camp at 8 o'clock. The results I do not know personally. I was not there.

Question. In the mean time did any orders come from General Curtis?

Answer. Not that I know of. I did ask Colonel Chivington that night if there was no hope that peace could be made with these Indians. He informed me that General Curtis had telegraphed him that it might be done on certain conditions; that is to say, they should deliver up property they had stolen, make restitution in ponies for those they had not got, and deliver up their desperadoes who had been making raids.

By Mr. Doolittle:

Question. You think about one-half of the Cheyennes and one-half of the Arapahoes were there in camp?

Answer. Yes, sir.

Question. Of these, what proportion were of their warriors?

Answer. I should think an equal portion of their warriors were with them.

By Mr. Ross:

Question. Half of the warriors of the two tribes?

Answer. I should think there were. So far as I know, the young men of the bands who were with them were there. There were warriors, and women and children too.

By Mr. Doolittle:

Question. The warriors belonging to these particular bands were not away?

Answer. Not to my knowledge. The other Indians, those who were away, were away with their families.

Question. Do they always take their women and children with them?

Answer. Not always. They leave their women and children when they go out on a war expedition. They were encamped at that time about eighty miles from the others on the Smoky Hill, in the buffalo country.

By Mr. Hubbard:

Question. When they go on a hunt, do they take their squaws and children?

Answer. They move their squaws and children to the buffalo country when they go to hunt. When they go on a war party they leave them behind.

By Mr. Ross:

Question. When you speak of a lodge, you mean a family?

Answer. Yes; a lodge will contain five on an average. We call a lodge five souls.

By Mr. Nesmith:

Question. Do you know anything about the attack?

Answer. I was not there. I only know what I heard from officers who were there.

Question. How did you regard those Indians who were in that encampment?

Answer. I regarded them as at that time friendly.

Question. What had been their conduct previous to that? Had they been murdering settlers, and robbing, and committing depredations?

Answer. These Cheyennes had not. They might have had some among them that had been.

Question. Colonel Chivington spoke to you of some desperadoes among the Indians; did you know of any of that character there?

Answer. I did not know of any of that character. There might have been some who were out with the Arapahoes. It was said there had been some there that were out.

Question. Was it your understanding that they made restitution of all stolen property prior to the attack?

Answer. The Arapahoes said they gave up all their government property. I think they had property belonging to citizens which they did not give up.

Question. Did they give up all their arms?

Answer. I am not able to say. I think it is doubtful whether they did. We did not think, at the time, that they did give up all their arms.

Question. How many guns did they give up?

Answer. But very few. They had not many guns. I thought they had more guns than they brought in and gave up.

By Mr. HUBBARD :

Question. Even if these desperate Indians were there among them, you would hardly have known it yourself?

Answer. No ; I did not know who were there, only as the chiefs informed me.

By Mr. NESMITH :

Question. Were those Indians, who gave up the young lady and three children, in that encampment?

Answer. One was there and was killed. The other was in the employ of the government at the time.

Question. Do you know that young lady's name?

Answer. Ropers.

By Mr. DOOLITTLE :

Question. Did any facts come to your knowledge as to the attack?

Answer. I have heard all the officers repeat it who were there.

Question. Give the current version.

Answer. I can state, according to the received version, that the command marched at 8 o'clock in the evening from Fort Lyon. They attacked the village, which was 30 miles distant, and fired into it about daylight. The Indians, for a while, made some resistance. Some of the chiefs did not lift an arm, but stood there and were shot down. One of them, Black Kettle, raised the American flag, and raised a white flag. He was supposed to be killed, but was not. They retreated right up the creek. They were followed up and pursued and killed and butchered. None denied that they were butchered in a brutal manner, and scalped and mutilated as bad as an Indian ever did to a white man. That is admitted by the parties who did it. They were cut to pieces in almost every manner and form.

Question. How many were killed there, according to the reports?

Answer. I will tell you how I got my information. There was a young half-breed who had been in Kansas. He had been educated here, and came out last summer, for the first time in a good many years, to the Indians. He had been about Fort Lyon a good portion of the summer When the command came down there, my first impulse was to get him to go up and tell these Indians that the troops were coming up there and might attack them, but he had gone, the day before, out to their camp He made an attempt to reach the command when they began to fire, but was deterred, fell back and jumped on to a pony, behind a squaw, and rode till he overhauled a drove of ponies that they were driving off. He rode with them to the camp and was with them 14 days after they got together on Smoky Hill. He said there were 148 missing when they got in. After that quite a number came in ; I cannot tell how many. There were eight who came into Fort Lyon to us, reducing it down to about 130 missing, according to the last information I had.

By Mr. NESMITH :

Question. Were you on the ground after the battle?

Answer. I was not.

By Mr. DOOLITTLE :

Question. Did you understand that any women or children were killed?

Answer. The officers told me they killed and butchered all they came to. They saw little papooses killed by the soldiers. Colonel Shupe was in command of the regiment ; Colonel Chivington in command of the whole force.

By Mr. ROSS :

Question. Who commanded the troops when this massacre took place?

Answer. Colonel Chivington was in chief command.

By Mr. HIGBY :

Question. Who was in immediate command of the party where the butchery took place? Who led the expedition?

Answer. Colonel Chivington led the expedition. I do not think there was anybody in command ; the soldiers appear to have pitched in without any command.

By Mr. NESMITH :

Question. What troops were they, and where were they raised?

Answer. They were the one-hundred-day regiment raised in Denver, with a portion of the first Colorado regiment. The one hundred-day men were Shupe's command as immediate colonel ; Chivington was colonel of the first regiment, and took command of the whole force.

By Mr. DOOLITTLE:

Question. As you learned, was it the first Colorado regiment that joined in this massacre, or was it the one-hundred-day men that were raised?

Answer. Officers of the first regiment told me they did not fire a gun, and would not or could not; some of their soldiers undoubtedly did.

Question. Were the men who actually made a rush on the village the one-hundred-day men?

Answer. That was so understood.

By Mr. ROSS:

Question. Do I understand you that the officers had nothing to do with it?

Answer. I was told by the officers that Colonel Chivington told the men to remember the wrongs the Indians had inflicted on the whites and to pitch in, and they just went at it pell-mell; forty of our troops were killed and wounded; fourteen died. The Indians would get their families ahead of them and then they would fall back, fighting as they went.

By Mr. DOOLITTLE:

Question. What about the property?

Answer. From five hundred to six hundred ponies were said to be brought in, having been taken from the Indians, and their whole property was destroyed and they left perfectly destitute without hardly even their clothing.

By Mr. NESMITH:

Question. Did you see any of the property brought in?

Answer. Yes, sir.

Question. What did it consist of?

Answer. It consisted of ponies principally, and Indian dresses, and the fixings natural about those wild Indians. They make their dresses out of skins and bead them off very nicely. The dresses were sold for from twenty to thirty dollars the dress.

Question. Was any of this property recognized as property stolen from the whites?

Answer. There were one or two things I saw that I knew had been stolen.

Question. Was any of the other property recognized as stolen property?

Answer. I saw a horse or two and a mule or two that were branded other brands than Indians'. Those Indians pick up a great many horses there, and sometimes they bring them in, but sometimes they do not. When they steal a horse their usual custom is to trade it right off to somebody else.

Question. Were there any Mexican dollars among that property?

Answer I do not know anything about that; I did not see any; they might have had some; I do not know. It must be a mistake to suppose, as has been said, that there were as many Mexican dollars as a mule could carry.

By Mr. DOOLITTLE:

Question. What is the condition of those tribes now?

Answer. I have not been able to see any of them, but this young man says they are all imbittered against the whites. He says that Black Kettle, the leading chief, laughed at him when he went out; said to him, "You are an old fool; you ought to have stood and been shot down as the rest of us" He made a great deal of fun of him for coming out there and coming under our protection. Two or three of their war councils said they had agreed first to strike the Platte and clean that out, and then strike towards Denver. They told him he had better leave the country there and get home as soon as possible, and furnished him a horse in the night to come home. This was the half-breed who was out this summer, of whom I have spoken.

By Mr. NESMITH:

Question. What was his name?

Answer. Edward Guerrier; and Major Wynkoop has his statement in writing, and I suppose it has been forwarded to the War Department.

By Mr. DOOLITTLE:

Question. What there is left of the tribe that escaped has gone north on to the Platte?

Answer. I suppose so.

By Mr. ROSS:

Question. Is that outside of the reservation?

Answer. Yes, sir; these Indians have not been on the reservation much; they only come in and see us; there is no camp there; they cannot live there; they have to go out and hunt, for in that country there is no settlement between the Platte and the Arkansas, and none for two hundred and forty miles below us on the Arkansas, and none south of the Platte from us, clear to Texas; it is a buffalo country; they roam there in bands and hunt and come into the agency two or three times a year.

By Mr. DOOLITTLE:

Question. What do you say of the reservation which has been set apart for the Arapahoes and Cheyennes?

Answer. I think we can never get them on to it again; they were killed there on it, and they are superstitious. The reservation is the best tract of land we have in Colorado for agricultural purposes, I think.

By Mr. ROSS:

Question. How is it as to hunting and game?

Answer. There is no hunting there and no game on it, only a few animals. No buffalo have been seen there for three or four years.

By Mr. DOOLITTLE:

Question. From your knowledge of the Arapahoes and Cheyennes and their character, do you think they can be brought to settle down and live a life of agriculture?

Answer. I do not think the present generation can, to any extent. Some few of them want to come in and live with the whites, but as a general thing they are opposed to settling down. They say their fathers hunted, lived, and roamed over the country; the country was all theirs, and they had plenty, but the white man has come and taken it. I think they have gone north now with their families toward the Yellowstone.

Question Have you an idea that they are uniting with the Sioux?

Answer. I think they are. The Sioux undoubtedly have been wanting them to unite the last two years. They have told me so. They have always disclaimed it and said they would not. They said they did not want to fight; the whites treated them well, and there was no use of their fighting. After the first fight of which I have spoken, they told me that if the whites let them alone they would be peaceable; that there was no object in fighting; but still they said there were young men in the party whom they could not control, which is the fact. The better portion of them cannot control all the young warriors, who are somewhat a political class of men and who make their capital out of their bravery, and if they have no Indians to fight they will fight somebody else.

By Mr. ROSS:

Question. I understood you to say that before this massacre there was a collision, and you could not tell which party commenced it; do you not know who shed blood first?

Answer. I heard officers there say that the Indians commenced it; and I heard others say they did not. I do not know. The Indians say they did not. They said they disarmed it; they came up and shook hands, and took their arms away, and that is like taking their life. That is their notion of it.

By Mr. DOOLITTLE:

Question. How many were in the camp that was attacked?

Answer. About 500. There were only a few lodges of the Arapahoes that were attacked, and before Chivington got there with his command they heard from those who escaped and got away. Only a few of the Arapahoes that were camped with the Cheyennes were attacked—eight lodges. Part of them have now escaped and gone to the Kioways and Comanches, south of Arkansas.

Question. Have you any other statement to make?

Answer. There was a good deal of misunderstanding among us there. At one time we supposed the Indians were all against us, and expected that they were. Indians would come in and try to get into the camp and see us, and see what was the matter, and after we got them in we learned these facts. An Indian whom I had two years ago, who speaks English, rode up to Fort Lyon, and he saw a soldier; he hallooed to that soldier and said he wanted to see Major Colley. He wanted to know what the fighting all meant, and to make peace. The soldier reported that he had been chased by an Indian and saw a number of others. We supposed they were coming to commit depredations and sent a command after them, who overhauled them, and got near enough to fire into them, but not near enough to hurt them. Since he has come in he has told me that he is the Indian who came there to throw down his bow and arrow and talk to me. We did not understand, and supposed he was coming with hostile designs. Then there is another thing. The people of Colorado are very much down on the Indians. As a general thing they want their land They are coming in contact universally with them. If they take anything to make a fire with, a conflict grows up. My opinion is that white men and wild Indians cannot live in the same country in peace.

Question. Are there any of the Indians in Colorado that you know who can be induced to live on and cultivate the soil?

Answer. I do not know much about the Utes. There is a tribe of Utes over there that I know nothing about. They are west of me in the mountains. I do not know whether they would cultivate the soil or not.

Question. But you think it would be next to impossible to get this generation of these Indians of the plains to settle down to cultivate the soil?

Answer. I do. They will stay with you if you feed them all the time, and there will be no trouble; but they will not work. The squaws do all their work that is done.

Question. Do the squaws of these nomadic tribes raise any corn or anything?

Answer. They do not raise anything. They depend on the buffalo. That is their great staple.

Question. What vegetables, if any, do they eat?

Answer. They like corn in any way, but they do not raise any. They are fond of pumpkins and potatoes; they will eat them when you give them to them, but they never raise anything. We attempted to get them to work on the reservation. We laid out a good deal of money in getting a farmer there last spring, and the crops looked very fine until this trouble broke out.

Question. How do you cultivate the crops there on the reservation; by irrigation?

Answer. By irrigation. We had 250 acres broken in corn on the Arkansas.

Question Is it a country where you have no rains during the summer season?

Answer. It rains in July. There are showers almost every day for a month.

Question. Cannot the country be cultivated without irrigation?

Answer. No, sir. Last season wheat might have been raised without irrigation, but there is no safety in it. As a general thing there is no attempt to raise anything without irrigation.

Question. At what time does the spring open there?

Answer. Earlier than in Wisconsin. We have but very little snow there. We have late frosts there. We can plant in April or the first of May.

Question. Do you have frosts late enough to injure corn planted as early as that?

Answer. We have not had.

Question. How early do the frosts come in the fall?

Answer. About as early as they do in Wisconsin—the last of September or first of October.

Question. With irrigation what productions can you raise: for instance, on the Arapaho and Cheyenne reservation?

Answer. Wheat, corn, oats, potatoes, barley, all kinds of vegetables.

Question. How is it as to fruit?

Answer. It has never been tried. Wild fruit is abundant; plums, wild grapes, and cherries.

Question. Would it be a good country for vines?

Answer. I think it would.

Question. Which way do your rains come from?

Answer. Our storms in winter come from the northeast altogether. Our rains are all showers coming from the mountains west and north.

By Mr. NESMITH:

Question. How is this reservation for timber?

Answer. There is very little of it; nothing for fencing or building, but enough for fire-wood. It is cottonwood entirely. There is beautiful stone, as handsome a stone quarry as I have ever seen, there, and plenty all along. We burnt lime last year. It was supposed to be sandstone, but we found it made excellent lime.

By Mr. DOOLITTLE:

Question. Are there any white settlers there?

Answer. A hundred miles above the reservation it is settled up the Arkansas towards Denver.

By MR. WINDOM:

Question. How far is the reservation from Denver?

Answer. The head of it is 150 miles.

By Mr. DOOLITTLE:

Question. Are the streams about there plenty?

Answer. There is hardly any stream that has any running, permanent water.

Question. So that it is only upon the Arkansas that you can irrigate?

Answer. We cannot on the reservation, except on the Arkansas.

Question. Is the country about there capable of a large settlement, a heavy population, in your opinion?

Answer. It is from the lower end of the reservation to the mountains on those streams. For stock-growing it is the best country I have ever seen. We do not feed at all in winter. The stock keep fat all winter without feeding—those that are not worked.

Question. How is it for sheep?

Answer. There is no finer country in the world for sheep, I think.

Question. Are the winters dry?

Answer. Very dry.

Question. But cold?

Answer. We have some cold days. A snow-storm lasts a day or so, but it is not wet snow; it is dry.

Question. How low does the thermometer go?

Answer. It has been as low as 20 degrees below zero. This winter more than half the time we slept with our doors and windows open. The nights are cool.

Question. So far as health and salubrity are concerned, what do you think of it for a people?

Answer. It cannot be beat in the United States for our white people. There is hardly anybody sick there, and I have known a great many cured of asthma and lung complaints.

Question. What is the nature of the country between this reservation and the Kansas settlements?

Answer. It is rather barren. There is hardly any timber after you get 50 miles below Fort Lyon.

Question Is that barrenness from a want of rain, or in the nature of the soil itself?

Answer. For want of rain. I say it is barren, although it produces grass. It is a good stock-growing country.

Question. Are there streams sufficient for stock growing purposes?

Answer. On the Arkansas, and as you go north on the Republican and the Smoky Hill, you find water there, and between that and the Platte.

Question. Do you think that all that country which we generally call the plains is adapted to a pastoral people and large stock-growing?

Answer. No doubt of it.

Question. And will hold a tolerably dense population?

Answer. It takes more country to grow stock there than it would in Wisconsin. You could have larger establishments.

By Mr. Higby:

Question. You say that through winter, stock lives well?

Answer. Yes, sir.

Question. When do the grasses of which you speak spring? Through what months do they grow, and when do they mature?

Answer. They commence in April. The grasses on the high lands generally mature in July, or soon after the rains. That which we call the buffalo and the gramma grass, the bunch grass here, is a different grass from any I have seen in the western country. They spring a little earlier than in other places.

Question. I understand you that there is no rain except in July?

Answer. I have known some in the fore part of August, but generally July is the rainy month.

Question. Then at the time your grasses spring there are no rains?

Answer. None.

Question. Is not that a natural vegetation?

Answer. It appears to be natural to that country; it grows every year.

Question. Do you say a crop cannot be raised annually with the season without irrigation?

Answer. They say that when the white man settles up a country it rains more.

Question. Have you tested it with the natural season by putting in agricultural seeds at the time of the springing of the natural vegetation?

Answer. They have done so about Denver and above me, and sometimes they raise a crop and sometimes they do not.

By Mr. Doolittle:

Question. Is there any coal on the Arapaho reservation?

Answer. Yes, sir; plenty of it on Sand creek. General Pierce, the surveyor general of the Territory, informed me that as he struck the creek he saw plenty of coal.

Question. What would you suggest or propose to do with these Indians?

Answer. My opinion is that they might have a hearing; that we might get at them in some way, and if we could make them believe what we told them they would be willing to go to some other country. There is a large country south of the Arkansas, between there and Texas, where the Kioways and Comanches roam. The Arapahoes might go there ; I think the Cheyennes would want to go where they came from, towards the Sioux.

Question. Are the Arapahoes and the Comanches and Kioways friendly ?

Answer. Yes, sir.

Question. Do they speak the same language?

Answer. Not the same language, but they can understand each other.

Question. Have they ever lived or hunted together ?

Answer. They have always hunted together and have intermarried.

Question. What is your suggestion as to the best thing to be done with them ?

Answer. It was my opinion after this affair that they would have to be annihilated ; that we could not get at them ; but Colonel Leavenworth tells me that he has seen the Kioways and Comanches, and they are willing yet to come into terms of peace and arrangement.

Question. Is there any other fact or suggestion which you desire to make in relation to the matter ?

Answer. The only fact is that, as I told you, the Colorado people are very much opposed to having peace with these Indians. It is almost as much as a man's life is worth to speak friendly of an Indian, and for that reason I do not believe they can live in that country.

By Mr. HUBBARD:

Question. From what does that feeling arise? Does it arise from the depredations and murders which the Indians have committed heretofore, or is it a natural antipathy which the whites there have against Indians?

Answer. There was a natural antipathy, and then the depredations and murders they have committed this year have outraged the people, and they think an Indian ought to be killed anyhow. It is my opinion that they cannot be got on to that reservation again. It is a pity the work was commenced there. Some came and complained that the government had not complied with treaty stipulations in building houses and completing the farm, and we were induced to commence last year.

By Mr. HIGBY :

Question From what you gathered, from all the information you received, did it seem to be a general desire among those engaged in the expedition to make the slaughter, or were they inflamed to it by some of their leaders?

Answer. The officers at Fort Lyon were opposed to going out, and represented to Colonel Chivington that they considered any men who would go out to fight those Indians, knowing the circumstances as they knew them, to be cowards.

Question. Did they so express themselves to Chivington and those men ?

Answer. Yes, sir.

Question. What answer, if any, was given?

Answer. Chivington threatened to put the officers under arrest. That was the answer, I believe.

Question. Were the officers who made those remarks officers of his command who did finally go with him ?

Answer. Some of them did finally go with him. They said that at Fort Lyon before they started.

By Mr. DOOLITTLE :

Question. In addition to your business as Indian agent, have you been prosecuting any other business there, any private business, farming, or anything of that sort ?

Answer. None at all. My son is settled there ; he went there in 1859, and put up some hay at Fort Lyon last summer.

Question. What has been usually the amount of annuities or presents that have passed through your hands to these Indians ?

Answer. The treaty of 1851 gave them about $17,000—I think that was the amount of it—in presents for the right of way through their country. In 1861 they made a permanent treaty and this reservation was assigned to them. By that treaty, under the direction of the Interior Department, they were to have $30,000 a year for fifteen years, to be expended in improvements, opening farms, building houses, and so on. Whether any of that has been given to them in goods or not, I do not know. We still continue to give them under the first treaty, which is not yet out, about $17,000 in the shape of presents.

Question. Of that appropriation of $17,000 a year, how much actually gets to and reaches the Indians and is distributed among them ?

Answer. The whole of it, so far as I know ; all that comes to me does.

Question. But where are the purchases made?
Answer. In New York, and the goods are shipped to Colorado.
Question Shipped by the overland route?
Answer. Contracts are made, and they are shipped by freighters from Atchison to Colorado. The bills of lading are sent on. The prices of the goods seem fair.
Question. How do they compare with the prices of the goods as sold in the markets of Colorado?
Answer. A great deal less than goods sold there.
Question. Are they furnished to the Indians cheaper than they could be purchased of dealers in Colorado?
Answer. A great deal cheaper.

By Mr. HUBBARD:

Question. Of what descriptions are the goods?
Answer. Blankets, sugar, coffee, flour, and some kinds of cloths, calicoes, and so on.
Question. Is much hardware sent out?
Answer. Not a great deal.
Question. Trinkets?
Answer. Yes; generally a little paint and a few beads.

By Mr. ROSS:

Question. Who fixes the prices?
Answer. I understand that the money is laid out in New York, and the government transports the goods to the Indians free of expense to them. The transportation does not come out of the annuities; it is let by contract.

By Mr. DOOLITTLE:

Question. The goods are purchased in New York, and the transportation is let by the government by contract?
Answer. Yes; the government contracts for hauling them to the agency.

By Mr. NESMITH:

Question. Have you been in the habit of receiving goods there for disbursement yourself?
Answer. I have received two parcels since I have been there. Last year I received none for these Indians.
Question. Have you ever made a requisition on the department here for goods?
Answer. Yes; every year I consult the Indians and see what they want, and make a requisition on the government, and send it on here.

By Mr. ROSS:

Question. You spoke of a price being fixed; is that the price of the goods when given by the government to the Indians?
Answer. I understand they have so much money to be expended for them, and the money is laid out in New York, and the goods are transported by the government.
Question. Then the goods would only be for distribution; there would be no price to be fixed?
Answer. There is no price fixed on the goods; we just give them to the Indians. When they come on I generally take them out of the wagons and tell the chiefs to give them to whom they belong, and they divide them up among their families.

By Mr. NESMITH:

Question. Have the goods generally been furnished according to the requisition you made?
Answer. Sometimes they say it is too large, and costs too much money.
Question. I mean in kind; do they send you what you ask for?
Answer. Yes, sir; they send the same articles.

By Mr. DOOLITTLE:

Question. As an illustration of the prices, what do blankets cost apiece out there?
Answer. So far as my knowledge extends, and I have seen the prices, they have been furnished cheaper than they could be bought there. Blue blankets, three-point as they call them, that Indians want, used to come at about $12 a pair in New York; I think they are higher now. They send out a good blanket; it is different from a soldier's blanket. I used to look over to see how the prices compared, and I always thought the prices were no higher than the goods were bought at.
Question. What kind of blankets did you get in fact?
Answer. Good blankets; I think the price two years ago—there were none sent last year—was $12 a pair. Since the trouble broke out it has not been safe to send them.

By Mr. ROSS:

Question. Did those Indians get anything last year?

Answer. Nothing at all.

By Mr. DOOLITTLE:

Question. What was the occasion of that?

Answer. I suppose on account of the troubles, and because they were fighting the whites there. The articles sent are good, fair articles.

Question. What does it cost a pound to get sugar there to the Indians?

Answer. The contract for freights was low. Two years ago I think it was five or six cents a pound. Freights now are higher than that.

By Mr. NESMITH:

Question. What is the difference between the contract price the government pays and private freight?

Answer. It was no higher than private freights, but generally lower, I think. I believe the freights on Indian goods were less than on soldiers' goods. I do not remember the amounts.

By Mr. DOOLITTLE:

Question. What has been spent of the money provided by the treaty?

Answer. About $20,000 has been expended in breaking up the land and building a house and warehouse at the reservation on the Arkansas, and for an acequia. Whether there has been any of that expended in goods sent out there I do not know.

Question. You think the Indians really will never live on the reservation?

Answer. I do not believe we can get them to live there now.

Question. What kind of a building has been made there?

Answer. They built a house for a blacksmith, that was about completed; then they were to build a house for the agent, and in that house there was to be a council-room, and also a store or warehouse, and that is about up to the windows. It is made of stone. It remains unfinished. They have broken the windows out of the blacksmith's house and out of the blacksmith's shop which was built. About 250 acres, or a little over, were broken up. The acequia was built also. We had a fine crop of corn there, which would have produced well if it had been taken care of.

By Mr. ROSS:

Question. Was it contemplated that the Indians themselves would work the land?

Answer. It was thought some would come in to work. We thought we could get some of them in to learn. The object was to teach and show them how to work.

Jesse H. Leavenworth sworn and examined.

By Mr. DOOLITTLE:

Question. Have you lived in Colorado?

Answer. Yes, sir.

Question. For what length of time?

Answer. I went to Colorado in 1860, and I was there until 1862, when I was authorized to raise the second regiment of Colorado volunteers, and was there till the fall of 1863 in command of that regiment on the frontier.

Question. What is about your age?

Answer. Near fifty.

Question. Are you the son of General Leavenworth?

Answer. Yes, sir; of General Henry Leavenworth, of the United States army.

Question. Did you graduate at West Point?

Answer. I did.

Question. During your father's lifetime, when he was in command upon the frontier, did you become well acquainted with Indian life and character on the border?

Answer. I did.

Question. During your stay in Colorado and since, have you become acquainted with the Cheyennes, Arapahoes, Kioways, Comanches, and Apaches?

Answer. Yes, sir; I believe I have a thorough acquaintance with each and every one of those tribes.

Question. Do you speak the language?

Answer. No, sir; I do not speak their language, but I talk with them by signs, more or less. I have no difficulty in communicating with them.

Question. From the best information you have, what do you estimate to be the number of the Arapahoes?

Answer. I think there is not to exceed from 1,500 to 1,700 of them. There is a band of Arapahoes that claim not to be connected with those of the Upper Arkansas—the North Platte Arapahoes. With that band I am not much acquainted; but with the Arapahoes of the Upper Arkansas, who have a reservation with the Cheyennes at Fort Lyon, I am well acquainted. I think there are about 280 lodges of them—that is the number I have counted many times—and I think there are from 1,500 to 1,700 of them, all told, men, women, and children.

Question. How many of the Cheyennes?

Answer. I have supposed there was about the same number, with the addition of eighty lodges of what are called Dog Soldiers, who have never associated much with the Indians of the Arkansas, but have kept aloof from them.

Question. What is the character of those who are called the Dog Soldiers?

Answer. They are a warlike, high-minded, savage people. They separated from the others on account of the Fort Lyon reservation, with which they were dissatisfied. They went north, and said they would never live on the reservation. They were dissatisfied with the treaty and went off on to the Smoky Hill, and kept between the Smoky Hill and the Powder river.

Question. How many of the Kioways do you estimate that there are?

Answer. I think there is just about the same number of them as there is of Cheyennes and of Arapahoes. I do not think there is much difference; there may be a hundred either way. There are from 1,500 to 1,700 of them.

Question. How many Apaches?

Answer. Forty lodges, and they average from four to five to a lodge.

Question. What is the character of the Apaches?

Answer. The Apaches are a small band of docile Indians dependent on their neighbors for protection. They first associated with the Arapahoes, but they thought the Arapahoes were not strong enough to protect them, and they separated from them and now run mostly with the Kioways, more for protection than anything else. They are led partly by the Kioways. For two years that I was in command of the southwestern frontier they would look upon the trains, but I never heard of any depredations committed. They would beg, but they would not do any wrong. They apparently felt their weakness and did not like to get into any trouble.

Question. What is the number of the Comanches?

Answer. There are nine bands of Comanches. Eight of them are what we call Union Comanches; the ninth band is the southern Comanches, residing in Texas, who are friendly with the Texans. I know that eight of the bands are friendly to the United States; the ninth band has never been north.

Question. How many of them are there?

Answer. I cannot state the exact number, but from the best information I can get they average from 500 to 700 warriors to a band. The old men, women, and children will average from three to five to each warrior. Mawwee has the largest band. It is a band composed mostly of young men. He has about 700 warriors, the largest band of all.

Question. You think, then, there would be about 3,500 souls in the largest bands, and that there are nine bands of them; would your estimate be that they amount altogether to about 30,000?

Answer. Not so many as that—from eighteen to twenty thousand, all told. I should like to state where I get most of my information about the Comanches. In 1834 my father went into the Comanche country with General Dodge, afterwards Governor Dodge, of Wisconsin, the commanding officer of the 1st regiment of dragoons. My father was the second officer in command. He went there to form a treaty, under General Jackson's orders, with the Comanches. On that expedition he died. He had with him a man by the name of Jesse Chisom, as guide and interpreter. Jesse Chisom has been with these Indians almost all the time since. He has been upon that frontier; he has traded with them; he speaks their language perfectly; and he is now my guide and interpreter for these Indians, and has helped me more since last fall than any one else in keeping them quiet and protecting them. His information in regard to them is perfect and complete, and I get most of my information from him. I have had a great deal to do myself with many of the bands, but my information is principally from him.

Question. Are all these bands, the Cheyennes, Arapahoes, Apaches, Kioways, and Comanches, of the nomadic tribes?

Answer. They are. They all live in lodges and move from place to place constantly over the plains. Wherever the grass fails them they remove to some other point. Where game is plenty they stay, and when it becomes scarce they move to some other point. They are the wild Arabs of America.

Question. Have the Comanches many horses?

Answer. A great many.

Question. In their movements do they go on foot or on horseback?

Answer. On horseback. A Comanche never moves except on horse, unless he is compelled to do so.

Question. Are they fine horsemen?

Answer. Splendid. There are no better horsemen in the world. They ride from the moment they can sit up straight. They are tied on the horse by the mother and the mother leads the horse, and that is the way they move from place to place.

Question. Are the Comanches a warlike people?

Answer. The most warlike we have on the continent, I think. They have fought the Texans for a great many years. Since the massacre at San Antonio—I do not remember in what year that was—they have been constantly at war with the Texans, and they are at war with them now. They have a great many Mexicans with them now as prisoners and servants or slaves.

Question. State the disposition of the Kioways, Comanches, and Apaches towards the United States at the present time.

Answer. Last summer I was appointed agent for the Kioways, Comanches, and Apaches, with instructions by the Indian department to meet them and to preserve peace between them and the United States, if possible. Owing to business outside of that I was unable to reach my agency until October. In October I arrived at Council Grove, the last town there is on the verge of civilization in the western part of Kansas. The Kioways, or the wild tribes, I cannot tell who they were, had ranged down within twenty miles of Council Grove last summer; had driven off stock and killed it, but committed no murders. General Curtis, a short time before that, had issued an order that no Indian should approach a military post. My headquarters were at Fort Larned, 240 miles east of Fort Lyon. Knowing that no Indian could approach Fort Larned, and having been in command of that frontier, and knowing all the chiefs and a great many of the braves of the Indian tribes, I felt very anxious to get in communication with them. To do it, it was impossible for me to go into their country with soldiers, because I could not approach any Indian in that way; and if I went alone, they, not knowing who was coming towards them, would of course ambush me; so that it was a very dangerous business. I therefore went south, down on to the Osage lands, where there were bands of Towacaros, Wacos, Keitchies, Wichitas, and Caddoes. These were Indians who had been run out of Texas some years ago, and when this war broke out were called refugee Indians. They had had more or less communication with the Comanches and were most of them very friendly with them. I went to them for the purpose of getting runners to go into the Comanche country and communicate with them, which was the only safe way I had to get to them. I made arrangements for some fifteen or twenty to go out. They started out and were gone a few days, and came back and said they had met some Osages, and the Osages had six spare horses and told them that they had killed six Comanches, and that if they, living on the Osage lands, went out the Comanches would kill them, and they did not dare to go. Before I could get another party started, the massacre at Fort Lyon, under Colonel Chivington, occurred, and then the Indians refused to go at all. They said there was treachery on the part of the whites, and if they went and anything should occur they would be blamed. I had some old acquaintances with the Caddoes. One was Jim Parkman, the chief, who was a very excellent, good man. He told them that he was well acquainted with me, and had been for a number of years; that whatever I might say they might rely upon; it was all straight. I finally succeeded in getting the Waco chief, with three or four of his brothers, two Towacaros, and a Keitchi to go out. They were gone twenty days, and came in with 96 Kioways and Comanches, and 9 Arapahoes that had escaped from Colonel Chivington's massacre. Little Raven's band of Arapahoes got away and six Apaches. When they came in and found who wanted to see them, they told me that they did not want to fight the whites, and had no wish to fight them, but were compelled to go to war. They said they would agree not to go into the Santa Fé road; they would not molest any more white men; they would get all the Indians together and meet me in four weeks and make a peace, and it should be a permanent peace; they did not want a war, but if the whites were determined to fight them on the Santa Fé road or above, they would join hands with the Texans, and go south. I agreed to meet them in four weeks. I came out to Council Grove, and from there to Fort Riley, and saw Colonel Ford, who commands the district. He at once agreed with me that it was right to make peace with them and stop the war. He sent my letter that I addressed to him to General Dodge, at St. Louis, who commanded the department, and telegraphed to him. General Dodge telegraphed back to Colonel Ford that the military have no authority to make peace with Indians; their duty is to make them keep peace by punishing them for hostility; and to keep posted as to their location, so that when they were ready they could strike them. Having been down there as a white man, and almost the only white man that had spoken to these Indians for nearly eight or ten months, I felt that I was doing wrong to the red man to get him to stop his war and then let the whites jump upon him, as Colonel Chivington had upon the Cheyennes, and I immediately started for Washington, in hopes that the military might be stopped and that the Indians might be protected. They do not want a war; they do not want to fight the whites; they want to be let alone.

Question. Have you a copy of the order of General Dodge?

Answer. I have. I have not a copy of my letter to Colonel Ford. I gave it to Colonel Ford for some purpose. I do not remember for what he wanted it.

Question. Will you please read General Dodge's telegraph?

Answer. It is—

"FEBRUARY 23, 1865.

"[By telegraph from St. Louis.]

"*To Colonel Ford, Fort Riley:*

"The military have no authority to treat with Indians. Our duty is to make them keep the peace by punishing them for their hostility. Keep posted as to their location, so that as soon as ready we can strike them. 400 horses arrived here for you.

"G. M. DODGE, *Major General.*"

I will say that, with all the information I can get, I have not learned that the Comanches have raised a hand hostile to the whites the past season. I know from report that Mawwee and Little Buffalo, the two leading chiefs of two bands, were at Fort Larned at the time the outbreak occurred between the Kioways and the post, and they immediately took their bands and went south, and I have no evidence that any Comanche has been north of the Arkansas this summer; I do not believe any of them have been. In conversation with General Curtis when I first got there, he told me that he did not think the Comanches had committed any depredations, and I do not think they have. I cannot learn that they have committed a single depredation. I think that all the depredations have been committed by Kioways and Cheyennes, with the Sioux from the north, and probably some Arapahoes, but I do not believe that any of the bands as a tribe have been united in a general war.

Question. Suppose that yourself and Major Colley were authorized to go out and meet these Indians and to make some presents to show the amicable feelings of the United States, rather than hostile feelings on the part of the government, do you believe you could reach them in a way to negotiate or to come to peace with them without any further hostilities?

Answer. In 1862 I was in command of the Santa Fé road from the Great Bend of the Arkansas to the Rattoon mountains, a distance of nearly 760 miles. I was sent there by General Blunt, with all the force at my command, to protect the frontier. I had 102 infantry and one section of artillery, and these were recruits. There were 18 men, all told, at Fort Lyon at the time I arrived there. Major Colley was then the Indian agent. I arrived there about the last of June. I had occasion to go south to Santa Fé to co-operate with General Canby, and I got back to Fort Lyon on the 31st of July. On the 1st day of August Major Colley received an express from Fort Larned saying that the Kioways, Comanches, Apaches, Arapahoes, and Cheyennes were in full force at Fort Larned, and that they had corralled a government train of goods, and asking for re-enforcements. I had no men that I could send. I started with Major Colley and his interpreter, and I went to Fort Larned and found that there was not one dozen of those Indians with whom I was acquainted; they were strangers to me. With the assistance of Major Colley and John Smith, the interpreter, in three days' time I had every one of those Indians off to their hunting-grounds, and the train was started under an escort of twenty men and went through to Fort Lyon, with the Indians camping almost every night around it, in perfect safety; and for two years those Indians never committed a depredation that I know of, and neither the government nor any individual lost a dollar by them. I left there in October, and the outbreak occurred in May following. I have not seen these Indians since I left there, until the 15th of February. I know them well. When I met them they agreed at once to quit hostilities. They said they did not want to fight; that I might make the road and they would travel it. I feel now that I can say with safety that I can go to them with Major Colley, and in thirty days the war will be ended, and it will save millions of money. I say it also because Major Whalley, of the regular army, wrote, last spring, to the department that if Colonel Chivington was not stopped in his course the government would be involved in a war that would cost millions of money. It has occurred. I told the department, last spring, that if Lieutenant Ayres was not stopped in hunting the Cheyennes from camp to camp they would get into a war. It has come. I know all the chiefs and a great many of the braves; I know them to be kind-hearted. I know there are bad men among them, but I know the Cheyennes so well that I am satisfied they can rule those bad men, and there is no necessity for this war. If the soldiers are stopped from hunting the Indians, I will guarantee peace in thirty days, and I will not ask $50,000 to do it with. They want to know that their Great Father will protect them. They want some man that they have confidence in to say that they shall be righted. They never came to me with a complaint that I did not right them if possible.

Question. As our white men are going and gathering into that country, and travelling all around about it, is not the game becoming scarcer?

Answer. It is.

Question. As the game diminishes, what do you suggest is to be done with the wild hunting Indians?

Answer. There is the finest country in the world for agricultural purposes south of the Arkansas, on the Red river, near Fort Cobb and the Wichita mountains, on the north fork of the Red river, where they can live and raise almost anything they want. It is now literally alive with cattle. They can go there now, and if the whites are kept away from them, with the abundance of cattle they can live without coming in contact with the whites. All along under the Staked Plain, in the northern part of Texas and eastern New Mexico, there is fine water and fine grazing.

Question. What is your opinion, based on your practical knowledge and experience of this matter? What would you advise the government to do?

Answer. I would advise them to let some individual in whom these Indians have confidence go there and tell them that they shall be protected; take them down south, where I have got Kioways, Comanches, and two bands of Arapahoes now, and let them remain there. I think the Cheyennes can be induced to go down there; but they will never go on to their reservation again.

Question. Do you think the Kioways and Comanches who live down there would be willing to let the Arapahoes and Cheyennes go among them?

Answer. Yes, sir; they would have no objection. The head chief of the Arapahoes is a half-Comanche; he speaks the Comanche language just the same as he does the Arapaho.

Question. From your knowledge of all these tribes of Indians, do you think they could be induced to abandon the hunter's life and live by pasturage or by cultivation of the soil?

Answer. They cannot at present. They may live by grazing, and gradually come into it; but at present it would be out of the question.

Question. They would be like the Arabs in that respect?

Answer. Yes; they would have to come to it gradually, and they may come to raising cattle, and as the buffalo disappeared begin upon the beef. I think they would make excellent graziers.

Question. Do you mean that they should be put in that part of Kansas, as well as the Indian Territory and Texas, that lies south of the Arkansas?

Answer. I would not bring them anywhere near Kansas if I could help it. There is a little band of refugee Indians called the Caddoes, who, when the rebellion broke out, were driven from Fort Cobb up north and came in almost to Fort Lyon. They came in destitute, freezing, and almost perishing. They brought a few cattle with them, a few hens, a few pigs, and a few calves. Major Colley received them. They were loyal; they were half-civilized; they lived in houses; and a better set of men I never met in my life, well-disposed, kind-hearted. They are like the Pueblos of Mexico. They were more than half-civilized. Their women dressed in long dresses, the same as our American women do; they made good bread; everything was neat and clean about them. They lived at Fort Larned. The government gave them $5,000 annuity two years ago. Last year the government authorized me to issue to them some goods to the amount of $5,000. I found them at the mouth of the Arkansas river. Last year they lost over 100 by small-pox. There were only 425 of them when they first came up. Parkman, their head chief, is one of the most intelligent men I ever met; he is correct in every particular. He told me that he could not live on the borders there; that the whites were stealing his horses all the time, and he moved across the Arkansas, on to what is called the Minisqua, and they followed him over there and stole quite a number of his horses there. He then moved on to the Chickasaqua. Since this Chivington massacre he has become alarmed, and he is now living with his little band away down between the Salt Plains and the Brushy mountains, as near Texas as he can go. Parkman, if he dared to return to the rebel States to-morrow, would be killed; he dare not return there, and he dare not come back here, the whites abuse him so and steal his horses. He has nothing left but a few ponies, and his men are suffering; they are dying almost every day from small-pox. John Leonard, the doctor and priest, died since I left, and his wife too. This is an illustration of the way they are treated.

WASHINGTON, *Wednesday, March* 8, 1865.

John S. Smith sworn and examined.

By Mr. DOOLITTLE :

Question. What is your age?

Answer. I was born in December, 1810.

Question. How long have you lived in the country west of Kansas, in Colorado?

Answer. I went to that country first in 1830.

Question. Do you know the language of the Arapahoes and Cheyennes?

Answer. I do that of the Cheyennes.

Question. Have you acted as interpreter for the Indian agent to the Cheyennes?

Answer. I have.

Question. Were you in the Indian camp of the Cheyennes when Colonel Chivington made his attack upon it?

Answer. I was.

Question. State when it was.

Answer. I left Fort Lyon for the Cheyenne village on the 26th of November; on the 27th I reached the village; on the 28th I remained there; and on the 29th the attack was made.

Question. How many Indians were there in camp?

Answer. I think about 500, men, women, and children.

Question. What number of warriors or men?

Answer. About 200. They will average two warriors to a lodge, and there were 100 lodges.

Question. What portion of the Cheyenne tribe was that?

Answer. The southern band, led by the main chief of the nation, Black Kettle.

Question. Where was the northern band at this time?

Answer. They were supposed to be over on the North Platte, between the North Platte and the Smoky Hill.

Question. What time in the day or night was the attack made?

Answer. Between daybreak and sunrise.

Question. State now the circumstances of the attack; just describe them in brief words.

Answer. As soon as the troops were discovered, very early in the morning, about daybreak, the Indians commenced flocking to the head chief's lodge, about the camp where I was—the camp over on Sand creek; it is called Big Sandy, about forty miles northeast of Fort Lyon. When the attack was made the Indians flocked around the camp of the head chief and he ran out his flag. He had a large American flag which was presented to him, I think, by Colonel Greenwood some years ago, and under this American flag he had likewise a small white flag.

Question. Was it light, so that the flags could be plainly seen?

Answer. Yes; they could be plainly seen.

Question. How long was this before any firing was heard?

Answer. A very few minutes; they were but a short time coming into camp after they were first discovered. They came on a charge. When I first saw them they were about three-quarters of a mile from the camp, and then the flag was run up by Black Kettle.

Question. Go on and state what occurred.

Answer. The firing commenced on the northeast side of Sand creek; that was near Black Kettle's lodge. The men, women, and children rushed to the upper end of the village, and ran to the lodge of another chief at the other end, War Bonnet.

Question. Were the Indians then armed?

Answer. Some of them were; some of them left their arms in their lodges; some few picked up their bows and arrows and lances as they left their lodges; the younger men did.

Question. Did they form in any battle array or with a view to oppose the charge?

Answer. No, sir; they just flocked in a promiscuous herd, men, women, and children together. The bed of Sand creek ran right up; there was little or no water in it at this place. Then they came to some breaks in the banks about where the troops overtook them, and the slaughter commenced; I suppose about three hundred yards above the main village. White Antelope was the first Indian killed, within a hundred yards of where I was in camp at the time. They fought them from very early in the morning, as I have stated, until about eleven o'clock that day before they all got back together in camp. The troops then returned to the Indian village, followed the Indians up the creek two or three miles firing on them, then returned back to the Indian camp and destroyed everything there was there—the entire village of one hundred lodges. I had a son there, a half-breed; he gave himself up. In this stampede of the Indians he started to go with them, but when he found there was a fair show for him he turned around and came back to our camp where the troops were. I made several efforts to get to the troops, but was fired on myself by our own troops. My son stayed in the camp of our soldiers one day and a night, and then was shot down by the soldiers. My life was threatened, and they had to put a guard around me to save my life.

Question. After you surrendered to the troops?

Answer. Yes, sir.

Question. How many were killed?

Answer. I think about seventy or eighty, including men, women, and children, were killed; twenty-five or thirty of them were warriors probably, and the rest women, children, boys, and old men.

Question. Were any Indian barbarities practiced?

Answer. The worst I have ever seen.

Question. What were they in fact?

Answer. All manner of depredations were inflicted on their persons; they were scalped, their brains knocked out; the men used their knives, ripped open women, clubbed little children, knocked them in the head with their guns, beat their brains out, mutilated their bodies in every sense of the word.

Question. Do you know which troops those were that actually did this work; whether they were the hundred-day men who came from Denver, or the regular first Colorado regiment?

Answer. I am not able to say; they were all in a body together, between eight hundred and one thousand men I took them to be. It would be hard for me to tell who did these things; I saw some of the first Colorado regiment committing some very bad acts there on the persons of Indians, and I likewise saw some of the one-hundred-day men in the same kind of business.

Question. You say the troops pursued the Indians until about eleven o'clock, the Indians fleeing all the while?

Answer. Yes, sir.

Question. When they came back to the Indian village were there any of the Indians there, men, women, or children, left?

Answer. No, sir; they were all gone except a few children who came into our camp an hour after we had all returned to this Indian camp. There were a couple of women there, white men's women, Indian women who had married white men, and they were not hurt. I think there were seven in number saved from the entire village, women and children, and they were taken to Fort Lyon.

Question. When those Indians were there in camp do you know in what relation they were to our forces at Fort Lyon?

Answer. Yes, sir; some of them had just returned from an interview with Governor Evans and Colonel Chivington at Denver city. We had seven of the chiefs up there with us at Denver city; I went as interpreter with them. They returned and were sent out for their families to move in near Fort Lyon, where they could be protected and taken care of; they were told that if the troops from Denver city or the Platte should meet them over in that direction they would probably hurt them, and it was supposed they would be better off in the vicinity of Fort Lyon, where they could be watched, than out further north, and they went there with all the assurances in the world of peace promised by the commanding officer, Major Wynkoop.

Question. Did he, in the mean time, issue some rations to them?

Answer. Yes, sir.

Question. Did they, so far as you know, remain there?

Answer. They did.

Question. And you, as interpreter of the United States, were in camp with them?

Answer. I was in camp with them at the time.

Question. Had this band, so far as you know, committed any depredations on our people after this interview at Denver?

Answer. None that I heard of; I heard of none until after this raid of Colonel Chivington.

Question. From your knowledge of these Indians, and all about them, and of that place which is set apart as their reservation, do you think they can be brought to settle down upon that Cheyenne reservation?

Answer. Yes, sir; with diligent workers there with them it could be done in some time; probably it would take all summer to do it.

Question. Do you think those Indians could be induced to leave off their wild hunting life and go into agricultural pursuits or the raising of cattle?

Answer. Not all of them; there are a few that are best acquainted with the whites who would be willing to do it; they have told us so; I think that in time, with encouragement, they could be brought to it. I have been twenty-seven successive years with the Cheyennes myself.

Question. During those twenty-seven years how have they been as a tribe generally towards our citizens?

Answer. They have been very peaceable until quite recently. In 1857 they had some trouble over on the Platte, but I never understood the particulars of it; that was when Colonel Sumner went out and had a little fight with them, but they came to immediately, and from that time until about twelve months ago, when they had a falling out with white settlers in the vicinity of Denver and below Denver on the Platte, they were peaceable; but this thing has been growing ever since that time, until Chivington made this raid. They have been followed up from the Platte to the Smoky Hill, and from the Smoky Hill to the Arkansas, and south of the Arkansas river; they went clear over south of Salt Springs, where Colonel Leavenworth is acquainted. Governor Evans then issued some circulars that were taken to them there, and explained to them that if they wanted to return in peace they could do so; that those who were friendly disposed could return to their reservation. As soon as they learned this, the body of them returned. This band that I speak of, that purchased some white prisoners from the Sioux and some of the northern band of Cheyennes, sent us word at Fort Lyon that if we would go out to them they would turn them over to us. I went with Major Wynkoop there as his interpreter, and they turned over four of them, whom they had got from the Sioux and from the northern band of Cheyennes

Question. Even now what is your opinion? Do you think, for instance, that if persons like Major Colley, yourself, or Colonel Leavenworth were to go to these Indians now, peaceable relations could be established between them and the United States, notwithstanding all that has occurred?

Answer. I say yes; I think so from the fact that they never wanted to fight the whites. They have lost certainly a great deal of the confidence that they used to have in the white man, but with proper exertions I think they might be brought back, with correct assurances.

Question. Did they have many ponies and horses?

Answer. Yes, sir.

Question. How many were taken away from them?

Answer. About six hundred head.

Question. And all their lodges?

Answer. Everything they had.

Question. These lodges of theirs are made of skins?

Answer. Of buffalo hides; a lodge is made after the pattern of a Sibley tent; when they move from one place to another they take their tents or lodges with them.

Question. Would you feel yourself any personal apprehensions if you were sent to go among them and converse with them?

Answer. I would not like to go without some Indian protectors; I could get some of our other friendly Indians and would readily go with them, sending them on probably as runners ahead of me, so as to let them know my business, and then I would not feel at all apprehensive of losing my life.

Question. But you think the result has been such that now they would kill any white man they should see.

Answer. Yes, sir; anybody.

Question. What is the number of the Cheyennes?

Answer. There are about four hundred and eighty or five hundred lodges, and they will average five souls to a lodge; there are about two thousand five hundred Cheyennes altogether; this includes the northern band.

Question. Is the northern band the same that are commonly called the Dog soldiers?

Answer. No, sir; the Dog soldiers are mixed up promiscuously; this is a band that has preferred the North Platte and north of the North Platte, and lives over in what is called the bad land, *mauvais terre.*

Question. How long have you been with these Indians?

Answer. Since I went there I have resided with these Indians off and on every year; I have generally been employed as United States interpreter; prior to that I was a trader in that country for St. Vrain & Co., and in that way I first learned the Cheyenne language.

John Evans sworn and examined.

By Mr. DOOLITTLE:

Question. Are you governor of the Territory of Colorado?

Answer. I am.

Question. How long have you been in that Territory?

Answer. Since the spring of 1862. I went there in May of that year.

Question. What is the state of the Indian tribes generally in your Territory at this time?

Answer. There are three tribes or bands of Utes which are in the mountains west of us, the Tabahuaches, the Uintas, and the Yampah or Bear River Indians. These Indians have not committed any depredations since the summer of 1863. They committed depredations upon the overland stage line between Denver and Salt lake at that time. In fact, they attacked a party of soldiers who went after them to procure some stock stolen from the stage stations, and killed two or three of the soldiers. I think the Indians did not get worsted any; perhaps one or two were wounded, but they made their escape with the stock, a portion of which, however, has since been returned by them.

Question. What is the condition of the Tabahuache bands?

Answer. They were together at this time.

Question. Are they now in peaceable relations with us?

Answer. Yes, they all have been since that time. Just before that treaty, Major Wynkoop went after them, at the time they made this raid upon the stage line, with quite a large expedition, and followed them down the San Luis valley. He followed their trail, but did not overtake them; ran out of subsistence, and returned. In the mean time I informed Agent Head, the agent of the Tabahuaches, of the difficulty. He had just returned from Washington with a party of chiefs of that band, who had been on a visit here, and he was instructed to get information to these Indians as rapidly as possible, and try to satisfy them until an explanation could be made in regard to this pursuit. They came down there very much alarmed, and at the same time intent upon going to war, and went to the Capotes and Muhuaches, who were near neighbors just over the line in New Mexico, asking them to join and go to war. Agent Head sent immediately to them the chiefs who had been here, and one of those chiefs, Ura, who is a very intelligent and very sharp and shrewd Indian, who speaks the English language fluently, went among them and explained to them the folly of going to war. He and his associates had seen the army of the Potomac, and one of his strong points with the Indians was, that the whites had soldiers enough to surround all their country and close them in and wipe them out. Through the representations of these chiefs difficulty was prevented, and they were induced to meet in council for the purpose of making the treaty of Conejos. That was the treaty with the Tabahuache band. That treaty was amended by the Senate, and last fall I met the band again in council to ratify the Senate amendments, and succeeded after a great deal of earnest effort to get their assent to the diminution of their hunting-grounds, all of which is matter of record. The Uintas, immediately subsequent to this expedition, were seen by Major Whitely and his interpreter, and they made an appointment with them last fall to have some presents for them this summer. They agreed to be peaceable and friendly and meet him in the spring. The waters, however, were so high and the snows were so deep that they could not meet him at the time appointed; they could not get there, nor could he, in the Middle Park, to the place appointed; but afterwards the major went over and found them and induced them to meet at the council ground of Conejos with the other tribes, to receive presents, in conjunction with the Tabahuache band, which they did, and went away very abundantly satisfied. We gave them a very nice distribution of goods. I gave them a lecture on obedience to their chiefs and on the necessity of going immediately to the agent as soon as any difficulty occurred, to report it to him and have it adjusted, instead of committing depredations or exciting any spirit of hostility amongst their men, which they were all satisfied with.

Question. So far as they are concerned, do you think they are on friendly terms now?

Answer. They are; and I understand that since my absence they have been down and offered their services to the commander of the department, if he should need them, as soldiers in the war against the Cheyennes.

Question. Are the Tabahuaches hostile to the Cheyennes and Arapahoes?

Answer. The Indians in the mountains all through New Mexico and Colorado have been at war with the Indians on the plains, as classes, from time immemorial; whenever they meet they fight.

Question. Is that so when they go to hunt on common hunting-grounds?

Answer. They get up their war parties. When I first went there I thought it would be a very humane and good idea to get those Indians to quit fighting one another, and I gave them a great many lectures on the impropriety of these war parties, but I found, after I had done it, that it gave a great deal of offence to them. One of them said he had been brought up to war, and to quit fighting was a thing he could not think of, and he thought it was an unworthy interference on my part. They were for non-intervention. I found that my plan was not working well, and I concluded to let them alone.

Question. Now, to come down more particularly to the difficulties with the Cheyennes and Arapahoes, will you state, in as brief terms as you can, your view of the matter and all you know about it; how the difficulty arose; how it has been managed, and the part the force of Chivington took in it?

Answer. When I went there, the first band of Indians that I met was a band of Arapahoes, under the command of Little Owl. They came in and gave me a visit; we had a friendly smoke, and they went off with this dissatisfaction: They said that the white people had taken their gold—this was Little Owl's speech; I do not know but that I have a copy of it. He said the white people had taken their gold and their lands; that they wanted their own lands, they did not care about the gold particularly. I told them that they had made a treaty at Fort Wise. He claimed that he was not there, and a good many of his party said they were not there, but some of them had been there. I told them that that treaty provided for their joining in the benefits that were conferred by the government. He said they would not settle on the Arkansas. There is mention in the treaty of one of the bands not being present. He and his band were perhaps as friendly then, and are now, as any other of the Indians of the plains. Friday, who was the chief talker of his band, had been brought up by Major Fitzpatrick, one of the old Indian agents there, and lived in St. Louis for some time, and he speaks English very well. He has, during all the difficulties, with a portion of his band, remained friendly. He came in and remained at Camp Collins under our protection, and has been subsisted by the government to a large extent, because it was unsafe for him to go out and hunt. Another portion of that band was among those young men who wanted to fight. In 1863, the spring next after my arrival, and after this interview, the head man after Little Owl's death—he died the winter after I arrived there—came in and told me there was a party of Sioux who had been down with them and had held a council, in which the question of driving the whites out of the country was the topic of discussion. The Sioux are at the Fort Laramie agency, which is not in Colorado Territory, but the Indians are in the habit of passing to and fro. These Indians are entirely nomadic; they have no definite home; they range generally in certain parts of the Territory, but they interchange in their hunts extensively. He told me that the Sioux had been down with them and they had held a council on Horse creek, as he reported, in which the question of driving the whites out of the country and preventing them from settling was the chief discussion. His claim was that he and a good portion of his band were opposed to anything of the kind, but some of them were very much in favor of going to war. Soon after that, Major Lorey, the agent of the Sioux Indians, came to Denver and saw me in regard to the same thing. He said there was dissatisfaction among the Indians; that he was satisfied that it was important to get them together and hold a council, or they would go to war. They were committing occasional depredations at that time which were reported, and which, in my report for 1863 to the Indian Bureau, are mentioned. I saw the impending danger from the talk I had had with the Arapahoes; I was satisfied that a portion of them did not feel well, and a portion of the Cheyennes had been in to see me once, some of the Dog soldiers on a war party, and they had gone after the Utes. I advised them not to go. That was at the time I was trying to make friends among them. They promised me that they would not, and started off as though they were going back to their own hunting-grounds, took a circuitous route, and in a day or two the settlers on the road to the South Park, in the southern mines, as they are called, came in and reported that this war party were committing depredations; they had outraged a woman at one of the ranches, and were in the habit generally of going to a ranch and taking what they wanted without injuring anybody, but they treated one hotel-keeper's wife very improperly. The man happened to be away, and they went into her bed-room and proposed to make her get up out of a sick-bed and get them something to eat, which was their custom. The settlers sent in for defence; they were alarmed and anticipated an attack. A squad of some half a dozen soldiers went after the Indians; Captain Wagner commanded the soldiers, but the Indians fled more rapidly than he pursued; he did not see them. He went up to get them to come out of the settlement and go back to their hunting-grounds again, but he saw no Indians, and while he came out at Colorado City, seventy-five miles south of Denver, the Indians went out on their way to the plains again. That was in July, 1862.

Question. Did any troubles occur in 1863?

Answer. This should have been told prior to what I have stated in regard to Little Owl's reporting to me the proposition to go to war. I will return now to that. In 1863, upon Major Lorey's representation, I wrote a letter, a very urgent letter, to the department here for active measures to try to prevent these Indians from becoming hostile and going to war, showing them the danger, that the Sioux Indians were in connexion with the hostile Sioux of Minnesota. A party from Minnesota had been with these Indians at the council on Horse creek. I sent Agent Lorey a despatch and got him to come in person to the Secretary of the Interior. He did so, and laid the matter before the department, with my letter, and they appointed a commission, consisting of Agent Colley, Agent Lorey, and myself, to get the Arapahoes and Cheyennes in council, and especially the northern bands, for the purpose of making an adjustment. I got his return and got the commission, I think in July, 1863. I sent for Major Colley, and we arranged for a council on the head of the Republican in the fall of 1863, on the 1st day of September, or thereabouts. I employed Elbridge Gerry, who has been about twenty-five years among them and has a Cheyenne wife, (and, by the way, he is a grandson of Elbridge Gerry who signed the Declaration of Independence, and a scholar and a man of very good mind,) and Antoine Jaunice, to go to the Indians on the head of the Republican and on the Platte, and up and above Major Lorey's agency, to find all the Arapahoes and Cheyennes they could. They started and notified them of the council and induced them to agree to come. They spent the time up to the 1st of September in these efforts. They met various bands and got promises from them to be at the council. Major Colley and Mr. Smith, together, undertook to notify the Indians of the Arkansas, the Arapahoes and Cheyennes, of this council, and induce them to come. They went in person and visited their principal bands and urged the importance and necessity of coming. At the time of the council, however, they declined to come, on account of their horses being poor, they being at work making their lodges, and the journey being such a long one. It was supposed to be about a medium ground between the different bands, so that we could get them all together. That was advised by Gerry and others, as will be seen in his report of this expedition. Mr. Gerry met the Cheyennes more particularly, where nearly all their chiefs were together, at the head of the Smoky Hill, on Beaver creek, and they promised to meet him at the time. He came out to the Platte river and escorted us to the Upper Timber, on the Rickaree fork of the Platte river, where we went; and after he had escorted us so that he could give us directions to find the place within two days' travel, he left us, in order to conduct the Indians to the same place. We waited two weeks for the Indians and Mr. Gerry's return, and we got quite uneasy about his safety. He came in finally with a report, which is published in my annual report for 1863, showing the reasons why they declined to come. I think all or nearly all the chiefs that signed the treaty of Fort Wise were in the party at the time. Mr. Gerry says that one of them, Bull Bear by name, agreed to come in on his promising to give him a horse if he would do so, but they held a council and decided that he should not do it; that they did not want anything more to do with the whites; that they did not want any presents, but they wanted their lands, and would have their lands. Mr. Gerry argued very sensibly, as will be seen by referring to his statement, which I hope the committee will read. After his report we had nothing to do. The chief of one of the northern bands, Spotted Horse, came in. Major Lorey saw Friday, and he promised to come, but did not get there. I saw several small parties of Cheyennes myself, who told me that they had decided not to hold a council. One was Yellow Wolf's band that I met on the Platte as I was on this expedition. They said, however, they meant to be friendly; they did not mean to fight, but they meant to have their lands. They took the ground that they had never sold their lands. Mr. Gerry argued with them that they had better recognize that, but the chiefs who signed that treaty told Gerry that they were obliged to repudiate the signing of that treaty of Fort Wise, or the Dog soldiers would kill them.

I returned home and was under the necessity of going as far in the opposite direction to meet the Tabahuache band of Utah Indians, which I had made arrangements to meet on the 1st of October. After I got back from Conejos, which took me until the latter part of October, I think the 16th or 20th of October, a party of Indians near Denver made a raid, and they stole Mr. Van Wirmer's horses. I sent out for them to come in and see me, counselled them against difficulty, and told them they must give up the horses they had stolen and try to remain peaceful. I sent to the department statements of these matters, which were published in the report for 1863. These were Arapahoes, I think, altogether; I do not think there were any Cheyennes among them I sent for the Indians to come in, and they gave up the horses that had been stolen, or made recompense for them to Mr. Van Wirmer. I found a white man, Mr. North, among them, who had been living with them for years and had a squaw wife, who sent me word that he could give me some advice that would be very important. I sent for him to come in, and his statement as made to me I communicated to the Interior Department and to the War Department at the time, and it will be found in my report for this year. His statement that a council of war had been held, and a confederation of the Indians had agreed to go to war in the spring, was laid before the War Department, and a request made that our military posts be strengthened instead of withdrawing troops, as the War Department was then withdrawing them on account of the danger. In the spring these Indians stole 175 head of cattle from Irvin & Jackman, government contractors, about thirty-five or forty miles from Denver, where they were herding them.

Question. What Indians took those cattle?

Answer. They were Cheyennes, I suppose. That is, the Indians who came in to make peace with Major Wynkoop gave me the statement of the particular bands that had committed the depredations, a memorandum of which I have. I do not recollect the facts well enough to state which Indians they were, but I can furnish them in detail as reported by the Indians themselves in this council. I got Major Whitely to take a record of the sayings of the council when they were at Denver, when Colonel Chivington and Colonel Shoop and other officers were present. That is the same council referred to by Captain Smith. Very nearly at the same time they committed the depredations on the Platte, and there were several depredations of this kind committed on the Arkansas and at different points, in pursuance of the arrangement that they had made with one another. The plan was laid down in Mr. North's statement. Wherever there were depredations the people were alarmed and ran in for military protection, and the soldiers went off while there were any to send. But early in the spring not only were our posts not re-enforced, but General Curtis ordered our troops all to Kansas, to rendezvous in the southeast corner of the Territory, on the Arkansas, with the understanding that they were to go to Kansas, as the general said, to fight rebels. I not only made application for re-enforcements, but protested against this, as I knew that the Indians, seeing the troops going away, would become more troublesome and we should have more difficulty in keeping them quiet. Major Colley labored very earnestly to try to pacify and keep them quiet; but these circumstances emboldened them. You will find a portion of my correspondence on the subject in my annual report for this year. I was unable to collect the facts as to all the depredations that were committed at various points. They were not all reported to my office, and I made application at the office of the commander for the information so as to embody it in my report—I mean the depredations that we had heard of as occurring at various points during the spring and summer—and the commander said he was not allowed to furnish the evidence. I suppose the reports will be found on the files of the War Department.

Question. At the time of the interview at Denver, when these chiefs were up there in behalf of the Cheyennes, were assurances given by you and Colonel Chivington that if they returned and went into camp in the neighborhood of Fort Lyon and did not commit depredations, they would have no difficulty?

Answer. After a long talk, by which I endeavored to get all the information that was practicable in regard to who had been doing mischief and what mischief they had been doing, I asked them what assurance they would give that they were going to be friendly. I said that it was no part of our intention to continue a war; that their disposition to be friendly was manifested by their coming up, but I wanted to know what they were willing to do to assure us of their continued friendship; whether they would be willing to join us in fighting the Sioux, a large party of whom, from the north of the Platte, they told us, were then threatening the Platte river, and were on the head of the Republican. I have here the minutes of that council at Denver, as taken down by Major Whitely.

Question. For a more specific statement you may refer to the minutes; but you can give us now the substance of the thing, and subsequently furnish the minutes if you wish.

Answer. After a talk the Indians said they desired to make peace, and they asked if I could give them any assurance that their band, which was on the head of the Republican, would be safe. I told them that I could not; that the soldiers might come across them there and attack them; I could not say anything about that; that their best course would be to get out of the way—to bring them in. In general terms they were advised that they had been at war; that they had been committing a great many depredations by their own confession; that I was not the peace-making power; that the War Department claimed the right to say when the troops should make war and when they should make peace, and that I turned them over to the War Department for this purpose. They professed to be willing not only to make peace, but to join with the whites in fighting the Sioux, the Kioways, and the Comanches, all of whom had been with them in their war parties.

Question. Was it not said by Colonel Chivington and yourself that if they would withdraw out of the way and go into the neighborhood of Fort Lyon they would be safe?

Answer. No, sir.

Question. What was the substance of what you told them on that subject?

Answer. The substance of my assurance was that they should show their peaceable intentions, and that I had little doubt they would be able to make and retain friendly relations with the military department.

Question. Was it not suggested to them to go to the neighborhood of Fort Lyon with their camp?

Answer. Colonel Chivington was there; he was commanding the district. Fort Lyon was not in his district. I asked him if he had anything to say, and he simply remarked to them that his way of making peace was for them to lay down their arms; that the soldiers were still out on the war-path. That, I think, was about the substance of his expression. That is also found in Major Whitely's report. Colonel Chivington simply remarked that they were out of his command; that Major Wynkoop would take them back and that he was competent to take care of them, or something to that effect.

Question. Was Major Wynkoop there with them?

Answer. He was there at the council. Immediately after that council I suggested to Major Wynkoop, through Colonel Shoop—I did not see him myself—that my judgment was, that for the time being it was better to treat them as prisoners of war, surrendered prisoners. I had no business to advise him about it; it was simply an extra-official suggestion that I made. I understood, however, that Major Wynkoop did treat them in that way.

By Mr. Ross:

Question. Did these men come in by your request?

Answer. No. The council was held by my request, as I before stated. These were brought in by Major Wynkoop, who went out to their camp to rescue some white prisoners from them, and when he got there he suggested to them to make peace and come in, and they came with him to see me.

By Mr. DOOLITTLE:

Question. Looking at the whole transaction as it was, did you not understand that when these Indians came and proposed to surrender the white prisoners, it was an overture on their part to do something to try and make peace with us?

Answer. I did.

Question. Did you not understand from what occurred at the council when Major Wynkoop was there, and on their going back, that, as they had surrendered these white prisoners, if they went back and remained where they were located, they were to have peace?

Answer. I supposed that they were.

Question. Major Wynkoop so understood, as far as you know?

Answer. Yes, sir; I supposed they were to have peace. What occurred after they went away from Denver I have nothing but flying rumors about. The next day after that council I started for the Conejos treaty-ground, 250 miles off.

By Mr. Ross:

Question. Can you give us any explanation of the orders under which the massacre occurred?

Answer. In regard to the massacre I gave no orders. I came away from the Territory before it occurred, and had no knowledge of any intention to make such an attack. I knew the soldiers were to go after the hostile Indians, but that they were actually going I had no knowledge whatever.

Question. Did you, as governor, make any order about following them up?

Answer. I made no orders except what will be found in my annual reports. There is a proclamation there to which some have taken exception. I will simply say in regard to it that it was at a time when our troops were all taken away or under orders to go away. The last company was on the march down to the Arkansas when several murders of families and burnings of houses occurred close to the capital. The people were terribly excited and making a great cry that I did not do anything for them. It was impossible to secure the militia. It was out of the question, on account of the state of the militia law, to get the militia out. We had no means of equipping such as would volunteer to go. In that state of the law, as the only means I could think of to justify the people in defending themselves was to issue a proclamation authorizing them to do, so I issued the proclamation, and it is part of my report. I may say further in regard to it that, in reference to pursuing, capturing, and destroying the enemy, I quoted the language of the Secretary of War in his complimentary order to General Rosecrans. The same language which he used in regard to the rebels I used in regard to the Indians. There was nothing said about massacring. The troops were strictly prohibited from interfering with friendly Indians, as will be seen by the document. That proclamation was issued before we commenced raising the third regiment, which I subsequently got authority from the Secretary of War to do. I had made application a month before for authority to raise them, but did not get it until this time. At the time I issued this proclamation I renewed my application to him for the means of defending ourselves, and he granted the privilege of raising a regiment, which was done very promptly by our people, for there was a great state of alarm and excitement at the time.

Question. Had you anything to do with directing the troops when this attack was made?

Answer. Nothing. I had no more command of those troops than I had of the army of the Potomac. I did not advise it in any way. Whenever anybody has said anything to me about troops, I have said that what they were raised for was to fight the Indians. I never had any knowledge that that particular attack was contemplated or that it occurred until I was in the States, after having left the Territory.

By Mr. WINDOM:

Question. Do you know of any palliation or excuse for that massacre except what you have stated before in general terms?

Answer. There are two stories in regard to it. I do not know what the testimony brought before you is in reference to it, but I see by my Denver papers and some others which I have received that they justify the attack on the ground that those Indians had left the fort and gone off with hostile intentions. I have seen one letter of that kind in the Denver papers.

Question. But you do not know any facts yourself?

Answer. I know no facts either justifying or condemning it except what I have heard here to-day—some of the statements made by Captain Smith. It would be a matter of interest, I have no doubt, to the committee if we were to collect a statement of the progress of the war so as to give the depredations committed, and show the inauguration of it. I have no doubt, as is stated in my annual report, that emissaries from the hostile tribes who were driven out of Minnesota have got us into these difficulties. The restlessness that is among our Indians would probably have amounted to nothing if it had not been for those Sioux coming down there and telling them—this is their common expression—"Now, whilst the whites are fighting among themselves, we can join together and drive them out of this country." I think that is a very general opinion among the Indians.

FORT LYON, C. T., *January* 15, 1865.

Personally appeared before me John Smith, Indian interpreter, who, after being duly sworn, says: That on the fourth day of September, 1864, he was appointed Indian interpreter for the post of Fort Lyon, and has continued to serve in that capacity up to the present date; that on the fourth day of September, 1864, by order of Major E. W. Wynkoop, commanding post of Fort Lyon, he was called upon to hold a conversation with three Cheyenne Indians, viz, One Eye and two others, who had been brought into the post that day; that the result of the interview was as follows: One Eye, Cheyenne, stated that the principal chiefs and sub-chiefs of the Cheyenne and Arapaho nations had held a consultation and agreed to send in himself, One Eye, with a paper written by George Bent, half-breed, to the effect that they, the Cheyennes and Arapahoes, had and did agree to turn over to Major E. W. Wynkoop, or any military authority, all the white prisoners they had in their possession, as they were all anxious to make peace with the whites, and never desired to be at war.

Major E. W. Wynkoop then asked One Eye, he having lived among whites and known to have always been friendly disposed toward them, whether he thought the Indians were sincere, and whether they would deliver the white persons into his (Major Wynkoop's) hands. His reply was, that at the risk of his life he would guarantee their sincerity.

Major Wynkoop then told him that he would detain him as a prisoner for the time, and if he concluded to proceed to the Indian camp, he would take him out with him and hold him as a hostage for their (the Indians') good faith.

One Eye also stated that the Comanche and Arapaho nations were congregated to the number of two thousand on the headwaters of the Smoky Hill, including some forty lodges of Sioux; that they had rendezvoused there and brought in their war parties for the purpose of hearing what would be the result of their message, by which they had sued for peace, and would remain until they heard something definite.

Major Wynkoop told One Eye that he would proceed to the Indian camps and take him with him. One Eye replied that he was perfectly willing to be detained a prisoner, as well as to remain a hostage for the good faith of the Indians, but desired the major to start as soon as possible for fear the Indians might separate. On the sixth day of September I was ordered to proceed with Major Wynkoop and his command in the direction of the Indian encampment. After a four days' march we came in sight of the Indians, and one of the three Indians before mentioned was sent to acquaint the chiefs with what was the object of of the expedition, with the statement that Major Wynkoop desired to hold a consultation with the chiefs.

On the tenth day of September the consultation was held between Major Wynkoop and his officers and the principal chiefs of the Cheyenne and Arapaho nations. Major Wynkoop stated through me to the chiefs apart that he had received their message; that acting on that, he had come up to talk with them; asked them whether they had all agreed to and indorsed the contents of the letter which he had in his possession, and which had been received from One Eye. Receiving an answer in the affirmative, he then told the chiefs that he had not the authority to conclude terms of peace with them, but he desired to make a proposition to them to the effect that if they would give him evidence of their good faith by delivering into his hands the white prisoners they had in their possession, he would endeavor to procure for them peace, which would be subject to conditions;

The expressions of other chiefs were to the effect that they insisted upon peace as the condition of their delivering up the white prisoners.

Major Wynkoop finally replied that he repeated what he had said before—that it was not in his power to insure them peace, and that all he had to say in the closing was, that they might think about his proposition; that he would march to a certain locality distant twelve miles, and there await the result of their consultation two days, advising them at the same time to accede to his proposition, as the best means of procuring that peace for which they were anxious.

The white prisoners were brought in and turned over to Major Wynkoop before the time had expired set by him; and Black Kettle, White Antelope and Bullbeef, of the Cheyenne nation, as well as Nevah Nattune, Bovea, and Hieys Buffalo, of the Arapaho nation, all these chiefs, delivered themselves over to Major Wynkoop. We then proceeded to Fort Lyon, and from there to Denver, Colorado Territory, at which place Governor Evans held a consultation with the chiefs, the result of which was as follows: He told them he had nothing to do with them; that they would return with Major Wynkoop who would reconduct them in safety, and they would have to await the action of the military authorities. Colonel Chivington, then in command of the district, also told them that they would remain at the disposal of Major Wynkoop until higher authority had acted in their case The Indians appeared perfectly satisfied, presuming that they would eventually be all right as soon as those authorities could be heard from, and expressed themselves so. Black Kettle embraced the governor and Major Wynkoop, and shook hands with all the other officials present, perfectly contented, deeming that the matter was settled. On our return to Fort Lyon I was told by Major Wynkoop to say to the chiefs that they could bring their different bands, including their families, to the vicinity of the post until he had heard from the big chief; that he preferred to have them under his eye and away from other quarters where they were likely to get into difficulties with the whites. The chiefs replied that they were willing to do anything Major Wynkoop might choose to dictate, as they had perfect confidence in him. Accordingly the chiefs went after their families and villages and brought them in. They seemed satisfied that they were in perfect security and safety. After their villages were located and Major Wynkoop had sent an officer to headquarters for instructions, he (Major Wynkoop) was relieved from command of the post by Major Scott J. Anthony, and I was ordered to interpret for him (Major Anthony) in a consultation he desired to hold with the Indians. The consultation that there took place between Major Anthony and the Indians was as follows: Major Anthony told them that he had been sent here to relieve Major Wynkoop, and that he would from that time be in command of this post; that he had come here under orders from the commander of all the troops in this country, and that he had orders to have nothing to do with Indians whatever, for they had heard at headquarters that the Indians had lately been committing depredations, &c., in the very neighborhood of this post; but that, since his arrival, he had learned that these reports were all false; that he would write to headquarters himself and correct the rumor in regard to them, and that he would have no objection to their remaining in the vicinity of Sand creek, where they were then located, until such a time as word might be received from the commander of the department; that he himself would forward a complete statement of all that he had seen or heard of them, and that he was in hopes that he would have some good news for the Indians upon receiving an answer; but he was sorry that his orders were such as to render it impossible for him to make them any issues whatever. The Indians then replied that it would be impossible for them to remain any great length of time, as they were short of provisions. Major Anthony then told them they could let their villages remain where they were, and could send their young men out to hunt buffalo, as he had understood that the buffalo had lately come close in. The Indians appeared to be a little dissatisfied at the change in commanders of the post, fearing that it boded them no good; but, having received assurances of safety from Major Anthony, they still had no fears of their families being disturbed.

On the twenty-sixth of November I received permission from Major Scott J. Anthony, commanding post, to proceed to the Indian villages on Sand creek, for the purpose of trading with the Indians, and started, accompanied by a soldier named David Louderback, and a citizen, Watson Clark. I reached the village and commenced to trade with them On the morning of the twenty-ninth of November the camp was attacked by Colonel J. M. Chivington, with a command of from nine hundred to one thousand men. The Indian village numbered about one hundred lodges, counting altogether about five hundred souls, two-thirds of whom were women and children, all of whose bodies had been mutilated in the most horrible manner. When the troops first approached, I endeavored to join them, but was repeatedly fired upon; also the soldier and citizen with me. When the troops began approaching, I saw Black Kettle, the head chief, hoist the American flag, fearing there might be some mistake as to who they were.

After the fight Colonel Chivington returned with his command in the direction of Fort Lyon, and then proceeded down the Arkansas river.

JOHN S. SMITH, *United States Interpreter.*

Sworn and subscribed to at Fort Lyon, C. T., this 27th day of January, 1865.

W. P. MINTON,
Second Lieutenant First New Mexico Volunteers, Post Adjutant.

A true copy:

J. E. TAPPAN,
Acting Assistant Adjutant General.

FORT LYON, COLORADO, *January* 27, 1865.

Personally appeared before me Samuel G. Colley, who, being duly sworn, on oath deposes and says: That he is now, and has been for the past three years, United States agent for the Arapahoes and Cheyenne Indians; that in the month of June last he received instructions from Hon. John Evans, governor and ex-officio superintendent of Indian affairs for Colorado Territory, directing him to send out persons into the Indian country to distribute printed proclamations (which he was furnished with) inviting all friendly Indians to come into the different places designated in said proclamation, and they would be protected and fed; that he caused the terms of said proclamation to be widely disseminated among the different tribes of Indians under his charge, and that in accordance therewith a large number of Arapahoes and Cheyennes came into this post, and provisions were issued to them by Major E. W. Wynkoop, commanding, and myself; that on the 4th day of September last two Cheyenne Indians (One-Eye and Manimick) came into this post with information that the Arapahoes and Cheyennes had several white prisoners among them that they had purchased, and were desirous of giving them up and making peace with the whites; that on the 6th day of September following Major E. W. Wynkoop left this post with a detachment of troops to rescue said prisoners, and that, after an absence of several days, he returned, bringing with him four white prisoners, which he received from the Arapaho and Cheyenne Indians; he was accompanied on his return by a number of the most influential men of both tribes, who were unanimously opposed to war with the whites, and desired peace at almost any terms that the whites might dictate; that immediately upon the arrival of Major Wynkoop at this post, large numbers of Arapahoes and Cheyennes came in and camped near the post; Major Wynkoop selected several of the most prominent chiefs of both nations and proceeded to Denver to counsel with Superintendent Evans; after his return he held frequent councils with the Indians, and at all of them distinctly stated that he was not empowered to treat with them, but that he had despatched a messenger to the headquarters of the department stating their wishes in the matter, and that as soon as he received advices from there he would inform them of the decision of General Curtis respecting them; that until that time, if they placed themselves under his protection, they should not be molested; that the Indians remained quietly near the post until the arrival of Major Anthony, who relieved Major Wynkoop; Major Anthony held a council with the Indians and informed them that he was instructed not to allow any Indians in or near the post, but that he had found matters here much better than he expected, and advised them to go out and camp on Sand creek until he could hear from General Curtis; he wished them to keep him fully advised of all movements of the Sioux, which they promptly did; he also promised them that as soon as he heard from General Curtis he would advise them of his decision; from the time that Major Wynkoop left this post to go out to rescue the white prisoners until the arrival of Colonel Chivington here, which took place on the 28th of November last, no depredations of any kind had been committed by the Indians within two hundred miles of this post; that upon Colonel Chivington's arrival here with a large body of troops he was informed where these Indians were encamped, and was fully advised under what circumstances they had come into this post, and why they were then on Sand creek; that he was remonstrated with both by officers and civilians at this post against making war upon these Indians; that he was informed and fully advised that there was a large number of friendly Indians there, together with several white men, who were there at the request of himself (Colley) and by permission of Major Anthony; that notwithstanding his knowledge of the facts as above set forth, he is informed that Colonel Chivington did, on the morning of the 29th of November last, surprise and attack said camp of friendly Indians and massacre a large number of them, (mostly women and children,) and did allow the troops of his command to mangle and mutilate them in the most horrible manner.

S. G. COLLEY, *United States Indian Agent.*

Sworn and subscribed to before me this 28th day of January, 1865, at Fort Lyon, Colorado Territory.

W. P. MINTON,
Second Lieutenant First New Mexico Volunteers, Post Adjutant.

A true copy :

J. E. TAPPAN,
Acting Assistant Adjutant General.

FORT LYON, COLORADO TERRITORY, *January* 16, 1865.

Personally appeared before me Lieutenant James D. Connor, first New Mexico volunteer infantry, who, after being duly sworn, says: That on the 28th day of November, 1864, I was ordered by Major Scott J. Anthony to accompany him on an expedition (Indian) as his battalion adjutant; the object of that expedition was to be a thorough campaign against hostile Indians, as I was led to understand. I referred to the fact of there being a friendly camp of Indians in the immediate neighborhood, and remonstrated against simply attacking that camp, as I was aware that they were resting there in fancied security under promises held out to them of safety from Major E. W. Wynkoop, former commander of the post of Fort Lyon, as well as by Major S. J. Anthony, then in command. Our battalion was attached to the command of Colonel J. M Chivington, and left Fort Lyon on the night of the 28th of November, 1864; about daybreak on the morning of the 29th of November we came in sight of the camp of the friendly Indians aforementioned, and were ordered by Colonel Chivington to attack the same, which was accordingly done. The command of Colonel Chivington was composed of about one thousand men; the village of the Indians consisted of from one hundred to one hundred and thirty lodges, and, as far as I am able to judge, of from five hundred to six hundred souls, the majority of which were women and children; in going over the battle-ground the next day I did not see a body of man, woman, or child but was scalped, and in many instances their bodies were mutilated in the most horrible manner—men, women, and children's privates cut out, &c.; I heard one man say that he had cut out a woman's private parts and had them for exhibition on a stick; I heard another man say that he had cut the fingers off an Indian to get the rings on the hand; according to the best of my knowledge and belief these atrocities that were committed were with knowledge of J. M Chivington, and I do not know of his taking any measures to prevent them; I heard of one instance of a child a few months old being thrown in the feed-box of a wagon, and after being carried some distance left on the ground to perish; I also heard of numerous instances in which men had cut out the private parts of females and stretched them over the saddle-bows, and wore them over their hats while riding in the ranks. All these matters were a subject of general conversation, and could not help being known by Colonel J. M. Chivington.

JAMES D. CONNOR,
First Lieutenant First Infantry New Mexico Volunteers.

Sworn and subscribed to before me this 27th day of January, 1865, at Fort Lyon, Colorado Territory.

W. P. MINTON,
Second Lieutenant First New Mexico Volunteers, Post Adjutant.

A true copy:

J. E. TAPPAN,
Acting Assistant Adjutant General United States Volunteers.

FORT LYON, COLORADO TERRITORY, *January* 27, 1865.

Personally appeared before me Private David Lauderbock, first cavalry of Colorado, and R. W. Clark, citizen, who, after being duly sworn, say: That they accompanied John Smith, United States Indian interpreter, on the 26th day of November, 1864, by permission of Major Scott J. Anthony, commanding post, Fort Lyon, Colorado Territory, to the village of the friendly Cheyenne and Arapaho Indians, on Sand creek, close to Fort Lyon, Colorado Territory, he, John Smith, having received permission to trade with the aforesaid friendly Indians; that on the morning of the 29th day of November, 1864, the said Indian village was attacked while deponents were in the same, by Colonel J. M Chivington, with a command of about one thousand (1,000) men; that according to their best knowledge and belief the entire Indian village was composed of not more than five hundred (500) souls, two-thirds of which were women and children; that the dead bodies of women and children were afterwards mutilated in the most horrible manner; that it was the understanding of the deponents, and the general understanding of the garrison of Fort Lyon, that this village were friendly Indians; that they had been allowed to remain in the localities they were then in by permission of Major Wynkoop, former commander of the post, and by Major Anthony, then in command, as well as from the fact that permission had been given John Smith and the deponents to visit the said camp for the purpose of trading.

DAVID H. LAUDERBOCK.
R. W. CLARK.

Sworn and subscribed to before me this 27th day of January, 1865.

W. P. MINTON,
Second Lieutenant New Mexico Volunteers, Post Adjutant.

A true copy:

J. E. TAPPAN,
Acting Assistant Adjutant General.

FORT LYON, COLORADO TERRITORY, *January* 27, 1865.

Personally appeared before me Second Lieutenant W. P. Minton, first regiment New Mexico infantry volunteers, and Lieutenant C. M. Cossitt, first cavalry of Colorado, who, after being duly sworn, say: That on the 28th day of November, 1864, Colonel J. M. Chivington, with the third regiment of Colorado cavalry, one-hundred-day men, and a battalion of the first cavalry of Colorado, arrived at this post, and on the 29th of November attacked a village of friendly Indians in the vicinity, and, according to representations made by others in our presence, murdered their women and children, and committed the most horrible outrages upon the dead bodies of the same; that the aforesaid Indians were recognized as friendly by all parties of this post, under the following circumstances, viz: that Major E. W. Wynkoop, formerly commander of the post, had given them assurances of safety until such time as he could hear from the commanding general of the department, in consequence of their having sued for peace and given every evidence of their sincerity by delivering up the white prisoners they had in their possession, by congregating their families together, and leaving them at the mercy of the garrison at Fort Lyon, who could have massacred them at any moment they felt so disposed; that upon Major Wynkoop's being relieved from the command of Fort Lyon, and Major Scott J. Anthony's assuming command of the same, it was still the understanding between Major Anthony and the Indians that they could rest in the security guaranteed them by Major Anthony; also that Colonel J. M. Chivington, on his arrival at the post of Fort Lyon, was aware of the circumstances in regard to the Indians, from the fact that different officers remonstrated with him, and stated to him how these Indians were looked upon by the entire garrison; that notwithstanding these remonstrances, and in the face of all these facts, he committed the massacre aforementioned.

W. P. MINTON,
Second Lieutenant First New Mexico Volunteers.
C. M. COSSITT,
First Lieutenant First Cavalry of Colorado.

Sworn and subscribed to before me this 27th day of January, 1865.

W. W. DENNISON,
Second Lieutenant First Colorado Veteran Cavalry,
Acting Regimental Adjutant.

A true copy:

J. E. TAPPAN,
Acting Assistant Adjutant General.

FORT LYON, COLORADO TERRITORY, *January* 16, 1865.

Personally appeared before me Captain R. A. Hill, first New Mexico volunteer infantry, who, after being duly sworn, says: That, as an officer in the United States service, he was on duty at Fort Lyon, Colorado Territory, at the time there was an understanding between the chiefs of the Arapaho and Cheyenne nations and Major E W. Wynkoop, with regard to their resting in safety with their villages in the vicinity of Fort Lyon until such time as orders in regard to them could be received from the commanding general of the department; that after Major Wynkoop being relieved from the command of Fort Lyon, Colorado Territory, the same understanding existed between Major Scott J. Anthony and the aforesaid Indians; that to the best of his knowledge and belief the village of Indians massacred by Colonel J. M. Chivington on the 29th day of November, 1864, were the same friendly Indians heretofore referred to.

R. A. HILL,
Captain First New Mexico Volunteers.

Sworn and subscribed to before me this 27th day of January, 1865.

W. P. MINTON,
Second Lieut. First Infantry New Mexico Volunteers, Post Adjutant.

A true copy:

J. E. TAPPAN,
Acting Assistant Adjutant General.

EXECUTIVE DEPARTMENT, COLORADO TERRITORY,
Denver, June 29, 1864.

DEAR SIR: I enclose a circular to the Indians of the plains. You will, by every means you can, get the contents to all these Indians, as many that are hostile may come to the friendly camp, and when they all do the war will be ended. Use the utmost economy in providing for those that come in, as the Secretary of the Interior confines me to the amount of our appropriations, and they may be exhausted before the summer is out. You will arrange to carry out the plan of the circular at Lyon and Larned.

You will use your utmost vigilance to ascertain how many of your Indians are hostile, where they are, and what plans they propose, and report to me by every mail at least. For this purpose you will enlist the active aid of Mr. John Smith and his son, and of such other parties as you may judge can be of essential service. Mr. C. A. Cook reports to me that Mr. Bent has given you important information in regard to the plans and strength of the hostile combinations on the plains. Please be careful and report to me in detail all of the reliab'e information you can get, promptly, as above directed.

I have the honor to be, respectfully, your obedient servant,

JOHN EVANS,
Governor of Colorado Territory and Sup't Indian Affairs.

Major S. G. COLLEY,
United States Indian Agent, Fort Lyon, C. T.

A true copy:

W. W. DENNISON,
2d Lieut. 1st Colorado Vet. Cavalry, Act'g Regt'l Adj't.

A true copy:

J. E. TAPPAN,
Acting Assistant Adjutant General.

COLORADO SUPERINTENDENCY OF INDIAN AFFAIRS,
Denver, June 27, 1864.

To the friendly Indians of the plains:

Agents, interpreters, and traders will inform the friendly Indians of the plains that some members of their tribes have gone to war with the white people. They steal stock and run it off, hoping to escape detection and punishment; in some instances they have attacked and killed soldiers, and murdered peaceable citizens. For this the Great Father is angry, and will certainly hunt them out and punish them, but he does not want to injure those who remain friendly to the whites; he desires to protect and take care of them. For this purpose I direct that all friendly Indians keep away from those who are at war, and go to places of safety.

Friendly Arapahoes and Cheyennes, belonging to the Arkansas river, will go to Major Colley, United States Indian agent, at Fort Lyon, who will give them provisions and show them a place of safety. Friendly Kiowas and Comanches will go to Fort Larned, where they will be cared for in the same way. Friendly Sioux will go to their agent at Fort Laramie for directions. Friendly Arapahoes and Cheyennes of the Upper Platte will go to Camp Collins, on the Cache-la-Poudre, where they will be assigned a place of safety, and provisions will be given them. The object of this is to prevent friendly Indians from being killed through mistake; none but those who intend to be friendly with the whites must come to these places. The families of those who have gone to war with the whites must be kept away from the friendly Indians. The war on hostile Indians will be continued until they are all effectually subdued.

JOHN EVANS,
Governor of Colorado and Superintendent of Indian Affairs.

A true copy:
W. W. DENNISON,
2d Lieut. 1st Colorado Vet. Cavalry, Act'g Regt'l Adj't.

A true copy:
J. E. TAPPAN,
Acting Assistant Adjutant General.

COLORADO SUPERINTENDENCY,
Denver, C. T., June 16, 1864.

SIR: You will immediately make necessary arrangements for the feeding and support of all the friendly Indians of the Cheyenne and Arapaho Indians at Fort Lyon, and direct the friendly Comanches and Kiowas, if any, to remain at Fort Larned ; you will make a requisition on the military commander of the post for subsistence for the friendly Indians o his neighborhood. If there is no agent there to attend to this, deputize some one to do it. These friendly Indians must be collected at places of rendezvous, and all intercourse between them and tribes or individuals engaged in warfare with us prohibited.

This arrangement will tend to withdraw from the conflict all who are not thoroughly identified with the hostile movement, and, by affording a safe refuge, will gradually collect those who may become tired of war and desire peace.

The war is opened in earnest, and upon your efforts to keep quiet the friendly Indians, as nucleus for peace, will depend its duration to some extent at least. You can send word to all these tribes to come as directed above, but do not allow the families of those at war to be introduced into the friendly camp. I have established a camp for our northern friendly bands on Cache-la-Poudre, and as soon as my plan is approved by the military I will issue a proclamation to the Indians.

Please spare no effort to carry out this instruction, and keep me advised by every mail of the situation.

Very respectfully, your obedient servant,

JOHN EVANS,
Governor and Ex-officio Sup't Indian Affairs.

A true copy:
W. W. DENNISON,
2d Lieut. 1st Colorado Vet. Cavalry, Act'g Regt'l Adj't.

A true copy:
J. E. TAPPAN,
Acting Assistant Adjutant Ganeral.

FORT LYON, COLORADO TERRITORY, *January* 16, 1865.

Personally appeared before me Private David Louderback, 1st cavalry of Colorado, and R. W. Clark, citizen, who, after being duly sworn according to law, say: That they accompanied John Smith, Indian interpreter, on the 26th day of November, 1864, by permission of Major Scott J. Anthony, commanding post of Fort Lyon, to the village of the friendly Indians, Cheyennes and Arapahoes, on Sand creek, close to Fort Lyon, he, John Smith, having received permission to trade with the aforesaid Indians ; that on the morning of the 29th of November the said Indian village, while the deponents were in the same, was attacked by Colonel J. M. Chivington with a command of about one thousand men ; that, according to their best knowledge and belief, the entire Indian party was composed of not more than five hundred souls, two-thirds of which were women and children ; that the dead bodies of children were afterwards mutilated in the most horrible manner ; that this village were friendly Indians ; that it was the understanding of the deponents, and the general understanding of the garrison at Fort Lyon, they were allowed to remain in the locality they were then in by Major E. W. Wynkoop, former commander of the post, and by Major Scott J. Anthony, then in command, as well as from the fact that permission had been given to John Smith and the deponents to visit the said camp for the purpose of trading.

DAVID LOUDERBACK.
R. W. CLARK.

Sworn and subscribed to before me this 16th day of January, 1865.
W. P. MINTON, *Post Adjutant.*

FORT LYON, COLORADO TERRITORY, *January* 16, 1865.

Personally appeared before me Lieutenant James D. Cannon, 1st New Mexico volunteer infantry, who, after being duly sworn, says: That on the 28th day of November, 1864, I was ordered by Major Scott J. Anthony to accompany him on an Indian expedition as his battalion adjutant; the object of the expedition was to be a thorough campaign against hostile Indians, as I was led to understand. I referred to the fact of there being a friendly camp of Indians in the immediate vicinity, and simply remonstrated against attacking that camp, as I was aware that they were resting there in fancied security, under promises held out to them of safety by Major E. W. Wynkoop, formerly commander of Fort Lyon, and by Major Scott J. Anthony, then in command. Our battalion was attached to the command of Colonel J. M. Chivington, and left Fort Lyon on the night of the 28th of November, 1864; about daybreak on the morning of the 29th of November came in sight of the camp of friendly Indians aforementioned, and was ordered by Colonel Chivington to attack the same, which was accordingly done. The command of Colonel Chivington was composed of about one thousand men; the village of Indians consisting of from one hundred to one hundred and thirty lodges, and, as far as I am able to judge, of from five to six hundred souls, the majority of them were women and children. In going over the battle-ground the next day I did not see a body of man, or woman, or child, but what was scalped, and in many instances their bodies were mutilated in the most horrible manner—men, women and children's privates cut out. I heard one man say that he had cut a woman's private parts out and had them for exhibition on a stick; I heard another man say that he had cut the fingers off of an Indian to get the rings on his hands. According to the best of my knowledge and belief, these atrocities that were committed were with the knowledge of Colonel J. M. Chivington, and I do not know of him taking any measure to prevent them. I heard of one instance of a child, a few months old, being thrown into the feed-box of a wagon, and after being carried some distance, left on the ground to perish; I also heard of numerous instances in which men had cut out the private parts of females and stretched them over their saddle-bows, and some of them over their hats. While riding in ranks, all these matters were a subject of general conversation, and could not help being known to Colonel J. M. Chivington.

JAMES D. CANNON.

Sworn and subscribed to before me this 16th day of January, 1865.

W. P. MINTON, *Post Adjutant.*

FORT LYON, COLORADO TERRITORY, *January* 16, 1865.

Personally appeared before me Captain R. H. Hill, 1st New Mexico volunteer infantry, who, after being duly sworn, says: That, as an officer in the service of the United States, he was on duty at Fort Lyon, Colorado Territory, at the time there was an understanding between the chiefs of the Arapahoes and Cheyenne nation and Major Wynkoop with regard to their resting in safety with these villages in the vicinity of Fort Lyon until such a time as orders in regard to them could be received from the commanding general of the department; that after Major Wynkoop being relieved from the command of Fort Lyon, the same understanding existed between Major S. J. Anthony and the aforementioned Indians; that, to the best of his belief, the village of Indians massacred by Colonel J. M. Chivington, on the 29th day of November, 1864, were the same friendly Indians heretofore referred to.

R. H. HILL.

Sworn and subscribed to this 16th day of January, 1865.

W. P. MINTON, *Post Adjutant.*

FORT LYON, COLORADO TERRITORY, *January* 16, 1865.

Personally appeared before me Second Lieutenant W. P. Minton, 1st New Mexico volunteer infantry, and Lieutenant C. M. Cossitt, 1st cavalay of Colorado, who, after being duly sworn, says: That on the 28th day of November, 1864, Colonel J. M. Chivington, with the 3d regiment Colorado cavalry, (one-hundred-days men,) and a battalion of the 1st cavalry of Colorado, arrived at this post, and on the 29th of November, 1864, attacked a village of friendly Indians in the vicinity, and, according to representations made by others in our presence, murdered their women and children, and committed the most horrible outrages upon the dead bodies of the same; that the aforesaid Indians were recognized as friendly Indians by all parties at this post, under the following circumstances, viz: That

Major E. W. Wynkoop, formerly commander of the post, had given them assurances of safety until such a time as he could hear from the commanding general of the department, in consequence of their having sued for peace, and given every evidence of their sincerity, by delivering up white prisoners they had in their possession, by congregating their families together and leaving them at the mercy of the garrison of Fort Lyon, Colorado Territory, who felt so disposed; that upon Major Wynkoop being relieved of the command of Fort Lyon, Colorado Territory, and Major Scott J. Anthony assuming command of the same, it was still the understanding between Major Anthony and the Indians that they could rest in that security guaranteed them by Major E. W. Wynkoop; also that Colonel J. M Chivington, on his arrival at the post of Fort Lyon, Colorado Territory, was made aware of the circumstances in regard to these Indians, from the fact that different officers remonstrated with him and stated to him how these Indians were looked upon by the entire garrison; that notwithstanding these remonstrances, and in the face of all true facts, he committed the massacre aforementioned.

C. M. COSSITT.
W. P. MINTON.

Sworn and subscribed to before me this 16th day of January, 1865.

W. W. DENNISON,
Acting Regimental Adjutant.

FORT LYON, COLORADO TERRITORY, *January* 16, 1865.

Personally appeared before me John Smith, United States Indian interpreter, who, after being duly sworn, says: That on the 4th day of September, 1865, he was appointed Indian interpreter for the post of Fort Lyon, Colorado Territory, and has continued to serve in that capacity up to the present time; that on the 4th day of September, 1865, by order of Major E. W. Wynkoop, commanding post of Fort Lyon, he was called upon to hold a conversation with three Cheyenne Indians, "One Eye" and two others, who had been brought into the fort that day; that the result of the interview was as follows: "One Eye" (Cheyenne) stated that the principal chiefs and sub-chiefs of the Cheyenne and Arapaho nations had held a consultation and agreed, to a man, of the chiefs and sub-chiefs to come or send in some one who was well acquainted with parties at the post, and finally agreed to send in himself, "One Eye," with a paper, written by George Bent, half-breed, to the effect that the Cheyenne and Arapaho chiefs would and did agree to turn over to Major E W. Wynkoop or any other military commander all the white prisoners they had in their possession, as they were anxious to make peace with the whites, and never desired to be at war. Major Wynkoop then asked "One Eye," he having lived among the whites and known to have always been friendly disposed towards them, whether they would deliver the prisoners into his (Wynkoop's) hands; his reply was that, at the risk of his life, he would guarantee their sincerity. Major Wynkoop then told him that he would deliver him as a prisoner for the time, and if he concluded to go to the Indian camp he would take him along as a hostage for their (the Indians') good faith. "One Eye" also stated that the Cheyenne and Arapaho nation were congregated, to the number of two thousand Indians, on the headwaters of Smoky Hill, including some forty lodges of Sioux; that they had rendezvoused there and brought in their war parties for the purpose of hearing what would be the result of their message by which they had sued for peace, and would remain until they heard something definite. Major Wynkoop told "One Eye" that he would proceed to the Indian camp and take him with him. "One Eye" replied that he was perfectly willing to remain a prisoner, as well as a hostage for the good faith of the Indians, but desired the major to start as soon as possible for fear the Indians might separate. On the 26th day of September I was ordered by Major Wynkoop to proceed, with his command, in the direction of the Indian encampment. After a four days' march we came in sight of the Indians, and one of the three Indians aforementioned was sent to acquaint the chiefs with what was the object of the expedition, with the statement that Major Wynkoop desired to hold a consultation with them (the chiefs) on the 10th day of September, 1864. The consultation was held between Major Wynkoop and his officers and the principal chiefs of the Cheyenne and Arapaho nations. Major Wynkoop stated, through me, to the chiefs, that he had received their message; that acting on that he had come to talk with them; asked them whether they all agreed to and indorsed the contents of the letter which he had in his possession, and which had been brought in by "One Eye." Receiving an answer in the affirmative, he then told the chiefs that he had not the authority to conclude terms of peace with them, but that he desired to make a proposition to them to the effect that if they would give him evidence of their good faith by delivering into his hands the white prisoners they had in their possession he would endeavor to procure for them peace, which would be subject to conditions; that he would take with him what principal chiefs they might select, and conduct them in safety to the governor of Colorado, and whatever might be the result of their interview, he would conduct them in safety to their tribe. "Black Kettle," the head chief of the Cheyenne nation, replied as follows: that the Cheyenne and Arapaho nation had always endeavored to observe the terms of their treaty with the United States government; that some years previously, when the whole emigration first commenced coming to what is now the Territory of Colorado, the country which was in possession of the Cheyenne and Arapaho nations, they could have successfully made war against them, the whites; they did not desire to do so; had invariably treated them with kindness, and have never, to his knowledge, committed any depredations whatever; that until within the last few months they had got along in perfect peace and harmony with their white brethren; but while a hunting party of their young men were proceeding north, in the neighborhood of the South Platte river, having found some loose stock belonging to white men, which they were driving to a ranch to deliver up, they were suddenly confronted by a party of United States soldiers and ordered to deliver up their arms; a difficulty immediately ensued, which resulted in killing and wounding several on both sides. A short time after an occurrence took place at a village of pappooses, squaws, and old men, located in what is known as the "Cedar cañon," a short distance north of the South Platte, who were perfectly unaware of any difficulty having occurred between the whites and a portion of their tribe, (Cheyenne;) were attacked by a large body of United States soldiers, some of them killed and their ponies driven off. After this, while a body of soldiers were proceeding from the Smoky Hill to the Arkansas, they reached the neighborhood of "Lou. Bear's" band of Cheyennes. "Lou. Bear," 2d chief of the Cheyenne nation, approached the column of troops alone, his warriors remaining off some distance, he not deeming that there was any hostility between his nation and the whites; he was immediately shot down and fire opened upon his band, the result of which was a fight between the two parties. Presuming from all these circumstances that war was inevitable, the young men of the Cheyenne nation commenced to retaliate by committing various depredations at all times, which he, "Black Kettle," and other principal chiefs of the Cheyenne nation, were opposed to, and endeavored by all the means in his power to restore pacific relations between that tribe and their white brethren, but at various times, when endeavoring to approach military posts for the purpose of accomplishing the same, was fired upon and driven off. In the meanwhile their brothers and allies, the Arapahoes, were on perfectly friendly terms with the whites, and Left Hand, one of the principal chiefs of the Arapaho nation, learning that it was the intention of the Kioways on a certain day to run off the stock from Fort Larned, proceeded to the commanding officer of that post and informed him of the fact. No attention was paid to the information he gave, and on the day anticipated the stock was run off by the Kioways. Left Hand again approached the post with a portion of his warriors for the purpose of offering his services to the commanding officer to pursue and endeavor to regain the stock from the Kioways, when he was fired upon and obliged hastily to leave. The young men of the Arapaho nation supposing it was the intention of the whites to make war upon them as well as the Cheyennes, also commenced retaliating as well as they were able, and against the desire of most of their principal chiefs, who, as well as Black Kettle and other chiefs of the Cheyennes, were bitterly opposed to hostilities with the whites. He then said that he had lately learned of the proclamation issued by the governor of Colorado, inviting all friendly disposed Indians to come to the different military posts and they would be protected by the government. Under these circumstances, nothwithstanding he thought the whites had been the aggressors and had forced the trouble on the Indians, anxious altogether for the welfare of his people, he had made this last effort to communicate again with the military authorities, and he was glad to have succeeded. He then arose, shook hands with Major Wynkoop and his officers, stating that he was still, as he had always been, a friend to the whites, and that, as far as he was concerned, he was willing to deliver up the white prisoners or do anything that was required of him to procure "peace," knowing it to be for the best of his people; but that there were other chiefs who still thought that they were badly treated by their brethren, but who were willing to make peace, but who felt unwilling to deliver up the white prisoners simply upon the promise of Major Wynkoop that he would endeavor to procure them peace; they desired that the condition of their delivering up the white prisoners would be an assurance of peace; he also stated that even if Major Wynkoop's propositions were not accepted then by the chiefs assembled, and although they had sufficient force to entirely overpower Major Wynkoop's small command, that from the fact that he had come in good faith to hold a consultation in consequence of the letter received, he should return to Fort Lyon, Colorado Territory, without being molested. The expressions of the other chiefs were to the effect that they insisted upon peace on the condition of their delivering up the white prisoners. Major Wynkoop finally replied, that he repeated what he had said, that it wa out of his power to insure them peace, and that all he had to say was, that they might think about his proposition; that he would march to a certain locality, distant twelve miles, and there await the result of their consultation for two days, advising them at the same time to accede to his proposition as the best means of procuring that peace for which they were anxious. The white prisoners were brought in and delivered up before the time had expired set by him, and Black Kettle, White Antelope, and Bull Bear, of the Cheyenne nation, as well as Nevah, Natance, Boisee, and Hip Buffalo, chiefs of the Arapahoes, delivered themselves over to Major Wynkoop. We then proceeded to Fort Lyon, and from thence to Denver, at which place Governor Evans held a consultation with the chiefs, the result of which was as follows: He told them they could return with Major Wynkoop, who would reconduct them in safety, and they would have to await the action of the military authorities. Colonel Chivington, then in command of the district of Colorado, also told them that they would remain at the disposal of Major Wynkoop until higher authorities had acted in their case. The Indians appeared to be perfectly satisfied, presuming that they would eventually be all right, as soon as those authorities could be heard from, and expressed themselves so. Black Kettle embraced the governor and Major Wynkoop, and shook hands with all the other officers present, perfectly contented, deeming the matter was settled. On our return to Fort Lyon I was told by Major Wynkoop to say to the chiefs that they could bring their different bands, including their families, to the vicinity of the post until he had heard from the big chief; that he preferred to have them under his eye, and away from other quarters where they were likely to get into difficulty with the whites. The chiefs replied that they were willing to do anything that Major Wynkoop might choose to dictate, as they had perfect confidence in him, and accordingly immediately brought their villages, their squaws, and pappooses, and appeared satisfied that they were in perfect safety. After their villages were located here, and Major Wynkoop had sent an officer to headquarters for instructions, then Major Wynkoop was relieved from command of the post by Major Scott J. Anthony, and I was ordered to interpret for him (Major Anthony) in a consultation he desired to hold with these Indians. The consultation that then took place between Major Anthony and these Indians was as follows: Major Anthony told them that he had been sent here to relieve Major Wynkoop, and that he would be from that time in command of the post; that he had come here under orders from the commander of all the troops in this country, and that he had orders to have nothing to do with the Indians whatever, as they had heard at headquarters that they had been committing depredations, &c., in the neighborhood of this post; but that, since his arrival, he had learned that these reports were all false; that he would write to headquarters himself and correct these errors in regard to them, and that he would have no objections to their remaining in the vicinity of Sand creek, where they were located, until such time as word might be received from the commander of the department; that he himself would forward a complete statement of all that he had seen and heard, and that he was in hopes that he would have some good news for the Indians upon receiving an answer; but that he was sorry that his orders were such as to render it impossible for him to make them any issues whatever. The Indians then replied that it would be impossible for them to remain where they were located any length of time, as they were short of provisions. Major Anthony then told them that they could let their villages remain where they were, and could send their young men out to hunt buffaloes, as he understood that the buffalo had lately come in very close. The Indians appeared to be a little dissatisfied in regard to the change of the commanders of the post, fearing that it boded them no good; but, having received assurances of safety from Major Anthony, they still had no fear of their families being disturbed. On the twenty-sixth day of November, 1864, I received permission of Major Scott J. Anthony, commander of the post, to proceed to the Indian village on Sand creek for the purpose of trading with the Indians, and started, accompanied by a soldier named Daniel Louderback and a citizen, Watson Clark. I reached the village and commenced to trade with them. On the morning of the twenty-ninth of November, 1864, the village was attacked by Colonel J. M. Chivington, with a command of from nine hundred to one thousand men. The Indian village was composed of about one hundred lodges, numbering altogether some five hundred souls, two-thirds of which were women and children. From my observation I do not think there were over sixty warriors that made any defence. I rode over the field after the slaughter was over and counted from sixty to seventy bodies of dead Indians, a large majority of which were women and children, all of whose bodies had been mutilated in the most horrible manner. When troops first appeared I endeavored to go to them, but was repeatedly fired upon; also the soldier and citizen that were with me. When the troops began approaching in a hostile manner. I saw Black Kettle hoist the American flag over his lodge, as well as a white flag, fearing that there might be some mistake as to who they were. After the fight Colonel Chivington returned with the command in the direction of Fort Lyon, and then proceeded by the road down the Arkansas river.

JOHN SMITH.

Sworn and subscribed to before me this sixteenth day of January, 1865.

W. P. MINTON, *Post Adjutant.*

FORT LYON, COLORADO TERRITORY, *April* 20, 1865.

Personally appeared before me Lieutenant James Olney, veteran battalion first Colorado cavalry, who, after being duly sworn, deposes and says: That he was present at the massacre of the Indians at Sand creek by Colonel Chivington, on the twenty-ninth day of November, 1864; that during that massacre he saw three squaws and five children, prisoners in charge of some soldiers; that, while they were being conducted along, they were approached by Lieutenant Harry Richmond, of the third Colorado cavalry; that Lieutenant Richmond thereupon immediately killed and scalped the three women and the five children while they (the prisoners) were screaming for mercy; while the soldiers in whose charge these prisoners were shrank back, apparently aghast.

JAMES OLNEY.

Sworn and subscribed to before me at Fort Lyon, Colorado Territory, this twentieth day of April, 1865.

CHARLES WHEELER,
Adjutant Veteran Battalion First Colorado Cavalry, Adjutant Fort Lyon.

Official copy respectfully furnished to headquarters. Fort Lyon, Colorado Territory, eleventh June, 1865.

CHARLES WHEELER,
First Lieutenant Veteran Battalion First Colorado Cavalry, Adjutant Fort Lyon.

FORT LYON, COLORADO, *January* 27, 1865.

Personally appeared before me Samuel G. Colley, who being duly sworn, on oath deposes and says: That he is now, and has been for the past three years, United States agent for the Arapaho and Cheyenne Indians; that in the month of June last he received instructions from honorable John Evans, governor and ex officio superintendent of Indian affairs for Colorado Territory, directing him to send out persons into the Indian country to distribute printed proclamations, (which he was furnished with,) inviting all friendly Indians to come into the different places designated in said proclamation, and they would be protected and fed; that he caused the terms of said proclamation to be disseminated among the different tribes of Indians under his charge, and that in accordance therewith a large number of Arapahoes and Cheyennes came in to this post, and provisions were issued to them by Major E. W. Wynkoop, commanding, and myself; that on the fourth day of September last two Cheyenne Indians (One Eye and Manimick) came in to this post with information that the Arapahoes and Cheyennes had several white prisoners among them that they had purchased, and were desirous of giving them up and making peace with the whites; that on the sixth day of September following Major E. W. Wynkoop left this post with a detachment of troops to rescue said prisoners, and that after an absence of several days he returned, bringing with him four white prisoners, which he received from the Arapaho and Cheyenne Indians. He was accompanied on his return by a number of the most influential men of both tribes, who were unanimously opposed to war with the whites, and desired peace at almost any terms that the whites might dictate; that immediately upon the arrival of Major Wynkoop at this post large numbers of Arapahoes and Cheyennes came and camped near the post. Major Wynkoop selected several of the most prominent chiefs of both nations and proceeded to Denver to counsel with Superintendent Evans. After his return he held frequent councils with the Indians, and at all of them distinctly stated that he was not empowered to treat with them; but that he had despatched a message to the headquarters of the department, stating their wish in the matter, and that as soon as he received advices from there he would inform them of the decision of General Curtis respecting them; that until that time, if they placed themselves under his protection they should not be molested; that the Indians remained quietly near the post until the arrival of Major Anthony, who relieved Major Wynkoop. Major Anthony held a council with the Indians and informed them that he was instructed not to allow any Indians in or near the post, but that he had found matters much better here than he had expected, and advised them to go out and camp on Sand creek until he could hear from General Curtis. He wished them to keep him fully advised of all the movements of the Sioux, which they promptly did. He also promised them that as soon as he heard from General Curtis he would advise them of his decision. From the time that Major Wynkoop left this post to go out to rescue the white prisoners until the arrival of Colonel Chivington here, which took place on the twenty-eighth day of November last, no depredations of any kind had been committed by the Indians within two hundred miles of this post; that upon Colonel Chivington's arrival here with a large body of troops, he was informed where the Indians were encamped, and was fully advised under what cirumstances they had come in to this post, and why they were then on Sand creek; that he was remonstrated with, both by officers and civilians at this post, against making war upon these Indians; that he was informed and fully advised that there was a large number of friendly Indians there, together with several white men, who were there at the request of himself (Colley) and by permission of Major Anthony; that notwithstanding his knowledge of the facts as above set forth, he is informed that Colonel Chivington did, on the morning of the twenty-ninth day of November last, surprise and attack said camp of friendly Indians and massacre a large number of them, mostly women and children, and did allow the troops under his command to mangle and mutilate them in the most horrible manner.

S. G. COLLEY,
United States Indian Agent.

Sworn and subscribed to before me this twenty-eighth day of January, at Fort Lyon, Colorado Territory.

W. P. MINTON,
Second Lieutenant New Mexico Volunteers and Post Adjutant.

FORT LYON, COLORADO TERRITORY, *January* 16, 1865.

SIR: In pursuance of Special Order No. 43, headquarters district of the Upper Arkansas, directing me to assume command of Fort Lyon, Colorado Territory, as well as to investigate and immediately report in regard to late Indian proceedings in this vicinity, I have the honor to state that I arrived at this post on the evening of the 14th of January, 1865, assumed command on the morning of the 18th, and the result of my investigation is as follows, viz:

As explanatory, I beg respectfully to state, that while formerly in command of this post, on the 4th day of September, 1864, and after certain hostilities on the part of the Cheyenne and Arapaho Indians, induced, as I have had ample proof, by the overt acts of white men, three Indians, Cheyennes, were brought as prisoners to myself, who had been found coming towards the post, and who had in their possession a letter, written, as I ascertained afterwards, by a half-breed in the Cheyenne camp, as coming from Black Kettle and other prominent chiefs of the Cheyenne and Arapaho nation, the purport of which was that they desired peace, had never desired war with the whites, and as well as stating they had in their possession some white prisoners, women and children, whom they were willing to deliver up, providing that peace was granted them; knowing that it was not in my power to insure and offer them peace for which they sued, and at the same time anxious, if possible, to accomplish the rescue of the white persons in their possession, I finally concluded to risk an expedition, with a small command I could raise, numbering one hundred and twenty-seven men, to the rendezvous where I was informed they were congregated to the number of two thousand, and endeavor by some means to procure the aforesaid white persons, and to be governed in my course of accomplishing the same entirely by circumstances, having formerly made a lengthy report in regard to the same. In my expedition I have but to say that I succeeded, procuring four white captives from the hands of these Indians, simply giving them, in return, a pledge that I would endeavor to procure for them the peace for which they so anxiously sued; feeling that under the proclamation issued by John Evans, governor of Colorado and superintendent of Indian affairs, a copy of which becomes a portion of this report, by virtue of my position as a United States officer highest in authority in the country included within the bounds prescribed as the country of the Arapaho and Cheyenne nations, I could offer them protection until such time as some measures might be taken by those higher in authority than myself in regard to them. I took with me seven of the principal chiefs, including Black Kettle, to Denver City for the purpose of allowing them an interview with the governor of Colorado, by that means making a mistake of which I have since become painfully aware, that of proceeding with these chiefs to the governor of Colorado Territory instead of to the headquarters of my district to my commanding officer. In the consultation with Governor Evans the matter was referred entirely to the military authorities. Colonel J. M. Chivington, at that time commander of the district of Colorado, was present at the council held with these Indian chiefs, and told them that the whole matter was referred to myself, who would act towards them according to the best of my judgment, until such time as I could receive instructions from the proper authority. Returning to Fort Lyon, Colorado Territory, I allowed the Indians to bring their villages to the vicinity of the fort, including their squaws and papooses, and in such a position that I could at any moment, with the garrison, have annihilated them had they given any evidence of hostility of any kind in any quarter.

I then immediately despatched my adjutant, Lieutenant W. W. Dennison, with a full statement, to the commanding general of the department, asking for instructions, but in the meanwhile various false rumors having reached district headquarters in regard to my course, I was relieved from the command of Fort Lyon, Colorado Territory, and ordered to report to district headquarters; Major Scott J. Anthony, 1st cavalry of Colorado, who had been ordered to assume command of Fort Lyon, Colorado Territory, previous to my departure, held a consultation with the chiefs in my presence, and told them that though acting under strict orders, under the circumstances, could not materially differ from the course which I had adopted, and allowed them to remain in the vicinity of the post with their families, assuring them of perfect safety until such time as positive orders should be received from headquarters in regard to them. I left the fort on the 26th of November, 1864, for the purpose of reporting to district headquarters; on the second day after leaving Fort Lyon, while on the plains, I was approached by three Indians, one of whom stated to me that he had been sent by Black Kettle to warn me that about two hundred Sioux warriors had proceeded down the road between where I was and Fort Larned to make war, and desired that I should be careful, another evidence of these Indians' good faith; all of his statement proved afterwards to be correct. Having an escort of twenty-eight men, I proceeded on my way, but did not happen to fall in with them.

From evidence of officers at this post I understand that on the 28th day of November, 1864, Colonel J. M. Chivington, with the 3d regiment of Colorado cavalry (one-hundred-days men) and a battalion of the 1st Colorado cavalry arrived at this post, ordered a portion of the garrison to join him, under the command of Major Scott J. Anthony, against the remonstrances of the officers of the post, who stated circumstances of which he was well aware, attacked the camp of friendly Indians, the major portion of which were composed of women and children. The affidavits which become a portion of this report will show more particulars of that massacre; any one whom I have spoken to, whether officers or soldiers, agree in the relation that the most fearful atrocities were committed that was ever heard of; women and children were killed and scalped, children shot at their mother's breast, and all the bodies mutilated in the most horrible manner. Numerous eye-witnesses have described scenes to me, coming under the notice of Colonel Chivington, of the most disgusting and horrible character, the dead bodies of females profaned in such a manner that the recital is sickening. Colonel J. M. Chivington all the time inciting his troops to these diabolical outrages previous to the slaughter; commencing, he addresed his command, arousing in them, by his language, all their worst passions, urging them on to the work of committing all these diabolical outrages, knowing himself all the circumstances of these Indians resting on the assurances of protection from the government given them by myself and Major S. J. Anthony; he kept his command in entire ignorance of the same, and when it was suggested that such might be the case, he denied it positively, stating that they were still continuing their depredations and lay there threatening the fort. I beg leave to draw the attention of the colonel commanding to the fact, established by the enclosed affidavits, that two-thirds or more of that Indian village were women and children. I desire also to state that Colonel J. M. Chivington is not my superior officer, but is a citizen mustered out of the United States service, and also to the time this inhuman monster committed this unprecedented atrocity he was a citizen by reason of his term of service having expired, he having lost his regulation command some months previous. Colonel Chivington reports officially that between five and six hundred Indians were left dead upon the field. I have been informed by Captain Booth, district inspector, that he visited the field and counted but sixty-nine bodies, and by others who were present, but that few, if any, over that number were killed, and that two-thirds of them were women and children. I beg leave to further state, for the information of the colonel commanding, that I talked to every officer in Fort Lyon, and many enlisted men, and that they unanimously agree that all the statements I have made in this report are correct. In conclusion, allow me to say that from the time I held the consultation with the Indian chiefs, on the headwaters of Smoky Hill, up to the date of the massacre by Colonel Chivington, not one single depredation had been committed by the Cheyenne and Arapaho Indians; the settlers of the Arkansas valley had returned to their camps and had been resting in perfect security, under assurances from myself that they would be in no danger for the present, by that means saving the country from what must inevitably become a famine were they to lose their crops; the lines of communication to the States were opened, and travel across the plains rendered perfectly safe through the Cheyenne and Arapaho country. Since this last horrible murder by Chivington the country presents a scene of desolation; all communication is cut off with the States, except by sending large bodies of troops, and already over a hundred whites have fallen as victims to the fearful vengeance of these betrayed Indians. All this country is ruined; there can be no such thing as peace in the future but by the total annihilation of all these Indians on the plains. I have most reliable information to the effect that the Cheyennes and Arapahoes have allied themselves with the Kiowas, Comanches and Sioux, and are congregated to the number of ——— thousand on the Smoky Hill. Let me also draw the attention of the colonel commanding to the fact stated by the affidavits, that John Smith, United States interpreter, a soldier and citizen were presented in the Indian camp by permission of the commanding officer of this camp, another evidence to the fact of these same Indians being regarded as friendly Indians; also, that Colonel Chivington states in his official report that he fought from nine hundred to one thousand Indians, and left from five to six hundred dead upon the field, the sworn evidence being that there were but five hundred souls in the village, two thirds of them being women and children, and that there were but from sixty to seventy killed, the major portion of whom were women and children. It will take many more troops to give security to the travellers and settlers in this country and to make any kind of successful warfare against the Indians. I am at work placing Fort Lyon in a state of defence, having all, both citizens and soldiers located here, employed upon the works, and expect to have them soon completed and of such a nature that a comparatively small garrison can hold the fort against any attack by Indians. Hoping that my report may receive the particular attention of the colonel commanding, I respectfully submit the same.

Your obedient servant,

E. W. WYNKOOP,
Major, Com'dg 1st Veteran Cavalry and Fort Lyon, C. T.

Lieutenant J. E. TAPPAN,
A. A. A. General, District of Upper Arkansas.

FORT LARNED, *May* 31, 1865.

Colonel Ford sworn:

I am colonel of the 2d Colorado regiment of cavalry and brevet brigadier general in command of the district of the Upper Arkansas. I have been in command since about the 1st of September last. I relieved Major Henning. From the best of my information all the tribes of Indians are hostile. The Kioways, Cheyennes, Comanches, Arapahoes, and parts of other tribes, with their families, are now south of the Arkansas, on the Red river, which is one of its tributaries. In February last a large number of them were about one hundred and fifty miles west of south of this point. From the best information I can get, there are about seven thousand warriors well mounted, some on fleet Texan horses. On horseback they are the finest skirmishers I ever saw. How large a force, mounted and infantry, would be required to defend the Santa Fé road and wage a successful war against the Indians south of the Arkansas? It would require at least ten thousand men—four thousand constantly in the field, well mounted; the line of defence to extend from Fort Lyon to Fort Riley and south about three hundred miles. All supplies would have to come from the States. Contract price for corn delivered at this point was $5.26 per bushel. I do not know how the Indian difficulties originated. I believe the Cheyennes are trying to keep all the Indian tribes in hostility. I have no doubt the attack of Colonel Chivington on the Cheyennes had a very bad effect. There are no Indians north of the Arkansas in my district except some small roving bands. I think, without moving south of the Arkansas, it would require four thousand men to defend the line of this road. I could not swear what Indians have committed the hostilities. Colonel Leavenworth has, in my opinion, the only feasible plan for procuring an interview with the hostile tribes. I received my information from some Mexicans who were trading with the Indians under a pass from General Carleton. If a treaty were made by which the Indians would agree to keep south of the Arkansas and east of Fort Bascom, would it protect this route? It would if the northern Indians did not come on to the road. The time has been when travelling over these plains was safe; the travel was as great then as now. There seems to be no reason why that state of affairs could not be brought about by making or conquering a treaty of peace. I think the mouth of Cow creek would be a good point to meet the Indians. General Dodge's orders were to the effect that the military authorities were not to make peace, but to punish the offenders. I am of the opinion that no permits to trade with the Indians should be given while we are carrying on hostilities against them; and no presents should be given by the agent without the concurrence of the military authorities. I am of the opinion that if a peace could be made by which the Indians would agree to keep south of the Arkansas it would be better than to conquer one. My plan of operations would be to capture their villages, women and children, killing the warriors found. I understand Kit Carson last winter destroyed an Indian village. He had about four hundred men with him, but the Indians attacked him as bravely as any men in the world, charging up to his lines, and he withdrew his command. They had a regular bugler, who sounded the calls as well as they are sounded for troops. Carson said if it had not been for his howitzers few would have been left to tell the tale. This I learned from an officer who was in the fight. From information I learn that Captain Parmeter, at Fort Larned, ordered soldiers to fire on Left Hand and party when they came to offer their services to recover the stock run off by other Indians. There is a general order in this district that no Indian shall be permitted to enter any fort or post without being blindfolded. I am satisfied that the Sand creek affair has made the Indians more bitter and harder to get at.

FORT LARNED, *May* 31, 1865.

John T. Dodds affirms:

I am fifty-four years old. Have spent six years among the Indians of Ohio and seven years here. Have been engaged, in company with another man, trading with the Indians. The Cheyennes complain that the Great Father was to give them a certain amount for the privilege of passing through their country. Heretofore they have had their presents delivered to them at a point designated by themselves; that they requested their agent, Major Colley, to make the delivery at Walnut creek, but instead the agent carried them on to Fort Lyon; that they could not go there for them without losing more horses than the goods were worth. Part of the Arapahoes, under Little Raven, went to Fort Lyon, but lost their ponies; and they all complain that if the Great Father intends giving them anything he should give it when it arrives in their country, and not put them to so much trouble. They complain further that they have to pay for the goods intended by the Great Father to be given them. The above is the statement of Black Kettle, Lean Bear, Left Hand, and Raven. They complain generally that the whites are encroaching on their lands and killing their buffalo. I think that before the Sand creek affair they were willing to settle on their reservations; but they now feel that they have been badly treated. The Comanches claim that until lately they have been at peace. A Kioway chief stated that if they went to war the Comanches would join them. Stante stated that the Kioways divided with the Comanches the stock run off from Fort Larned. I think if Satank and Stante, of the Kioways, were out of the way there would be peace, but not until. After the stock was run off from Fort Larned, Lean Bear started to go into the fort under a flag of truce, but was fired on by order of Captain Parmeter. He left, tearing up his flag. Mauwee, One-Eye, Lou Bears, and Two Buttes, chiefs of the Comanche tribe, were present at the fort when the stock was run off, and have not since been seen.

FORT RILEY, *May* 25, 1865.

Edmond G. Guerrier, being duly sworn, says:

I am the person referred to by Mr. Mayer in his statement. I speak English well; I can speak Cheyenne some, though from long absence I have forgotten a good deal of Cheyenne. My father was a Frenchman and my mother a Cheyenne. I am twenty-five years of age. I was in the camp of the Cheyennes when Chivington made his attack upon them. I had been with them about three days before the attack. There were, I think, about eighty lodges; there are four or five in a lodge on the average; can't tell precisely the number. After the attack I remained with them about four weeks. I do not know how many warriors there were in the lodges. I do not think there were over two hundred warriors in the camp. Last spring I met John Smith, the interpreter, to go out with him; about the time we got out there the Cheyennes were at war with the whites; but the Kioways, Comanches, and Arapahoes were friendly to the whites. I drove team out for Major Colley, the Indian agent. I took my discharge at Fort Lyon, came back to Fort Larned and hired to another man to trade with the Indians, and lay in camp at Walnut creek and Fort Garah a few days after the Kioways, Comanches, and Arapahoes broke out into hostilities, and came into our camp at Fort Garah. There were two Cheyennes in the camp with us that night, and they saved us, saved our lives, myself and a trader. That night I left with the two Cheyenne Indians. This was in July some time. I was out with them until September, when they sued for peace. I wrote the propositions for them to send into Fort Lyon, as the terms of peace. Major Colley, the Indian agent, was there. Major Wynkoop, then in command of Fort Lyon, came out into the prairie and met the Indians. Before he came he replied to my letter. His letter was directed to the chiefs. I read the letter to the chiefs. I think they have the letter still if it was not lost at the fight. The substance of the letter which I wrote and signed by order of the chief was this : That the Indians held some prisoners, three women and four children, and that they were ready to surrender them; that the Indians desired peace, and to have all the other Indians come too, and have a general peace. He does not now remember all the contents of the letter. One thing more I remember about the prisoners; they had heard there were some Indian prisoners at Denver, and they wanted to have them given up also. The substance of Wynkoop's letter, as I now recollect, was this: He stated there were no Indian prisoners, to his recollection or knowledge, at Denver; that he would come out to talk with the Indians, and wanted them to meet him on one of the branches of the Smoky Hill; he did not come out to fight, but to talk, and wanted them to bring the prisoners along. I read the letter to the Indians; they saddled up their horses and started immediately and met him that night, but had no interview until the next morning. He told them he was not big chief enough to make a treaty; he had no orders of that kind, but told them he would do all he could, and use his influence if some of the chiefs would go to Denver and see the governor, and told them that by giving up their prisoners to him it would go to show they were in earnest for peace. The Indians agreed to do so, and started the same day to go after the prisoners. In three days they brought in one young woman, and in a day or two after that brought in three children; the other three had gone north with another party of the band on to the Powder river. The chiefs who brought in the prisoners went with Wynkoop to see the governor at Denver. After Wynkoop and the chiefs returned, Wynkoop desired that the Indians who wished to be friendly should all come in and camp near Fort Lyon. If they did so it would show, if there were depredations committed they had no part in them; and if they did so, as long as they would behave, he would issue them rations. He was expecting some expeditions, and if they were found outside they would be treated by them like hostile Indians. He told them as long as they would stay there and behave themselves he would protect them and see that no troops should hurt them. I am sure and positive of this. Black Kettle and White Antelope, Cheyenne chiefs, also told me that Wynkoop had promised protection if they would come in, and they had promised to do so; and that Wynkoop had acted like a gentleman, more so than any other white man who had dealt with them, and they had promised to come in, and they did so. Before they came in Wynkoop was relieved of his command, and Major Anthony took command. Wynkoop left and came east. They were encamped on Sand creek, about twenty-five or thirty miles from Fort Lyon. A few days after Wynkoop left I went out with John Smith from Fort Lyon to the camp to trade. Smith had a Cheyenne wife at the camp; he also had a son with him, full grown. About three days after that the camp was attacked early in the morning. David Louderback was also in the camp; also a young man by the name of Watt Clark; these were white men. I was, at the time of the attack, sleeping in a lodge. I heard, at first, some of the squaws outside say there were a lot of buffalo coming into camp; others said they were a lot of soldiers. The squaws in my lodge looked out and then called to me to get up; "there were a lot of soldiers coming." I did so, went out, and went towards Smith's tent, where he traded; I ran and met him. Louderback, the soldier, proposed we should go out and meet the troops. We started; before we got outside the edge of the tent I could see soldiers begin to dismount. I thought they were artillerymen and were about to shell the camp. I had hardly spoken when they began firing with their rifles and pistols. When I saw I could not get to them, I struck out; I left the soldier and Smith; I went to the northeast; I ran about five miles, when I came across an Indian woman driving a herd of ponies, some ten or fifteen. I got a pony. She was a cousin of mine—one of White Antelope's daughters. I went on with her to Smoky Hill. I saw as soon as the firing began, from the number of troops, that there could be no resistance, and I escaped as quick as I could. From all I could learn at the council held by the Indians, there were one hundred and forty-eight killed and missing; out of the one hundred and forty-eight, about sixty were men—the balance women and children. From all I heard before and after the attack, I am sure that the Indians were encamped at the place where they were attacked in full faith and assurance that they would be protected as friendly Indians. George Bent, a half-Cheyenne, helped me in writing the letter to Wynkoop to make terms of peace.

E. G. GUERRIER.

Henry F. Mayer:

I am sutler to the post, and have been such for two and a half years. I am forty seven years of age. I know Edmond G. Guerrier, a son of William Guerrier, formerly an Indian trader, a Frenchman, and trader at Fort Laramie, by a Cheyenne woman. He is now about twenty-five years of age. I know him intimately. I was the executor of his father's estate, and am his guardian. His father died in February, 1858. Edmond has been with me most of the time since I know him to be an upright, intelligent, correct young man. He is entirely reliable. I trust every word he says.

H. F. MAYER.

Sworn to this 25th day of May, 1865, before me.

J. R. DOOLITTLE.

Captain L. Wilson, 1st Colorado cavalry, sworn:

I arrived in Colorado in May, 1860, from Omaha, Nebraska; was raised in Pennsylvania; I have been in the service since August, 1861; I entered the service as a private, was promoted to second lieutenant, and then to captain. The only fight with Indians I have been engaged in was the Sand creek affair. I was first lieutenant commanding a battalion at Sand creek; I think there were about eight hundred troops engaged, under the command of Colonel Chivington. The fight occurred on the 29th of November, 1864; the column concentrated at Fort Lyon and moved from there. No pickets were thrown around the post by the command, and nothing done to prevent any one from passing out. We reached Fort Lyon about 10½ o'clock on the morning of the 28th; we received no information that the Indians at Sand creek were considered under the protection of the government. Major Scott Anthony was in command of the post; the column moved about 9½ o'clock in the evening; the command was composed of cavalry with six pieces of 12-pound howitzers. We reached the Indian village at daybreak the next morning, surprising the Indians. I was ordered with my battalion to cut the Indians off from their ponies. The advance was made from the southeast side by the whole column. My orders from Colonel Chivington were to cut the herd off, and in doing that I was compelled to fire on the Indians. The first firing was by our troops; I detached H company of my battalion, which was engaged some five minutes before the action became general. The artillery opened on the Indians, who had approached me under a bank as if they were going to fight. The Indians returned our first fire almost instantaneously. I was wounded in the early part of the action; the general action lasted about two hours. I saw no flag of any kind among the Indians. I heard the loss of the enemy estimated by some of the officers engaged at from 300 to 500; I should judge there were from 600 to 800 Indians in all. I heard no orders given in relation to taking prisoners, but it was generally understood among the officers and men, that no prisoners would be taken. Young Jack Smith and young Bent, half-breeds and two or three squaws, were the only prisoners taken. Young Bent was sent as a prisoner to Fort Lyon; Jack Smith was afterwards killed in camp. The squaws and pappooses followed the column to Fort Lyon; one young infant was picked up on the field; when we got into camp it was given to one of the squaws, but afterwards died and was buried. I saw some Indians that had been scalped, and the ears were cut off of the body of White Antelope. One Indian who had been scalped had also his skull all smashed in, and I heard that the privates of White Antelope had been cut off to make a tobacco bag out of. I heard some of the men say that the privates of one of the squaws had been cut out and put on a stick. There was a herd of about 600 ponies, mules and horses captured, whose average value per head was, I think, about $100; the Indians did not succeed in getting away with more than half a dozen of them. The herd was placed in charge of Captain Johnson, provost marshal of the column, and sent into Fort Lyon. When I reached Fort Lyon, I heard from the quartermaster that the main portion of the herd had been stolen by the troops; there were about 250 head recovered and brought to Denver with the command. Of the whole number captured the government derived no benefit, the stock being stolen and generally distributed throughout the country. In the Indian camp I saw one new scalp, a white man's, and two old ones. Some clothing was found, women's shoes and dresses, and officers' uniforms and other articles. The men helped themselves to what they wanted, and the balance was burned in the village. All the force, with the exception of about two hundred and forty of the veteran battalion, were one-hundred-days men; this was their only engagement. I do not know of its being an Indian custom to scalp their own dead, but am of the opinion that the Indians at Sand creek were scalped by our soldiers.

Pressly Talbott sworn:

Have resided in the Territory since 1859; I came from Kentucky; have become pretty well acquainted with Indian affairs; the difficulties arise from depredations committed by the Indians. The first year I was here there was no difficulty with the Indians; since then they have been committing depredations. I entered the service as captain in the 3d regiment Colorado one-hundred-days men; the only battle I was engaged in was at Sand creek. I was at Fort Lyon the day before the battle; I had a conversation with Major Anthony, who expressed himself glad that we had come, saying that he would have attacked the Indians himself had he had sufficient force. I did not understand from any source that the Indians had been placed there at Sand creek under the protection of the government. Colonel Chivington gave orders that no parties, either military or civil, should be allowed to leave or enter Fort Lyon without his consent, and he stationed pickets to enforce the order. I believe the object of the order was to prevent any one from giving the Indians information that troops were coming. I think we moved from Fort Lyon with about 650 men and four pieces of artillery, passing a distance of about forty-five miles, reaching the Indian village about sun up, surprising the Indians; Colonel Chivington ordering that the ponies be first secured, and Captain Wilson was intrusted with stampeding the ponies with Colonel Shoup. I received orders to march up the right side of the creek and attack, which I obeyed; the troops on the other side of the creek had commenced firing before; the artillery was also playing on the Indians. My company was permitted to charge the banks and ditches. No orders were given about taking prisoners. I was wounded and taken from the field about half an hour after the battle began, and know nothing of the fight after that time; I was shot through with a bullet. I did not see any flags displayed by the Indians. I do not know what disposition was made of the captured stock. I occupied a room while wounded adjoining the room of Major Colley, and was shown papers by John Smith against the government for 105 buffalo robes, two white ponies, and a wagon-load of goods. This account was made out in favor of Smith and Colley for $6,000. They claimed they had other demands against the government, and Smith said they would realize $25,000 out of it, and damn Colonel Chivington. They were very bitter in their denunciations of Colonel Chivington and Major Downing. Private Louderback swore to the accounts; he was detailed as a nurse for me, but did writing for Smith and Colley.

DENVER, *July* 21, 1865.

Jacob Downing sworn:

I have resided in Colorado since the spring of 1860; am a native of Albany, New York, a lawyer by profession, and about thirty-three years of age. I was major of the first cavalry of Colorado; was in service from August, 1861, to January, 1865. A portion of the time I acted as inspector of the district of Colorado. The first collision between the troops and the Indians was at Fremont's orchard, near Camp Sanborn, on the north side of the South Platte river, about the twelfth of April, 1864. I was at Camp Sanborn, inspecting troops. In the evening, about 9 o'clock, a man by the name of Ripley, a ranchman on the Kioway creek, came into Camp Sanborn and stated that the Indians had taken from him all his stock, and that he had narrowly escaped with his life. He did not know what tribe of Indians, and said that they were driving the people off from the Kioway, Bijout, and other creeks. He requested Captain Sanborn, the commander of the post, to give him the assistance of a few troops, stationed there, to recover the stock, saying that he knew the Indians; that they would go north, and he thought he could find them. Captain Sanborn consented. Next morning Lieutenant Dunn, with about forty men, was ordered to go in pursuit and recover the stock, if possible, taking Mr. Ripley as guide; with instructions also, as I understood, to disarm the Indians if he found them in possession of the stock, but to use every means to avoid a collision with them. He started that morning and returned about ten o'clock that evening, stating that he had had a fight with the Indians; that they first fired upon him. After marching until four o'clock in the afternoon he came in sight of the Indians, near Fremont's orchard. He was then on the south side of the Platte; the Indians were crossing to the north side, some of whom were driving a herd of stock—horses, mules, &c. In the river he halted his command to allow the horses to drink, they not having had water since morning, when Mr. Ripley and a soldier went ahead of the command to see what the Indians were driving, and to see if they could see Ripley's stock in the herd of the Indians. They soon returned, when Ripley stated that he recognized the Indians as those who drove off his stock, and had seen his horses in their herd, which they were rapidly driving towards the bluffs. The soldier stated that he thought the Indians intended to fight; that they were loading their rifles. When Lieutenant Dunn arrived on the north bank of the Platte, where he could see the Indians, he found them with their bows strung and their rifles in their hands. He directed

Mr. Ripley and four soldiers to stop the herd the Indians were driving, halted his command, and alone rode forward to meet the Indians; talked with them, endeavoring to obtain the stock without any difficulty, and requested one or two of the Indians to come forward and talk with him. They paid no attention to him, but together and in line rode towards him. Finding them determined not to talk with him, he rode slowly back to his command, and when the Indians were within about six or eight feet, he ordered his men to dismount and disarm the Indians. As soon as his men had dismounted the Indians fired upon them, and a fight commenced, which lasted about an hour. He succeeded in driving them into the bluffs, and followed them that night about twenty miles. He had four wounded, two of whom afterwards died. He thought he killed a number of Indians. The Indians, being greatly superior in numbers, succeeded in getting their dead and wounded away. At the commencement of the fight a small party of Indians drove the stock into the bluffs, and Ripley's stock was never recovered. He afterwards learned they were southern Cheyennes. He learned it from spears, bows, arrows, and other things left on the ground where the fight occurred, and by statements of some of the Indians of the Cheyennes; this is hearsay. Major Whitely took the statement of Indians at Camp Welles Lieutenant Dunn had separated his command, and had only sixteen men with him. He thought there were from eighty to one hundred Indians. He returned to camp, and next morning, having obtained a man named Geary as a guide, with a fresh mount, he started in pursuit. It having snowed in the night, the trail was obliterated so they could not follow it. The next was a fight I had with them at Cedar Bluffs. I came to Denver and requested Colonel Chivington to give me a force to go against the Indians. He did so. I had about forty men I captured an Indian and required him to go to the village, or I would kill him. This was about the middle of May. We started about eleven o'clock in the day; travelled all day and all that night. About daylight I succeeded in surprising the Cheyenne village of Cedar Bluffs, in a small cañon about sixty miles north of the South Platte river. We commenced shooting; I ordered the men to commence killing them. We soon found a cañon on the edge of the brinks, occupied by warriors with rifles. I arranged my men the best, as I thought, under the circumstances, and commenced shooting at them, and they at us The fight lasted about three hours. They put their dead under the rocks. They lost, as I was informed, some twenty-six killed and thirty wounded. My own loss was one killed and one wounded I burnt up their lodges and everything I could get hold of. There were fifteen large lodges and some smaller ones, but I was informed that there were some warriors who had no lodges. I took no prisoners. We got out of ammunition and could not pursue them. There were women and children among the Indians, but, to my knowledge, none were killed. We captured about one hundred head of stock, which was distributed among the boys. The stock consisted of ponies, for which I would not have given $5 per head. They were probably worth in this market $15 per head I distributed the stock among the men for the reason that they had been marching almost constantly day and night for nearly three weeks, and with the understanding that if Major General Curtis, commanding the department, would not consent to it, they would turn the stock over to the government—having seen such things done in New Mexico, under the command of General Canby, commanding the department. General Curtis would not allow this to be done, and I ordered the men to turn the ponies over to Lieutenant Chase, acting battalion quartermaster, which, to the best of my knowledge and belief, was done; and by Lieutenant Chase, as I was informed, the ponies were turned over to the government. About the same time I heard Lieutenant Ayres had a collision with the Indians. I made my attack on the Indians from the fact that constant statements were made to me by the settlers of the depredations committed by the Indians on the Platte, and the statements of murders committed; and I regarded hostilities as existing between the whites and Cheyennes before I attacked them at Cedar Bluffs, and before Lietuenant Dunn had a collision with them; and continue up to the present time I was under Colonel Chivington when he went to Fort Lyon, and when he made the attack at Sand creek. I have no knowledge of what occurred between the Indians and Major Wynkoop, commander of the post of Fort Lyon, but heard Major Anthony's statement Colonel Chivington marched with about five hundred men from Camp Fillmore; upon arriving at Fort Lyon he surrounded the place with pickets to prevent any one from leaving. He met Major Anthony at the officers' quarters. I was not present at the commencement of the interview, but came up soon after. I heard Colonel Chivington ask Major Anthony how the Indians were. The major said he wished Colonel Chivington would go out and attack them; that every man in Fort Lyon would go with him that had the opportunity; that he would have attacked them long before if he had had a sufficient number of troops. He stated that the Indians were on Sand creek, about twenty miles from Fort Lyon; but afterwards understood that he was mistaken, as they were about forty miles from Fort Lyon He urged an immediate attack upon the Indians, stating that he would like to save out of the number a few who he believed to be good Indians; mentioning the names of One Eye, Black Kettle, and one other, stating that the rest ought all to be killed. He said, in substance, that he had ordered the Indians at one time to give up their arms, and that he had intended to treat them as prisoners of war; that they gave him a few bows and arrows used by boys, and perfectly useless for warriors; that they gave up a Hawkins rifle without any lock on it; and, in fact, all the arms they surrendered were useless. Then, believing that they were insincere in their professions of friendship, he had returned their arms, ordered them away from the post, and directed the guard to fire upon them if they attempted to come into the fort. In fact, all his statements were urging Colonel Chivington to attack the Indians; that they were hostile. The command arrived at Fort Lyon in the forenoon, and that evening about 9 o'clock Colonel Chivington's command started for Sand creek. I should judge he took with him some one hundred or one hundred and twenty men from Fort Lyon. We reached Sand creek about sunrise next morning. A battalion was immediately ordered to place themselves between the village and the ponies; the other battalions were brought up and nearly surrounded the village. The horse of a man named Pierce was apparently running away with him; the horse ran into the village and fell, but got up; when an Indian fired and killed Pierce; this was the first shot fired, to my knowledge. I rode forward to the village at the head of what was left of my battalion, some having been sent away, and when near the village an Indian fired at me from under the bank of the creek. After looking at the arrangement of the village, I went back to Major Anthony, who had his battalion in line, and, under the supposition that he was going to charge the village with his cavalry, advised him not to do it, believing that the horses were liable to become entangled among the ropes and fall. Immediately after Pierce was killed the battalion on the right commenced firing into the village. Major Anthony was on the east of the village, on the north side of the creek; most of the command were dismounted, and fought in that way. The Indians took refuge in trenches under the banks, which had evidently been dug before our arrival. The fighting became general; we killed as many as we could; the village was destroyed and burned. The surgeon informed me that some forty were killed and wounded in Colonel Chivington's command. My own belief is, that there were some five hundred or six hundred Indians killed; I counted two hundred and odd Indians within a very short distance of where their village stood, most of whom were in these trenches, and Indians were killed five and six miles from the village; but of the two hundred killed, I counted about twelve or fifteen women and a few children, who had been killed in the trenches. I did not see any flag over the village, but afterwards saw a man with a small flag, who said he got it out of a lodge; I saw no person advancing with a white flag, but think I should have seen it had it happened. The Indians were not buried by our men. I saw no soldier scalping anybody, but saw one or two bodies which had evidently been scalped. I understand two or three squaws were taken prisoners, and carried to Fort Lyon. A half breed named Smith was taken prisoner, but was afterwards shot, the man who shot him afterwards deserting. I remember seeing John Smith after the attack was made. Major Anthony ordered his men to cease firing, and called to Smith to come towards him. I saw no mutilated bodies besides scalping, but heard that some bodies were mutilated. I don't know that I saw any squaw that had been scalped. I saw no scalps or other parts of the person among the command on our return I saw no papoose in a feed-box. I think I saw one with a squaw the night of our first camp, but understood they abandoned it the next morning, when the command moved. I heard Colonel Chivington give no orders in regard to prisoners. I tried to take none myself, but killed all I could; and I think that was the general feeling in the command. I think and earnestly believe the Indians to be an obstacle to civilization, and should be exterminated. I think there were some five hundred or six hundred head of ponies, horses, and mules. Colonel Chivington ordered the provost marshal, Captain J. J. Johnson, to take charge of them and turn them over to the quartermaster at Denver. Captain Johnson took charge of them and, I think, turned them over. I do not know of any being distributed among the men. I acted as attorney for Colonel Chivington in the late investigation.

DENVER, *July* 27, 1865.

Oliver A. Williard:

Is a clergyman of the Methodist Episcopal church, residing in Denver, and have resided here three years nearly; I know Colonel Chivington, and also Governor Evans; I have had conversation with Colonel Chivington more than once upon the subject of Governor Evans's connexion with the affair at Sand creek last year; Colonel Chivington said that Governor Evans had no knowledge of when he was to strike, or where, nor what was the object of his expedition; he said this more than once; he said it was necessary to keep secrecy in such expeditions, and the governor knew nothing of it when he went to the States; the governor was absent when the attack took place; both Colonel Chivington and Governor Evans are my friends, and members of my church.

Major Simeon Whitely sworn:

I have resided in Colorado since April, 1863; I came here from Wisconsin; there was no outbreak among the Plain Indians until a year ago last spring; since then there has been continual trouble; I was present at a council held between Governor Evans and seven or nine chiefs of the Cheyenne and Arapaho tribes in September, 1864; copies of what was said at the council are on file in the Senate Committee on Indian Affairs, and in the commission to investigate the conduct of Colonel Chivington; the original draught is in the possession of Governor Evans; I did not hear Governor Evans say that he did not want to see the Indians, or to make peace with them; he told them that the power to make peace had passed out of his hands; I did not hear him at any time say that if he made peace he would not know what to do with the regiment he had raised; in making the report of what transpired at the council I took great pains, and am sure that it is a correct and truthful account of the whole transaction; when the third Colorado regiment came back from Sand creek I saw in the hands of a good many of the privates a great many scalps, or parts of scalps, said to have been taken in that fight; at a theatrical performance held in this city I saw a great many scalps exhibited; at various times in the city I must have seen as many as a hundred scalps.

S. E. Browne sworn:

I have lived in Colorado since May, 1862, during which time have been United States attorney for the Territory; I have no doubt that if the military and civil management of Indian affairs were in discreet and competent hands Indian difficulties might be avoided; I personally know of no frauds or peculations committed against the government or Indians by any civil or military officers; in February last I was elected colonel of a mounted regiment raised in this Territory to serve for ninety days; late in the month of February I was in General Moonlight's headquarters, who was in command of the district of Colorado at that time, and heard him say that from the first and third Colorado cavalry then mustered out, and the horses and ponies taken at Sand creek, there were two thousand two hundred head to be accounted for to the government, but of that number only four hundred and twenty-five or four hundred and seventy-five had been accounted for, leaving a deficit of over seventeen hundred that he knew not what had become of; a comparatively small number, I have been informed, have since been recovered; I have seen over a hundred scalps in the city and through the country, said to have been taken at Sand creek; early in September or late in August last I heard Colonel Chivington in a public speech announce that his policy was to "kill and scalp all, little and big; that nits made lice;" one of the main causes of our difficulties with the Indians comes from the delay in paying the Indians their annuities according to law.

Colonel Potter sworn:

Am colonel of the sixth United States volunteers; I have been in Colorado nearly two months; am in command of the south sub-district of the plains; off from the stage lines I have received no reports; on the line south to Forts Garland and Fillmore, and the line into the States, I have had no difficulty, but on the line to Green river, towards Salt lake, the Indians have been troublesome, killing men, &c.; the Indians, as near as I can find out, are the Arapahoes, who have committed depredations between Fort Collins and the North Platte; they have driven off stage stock from some of the stations, and have also killed one sergeant and five men, burnt Foot's ranch, attacked a train near the ranch, capturing two wagons and running off some sixty head of stock; the train was escorted by soldiers, who fought as well as men could until their ammunition gave out; it requires from twenty-five to thirty men to guard the stage from Virginia Dale to the North Platte; these depredations I believe to have been committed by the Arapahoes, who, while their families are fed and protected by the government, prey upon the trains; I know of no other Indians who have committed depredations this side of the North Platte; north of the North Platte depredations have been committed by the Sioux and Cheyennes; General Connor, commanding the district, is now at Fort Laramie; I do not know the strength of his force; I have at present twelve hundred and eighty-eight men under my command; I don't think there is any possibility of making any lasting peace with the Indians; I think there is only one of three things to do—either abandon the country to the Indians, forcibly place the tribes on reservations surrounded by soldiers, or exterminate them; my orders are to kill every male Indian over twelve years of age found north of the South Platte, but to disturb no women and children; as far as I know the policy of the military department here, it is to exterminate the Indians; Utah is within General Connor's district; I know of no depredations committed in Utah.

Dr. Caleb S. Birtsell sworn:

I have resided in Colorado since 1859; I came from Ohio originally; I was at the battle of Sand creek as assistant surgeon of the third Colorado cavalry; it commenced by our men corralling the ponies; Colonel Chivington and Colonel Shoup gave orders to form in line of battle, but it could not be kept; firing commenced, and I was soon after engaged attending to the wounded; I saw very little of what occurred; I reserved some of the lodges for hospital tents, and my time was occupied that day and night and the next day caring for the wounded; on the afternoon of the 29th of November, while in one of the lodges dressing wounded soldiers, a soldier came to the opening of the lodge and called my attention to some white scalps he held in his hand; my impression, after examination, was that two or three of them were quite fresh; I saw in the hands of soldiers silk dresses and other garments belonging to women; I saw some squaws that were dead, but did not go over the ground; I did not see any Indians scalped, but saw the bodies after they were scalped; I saw no other mutilations; I did not see any kind of a flag in the Indian camp; there were none left wounded on the field; I know of none being killed after being taken prisoner; soon after the battle, on the march, and here in Denver, I have seen soldiers with Indian scalps; of the stock captured a great many died, and some were distributed among the troops, and some, I think, were sold; I heard Major Anthony say that he had given the Indians back what arms they had delivered up, and told them they must take care of themselves—that he would issue no more provisions to them—and that they dared the soldiers out to fight; my impression is that orders were given to take no prisoners; I think Colonel Chivington was in a position where he must have seen the scalping going on.

Asbury Bird, company D, 1st Colorado cavalry, sworn:

I was present at the engagement between Lieutenant Ayres and the Indians, composed of Cheyennes, Arapahoes, and some Kioways. There was some cattle stolen on the head of Beaver creek. We were sent to recover it; encountered a band of five lodges; two of the Indians came towards us armed with rifles; when about sixty yards off we hollered "how" to them, and they to us; before we got clear up to them they saw the command about half a mile in rear of us coming up on a lope, and put off to their village and took their squaws and left. Lieutenant Ayres took round a hill to catch the Indians. On our left there was one Indian, and Lieutenant Ayres sent two men to capture him; but the Indian shot one of the men and the other ran off. The ground being too rough to get the artillery up, we returned to the Indian camp, took all the meat, &c., and burned the lodges. We got on the Indian trail the next morning and pressed them so close they abandoned many things, and we recovered twenty of the stolen cattle. We then returned to Denver. We were ordered out again; met some Indians of the Sioux tribe; held a talk with them; they said they did not wish to fight; did not feel strong enough; they stayed in our camp that night, we sharing our provisions with them. The next morning, about 9 o'clock, we were attacked by about seven hundred Indians, and fought them until dark; we lost four men killed. We had no interpreter along with us. When the two Indians came to meet me they appeared friendly, but when they saw the command coming on a lope, they seemed frightened and ran off. No effort was made by Lieutenant Ayres to hold a talk with the Indians. I was with the train at Sand creek, but did not see the fight. I went over the ground soon after the battle. I should judge there were between 400 and 500 Indians killed. I counted 350 lying up and down the creek. I think about half the killed were women and children. Nearly all, men, women, and children, were scalped. I saw one woman whose privates had been mutilated. The scalps were carried away mostly by the 3d regiment, one-hundred-day men. I saw but one Indian infant killed. Two children were brought to the fort. I think about 500 head of stock was taken; about 400 were turned over to the quartermaster at Fort Lyon. A great portion of all the stock became scattered through the country. In a conversation with Dick Colley, in the month of November, 1864, he told me they had sent $2,000 worth of the Indian goods to Denver, and expected the money every day. I heard John Smith say he had some goods that did not cost him anything; that he was going to trade with the Indians, and if he lost them would not be out anything.

Mr. Bouser sworn:

The first difficulty between the Cheyennes and Arapahoes and whites occurred on the 11th day of April, 1864. A white man came into Camp Sanborn and reported that he had cattle stolen. A detail of twenty men was sent after the Indians to get the cattle. The commander of the detail, Lieutenant Clark Dunn, had orders to disarm and fetch in the Indians; if they refused, to sweep them off the face of the earth. A fight occurred, and some Indians were wounded, also four soldiers, two of whom afterwards died. There was no interpreter along with the detail. The Indians, so Lieutenant Dunn told me, shook hands, and appeared as though they wanted to say or do anything. I know an Indian named Spotted Horse, part Cheyenne and part Sioux; he is now dead; he told me that he was in the affair with Lieutenant Dunn. He said the Indians took three head of cattle; there were 100 warriors. There was snow on the ground, and the Indians were hungry and took the cattle; they would have come into Denver if their horses had been in condition. They went south of the river with the cattle, intending if the soldiers came after them to settle for the cattle by giving some of their ponies Before they had time to cross the river and kill the cattle the soldiers overtook them. The soldiers had no interpreter, held no talk with the Indians, gave them no time even to deliver the cattle, but pitched into them. He also told me that had he been up in time, as he speaks English, or had there been an interpreter, the whole matter might have been settled without a fight. As it was, the Indians rode up close to the soldiers, dismounted, and shook hands with them. Lieutenant Dunn's men then took hold of some of the Indians' weapons and tried to wrest them away. The Indians did not know what it meant, and refused to give up their arms, when they were fired upon by the soldiers. Spotted Horse, seeing that there was going to be a war, threw up his chieftainship, and with it some one hundred head of ponies, and came in to Governor Evans. I acted as interpreter, and he told substantially to Governor Evans the above. This same chief traded four of his ponies to ransom a white woman—Mrs. Kelly. The next collision was under Major Downing, at Cedar cañon. I have a Brulé Sioux woman for a wife. I am of opinion that a lasting peace could be made with all the southern Sioux without any more fighting.

FORT LYON, COLORADO TERRITORY.

Lieutenant Cramer sworn:

I am stationed at this post, 1st lieutenant company C, veteran battalion Colorado cavalry. I was at this post when Colonel Chivington arrived here, and accompanied him on his expedition. He came into the post with a few officers and men, and threw out pickets, with instructions to allow no one to go beyond the line. I was then in command of company K. He brought some eight or nine hundred men with him, and took from this post over a hundred men, all being mounted. My company was ordered along to take part. We arrived at the Indian village about daylight. On arriving in sight of the village a battalion of the 1st cavalry and the Fort Lyon battalion were ordered on a charge to surround the village and the Indian herd. After driving the herd towards the village, Lieutenant Wilson's battalion of the 1st took possession of the northeast side of the village, Major Anthony's battalion took position on the south, Colonel Chivington's 3d regiment took position in our rear, dismounted, and after the fight had been commenced by Major Anthony and Lieutenant Wilson, mounted, and commenced firing through us and over our heads. About this time Captain John Smith, Indian interpreter, attempting to come to our troops, was fired on by our men, at the command of some one in our rear, "To shoot the damned old son of a bitch." One of my men rode forward to save him, but was killed. To get out of the fire from the rear, we were ordered to the left. About this time Colonel Chivington moved his regiment to the front, the Indians retreating up the creek, and hiding under the banks. There seemed to be no organization among our troops; every one on his own hook, and shots flying between our own ranks. White Antelope ran towards our columns unarmed, and with both arms raised, but was killed. Several other of the warriors were killed in like manner. The women and children were huddled together, and most of our fire was concentrated on them. Sometimes during the engagement I was compelled to move my company to get out of the fire of our own men. Captain Soule did not order his men to fire when the order was given to commence the fight. During the fight, the battery on the opposite side of the creek kept firing at the bank while our men were in range. The Indian warriors, about one hundred in number, fought desperately; there were about five hundred all told. I estimated the loss of the Indians to be from one hundred and twenty-five to one hundred and seventy-five killed; no wounded fell into our hands, and all the dead were scalped. The Indian who was pointed out as White Antelope had his fingers cut off. Our force was so large that there was no necessity of firing on the Indians. They did not return the fire until after our troops had fired several rounds. We had the assurance from Major Anthony that Black Kettle and his friends should be saved, and only those Indians who had committed depredations should be harmed. During the fight no officer took any measures to get out of the fire of our own men. Left Hand stood with his arms folded, saying he would not fight the white men, as they were his friends. I told Colonel Chivington of the position in which the officers stood from Major Wynkoop's pledges to the Indians, and also Major Anthony's, and that it would be murder, in every sense of the word, if he attacked those Indians. His reply was, bringing his fist down close to my face, "Damn any man who sympathizes with Indians." I told him what pledges were given the Indians. He replied, "That he had come to kill Indians, and believed it to be honorable to kill Indians under any and all circumstances;" all this at Fort Lyon. Lieutenant Dunn went to Colonel Chivington and wanted to know if he could kill his prisoner, young Smith. His reply was, "Don't ask me; you know my orders; I want no prisoners." Colonel Chivington was in position where he must have seen the scalping and mutilation going on. One of the soldiers was taking a squaw prisoner across the creek, when other soldiers fired on him, telling him they would kill him if he did not let her go. On our approach to the village I saw some one with a white flag approaching our lines, and the troops fired upon it; and at the time Captain Smith was fired upon, some one wearing a uniform coat was fired upon approaching our lines. Captain Smith was wearing one. After the fight I saw the United States flag in the Indian camp. It is a mistake that there were any white scalps found in the village. I saw one, but it was very old, the hair being much faded. I was ordered to burn the village, and was through all the lodges. There was not any snow on the ground, and no rifle-pits. I was present at the interview on the Smoky Hill between Major Wynkoop and the Indians, and it is correctly set out in his report, which I have read. I was also present at the interview between the Indian chiefs and Major Anthony, after he had assumed command. The chiefs desired to come into the post for protection, as they had heard through the Sioux that the 3d regiment Colorado troops was advancing in their direction. Major Anthony declined to permit them, saying he had not provisions to feed them. They must stay where they were, and their young men must go out and hunt buffalo. This was only three days before the massacre.

FORT LYON, COLORADO TERRITORY.

C. M. Cossitt:

Is acting quartermaster at this post; was here when Colonel Chivington came in from Sand creek after the fight or massacre there. He used to stop with me when he came here. In my room several present, among others Major Colley, Indian agent. He thought he had done a brilliant thing which would make him a brigadier general. I think the expression was, "that he thought that would put a star on his shoulder." This would do for a second Harney as an Indian fighter. This is the substance of the conversation.

C. M. COSSITT,
Lieut. Vet. Battalion 1st Colorado Cavalry, A. A. Q. M.

Lucien Palmer sworn:

Am sergeant of company C, veteran battalion 1st Colorado cavalry. I was such at the time of the attack on the Cheyennes by Chivington; I was in the midst of the fight; I counted 130 bodies, all dead; two squaws and three papooses were captured and brought to Fort Lyon. I think among the dead bodies one-third were women and children. The bodies were horribly cut up, skulls broken in a good many; I judge they were broken in after they were killed, as they were shot besides. I do not think I saw any but what was scalped; saw fingers cut off, saw several bodies with privates cut off, women as well as men. I saw Major Sayre, of the 3d regiment, scalp an Indian for the scalp lock ornamented by silver ornaments; he cut off the skin with it. He stood by and saw his men cutting fingers from dead bodies. This was the morning after the fight. All I saw done in mutilating bodies was done by the members of the 3d regiment. I counted the number of dead bodies, but did not count the women and children separate from the men to learn the proportion of each. I speak only from my impression as to the women and children being one-third of the number killed. I was with the battery.

Amos C. Miksch sworn:

Am a corporal in company E, veteran battalion, 1st Colorado cavalry; was born in Pennsylvania, but my home is in Ohio. I was in the battery; did not see the first attack; after we came up we opened on the Indians; they retreated and we followed and stayed until all were killed we could find. Next morning after the battle I saw a little boy covered up among the Indians in a trench, still alive. I saw a major in the 3d regiment take out his pistol and blow off the top of his head. I saw some men unjointing fingers to get rings off, and cutting off ears to get silver ornaments. I saw a party with the same major take up bodies that had been buried in the night to scalp them and take off ornaments. I saw a squaw with her head smashed in before she was killed. Next morning, after they were dead and stiff, these men pulled out the bodies of the squaws and pulled them open in an indecent manner. I heard men say they had cut out the privates, but did not see it myself. It was the 3d Colorado men who did these things. I counted 123 dead bodies; I think not over twenty-five were full-grown men; the warriors were killed out in the bluff; altogether I think there were about 500. There were 115 lodges, from four to five in a lodge. In the afternoon I saw twenty-five or thirty women and children; Colonel Chivington would not allow them to come in; a squad of the 3d Colorado was sent out; I don't know what became of them; it was about four miles off. The Indians were generally scalped as they fell. Next day I saw Lieutenant Richmond scalp two Indians; it was disgusting to me; I heard nothing of a fresh white scalp in the Indian camp until I saw it in the Dunn papers. There was no snow on the ground; there were no rifle-pits except what the Indians dug into the sand-bank after we commenced firing. I saw them digging out sand with their hands while firing was going on; the water came into the trenches they dug in this manner.

FORT LYON, *June* 9, 1865.

Major Wynkoop sworn:

I am in command of this post; I was in command in May, 1864, and until within a short time previous to the Sand creek affair.

Question. Do your report and the accompanying affidavits state the facts of that affair?

Answer. They do so far as they go. I have been a resident of this Territory since October, 1858. I have been familiar with the state of affairs with the Cheyenne and Arapaho Indians. Previous to the Chivington affair hostilities were open about four months. From my own personal knowledge I have no doubt that the hostilities were commenced by a detachment of soldiers under the command of Lieutenant Dunn, who was sent in search of some cattle supposed to have been stolen and driven away by some Cheyenne Indians. A conflict occurred between Lieutenant Dunn and the Indians. Captain Sanborn sent out the detachment. A rumor had reached district headquarters that the cattle had been stolen by the Indians, and Colonel Chivington issued orders that a detachment should be sent out to recover the stock and disarm the Indians. The attempt to disarm the Indians resulted in a conflict; there was one killed and three wounded on our side. That was the first difficulty I know of between the Cheyennes, Arapahoes and whites since my residence in the country, seven years. The next difficulty was an attack on a Cheyenne village by Major Downing, under Chivington's orders. The major reported he had killed over forty warriors, but the Cheyenne chiefs stated to me that their loss consisted of two squaws and two pappooses. Our loss was one killed. Lieutenant Ayres, of the Colorado battery, had the next conflict with the Indians. He had been ordered by Colonel Chivington, as he stated to me, to kill all Indians he came across. He marched from Fort Larned, about forty miles, until he came to Lean Bear's band of Cheyennes, a few of whom were some distance from the column, hunting buffalo. Sergeant Fribbley was approached by Lean Bear, and accompanied by him into our column, leaving his warriors at some distance. A short time after Lean Bear reached our command he was killed, and fire opened upon his band. I am not aware of any hostilities committed by Lean Bear's command previous to this time. A running fight for a couple of hours ensued, in which we lost several killed, the Indians getting possession of the bodies. My information has been derived from information received and reports made to me, also from the Cheyennes. At and previous to the fight of Lieutenant Ayres, a band of Arapahoes were situated about twenty-five miles from here, on Sand creek; they had been in the habit of coming into the fort frequently, and having communication with their agent, Major Colley, and myself. I had been in the habit of issuing rations to them when I found them in want. They had given every evidence of friendship for the whites, and were in the habit of bringing in and delivering to me government stock found loose on the prairie. In consequence of this friendly feeling on their part, and desirous to keep them friendly, as we were at war with the Cheyennes. I issued rations to them every ten days. About this time I made the proposition to them. Colonel Chivington was temporarily at this post, and in the presence of several officers I submitted the proposition to him, and he heartily indorsed the same, and was present at one or two issues. This post was then in the district of the Upper Arkansas; Colonel Chivington was here, but dated his orders headquarters in the field. Left-Hand's band was at this time camped near Fort Larned; near them was a band of Kiowas. Left-Hand, who had always been friendly to the whites, learned that the Kiowas, on a certain day, intended to run off the stock from Fort Larned, and he accordingly stated that fact to the commanding officer of that post, Captain Parmeter. No apparent attention was paid to the information given by Left-Hand, and on the day indicated by him the stock was driven off by the Kiowas. Immediately after this Left-Hand and his band approached the post to offer his services and the services of his young men to pursue the Kiowas and recover the stock. Meeting a soldier a short distance from the post, he requested him to state to the commanding officer his object. I am personally acquainted with Left-Hand; he speaks English. Left-Hand continued to approach the post, at the same time exhibiting a white flag, when fire was opened upon them by the battery, which drove them off After sufficient time had elapsed for the news to reach this vicinity, the band of Arapahoes camped here suddenly disappeared. Not a great while afterwards a citizen, a quartermaster's teamster, and his wife, while travelling from Denver here, were attacked by Indians; the man killed and the woman carried off I have reliable information that this act was committed by Little Raven's band of Arapahoes. A short time after that, two citizens on their way to this post to testify before a military commission, sixteen miles from here, were attacked by Indians and killed. My information is, that this outrage was committed by Little Raven's band. I know of no outrages committed by any of Left-Hand's band. While a small detachment of my regiment, some thirty men, were encamped near the mouth of the Cimarron crossing, their stock was run off. Lieutenant Chase, encamped at Jimmy's camp, had his stock driven off The letter I received from the Indians is correctly printed in the Commissioner's report. I do know that the Indians encamped on Sand creek felt that they were under the protection of the government, and were friendly; have driven my family down to their camp and sat in their lodges, without an escort. Colonel Chivington had no orders to attack the Cheyenne camp; I never have received any instructions in regard to Indians and their treatment. Since the Sand creek affair there has existed the deadliest hostility between those tribes and the whites; they have killed many persons on the Platte, and captured and destroyed much property. I know of no depredations committed on this route by the Cheyennes and Arapahoes since; I have reason to know that the Kiowas and Comanches have joined them in hostilities; I know that the Sioux are anxious, with the other tribes, to make peace, if the Cheyennes and Arapahoes do, and I think before the Sand creek affair a lasting peace could have been made with all the Indians. Since the massacre I have not been able to hold any communication with the Indians. I have in my possession a statement made by a half-breed, who had been in their camp since the massacre. He was in during the attack, and was among those who escaped; he was also in their camp when the remnant of the tribe got together on the Smoky Hill. Black Kettle, head chief of the Cheyennes, was there, but in disgrace with his tribe; was recognized no longer, and was taunted for having, by putting too much faith in the white man, their women and children murdered. They insulted him and threatened his life, asking him why he did not stay and die with his brother, White Antelope. The Indians told him that altogether there were one hundred and forty missing, but some wounded afterwards came in. Black Kettle is the only chief left who was in favor of peace. White Antelope folded his arms stoically and was shot down, refusing to leave the field, stating that it was the fault of Black Kettle, others, and himself that occasioned the massacre, and he would die. Black Kettle refusing to leave the field, was carried off by his young men. I gave to the head chiefs of the Cheyennes and Arapahoes a written statement that I had, in consequence of their delivering up some white prisoners, come to an understanding as a United States officer to cease hostilities until such a time as something definite could be concluded by the proper authorities, and warned all officers from interfering with them in a hostile manner until such time should elapse. I pledged myself to give them an interview with the governor of Colorado, and, whatever might be the result, I would return them in safety. This post, at the time of Chivington's attack, was not in his department; but he went out of his district to make the attack. There was force enough at this post, if necessary, to have whipped the Indians I do not think this reservation is very good, not as good as on the Beaver creek or Smoky Hill Fork. The latter place is midway between the travelled routes, and the Indians would much prefer land there. There is a great scope of country south of the Arkansas; the Smoky Hill is the best section of country for the buffalo. In 1858 I travelled with one companion down the Platte, through all the tribes, and was fed and lodged in their camps, encountering no difficulty. I think we might make peace if we could meet the Indians, with the exception of the Dog soldiers of the Cheyennes. But it would be difficult, in consequence of the massacre, to obtain their confidence. I think it a matter of justice to the Indians, and of a decent self-respect to the government, that an effort should be made to make peace. At the time I met the Indians I had but 130 men, and the Indians had some 700 armed warriors. I think had a fight occurred I should have been defeated After Major Anthony assumed command of the post, he proceeded with a command of cavalry to an Arapaho village, containing the bands of Little Raven and Left-Hand. I had gone down to the village simply as a looker-on, and was there when Major Anthony arrived. He told Little Raven and Left-Hand that he had come for the purpose of taking their arms, as it became necessary to consider them prisoners; he did not wish any of them to leave camp without permission from him; he said he would count the number of souls in their camp, and would send an officer every day to verify their presence. The chiefs both appeared willing to deliver up their arms, Little Raven stating he did not desire to be at war with the whites, but was willing to submit to whatever Major Anthony might impose on him. Left-Hand coincided, but requested that he would like to have the Indian boys retain their bows and arrows, as they were in the habit of shooting prairie dogs and jack rabbits, which proved of benefit to them in consequence of their destitute situation. Major Anthony refused to accede to his request, and ordered all the arms to be turned over to him, which was accordingly done, and I saw them placed in a wagon and conveyed to Fort Lyon. This occurred about ten days previous to the fight on Sand creek; Left-Hand joining the Cheyennes, and Little Raven going to Camp Wynkoop.

I proceeded from this post with a detachment of cavalry under charge of Lieutenant Cramer. At Booneville I left the detachment, and proceeded ahead with the white prisoners, expecting the cavalry having the Indian chiefs in charge would reach Denver two days after my arrival. My object in proceeding ahead was to have an interview with Governor John Evans, ex-officio superintendent of Indian affairs, previous to the arrival of the chiefs. On my arrival I was informed that the governor was sick in bed, and on that evening I did not see him. The next morning he called on me at my hotel. Upon entering the parlor I found him in conversation with Dexter Colley, son of the Indian agent for the Cheyennes and Arapahoes, who was present during our whole interview. I told the governor I had come up in accordance with my report; had brought the rescued white prisoners with me, and that the chiefs would be in in a few days, for the purpose of having an interview with him. He intimated that he was sorry I had brought them; that he considered he had nothing to do with them; that they had declared war against the United States, and he considered them in the hands of the military authorities; that he did not think, anyhow, it was policy to make peace with them until they were properly punished, for the reason that the United States would be acknowledging themselves whipped. I said it would be strange if the United States would consider themselves whipped by a few Indians, and drew his attention to the fact that, as a United States officer, I had pledged myself to these Indians to convey them to Denver, to procure an interview with himself, being the Indian superintendent, upon conditions communicated to him in my report; that I had brought these Indians a distance of nearly four hundred miles from their village with that object in view; and desired that he would furnish them an audience. He replied querulously that he was to start next day to visit the Ute agency on business; besides, he did not want to see them, anyhow. I endeavored to explain to him the position in which I was placed, and earnestly requested that he would await their arrival. He then referred to the fact that the third regiment of one-hundred-day men having been raised, and in camp, were nearly ready to make an Indian campaign. He further said that the regiment was ordered to be raised upon his representations to Washington that they were necessary for the protection of the Territory, and to fight hostile Indians; and now, if he made peace with the Indians, it would be supposed at Washington that he had misrepresented matters in regard to the Indian difficulties in Colorado, and had put the government to a useless expense in raising and equipping the regiment; that they had been raised to kill Indians, and they must kill Indians. Several times in our conversation in regard to the object of the Indians who were coming to see him, he made the remark, "What shall I do with the third regiment, if I make peace?"

I have recently been over the battle-field of Sand creek: I saw no evidences of any intrenchments. I do not think the location is suitable for defence.

DENVER, COLORADO TERRITORY, *September* 13, 1865.

DEAR SIR: Enclosed please find a copy of my reply to the "Committee on the Conduct of the War." I hope you will find in it a vindication against their unjust implication of my name in the "Sand creek affair."

I fain would hope that, in your report, my administration of Indian affairs might have such mention as the faithfulness of which I am conscious entitles me to receive. I ask nothing but justice, and feel confident that I shall receive this. But the circumstances in which I am placed by the Committee on the Conduct of the War make me anxious for more at the hands of your committee than a mere passing notice. If there is any point in my administration not fully and satisfactorily explained I shall be happy to give the facts as they are.

I have, from what was said to me, assumed that the account of my stewardship was satisfactory to you. I trust I have not been hasty in this.

I am gratefully obliged for the kind words in my behalf you were pleased to express at Washington, which have been communicated to me by a friend.

I have the honor to be, very respectfully, yours, &c.,

JOHN EVANS.

Hon. J. R. DOOLITTLE.

Reply of Governor Evans, of the Territory of Colorado, to that part, referring to him, of the report of the "Committee on the Conduct of the War," headed "Massacre of Cheyenne Indians."

EXECUTIVE DEPARTMENT AND SUPERINTENDENCY OF INDIAN AFFAIRS, C. T.,
Denver, August 6, 1865.

To the Public:

I have just seen, for the first time, a copy of the report of the Committee on the Conduct of the War, headed "Massacre of Cheyenne Indians."

As it does me great injustice, and by its partial, unfair, and erroneous statements will mislead the public, I respectfully ask a suspension of opinion in my case until I shall have time to present the facts to said committee or some equally high authority, and ask a correction. In the mean time I desire to lay a few facts before the public.

The Committee on the Conduct of the War, as shown by the resolution of the House of Representatives heading the report, had power "to inquire into and report all the facts connected with the late attack, by the 3d regiment Colorado volunteers, under Colonel Chivington, on a village of the Cheyenne tribe of Indians, near Fort Lyon."

They had no power to inquire into my management of Indian affairs except in so far as it related to this battle; and the chairman of the committee assured me that they would not inquire into such general management. Having no connexion whatever with the battle, and, at the time, knowing nothing of the immediate facts connected therewith, I so stated to the committee, and, relying upon the above assurance of the chairman, addressed myself to another committee which had been appointed to investigate the management of Indian affairs generally in the United States. Of this committee, Senator Doolittle was chairman, and to it, I believe, I have rendered a satisfactory account of my stewardship.

The Committee on the Conduct of the War, however, have seen fit to go beyond the scope of their powers, and to enter into a hasty and general investigation of Indian affairs in this superintendency, and in their report attack matters occurring at remote periods from, and entirely disconnected with, the subject-matter of investigation.

Under these circumstances, having been censured unheard, I claim the privilege of presenting proof of the falsity of their charges, in order that, so far as it can be done, the committee, or equally high authority, may repair the great injury done me. And I pledge myself to prove, by official correspondence and accredited testimony, to their satisfaction, and that of all fair-minded men, the truth and justice of my complaint.

I do not propose to discuss the merits or demerits of the Sand creek battle, but simply to meet the attempt, on the part of the committee, to connect my name with it, and to throw discredit on my testimony. I shall not ask the public to take my assertions, except so far as I shall sustain them by undoubted authority, a large part of which is published in government documents by the authority of the honorable body of which the committee are members. The report begins:

"In the summer of 1864 Governor Evans, of Colorado Territory, as acting superintendent of Indian affairs, sent notice to the various bands and tribes of Indians within his jurisdiction that such as desired to be considered friendly to the whites should repair to the nearest military post in order to be protected from the soldiers who were to take the field against the hostile Indians."

This statement is true as to such notice having been sent, but conveys the false impression that it was at the beginning of hostilities, and the declaration of war. The truth is, it was issued by authority of the Indian department months after the war had become general, for the purpose of inducing the Indians to cease hostilities, and to protect those who had been or would become friendly, from the inevitable dangers to which they were exposed. This "notice" may be found published in the report of the Commissioner of Indian Affairs for 1864, page 218.

The report continues:

"About the close of the summer some Cheyenne Indians, in the neighborhood of the Smoky Hill, sent word to Major Wynkoop, commanding at Fort Lyon, that they had in their possession, and were willing to deliver up, some white captives they had purchased of other Indians. Major Wynkoop, with a force of over one hundred men, visited those Indians and recovered the white captives. On his return he was accompanied by a number of the chiefs and leading men of the Indians, whom he had brought to visit Denver for the purpose of conferring with the authorities there in regard to keeping the peace. Among them were Black Kettle and White Antelope, of the Cheyennes, and some chiefs of the Arapahoes. The council was held, and these chiefs stated that they were friendly to the whites and had always been."

Again they say:

"All the testimony goes to show that the Indians under the immediate control of Black Kettle and White Antelope, of the Cheyennes, and Left-Hand, of the Arapahoes, were and had always been friendly to the whites, and had not been guilty of any acts of hostility or depredations."

This word which the committee say was sent to Major Wynkoop was a letter to United States Indian Agent Major Colley, which is published in the report of the Commissioner of Indian Affairs for 1865, page 233, and is as follows:

"CHEYENNE VILLAGE, *August* 29, 1864.

"MAJOR COLLEY: We received a letter from Bent, wishing us to make peace. We held a council in regard to it. All come to the conclusion to make peace with you, providing you make peace with the Kiowas, Comanches, Arapahoes, Apaches, and Sioux. We are going to send a messenger to the Kiowas and to the other nations about our going to make peace with you. We heard that you have some [prisoners] in Denver. We have seven prisoners of yours which we are willing to give up, providing you give up yours. There are three war parties out yet, and two of Arapahoes. They have been out some time and expected in soon. When we held this council there were few Arapahoes and Sioux present. We want true news from you in return. That is a letter.

"BLACK KETTLE, *and other Chiefs*."

Compare the above extract from the report of the committee with this published letter of Black Kettle and the admission of the Indians in the council at Denver.

The committee say, the prisoners proposed to be delivered up were *purchased of other Indians*. Black Kettle, in his letter, says: "We have seven prisoners of yours, which we are willing to give up, providing you give up yours."

They say nothing about prisoners whom they had *purchased*. On the other hand, in the council held in Denver, Black Kettle said:

"Major Wynkoop was kind enough to receive the letter, and visited them in camp, to whom they delivered four white prisoners, one other (Mrs. Snyder) having killed herself; that there are two women and one child yet in their camp whom they will deliver up as soon as they can get them in; Laura Roper, 16 or 17 years; Ambrose Asher, 7 or 8 years; Daniel Marble, 7 or 8 years; Isabel Ubanks, 4 or 5 years. The prisoners still with them [are] Mrs. Ubanks and babe, and a Mrs. Norton, who was taken on the Platte. Mrs. Snyder is the name of the woman who hung herself. The boys were taken between Fort Kearney and the Blue."

Again: they did not deny having captured the prisoners, when I told them that having the prisoners in their possession was evidence of their having committed the depredations when they were taken. But White Antelope said: "We (the Cheyennes) took two prisoners west of Kearney, and destroyed the trains." Had they *purchased* the prisoners they would not have been slow to make it known in this council.

The committee say the chiefs went to Denver to confer with the authorities about *keeping the peace*. Black Kettle says: "All come to the conclusion to *make peace* with you providing you will *make peace* with the Kiowas, Comanches, Arapahoes, Apaches, and Sioux."

Again, the committee say:

"All the testimony goes to show that the Indians under the immediate control of Black Kettle and White Antelope, of the Cheyennes, and Left-Hand, of the Arapahoes, *were, and had been, friendly to the whites, and had not been guilty of any acts of hostility or depredations*"

Black Kettle says, in his letter: "We received a letter from Bent, wishing us to make peace." Why did Bent send a letter to *friendly* Indians, and want to make peace with Indians "*who had always been friendly?*" Again, they say, "We have held a council in regard to it." Why did they hold a council in regard to making peace, when they were already peaceable? Again, they say, "All come to the conclusion to *make peace* with you, *providing* you make peace with the Kiowas, Comanches, Arapahoes, Apaches, and Sioux. We have seven prisoners of yours, which we are willing to give up, providing you give up yours. There are three *war* [not *peace*] *parties* out yet, and two of Arapahoes."

Every line of this letter shows that they were and had been at war. I desire to throw additional light upon this assertion of the committee that these Indians "were and had been friendly to the whites, and had not been guilty of any acts of hostility or depredations;" for it is upon this point that the committee accuse me of prevarication.

In the council held at Denver, White Antelope said: "We (the Cheyennes) took two prisoners west of Kearney, and destroyed the trains." This was one of the most destructive and bloody raids of the war. Again, Neva (Left-Hand's brother) said: "The Comanches, Kiowas, and Sioux have done much more harm than we have."

The entire report of this council, which is hereunto attached, shows that the Indians had been at war, and had been "guilty of acts of hostility and depredations."

As showing more fully the status and disposition of these Indians, I call attention to the following extract from the report of Major Wynkoop, published in the report of the Commissioner of Indian Affairs for 1864, page 234, and a letter from Major Colley, their agent; same report, page 230. Also statement of Robert North; same report, page 224.

"Fort Lyon, Colorado Territory, *September* 18, 1864.

"Sir: * * * * * * Taking with me, under strict guard, the Indians I had in my possession, I reached my destination, and was confronted by from six to eight hundred Indian warriors, drawn up in line of battle, and prepared to fight.

"Putting on as bold a front as I could under the circumstances, I formed my command in as good order as possible for the purpose of acting on the offensive or defensive, as might be necessary, and advanced towards them, at the same time sending forward one of the Indians I had with me, as an emissary, to state that I had come for the purpose of holding a consultation with the chiefs of the Arapahoes and Cheyennes, to come to an understanding which might result in mutual benefit; that I had not come desiring strife, but was prepared for it if necessary, and advised them to listen to what I had to say, previous to making any more warlike demonstrations.

"They consented to meet me in council, and I then proposed to them that if they desired peace to give me palpable evidence of their sincerity by delivering into my hands their white prisoners. I told them that I was not authorized to conclude terms of peace with them, but if they acceded to my proposition I would take what chiefs they might choose to select to the governor of Colorado Territory, state the circumstances to him, and that I believed it would result in what it was their desire to accomplish—'peace with their white brothers.' I had reference, particularly, to the Arapaho and Cheyenne tribes.

"The council was divided—undecided—and could not come to an understanding among themselves. I told them that I would march to a certain locality, distant twelve miles, and await a given time for their action in the matter. I took a strong position in the locality named, and remained three days. In the interval they brought in and turned over four white prisoners, all that was possible for them at the time being to turn over, the balance of the seven being (as they stated) with another band far to the northward.

* * * * * * * * * * * *

"I have the principal chiefs of the two tribes with me, and propose starting immediately to Denver, to put into effect the aforementioned proposition made by me to them.

"They agree to deliver up the balance of the prisoners as soon as it is possible to procure them, which can be done better from Denver City than from this point.

"I have the honor, governor, to be your obedient servant,

"E. W. WYNKOOP,

"*Major First Col. Cav., Comd'g Fort Lyon, C. T.*

"His Excellency John Evans,

"*Governor of Colorado, Denver, C. T.*"

"Fort Lyon, Colorado Territory, *July* 26, 1864.

"Sir: When I last wrote you I was in hopes that our Indian troubles were at an end. Colonel Chivington has just arrived from Larned, and gives a sad account of affairs at that post. They have killed some ten men from a train, and run off all the stock from the post.

"As near as they can learn, all the tribes were engaged in it. The colonel will give you the particulars. There is no dependence to be put in any of them. I have done everything in my power to keep the peace; I now think a little powder and lead is the best food for them.

"Respectfully, your obedient servant,

"S. G. COLLEY, *United States Indian Agent.*

"Hon. John Evans,

"*Governor and Superintendent Indian Affairs.*"

The following statement, by Robert North, was made to me:

"NOVEMBER 10, 1863.

"Having recovered an Arapaho prisoner (a squaw) from the Utes, I obtained the confidence of the Indians completely. I have lived with them from a boy, and my wife is an Arapaho.

"In honor of my exploit in recovering the prisoner, the Indians recently gave me a 'big medicine dance,' about fifty miles below Fort Lyon, on the Arkansas river, at which the leading chiefs and warriors of several of the tribes of the plains met.

"The Comanches, Apaches, Kiowas, the northern band of Arapahoes, and all of the Cheyennes, with the Sioux, have pledged one another to go to war with the whites as soon as they can procure ammunition in the spring. I heard them discuss the matter often, and the few of them who opposed it were forced to be quiet, and were really in danger of their lives I saw the principal chiefs pledge to each other that they would be friendly and shake hands with the whites until they procured ammunition and guns, so as to be ready when they strike. Plundering, to get means, has already commenced; and the plan is to commence the war at several points in the sparse settlements early in the spring. They wanted me to join them in the war, saying that they would take a great many white women and children prisoners, and get a heap of property, blankets, &c.; but while I am connected with them by marriage, and live with them, I am yet a white man, and wish to avoid bloodshed. There are many Mexicans with the Comanche and Apache Indians, all of whom urge on the war, promising to help the Indians themselves, and that a great many more Mexicans would come up from New Mexico for the purpose in the spring."

In addition to the statement showing that all the Cheyennes were in the alliance, I desire to add the following frank admission from the Indians in the council:

"Governor Evans explained that smoking the war-pipe was a figurative term, but their conduct had been such as to show they had an understanding with other tribes.

"SEVERAL INDIANS. We acknowledge that our actions have given you reason to believe this."

In addition to all this, I refer to the appended statement of Mrs. Ewbanks. She is one of the prisoners that Black Kettle, in the council, said they had. Instead of *purchasing* her, it will be observed that they first *captured* her on the Little Blue, and then *sold* her to the Sioux.

Mrs. Martin, another rescued prisoner, was *captured* by the *Cheyennes* on Plum creek, *west* of *Kearney*, with a boy nine years old. These were the prisoners of which White Antelope said, in the council, "We took two prisoners west of Kearney, and destroyed the trains." In her published statement she says the party who captured her and the boy killed eleven men and destroyed the trains, and were mostly *Cheyennes*.

Thus I have proved, by the Indian chiefs named in the report, by Agent Colley and Major Wynkoop, to whom they refer to sustain their assertion to the contrary, that these Indians had "been at war, and had committed acts of hostility and depredations."

This documentary evidence could be extended much further, but enough has been produced to show the utter recklessness of their statements; and because I would not admit, in the face of these published facts, that these Indians "were, and always had been, friendly, and had not been guilty of any acts of hostility or depredations," the committee accuse me of "prevarication." They say that I prevaricated "for the evident purpose of avoiding the admission that he was fully aware that the Indians massacred so brutally at Sand creek were then, *and had been, actuated by the most friendly feelings towards the whites.*"

I had left the Indians in the hands of the military authorities, as I shall presently show. There were many conflicting rumors as to the disposition made of them. I was absent from the Territory, and could state nothing positive in regard to their status after the council.

In regard to their status prior to the council at Denver, the foregoing public documents which I have cited show how utterly devoid of truth or foundation is the assertion that these Indians "had been friendly to the whites, and had not been guilty of any acts of hostility or depredations." Ignorance of the facts contained in the report of the Commissioner of Indian Affairs for 1864 is inexcusable on the part of the committee, for I particularly referred them to it.

I am obliged to the committee, however, for stating wherein I prevaricated, for I am thus enabled to repel their gross attack on my character as a witness, by showing that they were *mistaken* and I was *correct* in my testimony.

The next paragraph of the report is as follows:

"A northern band of the Cheyennes, known as the 'Dog Soldiers,' had been guilty of acts of hostility; but all the testimony goes to prove that they had no connexion with

Black Kettle's band, and acted in spite of his authority and influence. Black Kettle and his band denied all connexion with, or responsibility for, the Dog Soldiers, and Left-Hand and his band were equally friendly."

The committee and the public will be surprised to learn the fact that these Dog Soldiers, on which the committee throw the *slight* blame of acts of hostility, were really among Black Kettle and White Antelope's own warriors, in the "*friendly*" camp to which Major Wynkoop made his expedition, and their head man, Bull Bear, was one of the prominent men of the deputation brought in to see me at Denver. By reference to the accompanying report of the council with the chiefs, to which I referred the committee, it will be observed that Black Kettle and all present based their propositions to *make peace* upon the assent of *their bands*, and that these Dog Soldiers were especially referred to.

The report continues:

"These Indians, at the suggestion of Governor Evans and Colonel Chivington, repaired to Fort Lyon and placed themselves under the protection of Major Wynkoop," &c.

The connexion of my name in this is again wrong. As will be seen by the accompanying report of the council, to which I referred in my testimony, I simply left them in the hands of the military authorities, where I found them, and my action was approved by the Indian bureau.

The following extracts from the accompanying report of the council will prove this, conclusively. I stated to the Indians:

* * * "Another reason that I am not in a condition to make a treaty is, that the war is begun, and the power to make a treaty of peace has passed from me to the great war chief."

I also said: "Again, whatever peace they may make must be with the soldiers, and not with me."

And again, in reply to White Antelope's inquiry, "How can we be protected from the soldiers on the plains?" I said: "You must make that arrangement with the military chief."

The morning after this council I addressed the following letter to the agent of these Indians, which is published in the report of the Commissioner of Indian Affairs for 1864, page 220:

"COLORADO SUPERINTENDENCY INDIAN AFFAIRS,
"*Denver*, *September* 29, 1864.

"SIR: The chiefs brought in by Major Wynkoop have been heard. I have declined to make any peace with them, lest it might embarrass the military operations against the hostile Indians of the plains. The Arapaho and Cheyenne Indians being now at war with the United States government, must make peace with the military authorities. Of course this arrangement relieves the Indian bureau of their care until peace is declared with them; and as these tribes are yet scattered, and all except Friday's band are at war, it is not probable that it will be done immediately. You will be particular to impress upon these chiefs the fact that my talk with them was for the purpose of ascertaining their views, and not to offer them anything whatever. They must deal with the military authorities until peace, in which case, alone, they will be in proper position to treat with the government in relation to the future.

"I have the honor to be, very respectfully, your obedient servant,
"JOHN EVANS,
"*Governor Colorado Territory and ex-officio Superintendent Indian Affairs.*

"Major S. G. COLLEY,
"*United States Indian Agent, Upper Arkansas.*"

That this course accorded with the policy of the military authorities was confirmed by a telegram from the department commander, sent from headquarters at Fort Leavenworth to the district commander, on the day of the council, in which he said: "I fear agent of the Interior Department will be ready to make presents too soon. It is better to chastise, before giving anything but a little tobacco to talk over. No peace must be made without my directions."

It will thus be seen that I had, with the approval of the Indian bureau, turned the adjustment of difficulties with hostile Indians entirely over to the military authorities; that I had instructed Agent Colley, at Fort Lyon, that this would relieve the bureau of further care of the Arapahoes and Cheyennes, until peace was made, and having had no notice of such peace, or instructions to change the arrangement, the status of these Indians was in no respect within my jurisdiction or under my official inspection.

In the face of all these facts—matters of public record—the committee attempt to make me responsible for the care of these Indians at the time of the battle.

It may be proper for me to say, further, that it will appear in evidence that I had no intimation of the direction in which the campaign against the hostile Indians was to move, or against what bands it was to be made, when I left the Territory last fall, and that I was absent from Colorado when the Sand creek battle occurred.

The report continues :

"It is true that there seems to have been excited among the people inhabiting that region of country a hostile feeling towards the Indians. Some had committed acts of hostility towards the whites, but no effort seems to have been made by the authorities there to prevent these hostilities, other than by the commission of even worse acts."

"*The people inhabiting that region of country!*" A form of expression of frequent occurrence in the reports of exploring expeditions, when speaking of savages and unknown tribes, but scarcely a respectful mode of mention of the people of Colorado.

"*Some* had committed acts of hostility towards the whites!" Hear the facts: In the fall of 1863 a general alliance of the Indians of the plains was effected with the Sioux, and in the language of Bull Bear, in the report of the council, appended, "Their plan is to clean out all this country."

The war opened early in the spring of 1864. The people of the east, absorbed in the greater interest of the rebellion, know but little of its history. Stock was stolen; ranches destroyed, houses burned, freight trains plundered, and their contents carried away or scattered upon the plains; settlers in the frontier counties murdered, or forced to seek safety for themselves and families in block-houses and interior towns; emigrants to our Territory were surprised in their camps, children were slain, and wives taken prisoners; our trade and travel with the States were cut off; the necessaries of life were at starvation prices; the interests of the Territory were being damaged to the extent of millions; every species of atrocity and barbarity which characterizes savage warfare was committed. This is no fancy sketch, but a plain statement of facts, of which the committee seem to have had no proper realization. All this history of war and blood—all this history of rapine and ruin—all this story of outrage and suffering on the part of our people—is summed up by the committee, and given to the public, in one mild sentence, "*Some* had committed acts of hostility against the whites."

The committee not only ignore the general and terrible character of our Indian war, and the great sufferings of our people, but make the grave charge that "no effort seems to have been made by the authorities there to prevent all these hostilities."

Had the committee taken the trouble, as they certainly should have done before making so grave a charge, to have read the public documents of the government, examined the record and files of the Indian bureau of the War Department, and of this superintendency, instead of adopting the language of some hostile and irresponsible witness, as they appear to have done, they would have found that the most earnest and persistent efforts had been made on my part to prevent hostilities. The records show that, early in the spring of 1863, United States Indian Agent Loree, of the Upper Platte agency, reported to me in person that the Sioux under his agency, and the Arapahoes and Cheyennes, were negotiating an alliance for war on the whites. I immediately wrote an urgent appeal for authority to avert the danger, and sent Agent Loree as special messenger with the despatch to Washington. In response, authority was given, and an earnest effort was made to collect the Indians in council. The following admission, in the appended report of the council, explains the result:

"GOVERNOR EVANS. * * * Hearing last fall that they were dissatisfied, the Great Father at Washington sent me out on the plains to talk with you and make it all right. I sent messengers out to tell you that I had presents, and would make you a feast; but you sent word to me that you did not want to have anything to do with me, and to the Great Father at Washington that you could get along without him. Bull Bear wanted to come in to see me, at the head of the Republican, but his people held a council and would not let him come.

"BLACK KETTLE. That is true.

"GOVERNOR EVANS. I was under the necessity, after all my trouble, and all the expense I was at, of returning home without seeing them. Instead of this, your people went away and smoked the war pipe with our enemies."

Notwithstanding these unsuccessful efforts, I still hoped to preserve peace.

The records of these offices also show that, in the autumn of 1863, I was reliably advised from various sources that nearly all the Indians of the plains had formed an alliance for the purpose of going to war in the spring, and I immediately commenced my efforts to avert the imminent danger. From that time forward, by letter, by telegram, and personal representation to the Commissioner of Indian Affairs, the Secretary of War, the commanders of the department and district; by travelling for weeks in the wilderness of the plains; by distribution of annuities and presents; by sending notice to the Indians to leave the hostile alliance; by every means within my power, I endeavored to preserve peace and protect the interests of the people of the Territory. And in the face of all this, which the records abundantly show, the committee say: "No effort seems to have been made by the authorities there to prevent these hostilities, other than by the commission of even worse acts."

They do not point out any of these acts, unless the continuation of the paragraph is intended to do so. It proceeds:

"The hatred of the whites to the Indians would seem to have been inflamed and excited to the utmost. The bodies of persons killed at a distance—whether by Indians or not is not certain—were brought to the capital of the Territory and exposed to the public gaze, for the purpose of inflaming still more the already excited feeling of the people."

There is no mention in this of anything that was done by authority, but it is so full of misrepresentation, in apology for Indians, and unjust reflection on a people who have a right, from their birth, education, and ties of sympathy with the people they so recently left behind them, to have at least a just consideration. The bodies referred to were those of the Hungate family, who were brutally murdered by the Indians, within twenty-five miles of Denver. No one here ever doubted that the Indians did it, and it was admitted by the Indians in the council. This was early in the summer, and before the notice sent in June to the friendly Indians. Their mangled bodies were brought to Denver for decent burial. Many of our people went to see them, as any people would have done. It did produce excitement and consternation, and where are the people who could have witnessed it without emotion? Would the committee have the people shut their eyes to such scenes at their very doors?

The next sentence, equally unjust and unfair, refers to my proclamation, issued two months after this occurrence, and four months before the "attack" they were investigating, and having no connexion with it or with the troops engaged in it. It is as follows:

"The cupidity was appealed to, for the governor, in a proclamation, calls upon all, either individually, or in such parties as they may organize, to kill and destroy, as enemies of the country, wherever they may be found, all such hostile Indians; authorizing them to hold, to their own use and benefit, all the property of said hostile Indians they may capture. What Indians he would ever term friendly it is impossible to tell."

I offer the following statement of the circumstances under which this proclamation was issued, by the Hon. D. A. Chever. It is as follows:

"EXECUTIVE DEPARTMENT, COLORADO TERRITORY, *August* 21, 1865.

"I, David A. Chever, clerk in the office of the governor of the Territory of Colorado, do solemnly swear that the people of said Territory, from the Purgatoire to the Cache a la Poudre rivers, a distance of over two hundred miles, and for a like distance along the Platte river, being the whole of our settlements on the plains, were thrown into the greatest alarm and consternation by numerous and almost simultaneous attacks and depredations by hostile Indians early last summer; that they left their unreaped crops, and, collecting into communities, built block-houses and stockades for protection at central points throughout the long line of settlements; that those living in the vicinity of Denver City fled to it, and that the people of said city were in great fear of sharing the fate of New Ulm, Minnesota; that the threatened loss of crops, and the interruption of communication with the States by the combined hostilities, threatened the very existence of the whole people; that this feeling of danger was universal; that a flood of petitions and deputations poured into this office, from the people of all parts of the Territory, praying for protection, and for arms and authority to protect themselves; that the defects of the militia law and the want of means to provide for defence was proved by the failure of this department, after the utmost endeavors, to secure an effective organization under it; that reliable reports of the presence of a large body of hostile warriors at no great distance east of this place were received, which reports were afterwards proved to be true, by the statement of Elbridge Gerry, (page 232, Report of Commissioner of Indian Affairs for 1864;) that repeated and urgent applications to the War Department, for protection and the authority to raise troops for the purpose, had failed; that urgent applications to department and district commanders had failed to bring any prospect of relief, and that in the midst of this terrible consternation, and apparently defenceless condition, it had been announced to this office, from district headquarters, that all the Colorado troops in the service of the United States had been peremptorily ordered away, and nearly all of them had marched to the Arkansas river, to be in position to repel the threatened invasion of the rebels into Kansas and Missouri; that reliable reports of depredations and murders by the Indians, from all parts of our extended lines of exposed settlements, became daily more numerous, until the simultaneous attacks on trains along the overland stage line were reported by telegraph, on the 8th of August, described in the letter of George K. Otis, superintendent of overland stage line, published on page 254 of Report of Commissioner of Indian Affairs for 1864. Under these circumstances, on the 11th of August, the governor issued his proclamation to the people, calling upon them to defend their homes and families from the savage foe; that it prevented anarchy; that several militia companies immediately organized under it, and aided in inspiring confidence; that under its authority no act of impropriety has been reported, and I do not believe that any occurred; that it had no reference to or connexion with the third regiment one-hundred-days men that was subsequently raised by authority of the War Department, under a different proclamation, calling for volunteers, or with any of the troops engaged in the Sand creek affair, and that the reference to it in such connexion, in the report of the Committee on the Conduct of the War, is a perversion of the history and facts in the case.

"DAVID A. CHEVER.

"TERRITORY OF COLORADO, *Arapaho County, City of Denver*, *ss:*

"Subscribed and sworn to before me this 21st day of August, A. D. 1865.

"ELI M. ASHLEY, *Notary Public.*"

I had appealed by telegraph, June 14, to the War Department, for authority to call the militia into the United States service or to raise one-hundred-day troops; also had written to our delegate in Congress to see why I got no response, and had received his reply to the effect that he could learn nothing about it; had received a notice from the department commander, declining to take the responsibility of asking the militia for United States service, throwing the people entirely on the necessity of taking care of themselves.

It was under these circumstances of trial, suffering and danger on the part of the people, and of fruitless appeal upon my part to the general government for aid, that I issued my proclamation of the 11th August, 1864, of which the committee complain.

Without means to mount or pay militia, and failing to get government authority to raise forces, and under the withdrawal of the few troops in the Territory, could any other course be pursued?

The people were asked to fight on their own account—at their own expense—and in lieu of the protection the government failed to render. They were authorized to kill only the Indians that were murdering and robbing them in hostility, and to keep the property captured from them. How the committee would have them fight these savages, and what other disposition they would make of the property captured, the public will be curious to know. Would they fight without killing? Would they have the captured property turned over to the government, as if captured by United States troops? Would they forbid such captures? Would they restore it to the hostile tribes?

The absurdity of the committee's saying that this was an "appeal to the cupidity," is too palpable to require much comment. Would men leave high wages, mount and equip themselves at enormous expense, as some patriotically did, for the poor chance of capturing property, as a mere speculation, from the prowling bands of Indians that infested the settlements and were murdering their families? The thing is preposterous.

For this proclamation I have no apology. It had its origin and has its justification in the imperative necessities of the case. A merciless foe surrounded us. Without means to mount or pay militia, unable to secure government authority to raise forces, and our own troops ordered away, again I ask, could any other course be pursued?

Captain Tyler's and other companies organized under it, at enormous expense, left their lucrative business, high wages and profitable employment, and served without other pay than the consciousness of having done noble and patriotic service; and no act of impropriety has ever been laid to the charge of any party acting under this proclamation. They had all been disbanded months before the "attack" was made that the committee were investigating.

The third regiment was organized under authority from the War Department, subsequently received by telegraph, and under a subsequent proclamation issued on the 13th of August, and were regularly mustered into the service of the United States about three months before the battle the committee were investigating occurred.

Before leaving this subject, I desire to call attention to the following significant fact; the part of my proclamation from which the committee quote reads as follows:

"Now, therefore, I, John Evans, governor of Colorado Territory, do issue this, my proclamation, authorizing all citizens of Colorado, either individually or in such parties as they may organize, to go in pursuit of all hostile Indians on the plains, *scrupulously avoiding those who have responded to my call to rendezvous at the points indicated.* Also to kill and destroy, as enemies of the country, wherever they may be found, all such hostile Indians."

The language which I have italicised in the foregoing quotation shows that I forbade, in this proclamation, the disturbance of the friendly Indians and only authorized killing the hostile.

The committee, in their censorious mention of the proclamation, omit this sentence which I have italicised, although they quote the language immediately in connexion with it, and add the exclamation, "What Indians he would ever term friendly it is impossible to tell." Had they not suppressed this sentence their exclamation would have been awkward. Had they not suppressed it, its appearance in its proper connexion would have answered one of their most serious charges against me.

Why is this? Does it not look like a persistent determination on their part to place me before the public in an improper and unjust position? If such a thing is possible, from so high a source, where is there any safety for the character of public men?

Before closing this reply, it is perhaps just that I should say that when I testified before the committee the chairman and all its members, except three, were absent, and I think, when the truth becomes known, this report will trace its parentage to a single member of the committee.

I have thus noticed such portions of the report as refer to myself, and shown conclusively that the committee, in every mention they have made of me, have been, to say the least, mistaken.

First. The committee, for the evident purpose of maintaining their position that these Indians had not been engaged in the war, say the prisoners they held were purchased. The testimony is to the effect that they captured them.

Second. The committee say that these Indians were and always had been friendly, and had committed no acts of hostility or depredations. The public documents to which I refer show conclusively that they had been hostile, and had committed many acts of hostility and depredations.

Third. They say that I joined in sending these Indians to Fort Lyon. The published report of the Commissioner of Indian Affairs, and of the Indian council, show that I left them entirely in the hands of the military authorities.

Fourth. They say nothing seems to have been done by the authorities to prevent hostilities. The public documents and files of the Indian bureau, and of my superintendency, show constant and unremitting diligence and effort on my part to prevent hostilities and protect the people.

Fifth. They say that I prevaricated for the purpose of avoiding the admission that these Indians "were and had been actuated by the most friendly feelings towards the whites." Public documents cited show conclusively that the admission they desired me to make was false, and that my statement, instead of being a prevarication, was true, although not in accordance with the preconceived and mistaken opinions of the committee.

Those who read this will be curious for some explanation of this slanderous report. To me it is plain. I am governor of Colorado, and, as is usual with men in public position, have enemies. Many of these gentlemen were in the city of Washington last winter, endeavoring to effect my removal, and were not particular as to the character of the means they employed, so that the desired result was accomplished. For this purpose, they conspired to connect my name with the Sand creek battle, although they knew that I was in no way connected with it. A friend in that city, writing to me in regard to this attempt, and mentioning the names of certain of these gentlemen, said: "They are much in communication with ——, a member of the committee charged with the investigation of the Chivington affair." These gentlemen, by their false and unscrupulous representations, have misled the committee.

I do not charge the committee with any intentional wrong. My charge against the committee is that they have been culpably negligent and culpably hasty; culpably negligent in not examining the public documents to which I called their attention, and which would have exonerated me, and saved them from many serious, unjust and mistaken representations; culpably hasty in concluding that I had prevaricated, because my statement did not agree with the falsehoods they had embraced.

If my statement did not agree with what they supposed to be the truth, my position was such as to demand that they should at least go to the trouble of investigating the public documents to which I called their attention before publishing a report containing charges of so grave a character.

That the Committee on the Conduct of the War should have published a report containing so many errors is to be regretted. It is composed of honorable gentlemen—members of the Congress of the United States—to whom have been intrusted duties of the gravest character, and from whom is expected, first, thorough investigation, and then careful statement, so that their reports may be relied upon as truth, so far as truth is ascertainable by human means.

This report, so full of mistakes which ordinary investigation would have avoided; so full of slander, which ordinary care of the character of men would have prevented, is to be regretted, for the reason that it throws doubt upon the reliability of all reports which have emanated from the same source, during the last four years of war.

I am confident that the public will see, from the facts herein set forth, the great injustice done me; and I am further confident that the committee, when they know these and other facts I shall lay before them, will also see this injustice, and, as far as possible, repair it.

Very respectfully, your obedient servant,

JOHN EVANS,
Governor of the Territory of Colorado and ex-officio Sup't Ind. Affairs.

Report of council with Cheyenne and Arapaho chiefs and warriors, brought to Denver by Major Wynkoop; taken down by United States Indian Agent Simeon Whiteley as it progressed.

CAMP WELD, DENVER, *Wednesday, September* 28, 1864.

Present: Governor John Evans; Colonel Chivington, commanding district of Colorado; Colonel George L. Shoup, third Colorado volunteer cavalry; Major E. Wynkoop, Colorado first; S. Whiteley, United States Indian agent; Black Kettle, leading Cheyenne chief; White Antelope, chief central Cheyenne band; Bull Bear, leader of Dog Soldiers, (Cheyenne;) Neva, sub-Arapaho chief, (who was in Washington;) Bosse, sub-Arapaho chief; Heap of Buffalo, Arapaho chief; Na-ta-nee, Arapaho chief; (the Arapahoes are all relatives of Left-Hand, chief of the Arapahoes, and are sent by him in his stead;) John Smith, interpreter to the Upper Arkansas agency; and many other citizens and officers.

His Excellency Governor Evans asked the Indians what they had to say.

Black Kettle then said: On sight of your circular of June 27, 1864, I took hold of the matter, and have now come to talk to you about it. I told Mr. Bent, who brought it, that I accepted it, but it would take some time to get all my people together—many of my young men being absent--and I have done everything in my power, since then, to keep peace with the whites. As soon as I could get my people together we held a council, and got a half-breed, who was with them, to write a letter to inform Major Wynkoop, or other military officer nearest to them, of their intention to comply with the terms of the circular. Major Wynkoop was kind enough to receive the letter, and visited them in camp, to whom they delivered four white prisoners—one other (Mrs. Snyder) having killed herself; that there are two women and one child yet in their camp, whom they will deliver up as soon as they can get them in—Laura Roper, sixteen or seventeen years; Ambrose Asher, seven or eight years; Daniel Marble, seven or eight years; Isabel Ubanks, four or five years. The prisoners still with them [are] Mrs. Ubanks and babe, and a Mrs. Morton, who was taken on the Platte. Mrs. Snyder is the name of the woman who hung herself. The boys were taken between Fort Kearney and the Blue. I followed Major Wynkoop to Fort Lyon, and Major Wynkoop proposed that we come up to see you. We have come with our eyes shut, following his handful of men, like coming through the fire. All we ask is that we may have peace with the whites. We want to hold you by the hand. You are our father. We have been travelling through a cloud. The sky has been dark ever since the war began. These braves who are with me are all willing to do what I say. We want to take good tidings home to our people, that they may sleep in peace. I want you to give all these chiefs of the soldiers here to understand that we are for peace, and that we have made peace, that we may not be mistaken by them for enemies. I have not come here with a little wolf bark, but have come to talk plain with you. We must live near the buffalo or starve. When we came here we came free, without any apprehension, to see you, and when I go home and tell my people that I have taken your hand, and the hands of all the chiefs here in Denver, they will feel well, and so will all the different tribes of Indians on the plains, after we have eaten and drank with them.

Governor Evans replied: I am sorry you did not respond to my appeal at once. You have gone into an alliance with the Sioux, who were at war with us. You have done a great deal of damage—have stolen stock, and now have possession of it. However much a few individuals may have tried to keep the peace, as a nation you have gone to war. While we have been spending thousands of dollars in opening farms for you, and making preparations to feed, protect, and make you comfortable, you have joined our enemies and gone to war. Hearing, last fall, that they were dissatisfied, the Great Father at Washington sent me out on the plains to talk with you and make it all right. I sent messengers out to tell you that I had presents, and would make you a feast, but you sent word to me that you did not want to have anything to do with me, and to the Great Father at Washington that you could get along without him. Bull Bear wanted to come in to see me at the head of the Republican, but his people held a council and would not let him come.

BLACK KETTLE. That is true.

Governor Evans. I was under the necessity, after all my trouble and all the expense I was at, of returning home without seeing them. Instead of this, your people went away and smoked the war-pipe with our enemies.

Black Kettle. I don't know who could have told you this.

Governor Evans. No matter who said this, but your conduct has proved to my satisfaction that was the case.

Several Indians. This is a mistake; we have made no alliance with the Sioux or any one else.

Governor Evans explained that smoking the war-pipe was a figurative term, but their conduct had been such as to show they had an understanding with other tribes.

Several Indians. We acknowledge that our actions have given you reason to believe this.

Governor Evans. So far as making a treaty now is concerned, we are in no condition to do it. Your young men are on the war-path. My soldiers are preparing for the fight. You, so far, have had the advantage; but the time is near at hand when the plains will swarm with United States soldiers. I understand that these men who have come to see me now have been opposed to the war all the time, but that their people have controlled them and they could not help themselves. Is this so?

All the Indians. It has been so.

Governor Evans. The fact that they have not been able to prevent their people from going to war in the past spring, when there was plenty of grass and game, makes me believe that they will not be able to make a peace which will last longer than until winter is past.

White Antelope. I will answer that after a time.

Governor Evans. The time when you can make war best is in the summer-time; when I can make war best is in the winter. You, so far, have had the advantage; my time is just coming. I have learned that you understand that as the whites are at war among themselves, you think you can now drive the whites from this country; but this reliance is false. The Great Father at Washington has men enough to drive all the Indians off the plains, and whip the rebels at the same time. Now the war with the whites is nearly through, and the Great Father will not know what to do with all his soldiers, except to send them after the Indians on the plains. My proposition to the friendly Indians has gone out; shall be glad to have them all come in under it. I have no new propositions to make. Another reason that I am not in a condition to make a treaty is that war is begun, and the power to make a treaty of peace has passed from me to the great war chief. My advice to you is to turn on the side of the government, and show by your acts that friendly disposition you profess to me. It is utterly out of the question for you to be at peace with us while living with our enemies, and being on friendly terms with them.

Inquiry made by one Indian. What was meant by being on the side of the government?

Explanation being made, all gave assent, saying: "All right."

Governor Evans. The only way you can show this friendship is by making some arrangement with the soldiers to help them.

Black Kettle. We will return with Major Wynkoop to Fort Lyon; we will then proceed to our village and take back word to my young men every word you say. I cannot answer for all of them, but think there will be but little difficulty in getting them to assent to help the soldiers.

Major Wynkoop. Did not the Dog Soldiers agree, when I had my council with you, to do whatever you said, after you had been here?

Black Kettle. Yes.

Governor Evans explained that if the Indians did not keep with the United States soldiers, or have an arrangement with them, they would be all treated as enemies. You understand, if you are at peace with us it is necessary to keep away from our enemies. But I hand you over to the military, one of the chiefs of which is here to-day, and can speak for himself to them, if he chooses.

White Antelope. I understand every word you have said, and will hold on to it. I will give you an answer directly. The Cheyennes, all of them, have their eyes open this way, and they will hear what you say. He is proud to have seen the chief of all the whites in this country. He will tell his people. Ever since he went to Washington and received this medal, I have called all white men as my brothers. But other Indians have since been to Washington and got medals, and now the soldiers do not shake hands, but seek to kill me. What do you mean by us fighting your enemies? Who are they?

Governor Evans. All Indians who are fighting us.

White Antelope. How can we be protected from the soldiers on the plains?

Governor Evans. You must make that arrangement with the military chief.

White Antelope. I fear that these new soldiers who have gone out may kill some of my people while I am here.

GOVERNOR EVANS. There is great danger of it.

WHITE ANTELOPE. When we sent our letter to Major Wynkoop, it was like going through a strong fire or blast for Major Wynkoop's men to come to our camp; it was the same for us to come to see you. We have our doubts whether the Indians south of the Arkansas, or those north of the Platte, will do as you say. A large number of Sioux have crossed the Platte, in the vicinity of the Junction, into their country. When Major Wynkoop came, we proposed to make peace. He said he had no power to make a peace, except to bring them here and return them safe.

GOVERNOR EVANS. Again, whatever peace they make must be with the soldiers, and not with me. Are the Apaches at war with the whites?

WHITE ANTELOPE. Yes, and the Comanches and Kiowas as well; also a tribe of Indians from Texas, whose names we do not know. There are thirteen different bands of Sioux who have crossed the Platte, and are in alliance with the others named.

GOVERNOR EVANS. How many warriors with the Apaches, Kiowas, and Comanches?

WHITE ANTELOPE. A good many; don't know.

GOVERNOR EVANS. How many of the Sioux?

WHITE ANTELOPE. Don't know; but many more than of the southern tribes.

GOVERNOR EVANS. Who committed the depredation on the trains near the Junction about the first of August?

WHITE ANTELOPE. Do not know; did not know any was committed; have taken you by the hand and will tell the truth, keeping back nothing.

GOVERNOR EVANS. Who committed the murder of the Hungate family on Running creek?

NEVA. The Arapahoes; a party of the northern band, who were passing north. It was Medicine Man, or Roman Nose, and three others. I am satisfied from the time he left a certain camp for the north, that it was this party of four persons.

AGENT WHITELEY. That cannot be true.

GOVERNOR EVANS. Where is Roman Nose?

NEVA. You ought to know better than me; you have been nearer to him.

GOVERNOR EVANS. Who killed the man and boy at the head of Cherry creek?

NEVA. (After consultation.) Kiowas and Comanches.

GOVERNOR EVANS. Who stole soldiers' horses and mules from Jimmy's camp twenty-seven days ago?

NEVA. Fourteen Cheyennes and Arapahoes together.

GOVERNOR EVANS. What were their names?

NEVA. Powder Face and Whirlwind, who are now in our camp, were the leaders.

COLONEL SHOUP. I counted twenty Indians on that occasion.

GOVERNOR EVANS. Who stole Charley Autobee's horses?

NEVA. Raven's son.

GOVERNOR EVANS. Who took the stock from Fremont's orchard and had the first fight with the soldiers this spring north of there?

WHITE ANTELOPE. Before answering this question I would like for you to know that this was the beginning of war, and I should like to know what it was for. A soldier fired first.

GOVERNOR EVANS. The Indians had stolen about forty horses; the soldiers went to recover them, and the Indians fired a volley into their ranks.

WHITE ANTELOPE. This is all a mistake; they were coming down the Bijou, and found one horse and one mule. They returned one horse before they got to Geary's to a man, then went to Geary's expecting to turn the other one over to some one. They then heard that the soldiers and Indians were fighting somewhere down the Platte; then they took fright and all fled.

GOVERNOR EVANS. Who were the Indians who had the fight?

WHITE ANTELOPE. They were headed by the Fool Badger's son, a young man, one of the greatest of the Cheyenne warriors, who was wounded, and though still alive he will never recover.

NEVA. I want to say something; it makes me feel bad to be talking about these things and opening old sores.

GOVERNOR EVANS. Let him speak.

NEVA. Mr. Smith has known me ever since I was a child. Has he ever known me commit depredations on the whites? I went to Washington last year; received good counsel; I hold on to it. I determined to always keep peace with the whites. Now, when I shake hands with them, they seem to pull away. I came here to seek peace, and nothing else.

GOVERNOR EVANS. We feel that they have, by their stealing and murdering, done us great damage. They come here and say they will tell me all, and that is what I am trying to get.

NEVA. The Comanches, Kiowas, and Sioux have done much more injury than we have. We will tell what we know, but cannot speak for others.

GOVERNOR EVANS. I suppose you acknowledge the depredations on the Little Blue, as you have the prisoners then taken in your possession.

WHITE ANTELOPE. We (the Cheyennes) took two prisoners west of Fort Kearney, and destroyed the trains.

GOVERNOR EVANS. Who committed depredations at Cottonwood?

WHITE ANTELOPE. The Sioux; what band, we do not know.

GOVERNOR EVANS. What are the Sioux going to do next?

BULL BEAR. Their plan is to clean out all this country; they are angry, and will do all the damage to the whites they can. I am with you and the troops, to fight all those who have no ears to listen to what you say. Who are they? Show them to me. I am not yet old; I am young. I have never hurt a white man. I am pushing for something good. I am always going to be friends with the whites; they can do me good.

GOVERNOR EVANS. Where are the Sioux?

BULL BEAR. Down on the Republican, where it opens out.

GOVERNOR EVANS. Do you know that they intend to attack the trains this week?

BULL BEAR. Yes; about one-half of all the Missouri River Sioux and Yanktons, who were driven from Minnesota, are those who have crossed the Platte. I am young and can fight. I have given my word to fight with the whites. My brother (Lean Bear) died in trying to keep peace with the whites. I am willing to die in the same way, and expect to do so.

NEVA. I know the value of the presents which we receive from Washington; we cannot live without them. That is why I try so hard to keep peace with the whites.

GOVERNOR EVANS. I cannot say anything about those things now.

NEVA. I can speak for all the Arapahoes under Left-Hand. Raven has sent no one here to speak for him. Raven has fought the whites.

GOVERNOR EVANS. Are there any white men among your people?

NEVA. There are none except Keith, who is now in the store at Fort Larned.

COLONEL CHIVINGTON. I am not a big war chief, but all the soldiers in this country are at my command. My rule of fighting white men or Indians is to fight them until they lay down their arms and submit to military authority. They are nearer Major Wynkoop than any one else, and they can go to him when they get ready to do that.

The council then adjourned.

I certify that this report is correct and complete; that I took down the talk of the Indians in the exact words of the interpreter, and of the other parties as given to him, without change of phraseology or correction of any kind whatever.

SIMEON WHITELEY.

Statement of Mrs. Ewbanks, giving an account of her captivity among the Indians. She was taken by the Cheyennes, and was one of the prisoners proposed to be given up by Black Kettle, White Antelope and others, in the council at Denver.

JULESBURG, COLORADO TERRITORY, *June* 22, 1865.

Mrs. Lucinda Ewbanks states that she was born in Pennsylvania; is 24 years of age; she resided on the Little Blue, at or near the Narrows. She says that on the 8th day of August, 1864, the house was attacked, robbed, burned, and herself and two children, with her nephew and Miss Roper, were captured by the Cheyenne Indians. Her eldest child, at the time, was three years old; her youngest was one year old; her nephew was six years old. When taken from her home was, by the Indians, taken south across the Republican, and west to a creek the name of which she does not remember. Here, for a short time, was their village or camping place. They were travelling all winter. When first taken by the Cheyennes she was taken to the lodge of an old chief whose name she does [not] recollect. He forced me, by the most terrible threats and menaces, to yield my person to him. He treated me as his wife. He then traded me to Two Face, a Sioux, who did not treat me as a wife, but forced me to do all menial labor done by squaws, and he beat me terribly. Two Face traded me to Black Foot, (Sioux,) who treated me as his wife, and because I resisted him his squaws abused and ill-used me. Black Foot also beat me unmercifully, and the Indians generally treated me as though I was a dog, on account of my showing so much detestation towards Black Foot. Two Face traded for me again. I then received a little better treatment. I was better treated among the Sioux than the Cheyennes—that is, the Sioux gave me more to eat. When with the Cheyennes I was often hungry. Her purchase from the Cheyennes was made early last fall, and she remained with them until May, 1865. During the winter the Cheyennes came to buy me and the child, for the purpose of burning us, but Two Face would not let them have me. During the winter we were on the North Platte the Indians were killing the whites all the time and running off their stock. They would bring in the scalps of the whites and show them to me and laugh about it. They ordered me frequently to wean my baby, but I always refused; for I felt convinced if he was weaned they would take him from me, and I should never see him again. They took my daughter from me just after we were captured, and I never saw her after. I have seen the man to-day who had her; his name is Davenport. He lives in Denver. He received her from a Dr. Smith. She was given up by the Cheyennes to Major Wynkoop, but from injuries received while with the Indians, she died last February. My nephew also was given up to Major Wynkoop, but he, too, died at Denver. The doctor said it was caused by bad treatment from the Indians. While encamped on the North Platte, Elston came to the village, and I went with him and Two Face to Fort Laramie. I have heard it stated that a story had been told by me to the effect that Two Face's son had saved my life. I never made any such statement, as I have no knowledge of any such thing, and I think if my life had been in danger he would not have troubled himself about it.

LUCINDA EWBANKS.

Witness:
J. H. Triggs, *1st Lieut. Comd'g Co. D, 7th Iowa Cavalry.*
E. B. Zabriskie, *Capt. 1st Cav. Nev. Vol., Judge Advocate Dis't of the Plains.*

Senator: Since you were here I have had another talk with Major Anthony, who was in command of Fort Lyon at the time Colonel Chivington arrived there, having relieved Major Wynkoop. He says, among a great many other things:

"As I told you before, but two days before Colonel Chivington came down, they [Cheyennes] sent word to me, *after I had fired on them*, that if that little G—d d—d red-eyed [Major Anthony's eyes and eyelids are red from having had the scurvy] chief wanted a fight out of them, if he would go up to their camp they would give him all he wanted."

And Major Anthony says to me: "I told Colonel Chivington I was glad he had come; that I would have gone before and cleaned out the sons of guns if I had had force enough; but there were some of them I should have saved if possible."

Again, he says: "This whole row has been caused by jealous officers and civilians who conspired to get 'Old Chiv.' out of the way."

I have no note or comment to make on this, only that it is a repetition of what the major said to me on the cars last spring, between Atchison and Leavenworth, and accords with what officers in Denver say he told them before the battle.

Truly yours,

SIMEON WHITELEY.

Hon. J. R. Doolittle, *U. S. Senate.*

EXTRACTS FROM THE ROCKY MOUNTAIN NEWS, DECEMBER, 1864.

Despatch from Colonel Chivington.

Headquarters District of Colorado,
Denver, December 7, 1864.

Editors News: The following despatch has been received at this office and forwarded to department headquarters:

Headquarters District of Colorado, in the Field,
Cheyenne Country, South Bend, Big Sandy, November 29.

General: In the last ten days my command has marched three hundred miles—one hundred of which the snow was two feet deep. After a march of forty miles last night, I, at daylight this morning, attacked a Cheyenne village of one hundred anc thirty lodges, from nine hundred to one thousand warriors strong. We killed chiefs Black Kettle, White Antelope, and Little Robe, and between four and five hundred other Indians; captured between four and five hundred ponies and mules. Our loss is nine killed and thirty-eight wounded. All did nobly. I think I will catch some more of them about eighty miles on Smoky Hill. We found a white man's scalp, not more than three days old, in a lodge.

J. M. CHIVINGTON,
Colonel, Commanding District of Colorado and First Indian Expedition.

Major General S. R. Curtis, *Fort Leavenworth.*

I am, gentlemen, very respectfully, your obedient servant,

CHARLES WHEELER,
A. A. A. General.

Letter from Colonel Shoup—About the big fight.

[The following private letter from Colonel Shoup was politely handed us for publication.

SOUTH BEND OF BIG SANDY, BATTLE GROUND,
Cheyenne Country, December 3, 1864.

DEAR SIR: I have the pleasure of informing you that we engaged the Indians on yesterday, on the Big Sandy, about forty (40) miles north of Fort Lyon. The engagement commenced at sunrise, and lasted to about 2½ o'clock p. m., completely routing the Indians.

Our loss is eight (8) killed, one missing, and about forty wounded. The Indian loss is variously estimated at from 300 to 500—I think about 300—between 500 and 600 Indian saddles, and over 100 lodges, with all their camp equipage. Black Kettle, White Antelope, One Eye, and other chiefs, are among the killed. I think this the severest chastisement ever given to Indians in battle on the American continent.

Our men fought with great enthusiasm and bravery, but with some disorder. There are plenty more Indians within a few days' march. I fear, however, they will lose their assumed bravery when they hear of the defeat of their allies in arms. The story that Indians are our equals in warfare is nailed. This story may do to tell to down-easters, but not to Colorado soldiers. About one hundred and seventy-five men of the first Colorado, a small detachment of the first New Mexico, and about six hundred and fifty of my regiment were in the engagement. I might, if time would permit, give you many interesting incidents that came under my notice during the battle, but I will have to close. Your son, the lieutenant, behaved well in the fight, and came out without a wound.

Your friend,

GEO. L. SHOUP.

Captain SOPRIS.

—

Letter from Major Anthony—About the Indian fight.

[The following from the major to his brother, in this city, we are permitted to publish:]

SAND CREEK, 25 MILES ABOVE FORT LYON,
December 1, 1864.

DEAR WEBB: I am here with the command. We have just had, day before yesterday, an Indian fight. We have nearly annihilated Black Kettle's band of Cheyennes and Left-Hand's Arapahoes.

* * * * * * * * * * * *

I did my share, and I think my command did as well as any in the whole brigade, notwithstanding I lost one man killed and two slightly wounded; I was one of the first in the fight and among the last to leave, and my loss is less than any other battalion. We have forty-seven persons killed and wounded.

* * * * * * * * * * * *

I will give particulars when I see you. We start for another band of red-skins, and shall fight differently next time. I never saw more bravery displayed by any set of people on the face of the earth than by those Indians. They would charge on a whole company singly, determined to kill some one before being killed themselves. We, of course, took no prisoners, except John Smith's son, and he was taken suddenly ill in the night, and died before morning.

Lieutenant Baldwin, of my command, lost his horse. I had one horse shot under me, but came off with a whole "hide." I did not sleep for three days and two nights until last evening.

S. J. ANTHONY.

—

Additional about the Indian fight.

HEADQUARTERS DISTRICT OF COLORADO, IN THE FIELD,
On Big Bend of Sandy Creek, Colorado Territory, November 29, 1864.

SIR: I have not the time to give you a detailed history of our engagement of to-day, or to mention those officers and men who distinguished themselves in one of the most bloody Indian battles ever fought on these plains. You will find enclosed the report of my surgeon in charge, which will bring to many anxious friends the sad fate of loved ones, who are and have been risking everything to avenge the horrid deeds of those savages we have so severely handled. We made a forced march of forty miles and surprised, at break of day, one of the most powerful villages of the Cheyenne nation, and captured over five hundred animals; killing the celebrated chiefs One Eye, White Antelope, Knock-Knee, Black Kettle, and Little Robe, with about five hundred of their people, destroying all their lodges and equipage, making almost an annihilation of the entire tribe.

I shall leave here, as soon as I can see our wounded safely on the way to the hospital at Fort Lyon, for the villages of the Sioux, which are reported about eighty miles from here on the Smoky Hill, and three thousand strong—so look out for more fighting. I will state for the consideration of gentlemen who are opposed to fighting these red scoundrels, that I was shown by my chief surgeon the scalp of a white man, taken from the lodge of one of the chiefs, which could not have been more than two or three days taken; and I could mention many more things to show how these Indians, who have been drawing government rations at Fort Lyon, are and have been acting.

Very respectfully, your obedient servant,

J. M. CHIVINGTON,
Colonel, Commanding Colorado Expedition against Indians on Plains.

CHARLES WHEELER,
A. A. A. General, Headquarters District of Colorado, Denver.

Colonel Bent sworn:

Having been living near the mouth of the Purgatoire on the Arkansas river in Colorado Territory for the last thirty-six years, and during all that time have resided near or at what is known as Bent's Old Fort, I have had considerable experience in Indian affairs from my long residence in the country. Since I have been there nearly every instance of difficulties between the Indians and the whites arose from aggressions on the Indians by the whites. Some of these aggressions are of recent date. About three years ago the Arapahoes were encamped near Fort Lyon; a soldier had obtained some whiskey and went to the Arapaho village after dark; he met an Indian or two outside and told them he wanted a squaw for the whiskey; that is, he wanted a squaw to sleep with for the whiskey. The Indian told him that if he would give him the whiskey he would get him a squaw; he gave him the whiskey, and the Indian started off and went into a lodge of his friends, and commenced drinking the whiskey with them, without bringing the squaw. The soldier started on a search for the Indian and whiskey, and found them in a lodge. The Indian refused to return the whiskey, when the soldier pulled out his revolver, fired and broke the Indian's arm; the soldier then made his escape and could never be identified by his officers or by the Indians. The matter created great confusion among the Indians, but was finally settled without a fight. I understood from some officers under Colonel Chivington that the hostilities between the Cheyennes and the whites were commenced by Colonel Chivington's orders, who sent an officer down the Platte to see some Indians who, it was said, had stolen some stock, with orders to disarm all the Indians he met. The officer proceeded until he met some Indians coming in with some animals they had found, belonging to the whites; he rode up to the Indians in what they thought to be a friendly manner, and, I think, shook hands with the Indians, and after doing that, he and his men made a grab for the Indians' arms. The Indians tried to run; the soldiers fired at them, wounding two; one fell from his horse, but the Indians rallied and got him off before the whites could get hold of them. This was a party of Cheyennes, I think seven in number. This was the first actual conflict between this tribe and the whites. Very soon after Lieutenant Ayres was sent down to pursue the Cheyennes; to continue down the Republican and Smoky Hill fork to Fort Larned. He met a party of Cheyennes on Smoky Hill, who were going out on a hunt; they had just left Fort Larned. One of the chiefs who had been on to Washington the spring previous was with the party. He went up to the soldiers, shook hands with them, showed the lieutenant the medal he got from the President, stating that his Great Father, when giving him the medal, told him to be always friendly to the whites. This chief, Lean Bear, was then shot by one of the soldiers; a fight then commenced; there were two other Indians killed, three soldiers killed and ten or twelve wounded. The troops then commenced retreating, and a running fight was kept up for ten or fifteen miles; the Indians finally left them, the soldiers going to Fort Larned. Lieutenant Ayres left his troops at Fort Larned and started for Fort Lyon. I met him on my way to the States, near Fort Lyon. He told me he had had a fight with the Cheyennes, and some Sioux connected with them, on the Smoky Hill, killing some seventeen of them. I continued on my journey the next morning and met an express from the Indian village, where the fight was, stating they had had a fight on the Smoky Hill, but did not know what it was about or for, and that they would like to see me and converse with me on the subject. I sent the express back, stating I would meet the chief on Coon creek. Seven days after this I met the chief on Coon creek; he stated to me that he did not know the cause of the attack; that it was not his intention or wish to fight the whites; that he wanted to be friendly and peaceable and keep his tribe so. He felt he was not able to fight the whites, and wanted to live in peace. I then asked him if he would prevent his young men from committing any depredations for twenty days, by which time I thought I should be able to go to Leavenworth, see General Curtis, then in command of the department, and return. After leaving the chief I altered my mind, and concluded I could do better by seeing the authorities in Colorado at Fort Lyon. I returned next morning towards Fort Lyon. On my arrival there I met Colonel Chivington, related to him the conversation that had taken place between me and the Indians, and that the chiefs desired to be friendly. In reply he said he was not authorized to make peace, and that he was then on the war path—I think were the words he used. I then stated to him that there was great risk to run in keeping up war; that there were a great many government trains travelling to New Mexico and other points, also a great many citizens, and that I did not think there was sufficient force to protect the travel, and that the citizens and settlers of the country would have to suffer. He said the citizens would have to protect themselves. I then said no more to him. I then went up to my ranch, twenty-five miles from Fort Lyon; was there about seven days, when I received a letter from Major Colley, the Indian agent, stating he wished to see me immediately on business. I went to the fort, and he (Major Colley) showed me Governor Evans's proclamation, also a letter from Governor Evans to him, directing him to get some one to go immediately to the different tribes of Indians and fetch all of the different tribes of Indians into the forts, Lyon and Larned—that is, all who desired to be friendly; that they should be protected by the government of the United States, and at the same time have rations issued to them. Governor Evans at that time was ex-officio superintendent of Indian affairs. I immediately started on my way in search of the Indians, alone; I found all the different tribes in the vicinity of Fort Larned; the Cheyennes, Arapahoes, Kiowas, Comanches, and Apaches. I then immediately brought the Cheyenne chiefs within four miles of Fort Larned, they being at war with the whites; the other tribes were at peace. I had an interview with the Cheyennes—translated to them the governor's proclamation; they expressed a great desire to make peace and to keep it, and appeared to be perfectly well satisfied with the governor's proclamation. They went up with me the next morning and had an interview with the commanding officer of the post, and everything was settled satisfactorily on both sides. The Indians then returned to their villages on the Arkansas, some twenty-five miles from Fort Lyon. I then mentioned to the commanding officer that I thought from the movements and actions of the Kiowas they would break out in a short time, which proved to be the case. In two or three days afterwards the Kiowas went up to Fort Larned and ran off the stock, at the same time wounding a sentinel. They resorted to a stratagem to obtain the stock: the squaws went into the fort and commenced a dance to attract the attention of the troops, while the war party got the horses, and when the alarm was given the squaws jumped on their horses and ran off. The Arapaho chief, Left-Hand, then took twenty-five of his men and went to Fort Larned, with the intention of offering his services to the United States, to assist them in fighting the Kiowas and recovering the stolen stock. He got within four hundred yards of the fort, met a soldier, and sent him to the commanding officer, to state that he wished to have an interview with him, but the first salute he received was a cannon shot fired at himself and party. Left-Hand carried a white flag, and could speak English very well. He was afterwards killed in the massacre on Sand creek. This was the commencement of the Arapaho war. The Arapahoes, who had committed no hostile acts previously, now commenced and committed more depredations than the Cheyennes. From information, I know of what occurred in the Sand creek fight; I had two sons in the village, and one who acted as guide and interpreter for the government, and was with Colonel Chivington. The attack at Sand creek on the Indians produced great excitement among them; they even deposed their head chief, Black Kettle, stating that he had brought them in there to be betrayed; they also stated that they had always heard that white men would not kill women and children, but they had now lost all confidence in the whites. Since that time the Cheyennes, Arapahoes, Kiowas, and a portion of the Comanches, have been at war with the whites. I have no doubt but for the firing on the Arapahoes at Fort Larned, and the affair at Sand creek, we might have had peace with all the Indians on the Arkansas. I have no doubt if proper persons (and by proper persons I mean those who would be honest and not try to defraud the Indians or the government, and they should be acquainted with the Indian character) were appointed agents, and if officers from the regular army, with troops from the same, were stationed at the posts near the Indians, I think there would be no difficulty. Volunteer officers, the Indians can see, have no control over their men—no discipline, and the soldiers cannot be punished for abusing the Indians. The last great difficulty previous to the one I have mentioned, grew out of the Sioux war. This war originated as follows: Some Mormons on their way to Salt lake were driving some stock; either a cow or an ox gave out, the Indians killed the animal, and the Mormons reported the fact to the commanding officer at Fort Laramie; the officer sent down for the Indian who killed the animal, but the Indians refused to send him, as he was not present and could not be found, offering at the same time to pay for the animal killed; the officer then sent Lieutenant Grattan, with eighteen men, to the Indian camp, where there were some three hundred warriors, to fetch the Indian away; he demanded that the Indian should be delivered in fifteen minutes, or he would fire on them; the Indian not being forthcoming at the time, Lieutenant Grattan fired on the Indians, and in a few minutes he and his command were all massacred. This occurred in 1854, and was the commencement of the Sioux war, which lasted some time, the Cheyenne band of the North Platte becoming involved in it. Two campaigns were carried on against them; one under General Harney, and the other under Colonel Sumner. In answer to your inquiry, I must say there have been a good many goods sent by the government to the Indians which never were delivered. These goods are withheld in various ways. For instance, an Indian will come in and make the agent a present of a poney another will make him a present of a mule, another will present four or five buffalo robes, all of which the agent will receive to himself, when he has no right to. The agent then pays these Indians out of the annuity goods, which causes a great deal of dispute among the other Indians, who see the goods which ought to come to them given in payment to other Indians. The Indians never make presents without expecting to receive something more than its value in return, so in the long run it is nothing more nor less than a trade. I believe there are agents, or agents' relatives, in this country who have made very good speculations. The son of Major Colley, the Indian agent of the Cheyennes and Arapahoes, was an Indian trader for the Cheyennes, Arapahoes, Kiowas, and Comanches. He came to this country the fall after his father was appointed agent. When he first came here he could not have had property of the value to exceed fifteen hundred dollars, which consisted of some thirty or forty head of cows. From what he said to me he must have made twenty-five or thirty thousand dollars in the two or three years he was trading with the Indians. John Smith acted as the Indian trader, and was considered as a partner in the business. It is hard to identify Indian goods, but I am satisfied that a portion of the goods traded with the Indians were annuity goods. From comparison of the goods traded and the annuity goods, I am satisfied they were identically the same goods. The Indians knew they were purchasing their own goods, but did not complain about it. At the time I was trading in the same village with Mr. Colley, one of my men went into his lodge and brought back to me a top of a box marked "U. S. Upper Arkansas Agency." I have heard it stated that sometimes agents give the Indian goods to white traders in the country to trade them on shares. To procure vouchers for the goods the agent will send out to have the tribe come in and get their annuity goods. The goods thought proper to be given them are piled in a heap on the prairie, the Indians sit round in a large circle, and the agent then tells them, "There are your annuity goods—divide them among yourselves." The agent then gets four or five of the principal chiefs to come in and sign the vouchers; as a matter of course the Indians do not know what or how much they are signing for. I would suggest that the Indians be allowed by law to select some white man to be present at the distribution, with power to examine all bills and vouchers, and see that the Indians are not defrauded. All the agents on the Arkansas have been in the habit of distributing the goods in the manner above described, and the poor and needy Indians do not get their share, which falls to the richer and more powerful ones. If the matter were left to me I would guarantee with my life that in three months I could have all the Indians along the Arkansas at peace, without the expense of war. These would include the Cheyennes, Arapahoes, Kiowas, Comanches, and Apaches. Some Cheyennes in whom I have confidence stated to me that they had no confidence in Major Colley, knowing he was swindling them out of their goods, and they did not care to come in and receive them, but when Major Fitzpatrick was their agent they had confidence and always came in for their annuities. There was a treaty made between the Cheyennes and Arapahoes and Colonel Boone. In my opinion the reservation now set apart for the Cheyennes and Arapahoes is not suitable. The best place for a reservation for them, in my opinion, would be on Beaver creek, between the Smoky Hill and the Republican. This would be in their own country, where the buffalo abound, and where they will probably last be seen. This reservation would be off from all the roads and all the great thoroughfares, and distant from all settlements. The land would be suitable for them, but not for the whites, and contains no minerals. On this reservation the agency should be established, and the agent should always be with them; grass and timber abound.

Robert Bent sworn:

I am twenty-four years old; was born on the Arkansas river. I am pretty well acquainted with the Indians of the plains, having spent most of my life among them. I was employed as guide and interpreter at Fort Lyon by Major Anthony. Colonel Chivington ordered me to accompany him on his way to Sand creek. The command consisted of from nine hundred to one thousand men, principally Colorado volunteers. We left Fort Lyon at eight o'clock in the evening, and came on to the Indian camp at daylight the next morning. Colonel Chivington surrounded the village with his troops. When we came in sight of the camp I saw the American flag waving and heard Black Kettle tell the Indians to stand round the flag, and there they were huddled—men, women, and children. This was when we were within fifty yards of the Indians. I also saw a white flag raised. These flags were in so conspicuous a position that they must have been seen. When the troops fired the Indians ran, some of the men into their lodges, probably to get their arms. They had time to get away if they had wanted to. I remained on the field five hours, and when I left there were shots being fired up the creek. I think there were six hundred Indians in all. I think there were thirty-five braves and some old men, about sixty in all. All fought well. At the time the rest of the men were away from camp, hunting. I visited the battle-ground one month afterwards; saw the remains of a good many; counted sixty-nine, but a number had been eaten by the wolves and dogs. After the firing the warriors put the squaws and children together, and surrounded them to protect them. I saw five squaws under a bank for shelter. When the troops came up to them they ran out and showed their persons to let the soldiers know they were squaws and begged for mercy, but the soldiers shot them all. I saw one squaw lying on the bank whose leg had been broken by a shell; a soldier came up to her with a drawn sabre; she raised her arm to protect herself, when he struck, breaking her arm; she rolled over and raised her other arm, when he struck, breaking it, and then left her without killing her. There seemed to be an indiscriminate slaughter of men, women, and children. There were some thirty or forty squaws collected in a hole for protection; they sent out a little girl about six years old with a white flag on a stick; she had not proceeded but a few steps when she was shot and killed. All the squaws in that hole were afterwards killed, and four or five bucks outside. The squaws offered no resistance. Every one I saw dead was scalped. I saw one squaw cut open with an unborn child, as I thought, lying by her side. Captain Soulé afterwards told me that such was the fact. I saw the body of White Antelope with the privates cut off, and I heard a soldier say he was going to make a tobacco-pouch out of them. I saw one squaw whose privates had been cut out. I heard Colonel Chivington say to the soldiers as they charged past him, "Remember our wives and children murdered on the Platte and Arkansas." He occupied a position where he could not have failed to have seen the American flag, which I think was a garrison flag, six by twelve. He was within fifty yards when he planted his battery. I saw a little girl about five years of age who had been hid in the sand; two soldiers discovered her, drew their pistols and shot her, and then pulled her out of the sand by the arm. I saw quite a number of infants in arms killed with their mothers. There were trading in the village at the time John Smith, a soldier named Louderback, and a teamster of young Colley's named Clark. They were trading goods said to belong to Dexter Colley and John Smith. The goods traded were similar to those they had been in the habit of trading before. I have heard the Indians charge Major Colley with trading their own goods to them.

Colonel Kit Carson sworn:

I have heard read the statement of Colonel Bent, and his suggestions and opinions in relation to Indian affairs coincide perfectly with my own. I came to this country in 1826, and since that time have become pretty well acquainted with the Indian tribes, both in peace and at war. I think, as a general thing, the difficulties arise from aggressions on the part of the whites. From what I have heard, the whites are always cursing the Indians, and are not willing to do them justice. For instance, at times large trains come out to this country, and some man without any responsibility is hired to guard the horses, mules, and stock of the trains; these cattle by his negligence frequently stray off; always, if anything is lost, the cry is raised that the Indians stole it. It is customary among the Indians, even among themselves, if they lose animals, as Indians go everywhere, if they bring them in they expect to get something for their trouble. Among themselves they always pay; but when brought in to this man, who lost them through his negligence, he refuses to pay, and abuses the Indians, striking or sometimes shooting them, because they do not wish to give up the stock without pay; and thus a war is brought on. That is the way in which difficulties frequently arise. I have heard read the statement of how the Sioux war arose, which agrees word for word with what I have heard, and what I believe to be the facts. And in relation to the war with the Cheyennes, I have heard it publicly stated that the authorities of Colorado, expecting that their troops would be sent to the Potomac, determined to get up an Indian war, so that the troops would be compelled to remain. I know of no acts of hostility on the part of the Cheyennes and Arapahoes committed previous to the attacks made upon them, as stated by

Colonel Bent. In 1830, or '31, I was one of a party who made peace with the Arapahoes, and since that time I know of no difficulty with them until that described by Colonel Bent. I know of no other great difficulties on the Arkansas route than the Sioux war and the present war. I think the Kiowas are hostile against the government without cause. The other tribes, I think, are rather compelled to be so. Most of the Comanches, I think, are friendly disposed. I think if proper men were appointed and proper steps taken, peace could be had with all the Indians on and below the Arkansas, without war. I believe that, if Colonel Bent and myself were authorized, we could make a solid, lasting peace with those Indians. I have much more confidence in the influence of Colonel Bent with the Indians than in my own. I think if prompt action were taken the Indians could be got together by the tenth of September. I know that even before the acquisition of New Mexico there had about always existed an hereditary warfare between the Navajoes and Mexicans; forays were made into each other's country, and stock, women, and children stolen. Since the acquisition, the same state has existed; we would hardly get back from fighting and making peace with them before they would be at war again. I consider the reservation system as the only one to be adopted for them. If they were sent back to their own country to-morrow, it would not be a month before hostilities would commence again. There is a part of the Navajoes, the wealthy, who wish to live in peace; the poorer class are in the majority, and they have no chiefs who can control them. When I campaigned against them eight months I found them scattered over a country several hundred miles in extent. There is no suitable place in their own country—and I have been all over it—where more than two thousand could be placed. If located in different places, it would not be long before they and the Mexicans would be at war. If they were scattered on different locations, I hardly think any number of troops could keep them on their reservations. The mountains they live in in the Navajo country cannot be penetrated by troops. There are cañons in their country thirty miles in length, with walls a thousand feet high, and when at war it is impossible for troops to pass through these cañons, in which they hide and cultivate the ground. In the main Cañon de Chelly they had some two or three thousand peach trees, which were mostly destroyed by my troops. Colonel Sumner, in the fall of 1851, went into the Cañon de Chelly with several hundred men and two pieces of artillery; he got into the cañon some eight or ten miles, but had to retreat out of it at night. In the walls of the cañon they have regular houses built in the crevices, from which they fire and roll down huge stones on an enemy. They have regular fortifications, averaging from one to two hundred feet from the bottom, with portholes for firing. No small-arms can injure them, and artillery cannot be used. In one of these crevices I found a two-story house. I regard these cañons as impregnable. General Canby entered this cañon, but retreated out the next morning. When I captured the Navajoes I first destroyed their crops, and harassed them until the snow fell very deep in the cañons, taking some prisoners occasionally. I think it was about the 6th of January, after the snow fell, that I started. Five thousand soldiers would probably keep them on reservations in their own country. The Navajoes had a good many small herds when I went there. I took twelve hundred sheep from them at one time, and smaller lots at different times. The volunteers were allowed one dollar per head for all sheep and goats taken, which were turned over to the commissary. I think General Carleton gave the order as an encouragement to the troops. I think from fifteen hundred to two thousand could subsist themselves in the Valley de Chelly. At this point it took me and three hundred men most one day to destroy a field of corn. I think probably fifteen hundred could subsist on the northeastern slope of the Tunacha mountain. I know of no other place near by where any considerable number could subsist themselves. I was in the valley of the San Juan, but can give no idea of the number that could subsist themselves in it. While I was in the country there was continual thieving carried on between the Navajoes and Mexicans. Some Mexicans now object to the settlement of the Navajoes at the Bosque, because they cannot prey on them as formerly. I am of the opinion that, in consequence of the military campaign and the destruction of their crops, they were forced to come in. It appears to me that the only objection to the Bosque is on account of the wood, which consists of mesquite roots; but I am not sufficiently acquainted with the character of it to give an opinion of it, and the time it would last, but it is rather hard to dig. Many of the Apaches understand farming, and they should be put on a reservation. I think the Jicarrilla Apaches would object to being put on the Bosque. The Apaches in Arizona, I think, would make very little objection to being placed on a reservation. With the Utes it would be more difficult, as they know nothing of planting, and when spoken to on the subject have invariably objected. They are a brave, warlike people; they are of rather small size, but hardy, and very fine shots. I would advise, however, that they be put on a reservation, as they cannot live much longer as now; they are generally hungry, and killing cattle and sheep, which will bring on a war. They are now at peace, and it would be the wiser

7

policy to remain at peace with them. I think there is a good place for a reservation north of the San Juan in Utah. I think that justice demands that every effort should be made to secure peace with the Cheyennes and Arapahoes before any war was prosecuted against them, in view of the treatment they have received.

HEADQUARTERS DISTRICT OF NEW MEXICO,
Santa Fé, New Mexico, October 22, 1865.

SIR: I have the honor herewith to enclose for the information of the congressional committee, of which you are the chairman, letters of instruction and advice from myself to various commanders and to different departments of the public service in relation to Indians, Indian wars, &c., &c., within my official jurisdiction and controlled by myself.

Among these letters will be found two or three relating to the wealth of this part of the country in precious metals. These are sent to you in order that the committee may see the national importance of settling Indians upon reservations, so that the country now inhabited by many bands of them may be left open to the enterprise and skill of the miner. The Indians will not themselves work the mines: they should not be permitted to lie in wait to murder the prospecter who comes with much toil and many privations to explore their country for its hidden wealth. This they will surely do unless they are exterminated or placed upon reservations. The miners *will* go to their country, and the question which comes up is, shall the miners be protected and the country be developed, or shall the Indians be suffered to kill them and the nation be deprived of its immense wealth?

In all that I have had to do in this command, so far as the Indians are concerned, I have endeavored to treat them justly, and I point to this record of over three years of anxiety and toil, mostly on their account, as one of which I do not feel ashamed.

I have the honor to be, very respectfully, your obedient servant,

JAMES H. CARLETON,
Brigadier General, Commanding.

Hon. JAMES R. DOOLITTLE,
United States Senate, Washington, D. C.

LETTERS RELATING TO INDIAN AFFAIRS IN THE DEPARTMENT OF NEW MEXICO DURING THE YEARS 1862 AND 1863.

[Extract.]

HEADQUARTERS DEPARTMENT OF NEW MEXICO.
Santa Fé, N. M., September 30, 1862.

GENERAL: I have the honor to inform you that I relieved General Canby in the command of this department on the 18th instant, and he left this city for Washington, D. C., four days afterwards. I find that during the raid which was made into this Territory by some armed men from Texas, under Brigadier General Sibley, of the army of the so-called Confederate States, the Indians, aware that the attention of our troops could not, for the time, be turned toward them, commenced robbing the inhabitants of their stock, and killed, in various places, a great number of people; the Navajoes on the western side, and the Mescalero Apaches on the eastern side of the settlements, both committing these outrages at the same time, and during the last year that has passed have left the people greatly impoverished. Many farms and settlements near Fort Stanton have been entirely abandoned.

To punish and control the Mescaleros, I have ordered Fort Stanton to be reoccupied. That post is in the heart of their country, and hitherto when troops occupied it those Indians were at peace. I have sent Colonel Christopher Carson, (Kit Carson,) with five companies of his regiment of New Mexican volunteers, to Fort Stanton. One of these companies, on foot, will hold the post and guard the stores, while four companies mounted, under Carson, will operate against the Indians until they have been punished for their recent aggressions. The lieutenant colonel, with four companies of the same regiment, will move into the Navajo country and establish and garrison a post on the Gallo, which was selected by General Canby; it is called Fort Wingate. I shall endeavor to have this force, assisted by some militia which have been called out by the governor of the Territory, perform such service among the Navajoes as will bring them to feel that they have been doing wrong.

* * * * * * * * * * *

I am, general, very respectfully, your obedient servant,

JAMES H. CARLETON,
Brigadier General, Commanding.

Brigadier General LORENZO THOMAS,
Adjutant General U. S. A., Washington, D. C.

Official:

ERASTUS W. WOOD,
Captain 1st Vet. Inf. C. V., A. A. A. General.

Confidential.]

HEADQUARTERS DEPARTMENT OF NEW MEXICO,
Santa Fé, N. M., October 11, 1862.

COLONEL: I have ordered Colonel Carson, with five companies of his regiment, to reoccupy Fort Stanton. These troops are already en route to that point; they will immediately commence hostile operations against the Mescalero and Navajo Indians who may be in that vicinity and southward of it.

You will order the following troops into the Mescalero country to co-operate with Colonel Carson, yet to be independent of him: Captain McCleave you will place in command of one expedition, to be composed of his own and one company of your regiment. He will start with this force, increased by twenty good Mexican spies and guides which you are authorized to employ at reasonable rates, on the 15th of next month, and be absent until the 31st day of December, 1862. He will proceed by the way of Dog Cañon and operate to the eastward and southeastward of that noted haunt of the Mescaleros.

You will order Captain Roberts of your regiment to command another expedition against these Indians. His force will be composed of all the effective men of his own company, all the effective men of Captain Pishon's company now in the valley of the Rio Grande, north of Fort Quitman, and twenty first-rate Pueblo Indians or Mexicans, whom you are authorized to employ at Isletta, Socorro, and San Elizario. These last twenty I would suggest you employ Don Gregorio Garcia, of San Elizario, to command. He has often been on expeditions against the Mescaleros and had good luck; he knows the country well. Captain Roberts will start from Franklin, Texas, on the 15th of November next, and be absent until December 31, 1862. He will proceed by the Wacco Tanks and thence northwestwardly to such points as will be most likely to be occupied by Apaches. Assistant Surgeon Kittridge will accompany Captain McCleave; Assistant Surgeon McKee will accompany Captain Roberts. There is to be no council held with the Indians, nor any talks. The men are to be slain whenever and wherever they can be found. The women and children may be taken as prisoners, but, of course, they are not to be killed.

From Dog Cañon and from the Wacco Tanks, subsistence stores and ammunition, &c., will doubtless have to be transported on pack-mules. I have ordered seventy-five pack-saddles to be sent down from Fort Union for the use of the two expeditions.

I would suggest a depot being formed by each expedition well out into the Mescalero country, further out than Dog Cañon or Wacco Tanks, if practicable—a depot that may be reached by wagons—and thence operate with pack-mules, leaving a few men in depot to guard the supplies not immediately required.

I send a copy of this letter to Colonel Carson, that he may know when you are to act, and where your forces are to operate, and he will shape his plans accordingly.

Much is expected of the California troops. I trust that these three demonstrations will give those Indians a wholesome lesson. They have robbed and murdered the people with impunity too long already.

If the movements are kept from being made public, so the Indians through the Mexicans may not know of your plans until the troops take the field, it will be better so. If the Indians want to negotiate, Carson will send the chief, under a flag, to Santa Fé for that purpose.

While Captain Roberts's company is in the field, you will station Captain Willis, with a portion of his company, at Franklin, and leave another portion, under Lieutenant Whittemore, to guard Hart's Mills.

Both McCleave and Roberts will be instructed to keep a journal of every day's march and work; of the estimated courses and distances travelled; of the kind of country passed over; of the water courses, springs, grass, &c., which they find.

These journals will be forwarded to department headquarters as soon as the campaign is over, and copies of them to Washington.

The several commands will be entirely independent of each other, unless they "happen to join to do duty together," and the commanding officers will have full powers to subdivide their forces, when once they have got into the Indian country, in such manner as in their judgment will be the best, having in view the punishment of the Indians.

I am, colonel, very respectfully, your obedient servant,

JAMES H. CARLETON,
Brigadier General, Commanding.

Colonel JOSEPH R. WEST,
Commanding the District of Arizona, Mesilla.

If necessary, Captain Willis can employ the doctor in El Paso to attend his sick during McKee's absence.

Official:

ERASTUS W. WOOD,
Captain 1st Vet. Inf. C. V., A. A. A. General.

HEADQUARTERS DEPARTMENT OF NEW MEXICO,
Santa Fé, N. M., October 12, 1862.

COLONEL: Enclosed you will find a confidential communication to Colonel West, commanding the district of Arizona; it is dated the 11th instant, and directs him to send two expeditions against the Mescalero Apaches, starting them on the 15th of next month.

I desire you to send one of your mounted companies down to the junction of the Rio Hondo with the Pecos, to act as an outpost to this country; to keep scouts well down the river towards Delaware creek to see that no force advances up the Pecos from the direction of Fort Lancaster, in Texas, without your having timely notice of the fact, so that you can send me word.

As your scouts from this company come near the mouth of the Peñasco they will, doubtless, find a plenty of Mescaleros. It was near that point where Captain Stanton was killed by them. In this case you could, if you thought it advisable, move the company down to the mouth of the Peñasco to produce an impression upon the Indians, at the same time it watched the approaches to New Mexico by the way of the Pecos; but under no circumstances will it leave the valley of the river unwatched.

The other three companies you can divide as you please, but with these you will make war upon the Mescaleros and upon all other Indians you may find in the Mescalero country, until further orders. All Indian men of that tribe are to be killed whenever and wherever you can find them. The women and children will not be harmed, but you will take them prisoners, and feed them at Fort Stanton until you receive other instructions about them. If the Indians send in a flag and desire to treat for peace, say to the bearer that when the people of New Mexico were attacked by the Texans, the Mescaleros broke their treaty of peace, and murdered innocent people, and ran off their stock; that now our hands are untied, and you have been sent to punish them for their treachery and their crimes; that you have no power to make peace; that you are there to kill them wherever you can find them; that if they beg for peace, their chiefs and twenty of their principal men must come to Santa Fé to have a talk here; but tell them fairly and frankly that you will keep after their people and slay them until you receive orders to desist from these headquarters; that this making of treaties for them to break whenever they have an interest in breaking them will not be done any more; that that time has passed by; that we have no faith in their promises; that we believe if we kill some of their men in fair, open war, they will be apt to remember that it will be better for them to remain at peace than to be at war. I trust that this severity, in the long run, will be the most humane course that could be pursued toward these Indians.

You observe that there is a large force helping you. I do not wish to tie your hands by instructions; the whole duty can be summed up in a few words: The Indians are to be soundly whipped, without parleys or councils except as above. Be careful not to mistake the troops from below for Texans. If a force of rebels comes, *you* know how to annoy it; how to stir up their camps and stock by night; how to lay waste the prairies by fire; how to make the country very warm for them, and the road a difficult one. *Do this*, and keep me advised of all you do.

I am, colonel, respectfully, your friend,

JAMES H. CARLETON,
Brigadier General, Commanding.

Colonel CHRISTOPHER CARSON,
1st New Mexico Vol, en route to Fort Stanton, N. M.

Official:

ERASTUS W. WOOD,
Captain 1st Vet. Inf. C. V., A. A. A. General.

[Extract.

HEADQUARTERS DEPARTMENT OF NEW MEXICO,
Santa Fé, N. M., November 9, 1862.

GENERAL: * * * * * * * * * *
You are aware of the hostile attitude of the Mescalero Apaches, the Pino Alto Apaches, and the Navajoes, and also of the rumors of another Texan raid. I shall endeavor to accomplish everything possible with the handful of men which are left. Five companies of Colonel Carson's regiment are now at Fort Stanton and in the Mescalero country, and four companies of the California volunteers enter that country from Fort Fillmore and from Franklin, Texas. These nine companies will, I trust, punish the Mescaleros well. Already, in one small affair, Carson's men have killed José Largo and Manuelita, two of the principal chiefs, and nine of the men, besides wounding several, and besides capturing, as I learn, some seventeen horses. By establishing Fort Sumner at the Bosque Redondo, I shut up the door through which the Kiowas and Comanches have hitherto entered New Mexico, and cut off a great thoroughfare northward of the Mescaleros. Another very important consideration in establishing this post was to open a portion of the country where good grass is found all winter for our worn-down animals to keep them from perishing. We could not buy hay enough to subsist them even if we had the money. The saving on hay alone, this winter, will more than build the post in the spring. During the winter the troops will live in tents or under canvas.

I beg to call your attention again to the practicability of sending the regiment of infantry and five companies of cavalry (at all events the former) which were asked for, to be sent from California, by General Canby.

The provisions are already in abundance at Fort Yuma and at Tucson, the medical stores and ammunition here, and the transportation all ready to convey the baggage of those troops from Fort Yuma to the Rio Grande.

The weather is now cool, and no discomfort would be experienced in passing the Gila desert.

I beg, respectfully, to ask that I have authority to incorporate the troops from California with those belonging to this department. Under War Department Orders No. 29, series for 1862, they are still borne as belonging to the column from California. This leads to great embarrassment in making up the returns, as the withdrawal of so many troops from this department renders it necessary to distribute the California troops throughout the department.

I trust the importance of this change, and the greater importance of sending more troops without delay into this department, will merit and receive your serious attention.

I am, general, very respectfully, your obedient servant,

JAMES H. CARLETON,
Brigadier General, Commanding.

Brigadier General LORENZO THOMAS,
Adjutant General U. S. A., Washington, D. C.

NOTE.—I herewith enclose a copy of a letter from Captain Archer, commanding at Fort Craig, New Mexico, in relation to an attack by Indians of a train on the Jornado del Muerto. The Indians are said to have been Navajoes; the party numbering about two hundred.
J. H. C.

Official:
ERASTUS W. WOOD,
Captain 1st Vet. Inf. C. V., A. A. A. General.

HEADQUARTERS DEPARTMENT OF NEW MEXICO,
Santa Fé, N. M., November 25, 1862.

COLONEL: I have the honor to acknowledge the receipt of your letter in relation to the Mescalero chiefs who have come to this city with Mr. Labadie, the Indian agent, to sue for peace.

Yesterday, in presence of the governor, the superintendent of Indian affairs, and other gentlemen, I had an interview with the chiefs above alluded to, and told them that if they and their part of the tribe desired to have peace they must come out of the Mescalero country, so that we should not mistake them for those who were hostile, and so that we would be sure that they conveyed no intelligence of our movements to those who did not come in. I told them I would send them and their families to Fort Sumner, at the Bosque Redondo, on the Pecos river, and there feed and protect them until we had punished those who were still at war, and until these latter come in and beg for peace likewise.

A train of government wagons will leave Fort Union, with subsistence stores, for Fort Stanton, in a few days. When this train starts to return, have all the Mescalero men, women, and children, *of the peace party*, with all of their effects, come with this train. The women and children and baggage will be hauled in the wagons, and you will see that they have provisions enough to last them all to the Bosque Redondo, by the way of Agua Negra. The meat portion of the ration will be beef on the hoof. The commanding officer at Fort Sumner will be instructed to feed and protect them after their arrival at the Bosque Redondo.

After these Indians have been sent to the Bosque Redondo you will continue to make war on the others, as heretofore instructed. If they sue for peace, (any one small band of the Mescaleros,) send that band to Fort Sumner to await there until the remainder come in. The result of this will be that, eventually, we shall have the whole tribe at the Bosque Redondo, and then we can conclude a definite treaty, and let them *all* return again to inhabit their proper country.

If you are satisfied that Graydon's attack on Manuelita and his people was not fair and open, see that all the horses and mules, including two said to be in the hands of one Mr. Beach, of Manzana, are returned to the survivors of Manuelita's band.

These arrangements seem to be just. When any band comes in for peace, send me a list of the names of all the men, and the number of the women and children, so that I may know the additional number to provide for at Fort Sumner.

I am, respectfully,

JAMES H. CARLETON,
Brigadier General, Commanding.

Colonel CHRISTOPHER CARSON,
Commanding Expedition against the Mescalero Apaches, Fort Stanton, N. M.

Official:

ERASTUS W. WOOD,
Captain 1st Vet. Inf. C. V., A. A. A. General.

HEADQUARTERS DEPARTMENT OF NEW MEXICO,
Santa Fé, N. M., November 26, 1862.

CAPTAIN: Enclosed herewith is an authentic copy of a letter from myself to Colonel Carson in relation to sending to Bosque Redondo certain men, women, and children of the Mescalero Apache Indians, who desire peace.

When these Indians come to Fort Sumner you will have them encamp sufficiently near your garrison to have them feel secure from attacks by Comanches and Kiowas, of whom they are much afraid; and sufficiently near for you to know that none of them leave for the Mescalero country without authority.

These Indians are to be fed by your commissary; are to be treated kindly; are not to be annoyed by soldiers visiting their camp at improper times.

As you see by my instructions to Colonel Carson, others of this tribe will doubtless soon be sent to join these. You will have all the parties that come in provided for and carefully protected from harm until further orders.

Send me by every express a list of the names of the men and the number of women and children which you are thus called upon to feed and protect, so that provision may be made for them.

I am, captain, very respectfully,

JAMES H. CARLETON,
Brigadier General, Commanding.

Captain JOSEPH UPDEGRAFF,
Commanding Fort Sumner, Bosque Redondo, N. M.

Official:

ERASTUS W. WOOD,
Captain 1st Vet. Inf. C. V., A. A. A. General.

[Extract.]

HEADQUARTERS DEPARTMENT OF NEW MEXICO,
Santa Fé, N. M., November 26, 1862.

SIR: If in your investigations of the matters relating to the attack by Graydon on Manuelita's band of Mescaleros it shall appear that one Charles Beach, of Manzana, is implicated to a criminal extent, arrest Beach and hold him securely until further orders. The horse and mule which Beach is said to have received as a part of the booty taken from the Indians must be restored to *you*, or Beach kept in confinement until this restoration is made. I consider Mr. Beach an improper person to reside in the Mescalero country, so he will be forbidden under any circumstances from settling there.

* * * * * * * * *

I am, captain, very respectfully, your obedient servant,

JAMES H. CARLETON,
Brigadier General, Commanding.

Colonel CHRISTOPHER CARSON, or,
Officer commanding Fort Stanton, N. M.

Official:

ERASTUS W. WOOD,
Captain 1st Vet. Inf. C. V., A. A. A. General.

HEADQUARTERS DEPARTMENT OF NEW MEXICO,
Fort Union, N. M., December 9, 1862.

SIR: I learned a week since, unofficially, that an Indian of the Utah tribe was in Taos recently, where certain parties are said to have gotten him drunk, then to have saturated some parts of his garments with spirits of turpentine and set fire to the clothing thus saturated. From the effects of this burning the Indian is said to have died. The Utah tribe to which he belonged is said to be very much incensed at this inhuman outrage, and to threaten to be avenged.

In your capacity as judge of this district it occurred to me that you are the proper person to institute inquiries into this matter, and if the rumor be true, to make it your especial business to cause the offenders to be brought to punishment.

As one of the United States officers in New Mexico, and as one whose particular calling is to see justice done, I trust I have but to call your attention to this alleged crime to awaken your zeal in the cause of justice and humanity.

In many years' experience in affairs connected with Indians, I think it never has been my lot to have heard of such horrible barbarity before on the part of white men toward Indians.

I am, sir, very respectfully, your obedient servant,

JAMES H. CARLETON,
Brigadier General, Commanding.

Hon. Judge KNAPP, *at Barclay's Fort, N. M.*

NOTE.—I beg you will acknowledge the receipt of this letter.

Official:

ERASTUS W. WOOD,
Captain 1st Vet. Inf. C. V., A. A. A. General.

[Extract.]

HEADQUARTERS DEPARTMENT OF NEW MEXICO,
Santa Fé, N. M., December 20, 1862.

* * * * * * * * * * *

A delegation of eighteen Navajo chiefs have been in asking for peace. They have heard of our demonstrations against the Mescalero Indians, and see that Fort Wingate is established in their own country, and imagine that our attention will soon be turned toward them.

I told them that they could have no peace until they would give other guarantees than their word that the peace should be kept; to go home and tell their people so; that we had no faith in their promises; that if they did not return we should know they had chosen the alternative of war; that in this event the consequences rested on them. With this they returned to their people.

* * * * * * * * * * * *

I am, general, very respectfully, your obedient servant,

JAMES H. CARLETON,
Brigadier General, Commanding.

Brigadier General LORENZO THOMAS,
Adjutant General U. S. A., Washington, D. C.

Official:

ERASTUS W. WOOD,
Captain 1st Vet. Inf. C. V., A. A. A. General.

HEADQUARTERS DEPARTMENT OF NEW MEXICO,
Fort Craig, N. M., January 2, 1863.

GENERAL: I have the honor to report that I am strengthening the defences of this post by fatigue parties and with the help of the citizens, so that should it ever be invested by the rebels, I trust to be able to hold it and its magazines of supplies.

To-morrow I leave for the Mesilla valley, and for the northwestern portion of Texas. Unless I hear beyond a doubt that Baylor's forces are coming, I shall organize and send into the country, around the headwaters of the Gila, an expedition to punish for their frequent and recent murders and depredations the band of Apaches which infest that region. The Pino Alto gold mines can then be worked with security. From all I can learn, that is one of the richest auriferous countries in the world—one whose development will tend greatly to the prosperity of this Territory.

Should I be so successful as to whip those Indians, I purpose at once to establish a military post near the Pino Alto mines, not only to furnish protection to the miners already working there, but to have a moral effect in preventing the Indians from further depredations.

A military road should be opened from Socorro, or Fort Craig, through by the copper mines, to intersect the road leading from Mesilla to Tucson at Ojo de la Vaca. This would shorten the distance from Santa Fé to Tucson at least one hundred miles; would avoid the Jornado del Muerto; and in a strategical point of view would render western Arizona less isolated and less in danger of being cut off by an enemy occupying the Mesilla valley; besides, it would make the Pino Alto gold region more accessible from the settled portion of New Mexico. You may rely upon it, the attention of the government may be worthily drawn to the importance of this road. It would doubtless cost one hundred thousand dollars to build it. I shall return to Santa Fé by the 25th instant.

I am, general, respectfully, your obedient servant,

JAMES H. CARLETON,
Brigadier General, Commanding.

Brigadier General LORENZO THOMAS,
Adjutant General U. S. A., Washington, D. C.

Official:

ERASTUS W. WOOD,
Captain 1st Vet. Inf. C. V., A. A. A. General.

HEADQUARTERS DEPARTMENT OF NEW MEXICO.
Santa Fé, N. M., February 1, 1863.

GENERAL: I have just returned from San Elizario and Franklin, in northwestern Texas, whither I went to confer with the people, who, in their alarm at the rumors of another invasion from the eastern part of that State, were fleeing into Chihuahua, and leaving their fields to lie uncultivated. The commander of the district of Arizona had issued an order that all lands thus abandoned should, for the year, be given to others who would cultivate them. This had a good effect. I am assured that they will all return.

There are no new rumors of an advance of rebels from Texas. They could have but little to gain by such an expedition, except the right of way to the Pacific, to which great importance is said to be attached by the southern confederacy. As, in the event of a separation, to use their argument, *they could not claim territory which they did not occupy*, it is possible that an effort will be made to recover and hold New Mexico and Arizona. Besides, it is perhaps a part of the plan to persuade, if possible, Chihuahua and Sonora to secede from Mexico and join the southern confederacy. For this purpose it is alleged that Colonel Reilly was sent by General Sibley last winter to confer with the governors of those States.

Leaving out of the question these reasons for recovering this country by troops of the so-called southern confederacy, the probabilities of an invasion cease. At this moment I consider such probabilities so remote as to justify me in employing the troops under my command in chastising the hostile tribes of Indians by which the settled portion of the Territory are surrounded. The Mescalero Apaches have been completely subdued. I have now three hundred and fifty of that tribe at Fort Sumner and *en route* thither. These comprise all that are left of those Indians, except a few who have either run off into Mexico or joined the Gila Apaches. I shall try to settle what have come in on a reservation near Fort Stanton, and have them plant fields for their subsistence the coming year.

The expedition ordered into the Gila country has already been quite successful. Mangus Colorado, doubtless the worst Indian within our boundaries, and one who has been the cause of more murders and of more torturing and of burnings at the stake in this country than all others together, has been killed; and in one battle a few days since over twenty of his followers were killed, (the bodies counted,) and quite an amount of stock captured. Among this stock were found some of the United States mules captured from one of our trains in an attack made on it by these Indians last November on the Jornado del Muerto. Hostilities against the Gila Apaches are now prosecuted with vigor, and will be productive of lasting benefits.

The evidences of rich gold fields, and of veins of silver, and of inexhaustible mines of the richest copper in the country at the head of the Mimbres river and along the country drained by the upper Gila, are of an undoubted character. It seems providential that the practical miners of California should have come here to assist in their discovery and development.

I have sent four companies of California volunteers to garrison Fort West, in the Pinos Altos gold region. I beg to ask authority to let, say, one-fourth of the command at a time have one month's furlough to work in the gold mines on their own account. In this way the mines and the country will become developed, while the troops will become contented to remain in service where the temptation to leave is very great.

By the time the spring opens the Apaches of the Gila will doubtless have been subdued, when I propose to punish the Navajo Indians for their recent murders and wholesale robberies. It is not practicable with my present force and amount of means to make effective demonstrations on more than one tribe at a time. It may be set down as a rule that these Navajo Indians have long since passed that point when talking would be of any avail. They must be whipped and fear us before they will cease killing and robbing the people.

All of the Colorado volunteers have been ordered home.

All of which is respectfully submitted.

JAMES H. CARLETON,
Brigadier General, Commanding.

Brigadier General LORENZO THOMAS,
Adjutant General U. S. A., Washington, D. C.

Official:

ERASTUS W. WOOD,
Captain 1st Vet. Inf. C. V., A. A. A. General.

[Extract.]

HEADQUARTERS DEPARTMENT OF NEW MEXICO,
Santa Fé, N. M., March 13, 1863.

GENERAL: * * * * * * * * * *

Your plan not to stay for one moment hostilities against the Apaches meets with my views and carries out my exact wishes. I do not look forward to any peace with them, except what we must command. They must have no voice in the matter. Entire subjugation, or destruction of all the *men*, are the alternatives.

Very respectfully, your obedient servant,

JAMES H. CARLETON,
Brigadier General, Commanding.

Brigadier General JOSEPH R. WEST,
Commanding District of Arizona, Mesilla, A. T.

Official:

ERASTUS W. WOOD,
Captain 1st Vet. Inf. C. V., A. A. A. General.

[Extract.]

HEADQUARTERS DEPARTMENT OF NEW MEXICO,
Santa Fé, N. M., March 16, 1863.

GENERAL: * * * * * * * * * *

Give orders that the company of cavalry that will return with Captain Anderson from Fort West to the Cienega (as directed in paragraph V of Special Orders No 17, current series, from these headquarters, which paragraph is herewith enclosed) have tools and help work the road to that point. These companies exploring for, locating, working on, or passing over the road in question, will attack any and all Indians they may find, except women and children. This will be a part of their instructions. There must be no peace, or conference, with any Indians living on any of the tributaries of the Mimbres, or the headwaters of the Gila, down as far as Fort Stanford, until they are completely subdued; and not then, until the subject has been duly considered and decided upon at these headquarters. If possible, the present war upon the Apaches, and the one about to be inaugurated against the Navajoes, will be continued *without intermission* to that point where a prospect is opened which may disclose that no other war will be necessary. So all instructions, operations, and efforts will look to no other conclusion.

The campaign sweeping the Florida mountains, about which I have twice written to you, should be borne in mind. Information should be gathered concerning that region, the best guides known, and the work done at the earliest practicable moment. This is a settled purpose, and will, I am sure, meet with a prompt and hearty co-operation on your part. Driven from the Gila, the Apaches will naturally seek asylum in those mountains. There the *maguey* grows, which is their principal food, and in the month of May they will begin to prepare it.

* * * * * * * * * * *

Very respectfully, your obedient servant,

JAMES H. CARLETON,
Brigadier General, Commanding.

Brigadier General JOSEPH R. WEST,
Commanding District of Arizona, Mesilla.

Official: ERASTUS W. WOOD,
Captain 1st Vet. Inf. C. V., A. A. A. General.

HEADQUARTERS DEPARTMENT OF NEW MEXICO,
Santa Fé, N. M., March 19, 1863.

GENERAL: I have the honor to inform you that the operations of the troops against the Mescalero Apaches have resulted in bringing in as prisoners about four hundred men, women and children of that tribe, from their fastnesses in the mountains about Fort Stanton, to Fort Sumner, at the Bosque Redondo, on the Pecos river. This leaves about one hundred, the remainder of that tribe, who are reported as having fled to Mexico and to join the Gila Apaches. Against these last, the Gila Apaches, vigorous hostilities are prosecuted, as I have already informed you. Want of troops and of forage has prevented any operations against the Navajoes. Now that the Mescaleros are subdued, I shall send the whole of Colonel Carson's regiment against the Navajoes, who still continue to plunder and murder the people. This regiment will take the field against them early in May. Already I have commenced drawing the companies in from the Mescalero country preparatory to such movement.

It is my purpose to induce the Mescaleros to settle on a reservation near Fort Sumner at the Bosque Redondo, on the Pecos river. The superintendent of Indian affairs for New Mexico and myself proceed to that point, starting to-day, to have "the talk" with them with reference to this matter. My purpose is to have them fed and kept there under *surveillance;* to have them plant a crop this year; to have them, in short, become what is called in this country a *pueblo.* If they are once permitted to go at large again, the same trouble and expense will again have to be gone through with to punish and subdue them. They *will* murder and rob unless kept from doing it by fear and force.

The bishop of Santa Fé will go down with the superintendent and myself, and, if the Indians agree to my terms, will have a talk with them about sending a priest down to teach them the gospel and open a school for the children. The superintendent will take down farming implements and other useful articles for the Indians, and an agent will remain with the Indians to instruct them in the use of these things.

You will feel pleased to learn that this long-dreaded tribe of murderers and robbers is brought to so promising a condition. Their country around Fort Stanton is fast filling up with settlers.

I shall return to Santa Fé on the 6th proximo.

I am, general, very respectfully, your obedient servant,

JAMES H. CARLETON,
Brigadier General, Commanding.

Brigadier General LORENZO THOMAS,
Adjutant General U. S. Army, Washington, D. C.

Official: ERASTUS W. WOOD,
Captain 1st Vet. Inf. C. V., A. A. A. General

HEADQUARTERS DEPARTMENT OF NEW MEXICO,
Santa Fé, N. M., April 10, 1863.

CAPTAIN: I herewith enclose for your information a copy of a report made by Major Arthur Morrison, 1st New Mexico volunteers, in relation to a dreadful massacre of a party of Mexicans, who went to gather salt on the plains west of Fort Stanton. Thus you see the remainder of that tribe, still at large, are as hostile as ever. This will admonish you to be doubly on your guard against the clandestine departure of any of those now at the Bosque Redondo. Should any of the men of those Mescaleros now at Bosque Redondo attempt to escape, after their promises to me to remain quietly there, you will be sure to cause them to be shot. If they give you much trouble in this respect, seize every animal they have and have all of them sent to Fort Union, and disarm all the men, even of their bows and arrows. Colonel Collins sends down another plough.

I have ordered the part of my escort which belonged to Captain Cremony's company to Fort Sumner, to strengthen the cavalry portion of your command. Lieutenant Muller is to return to Santa Fé

It is possible that Mr. Labadie, the Indian agent, will wish to be absent from his duties a good deal, to the great detriment of the public service. In this event you will report the fact to these headquarters. He is a good agent if he attends to his business; if he does not stay at his post I shall ask for his removal. You had better let him know it.

Large quantities of melons and pumpkins should be planted. The pumpkins dried are not only a fine article of diet, but are anti-scorbutic to a great degree.

The prospects in the east seem to be brightening. I shall be down in June.

Very respectfully, your obedient servant,

JAMES H. CARLETON,
Brigadier General, Commanding.

Captain JOSEPH UPDEGRAFF, U. S. A.,
Fort Sumner, New Mexico.

Official:

ERASTUS W. WOOD,
Captain 1st Vet. Inf. C. V., A. A. A. General.

HEADQUARTERS DEPARTMENT OF NEW MEXICO,
Santa Fé, N. M., April 10, 1863.

SIR: I have the honor to enclose herewith the copy of a report made by Major Arthur Morrison of some dreadful murders by Mescalero Indians on the plains west of the Sierra Blanca, near Fort Stanton.

You will be sure to have slain every Mescalero Indian who may be met with at large in the vicinity of your post. No woman or child of the tribe will be injured, but such will be sent as prisoners to Fort Sumner. I have had a talk with the Indians of this tribe now at Fort Sumner, and told them that if they left that point to return to Fort Stanton or its vicinity without written permission from the commander at Fort Sumner, they would be shot; that you would have orders to that effect. These are the orders; be sure they are rigidly executed.

Send Captain Abreü's company out, or as much of it as can be spared, and endeavor to recover the stock of Mr. Lugan, of Socorro, Texas, a very worthy man. He seemed to have owned the "outfit" of the party sent for the salt.

Detachments must be kept scouting about the Sacramento and Blanca mountains all the time, in search of Indians. As soon as more troops arrive, now *en route* from California, the strength of your garrison will be increased. Great care should be bestowed on the gardens for your post. It would be well to put in a good crop of corn at what is known as the Beach farm, watered by a spring, some ten or fifteen miles below Fort Stanton. This could be planted by the companies at odd times, and sold for the benefit of the company fund.

Respectfully, &c.,

JAMES H. CARLETON,
Brigadier General, Commanding.

COMMANDING OFFICER, *Fort Stanton.*

Official:

ERASTUS W. WOOD,
Captain 1st Vet. Inf. C. V., A. A. A. General.

HEADQUARTERS DEPARTMENT OF NEW MEXICO,
Santa Fé, N. M., April 11, 1863.

COLONEL: There is said to be a man in Taos, or near there, who was for a great many years a captain with the Navajo Indians, against whom you are about to take the field. Mr. Manzaneres, of Abiquiu, says he knows their country thoroughly; it will be well for you to secure his services as a guide. Some of the Ute Indians from the neighborhood of Abiquiu would like to be employed as trailers, &c. You have my authority to secure the services of, say, ten of the *best* Ute warriors, and say four of the *best* Mexican guides, as spies and guides for the contemplated campaign against the Navajoes, their services to commence when the campaign commences; a reasonable compensation will be allowed them. It is said several fine guides live near Abiquiu; we will have none but the best; our work is to be thorough, and we must have *men* to do it.

I shall leave for Fort Wingate on the 13th instant, and shall be gone some twelve days. When I return you will doubtless be in Santa Fé.

I am, colonel, very respectfully, your obedient servant,

JAMES H. CARLETON,
Brigadier General, Commanding.

Colonel CHRISTOPHER CARSON,
1st New Mexico Volunteers, Taos, N. M.

Official:

ERASTUS W. WOOD,
Captain 1st Vet. Inf. C. V., A. A. A. General.

HEADQUARTERS DEPARTMENT OF NEW MEXICO,
Santa Fé, N. M., April 12, 1863.

GENERAL: I have the honor to report that I returned from Fort Sumner, at the Bosque Redondo, on the Pecos river, on the 5th instant. I found, gathered in at that point, four hundred and fifteen men, women, and children of the Mescalero Apaches, of whom I have heretofore written to you. The rest of the tribe is still hostile. Those at the Bosque Redondo have been told that if they behave themselves, and remain quietly at that point, they will be well cared for and fed until they can raise food for themselves. This they have promised to do. They have also been told that if they attempt to leave they will be shot.

It is very important that Fort Sumner be named as a chaplain post. If this is done, the bishop will send a minister to that point who will teach the Indian children Christianity, and to read and write. I earnestly beg that the Secretary will attend to this request at once, as great good will doubtless result from it.

To-morrow I proceed to Fort Wingate, in the Navajo country, to take preliminary measures, and gather information for a campaign against the Navajoes as soon as the grass starts sufficiently to support stock.

I am, general, very respectfully, your obedient servant,

JAMES H. CARLETON,
Brigadier General, Commanding.

Brigadier General LORENZO THOMAS,
Adjutant General U. S. A., Washington, D. C.

Official:

ERASTUS W. WOOD,
Captain 1st Vet. Inf. C. V., A. A. A. General.

HEADQUARTERS DEPARTMENT OF NEW MEXICO,
Santa Fé, N. M., April 27, 1863.

CAPTAIN: I authorized the quartermaster at Fort Sumner to let the superintendent of Indian affairs have some beef cattle belonging to the quartermaster's department, with which to feed Apache Indians, now held near Fort Sumner, New Mexico. The superintendent was to pay whatever price these cattle should prove to be worth, the price to be determined by yourself. Please have this matter adjusted, and the funds received from the sale incorporated with the funds pertaining to your department.

I am, captain, respectfully, your obedient servant,

JAMES H. CARLETON,
Brigadier General, Commanding.

Captain JOHN C. MCFERRAN,
Chief Quartermaster Department of New Mexico, Santa Fé, N. M.

Official:

ERASTUS W. WOOD,
Captain 1st Vet. Inf. C. V., A. A. A. General.

HEADQUARTERS DEPARTMENT OF NEW MEXICO,
Santa Fé, N. M., April 27, 1863.

SIR : Your letter of March 18, 1863, in relation to gentlemen who have made inquiries of you whether *Fort West* is to be permanently garrisoned, as in this event those gentlemen are desirous of investing in and working the mines of precious metals near the head of the Gila, I have had the honor to receive ; and I beg to reply that unless I am compelled by confederate forces to abandon the rich country about Pinos Altos and on the Rio Prieta, it will be held permanently. Our troops have already killed Mangus Colorado, his son, his brother, and some sixty of his braves, and I am still prosecuting hostilities against the Gila Apaches, and propose to continue doing so until people can live in that country, and explore and work the veins of precious metals which we know abound there, with safety.

The country along the Rio Prieta, and further down the Gila, gives promise of wonderful richness in gold and silver. I have two companies out now surveying a road from Fort Craig to Fort West.

I am, sir, very respectfully, your obedient servant,

JAMES H. CARLETON,
Brigadier General, Commanding.

SAMUEL J. JONES, Esq., *Kansas City, Missouri.*

Official :

ERASTUS W. WOOD,
Captain 1st *Vet. Inf. C. V., A. A. A. General.*

[Extract]

HEADQUARTERS DEPARTMENT OF NEW MEXICO,
Santa Fé, N. M, *May* 1, 1863.

MAJOR : No Mescaleros will have a right, even with a pass, to come back from Fort Sumner into their country to make *mescal.* I wish you would write this to Captain Updegraff. Nor will any woman or child return from Fort Sumner. One or two were to be permitted to come to tell the rest of the tribe to come in.

* * * * * * * * * * *

You will kill every Mescalero *man* that can be found without a passport.

I am, major, very respectfully,

JAMES H. CARLETON,
Brigadier General, Commanding.

Major JOSEPH SMITH,
5th Inf. Cal. Vols., Commanding Fort Stanton, N. M.

Official :

ERASTUS W. WOOD,
Captain 1st *Vet. Inf. C. V., A. A. A. General.*

HEADQUARTERS DEPARTMENT OF NEW MEXICO,
Santa Fé, N. M., May 10, 1863.

GENERAL : I am officially informed by the superintendent of Indian affairs for New Mexico, under date of the 9th instant, that persons who have just crossed the plains to this Territory from Missouri state that there is evidence of hostile intentions towards the whites among the Indians of the great prairies lying between New Mexico and the frontier of Kansas, Missouri, &c. This feeling, it seems, has manifested itself so far that the agent in charge of some of these Indians has written to traders and expressed the belief that there would be a general uprising among those tribes unless steps are taken to prevent it. If the War Department will station one *good* regiment of cavalry at old Fort Atkinson, below the lower crossing of the Arkansas, at the lower Cimarron Springs, and on the headwaters of the Cimarron, near Cold Spring, on the old Cimarron route, say four companies at each point, it would be a timely precaution so far as these Indians are concerned.

This year the merchants of New Mexico have sent larger and more trains to the States for goods than ever before. Indeed, nearly all of the available capital in this country invested in means of transportation and goods will, in six weeks, be afloat, as it were, on the great plains. Besides, all of the army supplies for the troops in this Territory will shortly be on the way out. The danger from attacks by Indians is not the least danger to provide against. The rebels in Arkansas under Price, and the rebels in Texas, know as well as we do just what will be upon the road; just how vital all those supplies are to us; just how poorly they may be guarded; and, if they have the enterprise which I believe they have, they will give us a good deal of trouble by cavalry raids after the grass has grown; therefore I beg the department to send the force indicated, and keep the garrisons at Fort Larned and Fort Wise in good strength in the number and *quality* of the troops. This should, in my opinion, be done without delay.

I am, general, very respectfully, your obedient servant,

JAMES H. CARLETON,
Brigadier General, Commanding.

Brigadier General LORENZO THOMAS,
Adjutant General U. S. A., Washington, D. C.

Official:

ERASTUS W. WOOD,
Captain 1st Vet. Inf. C. V., A. A. A. General.

Private.]

HEADQUARTERS DEPARTMENT OF NEW MEXICO,
Santa Fé, N. M., May 10, 1863.

MY DEAR GENERAL: I am aware that every moment of your time is of value to the country, and I would not presume to ask you even to read this note did I not believe that what is herewith enclosed would be of interest to you as a general, and, therefore, as a statesman. Among all my endeavors since my arrival here, there has been an effort to brush back the Indians, as you have seen from official correspondence, so that the people could get out of the valley of the Rio Grande, and not only possess themselves of the arable lands in other parts of the Territory, but, if the country contained veins and deposits of the precious metals, that they might be found. So I re-established Fort Stanton, and at least a hundred families have gone to that vicinity to open farms, and they are commencing to find gold there.

I established Fort West, and have driven the Indians away from the head of the Gila, and they are finding gold and silver and cinnabar there. There is no doubt in my mind that one of the richest gold countries in the world is along the affluents to the Gila, which enter it from the north along its whole course. Thus you can see one reason why the rebels want, and why we may not permit them ever to have, a country evidently teeming with millions on millions of wealth.

Last winter I asked for one hundred thousand dollars to make a wagon road from near Fort Craig to the Gila. My request was not listened to, and I endeavored to open the road without help. Strategically, you will see its value. Intrinsically, as I then anticipated, it would be beyond price. My preliminary survey has been unsuccessful, as you observe by Captain Anderson's letter, herewith enclosed. But I do not despair of success. You will also see by the enclosed notes what signs of mineral wealth are already discovered. If I only had one more good regiment of California infantry, composed, as that infantry is, of practical miners, I would place it in the Gila country. While it would exterminate the Indians, who are a scourge to New Mexico, it would protect people who might wish to go there to open up the country, and would virtually be a military colony when the war ended, whose interests would lead the officers and soldiers to remain in the new El Dorado. Pray give all this a thought. It is not a chimera, but a subject that is worthy of the attention of the government *now*. California, you remember, was not considered as valuable an acquisition until its gold startled the whole world. Do not despise New Mexico, as a drain upon the general government. The money will all come back again.

The report of Captain McCleave I allowed to be printed to make others emulous of the self-denial, fixedness of purpose, and hard work of these Californians. This McCleave is the officer I wrote to you about as one who would not draw his pay while he was a prisoner with the rebels. As a *soldier* you will see he has tolerably fair qualities.

I am, general, very sincerely yours,

JAMES H. CARLETON, *Brigadier General.*

Major General HENRY W. HALLECK,
General-in-Chief, &c., Washington, D. C.

Official:

ERASTUS W. WOOD,
Captain 1st Vet. Inf. C. V., A. A. A. General.

HEADQUARTERS DEPARTMENT OF NEW MEXICO,
Santa Fé, N. M., May 11, 1863.

CAPTAIN: Lieutenant Mills will be retained on duty at Fort Sumner until further orders. Call in Lieutenant Bennet and his picket-guard. Let your interpreter and guide take turns in watching on the routes from Texas. If the Indians give you any trouble, take and burn all their bows and arrows; take and send to Fort Union all their rifles and horses. I cannot, for a short time, send you any more men. So you must work the harder and watch the closer with what you have got.

I am, captain, respectfully,

JAMES H. CARLETON,
Brigadier General, Commanding.

Captain JOSEPH UPDEGRAFF,
Commanding Fort Sumner, N. M.

Official:

ERASTUS W. WOOD,
Captain 1st Vet. Inf. C. V., A. A. A. General.

HEADQUARTERS DEPARTMENT OF NEW MEXICO,
Santa Fé, N. M., May 29, 1863.

CAPTAIN: Enclosed herewith you will find a copy of a letter from these headquarters, dated the 24th instant, to Colonel Collins, superintendent of Indian affairs, informing him of the inability of the military department to furnish subsistence stores to the Apache Indians at Bosque Redondo after the 31st instant.

The general commanding directs that you be governed accordingly. Colonel Collins reports that Mr. Labadie has been instructed to purchase some sheep, which are said to be in the neighborhood, for these Apache Indians. If Mr. Labadie fails to supply these Indians you will report the fact to Colonel Collins.

I have the honor to be, captain, very respectfully, your obedient servant,

CYRUS H. DE FORREST, *Aide-de-Camp.*

Captain JOSEPH UPDEGRAFF, U. S. A.,
Commanding Fort Sumner, N. M.

Official:

ERASTUS W. WOOD,
Captain 1st Vet. Inf. C. V., A. A. A. General.

[Extract.]

HEADQUARTERS DEPARTMENT OF NEW MEXICO,
Santa Fé, N. M., May 30, 1863.

GENERAL: * * * * * * * * * *
Please publish an order complimenting the command of Captain Tidball, including Doctor Cox, 5th infantry California volunteers, and the citizens who accompanied Captain Tidball, for their zeal, energy, and gallantry in their attack upon the band of Apaches in the Aravayha cañon in Arizona. (Give the exact date of the battle.) Mr. C. Trumbull Hayden seems to have done well in helping punish these savages who delight in roasting their victims. I remember seeing and burying the bones and ashes of one of the victims they had tortured by fire, and of burying the bodies of six more, near Apache cañon, on the 31st of July, 1862. Poor Sergeant Wheeling and the guide Chaves, whom we lost, have begun to be avenged.

* * * * * * * * * *

I am, general, very respectfully, your obedient servant,

JAMES H. CARLETON,
Brigadier General, Commanding.

Brigadier General JOSEPH R. WEST,
U. S. Vols., Commanding District of Arizona, Hart's Mills, Texas.

Official:

ERASTUS W. WOOD,
Captain 1st Vet. Inf. C. V., A. A. A. General.

HEADQUARTERS DEPARTMENT OF NEW MEXICO,
Santa Fé, N. M., June 11, 1863.

CAPTAIN: In reply to your communication of May 29, I am directed by the department commander to say to you that he wishes you to have the Indians at the Bosque Redondo continue to plant corn until the 4th day of July. So much of the corn as does not fully ripen will be purchased by the government for fodder.

The general desires also to know how many acres the Indians have already planted, and how much ground is under cultivation for the use of the command at your post. In such a climate crops planted very late in the season come to maturity with great rapidity.

I am, captain, very respectfully, your obedient servant,

BEN. C. CUTLER, *A. A. General.*

Captain JOSEPH UPDEGRAFF,
U. S. 5th Infantry, Commanding Fort Sumner, N. M.

Official: ERASTUS W. WOOD,
Captain 1st Vet. Inf. C. V., A. A. A. General.

HEADQUARTERS DEPARTMENT OF NEW MEXICO,
Santa Fé, N. M., June 12, 1863.

MOST REVEREND SIR: Enclosed herewith please find an order from the Secretary of War, creating Fort Sumner a chaplain post. I beg respectfully that you will name some clergyman of energy, and of all those qualities of patience, good temper, assiduity and interest in the subject so necessary in one who is wanted to teach the Indian children now at Fort Sumner, not only the rudiments of an education, but the principles and truths of Christianity.

The person whom you might select for so important and interesting a trust will doubtless be selected by the council.

Respectfully, your obedient servant,

JAMES H. CARLETON,
Brigadier General, Commanding.

Right Reverend Bishop LAMEZ, *Santa Fé, N. M.*

Official: ERASTUS W. WOOD,
Captain 1st Vet. Inf. C. V., A. A. A. General.

HEADQUARTERS DEPARTMENT OF NEW MEXICO,
Santa Fé, N. M., June 12, 1863.

GENERAL: I beg that you will leave no stone unturned to get the troops which are ordered up the country from your district on the march to their several destinations at once. I have written to Colonel Rigg to send Hind's company to Franklin with all practicable despatch. The organization of the expedition against the Navajoes has been approved by the War Department, and it is desirable to have the troops in the field before the grain is gathered. So I count on celerity of movement from below.

I am, general, respectfully,

JAMES H. CARLETON,
Brigadier General, Commanding.

Brigadier General JOSEPH R. WEST,
U. S. Vols., Commanding District of Arizona, Hart's Mills, Texas.

Official: ERASTUS W. WOOD,
Captain 1st Vet. Inf. C. V., A. A. A. General.

HEADQUARTERS DEPARTMENT OF NEW MEXICO,
Santa Fé, N. M., June 13, 1863.

CAPTAIN: Enclosed herewith please find the copy of a letter to the chief commissary to send to the *Pueblo Colorado*, Navajo country, a certain amount of subsistence stores which will weigh, in gross weight, 236,813 pounds. For these stores transportation will be required. The stores should be at Los Pinos so as to move thence under the escort of troops on the 1st proximo.

I am, captain, very respectfully, your obedient servant,

JAMES H. CARLETON,
Brigadier General, Commanding.

Captain JOHN C. MCFERRAN,
Chief Quartermaster, Santa Fé, N. M.

Official:

ERASTUS W. WOOD,
Captain 1st Vet. Inf. C. V., A. A. A. General.

[Extract.]

HEADQUARTERS DEPARTMENT OF NEW MEXICO,
Santa Fé, N. M., June 14, 1863.

GENERAL: * * * * * * * * * *

There are rumors, coming through the Comanches, that a force of Texans will attack the trains en route to New Mexico from the western frontiers. It would be a wise precaution, in my opinion, to station a regiment of cavalry as indicated in my letter to yourself, dated May 17, 1863.

The troops destined to operate against the Navajoes, will take the field on the 1st proximo.

I am, general, very respectfully, your obedient servant,

JAMES H. CARLETON,
Brigadier General, Commanding.

Brigadier General LORENZO THOMAS,
Adjutant General U. S. A., Washington, D. C.

Official:

ERASTUS W. WOOD,
Captain 1st Vet. Inf. C. V., A. A. A. General.

Private.]

HEADQUARTERS DEPARTMENT OF NEW MEXICO,
Santa Fé, N. M., June 14, 1863.

MY DEAR GENERAL: I enclose herewith for your perusal copies of two letters just received by Chief Justice Benedict from a kinsman who is a member of a prospecting party which left the Rio Grande, under the leadership of old Captain Walker of Rocky mountain and California celebrity.

There is no doubt, from Benedict's character, that all he says of the mineral wealth of the region southwest of the San Francisco mountains is under rather than over the mark.

I have seen the gold he sent to Judge Benedict; it is coarse and seems to be of the first quality. By taking Whipple's wagon-road *via* Zuñi, the Cosnino caves, and thence across the headwaters of the Rio Verde to a stream marked on the map of New Mexico, published by the War Department in 1859, *Val de Chino*, I believe this gold region would be reached by a fine practicable wagon-road within three hundred and fifty miles from Albuquerque.

I will send word to this Mr. Benedict that if he and Walker will come through from these gold fields to Albuquerque, I will employ Walker as guide, and send a military force of, say, two companies of California volunteers through to that point, and there establish a military post for the protection of miners until they become strong enough to protect themselves. In this case it would be well to have a first-rate topographical engineer to make an authentic map of this *terra incognita*, and fix its principal geographical features instrumentally. This, general, is a matter that, in all laudable ways, should have the immediate help and fostering care of the government. I trust, amid all your cares and anxieties, you will have time to give this subject a thought. There is every evidence that a country as rich if not richer in mineral wealth than California, extends from the Rio Grande, northwestwardly, all the way across to Washoe. If I could have but one first-rate regiment more of infantry I could brush the Indians away from all that part of it east of the Colorado river.

The troops for the campaign against the Navajoes take the field on the 1st proximo.

I am, general, very truly, yours,

JAMES H. CARLETON,
Brigadier General, Commanding.

Major General HENRY W. HALLECK,
General-in-Chief U. S. A., Washington, D. C.

Official:

ERASTUS W. WOOD,
Captain 1st Vet. Inf. C. V., A. A. A. General.

HEADQUARTERS DEPARTMENT OF NEW MEXICO,
Santa Fé, N. M., June 14, 1863.

GENERAL: I beg respectfully that you will order Major Mayer, 1st New Mexico volunteers, (who went east without proper authority, and who was afterwards on sick leave in New York, and who now figures somewhere as an assistant provost marshal, as I learn,) to join his regiment without delay. The regiment, Colonel Carson's, is ordered to take the field against the Navajoes, and Major Mayer's services are greatly needed. If he cannot join, (it is understood that he will resign rather than return to this country,) some other major should be appointed to fill his place.

I am, general, respectfully, &c.,

JAMES H. CARLETON,
Brigadier General, Commanding.

Brigadier General LORENZO THOMAS,
Adjutant General U. S. A , Washington, D. C.

Official:

ERASTUS W. WOOD,
Captain 1st Vet. Inf. C. V., A. A. A. General.

HEADQUARTERS DEPARTMENT OF NEW MEXICO,
Santa Fé, N. M., June 17, 1863.

GENERAL: Enclosed herewith please find an order organizing an expedition against the Navajoes, and likewise a request from Colonel Carson, the distinguished commander of the expedition, asking authority to employ one hundred Ute Indians to act as auxiliaries to his force. I beg respectfully to submit, with my approval, this request to the Adjutant General, for the consideration of the War Department, believing the money expended in the employment of these Indians for the purpose indicated will be profitably laid out. The Utes are very brave, and fine shots, fine trailers, and uncommonly energetic in the field. The Navajoes have entertained a very great dread of them for many years. I believe one hundred Ute Indians would render more service in this war than more than double their number of troops. They could be mustered as a company, or, preferably, could be employed as spies and guides.

It is important, if the employment of these Indians be authorized, that I be so informed at the earliest practicable date.

I have the honor to be, general, very respectfully, your obedient servant,

JAMES H. CARLETON,
Brigadier General, Commanding.

Brigadier General LORENZO THOMAS,
Adjutant General U. S. A., Washington, D. C.

Official:

ERASTUS W. WOOD,
Captain 1st Vet. Inf. C. V., A. A. A. General.

HEADQUARTERS DEPARTMENT OF NEW MEXICO,
Santa Fé, N. M., June 22, 1863.

MY DEAR CAPTAIN: I have seen two letters written by Mr. Benedict to Judge Benedict, setting forth the wonderful discoveries which yourself and party have made. I have written to the War Department and to General Halleck on the subject. The surveyor general of New Mexico proceeds to visit your new gold regions, and when he returns will make an official report on their probable extent and value, so that the government can be well informed on the subject. If you can do so, when General Clark has completed his observations, I desire that you will come by Whipple's route, by Zuñi to Albuquerque, with General Clark and escort, so that I may employ you as a guide for a couple of companies of troops which I will send to establish a military post in the very heart of the gold country. These companies you can guide back by the best practicable route for wagons. I am satisfied that Albuquerque will be the point from which you will draw your supplies. The people who will flock into the country, around the San Francisco mountains, will soon open farms and have stock enough for the mines. All they want is military protection on the road and in that country until they have got a good foothold, then they will take care of themselves.

I am just commencing active operations against the Navajoes. I enclose an order which organizes the expedition. You see the new fort will be at Pueblo, Colorado, about twenty-eight miles southwest of old Fort Defiance, and this will be the nearest point for your people to get supplies in case of accident. The sutler there will doubtless have a large stock of goods, and I will tell him about keeping on hand such articles of prime necessity as you all might require. I send you a map of the country, so that you may know about where Fort Canby will be situated. I send you another similar map, on which you can trace your new gold fields.

If I can be of any service to yourself or party, it will afford me pleasure to help you. If I can help others to a fortune, it will afford me not quite as much happiness as finding one myself, it is true—but nearly as much. My luck has always been not to be at the right place at the right time for fortunes. I have been a little too far ahead, or else a little too much behind, for that. Yourself and your party deserve success for your industry and perseverance. Hoping that each of you will receive abundant reward for your past toil and hardships and danger,

I am, captain, very respectfully, your obedient servant,

JAMES H. CARLETON,
Brigadier General, Commanding.

Captain JOSEPH WALKER,
At the Walker mines, Arizona.

Official:

ERASTUS W. WOOD,
Captain 1st Vet. Inf. C. V., A. A. A. General.

HEADQUARTERS DEPARTMENT OF NEW MEXICO,
Santa Fé, N. M., June 22, 1863.

CAPTAIN: I send you a map of New Mexico, on which I desire that you will trace your route to and from the new gold fields, in obedience to orders to go as an escort to Surveyor General Clark.

Have great care taken of your animals. When you arrive at the new diggings, I want each of your men to prospect and wash, and I want you to report the exact time they severally work and the amount of gold each one obtains in return for his labor during that time. Much reliance will be placed upon these statistics. The people must not be deceived, nor be inveigled into that distant desert country without knowing well what they may expect to find. If the country is as rich as represented—and of this I have no doubt—there will, on your return, be a revolution in matters here which no man now can even dream of. I have written to the authorities at Washington, that if the country is rich as reported, on your return I shall send two companies of California troops to establish a post right in the heart of the gold region. Your company may perhaps be one of them. So you will have an eye to the best location for a post of one company of infantry and one of cavalry. In returning by the Whipple route to Albuquerque, mark the country well for the whole way from the gold region. Take your best men with you, and things to wash with. Send me a few specimens for the War Department on your return. Wishing you good fortune,

I am, captain, very respectfully, your obedient servant,

JAMES H. CARLETON,
Brigadier General, Commanding.

Captain NATHANIEL J. PISHON,
First Cavalry California Volunteers, Fort Craig, N. M.

Official:

ERASTUS W. WOOD,
Captain 1st Vet. Inf. C. V., A. A. A. General.

HEADQUARTERS DEPARTMENT OF NEW MEXICO,
Santa Fé, N. M, *June* 23, 1863.

COLONEL: I enclose herewith General Orders No. 15, current series from these headquarters, which organizes the expedition against the Navajo Indians. It is hoped now that the people of New Mexico will become more secure in their persons and property. As soon as the troops take the field, the small bands of Navajo robbers now infesting the settlements will doubtless return to their country to look after the safety of their women and children, and as long as the troops are engaged in active operations against their tribe they will not have a disposition to come in on the river.

You remember what I told Barboncito and Delgadito about what would be required of all Navajoes who did not want to engage in the war, or be sufferers from it: that while hostilities were progressing against their tribe no peace party of Navajoes could remain in the country; that all those Navajoes who claimed not to have murdered and robbed the inhabitants must come in and go to the Bosque Redondo, where they would be fed and protected until the war was over; that unless they were willing to do this, they would be considered hostile and would be proceeded against accordingly; that in this event, if they or their families suffered, these consequences would be the result of their refusing to accede to such a reasonable demand, and the responsibility would rest upon them, not upon me; that a time would be set for all those who desired to avail themselves of the offer to come in with their families to Fort Wingate; that they should be transported to Bosque Redondo in our trains, &c.

Send for Delgadito and Barboncito again and repeat what I before told them, and tell them that I shall feel very sorry if they refuse to come in; that we have no desire to make war upon them and other good Navajoes; but the troops cannot tell the good from the bad, and we neither can nor will tolerate their staying as a peace party among those against whom we intend to make war. Tell them they can have until the twentieth day of July of this year to come in—they and all those who belong to what they call the peace party; *that after that day every Navajo that is seen will be considered as hostile and treated accordingly*; that after that day the door now open will be closed. Tell them to say all this to their people, and that as sure as that the sun shines all this will come true.

I am, colonel, respectfully, your obedient servant,

JAMES H. CARLETON,
Brigadier General, Commanding.

Lieutenant Colonel J. FRANCISCO CHAVEZ,
First New Mexico Volunteers, commanding at Fort Wingate, N. M.

[Copy of this letter furnished Colonel Carson, June 23, 1863.]

Official:

ERASTUS W. WOOD,
Captain 1st Vet. Inf. C. V., A. A. A. General.

HEADQUARTERS DEPARTMENT OF NEW MEXICO,
Santa Fé, N. M., *June* 23, 1863.

SIR: Enclosed herewith please find an order from the War Department making Fort Sumner a chaplain post. As soon as I received this order, I addressed a letter to the Right Reverend Bishop Lamez, and requested that he would recommend some minister for this important position—it being the purpose in having a chaplain at Fort Sumner, for such chaplain, in addition to his other and regular duties, to instruct the Apache Indians in the truths and principles of the Christian religion, and to teach their children to read and write. Enclosed herewith I have the honor to send you a letter from the bishop recommending the Reverend Joseph Fialon to be appointed chaplain of your post. Mr. Fialon is now in France, but will be back in August. See for your guidance pages 209 and 210 of the revised regulations. As the duties will be very heavy, I trust the council will be considerate in the rate of pay recommended.

I am, sir, very respectfully, your obedient servant,

JAMES H. CARLETON,
Brigadier General, Commanding.

COMMANDING OFFICER, *Fort Sumner, N. M.*

Official:

ERASTUS W. WOOD,
Captain 1st Vet. Inf. C. V, A. A. A. General.

HEADQUARTERS DEPARTMENT OF NEW MEXICO,
Santa Fé, N. M., June 26, 1863.

GENERAL: I have written a letter to Captain Walker, which goes down to Fort Craig to your care. It is hoped and expected that he will come with you as guide on Whipple's route *via* Zuñi.

Since you left, I have seen a gentleman named Groom, who last fall came from the new gold diggings on the Colorado river, ascending Williams's fork to the San Francisco mountains, and thence in by Zuñi to Fort Wingate and Albuquerque. He is very anxious to return to the new gold fields, having always entertained the purpose of doing so as soon as he was able. I have told him to go to Fort Craig and consult with yourself, Colonel Rigg, and Captain Pishon on the subject of your journey. He is firmly of the opinion that he can guide the party to the point indicated in Mr. Benedict's letter as the one where most gold was found—by the route from Zuñi. *If this can be done*, a great distance will be saved, much very hot weather upon the desert avoided, and, better than all, much time gained. The subject is left wholly to your decision. In case you determine to go from Fort Craig *via* Zuñi, and so on on *Whipple's* route, Captain McFerran and myself have come to the conclusion that with three good wagons and teams you can take flour, bacon, sugar, coffee, salt, &c., enough for the party for seventy-odd days, and travel light. You should take some pack-saddles *complete*, with ropes, wanties, &c., perfect, that when near the San Francisco mountains, if it become necessary or advisable to leave a camp or leave your wagons, you can proceed on to the gold fields without embarrassment. Great care and forecast must be exercised to have everything which will be *indispensably* necessary, and not an ounce more. In case you conclude to go by the Zuñi route, then Mr. Groom can be employed by Colonel Rigg as a guide. From Fort Craig to Zuñi there is a wagon-road over which troops have travelled, and Captain McFerran says there are men living at Socorro, and in the neighborhood of Fort Craig, who know this route. One of them Colonel Rigg can employ to pilot you out on to the Whipple route wherever it may be necessary to strike it, whether at or this side of Zuñi. This guide can go through with you. Once on the Whipple route, then Mr. Groom's knowledge will be available. In case no such guide can be found for the country between Fort Craig and the Whipple route, your party can come up the river to Las Lunas and go out on the road *via* Fort Wingate. *In this event*, you need take from Fort Craig only rations enough to last to Wingate, and there lay in the supply for the remainder of the journey. This will save your stock for the rest of the work.

All these remarks have been made having in view the decision to go *via* Zuñi. In case you go by the Fort West route, as originally suggested, Mr. Groom, being an old and experienced packer, can be employed in that capacity. You will find him a very gentlemanly and intelligent man. He has had misfortunes and is entirely destitute, but from what I have seen of him, and what I have heard of him, he seems to be worthy of consideration, kindness, confidence, and help. He is known to Colonel Rigg.

Great care and vigilance must be exercised with regard to Indians. *Never* be off your guard; *never* become careless; be sure when your stock is grazing to have men *with arms in their hands* always with them, and *always* on the alert and *awake*. I cannot impress this matter too strongly upon your mind. In my experience I have found that to travel mornings and evenings, and to lie by in the heat of the day, keeps the stock in better order than to make the whole march without turning out to graze. I wish you luck.

I am, general, very respectfully, your obedient servant,

JAMES H. CARLETON,
Brigadier General, Commanding.

General JOHN A. CLARK,
Surveyor General of New Mexico, Fort Craig, N. M.

Official:

ERASTUS W. WOOD,
Captain 1st Vet. Inf. C. V., A. A. A. General.

HEADQUARTERS DEPARTMENT OF NEW MEXICO,
Santa Fé, N. M., June 26, 1863.

COLONEL: I send you this note by Mr. Groom, whom you know. I have written to General Clark that if, upon consultation with yourself and Captain Pishon and Mr. Groom, it shall seem expedient to go to the new gold fields *via* Zuñi, you are authorized to employ Mr. Groom as a guide, at a reasonable compensation. In the event of a decision among you to go that way, starting across the country *directly* from Fort Craig to the Whipple route, you are authorized to employ some good person as guide until that road is struck. This latter person's services will be continued throughout the journey to and from the gold fields. After the Whipple road is struck, he can act as a spy and herder, &c. In case it is concluded to go *via* Fort West and Tucson and the Pimo villages, you are authorized to employ Mr. Groom as a packer, at a reasonable compensation.

Great care should be taken to fit out this party down to the minutest detail. Some medicines should be taken along, some lint, bandages, a field tourniquet, &c., &c. The wagons should be *minutely* inspected, the boxes looked at, and extra linchpins, hame-strings, buckskins for mending harness, rope for packing, two lanterns made secure from breakage, (in case a man is wounded by night,) axle-grease, and auger, saw, some wrought nails, &c., &c.

I am, colonel, very respectfully, your obedient servant,

JAMES H. CARLETON,
Brigadier General, Commanding.

Colonel EDWIN A. RIGG,
Commanding at Fort Craig, N. M.

NOTE.—In case the party goes by Fort Wingate, provisions for the trip can be got there.
J. H. C.

Official:
ERASTUS W. WOOD,
Captain 1st Vet. Inf. C. V., A. A. A. General.

HEADQUARTERS DEPARTMENT OF NEW MEXICO,
Santa Fé, N. M., June 27, 1863.

MAJOR: I enclose herewith for your information a copy of a letter received from commanding officer at Fort McRae, New Mexico, giving an account of an attack made upon Captain Pfieffer, first New Mexico volunteers, by a party of Mescalero Apaches. The general commanding directs me to say to you that he considers it unnecessary to point out the course you should pursue in case any of these Indians should be found lurking around Fort Stanton. No measure, except one of great severity, should be resorted to with Indians such as those referred to in the enclosed communication.

I am, major, very respectfully, your obedient servant,

BEN. C. CUTLER,
Assistant Adjutant General.

Major JOSEPH SMITH,
Fifth Inf. C. V., Commanding Fort Stanton, N. M.

Official:
ERASTUS W. WOOD,
Captain 1st Vet. Inf. C. V., A. A. A. General.

HEADQUARTERS DEPARTMENT OF NEW MEXICO,
Santa Fé, N. M., June 28, 1863.

CAPTAIN: By reference to a letter to myself from the War Department, dated May 20, 1863, a copy of which was forwarded to you on the 12th instant, it is evidently contemplated that *all* subsistence stores intended for Indians, which are furnished by the military, should be furnished by the Subsistence department solely. Therefore, in order that these matters may not be complicated even indirectly by a sale of cattle by the Quartermaster's department to the Indian department, as heretofore authorized, the cattle which have been transferred to the Indian department by Lieutenant Barr, as acting assistant quartermaster at Fort Sumner, as well as all *quartermaster* cattle which had previously been slaughtered at that post for issue to Indians, will at once be paid for by the chief commissary. The chief commissary will then make the sale, and receive the money for all the cattle delivered to the Indian department on the hoof, as before mentioned, and will make the "abstracts of the issues" alluded to in the letter from the War Department of May 20, 1863, "to the Commissary General, in order that it may be submitted to the Secretary of the Interior for settlement."

I am, captain, very respectfully, your obedient servant,

JAMES H. CARLETON,
Brigadier General, Commanding.

Captain JOHN C. MCFERRAN, U. S. A.,
Chief Quartermaster Department of New Mexico, Santa Fé, N. M.

Official:

ERASTUS W. WOOD,
Captain 1st Vet. Inf. C. V., A. A. A. General.

[Extract.]

HEADQUARTERS DEPARTMENT OF NEW MEXICO,
Santa Fé, N. M., June 28, 1863.

GENERAL: Your letter of the 20th instant, announcing that Lieutenant Bargie, first New Mexico volunteers, had been killed by Miembres Indians, has just been received. The express for below waiting, I have but a moment in which to write. That you will take prompt and efficient measures to punish these Indians, and render the road more safe, I have no doubt. The presence of Fritz's company at Fort Stanton is greatly needed, as I have been obliged to call for Abreü's company for the Navajo campaign, which leaves Major Smith with but one company, and the Indians in that neighborhood are getting troublesome. I am expecting to hear of the arrival of Green's company at Fort McRae, and that companies C and H, first infantry, have arrived at or are near Los Pinos.

* * * * * * * * * * *

I am, general, very respectfully, your obedient servant,

JAMES H. CARLETON,
Brigadier General, Commanding.

Brigadier General JOSEPH R. WEST,
U. S. Vols., commanding District of Arizona, Hart's Mills, Texas.

Official:

ERASTUS W. WOOD,
Captain 1st Vet. Inf. C. V., A. A. A. General.

HEADQUARTERS DEPARTMENT OF NEW MEXICO,
Santa Fé, N. M., June 29, 1863.

GENERAL: Enclosed herewith please find the official copies of letters from the district of Arizona, giving an account of Indian murders on the Jornado del Muerto on the 16th and 20th instants.

Lieutenant L. A. Bargie, first New Mexico volunteers, who was murdered and mutilated, was from Washington city.

I am, general, very respectfully, your obedient servant,

JAMES H. CARLETON,
Brigadier General, Commanding.

Brigadier General LORENZO THOMAS,
Adjutant General of the Army, Washington, D. C.

Official:

ERASTUS W. WOOD,
Captain 1st Vet. Inf. C. V., A. A. A. General.

HEADQUARTERS DEPARTMENT OF NEW MEXICO,
Santa Fé, N. M., July 2, 1863.

MAJOR: When this reaches you, you will have heard of the murder by Indians of expressmen bringing mail from Fort Stanton to Santa Fé. Please to get all the particulars of these and other Indian atrocities recently committed in your vicinity, and report them officially and at length.

Captain Abreü's company must march at once to Los Pinos.

Report the amount of government stock lost by Indians near your post, and the exact amount remaining on hand. Have your command on the alert, and let us hear that any Indian men at large in your vicinity without a written pass have been destroyed. No mercy must be shown to them. We have suffered too much from them already. I understand they tortured by fire the expressmen.

Much reliance is placed upon your ability to rid your neighborhood of these murderers. When Captain Fritz comes you can use his company by detachments—*each one under an officer*—in scouring the country. Vigilance and energy and *continued* effort will sooner or later attain the desired end. The men, whether as scouts or herders, must *never* be off their guard.

I am, major, very respectfully, your obedient servant,

JAMES H. CARLETON,
Brigadier General, Commanding.

Major JOSEPH SMITH,
Fifth Inf. C. V., Commanding at Fort Stanton, N. M.

Official:

ERASTUS W. WOOD,
Captain 1st Vet. Inf. C. V., A. A. A. General.

HEADQUARTERS DEPARTMENT OF NEW MEXICO,
Santa Fé, N. M., July 29, 1863.

CAPTAIN: Colonel McMullen will relieve you in command of Fort Union on the fourth proximo. On the fifth proximo you will leave with your company for Camp Easton, and Captain Hollister will on that day leave Fort Union with company "C" United States 7th Infantry for Fort Stanton. This letter is written thus early, in advance of the receipt by you of the order, that you may have these two companies in readiness at all points to move promptly on the day specified. Each company will be provided with five thousand rounds of ammunition in boxes, besides twenty rounds of ammunition to be carried by each soldier in his cartridge-box. Great care must be taken, particularly with the company ordered to Fort Stanton, to have kegs or barrels sufficient to carry two gallons of water per man, as there are long distances on the Fort Stanton road where water is not to be found, unless we have a timely fall of rain.

The Indians are not only numerous but very hostile around Fort Stanton, and Major Smith, commanding at that post, asks for more troops successfully to pursue them, and at the same time garrison his post and guard his herd. The Indians are said to be bad on your route to Camp Easton. I mention this that you and Captain Hollister may be on your guard *all the time*, having reference to the safety of your animals by night and by day.

You will promptly attack and destroy any and all grown male Indians whom you may meet between Fort Union and Camp Easton. Women and children will not be harmed, but will be taken prisoners, and will be securely guarded until further orders.

A copy of this letter is herewith enclosed for Captain Hollister, who will be governed by the same rules with regard to any Indians he may meet between Fort Union and Fort Stanton.

Very respectfully, your obedient servant,

JAMES H. CARLETON,
Brigadier General, Commanding.

Captain PETER W. L. PLYMPTON, *U. S. A., Fort Union, N. M.*

Official:

ERASTUS W. WOOD,
Captain 1st Vet. Inf. C. V., A. A. A. General.

HEADQUARTERS DEPARTMENT OF NEW MEXICO,
Santa Fé, N M., July 29, 1863.

MAJOR: If Captain Abreü's company has not left Fort Stanton for the Navajo campaign when you receive this letter, detain it until further orders.

There is not, in my judgment, any necessity for a picket down the Pecos below your post, for the present. Your whole attention will be devoted to hunting and killing Indians, until none are to be found in your part of the Territory. Women and children are to be spared, to be sent to Fort Sumner as occasion may offer.

I send you company "C" United States 7th infantry. These officers and men have been a long time in garrison, and will not only hope to be kept in the field, *but will be kept in the field hunting and killing Indians until you are no more annoyed by the savages.* At that moment report the fact, as the company is greatly needed at another point.

This company and the California infantry company—seeing who can do the best—will have a generous emulation in scouring the Capitan, Blanco, and Sacramento mountains. The "California boys" must look out for their laurels.

I am, major, very respectfully, your obedient servant,

JAMES H. CARLETON,
Brigadier General, Commanding.

Major JOSEPH SMITH,
Commanding at Fort Stanton, N. M.

Official:

ERASTUS W. WOOD,
Captain 1st Vet. Inf. C. V., A. A. A. General.

HEADQUARTERS DEPARTMENT OF NEW MEXICO,
Santa Fé, N. M., July 30, 1863.

GENERAL: I have just received your letter of the 18th instant, giving an account of the capture by Indians of mules and wagons in Cook's cañon, and of the fine conduct of Sergeant Hoyt, of company "D" 1st infantry California volunteers. Please make a recommendation for Sergeant Hoyt's promotion in a letter having no reference to other matters. It will afford me great pleasure to aid in getting a commission for so gallant a soldier. Captain French's little fight was creditable; but *he* always does well.

Respectfully, &c.,

JAMES H. CARLETON,
Brigadier General, Commanding.

Brigadier General JOSEPH R. WEST,
U. S. Vols., Com. District of Arizona, Hart's Mills, Texas.

Official:

ERASTUS W. WOOD,
Captain 1st Vet. Inf. C. V., A. A. A. General.

HEADQUARTERS DEPARTMENT OF NEW MEXICO,
Santa Fé, N. M., July 31, 1863.

MAJOR: The general commanding directs me to say to you that, by the company which will leave Fort Union on the 5th of August next for your post, Captain McFerran will send twenty-five horses for Captain Fritz's company.

The general hopes to hear of your better success against the Indians in your vicinity, after the arrival of this re-enforcement of men and horses.

I am, major, very respectfully, your obedient servant,

CYRUS H. DE FORREST, *Aide-de-Camp.*

Major JOSEPH SMITH,
Commanding at Fort Stanton, N. M.

Official:

ERASTUS W. WOOD,
Captain 1st Vet. Inf. C. V., A. A. A. General.

HEADQUARTERS DEPARTMENT OF NEW MEXICO,
Santa Fé, N. M., August 1, 1863.

GENERAL: Enclosed herewith please find the last advices from Chihuahua, Mexico, received at these headquarters. Mr. Creel's letter, dated July 15, 1863, you will find to give the true feeling of the Mexican people in Chihuahua.

The extraordinary developments of gold and silver in Arizona, which I write to you about in another letter by this mail, are but one example of the gold and silver in Chihuahua, Sonora, and Sinaloa, which states the French want, and which *we* should never permit them to have.

Respectfully, I am, general,

JAMES H. CARLETON,
Brigadier General, Commanding.

Brigadier General LORENZO THOMAS,
Adjutant General U. S. A., Washington, D. C.

Official:

ERASTUS W. WOOD,
Captain 1st Vet. Inf. C. V., A. A. A. General.

HEADQUARTERS DEPARTMENT OF NEW MEXICO,
Santa Fé, N. M., August 2, 1863.

GENERAL: On the 21st of last June I wrote to you a letter, enclosing copies of several communications in relation to extraordinary discoveries of gold and silver in Arizona Territory, particularly at a point or region lying southwestwardly from the San Francisco mountains, west of Albuquerque, New Mexico. I now herewith enclose two other communications from Mr. Benedict and a man named Jack Swilling, both reliable men, on the same subject. These communications speak for themselves.

There cannot be a doubt, from these and from other reliable sources, that all that is said of these discoveries is true.

You will see by the last return of the troops in this department that the effective strength is less than three thousand men. Of these, nearly eleven hundred are in active operations in a campaign against the Navajo Indians, and many of the remainder are constantly employed in active operations against the Apaches, who are scattered through the country in small bands, committing murders and robberies almost daily. The cavalry force in this country is entirely inadequate to pursue successfully these lawless savages. There were seven companies of the 1st cavalry California volunteers, which, last winter, General Wright wrote should be sent one by one across the desert, to New Mexico, as fast as they were raised. Of these, *none have come*, nor do I hear of their coming. Even if they started soon, it would be winter before they would arrive. I beg respectfully to urge upon the War Department the absolute necessity of sending to this department, at the earliest practicable moment, one full regiment of cavalry. The forage here this year is more abundant than ever, and when our stores now *en route* arrive we shall have an abundance of everything for their wants.

As soon as the surveyor general, Clark, returns and makes an official report on the richness and extent of the new gold fields, *it will be absolutely necessary* to post troops in that section of the country; indeed, the capital of Arizona will be sure to be established *there.* All of the people of Tucson, our teamsters, and employés generally, who could possibly get away, have already left for that region. These troops, together with those we need here, additional to what we have, will fall below the mark of what are required. *There will be many desertions.* It is therefore incumbent on the War Department to take timely measures, so that troops to come may reach here before the grass is dry on the prairies or the winter sets in.

There is a rumor here that a fine regiment of Wisconsin cavalry is operating somewhere between this country and the States. Could not that regiment be sent here before the fall months are over?

The subject of these new discoveries demands the immediate and serious attention of the government.

Please, if any troops are ordered here, to reply by telegraph to Julesburg, to come by express from Denver, so that I may have hay cut while there is yet time.

I am, general, very respectfully, your obedient servant,

JAMES H. CARLETON,
Brigadier General, Commanding.

Brigadier General LORENZO THOMAS,
Adjutant General of the Army, Washington, D. C.

Official:
ERASTUS W. WOOD,
Captain 1st Vet. Inf. C. V., A. A. A. General.

HEADQUARTERS DEPARTMENT OF NEW MEXICO,
Santa Fé, N. M., August 3, 1863.

CAPTAIN: Send a company of infantry from your post to scour the eastern slope of the Sandia mountain country, from Tejerras cañon northwardly towards the Placer mountains, with instructions to kill every male Navajo or Apache Indian who is large enough to bear arms, and who may be living in the fastnesses of the region above described. You are authorized to hire two good guides at a reasonable compensation. The company will keep the field for thirty days. It will start at once.

I am, captain, very respectfully,

JAMES H. CARLETON,
Brigadier General, Commanding.

Captain WILLIAM H. LEWIS, U. S. A.,
Commanding at Albuquerque, N. M.

Official:
ERASTUS W. WOOD,
Captain 1st Vet. Inf. C. V., A. A. A. General.

HEADQUARTERS DEPARTMENT OF NEW MEXICO,
Santa Fé, N. M., August 3, 1863.

CAPTAIN: Send a company of infantry from your post to scour the country thoroughly from Abo Pass northwardly along the eastern slope of the Manzana mountains to Tejerras cañon. The troops will not go into any of the towns lying east of the Manzana mountains, but will be kept busily scouting, and will be instructed to kill every Navajo or Apache Indian large enough to bear arms whom they may find. No women or children will be killed; these will be captured and held until further orders. It is believed that in the fastnesses of those mountains are many of these Indians. They will doubtless be found well up toward or at the crest of the ridge. There are points along the western base where there is water which can be reached by wagons with rations from time to time. The subsistence to be carried in the mountains will be bacon, flour, sugar and coffee. These will be carried by the men in haversacks, and by a few pack-mules from one point to another, where a wagon can reach the base of the mountains, as the command progresses northward. The details how best to accomplish this are left to your good judgment. The company will be in the field for thirty days, and will start at once. You are authorized to hire two good guides, at a reasonable compensation, to go with it, and two or three packers.

Respectfully, your obedient servant,

JAMES H. CARLETON,
Brigadier General, Commanding.

Captain SAMUEL ARCHER, U. S. A.,
Commanding at Los Pinos, N. M.

Official:

ERASTUS W. WOOD,
Captain 1st Vet. Inf. C. V., A. A. A. General.

HEADQUARTERS DEPARTMENT OF NEW MEXICO,
Santa Fé, N. M., August 4, 1863.

COLONEL: I have been informed that there is a spring called *Ojo de Cibolo*, about fifteen miles west of Limitar, where the Navajoes drive their stolen cattle and "jerk" the flesh at their leisure. Cannot you make arrangements for a party of resolute men from your command to be stationed there for, say, thirty days, and kill every Navajo and Apache they can find? A cautious, wary commander, hiding his men, and moving about at night, might kill off a good many Indians near that point.

I am, colonel, very respectfully, your obedient servant,

JAMES H. CARLETON.
Brigadier General, Commanding.

Colonel EDWIN A. RIGG,
Commanding at Fort Craig, N. M.

Official:

ERASTUS W. WOOD,
Captain 1st Vet. Inf. C. V., A. A. A. General.

HEADQUARTERS DEPARTMENT OF NEW MEXICO,
Santa Fé, N. M., August 5, 1863.

MAJOR: In reply to your communication of July 31, 1863, relative to an extract from department Special Orders No. 33, current series, ordering Captain Abreü's company to Los Pinos, I am directed by the general commanding to say to you that, doubtless, the order for Captain Abreü to remain for the present at Fort Stanton was received before the company had left for Los Pinos; that the horses ordered to be sent from Fort Union for that company were not sent, from some unaccountable oversight or neglect at that post, but were sent in another direction.

The commanding general expects that you will clear the whole Bonita country of every Indian in it. The company of the 7th United States infantry must be kept in the field to help, as it is to go to another post as soon as this work is done.

I am, major, very respectfully, your obedient servant,

CYRUS H. DE FORREST, *Aide-de-Camp.*

Major JOSEPH SMITH,
Commanding at Fort Stanton, N. M.

Official:

ERASTUS W. WOOD,
Captain 1st Vet. Inf. C. V., A. A. A. General.

[Extract]

HEADQUARTERS DEPARTMENT OF NEW MEXICO,
Santa Fé, N. M., August 6, 1863.

COLONEL : I have the honor to acknowledge the receipt of your letter of the 1st instant. You will send the eleven recruits, 1st New Mexico volunteers, whom you report as just arrived at your post, to Los Pinos by the first practicable opportunity—say by the first train that comes up after the receipt of this communication. You will forward to the same point all recruits for that regiment received from below as soon as practicable after their arrival at Fort Craig. They are much needed in the Navajo country. Keep these headquarters advised of when you send such recruits, and transmit a list of their names.

* * * * * * * * * *

It is sincerely hoped, and expected, that you will be able to arrange some plan by which the predatory bands of Indians infesting your district may be destroyed. This is a subject that not only demands your attention, but your action. The troops must be kept after the Indians, not in big bodies, with military noises and smokes, and the gleam of arms by day, and fires, and talk, and comfortable sleeps by night; but in small parties moving stealthily to their haunts and lying patiently in wait for them; or by following their tracks day after day with a fixedness of purpose that never gives up. In this way, as large a command as that at Craig ought not to be run over or hooted at by a few naked Indians armed with bows and arrows. Some flour, bacon, a little coffee, and sugar, thrown on a pack-mule, with the men carrying, say, two or three days' rations in their haversacks, and it will surprise the country what a few resolute men can do. If a hunter goes after deer, he tries all sorts of wiles to get within gunshot of it. An Indian is a more watchful and a more wary animal than a deer. He must be hunted with skill; he cannot be blundered upon; nor will he allow his pursuers to come upon him when he knows it, unless he is the stronger.

I have made these few remarks because I desire you to impress upon your officers and men the utter folly of going after Indians unless these rules are observed. I once, in this country, with some good trackers under Kit Carson, followed a trail of Apaches for over a fortnight. I caught them. Others can do as well.

I am, colonel, respectfully, your obdient servant,

JAMES H CARLETON,
Brigadier General, Commanding.

Colonel EDWIN A RIGG,
Commanding at Fort Craig, N. M.

Official :

ERASTUS W. WOOD,
Captain 1st Vet. Inf. C. V., A. A. A. General.

HEADQUARTERS DEPARTMENT OF NEW MEXICO,
Santa Fé, N. M., August 6, 1863.

GENERAL : Cause the arms and ammunition sent from the department of the Pacific for the Pimo Indians to be placed in the hands of those Indians without delay, with such restrictions as will best subserve the interests of the government, and will insure that the Pimos use them in assisting to make war upon the Apaches, as far as it is practicable to get such assurance from Indians.

I am, general, very respectfully, your obedient servant,

JAMES H. CARLETON,
Brigadier General, Commanding.

Brigadier General JOSEPH R. WEST,
U. S. Vols., Com. District of Arizona, Hart's Mills, Texas.

Official :

ERASTUS W. WOOD,
Captain 1st Vet. Inf. C. V., A. A. A. General.

[Extract.]

HEADQUARTERS DEPARTMENT OF NEW MEXICO,
Santa Fé, N. M., August 6, 1863.

GENERAL : * * * * * * * * *

In reply to your note of July 27th ultimo, I have the honor to say that the letter asking for a company from Fort Craig, to co-operate with Major McCleave in his efforts against the Indians, was sent to Colonel Rigg, and your request ordered to be carried out. The following was the indorsement:

"July 15. This letter is respectfully referred to the commander at Fort Craig, who will send company K, 1st infantry California volunteers, to the points mentioned by Major McCleave, and this company will be instructed to proceed with great caution, without noise of trumpets or drums, or loud talking, or the firing of guns, except in battle; to march silently, *mostly by night;* to build fires of dry twigs. that no smoke may arise from them; to have no fires by night; to kill every Indian *man* they can find; to be gone thirty days; to have pack-mule transportation where wagons cannot go; to remember that California troops always find and whip the Indians; to excel in this respect all other California troops."

This indorsement was on a letter from Major McCleave to General West, dated June 25, and enclosed in a letter from General West to these headquarters.

* * * * * * * * * *

I am, general, very respectfully, your obedient servant,

JAMES H. CARLETON,
Brigadier General, Commanding.

Brigadier General JOSEPH R. WEST,
U. S. Vols., Com. District of Arizona, Hart's Mills, Texas.

Official: ERASTUS W. WOOD,
Captain 1st Vet. Inf. C. V., A. A. A. General.

HEADQUARTERS DEPARTMENT OF NEW MEXICO,
Santa Fé, N. M., August 7, 1863.

MAJOR: When Lieutenant Wardwell leaves your post to return scouting towards Santa Fé, it will be well for you to send along with him all persons casually at your post, who belong to other commands, if they are fit for duty. He must not be embarrassed by sick men, as he is ordered to hunt and fight Indians all the way back. Give him twenty days' rations and written orders that he will diligently spend that time in hunting Indians. He will go near no town or village on his way back He will keep notes of every day's marches and work, and make to these headquarters a detailed report on his return. Instruct him to do all this. * * * * * * * *

Your animals must be carefully herded by a guard of suitable strength and suitable vigilance. I hope not to hear that the United States herds have been run off again. If we cannot protect our own stock we can hardly protect that of the people. If one or two men make large circuits every day, morning and evening, about your post and about your herd, if they are at all expert, they will cut all trails in the neighborhood. There are a thousand ways to know if Indians are about which should be practiced. Thus far the Indians about Fort Stanton, I am sorry to say, have had rather the best of it.

* * * * * * * * * * *

The company of the 7th infantry *is to be kept in the field* until all the Indians have been driven from your part of the country; then it is to go to another post. Keep your command busy scouting. The Indians must not run over us rough-shod. It seems to me that we are as smart as they are, and *can* arrange some plan by which we can surprise and destroy them. It is said the few remaining Mescaleros in your country, numbering about seventy men, women, and children, have been joined by small parties of Navajoes, and that they are operating together. They talk the same language.

I am very anxious to hear that you have made an impression upon those Indians. Make a written report of all your command has done from the time one express left until you send the next, and so on.

I am, major, very respectfully, your obedient servant,

JAMES H. CARLETON,
Brigadier General, Commanding.

Major JOSEPH SMITH,
Commanding at Fort Stanton, N. M.

Official: ERASTUS W. WOOD,
Captain 1st Vet. Inf. C. V., A. A. A. General.

HEADQUARTERS DEPARTMENT OF NEW MEXICO,
Santa Fé, N. M., August 7, 1863.

COLONEL: I have heard a rumor that you have had some success against the Navajoes, and have felt surprised that an official report from you on the subject could not have reached me as soon as the rumor.

Make a note of this: You will send me a weekly report, in *detail*, of the operations of your command, a certified copy of which I desire to send to Washington by each mail, if possible. Let me know all about the crops destroyed, their extent and location ; all about the stock captured—when, where, by whom, and the kind and number; all about the Navajoes killed, and the exact number of captured women and children. The prisoners are all to be sent to Santa Fé, to my care, by every safe and practicable opportunity.

Be sure and make *timely* requisitions for supplies.

Keep me advised of just how you are getting along in all respects.

Major Morrison will be required to state what reason he had for delaying his command so long at and near Las Lunas. That officer will be kept in the field until he has become an experienced Indian fighter. When you can, pray give Major Blakeney a chance for distinction.

The value of time cannot be too seriously considered. Make *every* string draw. Much is expected of you, both here and in Washington.

I am, colonel, very respectfully, your obedient servant,

JAMES H. CARLETON,
Brigadier General, Commanding.

Colonel CHRISTOPHER CARSON,
Commanding Fort Canby, N. M.

Official:

ERASTUS W. WOOD,
Captain 1st Vet. Inf. C. V., A. A. A. General.

HEADQUARTERS DEPARTMENT OF NEW MEXICO,
Santa Fé, N. M., August 7, 1863.

SIR: I have waited anxiously to hear that the command at Fort Wingate had had some success against the Navajoes. It seems to me that if some thirty or forty men, with some flour, bacon, sugar, and coffee, in haversacks, and on a few pack-mules, should move by night, (hiding by day,) without noise, and very cautiously, they would be able to surprise parties of Navajoes at or near their fields, which fields, within a radius of seventy miles of Fort Wingate, must all be destroyed before the crops are gathered by the Indians. All captured women and children (none will be killed) will be sent, by every practicable opportunity, to Santa Fé.

I speak of thirty or forty men: one, two, or three such parties can be in the field at once, in different directions, if necessary and expedient. The Navajo Indians have got to be whipped, and I wish to hear that the Fort Wingate garrison has done its part. There is no peace party of Navajoes, unless such a party came in before the 20th of last July. The whole tribe is a war party, and as such will be treated alike. Every male Navajo able to bear arms will be attacked and destroyed or captured wherever he may be found, unless he came in before the 20th of last July. No women and children will be harmed, but will be sent to Santa Fé as prisoners. The rule is a plain one, and needs no future correspondence to define its meaning.

A weekly report, *in detail*, of what the command at Fort Wingate will have accomplished, week after week, until further orders, whether in building or in campaigning, will be made to these headquarters by the commanding officer of that post. Remember this, and be sure to be particular in making the report, a certified copy of which will be sent by mail to Washington as soon as received.

Be sure and make *timely* requisitions for supplies.

I am, sir, very respectfully, your obedient servant,

JAMES H. CARLETON,
Brigadier General, Commanding.

Lieutenant Colonel J. FRANCISCO CHAVEZ,
Or Officer Commanding Fort Wingate, N. M.

NOTE.—If *Barboncito, Delgadito,* or *Ché* wish to be employed as expressmen to and from Fort Canby, I have no objection. In this case their families may remain at the fort. If not, they will be sent here if captured alive. The old Navajo woman I saw at Wingate can remain there. J. H. C.

Official:

ERASTUS W. WOOD,
Captain 1st Vet. Inf. C. V., A. A. A. General.

[Extract.]

HEADQUARTERS DEPARTMENT OF NEW MEXICO,
Santa Fé, N. M., August 7, 1863.

GENERAL: * * * * * * * * * *
It is well to inform you that a trail of, say, two hundred Navajoes going south was passed three days since by a gentleman from Colonel Carson's command. The trail was fresh and was passed a short distance this side of Laguna. These Indians sometimes go as low or lower than Fort Thorn. As you are aware, they are a branch of the Apache family, talk the same language, and are said now to be mixed with predatory bands of the Apaches.

I am, general, very respectfully, your obedient servant,

JAMES H. CARLETON,
Brigadier General, Commanding.

Brigadier General JOSEPH R. WEST,
U. S. Vols., Commanding District of Arizona, Hart's Mills, Texas.

Official:

ERASTUS W. WOOD,
Captain 1st Vet. Inf. C. V., A. A. A. General.

HEADQUARTERS DEPARTMENT OF NEW MEXICO,
Santa Fé, N. M., August 14, 1863.

COLONEL: I shall write to Captain Shoemaker to send you twenty sets complete of the McClellan horse equipments.

Some three hundred head of cattle are on the way to Fort Craig, destined for the district of Arizona. As soon as they come report the fact, and guard them securely until further orders. If it takes your whole available force, the public animals must be guarded beyond a shade of danger from Indians.

All the troops that can be spared in the whole upper country are after Indians. Pettis sending for re-enforcements, thus losing time, augurs badly. I hope to hear that your troops have killed some Indians.

A good deal of study of how to get at them, and a good deal of caution and fixedness of purpose in carrying plans into execution, will be sure to produce good results eventually.

There are many Navajoes and Apaches prowling over the country. The troops and the people must all the time be on their guard.

I am, colonel, very respectfully, your obedient servant,

JAMES H. CARLETON,
Brigadier General, Commanding.

Colonel EDWIN A. RIGG,
Commanding at Fort Craig, N. M.

Official:

ERASTUS W. WOOD,
Captain 1st Vet. Inf. C. V., A. A. A. General.

HEADQUARTERS DEPARTMENT OF NEW MEXICO,
Santa Fé, N. M., August 15, 1863.

CAPTAIN: In reply to your communication of the 6th instant, relating to captured Indians, the general commanding directs me to send you a copy of a letter from these headquarters to Colonel Chavez, commanding Fort Wingate, dated August 7, 1863, and to say to you that captured Indians will be sent to Santa Fé by every practicable opportunity—if necessary, the men in irons; and in case any attempt to escape is made by them they will be shot down.

The copy of the letter herewith enclosed contains instructions which are sufficiently explicit to require no further correspondence on the subject.

I am, captain, very respectfully, your obedient servant,

CYRUS H. DE FORREST, *Aide-de-Camp.*

Captain RAFAEL CHACON,
1st N. M. Vols., Commanding at Fort Wingate, N. M.

Official:

ERASTUS W. WOOD,
Captain 1st Vet. Inf. C. V., A. A. A. General.

HEADQUARTERS DEPARTMENT OF NEW MEXICO,
Santa Fé, N. M., August 16, 1863.

GENERAL: On the 2d instant I wrote to you a letter showing the importance of sending more troops to this department. Fearing that letter may have been delayed or miscarried, I enclose herewith a duplicate of it.

You are aware that the Territories of Arizona and New Mexico are more extensive than, say, five or six such States as Ohio; that they swarm with hostile Indians; that the wealth of the country, consisting mainly in flocks and herds, is greatly exposed to depredations on a large scale. A man may have twenty thousand dollars' worth of stock, the result of a life of watching and care, and in one night become a beggar from a raid by a dozen Navajoes or Apaches.

Since Colonel Carson took the field many small bands of Navajoes have come into the settlements and are committing some murders and many robberies. I have all the troops in the field which can be spared from the various posts, but men on foot, in an open country, are not successful against these mounted savages. If I could have the full regiment of cavalry asked for, and could have authority to raise one independent company of native mounted volunteers in each county, to scout in that county, I really believe the Indian wars in New Mexico could be brought forever to a close. Pray send the regiment and grant the authority. These companies could be discharged as soon as their services were no longer required. The men of each county being familiar with all the trails and watering places of their own county, and being near the flocks and herds of their own neighbors, to get notice and give chase the moment hostile Indians made their appearance would, in my opinion, be a cheap and efficient auxiliary to the operations by the more permanently organized troops.

We have rumors of a guerilla force having been organized at San Antonio, Texas, under the notorious Baylor, to come here on a robbing and murdering expedition. This may be so; and if so, you can see, as well as I, the greater necessity of sending more troops here. Whatever is done should be done at once.

I am, general, very respectfully, your obedient servant,

JAMES H. CARLETON,
Brigadier General, Commanding.

Brigadier General LORENZO THOMAS,
Adjutant General U. S. A., Washington, D. C.

Official:

ERASTUS W. WOOD,
Captain 1st Vet. Inf. C. V., A. A. A. General.

HEADQUARTERS DEPARTMENT OF NEW MEXICO,
Santa Fé, N. M., August 18, 1863.

COLONEL: I have the honor to acknowledge the receipt of your letter of the 24th ultimo, in relation to the disposition to be made of captured Navajo women and children, and to say, in reply, that *all* prisoners which are captured by the troops or employés of your command will be sent to Santa Fé, by the first practicable opportunity after they are, from time to time, brought in as prisoners. *There must be no exception to this rule.* Here, the superintendent of Indian affairs and myself will make such dispositions as to their future care and destination as may seem most humane and proper.

All horses, mules, or other stock which the troops or employés under your command may capture belong to the United States, and will be reported to department headquarters. The horses and mules will be turned over to your chief quartermaster, who will have them carefully branded "U. S.," and used in the public service. These he will account for on his property returns. But to stimulate the zeal of the troops and employés who have captured horses and mules from the Navajoes, or who may hereafter make such captures from those Indians, a bonus of twenty dollars apiece will be paid to their captors as prize-money, on the delivery to the chief quartermaster of every sound, serviceable horse or mule. These will be accounted for as purchased.

All sheep captured will be turned over to the chief commissary of your expedition. These will be taken up on the returns of provisions; will be properly marked; will be killed from time to time and issued as fresh meat to the troops and employés. The chief commissary is authorized to pay the captors of such sheep one dollar per head as prize money, and as an encouragement to renewed exertions. Every lot captured will at once be reported to department headquarters. The sheep paid for, as here set forth, will be taken up as purchased.

All other property captured from the Indians will be reported, when orders will be given as to what disposition shall be made of it.

I am, colonel, very respectfully, your obedient servant,

JAMES H. CARLETON,
Brigadier General, Commanding.

Colonel CHRISTOPHER CARSON,
Commanding Expedition against the Navajoes, Fort Canby, N. M.

Official:

ERASTUS W. WOOD,
Captain 1st Vet. Inf. C. V., A. A. A. General.

HEADQUARTERS DEPARTMENT OF NEW MEXICO,
Santa Fé, N. M., August 19, 1863.

CAPTAIN: You will, immediately on receipt of this, send the 1st sergeant of Captain Cremony's company and twenty-five picked men of that company on a scout after Indians, up the Pecos as far as Agua Negra, and thence towards the Piedra Perdinales, on a road leading from Agua Negra to Albuquerque. The party will be absent thirty days, and will kill every Apache or Navajo Indian who is large enough to bear arms, whom it can find in that region. No women or children will be harmed. These will be taken and held captive until further orders.

There are small parties of Navajoes and Apaches prowling around that section of country which must be destroyed. Urge the sergeant to use his utmost endeavors to this end. There are other parties out from all the posts, and I trust the party from yours will try hard to obtain results which will be creditable to it. The party will be in the field scouting all the time for thirty days. You are authorized to employ two good trackers and guides for it. If one or two of your Apaches can do this, let the experiment be tried, and pay well, say two dollars a day cash, for his services. Little by little we will avail ourselves of their knowledge in ferreting out others, and in finding water and grass.

Report every week how you progress in building, and on all other matters which would be useful and interesting to be known here of your surroundings and of the condition of the Apaches.

I am, captain, very respectfully, your obedient servant,

JAMES H. CARLETON,
Brigadier General, Commanding.

Captain JOSEPH UPDEGRAFF, U. S. A.,
Commanding at Fort Sumner, N. M.

NOTE.—The sergeant will be instructed to keep a journal of his operations and marches, day by day, which will be sent to department headquarters when the service is done.

Official:

ERASTUS W. WOOD,
Captain 1st Vet. Inf. C. V., A. A. A. General.

[Extract.]

HEADQUARTERS DEPARTMENT OF NEW MEXICO,
Santa Fé, N. M., August 19, 1863.

MAJOR: I regret to learn of the capture, by Navajoes, of so large a flock of sheep as that seen in their possession by Lieutenant Higden. I suppose, of course, that you immediately sent troops to recapture the sheep and destroy the Indians.

* * * * * * * * * * *

You have a large command and an expensive one; and I hope to hear soon of some favorable reports in the way of destruction of Indians and the recovery of stock. Every Navajo or Apache man who may be found by your troops will be destroyed or taken prisoner. No women and children will be injured. These will be held until further orders.

Each command that leaves your post is to keep a journal of every day's operations, which journal, when the commands return to your post, is to be sent to me.

I shall be impatient until I hear of some success in your quarter of the country. There are now scouts out from every post in the department.

Respectfully, your obedient servant,

JAMES H. CARLETON,
Brigadier General, Commanding.

Major JOSEPH SMITH,
Commanding at Fort Stanton, N. M.

Official:

ERASTUS W. WOOD,
Captain 1st Vet. Inf. C. V., A. A. A. General.

HEADQUARTERS DEPARTMENT OF NEW MEXICO,
Santa Fé, N. M., August 19, 1863.

CAPTAIN: Immediately on the receipt of this letter you will send Lieutenant Brady, with twenty-five picked men from Captain Bergmann's company of 1st New Mexico volunteers, on a scout up Red river to Cañon Largo—the mouths of the Conchas and Mora—and to hunt up and destroy any parties of Navajoes or Apaches which may be found in that section of country. No women and children will be harmed; these will be taken and held as prisoners until further orders.

Lieutenant Brady is said to be a very energetic, determined man, and will doubtless perform this special service with marked credit to himself and to your command. Similar scouts are out from all the posts, and it is hoped that by activity and caution the Indians now infesting the country east of the Rio Grande will be destroyed. The party will be absent on this duty thirty days. A journal will be kept by Lieutenant Brady of each day's march and operations, which will be sent to me. While he is in the neighborhood of Cañon Largo it would be well for him to see if the road could be made off the *mesa* from the direction of Fort Union—the road I spoke to you about.

I am, captain, very respectfully, your obedient servant,

JAMES H. CARLETON,
Brigadier General, Commanding.

Captain P. W. L. PLYMPTON, U. S. A.,
Commanding at Fort Bascom, N. M.

HEADQUARTERS DEPARTMENT OF NEW MEXICO,
Santa Fé, N. M., August 23, 1863.

GENERAL: I have the honor to report that nearly all the troops in this department, certainly all that can possibly be spared, are now in the field endeavoring to chastise hostile Indians, as well as to protect the people in their persons, and their property in flocks and herds.

Colonel Carson, with all the available force from Fort Canby, and Major Willis, with two companies from Fort Wingate, are after Navajoes in the Navajo country. I have stationed a force in a pass in the Jemez mountains, known as El Valle Grande, to prevent stock being driven through that noted thoroughfare. Another force is at the Cibola Springs, west of Limitar, and companies and smaller detachments are scouting over the country east of the Rio Grande, from Forts Bascom, Sumner and Stanton, and from Albuquerque and Los Pinos. Four companies are operating against the Apaches near the heads of the Miembres and the Gila. Yet with all these exertions, *small* parties of fives, and tens, and twenties, of Navajoes and Apaches, most always well mounted, steal through the country and commit depredations. You will observe that the force here is entirely inadequate for the absolute necessities of the country. The plan suggested in my letter of last week of giving me authority to raise one independent company of volunteers in each county, mainly for the defence of the county, would, in my opinion, be entirely effective against these small predatory bands. The tribes in their country could then be attacked by the regularly organized troops. Another full regiment of cavalry should be sent here at once. I would not ask for a man, general, unless I knew it was absolutely necessary to have him.

Respectfully, your obedient servant,

JAMES H. CARLETON,
Brigadier General, Commanding.

Brigadier General LORENZO THOMAS,
Adjutant General U. S. A., Washington, D. C.

Official:

ERASTUS W. WOOD,
Captain 1st Vet. Inf. C. V., A. A. A. General.

HEADQUARTERS DEPARTMENT OF NEW MEXICO,
Santa Fé, N. M., August 26, 1863.

MAJOR: The Indians beginning to be troublesome about Fort Union, where there is no cavalry, I have been obliged to order Captain Fritz's company to that post. In case you have not transportation to move all the company property with the company now, you will have such property boxed up and forwarded by the first train coming from your post to Fort Union.

Let Captain Fritz transfer his new horse equipments complete to Captain Abreü; he will have them replaced at Fort Union. Captain Fritz will also transfer to Captain Abreü, of the new horses which he has received, enough to mount sixty of Captain Abreü's men. These will be replaced as soon as practicable after the Captain's arrival at Fort Union.

It is said that some eight thousand sheep were run off by Navajoes on the 24th instant, from Benguin valley, near Fort Union. Some troops, mounted on mules, are in pursuit. Should these not overtake them, it is calculated that parties from your post can intercept them on their way toward the Jornada, or to cross the Rio Grande at some place higher up. Having timely notice, I trust *this* flock will not get by you.

I am, major, very respectfully, your obedient servant,

JAMES H. CARLETON,
Brigadier General, Commanding.

Major JOSEPH SMITH,
Commanding at Fort Stanton, N. M.

Official:

ERASTUS W. WOOD,
Captain 1st Vet. Inf. C. V., A. A. A. General.

DEPARTMENT OF NEW MEXICO, ASSISTANT ADJUTANT GENERAL'S OFFICE,
Santa Fé, N. M., August 27, 1863.

MAJOR: The general commanding directs me to say to you that he expects that, in sending out scouting parties from Fort Stanton, you will be particular to give such instructions that a careful lookout will be kept up for Navajoes and Apaches in the neighborhood of the Salt lakes, which are situated in a northerly direction from the Gallinos mountains, and toward Manzana.

I am, major, very respectfully, your obedient servant,

BEN. C. CUTLER,
Assistant Adjutant General.

Major JOSEPH SMITH,
Commanding at Fort Stanton, N. M.

Official:

ERASTUS W. WOOD,
Captain 1st Vet. Inf. C. V., A. A. A. General.

DEPARTMENT OF NEW MEXICO, ASSISTANT ADJUTANT GENERAL'S OFFICE,
Santa Fé, N. M., August 27, 1863.

SIR: I have the honor to acknowledge the receipt of your communication of the 24th instant, and am directed by the department commander to say that he trusts you will use every exertion to intercept and destroy any parties of hostile Indians who may attempt to pass in the vicinity of your camp. He desires that you make the huts you are building for your men as substantial and as comfortable as you possibly can, and lay up a good supply of wood, and if possible have a supply of hay cut and stacked up for, say, eighteen government animals, in case your own party or any other party of troops are obliged to remain during the winter at Las Valles, and for, say, what ten beef cattle would consume in four months. Having this object in view, the general leaves it all to your own good judgment as to the place where, and the manner in which, you shall put up these huts, so that the men may be comfortable.

I am, sir, very respectfully, your obedient servant,

BEN. C. CUTLER,
Assistant Adjutant General.

First Lieutenant ERASTUS W. WOOD,
Commanding at Las Valles, N. M.

Official:

ERASTUS W. WOOD,
Captain 1st Vet. Inf. C. V., A. A. A. General.

HEADQUARTERS DEPARTMENT OF NEW MEXICO.
Santa Fé, N. M., September 2, 1863.

GOVERNOR: It becomes my melancholy duty to inform you that Major Joseph Cummings, 1st New Mexico volunteers, was killed by the Navajo Indians near Pueblo Colorado, in the Navajo country, on the 18th ultimo.

There was no better soldier than he within the department of New Mexico. He was brave and generous to a fault, and in manly attributes he had but few equals, and hardly a superior. His comrades in arms are overwhelmed with sorrow at his untimely fate, and from them there comes but one expression—that of admiration of his manly character, and grief at his loss.

I am, very respectfully, your excellency's obedient servant,

JAMES H. CARLETON,
Brigadier General, Commanding.

His Excellency HENRY CONNELLY,
Governor of New Mexico, Santa Fé, N. M.

Official:

ERASTUS W. WOOD,
Captain 1st Vet. Inf. C. V., A. A. A. General.

HEADQUARTERS DEPARTMENT OF NEW MEXICO,
Santa Fé, N. M., September 3, 1863.

GENERAL: I have to inform you that, from information I have received, it is probable the Navajo Indians in large numbers have gone southward and joined the Gila Apaches somewhere in the White mountains. If this is so, it will be well for you to be prepared, not only to whip them if they come into your district, but to be on your guard against increased depredations.

The troops in the Navajo country are pressing them sorely. By the time the snows of winter drive them down out of the mountains it is hoped we shall have better success.

I am, general, respectfully, &c.,

JAMES H. CARLETON,
Brigadier General, Commanding.

Brigadier General JOSEPH R. WEST,
U. S. Vols., Commanding District of Arizona, Las Cruces, N. M.

Official:

ERASTUS W. WOOD,
Captain 1st Vet. Inf. C. V., A. A. A. General.

HEADQUARTERS DEPARTMENT OF NEW MEXICO,
Santa Fé, N. M., September 4, 1863.

SIR: You will make a report every week of all that is done by the party under your command at the Valles. Although no sign of Indians may be seen, you must be sure to be on your guard against surprise, and teach parties of your men detached from the main body to be vigilant all the time.

As troops may stay in the Valles all winter, you will make *timely* preparation, to this end. A storehouse to contain three months' supply for forty men, and an oven, will be built.

I am, sir, respectfully, &c.,

JAMES H. CARLETON,
Brigadier General, Commanding.

Second Lieutenant PHILIP A. J. RUSSELL,
1st Infantry Cal. Vols., Santa Fé, N. M.

Official:

ERASTUS W. WOOD,
Captain 1st Vet. Inf. C. V., A. A. A. General.

[Extract.]

DEPARTMENT OF NEW MEXICO, ASSISTANT ADJUTANT GENERAL'S OFFICE,
Santa Fé, N. M., September 4, 1863.

GENERAL: I have the honor to transmit for your information duplicate copies of the various communications which were forwarded to you from this office by the mail which left Santa Fé on the 22d ultimo, under the supposition that the originals were all destroyed by the Indians who captured the mail on the Jornada del Muerto on the 26th ultimo.

* * * * * * * * * * * *

I am, general, very respectfully, your obedient servant,

BEN. C. CUTLER,
Assistant Adjutant General.

Brigadier General JOSEPH R. WEST, U. S. Vols.,
Commanding District of Arizona, Hart's Mills, Texas.

Official:

ERASTUS W. WOOD,
Captain 1st Vet. Inf. C. V., A. A. A. General.

HEADQUARTERS DEPARTMENT OF NEW MEXICO,
Santa Fé, N. M., September 5, 1863.

CAPTAIN: Your letter setting forth your inability to do much at building of your post has been received. I have given orders for fifty citizens to be employed to help you. It is hoped you take great interest in having your command comfortably sheltered before the winter sets in. There can be no good reason why this is not done. There seems to be as much indifference as to the progress of the work as there was to the setting out of trees. If so, this cannot be complimentary, in the long run, either to yourself or your command. It is difficult to conceive how, with three companies, with nine men for guard, and a small party on detached service, you have no men to help build your post.

Captain Hollister is reported to have said at Fort Stanton that you had told him that Ojo Blanco was not at Fort Sumner, and had been gone some time. I do not credit the report, because I take it for granted that if a single Indian which had been turned over to you for safe-keeping made his escape, you would, as it is made your duty to do, at once notify me of the fact.

I have sent you fifty-one Navajo men, women, and children, who are likewise to be retained near your post as prisoners. They will be allotted some place where they will be by themselves. They are to be fed by the Indian agent, as the Apaches are fed, and are to be treated with the greatest kindness. As fast as others are captured they will be sent to you. It is my purpose to have the whole Bosque Redondo part of the valley of the Pecos set apart as an Indian reservation, and place upon it all captured Navajoes and Apaches. They belong to the same family, and as a Pueblo under proper care and instruction, will soon again become a homogeneous people. Your chaplain will be here on his return from Europe, in about two weeks.

I am, captain, very respectfully, your obedient servant,

JAMES H. CARLETON,
Brigadier General, Commanding.

Captain JOSEPH UPDEGRAFF, U. S. A.,
Commanding at Fort Sumner, N. M.

Official:

ERASTUS W. WOOD,
Captain 1st Vet. Inf. C. V., A. A. A. General.

HEADQUARTERS DEPARTMENT OF NEW MEXICO,
Santa Fé, N. M., September 6, 1863.

GENERAL: I have the honor to report that I have this week sent fifty-one Navajo Indian men, women, and children to Fort Sumner, at the Bosque Redondo, on the Pecos river, where, as I have before informed you, I have four hundred and twenty-five Mescalero Apaches, held as prisoners.

The purpose had in view is to send all captured Navajoes and Apaches to that point, and there to feed and take care of them until they have opened farms and become able to support themselves, as the Pueblo Indians of New Mexico are doing. The War Department has already approved of this in the case of the Apaches, and authorized that Fort Sumner should be a chaplain post, so that the chaplain there could educate the Indian children. This year those Indians have been contented and happy. They planted, under the direction of their agent and with a little help, some large fields of corn; and now that they have their *acequia* dug, will next year raise quite enough to support themselves. This the Navajoes can be persuaded to do as well.

At the Bosque Redondo there is arable land enough for all the Indians of this family, (the Navajoes and Apaches have descended from the same stock and speak the same language,) and I would respectfully recommend, now that the war is vigorously prosecuted against the Navajoes, that the only peace that can ever be made with them must rest on the basis that they move on to these lands, and, like the Pueblos, become an agricultural people and cease to be nomads. This should be a *sine qua non.* As soon as the snows of winter admonish them of the sufferings to which their families will be exposed, I have great hopes of getting the most of the tribe. The knowledge of the perfidy of these Navajoes, gained after two centuries of experience, is such as to lead us to put no faith in their promises. They have no government to make treaties. They are a patriarchal people. One set of families may make promises, but the other set will not heed them. They understand the direct application of force as a law. If its application be removed, that moment they become lawless. This has been tried over and over, and over again, and at great expense. The purpose now is never to relax the application of force with a people that can no more be trusted than you can trust the wolves that run through their mountains; to gather them together, little by little, on to a reservation, away from the haunts, and hills, and hiding-places of their country, and then to be kind to them; there teach their children how to read and write; teach them the arts of peace; teach them the truths of Christianity. Soon they will acquire new habits, new ideas, new modes of life; the old Indians will die off, and carry with them all latent longings for murdering and robbing; the young ones will take their places without these longings; and thus, little by little, they will become a happy and contented people, and Navajo wars will be remembered only as something that belongs entirely to the past. Even until they can raise enough to be self-sustaining, you can feed them cheaper than you can fight them.

You will observe that the Bosque Redondo is far down the Pecos, on the open plains, where these Indians can have no lateral contact with settlers. If the government will only set apart a reservation of forty miles square, with Fort Sumner, at the Bosque Redondo, in the centre, all the good land will be covered, and keep the settlers a proper distance from the Indians.

There is no place in the Navajo country fit for a reservation; and even if there were, it would not be wise to have it there; for, little by little, the Indians would steal away into their mountain fastnesses again, and then, as of old, would come a new war, and so on *ad infinitum.*

I know these views are practical, practicable, and humane; are just to the suffering people, as well as to the aggressive, perfidious, butchering Navajoes. If I can have one more full regiment of cavalry, and authority to raise one independent company in each county in the Territory, they can soon be carried to a final result.

I am, general, very respectfully, your obedient servant,

JAMES H. CARLETON,
Brigadier General, Commanding.

Brigadier General LORENZO THOMAS,
Adjutant General U. S. A., Washington, D. C.

Official:

ERASTUS W. WOOD,
Captain 1st Vet. Inf. C. V., A. A. A. General.

HEADQUARTERS DEPARTMENT OF NEW MEXICO,
Santa Fé, N. M., September 6, 1863.

COLONEL: I have sent to Fort Union fifty-one Navajo men, women, and children, *en route* to Fort Sumner. They are escorted by some soldiers, under Lieutenant Holmes, of the first New Mexico volunteers. The Indians will be treated with great kindness while at your post. You will see that suitable provisions are made for their subsistence there, and for the journey to Fort Sumner, whither Lieutenant Holmes and escort is to accompany them. You will inform the depot quartermaster and commissary that if they have supplies to send to Fort Sumner, this same escort can guard them, and return with the train to Fort Union.

Respectfully, &c.,

JAMES H. CARLETON,
Brigadier General, Commanding.

Lieutenant Colonel WILLIAM McMULLEN,
Commanding Fort Union, N. M.

Official:

ERASTUS W. WOOD,
Captain 1st Vet. Inf. C. V., A. A. A. General.

HEADQUARTERS DEPARTMENT OF NEW MEXICO,
Santa Fé, N. M., September 6, 1863.

GENERAL: I enclose herewith the copy of a letter from Captain A. H. French, first cavalry California volunteers, himself an old practical miner. From all points I hear news confirmatory of the theory that from the head of the Gila northwestwardly to the Colorado river, near Fort Mojave, there is a region of country of unequalled wealth in the precious metals. I soon expect to hear of the return of Surveyor General Clarke, and the party I sent with him to the new Eldorado, when the government will then be officially as well as reliably informed, by an eye-witness, of the wealth so much written about.

I am, general, respectfully, &c.,

JAMES H. CARLETON,
Brigadier General, Commanding.

Brigadier General LORENZO THOMAS,
Adjutant General U. S. A., Washington, D. C.

Official:

ERASTUS W. WOOD,
Captain 1st Vet. Inf. C. V., A. A. A. General.

HEADQUARTERS DEPARTMENT OF NEW MEXICO,
Santa Fé, N. M., September 10, 1863.

SIR: The general commanding desires to be informed, without delay, what amount of money and other valuables came into your possession from the persons and the vicinity of the murdered express men you came across when *en route* from Fort Stanton to Santa Fé in the month of June last, and what disposition has been made of such valuables and money.

I am, sir, very respectfully, your obedient servant,

CYRUS H. DE FORREST, *Aide-de-Camp.*

Lieutenant WILLIAM H. HIGDON,
Fifth Infantry, California Volunteers, Fort Stanton, N. M.

Official:

ERASTUS W. WOOD,
Captain 1st Vet. Inf. C. V., A. A. A. General.

HEADQUARTERS DEPARTMENT OF NEW MEXICO,
Santa Fé, N. M., September 13, 1863.

GENERAL: I have the honor herewith to enclose, for the information of the War Department, copies of letters received from Samuel J. Jones, Charles O. Brown, and King. S. Woolsey, in relation to the new gold fields southwest from the San Francisco mountains, about which I have so frequently written to you. Brown and Woolsey are men whose statements are to be credited. Jones simply transmits Brown's letter.

Surveyor General Clarke, and the officer and men I sent with him, have not yet returned. They should be back before the end of the month, when their reports will be forwarded. It is unnecessary for me to take up the time of the War Department by making comments on the prospective results of such startling developments of treasure, whether to Arizona and New Mexico, or to the country at large; they will be apparent to all on a moment's reflection.

In other letters heretofore written, I have endeavored to impress upon your mind the importance of sending an additional regiment of cavalry—a full regiment—to this country. Authority has been received by the governor of New Mexico to raise in the Territory two regiments more of troops, but it is very doubtful if even one can now be raised: first, because of the real scarcity of men; second, because other more profitable pursuits interpose; third, because nearly all the floating population will go to the new gold fields. An effort will be made to raise one regiment of infantry, as there are not horses in the Territory which can be spared from other labor to mount a regiment of cavalry. If a full regiment of cavalry could at once be sent here from the States, I would have troops quite sufficient, I hope, to whip the Indians, and to protect the people going to and at the mines. The authority to raise one independent company in each county, for the protection of the people and flocks and herds of that county, should be given to me. I have no inclination to ask for more authority or more troops than I need. I beg respectfully to say, if I am considered worthy of commanding so remote a department, some confidence should be reposed in my judgment—being, as I am, upon the ground—of what is absolutely wanted. If troops cannot be sent, permit me to recruit in Colorado Territory. One thing should be borne in mind: Every regiment you send here, whether from the east or from California, will stay. Thus each one is a military colony, to people the vast uninhabited region between the Rio Grande and the Pacific. As winter is so near, time now is everything.

Pray let serious attention be given to the subject of these new discoveries of gold. A new revolution in all that pertains to this country is on the eve of commencing, and the government should provide for approaching emergencies. The people will flock to the mines, and should be protected.

Providence has indeed blessed us. Now that we need money to pay the expenses of this terrible war, new mines of untold millions are found, and the gold lies here at our feet, to be had by the mere picking of it up! The country where it is found is no fancied Atlantis; is not seen in golden dreams; but it is a real, tangible El Dorado, that has gold that can be weighed by the steelyards—gold that does not vanish when the finder is awake.

I hope I may not be considered visionary, and therefore be denied reasonable help. This is a great matter not only for our present wants, but for the future security of our country; for, henceforth, in place of a desert, dividing peoples, we find a treasure which will attract not only a population to live upon that desert, but which will, as sure as the sun shines, bring the great railroad over the 35th parallel, and thus unite the two extremes of the country by bars of steel, until, from the Atlantic to the Pacific, we become homogeneous in interest as in blood.

I beg you will send to New Mexico a first-rate topographical engineer to map the new gold fields, and fix their positions instrumentally. Congress should, by early legislation, determine whether the government shall have rights of seigniorage in these new treasures, and whether foreigners shall come and take gold from the country *ad libitum* and without tax.

I am, general, very respectfully, your obedient servant,

JAMES H. CARLETON,
Brigadier General, Commanding.

Brigadier General LORENZO THOMAS,
Adjutant General U. S. A., Washington, D. C.

Official:

ERASTUS W. WOOD,
Captain 1st Vet. Inf. C. V., A. A. A. General.

HEADQUARTERS DEPARTMENT OF NEW MEXICO,
Santa Fé, N. M., September 13, 1863.

SIR: I have had the honor frequently to write to the War Department of the new gold fields which have been discovered along the Gila river, and upon the line of the 35th parallel, between the Rio Grande and the Rio Colorado. Enclosed herewith please to find copies of letters upon this subject which I have just received.

You will at once perceive that the capital, as well as the population, of the new Territory of Arizona will be near that oasis upon the desert out of which rise the San Francisco mountains, and in and beside which are found these extraordinary deposits of gold; and not at the insignificant village of Tucson, away in the sterile region toward the southern line of the Territory. This will render absolutely indispensable a new mail route over the Whipple road to the new gold fields, and thence crossing the Colorado at old Fort Mojave, (now abandoned,) and thence up the Mojave river and through the Cajon Pass to Los Angeles, California. People flocking towards these mines will clamor for, and will deserve to have, mail facilities. They will go from the east; they will come from California; therefore liberal appropriations should be made early in the approaching session of Congress to prepare the road; to establish a post near the San Francisco mountains; to re-establish old Fort Mojave; to have a first-class permanent ferry across the Colorado at that point; and to provide for an overland mail from Albuquerque to Los Angeles. The reason why I have presumed to write to you upon this important matter is that you may give it timely consideration.

There is no doubt but the reports of these immense deposits of gold are true. As a statesman you will readily imagine all of the political results which must at once ensue from such startling developments when they obtain publicity. This should not be given to them until we have official reports from Surveyor General Clarke and a party I sent with him to see precisely into the matter. We know from various other sources what that report must be, at least sufficiently to make timely preparations for emergencies which will then at once arise.

For myself there comes no little satisfaction in the thought that, for all the toil through the desert of the troops composing the column from California, there will yet result a substantial benefit to the country; that if those brave fellows, who encountered their hardships so cheerfully and patiently, who endured and suffered so much, have not had the good fortune to strike a good, hard, honest blow for the old flag, they have, at least, been instrumental in helping to find gold to pay the gallant men who have had that honor. Somebody had to perform their part in the grand drama upon which the curtain is about to fall. The men from California accepted unmurmuringly the *rôle* that gave them an obscure and distant part upon the stage, where it was known they could not be seen, and believed they would hardly be heard from; but in the great tragedy so cruelly forced upon us, they tried to perform their duty, however insignificant it might be, and to the best of their ability; and now, a finger of that Providence who has watched over us in our tribulation, and who blesses us, lifts a veil, and there, for the whole country, lies a great reward.

I am, sir, very respectfully, your obedient servant,

JAMES H. CARLETON,
Brigadier General, Commanding.

Hon. MONTGOMERY BLAIR,
Postmaster General, Washington, D. C.

Offi cil:

ERASTUS W. WOOD,
Captain 1st Vet. Inf. C. V., A. A. A. General.

[Extract.]

HEADQUARTERS DEPARTMENT OF NEW MEXICO,
Santa Fé, N. M., September 18, 1863.

GENERAL: * * * * * * * * * *

You will issue instructions to all your posts that the protection of the government herds must be the first duty of every garrison. It is a mortifying thing to admit that the Indians run off the stock of the troops. A vigilant officer with vigilant men would want nothing better than for Indians to come and make an attempt to do this. It would save a hard march to go in search of the Indians. It is hoped we have heard the last of such misfortune.

The new post at Cook's Springs will need and should receive your immediate attention. By industry, and some help from other troops and a few citizens, it ought to be done before freezing weather comes. Hay can be got at the Mimbres; *vigas* from the ruins of Fort Thorn, if not nearer, and everything can be made snug and tidy and secure before winter comes. The spring should be dug out so that no muck will surround the water, and then be nicely stoned. The volume of water should be large, that whole trains need not exhaust it.

I am, general, respectfully, your obedient servant,

JAMES H. CARLETON,
Brigadier General, Commanding.

Brigadier General JOSEPH R. WEST,
U. S. Vols., Commanding District of Arizona, Las Cruces, N. M.

Official:

ERASTUS W. WOOD,
Captain 1st Vet. Inf. C. V., A. A. A. General.

[Extract.]

HEADQUARTERS DEPARTMENT OF NEW MEXICO,
Santa Fé, N. M., September 18, 1863.

MAJOR: You will take Captain Hollister's company and twenty other men from your command and proceed to the Gallinas mountains, and cause the spring there to be cleaned out and enlarged, so that water enough may accumulate for the use of trains and cavalry which may encamp there. While there your command will all the time be on the lookout for Indians, and you will attack all you can find or may encounter. Captain Hollister's company will be kept encamped at that point after the spring is prepared, until the 1st of December, to watch for and attack Indians. You will give him written instructions not to visit any town or settlement, or permit any of his command to do so, during that time. On the 1st day of December that company will return to Fort Stanton. You, yourself, will return as soon as the spring is properly prepared. It is possible you may have to have the reservoir for the water below the spring on account of the neighboring rocks.

* * * * * * * * * * *

Now that you find no Indians near Fort Stanton you should give careful instructions to your guards and herders to be on the lookout for them.

I am, major, respectfully, &c.,

JAMES H. CARLETON,
Brigadier General, Commanding.

Major JOSEPH SMITH,
Commanding at Fort Stanton, N. M.

Official:

ERASTUS W. WOOD,
Captain 1st Vet. Inf. C. V., A. A. A. General.

HEADQUARTERS DEPARTMENT OF NEW MEXICO,
Santa Fé, N. M., September 18, 1863.

CAPTAIN: You will send a party of thirty, rank and file, to be commanded by Lieutenant Speed, of your regiment, to proceed through the Abo Pass and scout along through the eastern portion of the Manzana mountains northward to Tijeras cañon, in search of Navajo and Apache Indians. The party will be instructed to kill all the male Indians of these tribes whom it may meet or can find. It will have the same instructions as regards supplies which the party recently returned had, except that under no circumstances will the commander of the scout leave it until it returns to your post.

The scout will keep the field thirty days, and will leave Los Pinos at once.

I am, captain, respectfully, &c.,

JAMES H. CARLETON,
Brigadier General, Commanding.

Captain SAMUEL ARCHER, U. S. A.,
Commanding at Los Pinos, N. M.

Official:

ERASTUS W. WOOD,
Captain 1st Vet. Inf. C. V., A. A. A. General.

HEADQUARTERS DEPARTMENT OF NEW MEXICO,
Santa Fé, N. M., September 18, 1863.

GENERAL: I have the honor herewith to enclose the reports of a scout against the Navajoes made recently from Fort Wingate by Captain Chacon, 1st New Mexico volunteers, and Captain Hargrave, 1st infantry California volunteers. You will be struck with the distances these troops have to march without water.

I am, general, respectfully, your obedient servant,

JAMES H. CARLETON,
Brigadier General, Commanding.

Brigadier General LORENZO THOMAS,
Adjutant General U. S A., Washington, D. C.

Official:

ERASTUS W. WOOD,
Captain 1st Vet. Inf. C. V., A. A. A General.

[Extract.]

HEADQUARTERS DEPARTMENT OF NEW MEXICO.
Santa Fé, N. M., September 19, 1863.

COLONEL: * * * * * * * * *

I recommend, unless you can produce the same result by more gentle measures, that you seize six of the principal men of the Zuñi Indians, and hold them as hostages until all Navajoes in and near their village are given up, and all stolen stock surrendered. You will assure the Zuñi Indians that if I hear that they help or harbor Navajoes, or steal stock from any white men, or injure the person of any white man, I will as certainly destroy their village as sure as the sun shines.

I have received the report of your operations in the vicinity of Cañon de Chelly. If any Indians desire to give themselves up, they will be received and sent to Fort Wingate, with a request that from that post they be sent to Los Pinos. No Navajo Indians of either sex, or of any age, will be retained at Fort Canby as servants, or in any capacity whatever. All must go to the Bosque Redondo.

You are right in believing that I do not wish to have these destroyed who are willing to come in. Nor will you permit an Indian prisoner, once fairly in our custody, to be killed, unless he be endeavoring to make his escape. There is to be no other alternative but this: Say to them—"Go to the Bosque Redondo, or we will pursue and destroy you. We will not make peace with you on any other terms. You have deceived us too often and robbed and murdered our people too long to trust you again at large in your own country. This war shall be pursued against you if it takes years, now that we have begun, until you cease to exist or move. There can be no other talk on the subject."

As winter approaches you will have better luck. I send your report to Washington.

I am, colonel, very respectfully, your obedient servant,

JAMES H. CARLETON,
Brigadier General, Commanding.

Colonel CHRISTOPHER CARSON,
Commanding Expedition against the Navajoes, Fort Canby, N. M.

Official:

ERASTUS W. WOOD,
Captain 1st Vet. Inf. C. V., A. A. A. General.

HEADQUARTERS DEPARTMENT OF NEW MEXICO,
Santa Fé, N. M., September 20, 1863.

GENERAL: I have the honor to report that Mr. John A. Clarke, the surveyor general of the Territory of New Mexico, has returned from his visit to the newly-discovered gold fields. He has written to me a letter giving a brief synopsis of his observations, a copy of which please to find herewith enclosed.

General Clarke is very careful to keep well within bounds in all he says about the gold, as he desires to give rise to no expectations which may not be realized. That there is a large and rich mineral region between the San Francisco mountains and the Colorado river there can be no doubt.

I am making preparations to establish a military post of two companies of infantry at or near the mines; and it is my purpose to have the troops leave the Rio Grande for that point some time about the 10th proximo.

I beg again respectfully to urge upon the War Department the expediency as well as the necessity of having an appropriation for the making of a road from the Rio Grande to the new gold fields, and thence to Fort Mojave on the Colorado river. From the latter point there is already a road up the Mojave river through the Cajon Pass to Los Angeles. Mail facilities should also be put upon the road. The new government of Arizona, if it ever come, will be at the gold fields, not at the insignificant village of Tucson.

I am, general, very respectfully, your obedient servant,

JAMES H CARLETON,
Brigadier General, Commanding.

Brigadier General LORENZO THOMAS,
Adjutant General U. S. A., Washington, D. C.

Official:

ERASTUS W. WOOD,
Captain 1st Vet. Inf. C. V., A. A. A. General.

HEADQUARTERS DEPARTMENT OF NEW MEXICO,
Santa Fé, N. M., September 20, 1863.

MY DEAR SIR: Knowing the great interest which you feel in all matters that will increase the prosperity of our country—and more particularly, at this time, in all matters that relate to its moneyed resources—I have ventured to write to you concerning the new gold fields recently discovered near the San Francisco mountains, on the 35th parallel, and between the Rio Grande and the Rio Colorado. Surveyor General Clarke, of this Territory, has just returned from these new gold fields, and has written a letter to myself, giving a brief account of what he saw. General Clarke is prudent in his expressions, lest extravagant expectations might be raised on what he says, leading to disappointment. From what he says, and from what I learn from other sources, a large region of country, extending from near the head of the Gila along the southern slope of the Sierra Blanca, Sierra Mogollon, (copper mountain,) San Francisco mountains, and thence to the Colorado, is uncommonly rich, even compared with California, in gold, silver, cinnabar, and copper. On the Prieta affluent to the Gila, from the north, gold was found by my scouting parties last winter as high as "forty cents to the pan." And veins of argentiferous galena were found which, I am informed by the best of authority, yielded more than a dollar to the pound of crude ore. If I can but have troops to whip away the Apaches, so that prospecting parties can explore the country and not be in fear all the time of being murdered, you will without the shadow of a doubt find that our country has mines of the precious metals unsurpassed in richness, number, and extent by any in the world. Rich copper, in quantity enough to supply the world, is found at the head of the Gila. Some of this copper abounds in gold. Some is pure enough for commerce with but very little refining. The gold is pure.

I send you herewith a specimen of copper from near Fort West, on the Gila, and two specimens of pure gold from the top of Antelope mountain, spoken of by General Clarke. These specimens were sent to me by Mr. Swilling, the discoverer of the new gold fields, near the San Francisco mountains. If it be not improper, please give the largest piece of the gold to Mr. Lincoln. It will gratify him to know that Providence is blessing our country, even though it chasteneth.

Now, would it not be wise for Congress to take early action in legislating for such a region; to open roads; to give force to subjugate the Indians; to give mail facilities; to claim rights of seigniorage in the precious metals, which will help pay our debts, &c.?

To so eminent a statesman as yourself it will be sure to occur that timely steps should be taken for the development and security of so rich a country.

Pray pardon my having trespassed upon your time, and believe me to be,

Very respectfully, your obedient servant,

JAMES H. CARLETON,
Brigadier General, Commanding.

Hon. SALMON P. CHASE,
Secretary of the Treasury, Washington, D. C.

Official:

ERASTUS W. WOOD,
Captain 1st Vet. Inf. C. V., A. A. A. General.

DEPARTMENT OF NEW MEXICO, ASSISTANT ADJUTANT GENERAL'S OFFICE,
Santa Fé, N. M., October 17, 1863.

COLONEL: In reply to your communication of this date, I am directed by the general commanding to state that the four horses and one mule belonging to the Navajo Indians are not to be taken from them, but that they be sent with these Indians to the Bosque Redondo.

I am, colonel, very respectfully, your obedient servant,

BEN. C. CUTLER,
Assistant Adjutant General.

Colonel M. STECK,
Superintendent of Indian Affairs, Santa Fé, N. M.

Official:

ERASTUS W. WOOD,
Captain 1st Vet. Inf. C. V., A. A. A. General.

DEPARTMENT OF NEW MEXICO, ASSISTANT ADJUTANT GENERAL'S OFFICE,
Santa Fé, N. M., October 21, 1863.

SIR: I have the honor to acknowledge the receipt of your communication of the 18th instant, reporting the arrival at your post of certain Navajo chiefs, who wish to make peace for their people.

In reply, I am directed by the department commander to say that the Navajo Indians have no choice in the matter: they must come in and go to the Bosque Redondo, or remain in their own country, at war. The commanding officer at Fort Wingate has received instructions to send by first practicable opportunity to Santa Fé all Navajo Indians who have been taken prisoners, or who may give themselves up. An exception will be made to this rule in the cases of the man Ché and his wife, and the woman Paulonia and her children. No other Navajoes will be allowed to remain at Fort Wingate, and if the large band of Indians of which you write are in the vicinity of your post they will be sent at once to Santa Fé, *en route* for Bosque Redondo. They will be fed, well cared for, and provided with a suitable escort. All stock of every description which may be brought in by, or taken with, these Indians, (except such as proves to be the property of the United States,) will be sent with them to the Bosque Redondo.

The department commander having decided that all Navajo Indians who desire peace must go to the Bosque Redondo, he directs me to say that further correspondence on this subject is unnecessary.

I am, sir, very respectfully, your obedient servant,

BEN. C. CUTLER,
Assistant Adjutant General.

COMMANDING OFFICER
At Fort Wingate, N. M.

Official:

ERASTUS W. WOOD,
Captain 1st Vet. Inf. C. V., A. A. A. General.

[Extract.]

DEPARTMENT OF NEW MEXICO, ASSISTANT ADJUTANT GENERAL'S OFFICE,
Santa Fé, N. M., October 22, 1863.

SIR: In reply to your communication of the 20th instant, asking for information concerning certain sum of money forwarded from Fort Stanton, New Mexico, to Santa Fé, by Sergeant Pablo Torres, company "A," 1st New Mexico volunteers, in June last, I am directed to inform you that the express to which you refer was attacked by Indians while *en route* to this place. On the 29th of last June Second Lieutenant W. H. Higdon, 5th infantry California volunteers, found the dead bodies of the two express men. He found several letters scattered around the bodies, some of them partially destroyed; he also found one hundred and nineteen dollars in legal tender notes, and some letters containing valuable papers which had been intrusted to his care by the sutler at Fort Stanton. The money was turned over to Captain E. B. Frink, 5th infantry California volunteers, the commanding officer of the company to which the murdered express man belonged, and the letters recovered were sent to their proper destination by Lieutenant Higdon. This officer made a statement to these headquarters regarding the money and valuables found on the bodies of the murdered express men.

* * * * * * * * * * *

I am, sir, very respectfully, your obedient servant,

BEN. C. CUTLER,
Assistant Adjutant General.

Hon. JOHN S. WATTS, *Santa Fé, N. M.*

Official:

ERASTUS W. WOOD,
Captain 1st Vet. Inf. C. V., A. A. A. General.

HEADQUARTERS DEPARTMENT OF NEW MEXICO,
Santa Fé, N. M., October 23, 1863.

COLONEL: You will cause to be said to all Navajoes that those who come in to go to Bosque Redondo—come in of their own accord—can bring with them, and take with them to the Bosque Redondo, all stock and other property of which they may be possessed. Stock will only be taken from those whom your parties may fall upon, not from those who voluntarily surrender. Tell them this by the first opportunity. It will doubtless have much influence with the rich men of the tribe.

I am, colonel, very respectfully,

JAMES H. CARLETON,
Brigadier General, Commanding.

Colonel CHRISTOPHER CARSON,
Com. Expedition against the Navajo Indians, Fort Canby, N. M.

Official:

ERASTUS W. WOOD,
Captain 1st Vet. Inf. C. V., A. A. A. General.

HEADQUARTERS DEPARTMENT OF NEW MEXICO,
Santa Fé, N. M., November 15, 1863.

SIR: Sixty or seventy Navajoes have come into San Miguel county and are robbing the people. They may come to attack and rob you. Be on your guard, and if small parties come about you be sure and destroy them. A spy on the summit of the mountain back of the spring could see any party coming across the plains from the north in the daytime. They will attempt to run out stock between you and Abo.

I am, sir, respectfully, &c.,

JAMES H. CARLETON,
Brigadier General, Commanding.

COMMANDER OF THE CAMP AT THE GALLINAS MOUNTAINS,
En route to Fort Stanton, N. M.

Official:

ERASTUS W. WOOD,
Captain 1st Vet. Inf. C. V., A. A. A. General.

HEADQUARTERS DEPARTMENT OF NEW MEXICO,
Santa Fé, N. M., November 15, 1863.

MAJOR: Some days since some sixty or seventy Navajoes crossed the country east of the Rio Grande and are now in San Miguel county. They have already captured one or two herds of sheep. They came on foot, but are doubtless by this time partially mounted. Now, these Indians will endeavor to escape with their booty down the plains east of Manzana, and will cross the river near La Joya or below Fort McRae. They will doubtless attempt to run off your stock; I trust they will not only not do this, but that you will destroy them.

I am, major, respectfully,

JAMES H. CARLETON,
Brigadier General, Commanding.

Major JOSEPH SMITH,
Commanding at Fort Stanton, N. M.

Official:

ERASTUS W. WOOD,
Captain 1st Vet. Inf. C. V., A. A. A General.

HEADQUARTERS DEPARTMENT OF NEW MEXICO,
Santa Fé, N. M., November 15, 1863.

GENERAL: I have the honor herewith to enclose a letter from the new superintendent of Indian affairs to the commander of Fort Sumner; a letter from the commander of Fort Sumner to myself, both in relation to Indians who have been collected at the Bosque Redondo. My indorsement on Captain Updegraff's letter is an order to Major Wallen, who has gone to Fort Sumner to relieve Captain Updegraff, as to what is to be done with the Mescalero Apaches.

The new superintendent of Indian affairs, Dr. Steck, who has gone to Washington, seems to have a confidence in the integrity of that noted band of murderers which is not entertained by myself. The troops have had much trouble in getting these Indians together. From his letter one would suppose that Mr. Labadie, the agent, had gotten them to move. You have been kept officially informed on all points connected with these Indians, and know that the agent has had nothing to do with the matter except to accompany the Indians from Fort Stanton to Fort Sumner, and to stay at the latter post with them. Mr. Labadie, however, I believe to be a good man and a good agent.

The superintendent seems not inclined to feed the Indians until they can get started upon their new ground sufficiently to support themselves. He seems to give himself but little anxiety about them, knowing that I will not see them starve.

I fear that, from some mistaken philanthropy, the experiment of having these Indians domesticated will be sadly interfered with. You may rest assured, if they be permitted to go back again to their mountains and cañons, everything in the way of subduing them will again have to be gone over with. Unless the War Department sends orders to the contrary, the Mescalero Apaches will remain where they are.

The point about their subsistence should be definitely determined. The Indian department here, I am satisfied, will not feed or care for them unless under positive instructions from Washington. When they need food I shall give it to them and send the abstracts to Washington, as heretofore directed by the Secretary of War.

It is to be very much regretted that there should be any conflict of opinion as to what is best to be done with these Indians.

Whatever the superintendent may desire to do, except to have them leave the Bosque Redondo, I shall certainly not oppose, but they shall not leave that point.

I am, general, very respectfully, your obedient servant,

JAMES H. CARLETON,
Brigadier General, Commanding.

Brigadier General LORENZO THOMAS,
Adjutant General U. S. A., Washington, D. C.

Official:

ERASTUS W. WOOD,
Captain 1st Vet. Inf. C. V., A. A. A. General.

HEADQUARTERS DEPARTMENT OF NEW MEXICO,
Santa Fé, N. M., November 22, 1863.

COLONEL: First Lieutenant William V. B. Wardwell, 1st cavalry California volunteers, leaves Santa Fé this morning, having under his charge one hundred and eighty-eight men, women and children of the Navajo tribe of Indians, *en route*, *via* Fort Union, for Fort Sumner. The transportation is ox-wagons as far as Fort Union. From that point they are to have such other transportation as the chief quartermaster may direct the depot quartermaster to give. It is important that they have no delay at Fort Union. They will be escorted thence to Fort Sumner by Captain Fritz, with thirty rank and file of his company. He will be charged especially to see that none of them escape. See that they have rations of flour, meat, salt, and half rations of sugar and coffee. See that they are treated with great kindness. Let Captain Fritz have four worn Sibley tents for the use of the women and children. These will be transferred to the acting assistant quartermaster at Fort Sumner.

The meat ration had better be beeves on the hoof as far as practicable. In this event gentle cattle should be selected.

You will please give your personal attention to see that these Indians are well cared for, and if you have not got the worn tents, this is your authority for drawing them from the depot quartermaster.

I am, colonel, very respectfully, your obedient servant,

JAMES H. CARLETON,
Brigadier General, Commanding.

Lieutenant Colonel WILLIAM MCMULLEN,
Commanding at Fort Union, N. M.

Official: ERASTUS W. WOOD,
Captain 1st Vet. Inf. C. V., A. A. A. General.

Through the chief quartermaster, who will please instruct Captain Davis as regards the transportation, and to have it ready when the Indians come.

HEADQUARTERS DEPARTMENT OF NEW MEXICO,
Santa Fé, N. M., November 22, 1863.

GENERAL: In my letter to you of September 6, 1863, the policy of moving the whole Navajo tribe of Indians on to a reservation at the Bosque Redondo, on the Pecos river, New Mexico, was advocated. Pursuant to that policy, all Navajoes whom we may capture, or who may voluntarily come in, are sent to Fort Sumner, which is at the Bosque Redondo. Enclosed herewith please find a list of Navajo captives who gave themselves up at Fort Wingate, and arrived here on the 21st instant. They number one hundred and eighty-eight men, women, and children. They leave for Fort Sumner this morning. Since they have surrendered I have heard of others who have come into Fort Wingate. When these have arrived at Fort Sumner, orders will be given to the commanding officer at that point to let four of the principal men among them return to the Navajo country, and tell all those of the tribe still at large what kind of a country they are to go to if they come in, and how those are treated who have surrendered and gone to that point. This will have a good effect, and I count confidently on getting the bulk of the tribe before the spring opens.

I beg to congratulate the War Department on the prospect now of ending forever all Navajo wars; and when once the tribe is quietly settled on the fine reservation alluded to, there is no reason why they will not be the most happy and prosperous and well-provided for Indians in the United States.

I am, general, very respectfully, your obedient servant,

JAMES H. CARLETON,
Brigadier General, Commanding.

Brigadier General LORENZO THOMAS,
Adjutant General U. S. A., Washington, D. C.

Official: ERASTUS W. WOOD,
Captain 1st Vet. Inf. C. V., A. A. A. General.

HEADQUARTERS DEPARTMENT OF NEW MEXICO,
Santa Fé, N. M., November 22, 1863.

MAJOR: To-day one hundred and eighty-eight men, women, and children of the Navajo tribe of Indians leave Santa Fé for the Bosque Redondo *via* Fort Union. I beg you will take particular pains to have these Indians located in a good place, and to see they have some shelter for their women and children. I learn that others have come in to Fort Wingate. These will soon be forwarded to you.

Among the Indians who leave here to-day is Delgadito. I have promised that he, and three others, named Cha-hay, Chiquito, and Tsee-é, shall return at once with the interpreter Jesus to the Navajo country, to let other Navajoes know what kind of a place the tribe is expected to move to, and to let the tribe know how those are treated who have gone to that point. Let those four Indians and Jesus have passports to return at once to Fort Wingate. The government seems to take great interest in this experiment of placing the nomadic Indians on reservations, and this exodus of the Navajo people from their country, to become a domesticated race, is an interesting subject to us all, and one fraught with great questions so far as the prospective wealth and advancement of New Mexico may go.

Of course, the subject of timely preparation of *acequias* and of grounds for next year's crops will demand and receive your earnest attention.

I am, major, very respectfully, you obedient servant,

JAMES H. CARLETON,
Brigadier General, Commanding.

Major HENRY D. WALLEN, U. S. A.,
Commanding Fort Sumner, N. M.

Official:

ERASTUS W. WOOD,
Captain 1st Vet. Inf. C. V., A. A. A. General.

HEADQUARTERS DEPARTMENT OF NEW MEXICO,
Santa Fé, N. M., November 23, 1863.

CAPTAIN: From the impossibility of transporting forage for your whole company in its journey as escort to Governor Goodwin to Fort Whipple, Arizona, you are hereby ordered to dismount all of the rank and file of your company, except twenty-five, and transfer the horses and horse equipments of all you thus dismount to the acting assistant quartermaster at Los Pinos, where they will be retained until you return. You will make out regular invoices of all this property to him and take regular receipts therefor. Sergeant Mandeville, and Privates Johnston, Reed, Spotts, Fletcher, Burk, and Tarrater, now here, are detailed to stay at Los Pinos, after they have come down to take care of your horses thus left behind, until you return. The men who are dismounted will proceed with you as part of the escort of Governor Goodwin.

I take this occasion to remind you of the necessity of the most thorough discipline among your men, and the greatest care of your horses. You will be sure that your horses are not ridden over one-third of the time by the watch, in order to keep them in strength ready for fighting.

You are admonished that you are to perform a most responsible duty through a country infested with hostile Indians from the moment you pass the Rio Grande; that constant vigilance, night and day, alone can save you from the great disaster of having the animals run off which belong to your company, as well as those which belong to the train and to the governor and suite. Your beef-cattle driven along upon the hoof you must guard with anxious care, or the Indians will get them, and with them your food. Your sentinels must be always on the alert—your men ready at all times to fall in at a moment's notice by night or day, to fight and defend your stock. You must inspect your men's arms the last thing at night and the last thing in the morning before the march is commenced. The men must sleep in their clothes with their arms by their side. You must have a few men in advance to see that there are no ambushes laid for your command to run into. You must have three or four men off on each flank to see that no enemy watches your movements. You must have a good rear-guard to bring up everything. Before you approach water, have a wide circuit made by yourself or trusty men, to see that no party lies in wait to pounce upon your stock when it is drinking. You and your company will be forever disgraced, if, after these instructions, you lose a hoof of stock.

All these rules must go into force the moment you cross the river, and must hold good until your return to Los Pinos. You yourself must never relax one moment in your vigilance. If this duty is performed well you will all have earned a high reputation; if ill, you are all sure to be disgraced, as I have said before.

10

Recollect that you and your men petitioned to be put upon this duty. Now let us all see the metal you are made of. Wishing you good fortune,

I am, captain, very respectfully, your obedient servant,

JAMES H. CARLETON,
Brigadier General, Commanding.

Captain JOHN H. BUTCHER,
Company H, 11th Mo. Cav. Vols., Los Pinos, N. M.

Through commanding officer.

Official:

ERASTUS W. WOOD,
Captain 1st Vet. Inf. C. V., A. A. A. General.

HEADQUARTERS DEPARTMENT OF NEW MEXICO,
Santa Fé, N. M., November 28, 1863.

MAJOR: Private Porter, of Cremony's cavalry company, has informed me that that company had found and was on the trail of Navajo Indians who were running off sheep a few days since, and that the company turned back and gave up the pursuit; that Sergeant Roberts offered to go on, even to the Rio Grande, if he could have only ten men. This has been a source of great mortification and pain to me. This is the first time Cremony has had a good chance to distinguish himself. Pray inquire into the facts. If he was not justified in turning back, your duty is plain. The troops in New Mexico had better quit the country if this is a sample of their perseverance.

If they had gotten out of rations they could have eaten horses. There was a prospect of some ten thousand sheep, as I am informed, which would have been good food if they had been caught.

This is the first instance on record where Californians, with Indians to track, have quit a warm trail. What reason can be given to justify such a course passes beyond my comprehension.

Respectfully, your obedient servant,

JAMES H. CARLETON,
Brigadier General, Commanding.

Major HENRY D. WALLEN,
Commanding Fort Sumner, N. M.

Official:

ERASTUS W. WOOD,
Captain 1st Vet. Inf. C. V., A. A. A. General.

HEADQUARTERS DEPARTMENT OF NEW MEXICO,
Santa Fé, N. M., December 5, 1863.

COLONEL: As I have before written to you, I have not authority to grant you a leave, but it is important that before long we have a consultation about further operations against the Navajoes. Therefore, as soon as you have secured one hundred captive Navajo men, women, and children, you will turn over the command of the troops and post of Fort Canby to Captain Casey, United States army, and come with those captives to Santa Fé. You will take all captives which may then be at Fort Wingate, and bring them in as well. Major Sena, Captain Pfeiffer, and Lieutenant Abeyta and Dr. Shout, may come as part of the escort to the Indians.

It is desirable that you go through the Cañon de Chelly before you come. It is also desirable that you try that murderer and have your court adjourn *sine die*. No other officers than those named will come with you. Captain Casey will be instructed to press the campaign against the Navajoes to the best of his ability while you are absent. If you have more than a hundred captives bring them all. Do not leave in Fort Canby, as servants or otherwise, one single Indian man, woman, or child of any tribe; and when you come by Fort

Wingate, make a clean sweep of every Indian man, woman, or child, whether held as servants or otherwise, at that post. Please forward no more applications for leaves of absence.

I am, colonel, very respectfully, your obedient servant,

JAMES H. CARLETON,
Brigadier General, Commanding.

Colonel CHRISTOPHER CARSON,
Commanding Navajo Expedition, Fort Canby, N. M.

Official:

ERASTUS W. WOOD,
Captain 1st Vet. Inf. C. V., A. A. A. General.

HEADQUARTERS DEPARTMENT OF NEW MEXICO,
Santa Fé, N. M., December 10, 1863.

SIR: I have had the honor to receive the proceedings of a board of officers assembled at Fort Bascom in November last, to make a schedule of property seized from persons who were believed to be violating the law regulating trade and intercourse with Indians.

You will confiscate the liquor and powder which they had, and deliver up to them all the rest of their property. You will inform them of the law, and of the penalty for breaking it. They were doubtless ignorant of its existence.

I am, sir, very respectfully, your obedient servant,

JAMES H. CARLETON,
Brigadier General, Commanding.

COMMANDING OFFICER *at Fort Bascom, N. M.*

Official:

ERASTUS W. WOOD,
Captain 1st Vet. Inf. C. V., A. A. A. General.

HEADQUARTERS DEPARTMENT OF NEW MEXICO,
Santa Fé, N. M., December 10, 1863.

COLONEL: Captain Greene will never cease his energetic course in recovering stock and in pursuing Indians. He hardly gives us time to talk over and admire his praiseworthy efforts before we get new information of some new and successful raid. No one in this department has a more substantial reputation for energy, perseverance, and dash than Captain Greene; and if he desires any help in any way from me, he has but to name it.

Do what is right and proper with regard to giving Don Pedro Garcia a part of the sheep alluded to in Captain Greene's letter of the 3d instant.

I am, colonel, very respectfully, your obedient servant,

JAMES H. CARLETON,
Brigadier General, Commanding.

Colonel EDWIN A. RIGG,
Commanding at Fort Craig, N. M.

Official:

ERASTUS W. WOOD,
Captain 1st Vet. Inf. C. V., A. A. A. General.

HEADQUARTERS DEPARTMENT OF NEW MEXICO,
Santa Fé, N. M., December 12, 1863.

GENERAL: Many of the Navajo women and children which we captured are quite naked, and the children, especially, suffer from the extreme cold. The superintendent of Indian affairs is away in the States, and neither money nor instructions have been left by him, with which or under which blankets or clothing can be procured for them. It is hard to see them perish. Will the War Department authorize the quartermaster department here to buy some cheap blankets for the destitute children, and to issue condemned clothing to these Indians until they can get a start at the Bosque Redondo towards clothing themselves? The Indian department here will do nothing unless under express and urgent instructions from Washington.

I am, general, very respectfully, your obedient servant,

JAMES H. CARLETON,
Brigadier General, Commanding.

Brigadier General LORENZO THOMAS,
Adjutant General U. S. A., Washington, D. C.

Official:

ERASTUS W. WOOD,
Captain 1st Vet. Inf. C. V., A. A. A. General.

HEADQUARTERS DEPARTMENT OF NEW MEXICO,
Santa Fé, N. M., December 18, 1863.

MAJOR: There are many Navajoes near Red river, who are sending off small parties with stock across the plains, by Galinas mountains, to cross the Rio Grande. See if you cannot intercept and destroy these small parties. Be on the lookout all the time. Unless you are careful they will get your stock.

I am, major, very respectfully, your obedient servant,

JAMES H. CARLETON,
Brigadier General, Commanding.

Major JOSEPH SMITH,
Commanding Fort Stanton, N. M.

Official:

ERASTUS W. WOOD,
Captain 1st Vet. Inf. C. V., A. A. A. General.

HEADQUARTERS DEPARTMENT OF NEW MEXICO,
Santa Fé, N. M., December 18, 1863.

SIR: On the receipt of this letter you will send all the effective men of Captain Shaw's company on a twenty days' scout, over in the Rita Quemado country and south of that, to kill every Navajo man that can be found in that section of the country. Women and children will be captured, but not harmed. If the troops start and march mostly by night, and are cautious about fires and noises, it is believed they will destroy many Indian warriors of this tribe. It is believed that just now there are parties of Indians going through by that way and south of there, from the Rio Grande, with stock.

Respectfully, your obedient servant,

JAMES H. CARLETON,
Brigadier General, Commanding.

COMMANDING OFFICER *Fort Wingate, N. M.*

Official:

ERASTUS W. WOOD,
Captain 1st Vet. Inf. O. V., A. A. A. General.

HEADQUARTERS DEPARTMENT OF NEW MEXICO,
Santa Fé, N. M., December 19, 1863.

GENERAL: Enclosed herewith I have the honor to forward a letter addressed to myself, which was written by the Reverend P. Equillon, vicar general of New Mexico, asking permission to have fifteen boys and ten girls of the captive Navajoes to educate in the Catholic schools at Santa Fé; and asks that, if the government will agree to this, it will authorize the food and clothing of these children be furnished at the expense of the United States.

This offer and request of the vicar general is a liberal one, and should, in my opinion, be accepted. Once these children become educated, they can be sent to teach others of their tribe on the reservation at Fort Sumner.

Mr. Equillon is a man of great piety and learning, and a practical philanthropist. He is very anxious to superintend the education of these children himself. He will be greatly disappointed if the government refuse his request. His rank in the church, his learning, and his pure and exalted character, are sufficient guarantees that he will do all that can be done for the benefit of these children if he may be permitted to have them.

I am, general, very respectfully, your obedient servant,

JAMES H. CARLETON,
Brigadier General, Commanding.

Brigadier General LORENZO THOMAS,
Adjutant General U. S. A., Washington, D. C.

Official :

ERASTUS W. WOOD,
Captain 1st Vet. Inf. C. V., A. A. A. General.

HEADQUARTERS DEPARTMENT OF NEW MEXICO,
Santa Fé, N. M., December 19, 1863.

SIR : Enclosed herewith is a letter from Governor Connelly about Navajo Indians being at or near La Sierra (Mesal.) Rica, on the Canadian. Go yourself, with the effective men of Bergmann's company, and pursue and destroy these Indians. Keep the field for twenty days, and report the result. Captain Fritz's company, from Union, and Cremony's, from Sumner, will be out on the same duty. Let me see who accomplishes the most.

I am, sir, very respectfully, your obedient servant,

JAMES H. CARLETON,
Brigadier General, Commanding.

COMMANDING OFFICER *at Fort Bascom, N. M.*

Official :

ERASTUS W. WOOD,
Captain 1st Vet. Inf. C. V., A. A. A. General.

HEADQUARTERS DEPARTMENT OF NEW MEXICO,
Santa Fé, N. M., December 19, 1863.

MAJOR : Please find enclosed herewith a letter from Governor Connelly about a band of Navajo Indians being at La Sierra (Mesal.) Rica, near the Canadian. Send the effective men of Cremony's company, with Cremony in command, on a twenty days' scout, (with bread, meat, sugar, and coffee,) to pursue and destroy these Indians. Fritz and Bergmann have been sent on the same duty. Let me know who does the most. Some Apaches might be permitted to go as trailers.

Respectfully, your obedient servant,

JAMES H. CARLETON,
Brigadier General, Commanding.

Major HENRY D. WALLEN, U. S. A.,
Commanding at Fort Sumner, N. M.

Official:

ERASTUS W. WOOD,
Captain 1st Vet. Inf. C. V., A. A. A. General.

HEADQUARTERS DEPARTMENT OF NEW MEXICO,
Santa Fé, N. M., December 19, 1863.

COLONEL : Enclosed herewith please find a copy of a letter, dated the 18th instant, from Governor Connelly in relation to Navajo Indians being at or near La Sierra (Mesal.) Rica, near the Canadian river. You will at once send the effective men of Captain Fritz's company to that point, with orders to pursue and destroy those Indians. The company will be out for twenty-five days. A similar letter to this is written to Bascom and to Sumner, and troops from those posts will be sent on the same duty. Give orders for all the details. Call on Captain Davis for the transportation. Don't let the troops be anchored to a train. They must go light or they will accomplish nothing. Tell Captain Fritz, *for once*, I hope he will catch the Indians. McCleave is ahead of him as yet.

Respectfully, your obedient servant,

JAMES H. CARLETON,
Brigadier General, Commanding.

Lieutenant Colonel WILLIAM MCMULLEN,
Commanding at Fort Union, N. M.

Official :

ERASTUS W. WOOD,
Captain 1st Vet. Inf. C. V., A. A. A. General.

HEADQUARTERS DEPARTMENT OF NEW MEXICO,
Santa Fé, N. M., December 20, 1863.

GENERAL : Enclosed herewith please find the official report of Colonel Carson's last scout after the Navajo Indians. I beg to call the attention of the War Department to what he says of the destitute condition of that peaceable and gentle tribe of Indians known as the Moquis.

A copy of a private letter from Major Henry D. Wallen, United States army, commanding at Fort Sumner, New Mexico, will be found enclosed herewith. It gives an interesting account of the feelings, condition, and prospects of the Apache and Navajo Indians gathered together at that point.

I am, general, very respectfully, your obedient servant,

JAMES H. CARLETON,
Brigadier General, Commanding.

Brigadier General LORENZO THOMAS,
Adjutant General U. S. A., Washington, D. C.

Official :

ERASTUS W. WOOD,
Captain 1st Vet. Inf. C. V., A. A. A. General.

HEADQUARTERS DEPARTMENT OF NEW MEXICO,
Santa Fé, N. M., December 20, 1863.

MAJOR : Your very interesting private letter, setting forth the feelings, condition, and prospects of the Indians under your charge, I have taken the liberty to send to the War Department.

You will exercise your own discretion on the subject of the diminution of the ration for the Indians. Mr. Labadie's views of that subject seem to be sound and practicable.

It is hoped this time that Captain Cremony will march with more judgment, and will report some results. That you have a plenty of hostile Navajoes near you there is no doubt. Did Cadetta, Blanco, and Chatto go out after the Mescaleros ?

I am, major, very respectfully, your obedient servant,

JAMES H. CARLETON,
Brigadier General, Commanding.

Major HENRY D. WALLEN, U. S. A.,
Commanding at Fort Sumner, N. M.

Official :

ERASTUS W. WOOD,
Captain 1st Vet. Inf. C. V., A. A. A. General.

HEADQUARTERS DEPARTMENT OF NEW MEXICO,
Santa Fé, N. M., December 21, 1863.

SIR : This will be handed to you by Don Anastacio Sandoval, of this city, who is a man of note here. He has just heard of the loss of his herd of 7,000 sheep from near Mesa Rica, on Red river. Mr. Sandoval knows all that section of country. You will send troops in pursuit of the Indians who stole these sheep. You will receive by mail an order to this effect. Mr. Sandoval will go with the troops. Care should be taken to not break down the horses before the Indians are come up with.

Now, I hope that we shall not hear that the troops turn back without the stock. The trail of these sheep can be followed. Give orders, if the party gets out of rations, for meat to be bought if any can be found; if none can be found, the troops can feed upon their pack-mules, and finally upon their horses; but they must not turn back, when once the trail is struck, until the stock is recovered, if they go to the furthest boundary of the Navajo country.

In case Fritz's company is already out, mount some infantry. Be careful, or the Indians will get your own and the herds of the depot quartermaster.

I am, sir, very respectfully, your obedient servant,

JAMES H. CARLETON,
Brigadier General, Commanding.

COMMANDING OFFICER *at Fort Union, N. M.*

Official:

ERASTUS W. WOOD,
Captain 1st Vet. Inf. C. V., A. A. A. General.

HEADQUARTERS DEPARTMENT OF NEW MEXICO,
Santa Fé, N. M., December 23, 1863.

GENERAL: Please find enclosed herewith a report by Major Henry D. Wallen, United States 9th infantry, commanding Fort Sumner, New Mexico, of a fight which took place within thirty-five miles of that post between parties sent out from the post and one hundred and thirty Navajo Indians. The result was, twelve Navajoes were left dead upon the field and one was taken prisoner. Many were doubtless wounded, but these were borne away. Our people captured nine thousand eight hundred and eighty-nine sheep and a good deal of other property.

I beg to call your attention to the conduct of Lieutenant Newbold, United States 5th infantry, who led the handful of cavalry, and also to the conduct of Mr. Lorenzo Labadie, Indian agent, and to the gallant chaplain of Fort Sumner, the Reverend Mr. Fialon. These two gentlemen, at the head of thirty Mescalero Apache Indians from the reservation at Fort Sumner, (Apaches who, one year ago, were our mortal enemies,) did most all the work, as they were fortunate in being the first to encounter the Navajoes.

Captain Bristol and Lieutenant McDermott, United States 5th infantry, at the head of their companies, manifested the utmost zeal and alacrity on this occasion, but were unable to get up in time to participate in the affair. It was a handsome little battle on the open plains.

The Apache chiefs, Cadella and Blanco, were very distinguished. One of their braves, named Alazan, was mortally wounded.

I beg to have authority to issue a suit of clothes to each of these thirty Apaches who took part in this fight. The government should give them some token of its appreciation of such fidelity and gallantry. They volunteered for the service, and fought without the hope of reward.

I am, general, very respectfully, your obedient servant,

JAMES H. CARLETON,
Brigadier General, Commanding.

Brigadier General LORENZO THOMAS,
Adjutant General U. S. A., Washington, D. C.

Official:

ERASTUS W. WOOD,
Captain 1st Vet. Inf. C. V., A. A. A. General.

HEADQUARTERS DEPARTMENT OF NEW MEXICO,
Santa Fé, N. M., December 23, 1863.

SIR: The interpreter at Fort Wingate, Jesus, with Delgadito, and three other Navajo Indians, who have been with Jesus to Fort Sumner, leave here this morning for Fort Wingate, *via* Jemez. I told Colonel Chavez that Jesus and Delgadito would go on with him, but, on reflection, I have concluded not to let them go. Jesus will be needed at Fort Wingate, and Delgadito is wanted to go out among other Navajoes to induce them to move. You will let Delgadito and the three Indians who are with him go out among their people, free to go where they please. But when they come back, if they should come back, they are not to be permitted to lurk around the post, but will be sent in with all the Indians who come in with them. I count on good results in letting these Indians run at large, for they will tell the others how we are treating those who have already surrendered. Let me know the day they leave your post to go out among their people. Jesus will stay at Fort Wingate.

I am, sir, respectfully, your obedient servant,

JAMES H. CARLETON,
Brigadier General, Commanding.

COMMANDING OFFICER *at Fort Wingate, N. M.*

Official:

ERASTUS W. WOOD,
Captain 1st Vet. Inf. C. V., A. A. A. General.

HEADQUARTERS DEPARTMENT OF NEW MEXICO,
Santa Fé, N. M., December 24, 1863.

DEAR SIR: I have the honor to enclose, for your information, a copy of a letter from myself to Major Wallen, commanding at Fort Sumner, and a copy of his reply. One of the first things to be got and sent out, and they should be sent by express, will be three strong "breaking-up ploughs." Pray send out a large lot of garden seeds, and get clothing and agricultural implements sent out *at once.* These matters demand your immediate attention. I will send you a paper giving an account of a late fight near Fort Sumner.

I am, sir, respectfully, your obedient servant,

JAMES H. CARLETON,
Brigadier General, Commanding.

MATHEW STECK,
Sup't of Indian Affairs, Territory of New Mexico, Santa Fé, N. M.

Official:

ERASTUS W. WOOD,
Captain 1st Vet. Inf. C. V., A. A. A. General.

HEADQUARTERS DEPARTMENT OF NEW MEXICO,
Santa Fé, N. M., December 24, 1863.

MAJOR: Dr. Bryan will send to Dr. Courtwright 50 bed-sacks and 100 blankets for the Indian hospital. They will be sent to Fort Union in a day or two.

There are no "breaking-up ploughs" here—not one. Borrow Giddings's. I shall send to Dr. Steck to buy and send send some out. This will take time. Shall send you down some small ploughs. If the ground be well wet small ploughs will do better than none. What with spades, hoes, small ploughs, the plough you have, and Giddings's, a good deal of land can be got ready to plant by April 1, 1864.

There are no Navajo goods here except some wool cards. Shall send you a lot of these. The owners of the sheep will come for them. You will require them to give to the Apaches who helped to recapture them enough wethers to be a suitable reward. The law allows a certain percentage, but I do not know how much. It is left to yourself to determine what would be right for the Apaches. The troops, of course, want nothing.

In consideration of the gallantry of the Apaches in the late affair, you are authorized to let a number of them, *not to exceed five,* have passports to go, first to Fort Stanton, and then from there, under new passports, out in the Mescalero country, *to try to induce the remainder of the tribe to come in.* You will send men who leave families behind. Their passes will be for sixty days, when they will report at Fort Sumner. They should be told how important it is for all who wish to come to come at once, to prepare for next year's planting. Write to Major Smith precisely what they go for, and so that he may give passes from his own post, and food to those coming in, when they reach his post.

If Captain Cremony, when out on the late scout, did not exercise energy in his pursuit of Indians, as is indicated in your letter, your duty is plain. It is very expensive keeping cavalry at Fort Sumner. He has a fine company, and if his men are properly led and handled would be of great service. You must keep that lower country free of hostile Navajoes. If Cremony is not the man to be at the head of his men to lead them, you must get some other leader. Of this you must judge ; but that company must keep all Navajoes off of a circuit of sixty miles' radius from your post.

I am, major, very respectfully, your obedient servant,

JAMES H. CARLETON,
Brigadier General, Commanding.

Major HENRY D. WALLEN, U. S. A.,
Commanding at Fort Sumner, N. M.

Official: ERASTUS W. WOOD,
Captain 1st Vet. Inf. C. V., A. A. A. General.

HEADQUARTERS DEPARTMENT OF NEW MEXICO,
Santa Fé, N. M., December 25, 1863.

SIR: It is important that you send a force, say of twenty mounted men, under a reliable, energetic officer, who, if he gets upon a trail of Indians, will not wish to turn back without some results, to the Abo Pass, to remain there and in that neighborhood twenty days, to watch for Navajoes coming from the direction of the Pecos, with or without stock, and to attack any and all parties it may find of these Indians. There are small bands of these Indians coming through to cross near the mouth of the Puerco. These may be intercepted. If Casa Colorado would be a better point, with pickets patrolling out towards the mountains to cut trails going east or west, you can send the party there.

It is hoped that this party may have as good luck as one had which was sent from Fort Sumner recently.

I am, sir, very respectfully, your obedient servant,

JAMES H. CARLETON,
Brigadier General, Commanding.

COMMANDING OFFICER *at Los Pinos, N. M.*

Official: ERASTUS W. WOOD,
Captain 1st Vet. Inf. C. V., A. A. A. General.

HEADQUARTERS DEPARTMENT OF NEW MEXICO,
Santa Fé, N. M., December 25, 1863.

SIR: I learn that Navajo Indians, in small parties, are crossing the Rio Grande near Alameda, and are depredating upon the stock in that neighborhood. You will send an efficient officer with twenty or thirty of your best men, mounted, (whether of artillery or infantry,) up to that part of the valley, or above, to stay there for twenty days, and to pursue and attack any parties of Navajoes which may have come in during that time. By having patrols moving up and down the river trails would be cut almost as soon as made. The party can remain at or near Bernalillo or Alameda, as shall be considered best.

I am, sir, very respectfully, your obedient servant,

JAMES H. CARLETON,
Brigadier General, Commanding.

COMMANDING OFFICER *at Albuquerque, N. M.*

Official: ERASTUS W. WOOD,
Captain 1st Vet. Inf. C. V., A. A. A. General.

HEADQUARTERS DEPARTMENT OF NEW MEXICO,
Santa Fé, N. M., December 31, 1863.

COLONEL: I regretted to hear that the Indians had run off thirty-eight of your best mules. It appears to me that if they prowl around your herds in this manner some stratagem might be used so as to decoy them to the neighborhood of a force strong enough to destroy them. It is hoped, hereafter, your command will be able to protect its own stock.

If Captain Casey can furnish mules to carry provisions for the expedition through the Cañon de Chelly, but not the men's blankets, you will not delay the expedition on account of lack of transportation. You will have the men carry their blankets and, if necessary, three or four days' rations in haversacks. The army of the Potomac carries eight days' rations in haversacks. Unless some fatigue and some privations are encountered by your troops the Indians will get the best of it.

Captain McFerran will soon send you some more mules. I sincerely hope we have had the last report of the Indians running off stock in the Navajo country.

Now, while the snow is deep, is the true time to make an impression on the tribe. You will give your chief quartermaster positive orders that, when expeditions leave Fort Canby for scouts, not to exceed twelve days, the men will be required to carry their blankets and greatcoats for the first eight days.

There is now a large party of citizens and Utes in the Navajo country after Indians. They started from Abiquia.

I am, colonel, very respectfully, your obedient servant,

JAMES H. CARLETON,
Brigadier General, Commanding.

Colonel CHRISTOPHER CARSON,
Commanding Navajo Expedition, Fort Canby, N. M.

Official: ERASTUS W. WOOD,
Captain 1st Vet. Inf. C. V., A. A. A. General.

LETTERS RELATING TO INDIAN AFFAIRS IN THE DEPARTMENT OF NEW MEXICO, DURING THE YEAR 1864.

HEADQUARTERS DEPARTMENT OF NEW MEXICO,
Santa Fé, N. M., January 11, 1864.

GENERAL: I have the honor to enclose the official report of a sharp little action with the Navajo Indians near Fort Sumner, New Mexico, on the Pecos river. You will see that great credit is due to Lieutenant Charles Newbold, United States 5th infantry, to Mr. Labadie, Indian agent, to Ojo Blanco, an Apache chief, and to several citizens and soldiers named in Major Wallen's report. The extreme severity of the weather doubtless was the reason why it happened that any of the Navajoes escaped.

Lieutenant Newbold's name is respectfully submitted for favorable consideration by the War Department.

I am, general, very respectfully, your obedient servant,

JAMES H. CARLETON,
Brigadier General, Commanding.

Brigadier General LORENZO THOMAS,
Adjutant General United States Army, Washington, D. C.

Official: ERASTUS W. WOOD,
Captain 1st Vet. Inf. C. V., A. A. A. General.

HEADQUARTERS DEPARTMENT OF NEW MEXICO,
Santa Fé, N. M., January 11, 1864.

SIR: I see that officers from your post go to Cubero. They have no duties there, and if they go "on leave," half their pay is stopped by the orders from the War Department. Send me an abstract of all officers of your command who have been absent at Cubero, or any other town, since October 31, 1863.

Every train going from Fort Wingate to Fort Canby will be escorted efficiently, and the escort will be commanded by an officer. The ammunition which will come to Fort Wingate with Captain Fritz will be strongly guarded to Fort Canby. The escort to each train should have spies on ahead, on the flanks, and in the rear, to prevent surprise. Shall the Indians *always* get the best of Fort Wingate troops?

Respectfully, &c.,

JAMES H. CARLETON,
Brigadier General, Commanding.

COMMANDING OFFICER, *Fort Wingate, N. M.*

Official: ERASTUS W. WOOD,
Captain 1st Vet. Inf. C. V., A. A. A. General.

HEADQUARTERS DEPARTMENT OF NEW MEXICO,
Santa Fé, N. M., January 12, 1864.

DEAR SIR: Your note of the 15th ultimo has just been received. Herewith you will find the message of the governor of New Mexico, indorsing the policy of putting the Navajo Indians on the reservation at Bosque Redondo. The legislature has unanimously approved this policy. Dr. Steck himself approved it before he left New Mexico, as I can prove. Every intelligent man in the country approves it. It will be the most unfortunate thing that ever happened to New Mexico and Arizona, the interfering with this policy. The Indians will go on as before. The great thoroughfare over the 35th parallel will be interrupted by them; people going to the new gold fields will be murdered; *and, after another fruitless season,* you will come to this policy at last. It is a pity that other motives, besides what is best for the country and the most humane for the Indians, should work to the disadvantage of the people, just now. We have made a good beginning, and if "let alone" this will be the last Navajo war.

Colonel Collins, who for years has been the superintendent, indorses the policy throughout, as you see by his paper. What motive influences Dr. Steck?

We had a sharp fight with the Navajoes on the 5th instant. You will see the account in the papers.

Very truly yours,

JAMES H. CARLETON,
Brigadier General, Commanding.

Hon. FRANCISCO PEREA,
Delegate in Congress from New Mexico, Washington, D. C.

Official:

ERASTUS W. WOOD,
Captain 1st Vet. Inf. C. V., A. A. A. General.

HEADQUARTERS DEPARTMENT OF NEW MEXICO,
Santa Fé, N. M., January 12, 1864.

GENERAL: I have just received a note from the Hon. Francisco Perea, delegate from New Mexico, in which he says: "Dr. Steck," (superintendent of Indian affairs for New Mexico,) "showed me a report which he is going to submit to the Indian department here, in which he disapproves your (my) policy to colonize the Navajo Indians, decidedly. He made several other allusions to your (my) campaign against them, which I did not like nor believe. He thinks it impossible to put the Navajo nation on the Pecos for the small space of irrigable lands at the Bosque," (Fort Sumner.)

I respectfully refer the War Department to the message of the governor of New Mexico, herewith enclosed, and which, with reference to Indian policy, was unanimously indorsed by the legislature. It is unhesitatingly indorsed by Colonel Collins, the late superintendent, and by Colonel Kit Carson, who has conduct of the campaign, and by every American and Mexican I have heard speak of the subject, Dr. Steck included, except Mr. Arny and Mr. Greiner, and I had not heard them say much for or against the policy.

It will be an unfortunate thing for New Mexico and Arizona if there be a change of policy, and you must come to this at last—depend upon it.

I am, general, very respectfully, your obedient servant,

JAMES H. CARLETON,
Brigadier General, Commanding.

NOTE.—As for the quantity of irrigable land at the Bosque Redondo, I believe there is more than enough; and even if there be not enough, the land at the Bosque Grande, twenty-five miles further down the river, can be used.

J. H. C.

Brigadier General LORENZO THOMAS,
Assistant Adjutant General U. S. A., Washington, D. C.

Official:

ERASTUS W. WOOD,
Captain 1st Vet. Inf. C. V., A. A. A. General.

HEADQUARTERS DEPARTMENT OF NEW MEXICO,
Santa Fé, N. M., January 12, 1864.

GENERAL: The general commanding this department addressed to you, this day, a communication in reference to a report about to be made by Dr. Steck, (superintendent of Indian affairs for this Territory,) disapproving of the policy now being pursued by the military authorities in this department towards colonizing the Navajo Indians.

I have the honor respectfully to state, for the information of the War Department, that on or about the last of October, 1863, I met Dr. Steck at Fort Union, New Mexico, *en route* for Washington city. I was present at the last interview Dr. Steck had with General Carleton. The doctor had that day arrived at Fort Union from Fort Sumner, at which post nearly eight hundred Apaches and Navajoes were collected. Dr. Steck, on this occasion, after having personally visited the Bosque Redondo and observed the condition of the Indians, approved, most cordially, the policy pursued towards them by General Carleton. He spoke of the Indians as being happy and contented; he gave it as his opinion that the Bosque Redondo was the only suitable place in New Mexico for a large Indian reservation; and the general tenor of his conversation was such as to impress me firmly with the belief that Dr. Steck intended to use his influence with the proper departments at Washington to have the policy of General Carleton, in this matter, carried out to the very letter.

I have the honor to be, general, very respectfully, your obedient servant,

BEN. C. CUTLER,
Assistant Adjutant General.

Brigadier General LORENZO THOMAS,
Adjutant General of the Army, Washington, D. C.

Official:

ERASTUS W. WOOD,
Captain 1st Vet. Inf. C. V., A. A. A. General.

HEADQUARTERS DEPARTMENT OF NEW MEXICO,
Santa Fé, N. M., January 15, 1864.

SIR: The general commanding directs me to say to you that Delgadito, having done so well in his recent trip into the Navajo country, need not be sent to the Bosque Redondo with the other Indians until further orders, but will be allowed to make other trips for the purpose of inducing more Navajoes to come in. The general thinks that if he would go to the Sierra Datil he would doubtless find some Navajoes there. Delgadito's family can remain at Fort Wingate until he goes to the Bosque if he so desires.

I am, sir, very respectfully, your obedient servant,

CYRUS H. DE FORREST, *Aide-de-Camp.*

COMMANDING OFFICER, *Fort Wingate, N. M.*

Official:

ERASTUS W. WOOD,
Captain 1st Vet. Inf. C. V., A. A. A. General.

DEPARTMENT OF NEW MEXICO, ASSISTANT ADJUTANT GENERAL'S OFFICE,
Santa Fé, N. M., February 2, 1864.

SIR: Colonel Carson, 1st cavalry New Mexico volunteers, will probably reach Los Pinos with about two hundred and forty Navajo Indians on the 5th instant.

I am directed by Major John C. McFerran, United States army, chief of staff at department headquarters, to say to you that it is the order of the general commanding that you send these Indians direct from Los Pinos to Fort Sumner, escorted by company K, 1st infantry California volunteers.

You will give the officer commanding the escort from Los Pinos, New Mexico, written instructions to use the utmost vigilance while these Indians are under his charge; he will see that they are well cared for, and that none of them escape on the road. After having taken the Indians safely to the Bosque Redondo, the commanding officer of company K, 1st infantry California volunteers, will report for duty, with his company, to the commanding officer of Fort Sumner, New Mexico.

I am, sir, very respectfully, your obedient servant,

BEN. C. CUTLER,
Assistant Adjutant General.

COMMANDING OFFICER, *Los Pinos, N. M.*

Official:

ERASTUS W. WOOD,
Captain 1st Vet Inf. C. V., A. A. A. General.

HEADQUARTERS DEPARTMENT OF NEW MEXICO,
Las Cruces, N. M., February 7, 1864.

GENERAL: I have the honor herewith to enclose a copy of the report of Colonel Christopher Carson, commanding the expedition against the Navajo Indians, of his success in marching a command through the celebrated *Cañon de Chelly*, the great stronghold of that tribe, and of the killing of twenty-three of the warriors and the capture of a large number of prisoners. These prisoners are now *en route* to the Bosque Redondo.

This report is accompanied by reports of Captain Asa B. Casey, United States army, and of Captain Albert H. Pfeiffer, of the 1st cavalry New Mexico volunteers, marked B and C. I also enclose a copy of a letter from Colonel Carson, written subsequent to his return to Fort Canby.

It will be seen by these papers that the operations of the troops during the severely cold weather has been of the most praiseworthy character, and been crowned with unparalleled success.

This is the first time any troops, whether when the country belonged to Mexico or since we acquired it, have been able to pass through the Cañon de Chelly, which, for its great depth, its length, its perpendicular walls, and its labyrinthine character, has been regarded by eminent geologists as the most remarkable of any "fissure" (for such it is held to be) upon the face of the globe. It has been the great fortress of the tribe since time out of mind. To this point they fled when pressed by our troops. Colonel Washington, Colonel Sumner, and many other commanders have made an attempt to go through it, but had to retrace their steps. It was reserved for Colonel Carson to be the first to succeed; and I respectfully request the government will favorably notice that officer, and give him a substantial reward for this crowning act in a long life spent in various capacities in the service of his country in fighting the savages among the fastnesses of the Rocky mountains.

Captain Asa B. Casey, of the United States 13th infantry, the chief quartermaster of the expedition against the Navajoes, volunteered for this march, and, as usual with this gallant and energetic officer, was particularly distinguished. I hope the government will reward him with the compliment of a brevet. He is entitled to a brevet for his gallantry in assisting the intrepid Captain William H. Lewis, United States 5th infantry, who burnt the Texan train in Apache cañon on the 28th of March, 1862, and richly deserves that and also a brevet for his distinguished services in the operations against the Navajoes. I am sure the government will not be unmindful of the labors of these officers and the brave soldiers who followed them, even though the field of their operations is far removed from the more important and brilliant events of the great war.

Sergeant Andreas Herrera, of company C, 1st cavalry New Mexico volunteers, it will be seen, has again distinguished himself, and it affords me great pleasure to call attention to his name.

I believe this will be the last Navajo war. The persistent efforts which have been and will continue to be made can hardly fail to bring in the whole tribe before the year ends. I beg respectfully to call the serious attention of the government to the destitute condition of the captives, and beg for authority to provide clothing for the women and children. Every preparation will be made to plant large crops for their subsistence at the Bosque Redondo the coming spring. Whether the Indian department will do anything for these Indians or not you will know. But whatever is to be done should be done at once. At all events, as I before wrote to you, "*we can feed them cheaper than we can fight them.*"

I am, general, very respectfully, your obedient servant,

JAMES H. CARLETON,
Brigadier General, Commanding.

Brigadier General LORENZO THOMAS,
Adjutant General U. S. A., Washington, D. C.

Official:

ERASTUS W. WOOD,
Captain 1st Vet. Inf. C. V., A. A. A. General.

DEPARTMENT OF NEW MEXICO, ASSISTANT ADJUTANT GENERAL'S OFFICE,
Santa Fé, N. M., February 14, 1864.

MAJOR: On the 8th instant Lieutenant Pettis, 1st infantry California volunteers, commanding company K of that regiment, started from Los Pinos, New Mexico, for the Bosque Redondo, having in charge about two hundred and thirty Navajo Indians. Lieutenant Pettis was directed to report to you for duty until further instructions were received from the general commanding.

I have received information from the commanding officer at Fort Wingate that about nine hundred Navajoes were at that post. Orders were sent, by last mail, that these Indians should be sent direct to Fort Sumner, escorted by company B, 1st cavalry California volunteers. The commanding officer of this company has orders to report to you for duty until the general commanding directs otherwise.

Captain A. F. Garrison, chief commissary, has been directed to send at once to Fort Sumner subsistence stores to feed at least fifteen hundred Indians in addition to those already at your post.

The expedition of Colonel Carson through the Cañon de Chelly has been a perfect success, and the Navajoes are coming in to Fort Canby in great numbers, and there is no doubt but that the greater portion of that tribe will proceed to the Bosque Redondo as soon as they can be furnished with transportation by the government.

Mr. Baker, who represents the superintendent of Indian affairs during his absence from this Territory, sent to the Indian agent at Fort Sumner, by a train which left Santa Fé yesterday, a quantity of goods to be distributed to the Indians at the Bosque Redondo—not a large supply, but all that he could spare.

The general commanding directs that you use every exertion to make these Indians as comfortable as circumstances will admit upon their arrival at Fort Sumner. Time is now precious, and having in view the approach of spring and the planting of a crop, the general directs that you see that the *acequias* are enlarged, and that such other steps are taken as you may deem proper to carry out what you know to be his views in regard to the Indians now being sent to the Bosque Redondo.

I am, major, very respectfully, your obedient servant,

BEN. C. CUTLER,
Assistant Adjutant General.

Major HENRY D. WALLEN, U. S. A.,
Commanding at Fort Sumner, N. M.

Official:

ERASTUS W. WOOD,
Captain 1st Vet. Inf. C. V., A. A. A. General.

HEADQUARTERS DEPARTMENT OF NEW MEXICO,
Albuquerque, N. M., February 19, 1864.

SIR: The general commanding directs me to say that as fast as practicable, after the Navajoes come in to your post, you will send them to Los Pinos, as it is cheaper to feed them on the Rio Grande than at your post.

You will also continue the campaign against that tribe as heretofore, that they may understand that hostilities are not discontinued against them on account of the number that have already delivered themselves up.

The general also directs that, by each express from your post, you send to department headquarters a statement showing the number of Navajoes captured, and who have delivered themselves up at your post, the number sent to Bosque Redondo, and the number remaining on hand. Each statement will include all who have come in and been sent away since the previous statement.

I am, sir, very respectfully, your obedient servant,

CYRUS H. DE FORREST, *Aide-de-Camp.*

COMMANDING OFFICER, *Fort Canby, N. M.*

Official:

ERASTUS W. WOOD,
Captain 1st Vet. Inf. C. V., A. A. A. General.

HEADQUARTERS DEPARTMENT OF NEW MEXICO,
Santa Fé, N. M., February 25, 1864.

MAJOR: In addition to the Indians already at the reservation at the Bosque Redondo, including those who went with Lieutenant Pettis, there are thirteen hundred now at Los Pinos, who will start for the Bosque to-day or to-morrow. Mr. Pettis will tell you how long they will probably be in coming.

You will be sure to make timely estimates for the bread and meat and salt required for all these Indians, and have a margin of food on hand of at least fifty days. There must be no mistake made about having enough for them to eat, even if we have to kill horses and mules for them. I have ordered Captain Garrison to get flour and meat to you as fast as possible. I count on your forecast, and shall endeavor to get everything which you may need and require; only you must make your requisitions, as you have the data. Count the Indians twice a month and report the number to these headquarters. Keep an exact history of the number and date of the arrival of all parties of Navajoes; of deaths and the cause; and of the births. Open a book for this purpose, that reference may be had to it from time to time for statistical information.

I hear this morning that there are thirteen hundred more at Canby and Wingate awaiting to come in. These must make over half of the whole tribe.

Major McFerran has caused to be sent to you two large ploughs, which were made here; two more are making at Fort Union, and we will endeavor to buy some. You should have at least eight ploughs running from now until the 10th of June for corn; until the 10th of July for beans, &c.

I am collecting large lots of seeds for you. Captain Craig has sent to Bascom to send over some yokes and chains with the cattle from that post. If they do not come soon send over for them, so as not to lose time.

The main thing to be done, while the ploughs are ruuuing, will be to have an *acequia-madre* of great capacity and length, so there will be no doubt of the supply of water being adequate to your wants. Estimate for hoes, spades, axes, kettles, &c., &c.

The responsibility resting upon you in starting properly this interesting colony is very great, but I know you to be equal to it. The government will not fail to appreciate and notice your labors. A copy of this letter will be sent to the War Department.

I am, major, very respectfully, your obedient servant,

JAMES H. CARLETON,
Brigadier General, Commanding.

Major HENRY D. WALLEN, U. S. A.,
Commanding at Fort Sumner, N. M.

Official:

ERASTUS W. WOOD,
Captain 1st Vet. Inf. C. V., A. A. A. General.

[Extract.]

HEADQUARTERS DEPARTMENT OF NEW MEXICO,
Santa Fé, N. M., February 26, 1864.

SIR: Send the two Mexican captives to the commanding officer at Los Pinos. Keep no people at your post awaiting advices from here. Send them all to Los Pinos. We cannot feed them at Wingate. Remember this, and make a weekly report of all you send. If Indians can come in to Fort Wingate they can be made to work along toward Los Pinos. If they are fed, and have food transported for them, they are well off. They must not be kept at Wingate. They must be employed in overcoming distance towards the Bosque Redondo.

Why has not the order been obeyed to send Captain Fritz's company in? Order it in at once. Feed corn or wheat to Indians, which otherwise Fritz's horses would have eaten. Issue, until further orders, only eighteen ounces of flour to a ration to your troops. Keep an account of the difference, so the companies can be paid money.

You must cut down on your rations in time. This sudden influx of Indians will embarrass us for a while. Keep none at your post. Move them at once towards the river. There we can provide for them. Send me a detailed report of all Navajoes who have surrendered at Wingate, with the date of coming in, and date of shipment to Los Pinos. Continue, then, these reports weekly. Keep all the statistics concerning them, so that the War Department may know exactly the history of their exodus.

* * * * * * * * * * *

I expect much from you. The great point to study is to save your own rations by getting the Indians away. If they could come to Wingate, they can come to Los Pinos.

Respectfully, your obedient servant,

JAMES H. CARLETON,
Brigadier General, Commanding.

COMMANDING OFFICER, *Fort Wingate, N. M.*

Official:

ERASTUS W. WOOD,
Captain 1st Vet. Inf. C. V., A. A. A. General.

DEPARTMENT OF NEW MEXICO, ASSISTANT ADJUTANT GENERAL'S OFFICE,
Santa Fé, N. M., February 26, 1864.

CAPTAIN: I have the honor to acknowledge the receipt of your communication of the 14th instant, reporting the arrival of large bodies of Navajo Indians at Fort Canby.

The general commanding directs that these Indians be sent with all practicable despatch to Los Pinos, New Mexico. Should your transportation be limited, or any of the Indians be unable to travel, you will send forward by every opportunity as many as you possibly can of the well ones, and allow those who are sick and crippled to remain at Fort Canby until they are able to stand the trip to the Rio Grande, or until you have transportation.

I have the honor to be, captain, very respectfully, your obedient servant,

BEN. C. CUTLER,
Assistant Adjutant General.

Captain ASA B. CASEY, U. S. A.,
Commanding at Fort Canby, N. M.

Official:

ERASTUS W. WOOD,
Captain 1st Vet. Inf. C. V., A. A. A. General.

DEPARTMENT OF NEW MEXICO, ASSISTANT ADJUTANT GENERAL'S OFFICE,
Santa Fé, N. M., February 26, 1864.

SIR: I am directed by the department commander to say to you, that as the Navajo Indians are now coming in and giving themselves up in great numbers, you will exercise a sound discretion in sending out scouting parties after them as long as they continue their present course. Indeed, you will not send out parties to attack them, unless in your judgment the exigencies of the case absolutely demand it.

I am, sir, very respectfully, your obedient servant,

BEN. C. CUTLER,
Assistant Adjutant General.

COMMANDING OFFICER, *Fort Wingate, N. M.*

Official:

ERASTUS W. WOOD,
Captain 1st Vet Inf. C. V., A. A. A. General.

HEADQUARTERS DEPARTMENT OF NEW MEXICO,
Santa Fé, N. M., February 27, 1864.

GENERAL: What with the Navajoes I have captured and those who have surrendered we have now over three thousand, and will, without doubt, soon have the whole tribe. I do not believe they number now much over five thousand, all told. You have doubtless seen the last of the Navajo war—a war that has been continued with but few intermissions for one hundred and eighty years, and which, during that time, has been marked by every shade of atrocity, brutality, and ferocity which can be imagined or which can be found in the annals of conflict between our own and the aboriginal race.

Our success, although hoped for and expected, has come upon us more suddenly than I anticipated. In consequence, it is found that our commissariat is hardly able to meet the large demands now made upon it. To provide against every contingency, I find it to be necessary to ask that you will telegraph to Fort Leavenworth to have sent thence by an express train two hundred thousand rations of subsistence at once.

We are bending all our energies to get corn, flour, meat, and salt to the Bosque Redondo, where the Indians are locating, and are making every effort to get lands ploughed and *acequias* dug preparatory to putting in a large crop at that point.

I beg to congratulate you and the country at large on the prospect that this formidable band of robbers and murderers have at last been made to succumb. To Colonel Christopher Carson, first cavalry New Mexico volunteers, Captain Asa B. Casey, United States army, and the officers and men who have served in the Navajo campaign, the credit for these successes is mainly due. The untiring labors of Major John C. McFerran, United States army, the chi f quartermaster of the department, who has kept the troops in that distant region supplied in spite of the most discouraging obstacles and difficulties—not the least of these the sudden dashes upon trains and herds in so long a line of communication—deserves the especial notice of the War Department.

I am, general, very respectfully, your obedient servant,

JAMES H. CARLETON,
Brigadier General, Commanding.

Brigadier General LORENZO THOMAS,
Adjutant General U. S. A., Washington, D. C.

Official:

ERASTUS W. WOOD,
Captain 1st Vet. Inf. C. V., A. A. A. General.

HEADQUARTERS DEPARTMENT OF NEW MEXICO,
Santa Fé, N. M., February 28, 1863.

MAJOR: Captain Bristol arrived here this morning. He said that flour seems to be unwholesome food for the Navajoes. It is, doubtless, because they do not cook their bread properly, and eat too much of it. They have been accustomed to food which had greater bulk in proportion to the nutriment it contained. I have ordered corn-meal to be sent to you for them, and have contracted for unbolted wheat-meal. Until this arrives issue wheat or corn to them as a change of food. They can make *matates*, and grind it as Mexicans do. You are admonished to see that the utmost economy is observed, both by troops and by the Indians, at your post. The drain now upon the commissariat is so great it will require every commander to give his personal attention to this matter, or we shall soon be upon diminished rations.

There are no more old tents to send you. The condemned tents have usually been ordered to be made up into sacks for corn. Your Navajoes must make wigwams. This brings me to the thought to ask you to plan a pueblo town for them. The buildings should be but one story high, and face to the *placitas*. By a proper arrangement—dead-wall on the outside, and the buildings arranged so as to mutually defend each other in fighting on the parapets—a very handsome and strong place could be made by the Indians themselves—that is, against small-arms. By having a judicious site selected, and the spare time of the families spent in putting up their houses, by next winter they can all be comfortably sheltered. Then to have trees planted to make shade, and I fancy there would be no Indian village in the world to compare with it in point of beauty. Over three thousand Navajoes have surrendered, and many are coming with stock which is their own. It was a condition, if they came voluntarily and surrendered with their stock, it should be theirs, and they should take it with them; if they held out, and we came and captured their stock, then the stock was ours. When these Indians with stock come, if they are willing to sell any that is not breeding stock, you can buy it, and pay what is fair for it, as fresh meat. This will alike teach them the relative value of stock and of money. In my opinion there are not over five thousand Navajoes in all. I believe I shall have them all at the Bosque within three months.

You have by far the most important command in this department. That you will exercise forecast and devote all your thoughts, time, and energy to the great work of colonizing this historic and formidable band of Indians, I fully believe.

I am, major, respectfully,

JAMES H. CARLETON,
Brigadier General, Commanding.

Major HENRY D. WALLEN, U. S. A.,
Commanding at Fort Sumner, N. M.

Official:

ERASTUS W. WOOD,
Captain 1st Vet. Inf. C. V., A. A. A. General.

HEADQUARTERS DEPARTMENT OF NEW MEXICO,
Santa Fé, N. M., February 29, 1864.

MAJOR: I desire that you give to the Indians at the Bosque Redondo all the hides and pelts of the cattle and sheep which are killed for them from flocks and herds sent for their subsistence, and not furnished by the contractor who delivers fresh beef at that post for the troops. If these hides do not furnish enough *parflesh* to make soles for their moccasins, you are authorized to purchase others from the contractor and issue for this purpose. An exact account must be made of these purchases by the quartermaster, and entered upon a separate abstract. The Indians to whom they are issued must receipt for them, and an officer witness their mark. It is possible that no one Indian will require a whole hide for himself and family; if not, he will receipt for one-fourth or one-half, as the case may be. These abstracts and receipt-rolls, sent through the chief quartermaster, will be approved by me.

I am, major, very respectfully, your obedient servant,

JAMES H. CARLETON,
Brigadier General, Commanding.

Major HENRY D. WALLEN, U. S. A.,
Commanding at Fort Sumner, N. M.

Official:

ERASTUS W. WOOD,
Captain 1st Vet. Inf. C. V., A. A. A. General.

HEADQUARTERS DEPARTMENT OF NEW MEXICO,
Santa Fé, N. M., March 3, 1864.

MAJOR: By the last advices from Captain Asa B. Casey, I learn that he has fifteen hundred Navajoes now at Fort Canby. I find it will be necessary to have made, at least, eight "breaking-up" ploughs, including those you have already had fabricated at Santa Fé and Fort Union, in order to have a sufficient amount of ground gotten ready for planting at the Bosque Redondo for those Indians. Please cause them to be made and sent to Fort Sumner at your earliest convenience.

Respectfully, your obedient servant,

JAMES H. CARLETON,
Brigadier General, Commanding.

Major JOHN C. MCFERRAN, U. S. A.,
Chief Quartermaster, Santa Fé, N. M.

Official:

ERASTUS W. WOOD,
Captain 1st Vet. Inf. C. V., A. A. A. General.

HEADQUARTERS DEPARTMENT OF NEW MEXICO,
Santa Fé, N. M., March 6, 1864.

GENERAL: I have the honor to enclose herewith, for the information of the War Department—

I. Letter dated February 20, 1864, from Second Lieutenant George W. Campbell, first cavalry New Mexico volunteers, in relation to a party of seven hundred and fifty Navajo Indians under his charge *en route* from the Navajo country to Bosque Redondo.

II. Letter dated February 21, 1864, from Captain Asa B. Casey, United States army, reporting that on the 18th of February he had forwarded one hundred and forty-seven Navajoes *en route* for the Bosque Redondo, and stating that he has fifteen hundred more Navajoes at the post of Fort Canby, New Mexico, awaiting transportation to go forward to the same locality, and that more are coming in.

III. Letter dated February 24, 1864, from Lieutenant Mullins, commanding at Los Pinos, New Mexico, stating that up to that date two thousand and nineteen Navajo Indians had arrived at that post. This number includes the party that came in under Lieutenant Campbell, and all who had gone by that post to the Bosque Redondo, but not those alluded to by Captain Casey.

[NOTE.—The number of Navajo prisoners in my hands by last advices is three thousand six hundred and fifty-six, and of Mescalero Apaches four hundred and fifty, making a total of four thousand one hundred and six.]

IV. Letter dated February 5, 1864, from Colonel Charles D. Posten, superintendent of Indian affairs for Arizona, giving an account of Indian difficulties near the southern line of that Territory, and asking military protection.

V. My reply to Colonel Posten's letter.

VI. Letter dated March 16, 1864, from Colonel James L. Collins, late superintendent of Indian affairs, to myself, suggesting what the government ought at once to do with reference to the captured Indians. Colonel Collins's views are worthy of great weight. You will see that they are fully indorsed by Governor Connelly and by Colonel Carson, who has been Indian agent in this country. All three of these gentlemen have great experience with Indians. They have resided in this country for thirty years. I beg to say that I fully concur in all that Colonel Collins has said.

By the subjugation and colonization of the Navajo tribe we gain for civilization their whole country, which is much larger in extent than the State of Ohio, and, besides being by far the best pastoral region between the two oceans, is said to abound in the precious as well as in the useful metals.

I beg to impress upon your mind, general, that the government should at once take some action for the immediate support and the prospective advancement of the Navajoes. Although they have been forced by military power to leave their country, yet the government is so greatly the gainer by their giving it up, that an annuity of at least one hundred and fifty thousand dollars should be given to them in clothing, farming implements, stock, seeds, storehouses, mills, &c., for ten years, when they will not only have become self-sustaining, but will be the happiest and most delightfully located pueblo of Indians in New Mexico—perhaps in the United States. Legislation to this end should be had at once. There should not be a week's delay.

Now, until laws be passed granting this annuity, somebody has got to feed and clothe these Indians. From what I have observed, the Indian department, as represented in this country, is slow to move in any matter looking towards the peaceful settlement of the Indians, thus freeing the country forever from their hostilities. There is no superintendent here; no goods or money belonging to the superintendency, as I am informed; and no agent to take care of and direct this interesting tribe.

I have had eight ploughs made, and am gathering up seed, opening acequias, and endeavoring to do all that I can possibly do to get in a crop for them this year. I wrote to the superintendent, now in Washington, to send out by express even two "breaking-up" ploughs; but he has not even answered my letter. The chief quartermaster has also bought blankets, and manta and kettles, hoes, axes, &c., &c., to help give them a start until you in Washington can come to their relief.

The troops have toiled hard to overcome this formidable tribe, and doubtless the operations against them will be entirely closed by the end of next May. It is a little hard that the Indian department does not stand ready to receive and provide for the captives, so that our attention and energies may be turned to other portions of the department where other bands of Apaches are killing and robbing the people with seeming impunity.

These Indians are upon my hands. They must be clothed and fed until they can clothe and feed themselves. I will not turn them loose again to war upon the people, and cannot see them perish either from nakedness or hunger.

I am, general, very respectfully, your obedient servant,

JAMES H. CARLETON,
Brigadier General, Commanding.

Brigadier General LORENZO THOMAS,
Adjutant General U. S. A., Washington, D. C.

Official:

ERASTUS W. WOOD,
Captain 1st Vet. Inf. C. V., A. A. A. General.

HEADQUARTERS DEPARTMENT OF NEW MEXICO,
Santa Fé, N. M., March 7, 1864.

MAJOR: I return herewith the charges against citizens Ramon, Lopez, and Mateo Sena, charged with violation of the intercourse law. Also enclosed you will find the proceedings of a board assembled to investigate matters concerning the selling of liquor to Indians.

The reservation of forty miles square, with Fort Sumner in the centre, has been duly set apart for Indian purposes, and approved by the President. No citizens, except those connected with the military establishment of Fort Sumner and with the Indian department, will be permitted to settle on the reservation; no persons shall be permitted to come within the lines to trade with Indians; no Indian will be permitted to sell to any person a single article of clothing, food, cooking utensils, agricultural implements, tools, or arms issued to him by the agent or by military officers; nor shall any Indian be permitted to sell any horse, ox, cow, sheep, goat, burro, mule, or other domestic animal, to any person outside of the military reservation, and to no person inside of the reservation, to be taken away from such reservation. You will at once establish such rules and take such measures as will give practical effect to this order.

The citizens against whom charges have been filed for violation of the intercourse law you will keep diligently at work planting or in digging acequias, or any other necessary labor looking towards raising a crop of corn, &c., for the Indians, until the district court for San Miguel county, or the county in which the offence was committed, meets, when you will cause them to be turned over to the civil authorities for trial.

I am, major, very respectfully, your obedient servant,

JAMES H. CARLETON,
Brigadier General, Commanding.

Major HENRY D. WALLEN, U. S. A.,
Commanding at Fort Sumner, N. M.

Official:

ERASTUS W. WOOD,
Captain 1st Vet. Inf. C. V., A. A. A. General.

HEADQUARTERS DEPARTMENT OF NEW MEXICO,
Santa Fé, N. M., March 9, 1864.

MAJOR: General Wright has requested me to send Captain Cremony's company to the department of the Pacific. You will at once have Captain Cremony turn in everything which will not be required on his march *via* Fort Stanton to Las Cruces. Give him three wagons to go as far as Fort Stanton, and rations only to last him to that post. The wagons will load at Stanton with wheat or corn for Sumner. Write to Major Smith to give Captain Cremony provisions and transportation to Las Cruces. There he will be provided for for the rest of his journey. Write to Major Smith to send the wagons, which must return from Las Cruces laden with flour to your post with the flour. Get Cremony off at once, not only to save the rations, but to save for Indians the corn and wheat his horses eat. This can be transferred to the subsistence department. You must get along with the very least cavalry you can, until the grass is high enough to maintain the horses without grain; and if you find you will run low on grain, you must not feed a cavalry horse an ounce of grain.

It will require the greatest effort and most careful husbandry to keep the Indians alive until the new crop matures. Every Indian—man, woman, or child—able to dig up the ground for planting, should be kept at work every moment of the day preparing a patch, however small. What with ploughing, spading, and hoeing up ground, with the labor of the troops and the Indians, you must endeavor to get in at least three thousand acres. It will surprise you to see how much can be done if the bands are properly organized, and all the officers go out and set the example of industry. The very existence of the Indians will depend upon it, and they should understand that now; for the country cannot support that number of mouths in addition to what we want for the troops. Everything depends on your efforts, and on your making every moment of time of every hand you can muster tell. The animals of the Indians must be bought and consumed before you kill a head of work-cattle; these you will need for ploughing. Atole will go a great ways even without meat. The Indians must live on the smallest possible quantity of food. The amount set in the order is in case we are fortunate in getting enough, which I greatly fear we shall have trouble in obtaining.

Very respectfully, your obedient servant,

JAMES H. CARLETON,
Brigadier General, Commanding.

Major HENRY D. WALLEN, U. S. A.,
Commanding at Fort Sumner, N. M.

Official:

ERASTUS W. WOOD,
Captain 1st Vet. Inf. C. V., A. A. A. General.

[Extract.]

Semi-official.]

HEADQUARTERS DEPARTMENT OF NEW MEXICO,
Santa Fé, N. M., March 10, 1864.

MY DEAR COLONEL: * * * * * * * * *
The cavalry at your post, and to come, must not be fed grain forage until I have time to see what all these human beings are to eat. Give them hay, and have large parties, headed by an officer, out on herd by day with them until further orders. There is no help for it. You must not have a worthless animal at your post. All such must be appraised and con-

demned, and sent to Los Pinos without delay as food for Indians. Work hard to help me carry out all this in letter and in spirit. I count on you, and all in your district. The rule applies to all cavalry, or mounted infantry.

Very sincerely yours,

JAMES H. CARLETON,
Brigadier General, Commanding.

Colonel EDWIN A. RIGG, *Fort Craig, N. M.*

Official:

ERASTUS W. WOOD,
Captain 1st Vet. Inf. C. V., A. A. A. General.

HEADQUARTERS DEPARTMENT OF NEW MEXICO,
Santa Fé, N. M., March 11, 1864.

MAJOR: I have heard that over five thousand of the Navajoes have surrendered, and within a few days you will have over two thousand of this tribe; the other three thousand are about leaving Fort Canby.

The question about sufficient food for them to support life, is one about which, as you may well suppose, I am very anxious. In conversing with Colonel Carson, Governor Connelly, and Major McFerran on this point, I find it is their opinion that one pound of flour, or of meat, or of meat, per day, to each man, woman, and child, if cooked as atole or porridge, or into soup, could be made to be enough, and is, probably, of more nutriment per day than they have been accustomed to obtain. Counting big and little, it is believed that this would feed them. On this basis, one pound of food per day—that is to say, of flour, or of corn, or of wheat, or of meat, made into soup or atole—I can barely see how they can be supported until we get provisions from the States, or their corn becomes ripe enough to pluck. The other day it occurred to me that it would not be well for you to sow much wheat; but I am told the wheat-crop will mature much sooner than corn, and therefore submit the question entirely to your judgment as to how much of each you will plant. You will at once commence the system of issuing the pound. The Indians themselves must be informed of the necessity of the restriction. Unless this plan be adopted, and at once, ultimate suffering must ensue. Soup and atole are the most nutritious, and the best way in which the food should be prepared to go a long way, and at the same time to be wholesome.

I am told the Navajoes never plough. I am told that corn can be planted (so the ground be prepared for irrigation) in hills, and that if afterwards the intermediate grass be cut down and the turf kept loosened, quite a good crop can be raised in that way. I have more anxiety about the length of your acequias than a little. If you only have water enough you can plant wheat, corn, beans, English turnips, in this order, until the summer be far advanced.

The Indian villages should be along the acequia, and each family, or band, have their separate lot, so that all could be spading up ground and getting it ready at the same time. Your acequia should be at least six miles in length, allowing that your land to be cultivated is one mile in width. If the land is narrower, the acequia should be longer. If you can get in six sections of crops, you can laugh at next winter. Working every hand every hour from morning until evening you will all be surprised at what you will accomplish.

Having sixty of the one hundred and forty-three cattle reserved for ploughing, you will run ten "breaking-up" ploughs. We have had eight new ones made. The ploughs can be in open ground away from the mesquite roots, and the spading in among the mesquite roots. I only make these hints as they occur to me. Being upon the ground, you will be the best judge of how best to employ your force. The troops, I know, will feel like lending a hand in so important a work. Again I recur to the length and breadth of the acequia. With plenty of water, and such a soil, I am sure you can raise a year's supply of bread this year. What an achievement! Pray let me count on the effort of every soul to attain such a vital point.

I will have two storerooms and a hospital for Indians made by contract, so as not to interfere with building the post, and have a doctor sent especially for Indians.

I am, major, very respectfully, your obedient servant,

JAMES H. CARLETON,
Brigadier General, Commanding.

Major HENRY D. WALLEN, U. S. A.,
Commanding at Fort Sumner, N. M.

Official:

ERASTUS W. WOOD,
Captain 1st Vet. Inf. C. V., A. A. A. General.

HEADQUARTERS DEPARTMENT OF NEW MEXICO,
Santa Fé, N. M., March 11, 1864.

MAJOR: Captain Cremony's company will, in a few days, come from Fort Sumner to your post *en route* to Las Cruces. Cremony will have three wagons from Sumner, which you will return to Sumner laden with wheat or corn, and escorted beyond danger. You will then give Cremony transportation to Las Cruces. The wagons which go with him to Cruces you will have return with flour from Cruces, and send this flour to Fort Sumner. Get some grain at Tulerosa for Cremony, so as not to haul any that way.

Report by return of mail how much grain you have on hand, and feed no more to cavalry horses until further orders. Have your cavalry horses sent under a strong guard, commanded by an officer, to some good grazing camp. Give such instructions that the men will not become careless and lose the horses. Have them (the horses) brought in every night and fed on hay, if you can. If the place for grazing is too far away for this, have them brought in every Saturday night. Every grain of corn and wheat has got to be saved for the five thousand captive Indians now on my hands. If I can see my way clear, and not require all the grain you have got, so much the better. Will the people at Tuleroso send wheat or corn to Fort Sumner? and if so, how much, and at how much a pound, and when will they deliver it? See about this, and let me know. Encourage everybody to plant all they can. We shall want more than they can raise. How many condemned and no-account animals have you at Stanton, of all sorts? Report.

I am, major, respectfully,

JAMES H. CARLETON,
Brigadier General, Commanding.

Major JOSEPH SMITH,
Commanding at Fort Stanton, N. M.

Official:

ERASTUS W. WOOD,
Captain 1st Vet. Inf. C. V., A. A. A. General.

HEADQUARTERS DEPARTMENT OF NEW MEXICO,
Santa Fé, N. M., March 12, 1864.

GENERAL: Since writing to you on the 6th instant in relation to the Navajo Indians, I have been informed that there are now three thousand of them—men, women, and children—who have surrendered at Fort Canby, and are about starting for the Bosque Redondo. These, with those now at that place and *en route* thither, will make five thousand five hundred, without including the captive Mescalero Apaches. There will doubtless be more Navajoes come in to Fort Canby—what are known as the *Ricos* of the tribe; men who have stock, and will doubtless be able to subsist themselves upon that stock until we are better prepared to take care of them. Colonel Carson has been instructed to send in the poor and destitute first. The Ricos will come in afterwards. Among the poor are nearly or quite all the ladrones and murderers, so that we have already in our hands the bad men of the tribe. An exact census will be taken of the Ricos, and a statement made of the probable amount of their stock, which has hitherto been greatly exaggerated, in my opinion. When this is done, Colonel Carson will himself come in from the Navajo country and go down to the Bosque Redondo to give the Indians the counsel they so much need just at this time as to how to start their farms and to commence their new mode of life. You have from time to time been informed of every step which I have taken with reference to operations against Indians in this country. I multiplied, as much as possible, the points of contact between our forces and themselves, and, although no great battle has been fought, still the persistent efforts of small parties acting simultaneously over a large extent of country has destroyed a great many and harassed the survivors until they have become thoroughly subdued. Now, when they have surrendered and are at our mercy, they must be taken care of—must be fed, clothed, and instructed. This admits neither of discussion nor delay. These six thousand mouths must eat, and these six thousand bodies must be clothed. When it is considered what a magnificent pastoral and mineral country they have surrendered to us—a country whose value can hardly be estimated—the mere pittance, in comparison, which must at once be given to support them, sinks into insignificance as a price for their natural heritage.

They must have two millions of pounds of breadstuffs sent from the States. This can be done by instalments—the first instalment to be started at once; say, five hundred thousand pounds of flour and corn, in equal parts. The next instalment to reach the Bosque in August next, and all to be delivered by the middle of next November. This amount will last them, with what we can buy here, until the crop comes off in 1865; when, from that time forward, so far as food may go, they will, in my opinion, be self-sustaining.

Add to these breadstuffs four thousand head of cattle, to come by instalments of five hundred each—the first to reach the Bosque by the first of July next, and all to be there by the middle of November. Salt can be bought here, but you cannot buy the breadstuffs or the meat; they are not in the country, and consequently cannot be got at any price. In view of the contingencies of delays, accidents, &c., I have put all the troops on half-rations, and, at most of the posts, ordered that no grain be issued to cavalry horses. These six thousand people must be fed until you can get us relieved by sending supplies, as above named, from the States. This matter, being of paramount importance, is alluded to here as the first which will claim your attention, or, rather, your action; for the matter is imperative—is self-evident; it needs no deliberation, as you will see, and admits of no delay.

Next comes the wherewithal to clothe these poor women and these little children. You will find in a duplicate of the letter which I wrote to you on the 6th of March, and which is herewith enclosed, a list of such articles as are absolutely needed now.

Then comes agricultural implements, which must be here to insure the crops Then the tools, cooking utensils, &c., &c., lists of which you will also find enveloped with this letter.

I beg to call your attention to that most important consideration—the management of the Navajoes upon the reservation. The amount of ability and business habits and tact necessary in one who should be selected to direct these people in their work, and in the systematic employment of their seasons of labor—in one having forecast to see their coming wants and necessities, and having resources of practical sense to provide for those wants and necessities—in one who would have the expending of the funds which must be appropriated for their support—cannot be commanded for the sum of fifteen hundred dollars per annum, given to an Indian agent. The law to be framed granting an annuity to the tribe should also provide for a *supervisor*, with a salary of at least three thousand dollars a year, and an *assistant supervisor*, with a salary equal to that of Indian agent. These men should be selected with great care. The assistant supervisor should be apt at accounts—practical as a man of business--of resources as a farmer and as a mechanic—of patience, industry, and temperance—one whose heart would be in his business, and who would himself believe that his time belonged to the government, and need not be spent mainly in "grinding axes" elsewhere at the expense of the United States. The superintendent need have, and should have, no further control than simply to audit the accounts.

If all this be set forth in the law, so far as salary and duties go, the whole plan will go into successful operation at once. If not set forth in the law, you may depend upon it, general, that, what with changes in superintendents—with diverse counsels and diverse interests, and lack of fixedness of purpose and system—the Indians will not be properly cared for, and, in room of becoming a happy, prosperous, and contented people, will become sad and desponding, and will soon lapse into idle and intemperate habits. You wish them to become a people whom all can contemplate with pride and satisfaction as *protegés* of the United States—a people who, in return for having given you their country, have been remembered and carefully provided for by a powerful Christian nation like ourselves. But unless you make in the law all the arrangements here contemplated, you will find this interesting and intelligent race of Indians will fast diminish in numbers, until, within a few years only, not one of those who boasted in the proud name of Navajo will be left to upbraid us for having taken their birthright, and then left them to perish.

With other tribes whose lands we have acquired, ever since the Pilgrims stepped on shore at Plymouth, this has been done too often. For pity's sake, if not moved by any other consideration, let us, as a great nation, for once treat the Indian as he deserves to be treated. It is due to ourselves, as well as to them, that this be done.

Having this purpose in view, I am sure the law-makers will not be ungenerous; nor will they be unmindful of all those essential points which, in changing a people from a nomadic to an agricultural condition of life, should be kept in view, in order to guard them against imposition, to protect them in their rights, to encourage them in their labors, and to provide for all their reasonable wants.

The exodus of this whole people from the land of their fathers is not only an interesting but a touching sight. They have fought us gallantly for years on years; they have defended their mountains and their stupendous cañons with a heroism which any people might be proud to emulate; but when, at length, they found it was their destiny too, as it had been that of their brethren, tribe after tribe, away back toward the rising of the sun, to give way to the insatiable progress of our race, they threw down their arms, and, as brave men entitled to our admiration and respect, have come to us with confidence in our magnanimity, and feeling that we are too powerful and too just a people to repay that confidence with meanness or neglect—feeling that for having sacrificed to us their beautiful country, their homes, the associations of their lives, the scenes rendered classic in their traditions, we will not dole out to them a miser's pittance in return for what they know to be and what we know to be a princely realm.

This is a matter of such vital importance that I cannot intrust to the accidents of a mail, but transmit this letter and its accompanying papers by a special messenger—Colonel James L. Collins, late superintendent of Indian affairs—who can be consulted with profit not only by the War and Interior Departments, but by the proper committees in Congress, whose attention will have to be called at once to the subject.

The War Department, general, has performed its whole duty in having brought these Indians into subjection, and now, in my opinion, stands ready to transfer them to the Department of the Interior. Other tribes along the Gila and in Arizona are murdering our people and committing robberies almost every week. We certainly should not be embarrassed with the care of Indians no longer hostile; so that it follows that laws should be at once passed to provide for them, and the proper officers be sent out immediately to receive them. We certainly, as soldiers, have come to that point where our services cannot properly be required any longer with anything which concerns the Navajoes, unless it be to station a guard in their midst for the preservation of order, and to protect them for a while from the nomads of the plains.

I am, general, very respectfully, your obedient servant,

JAMES H. CARLETON,
Brigadier General, Commanding.

Brigadier General LORENZO THOMAS,
Adjutant General U. S. A., Washington, D. C.

Official:

ERASTUS W. WOOD,
Captain 1st Vet. Inf. C. V., A. A. A. General.

[Extract.]

HEADQUARTERS DEPARTMENT OF NEW MEXICO,
Santa Fé, N. M., March 16, 1865.

CAPTAIN: * * * * * * * * * *

You will have corn or wheat issued to Indians, if practicable, at the rate of one pound a day to each. This, with transportation added, will be paid for by the subsistence department. The Indians will have no other food given to them except salt. In case meat is given to them at times, it will be in lieu of the wheat or corn, and at the same rate, i. e., one pound for each Indian, big and little.

Say to Colonel Carson that I think we can feed 6,000 Navajoes, but not to send in more, or feed additional numbers at Fort Canby. This 6,000 includes all you have sent, which now amounts to 5,000, including those left at the fort when you sent in the 2,000 and upwards, and includes those sent from Fort Wingate and elsewhere. So it will leave a thousand to send, supposing you have sent off the four hundred left at Canby when the 2,000 came away. Will not that be the most of the tribe? I hardly think they will overrun 6,000. The greatest care must be had of food; every ounce must be made to tell.

Keep up a perfect record of all Indians who come in—who are sent off—who are born, die, or desert, and the amount of stock sent to the Bosque. These statistics are absolutely necessary. You will furnish them on the 10th, 20th, and last days of the month.

Respectfully, your obedient servant,

JAMES H. CARLETON,
Brigadier General, Commanding.

Captain ASA B. CAREY, U. S. A.,
Fort Canby, N. M.

Official:

ERASTUS W. WOOD,
Captain 1st Vet. Inf. C. V., A. A. A. General.

HEADQUARTERS DEPARTMENT OF NEW MEXICO,
Santa Fé, N. M., March 19, 1864.

GENERAL: I have the honor to enclose herewith a copy of a letter from Dr. Steck, the superintendent of Indian affairs, to myself. It is dated at Washington, February 12, 1864. It is to be observed that he declines to feed the Navajoes. It is a fact that he went off to Washington without making provisions for subsisting the four hundred and fifty Mescalero Apaches which I had moved to the Bosque Redondo, and which Colonel Collins took off my hands last April, but which his successor, this Dr. Steck, let come back on to my hands again in November, 1863. And now, to cap the climax in the way of modesty, you will observe that he wishes me to help move the peaceable Jicarrillas to the Bosque *and to feed them as well.* If this be done, it would be curious to learn *what* Indian affairs Dr. Steck is superintending.

You will also find herewith enclosed a copy of a letter from Captain Bristol, United States army, written at my request, and sent to a Mr. Baker, who, I believe, assumes to be acting as Dr. Steck's vicegerent while the doctor is absent in Washington. He never answered the letter nor gave the articles enumerated, although, I am informed, he has many in store which he says are for the Pueblo Indians. It may not be amiss to state that the Pueblo Indians are all comfortably provided for; *that the Navajoes are utterly destitute,* and that he could have let these articles go to the Navajoes without detriment.

You will also find enclosed with this a letter from Major Wallen, United States army, who is in command of Fort Sumner, and is doing all he can to get the Indians located, to get in their crops, and to have them well cared for.

Last fall, as you have been informed, this superintendent desired that we should let the Mescalero Apaches go to their country again. This was positively forbidden by myself. Then he went to Washington and endeavored to oppose the Navajoes going to the Bosque Redondo, because *he* thought they should have a reservation in their own country. He knows well enough there is no one place in the Navajo country where there is tillable land enough for such a purpose; he knows they could not be kept on such a reservation; he knows the difference in cost of transportation of supplies alone for Indians and for the garrison in their midst would be against a reservation there equal to the support of the tribe at the Bosque Redondo. Last fall, at the Bosque, he held out the idea that the Indians (Mescaleros) then there should go to their country. When told by the military that if they attempted to go they would be shot, *it made trouble. Now* he writes to the agent there that it is an Apache reservation, (land enough to support 10,000 people given to 450!) and that the Navajoes will not be permitted to stay there. The poor Navajoes, as you see by Major Wallen's letter, who had thought they had finally got a home, feel unhappy at the prospect of moving again. And thus he makes more trouble; and all this time, it will be well to remark, he feeds neither the Navajoes nor the Apaches, and his vicegerent will not even lend us some hoes and brass kettles to help out a little when we have so many prisoners on our hands and are straining every point to feed them and to get in a crop this year for their support.

Dr. Steck wants to hold councils with Navajoes! It is mockery to hold councils with a people who are in our hands and have only to await our decisions. *It will be bad policy to hold any councils.* We should give them what they need—what is just, and take care of them as children until they can take care of themselves. The Navajoes should never leave the Bosque, and never shall if I can prevent it. I told them that that should be their home. They have gone there with that understanding. There is land enough there for themselves and the Apaches. The Navajoes themselves are Apaches, and talk the same language, and in a few years will be homogeneous with them.

I beg therefore to say, that unless the Navajoes are permitted to stay at the Bosque Redondo, *they have been treated in bad faith.* And I beg further to say that, judging from the manner in which this Dr. Steck has gone on, his superintendency of Indian affairs will not conduce either to the happiness or the prosperity of the Indians. Pray let us do what is right by the Indians without the mockery of a council, when, finally, we should have everything our own way. *And as I have promised the tribe that the Bosque should be their home, I trust the government will make good my promise.*

I am, general, very respectfully, your obedient servant,

JAMES H. CARLETON,
Brigadier General, Commanding.

Brigadier General LORENZO THOMAS,
Adjutant General U. S. A., Washington, D. C.

Official: ERASTUS W. WOOD,
Captain 1st Vet. Inf. C. V., A. A. A. General.

HEADQUARTERS DEPARTMENT OF NEW MEXICO,
Santa Fé, N. M., March 21, 1864.

CAPTAIN: You will send a list of all Indian prisoners which arrive at your post, made out on the day of their arrival, and showing their condition as regards clothing and cooking utensils; and you will make out a list of all who leave your post for the Bosque Redondo, made on the day of their departure. Keep a record of all deaths, births, and desertions among them while at your post, and send an abstract of it to these headquarters, and send a list of the stock arriving and departing which belongs to the Indians, and of what articles you issue to the Indians.

I am, captain, respectfully,

JAMES H. CARLETON,
Brigadier General, Commanding.

Captain THOMAS L. ROBERTS,
Commanding at Los Pinos, N. M.

Official:

ERASTUS W. WOOD,
Captain 1st Vet. Inf. C. V., A. A. A. General.

HEADQUARTERS DEPARTMENT OF NEW MEXICO,
Santa Fé, N. M., March 25, 1865.

MAJOR: On your list of persons composing the military establishment of Fort Sumner, who are entitled to draw rations, you put down six as belonging to the Indian department. Neither Mr. Labadie nor his employés having a right either to draw or buy rations, who are these six persons?

The Indians are to be fed at the rate of *one* pound for each man, woman and child per day, of fresh meat, or of corn, or of wheat, or of wheat-meal, or of corn-meal, or of flour, or of krout, or of pickles; or, in lieu of any one of these articles, half a pound of beans, or of rice, or of peas, or of dried fruit. Salt at the regulation allowance if necessary.

It is not only desirable on account of the health of the Indians, but to save the regular subsistence stores for the troops, that corn and wheat, and corn-meal and wheat-meal, and beans be issued to Indians. We have a good supply of beans, and as they are a wholesome and nutritious article of diet, you can cause them to be issued as often as practicable. If meat could be killed so as to have some meat and some farinaceous food made into soups, it would doubtless go further and be more acceptable to the Indians. Save the work-cattle for ploughing. Be sure that no wool or pelts are thrown away.

In future reports, the amount of food for Indians which you may have on hand will be rendered on a separate paper from that for troops, and the return of Indians will be on a separate paper from any account of troops. This will lead to no confusion in counting upon the duration of your supplies.

How many ploughs are you now running? Please report from time to time the progress you make in getting ground ready for cultivation. Some more ploughs, two at least, will soon be sent down.

I am, major, very respectfully, your obedient servant,

JAMES H. CARLETON,
Brigadier General, Commanding.

Major HENRY D. WALLEN,
Commanding at Fort Sumner, N. M.

NOTE.—I have mentioned the amount of food to be issued to Indians as an amount sufficient for their support, according to the judgment of Governor Connelly, Major McFerran, Colonel Carson, and others. But you are upon the ground, and can tell if this be enough or not. If not enough, in your opinion, give me your views of how much should be issued. The utmost economy must be observed, but there must be no want.

J. H. C.

Official:

ERASTUS. W. WOOD,
Captain 1st Vet. Inf. C. V., A. A. A. General.

[Extract.]

HEADQUARTERS DEPARTMENT OF NEW MEXICO,
Santa Fé, N. M., March 27, 1864.

DEAR MAJOR: * * * * * * * * * *
We shall want more long-handled shovels, and at least two hundred strong hoes, for the Indians. Wallen writes they break three spades a day. If, when this reaches you, you have already telegraphed to send out the five hundred thousand pounds of flour and two thousand head of cattle for Indians, you need not change it, as we can use the flour and cattle here

and for *the* expedition, but if you have not telegraphed as yet in relation to the matter, send this message: "We have succeeded in getting bread and meat enough for Indians. None need be sent."

If you can manage to get enough breaking-up ploughs to make twenty with what we have, send them through as soon as you can. What will a peck of English turnip-seed cost, good fresh seed?

* * * * * * * * * * *

Truly yours,

JAMES H. CARLETON,
Brigadier General, Commanding.

Major JOHN C. MCFERRAN,
Chief of Staff, &c., Denver City.

Official:

ERASTUS W. WOOD,
Captain 1st Vet. Inf. C. V., A. A. A. General.

HEADQUARTERS DEPARTMENT OF NEW MEXICO,
Santa Fé, N. M., March 30, 1864.

MAJOR: Mr. Robert Carley, of Albuquerque, had some mules run off by Indians last summer. He says the Navajoes who are coming in have some of these mules. We have told the Indians if they voluntarily surrendered they should retain their stock. The question arises whether they do not claim such stolen stock as their stock. I decided, in case of government mules found with them, that they should have ten dollars a head for recovering it, the price paid others, as we cannot tell whether the Indian *now* in possession of the animal is the one, or even belongs to the tribe of the one who stole it.

Mr. Carley in the same way should pay ten dollars a head for recovering his mules to the person who now has them in possession. This seems to be no more than right. Certainly it is the only just way by which I can reconcile the giving up of the stock with what is due to both parties.

It may be hard on the Indian, and is certainly hard on Mr. Carley. Better this, however, than not get his mule at all. So you will explain this matter to the Indians, have Mr. Carley identify the mule or mules, and when he pays the money, as indicated, to the Indian, the mule or mules will be given up.

I am, major, very respectfully, your obedient servant,

JAMES H. CARLETON,
Brigadier General, Commanding.

Major HENRY D. WALLEN, U. S. A.,
Commanding at Fort Sumner, N. M.

Official:

ERASTUS W. WOOD,
Captain 1st Vet. Inf. C. V., A. A. A. General.

HEADQUARTERS DEPARTMENT OF NEW MEXICO,
Santa Fé, N. M., April 1, 1864.

COLONEL: On the 10th instant I shall despatch a small train from Albuquerque with subsistence stores for Fort Whipple. It will take some seventy-two thousand pounds of assorted stores.

As soon as the Navajo war has finally closed, which will, I hope, be soon, as I already have six thousand prisoners of that tribe, operations will be commenced on the Apaches. I desire to establish a post, which will be a base of operations, on the Gila river, on that great bottom north of Fort Bowie. That must be the most important agricultural region in Arizona; and while it is central with regard to operations against Apaches, it will protect the farming interests there and the rich mineral region near the Prieta, affluent to the Gila from the north, opposite somewhere about the centre of the bottom alluded to. I desire that you proceed from Fort Bowie to that point and select the site of a four-company post. Have Captain Tidball or some other intelligent officer go with you, and have the ground so marked that he can direct the troops to the identical spot you select.

I enclose herewith a copy of a letter just received from Colonel Posten, superintendent of Indian affairs for Arizona. You will order, in my name, a board of officers to assemble to investigate and report upon the matters of which he complains. Let this be done at once. I trust that there is no disposition on the part of the military to embarrass Colonel

Posten, or to withhold any reasonable amount of help which he may properly require in the way of escorts. As for transportation, it seems to me that the Department of the Interior should furnish him with that, and not the Department of War. He surely has no right to claim that, and yet, when it can be spared, there must be no splitting of hairs. It is for the public service. I take it for granted that Colonel Posten will see how hard we are pushed for transportation, and not feel to ask for more than what is positively necessary to discharge his official duties as superintendent. The exigencies of the military service will first be considered by the military; but we must be neighborly, and it is our duty as well to help all the other branches of the government in that isolated and dangerous region.

At this season of the year, when transportation is scarce, an effective campaign against the Apaches of Arizona cannot be put afoot by the waving of a wand. Troops and supplies have to be collected from very distant points, and at great expense, and means of transportation have to be provided without leaving the rest of the department at a dead lock. Please inform the people of Arizona that they shall have help as soon as it can be given effectively. When I commence on the Apaches, as when I commenced upon the Navajoes, they must understand it is to be a serious war; not a little march out and back again. If there can be a post established at the point indicated by the middle of May, the troops can have some vegetables this year.

Let me know how far it is from Fort Bowie to that point, and whether it is a good wagon road, and if there be water mid-way.

I am, colonel, very respectfully, your obedient servant,

JAMES H. CARLETON,
Brigadier General, Commanding.

Lieutenant Colonel NELSON H. DAVIS,
Assistant Inspector General U. S. A., Tucson, Arizona.

Official:

ERASTUS W. WOOD,
Captain 1st Vet. Inf. C. V., A. A. A. General.

HEADQUARTERS DEPARTMENT OF NEW MEXICO,
Santa Fé, N. M., April 1, 1864.

COLONEL: We have succeeded so well in getting food for the Navajoes that the restriction can be removed with regard to feeding forage to cavalry horses. You will therefore feed as you had done up to the date of that restriction.

* * * * * * * * * * *

The Apaches in the mountains southwest of your post and at the head of the Mimbres are numerous and hostile. Cannot you send, say, two good, resolute parties of forty men each, by different routes, to hunt and destroy all but the women and children? Have Greene organize a third party and take a third route. Each party should go light; should depend mainly on beef on the hoof, or sheep if you have them, a little sugar and coffee and flour and salt. Let the parties be out for at least forty days, and go well into the country—go without noise, with spies in advance, with flankers, with men concealed in each camp when the troops leave it, to destroy all who follow on the trail. If you think forty too small a party, increase it.

In and around Fort West and the Burro mountains the Apaches are also numerous. I suppose they have just come back from their winter residence in Chihuahua. They have just run off seventy mules and horses from one of our trains at Cow Springs. Whitlock is after them from the Mimbres. I will try to send a force south from Wingate, and another from Canby. Picked men and officers, each striving to do his utmost, will accomplish a good deal. To move silently to hunt Indians is the only way to accomplish anything at all. For God's sake let the commands move light, as we want much transportation to get supplies south of the Jornado. Greene sets the example of moving light.

I am, colonel, very respectfully, your obedient servant,

JAMES H. CARLETON,
Brigadier General, Commanding.

Colonel EDWIN A. RIGG,
Commanding at Fort Craig, N. M.

Official:

ERASTUS W. WOOD,
Captain 1st Vet. Inf. C. V., A. A. A. General.

HEADQUARTERS DEPARTMENT OF NEW MEXICO,
Santa Fé, N. M., April 3, 1864.

GENERAL: Since writing to you on the 12th ultimo, the letter taken to Washington by Colonel James L. Collins, bearer of despatches, we have been able to secure more food for the captive Indians than I believed then to be possible, and therefore I directed Major McFerran, chief of staff, to telegraph to you from Denver City to send out but five hundred thousand pounds of flour and two thousand head of cattle, these to arrive in October.

We have been able to borrow some subsistence stores from the district of Colorado, and I have just heard of the arrival, at the mouth of the Colorado river, of a vessel with subsistence stores which will be taken to Fort Yuma, whence we can draw upon them to a certain extent for the troops in western Arizona. This vessel had been seventy days out! So that I can now see the way clear for the troops and the Indians to be fed until supplies can come out from the States. About this I was very anxious.

The Apaches in Arizona are very hostile, and efforts must be made to subdue them at the earliest practicable day. I was in hope that some answer would long before now have been given to my letter to you dated the 29th of last November, a duplicate of which was also forwarded on the 12th of last January, in relation to increasing the bounties to be paid to troops re-enlisting in this remote department. Some more men, perhaps, might have been gotten under the law for re-enlisting veterans, had it not expired so soon. Before the orders reached here extending the time to the first of March, there were only a few days left, not enough to let the fact be known at the remote posts where the troops are the most needed. The last extension to the first instant only reached here at noon on the 31st day of March, and could only be known in Santa Fé before the time expired. So, practically, it was of no avail except to secure the re-enlistment of eleven men.

* * * * * * * * * * *

Is it expected in Washington that I am to furnish transportation for Indian goods, and escorts and transportation for the superintendent of Indian affairs, and for other civil officers in Arizona? I will do all I can consistent with requirements in the military branch of the service. I am written to, and about, as if this could be demanded as a right.* Should not other departments furnish all but escorts?

I am, general, very respectfully, your obedient servant,

JAMES H. CARLETON,
Brigadier General, Commanding.

Brigadier General LORENZO THOMAS,
Adjutant General U. S. A., Washington, D. C.

* See enclosed letter from Colonel Posten, dated March 10, 1864, marked I; letter from Colonel Coult, commanding at Tucson, of March 18, 1864, marked II; letter from General Carleton to Lieutenant Colonel N. H. Davis, dated April 1, 1864, marked III.

Official:

ERASTUS W. WOOD,
Captain 1st Vet. Inf. C. V., A. A. A. General.

HEADQUARTERS DEPARTMENT OF NEW MEXICO,
Santa Fé, N. M., March 20, 1864.

MAJOR: I have received your letter in relation to Labadie's making the Navajoes unhappy by suggesting they would move. You have the Navajoes and Apaches under your charge, and Labadie, too, so far as seeing that he does and says nothing to make the Indians either unhappy or discontented. If he does either, you will at once order him off the reservation, and order any other person off, whatever be his rank in the Indian department, unless he will promise not to sow seeds of discontent among the Indians still under charge of the military and who are fed by us. You will be sure to let no Indian leave the reservation except by my authority, let whoever may desire it, until after the Indians are all transferred to the Department of the Interior. We have had trouble enough by these outside hostile, puerile, senseless interferences, and I propose to have no more of it. So you will be governed entirely by orders from me. You are responsible for the safety, care, feeding and work of the Apaches and Navajoes. Don't the Apaches eat our food? And you will be sure, as long as you have this responsibility, to let neither Labadie, nor Steck, nor anybody else, come there to breed mischief or make trouble. When the Indian department acts properly and feeds and clothes the Indians, we will let them do it in their own way; but when they throw the Indians on our hands, as they did the Apaches, to feed, then they must not meddle with them until they get them back. This matter has been represented to the War Department. Have neither nonsense nor child's play.

Have sent you seven ploughs. Will soon send you some more, if possible. Have sent to Craig for fifty each of shovels, spades, pickaxes. Will try to send you ten more ploughs and some farmers to help work. You must get in six sections. Tell Calloway, (who is a trump,) Colonel Collins has gone to Washington to look after matters for the Navajoes. There are 2,200 *en route* from Canby, besides those who came with Mullins, and 400 more at Canby awaiting transportation. Send me a copy of this letter. I shall be down as soon as I see you *all* have enough to eat; 6,000 is no joke.

Respectfully, &c.,

JAMES H. CARLETON, *Brigadier General, Commanding.*

Major HENRY D. WALLEN,
Commanding Fort Sumner, N. M.

Official:

ERASTUS W. WOOD,
Captain 1st Vet. Inf. C. V., A. A. A. General.

HEADQUARTERS DEPARTMENT OF NEW MEXICO,
Santa Fé, N. M., April 8, 1864.

MAJOR: I have the honor to inform you that I have ordered one hundred thousand pounds of subsistence stores from Albuquerque to Fort Whipple. They start the 10th instant. These stores will reach your post on the 15th or 25th of May next. The train will be escorted by the remainder of company "D" 1st cavalry California volunteers. When the train returns, send in to Albuquerque, New Mexico, (giving them rations only to Fort Wingate,) company "F" 1st infantry California volunteers. This will give you a company of infantry and nearly a company of cavalry for your garrison. The next train that goes out with rations will be escorted by a company whose time will not be out for a year or two. How you stand with reference to supplies, and the number of mouths to eat them, you should report by every express. You disappoint me by the paucity of your reports on all the subjects of which I spoke to you. You have doubtless got back from, and had time to give me, a full account of your explorations.

I am preparing to commence operations against the Apaches of Arizona. A post will be established in the great valley of the Gila, directly north of Fort Bowie, and from that point hostilities will be prosecuted. If possible the troops will be there by the 1st of June. The valley in which it is intended to put the post is said to be very fertile; to be some sixty miles long and a mile and a half broad. It will be the greatest agricultural locality in the Territory. The Prieta, a stream running through the richest gold region, comes into the Gila about midway the valley.

* * * * * * * * * *

I am, major, very respectfully, your obedient servant,

JAMES H. CARLETON, *Brigadier General, Commanding.*

Major EDWARD B. WILLIS,
Commanding Fort Whipple, Arizona.

Official:

ERASTUS W. WOOD,
Captain 1st Vet. Inf. C. V., A. A. A. General.

HEADQUARTERS DEPARTMENT OF NEW MEXICO,
Santa Fé, N. M., April 8, 1864.

COLONEL: I have noted what you have said about the rich Navajoes. If they can feed themselves you can send in even 10,000. If not, send in not over 8,000, including what we have. Those who have stock and can support themselves had better be told again that, if they come in, they shall have their own stock. If they compel us to force them in, we will have all we can take. I cannot believe but that 8,000 will cover all the tribe; and we can manage to feed that number. The Ricos can live on their stock at the Bosque as well as in their own country. Transfer your command to Captain Carey when you come in on the court that is to try Captain Everett.

I am, colonel, very respectfully, your obedient servant,

JAMES H. CARLETON,
Brigadier General, Commanding.

Colonel CHRISTOPHER CARSON,
Commanding Navajo Expedition, Fort Canby, N. M.

NOTE.—Captain Murphy can come. Captain Pfeiffer must stay with his company. Send in Indians by every opportunity. If the ricos come in soon they can plant some this year.

Official:

ERASTUS W. WOOD,
Captain 1st Vet. Inf. C. V., A. A. A. General.

HEADQUARTERS DEPARTMENT OF NEW MEXICO,
Santa Fé, N. M., April 9, 1864.

MAJOR: I have received your letter of the 1st of April, 1864, in relation to food for the Indians. It was well, if you found that a pound of breadstuffs a day, or its equivalent in meat, was not enough, to issue more. It is possible that we may be able to get meat so as to give them a pound apiece per day, if the whole animal, weighed just as it lies upon the ground after it is killed, the entrails taken out, but the animal not skinned, (for they eat the entrails, which will compensate for the skin,) be issued. If we cannot get the animals you will have to make close calculations, so as not to find yourself entirely without meat. You will, if necessary, have to issue less. The Indians will have beans issued to them once a week. Have them taught by the soldiers how to cook the beans. You are authorized to issue to the chiefs and principal men of the Navajoes and Apaches some coffee and sugar—in all not to exceed eighty rations per day—the Navajoes to have their just proportion, having reference to their superior numbers. You should have a good talk in council with the chiefs of both tribes in convention, and tell them that every effort is making to get food forward, but they must be prudent and see that not an ounce is wasted; that Colonel Collins has gone to Washington, at my request, to urge upon the government to send out blankets and other clothing, and tools, and utensils for farming and for cooking, and tobacco, and ornaments, &c., and that I hope soon to send them word that the articles have been bought and are upon the road; that the Indians must be patient and must believe we will do all we can to make them comfortable and happy; that the Indians have the best land in the country; that the Mexicans are jealous that they have such a beautiful place; that, if they work hard, in a few years they will be the richest *pueblo* in the country. This is all true; and if they could be made to see how they will prosper if they will only be patient, be prudent, and industrious, as I see it, they would be very happy and contented.

On the 25th of February you were directed to make timely estimates for food for Indians, so as to have fifty days' supply on hand. We have not yet received an estimate for this food. Make the estimates on the Indians you actually have on hand to feed. Why has it not been sent in?

Major McFerran has bought ten ploughs for you at Denver. Have the yokes and chains got in readiness. The ploughs will soon reach you. The Indians themselves should learn to plough. You should talk with the chiefs how important this is. They will have to do it some day. Now is the time to learn. You may even hire them as laborers to plough. We canot get citizens to do this.

You have by far the most important command in this Territory. Every one knows it and speaks about it. I should rather you would stay at Sumner than to send you to Bascom, because I believe you will take an interest in this great work. The post of Fort Sumner is uncommonly healthy, as all the records show. The water, although a little brackish, is proved to be most wholesome. When Fritz's company comes a cavalry camp must be formed down the river, and the horses kept on grass. We cannot get the corn to feed to cavalry at Fort Sumner. It must be reserved for the feeding of human beings. Remember this, and please to remember it in time.

I am, major, very respectfully, your obedient servant,

JAMES H. CARLETON,
Brigadier General, Commanding.

Major HENRY D. WALLEN, U. S. A.,
Commanding Fort Sumner, N. M.

Official:

ERASTUS W. WOOD,
Captain 1st Vet. Inf. C. V., A. A. A. General.

HEADQUARTERS DEPARTMENT OF NEW MEXICO,
Santa Fé, N. M., April 17, 1864.

GENERAL: Enclosed herewith please find—

1st A copy of a private letter from Governor Goodwin, of Arizona, to myself. This letter is dated at Tucson, Arizona, April 4, 1864. It shows that there is an immediate and pressing necessity for a military force to go to that country to punish the Indians, who are not only numerous, but very hostile. In this letter Governor Goodwin sustains the action of Colonel Davis, assistant inspector general United States army, about which Colonel Posten, the superintendent of Indian afiairs, so bitterly complained in a letter already sent to you.

2d. A copy of a letter from Lieutenant Colonel Davis, assistant inspector general, United States Army, dated at Fort Whipple, Arizona, March 20, 1864, in which, among other things, he treats at length of these Indian difficulties.

3d. A copy of a letter from Lieutenant Colonel Davis, assistant inspector general U. S. A., dated at Tucson, Arizona, April 4, 1864 In this will be seen what is said of Colonel Brown, of the 1st cavalry California volunteers, now *en route* to this department from that of the Pacifiic Colonel Brown has been ordered to Fort Craig, New Mexico, there to await further orders. What with political schemes and mining interests in Arizona, both of officers of volunteers, of civil officers, and citizens—which go to form not only springs of action, but which warp judgment, and sometimes strive to deflect the rays which should come direct from truth—it is difficult for any commander, who proposes to act with an eye to the interests of the government, to act justly by all, and to act with anything like vigor, to escape the most unmeasured abuse. You can depend on this. I shall expect at least my share, for I find that my ideas of what should be done conflict very directly with those of many of these gentlemen who have gone in one capacity or another to that Territory.

4th. Copies of extracts from private letters from Lieutenant Colonel Davis, United States Army, on affairs in Arizona.

The necessities which are shown by these letters to exist for immediate demonstrations against the Apaches of Arizona, have induced me to commence organizing an expedition to proceed against them. It will consist of, say, about five hundred men; will start from Las Cruces, New Mexico; will have its depot of supplies on the Gila river, north of Fort Bowie, whence small parties of twenties, and forties, and eighties, will radiate in all directions and follow any trail that may be found. We must trust to the gallantry of small parties against any numbers. Large parties move snail-like; are seen at once and are avoided; generally are laughed at by these Apaches. Small parties move secretly; cover more ground; move vith celerity; emulate to do better than all others, and, in the end, either destroy the Indians or worry them into submission.

It is very fortunate that the Navajo war is at that point toward a final ending as to give but little further uneasiness. If, by the help of Providence, we can have the same fortune in our demonstrations against the Apaches of Arizona, the great drain upon the treasury, which has been kept up by these Indian wars, will forever cease.

I am, general, very respectfully, your obedient servant,

JAMES H. CARLETON, *Brigadier General, Commanding.*

Brigadier General LORENZO THOMAS,
Adjutant General U. S. A, Washington, D. C.

Official:

ERASTUS W. WOOD,
Captain 1st Vet. Inf. C. V., A. A. A. General.

HEADQUARTERS DEPARTMENT OF NEW MEXICO,
Santa Fé, N. M., April 1, 1864.

COLONEL: There are many Apaches returned from Chihuahua, and are now in the Mogollon and White mountains, at the head of the Little Colorado, due south of Fort Canby. A few days since they stole 70 mules and horses from one of our trains at Cow Springs. Is it possible for you to send a force of one hundred picked men into these mountains, to scout for them for, say, fifty days? If so, do it at once. Two parties will be out from Craig, and two others from McRae, and one from the Mimbres. You will find some Navajoes in that way who have stock. The men should take mainly cattle or sheep on the hoof for food, a very little flour and sugar and coffee and salt. This is the way they will go from the other posts: as light as possible; as silently as possible; with spies well to the front; with flankers: with a few men secreted in camps to ambush Indians following the trail.

I think you overrate the numbers of the Navajoes. Get all the information you can from prisoners, Zuñi Indians, Moquois, of where they are; have this written down, and the probable numbers. We will then see what the chiefs at the Bosque say. Some of those we can then get for guides, and lay all our plans understandingly. You can send on 7,500 Navajoes, including what we have. That number we can feed.

* * * * * * * * * *

Respectfully, I am, colonel, your obedient servant,

JAMES H. CARLETON, *Brigadier General, Commanding.*

Colonel CHRISTOPHER CARSON,
Commanding Navajo Expedition, Fort Canby, N. M.

Official:

ERASTUS W. WOOD,
Captain 1st Vet. Inf. C. V., A. A. A. General.

HEADQUARTERS DEPARTMENT OF NEW MEXICO,
Santa Fé, N. M., April 20, 1864.

MY DEAR SIR: I have had the pleasure to read your letter to Lieutenant Colonel Coult, sent by Captain French, in which you kindly give us the privilege of receiving supplies at the port of Guaymas, and the privilege of transporting them through the sovereign State of Sonora to our Territory of Arizona, for the use of the troops of the United States serving in that Territory. You also give us the privilege of continuing the pursuit of hostile Apaches over the boundary line, if necessary, into your state; a corresponding privilege which we cordially extend towards the forces of your excellency, when following our common enemy, the Apaches.

These kindnesses are duly appreciated. They serve to make your people and our people still faster friends, and serve to make us feel that we have kind and obliging neighbors. We only trust your excellency will contrive some way by which we may have the pleasure of reciprocating the favors you have extended towards us.

There is one matter which should be called to the attention of your excellency at this time. I am about to commence hostile operations against the Apaches of Arizona. A force of five hundred men will leave Las Cruces, on the Rio Grande, about the 10th proximo, and will march to a point on the Gila north of the Chiricahui mountains; there establish a depot, and from that point, in small parties, commence operations upon those savages. I shall at the same time endeavor to get the Pimo and Maricopa Indians to help, and also the miners in Arizona. In this way a great many men, acting simultaneously against them, will make them suffer very greatly. Some of them will doubtless make their way into Sonora. If your excellency will put a few hundred men into the field on the first day of next June, and keep them in hot pursuit of the Apaches of Sonora, say for sixty or ninety days, we will either exterminate the Indians or so diminish their numbers that they will desire to cease their murdering and robbing propensities, and live at peace. Your excellency is well aware that the great obstacle which stands in the way of the immediate advancement towards prosperity of Sonora, Chihuahua, and Arizona, is this tribe of savages. When it is subdued that prosperity will come, but not till then. I beg you will write to the governor of Chihuahua on this point, so that we may make a combined effort against these Apaches. If we do this I am sure we shall succeed. It has been my good fortune, in making war upon the Mescalero Apaches and the Navajoes, to destroy a great many; and I have now 6,000 of them prisoners. They are upon a reservation at the Bosque Redondo, on the Pecos river, where they are now planting corn and wheat, and where they will form a *pueblo*. I sincerely trust I may count on the earnest and powerful co-operation of your excellency in prosecuting hostilities against the Apaches, which infest the country on both sides of the line west of the Rio Grande.

With sincere wishes for the health and happiness of your excellency, and for the happiness and prosperity of the good people of Sonora,

I have the honor to be your excellency's obedient servant,

JAMES H. CARLETON,
Brigadier General, Commanding.

His Excellency, Don YGNACIO PESQUIRA,
Governor of Sonora, Mexico.

Official:

ERASTUS W. WOOD,
Captain 1st Vet. Inf. C. V., A. A. A. General.

HEADQUARTERS DEPARTMENT OF NEW MEXICO,
Santa Fé, N. M., April 20, 1864.

MY DEAR SIR: I have ventured to trespass upon your time in order to call your attention to a plan I have in view, which looks toward a punishment for murders and robberies of the Apache Indians, who infest the states of Chihuahua and Sonora, and the Territory of Arizona, on our side of the line. About the 10th of May, or a little later, I shall send a command of troops, numbering, say, five hundred men, to a point on the Gila north of the Chiricahui mountains, where a depot of supplies will be established, and from which the troops, in small parties, will move in every direction, and follow up and attack every male Apache Indian able to bear arms whose trail may be met, or who may be overtaken. At the same time this is done it is my purpose to get the Pimos and Maricopa Indians, to whom I have given over two hundred muskets and ammunition in plenty for the same, to join in hostilities against the tribe. The miners at the gold fields in western Arizona say they will also turn out and help, if they can have some provisions from me, which I shall give them.

Now these active operations will cause many of these Indians to flee across the lines into Chihuahua and Sonora. If your excellency will turn out your militia and get a few hundred of them into the field by the 10th or 15th of June next, for, say, fifty or sixty days, we shall accomplish a great deal toward the destruction of the common enemy of all the citizens of your state as well as of Sonora, and the country on our side of the line. Not until this is done effectually can we hope for anything like prosperity. I hope your excellency will give your powerful co-operation in a matter of such grave importance. In this event, should your troops desire to come on our side of the line, come in welcome, when you please, and as far as you please.

A captive Mexican woman, whom we took away from the Apaches, and who is now at Pinos Altos, says the Apaches go into the town of Corralitas and buy powder and other ammunition from a Mexican resident of that place, whose name is Zoloaga. If this is so, I have but little doubt but that your excellency will cause Mr. Zoloaga to be shot; for it would be impossible to conceive of a crime of greater magnitude.

Hoping to hear a favorable response to my proposition, and ardently praying for the health and prosperity of your excellency, and the happiness and good fortune of the good people of the state of Chihuahua,

I have the honor to subscribe myself, with high regards, your excellency's obedient servant,

JAMES H. CARLETON,
Brigadier General, Commanding.

Don Louis Perrazas,
Governor of Chihuahua, Mexico.

Official:

ERASTUS W. WOOD,
Captain 1st Vet. Inf. C. V., A. A. A. General.

Headquarters Department of New Mexico,
Santa Fé, N. M., April 20, 1864.

My Dear Governor: About the 10th of May proximo a command of, say, five hundred men will start from Las Cruces, New Mexico, for a point to be selected on the Gila river, north of Fort Bowie, as the site of a new post. Here a depot will be formed, and from this place active hostilities will be commenced and continued against the Apache Indians of Arizona. The purpose of this letter is to urge upon your excellency the importance of getting every citizen of the Territory who has a rifle to take the field for, say, sixty days, and to co-operate with us in making war upon this tribe. The only hope we can have of speedy success must rest upon the combined efforts of every man who can be got to take the field. In this way, where many parties are in pursuit of Indians at the same time, the Indians, in endeavoring to escape from one, run into others. In this way, those who are not destroyed will soon be worried into acquiescence with our terms. I have written to the governors of Chihuahua and Sonora to endeavor to get them to turn out a few hundred men each, and to co-operate with us for sixty days, commencing, say, June 10, and have given them authority to pursue Indians over the line and as far into our Territory as they please.

I have given the Pimos and Maricopas over two hundred stand of arms, and ammunition for the same, for the purpose of enabling them to prosecute hostilities against the Apaches, and I desire that you will urge them to put four parties of, say, fifty men each in the field for the same sixty days. The Papagoes should also be induced to help their quota, and make the war general, and make it extend over as large a field as possible at the same moment of time. Here lies the great key to our success. While this is doing, troops will be directed to work eastward from Fort Whipple, southward from Fort Canby, southwestward from Fort Wingate, westward from Forts Craig and McRae. These movements will be simultaneous, and must produce favorable results. I will consult with Governor Connelly and try to get him to send a few militia from the southern part of the Territory to help.

Let me count on your active and energetic efforts in this matter, and in a few months we may hope to see Arizona free from the great impediment which stands in the way of her speedy development. Pray see the Papagoes, the Pimos, and the Maricopas, and have that part of the programme well and effectually executed. You will be able to secure the efforts of the miners without trouble. Let us work earnestly and hard, and before next Christmas your Apaches are whipped. Unless we do this you will have a twenty years war.

You may count on my doing all that can be done to clear your Territory of these terrible savages; but it will take hard work and persistent work. Every man who has the development and prosperity of Arizona at heart must put his shoulder not only to the wheel, but to the rifle.

I am, my dear governor, very respectfully, your obedient servant,

JAMES H. CARLETON,
Brigadier General, Commanding.

His Excellency JOHN N. GOODWIN,
Governor of Arizona, Tucson, Arizona.

Official:

ERASTUS W. WOOD,
Captain 1st Vet. Inf. C. V., A. A. A. General.

HEADQUARTERS DEPARTMENT OF NEW MEXICO,
Santa Fé, N. M., *April* 21, 1864.

COLONEL: * * * * * * * * * *
I am organizing a command of five hundred men to operate from a base to be established on the Gila, north of Fort Bowie. This command will take the field about the 10th proximo, and will be supplied with flour from mills in your district.

You are authorized to give the Indian ponies captured in the very handsome affair of the energetic and gallant Whitlock to his command. Let me assure you, colonel, that Captain Whitlock's success is regarded here as a great *coup* on the Apaches. I feel to thank him most heartily for his exertions, prudence, skill, perseverance, and gallantry. The officers and soldiers who went with him, and who shared alike his toil and his triumphs, deserve great praise.

The letter sent by this mail to the governor of Chihuahua I wish you to forward by express. It is left unsealed, that you may read it. Every effort must be made to have a general rising of both citizens and soldiers, on both sides of the line, against the Apaches. All, Mexicans and Americans, have a direct interest in this matter.

I hope you will have every company in your command put in immediate readiness for the field, prepared at all points.

If possible I will come down in May.

I am, colonel, very respectfully, your obedient servant,

JAMES H. CARLETON,
Brigadier General, Commanding.

Colonel GEORGE W. BOWIE,
Commanding District of Arizona, Franklin, Texas.

Official:

ERASTUS W. WOOD,
Captain 1st Vet. Inf. C. V., A. A. A. General.

HEADQUARTERS DEPARTMENT OF NEW MEXICO,
Santa Fé, N. M., *April* 24, 1864.

GENERAL: I have the honor herewith to enclose—

1st. An official copy of a letter from Captain J. Thompson, 1st cavalry New Mexico volunteers, giving the essential points of a march which he made from Fort Canby, in the Navajo country, to Fort Sumner, on the Pecos river, having in his charge, when he arrived at Fort Sumner, two thousand four hundred Navajo prisoners. The Adjutant General will see that one hundred and ninety-seven of these Indian prisoners of Captain Thompson's party, when he left Fort Canby, died *en route*. The weather was very inclement, with terrible gales of wind and heavy falls of snow; the Indians were nearly naked; and, besides, many died from dysentery, occasioned by eating too heartily of half-cooked bread, made of our flour, to which they were not accustomed.

2d. A copy of a letter from Major Henry D. Wallen, United States army, commanding at Fort Sumner, in the heart of the Indian reservation. This letter explains how the Navajo and Apache prisoners are getting along.

By next week we shall have some sixteen ploughs running near the post.

Both of these letters are dated the 15th instant.

I am, general, very respectfully, your obedient servant,

JAMES H. CARLETON,
Brigadier General, Commanding.

Brigadier General LORENZO THOMAS,
Adjutant General U. S. A., Washington, D. C.

Official:

ERASTUS W. WOOD,
Captain 1st Vet. Inf. C. V., A. A. A. General.

HEADQUARTERS DEPARTMENT OF NEW MEXICO,
Santa Fé, N. M., April 24, 1864.

GENERAL: I have the honor herewith to enclose—

1st. A copy of an official letter from Colonel Christopher Carson, 1st cavalry New Mexico volunteers, dated the 10th instant. In this letter the colonel expresses his convictions that we have not yet got one-half of the tribe of Navajoes. In this, from all I can learn, I think the colonel overestimates the number of those not come in. In my belief the *Ricos* not yet surrendered, but who, it is said, will soon come in, do not number over two thousand. We have now, in round numbers, six thousand, which would make the whole number of the nation to be eight thousand—a full estimate, I think. See in this letter what Colonel Carson says of the "wisdom" displayed in moving these Indians. I use the word wisdom without any reference to myself, but merely to contrast it against the utter folly of any measure looking toward putting the Navajoes on a reservation in the Navajo country.

2d. An official copy of a private letter from Colonel Carson, in which he speaks more fully of the propriety of removing the Indians, and of his desire to be at some post where he can have his family with him. Colonel Carson has labored hard, and is deserving of some respite. I sincerely trust the War Department will recognize his services in some substantial manner.

Captain Asa B Carey, who has labored so hard in this Navajo war, should be brevetted a lieutenant colonel. This recommendation is based upon the supposition that he will surely be brevetted a major for distinguished gallantry in assisting to burn the Texan train in Apache cañon, March 28, 1862.

Major John C. McFerran, United States army, should receive a brevet as lieutenant colonel for distinguished services as chief quartermaster of this department during the Navajo war. See a copy of my letter of February 27, 1864, on this subject.

I am, general, very truly and respectfully, your obedient servant,

JAMES H. CARLETON,
Brigadier General, Commanding.

Brigadier General LORENZO THOMAS,
Adjutant General U. S. A., Washington, D. C.

Official:

ERASTUS W. WOOD,
Captain 1st Vet. Inf. C. V., A. A. A. General.

HEADQUARTERS DEPARTMENT OF NEW MEXICO,
Santa Fé, N. M., April 24, 1864.

GENERAL: I have the honor herewith to enclose—

1st. A copy of a private letter from the Hon. Richard C. McCormick, secretary of Arizona, dated Fort Whipple, Arizona, March 26, 1864, in relation to Indian hostilities in that Territory. This will be proved to be a very interesting letter.

2d. A copy of the Arizona Miner, newspaper, which also tells of Indian troubles there.

3d. A copy of an official letter from Major Edward B. Willis, 1st infantry California volunteers, commanding at Fort Whipple, Arizona Territory. It is dated March 18, 1864. This letter gives an account of an extended scout in that distant *terra incognita* in search of a locality for the territorial capital. The description of the country, and the difficulty of travelling over it, will be found interesting and of historic value in connexion with the first settlement of what, at no distant day, will be a powerful and wealthy State.

4th. A copy of an official letter from the same officer. It is dated Fort Whipple, Arizona, March 28, 1864, and gives further intelligence of the hostilities of the Apaches in that section of country.

5th. Letter from myself to his excellency the governor of Chihuahua, Mexico. It is dated April 20, 1864.

6th. Letter from myself to his excellency the governor of the State of Sonora, Mexico.

7th. Letter of same date from myself to his excellency John H. Goodwin, governor of the Territory of Arizona.

These last three letters will inform the War Department of measures which are now taking towards commencing hostilities against the Apaches of Arizona. We are getting supplies and means of transportation down to Las Cruces as fast as practicable, and collecting troops there from other points for this service. We shall all do our best to put an end to these Indian troubles in Arizona. The War Department must know that all of Arizona north of the Gila for, say, two hundred miles, and covering the range of country infested by hostile Indians, is of the most difficult character over which to move troops. Every expedition must be made with pack-mules for transportation, and as the country may be said to be unknown with regard to practicable routes and to points where grass and water may be found, too much must not be expected from the labors of the troops. They will do their best; and if the plan of operations which is set forth in the letter to Governor Goodwin be carried out, hopes for good results may, with some reason, be entertained.

8th. A map of the country upon which Lieutenant Cyrus H. De Forrest, aide-de-camp, has laid down some of the principal points alluded to in these letters. It will be found to be useful as a map for reference.

I am, general, very respectfully, your obedient servant,

JAMES H. CARLETON,
Brigadier General, Commanding.

Brigadier General LORENZO THOMAS,
Adjutant General U. S. A., Washington, D. C.

Official:

ERASTUS W. WOOD,
Captain 1st Vet. Inf. C. V., A. A. A. General.

HEADQUARTERS DEPARTMENT OF NEW MEXICO,
Santa Fé, N. M., April 24, 1864.

GENERAL: On the 15th ultimo, about 3 p. m., the Apache Indians of Arizona stampeded a herd of government mules at Cow Springs, one march west of the Mimbres river, and succeeded in getting off with sixty of these mules and four public horses. This could not have been done had a company of infantry, which was escorting the train to which these animals belonged, been on the alert, and with sentinels posted well outside of the herd, which was grazing.

Enclosed herewith please find a letter from Colonel George W. Bowie, commanding district of Arizona, and a letter from Captain James H. Whitlock, commanding a company in Colonel Bowie's regiment, 5th infantry California volunteers, wherein you will see with what handsome results these Indians were followed. Captain Whitlock and the gallant men who accompanied him deserve an especial notice from the War Department.

A dozen or two of pursuits like Captain Whitlock's would give our troops the *morale* over these Ishmaelites of our deserts. Twenty-one Apache warriors left dead upon the ground, and a large amount of stock retaken, are results which the War Department may consider to be creditable.

I am, general, very respectfully, your obedient servant,

JAMES H. CARLETON,
Brigadier General, Commanding.

Brigadier General LORENZO THOMAS,
Adjutant General U. S. A., Washington, D. C.

Official:

ERASTUS W. WOOD,
Captain 1st Vet. Inf. C. V., A. A. A. General.

HEADQUARTERS DEPARTMENT OF NEW MEXICO,
Santa Fé, N. M., April 25, 1864.

COLONEL: Enclosed herewith you will find a telegram dated at San Francisco, the 7th instant. The companies which are to be sent by Yuma are the last three of the seven companies of the 1st cavalry California volunteers. Colonel Davis, United States army, who is supposed to be at or near Tucson, has this day been written to to send the best one of these companies to the Riventon, and the other two to await orders at the camp on the Mimbres. In case Colonel Davis has left Tucson when these companies come, you will see that these troops are distributed as I have directed. Have your whole command put in immediate order for field service. See that all your canteens, haversacks, water-kegs, pack-saddles, apacahoes, wagons, harness, &c., are in the best possible repair, so as to move your troops at a day's notice.

Depend on this, the present garrison at Tucson will be sure to take the field at a very early day, and I desire to have it move without delay and in splendid order for field service and fighting. When you come to have critical inspections of your material, of your clothing, camp and field equipage, of what needs repairs, of what is absolutely essential and what is not, you will find, as I have often found, that you have a great task on your hands. See that all of your books are posted up to date, and all accounts made up to date and sent off, that there be no after-claps about your records, whether of post or in any company or staff departments. Have everything snug and ship-shape and prepared, as a sailor might say, for a storm.

I am, colonel, very respectfully, your obedient servant,

JAMES H. CARLETON,
Brigadier General, Commanding.

Lieutenant Colonel THEODORE A. COULT,
Commanding at Tucson, Arizona.

Official:

ERASTUS W. WOOD,
Captain 1st Vet. Inf. C. V., A. A. A. General.

HEADQUARTERS DEPARTMENT OF NEW MEXICO,
Santa Fé, N. M., April 25, 1864.

COLONEL: You are authorized to let the camp on the Mimbres remain as it is until further orders. It will be a good strategic point, having reference to approaching operations against the Apaches of Arizona.

Please send some first-rate men and have Leitzendorfer's well enlarged, and made so as to hold a large volume of water. The troops will doubtless have to go by the Cienega de San Simon on account of a lack of water on the Stein's Peak route. Have Cow springs enlarged and cleaned out without delay.

Respectfully, I am, colonel, your obedient servant,

JAMES H. CARLETON,
Brigadier General, Commanding.

Colonel GEORGE W. BOWIE,
Commanding District of Arizona, Franklin, Texas.

Official:

ERASTUS W. WOOD,
Captain 1st Vet. Inf. C. V., A. A. A. General.

HEADQUARTERS DEPARTMENT OF NEW MEXICO,
Santa Fé, N. M., May 2, 1864.

CAPTAIN: Please find enclosed herewith General Orders No. 12, current series from these headquarters. You can have a picked command of sixty men, all told, got in readiness and move by the 20th instant, so as to be in position in time to perform your part of the programme. Of course, if this party comes across Navajoes who are not *en route* to surrender themselves at your post, they will be attacked. It seems to me you could get two or three Navajo guides who could take the troops directly to an Apache rancheria. Let us see whether parties of New Mexico volunteers can excel parties of Californians. Let officers and men be picked. * * * * * * * *

I am, captain, very respectfully, your obedient servant,

JAMES H. CARLETON,
Brigadier General, Commanding.

Captain Asa B. Carey, U. S. A.,
Commanding Navajo Expedition, Fort Canby, N. M.

Official:

ERASTUS W. WOOD,
Captain 1st Vet. Inf. C. V., A. A. A. General.

Department of New Mexico, Assistant Adjutant General's Office,
Santa Fé, N. M., May 3, 1865.

Captain: Your communication of the 29th ultimo has been received. The commanding general directs me to say that the course adopted by you with reference to the Mexicans and Indians who attacked the Navajoes that were *en route* to Fort Canby is approved. You will retake any stock or property thus taken from the friendly Navajoes and return it to them; and take prisoners, and send to Santa Fé, any Mexicans, Zuñi, Moquoi or Utah Indians who offend in that manner. Send word to the Zuñis and Moquis that if they allow this to occur again their villages will be attacked by our troops. If necessary, take some of the chiefs and principal men and hold them as hostages for the good behavior of the balance of the tribe.

The missing communication from the express package was probably one taken out by Colonel Carson, while *en route* from Fort Canby to Santa Fé. The express man had orders to give him a letter from the package if he should meet the colonel on the road.

Enclosed you will find a copy of department General Orders No. 12, current series. The general thinks it would be well, in executing that portion of paragraph V which refers to Fort Canby, to transport your supplies, if possible, by wagons to the base of the Mogollon mountains. By so doing you would save your pack-mules for the more active operations. If you can spare the wagons from the post they might remain until the return of the detachment. The guard left with them would have to intrench themselves to prevent being captured while the scouting parties were out.

I am, captain, very respectfully, your obedient servant,

CYRUS H. DE FORREST, *Aide-de-Camp.*

Captain Asa B. Carey, U. S. A.,
Commanding at Fort Canby, N. M.

Official:

ERASTUS W. WOOD,
Captain 1st Vet. Inf. C. V., A. A. A. General.

Headquarters Department of New Mexico,
Santa Fé, N. M., May 9, 1865.

General: Enclosed herewith I have the honor to send you an interesting report on affairs at Fort Sumner, as far as the Navajo and Apache Indians are concerned. This report is written by Major Henry D. Wallen, United States army, at present in command at Fort Sumner. It shows the progress of the work that has been done there preliminary to getting in a crop. Want of tools, want of clothing, want of almost everything, is severely felt; but we are hoping that the authorities at Washington will soon remedy all this.

I am, general, very respectfully, your obedient servant,

JAMES H. CARLETON,
Brigadier General, Commanding.

Brigadier General Lorenzo Thomas,
Adjutant General U. S. A., Washington, D. C.

Official:

ERASTUS W. WOOD,
Captain 1st Vet. Inf. C. V., A. A. A. General.

HEADQUARTERS DEPARTMENT OF NEW MEXICO,
Santa Fé, N. M., May 31, 1864.

GENERAL: I have the honor to enclose herewith—

1st. An official copy of a report dated May 5, 1864, made by Lieutenant Henry H. Stevens, 5th infantry California volunteers, and giving particulars of a handsome little fight which took place between company I, 5th infantry California volunteers, under Lieutenant Stevens's command, and one hundred Apache warriors. The Indians attacked the troops as they were passing through Doubtful Cañon, near Stein's Peak, in Arizona. Lieutenant Stevens deserves credit for the handsome manner in which he conducted this affair.

2d. An official copy of a report on the Navajo war, and other matters pertaining to the settlement upon a reservation of this formidable tribe. This report is made by Colonel Christopher Carson, 1st cavalry New Mexico volunteers, and is dated May 20, 1864.

I am, general, very respectfully, your obedient servant,

JAMES H. CARLETON,
Brigadier General, Commanding.

Brigadier General LORENZO THOMAS,
Adjutant General U. S. A., Washington, D. C.

Official:

ERASTUS W. WOOD,
Captain 1st Vet. Inf. C. V., A. A. A. General.

HEADQUARTERS DEPARTMENT OF NEW MEXICO,
Santa Fé, N. M., May 31, 1864.

GENERAL: Enclosed herewith please find a report made by Captain Francis McCabe, 1st cavalry New Mexico volunteers, of the movement of over eight hundred Navajo prisoners from their native country to the reservation at the Bosque Redondo. I am induced to send all these reports to the War Department that you may be in possession of the historical facts connected with the final exodus of this interesting people from the land of their birth to that set apart for their residence, henceforth, by the general government.

I am, general, very respectfully, &c., &c.,

JAMES H. CARLETON,
Brigadier General, Commanding.

Brigadier General LORENZO THOMAS,
Adjutant General U. S. A., Washington, D. C.

Official:

ERASTUS W. WOOD,
Captain 1st Vet. Inf. C. V., A. A. A. General.

HEADQUARTERS DEPARTMENT OF NEW MEXICO,
Santa Fé, N. M., June 17, 1864.

CAPTAIN: I have directed Colonel Rigg to establish Fort Goodwin in or near the Tuleroso valley. Colonel Davis suggests that you be selected to point out the exact spot. To save time proceed at once and join Colonel Rigg for this purpose, which, when completed, may leave no doubt upon so important a point. Give Colonel Rigg all possible information of the country, the San Carlos and Bonita valleys; of wheat and corn-fields belonging to Indians, that he may consume the grain before it is gathered by them, and then return as quickly as possible to your post and carry out effectively, as I know you will do, your part of the programme. I feel to congratulate you on your success. Pray thank the officers and men who were with you for their gallant conduct and their efficient services. Do this in my name.

My anxiety to do all that mortals can do to bring this Apache war to a speedy and final end is very great. Not until then will Arizona show the world her wonderful deposits of gold and silver.

I am, captain, respectfully,

JAMES H. CARLETON,
Brigadier General, Commanding.

Captain T. T. TIDBALL,
Commanding at Fort Bowie, Arizona.

Official:

ERASTUS W. WOOD,
Captain 1st Vet. Inf. C. V., A. A. A. General.

HEADQUARTERS DEPARTMENT OF NEW MEXICO,
Santa Fé, N. M., June 19, 1864.

GENERAL: I have the honor herewith to enclose—

1st. An official copy of a letter from Major Edward B. Willis, 1st infantry California volunteers, commanding at Fort Whipple, Arizona. It is dated the 27th ultimo, and gives the latest intelligence from the new gold fields in that vicinity. The general will see that the promise of mineral wealth in northern Arizona is becoming more than realized.

2d. An official copy of a letter from Lieutenant Colonel Nelson H. Davis, assistant inspector general United States army. It is dated at Tucson, Arizona, June 5, 1864.

Colonel Davis was ordered to select a site for a post to be established on the Gila river, northward from Fort Bowie, Arizona, and had an escort of about one hundred men, more or less, according to my recollection from previous reports. With a part of this escort he made a night march, and at daybreak attacked a rancheria of Apaches and killed forty-nine of them. This is decidedly the most brilliant success over that tribe of brutal murderers which has ever been won. Too much praise cannot be awarded to Colonel Davis and the handful of officers and men who so gallantly followed him, for this achievement.

I urgently request that Colonel Davis may receive the compliment of a brevet for such gallant and meritorious conduct.

Very respectfully, your obedient servant,

JAMES H. CARLETON,
Brigadier General, Commanding.

Brigadier General LORENZO THOMAS,
Adjutant General U. S. A., Washington, D. C.

Official:

ERASTUS W. WOOD,
Captain 1st Vet. Inf. C. V., A. A. A. General.

HEADQUARTERS DEPARTMENT OF NEW MEXICO,
Santa Fé, N. M., June 25, 1864.

GENERAL: I have the honor herewith to enclose a copy of a letter, dated the 9th instant, from Captain Henry B. Bristol, United States army, commanding at Fort Sumner, N. M. You will see that it gives very gratifying intelligence from the Navajoes and Apaches on the reservation at that post. The overflow of the river alluded to is over the lower bottom; the crops are quite all planted on a second bottom some four or five feet higher, and were not injured, I suppose. I think the estimate of three thousand acres already planted is too large, but do not doubt but that the number of acres which will be planted this year will come nearly up to three thousand—may exceed it. The Indians, as a general thing, are very docile and quite industrious.

I am general, very respectfully, your obedient servant,

JAMES H. CARLETON,
Brigadier General, Commanding.

Brigadier General LORENZO THOMAS,
Adjutant General U. S. A., Washington, D. C.

Official:

ERASTUS W. WOOD,
Captain 1st Vet. Inf. C. V., A. A. A. General.

HEADQUARTERS DEPARTMENT OF NEW MEXICO,
Santa Fé, N. M., June 26, 1864.

DEAR SIR: Your letter of the 16th instant was handed to me by Captain Benjamin C. Cutler, assistant adjutant general, last evening. I regret to hear that the Indians in Colorado are becoming hostile. Your excellency, perhaps, may not have heard that we are now in the midst of active operations against the numerous hordes of Apaches in Arizona, and that nearly all the available force in this department is now occupied in that campaign or in conducting captive Navajo Indians from their native country to the Bosque Redondo, on the Pecos river, a distance of more than three hundred miles, or in guarding near seven thousand of these captives at Fort Sumner and Fort Canby. A short time since a band of guerillas robbed some trains upon the Cimarron route, and I have troops in pursuit of them from Fort Union and from Fort Bascom. I mention these matters to show how the small number of men now under my command are employed. But when we were menaced and in trouble you came to help us, and you may be sure that should you need our assistance we will respond to your call, as far as possible, to the last man that can be spared. I will try to get some more troops to Fort Union at the earliest practicable day, and will help you all we can.

Be of good cheer, for if Colorado and New Mexico join in hostilities against the Utes, I believe by the end of next winter we could bring them to such a state as to make any other campaign unnecessary. It would be well to avoid a collision until the snow falls, if possible. The winter time is the most favorable for operations against Indians, as then no time is lost in trailing, and they soon become exhausted of supplies; and, being embarrassed by their families, cannot so well elude pursuit. Of course, a war with that or any other tribe is to be avoided altogether, if possible. When it is commenced, it should be commenced because they have been the aggressors and are clearly in the wrong. In this case the punishment should be very severe. I mention these matters to your excellency, so that all efforts for peace may be resorted to before war is resorted to; then, if we must have war in spite of our efforts, Colorado and New Mexico united may make it a war which they will remember.

I am, very respectfully, your excellency's obedient servant,

JAMES H. CARLETON,
Brigadier General, Commanding.

His Excellency John Evans,
Governor of Colorado, Denver, Col.

Official:

ERASTUS W. WOOD,
Captain 1st Vet. Inf. C. V., A. A. A. General.

Headquarters Department of New Mexico,
Santa Fé, N. M., June 30, 1864.

Colonel: By a communication from the War Department to these headquarters, dated January 9, 1864, it is forbidden for any of the military to adopt Indian children. This, in connexion with another communication from the same source on the giving up of Indians held by citizens, which communication is referred to in a recent proclamation by the governor of New Mexico to the people, induces me to believe that under no circumstances will the government tolerate the "binding out" of Indians to either officers or citizens; therefore I decide that all Apache captives be sent, properly guarded, to the Rio Grande, at Las Cruces, and thence to the reservation at the Bosque Redondo. Please to thank Captain French and his men, in my name, for their handsome campaign, made with good results, under discouraging circumstances.

It is to be hoped that the citizens of Tucson, who have so much interest in a successful termination of the Apache campaign, will go out and strike one good blow to help the cause. The troops operating from the north have had some beautiful little battles, and killed and captured quite a number of Apaches.

I am, colonel, very respectfully, your obedient servant,

JAMES H. CARLETON,
Brigadier General, Commanding.

Lieutenant Colonel Theodore A. Coult,
Commanding at Tucson, Arizona.

Official:

ERASTUS W. WOOD,
Captain 1st Vet. Inf. C. V., A. A. A. General.

Headquarters Department of New Mexico,
Santa Fé, N. M., July 8, 1864.

Major: I desire that you send to the Bosque with the next party of Navajoes all of the Apache prisoners who were brought in by Captain Pfeiffer's command. If there be danger of their escaping *en route*, the men of those prisoners should be ironed. By having some of the Arizona Apaches at the Bosque, I can, at the proper time, send some of them out into their own country with such intelligence as may induce others to come in. It is important that every Navajo Indian should be sent to the Bosque at the earliest practicable day. I wish to break up Fort Canby as soon as possible. Please send me an express the day the next party starts, with an account of its strength, the number and description of its stock, &c.

I am, major, respectfully,

JAMES H. CARLETON,
Brigadier General, Commanding.

Major P. W. L. Plympton,
Commanding at Fort Canby, N. M.

Official:

ERASTUS W. WOOD,
Captain 1st Vet. Inf. C. V., A. A. A. General.

Headquarters Department of New Mexico,
Santa Fé, N. M., July 8, 1864.

General: I have the honor to enclose herewith—

1st. A return of captive Indians now at the Bosque Redondo. This return is dated the 30th ultimo, and shows a total of 6,321. Information, not in an official form, has just been received here that there are now at Fort Canby 1,000 more Navajoes, awaiting transportation for the children, to go to the Bosque. Teams are now on the way to that post to move this party. I have reason to believe that we shall soon have them all; for the Navajoes who come in say that the Ute Indians are endeavoring to cut off all Navajoes who are still at large. This will hasten them in.

2d. A copy of a letter from Captain H. B. Bristol, United States army, conveying a letter to himself, written by Captain William P. Calloway, 1st infantry California volunteers, who has had charge of the planting at Fort Sumner. These letters show how much has been done towards raising a crop this year. If we could have had tools and farming utensils enough we could have raised twice as much this year. A field of 3,000 acres will help a good deal, however. I am very hopeful that next year there will be enough raised to support all the Indians at the Bosque Redondo.

Respectfully, your obedient servant,

JAMES H. CARLETON,
Brigadier General, Commanding.

Brigadier General Lorenzo Thomas,
Adjutant General U. S. A., Washington, D. C.

Official:

ERASTUS W. WOOD,
Captain 1st Vet. Inf. C. V., A. A. A. General.

Headquarters Department of New Mexico,
Santa Fé, N. M., July 17, 1864.

Captain: I desire that you make, once a week at least, a report of the progress made in building by the employés and troops, and of the progress made in planting and attending to crops, and the appearance of the crops belonging to the Indians. Some three or four hundred of hoes have recently been sent to you. Do you absolutely need more, and if so, how many?

The Reverend Mr. Hayes has come back and gives us the pleasing intelligence that he has engaged a priest and three lay brothers and some sisters to instruct the Indian children; and the Secretary of the Interior has written to the bishop of New Mexico that we shall have some assistance toward establishing of the schools at Fort Sumner. Tell the Indians this. Now, as the season is far advanced, and it is important to have school-rooms erected at the earliest practicable day, I wish you would consult with Colonel Carson, and get the Indians to make a sufficient quantity of adobes to put up, say, eight good rooms for school purposes and for the teachers to live in.

I want a site chosen for this school establishment near the post, and a plan carefully drawn for the different buildings. The rooms should, when all completed, occupy the four sides of a square. No one school-room should hold over one hundred scholars. Now all the rooms should face inward on the square or *placita*. Here the children could play. Suppose the square to be arranged so as to be to the same points of the compass as Fort Sumner. Now the first rooms to be built, this year, should be those on the northern side, and if possible some on the east and west sides. Next year we could complete the square. It follows, then, that the whole plan should be carefully made, and be framed, and be kept at Fort Sumner, to be built to from time to time, until completed. It must be remembered that for at least 800 children, with rooms for teachers, &c., the establishment when done will be quite extensive. I wish you to study out this matter carefully, and give expression to the idea by a well-considered plan with specifications. We will at once build as many of the rooms as we can. All we ask of the Indians is to make the adobes. If they help lay them they shall be paid for that part of the labor. The site should be so chosen that a fine, large piece of ground can be set apart as a garden, where the boys can be taught practically the art of raising fruit and vegetables. We have no time to lose.

I am, captain, very respectfully, your obedient servant,

JAMES H. CARLETON,
Brigadier General, Commanding.

Captain HENRY B. BRISTOL,
Commanding at Fort Sumner, N. M.

Official:

ERASTUS W. WOOD,
Captain 1st Vet. Inf. C. V., A. A. A. General.

HEADQUARTERS DEPARTMENT OF NEW MEXICO,
Santa Fé, N. M., July 21, 1864.

COLONEL: From information which I have received, I believe that many Apaches have left the mountains north of the Gila and are now in considerable numbers along the Sonora line, about and west of Lake Guzman. I am anxious that an officer of experience should command a small force and proceed against these Apaches. His operations in this respect will be independent of, but auxiliary to, the general movement now making against these Indians, which movement is under the command of Colonel Rigg, 1st infantry California volunteers. You are selected to command this force, and will proceed to Las Cruces, and, by my authority, require of Colonel Bowie, commanding the district of Arizona, the necessary number of troops, not to exceed seventy, rank and file of infantry, and not to exceed fifteen cavalry, with a proportionate number of officers. The necessary funds, subsistence stores, transportation, guides, and packers, will be furnished by the chief quartermaster and chief commissary of the district of Arizona on and according to your requisitions. The ordnance officer at Las Cruces will also furnish what ordnance and ordnance stores you may want. The time to be occupied on this expedition is left to your judgment; but it is presumed that you can accomplish all practicable purposes with regard to the Indians in, say, not to exceed sixty days from the time of departure from Las Cruces. I have heard that some rich *placers* of gold have recently been discovered on the Sonora line, somewhere northwestwardly from Corralitas; that these *placers* occupy the country on both sides of the line. I have also heard that in that neighborhood, or still further westward, there are some *very rich* mines of silver. You will get all the information you can in relation to the truth of these rumors, as to the existence and character of these mines, as the next important consideration, after the subjugation of the Indians, is the knowledge of the mineral wealth of the country. This is now of vast importance to the general government. Having completed all this, and returned the troops to their proper stations, you will come to department headquarters and report the result in writing for the information of the War Department.

If possible procure specimens of good size from any *placers* or mines which you may visit or discover, that they may be sent to Washington with your report.

I am, colonel, very respectfully, your obedient servant,

JAMES H. CARLETON,
Brigadier General, Commanding.

Lieutenant Colonel NELSON H. DAVIS,
Assistant Inspector General U. S. A., and chief commissary.

Official:

ERASTUS W. WOOD,
Captain 1st Vet. Inf. C. V., A. A. A. General.

HEADQUARTERS DEPARTMENT OF NEW MEXICO,
Santa Fé, N. M., July 23, 1864.

GENERAL: I have the honor herewith to enclose—

1st A copy of a letter dated July 12, 1864, at Fort Canby, by Major P. W. L. Plympton, United States seventh infantry, temporarily in command of that post. This letter shows that, say, one thousand and forty-four Navajo Indians are now *en route* from the Navajo country to the reservation at the Bosque Redondo. This nearly completes the whole tribe. As operations are concluded in the Navajo country, instructions have been given for the abandonment of Fort Canby as soon as the *matériel* can be gotten away.

2d. A copy of a letter dated at Fort Sumner, New Mexico, on the 14th instant, from Colonel Carson. This interesting letter shows the favorable condition of affairs at the reservation to which the Navajo tribe of Indians have been sent. It shows that there are now on the reservation six thousand three hundred and nine Indians. When those reach there who are now *en route*, there will be seven thousand three hundred and fifty-three. It is possible when all the stragglers come in the number will be swelled to eight thousand.

3d. A copy of a letter dated at Fort Sumner, New Mexico, on the 15th instant. This letter, written by Captain Henry B. Bristol, United States fifth infantry, in command of that post, gives a very satisfactory account of the condition of affairs at that important station.

I am, general, very respectfully, your obedient servant,

JAMES H. CARLETON,
Brigadier General, Commanding.

Brigadier General LORENZO THOMAS,
Adjutant General U. S. A., Washington, D. C.

Official:

ERASTUS W. WOOD,
Captain 1st Vet. Inf. C. V., A. A. A. General.

HEADQUARTERS DEPARTMENT OF NEW MEXICO,
Santa Fé, N. M., August 13, 1864.

CAPTAIN: I have not received your return of captive Indians made in tabular form, and showing loss and gain, for the month of July, 1864. Please send it at once, that a copy may be forwarded to the War Department. Hereafter enter upon the remarks on your post return the number of captive Indians of each tribe which you have on the last day of each month. I desire that a regular morning report be kept of these Indians, so that a history of the changes among them can always be at Fort Sumner. In the column of remarks of such report, enter arrivals, births, deaths, &c., &c., and events, such as when fields were ploughed, hoed, crops gathered, and amounts, acequias dug, &c., &c. Such a report will be exceedingly useful for future reference. Of course the report will only be approximately correct, except on days when you make a regular count of the Indians. Major Wallen, I believe, commenced a book of this kind If it is found impracticable to make a morning report, have it made weekly and on the last day of each month, when, of course, it will correspond with the total of the monthly return sent to department headquarters.

I am, captain, very respectfully, your obedient servant,

JAMES H. CARLETON,
Brigadier General, Commanding.

Captain HENRY B. BRISTOL,
Commanding at Fort Sumner, N. M.

Official:

ERASTUS W. WOOD,
Captain 1st Vet. Inf. C. V., A. A. A. General.

HEADQUARTERS DEPARTMENT OF NEW MEXICO,
Santa Fé, N. M., August 14, 1864.

SIR: Enclosed herewith is the ground-plan of a building for school-rooms and for quarters for some sisters and some lay brothers, who are coming to this Territory to assist in teaching the Navajo and Apache children how to read, write, &c. It is proposed to make this building near Fort Sumner, on the Navajo and Apache reservation. There we already have seven thousand five hundred of these Indians, and at least one thousand if not twelve hundred children among them. I have already expended, from quartermaster's funds, some eighteen thousand dollars for a hospital and for store-rooms for grain for these Indians. Those buildings are now nearly, if not quite, completed. If you could give twelve thousand dollars toward making this building, out of the one hundred thousand dollars just appropriated, we could soon have shelter for the teachers and rooms for the children and make a commencement in the great work in educating the youth of this interesting people. The twelve thousand dollars would be not even half what contractors would charge to put up the building and finish it complete, but that sum would pay for the *vigas* and the lumber, and for doors and windows. We hope to be able to get the Indians themselves to make the *adobes*, and to help lay up the walls. All of the expense of moving, clothing, feeding, and attending the sick of these Indians has thus far been thrown upon the War Department. I suppose the superintendent of Indian affairs has no authority to do anything for them.

If the twelve thousand dollars could at once be put at the disposal of Major John C. McFerran, the chief quartermaster of this department, I believe we could have all the arrangements completed for the school to go into operation before the first of next January.

I have been encouraged to address this note to you from having seen a letter which you wrote to Bishop Lanny on this subject.

I am, sir, very respectfully, your obedient servant,

JAMES H. CARLETON,
Brigadier General, Commanding.

Hon. J. P. Usher,
Secretary of the Interior, Washington, D. C.

Official:

ERASTUS W. WOOD,
Captain 1st Vet. Inf. C. V., A. A. A. General.

Headquarters Department of New Mexico.
Santa Fé, N. M., August 15, 1864.

Captain: I have heard that many Navajoes have had leave of absence. This is very hazardous just now when there are so many Indian troubles on the plains and in this country. If the report be true you will discontinue the practice until further authority from these headquarters.

* * * * * * * * * * *

Respectfully,

JAMES H. CARLETON,
Brigadier General, Commanding.

Captain Henry B. Bristol,
Commanding at Fort Sumner, N. M.

Official:

ERASTUS W. WOOD,
Captain 1st Vet. Inf. C. V., A. A. A. General.

Headquarters Department of New Mexico,
Santa Fé, N. M., August 15, 1864.

Colonel: Please give no more passes to Indians living on the reservation until further orders. There are now many Indian troubles, and the people will be alarmed even at seeing friendly Indians from the reservation.

The Comanches have, within a few days, killed five Americans at lower Cimarron springs, and run off cattle from a train of five wagons belonging to Mr. Allison, of this city. You will therefore have no word sent to them to come to make a treaty with Navajoes. Will two hundred Apaches and Navajoes go with troops to fight Comanches in case of serious troubles with the latter Indians?

Respectfully, your obedient servant,

JAMES H. CARLETON,
Brigadier General, Commanding.

Colonel Christopher Carson, *Fort Sumner, N. M.*

Official:

ERASTUS W. WOOD,
Captain 1st Vet. Inf. C. V., A. A. A. General.

HEADQUARTERS DEPARTMENT OF NEW MEXICO,
Santa Fé, N. M., August 16, 1864.

CAPTAIN: You are authorized to employ Navajoes to make adobes for their new schoolrooms by giving them a ration, as you suggested. They should commence at once. The site should be selected, and have the adobes made and carefully piled away near the site. A copy of your plan has been sent to the Secretary of the Interior, and he may give some help. If enough to buy the lumber and the doors and windows, we will do the rest. Let me count on your immediate and careful and continuous attention to this matter of the adobes. If these can be made at once, the building will be completed this fall, if Mr. Usher gives us help. Encourage the Indians to help.

Respectfully, your obedient servant,

JAMES H. CARLETON,
Brigadier General, Commanding.

Captain HENRY B. BRISTOL,
Commanding at Fort Sumner, N. M.

Official:

ERASTUS W. WOOD,
Captain 1st Vet. Inf. C. V., A. A. A. General.

DEPARTMENT OF NEW MEXICO, ASSISTANT ADJUTANT GENERAL'S OFFICE,
Santa Fé, N. M., August 22, 1864.

SIR: Enclosed herewith please find copy of letter to Captain E. H. Bergmann, first New Mexico cavalry, commanding Fort Bascom. Should the commanding officer of that post require help from you—a contingency contemplated in that letter—send to him as much as you can spare. The general suggests whether, in this event, it would not be well to send one hundred or more picked Apaches and Navajoes to help whip the Comanches, their hereditary enemies.

The chief quartermaster will direct that a set of blacksmith tools complete, and some iron, be sent to Fort Sumner for the use of the Navajoes. Tell them to go to work at once and make adobes to build the shop. You select the site near the post, and have the shop made long enough to have a forge in each end. It should not be too wide, on account of the difficulty of getting vigas of the proper length. You will furnish the vigas, in case the Navajoes cannot get them, by going to some place up the river. You will also furnish the window-casing and doors.

Have a board of officers go through the fields and make a careful examination to ascertain the probable per cent of corn which is injured. It is hoped that not so much of it has been destroyed as you feared.

I have the honor to be, very respectfully, your obedient servant,

BEN. C. CUTLER,
Assistant Adjutant General.

COMMANDING OFFICER, *Fort Sumner, N. M.*

Official:

ERASTUS W. WOOD,
Captain 1st Vet. Inf. C. V., A. A. A. General.

[Extract.]

DEPARTMENT OF NEW MEXICO, ASSISTANT ADJUTANT GENERAL'S OFFICE,
Santa Fé, N. M., August 22, 1864.

CAPTAIN: The general commanding the department directs that you take fifty rank and file and one officer, have them well mounted, and march without delay to Fort Union. Leave careful instructions with Captain Deüs about continuing the building of your post. You will leave behind the mechanics and men who will be most essential to that purpose. You will caution Captain Deüs about having a look-out party down the river to let him know whether any demonstration is about to be made against him by any large parties of Comanches, and if so, to send word to Fort Sumner in case those demonstrations are of an unmistakably hostile character, so as to get help from that post. The Comanches, Kiowas, and Cheyennes are attacking trains between the Cimarron and the frontier of Missouri, and some men have been killed by them upon the Cimarron. You will have thirty infantry added to your force at Fort Union, and remain at or near the upper Cimarron spring, Cold spring, or Cedar bluffs, according to how you find the best grazing. Each of the three points is a favorite place where Indians lie in wait to attack passing trains, and the purpose for which you are sent is to see that these trains are properly guarded until those points are safely passed. With the thirty infantry you can have your camp secure while you are making scouts, and are escorting with your cavalry. Major Joseph Updegraff, United States army, with fifty infantry and fifty cavalry, will be at or near the lower Cimarron spring. Should he need assistance from your party, he will send to you for it. If you need assistance from his, send to him.

* * * * * * * * * *

The general commanding thinks you had better take your guide, Mr. DeLisle, with you, as he knows all of the country around the upper Cimarron, and is familiar with all the Indians who frequent that part of the country.

I have the honor to be, captain, very respectfully, your obedient servant,

BEN. C. CUTLER,
Assistant Adjutant General.

Captain Edward H. Bergmann,
First New Mexico Cavalry, commanding at Fort Bascom, N. M.

Official: ERASTUS W. WOOD,
Captain 1st Vet. Inf. C. V., A. A. A. General.

Headquarters Department of New Mexico,
Santa Fé, N. M., August 24, 1864.

Colonel: I have the honor to inform you that the commanding officer at Fort Canby, New Mexico, writes to me that the Moqui and Oribi Indians have lost their crops from high winds and excessive drought, and are, from the statements of the Indians themselves, as well as from their famished appearance, already at the point of starvation.

Please to inform me by return of mail, or express, whether you will take measures at once to have them provided with food. If you will not do this, please state your determination to this end.

I have the honor to be, very respectfully, your obedient servant,

JAMES H. CARLETON,
Brigadier General, Commanding.

Colonel Charles D. Poston,
Sup't of Indian Affairs, Territory of Arizona, Tucson, or Prescott, Arizona.

Official: ERASTUS W. WOOD,
Captain 1st Vet. Inf. C. V., A. A. A. General.

Headquarters Department of New Mexico,
Santa Fé, N. M., August 27, 1864.

Sir: I have been furnished with copies of two letters written to the Hon. William P. Dole, Commissioner of Indian Affairs, by Matthew Steck, superintendent of Indian affairs for New Mexico. The letters are dated May 28 and June 25, 1864, and are in relation to the removal of the Navajo Indians from their country to the reservation set apart by law for these Indians and for the Apaches.

I have no disposition to have any controversy with Mr. Steck, nor do I wish to claim for the Indians anything that is not their just due, but truth and candor compel me to say that those letters are calculated greatly to mislead you with reference to this whole question.

Please find herewith enclosed a return of the number of Indians now at the reservation and *en route* thither. These comprise the principal chiefs and the most of the tribe, including nearly all the rich Indians. This fact is patent to every person in this country. The Indians on the reservation are the happiest people I have ever seen. They are industrious, and look forward with ardent hopes to the time when they can raise enough to support themselves. In room of committing depredations, they have gone out and attacked Indians who were attempting to run off the herds of the people. This fact is of public notoriety.

No board was ordered by the War Department. I, myself, ordered one. The board included provisions bought for troops and issued to Indians. No sixty men were ever employed by the quartermaster's department for Indians. Some public oxen were used for ploughing fields. The contracts for supplies for Indians included the cost of tansportation to Fort Sumner, where the supplies were to be delivered. The supplies were not for four months but for nearly a year. The whole cost of supplies, as ascertained by the board, was $414,852 66, total cost, and this for nearly or quite a years' supply, and not $700,000 for four months' supply and for labor, &c., as stated. Beef has risen greatly in price from the advance in the price of gold, and it is fortunate these purchases were made when they were. It was a saving to the government of more than $200,000. I have never heard of sheep being sold at four dollars per head, even at the highest, and one at a time. It is true that I had two storehouses made for the provisions, which cost $9,000, and a hospital for the Indians which cost $9,000.

The people are not opposed to the Indians being located at the Bosque Redondo; we all know that such an idea has been started and written upon for effect. I enclose for your perusal a New Mexican newspaper, with one of these supposed-to-be manufactured articles in it. No persons were killed by Indians from the reservation; no stock was run off by them. The stock was run off by the wild uncaught Apaches, it is thought, from Arizona, and was taken away from them by the troops. See the enclosed gazette.

I am sorry to trouble you about such matters, but let me assure you, as a gentleman, you are imposed upon by these letters, and the conduct of the military authorities here is not fairly represented. Time will prove all this to you. The proceedings of the board alluded to are in the War Department.

I enclose a letter from Colonel Carson in relation to the late raid upon the stock of the people by the Apaches.

We have had the Indians to contend with, and after much toil and suffering have brought this formidable tribe to terms. We hardly supposed that an officer of the government could sit down, and by such an array of misstatements endeavor to prejudice so high a public functionary as yourself against the only measure that can ever secure peace and prosperity to this impoverished country. I appeal to the proceedings of the board in question, to the archives of the quartermaster and subsistence departments, to the adjutant general of the army, to all the principal gentlemen in this country, commencing with the governor, the delegate, the chief justice, &c., &c., and to Colonel Carson, who commanded the expedition against the Navajoes, for the exactness of the statements here made.

I don't believe that, all told, there are one thousand Navajoes left in their country, and these, from the best information as yet ascertained, have fled away beyond the Little Colorado. You will perhaps, some time or other, learn the motives which have induced these statements by Dr. Steck. It is a pity, when so much has been accomplished for the country, that any one should come forward with a studied effort to undo it all.

I have the honor to be, very respectfully, your obedient servant,

JAMES H. CARLETON,
Brigadier General, Commanding.

Hon. J. P. Usher,
Secretary of the Interior, Washington, D. C.

Note.—Contrast the comparative expense between feeding and fighting these Indians, as set forth in Superintendent Steck's letter to the Commissioner of Indian Affairs, dated September 19, 1863. (See Report of Commissioner of Indian Affairs for 1863, p. 107; and also see the able Report of the Commissioner of Indian Affairs for 1863, pp. 13, 14 and 15.)

Official:

ERASTUS W. WOOD,
Captain 1st Vet. Inf. C. V., A. A. A. General.

Headquarters Department of New Mexico,
Santa Fé, N. M., August 27, 1864.

General: I have the honor to inform you that I have ordered a force of fifty cavalry and fifty infantry, under the command of Major Joseph Updegraff, to the lower Cimarron springs, to assist in giving protection to trains *en route* from and to the States; and fifty cavalry and thirty infantry to the upper Cimarron spring for a like purpose. I informed you on the 8th instant that fifty cavalry and fifty infantry had been sent, via the Cimarron route, to the upper crossing of the Arkansas to help the trains. These three parties, all that can be safely spared at this moment, will, it is to be hoped, effect good results. They are rationed for fifty days.

I am, general, very respectfully, your obedient servant,

JAMES H. CARLETON,
Brigadier General, Commanding.

Brigadier General LORENZO THOMAS,
Adjutant General U. S. A., Washington, D. C.

Official:

ERASTUS W. WOOD,
Captain 1st Vet. Inf. C. V., A. A. A. General.

HEADQUARTERS DEPARTMENT OF NEW MEXICO,
Santa Fé, N. M., August 27, 1864.

MAJOR: Under the peculiar circumstances in which you are placed with reference to Indian hostilities and a want of arms, the authority given to you by Colonel John C. McFerran, United States army, chief of staff at these headquarters, to take from Mr. Bryant's train fifteen boxes of Sharp's carbines and ten boxes of revolvers, with a reasonable amount of ammunition for the same, is hereby approved. Please call a board to count the articles and send triplicate receipts for them in favor of William R. Shoemaker, in charge of ordnance depot at Fort Union, New Mexico.

Enclosed herewith please find copies of orders sending two companies of infantry to give you help. I have to inform you that I have ordered fifty cavalry and fifty infantry, with two mountain howitzers, to the crossing of the Arkansas, fifty cavalry and fifty infantry to the lower Cimarron spring, and fifty cavalry and thirty infantry to the upper Cimarron spring. The first of these detachments has already arrived at its destination; the latter two will leave Fort Union within a week. It is important that your scouts should know this. These detachments have been rationed for fifty days. We will help all we can. We have the Apache war in Arizona on our hands, and nearly eight thousand Navajo prisoners to guard, but we do not forget that your gallant troops from Colorado came to our relief when we were sorely pressed. But for the fact that over half of the available force in this department is about to be mustered out of service, we would do even more.

I am, major, very respectfully, your obedient servant,

JAMES H. CARLETON,
Brigadier General, Commanding.

Major EDWARD W. WYNKOOP,
Commanding at Fort Lyon, District of Colorado.

Official:

ERASTUS W. WOOD,
Captain 1st Vet. Inf. C. V., A. A. A. General.

HEADQUARTERS DEPARTMENT OF NEW MEXICO,
Santa Fé, N. M., August 27, 1864.

GENERAL: I have the honor again to call your attention to the condition of this department with reference to its rapidly diminishing force from the mustering out of service now, and between this time and next November, of the most of the 1st cavalry, New Mexico volunteers, of five companies of the 1st cavalry, and the 1st and 5th regiments of infantry, California volunteers. As you will see, this leaves the department in a helpless condition. The Indians upon the plains are attacking our trains and killing our people. We are in active hostilities with the Apaches of Arizona, and have seven thousand six hundred and forty-one Indian prisoners upon the reservation, which, for the present, we are obliged to guard. I heard a rumor that it was the intention of the War Department to send Colonel Ford's regiment of Colorado volunteers for service in this department. If that regiment, now in Missouri, could be sent at once across the plains to New Mexico, the moral effect upon the hostile Indians *en route* would doubtless be so great that they would leave the road and thus let our trains come through in safety. The importance of these trains coming through without molestation, laden as they are with our subsistence stores, hospital stores, and supplies of ordnance and ordnance stores, cannot be too highly estimated. I beg this matter may have the immediate and serious attention of the War Department.

I am, general, very respectfully, your obedient servant,

JAMES H. CARLETON,
Brigadier General, Commanding.

Brigadier General LORENZO THOMAS,
Adjutant General U. S. A., Washington, D. C.

Official:

ERASTUS W. WOOD,
Captain 1st Vet. Inf. C. V., A. A. A. General.

DEPARTMENT OF NEW MEXICO, ASSISTANT ADJUTANT GENERAL'S OFFICE,
Santa Fé, N. M., August 27, 1864.

MAJOR: The commanding general directs me to say that you will exercise the greatest care, while out upon the Cimarron, that the Indians do not run off your stock. At night the animals must be tied to a picket line in camp, and grass cut and hauled into camp during the day and fed to them by night. This will keep things snug. Such articles as you may require to carry this order into execution you will obtain from the depot quartermaster at Fort Union, New Mexico.

I am, major, very respectfully, your obedient servant,

CYRUS H. DE FORREST, *Aide-de-Camp.*

Major JOSEPH UPDEGRAFF, U. S. A.,
Fort Marcy, N. M.

Official:

ERASTUS W. WOOD,
Captain 1st Vet. Inf. C. V., A. A. A. General.

HEADQUARTERS DEPARTMENT OF NEW MEXICO,
Santa Fé, N. M., August 29, 1864.

GENERAL: Colonel McFerran, chief of staff at these headquarters, has just come across the plains, and has submitted the enclosed communication, descriptive of the condition of affairs on the road, with reference to Indian troubles. I have ordered one company of infantry to Fort Lyon and another to Gray's ranch on the Purgatory river; have ordered fifty cavalry and fifty infantry to the Crossing of the Arkansas, by the Cimarron route, fifty cavalry and fifty infantry to the lower Cimarron spring, and fifty cavalry and thirty infantry to the upper Cimarron spring, to give all the help they can. You are aware that there are not enough troops here to guard properly the road.

If you will give me two thousand efficient men from the States, Ford's 2d Colorado regiment as part of them, and give me authority to employ our Utes, Apaches, and Navajoes, I feel quite sure that the Kiowas and Comanches, to say the least, can be so roughly handled as to make them refrain from these depredations for some years to come. The season is rapidly advancing, and unless the troops arrive here by the end of October their stock will be unfit for service this fall and winter. They should be ordered to guard trains *en route*. Once we can get all our supplies in, and get the merchants' trains off the road, we can commence upon the Indians in earnest. Our first care should be the defensive—the preservation of the trains. When they are secure, the offensive may be begun in earnest.

I am, general, very respectfully, your obedient servant,

JAMES H. CARLETON,
Brigadier General, Commanding.

Brigadier General LORENZO THOMAS,
Adjutant General U. S. A., Washington, D. C.

Official:

ERASTUS W. WOOD,
Captain 1st Vet. Inf. C. V., A. A. A. General.

HEADQUARTERS DEPARTMENT OF NEW MEXICO,
Santa Fé, N. M., August 29, 1864.

GENERAL: Enclosed herewith please find a return of Indian captives at Fort Sumner on the 31st ultimo, and a letter from the commander at Los Pinos of one thousand two hundred and nine Navajoes and twelve Apaches who left that post for the reservation on that day. Besides these, I have information of one hundred and fifty more Navajoes who have just reached Los Pinos. The last parties who have come in are of the rich men of the tribe. In my opinion one thousand more will cover every Navajo remaining back in their country, and these will come straggling in as soon as cold weather comes on. This war then may be considered as done. I have given orders for the breaking up of Fort Canby. We are bringing off the material as fast as we can.

Respectfully, your obedient servant,

JAMES H. CARLETON,
Brigadier General, Commanding.

Brigadier General LORENZO THOMAS,
Adjutant General U. S. A., Washington, D C.

Official:

ERASTUS W. WOOD,
Captain 1st Vet. Inf. C. V., A A. A. General.

DEPARTMENT OF NEW MEXICO, ASSISTANT ADJUTANT GENERAL'S OFFICE,
Santa Fé, N. M., September 2, 1864.

SIR: Major Edward B Willis, 1st infantry California volunteers, left at your post eight Apache Indians and one Mexican boy who was a captive in their hands. The general commanding desires to see and talk with these Indians; he therefore directs that you send this party, securely ironed (each Indian with ball and chain) and properly guarded, to department headquarters The general suggests that one non-commissioned officer and six trusty men would be a sufficient guard to prevent escape; also that the Mexican boy be kept separated as far as practicable from the Indians, for fear that he may receive some injury at their hands.

I am, sir, very respectfully, your obedient servant,

BEN. C. CUTLER,
Assistant Adjutant General.

COMMANDING OFFICER, *Los Pinos, N. M.*

Official:

ERASTUS W. WOOD,
Captain 1st Vet. Inf. C. V., A. A. A. General.

HEADQUARTERS DEPARTMENT OF NEW MEXICO,
Santa Fé, N. M., September 12, 1864.

CAPTAIN: On account of the difficulty for procuring cattle to be killed for meat, to issue to the Indians on the reservation at the Bosque Redondo, you will issue meat to those Indians at the rate of half a pound apiece per day to each Indian entitled to draw rations as heretofore, and in lieu of the half pound thus cut down, you will issue half a pound of corn or breadstuffs, so that each Indian will receive a pound and a half of breadstuffs and half a pound of meat per day. Explain this matter to the Indians, and commence the new rate of issue at once. You will assemble a board of officers to ascertain how much corn and grain was raised by Mr. Labadie by hands paid by the United States and by Indians upon the reservation, and have the product of such labor turned in to the public stores for issue to the Apaches. An exact account will be taken of such product, whether of grain, corn, beans, straw, fodder, &c., so that the records and statistics may be exact for reference in future. You will also make arrangements at once not to issue any food to those Navajoes who have made crops until all that they have raised has been consumed.

You are the guardian of the interests of the United States, and as such should long since have seen, when the Indians had a plenty for their support in their fields, that they were not fed by the government. It is understood that Mr. Labadie has a large flock of sheep on the reservation, and that he bought some sheep of the Indians. Mr. Labadie's sheep will not be permitted to stay within the limits of the reservation. He should not have been permitted to purchase an ounce of food of the Indians, nor under any circumstances a single sheep. Report the facts in the case.

From the receipt of this letter neither himself nor his employés will be permitted to buy subsistence stores or to draw such stores, or to buy them from the troops or from the Indians. I desire to be informed if there is any practical necessity for Mr. Labadie to live on the reservation while it is in charge of the military. You will see that no one buys a single article from the Indians except the quartermaster, who is authorized to buy their fodder at a fair price. You will at once have all the ploughs put in order, and continue breaking up new land. You will at once have the *acequia* properly enlarged. Pray, do not correspond about this matter, but have it done.

I am, captain, respectfully,

JAMES H. CARLETON,
Brigadier General, Commanding.

Captain HENRY B. BRISTOL,
Commanding at Fort Sumner, N. M.

NOTE.—I shall try to come to Fort Sumner about the 30th instant.

Official:

ERASTUS W. WOOD,
Captain 1st Vet. Inf. C. V., A. A. A. General.

HEADQUARTERS DEPARTMENT OF NEW MEXICO,
Santa Fé, N. M., September 16, 1864.

DEAR SIR: As you are doubtless aware, I have now nearly eight thousand Indians upon the reservation at the Bosque Redondo, who are almost entirely destitute of clothing and blankets, and now the cold weather is rapidly approaching. It is of vital importance that the articles which were to be purchased for these Indians with the hundred thousand dollars appropriated by Congress in its last session for this purpose, arrive at the Bosque Redondo and be distributed at the earliest practicable moment.

I write directly to yourself on the subject, that no time may be lost. I do this because I had heard it was possible these Indian goods might not come out this fall. Let me impress upon your mind that unless they come, hundreds of naked women and children will be likely to perish. A special train of wagons, escorted by a company of troops, can come through at all seasons.

I am, sir, very respectfully, your obedient servant,

JAMES H. CARLETON,
Brigadier General, Commanding.

Hon. WILLIAM P. DOLE,
Commissioner of Indian Affairs, Washington, D. C.

Official:

ERASTUS W. WOOD,
Captain 1st Vet. Inf. C V., A. A. A. General.

HEADQUARTERS DEPARTMENT OF NEW MEXICO,
Santa Fé, N. M., September 18, 1864.

COLONEL: I have received, through Brigadier General Crocker, United States volunteers, a message from Mr. Lucien B. Maxwell that some two hundred or more Ute Indians, now near Mr. Maxwell's place on the Little Cimarron, are willing and anxious to go out on the plains and attack the Kiowas and other Indians now depredating upon our trains and killing our people who are *en route* to and from the States and New Mexico, provided that they, the Utes, can be furnished with some rations, ammunition, perhaps a blanket apiece, and provided they may have whatever stock or other property they may be able to capture from the hostile Indians alluded to. I desire that you proceed without delay to Mr. Maxwell's, and if a strong party of these Utes, say two hundred, are willing to go on the service alluded to, under your direction and command, I wish them to do so on the terms above indicated, except that if they capture from the Indians of the plains any stock belonging to the United States or to the citizens, such stock shall be restored to the rightful owners on the owners paying to the said Utes a fair sum for the recovery of the animals, which sum per head must be agreed upon between yourself and the said Utes before they start upon the expedition. All stock belonging to the hostile Indians themselves, and which has not been captured from the United States troops or trains, or from citizens, the Utes shall receive as their own in case they can take it from the said hostile Indians. It is important to have these Utes start at once in case they go at all, and I desire that you should lead them. There are fifty cavalry and thirty infantry at or near Cold spring, under Captain Bergmann, and fifty cavalry and fifty infantry at the lower Cimarron spring, under Major Updegraff, and a like force at the crossing of the Arkansas, under Captain Davis; there is also a company of infantry on the road near Gray's ranch. Any one of these parties will co-operate with you on showing this authority to its commander.

In case the Utes will go, you will proceed to Fort Union and report to me the number and the length of time for which they should draw subsistence, &c. It is important that there be no unnecessary delay in this matter. It is believed that a demonstration of this kind, made at this time, will be productive of good results. The main object is to have the Utes commit themselves in hostility to the Indians of the plains, that there may be less chance for them to join in any league which the latter Indians may attempt to make for a general war by all the Indians between the mountains and the Missouri upon the whites.

Your knowledge of the haunts of the Indians of the plains, and the great confidence the Ute Indians have in you as a friend and as a leader, point to yourself as the most fitting person to organize, direct, and bring this enterprise to a successful issue.

I am, colonel, very respectfully, your obedient servant,

JAMES H. CARLETON,
Brigadier General, Commanding.

Colonel CHRISTOPHER CARSON,
1st Cavalry New Mexico Volunteers, Taos, N. M.

Official:

ERASTUS W. WOOD,
Captain 1st Vet. Inf. C. V., A. A. A. General.

DEPARTMENT OF NEW MEXICO, ASSISTANT ADJUTANT GENERAL'S OFFICE,
Santa Fé, N. M., September 27, 1864.

SIR: The commanding general directs that you say to the Kiowas and Comanches who came to your post under a flag of truce, that their people have attacked our trains, killed our people, and run off our stock; that we believe their hearts are bad, and that they talk with a forked tongue; that we put no confidence in what they say; that they must go away, as we regard them not as friends; that they need not come in with any more white flags until they are willing to give up all the stock they have stolen this year from our people, and also the men among them who have killed our people without provocation or cause; that we will not permit them to visit the Navajoes on the reservation, nor permit any treaty to be made with the Navajoes until the injuries done us have been atoned for to our satisfaction. This is what at once must be told them, and these emissaries must go away.

The general is fearful that these Indians came in only to spy out the strength of your command, &c., and have a strong force near to swoop off the stock, as was done at Fort Larned. I enclose a copy of a letter to Colonel Chaves, ordering him to proceed to and take command of Fort Bascom, New Mexico.

I am, sir, very respectfully, your obedient servant,

CYRUS H. DE FORREST,
Captain 2d Colorado Cavalry, A. A. A. General.

COMMANDING OFFICER, *Fort Bascom, N. M.*

Official:

ERASTUS W. WOOD,
Captain 1st Vet. Inf. C. V., A. A. A. General.

HEADQUARTERS DEPARTMENT OF NEW MEXICO,
Santa Fé, N. M., October 9, 1864.

GENERAL: I have had the honor to receive your very interesting letter of the 28th ultimo in relation to the condition of the Indians upon the reservation at the Bosque Redondo, and have this day forwarded certified copies of it to the Department of War and of the Interior.

Taking into consideration the requirements of par. 1, Special Orders No. 37, current series from these headquarters, and also the fact that Fort Sumner and its dependencies do not constitute a district, and taking into consideration the injunctions of the 62d article of war, I cannot see how you can avoid assuming command of the troops; for it is yourself who must "give orders for what is needful to the service." Captain

Bristol is an excellent officer, and has my fullest confidence, and you can place him in charge of any particular part or parts of the service at Fort Sumner; but, as you see, general, the orders and the law make you the responsible man, and as such I am obliged to recognize yourself as the commander of Fort Sumner.

Please forward a report similar to the one already forwarded, at the last of each month, showing the condition of affairs at the Bosque Redondo; the progress made in breaking up new ground; in opening *acequias*, and their length and capacity, and in setting out trees. Last winter nearly 1,400 trees were set out. Some of these died or were destroyed by horses, &c., this summer. Others must be planted in their place. This winter it is my desire to have 5,000 additional trees planted. The avenue should be extended as far as practicable, both up and down the river, and trees should be planted on each side of all the large *acequias*. When they get large they will shade the water, and their roots will strengthen the banks. But, mainly, it is required to have at least this number of trees planted every year to supply fuel to the thousands of Indians when the mesquit roots have all been consumed.

Please have a return rendered of all the serviceable ploughs, hoes, picks, spades, and shovels, which you have on hand, for the use of the Indians, at the end of every month.

I desire soon to come down and make a personal inspection of all matters pertaining to the reservation. Pray have every plough running, and every spade, shovel, and pick employed in enlarging *acequias*, in opening new ones, and in grubbing out roots where land must be ploughed, and in spading up land for cultivation.

I have information that 300 or 400 of the richest Navajoes are now near Fort Wingate, on their way in.

Very respectfully, general, I am your obedient servant,

JAMES H. CARLETON,
Brigadier General, Commanding.

Brigadier General MARCELLUS N. CROCKER, U. S. Vols.,
Commanding at Fort Sumner, N. M.

Official:

ERASTUS W. WOOD,
Captain 1st Vet. Inf. C. V., A. A. A. General.

HEADQUARTERS DEPARTMENT OF NEW MEXICO,
Santa Fé, N. M., October 14, 1864.

COLONEL: I have received your letter of the 10th instant in relation to the Utes and Apaches. You will issue to the men of those tribes, who will be sure to go, one and a quarter pound of beef and one pound of breadstuffs per man, each day, and the necessary amount of salt. You will send to Fort Union for the salt and get the meat and breadstuffs from Mr. Maxwell. Captain Bell will write to you on the subject. The amount of issues must not exceed the number of your party. Send me an exact list of the number who will be sure to go. As soon as I get off the Arizona mail and make arrangements for Thompson's company and a train of supplies which are to go to Fort Whipple, I will commence the organization of your party. General Crocker writes that some of the Apaches from the Bosque will go. They are the best fighting Indians we have. It is possible you will not be able to get off quite so soon as we talked, as I may have to wait for Bergmann to come back. But this I shall know in two or three days, and will write you by mail. The guns, ammunition, and blankets and shirts will be sent to you. At Taos we agreed on two hundred men and one hundred Indians as the strength of the party. You now say three hundred men. These I will try to raise, but the Apaches from Fort Sumner will have to be included. I will write by mail. Give me positive information of the number of Indians who will go. I believe you will have big luck.

Very respectfully, your obedient servant,

JAMES H. CARLETON,
Brigadier General, Commanding.

Colonel CHRISTOPHER CARSON,
At Maxwell's, on the Cimarron, N. M.

Official:

ERASTUS W. WOOD,
Captain 1st Vet. Inf. C. V., A. A. A. General.

HEADQUARTERS DEPARTMENT OF NEW MEXICO,
Santa Fé, N. M., October 20, 1864.

COLONEL: I have just received your letter of the 18th instant. It is impossible for me to issue rations to the families of the Utes; I have not the means or the right. The Indian department should do this. If the Utes will not agree to remain in the field forty-five days they had better not go.

You will be informed what troops will form your command as soon as I can get an express from Sumner and Bascom replying to communications sent there some four or five days since. I approve of Lieutenant Haberkom's going with you if Colonel Selden can spare him. You can have Lieutenant Taylor for your commissary and quartermaster; I cannot conjecture why he expected to go. But he is a capable officer, and if he tries can be distinguished. Your Utes and Apaches should have sugar and coffee from Fort Bascom. I will try to get the Apaches, some fifty, to go with you from Fort Sumner. An order was given to the quartermaster's department for the blankets and shirts to be sent to you. It has doubtless been received at Fort Union. Call on Captain Shoemaker for the rifles; show him this letter as your authority. Send me an exact list of all you receive for the Utes. Talk with Captain Carey how few mules you will want to go from Maxwell's to Bascom. Reduce the number down to the lowest. Your own things which you may need at Bascom had better be sent to Fort Union to go down on a wagon.

In haste, respectfully, your obedient servant,

JAMES H. CARLETON,
Brigadier General, Commanding.

Colonel CHRISTOPHER CARSON,
1st Cavalry New Mexico Volunteers, Fort Union, N. M.

Official:

ERASTUS W. WOOD,
Captain 1st Vet. Inf. C. V., A. A. A General.

HEADQUARTERS DEPARTMENT OF NEW MEXICO,
Santa Fé, N. M., October 21, 1864.

GENERAL: Mr. La Rue, sutler at Fort Sumner, has, I understand, several thousand pounds of pumpkins which he desires to sell. If these pumpkins were raised by Indians they should not have gone into his possession, as it is forbidden, positively, for any one to buy a single article of food, animate or inanimate, from Indians belonging to the reservation. If not raised by Indians, these pumpkins may be bought at what you consider a fair price per pound, and issued in lieu of other food. Did not the Indians themselves raise many pumpkins and turnips? If so, these articles must be consumed by them, and the breadstuff issues be diminished while these vegetables last. The money for the fodder should be used toward defraying the expenses of subsistence of Indians. Pray take this matter under consideration, and have it so arranged that all the fruit of the labor of the Indians on their farms will be sure to go toward feeding them, except a sufficient sum to buy them tobacco. An exact account of the money received for fodder, &c., and how expended, should be kept, so that a copy may be forwarded to the War Department once a quarter. You cannot be too particular in this matter.

Please to have an understanding with Mr. Labadie to this effect. The reservation is for the present under the exclusive control of the military. It follows that all persons residing upon it must be subject to that control.. If any person refuses to follow the injunctions of the commander of the reservation, of course he cannot remain upon that reservation. I trust Mr. Labadie will see the necessity of this rule and will conform to it, so that there may be no collision between yourself and himself, or necessity for him to move. He seems to be a clever man, and will do right, if he fully understands this matter, I have no doubt.

The board found that the present and proposed farms would make about four thousand acres. This will not be enough for the support of the Indians, nor will it be half what they can cultivate if their labors are well directed. Pray think of this, and see that every man and woman able to work be kept employed in preparing fields for cultivation from now until the next season for planting has passed by. This increased extension will carry with it the idea of lengthening and enlarging the main acequias. Please be sure to have enough acequias, and those of sufficient volume.

Are any of the Navajo horses fit for light cavalry service? If so, how many can be bought of this quality, and at what price per head? Some of them might do well for men in Colonel Carson's regiment, particularly for light Mexicans.

I shall leave for Franklin, Texas, about the first proximo, and shall endeavor to return *via* Fort Stanton and Fort Sumner.

I am, general, very respectfully, your obedient servant,

JAMES H. CARLETON,
Brigadier General, Commanding.

Brigadier General MARCELLUS M. CROCKER, U. S. Vols.,
Commanding at Fort Sumner, N. M.

Official:

ERASTUS W. WOOD,
Captain 1st Vet Inf. C. V., A A. A. General.

HEADQUARTERS DEPARTMENT OF NEW MEXICO,
Santa Fé, N. M., October 22, 1864.

GENERAL: But a few days since I wrote to you directing that the ration of breadstuffs to be issued until further orders, to each captive Indian, big and little, upon the reservation, must be cut down to one pound and a quarter per day.

Since that was written I have had consultations with the chief commissary with reference to his ability to get an adequate supply of stores to the Bosque, so that there would be no danger of running short, and I find that in my judgment it is all-important to reduce the ration of breadstuffs to twelve ounces per day, and to have issued eight ounces of meat per day—twenty ounces of solid food in all—until we can hear from the proposals for furnishing wheat, &c , which you will see in the enclosed gazette, and until we see what success the staff officers will have in getting corn. We shall strain every nerve to get a plenty ; but as we may encounter delays which would perhaps be fatal to the Indians, unless this precaution were taken, the Indians must see the necessity which compels it and be satisfied. Assemble the chiefs and tell them this:

1st. That we did not look for a loss of all their corn by the worms, but supposed that they would raise nearly enough this year to support themselves, which they have failed to do.

2d. That we have been greatly embarrassed in getting their supplies from the States because the Kiowas and Comanches attacked our trains.

3d. That the hail and frost killed nearly all the corn in Taos and Mora, the two places where we expected to get what the Indians would need.

4th. That more Indians have come in than we expected would come, which must be fed.

5th. That they must make their food into *atolé*, by which it will go much further, and use their pumpkins and melons, of which Mr. Labadie informs me there are yet many, to help out their meals. The Indians must be made to understand that we are doing our best for them, but cannot overcome impossibilities ; that unless we took this timely precaution they must starve.

Through all the clouds that now seem to surround this important, and, to them, vital matter, I hope soon to see some encouraging light, when you will be informed, so as to add, if necessary, to this diminished ration at the earliest moment.

While the expedition is out after Kiowas and Comanches, parties of Navajoes might be permitted to go eastward and southeastward to hunt. Each party should have a pass and be headed by a responsible chief. A good non-commissioned officer or soldier going with such a party would insure that it went for this purpose, and did not turn off its course to depredate upon the flocks and herds of the people.

This latter matter should be surrounded by all possible safeguards that it be not abused.

I am, general, very respectfully, your obedient servant,

JAMES H. CARLETON,
Brigadier General, Commanding.

Brigadier General MARCELLUS M. CROCKER, U. S. Vols ,
Commanding at Fort Sumner, N. M.

NOTE.—If the Indians murmur at these necessary measures for their own good, and to shield them from the possible danger of being out of food entirely, tell them that they must make up deficiencies from their own stock, which they will have to do if worse comes to worst.

J. H. C.

Official:

ERASTUS W. WOOD,
Captain 1st Vet. Inf. C. V., A. A. A. General.

HEADQUARTERS DEPARTMENT OF NEW MEXICO,
Santa Fé, N. M., October 22, 1864.

GENERAL: I received a letter from Major General Curtis, dated the 19th ultimo, in which he says, "General Blunt is at or near Fort Larned looking out for Indians, and may co-operate with you in crushing out some of the vile hordes that now harass our lines of communication."

This is to inform you that a report has reached me, coming through Mexicans, that the Kiowas and Comanches are now encamped on a creek called Palo Duro, some two hundred miles in a northeasterly direction from the mouth of Utah creek, on the Canadian or Colorado river, east of Fort Union, New Mexico. This would make them about, say, two hundred miles south of Fort Larned, or southwardly from that post.

I shall, within ten days, send a force of three hundred volunteer troops, two hundred mounted and one hundred on foot, with two mountain howitzers, and, say, one hundred Ute and Apache Indians, *i. e.*, four hundred in all, under Colonel Christopher Carson, to attack the Kiowas and Comanches. This force will move down the Colorado to within fifteen miles of Ute creek and there doubtless take a road running northeast toward the States, which road is said to come into the Arkansas from the southwest near the mouth of Walnut creek.

I hope you may be able to time your movements so as to reach the Indians on the Palo Duro or near there at the same moment with Colonel Carson, so that a blow may be struck which those two treacherous tribes will remember.

I will send a copy of this letter to Colonel Carson.

Very respectfully, your obedient servant,

JAMES H. CARLETON,
Brigadier General, Commanding.

Major General JAMES G. BLUNT, U. S. Vols.,
Commanding an Expedition against the Kiowas and Comanches, Fort Larned, Kansas.

NOTE.—I enclose herewith a copy of General Orders No. 32, current series from these headquarters

To be sent to the general by express from Fort Larned.

Official:

ERASTUS W. WOOD,
Captain 1st Vet. Inf. C. V., A. A. A. General.

HEADQUARTERS DEPARTMENT OF NEW MEXICO,
Santa Fé, N. M., October 23, 1864.

COLONEL: Enclosed herewith please find General Orders No. 32, current series from these headquarters, which organizes an expedition under your command to proceed against hostile Kiowas and Comanches. As you see, I have given you more men than you asked for, because it is my desire that you give those Indians, especially the Kiowas, a severe drubbing. Enclosed is also a copy of a letter which I send by mail to General Blunt. I do not wish to embarrass you with minute instructions. You know where to find the Indians; you know what atrocities they have committed; you know how to punish them. The means and men are placed at your disposal to do it, and now all the rest is left with you.

I need not repeat to you the orders given to all commanders whom I have sent out to fight Indians, that women and children will not be killed—only men who bear arms. Of course, I know that in attacking a village, women and children are liable to be killed, and this cannot, in the rush and confusion of a fight, particularly at night, be avoided; but let none be killed wilfully and wantonly. We make war upon men who have murdered and robbed our people.

I have written to General Crocker that if thirty of the Mescalero Apaches wish to go under Cadetta, they can come to Bascom with Captain Fritz and join you there. In this case the general will give them a blanket and shirt apiece and arm them. They complain that their horses are poor. They will be told that they can get better ones from the Kiowas. You had better come at once to Fort Union and see everything started to suit yourself, and then return to Maxwell's and go on with the Utes. Remember to take everything from Union which you will require for packing, as at Fort Bascom you will find little or nothing belonging to the post for this purpose.

Should you get among the buffaloes you can stay out, if necessary, a much longer time than you otherwise could.

Be sure and take some spades and axes, so as to form an intrenched camp for wounded men, and supplies, if necessary.

I am, colonel, very respectfully, your obedient servant,

JAMES H. CARLETON,
Brigadier General, Commanding.

Colonel CHRISTOPHER CARSON,
At Maxwell's Ranch on the Cimarron River, N. M.

NOTE.—I enclose a copy of a letter to Major General Blunt, dated the 22d instant.

Official:

ERASTUS W. WOOD,
Captain 1st Vet. Inf. C. V., A. A. A. General.

HEADQUARTERS DEPARTMENT OF NEW MEXICO,
Santa Fé, N. M., October 27, 1864.

SIR: Owing to the total failure of the crop at the Bosque Redondo, and the partial failure of the crop at Taos Mora, and in other places in the Territory, I find that we have now as many Navajoes and Apaches on the reservation as we can feed during the winter, so that no more will be permitted to come in until further orders. If necessary you will have runners sent to inform the Navajoes of this decision. As soon as provisions have been accumulated enough to warrant others in coming in without danger of suffering, word will be sent to that effect, so that the remnant of the Navajo tribe still at large may proceed to join their people. If any of those still at large commit either murders or robberies they will be pursued and destroyed wherever found. When the season for planting came, this year, those at large were invited to come in and help put in a crop, but then they would not come. Now that the winter is setting in, they are anxious to come and eat the fruit of the labor of others. It is true, their labors in planting would have had poor results, but they would have shown a disposition to help raise their own sustenance, which would have been praiseworthy. Now they must take care of themselves until another spring opens, when again they will have an opportunity to put in a crop. Tell them this.

Ascertain as nearly as possible how many Navajoes are still at large, and whether they are poor or rich, and report the facts. Get your horses into serviceable condition, and be on the look-out that no Apache from the White or the Mogollon mountains and that no Navajoes run off the flock of the people. I must count on your being always on the alert and ready to take the field to prevent any such consequences.

Very respectfully, your obedient servant,

JAMES H. CARLETON,
Brigadier General, Commanding.

COMMANDING OFFICER, *Fort Wingate, N. M.*

NOTE.—When did Captain Thompson leave? How long was the train detained at your post?

Official:

ERASTUS W. WOOD,
Captain 1st Vet. Inf. C. V., A. A. A. General.

HEADQUARTERS DEPARTMENT OF NEW MEXICO,
Santa Fé, N. M., October 28, 1864.

GENERAL: Colonel McFerran, chief of staff, has suggested that if we should take one of the two new storehouses made for the protection of Indian food, and arrange in it a system of ovens, according to the enclosed rough plan, and bake the wheatmeal and flour which we may, perhaps, be able to get for issue to the Indians, and issue bread instead of the flour, we could feed them with less trouble and more economically. I wish you would take this subject under consideration. You are upon the ground, and can judge of the practicability of such a plan, and what would be its success. A very important point will be the procuring of a sufficient and constant supply of oven-wood. A calculation of how many times each oven would have to be heated per day, and the quantity required each time, and a calculation as to where wood will have to be drawn from; how long the supply would last; how many loads could be got in a given time, &c., &c., should be well considered, and should be balanced against the present manner of issuing flour for the Indians themselves to cook in their style; and the report should show which would be the preferable mode, and the reasons therefor. It has always seemed to me that the cooking of the flour and meat as a soup would be by far the most nutritious. By cooking twenty ounces of solid food to each person, big and little, per day, in this way, would be as much as they could possibly require. There is one thing which you must rely upon: that amount is positively as much as we can get by the most strenuous efforts; and to *keep up* this supply until the crop matures next year gives me more anxious moments in thinking by what process it can be done than you can well imagine.

Send me an exact return of how much corn and grain Captain Morton has in the quartermaster's department, after having turned over the wheat in the quartermaster to the subsistence department, and exactly how many animals he feeds per day.

What we must do, owing to the scarcity of food and the difficulties in transportation, I see from my point of view more clearly than the Indians can see it. They must believe we are doing our best for them, and submit without murmuring to what cannot be helped. If they have more than the twenty ounces per day till corn comes from the States *certain starvation must ensue.* This matter must be looked squarely in the face, and they must meet it like men. It cannot be helped. As much wheat as possible must be sown. This they cannot consume before it ripens; it matures early, and a crop of beans can be planted on the same ground after the wheat is gathered.

I am, general, very respectfully, your obedient servant,

JAMES H. CARLETON,
Brigadier General, Commanding.

Brigadier General MARCELLUS M. CROCKER, U. S. Vols.,
Commanding at Fort Sumner, N. M.

Official:

ERASTUS W. WOOD,
Captain 1st Vet. Inf. C. V., A. A. A. General

HEADQUARTERS DEPARTMENT OF NEW MEXICO,
Santa Fé, N. M., October 28, 1864.

SIR: Let whatever captive Navajoes you now have at Los Pinos, or which may come to that post for their country, *en route* to Bosque Redondo, remain at Los Pinos until further orders. The difficulty of getting transportation for food to the Bosque Redondo makes it imperative to feed all we can nearer the source of supply until that difficulty is overcome.

The daily allowance, until further orders, of food for these Indians will be twelve ounces of breadstuff and eight ounces of meat, to large and small.

You will have the Indians required to stop at Los Pinos put in as sheltered a place as possible, and have them made as comfortable as circumstances will admit. Please report, if they require blankets, how many they require. In this connexion it is well to remark that you can doubtless procure at a fair price some sheep to issue for the meat ration. Should you do this, the Indians could be employed in making the wool into blankets for their children, as far as practicable. Please report in full all that you do to carry these instructions into effect. Are there not some buildings or corrals that could be used as shelter for the children? I trust greatly to your resources to have them well cared for, and am,

Respectfully, your obedient servant,

JAMES H. CARLETON,
Brigadier General, Commanding.

Lieutenant EDMUND BUTLER, U. S. A.,
Commanding at Los Pinos, N. M.

Official:

ERASTUS W. WOOD,
Captain 1st Vet. Inf. C. V., A. A. A. General.

HEADQUARTERS DEPARTMENT OF NEW MEXICO,
Santa Fé, N. M., October 29, 1864.

SIR: I have the honor to acknowledge the receipt of your official communication of the 26th instant. It would have been answered before but for the press of business which had to go by the southern mail. The information upon which your letter is based differs from that which has reached me through other channels, in regard to the complicity of the Comanches in the late robberies and murders on the plains. I am advised that these troubles first commenced with the Cheyennes and Arapahoes, and, in the attempt to conciliate those tribes, Colonel Bent and Indian Agent Colley, acting on the part of the government, issued to those Indians a liberal supply of stores. This excited the jealousy of the Comanches and Kiowas, who alleged that they did not understand why they, who had remained quiet, should be excluded from the bounty of the government, while those who had been murdering and robbing should be thus favored; and, as no attempt was made to remove this cause of complaint, they, too, commenced depredating, and I was not aware, until the receipt of your letter, that any doubt existed as to the guilt of the Comanches equally with the Kiowas. It is certainly understood that the interruption to our line of travel to the States is owing to the hostility of the Cheyennes, Arapahoes, Comanches, and Kiowas.

The attack upon the trains at Walnut creek, and the murder of our countrymen, was known to be by the Comanches and Kiowas. The horses taken from the mounted company on the long route between Forts Larned and Lyon were taken by the Comanches and Kiowas. The mules taken from Mr. Bryant's train near Fort Larned were, beyond a doubt, run off by the same Indians, who, it is alleged, crawled through a Mexican train and up to Bryant's train before they gave the yell which stampeded the mules. These mules other Comanches and Kiowas, mounted, were ready to take charge of as soon as they broke from the wagons—so it is said. The taking of oxen at Pawnee fork, where there were several men killed, is well known to have been by Comanches and Kiowas. The large number of mules taken from Don Ambrosio Armijo's train, this side of the upper crossing of the Cimarron, were taken by Comanches and Kiowas, for they were recognized as such by the teamsters in charge of the train. The outrage upon Mr. Allison's train, at the lower Cimarron spring, was, as I have been informed by eye-witnesses, committed by Comanches. The Mexicans with the train witnessed the whole transaction, and saw the five Americans taken out from among themselves and shot down in cold blood. The bodies of the sufferers were afterward buried by Captain Nicholas S. Davis, first infantry California volunteers, whom I sent to the crossing of the Arkansas, to render what assistance he could. When these Americans were thus brutally murdered and scalped, the Mexicans, their companions, were furnished by the Comanches with the means to return unharmed to the settlements. All the stock taken by the Indians at the points named along the Arkansas river was driven southward directly into the Comanche country, where, it is understood, those Indians have a large depot of stolen cattle, horses, and mules.

The expedition now on the plains under the command of General Blunt is for the purpose of making war upon the Comanches and Kiowas. For this purpose it is understood that expedition moved into the country of those Indians. There can hardly be a doubt, that while the Comanches were thus robbing and murdering at the points named, other parties of Comanches were depredating on the frontier settlements of Texas, and have brought herds of cattle away from that State, as well as out of the northeastern portion of Mexico; but these latter raids of these Bedouins of our plains do not prove the former not to have been made.

The discrimination which the Comanches have frequently made in favor of the people, natives of this Territory, and against Anglo-Americans, cannot be regarded in any other light than as an insult to the government and to our people, and I suppose there will be no doubt what it becomes my duty to do in reference to it. It seems to me that this favor shown to the Mexicans lessens the weight of the information which you have received. The Mexicans, finding themselves thus favored, of course feel inclined to favor the Indians in return; and the Mexicans would doubtless be further induced to this course from a desire to continue the trade which is carried on with these Indians by the very men from whom you get your information. I also feel myself compelled to differ with you in regard to the past conduct of the Comanches on our eastern frontier. I cannot venture for information upon this subject as far back as eighty years, but I am advised that in the year 1856 the Comanches, in connexion with a few Kiowas, made a raid through the settlements in the direction of the Navajo country, and it is said that on their return from the Rio Grande they robbed houses, violated women, and killed the stock of the citizens. After they had collected various small lots of mules and horses, they finally drove off from near Las Vegas fifty-odd mules, the property of our present Governor Connelly. I cannot enumerate all the robberies and outrages which they committed from time to time from 1851 to 1856, during my first sojourn in New Mexico, particularly about Chaparita and on the Pecos. I myself was sent in pursuit of them on one occasion. Then three Mexican captive boys got away from them, and these General Garland sent home to their friends in Mexico. I am informed that in 1860 they drove off one hundred and odd head of cattle from Mr. Giddings, and killed a number of his fine sheep, which, at great cost, he had brought from the

States. About this time, too, they attacked the grazing camp of Messrs. Moore and Rees on the Pecos, killed one man, and destroyed and ran off horses and cattle from that camp. In the early part of 1861 they drove off four hundred and fifty head of cattle belonging to the United States. To these robberies may be added a large list mentioned in a letter from Mr. Levi J. Keithly, which was published about the same date. In May, 1861, Colonel Collins, the superintendent of Indian affairs, in company with Captain Wainwright, of the army, met the Comanches at Alamo Gordo, when several chiefs were present, among them Esaquipa and Pluma de Aguila, who are known to be the principal chiefs of the band of Comanches which occupies the country along the Canadian. Stipulations of peace were agreed upon with those chiefs, and they promised not to return to the settlements again unless permitted to do so by the authorities of the government. This agreement, however, was violated in a few days after the council; the Indians returned to the settlements, and, after being warned off by Captain Duncan, United States army, were attacked by him, and one of their number was killed and several wounded. Since then I have not heard of their committing any depredations upon the settlements of New Mexico. But if you will contemplate the record of their atrocities upon our people on the plains *this* year, and count among those atrocities the going up to unoffending citizens travelling with trains, the shaking of hands with those citizens and then coolly shooting them down, the scalping of their victims, the scalping of two innocent boys yet living and now in the hospital at Fort Larned, the killing and the mutilating of the bodies of the five Americans with Allison's train, I think you can hardly fail to see that I should be derelict of my duty if I should refrain from making at least an attempt to avenge our slaughtered and plundered citizens. For all these reasons I have sent Colonel Carson into the field with as many men as can be spared to make such an attempt, and it is not proposed to embarrass him with such instructions as you have done me the honor to suggest. If, however, you are satisfied that any portion of the Comanche tribe have not participated in the late outrages, and who still seriously desire to be at peace, and will send a reliable agent with Colonel Carson to designate that portion, he will be charged to make the discrimination, unless he have information which may lead him to believe that such agent is mistaken.

I beg to apologize for the length of this communication, and in closing it to assure you that it has been with reluctance that I sent these troops into the field to make war; but I cannot see what else there is left for us to do, unless it be to bear all these outrages uncomplainingly, and as soon as spring opens witness their recurrence with increased barbarity; for these Indians would attribute our refraining to strike to our fears, and then kill and rob our people with impunity.

I have the honor to be, very respectfully, your obedient servant,

JAMES H. CARLETON,
Brigadier General, Commanding.

MATTHEW STECK, Esq.,
Superintendent of Indian Affairs, Santa Fé, N. M.

NOTE.—I append, for your information, a copy of a letter from Mr. Greenwood, Commissioner of Indian Affairs, to Mr. Secretary Thompson, in relation to depredations in San Miguel county, New Mexico, in November, 1859. J. H. C.

Official: ERASTUS W. WOOD,
Captain 1st Vet. Inf. C. V., A. A. A. General.

DEPARTMENT OF THE INTERIOR.
Office Indian Affairs, December 30, 1859.

SIR: I have the honor to transmit, for your information, the copy of a letter from Superintendent J. L. Collins, dated the 5th instant, covering the minutes of the proceedings of a meeting of the citizens of San Miguel county, assembled on the 1st instant, at Las Vegas, New Mexico.

The minutes show not only that the Comanches have, during November last, destroyed several ranches, but are now prowling upon the borders with the evident design of repeating their depredations upon the property of the settlers.

The superintendent says, in his communication, that he believes that the statements of the settlers are not exaggerated, and submits the propriety of calling the attention of the Secretary of War to the subject. He further says that the Indians of the plains will certainly have to be chastised before we can have any security in passing over the plains. He thinks that a large military force should be employed, and that three columns—one from Texas, one from New Mexico, and one from Kansas—should simultaneously enter the Indian country, and that a single column would, in his opinion, do nothing effective. I would respectfully suggest, provided it meets with your approbation, that copies of the enclosures be transmitted to the Secretary of War for his information, and such action thereon as in his judgment the exigencies of the case shall require.

Very respectfully, your obedient servant,

A. B. GREENWOOD, *Commissioner.*

Hon. JACOB THOMPSON, *Secretary of the Interior.*

Official :

ERASTUS W. WOOD,
Captain 1st Vet. Inf. C. V., A. A. A. General.

HEADQUARTERS DEPARTMENT OF NEW MEXICO,
Santa Fé, N. M., October 30, 1864.

GENERAL : I have delayed making a formal report on the important matter of subsisting the Navajo and Apache Indians, now on the reservation at the Bosque Redondo, until I could learn definitely the probable result of the harvest in this Territory. As you have already seen in a report of General Crocker on the condition of the Indians at the Bosque Redondo, everything there was a success, except the crop of corn. We had a field of nearly three thousand acres, which promised to mature finely, when, after it had tasselled and the ears formed, it was attacked by what they here call the cut-worm, or army-worm, and the whole crop destroyed. I enclose herewith the report of a board of survey on the subject. When this was known, I then hoped the corn, and grain, and bean crop in the Territory would prove adequate to the wants of the Indians, until the crop matures in 1865 ; but the wheat crop, when nearly ready for harvest, was drenched and beaten down by unprecedented storms of rain, and over half destroyed. In Taos, Mora, Rio Arriba, and San Miguel counties, whence we reasonably expected to get a good supply of corn, the hail-storms and early and severe frosts nearly destroyed the whole crop. This, too, was the case with the beans ; so that there is a great scarcity even for the people.

The reports which were sent to Washington that I had purchased last spring supplies enough to last the captive Indians for two years were unfounded in fact, as I wrote to you at the end of last June. The breadstuffs remaining of that purchase will all be consumed by the end of December of this year. We have advertised for wheat, wheat-meal, and beans enough to last until corn can be brought from the States ; but, in my opinion, we shall hardly be able to secure the requisite quantity in the country, for the reasons before stated.

This failure of the crop—a visitation of God—I could not contend against. It came, and now we must meet the consequences as best we may. The Indians could not be turned loose, or even taken back to their country, without being obliged to war upon the people, as heretofore, or perish. This is stated, not that I have any idea of either turning them loose or taking them back, but in answer to the senseless arguments which a few persons here, headed by the superintendent of Indian affairs, are making against the reservation at the Bosque Redondo. It then follows that we must feed them where they are, until at least the harvest of next year, which we may reasonably hope, judging from the past, will not be disastrous, as the one of this. The future of not only New Mexico, but of Arizona, depends on the determination and the ability of the general government to hold this formidable tribe, now that it has been subdued and gotten in hand, until it can support itself. Nothing should arise or conspire to let them go again. The axiom, "that that system is the cheapest and best which is cheaper and better than any other in the long run," should be borne in mind as having an exact fitness to the question of holding these Indians. The enclosed letter to General Crocker about reducing the amount of food to be issued until we can get some more ahead, I have not heard from in reply, but I hope he will be able to carry into effect my request without trouble.

You can hardly imagine, general, the great difficulties which have lain in the path leading toward the settlement of this nation. Congress passed a bill appropriating one hundred thousand dollars toward clothing them and getting them farming utensils, tools, &c. This was the first of July last, and, as yet, not a yard of cloth, or a blanket, or spade, or plough, has reached them. Now the cold weather is setting in, and I have thousands of women and children who need the protection of a blanket. It is said that the goods bought by this money left Leavenworth on the first of October, instant. With good luck they may be at the Bosque Redondo by the tenth of next December. All these things the Indians were told would be here long ago, and they have waited and hoped for them until now, when the winter is upon us, and they think we may be acting in bad faith. This has been very unfortunate. Add to this the complete destruction by the army-worm of their crops, which they had labored so hard to raise. Then, to fill the measure of their troubles, the failure of the crop elsewhere obliges me to cut down their ration. These are their troubles.

Ours have been manifold, but they have been met and overcome thus far. Now we have come to that point when we must have immediate help from the government. We must have our past requisitions for funds filled at once, and those which we shall be obliged to make promptly filled, else what little food the people have to sell will be held in their hands. You can better imagine the consequences resulting from our inability to get this food, and have it at the Bosque Redondo in time, than I describe them.

Again, it is absolutely necessary that two thousand five hundred head of good cattle be bought in Kansas or Missouri, and sent out at once. This the War Department should order to be done. There should be no time lost by advertising for proposals, but the stock on hand, if there be any, should be sent, or it should be bought in the open market and forwarded, one thousand two hundred and fifty at a time, without delay. Then, if we cannot get bread, we can give the Indians more meat, and at least keep them from perishing.

I trust the earnestness of my appeal will be measured by the necessities which surround me, and that there will be no delay in filling our requisitions for money, or in sending these cattle.

I am, general, very respectfully, your obedient servant,

JAMES H. CARLETON,
Brigadier General, Commanding.

Brigadier General LORENZO THOMAS,
Adjutant General U. S. A., Washington, D. C.

List of papers which accompanied this letter.

Proceedings of a board of survey convened at Fort Sumner, New Mexico, August 30, 1864.
Copy of a letter to General Crocker, dated October 22, 1864.
Copy of a letter from General Crocker, dated October 21, 1864.—(Extract.)
Copy of a letter from Captain Calloway, dated September 14, 1864.
Copy of a letter from Lorenzo Labadie, dated October 22, 1864.
Copy of a letter from Colonel John C. McFerran, chief quartermaster, to Major H. M. Enos, division quartermaster, dated October 29, 1864.

Official:

ERASTUS W. WOOD,
Captain 1st Vet. Inf. C. V., A. A. A. General.

HEADQUARTERS DEPARTMENT OF NEW MEXICO,
Santa Fé, N. M., October 31, 1864.

GENERAL: The cold weather admonishes me to write to you about what it appears to me would be the best plan to construct habitations for the Indians for the approaching winter. If you will have circular excavations made at the points where you will have the different villages—each one large enough for a family, and, say, four feet or more in depth, with the earth embanked some three or four feet high on the north side, with steps cut in the earth to descend to the floor—they would be very warm, even with a little fire. Pray have one made as a model, and, if they like it, encourage the Indians to follow the pattern. In this way the cold winds will be entirely escaped by the children. What is done should be at once, before the winter sets in. The Indians can spread the floors with coarse reed grass, or with hay, and can make beds of grass which will be very comfortable. Besides, they will have some green hides and skins to spread down. Such excavations require no timber, are warmer than the huts they have, and are soon made. They should be made north of the north acequia, and far enough removed to avoid dampness from it. I have ordered Captain Bell to buy if possible and send down from Fort Union, where he has gone, 4,000 sheep. These will furnish wool to weave into little blankets for the smaller children; the skins can be dressed for clothing, and the flesh issued for food at the present established rates. The whole animal, including what the butchers call the "head and pluck," must be issued.

You must pardon me for suggesting all these details, but my anxiety is so great to make this powerful nation, which has surrendered to us, as happy and as well cared-for as possible under all the adverse circumstances which encompass us, that every idea looking to this end which comes into my mind I send to you, fully believing that you will enter into the spirit which animates me for their good. The economy in the use of food in all things must be observed. The making of soups, which is by far the best way to cook what they have, must be inculcated as a religion. And let me observe that one pound of solid food made into nutritious soup—nutritious because well and thoroughly boiled—

for each man, woman, and child, per day—for a Frenchman—is more than he wants, and more than he gets, as a rule.

I hope the Indian goods will be at Fort Union by the twentieth of November, and at the Bosque by the end. Then they will have more tools to work with—some blankets, shirts, and cloth, for the children's nakedness. These articles, with the fleeces of the 4,000 sheep, will help keep the Indians comfortable. Tell them to be too proud to murmur at what cannot be helped. We could not foresee the total destruction of their corn crop, nor could we foresee that the frost and hail would come and destroy the crop in the country; but not to be discouraged; to work hard, every man and woman, to put in large fields next year, when, if God smiles upon our efforts, they will, at one bound, be forever placed beyond want, and independent. Tell them not to believe ever that we are not their best friends; that their enemies have told them that we would destroy them; that we had sent big guns there to attack them; but that those guns are only to be used against their enemies, if they continue to behave as they have done.

In relation to the excavations, it would be well to have them at the sites of the different villages, for this reason: the Indians will then be near where they will erect their houses, and will lose no time in going to their labors upon them.

If the Navajoes had the spirit with reference to the Comanches which they ought to have toward their hereditary enemies, a war party of 500 of the former could go out and get all the stock they wanted. It would add to the punishment which the Comanches deserve for their depredations and butcheries of this year.

Captain Bristol and Captain Calloway would be the best men to prepare a model for the temporary habitations for the Indians.

Colonel Collins tells me that some twenty wagons and sixty work-cattle are coming, as he understands, for the Indians. Colonel McFerran will have ten wagons—old and condemned—sent down from Fort Union. These will be given to them. Thus, little by little, they will have many conveniences. Tell them this, please. Some of their own horses should be broken to teaming and ploughing.

It is possible a committee of the legislature may come down to see how the Indians are getting on. Pray have them kindly received and shown everything. I know I can count on your constant thoughts and earnest and persistent efforts to second me in this important work, and shall always feel obliged to you for them.

Respectfully, general, your obedient servant,

JAMES H. CARLETON,
Brigadier General, Commanding.

Brigadier General MARCELLUS M. CROCKER, U. S. Vols.,
Commanding at Fort Sumner, N. M.

NOTE.—I shall start for Franklin about the 10th November.

Official:

ERASTUS W. WOOD,
Captain 1st Vet. Inf. C. V., A. A. A. General.

HEADQUARTERS DEPARTMENT OF NEW MEXICO,
Santa Fé, N. M., November 1, 1864.

SIR: We have in this department nearly 10,000 Navajo and Apache Indians whom we are endeavoring to establish upon a reservation and teach to till the earth for a support. You were kind enough last year to send us a few packages of seeds, for which we are very thankful. I pray that you will send us a large supply this year. If some came every mail from now until the planting season will be over next year, it will help us very much. They should be put up in the strongest possible wrappers, preferably in tin boxes, and be legibly marked. This year the army-worm totally destroyed the crop planted by the Indians, which was a calamity, and reduces us to great straits. With God's blessing, next year, we hope to raise enough for their support.

I am, sir, very respectfully, your obedient servant,

JAMES H. CARLETON,
Brigadier General, Commanding.

CHIEF OF THE AGRICULTURAL BUREAU, *Washington, D. C.*

Official:

ERASTUS W. WOOD,
Captain 1 t Vet. Inf. C. V., A. A. A. General.

HEADQUARTERS DEPARTMENT OF NEW MEXICO,
Santa Fé, N. M., November 6, 1864.

GENERAL: I beg again to impress upon your mind the planting of the 5,000 trees this winter on the reservation. If 10,000 can be planted and cared for, so much the better. Please give this important matter your personal attention. When the mesquite roots have all been consumed we shall have growing quite a forest of wood for fuel if we plant from 5,000 to 10,000 trees per annum. Captain Calloway informed me that immense numbers could be easily procured.

5 *p. m.*—Your letter of the 28th ultimo has just been received. The Indians must be contented with the amount of food now ordered to be issued to them; *id est*, twenty ounces per day of solid food to each individual. Major McCleave, 1st cavalry California volunteers, is the officer I propose to send to your post to act as commissary.

Please make arrangements to have a certain census of all captive Indians on the reservation made on the 30th instant by actual count. At that time it will be well to know the strength of each family, with age, sex, &c., of each. Report the number, age, sex, &c., of the orphan children, and what plan you have adopted with reference to their case. This will be an especial report required for the War Department. Pray let it be as full and complete as possible, and give the amount and kind of stock owned by each family or each Indian, as the case may be. If you require any more of the tin tickets to facilitate the issue of rations, please write to Captain Shoemaker to have them made, stating the number and size (with regard to the figures stamped upon them) of what you require. It is left with yourself to invest the money due to Indians for fodder as you may think will most conduce to their interests. A fund should be formed to provide grape cuttings and to pay for pumpkin, melon, chilé, and other seeds. Please let me know if many seeds have been saved for planting, and what you will require.

The seed wheat must be selected from the wheat you have on hand as far as possible. Suppose, for example, you cause to be sown, say, 3,000 acres. This will take from 4,500 bushels to 6,000 bushels, equal to 300,000 pounds, a frightful quantity, considering the scarcity. It will not do to trust too much to the corn crop. Besides, if the wheat is sown early, and matures early, beans can be raised on the same ground next summer—a great gain.

The Indians destroy a great deal of the corn crop by eating the corn before the ears are filled. Separate ground should be planted to be depredated on, so that the main fields would be left intact to ripen. Captain Bell, commissary of subsistence, has bought twelve new ploughs. These shall be sent down as soon as they come. If all the able-bodied Indians will keep busily at work now, and day by day, until the next planting season has passed, 10,000 acres can be put in seed with ease. The 4,000 sheep have been bought and are *en route* to you. The fleeces should be given to the poorest Indians. Please inform me of how much these sheep average in weight per head, taking every ounce that can be issued as food.

If the commissary would arrange to have all the blood of slaughtered cattle and sheep saved, to be made into haggies and blood puddings, it would be great food for the orphan children who go to the school. The scarcity of food in the country is very great, and every resource must be tried to economize, or there will be positive suffering before the next crop will be gathered.

Please have the land which is to be cultivated measured. A calculation can easily be made which will determine beyond a doubt the number of acres. Delays in the arrival of the mail have detained me from going below. I shall start some time this week, and shall endeavor to return *via* Fort Sumner.

I am, general, very respectfully, your obedient servant,

JAMES H. CARLETON,
Brigadier General, Commanding.

Brig. Gen. MARCELLUS M. CROCKER, U. S. Vols.,
Commanding at Fort Sumner, N. M.

Official:

ERASTUS W. WOOD,
Captain 1st Vet. Inf. C. V., A. A. A. General.

HEADQUARTERS DEPARTMENT OF NEW MEXICO,
Santa Fé, N. M., November 8, 1864.

SIR: I have the honor to acknowledge the receipt of your communication of the 5th instant, and to say, in reply, that it has hitherto seemed to be my duty, when Indians murdered our people and ran off their stock, to punish the aggressors if I could. The responsibility of all the consequences which may follow my acts it is expected will rest where it rightfully belongs—that is to say, upon myself. I was not aware, until so informed by yourself, that it was expected that investigations, with reference to Indian hostilities on our people, were to be made through your office before a blow could be struck. It is, however, acknowledged that you should be informed when hostile demonstrations are to be made against Indians within your superintendency, and, therefore, copies of orders in such cases have been sent to you. Utes and Apaches have had authority to go against the Comanches and Kiowas, with Colonel Carson, mainly because it was desirable, when so many coalitions are forming between the various Indian tribes against the whites, to have the savages of the mountains committed on our side as against the Indians of the plains. This subject seemed to be the peculiar province of the military department, which is charged with the protection of the people.

It may not be improper to inform you that I, myself, was in command of the troops at Albuquerque, in 1856, when the Comanches and Kiowas visited that town. I gave them an ox and some flour and sugar and coffee, and had a talk with them. Enclosed please find a copy of a letter from department headquarters to myself in relation to them.

It is to be regretted that, from no cause on the part of the military, there has come to exist a state of affairs between ourselves officially which seems to preclude the idea of much cordiality in consultation or in co-operation; but my earnest efforts shall continue and the whole of my ability be given to protect the persons and property of the people residing within this department from Indian aggressions, even though, unhappily, there be not such a condition of harmony between ourselves, as public officers, as might be desirable.

I have the honor to be, very respectfully, your obedient servant,

JAMES H CARLETON,
Brigadier General, Commanding.

MATTHEW STECK, Esq.,
Superintendent of Indian Affairs, Santa Fé, N. M.

Official:

ERASTUS W. WOOD,
Captain 1st Vet. Inf. C. V., A. A. A. General.

DEPARTMENT OF NEW MEXICO, ASSISTANT ADJUTANT GENERAL'S OFFICE,
Santa Fé, N. M., November 9, 1864.

GENERAL: The general commanding the department has been sorry to learn that some Indians from the reservation are reported to have killed a beef belonging to a citizen who lives near Mr. Giddings, or above there. If this be true, the general says that a stern example must be made by the punishment of the aggressors. If they cannot individually be identified, the chief of the particular band to which they belong should be imprisoned and kept as a hostage for the good behavior of his people until the offenders have been given up.

The general further directs that you call the chiefs together and tell them about this, and tell them you have orders to try and punish, if necessary by shooting, any Indian who depredates upon the property of the citizens This matter must be met at once, and met in a manner to prevent its recurrence. Pay the owner of the beef out of the money due the Indians for fodder, and have them see you do it. The commanding general trusts that you will be able to adopt such measures, by precept and by force, as shall forever put a stop to such acts. Forbid the Indians coming toward the settlements. They must herd their stock and hunt to the northeast, east, and southeast of the post.

I have the honor to be, general, very respectfully, your obedient servant,

BEN. C. CUTLER,
Assistant Adjutant General.

Brig. Gen. MARCELLUS M. CROCKER, U. S. Vols.,
Commanding at Fort Sumner, N. M.

Official:

ERASTUS W. WOOD,
Captain 1st Vet. Inf. C. V., A. A. A. General.

HEADQUARTERS DEPARTMENT OF NEW MEXICO,
Socorro, N. M., November 15, 1864.

MAJOR: On the 8th instant seven Indians, supposed to be Moqui, Zuñi, and Apache Indians from arrows found, attacked four shepherds near Limitar, killed three and ran off 3,000 head of sheep. They doubtless went to the Rita Quemado toward Zuñi and the

Moqui. Take a few resolute men, go yourself south, cut their trail and follow it and retake the sheep. I believe the Moquis, pressed by hunger, have committed the robbery. If you travel as well as you did on your late trip you will be sure to catch them and make some reputation. I am anxious for you to succeed in this. I have great faith in your energy and perseverance.

Send a copy of this letter to department headquarters for record.

I am, major, respectfully, your obedient servant,

JAMES H. CARLETON,
Brigadier General, Commanding.

Major ETHAN W. EATON,
Commanding at Fort Wingate, N. M.

Official:

ERASTUS W. WOOD,
Captain 1st Vet. Inf. C. V., A. A. A. General.

DEPARTMENT OF NEW MEXICO, ASSISTANT ADJUTANT GENERAL'S OFFICE,
Santa Fé, N. M., November 25, 1864.

GENERAL: Dr. M. Steck, superintendent of Indian affairs for the department of New Mexico, leaves Santa Fé on the 26th instant for Fort Union. He goes to that post for the purpose of receiving and conducting to Fort Sumner, New Mexico, a train of goods and presents intended for the Indians on the military reservation at the Bosque Redondo, about to arrive from the States. I am directed by the general commanding to say to you that it is his desire that you afford Dr. Steck every assistance in your power to enable him to carry out the wishes of the Commissioner of Indian Affairs in the distribution of these goods. Dr. Steck may take an escort from Fort Union; in case he should do so, you are directed to return the same to that post as soon as practicable. The general also directs that if the superintendent wishes to examine into the condition of the Indians under your charge and to go among and talk with them, you will permit him to do so, and have Captain Calloway and your interpreter go with him and show him the Indian farm, mode of working it, facilities for doing so, &c., &c., and how Indians are supplied with food, as well as any other information he may desire to obtain in relation to the Indians on the reservation.

I have the honor to be, general, very respectfully, your obedient servant,

BEN. C. CUTLER,
Assistant Adjutant General.

Brig. Gen. MARCELLUS M. CROCKER, U. S. Vols.,
Commanding at Fort Sumner, N. M.

Official:

ERASTUS W. WOOD,
Captain 1st Vet. Inf. C. V., A. A. A. General.

[Confidential.]

DEPARTMENT OF NEW MEXICO, ASSISTANT ADJUTANT GENERAL'S OFFICE,
Santa Fé, N. M., December 9, 1864.

GENERAL: I have just heard from the general commanding. He was at Las Cruces, New Mexico, on the 1st instant, and he directs me to write to you as follows:

About one year since, when Dr. Steck, superintendent of Indian affairs for New Mexico, went to the Bosque Redondo, he caused the Apaches to become discontented, by telling them that they could go to their own country to make *mescal*. If the doctor pursues any such course during his present visit, or talks with the Navajoes in any manner to make them unhappy or discontented, he will be required at once to leave the reservation.

I have the honor to be, general, very respectfully, your obedient servant,

BEN. C. CUTLER,
Assistant Adjutant General.

Brig. Gen. MARCELLUS M. CROCKER, U. S. Vols.,
Commanding at Fort Sumner, N. M.

Official:

ERASTUS W. WOOD,
Captain 1st Vet. Inf. C. V., A. A. A. General.

HEADQUARTERS DEPARTMENT OF NEW MEXICO,
Franklin, Texas, December 10, 1864.

DEAR GENERAL: Your private letter of 17th ultimo came to hand to-day. I have written to the chief commissary that if he can see his way clear to feed the Indians, if we add four ounces to the present meat ration, making it twelve ounces per day to each Indian, to write to you to that effect by the special express which will take this letter from Santa Fé, when you will give orders accordingly.

Whether the Indians understand the necessity of diminishing their rations or not, that necessity meets us at every turn from the great scarcity in the country, and they must be satisfied. If they proceed to any unpleasant extremes force must be used against them on the moment. They must do what we direct or perish. Besides, they must commence work upon their fields at once. Adopt the best plan to produce this result, but the result must be produced now before it is too late.

You can try this plan if the chief commissary finds he can make the additional four ounces to the meat ration per day. Issue the addition only to those who do good days' work.

Order a military commission to try the three Navajoes about whom you write. Have them have a fair trial. If they are sentenced to be hung or shot for what they have done as alleged, they will deserve the sentence. Your arrangement about having a part of the Indian hospital used for school purposes is a good one and approved by me.

It was my purpose to come to Fort Sumner *via* Fort Stanton from Las Cruces, but I fear I shall not have time. If not, I shall come as soon after my arrival at Santa Fé as possible. I shall leave here, *en route* to Las Cruces, on the 13th, and shall be obliged to remain there a day or two. Hoping that, by firmness and kindness combined, you will succeed in managing the Indians in a satisfactory manner,

I am, dear general, very truly yours,

JAMES H. CARLETON,
Brigadier General, Commanding.

Brig. Gen. MARCELLUS M. CROCKER, U. S. Vols.,
Commanding at Fort Sumner, N. M.

Official:

ERASTUS W. WOOD,
Captain 1st Vet. Inf. C. V., A. A. A. General.

HEADQUARTERS DEPARTMENT OF NEW MEXICO,
Franklin, Texas, December 10, 1864.

CAPTAIN: I have just received a letter from General Crocker, stating that the Indians make many daily complaints that their ration is too small. If you can see your way clear in getting supplies so that you can safely increase the meat ration to twelve ounces per day to each Indian, of meat—it is now eight ounces—and twelve ounces of breadstuffs, in all twenty-four ounces to the ration, write to General Crocker at once by special express to increase the issue of the meat ration to twelve ounces.

I am, captain, respectfully,

JAMES H. CARLETON,
Brigadier General, Commanding.

Captain WILLIAM H. BELL, U. S. A.,
Chief Commissary, Santa Fé, N. M.

Official:

ERASTUS W. WOOD,
Captain 1st Vet. Inf. C. V., A. A. A. General.

HEADQUARTERS DEPARTMENT OF NEW MEXICO,
Las Cruces, N. M., December 15, 1864.

COLONEL: I had the pleasure to receive your very interesting and satisfactory report of your battle with the Kiowas on 25th ultimo, and have sent a copy of it to the War Department.

I beg to express to you and to the gallant officers and soldiers whom you commanded on that occasion, as well as to our good auxiliaries, the Utes and Apaches, my thanks for the handsome manner in which you all met so formidable an enemy and defeated him. Please to publish an order to this effect.

This brilliant affair adds another green leaf to the laurel wreath which you have so nobly won in the service of your country.

That you may long be spared to be of still further service, is the sincere wish of your obedient servant and friend,

JAMES H. CARLETON,
Brigadier General, Commanding.

Colonel CHRISTOPHER CARSON,
Com'dg Expedition against the Kiowa and Comanche Indians, Fort Bascom, N. M.

Official:

ERASTUS W. WOOD,
Captain 1st Vet. Inf. C. V., A. A. A. General.

LETTERS RELATING TO INDIAN AFFAIRS IN THE DEPARTMENT OF NEW MEXICO DURING THE YEAR 1865.

HEADQUARTERS DEPARTMENT OF NEW MEXICO,
Whittemore's Ranche, N. M., January 5, 1865.

GENERAL: The general commanding the department directs me to write to you as follows: Send all men belonging to company A, 1st cavalry New Mexico volunteers, to Fort Stanton. It is supposed that some are at your post unless they left with Lieutenant Hubbell for Fort Stanton.

The general saw a Navajo woman, having with her a Navajo girl aged about twelve years, about three miles from this place. They had evidently followed an ox train which had brought flour to Fort Sumner from Mr. Moore a few days since, and this evening another Navajo woman, aged about eighteen, came into this ranche from the direction of Fort Sumner; this last one he has asked Mr. Whittemore to return to Fort Sumner by the first opportunity. The general is under the impression that a great many Navajo women are inveigled away from Fort Sumner by Mexicans who come there with supplies, and that others are perhaps wandering away towards the settlements. This must be effectually stopped at once, and he leaves it with you to adopt the means.

It is understood here that Dr. Steck told Mr. Taylor that the Navajoes are going off by fives and sixes every day; that the Indians told him so. One or two movable pickets commanded by a determined officer could soon ascertain whether this is true and put a stop to it An officer and a half dozen men stationed at this point to search trains might also do a great deal of good. In conclusion, the general suggests whether it would not be better to not permit any Indians to leave the post without a written passport, these to be delivered up on their return.

I am, general, very respectfully, your obedient servant,

ERASTUS W. WOOD, *Aide-de-Camp.*

Brig. Gen. MARCELLUS M. CROCKER, U. S. Vols.,
Commanding at Fort Sumner, New Mexico.

Official:

ERASTUS W. WOOD,
Captain 1st Vet. Inf. C. V., A. A. A General.

HEADQUARTERS DEPARTMENT OF NEW MEXICO,
Santa Fé, N. M., January 14, 1865.

GENERAL: I have the honor herewith to enclose for the information of the Secretary of War the proceedings of a board of officers assembled by Brigadier General Crocker, United States volunteers, at Fort Sumner, New Mexico, to make an examination of the quantity, quality and kind of goods issued by Matthew Steck, esq., superintendent of Indian affairs for New Mexico, to the Navajo Indians at the Bosque Redondo, in December, 1864.

You will also please find enclosed a letter from General Crocker on this subject, and likewise letters from Captain Lusby, assistant adjutant general, and of Mr. La Rue, the present sutler at Fort Sumner, setting forth their opinions of the value of the goods. You are aware that Congress passed a bill appropriating one hundred thousand dollars for the purchase of goods for these Indians. The result to the Indians is shown by these papers. Captain Bristol, who was on the board, informed me that Mr. Steck asked him not to count the pieces of prints.

If, general, this is to be considered as a specimen of the manner in which the intentions of Congress in making appropriations are to be carried into practical effect, it would be well for that honorable body, when considering the matter with reference to how much of that appropriation would reach the point aimed at by them, to leave a wide margin for what in target practice is technically called "the drift."

I have the honor to be, very respectfully, your obedient servant,

JAMES H. CARLETON,
Brigadier General, Commanding.

Brigadier General LORENZO THOMAS,
Adjutant General U. S. A., Washington, D. C.

NOTE.—The wagons and oxen, much needed, have not been turned over to the Indians, or to the commander at Fort Sumner for their use.

Official: ERASTUS W. WOOD,
Captain 1st Vet. Inf. C. V., A. A. A. General.

HEADQUARTERS DEPARTMENT OF NEW MEXICO,
Santa Fé, N. M., January 17, 1865.

SIR: I have been informed that an influential Mexican wrote to his brother in Valencia county, on the Rio Grande, that unless the people there opposed the colonization of the Navajoes at the Bosque Redondo, and unless they succeeded in having the Navajoes got back to their own county, all of the government business which has hitherto been so beneficial to that country by passing trains of supplies to the old Navajo country, and the employment of means of transportation for army purposes in that country, would cease. There can hardly be a doubt but that here are a set of demagogues who foresee that when the Indians are all colonized, there will be no further need of the immense expenditures which have hitherto been incurred in keeping troops in New Mexico, and make that one of the points to oppose so important a measure. It is well to remember the machinations of parties to keep up the Florida war. In my opinion, this idea of losing the government patronage for New Mexico when the Indian difficulties should come to an end, with a certain set who care nothing for the poor or the future of the country, is one great element of opposition to the measure. I can prove by figures, if necessary, that to place and keep the Indians on any reservation in their own country, for example on the San Juan—the only place which even those who wish them moved say they could occupy—would cost more than three times as much as to keep them where they are. If those who wish them moved will name the place west of the Rio Grande where they would put them, I will measure the distances, survey the ground, get bids for freight, calculate the cost of the forts, the number and cost of the various garrisons, the cost of food, and prove by positive data what, without going into minute details, I here state. You had better, by far, move them to Kansas or Missouri, for then you take them where provisions are cheap.

I am, sir, very respectfully, your obedient servant,

JAMES H. CARLETON,
Brigadier General, Commanding.

ADJUTANT GENERAL OF THE ARMY, *Washington, D. C.*

Official: ERASTUS W. WOOD,
Captain 1st Vet. Inf. C. V., A. A. A. General.

HEADQUARTERS DEPARTMENT OF NEW MEXICO,
Santa Fé, N. M., January 24, 1865.

GENERAL: I have the honor to enclose herewith a copy of Colonel Carson's report of his fight with the Kiowas and Comanches on his expedition as ordered by General Orders No. 32 of last year, from these headquarters. Had General Blunt gone on to the Palo Duro, near the scene of this fight, those two tribes would doubtless have received a severe punishment.

I find that it is impossible for me to guard the lines of communication hence to the States with the limited force at my command, and at the same time guard the nine thousand Indian prisoners I have and whip other hostile Indians within New Mexico and Arizona. It is simply impossible for me to do it. Therefore I must depend on your help to this end.

Permit me to suggest that if you will send six companies of cavalry and two of infantry and a section of artillery *via* the bend of the Arkansas near Walnut creek, to the Palo Duro, (there is a fine road leading to New Mexico by that route,) and there to encamp for the summer, the cavalry to scout, the infantry and artillery to hold an intrenched camp with the hospital and supplies, the efforts of the Comanches and Kiowas would be paralyzed; for that point is in the very heart of their country, is easy of access, and has an abundance of fine wood, water and grass. If then you would have two companies of infantry and four of cavalry at old Fort Atkinson, twenty-six miles below the Cimarron crossing of the Arkansas, and two companies of infantry, one section of artillery, and four companies of cavalry at Fort Larned, which, in all, would amount to one regiment of cavalry, six companies of infantry and two sections of artillery, I think that, with what I could do from Fort Union to the crossing of the Arkansas, the route would be rendered safe during the summer. I suggest what is here written from having some knowledge of the country and of the summer haunts of the Indians. I am getting troops prepared to occupy the lower Cimarron spring, Cold spring, Rabbit Ear and Whetstone creek. These will furnish escorts from point to point to the crossing of the Arkansas, a distance of three hundred and fifty miles from Fort Union. Unless what is here suggested be done, and done by the first of May next, there will be many lives sacrificed and much property destroyed. I beg that you will furnish at least what is here suggested. If you know of better points than those named where troops should be placed, having these objects in view, of course you will place them there. I only offer the result of my observation and experience on the road to be guarded, and would not be understood as desiring to influence your own judgment in the matter. General Sumner, when in command here, employed myself upon the road for two seasons, which gave me some knowledge of the country. I enclose herewith a newspaper having paragraph I of Special Orders No 2, current series from these headquarters, by which you will see that troops are moving toward Fort Union preparatory to taking up the positions upon the road here indicated. The government should at once make the continuation of the telegraph from Denver to Santa Fé; then we could act in concert and produce lasting results. If I had influence it should be exerted to this end. The proposition is self-evident. Once you bring the whole matter of the good results to be attained by having telegraphic communication with Santa Fé, movements can be combined and timed by the commanders of these two military departments which must result in the total subjection of the Indians of the plains. The economy of such an enterprise, when considered in connexion with the cross-purposes with which, for want of rapid communication, we now have necessarily to work, is its principal recommendation.

I have the honor to be, general, very respectfully, your obedient servant,

JAMES H. CARLETON,
Brigadier General, Commanding.

Major General SAMUEL R. CURTIS,
Commanding the Department of Kansas, Fort Leavenworth, Kansas.

Official: ERASTUS W. WOOD,
Captain 1st Vet. Inf. C. V, A. A. A. General.

HEADQUARTERS DEPARTMENT OF NEW MEXICO,
Santa Fé, N. M., January 29, 1865.

GENERAL: I have the honor herewith to enclose for the information of the War Department the following documents. I send the originals, so that those who may have them to consider and act upon may have positive evidence in their own hands:

1st. General Orders No. 32, series for 1864, from these headquarters.

2d. Original letter from Matthew Steck, esq., superintendent of Indian affairs, acknowledging receipt of General Orders No. 32, above named. It is dated October 26, 1864.

3d. Copy of my reply to Mr. Steck's letter.

4th. Original letter from Superintendent Steck to his excellency the governor of New Mexico, stating that since he received General Orders No. 32, he had not issued any passes for Mexicans to go and trade with the Comanches. This letter is dated November 23, 1864.

5th. Original letter from Captain Edward H. Bergmann, 1st cavalry New Mexico volunteers, dated November 26, 1864, enclosing an autograph passport signed by Superintendent Steck, and dated October 27, 1864.

6th. Original letter from Captain Bergmann, dated December 4, 1864, enclosing an autograph passport, dated October 27, 1864, and another dated November 15, 1864, also written by Superintendent Steck's own hand.

7th. Original of a letter written by Captain Bergmann, dated November 24, 1864, in relation to Mexican traders with passports from Superintendent Steck, going stealthily past the military lines after they had been warned not to do so, and giving information to the enemy of the movement of troops.

8th. Original of a letter written by Colonel Carson, commanding an expedition against the Indians, stating that he found powder and lead in their camp, which had been furnished, without a doubt, by Mexican traders.

9th. Original letter from Captain Murphy, enclosing an affidavit of the movements of Mexican traders with passports from Superintendent Steck, in defiance of warnings that we were at war with the Indians.

10th. Printed report by Colonel Carson of his battle with the Indians.

You are aware, general, that the Indians robbed our trains on the route hence to the States during nearly all of last summer. That in the winter, as those same Indians moved south with their booty in stock, the Mexicans here, whom the Indians have not harmed on the road as set forth in my letter to Dr. Steck, got passports from Dr. Steck to go out on the plains east of this Territory to buy the stock robbed from Americans. That they paid in part for this stock with ammunition which they knew would be used against Americans in a continuation of this iniquitous business, there is not the shadow of a doubt. How many of these passports were issued by Superintendent Steck after he had notice of hostilities and before he wrote to the governor that he had issued none since he got that notice, it is impossible to say. The enclosed three are all which thus far have been intercepted.

The military is doing its best to protect the people and the lines of communication from hostile Indians; but when a high civil functionary gives passports to men to carry on a nefarious traffic, when he knows in reason that those men will give information of the movements of the troops; and when he sits down and deliberately writes to the governor that he has not given such passports, you must know, general, that such conduct adds not a little, to say the least, to our many embarrassments.

Very respectfully, your obedient servant,

JAMES H. CARLETON,
Brigadier General, Commanding.

ADJUTANT GENERAL U. S. A., *Washington, D. C.*

Official:

ERASTUS W. WOOD,
Captain 1st Vet. Inf. C. V., A. A. A. General.

HEADQUARTERS DEPARTMENT OF NEW MEXICO,
Santa Fé, N. M., February 12, 1865.

SIR: Enclosed, herewith, please find a printed notice to the people that a company of troops will leave Fort Union on the 1st and 15th of each month, to escort trains from that post to Fort Larned, Kansas. You will detail the company which has been longest from field service to move on this duty on the 1st proximo. Every officer and effective man will go. It will have one hundred rounds of ammunition per man in boxes, and twenty rounds per man in cartridge-boxes. Each man will be allowed to take two blankets, one greatcoat, two extra shirts, two extra drawers, one pair extra shoes, one pair extra pants; and no more clothing, except what he wears. You yourself will make a personal inspection of each man's knapsack, after the company has marched off the parade, and see that this order is carefully observed. The company will take rations only to Fort Lyon, Colorado Territory. There it will draw enough to last it to Fort Larned. It is hoped the company commander is a man capable of looking out well for the safety of the animals and property he is to escort and guard, and that he does not need specific instructions on this point. It is hoped he and his men will be not only ready to fight, *but will fight* any number of hostile Indians they may meet, or who may attack or menace the company or the train, by night or by day, in storm or in fair weather. It is to be hoped that neither officers nor men will be off their guard, or idle away their time, but will attend to the business for which the government pays them. No man's musket will be carried in a wagon or in a feed-box. He must carry it himself *all the time.* Only two tents will be taken to a company. The chief quartermaster will send orders with reference to the transportation—not to exceed two six-mule teams.

Respectfully, &c.,

JAMES H. CARLETON,
Brigadier General, Commanding.

COMMANDING OFFICER, *Fort Union, N. M.*

Official:

ERASTUS W. WOOD,
Captain 1st Vet. Inf. C. V., A. A. A. General.

Headquarters Department of New Mexico,
Santa Fé, N. M., February 15, 1865.

This morning Herrera Grande and five other Navajo chiefs, and Jesus, the interpreter for whom I wrote to General Crocker, on the 22d of January, 1865, came to Santa Fé, *en route* to the old Navajo country. I had a talk with them in the presence of Governor Connelly and Don José Manuel Gallegos. It was to this effect:

"They were to go out into the old Navajo country and tell the Navajoes still remaining there that they must come in at once, and go to the reservation; that this is the last warning they will have; that, if they come in now, their stock shall remain as their own. But if, within five weeks from the time of the notice, they are not at Fort Wingate, the door will be shut, and we will then fight them, the people will fight them, and the Utes will fight them, and they will be destroyed. In this case their blood will be on their own heads, not on ours, as they have had fair warning. These Navajoes whom I send out as delegates with this warning are then to return to Santa Fé, and thence to the Bosque Redondo, without waiting for any others."

JAMES H. CARLETON,
Brigadier General, Commanding.

Official:

ERASTUS W. WOOD,
Captain 1st Vet. Inf. C. V., A. A. A. General.

Headquarters Department of New Mexico,
Santa Fé, N. M., February 20, 1865.

Sir: I send Lieutenant John Ayres, 1st cavalry New Mexico volunteers, with Herrera Grande and two other principal men of the Navajo nation, and with Jesus, the interpreter, to Fort Wingate, *en route* to inform Manuelito and the other Navajoes not yet surrendered, that they must now come in and go to the reservation, so as to help put in a crop this year. If you think it advisable, Lieutenant Ayres and his party can proceed with Herrera to Manuelito's camp. In this case some one should go who can talk Spanish fluently, so as to act as Lieutenant Ayres's interpreter, in case you think private Dorland cannot talk that language sufficiently well to make Jesus understand what Lieutenant Ayres may have to communicate. If it would be necessary to send half a dozen more picked men, you can do so. In case Lieutenant Ayres should go on with this delegation—and this is left with you to decide—see that he has a plenty of rations, and, if he take a team, plenty of forage. In case the Indians go on alone, give them animals to ride. You had better give them these, in either event, as they may be obliged to leave the road to hunt Manuelito. The remnant of the tribe still in the old Navajo country will be destroyed, unless they come in. The people of the country and the Utes will rob them first and capture their children for servants, and by degrees will completely exterminate them. Their only safety depends on their immediate surrender and removal to the Bosque Redondo. Be sure to impress this important truth upon the minds of all Navajoes still back. Not six months will go past before what is here stated will come true, and I wish to save them from such unhappy consequences, in case they persist in their folly of remaining behind. Herrera and the others, having given the warning, will not wait for the other Navajoes, but will return at once to Santa Fé, *en route* to Fort Sumner, where they are anxious to make preparations for planting.

Very respectfully, your obedient servant,

JAMES H. CARLETON,
Brigadier General, Commanding.

Commanding Officer, *Fort Wingate, N. M.*

Official:

ERASTUS W. WOOD,
Captain 1st Vet. Inf. C. V., A. A. A. General.

Headquarters Department of New Mexico,
Santa Fé, N. M., February 25, 1865.

Sir: Your note of this date I have had the honor to receive. We are not yet at peace with the Kiowas and Comanches. I hope soon to receive intelligence that a delegation from the latter tribe have come to Fort Bascom to make overtures for peace. I have authorized three parties to go out to their country to procure three American women and three children said to be held captive by them, and to procure one Mexican boy, stolen from Chihuahua. When these parties return we shall know more definitely whether any durable compact can be made, having in view a peace with those tribes, when you will be duly notified of the result.

I have the honor to be, very respectfully, your obedient servant,

JAMES H. CARLETON,
Brigadier General, Commanding.

MICHAEL STECK, Esq.,
Superintendent of Indian Affairs, Santa Fé, N. M.

Official:

ERASTUS W WOOD,
Captain 1st Vet. Inf. C. V., A. A. A. General.

HEADQUARTERS DEPARTMENT OF NEW MEXICO,
Santa Fé, N. M., February 26, 1865.

SIR: Mr. Delgado said he would send a party out to endeavor to buy the captives of whom I wrote to you yesterday. I cannot consent to traders going to the Comanche country for any other than the *bona fide* purpose of trying to get by purchase or otherwise the unfortunate persons now held captive by that people, or by the Kiowas. Passports having this purpose in view will be countersigned, and the parties permitted to pass through our pickets.

I am, sir, respectfully,

JAMES H. CARLETON,
Brigadier General, Commanding.

MICHAEL STECK, Esq.,
Superintendent of Indian Affairs, Santa Fé, N. M.

Official:

ERASTUS W. WOOD,
Captain 1st Vet. Inf. C. V., A. A. A. General.

DEPARTMENT OF NEW MEXICO, ASSISTANT ADJUTANT GENERAL'S OFFICE,
Santa Fé, N. M., March 10, 1865.

MAJOR: I send down by this express a small sack of apricot seeds, which the general desires to have planted at once.

The general commanding directs me to say that General Crocker was some time since instructed to feed to captive Indians one pound of fresh meat and three-quarters of a pound of breadstuff per head, each day, commencing March 1st; but owing to the cattle having fallen off during the late stormy weather you will cause to be fed, commencing at once, one pound of breadstuff and three-quarters of a pound of meat per head, each day, to the aforesaid Indians.

The general also directs that you fit out a party of about one hundred Indians, well provided with axes. Place them under the charge of some efficient officer—Lieutenant Fox, for instance—and send them up the Pecos river, to cut wood and let it float down for the use of the troops and Indians on the reservation. This wood can be stopped by running a boom out into the river at some point near the post; but great care should be used in order that it should not have the effect of causing the spring floods to overflow the river bottoms.

I have the honor to be, major, very respectfully, your obedient servant,

BEN. C. CUTLER,
Assistant Adjutant General.

Major WILLIAM MCCLEAVE,
1st Cavaly C. V., Com. at Fort Sumner, N. M.

Official:

ERASTUS W. WOOD,
Captain 1st Vet. Inf. C. V., A. A. A. General.

HEADQUARTERS DEPARTMENT OF NEW MEXICO,
Santa Fé, N. M., March 15, 1865.

MAJOR: I received yesterday your note of the 9th instant. I have written to Mr. Dold that if he desires his train to proceed the escort will go with it, as originally ordered. Let the company understand that it must be on the watch all the time and not be surprised. By having it understood how the train shall march, with advanced spies, and with flankers, and with men in rear to give the alarm; and have it understood how the wagons shall be corralled in case of alarm, so that a corral can be formed at a moment's notice; and by having it understood that the men are to fight to the last man in case of an attack—there will hardly be a doubt of their making a successful trip.

You will tell the Comanche chiefs that they will send runners to warn the Indians that if they attack our trains, either upon the Palo Duro, the Cimarron, or the Raton mountains route, we will put men enough in the field against them to destroy them. Tell them that the question of a bitter war is left with themselves; that we do not propose to have our trains stopped or our people murdered with impunity; that if they keep off the road we shall not harm them. But if they attack our trains we will make a war upon them which they will always remember. Tell the chiefs that if our trains are attacked we shall not wish to see them again; that we shall not believe ever in their sincerity, certainly not in their ability to control their people.

I will send you another company, and if you are attacked we expect, of course, that you will make a handsome defence.

I believe, if Deüs is not surprised, he can whip all the Indians which will dare to come against a train of wagons filled with soldiers, on the road, or against a well-formed corral, in camp. We must not have the commerce of the country stopped by rumors. We must go ahead, and, if worse comes to worst, fight it out. Let that be understood just now. And be sure and impress this idea upon those chiefs. It will be a sorry time for their people in the long run. Tell them of their helpless condition in winter, and that we shall not forget their summer rascalities.

Respectfully, your obedient servant,

JAMES H. CARLETON,
Brigadier General, Commanding.

Major EDWARD H. BERGMANN,
Commanding at Fort Bascom, N. M.

NOTE.—Have the trains take some water-barrels to hold water for the men, in case a corral is made to fight when the train is not near a stream. Give Captain Deüs orders to keep the barrels filled *all the time.*

Official:

ERASTUS W. WOOD,
Captain 1st Vet. Inf. C. V., A. A. A. General.

HEADQUARTERS DEPARTMENT OF NEW MEXICO,
Santa Fé, N. M., March 16, 1865.

SIR: I have had the honor to receive your letter of the 15th instant, stating, that you have received information that the Apache Indians, known as the Mimbres band of that tribe, desire peace; and that you propose to have a talk with them in their own country, and desire that I give you an escort as far as Fort West on the Gila river. In reply, I beg to say that I have been duly informed of the disposition of those Indians, and some weeks since gave directions as to the only terms on which peace could be had. I have hitherto considered, and am still of the opinion, that when we are at war with a band of Indians the military department of the government should and must manage all affairs connected with them until the war is ended; otherwise a superintendent or Indian agent might go and have talks and negotiate with them, when in the opinion of the military commander the proper time had come to prosecute hostilities with increased rigor; and thus the two branches of the government might act with cross-purposes.

The Indians to whom you allude have been long at war, and are now, it is believed, coming to that point where they wish to surrender. They are still in the hands of the military, *and will be, until the military commander makes peace with them upon his own terms.* Some of them have been captured and are kept as prisoners, so that when, in the opinion of the military commander, the proper time comes, if the present efforts to get the Indians fail, they will be sent as runners to tell their headmen to come in for a talk. Should the headmen thus come in, they will again be informed that the *ultimatum* is for their people to remove to the reservation at the Bosque Redondo; that they can have peace on no other basis; that we will continue the war until that result is produced, or the band is exterminated.

To have any person outside of the military go and hold talks with them would be productive of no good, and might lead to complications which should be avoided. I therefore trust you will suspend the prosecution of your contemplated journey with such an end in view. As soon as these Indians are at peace, and are removed to the reservation, and the Department of the Interior stands ready to feed and take care of them, in common with the Navajo Indians and the Mescalero Apaches, you will of course be notified, when it will afford me pleasure to turn them over to you. But until that time comes, the military will claim to manage them to the best of its ability, whether in making war or in making peace.

I have the honor to be, very respectfully, your obedient servant,

JAMES H. CARLETON,
Brigadier General, Commanding.

MICHAEL STECK, Esq.,
Superintendent of Indian Affairs, Santa Fé, N. M.

NOTE.—See enclosed indorsement, number 772, series of 1865, from these headquarters.

Official: ERASTUS W. WOOD,
Captain 1st Vet. Inf C. V., A. A. A. General.

HEADQUARTERS DEPARTMENT OF NEW MEXICO,
Santa Fé, N. M., March 21, 1865.

Herrera Grande, Fecundo, and the other Navajo chiefs who were sent as delegates on the 15th of February, 1865, to the old Navajo country to tell Manuelito and other Indians still in that country that they must go the Bosque, came back yesterday, and this morning came to department headquarters to report the result of their mission. His excellency Governor Connelly, Colonel James L. Collins, Hon. José Manuel Gallegos, Colonel Nelson H. Davis, assistant inspector general United States army, and Lieutenant Colonel Eaton, 1st cavalry New Mexico volunteers, were present when Herrera made his report, which was made in Navajo to Jesus, the interpreter, and was rendered in English by his excellency the governor. It was as follows:

Herrera Grande says: Three days and a half after he left Fort Wingate he got to Zuñi, where he met Manuelito. They embraced, when Herrera told Manuelito he had come to see him. Manuelito said his elder brother was the commander, and it would be better to go where his brother was. Next day Herrera started for the rancheria, and was overtaken at Ojo del Venado that afternoon by Manuelito, who had staid back at Zuñi for awhile. That night, in talking with Manuelito, the latter said he would be willing to go to the Bosque, but his animals were poor. Herrera said it was not his orders for him to go, but the commander's orders. They camped together, and the next day at 3 p. m they arrived at the camp of Manuelito. Next day after, Manuelito sent out to call in those who were absent. Many had scattered, owing to a recent attack of the Utes. They came in that evening, in all about fifty men, women and children; this is about half of Manuelito's band. Then Manuelito brought in his stock; there were about 50 horses and 40 sheep. He said: "Here is all I have in the world. See what a trifling amount. You see how poor they are. My children are eating roots," (palmillas). Manuelito said the stock was so poor it could not travel to the Bosque now. Herrera said he was not authorized to extend the time set for him to come in. The two men who went with Herrera joined the latter in saying that it was no use to discuss the matter; that if they did not go to the Bosque worse would come to them; that they need not remain behind thinking to have wealth in stock as they used to have; that they would lose not only their stock, if they staid, but their lives; that the dead could not be called back, and they had better think of this. The women and children, seeing that Manuelito was not disposed to come, commenced to cry, as they seemed to foresee the consequences of remaining behind. This conversation took place before the arrival of Manuelito's brother. But he soon came, when he said that *his* animals were too poor, and he wanted to remain. After this conversation, Herrera said it was no use to remain longer; that he had delivered his message and would now go back to the Bosque. They then asked for three months to get their stock in order so that they could go. Manuelito said then, upon reflection, he concluded not to go. That his God and his mother lived in the west and he would not leave them; that there was a tradition that his people should never cross the Rio Grande, the Rio San Juan, or the Rio Colorado; that he also could not pass three mountains, and particularly could he not leave the Chusca mountains, his native hills; that his intention was to remain; that he was there to suffer all the consequences of war or famine; that now he had nothing to lose but his life, and *that* they could come and take whenever they pleased, but he would not move; that he had never done any wrong to the Americans or the Mexicans; that he had never robbed, but had lived upon his own resources; that if he were killed innocent blood would be shed.

Herrera then said to him, "I have done all I could for your benefit; have given you the best advice; I now leave you as if your grave were already made." Here they parted, and Herrera and his companions then came to Zuñi, where five Navajoes overtook them, some of whom had heard what had been said in council, and told them that a good many Navajoes would come in; and that the commander at the fort should be told of it, so as to be prepared for them and not treat them as enemies; that they would try to be in in fifteen days; but the snow was deep, and if they failed they would send in runners to tell the reason. Herrera then came to Fort Wingate, and this was the end of his mission.

Jesus, the interpreter, then said that Manuelito told him, while the party was at Manuelito's rancheria, as follows:

"Last summer, when I had a talk with you at Cañon Bonita, I told you I would come in, but I told you falsely. Now I tell you what is true: I will not go, and it is no use in killing up horses in coming for me; I will never go voluntarily."

Herrera was then asked by General Carleton how many Navajoes he thought were still back in the old Navajo country? How many, of all who remain, west of the Rio Grande?

Answer. From our calculations there are now six small parties. The first one is beyond the Colorado Chiquito, and consists of fifty souls, all told—men, women and children. They are mostly all ladrones.

The next is Manuelito's band. It lives this side of Colorado Chiquito, about sixty miles beyond Zuñi. It consists of about one hundred souls, of all ages and sexes. There are about twenty-five warriors. Not over twenty-five of this party say they will stay in the old Navajo country, but will go to the Bosque.

The third party is at a place called Quelitas, south of Fort Canby. That band consists of sixty or seventy. They are living there on piñones. They had considerable stock, but the Utes have recently taken it. They now live entirely upon nuts and roots.

The fourth party lives at Pueblo Colorado. This party is poor, and lives also on piñones. This party has a hundred or more souls, with from thirty to thirty-five men who could bear arms.

The fifth party is in Cañon de Chellé. This party numbers sixty persons—men, women, and children. Has about twenty men.

There is a sixth party at the Mesas de Calabazas, which has some stock—say 2,000 head of sheep and 100 horses. This party is friendly with the Pah-Utes, and numbers about one hundred. This makes four hundred and eighty in all, at the outside. We think there are less.

Question by General Carleton. In your judgment, how many of these will voluntarily come in?

Answer. We cannot tell how many, but probably seventy or eighty, or perhaps more.

Here the interview ended, and, on the 22d day of March, Herrera and party left for the Bosque Redondo.

JAMES H. CARLETON,
Brigadier General, Commanding.

Official:

ERASTUS W. WOOD,
Captain 1st Vet. Inf. C. V., A. A. A. General.

HEADQUARTERS DEPARTMENT OF NEW MEXICO,
Santa Fé, N. M., March 21, 1865.

[By the hands of Michael Steck, esq., superintendent of Indian affairs in New Mexico.]

MAJOR: I herewith enclose for your information a copy of a letter which I wrote to Superintendent Steck on the 18th instant; also a copy of his reply. Dr. Steck will cause to be transferred to Captain William L. Rynerson, assistant quartermaster United States volunteers, certain articles of property belonging to the Indian department, for the use of the Apaches and Navajoes upon the reservation. You will direct Captain Rynerson to receipt for them and to account for them through the proper department to the treasury of the United States. Dr. Steck will give him information as to necessary details in making out the accounts, and the usual channel of communication. Of course these accounts will be distinct from all army property accounts, and, so far as this property is concerned, Captain Rynerson will be an acting Indian agent. Should Dr. Steck visit the Bosque Redondo, I bespeak for him at your hands the hospitality and consideration and kindness to which he is entitled as the head of the Indian department in New Mexico.

I am, major, very respectfully, your obedient servant,

JAMES H. CARLETON,
Brigadier General, Commanding.

Major WILLIAM McCLEAVE,
Commanding at Fort Sumner, N. M.

Official:

ERASTUS W. WOOD,
Captain 1st Vet. Inf. C. V., A. A. A. General.

HEADQUARTERS DEPARTMENT OF NEW MEXICO,
Santa Fé, N. M., March 22, 1865.

GENERAL: I felt it to be my duty to order that Mr. Lorenzo Labadie, Indian agent for the Mescalero Apaches, be required to leave the reservation at the Bosque Redondo. He has, without a doubt, been engaged in buying cattle which had been delivered at Fort Sumner for subsistence for Indians. Captain Morton was not found guilty on the specification charging him with sending government cattle to Labadie's herd; but in General Crocker's opinion, as well as in my own, there can hardly be a doubt that Labadie and he were concerned in defrauding the government. I send the original record of the proceedings of the general court-martial, which tried Captain Morton, to you for your perusal. I beg, respectfully, that the Secretary of War ask of the Secretary of the Interior that Mr. Labadie be removed as Indian agent. He is not fit to hold office under the government.

Very respectfully, your obedient servant,

JAMES H. CARLETON,
Brigadier General, Commanding.

ADJUTANT GENERAL OF THE ARMY, *Washington, D. C.*

Official:

ERASTUS W. WOOD,
Captain 1st Vet. Inf. C. V., A. A. A. General.

HEADQUARTERS DEPARTMENT OF NEW MEXICO,
Santa Fé, N. M., March 23, 1865.

SIR: I understand if Manuelito, the Navajo chief, could be captured his band would doubtless come in; and that if you could make certain arrangements with the Indians at the Zuñi village, where he frequently comes on a visit and to trade, they would co-operate with you in his capture. Whatever honorable arrangements can be made for his capture would doubtless save his people from being robbed and perhaps exterminated. Send runners to tell all Navajoes who want to come in to get to Fort Wingate as soon as possible. I believe many wish to come and will come. Owing to the deep snows which have fallen, and the weakness of their animals, consequent upon the late severe winter, the time in which they may come in before hostile demonstrations will again be commenced against those who positively refuse to come is extended to May 1, 1865. Try hard to get Manuelito. Have him securely ironed and carefully guarded. It will be a mercy to others whom he controls to capture or kill him at once. I prefer he should be captured. If he attempt to escape when again in our power, as he did from Fort Canby, he will be shot down.

As fast as Indians come in to Fort Wingate send them to Los Pinos, where provisions are cheaper. Send some of those who come as runners to warn the rest to come in, not only to avoid danger, but to help put in a crop this year. Keep me promptly advised of all you do.

I am, sir, respectfully, your obedient servant,

JAMES H. CARLETON,
Brigadier General, Commanding.

Major JULIUS C. SHAW,
Commanding at Fort Wingate, N. M.

Official:

ERASTUS W. WOOD,
Captain 1st Vet Inf. C. V., A. A. A. General.

HEADQUARTERS DEPARTMENT OF NEW MEXICO,
Santa Fé, N. M., March 30, 1865.

SIR: I have the honor herewith to enclose for your information printed copies of General Orders No. 3, series of 1864, and General Orders No. 4, series for 1865, from these headquarters, which give an epitome of operations against Indians within the department of New Mexico for the last two years.

You will observe in the summing up, in General Orders No. 4, that we have three thousand Indian children now upon the reservation. It is in reference to these children that this communication is written.

Last year I had the honor to request of the Secretary of the Interior that that department furnish funds for the building of school-houses in which these children may be educated, but no answer was ever made to the letter. I now beg that you will take this important matter under consideration. It lies at the bottom of all our efforts to civilize these Indians. The education of these children is the fundamental idea on which must rest all our hopes of making the Navajoes a civilized and Christian people. It is unnecessary for me to put on paper the many arguments which I could use to convince you of the importance of having schools for these children. You can figure to your own mind 3,000 intelligent boys and girls with no one to teach them to read or write. Here is a field for those who are philanthropic which is ample enough to engage their attention and be the object of their charities for many years. Without money to build school-houses and to buy books, my hands are tied. The bishop of New Mexico has promised help in the way of teachers, but, in my opinion, this important subject should receive the fostering care of the government. These children properly belong to your department, and now, as well as when they have become men and women, are and will be objects which must engage your solicitude. I trust, therefore, that my appeal to you in their behalf will not be in vain.

There is another point to which I beg to call your immediate attention. Last year I requested of you that the surveyor general of New Mexico should cause to be surveyed the Indian reservation. This should be done at once. Not only should the exterior lines be run and be marked by durable mounds, but the irrigable lands should be laid off in ten acre lots for assignment to different families. Perhaps even lots of a smaller size may be necessary. No permanent organization of the tribes into bands, nor identity of lands, with particular fields, can be made fairly and justly until this survey is made. You are aware that there are no public surveys making either in this Territory or in Arizona which would interfere with this work. Not one rood of land has been surveyed in New Mexico since September, 1862, to my knowledge; the reason was, perhaps, on account of Indian difficulties. But there exists no reason why this important reservation may not at once be surveyed and be cut up into lots. I pray that this may be done at an early day.

Very respectfully, your obedient servant,

JAMES H. CARLETON,
Brigadier General, Commanding.

Hon. SECRETARY OF THE INTERIOR, *Washington, D. C.*

Official:

ERASTUS W. WOOD,
Captain 1st Vet. Inf. C. V., A. A. A. General.

HEADQUARTERS DEPARTMENT OF NEW MEXICO,
Santa Fé, N. M., April 24, 1865.

GENERAL: I returned yesterday from the Bosque Redondo. It will be impossible to organize into bands and systematically direct the labors of the 9,000 Indians we have at that point unless the lands are properly surveyed. I have written two letters to the Secretary of the Interior on the subject. The last one is herewith enclosed. The surveyor general of New Mexico is now in Arizona, and it is uncertain when he will return. Even if he were here there are no practical surveyors here who could do the work. So I beg respectfully to recommend that the War Department, unless the Department of the Interior will do it, will employ and send out at once some practical surveyors to divide this land so that particular lots can be given to particular bands and families. To do this by guess is going to lead to endless quarrels. Once I can divide up the land so as to let a given quantity be set apart for a certain number of Indians, and have it defined by a wall which they can make, once the lines are drawn, the great step towards organization will at once commence. Now, I have but a mass of Indians with no acknowledged head, and no subdivisions. The question about the schools for the 3,000 children I have written much about, but can do nothing without authority from Washington to erect the school-houses.

Very respectfully, your obedient servant,

JAMES H. CARLETON,
Brigadier General, Commanding.

ADJUTANT GENERAL U. S. A., *Washington, D. C.*

Official:

ERASTUS W. WOOD,
Captain 1st Vet. Inf. C. V., A. A. A. General.

HEADQUARTERS DEPARTMENT OF NEW MEXICO,
Santa Fé, N. M., April 26, 1865.

MAJOR: I desire that you have a careful examination made of the amount of subsistence stores on hand for issue to Indians at Fort Sumner. This subject gives me great anxiety. Should there be any accident to prevent the arrival of corn from the States, we shall have to diminish the ration, and must know to what extent this must be done before the stock runs low.

Should the priest, who has been elected chaplain, come with Paymaster Watts, who will be at your post to pay off in a few days, give him for religious and school purposes the three rooms in the Indian hospital which I looked at when there. The steward knows the three. They are contiguous and are of the following dimensions: two rooms in the west wing, each 18 by 20 feet; and one front room, 20 by 30 feet. He is a fine young man, and I bespeak for him your kind consideration, help, and encouragement. I believe it would be better for him to have the care of as many children who are orphans as possible. He will then know if they get enough to eat.

I enclose herewith a copy of a letter from myself to Mr. Labadie, and a copy of his reply. Your own judgment will dictate what is best to be done. If that woman has sold or is selling grain, the matter can be soon ascertained. Woodworth can be sent for, questioned, and, if guilty, tried. You have one or two links; you can now follow up the chain. See what Labadie told Mr. Edgar in this connexion.

Respectfully, &c.,

JAMES H. CARLETON,
Brigadier General, Commanding.

Major WILLIAM MCCLEAVE,
Commanding at Fort Sumner, N. M.

Official:

ERASTUS W. WOOD,
Captain 1st Vet. Inf. C. V., A. A. A. General.

HEADQUARTERS DEPARTMENT OF NEW MEXICO,
Santa Fé, N. M., May 4, 1865.

COLONEL: I received your note of the 12th of April. It is my purpose to establish a camp of three companies during the summer at or near Cedar Bluffs or near Cold spring, on the Cimarron route, to give assistance to trains *en route* to and from the States. I believe if you go upon duty at that point you will be able to have a talk with some of the chiefs of Cheyennes, Kiowas, and Comanches, and impress them with the folly of continuing this bad course. The troops would have been ordered out to that point before now, but the spring was so backward the grass would not sustain the animals. Pfeiffer, perhaps, may be spared to go. It would be well for you to get ready to go from Fort Union by the 20th instant.

Please talk with Colonel St. Vrain about purchasing the beaver skins for me.

Respectfully, your obedient servant,

JAMES H. CARLETON,
Brigadier General, Commanding.

Colonel CHRISTOPHER CARSON, *Taos, N. M.*

NOTE.—It would be well if Mr. Benthner would send out to your camp some necessaries to sell to your soldiers, and canned fruit, which would keep them healthy. Besides, he would sell much to passing companies and trains.

Official:

ERASTUS W. WOOD,
Captain 1st Vet. Inf. C. V., A. A. A. General.

HEADQUARTERS DEPARTMENT OF NEW MEXICO,
Santa Fé, N. M., May 8, 1865.

COLONEL: I received last evening your note of the 6th instant, and enclose herewith the order for your movement. In my opinion your consultations and influence with the Indians of the plains will stop the war. Be sure and move on the appointed day. I have full faith and confidence in your judgment and in your energy.

To have a fine camp, with ovens; a comfortable place for the sick; good store-rooms; some defences thrown up to prevent surprise; pickets established at good points for observation; hay cut and hauled to feed of nights or in case the Indians crowd you; large and well-armed guards, under an officer, with the public animals when herding; promptness in getting into the saddle and in moving to help the trains; a disposition to move quick, each man with his little bag of flour, a little salt and sugar and coffee, and not hampered by packs; arms and equipments always in order; tattoo and reveille roll-calls invariably under arms, so that the men shall have their arms on the last thing at night and in their hands the first thing in the morning; to have an inspection by the officers at tattoo and at reveille of the arms, and to see that the men are ready to fight, never to let this be omitted; to have, if possible, all detachments commanded by an officer, to report progress and events from time to time—these seem to be some of the essential points which, of course, you will keep in view. If the Indians behave themselves, that is all the peace we want, and we shall not molest them; if they do not, we will fight them on sight and to the bitter end. The war is over now, and, if necessary, 10,000 men can at once be put into the field against them. Tell them this. It is a short speech, but it covers all the ground. You know I don't believe much in smoking with Indians. When they fear us, they behave They must be made to fear us or we can have no lasting peace. They must not think to stop the commerce of the plains, nor must they imagine that we are going to keep up escorts with trains. We do this now until we learn whether they will behave or not. If they will not, we will end the matter by a war which will remove any further necessity for escorts. Keep up discipline from the start and all the time. After you have established your camp and got matters in training, please report in full.

Very respectfully and truly,

JAMES H. CARLETON,
Brigadier General, Commanding.

Colonel CHRISTOPHER CARSON,
1st Cavalry New Mexico Volunteers, Taos, N. M.

Official:

ERASTUS W. WOOD,
Captain 1st Vet. Inf. C. V., A. A. A. General.

HEADQUARTERS DEPARTMENT OF NEW MEXICO,
Santa Fé, N. M., May 8, 1865.

GENERAL: I am anxious that some five or six of the principal chiefs of the Navajo nation of Indians, and some three or four of the principal men of the Mescalero Apache Indians, from the nine thousand of these two peoples now upon the reservation at the Bosque Redondo, New Mexico, should go to Washington to see and talk with the President, the Secretary of War, and the Secretary of the Interior. They are very anxious, themselves, to go, and I am confident that for them to see our authorities and to see our country *en route* to the seat of government, will have a beneficial result. I respectfully beg leave from the War Department to send them on under the charge of Captain Henry B. Bristol, United States 5th infantry, who has for a long time been stationed in their midst, has directed their labors, settled their little differences, has taken uncommon interest in their welfare and advancement, and whom they look upon with great affection and confidence. This can be done with but a trifling expense, as they can go to Leavenworth in public wagons. I trust the honorable Secretary will be pleased to know that they wish to see him and to take him by the hand. He cannot fail to have his feelings interested in their behalf, once he has seen what intelligent and manly fellows they are. And once they know that the heads of the government take an earnest interest in their welfare, and are disposed to be generous to them and their people, they will return satisfied and happy.

I am, general, very respectfully, your obedient servant,

JAMES H. CARLETON,
Brigadier General, Commanding.

ADJUTANT GENERAL OF THE ARMY, *Washington, D. C.*

Official:

ERASTUS W. WOOD,
Captain 1st Vet. Inf. C. V., A. A. A. General.

DEPARTMENT OF NEW MEXICO, ASSISTANT ADJUTANT GENERAL'S OFFICE,
Santa Fé, N. M., June 3, 1865.

SIR: It has been officially reported to the governor that yesterday a party of Indians, supposed to be the band of the Jicarilla Apache chief José Largo, attacked the herders of Mr. Alexander Valle and Donaciano Vigil, at the Rio de la Vaca, about twelve miles from Mr. Valle's ranch on the Pecos, but between his place and Tecalote. Two herders were killed, their arms taken from them, also their horses and other animals.

The general commanding directs that you at once start out a picked party of two officers and thirty men, one-half cavalry and the remainder infantry, well armed, and with twenty days' rations on pack animals. The officer in command will be directed to use every effort to get on the trail of these Indians, but before attacking them to be sure that they are the guilty parties. Should it appear beyond a doubt that these Indians are the ones who killed the herders and drove off the stock, they will be pursued until caught and punished, even if the men are compelled to go upon half-rations, and if the stock and property is retaken it will be returned to the owners.

A man from the Pecos will meet the troops at Tecalote and guide them from there to the place where the men were killed, and Mr. Valle goes to his home in the morning and will get up a party of citizens to co-operate with the military and act as scouts, &c.

The officer who goes in command of this party should be particularly careful in guarding his own stock and in providing against a surprise, as this Indian, José Largo, is perfectly acquainted with the country over which the troops will travel, and has with him generally about thirty warriors.

I have the honor to be, sir, very respectfully, your obedient servant,

BEN. C. CUTLER,
Assistant Adjutant General.

COMMANDING OFFICER, *Fort Union, N. M.*

Official:

ERASTUS W. WOOD,
Captain 1st Vet. Inf. C. V., A. A. A. General.

HEADQUARTERS DEPARTMENT OF NEW MEXICO,
Tecalote, N. M., June 19, 1865.

MAJOR: I have learned by a private letter from Captain Henry B. Bristol to Captain Cutler, dated June 16, 1865, that Ganado Blanco, Barboucito Blanco, and some ten or twelve Navajoes, with their herds of horses and sheep, left the reservation for Chusca, ther place of abode before coming to the Bosque. Major Fritz and Captain Fox, with forty cavi alry, are in pursuit, and Captain Gorham, with the interpeter Jesus and a small party, are out. Captain Bristol could not ascertain positively the number gone until he could have another count. The Indians say that nearly all the Indians that had stock to carry them had left. No reason is assigned for this unfortunate step except that it was sickly there. I hope the Indians have not been incited to this step by parties opposed to the reservation system. These Indians must be recaptured or destroyed before they cross the Rio Grande. It is unfortunate that we have not sufficient troops to do this, and we must call upon the people for help; but we will concentrate all the troops possible. Send an order for all the mounted men at Las Cruces, Fort Selden and Fort McRae, to march at once to Fort Craig; for Colonel Rigg, with Samburn's company of cavalry and the company of infantry formerly commanded by Captain Haskell, to march at once to Los Pinos. Tell Colonel Rigg to say to General Montoya to raise one hundred well armed, well mounted men, and go with Colonel Rigg or follow him as quickly as possible. All these troops will be cautioned to take with them an abundant supply of ammunition. Unless the presence of these Navajoes near the Rio Grande should render it otherwise necessary, Colonel Rigg will move immediately with this force from Los Pinos to the pass of Abo. You will send an express to Brady to join with all his company, mounted and on foot, Colonel Rigg at that point, or at such other point as circumstances may render it necessary for Colonel Rigg to go. Send to Colonel Davis to send Captain Nichols with fifty of the picked and best mounted men of his company, at once, to Fort Stanton by the shortest route, taking the soldiers now at the Tularosa saw-mill in to Fort Stanton, as he passes that point.

Have Captain Shinn move at once with all the effective men of his command, and through the Camwell pass to some point east of the mountains, where he can, by means of spies, observe the plains towards the Bosque. Order Colonel Shaw to send fifty mounted men to join Captain Shinn at once by way of Los Pinos.

Get Don Ambrosio Ameijo to raise one hundred picked, well mounted men, Americans and Mexicans, with Blas Lucero for guide, and to go with, or as soon as practicable join, Captain Shinn. Get General Clever to raise one hundred men, Mexicans and Americans, and proceed to Galisteo, or some point fifteen or twenty miles from there in the direction of Anton Chico, where, through his spies, he can get an idea as to the whereabouts of the Indians, with a view of attacking them or of joining Captain Shinn, or the armed party nearest to him, as circumstances may require. I wish Colonel Brown to raise another hundred men, including the men he can get at Fort Marcy, and proceed with them to Don Serafin Ramirez's place beyond the Placer mines, and there throw out spies toward the east to observe the motions of the Indians, and to attack any and all parties of Navajoes of which he can obtain information and can reach. Dr. Brown will go with Colonel Brown.

See the governor and get him to confirm all this, and get him to write to all the principal citizens to aid in this matter at once. I hope it will be the last, as it has been the first, time that Navajoes will attempt to escape from the reservation. Do all this promptly; if necessary, hire transportation; furnish rations from the government supplies; then place yourself with the command of Captain Shinn, and there, in my name, give such orders for the combination and supply of these forces, the sending out of spies, the attacking of the Navajoes, the protection of the people, and the getting such Navajoes as may be captured back to the Bosque Redondo as in your judgment may be for the best until you hear further from me.

Say to the governor that the hundred men that may be called out under General Montoya Ambrosio Amijo, General Clever, and Colonel Brown, I will endeavor to get paid by the government. Such other parties of citizens as may go out to attack these Indians shall be rewarded with all the stock they can recover from them. It is probable that the Indians, many of them, are embarrassed with their women and children and cannot travel as fast as war parties. Tell the governor to send word to owners of stock to get their stock to places of security until this matter is ended. It is likely that many of the Indians of Santa Domingo, Ysleta, San Dia, and San Felipe may desire to go, if so, authorize and urge them to do so.

Let everything be done quickly, but let there be nothing like a stampede. I shall go to Fort Union to-morrow, and, having seen the congressional committee, shall go to the Bosque as soon as possible; when, having learned more definitely about the matter, will give you further information.

Have some spies, to be sure that the Indians do not pass down the river, with a view of crossing the Rio Grande at some point on the Jornada. Captain Fountain, at Paraje, would be one good man to employ on this business.

The people of Chilili, Manzana, Toren, and Punta del Agua are well acquainted with the country to the east of those places, and good spies can be got from among them.

I have the honor to be, major, very respectfully, your obedient servant,

JAMES H. CARLETON,
Brigadier General, Commanding.

Major WILLIAM H. LEWIS, U. S. A.,
Santa Fé, N. M.

NOTE.—You will order Doctor Foye to accompany Rigg. I beg you to bear in mind that in this matter time is precious. Colonel Rigg will be ordered to start at once, without waiting for the troops ordered from below to arrive at Fort Craig. Give directions that no women nor children be killed.

J. H. C.

Official:

ERASTUS W. WOOD,
Capatin 1st Vet. Inf. C. V., A. A. A. General.

HEADQUARTERS DEPARTMENT OF NEW MEXICO,
Fort Sumner, N. M., June 25, 1865.

MAJOR: Your letter of the 22d instant was received this evening, and I am directed by the general commanding to say that your action, as stated therein, is approved by him.

The Navajoes who ran away from the reservation have returned, with the exception of a small party not exceeding twenty-eight or thirty in number, as reported. Many are said to have died from starvation and want of water, and those who could get back were glad to do so, and it appears that all are now more contented than ever.

The general desires you to send at once, by express, and order the troops detailed from Forts Wingate, Craig, Selden, and Las Cruces back to their respective posts. Captain Shinn, with the troops from Albuquerque and Fort Stanton, will remain out until further orders. If it happen that citizen parties are in the field they should be informed that they can return to their homes.

It is believed by many officers here that these Navajoes have been tampered with by men who, for political purposes, have opposed the reservation, and would be willing to see the interests of the country suffer, provided they could advance their own.

I have the honor to be, major, very respectfully, your obedient servant,

BEN. C. CUTLER,
Assistant Adjutant General.

Major WILLIAM H. LEWIS, U. S. A.,
Santa Fé, N. M.

Official:

ERASTUS W. WOOD,
Captain 1st Vet. Inf. C. V., A. A. A. General.

HEADQUARTERS DEPARTMENT OF NEW MEXICO,
Santa Fé, N. M., July 13, 1865.

MAJOR: In view of the evident shortness of the crop of breadstuffs throughout the Territory this year, I find that it will be much cheaper and much safer to diminish the amount of breadstuff to be issued to captive Indians to three-fourths of a pound per head per diem, and to increase the meat ration for said Indians to one pound per head per diem, from the date when you receive this letter until further orders.

The ration of solid food in gross will, by this measure, be the same, only there will be one-fourth of a pound more meat, and one-fourth of a pound less breadstuff to the ration.

Respectfully, &c,

JAMES H. CARLETON,
Brigadier General, Commanding.

Major WILLIAM MC CLEAVE,
Commanding at Fort Sumner, N. M.

Official:

ERASTUS W. WOOD,
Captain 1st Vet. Inf. C. V., A. A. A. General.

HEADQUARTERS DEPARTMENT OF NEW MEXICO,
Santa Fé, N. M., July 18, 1865.

MAJOR: I have been informed by Mr. Parker that the corn worm has made its appearance at the Bosque, and this causes me great anxiety. As I understand it, the butterfly or moth, which lays the egg that produces this worm, lays that egg in the moist silk of the growing ear. Each thread of that silk goes down to the embryo kernel of corn, and becoming impregnated by the pollen or seed, which, like dust, floats from the spindle, the kernel comes to maturity. If I am correctly informed, once you destroy a thread of that silk, before impregnation takes place, no kernel of corn will grow at the point where that thread had root upon the ear. So, if to destroy the worm, which is at first found at the tip of the ear, you cut off or break the thread of silk, you prevent the growth of a corresponding number of kernels of corn. But if each ear, at its upper extremity, could be carefully opened and the worm removed without breaking the threads of silk, the corn would be saved, in my opinion. So much is at stake in this matter that I wish you would make the attempt and let me know the result. The moth that lays the egg looks like a small butterfly; and if some plan could be had to destroy that, the evil would be attacked at the proper place. In Kansas, it is said, that plates, with molasses in them, were placed on posts in corn-fields, and at these the moths would come, when they could be destroyed. It would be well to try this experiment in three or four places. Of course in your extended farm it would be impossible to carry it out effectually.

Every ounce of food should be carefully husbanded. Famine literally stares the people of the Territory in the face this year. I am devising every plan possible to get extra amounts of hay and mesquite beans, &c., for our animals, so as to leave to the people all they can raise. You should tell the Indians what a dreadful year it is, and how they must save everything to eat which lies in their power, or starvation will come upon them. Have large parties at work with those hoes. Corn, well hoed, will produce twice as much as corn indifferently attended to.

Let me now give you notice of the importance of saving all the melon and pumpkin seeds possible. Make it a business of some to do this. A seed-room should be made now. Have the shelves, on which the bags of seed are to be placed, suspended by wires from the ceilings, that the mice may not be able to get upon the shelves to depredate upon the seeds.

Very respectfully, your obedient servant,

JAMES H. CARLETON,
Brigadier General, Commanding.

Major WILLIAM McCLEAVE,
Commanding at Fort Sumner, N. M.

Official:

ERASTUS W. WOOD,
Captain 1st Vet. Inf. C. V., A. A. A. General.

HEADQUARTERS DEPARTMENT OF NEW MEXICO,
Santa Fé, N. M., July 20, 1865.

GENERAL: About the 15th ultimo two of the Navajo chiefs, named Ganado Blanco and Barboucito, with quite a large number of their followers, left the reservation at the Bosque Redondo, and started in the direction of the old Navajo country. There came to Santa Fé many rumors swelling the number who had escaped as high as three thousand. There was not cavalry enough at Fort Sumner to pursue and bring back all the reported fugitives; and to make it certain that all the main points along the Rio Grande should be watched and guarded, I authorized that some citizens should be called out to help the few troops along the river to check and drive back these Indians. You doubtless know that much of the available force in this department was then, and is now, off on the plains endeavoring to protect trains *en route* to this country from the hostile Indians in that quarter. This rendered a call for help on the citizens imperative. (See the enclosed circular.)

It so happened that many of the Indians who attempted to escape returned of their own accord to the Bosque, as they got out of provisions and suffered greatly for the want of water. The others were both pursued and headed off, so it is doubtful if a single one was able to cross the river. Ganado Blanco and some of his followers were killed, and much of their stock captured. (See the accompanying reports of Major Fritz, Captain Brady, Captain French, and of General Montoyo.) It is doubtful if another attempt will soon be made by parties of Navajoes to escape.

Enclosed, also, is a roll of some of the citizens who abandoned their work and went into the field. I have directed that they be named as spies and guides, that, if the War Department so orders, they can be paid by the quartermaster department, as the pay department can only pay legally and regularly organized companies. You will see how few days they were employed. No price was fixed for their services. That is left with the War Department. I think these men should be paid. If paid, in case of a sudden emergency every citizen hereafter will take the field with alacrity.

Respectfully, your obedient servant,

JAMES H. CARLETON,
Brigadier General, Commanding.

ADJUTANT GENERAL, U. S. A., *Washington, D. C.*

Official:

ERASTUS W. WOOD,
Captain 1st Vet. Inf. C. V., A. A. A. General.

HEADQUARTERS DEPARTMENT OF NEW MEXICO,
Santa Fé, N. M., July 24, 1865.

MAJOR: The plan adopted by you to let the quartermaster at your post have unthreshed grain to feed his animals and to cavalry horses, and take therefor to issue as breadstuffs to Indians grain which he has in sacks that is already cleaned up, seems to be wise and labor-saving. The accounts of these exchanges should be rigidly kept, so as to challenge scrutiny on the part of those who fancy wrong where all is right. The straw, which goes with the grain thus exchanged, should be weighed, and, if it answer the place of hay, should be paid for at a fair valuation, so that the Indian farm should give all the fair returns toward the support of the Indians which may be possible.

I have sent for a bell, to be used as a signal for hours of labor and repose for the Indians. This will weigh one thousand pounds, and cost in St. Louis two hundred and fifty dollars

This must be paid for out of a fund accruing from sales of straw and fodder from the Indian farm. Then there are soldiers to pay for the extra clothing worn out in their unusual labors upon that farm, and garden-seeds, and grape-shoots, &c., to say nothing of getting sheep and wool for the Indians. This must come out of the proceeds of the sales of the straw and fodder; so that I hope you will have a book opened and an account kept of all straw or fodder sold, date of sale, price agreed upon, amount received, &c.

I am, major, very respectfully, your obedient servant,

JAMES H. CARLETON,
Brigadier General, Commanding.

Major WILLIAM McCLEAVE,
Commanding at Fort Sumner, N. M.

Official:

ERASTUS W. WOOD,
Captain 1st Vet. Inf. C. V., A. A. A. General.

HEADQUARTERS DEPARTMENT OF NEW MEXICO,
Santa Fé, N. M., July 25, 1865.

To whom it may concern:

Two Navajo women—Not-li-ar-pa and Es-nart-so, or, as they are called in Spanish, Maria and Guadalupe—came to department headquarters to-day, and in presence of his excellency Governor Henry Connelly and of the superintendent of Indian affairs, Don Felipe Delgado, said that they desired to live in the family of Don Antonio José Mora, of Cieneguilla, near Santa Fé. This I have agreed that they may do so, as it is their wish voluntarily made. But it is understood by all the parties that the said women, or either of them, may depart from said family and go where they please, without hindrance from the said Mora, or any other person, provided they do not go to the old Navajo country, or commit crimes or misdemeanors against any person or persons in this Territory, or within the boundaries of the United States. Each one of the women named herein is furnished with a copy of this paper, and it is recorded at department headquarters.

JAMES H. CARLETON,
Brigadier General, Commanding.

Signed in presence of—
HENRY CONNELLY.
FELIPE DELGADO.

Official:

ERASTUS W. WOOD,
Captain 1st Vet. Inf. C. V., A. A. A. General.

HEADQUARTERS DEPARTMENT OF NEW MEXICO,
Santa Fé, N. M., July 29, 1865.

MAJOR: Owing to the threatened scarcity of breadstuffs, and the difficulty there will doubtless be to procure enough for the subsistence of the Indians upon the reservation, in case their own crop fail, from and after the date of the receipt by yourself of this letter, you will cause to be issued to each Indian upon the reservation, per day, until further orders, half a pound of breadstuffs and one and a quarter pound of meat—in all, one pound and three-quarters of solid food. This can the more economically be done now, when cattle are fat; and, besides, the Indians can eke out their meals at this season of the year with melons, pumpkins, &c.

Respectfully, your obedient servant,

JAMES H. CARLETON,
Brigadier General, Commanding.

Major WILLIAM McCLEAVE,
Commanding at Fort Sumner, N. M.

Official:

ERASTUS W. WOOD,
Captain 1st Vet. Inf. C. V., A. A. A. General.

HEADQUARTERS DEPARTMENT OF NEW MEXICO,
Santa Fé, N. M., July 30, 1865.

GENERAL: I had the honor to receive your letter of the 30th ultimo, which gives your views in reference to the protection of the Santa Fé road from Indians, and gives information of expeditions which you are about starting against Indians south of the Arkansas river.

My opinion is, while the trains are exposed upon the plains in the summer season, our force should be so distributed as to give them protection. When they cease to run in the fall and winter, the Indians being then in known haunts with their families, can be more readily attacked, and without the danger, as now, of their dodging the troops, and, while the latter are off the road, of their pouncing upon the trains left unguarded.

From lack of troops it will be entirely out of my power to co-operate in your contemplated movements. The Indians within this Territory occupy the attention of every man that can be spared to take the field.

I am, general, very respectfully, your obedient servant,

JAMES H. CARLETON,
Brigadier General, Commanding.

Brigadier General JAMES H. FORD,
Commanding District of Upper Arkansas, Fort Larned, Arkansas.

Official:

ERASTUS W. WOOD,
Captain 1st Vet. Inf. C. V., A. A. A. General.

HEADQUARTERS DEPARTMENT OF NEW MEXICO,
Santa Fé, N. M., August 2, 1865.

SIR: It is said that a party of Indians crossed the Rio Grande, near Stapleton's ranch, doubtless, if true, going west; and some troops were ordered, with ten days' rations, on the 21st ultimo from Fort Craig, to take the trail and follow it up.

These Indians may be Navajoes, and, if so, they will doubtless, if not before killed or captured, go through the Rita Quemada toward the old Navajo country.

It is expected that they will not only not get any of your stock, but that you will have a good account given of them. Kill or capture all Navajo men you can find in the old Navajo country without proper passports.

Respectfully,

JAMES H. CARLETON,
Brigadier Generol, Commanding.

COMMANDING OFFICER, *Fort Wingate, N. M.*

Official:

ERASTUS W. WOOD,
Captain 1st Vet. Inf. C. V., A. A. A. General.

HEADQUARTERS DEPARTMENT OF NEW MEXICO,
Santa Fé, N. M., August 6, 1865.

COLONEL: I had the honor to receive your letter of August 2, 1865, enclosing a letter to yourself from the Hon. J. R. Doolittle, United States Senate, chairman of the congressional committee to inquire into Indian affairs, and also enclosing two telegraphic despatches from the Secretary of War to Mr. Doolittle, with reference to holding councils with the Indians. Mr. Doolittle's letter, and Mr. Stanton's despatches, I herewith return for your guidance in your special mission upon the plains, made at the request of Mr. Doolittle. Your knowledge of what Mr. Doolittle desires and hopes you will be able to effect with the Indians of the plains, which knowledge you have derived in conversation with that gentleman, precludes the necessity of special instructions from me. Indeed, in this matter, where, as I understand it, the great object to be had in view by yourself is to make preliminary arrangements, if possible, with the Comanches, Kiowas, and Cheyennes and Arapahoes, so that hostilities on their part will cease, and so that their chiefs and principal men will meet commissioners in council to make a treaty of peace. Your great knowledge of the Indians—your knowledge of what is desired on the part of the government—your knowledge of the danger to be apprehended that the Indians may believe our overtures proceed rather from our fears of them than from a sincere desire not to make war upon them on our part, unless they compel us to do so—your knowledge of how to talk with them, so that they may not suffer from any such delusion—these considerations you understand so much better than myself, that it is unnecessary for me to give you, or attempt to give you, any instructions in the case.

I wish you to keep a journal of each day's march, and of each day's events, and of what Indians you meet. Please report your talks with them, and all they say in reply. This information is required for the War Department. If you go by Fort Bascom, you have my authority to take Mr. DeLisle, the guide at that post, with you. He knows well the country between the Canadian and the Arkansas rivers.

Please look well to the country you pass over, with an eye to the site of a large post to be built in the place where the Kiowas and Comanches spend their winters—a ten-company post, with six of the companies cavalry.

I enclose herewith the order for your escort, and for Adjutant Tanfield to join you. That you may have good luck and return in health and safety, is the earnest wish of your sincere friend,

JAMES H. CARLETON,
Brigadier General, Commanding.

Colonel CHRISTOPHER CARSON, *Fort Union, N. M.*

Official: ERASTUS W. WOOD,
Captain 1st Vet. Inf. C. V., A. A. A. General.

HEADQUARTERS DEPARTMENT OF NEW MEXICO,
Santa Fé, N. M., August 6, 1865.

SIR: The bearer of this letter is Colonel Theodore H. Dodd, a distinguished soldier during the late rebellion, but who, since he retired from service, has been, as you are aware, appointed Indian agent for the Navajoes. Colonel Dodd came out to New Mexico with the Hon. James R. Doolittle, chairman of Indian affairs in the Senate, and went to the Bosque Redondo to enter upon his duties. He expected to find his commission here, but he has not yet received it. From the 25th day of last June, the day when Colonel Dodd arrived at the Bosque Redondo, he is, as yourself I hope will decide, clearly entitled to pay.

We have learned, unofficially, that in the last session of Congress one hundred thousand dollars were appropriated for the Navajo Indians. Not one line of official information has been received on the subject, so far as I can learn, and here it is in August, with the fall and winter so near at hand, when the women and children will be suffering for the want of clothing. In order to insure that there shall be no delay either in making the purchases of necessary articles for the Indians, and in getting them out here before the winter sets in, I have advised Colonel Dodd to go directly through to Washington and to see personally after these important matters, in which the health and comfort of nine thousand Indians, entirely dependent upon the government for everything, are concerned. I hope you will approve of his coming. Indeed, there was nothing else left for him to do, unless to sit down and see the people whose wants he is in duty bound to look after perish, when the snows come, for want of clothing.

You will find Colonel Dodd, whom I have known for some years, to be a fine gentleman, and one who is conscientious to the last degree in the discharge of his official duties. He has fine business capacity, and I have to congratulate you in having secured his valuable services.

I have the honor to be, very respectfully, your obedient servant,

JAMES H. CARLETON,
Brigadier General, Commanding.

Hon. COMMISSIONER OF INDIAN AFFAIRS, *Washington, D. C*

Official: ERASTUS W. WOOD,
Captain 1st Vet. Inf. C. V., A. A. A. General.

HEADQUARTERS DEPARTMENT OF NEW MEXICO,
Santa Fé, N. M., August 9, 1865.

MAJOR: I regret exceedingly to learn that the Indians cannot be prevented either from depredating upon the crops, or of leaving the reservation without passports. Pray urge upon every officer and soldier and Indian the great importance of letting the crops ripen. This is a year of great scarcity all over the country, and every ounce of food which can possibly be saved for winter must be saved. You should impress this matter at once upon the minds of the Indians.

The question of saving and taking care of seeds, as heretofore ordered, now has force. Make it a business to save all the seeds possible. Have an Indian prisoner detailed to pick up, sort, and wash all loose seeds found about the post. Please have a report made at the end of each month until November 30 next of the amount and kind of seed saved. This year I do not wish to be disappointed in this all-important matter. Pray give it your personal attention. If every officer and soldier, and every Indian, becomes impressed with the importance of the matter, great results will follow. I know you and Bristol will enter into the spirit of the matter.

Again, tell the Indians I will cause to be killed every Indian I find off the reservation without a passport. A great many have been killed in the Navajo country. The troops are now fast coming in from the plains, and we will be sure to catch them. Tell them this. Make suitable forms for your returns of captive Indians and for Indian passports, and send the forms to me, so that I can have some blanks printed for you. The count for August 31 will be the one which will appear in the printed reports in Washington. Please have that made with great care.

Respectfully, &c.,

JAMES H. CARLETON,
Brigadier General, Commanding.

Major WILLIAM McCLEAVE,
Commanding at Fort Sumner, N. M.

Official:

ERASTUS W. WOOD,
Captain 1st Vet. Inf. C. V., A. A. A. General.

HEADQUARTERS DEPARTMENT OF NEW MEXICO,
Santa Fé, N. M., August 15, 1865.

On the 15th of August, 1865, came to Santa Fé Miguel, the one-eyed chief of the Coyotero Apaches. He had with him Es-ka-la-natz-ah, (in Spanish Guapo, in English Brave,) Es-kel-tatz-ze-joms, (The Rolling,) Es-ka-cho-yer, (The Lost,) El Perdido. They wished to go to the Bosque to see their friends, seven women and six men, now retained there as prisoners. These Indians with Miguel were told of the consequences of their people remaining in the Sierra Blanca. That they had better all come and go to the Bosque. It was the only means of saving them, as the miners would come, and the troops would come, and there would be wars until all of them would be destroyed. That by moving to the Bosque they would be protected and be happy. They said they would go back and tell their people what was said. I told them they might go to the Bosque and remain there until I wrote to the commanding officer about them and their friends, now prisoners there. It is proposed to let all the Coyoteros held as prisoners return to their country, as they have now seen how we treat those who have surrendered. This will have an effect upon the tribe when pressed in war, as it surely will be.

JAMES H. CARLETON,
Brigadier General, Commanding.

Interpreted through Conception Aquierra, Coyotero interpreter.

Official:

ERASTUS W. WOOD,
Captain 1st Vet. Inf. C. V., A. A. A. General.

HEADQUARTERS DEPARTMENT OF NEW MEXICO,
Santa Fé, N. M., August 16, 1865.

SIR: This letter will be brought to you by Miguel, the one-eyed Coyotero chief, who returned from the Bosque to his own country, starting last spring. He wants all the Coyotero men and women at the Bosque to go back to their own country with him. He says there are six men and seven women, exclusive of himself and the three Indians now with him. Please report if they are more or less of that number. It is my purpose to let the Indians of this tribe return, for they will all be disciples for the Bosque when the tribe is pushed by war and hunger, as it is sure to be, for they will murder and steal from the people, and will have to be made war upon systematically until they are subdued and moved to the reservation or are destroyed. This is all simply a question of time. When that time comes then these Indians will all be advocates for the reservation. Let me know your views on the subject.

I am, sir, very respectfully, your obedient servant,

JAMES H. CARLETON,
Brigadier General, Commanding.

COMMANDING OFFICER, *Fort Sumner, N. M.*

Official:

ERASTUS W. WOOD,
Captain 1st Vet. Inf. C. V., A. A. A. General.

HEADQUARTERS DEPARTMENT OF NEW MEXICO,
Santa Fé, N. M., August 30, 1865.

MAJOR: I am very anxious in relation to the matter of the saving of the seeds of pumpkins, melons, cantelupe, chili, and of garden vegetables generally, at the Bosque. We should have at least twice as much of each kind as will be required for planting another year, to provide against the necessity of replanting and for damage to some of the seeds in drying. They should be dried in the shade. Give an order in reference to this important matter and see that it is strictly enforced. Have the seed-room made.

Respectfully,

JAMES H. CARLETON,
Brigadier General, Commanding.

Major WILLIAM MCCLEAVE,
Commanding at Fort Sumner, N. M.

Official:

ERASTUS W. WOOD,
Captain 1st Vet. Inf. C. V., A. A. A. General.

HEADQUARTERS DEPARTMENT OF NEW MEXICO,
Santa Fé, N. M., September 11, 1865.

To whom it may concern:

The bearer of this is a Coyotero Apache chief named Miguel in Spanish, or Es-chá-pa in Apache. If he desires to come to Santa Fé to talk with the chief military officer in New Mexico, he will be permitted to come without molestation.

JAMES H. CARLETON,
Brigadier General, Commanding.

Official:

ERASTUS W. WOOD,
Captain 1st Vet. Inf. C. V., A. A. A. General.

HEADQUARTERS DEPARTMENT OE NEW MEXICO,
Santa Fé, N. M., September 11, 1865.

To whom it may concern:

The bearer of this is a Coyotero Apache chief named Esh-kel-a-ná-sta. If he desires to come to Santa Fé to talk with the chief military officer in New Mexico, he will be permitted to come without molestation.

JAMES H. CARLETON,
Brigadier General, Commanding.

Official:

ERASTUS W. WOOD,
Captain 1st Vet. Inf. C. V., A. A. A. General.

HEADQUARTERS DEPARTMENT OF NEW MEXICO,
Santa Fé, N. M., September 11, 1865.

SIR: The bearer of this is Miguel, the chief of the Coyotero Apaches. He returns to his country with some men, women and children of his tribe, nineteen in all, who are named on the enclosed list. These Indians know now all about the Bosque. They promise to be friends and not to molest the whites. They live in the White mountains south of Zuñi. Give them rations and send them on to Zuñi and let them go free. Send word to the governor of Zuñi to give Miguel the three horses and equipments taken from him when he was captured. The interpreter can go on with them to their country if he pleases, or return from Zuñi. Should it become necessary hereafter to make war upon these Coyotero Apaches, knowing the Bosque reservation as all these now do, the tribe will be easily induced to remove. This was the object had in view in sending these prisoners to that point and then returning them in this manner to their people.

Respectfully, your obedient servant,

JAMES H. CARLETON,
Brigadier General, Commanding.

COMMANDING OFFICER, *Fort Wingate, N. M.*

NOTE.—Copy the enclosed and send the original back.

Official:

ERASTUS W. WOOD,
Captain 1st Vet. Inf. C. V., A. A. A. General.

[Extract.]

HEADQUARTERS DISTRICT OF NEW MEXICO,
Santa Fé, N. M., September 15, 1865.

COLONEL: * * * * * * * * * * *
The Navajo and Apache reservation is at Fort Sumner, and here I have seven thousand six hundred and twenty-two prisoners of those tribes which are fed by the subsistence department, and will be thus supplied with food until they can raise enough to sustain themselves. The reserve has been made by Congress, and is forty miles square with Fort Sumner in the centre. Captain John B. Shinn, United States 3d artillery, has been ordered by General Grant to survey it, and he is now *en route* from Albuquerque to fulfil his instructions to this end. The care and management of this number of wild Indians and the system to be inaugurated and carried out which shall gradually change them from lawless savages to a people who are to obey necessary rules for their good behavior and general tranquillity, and show them as well the necessity of earning their bread by the labor of their hands, will doubtless engage the attention and have the solicitude of the commander of the department. I think it would be well for him to come here and give this matter a personal inspection. No written account of what has been done or what should be done would impress upon his mind a proper idea of the subject.

A congressional committee, consisting of Senator J. R. Doolittle, chairman, Vice-President Foster, and Representative Ross, visited the reservation in June of this year, but their stay was so short and their inspection so cursory, that much remains to be considered and acted upon which cannot be considered in their report If the commanding general would come here and look into the matter himself he would then be able to give detailed instructions with reference to this very important and interesting experiment of colonizing the wild Indians of New Mexico. If I am to remain in command here it would help me very much to have the benefit of his counsel and instruction in a matter involving such immense interests and now of considerable expense to the government, and besides, would lighten not a little the burden of responsibility of such a charge. * * * * * *

It is my intention this fall and next winter to make war upon the Mimbres Apaches, a small band of very bad and aggressive Indians. For this purpose a camp will be established on the Mimbres river where hay will be put up. The subsistence stores to furnish, say, four companies to be sent on this duty, are nearly all *en route* to Fort Cummings, where they will be kept in store and be drawn upon from time to time as they may be needed by the troops in camp on the Mimbres or those scouting against the Indians from the latter point. This is the only hostile operation at present determined upon. Sudden outbreaks of Indian prisoners, or inroads or aggressions of tribes around and in the Territory, may necessitate other movements. But these are only contingencies; they may not occur.

I enclose herewith a return of the troops in, and pertaining to, this district. I also enclose an order showing distances between important points in and connected with New Mexico.

I beg to be informed fully of the wishes of the commanding general with reference to what he desires to have done, and to say that I will endeavor to carry out all his views to the best of my ability.

I am, colonel, very respectfully, your obedient servant,

JAMES H. CARLETON,
Brigadier General, Commanding.

Colonel RICHARD C. DRUM,
Assistant Adjutant General, San Francisco, California.

Official:

ERASTUS W. WOOD,
Captain 1st Vet. Inf. C. V., A. A. A. General.

HEADQUARTERS DISTRICT OF NEW MEXICO,
Santa Fé, N. M., September 20, 1865.

COLONEL: The enclosed extract of Special Orders No. 2, current series from these headquarters, which have reference to the past field and distant service of some of the companies, and the prospective field and distant service of other companies which have been some time in garrison, I wish you would assist in carrying into operation so that no loss of time may occur. The companies ordered now to leave Fort Union should leave at once, because the movement of the troops against the Mimbres Indians depends on the early arrival to the places designated of those here named.

Please do me the favor to see, by personal inspection, that they are carefully fitted out. If they have any unserviceable property it will not be taken along. See that their arms are in good fighting order. In case any of them are out of repair have Captain Shoemaker exchange good ones for them. I will make the matter all right when the work has been done, whenever he wants my signature. This will save time. Give orders that each company takes hard bread enough to last for its whole march. This will ease your storehouses. There will be at least four companies operating against the Mimbres Indians while one guards camp—five in all. They will want a reasonable amount of transportation in the shape of wagons, for camp purposes, and pack-mules, saddles, wanties, packing-rope, lariats, paulins to cover stores for, say, a month's supply, as the main stores will be in Fort Cummings; two good hospital tents, &c., &c., and one or two of those ambulances you have at Union, in case there are none like them below. The ambulances should go with Colonel Abreü. It is likely you have all the articles needed at Fort Craig, or below there, or at Fort Cummings. I wish to use the articles nearest the scene of operations to save transportation. There must be nearly or quite enough at Las Cruces or Selden. There will be some axes, spades, picks, blacksmith tools, &c., wanted. All this will be left to your judgment. The supplies can be invoiced and sent at once to acting assistant quartermaster, Camp Mimbres.

Respectfully, your obedient servant,

JAMES H. CARLETON,
Brigadier General, Commanding.

Colonel HERBERT M. ENOS, U. S. A.,
Chief Quartermaster, Fort Union, N. M.

Official:

ERASTUS W. WOOD,
Captain 1st Vet. Inf. C. V., A. A. A. General.

SPECIAL ORDERS ISSUED DURING THE YEARS 1862, 1863, 1864, AND 1865, RELATING TO INDIANS IN THE DEPARTMENT OF NEW MEXICO.

[Special Orders No. 176.—Extract.]

DEPARTMENT OF NEW MEXICO, ASSISTANT ADJUTANT GENERAL'S OFFICE,
Santa Fé, N. M., September 27, 1862.

* * * * * * * * * * *

III. Fort Stanton, on the Bonito river, in the country of the Mescalero Apaches, will without delay be reoccupied by five companies of Colonel Christopher Carson's regiment of New Mexico volunteers. * * * * * * * Colonel Carson will receive written instructions as to the particular duties expected of his command while serving in the Mescalero country. The world-wide reputation of Colonel Carson as a partisan gives a good guaranty that anything that may be required of him, which brings into practical operation the peculiar skill and high courage for which he is justly celebrated, will be well done.

* * * * * * * * * * *

By command of Brigadier General Carleton:

BEN. C. CUTLER,
First Lieutenant C. V., A. A. A. General.

Official:

BEN. C. CUTLER,
Assistant Adjutant General.

[Special Orders No. 180.—Extract.]

DEPARTMENT OF NEW MEXICO, ASSISTANT ADJUTANT GENERAL'S OFFICE,
Santa Fé, N. M., October 7, 1862.

* * * * * * * * * * *

V. A board of officers, to consist of Captain Henry R. Selden, United States 5th infantry, Assistant Surgeon Joseph C. Bailey, medical department United States army, and First Lieutenant Allen L. Anderson, 5th United States infantry, acting as lieutenant of engineers, will proceed to the Navajo country, and, near the headwaters of the Gallo, select the exact site on which Fort Wingate should be established.

* * * * * * * * * * *

By command of Brigadier General Carleton:

BEN. C. CUTLER,
First Lieutenant C. V., A. A. A. General.

Official:

BEN. C. CUTLER,
Assistant Adjutant General.

[Special Orders No. 186.—Extract.]

DEPARTMENT OF NEW MEXICO, ASSISTANT ADJUTANT GENERAL'S OFFICE,
Santa Fé, N. M., October 19, 1862.

* * * * * * * * * * *

II. Lieutenant Colonel Edwin A. Rigg will proceed to Franklin, Texas, and carefully fit out for field service against the Mescalero Apaches company E, 1st infantry and company D, 1st cavalry California volunteers, and twenty spies and guides. Colonel West will give Lieutenant Colonel Rigg detailed instructions as to what this force is to do, and all other information necessary to have it completely prepared for the service it has to perform.

* * * * * * * * * * *

By command of Brigadier General Carleton:

BEN. C. CUTLER,
Captain and A. A. General.

Official:

BEN. C. CUTLER,
Assistant Adjutant General.

[Special Orders No. 193.—Extract.]

DEPARTMENT OF NEW MEXICO, ASSISTANT ADJUTANT GENERAL'S OFFICE,
Fort Union, N. M., November 4, 1862.

I. A board of officers, to consist of Lieutenant Colonel Dodd, 2d Colorado volunteers, Surgeon James M. McNulty, 1st infantry California volunteers, and First Lieutenant Cyrus H. De Forrest, 2d Colorado volunteers, will convene at Bosque Redondo, on the Pecos river, New Mexico, on the 15th of November, 1862, or as soon thereafter as practicable, and proceed to select the exact site for Fort Sumner, the new post recently ordered to be established. Lieutenant De Forrest will prepare a map of the site and its surroundings. The map will embrace the valley of the Bosque Redondo from the bluffs at its upper termination to a point eighteen miles below the bluffs.

* * * * * * * * * *

JAMES H. CARLETON,
Brigadier General, Commanding.

Official:

BEN. C. CUTLER,
Assistant Adjutant General.

[Special Orders No. 6.—Extract.]

DEPARTMENT OF NEW MEXICO, ASSISTANT ADJUTANT GENERAL'S OFFICE,
Fort Craig, N. M., January 21, 1863.

Lieutenant Colonel Edwin A. Rigg 1st infantry California volunteers, will organize an expedition of one hundred and twenty-five infantry and cavalry California volunteers, to punish the Gila and Mimbres Apaches, parties of whom are almost daily committing depredations upon the people along the Rio Grande, in the vicinity of Fort Craig. This expedition will move with wagons on the morning of the 22d instant, in a westerly direction from that post to a post known as El Tularoso, where a depot will be formed, to be guarded by an officer and twenty-five rank and file. From this depot the remaining one hundred men, with pack-mules for transportation, will operate against the Apaches named above, who inhabit the mountain region about the headwaters of the Mimbres and Gila rivers. The troops are to remain in the field for thirty days.

* * * * * * * * * * *

JAMES H. CARLETON,
Brigadier General, Commanding.

Official: BEN. C. CUTLER,
Assistant Adjutant General.

[Special Orders No. 40.—Extract.]

DEPARTMENT OF NEW MEXICO, ASSISTANT ADJUTANT GENERAL'S OFFICE,
Santa Fé, N. M., August 17, 1863.

I. First Lieutenant Erastus W. Wood, with one non-commissioned officer and four mounted men from the general's escort, and four non-commissioned officers and thirty-one privates from Company A, 1st infantry California volunteers, will proceed with all practicable despatch to a locality forty miles from Santa Fé, known as the Valles, and there, and in that vicinity, lie in wait for thirty days, to kill every Navajo or Apache Indian who attempts to go through that noted thoroughfare. No women and children will be harmed: these will be captured.

* * * * * * * * * * *

By command of Brigadier General Carleton:

BEN. C. CUTLER,
Assistant Adjutant General.

Official: BEN. C. CUTLER,
Assistant Adjutant General.

[Special Orders No. 43.—Extract.]

DEPARTMENT OF NEW MEXICO, ASSISTANT ADJUTANT GENERAL'S OFFICE,
Santa Fé, N. M., September 4, 1863.

* * * * * * * * * * *

V. Second Lieutenant Thomas Holmes, of the first New Mexico volunteers, with a detachment of men from Fort Wingate, will proceed to Fort Sumner, New Mexico, *via* Fort Union, in charge of fifty-one Navajo Indian prisoners. These prisoners will be carefully guarded and properly cared for in all respects while on the way. When they have arrived at Fort Sumner, the commanding officer of that post will be held responsible that they are retained there, and are fed and cared for in all respects as the Apache Indians are whom he has in charge.

* * * * * * * * * * *

By command of Brigadier General Carleton:

BEN. C. CUTLER,
Assistant Adjutant General.

Official: BEN. C. CUTLER,
Assistant Adjutant General.

[Special Orders No. 5.—Extract.]

DEPARTMENT OF NEW MEXICO, ASSISTANT ADJUTANT GENERAL'S OFFICE,
Santa Fé, N. M., February 23, 1864.

* * * * * * * * * * *

IV. Company E, 1st infantry California volunteers, now at Fort Craig, New Mexico, will, without delay, take post at Los Pinos. As soon as it arrives at that station, company E, 5th United States infantry, will be prepared to escort from Los Pinos the next party of Navajo Indians which are sent from thence to Fort Sumner after that date. This company will form a part of the garrison of Fort Sumner.

* * * * * * * * * * *

By command of Brigadier General Carleton:

BEN C. CUTLER,
Assistant Adjutant General.

Official:

BEN. C. CUTLER,
Assistant Adjutant General.

[Special Orders No. 8.—Extract.]

DEPARTMENT OF NEW MEXICO, ASSISTANT ADJUTANT GENERAL'S OFFICE,
Santa Fé, N. M., March 14, 1864.

I. Colonel James L. Collins, late the superintendent of Indian affairs for New Mexico, will proceed from Santa Fé to Washington city, D. C., as bearer of important despatches to the War Department, having reference to the immediate support, settlement, and prospective care and maintenance of the more than five thousand Navajo prisoners, who have been captured, or who have voluntarily surrendered to the military within this department within the last four months. Colonel Collins will receive written instructions as to the particular points to which he is to call the attention of the authorities in Washington with regard to this grave matter, now become so vital to the Indians, and filled with such mighty issues to the people of the Territory. The chief quartermaster will provide Colonel Collins with funds for the necessary transportation of himself to Washington city and back to Santa Fé.

* * * * * * * * * * *

By command of Brigadier General Carleton:

CYRUS H. DE FORREST, *Aide-de-Camp.*

Official:

BEN. C. CUTLER,
Assistant Adjutant General.

[Special Orders No. 12.—Extract.]

DEPARTMENT OF NEW MEXICO, ASSISTANT ADJUTANT GENERAL'S OFFICE,
Santa Fé, N. M., April 11, 1864.

* * * * * * * * * * *

VI. Captain William H. Bell, commissary of subsistence United States army, will without delay transfer all subsistence stores, property, funds, and records which pertain to the subsistence depot at Fort Union, New Mexico, to Lieutenant Benjamin Taylor, jr., United States 5th infantry, and will then take post at Santa Fé, New Mexico, where, until further orders, he will be charged with the especial duty of providing subsistence for all Navajo and Apache Indians who may now be at the reservation at the Bosque Redondo, or who are, or may be, *en route* to that point from the country where they are taken, or voluntarily give themselves up.

* * * * * * * * * * *

By command of Brigadier General Carleton:

CYRUS H. DE FORREST, *Aide-de-Camp.*

Official:

BEN. C. CUTLER,
Assistant Adjutant General.

[Special Orders No. 30.—Extract.]

DEPARTMENT OF NEW MEXICO, ASSISTANT ADJUTANT GENERAL'S OFFICE,
Santa Fé, N. M., August 8, 1864.

* * * * * * * * * * *

III. Second Lieutenant William R. Savage, 1st cavalry California volunteers, will proceed to Fort Sumner with the Arizona Apache Indian prisoners now under his charge, and deliver them to the commander of that post, when Lieutenant Savage, with his party and means of transportation, will return to Santa Fé. The commander at Fort Sumner will enter upon his report of Indian captives all Arizona Apaches in a separate line.

* * * * * * * * * * *

By command of Brigadier General Carleton:

BEN. C. CUTLER,
Assistant Adjutant General.

Official:

BEN. C. CUTLER,
Assistant Adjutant General.

[Special Orders No. 32.—Extract.]

DEPARTMENT OF NEW MEXICO, ASSISTANT ADJUTANT GENERAL'S OFFICE,
Santa Fé, N. M., August 20, 1864.

* * * * * * * * * * *

V. Immediately upon having relinquished the command of the 5th United States infantry, Major Updegraff, with company A of that regiment, will proceed with all practicable despatch to Fort Union, New Mexico, where he will be joined by fifty rank and file of company K, 1st cavalry California volunteers, under the captain of that company, when he will proceed to the Lower Cimarron springs, on the road to Missouri, to give protection to trains now *en route* to and from the States. Major Updegraff's command will take sixty days' rations of subsistence from Fort Union. The chief quartermaster will provide the necessary transportation.

* * * * * * * * * * *

By command of Brigadier General Carleton:

BEN. C. CUTLER,
Assistant Adjutant General.

Official:

BEN. C. CUTLER,
Assistant Adjutant General.

[Special Orders No. 34.—Extract.]

DEPARTMENT OF NEW MEXICO, ASSISTANT ADJUTANT GENERAL'S OFFICE,
Santa Fé, N. M., August 28, 1864.

* * * * * * * * * * *

II. All of the effective men of Captain Louis Felsenthal's company C, of the first infantry, New Mexico volunteers, will proceed with all practicable despatch to Gray's ranch, on the Purgatory river, or to some other more eligible point near that place, and will furnish escorts to the United States mail from Gray's ranch to Fort Lyon and back, and from Gray's ranch to Mr. Maxwell's, on the Little Cimarron and back. The company will be on this duty sixty days, and will be provided with subsistence for that period, and with one hundred and fifty rounds of ammunition per man.

The chief quartermaster will furnish the necessary transportation, and make provision for suitable transportation for the escorts and for forage. The chief commissary will give orders for such fresh meat as may be needed by the troops who are thus detached.

* * * * * * * * * * *

By command of Brigadier General Carleton:

BEN. C. CUTLER,
Assistant Adjutant General.

Official:

BEN. C. CUTLER,
Assistant Adjutant General.

[Special Orders No. 34.—Extract.]

DEPARTMENT OF NEW MEXICO, ASSISTANT ADJUTANT GENERAL'S OFFICE,
Santa Fé, N. M., August 28, 1864.

I. Captain Reuben A. Hill, with all the effective men of his company K, first infantry, New Mexico volunteers, will march with all practicable despatch to Fort Lyon, district of Colorado, and there report for duty for sixty days from date of arrival at that post.

This movement is considered necessary to render all possible help against the Indians of the plains, who are now openly hostile to passing trains, as well as to the United States mails. The company will be provided at Fort Union depot with one hundred and fifty rounds of ammunition per man, and with subsistence to Fort Lyon, Colorado Territory.

The chief quartermaster will furnish the necessary transportation.

* * * * * * * * * * *

By command of Brigadier General Carleton:

BEN. C. CUTLER,
Assistant Adjutant General.

Official:

BEN. C. CUTLER,
Assistant Adjutant General.

[Special Orders No. 37.—Extract.]

DEPARTMENT OF NEW MEXICO, ASSISTANT ADJUTANT GENERAL'S OFFICE,
Santa Fé, N. M., September 19, 1864.

I. Brigadier General M. M. Crocker, United States volunteers, will take post at Fort Sumner, New Mexico, where, in addition to commanding the troops, General Crocker will have the care and supervision of the eight thousand captive Indians now upon the reservation at the Bosque Redondo, and of all other captive Indians who may come to be located at that point. The general will cause the lands at once to be fairly allotted to the different bands and families of Indians;* the acequias to be enlarged and new ones dug; the fields to be cleared and ploughed and gotten ready for planting; the sites to be chosen for the villages of the different bands on elevated lands which are not irrigable, but along which an acequia can be constructed that will keep up a continuous supply of water.

The general will also see that no rations of food are issued to Indians who have food on hand, which they themselves have raised, until the latter food be exhausted, and that the utmost economy be exercised in all matters pertaining to the subsistence and the support of the Indians; and he will see that patience, kindness, moderation, justice, and firmness be exercised toward them until they have gradually become accustomed to the restraints and requirements to which they must be subjected and observe in their transition from a nomadic to an agricultural mode of life, and from a savage to a civilized state of existence.

* * * * * * * * * * *

By command of Brigadier General Carleton:

BEN. C. CUTLER,
Assistant Adjutant General.

Official:

BEN. C. CUTLER,
Assistant Adjutant General.

*This could not be done, and cannot be done, until surveys are made. See letter to Secretary of the Interior on this subject. J. H. C.

[Special Orders No. 41.—Extract.]

DEPARTMENT OF NEW MEXICO, ASSISTANT ADJUTANT GENERAL'S OFFICE,
Santa Fé, N. M., October 26, 1864.

* * * * * * * * * * *

V. It is reported that there is at Mora and Las Vegas, New Mexico, something like one hundred and forty thousand pounds of flour and shorts, which the exigencies of service require should be bought at once in open market as subsistence for Navajo Indians.

The chief commissary will proceed to those places and make the purchase, if the articles can be bought at all for anything like a fair price.

By command of Brigadier General Carleton:

BEN. C. CUTLER,
Assistant Adjutant General.

Official:

BEN. C. CUTLER,
Assistant Adjutant General.

DEPARTMENT OF NEW MEXICO, ASSISTANT ADJUTANT GENERAL'S OFFICE,
Santa Fé, N. M , February 8, 1865.

To the people:

Owing to Indian difficulties upon the roads leading from New Mexico to the States, a company of troops will leave Fort Union, New Mexico, for Fort Larned, Kansas, on the first and fifteenth of every month, until further orders, commencing on the first day of March, 1865. The first company will go by the Raton mountain route, the second by the Cimarron route, and so on, alternately. The merchants and others who wish to send trains in after goods can assemble their trains at such points near Fort Union as may be desired by them, so as to have the protection of these periodical escorts, if such be their wish. Arrangements will be made with Major General Curtis, commanding the department of Kansas, so as to send these companies back from Fort Larned at such times as may best promote the interests and safety of all who may have trains upon the road coming in this direction.

By command of General Carleton:

BEN. C. CUTLER,
Assistant Adjutant General.

Official:

BEN. C. CUTLER,
Assistant Adjutant Genera.

[Special Orders No. 6.—Extract.]

DEPARTMENT OF NEW MEXICO, ASSISTANT ADJUTANT GENERAL'S OFFICE,
Santa Fé, N. M., February 16, 1865.

* * * * * * * * * * *

VIII. Second Lieutenant John Ayers, first cavalry New Mexico volunteers, is hereby detailed to proceed with a delegation of four Navajo chiefs, who are to proceed to the old Navajo country to give warning to those of that tribe who have not surrendered, that they must now come in. Lieutenant Ayers will have four good cavalry soldiers furnished from the commanding general's escort, and will take a tent and rations for his men, as well as for these chiefs. When Lieutenant Ayers arrives at Fort Wingate, he will receive further orders. The chief quartermaster will cause the necessary transportation to be furnished.

* * * * * * * * * * *

By command of Brigadier General Carleton:

BEN. C. CUTLER,
Assistant Adjutant General.

Official:

BEN. C. CUTLER,
Assistant Adjutant General.

[Special Orders No. 8.—Extract]

DEPARTMENT OF NEW MEXICO, ASSISTANT ADJUTANT GENERAL'S OFFICE,
Santa Fé, N. M., March 11, 1865.

* * * * * * * * * * *

IX. In compliance with Special Orders No. 477, series for 1864, from the headquarters of the army, Brigadier General Marcellus M. Crocker, United States volunteers, is relieved from further duty in the department of New Mexico, and will proceed without delay and report in person to the general commanding the army of the Cumberland for assignment to duty.

The general commanding the department of New Mexico takes this occasion to express his warmest thanks for the efficient and judicious manner in which General Crocker has conducted the affairs pertaining to the important post of Fort Sumner, and to the reservation at the Bosque Redondo with its nine thousand captive Indians—a duty which required an exercise of great judgment, moderation, firmness, and forecast, and a duty which has been performed in such a manner as not only to give the utmost satisfaction to those connected professionally with the military affairs of that post and of the department, but to win the affectionate regard of the Indians themselves, who are there receiving their first impressions of civilization, and their first lessons in the art, literally, of earning their bread by the sweat of their brow. General Crocker carries with him to the new field of duty to which he has been called, the earnest wishes on the part of the comrades he leaves behind, not only that he will be soon restored to health, but have an opportunity to add renewed lustre to his already brilliant reputation as a soldier.

* * * * * * * * * * *

By command of Brigadier General Carleton:

BEN. C. CUTLER,
Assistant Adjutant General.

Official:

BEN. C. CUTLER,
Assistant Adjutant General.

[Special Orders No. 10.—Extract.]

DEPARTMENT OF NEW MEXICO, ASSISTANT ADJUTANT GENERAL'S OFFICE,
Santa Fé, N. M., March 24, 1865.

I. N. H. Davis, assistant inspector general, United States army, will proceed hence as soon as practicable, after first completing reports of inspections on which he is now engaged, to Fort McRae and Roblero, New Mexico, and select a site at or near each of these points, for a military post there to be established. * * * * * *

II. Having completed this duty, he will proceed *via* Las Cruces and Fort Cummings to Pinos Altos, New Mexico, and make arrangements for having an interview with the principal men of the Mangas Colorado band of Apache Indians, with the object of advising this band to remove in peace to the Indian reservation at the Bosque Redondo. Special verbal instructions will be given him from these headquarters.

III. The commissary at Las Cruces will furnish subsistence stores for issue to these Indians, at the council, should it be thought advisable to give them any.

* * * * * * * * * * *

By command of Brigadier General Carleton:

BEN. C. CUTLER,
Assistant Adjutant General.

Official:

BEN. C. CUTLER,
Assistant Adjutant General.

[Special Orders No. 13.—Extract.]

DEPARTMENT OF NEW MEXICO, ASSISTANT ADJUTANT GENERAL'S OFFICE,
Santa Fé, N. M., April 15, 1865.

* * * * * * * * * * *

V. A board of officers, to consist of Major William McCleave, first cavalry California volunteers, Captain Henry B. Bristol, United States army, Captain William L. Rynerson, United States volunteers, Captain Emil Fritz, first cavalry California volunteers, and Captain Laurence G. Murphy, first cavalry New Mexico volunteers, will assemble at Fort Sumner, New Mexico, at 10 o'clock, a. m., on Wednesday, the 26th of April, 1865, or as soon thereafter as practicable, to consider and report upon the subject of the better organization of the Navajo tribe of Indians, to the end that more easy control can be had of their labor, and that the fruits of that labor may best conduce to their permanent support. The board will take great pains so to effect the purpose for which it is organized, as to present a clear and practical plan of organization, &c., which may be definitely understood in all its details by the War Department, to which the report of the board will be submitted.

* * * * * * * * * * *

By command of Brigadier General Carleton:

BEN. C. CUTLER,
Assistant Adjutant General.

Official:

BEN. C. CUTLER,
Assistant Adjutant General.

DEPARTMENT OF NEW MEXICO, ASSISTANT ADJUTANT GENERAL'S OFFICE,
Santa Fé, N. M., May 4, 1865.

To the people:

After the 15th instant, no more companies can be spared from Fort Union to escort trains until some of those now absent on this duty return, when due notice will be given of the time of departure of the next company. It is well for the people to know that Colonel Carson will establish, at or near Cedar bluffs or Cold springs, a camp of three companies for the summer, so as to afford all possible protection to trains passing that dangerous neighborhood on the Cimarron route. These troops will leave Fort Union on the 20th instant.

By command of Brigadier General Carleton:

BEN. C. CUTLER,
Assistant Adjutant General.

Official:

BEN. C. CUTLER,
Assistant Adjutant General.

[Special Orders No. 15.—Extract.]

DEPARTMENT OF NEW MEXICO, ASSISTANT ADJUTANT GENERAL'S OFFICE,
Santa Fé, N. M., May 7, 1865.

* * * * * * * * * * *

IV. Colonel Christopher Carson, with Major Albert H. Pfeiffer and companies C and L of his regiment and company F, first cavalry California volunteers, will proceed from Fort Union, New Mexico, starting on the 20th instant, to Cedar bluffs or Cold spring, on the Cimarron route to the States, where, at or near one of these places, Colonel Carson will select and establish a camp to be occupied until the first day of November next, unless otherwise ordered from these headquarters. The object of establishing this camp is to have troops at that dangerous part of the route, in order to give protection to trains passing to and from the States. The details as to how this force can best effect that object are left entirely with Colonel Carson.

* * * * * * * * * * *

By command of Brigadier General Carleton:

BEN. C. CUTLER,
Assistant Adjutant General.

Official:

BEN. C. CUTLER,
Assistant Adjutant General.

[General Orders No. 15.]

HEADQUARTERS DEPARTMENT OF NEW MEXICO,
Santa Fé, N. M., June 15, 1863.

I. For a long time past the Navajo Indians have murdered and robbed the people of New Mexico. Last winter, when eighteen of their chiefs came to Santa Fé to have a talk, they were warned, and were told to inform their people that, for these murders and robberies, the tribe must be punished, unless some binding guarantees should be given that in future these outrages should cease. No such guarantees have yet been given; but, on the contrary, additional murders and additional robberies have been perpetrated upon the persons and property of our unoffending citizens. It is therefore ordered that Colonel Christopher Carson, with a proper military force, proceed without delay to a point in the Navajo country known as Pueblo Colorado, and there establish a defensible depot for his supplies and hospital, and thence to prosecute a vigorous war upon the men of this tribe until it is considered, at these headquarters, that they have been effectually punished for their long-continued atrocities.

The following comprises the force alluded to above:

Field and staff.

Colonel Christopher Carson, 1st New Mexico volunteers, commanding.
Captain A. B. Carey, United States army, chief quartermaster.
First Lieutenant Richard S. Barrett, 1st infantry California volunteers, chief commissary.
First Lieutenant Lawrence G. Murphy, adjutant, 1st New Mexico volunteers.
Major Joseph Cummings, 1st New Mexico volunteers.
Major Arthur Morrison, 1st New Mexico volunteers.
Surgeon Allen F. Peck, 1st New Mexico volunteers.
Rev. Damaso Taladrid, chaplain 1st New Mexico volunteers.

Companies.

Number.	Captains.	Letter of company.	Number of officers.	Rank and file.	Aggregate.	Mounted.	Dismounted.
1	F. P. Abreü	A	3	75	76	78	......
2	A. H. Pfeiffer	H	3	76	79	79	......
3	J. L Barbey	G	3	61	64	64	......
4	Charles Deus	M	3	90	93	93	......
5	John Thompson	K	3	54	57	57	......
6	Joseph Birney	D	3	102	105	105	......
7	Francis McCabe	L	3	86	89	......	89
8	Eben Everett	B	3	80	83	......	83
9	José de Sena	C	3	85	88	......	88
			27	709	736	476	260

Companies K, L, and M will proceed from Fort Union, New Mexico, to Los Pinos, New Mexico, starting the day after the military commission adjourns which has been ordered to assemble at Fort Union.

Companies A, H, and G have heretofore been ordered to rendezvous at Los Pinos.

Companies B and C, now at Fort Wingate, will be in readiness to move at a day's notice.

Colonel Carson will require, and receive, two mountain howitzers on prairie carriages, with an adequate supply of ammunition, &c., to be used in defence of his depot at Pueblo Colorado.

These troops will march from Los Pinos for the Navajo country on Wednesday, July 1, 1863.

The chiefs of the quartermaster, subsistence, medical, and ordnance departments will furnish, on Colonel Carson's requisition, such spies and guides, means of transportation, intrenching tools, quartermaster property, clothing, camp and garrison equipage, subsistence stores, hospital stores, medicines, arms, and ammunition as may be necessary to equip and provide completely for his command to insure to it the cardinal requirements of health, food, mobility, and power.

II. The post of Fort Wingate, at the headwaters of the Gallo, in the Navajo country, will be garrisoned, until further orders, by the following troops:

Field and staff.

Lieutenant Colonel J. Francisco Chaves, 1st New Mexico volunteers.

Major Edward B. Willis, 1st infantry California volunteers.

Assistant Surgeon J. H. Shout, 1st New Mexico volunteers.

First Lieutenant Benjamin Stevens, regimental quartermaster, 1st New Mexico volunteers.

First Lieutenant Archibald McEachran, regimental commissary of subsistence, 1st New Mexico volunteers.

Companies.

Number.	Captains.	Letter of company.	Number of officers.	Rank and file.	Aggregate.	Mounted.	Dismounted.
1	J. C. Shaw	F	3	84	87	......	87
2	Rafael Chacon	E	3	81	84	84	......
3	J. P. Hargrave	C	3	69	72	......	72
4	Lafayette Hammond	H	2	81	83	......	83
			11	315	326	84	242

These troops are likewise to operate against the Navajo Indians, and will alternate in their scouts, so as to have at least two companies in the field all the time.

III. A board of officers, to consist of Colonel Christopher Carson, 1st New Mexico volunteers; Major Henry D Wallen, United States army, acting inspector general; Surgeon James M. McNulty, United States volunteers, medical inspector; Brevet Captain Allen L. Anderson, United States army, acting engineer officer; and Captain Benjamin C. Cutler, assistant adjutant general United States volunteers, will proceed with Colonel Carson's command to the locality known as Pueblo Colorado, in the Navajo country, and select and mark out, at or as near that place as practicable, the exact site for a military post, to be garrisoned by four companies of cavalry and four companies of infantry.

A map of the surrounding country will accompany the report of the board, as well as a ground-plan of the post, an estimate of its cost, and its measured distance from the Rio Grande.

The geographical position of the post will be fixed instrumentally.

Unless otherwise ordered by competent authority, this new post will be known as Fort Canby, in honor of Brigadier General E. R. S. Canby, United States army, the recent commander of the department of New Mexico.

By command of Brigadier General Carleton.

BEN. C. CUTLER,
Assistant Adjutant General.

[General Orders No. 3.]

HEADQUARTERS DEPARTMENT OF NEW MEXICO,
Santa Fé, N. M., February 24, 1864.

The following notices of combats with hostile Indians in New Mexico, and synopsis of Indian depredations, as well as operations generally against them, during the year 1863, are published for the information of all concerned. Perhaps not over one scout in four, which was made against the Indians during that period, was at all successful; but no notice is made except of scouts which had results for or against us. This fact is stated to convey a better idea of the labor of the troops:

January 4.—Colonel Carson, commanding Fort Stanton, reports arrival of two Mescalero Indians, who stated that, in six days, one hundred Mescalero Indians would deliver themselves up at Fort Stanton; that this number comprised all the Mescaleros not already at Bosque Redondo.

January 9.—Captain Updegraff, commanding Fort Sumner, reports that two men of the picket stationed at Bosque Grande left the picket contrary to orders, to hunt, and that one of them, Private Samuel Strunk, company M, 1st New Mexico volunteers, was killed by Indians; that the number of Indians then at Bosque Redondo was 248.

January 17.—Colonel Carson reports the arrival at Fort Stanton of one hundred Mescaleros mentioned in his communication of the 4th instant, under the following named chiefs: Ojo Blanco, Janero Viejo, Janero Pablo, Janero Francisco, José La Paz, Mancos Son, Schat-hi.

January 17.—Captain E. D. Shirland, 1st cavalry California volunteers, brought Mangus Colorado, an Apache chief, into Fort McLean, a prisoner. On the morning of the 18th, in attempting to escape, Mangus was killed by the guard.

January 20.—Captain Shirland came upon an Indian rancheria, surprised and defeated the Indians, killing nine and wounding many more, and capturing from them thirty-four head of stock, a portion of which were government mules. The rancheria and all that pertained to it was destroyed.

January 19.—Captain William McCleave, 1st cavalry California volunteers, reports that, in obedience to orders, he started from Fort McLean and proceeded to the Pinos Altos mines; arriving at the latter place, a party of Mangus Colorado's band of Apaches approached; the men were ordered to attack them, which was done; eleven Indians were killed and one wounded; the latter proved to be the wife of the chief, Mangus Colorado. Three horses were captured, but, being in poor condition, the people at the mines were permitted to keep them. Eleven Indians killed, one wounded, and three horses captured.

January 29.—On the 29th January the Indians attacked two hunting parties of company A, 5th infantry California volunteers, at Pinos Altos mines, killed private Hussey and wounded Sergeant Sitton. The Indians were driven off with a loss of 20 killed and 15 wounded. Sergeant Sitton behaved gallantly in this affair.

February 16.—L. M. Vaca reports that 4,000 sheep were stolen from the neighborhood of Limitar by Navajoes, and reports that the Navajoes stole 2,000 sheep which he recaptured at the Sierras Oscuras, (Black Hills,) killing three and wounding several Indians, and capturing all their saddles, provisions, &c.

February 25.—José L Perea reports that a band of 40 Navajoes attacked and drove off 6,000 sheep 25 miles south of Pope's artesian well.

March 4.—L. M. Vaca reports that since February 26, 310 head of horses and cattle have been stolen by Indians from the neighborhood of Limitar.

March 5.—Major Morrison reports departure of Indians mentioned in Colonel Carson's communication of January 17, 1862, from Fort Stanton to Bosque Redondo; also the departure of 15 additional Indians who had given themselves up.

March 12.—Indians captured near Sabinal 2,300 head of sheep; were followed by Mexicans, who recaptured them on the Jornada on the night of the 12th or 13th.

March —.—A band of 40 Indians pursued two expressmen going from Fort Stanton to Fort Union. These Indians had a large herd of sheep. Captain Abreü, commanding Fort Stanton, sent Lieutenant McAllister and thirty men, with ten days' rations, to the Sierras Oscuras, to intercept them. The expedition failed to recover the stock.

March 22.—On the afternoon of March 22 the Gila Apaches made a descent upon the public herd which was grazing near Fort West, and succeeded in running off some 60 head of horses. Indians numbered —. At 8 o'clock p. m. the gallant Major William McCleave, 1st cavalry California volunteers, started in pursuit, with a command consisting of Lieutenants French and Latimer, 1st cavalry California volunteers, 40 men of company A, 25 men of company B, and 14 men of company C, 1st cavalry California volunteers. Major McCleave followed trail of Indians in a westerly course about seventy miles, and down the Gila five miles, then across a divide to Rio Negro, where he arrived at 9 a. m. on the 26th, and then moved up the stream a short distance; signs at this point indicated the close proximity of Indians and a rancheria. During twilight command moved up the stream two miles and made camp. Thirty men were mounted on only serviceable animals left, under Lieutenant Latimer, and 30 dismounted, under Major McCleave, started in search of rancheria, leaving remainder of command, with Lieutenant French, in charge of broken-down animals, pack-animals, provisions, &c. Leaving the camp at 8 o'clock p. m., the command ascended a mountain on west side of stream and travelled about twelve miles without meeting with any success; here command rested from 1 o'clock of the 27th until dawn of day, it raining all the time. When light enough to see, Major McCleave discovered, from an elevated position, trees, which indicated presence of water, and a horse grazing in neighborhood also indicated that the rancheria was near by. Lieutenant Latimer was ordered ahead with his command; discovered rancheria and gallantly charged upon it. Part of the dismounted men immediately commenced gathering in and guarding the horses, to prevent the escape of the Indians, while the others were skirmishing and fighting on the bluffs. The fight lasted for twenty minutes, and resulted in the complete routing of the Indians, the capture of all our own horses that could be found, and many Indian horses; the killing of twenty-five Indians, and the complete destruction of the rancheria, provisions, and all they possessed. Private Hall, of company B, 1st cavalry California volunteers, was wounded in this fight. The command then returned to camp, and soon after noon started on return trip by a route supposed more direct than the one by which the Indians were followed from the fort. This route led up a cañon from sides of which the Indians attacked rear guard of command, wounding Lieutenant French, killing two horses and wounding one. As soon as the attack was made, the soldiers ascended the perpendicular walls of the cañon by climbing one over the other. This was done amidst showers of arrows. As soon as they reached the top the Indians fled in every direction. The superiority of the Californians over the Apaches, at their own style of fighting, was shown in the case of Corporal Ellis, of company A, who crawled unseen to a rock, behind which was an Indian, and giving a short cough the Indian raised his head to discover its cause, when a bullet from Ellis's rifle dashed through his brain. The Indians lost in this attack three killed.

On the 30th, provisions giving out, a sergeant and five men were sent to the fort for a supply. Until their return the party subsisted on horse-flesh.

On the 4th of April the command reached fort. On 5th, Private Hall died from the wounds received in the fight.

Indian loss, twenty-eight killed; troops, one.

March 24.—Major Morrison, with Captain Pfeiffer's company New Mexico volunteers, *en route* from Fort Stanton to Fort McRae, at San Nicolas spring came upon a wounded Mexican, who stated he belonged to a train belonging to Martin Lujan, of Socorro, Texas; that the train had been attacked by Indians and nearly all the party killed, he being wounded in three places and left for dead. Major Morrison, with Lieutenant Bargie and 18 men of the company, went in pursuit, came to the salt marshes at daybreak of the 25th, found ten wagons stripped of everything portable, and, within a circuit of three miles, seven dead bodies of Mexicans, which they buried. They then followed the trail of the Indians towards the Sacramento mountains, then towards the Sierra Blanca until noon, when they met a party of Mexicans, from Tularosa, in pursuit of the same Indians; they had been informed of the massacre by another wounded Mexican, who had escaped. The Indians had at this time twenty hours' start and were hidden in the recesses of the Sierra Blanca. Major Morrison returned to San Nicolas spring, arriving there on the evening of the 25th, having travelled 150 miles. Lieutenant Bargie's conduct is spoken of as deserving of praise. Estimated number of Indians, 45 in all, 20 of whom were warriors; arrows indicate they were Apaches; seven Mexicans killed and 70 head of cattle stolen.

April 25.—Captain Benjamin F. Harrover, 5th infantry California volunteers, reports that he attacked, at Apache pass, a band of Apache Indians, numbering about two hundred, thirty of them mounted and several of them armed with guns. At the first fire the Indians fell back, but kept up the fight for nearly two hours. In this affair Private Wilcox, of company E, 5th infantry California volunteers, was wounded. Indian loss, three killed, — wounded; troops, one private wounded.

May —.—Major Joseph Smith, commanding Fort Stanton, reports that a party of Indians made a descent on the farmers of Ruidoso and killed a man named Harding, robbed his house, and drove off ten or twelve head of stock.

May 1.—Cesario Duran, a citizen, reports that a party, under his command, had a hard fight with the Apaches in the San Andreas mountains, and succeeded in killing and wounding many Indians; the party lost two men killed; the party recovered several animals and captured seven horses.

May 8.—Lieutenant Colonel J. F. Chaves, 1st New Mexico volunteers, reports that an Indian named Gordo was seized and turned over to Lieutenant B. Stevens on the morning of 11th instant. The Indian unbound himself and attempted to escape; the sentinel in charge shot and killed him.

May 16.—On the night of the 15th the Navajoes stole from Jemez six head of horses.

May —.—Charles T. Hayden, citizen, reports that the Indians attacked his train near the line of Chihuahua; they were defeated, with a loss of eleven killed, including the renowned Copinggan. Three horses were captured in this fight.

May —.—Captain T. T. Tidball, 5th infantry California volunteers, with 25 men of his company and a small party of citizens, attacked a rancheria in Cajon de Arivaypa, killing over 50 Indians, wounding as many more, taking 10 prisoners, and capturing 60 head of stock, with the loss of only one man—Thomas McClelland. The party marched five days without lighting a fire, maintaining silence, hiding by day and travelling by night, over a country hitherto untrod by white men.

June —.—Major Joseph Smith, commanding Fort Stanton, reports that the Indians attacked the expressmen on the 21st of June, near the Galinas, and compelled them to abandon their mules and express matter and take to the mountains. The mules and express lost.

June 24.—Major Morrison reports an attack on Lieutenant Bargie and escort on the Jornada, in which Lieutenant Bargie, while fighting gallantly, was killed. The conduct of Sergeants Peña and Ulisari, and the two prisoners they had in charge, is highly praised.

June 26.—Major Morrison reports further, in regard to the fight on the Jornada, that Private Lucero, 1st New Mexico volunteers, was killed.

June 20.—Captain A. H. Pfeiffer, wife, and two servant girls, with escort of six men of the 1st New Mexico volunteers, were attacked by a party of Apache Indians, numbering 15 or 20, at a hot spring near Fort McRae. The captain was bathing at the time, when the Indians made a rush upon the party, killing two men, Privates Nestor Quintana and Mestas. Captain Pfeiffer was wounded in his side by an arrow, and Private Dolores received two shots in his right arm and hand. A citizen named Betts, who was with Captain Pfeiffer, was also wounded. The remainder of party, except the women, succeeded in reaching Fort McRae unharmed, and reported facts to Major Morrison, commanding post. He immediately started in pursuit, with 20 mounted men, but did not succeed in overtaking the Indians. Mrs. Pfeiffer and the servant girls were found in the trail, badly wounded. Mrs. Pfeiffer and one of the servants have since died; the other doing well. Loss in this affair, two privates killed; two women mortally wounded; one officer, one private, one woman, and a citizen wounded; seven horses and two mules taken by the Indians. Indian loss unknown.

June 27.—Major Joseph Smith, commanding Fort Stanton, reports the loss of part of his herd of horses and mules, stolen by Indians. An infantry company sent in pursuit.

June 28.—Lieutenant W. H. Hi_don, 5th infantry California volunteers, reports that on his way from Fort Stanton to Santa Fé, near Gallinas springs, he found the bodies of Privates Nicolas Quintana, of company A, 1st New Mexico volunteers, and John Hinckley, of company A, 5th California volunteers, who had been murdered by the Indians. The Indians had evidently wounded Private Quintana, tied him to a stake and burned him. Some legal-tender notes and several letters were found near the body of Hinckley.

July 2.—Lieutenant Colonel Chaves reports that Captain Rafael Chacon, 1st New Mexico volunteers, with 22 men, was sent in pursuit of a band of Indians who had stolen some horses and oxen from Fort Wingate. The oxen were recaptured near the post; the troops followed the trail of the Indians for three days, and finally overtook them, when a sharp fight ensued. The Indians fought with great bravery, but were finally driven from their cover and fled. The conduct of Sergeant Antonio José Tresquez in this affair is highly spoken of by Captain Chacon. Indian loss unknown. Troops, one private wounded.

July 4.—Captain N. J. Pishon reports that, with 27 men of his company, D, 1st cavalry California volunteers, he pursued a party of eight Indians, who had driven off 104 government mules from Fort Craig, overtook them a few miles from the post, and killed four Indians and recovered all the mules. Captain Jules L. Barbey, who accompanied the command, was shot through the wrist by an arrow. Privates Jackson and Bancroft were also slightly wounded.

July 12.—Captain A. H. French, 1st cavalry California volunteers, with twenty-seven men of his company, attacked and routed, near Fort Thorne, a band of Apache Indians, supposed to number sixty warriors. Indian loss, ten killed and four horses captured. Sergeant Walsh and Farrier Burns were wounded.

July 11.—Sergeant E W. Hoyt, of company D, 1st infantry California volunteers, with three men of company B and three men of company D, 1st infantry California volunteers, having in charge four wagons *en route* to Las Cruces, was attacked by Indians in Cook's pass and forced to abandon three wagons and nineteen mules, and had four men slightly wounded. Four Indians are known to have been killed and a number wounded. Sergeant Hoyt acted with the greatest coolness in this affair.

July 19.—Lieutenant Juan Marques, 1st New Mexico volunteers, while returning from Horse Head crossing of the Pecos, with 15 men of company A, 1st New Mexico volunteers, was attacked at the Rio Honda by about 50 Indians, while in camp at that point. The Indians gained possession of the camp, but were finally driven across the river, carrying with them their wounded. They soon after recrossed the river and charged on the herd, but were again driven back with loss. In this charge, Private José Chaves was killed. For several hours the fight was continued. The Indian force rapidly increased, and at last numbered some 200. The ammunition gave out and the soldiers were ordered to break their rifles and make their escape, which they did.

Lieutenant Marquez reports the conduct of the following named men as worthy of mention: Corporals Brigaloa and José G. Gonzales, and Privates Santiago Torres, G. Romero, Antonio Archuleta, José D. Tresquez, and Jesus Lopez. All the public animals (including 10 mules) were lost in this affair. Indian loss, six killed.

July 22.—Captain F. P. Abreü, 1st New Mexico volunteers, and Captain Emil Fritz, 1st cavalry California volunteers, with a detachment of New Mexico and California volunteers, left Fort Stanton for the Rio Pecos to overtake and chastise the Indians who had attacked Lieutenant Marques.

After following the Indians for forty-five miles, Captain Fritz came upon their camp and captured two horses, six mules, and all the plunder of the camp; the Indians made their escape.

July 30.—Lieutenant W. H. Higdon reports that on the 30th of July, *en route* from Fort Union to Fort Stanton, he saw about seventy-five Indians driving a large herd of sheep, judged to number twenty thousand. Believing his party too small to attack so large a band of Indians, they were allowed to pass unmolested.

July 24.—Lieutenant John Lambert, 5th infantry California volunteers, reports that the Indians attacked a detachment under his command in Cook's cañon; at the first fire Sergeant Hance, of company H, 5th infantry, was wounded in his shoulder and hand; soon after Private Queen, of company F, was mortally wounded. Two wagons were abandoned to the Indians, also twelve mules. Private Queen died before the fight ended.

July 19.—Lieutenant Colonel McMullen's ambulance was attacked by Indians near Paraje and Assistant Surgeon E. S. Watson, 1st infantry California volunteers, and Private Johnson, company G, 1st infantry California volunteers, were killed. The escort killed two Indians and wounded others. Colonel McMullen's horse was captured by the Indians. Our loss, one commissioned officer and one private killed; one horse lost. Indian loss, three killed and —— wounded.

August 4.—Lieutenant B Stevens, 1st New Mexico volunteers, reports that when returning from Cuvero to Fort Wingate, he came upon a party of Navajo Indians, seven men and two boys, took them prisoners and placed them in the guard-house at Fort Wingate.

August 6.—M. Steck, superintendent of Indian affairs, reports that a portion of the Utahs, Mohuaches and Tabahuaches had killed nine Navajoes and captured twenty-two horses.

August 6.—Captain E. H. Bergmann reports that a party of company I, 1st New Mexico volunteers, in charge of a herd of beef cattle, were attacked by a body of Navajoes on the 22d July, near Conchas springs. The party consisted of Sergeant José Lucero and Privates Juan F. Ortiz and José Banneras, who fought the Indians from 11 a. m. until after sundown, killing and wounding several of them. The Indians succeeded in killing Sergeant

Lucero and Private Ortiz. Private Banneras being severely wounded by eight arrow-shots, gathered up the muskets and pistols of his dead comrades and threw them into the springs. The Indians fractured his skull with rocks and left him for dead, but he recovered towards morning and made his way to Chaparita. The Indians drove off the cattle; (number not stated.)

Captain Bergmann learning that the Indians had driven off ten thousand sheep, mounted thirty men and endeavored to intercept them at the crossing of the Pecos. Corporal Martinez came close to their rear and succeeded in killing two and wounding several. The corporal destroyed their camp utensils and captured three beeves.

August 11.—M. Steck, superintendent of Indian affairs, reports that the Utahs have during the last ten days killed thirty Navajoes, and captured and brought in sixty children of both sexes, and captured thirty horses and two thousand sheep. On the 11th instant four Utahs came in with three scalps and six captives. Total, thirty-three killed, sixty-six captured, and thirty horses and two thousand sheep taken.

August 19.—Colonel Christopher Carson reports that he left camp near Cañon Bonita, August 5, 1863, on a scout for thirty days. On the first day out sent Sergeant Romero with fifteen men after two Indians seen in the vicinity; he captured one of their horses; the Indians made their escape. On the night of the 4th instant Captain Pfeiffer captured eleven women and children, besides a woman and child, the former of whom was killed in attempting to escape, and the latter accidentally. Captain Pfeiffer's party also captured two other children, one hundred sheep and goats, and one horse. The Utes captured in the same vicinity eighteen horses and two mules, and killed one Indian. Captain Pfeiffer wounded an Indian, but he escaped. On the 16th, a party who were sent for some pack-saddles brought in one Indian woman. At this camp the brave Major Cummings, 1st New Mexico volunteers, was shot through the abdomen by a concealed Indian, and died instantly. One of the parties sent out from this camp captured an Indian woman. Total Indians killed, three; captured, fifteen; wounded, one; twenty horses, two mules, and one hundred sheep and goats captured. Troops, one commissioned officer killed.

August 19.—Captain Henry A. Greene, 1st infantry California volunteers, having received information that a party of Indians with a large herd of sheep had crossed the Rio Grande on the morning of the 8th instant, mounted twenty men and started in pursuit, and after following their trail for nearly two hundred miles, came upon them and opened fire. The Indians fled, and the command recovered sixteen hundred to eighteen hundred sheep, and drove them to Fort Craig.

August 24.—Captain W. Craig reports that a party of sixteen Indians attacked his herders, near Fort Union, and drove off eighteen government mules.

August 27.—Captain V. Drescher, 1st infantry California volunteers, reports the horses and mules at Fort West were stampeded by Indians; animals not recovered—Indians not pursued. Twenty-six mules and one horse lost.

August 29.—Captain Henry A. Greene, 1st infantry California volunteers, reports that the Indians attacked the mail stage on the Jornada near the Point of Rocks, and captured seven mules. As soon as the information was received fifteen mounted men were sent in pursuit, and nine men detailed to escort the stage through. The mounted party, on coming in view of the Rio Grande, saw three Indians on the bank; the balance of the band were back in the brush; the three Indians were fired upon; one of them fell, but recovered again. A part of the command under Lieutenant Fountain charged across the river; the Indians ran and concealed themselves. The party then dismounted and commenced to skirmish through the bushes. While on this duty Private George Dickey was mortally wounded by the only shot fired by the Indians during the affair. Dickey saw an Indian jump into the river, and shot him; the Indian turned after being shot and gave Dickey the wound which caused his death. Indian loss, one killed, three wounded. Our loss, one private killed.

August —.—Colonel Christopher Carson with his command left Pueblo Colorado on the 20th day of August for Cañon de Chelly with the main force, secreting twenty-five men under Captain Pfeiffer in the cañon to watch for Indians. Soon after, two Indians were seen approaching the cañon, and were fired upon, and although badly wounded succeeded in getting away. On the same day the advance guard pursued and killed an Indian. On the 31st the command returned to Fort Canby. Indian loss, one killed, two wounded.

August 27.—Two Navajo Indian prisoners attempted to escape from the guard-house at Fort Defiance; one was killed by the guard and the other mortally wounded.

August 31.—Lieutenant Colonel Chaves, commanding Fort Wingate, reports that a large party of Navajoes attacked the escort to the wood wagons about five miles from the post, wounding Private Luciano Pais and driving off twelve mules. The Indians were pursued, but not overtaken. Our loss, one man wounded; twelve mules taken.

August 23.—Captain R. Chacon, 1st cavalry New Mexico volunteers, left Fort Wingate with forty enlisted men on a scout after Indians. On the 27th, when near the salt lakes, the party espied a band of Navajoes, and succeeded in killing two and capturing eight. On the same day one of the Indians in attempting to escape was killed by the soldier who had him in charge. On the 28th the party attacked 150 Indians, who fled in all directions; the party here captured seven children, and recovered a captive Mexican boy, named Agapeto Apodaca; killed three Indians, and captured fifteen hundred head of sheep and goats, seventeen head of horses, mules, burros and colts. On this scout there were six Indians killed, fourteen captured, one Mexican boy rescued; fifteen hundred head of sheep, seventeen horses, mules, burros, and colts captured.

August 27.—Captain T. T. Tidball, 5th infantry California volunteers, commanding Fort Bowie, reports that the Apache Indians ran off six horses and one mule from that post.

September 8.—Captain Joseph P. Hargrave, 1st infantry California volunteers, reports that he left Fort Wingate on the 22d of August, on an expedition against the Navajoes. On the 26th August saw forty Indians on the Little Colorado; charged on them, but they fled before the troops got within gunshot of them. At this place captured five hundred head of sheep. On the 30th August the mules belonging to command (number unknown) were driven off by the Indians. A party of mounted men were sent in pursuit, but failed to overtake them.

September 5.—M. Steck, superintendent of Indian affairs, reports that a party of Utahs have killed nine Navajoes and captured forty children, and that the Pueblo Indians have killed a Navajo warrior, and that the governor of Jemez had killed one Navajo. Indian loss, 11 killed, 40 captured.

September 5.—Captain J. H. Whitlock, 5th infantry California volunteers, reports that he found an Indian camp, surprised it, and captured two mules, one Sharp's carbine, one United States blanket, and one thousand pounds of mescal; burned the camp, including all that pertained to it. On the 8th of September found Indians in force and had a spirited fight with them for fifteen minutes. One man and the guide severely wounded, and one horse killed. Indian loss unknown. Our loss, one soldier and one citizen wounded, and one horse killed.

September 8.—The Indians made an attack on Puertecito de las Salinas. Three Mexicans who went in pursuit of them were killed.

September 26.—Captain Henry A. Greene, the indefatigable, commanding Fort McRae, learning that a band of Indians with ten head of stock had crossed the Rio Grande near the Rio de los Alimosos, and that Corporal Argust with three men had gone in pursuit, immediately mounted eight men and started for the town of Alimosa; arriving at this point, eighteen mounted Mexicans joined his party. The whole party then travelled to Cañada Palomas crossing. At this point the stock was found, having been abandoned by the Indians

Corporal Argust, and Privates Daniel D. Tompkins, Alonzo C. Mullen, and William Lockhart, are highly praised by Captain Greene for their zeal and energy on this occasion.

September 27.—Lieutenant P. A. J. Russell, 1st infantry California volunteers, with four mounted men and a party of Pueblo Indians, started from Valles Grande on the trail of a band of Navajoes who had stolen a lot of stock from the Pueblos. The trail was followed into the town of Jemez, where the party recaptured one hundred and twenty-five head of sheep and two horses. Killed eight Navajoes and took twenty women and children prisoners.

September 28.—Baltasar Montaño, citizen, reports the result of a campaign against the Navajoes, as follows: Two Indians killed, five wounded, eleven or twelve animals captured. Two horses and one mule lost.

October 5.—Colonel Carson reports that on the 22d of September his command pursued a party of Indians, but, owing to the broken-down condition of his animals, they only succeeded in capturing one. On the 2d day of October discovered a small Indian village which had just been abandoned; this was destroyed, nineteen animals captured, seven of which got away. Three men left camp to hunt up the animals which had escaped; they did not return until after the command had returned to Fort Canby; they state that they were attacked by a party of Indians when within five miles of the post, one of whom they killed. One of the men, named Artin, was severely wounded and the Indians captured his mule. On the 3d day of October Lieutenant Postle discovered an Indian, pursued him and wounded him in three places; the lieutenant was slightly wounded by the Indian. Indian loss, one killed, one wounded, and one captured, twelve animals captured. Our loss, one officer and one private wounded and one mule lost.

October 5.—Ramon Luna, agent for the Pueblo Indians, reports that the Pueblos in a recent campaign against the Navajoes killed twenty-two of them, captured fifty-one prisoners, one thousand two hundred sheep and forty mules; some of the mules had the U. S. brand.

October 6.—Major Edward B. Willis, 1st infantry California volunteers, left Fort Wingate on the 15th day of September on an expedition against the Indians, with forty men each of company H, 1st infantry California volunteers, and company F, 1st New Mexico volunteers. At the Cienega Amarilla the command captured one horse and one mule; at Jacob's Well found a few Indians and captured two of them. At this point found and destroyed several fields of pumpkins and watermelons. The command then returned to Fort Wingate. Major Willis in his report says: "I cannot speak in too high terms of the officers and men of this command; no men could be more anxious to do their duty or more cheerfully incur the hardships of a campaign; after a march of twenty-five or thirty miles, the whole command would cheerfully volunteer and march the whole night on the slightest prospect of doing any service." Two Indians, one horse, and one mule captured.

October 13.—Two wagons which had been sent about a mile from Fort Canby for wood, in charge of a non-commissioned officer and five men, were attacked by the Indians; the escort and teamsters ran at the first fire, leaving the wagons and teams in possession of the Indians; ten mules were lost, two mules and the wagons were left. One of the soldiers, in his hurry to escape, left his musket at the wagons; the Indians carried it off.

October 15.—The train of Miguel Romero, hay contractor, was attacked by Indians while on its way from hay camp to Fort Canby; the non-commissioned officer in charge of the escort was wounded and one teamster severely wounded. The Indians drove off five mules and one pony.

October 16.—Lieutenant Thomas Henderson, 1st cavalry New Mexico volunteers, reports that while *en route* from Fort Stanton to Santa Fé he met three Indians with a lot of mules, near the Buffalo spring. The Indians, on being discovered, abandoned nineteen mules and escaped.

October 18.—Lieutenant Dowlin, 1st cavalry New Mexico volunteers, reports that a party under his command killed two Indians near the Laguna Negra.

October 22.—Captain Rafael Chacon, with his company, pursued a band of Indians who had run off stock near Fort Wingate, and captured from them two mules and two horses.

October 25.—Lieutenant Charles H. Fitch, on an Indian scout, captured two horses and one mule.

October 21.—Lieutenant Nicholas Hodt, 1st New Mexico volunteers, with forty men, left Fort Canby, October 21, on a scout against the Indians. On the 22d saw a party of Indians who succeeded in escaping to the mountains; near Cañada Colorado the command captured one woman.

October 31.—Lieutenant E. Latimer, 1st cavalry California volunteers, left Fort Union with a detachment of nine men for Fort Sumner, having in charge twenty-one Indian prisoners. On the night of November 4, while encamped at the mouth of Gallina river, sixteen of the Indians succeeded in making their escape. They were pursued but not recaptured.

November 9.—A party of Mexicans passed through Fort Wingate on the 1st instant in pursuit of Indians. At the Sierra Negra the party had a fight with a band of Navajoes; killed five and took sixteen prisoners. About two leagues from Sierra the party had another fight with the Indians; killed two and took two prisoners. At the Sierra de Chusca had a skirmish with the Indians and captured twenty-four prisoners, twenty horses and mules, and twenty-five sheep and goats. At Carriso springs the party came upon a band of Indians numbering from two to three hundred, with several thousand head of stock; the captain of the party, being fearful of losing his prisoners, allowed this band to pass unmolested. Indian loss—killed, seven; prisoners, forty-two; twenty horses and mules and twenty-five sheep and goats captured.

November 4.—Captain A. L. Anderson reports that while in camp on the Gila river near the Pinal mountains, the Indians crept to within range of his picket line and discharged several volleys of arrows at the animals, sentinels, and the men sleeping near. Four horses were so badly wounded that it became necessary to kill them. A squad of men was left concealed in the camp, and after the column had marched they succeeded in killing one of a party of Indians who approached them. Indian loss, one killed; our loss, four horses killed.

November 5.—Captain Henry A. Greene, commanding Fort McRae, reports that a band of Indians crossed the Rio Grande near the Rio Plumas, with several hundred sheep, on the 4th of November. As soon as the information was received at Fort McRae, Captain Greene mounted seven men and started for the point it was reported the Indians had crossed; arriving there he found that the men at the Vidette station had already started in pursuit. Captain Greene took up the trail, and on the 5th instant overtook the men from the station. After travelling with them one hundred and fifty miles, Captain Greene returned to Fort McRae, leaving Sergeant Rhodes and Corporal Argust to follow the trail On the 12th November Sergeant Rhodes returned and reported that he overtook the Indians about two hundred and twenty-five miles from the Rio Grande, and after a sharp skirmish routed them and recovered one hundred and seventy sheep. Private Atkinson was wounded by an arrow in this affair. The sergeant and the men who were with him are highly commended by Captain Greene. Indian loss, one killed and four wounded. Captain Greene states that the Indians could not have crossed the river with the sheep, within two miles of Lieutenant Whittemore's camp, had that officer used proper vigilance. Our loss, one private wounded.

November 5.—Lieutenant Nicholas Hodt, 1st cavalry New Mexico volunteers, left Fort Canby October 27 on a scout after Indians. Result of this scout, four government mules worn out and shot.

November —.—E. Montoya, Brigadier General New Mexico militia, reports that Captain Tafolla overtook a party of Indians near the Sierra del Datil and took from them twenty-six head of cattle, four burros, and three horses.

November —.—E. Montoya reports that his party attacked a band of Indians at the "Three Brothers," and recovered forty-two head of cattle—no Indians killed.

November 15.—Colonel Carson with his command left Fort Canby for the country west of the Oribi villages, for the purpose of chastising the Navajo Indians inhabiting that region. On the 16th a detachment, under Sergeant Andres Herrera, overtook a small party of Inans, two of whom were killed and two wounded; fifty sheep and one horse were captured; Colonel Carson speaks in high terms of the zeal and energy displayed by Sergeant Herrera.

On the 25th the command captured one boy and seven horses and destroyed an encampment; on the same day captured one woman and one child, and about five hundred head of sheep and goats, seventy horses, and destroyed an Indian village. On the 3d of December surprised an Indian encampment, capturing one horse and four oxen. The Indians escaped. Indian loss, two killed, two wounded, three captured; 550 sheep and goats, nine horses, and four oxen captured.

November 27.—Roman A. Baca reports that he left Ceboileta with a party of one hundred and sixteen mounted Mexicans and travelled in a northwesterly direction for six days; when about fifty miles from Chusca, on the sixth day out, the party encountered about two hundred Indians; killed six, and took three prisoners, who are now in the custody of Lieutenant Stevens; the party also captured three Indian ponies.

November 30.—L. M. Baca, judge of probate, reports that on the night of the 27th November, three miles from La Joya, the people at that place captured from sixty-one Navajoes 1,907 head of sheep.

November 30.—Lieutenant J. Laughlin, while *en route* from Fort Wingate to Los Pinos, on the night of November 30 surprised a party of six or seven Indians at the Rio Puerco; the Indians fled, leaving seventy head of cattle, which were taken to Los Pinos and turned over to the owner.

On the 4th of November ten head of cattle belonging to the command at Valles Grande were driven off by the Indians.

On the 9th day of November José Ignacio Valencia, in charge of a herd of sheep, had a fight with the Indians at Cañoncitas of the Conchas. One Indian was killed.

December 1.—Captain Henry A. Greene, 1st infantry California volunteers, receiving information that a band of Indians had crossed the Jornada with two hundred sheep, took seven men of his company and started on their trail. The party overtook the sheep on the summit of the Sierra Caballo, on the east side of the Rio Grande. The sheep were taken to Fort McRae.

December 16.—Major Henry D. Wallen, United States 7th infantry, commanding Fort Sumner, reports that on the morning of the 16th instant Mr. Labadie and Rev. Mr. Fialon reported to him that a large number of Indians with an immense herd of sheep were at the Carretas; the officers and men of company D, 5th, and company C, 7th infantry, were awakened and prepared to take the field with two days' rations; a lieutenant with eight mounted men of company B, 2d cavalry California volunteers, was also got in readiness; Mr. Labadie, Mr. Fialon, and thirty Apache Indians also started in pursuit. The party left the post at 5½ a m. for the Carretas; the mounted men and Indian agent, with the Indians, outstripped the party on foot and took up the Navajo trail on the west bank of the Pecos river. At thirty-five miles northwest from Fort Sumner they overtook the Navajoes, in number about one hundred and thirty, ten mounted, and twenty armed with rifles. A severe contest ensued, in which the Navajoes lost twelve killed and left on the field, and a number killed and wounded who were carried off; one prisoner taken, all the sheep recovered, amounting to five thousand two hundred and fifty-nine, thirteen burros, four rifles, one horse, their provisions, blankets, one hundred and fifty pairs of moccasins, and nearly all the effects taken from Mr. Labadie's train.

Major Wallen calls the attention of the general commanding to the gallant conduct of Mr. Labadie, Privates Loser and Osier of company B, 2d cavalry California volunteers, Ojo Blanco and Cadetta, the chiefs of Apaches, Alazan, an Apache, who was badly wounded, and the Apaches generally, who rendered signal service. Lieutenant Newbold with three men pursued the flying Navajoes three miles beyond the scene of action, but owing to the exhausted condition of his animals was obliged to desist from further pursuit.

The Navajoes, just before reaching the Pecos, were alarmed by some pistol shots discharged from a wagon train, and abandoned four thousand six hundred and thirty sheep, which were secured by the Mexicans attached to the train. Lieutenant McDermott with ten mounted men and six Apaches were sent to collect the herd and bring it to the post. Before reaching the camp, Alazan, the Apache named above, died.

December 16.—Thirty-five Navajo Indians were sent to Fort Sumner this day; this party gave themselves up at Fort Wingate as prisoners of war.

December 20.—First Lieutenant D Montoya, 1st cavalry New Mexico volunteers, in accordance with instructions received from Colonel Carson, left Fort Canby in pursuit of a party of Navajo Indians. On the second day out marched through a heavy snow-storm. On the third day came upon an Indian encampment, attacked it, and succeeded in killing one Indian and capturing thirteen women and children, besides a lot of Navajo blankets, moccasins, &c.

Near the Pueblo Colorado the command pursued two Indians, (man and woman,) and wounded the Indian and captured the woman.

Lieutenant Montoya recommends to the notice of the colonel commanding the good conduct and soldierly bearing of First Lieutenant C. M. Hubbell, and First Sergeant Antonio Mora, of company C 1st cavalry New Mexico volunteers, who were severely wounded in the last affair. Corporal Marcos, of company C, was particularly conspicuous on this scout; he was also wounded. Sergeant José Ortiz was also very active in pursuing and engaging the Indians.

December 7.—Lieutenant Benjamin F. Stevens reports that he saw three Mexicans near Cebolleta, having three Indian captives in their possession; the whole party were taken prisoners by him. The Mexicans soon after made their escape. The captives were sent to Fort Sumner.

December 22.—Captain John Thompson, 1st cavalry New Mexico volunteers, left Fort Canby with one hundred men on a scout after Indians. On the 26th, at Mesa la Baca, sent out Sergeant Romero with thirty men, who came upon a party of Indians; killed one, and captured twelve. On the same day a party under Sergeant Dorsette discovered two Indians; wounded one, and captured the other. Indian loss, one killed, thirteen captives, and one wounded.

On the 6th of December the Navajoes ran off some cows from the Pueblo Santa Ana; the Indians of the Pueblo went in pursuit, recovered their stock, and killed two Navajoes.

On the 11th of December José Ma. Martin with a party of Mexicans went in pursuit of Navajoes who had been stealing stock; the stock was recovered and two Indians killed.

On the 28th December the people of San Miguel and Pueblo overtook and surprised a party of Indians, and recovered a lot of cattle, and took the arms of the Indians.

The zeal and energy shown by the officers and soldiers, and the fortitude with which they have encountered hunger, thirst, fatigue and exposure, in their pursuit of hostile Indians within this department during the past year, are deserving of the highest admiration. Not less is this due to those parties who were so unfortunate as not to overtake the Indians than to those who came up with them. All toiled and suffered alike. The gallantry which every one has shown when there was an opportunity to close with the enemy, proves that that virtue among the troops in New Mexico is common to all.

The alacrity with which citizens of New Mexico have taken the field to pursue and encounter the Indians is worthy of all praise. Many of them have been conspicuous for their courage, and *all* have shown a settled determination to assist the military in their efforts to rid the country of the fierce and brutal robbers and murderers who for nearly two centuries have brought poverty to its inhabitants, and mourning and desolation to nearly every hearth throughout the Territory.

The department commander congratulates the troops and the people on the auspicious opening of the year 1864. For one hundred and eighty years the Navajo Indians have ravaged New Mexico, but it is confidently expected that the year 1864 will witness the end of hostilities with that tribe. Then New Mexico will take a stride towards that great prosperity which has lain within her grasp, but which hitherto she has not been permitted to enjoy.

By command of Brigadier General Carleton:

BEN. C. CUTLER,
Assistant Adjutant General.

Recapitulation.

Month.	TAKEN FROM INDIANS.					TAKEN BY INDIANS.					CITIZENS.		INDIANS.			COMM'D OFFI'RS.		ENLIS'D MEN.	
	Sheep.	Horses.	Mules.	Cattle.	Burros.	Sheep.	Horses.	Mules.	Cattle.	Burros.	Killed.	Wounded.	Killed.	Wounded.	Captured.	Killed.	Wounded.	Killed.	Wounded.
1863.																			
January															248			1	
Do															100				
Do													20	15				1	1
Do													1						
Do			34										9						
Do		3											11	1					
February						4,000													
Do	2,000					2,000							3						
Do...25						6,000													
March									310										
Do															15				
Do	2,300					2,300													
Do											7		28				1	1	
April									70		1		3						1
May											2								
Do									12										
Do		7											1						
Do							6												
Do		3											11						
Do				60							1		50	50	10				
June								2								1			
Do																		1	
Do							7	2			2	2					1	2	1
Do																		2	
July																			1
Do			104					104					4				1		2
Do		4											10						2
Do								19					4						4
Do								10					6					1	
Do							1						2			1		1	
Do		2	6																
Do								12							9			1	1
August													9						
Do		22											2						
Do				3		10,000							33		66			2	1
Do	2,000	30											3	1	15	1			
Do	100	20	2																
Do	1,800																		
Do			18																
Do							1	26					1	3				1	
Do								7					1	2					
Do													1	1					1
Do								12											
Do	1,500	17											6		14				
Do							6	1											
September	500																		
Do													11		40				
Do																			1
Do												1							
Do				10							3								
Do	125	2											8		20				
Do													2	5					1
October													1	1	1		1		
Do	1,200		40										22		51				
Do		1	1												2				
Do								10											1
Do		1	5																
Do...16			19									1							
Do													2						
Do		2	2																
Do		2	1																
Do						89													
Do															1				
November	25	20											7		42				
Do													1						1
Do	170												1	4					
Do		3		26	4														
Do				42															
Do	550	9		4									2	2	3				
Do		3											6		3				
Do	1,907																		
Do				70															

Recapitulation—Continued.

Month.	TAKEN FROM INDIANS.					TAKEN BY INDIANS.					CITIZENS.		INDIANS.			COMM'D OFFI'RS.		ENLIS'D MEN.	
	Sheep.	Horses.	Mules.	Cattle.	Burros.	Sheep.	Horses.	Mules.	Cattle.	Burros.	Killed.	Wounded.	Killed.	Wounded.	Captured.	Killed.	Wounded.	Killed.	Wounded.
1863.																			
November	......	....	....	....	....	......	....	....	10	....	....	....	....	....	....	....	....	....	....
Do	......	....	....	....	....	......	....	....	....	....	....	....	....	....	....	....	....	....	....
December	200	....	....	....	....	......	....	....	....	....	....	....	1	....	....	....	....	....	....
Do	......	....	....	....	....	......	....	....	....	....	....	....	....	....	....	....	....	....	....
Do	9, 889	1	....	....	13	......	....	....	....	....	....	....	2	....	....	....	....	....	....
Do	......	....	....	....	....	......	....	....	....	....	....	....	12	....	1	....	....	....	....
Do	......	....	....	....	....	......	....	....	....	....	....	....	2	....	....	....	....	....	....
Do	......	....	....	....	....	......	....	....	....	....	....	....	....	....	35	....	....	....	....
Do	......	....	....	....	....	......	....	....	....	....	....	....	1	1	13	....	....	....	....
	......	....	....	....	....	......	....	....	....	....	....	....	1	1	14	....	....	....	2
	24, 266	152	232	215	17	24, 389	21	205	402	....	16	4	301	87	703	3	4	14	21

Official :

CYRUS H. DE FORREST, *Aide-de-Camp*.

[General Orders No. 8.]

HEADQUARTERS DEPARTMENT OF NEW MEXICO,
Santa Fé, N. M., March 25, 1864.

I. It is announced to the troops in this department, that by the active efforts of the officers of the general staff, a sufficient quantity of food for some seven thousand captive Indians has been secured to last until supplies come from the States, or the crops of the present year shall ripen and come into market. About six thousand Indians have already been captured, or have voluntarily given themselves up, and are at or on their way to the reservation at Fort Sumner, on the Pecos river, where we must feed them until they can raise food enough to support themselves. This they will, in a great measure, be able to do the coming summer; next year, without a doubt, they will produce as much as they can consume. It is believed that when the last Navajo Indian has surrendered, or been captured, the number to be fed of this tribe will not exceed seven thousand. Anxiety with regard to our ability to get this food was the reason why, a short time since, the troops were placed upon half-rations, until the result of efforts to this end should become known. An account of subsistence stores on hand exhibits the gratifying fact that we can not only feed the Indians, but that the troops can resume the drawing of their full rations, except of the articles of coffee and candles; of these, two-thirds rations will be issued until further orders.

II. Hereafter, on the last day of each month, the commander of every military post and camp within the department will send direct to department headquarters an exact account of all subsistence stores on hand, and a list of all troops, employés, laundresses, and servants, who receive rations by issue, purchase, or otherwise, at his post, with an exhibit placed against each article of stores showing how many days it will last.

III. Officers will be permitted to purchase a reasonable quantity of stores for the use of themselves and their families, and their authorized servants. This authority has heretofore been grossly abused in several instances, which have been brought to the notice of the commanding general. Commanders of posts will promptly arrest and file charges against any officer who purchases more than this reasonable allowance of subsistence stores, or who, if he have no family, procures such stores for the subsistence of others besides himself and authorized servants.

IV. Commanding officers at stations distant from the source of supply will exercise great forecast, to the end that requisitions are sent for stores in time, and will carefully watch over and husband their provisions, and if there is danger of running short before others can be received, to diminish the amount to be issued to their command at such a seasonable date as to prevent any serious privation or want.

V. Hereafter, to save time and provide against accidents, commanders of posts will send all estimates for supplies or funds direct to the proper staff officers at department headquarters. At the same time duplicates of such estimates will be forwarded to the district commander, who, before he transmits them, will make such comments upon them as he may deem necessary for a full understanding of the matter as regarded from his point of view.

By command of Brigadier General Carleton:

ERASTUS W. WOOD, *Aide-de-Camp.*

[General Orders No. 4.]

HEADQUARTERS DEPARTMENT OF NEW MEXICO,
Santa Fé, N. M., February 18, 1865.

I. The following record of combats with Indians on the part of the troops, as well as on that of citizens of New Mexico and Arizona, during the year 1864, is published for the information of all concerned. Only those operations are mentioned which were attended with results either in our favor or against us, and they are about as one to four, so that the account which follows shows but a faint idea of the work performed. It is possible that there may have been some robberies, which are not mentioned here; but if so, no authentic report of them has been received.

II. The number of Indians on the reservation at the Bosque Redondo, as shown by General Orders No. 3, series for 1864, from these headquarters, was seven hundred and three Apaches and Navajoes on the 31st day of December of that year.

January —.—Major Sena, 1st cavalry New Mexico volunteers, with his command, arrived at Fort Canby, bringing in three hundred and forty-four Navajo prisoners.

January 3.—Wagonmaster Russell's train *en route* to Fort Canby, New Mexico, was attacked near the Puerco by about one hundred and fifty Navajo Indians. Mr. Russell was killed; Mr. Strong and two teamsters wounded. The three lead wagons were cut off and twenty mules were taken by the Indians, together with some corn, blankets, &c. This information was forwarded to the commanding general of the department by Major John C. McFerran, chief quartermaster, with the following remarks: "Respectfully referred to the department commander for his information. This Wagonmaster Russell is Powell Russell, who entered the service of the Quartermaster's department as a teamster, a poor, illiterate boy, in 1853. By his honesty, industry, modesty, truth, and energy, he rose to be the principal or head wagonmaster in the department. This position he has filled to the perfect satisfaction of every one, and has now fallen like a true man, as he was, at his post and doing his duty. It will be very, very difficult to replace him."

January 5.—Major Edward B. Willis, 1st infantry California volunteers, commanding Fort Whipple, Arizona, reports that the Penal Apaches ran off eleven head of government cattle at Walker's mines. A party under Captain Hargrave was sent in pursuit, but failed to overtake the Indians.

January 6—Captain Julius C. Shaw, 1st cavalry New Mexico volunteers, commanding Fort Wingate, reports that four Navajo Indians surrendered themselves at that post.

January 6.—Major Henry D. Wallen, United States 7th infantry, commanding Fort Sumner, New Mexico, reports that on the morning of the 5th instant the Navajoes ran off the Apache herd from that post. Lieutenant Newbold, 5th United States infantry, with ten mounted men of the 2d cavalry California volunteers and 5th United States infantry, were sent in pursuit, accompanied by Mr Labadie, Indian agent, Mr. Carillo, Mr. Whittemore, and twenty-five Apaches from the reservation. Captain Calloway and his company I, first infantry California volunteers, was directed to follow the trail of the mounted party. Lieutenant Newbold encountered over one hundred Navajoes, mounted and on foot, about twelve miles from the post. A sharp fight ensued, in which nine Navajoes were left dead on the field. The Navajoes then broke into two parties and fled, and a running fight was kept up for about ten miles. Part of the force pursued one party to the Pecos river. Of this party only eight escaped. Of the other party of Indians only seventeen escaped, and some of these were wounded. Forty Indians are reported to have been left dead on the field, and at least twenty-five wounded. It is believed that nearly all the Navajoes would have been killed had it not been for the extremely cold weather. The mercury was ten degrees below zero. The men could with difficulty cap their pieces, their fingers being so numb. Some were frost-bitten. About fifty head of horses and mules were recovered in this fight, all belonging to the Apaches. Major Wallen calls the attention of the general commanding to the handsome manner in which Lieutenant Newbold managed this successful engagement, also to the meritorious conduct of the soldiers, citizens, and Apaches engaged.

January 8.—Mr. George Cooler, wagon and forage master at Fort Craig, New Mexico, with ten infantry soldiers and a party of Mexican citizens, while on a scout after Indians, recovered one Mexican boy named Vincente Urbano, who was stolen by the Indians near the Pecos river, one rifle, and fifty-eight goats. On the 11th instant came upon a party of Indians and succeeded in killing one and capturing one squaw and one child. In this skirmish two of Cooler's party were wounded; one of them, José Garcia, died the next day. On the 12th found seven horses and one mule, and captured two Indian women.

January 12.—Captain Julius C. Shaw, 1st cavalry New Mexico volunteers, commanding Fort Wingate, reports that Lieutenant José M. Sanchez, with a detachment of company F, 1st cavalry New Mexico volunteers, attacked a party of Indians near the Datil mountains, and killed three men, captured two women and one boy and eighteen Navajo horses and sixty-two head of sheep and goats. The chief, Sordo, was killed in this fight. Captain Shaw also reports that sixty Navajoes have given themselves up at that post since the 1st instant.

January 14.—Sergeant Joseph Felmer, 1st cavalry California volunteers, reports that he recovered seven head of cattle while in pursuit of a party of Indians and turned them over to Don Pablo, of La Joya, New Mexico.

January 15.—Serafin Ramirez, a citizen of New Mexico, reports that the Navajo Indians drove off twelve head of cattle and two mules belonging to him, between the 25th of December and 9th of January, and during the same time they killed three of his cattle.

January 21.—Captain Julius C. Shaw, commanding Fort Wingate, New Mexico, reports that twenty-three Navajo Indians have surrendered at that post since his last report.

January —.—On the 6th instant, Colonel Christopher Carson, commanding the Navajo expedition, left Fort Canby, New Mexico, with fourteen commissioned officers and three hundred and seventy-five enlisted men, on an expedition to the Cañon de Chelly. On the 8th instant one warrior was killed by the colonel's escort. On the 12th Sergeant Andres Herrera, with fifty men, who was sent out the previous night, returned bringing into camp two women and two children prisoners and one hundred and thirty head of sheep and goats, and reported that his command had killed eleven and wounded five Indians. On the 14th instant Captain Pfeiffer and party, who had been sent out from Fort Canby some days previous to operate in the east opening of the cañon, came into camp and reported having passed through the cañon without a single casualty in his command. He killed three Indians and brought in nineteen prisoners, women and children. On the 15th instant sixty Indians arrived in camp and surrendered themselves as prisoners. On the same day a party under command of Captain Joseph Berney killed two Indians and captured four. One hundred and ten Indians surrendered to Captain Carey's command while upon its return march to Fort Canby. Result of this expedition: Indians killed, twenty-three; wounded, five; prisoners, thirty-four; voluntarily surrendered, two hundred; and two hundred head of sheep and goats captured.

January 24.—A party of thirty Americans and fourteen Maricopa and Pimo Indians under Colonel King S. Woolsey, aid to the governor of Arizona, attacked a band of Gila Apaches sixty or seventy miles northeast of the Pimo villages, and killed nineteen of them and wounded others. Mr. Cyrus Lennon, of Woolsey's party, was killed by a wounded Indian.

January 26.—Lieutenant Thomas A. Young, 5th infantry California volunteers, with one sergeant and eleven privates of the California volunteers, started from Fort Craig, New Mexico, on a scout after Indians. On the 28th instant the party was attacked by about sixty Indians, who wounded Lieutenant Young, Sergeant Thomas Richards, and Privates Harvey McConkey, Thomas Clark, and Louis Mann, of company D, first cavalry California volunteers. In this affair seven Indians were killed. The party, not being strong enough to continue the fight, returned to Fort Craig on the 30th instant.

January —.—The militia of Socorro county, New Mexico, under General Stanislaus Montoya, on a scout near Sierra Datil, killed twenty Indians and took twenty prisoners.

February 2.—Major E. W. Eaton, commanding Fort Wingate, sent two hundred Indians from that post to Los Pinos, *en route* to the Bosque Redondo. The chief, Delgadito, arrived at Fort Wingate this day with six hundred and eighty Indians.

February 14.—Captain A. B. Carey, United States army, commanding Fort Canby, New Mexico, reports the arrival at that post of Soldado Serdo, with his herd; also, that there are one thousand prisoners now at that post.

February 14.—Captain Joseph Berney, 1st cavalry New Mexico volunteers, arrived at Los Pinos this day, bringing in one hundred and seventy-five Navajo prisoners.

February 24.—Captain A. B. Carey, commanding the Navajo expedition, reports that he has forwarded one hundred and seventy-five Navajoes to the Bosque Redondo since last report, and that there are now fifteen hundred Navajoes at Fort Canby awaiting transportation.

February 24.—Lieutenant Martin Mullins, United States army, commanding at Los Pinos, New Mexico, reports that to present date two thousand and nineteen Navajoes have arrived at that post *en route* to Fort Sumner, and that there are fourteen hundred and forty-five now at that post awaiting transportation.

February 24.—Captain James H. Whitlock, with twenty-one men of his company F, 5th infantry California volunteers, left camp on the Mimbres, New Mexico, on the 24th day of February, on a scout after Apache Indians. At about 5 o'clock p. m. on the 25th he came up to a party of nineteen Indians, attacked and killed thirteen of them and wounded the others, and captured one Indian pony. The command returned to camp on the 29th, without the slightest accident of any kind.

February 25.—Three Indian women escaped from the detachment commanded by Lieutenant W. B. Smith, 1st infantry California volunteers, while *en route* from Fort Union to the Bosque Redondo.

February 28.—Captain A. B. Carey reports that there are two thousand five hundred Navajoes at Fort Canby awaiting transportation to the Bosque Redondo.

March 4.—Two thousand one hundred and thirty-eight Navajoes were this day forwarded from Fort Canby to the Bosque Redondo, having in their possession four hundred and seventy-three horses and three thousand sheep. One hundred and twenty-six Indians died at Fort Canby between the 20th of February and March 4.

March 7.—Lieutenant Hodt, 1st cavalry New Mexico volunteers, with twenty-five enlisted men, left Fort Canby on a scout in search of Indians who had stolen eighteen horses and mules from Caballo Prieto, chief, who had surrendered. The thieves, four in number, were captured near Zuñi, and eleven head of the stock recovered.

March 8.—Captain Quirino Maes, from Conejos, Colorado Territory, with an independent company of sixty-seven men, arrived at Pueblo, Colorado. This company had been operating against the Navajoes since the 1st of January, 1864, and had killed twenty-six Indians and captured four. Five horses were taken from the Indians.

March 14.—Captain Joseph Berney arrived at Fort Sumner with fourteen hundred and thirty Navajo prisoners. Ten Indians died on the road from Los Pinos.

March 18.—Eight mounted Indians made an attack upon a government herd at Cow springs, New Mexico, and drove off sixty-eight mules, four government and two private horses. The Indians were pursued by Lieutenant H. H. Stevens, 5th California infantry, with nine men, for a considerable distance, but they escaped with the stock.

March 18.—Major Edward B. Willis, 1st infantry California volunteers, with forty enlisted men and fourteen citizens, fell in with a party of Apaches near the San Francisco river, Arizona, killed five Indians and lost one man, Private Fisher, of company D, first cavalry California volunteers.

March 27.—Fifty-five Navajoes surrendered at Fort Canby, New Mexico, eight of whom died. They had sixty-two head of sheep and goats.

March 29.—Eighty-six Navajoes arrived at Los Pinos, New Mexico, *en route* to Fort Sumner, having with them six horses and two mules.

March —.—The Apache Indians attacked Mr. Goodhue and four other persons, between the Hasiampa and Granite creek. Goodhue was killed. The men with him succeeded in driving the Indians off. The Indians also attacked a train of wagons near Weaver, Arizona, and mortally wounded a Mr. Rykman and a Mexican; another of the party was slightly wounded. The Indians took all the stock, and plundered the wagons.

April 3.—Eighty-six Navajoes surrendered at Fort Canby, two of whom died These Indians have one hundred and twenty sheep and goats, and six horses.

April 5.—Captain Francis McCabe, 1st cavalry New Mexico volunteers, arrived at Los Pinos, New Mexico, bringing seven hundred and twenty Navajo Indians.

April 7.—Captain James H. Whitlock, 5th infantry California volunteers, with a command consisting of twenty-six enlisted men of company F and twenty enlisted men of company I, under Lieutenant Burkett, and ten enlisted men of company C, first cavalry California volunteers, attacked about two hundred and fifty Indians near Mount Grey, or Sierra Bonita, Arizona, and after a spirited fight of over one hour routed the Indians, killing twenty-one of them left on the ground and wounding a large number. Forty-five head of horses and mules were captured from the Indians, and all their provisions and camp equipage destroyed.

April 10.—Seventy-eight Navajoes surrendered at Fort Canby, having in their possession one horse and one hundred and fifty head of sheep and goats.

April 11.—Major Edward B. Willis, commanding Fort Whipple, Arizona, reports that Colonel King S. Woolsey, with his party, surprised an Indian rancheria, killing fourteen Indians, who were left on the ground, and wounding others who escaped. A small party of California volunteers, who were sent with Colonel Woolsey, behaved well—Privates Beach and Holman, of company F, killing five of the Indians.

April —.—Lieutenant Martin Quintana, 1st cavalry New Mexico volunteers, reports that while *en route* from Moqui to Fort Canby four Indians delivered themselves up to his command.

April 24.—One hundred and nine Navajoes surrendered themselves at Fort Canby between April 18 and April 24. These Indians had one hundred and fifty-nine head of horses and two hundred and thirty head of sheep and goats.

May 1.—Three hundred and ninety-two Navajoes surrendered themselves at Fort Canby since last report, making the total number on hand at that post six hundred and twenty-three. They have, altogether, three hundred and twenty head of horses and six hundred and fifty head of sheep.

May 1.—Forty-two Mescalero Apaches, including Ojo Blanco, escaped from the Indian reservation at Fort Sumner, and returned to their own country.*

May 3.—Lieutenant Henry H. Stevens, 5th infantry California volunteers, with a command of fifty-four men, California volunteers, while on the march from Fort Cummings to Fort Bowie, Arizona, was attacked in Doubtful Cañon, near Steen's peak, by about one hundred Apache Indians. The fight lasted for nearly two hours, and resulted in the killing of ten Apaches, who were left on the ground, and wounding about twenty. The troops lost in this affair one man missing and five wounded—one mortally; one horse killed and one wounded.

May 9.—Captain Charles P. Marion reports that while on a scout near Zuñi, five hundred Navajoes surrendered themselves to his command. These Indians had in their possession one thousand horses and over five thousand sheep and goats.

May 11.—The Apache Indians ran off two horses from the ranch of Mr. Stipich, a farmer on the Rio Bonito. They were pursued by Second Lieutenant S. L. Snyder and thirteen men of company A, first cavalry New Mexico volunteers, but were not overtaken.

May 13.—Seven hundred and seventy-seven Navajo Indians arrived at Fort Sumner this day.

May 25.—Lieutenant Colonel Nelson H. Davis, assistant inspector general United States army, with Captain T. T. Tidball, fifth infantry California volunteers, two commissioned officers and one hundred and two enlisted men, cavalry and infantry, started from Fort Bowie on a scout after Indians. On the 25th instant surprised a rancheria, and killed one Indian; later the same day, killed one Indian and captured one.

May 26.—On the 26th instant came upon a rancheria, killed one Indian and destroyed several acres of corn. In this skirmish First Sergeant Christian Foster, of company K, fifth infantry California volunteers, was severely wounded. On the same day, one woman and two children were captured. On the 28th, captured five women and two children.

May 29.—On the 29th instant the command surprised a rancheria, and killed thirty-six, wounded four, and took two prisoners; captured six hundred and sixty dollars in gold coin, one Sharp's carbine, one Colt's revolver, one shot-gun, one saddle, one thousand pounds of mescal, and a lot of horse equipments, powder, powder-horns, &c. Sergeant Charles Brown, of company K, fifth infantry California volunteers, is mentioned in Captain Tidball's report for his zeal and energy in this scout.

May 29.—Captain George A. Burkett, with thirty-three enlisted men of company I, 5th infantry California volunteers, surprised an Indian rancheria on the Rio de Mescal, and killed thirteen, wounded thirteen, and took three prisoners; captured one mule, three horses, one Sharp's carbine, one saddle and saddle-bags, one ton of mescal, and a small quantity of powder. The command destroyed some fields of corn and wheat. A portion of the mescal was kept to feed the prisoners; the balance was destroyed.

June 3.—Five hundred and fifty Navajoes arrived at Los Pinos this day, who had one hundred and ninety horses and two hundred and ninety-four sheep and goats. These Indians, with two hundred others, were forwarded to Fort Sumner.

June 3.—The Apache Indians attacked a party of five miners near Fort Whipple, Arizona, and wounded every man of the party.

June 7.—Captain Julius C. Shaw, 1st cavalry New Mexico volunteers, with his command, attacked a rancheria near Apache spring. Two Indians were mortally wounded.

June 11.—Four Apaches attacked a party of soldiers under Captain T. T. Tidball, near San Pedro crossing, but did not succeed in doing any damage. The troops wounded one of the Indians.

June 20.—Major Edward B. Willis, 1st infantry California volunteers, reports that a detachment under his command attacked a party of Apache Indians near Salinas river, Arizona, and killed four of them.

June 20.—The express escort between Camp Goodwin and Fort Bowie was attacked by a party of Indians, while crossing the Chiricahui mountains. The Indians were whipped off by the escort. Several Indians reported wounded. Four burros were taken from the Indians.

---

* This party voluntarily returned to the reservation on the 16th of September. Shortly afterward Ojo Blanco died.

June.—Captain Henry M. Benson, 1st infantry California volunteers, left Fort Whipple, Arizona Territory, with his company F, first California infantry, on a scout after Indians. Five Indians were killed and two wounded by this command, and large quantities of corn and beans destroyed.

June —.—Captain Albert H. Pfeiffer, 1st cavalry New Mexico volunteers, with one lieutenant and sixty-four enlisted men, attacked a band of Indians near the Colorado Chiquito, Arizona, and in a running fight of eight miles killed five and wounded seven of them. After the fight was over two Indians came into camp with signs of peace, but in a moment fired their guns, severely wounding Captain Pfeiffer and Private Pedro Rael. The Indians were instantly killed. When the shots were fired, a large party of Indians came running towards the camp. A volley was fired into them, when they scattered in all directions. This volley wounded several.

June 28.—Captain James H. Whitlock, commanding Camp Miembres, reports that he left the post on the 21st instant on a scout after Indians. On the 22d came upon a party of three Indians, two of whom were killed and the other captured.

July 10.—Lieutenant Antonio Abeyta, 1st cavalry New Mexico volunteers, while *en route* from Fort Wingate to Los Pinos, New Mexico, with twenty-six Navajo and seven Apache Indian prisoners, came upon a party of Navajoes at Fish spring, numbering three hundred and seventy-five, coming in to surrender themselves and go to the reservation. These Indians had in their possession three hundred horses, sixteen mules, one thousand and eighty-five sheep, and three hundred and fifty goats. This party was turned over to the commanding officer at Los Pinos.

July —.—Captain Saturnino Baca, 1st cavalry New Mexico volunteers, with fifty-three enlisted men, left Fort Canby on the 9th instant, on a scout after Indians. Marched to the Little Colorado river. He returned to Fort Canby on the 21st instant. On this scout six Indians were killed and six taken prisoners, two horses and two mules captured, and large quantities of corn, wheat, beans, &c., destroyed.

August 1.—Captain T. T. Tidball, 5th infantry California volunteers, returned from a scout of twenty-three days. He reports that he saw but few Indians, and killed but one—an Apache chief called "Old Plume."

August 1.—Four Mexican citizens are reported as having been killed by the Apache Indians at the Conchas.

August 1.—Twelve hundred and nine Navajoes and twelve Apaches left Los Pinos, New Mexico, for the Bosque Redondo. These Indians had in their possession three hundred and fifty-seven horses, nineteen mules, and two thousand and five sheep and goats.

August 3.—A band of Apache Indians, having captives, sheep, horses, burros and cattle, were discovered near Alamo Gordo by Delgadito Chiquito, Navajo chief, who sent a messenger to Fort Sumner to inform the commanding officer of the fact. Thirty-five men of the California cavalry were sent in pursuit, also a strong party of Navajoes from the reservation. In the mean time Delgadito's party attacked the Apaches and were defeated with a loss of one killed and three wounded, among the latter Delgadito himself. The party of Navajoes from the post came upon the Apaches and took from them five hundred sheep and thirteen burros.

August 6.—Mr. Charles G. Parker's train, *en route* to Chihuahua, Mexico, was attacked by the Mescalero Apaches, twenty miles below the Gallinas mountains. The Indians drove off about fifty mules. They were followed by the wagon-master and some teamsters, but succeeded in driving off the animals. Two men were severely wounded.

August 7.—Sergeant B. F. Fergusson, of company E, 5th infantry California volunteers, with a party of men, attacked fifteen Apaches who were seen approaching the camp on the Rio Carlos, and killed five of them.

August —.—The command which left Fort Cummings on the 5th day of August, on a scout to Lake Guzman, killed one Indian near the Florida mountains. Very few Indians were seen, they having evidently deserted the country on the approach of the troops, who, on this scout, marched twelve hundred miles.

August 13.—Lieutenant Henry Becker, 1st cavalry New Mexico volunteers, left Fort Canby, New Mexico, with ninety-two Indian prisoners and eight hundred head of sheep. On the route to Los Pinos he was joined by one hundred and fifty-one Indians, having in their possession seven hundred sheep and eighty-five horses. The Indians and stock were turned over to the commanding officer at Los Pinos.

August —.—Colonel King S. Woolsey reports that while on a scout after Indians near the Rio Prieto, one of his men, named J. W. Beauchamp, was waylaid and killed by the Apache Indians.

August —.—Major Thomas J. Blakeney, 1st cavalry California volunteers, on a scout of thirty days after Apache Indians, killed ten and captured two Indians, and destroyed twenty acres of corn and large quantities of pumpkins, beans, &c

August —.—Captain Henry A. Greene, 1st infantry California volunteers, on a scout after Indians from Fort McRae, New Mexico, killed five Indians and captured six. Nineteen head of beef cattle were recovered from the Indians

August —.—Captain John S. Thayer, 5th infantry California volunteers, left Fort Goodwin, Arizona Territory, with his company, on a scout after Indians. On the fourth day out the company destroyed about seventy acres of corn, also several small fields of beans and pumpkins. On the sixth day came upon a party of Indians—wounded several and captured one, who was afterwards shot while attempting to escape. A Mexican captive was rescued from these Indians. On the eighth day out attacked a party of Indians and killed six and wounded two.

August 25.—Captain Francis McCabe, 1st cavalry New Mexico volunteers, reports that while on a scout after Indians in the Sacramento mountains, he detached a party under Lieutenant Henry W. Gilbert, of the same regiment, to follow the trail of the Indians. Lieutenant Gilbert took with him twenty men. The party, although warned by the guide, marched in a body directly into an ambush, when Lieutenant Gilbert was killed at the first fire. The guide Sanches and Private Ma. Sandoval were killed and three men wounded. One Apache killed and five wounded. This command were leading their horses when the attack was made. The men, after the fall of their officer, shamefully abandoned their horses. The Indians got the most of the horses and equipments.

September 19.—Lieutenant Patrick Healy, 1st infantry New Mexico volunteers, with a detachment of ten men, while in pursuit of Indians, entered the town of Cañada de Alamosa, New Mexico, where five Indians were captured. One of the Indians afterwards made his escape.

September 25.—Captain William Ayers, 1st infantry New Mexico volunteers, learning that a party of Indians were at Cañada de Alamosa, started in pursuit of them and succeeded in capturing one man, four women and one child. The others made their escape to the mountains.

October 20.—A band of Navajo Indians attacked Mr. Huning's train on the Colorado Chiquito, and succeeded in driving off seven or eight hundred head of sheep, the property of Captain Joseph P. Hargrave

November 6.—Some Indians are said to have run off five hundred sheep from the headwaters of the Rio Puerco, belonging to Don Inez Perea.

November 8.—On the 8th of November some Navajoes and Apaches from the west ran off three thousand head of sheep belonging to Don José Pino y Vaca, four miles from Limitar, New Mexico, and killed four pastores who had the sheep in charge. Their names were Antonio Gallegos, Romaldo Peralta, Francisco Capillo, and Lenovio Sarcilla. Instructions were sent to Major Eaton, commanding at Fort Wingate, to cross the country to the Rio Quemado and endeavor to cut the trail of the Indians.

November 9.—A Navajo Indian found lurking near the government herd at Fort Sumner was arrested by the herd guard, and in attempting to make his escape was killed.

November 25.—Colonel Christopher Carson, 1st cavalry New Mexico volunteers, with a command consisting of fourteen commissioned officers, three hundred and twenty-one enlisted men and seventy-five Indians, Apaches and Utes, attacked a Kiowa village of about one hundred and fifty lodges, near the Adobe fort, on the Canadian river, in Texas, and after a severe fight compelled the Indians to retreat, with a loss of sixty killed and wounded. The village was then destroyed. The engagement commenced at 8½ a. m., and lasted without intermission until sunset.

In this fight Privates John O'Donnell and John Sullivan, of company M, 1st cavalry California volunteers, were killed, and Corporal N. Newman, Privates Thomas Briggs, J. Jameson, —— Mapes, Jasper Winant, J. Horsley. of company B, and Holygrafer, of company G, 1st cavalry California volunteers, Antonio Duro and Antonio Sanches, of company M, and H. Romero, of company I, 1st cavalry New Mexico volunteers, were wounded. Four Utes wounded.

Colonel Carson, in his report, mentions the following officers as deserving the highest praise: Major McCleave, Captain Fritz and Lieutenant Heath, of the 1st cavalry California volunteers, Captains Deus and Berney, 1st cavalry New Mexico volunteers, Lieutenant Pettis, 1st infantry California volunteers, Lieutenant Edgar, 1st cavalry New Mexico volunteers, and Assistant Surgeon George S. Courtright, United States volunteers.

The command destroyed one hundred and fifty lodges of the best manufacture, a large amount of dried meats, berries, buffalo robes, powder, cooking utensils, &c., also a buggy and spring wagon, the property of Sierrito, or Little Mountain, the Kiowa chief.

November 27.—An Apache Indian, in attempting to escape from Captain Thompson's company, 1st cavalry New Mexico volunteers *en route* to Fort Whipple, was killed by the guard.

November 27.—Colonel Oscar M. Brown, 1st cavalry California volunteers, with one hundred men, returned from a scout to the Apache country. Four squaws were captured by

Colonel Brown's command. Although this scout of nearly sixty days was unsuccessful, it was one of the hardest of the year.

December 2.—One thousand and twenty Navajo Indians, having in their possession three thousand five hundred sheep and goats, four hundred horses and thirty mules, arrived at Fort Sumner.

December —.—Major E. W. Eaton, 1st cavalry New Mexico volunteers, on a scout after Indians, came upon their camp near Red river; killed one Indian and took two prisoners and recovered one hundred and seventy-five sheep, one horse and one burro. These were the Indians who helped to run off sheep from Limitar on the 8th November.

December 15.—Captain Allen L. Anderson, 5th United States infantry, with a small party of men, attacked an Indian rancheria near the Weaver Mines, Arizona, killed three and wounded three Apache Indians.

December 15.—Captain John Thompson, 1st cavalry New Mexico volunteers, with a party of twelve enlisted men, attacked an Apache rancheria near Weaver, Arizona, and killed eleven and wounded four.

December 24.—Lieutenant Paul Dowlin, 1st cavalry New Mexico volunteers, reports that on his return trip from Fort Whipple, Arizona, the Navajo Indians ran off fourteen of his mules.

December 25.—A band of Apache Indians made an attack on the town of Rincon, near Fort McRae, New Mexico; took a Mexican boy prisoner, and drove off nine head of cattle. A party was started in pursuit and succeeded in recovering three head of cattle. The Mexican boy's body was found, lanced in several places.

December 29.—Captain William Brady, 1st cavalry New Mexico volunteers, reports that he found the body of Reyes Flores, the guide, near the Tuleroso saw-mill. Whether he had been killed by Indians or by others is not certain.

December 31.—Lieutenant Samuel L. Barr, with company F, 5th United States infantry, and a detachment of 1st cavalry New Mexico volunteers, surprised an Indian camp near Sycamore springs, Arizona; killed four Indians and captured two head of cattle.

Recapitulation of a census of the Navajo Indians on the reservation at the Bosque Redondo, New Mexico, on the 31*st day of December*, 1864, *their stock, &c.; taken by Captain Francis McCabe,* 1*st cavalry, New Mexico volunteers:*

Number of lodges, 1,276; number of families, 1,782.

Number of males from 50 to 80 years of age	300
Number of males from 18 to 50 years of age	2,129
Number of males from 5 to 18 years of age	1,525
Number of male infants	134
Number of females from 50 to 80 years of age	373
Number of females from 18 to 50 years of age	2,187
Number of females from 5 to 18 years of age	1,418
Number of female infants	288
Total population	8,354

Number of horses, 3,038; number of mules, 143; number of sheep, 6,962; number of goats, 2,757; number of looms, 630.

Average number of persons to each family is near 5; average number of horses to each family is near 2; average number of sheep to each family is near 4.

AGGREGATES.

Number of Apache Indians at the Bosque Redondo reservation on the 31st day of December, 1864.

Mescalero Apaches:

Men	113
Women	153
Children	139
Total	405

Gila Apaches:

Men	5
Women	5
Children	10
Total	20

Gila Apaches *en route* to the reservation:

Men	8
Women	6
Total	14

Making the total number of captive Indians as follows:

Number of Indian captives on the reservation on the 31st of December, 1863	703
Number who were captured and who surrendered themselves during the year 1864	8,090
Total	8,793

During the year 1864, the few troops serving within the department of New Mexico were obliged to undergo extraordinary labors, privations and hardships in following the line of their duty. Early in the year, while the country was still covered with snow, their marches in pursuit of Navajo Indians, in continuation of the campaign begun in the summer of 1863, the frequent combats with bands of that tribe, not only in the Navajo country but in the open plains to the east of the Rio Grande, exhibited courage, self-denial, perseverance, ability, and the will to encounter and to endure protracted hardships, on the part of both officers and men. which would be very creditable to any troops in the army.

It was often their lot to be compelled, from the nature of the country, and sometimes from limited means of transportation, to carry their blankets and provisions on their backs, and to struggle for days through deep snows, over mountains, through forests, and down through the deep mazes of the most wonderful cañons in the world, in pursuit of a wily and active enemy, who was familiar with every rod of that distant and, in many places, hitherto considered inaccessible region.

It was their lot to feel that even though they were successful in their efforts, far beyond the success which had attended the labors of others who had preceded them in campaigns against these Indians, still they would win none of that *éclat* which those receive for, perhaps, no harder service on other fields. It was their lot to show fidelity, and integrity, and earnestness in their labors for the public good—prompted to this course, not by the expectation of applause or advancement, but by a feeling honestly to discharge their duty, though no approving eye witnessed their labors or their sufferings, and they had no credit save that shown in the mirror of a clear conscience, or by the approval of their own hearts. The results which followed such labors will be considered as remarkable in the annals of Indian warfare.

The Navajoes soon found that they had no place of security from such determined adversaries, and, being pressed on every hand by unexampled rigor, the spirit of the tribe was soon broken. Many were captured, and more voluntarily surrendered, when, in bands of fifty to one and two thousand, they commenced their pilgrimage to the Bosque Redondo, a place selected for them by the government, and situated upon the open plains east of the Rio Grande, and more than four hundred miles from their native valleys and mountains. The exodus of this whole people, men, women and children, with their flocks and herds, leaving forever the land of their fathers, was an interesting but a touching sight.

Then came the operations of the troops against the Apaches of Arizona. To those acquainted with the difficulties of campaigning in that distant country—formidable against the movement and supply of troops in every way in which a country can be formidable, whether considered on account of its deserts, its rugged and sterile mountains, its frequent and often impassable defiles, and, in widely extended regions, the scarcity of water and grass—the wonder will be that the troops were ever able to overtake the Indians at all. Although the results of operations in that Territory were not so great as hoped for, yet they were creditable, and were won at an expense of toil and privation of which any description could give but a faint idea to one who had never traversed this very singular country. The marches of the troops were long, and sometimes repaid by but poor results. For example: on one expedition, under one of our most distinguished officers, the troops marched 1,200 miles, and actually killed but one Indian. Oftentimes long scouts would be made, and not an Indian, or even the track of one, would be discovered; yet the movements of the troops in every direction through the country of the Arizona Apaches, and a few partial encounters with them, attended by great good fortune, gave us the *morale* over them, until now they are inclined to flee at the sight of our armed parties, and scatter in all directions, and not to stand upon hill-tops and crags and jeer at our men by insulting cries and gestures, as they did when we first began war upon them. It is hoped that in a short time they too will be sufficiently subdued to surrender and go upon a reservation.

While all this was doing, the Indians of the plains commenced their attacks upon the trains of the government and of citizens coming out with supplies. This required that troops should be sent out to help these trains past the points of danger. Once this was done, and the most of the trains secure, an expedition was formed to punish even these Indians for their conduct. The Kiowas had been the most hostile, and had committed some of the most atrocious of the murders. It so happened that in Colonel Carson's brilliant affair with the Comanches and Kiowas, on the 25th of November, the Kiowas suffered the most loss, and had their beautiful village of 150 lodges, together with all their property and reserve of food, entirely destroyed.

Not only have the troops thus followed and punished the Indians, but they have opened new roads, repaired others which had become destroyed by floods, have built posts, guarded trains through the interior of Arizona and New Mexico, and conducted the thousands of captive Indians from the old Navajo country to the reservation, and not only guarded them there, but have directed their labors in opening up what will be one of the most magnificent farms in the United States.

The general commanding the department takes great pleasure in being able to congratulate the troops on such a record. The increased security of life and property throughout this widely extended department, attests the beneficial results which spring from these efforts. The prosperity of New Mexico and Arizona will be sure to follow. So it must ever be a source of gratification and pride to every officer and soldier engaged in this great labor to know that the people for whom he has toiled are getting to be more secure in their lives, and to be better off in their worldly condition.

All this has been done quietly and without ostentation on the part of the troops. In the great events which have marked the struggle of our country to preserve intact the union of all the States, it was not expected that such labors would receive the attention of the general government; but the fact that two great States will yet date their rise, progress, and the commencement of their prosperity from this subjugation of hostile Indians, will always be most gratifying to remember by those who so nobly did the work.

By command of Brigadier General Carleton:

BEN. C. CUTLER,
Assistant Adjutant General.

Recapitulation.

Month.	TAKEN FROM INDIANS.					TAKEN BY INDIANS.				KILLED AND WOUNDED.								Captured and surrendered.
										Comm'd officers.		Enlisted men.		Citizens.		Indians.		
	Sheep.	Horses.	Mules.	Cattle.	Burros.	Sheep.	Horses.	Mules.	Cattle.	Killed.	Wounded.	Killed.	Wounded.	Killed.	Wounded.	Killed.	Wounded.	
1864.																		
Jan. 3								20						1	3			
Jan. 5									11									
Jan. 6		50														40	25	
Jan. 11																1		
Jan. 12	62	25	1													3		
Jan. —														1	1	1		
Jan. 14				7														
Jan. 15								2	12									
Jan. —	200															23	5	
Jan. 24														1		19		
Jan. 26											1		4			7		
Jan. —																20	6	
Feb. 24		1														13		
March 4	3,000	473																
March 7		11					18											
March 8		5														26		
March 18							6	68										
March —												1				5		
March 27	62																	
March —														2	2			
April 3	120	6																
April 7		30	15													21		
April 10	150	1																
April 11																14		
April 24	230	159																
May 1	650	320																
May 3												2	5			10	20	
May 9	5,000	1,000																
May 11							2											
May 25													1			38	4	
May 29		3	1													13	13	
June 3															5			
June 11																2	1	
June 20					4											4	5	
June —																5	2	
June —											1		1			7	12	
June —																2		
June 28																2		
July 10	1,435	302	18													6		
Aug. 1																1		
Aug. —														4				
Aug. 3	500				13													
Aug. 6								50							2			
Aug. 7																5		
Aug. 13	700	85																
Aug. —														1		1		
Aug. —																10		
Aug. —				19												5		
Aug. —																7	5	
Aug. 25										1			3	2		1	5	
Oct. 20						750												
Nov. 6						500												
Nov. 8						3,000								4				
Nov. 9																1		
Nov. 25												3	9			30	30	
Nov. 27																1		
Dec. —	175	1			1											1		
Dec. 15																14	7	
Dec. 24								14										
Dec. 25				3					9					1				
Dec. 29														1				
Dec. 31				2												4		
Total..	12,284	2,472	35	31	18	4,250	26	154	32	1	2	6	23	18	13	363	140	8,090

Official:

ERASTUS W. WOOD, *Aide-de-Camp.*

[General Orders No. 32.]

HEADQUARTERS DEPARTMENT OF NEW MEXICO,
Santa Fé, N. M., October 22, 1864.

An expedition will be organized, without delay, to move against the Kiowa and Comanche Indians, who, during the last summer, attacked trains on the roads leading from New Mexico to the States. This expedition is designed to co-operate with one moving from near Fort Larned, under the command of Major General Blunt, with a view to the punishment of the same Indians. Its organization will be as follows:

Colonel Christopher Carson, 1st cavalry New Mexico volunteers, commanding.
Lieutenant Colonel Francisco P. Abreü, 1st infantry New Mexico volunteers, to command the infantry.
Major William McCleave, 1st cavalry California volunteers, to command the cavalry.
First Lieutenant Benjamin Taylor, jr., United States 5th infantry, acting assistant quartermaster and acting commissary of subsistence.
Assistant Surgeon George S. Courtright, United States volunteers.

Captain Birney's company, mounted	42
Lieutenant Heath, with all of Johnson's men now at Fort Union and at Fort Bascom.	39
Captain Witham's cavalry, now *en route* to Fort Union	66
Captain Fritz, with thirty of the best cavalry from Fort Sumner, New Mexico	30
Captain Deus's company at Fort Bascom	69
Lieutenant Edmiston, with the effective men of company A, 1st veteran infantry California volunteers	62
Lieutenant Pettis, with all the effective men of company K, 1st infantry California volunteers, with two mountain howitzers	45
Total, say	353

To these will be added, of Ute Indians and Jicarilla Apache Indians, say 100. These will proceed to Fort Bascom, New Mexico, direct from Mr. Maxwell's ranche, on the Cimarron, and there join the troops.

Captain Marion's company C and Captain Baca's company E, 1st cavalry New Mexico volunteers, and Captain Bergmann's men, now on the plains, will garrison Fort Bascom until further orders. All these troops will concentrate at once at Fort Bascom, and have that post as their base of operations, and thence commence the movement against the Kiowas and Comanches. As the season is now getting late, every moment becomes more and more precious. Every officer and soldier must therefore do his utmost, not only to take the field promptly, but to accomplish all that can be accomplished in punishing these treacherous savages before the winter fairly sets in. They have wantonly and brutally murdered our people without cause, and robbed them of their property; and it is not proposed that they shall talk and smoke and patch up a peace until they have, if possible, been punished for the atrocities they have already committed. To permit them to do this would be to invite further hostile acts from them as soon as the spring opens and our citizens once more embark in their long journeys across the plains.

The various chiefs of the staff departments will furnish Colonel Carson with the means of transportation and supplies necessary to give this order practical effect.

By command of Brigadier General Carleton:

BEN. C. CUTLER,
Assistant Adjutant General.

[General Orders No. 2.]

HEADQUARTERS DEPARTMENT OF NEW MEXICO,
Santa Fé, N. M., January 31, 1865.

On the 22d day of last October an order was published at these headquarters which organized an armed expedition against the Kiowa and Comanche Indians. Their depredations upon our trains, and their murdering of our people on the roads leading to the States, during the last year, was the reason why this was done.

After that order was published and issued, and its receipt acknowledged, passports were issued to citizens to go out upon the plains to trade with these very Indians. The traders to whom these passports were given were warned, on their arrival at Fort Bascom, New Mexico, by Lieutenant Colonel Abreü, the commanding officer, of the state of hostility which existed between our troops and the Kiowas and Comanches ; and these traders were ordered not to proceed further toward the Indian country while the present condition of affairs existed. These orders were utterly disregarded ; the traders got stealthily past our pickets, and, the Indians themselves say, brought them news of the approaching troops. Also, there cannot be a doubt that these traders sold the Indians the very powder and lead with which our brave soldiers were killed and wounded. These matters have been so clearly developed as not to leave the shadow of a doubt on the subject.

It is therefore ordered that no citizen trader will hereafter be allowed to pass any military post or picket, along the eastern frontier of New Mexico, for the purpose of trafficking with the Kiowas and Comanches, unless it shall have been announced in orders by the military authorities that we are no longer at war with those Indians, or unless his passport be *viséd* and countersigned at these headquarters ; and all commanders of posts, pickets, and bodies of troops are hereby ordered to arrest and hold as prisoners any person or persons without such passport who may be found trafficking with Kiowas and Comanches, or found proceeding to the country of those Indians for the purpose of such traffic, until notice be duly given that we are at peace with those tribes, as above stated.

The general commanding the department is charged with the protection of the lives and property of the people from hostile Indians, and he regrets to be compelled, for the reasons given, to pursue the course here indicated. He had a right to suppose, on general principles, that no such passports would either be asked for or given, and that no such illicit commerce would be carried on with our enemies. Such a course, it will readily be seen, tends not only to embarrass the military, but to paralyze their efforts to punish those savages for their repeated crimes.

By the 57th article of the act of Congress entitled "An act for establishing rules and articles for the government of the armies of the United States," approved April 10, 1806. holding correspondence with, or giving intelligence to, the enemy, either directly or indirectly, is made punishable by death, or such other punishment as shall be ordered by the sentence of a court-martial.

By command of General Carleton :

BEN. C. CUTLER,
Assistant Adjutant General.

Abstract of all provisions which have been issued to captive Indians in the department of New Mexico from March 31, 1865, to June 30, 1865, compiled from returns and reports in the office of the chief commissary of subsistence, department of New Mexico, in accordance with department General Orders No. 17, of June 8, 1864, by Captain W. H. Bell, C. S., chief commissary of subsistence, department of New Mexico.

Date.	Name of post.	Name of commissary.	On what return of provisions accounted for.	Fresh beef.	Beef pluck.	Mutton.	Mutton pluck.	Bacon.	Flour.	Corn meal.	Wheat meal.	Wheat.
1864.				*lbs. oz.*	*lbs.*	*lbs.*	*lbs.*	*lbs. oz.*	*lbs. oz.*	*lbs.*	*lbs.*	*lbs.*
March	Fort Sumner, N. M.	Capt. W.L. Rynerson, a.c.s.	March	125,778 4	3,029	78,803	6,205	21 0	169 08		113,384	
April	do	do do	April	193,648 8	6,505			91 8	910 00		179,040	
May	do	do do	May	180,800 4	6,240				2,187 06	9,956	173,042	
June	do	do do	June	40,833 0	741	121,593	9,168	65 4	1,079 12	477	18,377	85,781
April	Fort Wingate, N. M.	Lieut. G. McDermott, a.c.s.	April	192 0								
May	do	do do	May			10		5 0	20 00			
April	Los Pinos, N. M.	Lieut. N. Thomasson, a. c. s	April	790 0					510 00			
May	do	do do	May	1,147 0					1,147 00			

Abstract of provisions, &c.—Continued.

Date.	Name of post.	Name of commissary.	On what return of provisions accounted for.	Corn.	Hominy.	Beans.	Rice.	Coffee, green.	Coffee, roasted.	Sugar.	Soap.	Salt.	Amount.
1864.				*lbs.*	*lbs.*	*lbs. oz.*	*lbs.*	*lbs. oz.*	*lbs. oz.*	*lbs. oz.*	*lbs. oz.*	*lbs. oz.*	
March	Fort Sumner, N. M.	Capt. W. L. Rynerson, a. c. s.	March	171,526	......	......	....	232 8	....	350 04	......	123 12	*$70,578 30
April	....do	.... do ....do	April	86,903	......	60 00	....	251 8	....	377 04	......	124 08	72,704 97
May	....do	.... do ....do	May	64,202	......	231 12	....	211 4	107 12	519 04	......	1,707 12	72,861 15
June	....do	.... do ....do	June	124,006	......	54 00	....	164 9	....	300 12	......	4,098 08	53,519 04
													†199,085 16
April	Fort Wingate, N. M.	Lieut. G. McDermott, a. c. s.	April	....	331¾	60 00	....	....	....	....	......	....	53 83¼
May	....do	.... do ....do	May	....	......	......	....	....	....	....	......	1 00	6 10
													‡59 93¼
April	Los Pinos, N. M.	Lieut. N. Thomasson, a. c. s.	April	....	......	......	85	....	....	....	4 12	26 04	160 65
May	....do	.... do ....do	May	....	......	......	....	....	....	....	5 14	42 12	265 74
													§426 39

* Reservation, part of 1st quarter 1865. † Reservation, 2d quarter 1865. ‡ Fort Wingate, 2d quarter 1865. § Los Pinos, N. M., 2d quarter 1865.

OFFICE CHIEF COMMISSARY OF SUBSISTENCE, DEPARTMENT OF NEW MEXICO,
Santa Fé, New Mexico, August 30, 1865.

I certify that the above abstract is correct.

W. H. BELL, *Capt. and. S., U. S. A.*

DEPARTMENT OF NEW MEXICO, ASSISTANT ADJUTANT GENERAL'S OFFICE,
Santa Fé, New Mexico, September 1, 1865.

Official:

BEN. C. CUTLER, *Assistant Adjutant General.*

OFFICE CHIEF COMMISSARY OF SUBSISTENCE, DEPARTMENT OF NEW MEXICO,
Santa Fé, N. M., July 4, 1865.

SIR: Please find, herewith, a statement of all purchases of subsistence stores procured for the Navajo and Apache Indians located on the Indian reservation at the Bosque Redondo.

The abstracts show the purchases up to the 30th June, 1865. These papers form part of my evidence as given before the honorable committee.

I have the honor to be, sir, most respectfully, your obedient servant,

W. H. BELL,
Captain and Commissary of Subsistence U. S. A.

Abstract of purchases for captive Indians in the month of May, 1864, *by Captain W. H. Bell, commissary of subsistence United States army.*

Date.	From whom purchased.	Beef-cattle.		Wheat.	Wheat meal.	Amount.
		No.	*Pounds.*	*Pounds.*	*Pounds.*	
1864.						
May 19	H. B. Denman	250	125,083⅔			$15,635 41½
19	D. B. Maxwell			23,991		1,449 45
26	W. H. Moore & Co				19,938	1,694 73
	Quantity and amount	250	125,083⅔	23,991	19,938	18,779 59½

I certify that the above abstract is correct.

W. H. BELL,
Captain and Commissary of Subsistence U. S. A.

OFFICE CHIEF COMMISSARY OF SUBSISTENCE,
Santa Fé, N. M., May 30, 1864.

Abstract of stores transferred to officers for captive Indians in the month of May 1864, *by Captain W. H. Bell, commissary of subsistence.*

Date.	No.	To whom issued.	Beef-cattle.		Wheat.	Wheat meal.
			No.	*Pounds.*	*Pounds.*	*Pounds.*
1864.						
May 19	1	Capt. P. G. D. Morton, A. C. S.	250	125,083⅔		
19	2	Capt. P. G. D. Morton, A. C. S.			23,991	
26	3	Capt. P. G. D. Morton, A. C. S.				19,938
		Quantity and amount	250	125,083⅔	23,991	19,938

I certify that the above abstract is correct.

W. H. BELL,
Captain and Commissary of Subsistence U. S. A.

OFFICE CHIEF COMMISSARY OF SUBSISTENCE,
Santa Fé, N. M., May 30, 1864.

Abstract of stores transferred to officers for the use of captive Indians in the month of June, 1864, by Captain W. H. Bell, commissary of subsistence United States army.

Date.	No	To whom issued.	Beef cattle		Sheep.	Mutton.	Corn meal.	Wheat meal.
1864.			*No*	*Pounds.*	*No*	*Pounds*	*Pounds*	*Pounds.*
May 18	1	Capt. P. G D Morton, A. C. S.	34	9,690	619	10,832	-------	--------
28	2	---do-----do----	----	-------				27,365
30	3	---do-----do----		-------	-------	-------	3,950	14,901
June 3	4	---do-----do----	53	15,913	-------	-------	-------	--------
13	5	---do-----do----	..	-------	-------	-------	-------	14,000
18	6	---do-----do----	703	324,537	------	-------	-------	--------
			790	350,140	619	10,832	3,950	56,266

I certify that the above abstract is correct.

W. H BELL,
Captain and Commissary of Subsistence, U. S. A.

OFFICE CHIEF COMMISSARY OF SUBSISTENCE,
Department of New Mexico, Santa Fé N. M, June 30, 1864.

Abstract of purchases on account of subsistence for captive Indians in the month of June, 1864, by Captain W. H. Bell, commissary of subsistence United States army.

Date.	No.	From whom purchased.	Beef-cattle.		Sheep.		Corn meal	Wheat meal.	Amount.
1864			*No*	*Pounds*	*No*	*Pounds*	*P'ds*	*Pounds*	
May 18	1	L. B. Maxwell.	34	9,690	619	10,832	-----	------	$2,395 37½
28	2	Cuan St. Vrain.	----	-------	--	-------	-----	27,365	2,326 02½
30	3	W. H. Moore & Co	----	-------	----	-------	3,950	14,901	1,612 21
June 3	4	Peter Allison..	53	15,913	----	-------	-----	-------	2,068 69
13	5	W. H. Moore & Co.	----	-------	----	-------	-----	14,000	1,190 00
18	6	H. B. Denman.	703	324,537	---	-------	-----	-------	40,567 12½
		Total........	790	350,140	619	10,832	3,950	56,266	50,160 42½

I certify that the above abstract is correct.

W H BELL,
Captain Candommissary of Subsistence U. S. A.

OFFICE CHIEF COMMISSARY OF SUBSISTENCE,
Santa Fé, N. M., June 30, 1864.

Abstract of subsistence stores transferred to officers for the use of captive Indians in the month of July, 1864, *by Captain W. H. Bell, commissary of subsistence United States army.*

Date.		No.	To whom issued.	Beef-cattle.		Sheep.		Flour.	Corn meal.	Wheat meal.	Wheat.	Corn.
				No.	*Pounds.*	*No.*	*Pounds.*	*Pounds.*	*Pounds.*	*Pounds.*	*Pounds.*	*Pounds.*
1864.												
April	2	1	Capt. P. G. D. Morton, A. C. S.								*61,443	
	2	2	do do					*27,400				
	5	3	do do								*83,314	
	6	4	do do						*21,588			
	6	5	do do					30,100				
	17	6	Lieut. N. Thomasson, A. C. S.			2,868	*43,020					
June	13	7	Capt. P. G. D. Morton, A. C. S.						9,875	15,500		
	18	8	do do							20,000		
	18	9	Lieut. N. Thomasson, A. C. S.							*10,150		
	18	10	Capt. P. G. D. Morton, A. C. S.							41,600		
	29	11	do do							49,600		
	30	12	do do							18,000		
July	1	13	do do									197,357
	2	14	do do	157	77,862							
	4	15	do do									64,872
	7	16	do do						8,291	9,073		
	8	17	Lieut. N. Thomasson, A. C. S.							3,000		
	8	18	Capt. P. G. D. Morton, A. C. S.							14,821		
	11	19	do do					20,500				
	11	20	do do							26,000		
	12	21	do do							10,019		
	13	22	do do							30,100		
	13	23	do do							19,975		
	13	24	do do									110,580
	14	25	do do							26,500		

15	26	Lieut. N. Thomasson, A. C. S.	----	----------	-----	---------	---------	---------	6,680	---------	---------
16	27	Capt. P. G. D. Morton, A. C. S.	----	----------	-----	---------	---------	---------	---------	---------	20,813
21	28	------do--------do	343	199,511$\frac{2}{3}$	-----	---------	---------	---------	---------	---------	---------
21	29	------do--------do	19	11,051$\frac{2}{3}$	-----	---------	---------	---------	---------	---------	---------
21	30	------do--------do	47	26,648$\frac{1}{3}$	-----	---------	---------	---------	---------	---------	---------
25	31	------do--------do	----	----------	-----	---------	---------	---------	---------	---------	21,045
			566	315,073$\frac{2}{3}$	2,868	43,020	78,000	39,754	301,038	144,757	414,667

* Stores marked thus were purchased by Captain Garrison, but not paid for by him.

I certify that the above abstract is correct.

W. H. BELL.
Captain and Commissary of Subsistence, U. S. A.

OFFICE CHIEF COMMISSARY OF SUBSISTENCE,
Department of New Mexico, July 31, 1865.

Abstract of purchases on account of subsistence for captive Indians in the month of July, 1864, by Captain W. H. Bell, C. S. U. S. A.

Date.		No.	From whom purchased.	Beef-cattle.		Sheep.		Flour.	Corn meal.	Wheat meal.	Wheat.	Corn.	Amount.
				No.	*Pounds.*	*No.*	*Pounds.*	*Pounds.*	*Pounds.*	*Pounds.*	*Pounds.*	*Pounds.*	
1864.													
July	22	1	Ceran St. Vrain							124, 200			$10, 557 00
	22	2	Ceran St. Vrain					57, 500					5, 750 00
	22	3	Ceran St. Vrain							67, 600			5, 746 00
	25	4	Anastacio Sandoval							19, 830			1, 784 70
	28	5	Andres Dold					20, 500					1, 947 50
	28	6	Andres Dold								144, 757		8, 395 90
	28	7	Andres Dold									64, 872	7, 135 92
	28	8	Hunter & Kitchen	343	199, 511⅔								24, 739 44
	31	9	W. H. Moore & Co						8, 291	23, 894			2, 756 44
	31	10	W. H. Moore & Co						21, 588				1, 888 95
	31	11	W. H. Moore & Co.						9, 875	15, 500			2, 181 56
	31	12	Watrous & Tipton									110, 580	12, 163 80
	31	13	C. W. Kitchen									197, 357	21, 709 27
	31	14	Hunter & Kitchen	157	77, 862								9, 654 88
	31	15	James Hunter									20, 813	2, 289 43
	31	16	H. B Denman	47	26, 648⅓								3, 331 04
	31	17	Peter Allison	19	11, 051⅔								1, 436 71
April	17		Juan Perea			2,868	43, 020						*5, 736 00
June	18		W. H. Moore & Co.							20, 000			*1, 700 00
July	12		W. H. Moore & Co.							10, 019			*851 61½
	13		W. H. Moore & Co							19, 995			*1, 699 57
	25		W. H. Moore & Co.									21, 045	*2, 314 95
				566	315, 073⅔	2,868	43, 020	78, 000	39, 754	301, 038	144, 757	414, 667	135, 770 67½

* Not paid for in the month.

I certify that the above abstract is correct.

W. H. BELL,
Captain and Commissary of Subsistence U. S. A.

OFFICE CHIEF COMMISSARY OF SUBSISTENCE,
Santa Fé, N. M., July 31, 1865.

Abstract of purchases on account of subsistence for captive Indians in the month of August, 1864, *by Captain W. H. Bell, commissary of subsistence United States army.*

Date.		No.	From whom purchased.	Beef-cattle.	Fresh beef.	Sheep	Mutton.	Wheat meal.	Wheat.	Corn.	Amount.
1864.				*Head.*	*Pounds.*	*Head*	*Pounds.*	*Pounds.*	*Pounds.*	*Pounds.*	
August	9	1	L. B. Maxwell	181	85,492				75,844		$12,062 79
	9	2	L. B. Maxwell						48,257		2,915 52
	9	3	L. B. Maxwell							79,962	8,795 82
	9	4	L. B. Maxwell							31,851	3,503 61
	10	5	Andres Dold							100,846	11,093 06
	12	6	James Hunter							132,233	14,546 63
	22	7	Ceran St. Vrain					10,800			918 00
	23	8	Ceran St. Vrain					102,242			8,690 57
	23	9	Andres Dold							73,414	8,073 54
	25	10	W. H. Moore & Co.							120,181	13,219 91
	28	11	John Dold	284	85,768						7,933 54
	31	12	W. H. Moore & Co.							32,128	3,534 08
	31	13	Ceran St. Vrain					89,700			7,624 50
	31	14	Ceran St. Vrain					24,931			2,119 13½
	31	15	James Hunter							4,456	490 16
	10		Mariana Urissario			400	8,000				950 00
	18		Andres Dold							23,808	2,618 88
	24		Andres Dold							14,503	1,595 33
			Quantity.	465	171,260	400	8,000	227,673	124,101	613,382	110,687 07½

I certify that the above abstract is correct.

W. H. BELL,
Captain and Commissary of Subsistence U. S. A.

OFFICE CHIEF COMMISSARY OF SUBSISTENCE,
Department of New Mexico, Santa Fé, N. M., August 31, 1864.

Abstract of provisions transferred to officers at Santa Fé, N. M., for the use of captive Indians in the month of August, 1864, *by Captain W. H. Bell, Com. Sub. U. S. A.*

Date.	No. of voucher.	To whom issued.	Beef-cattle.	Fresh beef.	Sheep.	Mutton.	Wheat meal.	Wheat.	Corn.
1864.									
April 20	1	Captain P. G. D. Morton, A. C. S						75,844	
23	2	do do	181	85,492					
June 23	3	do do						48,257	
July 2	4	do do							79,962
6	5	do do							7,921
15	6	do do							23,930
25	7	do do							132,233
27	8	do do							100,846
August 1	9	do do							64,072
3	10	do do					9,142		
3	11	do do							120,181
4	12	do do					10,800		
5	13	do do					30,500		
6	14	do do					29,600		
8	15	Captain T. J. Copp, C. S	284	85,768					
8	16	Captain P. G. D. Morton, A. C. S					33,000		
8	17	do do							9,342
10	18	do do			*400	*8,000			
11	19	do do					54,900		
18	20	do do					34,800		
18	21	do do							*23,808
20	22	do do							32,128
22	23	do do					9,931		
24	24	do do							4,456
24	25	do do					15,000		
24	26	do do							14,503
		Total issued	465	171,260	400	8,000	227,673	124,101	613,382

* Not paid for.

I certify that the above abstract is correct.

W. H. BELL,
Captain and Commissary of Subsisten ce U. S. A.

OFFICE CHIEF COMMISSARY OF SUBSISTENCE, *Santa Fé, N. M., August* 31, 1864.

Abstract of purchases on account of subsistence for captive Indians in the month of September, 1864, by Captain W. H. Bell, commissary of subsistence United States army.

Date.	From whom purchased.	Beef-cattle.		Sheep.		Flour.	Wheat meal.	Wheat.	Corn.	Amount.
		No.	*Pounds.*	*No.*	*Pounds.*	*Pounds.*	*Pounds.*	*Pounds.*	*Pounds.*	
1864.										
August 31	W. H. Moore & Co.								12,901	$1,419 11
September 6	James Hunter								27,917	3,070 87
12	John Dold			541	14,877½					1,376 16¾
12	John Dold	95	38,356¼							3,547 95¼
15	L. B. Maxwell							35,890		2,168 35
17	C. S. Hinckley	103	65,199							11,735 82
21	Ceran St. Vrain					2,300	1,700			374 50
	Quantity and amount	198	103,555¼	541	14,877½	2,300	1,700	35,890	40,818	23,692 77

I certify that the above abstract is correct.

W. H. BELL,
Captain and Commissary of Subsistence U. S. A.

OFFICE CHIEF COMMISSARY OF SUBSISTENCE,
Department of New Mexico, September 30, 1865.

Abstract of stores transferred to officers for captive Indians in the month of September, 1864, by Captain W. H. Bell, commissary of subsistence United States army.

Date.	No.	To whom issued.	Beef-cattle.		Sheep.		Flour.	Wheat meal.	Wheat.	Corn.
			No.	*Pounds.*	*No.*	*Pounds.*	*Pounds.*	*Pounds.*	*Pounds.*	*Pounds.*
1864.										
August 31	1	Captain P. G. D. Morton, A. C. S.								12,901
September 6	2	Captain P. G. D. Morton, A. C. S.								27,917
12	3	Captain P. G. D. Morton, A. C. S.			541	14,877½				
12	4	Captain T. J. Copp, A. C. S.	95	38,356¼						
15	5	Captain P. G. D. Morton, A. C. S.							35,890	
17	6	Captain P. G. D. Morton, A. C. S.	103	65,199						
21	7	Captain P. G. D. Morton, A. C. S.					2,300	1,700		
		Quantity and amount	198	103,555¼	541	14,877½	2,300	1,700	35,890	40,818

I certify that the above abstract is correct.

W. H. BELL,
Captain and Commissary of Subsistence U. S. A.

OFFICE CHIEF COMMISSARY OF SUBSISTENCE,
Santa Fé, New Mexico, September 30, 1865.

Abstract of purchases on account of subsistence for captive Indians in the month of October, 1864, by Captain W. H. Bell, commissary of subsistence United States army.

Date.		From whom purchased.	Beef-cattle.		Flour.	Corn.	Amount.
1864.			*Head.*	*Pounds.*	*Pounds.*	*Pounds.*	
Sept.	1	John Dold	80	44,800			$4,144 00
	22	C. S. Hinckley	111	48,117			8,661 06
	28	C. S. Hinckley	308	209,070 $\frac{4}{10}$			37,632 60
	30	C. S. Hinckley	165	110,917 $\frac{1}{8}$			19,965 06
Oct.	3	W. H. Moore & Co.				4,074	448 14
	15	Andres Dold			24,400		2,318 00
	17	C. S. Hinckley	127	88,195			15,875 10
	18	C. S. Hinckley	160	123,200			22,176 00
	21	C. S. Hinckley	340	198,475			35,725 50
	24	C. S. Hinckley	186	106,020			19,083 60
		Quantities	1,477	928,794 $\frac{1}{2}$	24,400	4,074	166,029 06

I certify that the above abstract is correct.

W. H. BELL,
Captain and Commissary of Subsistence U. S. A.

OFFICE CHIEF COMMISSARY OF SUBSISTENCE,
Department of New Mexico, Santa Fé, N. M., October 31, 1864.

Abstract of stores transferred to officers at Santa Fé, New Mexico, for the use of captive Indians during the month of October, 1864, by Captain W. H. Bell, commissary of subsistence United States army.

Date.		No of voucher.	To whom issued.	Beef-cattle.	Fresh beef.	Flour.	Corn.
1864.				*Head.*	*Pounds.*	*Pounds.*	*Pounds.*
Sept.	1	1	Capt. T. J. Copp, C. S.	80	44,800		
	22	2	Capt. P. G. D. Morton, A. C. S.	111	48,117		
	28	3	Capt. T. J. Copp, C. S.	308	209,070 $\frac{4}{10}$		
	30	4	Capt. T. J. Copp, C. S.	165	110,917 $\frac{1}{8}$		
Oct.	3	5	Capt. P. G. D. Morton, A. C. S.				4,074
	15	6	Capt. P. G. D. Morton, A. C. S.			24,400	
	17	7	Capt. T. J. Copp, C. S.	127	88,195		
	18	8	Capt. T. J. Copp, C. S.	160	123,200		
	21	9	Capt. T. J. Copp, C. S.	340	198,475		
	24	10	Lieut. W. H. Higdon, A. C. S.	186	106 020		
			Total issued	1,477	928,794 $\frac{1}{2}$	24,400	4,074

I certify that the above abstract is correct.

W. H. BELL,
Captain and Commissary of Subsistence U. S. A.

OFFICE CHIEF COMMISSARY OF SUBSISTENCE,
Department of New Mexico, Santa Fé, N. M., October 31, 1864.

Abstract of purchases of subsistence for captive Indians in the month of November, 1864, *by Captain W. H. Bell, commissary of subsistence United States army.*

Date.	From whom purchased.	Beef-cattle.		Flour.	Corn.	Wheat.	Grain sacks.	Amount.
		No.	*Pounds.*	*Pounds*	*Pounds.*	*Pounds.*	*No.*	
1864. Nov. 2	L. B. Maxwell	235	106,925					$9,355 93¾
3	Major H. M. Enos, Q. M.				140,000			11,200 00
10	L. B. Maxwell		5,050	2,300				964 50
15	Capt. A. B. Carey, A. Q. M.				22,120	28,501	345	4,798 70
	Quantity	235	111,975	2,300	162,120	28,501	345	26,319 13¾

I certify that the above abstract is correct.

W. H. BELL,
Captain and Commissary of Subsistence U. S. A.

OFFICE CHIEF COMMISSARY OF SUBSISTENCE,
Santa Fé, New Mexico, November 30, 1864.

Abstract of stores transferred to officers for the use of captive Indians in the month of November, 1864, *by Captain Bell, commissary of subsistence United States army.*

Date.	No.	To whom issued.	Beef cattle.		Flour.	Corn.	Wheat.	Grain sacks.
			No.	*Pounds.*	*P'ds.*	*Pounds*	*Pounds.*	*No.*
1864. Nov. 2	1	Captain P. G. D. Morton, A. C. S.	235	106,925				
3	2	do do				140,000		
10	3	do do		5,050	2,300			
15	4	do do				22,120	28,501	345
		Quantity and amount	235	111,975	2,300	162,120	28,501	345

I certify that the above abstract is correct.

W. H. BELL, *Captain and C. S. U. S. A.*

OFFICE CHIEF COMMISSARY OF SUBSISTENCE,
Santa Fé, N. M., November 30, 2864.

Abstract of purchases on account of subsistence for captive Indians during the month of December, 1864, by Captain W. H. Bell, commissary of subsistence United States army.

Date.	No. of voucher.	From whom purchased.	Beef-cattle.		Sheep.		Flour.	Wheat.	Corn.	Grain sacks.	Amount.
			Head.	*Pounds.*	*Head.*	*Pounds.*	*Pounds.*	*Pounds.*	*Pounds.*	*No.*	
1864.											
Nov. 15	....	Quartermaster's department						124,319			$7,251 94
15	....	Quartermaster's department								1,042	521 00
Dec. 3	....	Andres Dold							22,557		2,481 27
3	....	C. W. Kitchen							35,279		3,880 69
5	....	Lewis & Brother						7,077	7,498		661 03
9	....	C. S. Hinckley	435	183,461							33,022 78
12	....	C. E. Cooley			4,331	129,930					15,158 50
12	....	Andres Dold					14,900				2,533 00
13	....	H. B. Denman	642	279,270							41,890 50
13	....	C. S. Hinckley	586	332,010							59,761 80
16	....	S. B. Maxwell							30,071		3,307 81
20	....	Quartermaster's department						41,759		385	4,633 61
24	....	Andres Dold					15,000				2,550 00
		Quantity	1,661	794,741	4,331	129,930	29 900	173 155	95,405	1,427	177,654 13

I certify that the above abstract is correct.

W. H. BELL,
Captain and Commissary of Subsistence U. S. A.

OFFICE CHIEF COMMISSARY OF SUBSISTENCE,
Department of New Mexico, Santa Fé, N. M., December 31, 1865.

Abstract of stores transferred to officers at Santa Fé, New Mexico, for captive Indians during the month of December, 1864, by Captain W. H. Bell, commissary of subsistence United States army.

Date.	No. of voucher.	To whom issued.	Beef-cattle.	Fresh beef.	Sheep.	Mutton.	Flour.	Wheat.	Corn.	Grain sacks.
1864.			*Head.*	*Pounds.*	*Head.*	*Pounds.*	*Pounds.*	*Pounds.*	*Pounds.*	*No.*
Nov. 15	1	Captain P. G. D. Morton, A. C. S						124,319		
15	2	do do								1,042
19	3	do do						24,497		
Dec. 3	4	do do							22,557	
3	5	do do							35,279	
5	6	Lieutenant Edmund Butler, A. C. S.						7,077	7,498	
9	7	Captain P. G. D. Morton, A. C. S.	433	183,461						
12	8	do do			4,331	129,930				
12	9	do do					14,900			
13	10	do do	642	279,270						
13	11	do do	586	332,010						
15	12	do do						17,069		
16	13	do do							30,071	
24	14	do do					15,000			
20	15	do do								385
		Total issued	1,661	794,741	4,331	129,930	29,900	*172,962	95,405	1,427

* For difference see abstract, February, 1865.

I certify that the above abstract is correct.

W. H. BELL,
Captain and Commissary of Subsistence U. S. A.

OFFICE CHIEF COMMISSARY OF SUBSISTENCE.
Department of New Mexico, Santa Fé, N. M., December 31, 1864.

Abstract of purchases on account of subsistence for the captive Indians in the month of January, 1865, *by Captain W. H. Bell, commissary of subsistence, United States army.*

Date.	From whom purchased.	Wheat meal.	Wheat.	Corn.	Amount.
January 2	W. H. Moore & Co	39,700			$5,796 20
4	do	10,000			1,460 00
6	do	37,600			5,489 60
12	Ceran St. Vrain	40,000			5,840 00
12	W. H. Moore & Co			14,869	1,635 59
13	J. Fuindenthal			87,500	5,000 00
16	Lewis & Brother		13,048		913 36
17	W. H. Moore & Co	44,000			6,424 00
26	D. B. Maxwell			31,828	3,501 08
	Total	171,300	13,048	134,197	36,059 83

I certify that the above abstract is correct.

W. H. BELL,
Captain and Commissary of Subsistence U. S. A.

OFFICE CHIEF COMMISSARY OF SUBSISTENCE,
Santa Fé, N. M., January 31, 1865.

Abstract of stores transferred to officers for captive Indians in the month of January, 1865, *by Captain W. H. Bell, commissary of subsistence United States army.*

Date.	No.	To whom issued.	Wheat meal.	Wheat.	Corn.
1865.			*Pounds.*	*Pounds.*	*Pounds.*
January 2	1	Capt. P. G. D. Morton, A. C. S	39,700		
4	2	do do	10,000		
6	3	do do	37,600		
12	4	Major Wm. McCleave, A. C. S	40,000		
12	5	do do			14,869
13	6	Capt. Edmund Butler, A. C. S			87,500
16	7	do do		13,048	
17	8	Major Wm. McCleave, A. C. S	44,000		
26	9	do do			31,828
		Total	171,300	13,048	134,197

I certify that the above abstract is correct.

W. H. BELL,
Captain and Commissary of Subsistence U. S. A.

OFFICE CHIEF COMMISSARY OF SUBSISTENCE,
Santa Fé, New Mexico, January 31, 1865.

Abstract of purchases on account of subsistence for captive Indians in the month of February, 1865, by Captain W. H. Bell, commissary of subsistence U. S. A.

Date.		From whom purchased.	Beef-cattle.		Sheep.		Wheat.	Wheat meal.	Corn.	Apricot seed.	Amount.
1865.			*Head.*	*Pounds.*	*Head.*	*Pounds.*	*Pounds.*	*Pounds.*	*Pounds.*	*Pounds.*	
Jan.	18	Quartermaster's department					10,000			20	$751 00
	28	Lazaro Senna									3 25
Feb.	1	Thomas C. Bull						95,000			11,400 00
	9	W. H. Moore & Co						38,964			6,994 03¾
	17	C. S. Hinckley	543	213,806¼							38,485 12½
	22	S. A Hubbell			4,376	127,998					19,839 69
	27	Andres Dold							34,580		8,472 10
		Total	543	213,806¼	4,376	127,998	10,000	133,964	34,000	20	85,945 20¼

I certify that the above abstract is correct.

W. H. BELL,
Captain and Commissary of Subsistence U. S. A.

OFFICE CHIEF COMMISSARY OF SUBSISTENCE,
Department of New Mexico, Santa Fé, N. M., February 23, 1865.

Abstract of stores transferred to officers for captive Indians in the month of February, 1865, by Captain W. H. Bell, commissary of subsistence United States army.

Date.		No. of voucher.	To whom issued.	Beef-cattle.		Sheep.		Wheat.	Wheat meal.	Corn.	Apricot seed.
				Head.	*Pounds.*	*Head.*	*Pounds.*	*Pounds.*	*Pounds.*	*Pounds.*	*Pounds.*
1864.											
Dec.	20	1	Captain P. G. D. Morton, A. C. S					193			
1865.											
Jan.	18	2	Captain P. G. D. Morton, A. C. S					10,000			
	28	3	Major Wm. McCleave, A. S. C								20
Feb.	1	4	Captain Rufus C. Vose, A. C. S						95,000		
	9	5	Major Wm. McCleave, A. C. S						38,964		
	17	6	Major Wm. McCleave, A. C. S	543	213,806¼						
	22	7	Major Wm. McCleave, A. C. S			4,376	127,998				
	27	8	Major Wm. McCleave, A. C. S					(*)		34,580	
			Total isssued	543	213,806¼	4,376	127,998	10,193	133,964	34,580	20

* For difference see abstract, December, 1864.

I certify that the above abstract is correct.

W. H. BELL,
Captain and Commissary of Subsistence U. S. A.

OFFICE CHIEF COMMISSARY OF SUBSISTENCE,
Department of New Mexico, Santa Fé, N. M., February 28, 1865.

Abstract of purchases on account of subsistence for captive Indians during the month of March, 1865, *by Captain W. H. Bell, commissary of subsistence United States army.*

Date.	From whom purchased.	Corn.	Wheat meal.	Amount.
1865.		*Pounds.*	*Pounds.*	
Feb. 10	Andres Dold	28,747	....	$27,043 01½
March 6	W. H. Moore & Co	....	29,600	5,313 00
	Quantity	28,747	29,600	12,356 01½

I certify that the above abstract is correct.

W. H. BELL,
Captain and Commissary of Subsistence U. S. A.

OFFICE CHIEF COMMISSARY OF SUBSISTENCE,
Department of New Mexico, Santa Fé, N. M., March 31, 1865.

Abstract of stores transfered to officers for captive Indians during the month of March, 1865, *by Captain W. H. Bell, commissary of subsistence United States army.*

Date.	No. of voucher.	To whom issued.	Coal.	Wheat meal.
1865.			*Pounds.*	*Pounds.*
Feb. 18	1	Major Wm. McCleave, United States army	28,747	....
March 6	2	Captain W. L. Rynerson	....	29,600
		Total issued	28,747	29,600

I certify that the above abstract is correct.

W. H. BELL,
Captain and Commissary of Subsistence U. S. A.

OFFICE CHIEF COMMISSARY OF SUBSISTENCE,
Department of New Mexico, Santa Fé, N. M., March 31, 1865

Abstract of purchases on account of subsistence for captive Indians during the month of April, 1865, by Captain W. H. Bell, commissary of subsistence United States army.

Date.	From whom purchased.	Beef-cattle.		Wheat meal.	Corn meal.	Corn.	Amount.
1865.		*Head.*	*Pounds.*	*Pounds.*	*Pounds.*	*P'ds.*	
Feb. 16	W. H. Moore & Co.	......	....	30,100	....	......	$4,394 60
Mar. 14	W. H. Moore & Co.	......	....	27,016	....	......	3,944 33
17	L B. Maxwell	......	....	....	....	1,000	110 00
April 12	W. H. Moore & Co.	......	....	61,436	....	......	11,027 76
	Vicente Romero	......	....	....	23,602	......	3,540 30
25	Vicente Romero	......	....	....	23,470	......	3,520 50
	H. B. Denman	26	9,620	....	....	......	1,443 00
	C. S. Hinckley	14	5,180	....	....	......	932 40
	Quantity	40	14,800	118,552	47,072	1,000	28,912 89

I certify that the above abstract is correct.

W. H. BELL,
Captain and Commissary of Subsistence U. S. A.

OFFICE CHIEF COMMISSARY OF SUBSISTENCE,
Department of New Mexico, Santa Fé, N. M, *April* 30, 1865.

Abstract of stores transferred to officers at Santa Fé, N. M., for captive Indians, during the month of April, 1865, by Captain W. H. Bell, commissary of subsistence United States army.

Date.	No. of voucher.	To whom issued.	Beef-cattle.		Wheat meal.	Corn meal.	Corn.
1865			*Head.*	*Pounds.*	*Pounds.*	*Pounds.*	*Pounds.*
Feb. 16	1	Maj. Wm. McCleave, A. C. S.	......	....	30,100	....	....
Mar. 14	2	Capt W. L. Rynerson, A. C. S	......	....	27,016	....	....
17	3	......do	......	....	....	....	1,000
April 12	4	......do	......	....	61,436	....	....
12	5	......do	......	....	....	23,602	....
25	6	......do	......	....	....	23,470	....
25	7	......do	26	9,620	....	....	....
25	8	......do	14	5,180	....	....	....
		Total issued	40	14,800	118,552	47,072	1,000

I certify that the above abstract is correct.

W. H. BELL,
Captain and Commissary of Subsistence U. S. A.

OFFICE CHIEF COMMISSARY OF SUBSISTENCE,
Department of New Mexico, Santa Fé, N. M., *April* 30, 1865.

Abstract of purchases on account of subsistence for captive Indians in the month of May, 1865, by Captain W. H. Bell, commissary of subsistence United States army.

Date.		From whom purchased.	Flour.	Corn meal.	Wheat meal.	Tomato seed.	Chili seed.	Garden seed, in papers.	Pumpkin seed.	Grain sacks.	Watermelon seed, assorted.	Amount.
1865.			*Pounds.*	*Pounds.*	*Pounds.*	*P'ds.*	*P'ds.*	*Pap's.*	*P'ds.*	*No.*		
April	12	W. H. Moore & Co			18,396							$2,685 81¼
	30	Captain R. C. Vose, A. C. S.		49,640								6,301 06¾
May	10	W. H. Moore & Co			43,158						60	85 50
	11	George T. Beall*				14	30					15 16⅔
	11	Augustin M. Hunt*					40	91			60	77 70
	11	George T. Beall										1,435 03
	11	W. H. Moore & Co			9,829							3,609 00
	15	Vicente Romero		24,060								2,034 07
	15	W. H. Moore & Co			13,932					151		113 25
	18	Quartermaster's department										7,354 95
	24	Ceran St. Vrain	49,033								50	43 25
	31	George T. Beall							26			
	31	Webb & Cuniffe									19	60 80
	31	Charles Blumner									2 13/16	3 00
	31	Hartford Gooch										
		Quantity and amount	49,033	73,700	85,315	14	70	91	26	151	191 13/16	

*On one receipt.

I certify that the above abstract is correct.

W. H. BELL, *Captain and Commissary of Subsistence U. S. A.*

OFFICE CHIEF COMMISSARY OF SUBSISTENCE,
Santa Fé, N. M., May 31, 1865.

Abstract of stores transferred to officers for the use of captive Indians in the month of May, 1865, by Capt. W. H. Bell, C. S. U. S. A.

Date.		No.	To whom issued.	Flour.	Corn meal.	Wheat meal.	Tomato seed.	Chili seed.	Garden seed, papers of.	Pumpkin seed, papers of.	Grain sacks.	Watermelon seed, assorted.	Amount.
1865.				*Pounds.*	*Pounds.*	*Pounds.*	*P'ds.*	*P'ds.*	*Papers.*	*P'ds.*	*No.*	*P'ds.*	
April	12	1	Captain W. L. Rynerson, A. C. S			18,396							
	30	2	do do		49,640	43,158							
May	10	3	do do				14	30				60	
	11	3	do do						91				
	11	4	do do					40				60	
	11	5	do do			9,829							
	11	6	do do		24,060								
	15	7	do do			13,932							
	15	8	do do								151		
	18	9	Lieutenant Paul Dowlin, A. C. S	49,033									
	24	10	Captain W. L. Rynerson, A. C. S									50	
	31	10	do do							26			
	31	10	do do									19	
	31	11	do do									$2\frac{13}{16}$	
			Total	49,033	73,700	85,315	14	70	91	26	151	$191\frac{13}{16}$	

W. H. BELL, *Captain and Commissary of Subsistence U. S. A.*

OFFICE CHIEF COMMISSARY OF SUBSISTENCE,
Department of New Mexico, Santa Fé, N. M., May 31, 1865.

Abstract of purchases on account of subsistence for captive Indians during the month of June, 1865, by Captain W. H. Bell, commissary of subsistence U. S. A.

Date.	From whom purchased.	Beef-cattle.		Sheep.		Wheat meal.	Corn meal.	Flour.	Amount.
		Head.	*Pounds.*	*Head.*	*Pounds.*	*Pounds.*	*Pounds.*	*Pounds.*	
1865.									
June 1	Vicente Romero						30,643		$4,596 45
3	C. S. Hinckley	437	185,725						33,430 50
4	Santiago L. Hubbell			4,880	103,700				18,406 75
10	W. H. Moore & Co					24,108			3,519 76¾
13	Ceran St. Vrain					52,493			7,663 97¾
3	W. H. Moore & Co					14,844			2,167 22¼
16	W. H. Moore & Co					90,623			13,230 95¾
17	José Ma. Gallegos			4,105	89,283				15,847 73¼
22	Ceran St. Vrain					12,549			1,832 15¼
12	Ceran St. Vrain							41,069	6,160 35
	Quantity	437	185,725	8,985	192,983	194,617	30,643	41,069	106,855 86

I certify that the above abstract is correct.

W. H. BELL,
Captain and Commissary of Subsistence U. S. A.

OFFICE CHIEF COMMISSARY OF SUBSISTENCE,
Department of New Mexico, Santa Fé, N. M., June 30, 1865.

Abstract of stores transferred to officers at Santa Fé, New Mexico, for captive Indians, during the month of June, 1865.

Date.	No. of voucher.	To whom issued.	Beef-cattle.		Sheep.		Wheat meal.	Corn meal.	Flour.
			Head.	*Pounds.*	*Head.*	*Pounds.*	*Pounds.*	*Pounds.*	*Pounds.*
1865. June 1	1	Captain W. L. Rynerson, A. C. S						30,643	
3	2	do do					14,844		
3	3	do do	437	185,725					
4	4	do do			4,880	103,700			
10	5	do do					24,108		
12	6	Lieutenant Paul Dowlin, A. C. S							41,069
13	7	Captain W. L. Rynerson, A. C. S					52,493		
16	8	do do					90,623		
17	9	do do			4,105	89,283			
22	10	do do					12,549		
		Total issued	437	185,725	8,985	192,983	194,617	30,643	41,069

I certify that the above abstract is correct.

W. H. BELL,
Captain and Commissary of Subsistence U. S. A.

OFFICE CHIEF COMMISSARY OF SUBSISTENCE,
Department of New Mexico, Santa Fé, N. M., June 30, 1865.

DISTRICT OF NEW MEXICO, ASSISTANT ADJUTANT GENERAL'S OFFICE,
Santa Fé, N. M., October 22, 1865.

MAJOR: Mr. Lorenzo Labadie, Indian agent, has written a letter in which the following sentence occurs:

"In March last I was informed by the officer in command at Fort Sumner that, under superior orders, my services as agent were not any more needed at the reservation, as all control over the Indians was conferred to the military department of New Mexico, which order, in my opinion, was given by the military in consequence of my solemn protest made against the unwholesome food furnished by the military department to the Navajo Indians, *who were frequently fed on meat from cattle that died of disease, and meat of horses and mules.*"

The general commanding directs that you have this matter thoroughly investigated, and report the result in writing to these headquarters.

I am, major, very respectfully, your obedient servant,

ERASTUS W. WOOD,
Captain 1st Vet. Inf. C. V., A. A. A. General.

Major WILLIAM MCCLEAVE,
Commanding Fort Sumner, N. M.

Official: CYRUS H. DE FORREST, *Aide-de-Camp.*

HEADQUARTERS FORT SUMNER, NEW MEXICO,
November 3, 1865.

MAJOR: I have the honor to acknowledge the receipt, from district headquarters, of a communication dated Santa Fé, New Mexico, October 22, 1865, relative to a letter written by Mr. Lorenzo Labadie, Indian agent, and in which he states that the Indians on this reservation were frequently fed on meat from cattle that died of disease, &c. In reply to the above, I will state that since my arrival at this post, on the 7th of last January, this is the first intimation I have had that diseased meat had ever been issued to the Indians, or that Mr. Labadie had made any protest in the matter. As an offset to all such slanderous statements, I herewith enclose affidavits of the men in charge of the principal herder on the reservation, who delivers all the animals for slaughter, and weighs the meat before it is issued to the Indians. So far as I am concerned, or could discover, the military authorities at this post have always been at much pains, not to say expense, to ameliorate the condition of the Indians. It was, perhaps, owing to friends of the reservation of Mr. Labadie's stripe that on yesterday the Indians were afraid to attend the feast, (harvest home,) lest a trap had been set to poison them. This Territory is much indebted to citizens who will condescend to lead the savage mind astray, and to such the blame of many of the atrocities committed may justly be attributed. Mr. Labadie states that his removal from here was caused in consequence of his protesting against the Navajo Indians being furnished unwholesome food. This, so far as I know, has not been the case. The prevailing opinion here on that occasion was, that he (Labadie) was removed for the reason that some seventy-seven head of government oxen, select ones, were discovered in his (Mr. Labadie's) herd. This at a distance of probably forty miles from this post. To speak plain, and call things by their proper names, this looked like stealing. However, Mr. Labadie may have been innocent of any knowledge of the fact, notwithstanding, on the 27th of last March, he acknowledged to Lieutenant E. Edgar that he had intended and agreed to purchase from Captain Morton the cattle alluded to above.

The officers at this post, regardless of the opinions or slanders of others, as they have heretofore, will continue to perform their duties toward the Indians in a proper manner. Nevertheless, they trust the time is not far distant when they will be relieved of all such disagreeable and unmilitary duties as they are now obliged to perform regarding the Indians.

I am, major, respectfully, your obedient servant,

WILLIAM MCCLEAVE,
Major 1st California Cavalry, Commanding.

Major BEN. C. CUTLER,
Ass't Adj't General, District of New Mexico, Santa Fé, N. M.

HEADQUARTERS DISTRICT OF NEW MEXICO,
Santa Fé, N. M., November 8, 1865.

Official:

CYRUS H. DE FORREST, *Aide-de-Camp.*

TERRITORY OF NEW MEXICO, *County of San Miguel:*

This 2d day of November, 1865, before me, R. E. Comins, second lieutenant 1st California cavalry, post adjutant at Fort Sumner, New Mexico, personally came Charles Hardison, who, being duly sworn according to law, doth declare and say: That he has been in charge of a large herd of government beef-cattle for issue to Indians on this reservation since the 11th day of January, 1865, and that to the best of his knowledge and belief no diseased meat of any description has been issued to the Indians, and that some time since, when a number of beef-cattle died of disease, the commanding officer ordered deponent to prevent the Indians taking away the meat lest it should make them sick.

CHARLES HARDISON.

Sworn and subscribed to before me, at Fort Sumner, New Mexico, the day and date first written.

R. E. COMINS,
Second Lieutenant 1st California Cavalry, Post Adjutant.

HEADQUARTERS DISTRICT OF NEW MEXICO,
Santa Fé, N. M., November 8, 1863.

Official:

CYRUS H. DE FORREST, *Aide-de-Camp.*

TERRITORY OF NEW MEXICO, *County of San Miguel:*

This 2d day of November, 1865, before me, R. E. Comins, second lieutenant 1st California cavalry, post adjutant at Fort Sumner, New Mexico, personally came Philip W. Sampson, and does solemnly swear that he has had charge of all the cattle and sheep on this reservation for issue to Indians since the 27th day of last January, and that during the whole period no diseased meat of any description has been issued to the Indians, and that during the past summer, when some cattle in the herds died of disease, the commanding officer, Major William McCleave, upon learning that the Indians took away part of the meat, told deponent to give orders to the herders not to allow the Indians to carry away such meat, lest it should cause sickness among them Deponent further states that he has delivered all the cattle and sheep for slaughter since the date above mentioned.

PHILIP W. SAMPSON.

Sworn and subscribed to before me, at Fort Sumner, New Mexico, the day and date first written.

R. E. COMINS,
Second Lieutenant 1st California Cavalry, Post Adjutant.

HEADQUARTERS DISTRICT OF NEW MEXICO,
Santa Fé, N. M., November 8, 1865.

Official:

CYRUS H. DE FORREST, *Aide-de-Camp.*

TERRITORY OF NEW MEXICO, *County of San Miguel:*

This 2d day of November, 1865, before me, R. E Comins, second lieutenant 1st California cavalry, post adjutant at Fort Sumner, New Mexico, personally came Hugh Collum, who, being duly sworn according to law, doth declare and say: That he has been in charge of a large herd of government beef-cattle for issue to Indians on this reservation since the 1st day of March, 1865, and that to the best of his knowledge and belief no diseased meat of any description has been issued to the Indians, and that some time since, when a number of cattle died of disease, the commanding officer ordered deponent to prevent the Indians taking away the meat, lest it should make them sick.

his
HUGH + COLLUM.
mark.

Witness: PHILIP W. SAMPSON.

Sworn and subscribed to before me, at Fort Sumner, New Mexico, the day and date first written.

R. E. COMINS,
Second Lieutenant 1st California Cavalry, Post Adjutant.

HEADQUARTERS DISTRICT OF NEW MEXICO,
Santa Fé, N. M., November 8, 1865.

Official:

CYRUS H. DE FORREST, *Aide-de-Camp.*

TERRITORY OF NEW MEXICO, *County of San Miguel:*

This 2d day of November, 1865, before me, R. E. Comins, second lieutenant 1st California cavalry, post adjutant at Fort Sumner, New Mexico, personally came José Jaramillo, and does solemnly swear that he has been in charge of a herd of government beef-cattle and sheep for issue to Indians on this reservation since the 1st day of January, 1865, and that to the best of his knowledge and belief no diseased meat of any description has been issued to the Indians, and that some time since, when a number of cattle died of disease, deponent received instructions from the commanding officer, Major William McCleave, to prevent the Indians taking away the meat, lest it should cause sickness among them.

his
JOSÉ × JARAMILLO.
mark.

Witness: PHILIP W. SAMPSON.

Sworn and subscribed to before me, at Fort Sumner, New Mexico, the day and date first written.

R. E. COMINS,
Second Lieutenant 1st California Cavalry, Post Adjutaut.

HEADQUARTERS DISTRICT OF NEW MEXICO,
Santa Fé, N. M., November 8, 1865.

Official:

CYRUS H. DE FORREST, *Aide-de-Camp.*

Abstract of money expenditure by the quartermaster's department, in the military department of New Mexico, for the transportation of Navajo Indians from the Navajo country to the Bosque Redondo, and the money value of quartermaster's stores issued to said Indians.

Date.	To whom paid.	By whom paid.	At what post.	Amount.	Remarks.
1864.					
Mar. 8	J. W. Whitenton	A. A. quarterm'r	Los Pinos, N. M.	$1,200 00	
8	José Jaramillo	..do.... do	....do..... do	2,000 00	
21	Salvador Armijo	..do.... do	....do..... do	500 00	
21	Ambrosio Armijo	..do.... do	....do..... do	1,000 00	
5	J. M. Luna	..do.... do	....do..... do	900 00	Train took wheat from Los Pinos to Fort Canby.
5	Rafael Luna	..do.... do	....do..... do	1,875 00	Do. do. do.
May 1	J. Placido Romero	..do.... do	....do..... do	300 00	
1	José de Jesus Castillo	..do.... do	....do..... do	375 00	
1	Santiago Luna	..do.... do	....do..... do	375 00	
1	Santiago Luna	..do.... do	....do..... do	960 00	
July 31	J. W. Whitenton	..do.... do	....do..... do	252 00	
Aug. 25	José Anto. Otero	..do.... do	....do..... do	50 00	
31	J. M. Luna	..do.... do	....do..... do	1,020 00	Took Co. E, 5th U. S. inf., to Fort Sumner, N. M.
31	J. M. Luna, (demur'ge)	..do.... do	....do..... do	200 00	Paid on certificate of Capt. I. Thompson, 1st N. M. cav., by order of Capt. Enos.
31	Felipe Chaves	..do.... do	....do..... do	1,800 00	
31	Bonifacio Chaves	..do.... do	....do..... do	900 00	
31	Desidero Sanches	..do.... do	....do..... do	200 00	
	Money value of quartermaster's stores	..do.... do	....do..... do	7,427 35	Consisted of blankets, brass kettles, camp kettles, and domestic, transferred by Col. McFerran, Capt. Enos, and Lieut. Butler.
Dec. 10	Rafael Chaves	..do.... do	Ft. Wingate, N. M.	300 00	5 wagons, at $60 each, took Indians to Bosque Redondo.
31	Pablo Pino	..do.... do	....do..... do	240 00	4 do. do. do.
Mar. —	Money value of quartermaster's stores	..do.... do	....do..... do	571 95	620 lbs. wheat, at 8 3-5 cents per lb.; 62 grain sacks, at 62 cents each, by order of department commander.
	Money value of quartermaster's stores	..do.... do	Ft. Canby, N. M.	131 80	Issued during 1864.
	Governme't transportation used in moving Indians			25,000 00	
	Total amount paid and money value of stores issued			47,578 10	

A. B. CAREY, *Capt. 13th Inf., U. S. A.,*
For H. M. ENOS, *Col. and Chief Quartermaster.*

SANTA FÉ, N. M., *July* 31, 1865.

NAVAJO FARM, *February* 4, 1865.

GENERAL: I have the honor to submit the following report, showing you the progress made, day by day, in ploughing on the Indian farm from the 7th day of last month (the date of last report) to date:

Amount of land ploughed last report, 495 acres.

Tuesday, January 10—ground ploughed in the afternoon with 5 ox ploughs	2½ acres.
Wednesday, January 11—ground ploughed in the afternoon with 5 ox ploughs	2½ acres.
Amount of land ploughed this week	5 acres.
Monday, January 16—land ploughed this afternoon with 21 ploughs	11 acres.
Tuesday, January 17—land ploughed this afternoon with 21 ploughs	11 acres.
Wednesday, January 18—land ploughed this afternoon with 22 ploughs	11½ acres.
Thursday, January 19—land ploughed this afternoon with 22 ploughs	11½ acres.
Friday, January 20—land ploughed all day with 21 ploughs	21 acres.
Amount of land ploughed this week	66 acres.

Monday, January 23—nothing done this week.

Monday, January 30—land ploughed this afternoon, 3 ox ploughs	1½ acres.
Tuesday, January 31—land ploughed all day, 28 ploughs	28 acres.
Wednesday, February 1—land ploughed all day, 28 ploughs	28 acres.
Thursday, February 2—land ploughed all day, 27 ploughs (man sick)	27 acres.
Friday, February 3—land ploughed all day, 29 ploughs	29 acres.
Saturday, February 4—storming.	
Total amount of land ploughed this week	113½ acres.

Total amount of land ploughed to date above on the old Apache Indian farm, 679½ acres.

Remarks.—I find that my estimate of one acre per day to the plough is too low. I am of the opinion that the ploughs are doing from one-third to one-half more than I have set them at.

By exchanging six or eight mules that I now have for better ones, and allowing for the necessary loss of time in repairing ploughs, I can run thirty ploughs every day, and with this number of ploughs I am quite sure that from two hundred and fifty to two hundred and eighty acres of ground can be ploughed per week, when the animals get stronger and the weather favorable for work. Much time has been lost on account of the manner in which the blacksmiths do their work. Some of them, it seems, neither know how nor care to make their work good and substantial. New work that they turn out is heavy in metal, and to look at it you would pronounce it serviceable, but the iron is burnt and made worthless before the article is finished. If this could be remedied much time could be saved.

There has been but little work done on the ditches since my last report. The weather has been cold, and all the Indian labor has been used in preparing the land for the plough.

Respectfully, your most obedient servant,

WILLIAM P. CALLOWAY,
Superintendent of Labor on Indian Farm.

Brigadier General M. M. Crocker,
Commanding Fort Sumner.

Navajo Farm, *February* 11, 1865.

General: I have the honor to submit the following report of the amount of land ploughed for the week ending February 11, to wit:

Amount ploughed last report, 679½ acres.
Monday, February 6—ground froze.
Tuesday, February 7—ground froze.
Wednesday, February 8—ground froze.
Thursday, February 9—ground froze.
Friday, February 10—ground froze.
Saturday, February 11—ground froze.
Total amount of land ploughed, 679½ acres.

I have the honor, general, to be your most obedient servant,

WILLIAM P. CALLOWAY,
Superintendent of Labor on Indian Farm.

Navajo Farm, *February* 18, 1865.

General: I have the honor to submit the following report of the amount of land ploughed for the week ending February 18:

Whole amount of land ploughed last report, 679½ acres.

Monday, February 13—ploughs 29	29 acres.
Tuesday, February 14—ploughs 30	30 acres.
Wednesday, February 15—ploughs 30	30 acres.
Thursday, February 16—ploughs 29	29 acres.
Friday, February 17—ploughs 29	29 acres.
Saturday, February 18—ploughs 29	29 acres.
Amount ploughed this week	176 acres.

Whole amount ploughed, 855½ acres.

I have the honor to be your obedient servant,

WILLIAM P. CALLOWAY,
Superintendent of Labor on Indian Farm.

NAVAJO FARM, *February* 25, 1865.

MAJOR: I have the honor to submit the following report for the week ending February 25, showing the amount of land ploughed for the week:

Amount ploughed last report, 855½ acres.

Monday, February 20—ploughs 30	30 acres.
Tuesday, February 21—ploughs 30	30 acres.
Wednesday, February 22—ploughs 30	30 acres.
Thursday, February 23—snowing.	
Friday, February 24—snowing.	
Saturday, February 25—snow too deep to plough.	
Amount of land ploughed this week	90 acres.

Whole amount ploughed, 945½ acres.

Respectfully submitted:

WILLIAM P. CALLOWAY,
Superintendent of Labor on Indian Farm.

NAVAJO FARM, *March* 4, 1865.

MAJOR: I have the honor to submit the weekly report showing the amount of land ploughed for the week ending March 4, 1865:

Amount ploughed last report, 945½ acres.

Monday, February 7—snow too deep to plough.	
Tuesday, February 28—snow too deep to plough.	
Wednesday, March 1—with 26 ploughs	26 acres.
Thursday, March 2—with 30 ploughs	30 acres.
Friday, March 3—with 13 ploughs; afternoon Indians left	7 acres.
Saturday, March 4—with 26 ploughs; 3 ploughs lent to companies to plough company gardens; forenoon ground froze	14 acres.
Amount ploughed this week	77 acres.

Whole amount ploughed, 1,022½ acres; 15 acres was sown in Pimo wheat.

Respectfully submitted:

WILLIAM P. CALLOWAY,
Superintendent of Indian Farm.

NAVAJO FARM, *March* 11, 1865.

MAJOR: I have the honor to submit the following weekly report, showing the progress made in ploughing for the week ending March 11, 1865:

Amount ploughed last report, 1,022½ acres.

Monday, March 6—with 28 ploughs	28 acres.
Tuesday, March 7—with 20 ploughs; 8 men relieved	20 acres.
Wednesday, March 8—with 28 ploughs	28 acres.
Thursday, March 9—with 28 ploughs	28 acres.
Friday, March 10—with 29 ploughs	29 acres.
Saturday, March 11—with 29 ploughs	29 acres.
Amount ploughed this week	162 acres.

Total amount ploughed, 1,184½ acres.

Of the amount ploughed this week sixty acres was sowed in wheat.

I have the honor to be your most obedient servant,

WILLIAM P. CALLOWAY,
Superintendent of Labor on Indian Farm.

NAVAJO FARM, *March* 18, 1865.

MAJOR: I have the honor to submit the following weekly report, showing the amount of land broken up for the week ending March 18, 1865:

Whole amount last report, 1,148 acres.

Monday, March 13—twenty-seven ploughs, all day	27 acres.
Tuesday, March 14—twenty-seven ploughs, all day	27 acres.
Wednesday, March 15—twenty-six ploughs, all day	26 acres.

Thursday, March 16—twenty-five ploughs, all day .... 25 acres.
Friday, March 17—twenty-three ploughs, all day .... 23 acres.
Saturday, March 18—twenty-two ploughs, all day .... 22 acres.

Amount ploughed this week .... 150 acres.

Respectfully submitted:

WILLIAM P. CALLOWAY,
Superintendent of Labor on Navajo Farm.

NAVAJO FARM, *March* 25, 1865.

MAJOR: I have the honor to submit the weekly report showing the amount of land ploughed for the week ending March 25:

Whole amount last report, 1,298 acres.
Monday, March 20—too windy to work.
Tuesday, March 21—twenty-three ploughs, all day .... 23 acres.
Wednesday, March 22—twenty-three ploughs, all day .... 23 acres.
Thursday, March 23—twenty-one ploughs, all day .... 21 acres.
Friday, March 24—twenty-three ploughs, all day .... 23 acres.
Saturday, March 25—twenty-five ploughs, all day .... 25 acres.

Amount ploughed this week .... 115 acres.

Respectfully submitted:

WILLIAM P. CALLOWAY,
Superintendent of Labor on Indian Farm.

NAVAJO FARM, *April* 1, 1865.

MAJOR: I have the honor to submit the following weekly report of ploughing done on the Navajo farm for the week ending April 1, 1865:

Whole amount ploughed last report, 1,413 acres.
Monday, March 26—twenty-four ploughs .... 24 acres.
Tuesday, March 27—seventeen ploughs; moved camp to-day .... 17 acres.
Wednesday, March 28—twenty-three ploughs .... 23 acres.
Thursday, March 29—twenty-three ploughs .... 23 acres.
Friday, March 30—twenty-three ploughs .... 23 acres.
Saturday, April 1—twenty-three ploughs .... 23 acres.

Amount ploughed this week .... 133 acres.

Respectfully, your obedient servant,

WILLIAM P. CALLOWAY,
Superintendent of Labor on Indian Farm.

Major WILLIAM MCCLEAVE,
1st California Cavalry, Commanding Fort Sumner, N. M.

NAVAJO FARM, *April* 8, 1865.

MAJOR: I have the honor to submit the following weekly report of the amount of ploughing done on the Navajo farm for the week ending April 8, 1865:

Amount last report, 1,546 acres.
Monday, April 3—twenty-five ploughs .... 25 acres.
Tuesday, April 4—twenty-four ploughs .... 24 acres.
Wednesday, April 5—too windy to work.
Thursday, April 6—twenty-four ploughs .... 24 acres.
Friday, April 7—twenty-three ploughs .... 23 acres.
Saturday, April 8—twenty ploughs; three teams sent to plough for Captain Rynerson .... 20 acres.

Amount ploughed this week .... 116 acres.

Respectfully submitted:

W. P. CALLOWAY,
Superintendent of Labor on Indian Farm.

HEADQUARTERS FORT SUMNER, N. M., *April* 13, 1865.

NAVAJO FARM, *April* 15, 1865.

MAJOR: I have the honor to submit the following report, showing the amount of land ploughed for the week ending April 15, 1865:

Amount last report, 1,662 acres.

Monday, April 10—twenty-two ploughs; three ploughs sent to Captain Rynerson	19 acres.
Tuesday, April 11—twenty-one ploughs; three ploughs sent to Captain Rynerson	18 acres.
Wednesday, April 12—nineteen ploughs; three ploughs sent to Captain Rynerson	16 acres.
Thursday, April 13—twenty-two ploughs; three ploughs sent to Captain Rynerson	19 acres.
Friday, April 14—twenty-three ploughs	23 acres.
Saturday, April 15—twenty-three ploughs	23 acres.
	118 acres.

Respectfully submitted:

WILLIAM P. CALLOWAY,
Superintendent of Labor on Indian Farm.

Major WILLIAM MCCLEAVE,
1st California Cavalry, Commanding Fort Sumner.

NAVAJO FARM, *April* 22, 1865.

MAJOR: I have the honor to submit the following weekly report of the ploughing done on the Navajo farm for the week ending April 22, 1865:

Amount last report, 1,780 acres.

Monday, April 17—twenty-four ploughs	24 acres.
Tuesday, April 18—twenty-five ploughs	25 acres.
Wednesday, April 19—twenty-four ploughs	24 acres.
Thursday, April 20—snowing.	
Friday, April 21—twenty-two ploughs	22 acres.
Saturday, April 22—twenty-two ploughs	22 acres.
Amount ploughed this week	117 acres.

Respectfully submitted:

WILLIAM P. CALLOWAY,
Superintendent of Labor on Indian Farm.

Major WILLIAM MCCLEAVE,
1st California Cavalry, Commanding Fort Sumner.

NAVAJO FARM, *April* 29, 1865.

MAJOR: I have the honor to submit the following weekly report for the week ending April 29, 1865:

Amount ploughed last report, 1,897 acres.

Monday, April 24—twelve ploughs	12 acres.
Tuesday, April 25—twelve ploughs	12 acres.
Wednesday, April 26—twenty ploughs	20 acres.
Thursday, April 27—seventeen ploughs, (three planting corn)	17 acres.
Friday, April 28—fifteen ploughs, (four planting corn)	15 acres.
Saturday, April 29—sixteen ploughs, (four planting corn	16 acres.
Amount of land broke this week	92 acres.

Respectfully submitted:

WILLIAM P. CALLOWAY,
Superintendent of Labor on Indian Farm.

Major WILLIAM MCCLEAVE,
1st California Cavalry, Commanding.

DEPARTMENT OF NEW MEXICO, ASSISTANT ADJUTANT GENERAL'S OFFICE,
Santa Fé, N. M., July 7, 1865.

Official:

BEN. C. CUTLER,
Assistant Adjutant General.

FORT CRAIG, NEW MEXICO, *June* 23, 1865.

CAPTAIN: I have the honor to report that I left Fort Sumner on the 15th instant, per special order from Major McCleave, commanding Fort Sumner, with Captain B. Fox and forty-five enlisted men of the 1st California cavalry, in pursuit of Navajo Indians, reported to have escaped from the reservation. I took the direct route to Fort Stanton, saw but one small trail leading south, some fifteen or eighteen horses, about fourteen miles from Sumner. At Fort Stanton I drew ten days' rations and started for the Oscura mountains, as per agreement with Major McCleave. I left the Ojo Milagno June 20, at 6 a. m., crossed the Mal Pais, and in the afternoon at the Tanks at the foot of the Oscura found an Indian trail. The Indians had used up all the water. I followed them up the mountain and found a great many more tracks coming in. About 5 o'clock p. m. I came up with the rancherio, captured four horses, one mule and one burro, and one child about three years old. The Indians all made their escape, their camp being in a very rough cañon. I destroyed everything in the village, broke up some twenty-five bows and a great many arrows.

The only water I could find was some the Indians had in camp, gathered from rocks and a small spring. Not being able to procure water for my horses, I started for the Rio Grande at 1 o'clock a. m., and arrived at San Pedro at 11½ a. m., June 21. I had to leave both men and horses, given out for want of water, but got them all in in the afternoon by sending them water from San Pedro. Some forty or fifty mounted Indians started in the direction of San Andreas. The Indians evidently suffered from the want of water, as they dug holes in every ravine, but without success. In my opinion it is impossible for a large number to cross lower down than the Oscura mountains, as the whole country is dried up and no grass on the prairie. On arriving at San Pedro my horses had travelled nearly a hundred miles without water. On the 22d I encamped near La Mesa and reported to Colonel Rigg, who has ordered me to proceed to La Joya and Abo Pass to-morrow morning.

A Navajo boy of the Cebolleta tribe, with me, tells me that most of the Indians of the village I destroyed belong to Delgadita Largo's tribe. There were from twenty to twenty-two camp-fires, and there must have been about eighty or ninety Indians at this camp.

Very respectfully, your obedient servant,

EMIL FRITZ,
Major 1st California Cavalry.

Captain BEN. C. CUTLER, A. A. G.,
Department of New Mexico, Santa Fé, N. M.

HEADQUARTERS FORT CRAIG, NEW MEXICO, *July* 2, 1865.

MAJOR: Pursuant to orders received from department headquarters on the 23d of June, 1865, I have the honor to state that I left this post on the following day for Los Pinos, where I arrived on the 27th ultimo, having received information there that five hundred Navajoes, with Captain Brady and his company of 1st New Mexico cavalry in pursuit, were making toward San Andreas Pass. I left immediately for La Joya, where Lieutenant Crouch, 1st veteran infantry California volunteers, and company was stationed. On arriving at that point I made the following disposition of the troops, having induced Captain Juan Carrio at that place with thirty of his men (militia) to take the field: I ordered Lieutenant Crouch to proceed with a detachment of his company to Abo Pass, taking with him some of the militia to act as guides, and eight men of company H, 1st cavalry California volunteers, and the remainder to patrol and guard the crossings of the river in conjunction with the balance of his company left from San Pedro to Los Pinos.

A detachment of cavalry, under the command of Lieutenant William Oman, 1st veteran infantry California volunteers, guards the crossings from San Pedro to La Mesa; Captain Fountain and party of militia at Paraje connects with the detachment of men under command of Lieutenant Billings, 1st cavalry California volunteers, on the Jornado del Muerto; and with General Montoya's sixty militia stationed at the Sierra Caballos to intercept any Indians attempting to cross the river above or below, and Captain French at Fort McRae, with the pickets at the different crossings of the river, and the command at this post under Captain Chapman, 1st veteran infantry California volunteers, ready to act in any direction, every avenue of escape across is closed from San Diego crossing to Los Pinos. Lieutenant John E. Oliphant, with a detachment of companies H and M, of the 1st cavalry California volunteers, amounting to thirty-six men, have left this day to join Lieutenant Sanburn's command of twenty cavalry at the Cienega, Navajo, Tularosa, or Rita Quamado, bearing westerly from this post; at the Tularosa a depot of supplies will be established.

Major Fritz's command goes with myself to scour the mountains east and drive out or kill all and any of these renegades who have made them their places of covert. So, with all the troops at the river on the alert and my command in the mountains, it is my most sanguine hope to be able, if we find any party or parties of Indians, to give them a sound thrashing Having made the dispositions I did of Lieutenant Sanburn's company H, 1st cavalry California volunteers, on the first intimation I had that the Indians had escaped, and Major Fritz having reported to me for orders, I used his command instead of H company.

I am, major, very respectfully, your obedient servant,

EDWIN A. RIGG,
Lieut. Col. 1st Vet. Inf. C. V., Commanding.

Major BEN. C. CUTLER, A. A. G.,
Department of New Mexico, Santa Fé, N. M.

HEADQUARTERS FORT CRAIG, NEW MEXICO, *July* 3, 1865.

GENERAL: On the receipt of the news that a number of Indians had left the reservation at the Bosque, I disposed of all the available troops at the post to intercept them. I ordered Lieutenant Sanburn out towards the Tularosa west, that, if they crossed the river below the crossings at or near La Joya and south, he could capture them; his command of twenty men would then be fresh and his horses also. When I received the order to move with Lieutenant Sanburn's company, company B, 1st veteran infantry California volunteers, I had disposed of the latter company in the direction that you directed. Major Fritz, 1st cavalry California volunteers, arrived here from the Bosque and reported the number of Indians that he supposed had left, and his destroying a rancherio in the Oscura mountains. Major Fritz destroyed all the ojos and other traps that those Indians had, capturing and bringing in a little girl papoose, which is now in my possession here. After receiving the order to move to Los Pinos, I directed Major Fritz, in the absence of other troops, to move up on the east bank of the river as far as La Joya, leaving detachments of his command at all the prominent or usual crossings between the La Mesa and La Joya. I left at once myself for Los Pinos, going up on the west bank of the river with a view to meet General Montoya and ascertain what portion of the militia could be depended upon to turn out. The general I met on his way to the post; he had already issued his orders and expected that each pueblo would turn out their ratio. I then directed him verbally to get all the men he could within twenty-four hours and proceed to the Sierra Caballos; he thought, as I did, that our troops being on the trail and the Jornado guarded, these mountains were the best place for him and command, and that, in the event of Indians crossing the Jornado, they must pass by that mountain or by the Polomas, and if they succeeded in passing his command to get to their homes, they would necessarily fall into the hands of Lieutenant Sanburn either at Carriso, Cienega, Navajo, Tularosa, or the Rita Quamada. At Socorro, Limitar, Sabinel, and other points, the militia were evidently making preparations to join General Montoya. I directed one party to picket the river to relieve the men placed there by Major Fritz. I arrived at Los Pinos and there learned that most of the Indians had returned to the Bosque. When the express arrived from Craig informing me that Captain Brady had arrived and reported that he had cut the trail and that the bulk of the Indians, some five hundred, had gone toward San Andreas Pass, I at once moved for the Jornado. My instructions were to go to Abo Pass unless the appearance of Indians on the river would change my disposition of troops. I at once moved down to La Joya and directed Lieutenant Crouch, with company B, 1st veteran infantry, and eight cavalry of company H, who had joined him, to move up to Abo Pass, with a detail of company B, 1st veteran infantry California volunteers, and with the balance of his company to picket the river down below San Pedro. I succeeded in getting out from La Joya some thirty men, (at least they promised to furnish that number,) who were to assist company B men in guarding the important crossings between La Joya and San Pedro, and relieve the men of Major Fritz's command. I then pushed on down the east bank of the river to El Sabino, where we swam our horses and arrived at Craig at daylight on the morning of the 1st July. I had the horses shod and crossed again on the afternoon of the 2d and sent forward to the Ojo de Anillas, expecting to follow them to-day and join the command there. The mail arriving brought me orders to direct troops from Wingate, Craig, Selden and Las Cruces to return to their proper posts. I have sent, in accordance with this order, expresses enclosing copy of the order to where I supposed these troops could be found. With the exception of the mounted troops from Las Cruces, company M, 1st cavalry California volunteers, I have had none to report to me either from Wingate, Stanton or Selden, and my own, viz, company B, 1st veteran infantry California volunteers, had already taken the field, also company H, 1st cavalry California volunteers, except twelve men who are left at the grazing camp at the saw-mill, twenty-two miles distant, and who joined me at Socorro. Major Fritz's command, consisting of detachments of company B and Captain Fox's companies 1st cavalry California volunteers, are the only troops that I have had. By express to-day Captain French informed me that General Montoya has had a fight with the Indians in the Sierra Caballos, and that he is following them up. At Limitar two Indians rode out of the mountains and took two horses from men working in the fields, stripping the men and lancing a third party, taking from him a sack of flour. The apathy exhibited by the people even when promised pay, rations and ammunition, is surprising. After General Montoya issued his order, many men, or what one would suppose were men, left the towns and hid themselves, or, as Davis did, used their wives' petticoats to hide or escape in. If the governor will send an inspector general among them he will find a large percentage of the territorial arms have been disposed of and not to be found. General Montoya, Don Pedro Berda, and Pablo Cordova and Emanuel Virgil are the only citizens who seemed to feel any interest in the matter. General Montoya, as he always does when called upon, took the field in person, and I expect is the only commander who has had the good fortune to have a fight. I am of the opinion that some one or two hundred Indians are straggling through the mountains east, and will try to cross. The Apaches are coming up also in small bands. The escort to the mail from Las Cruces reports that between the Point of Rocks and Fort Selden they crossed a trail of Indians driving some two or three hundred sheep, and from the direction of the trail were making for the San Diego crossing and Fort Thorn. Not having any command outside of this post, and having but few troops after deducting for escorts and guard, I cannot follow up or cut off Indians. If at this time two good cavalry companies could be spared, I will guarantee that the limits from La Joya to the San Diego crossing no Indians will cross, or if they do either way, that but few will have an interesting tale to tell to their people.

I am, general, very respectfully, your obedient servant,

EDWIN A. RIGG,
Lieut. Colonel 1st Vet. Inf. C. V., Commanding.

Brigadier General JAMES H. CARLETON,
Commanding Department of New Mexico, Santa Fé, N. M.

DEPARTMENT OF NEW MEXICO,
Santa Fé, N. M., July 7, 1865.

Official:

BEN. C. CUTLER,
Assistant Adjutant General.

ALBUQUERQUE, N. M., *July* 1, 1865.

CAPTAIN: I have the honor to report that, on the 29th ultimo, I saw an Indian woman, lately escaped from the Bosque Redondo, at the house of Juan C. Ysidro, the brother of the alcalde at Bernalillo. The woman escaped with several other Indians. She says that a party of Mexicans captured herself and killed her husband and seven others. This woman wants to be sent back to the Bosque, and could, in my opinion, give valuable information as to the escaped Indians.

The person who holds her a prisoner says that he bought her, about ten days ago, for a cow and ten goats.

I give you this information to enable the military authorities to recover her, and send her to the Navajo reservation.

I was also informed that several escaped Navajoes are harbored by parties living at Bernalillo.

Respectfully, your obedient servant,

WM. P. CALLOWAY.

Captain F. McCABE,
Commanding Officer, Albuquerque, N. M.

A true copy:

ERASTUS W. WOOD,
Captain 1st Vet. Inf. C. V., A. A. A. General.

INSPECTOR GENERAL'S DEPARTMENT, DEPARTMENT OF NEW MEXICO,
Santa Rita Copper Mines, N. M., May 3, 1865.

CAPTAIN: I have the honor to report, for the information of the department commander, that, in obedience to Special Orders No. 10, from department headquarters of March 24, 1865, I arrived at Fort Cummings, New Mexico, the 13th instant.

From information obtained from Captain Burkett and Lieutenant Houston, at this post, the latter having had a talk with the Chief Victoria, I fixed upon this place as the most eligible for meeting and holding a council with the Indians living about the Mimbres river and in the Pinos Altos region. Accordingly, on the following day, April 14, from my camp on the Mimbres, I addressed a note to J. M. Hunt, of Pinos Altos, requesting him to have the Indians notified that I wished to see their principal men in council, at this place, on this date. The day after my arrival here, April 17, I sent the Mexican, of Captain Cook's company, and one Apache Indian, (both brought along for the purpose,) out to the north, east, and west, to inform all Indians they could find of the time and place of the proposed council.

On the 18th instant Indians commenced to come in in small numbers, including squaws and children. On the 19th I despatched the other of the two Apaches with me to Pinos Altos, with a letter to Mr. Hunt, informing him that I desired he would have the Indians notified that I wanted the chiefs and principal men only, and not the squaws and children; that it was to be a council and not a feast; that I was not prepared to feed them.

The next morning I received a letter from him, by the Apache, that he would be here on the 21st, with Victoria and others; that he could not well detain them longer, and that it would be impossible to keep the squaws and children from coming; that they had little or nothing to eat, and were eating the people of Pinos Altos out of provisions.

On the 20th instant some fifty-six were reported here present. April 21, Mr. Hunt, with Victoria and others of his band, arrived, making the whole number present probably about one hundred. Victoria and his people said they were poor and hungry; that they were not all here, and he put himself in my power, and was ready to drink fresh water from my hand. He (Victoria) was told that while here he and his people should not be harmed, and they would be allowed to go away without injury; that they would be treated in good faith. Hard bread and bacon were given them, and a little coffee and sugar to a few of the principal men, and the council appointed for the afternoon. At 2 o'clock p. m. a council was held with Victoria, the principal chief; Paskeen, Cassari, and Salvador, sons of the late Mangus Colorado; Nané, one of the principal men of the tribe and a friend of Victoria; Acostá, and some thirty others, three of whom were from the band of Capitan Chiquito, whose rancheria was reported three days' travel north from Pinos Altos.

It was evident they were quite destitute of food and clothing; the three from Chiquito's band were the best clad, in buckskins. The council was held from 2 p. m. until 4½, in the presence of Captain Cook, 1st New Mexico volunteers; A. H. French, late captain 1st California cavalry; Mr. Amberg, who very kindly acted as interpreter; Mr. Hunt, and Maria Mendez, a woman who had been a captive among them since a child, (from Sonora,) until within some six years, who acted as interpreter, speaking the Spanish and Apache languages fluently. They were told, in substance, as follows, to wit: "I have something to say to Victoria and his people present of much importance to them. I came by authority of the general commanding all the troops in their country and the government. I shall talk to them truly and plainly; I did not speak with two tongues; they could rely upon what I told them; I heard they wanted peace, and I came to see and talk with them to know if it was so, and if true, to tell them on what terms they could have peace; they need not be afraid, for while here I would protect them; the government has made a reservation at the Bosque Redondo ample for all the Indians who wanted peace and would go there; it would not make another one for them; it had cost much to get supplies at the Bosque to feed all who would go and live there; they could be fed there; they could not be fed here; there was land there sufficient for all; enough to raise what they required to eat and more, and to graze their herds; there they could live in peace and plenty; although they would make peace here, and most of them keep it, there would be some bad men among them, as there were with other people, who would steal and kill, and the government could not know and tell who they were unless the good and peaceable men were at the reservation; all others would be considered bad men, at war with the white man, and so treated; I do not come to ask them to make peace, but to tell them they could have peace by going to the reservation at the Bosque; if they did not go they would be at war with the government; it was for them to decide which they would have, war or peace; if war, they should have it to their hearts' content; they must think well of what I told them now, and not come for peace too late, when the door was shut; I did not tell them this to threaten them or to boast of what would be done, but to let them know what they might expect, so that afterwards they could not say I had not told them plainly what the government meant; it was for them to say whether they would have war, be hunted from place to place, be poor and destitute and without a home, to be killed wherever found, or to live with their families, at peace with the white people, and have plenty to eat and wear; if they were not prepared to go now with their families to the Bosque, and wished to send some of their number there first to see the place and report upon it to their people, they could do so, and those who went should be protected and fed while going to and returning from the reservation; but, on their return, if they concluded to go, their people must be ready to go there at once; any who would go now with their families would be

20

fed, and those who should go after the delegation had returned would be fed while going there; they must understand that the government would feed them only on these terms; also that if they did not go they would be considered at war with us; more soldiers were coming to Arizona, and more would be sent after them here; I had told them what I was directed to tell them; it was for them to decide now what to do."

Victoria replied, in substance, as follows, to wit: "I and my people want peace; we are tired of war; we are poor and have little for ourselves and our families to eat or wear; it is very cold; we want to make a peace, a lasting peace, one that will keep; we would like to live in our country, and will go on to a reservation where the government may put us, and those who do not come in (of our people) we will go and help fight them; he said his people were not now all together, and were not ready to go to the Bosque; that he wanted to see the reservation first and know how the Indians live there, and if there was plenty of land for them all; he was willing to go himself, and any others I would name would go with him; he asked for protection while going and returning, which was promised him; he said he would have his people ready to go soon after his return if they concluded to go there; he said he was pleased with what I had told him and his people; it was plain and they could understand it; it was like talking to men and not to women; they knew now what to expect; he felt better; he had confidence in what I told him; he wanted peace and he meant it; I could rely upon what he said and promised; he had washed his hands and mouth with cold fresh water, and what he said was true; he said he spoke for all present; what he said all present consented to."

Victoria and Salvador, Nané and Acosta were named as the delegation to visit the reservation, the first two by myself, the latter two by Victoria.

They promised that in the mean time their people should keep peace with the whites, and would not kill or steal from them. They wanted me to have my people told that they were now at peace, so that when hunting they should not be hurt. I told them they would not be hurt if they kept their promise. If any of their men should kill or steal, and they would give up the guilty ones to the government, the others should not be molested; if not, all would be held responsible for their acts.

Victoria and others asked if their families would be fed while this peace lasted. They were told all who will go to the reservation should be fed, otherwise not. This I had before told them, and they must now so understand. Those present expressed themselves satisfied. Nané said, I could trust them; that I could now lie down beside the road and not be afraid, there was no danger of my animals; that he had no pockets to put what I said in, but the words had sunk deep into his heart, and they would not be forgotten.

Those from Capitan Chiquito's band said, they would return and tell their chief what they had heard, and that there was now peace, and they should not kill or steal from the white man; they would be ready to hear what Victoria said, on his return, and if he went to the Bosque, they thought their chief and people would go there to.

These men, as well as Victoria and his own men, said it was the Coyotero Apaches who stole mules from Paraje last October, and took a boy from there, captive; that they were not on friendly terms with the Coyoteros; they did not know where the boy was.

Victoria said his express had returned from Churchia's rancheria, and that he was out on a scout. He told Mr. Hunt that this was the first time he had ever asked for peace; heretofore he had opposed peace; that now he wanted peace and did not want to fight, they are suffering from hunger.

The result of the conference with these Indians, if they are to be believed, is more satisfactory than was anticipated, from what I had heard *en route* hither. I believe some want peace, and are disposed to yield much to the demands of the government with regard to them. I am encouraged to believe they will go to the reservation at the Bosque, if judiciously managed. Should they do so, it will be of great advantage to this rich section of mineral country; should they not conclude to go, I think now is the time to make war upon them as vigorously as possible.

On the 23d of April I moved my camp to near Pinos Altos, at which point, as previously agreed, the delegation to go to the reservation was to meet me. Not an Indian made his appearance. From all the information I could gather respecting them, I concluded they were acting in bad faith. Victoria sent me word, however, that some of their horses had been stolen, and his people had gone after them, and they could not meet me, as was agreed. Their rancherias were moved. I gave orders to my men to capture or kill every Indian (buck) they found. I remained in this camp three days. We scouted freely through the hills and surrounding country; no Indians seen. Four squaws came to the town ostensibly to trade, and see me, as reported. I did not see them.

On the 27th of April I left *en route* for Fort Cummings. At one o'clock at night I received an express from Mr. Hunt at Pinos Altos, informing me that some sixty armed Indians came into town on the p. m. of the day I left. That they evidently were ready for mischief; that the miners were collected as soon as possible. The Indians are reported to have got whiskey and powder of an Italian, (Don Carlos.) Whiskey had been given or sold them at different times previously by different persons in Pinos Altos. An Indian in attempting to drive off animals from the plaza was shot dead, when they all disappeared. Two children came in and said the squaws had gone off. An attack upon the town is apprehended at daylight

I sent immediately all the infantry I had (thirteen) except two, with instructions to reach Pinos Altos by daylight, if possible, and for the sergeant to consult with the citizens of the place as to the best steps to take. To seize all the ammunition and whiskey the Italian had, and arms; shut up his store and make him prisoner. The arms to be given to the citizens for their defence, if they had not already taken them.

An express was sent to Captain Burkett to make a short campaign of ten to twenty days, with some thirty men, against these Indians. He moved promptly, and on the 29th ultimo was to have arrived at Pinos Altos. He had instructions to make prisoners of such persons as it should be proven had given or sold to Indians powder and whiskey, and especially the Italian, (Don Carlos.) See enclosures marked A, B and C, being respectively a prohibition to the citizens of Pinos Altos to trade powder, whiskey, &c., to the Indians, as they were considered at war with the United States; and affidavits of James L. Homer and Richard A. Sarle, relative to certain persons giving or selling to Indians whiskey.

In conclusion, I would state that I believe a portion of these Gila Apaches are anxious for peace and are willing to go to the Indian reservation; that others, among whom are the principal men, do not intend to go there; are as bad at heart as ever, and have been endeavoring merely to put off any hostile movements towards them on the part of the government until they were better prepared for war and warm weather came. They are just about as friendly and peaceable and as much to be trusted as a rattlesnake when his tail is trodden upon. A vigorous and unrelenting war upon this savage and treacherous foe is the true policy to be pursued towards them, in my judgment. No good and lasting benefits to this country will result from a different course in regard to them.

The penalties of the law should be strictly enforced for its violation relative to Indian trade; the man who would give or sell to a hostile Apache that which would in any way aid or be the means of his killing the citizens of the country, should be hung without ceremony or absolution.

The Apaches are reported bad in Arizona, Chihuahua, and Sonora. Much stock is reported to have been stolen and killed, and many persons attacked, wounded and killed. The very Indians who talked so well in council, whose mouths were just purified with cold water, who were, like Uriah Heap, *very humble*, and whose hearts were imbued with a devout desire for peace, are the same *hombres* who are robbing and killing as opportunity offers.

Death to the Apache, and peace and prosperity to this land, is my motto.

I am, captain, very respectfully, your obedient servant,

N. H. DAVIS,
Assistant Inspector General, U. S. A.

Captain BEN. C. CUTLER, A. A. G.,
Department of New Mexico, Santa Fé, N. M.

DEPARTMENT OF NEW MEXICO,
Santa Fé, N. M., August 1, 1865.

Official:
BEN. C. CUTLER,
Assistant Adjutant General.

Proceedings of a board of officers which assembled at Fort Sumner, New Mexico, by virtue of the following order, viz:

[Special Orders, No. 13.—Extract.]

"DEPARTMENT OF NEW MEXICO, ASSISTANT ADJUTANT GENERAL'S OFFICE,
"*Santa Fé, N. M., April* 15, 1865.

"V. A board of officers, to consist of Major William McCleave, 1st cavalry California volunteers, Captain Henry B. Bristol, United States army, Captain Emil Fritz, 1st cavalry California volunteers, and Captain Lawrence G. Murphy, 1st cavalry New Mexico volunteers, will assemble at Fort Sumner, New Mexico, at 10 o'clock a. m., on Wednesday, the 26th day of April, 1865, or as soon thereafter as practicable, to consider and report upon the subject of the better organization of the Navajo tribe of Indians, to the end that more easy control can be had of their labor, and that the fruits of that labor may best conduce to their permanent support.

"The board will take great pains so to effect the purpose for which it is organized as to present a clear and practical plan of organization, &c., which may be definitely understood in all its details by the War Department, to which the report of the board will be submitted.

"By command of Brigadier General Carleton:

"BEN. C. CUTLER,
"*Assistant Adjutant General.*"

FORT SUMNER, NEW MEXICO,
April 26, 1865.

The board met pursuant to the foregoing order—all the members present—and after a careful consideration of the subjects presented for its action, respectfully submits the following report:

Bearing in mind the fact that the government of the Navajoes has always been patriarchal, without a recognized or acknowledged head of the nation, and that each chief had supreme control of his own family or band, it became apparent to the board that this form of government should be adopted as far as practicable and consistent with the interests of the government and the good of the tribe.

The first step towards this end is the dividing them off into villages, at say half a mile apart, the farm of each village to be in its immediate front, and the number of villages to be twelve, this being the number of principal men having families or bands. To each village there should be one principal chief, whose duty it will be to carry out and enforce all laws given him for the government of his village, or any instructions which he may receive at any time from the commanding officer, both to be fully and clearly explained to him by the interpreters. He will be held responsible for the order and police of his village. He will make a report at retreat every evening of the state of his village during the day, and if there are any absentees. Should any of his people leave the reservation during the day he will immediately report the fact to the commanding officer or officer of the day. He will see that none of his people leave their village between the hours of 7 o'clock p. m. and 5 o'clock a. m. in winter, and 7 o'clock p. m. and 4 o'clock a. m. in summer.

To each village there will be sub-chiefs at the rate of one to every one hundred souls. They will be appointed by the chief, and will retain their offices during good behavior. Their duties will consist in aiding the chief to execute the laws, and, in conjunction with him, as president, will form a court for the trial of minor offences, and for arbitration, in their respective villages.

The head chiefs of the respective villages will form a superior court, presided over by the commanding officer, or some officer especially appointed, who will be furnished with a clerk and the necessary interpreters. This court will be, in jurisdiction, analogous to a general court-martial, as will the inferior or village court to that of a regimental or garrison court-martial.

The indictment, finding, and sentence of the court will be duly recorded in a book to be kept for that purpose, a correct attested copy of which will be submitted to the department commander, through the commanding officer, at least one week after each trial.

The department commander has power to pardon or mitigate the sentence of the court.

The chiefs or members of the court will be the jurors, and the presiding officer the judge.

Appeals from decisions of the inferior or village courts will be heard and determined by this court.

It is the desire of the board to have the system of jurisprudence as simple as possible, and therefore think that from the decision of this court there should be no appeal, as there is still left a power to mitigate or pardon.

These courts organized, as in the foregoing, will decide upon all questions in law and equity, the inferior court confining itself to cases within its jurisdiction.

The court should assemble every three months on simple notification of day by the judge.

The twelve chiefs will also form a superior council, to be presided over by an officer, who will control their proceedings, and prevent the discussion of any matters dangerous to the peace and welfare of the reservation. Its functions will be exclusively deliberative, and it can entertain no question which should properly come before one of the courts. It should assemble every three months for the transaction of business, but may be assembled at any time the commanding officer may think necessary.

A chief may be removed from office by the commanding officer, whenever in his judgment the public service demands it, or he may be removed for misconduct by a two-thirds vote of his peers.

When a vacancy occurs in the position of chief, it will be filled by appointment by the commanding officer, but his choice is restricted to the sub-chief of the village in which the vacancy occurs.

In submitting the following articles the board wishes it understood that it has embraced only such offences as are peculiarly applicable to these people in their present transition state. It would be impracticable to provide in a report of this description for the punishment of all the crimes and offences known to our laws, nearly all of which are equally incidental to these people as to the same numbers of a more civilized community, under similar circumstances. But to guard against the permitting of offenders to go unpunished, and to establish a gradual and wholesome dread of outraging the law, it is recommended that the criminal laws of the Territory be so amended as to somewhat modify the penalties, and furnished to the officer designated to preside over their courts for his guidance in all cases which might arise. It may appear unjust to punish people for a violation of laws which they do not only not understand, but have heretofore been taught to regard as the highest virtue to break. But it must be recollected that these Indians have got to be made to respect the bonds which unite civilized society, and the only practical way of doing this is by inflicting a punishment, however light, for the first offence, and increasing the punishment in proportion to the increase of knowledge, until its severity would prevent further repetition. This is the only possible mode of instructing them on the subject of the laws:

ARTICLE 1. Any adult Indian guilty of murder in the first or second degree will be punished by hanging by the neck until dead, by lashes, or by fine or imprisonment with hard labor, according to the degree of the offence.

ARTICLE 2. Theft will be punished with lashes, fines, or imprisonment with hard labor, according to the decree of the offence.

ARTICLE 3. Any able-bodied Indian absenting himself from the necessary work on his farm, or the acequia, or who shall refuse to perform such work, shall be confined at hard labor for a period not less than one week nor more than two months.

ARTICLE 4. Any Indian who shall wantonly destroy the tools or implements furnished him by the government, or who shall lose the same through neglect, shall forfeit from the proceeds of his farm an amount equal to the damage sustained, and shall be confined at hard labor, as in the preceding article.

ARTICLE 5. Any Indian who shall wantonly destroy any trees or farm produce on the reservation shall be confined at hard labor as in article 3.

ARTICLE 6. Any adult Indian who shall be found absent from his or her village between the hours of 7 o'clock p. m. and 5 o'clock a. m. in winter, and 8 o'clock p. m. and 4 o'clock a. m. in summer, shall be imprisoned as in article 3.

ARTICLE 7. Any Indian who shall absent himself from the reservation without permission from the proper authority shall be confined at hard labor as in article 3.

ARTICLE 8. Females shall not be subject to capital punishment or the infliction of lashes.

The Indians of this reservation have been more than once unjustly charged with the commission of offences against the citizens outside of the reserve, and with a view to prevent the probability of cause for such complaints, as well as to secure the presence of the Indian and his labor, some of the foregoing articles were framed.

RECOMMENDATIONS.

1. That as capital punishment for the crime of murder is unknown among them, it be resorted to only in extreme cases.

2. That there be employed one factor and six assistants to each village. The duties of the factor will be to take charge of, and be responsible for, all tools, implements, and seeds belonging to the village; to superintend and direct the labor on the farm; to receive and keep an accurate account of the produce of each Indian's garden, and to issue it back to them in such quantities and under such regulations as the commanding officer may direct. He will be under the control of the commanding officer, to whom he will render his accounts for examination.

3. That the factor and his assistants receive a liberal compensation, so as to secure the services of competent and reliable men.

4. That the compensation of the factor and assistants, as well as all other incidental expenses, be deducted from the surplus produce of the farms, but that in case of total failure of the crops, or in the event of there being no surplus, then the employés will be paid with government funds, provided such failure of the crops or lack of surplus was not the result of their neglect, in which case they should be discharged, forfeiting all pay due them.

5. Should it become necessary at any time, from total or partial failure of the crops, for the government to issue the Indians rations, pay the employés, or be at any other incidental expense, that the government be reimbursed by a gradual tax on the produce of the farms, the tax to be uniform, so as not to bear too heavy on the industrious, and the assessment to be made by a board of officers.

6. That for each village there be erected a substantial store-house for tools, implements, seeds, and produce, with accommodations for the factor and his assistants.

7. That a suitable building be erected in a central place for a court-house and council-room, with accommodations for prisoners, guard, &c.

8. That the chief of each village, willing to live in a house, have a suitable one built for him, and that where they prefer lodges, assistance be rendered them to build ones of a superior description.

9. That, when establishing the villages, the lodges be erected so that they be made as comfortable and commodious as their peculiar formation will permit.

10. That an appropriate and comfortable uniform be furnished the chiefs semi-annually.

11. That, in order to give authority and consequence to the chiefs, they should be treated with the utmost consideration by the military authorities; and, that they may be induced to value their positions, they should receive occasional presents, and thereby insure a strict and faithful discharge of their duties.

12. In order to wean the Indians from their present helpless dependence on the military power, that in future all complaints must be submitted to the respective chiefs and their courts for redress and settlement, and not as heretofore to the post commander.

13. That, with the same object in view, the direct issue of rations by the military authorities be discontinued as speedily as possible. So long as the present system continues the Indian is well aware that he will not be permitted to want, whether he works or not, and takes advantage of the fact to satisfy his natural inclination to idleness.

14. That immediate measures be taken to erect a suitable church and school-house.

15. That as some of these Indians, known as "Cebolletanos," are now professedly Roman Catholics, as this is the religion of the country, and as this church alone possesses the necessary organization and means to accomplish the reformation and education of these Indians, that the church and school-house be placed under the control of ministers of that denomination.

16. That in the event of the church being willing to put up, at its own expense, the necessary buildings, a suitable site be selected, and the ground be granted by the government without cost or taxes to the head of the church in New Mexico; provided that it can never be transferred or disposed of, nor used for any other purpose; and providing, also, that the buildings are erected in a reasonable time, and will revert to the government, with all improvements, whenever they cease to be used for religious and educational purposes.

17. That a board of visitors be appointed semi-annually to inspect the schools and report upon their condition, and the progress of the scholars.

18. That no traders be permitted to enter the reservation for purposes of traffic, except by special permission of the commanding officer, with the approval of the department commander, and then only under such regulations as will secure the Indians against the possibility of fraud.

19. That all articles be considered contraband, except such as contribute to their health and comfort.

20. That the sale to the Indians of arms, ammunition, and intoxicating liquors be positively prohibited.

21. That the purchase of horses by the Indians be prohibited, and the raising of them be discouraged, being unprofitable, and only used by them as a means of locomotion, when the object is to confine them to the reservation.

22. That there be an annual prize given to the Indian who raises the largest and best crop of cereals in proportion to the size of his farm.

23. That all expenses, of whatever description, which the government may be at in the future for the benefit of these Indians, be deducted from the surplus produce of their farms and refunded.

24. As the Indians depend almost entirely for clothing of every description on the wool of the sheep, that for the next three years the produce of their farms, over and above the amount required for their support, and to defray incidental expenses, be converted into sheep, under the direction of the subsistence department. This will be the means of supplying a great want of these people, and, by giving proper occupation to the females, tend to promote industry and virtue.

Owing to the illness of one of the members, the board has been prevented in furnishing their report at an earlier day. It is now respectfully submitted.

WM. McCLEAVE,
Major 1st Cal. Cav., President.
LAWRENCE G. MURPHY,
Captain 1st Cav. New Mexico Vols, Recorder.

There being no further business before the board, it adjourned *sine die.*

WM. McCLEAVE,
Major 1st Cal. Cav., President.
LAWRENCE G. MURPHY,
Captain 1st Cav. New Mexico Vols., Recorder.

DEPARTMENT OF NEW MEXICO,
Santa Fé, N. M., July 5, 1865.

Official:

BEN. C. CUTLER,
Assistant Adjutant General.

HEADQUARTERS DEPARTMENT OF NEW MEXICO,
Santa Fé, N. M., March 30, 1865.

SIR: I have the honor herewith to enclose for your information printed copies of General Orders No. 3, series of 1864, and General Orders No. 4, series for 1865, from these headquarters, which give an epitome of operations against Indians within the department of New Mexico for the last two years. You will observe in the summing up in General Orders No. 4, that we have three thousand Indian children now upon the reservation. It is in reference to these children that this communication is written.

Last year I had the honor to request of the Secretary of the Interior that that department furnish funds for the building of school-houses in which these children may be educated, but no answer was ever made to the letter. I now beg that you will take this important matter under consideration. It lies at the bottom of all our efforts to civilize these Indians. The education of these children is the fundamental idea on which must rest all our hopes of making the Navajoes a civilized and Christian people. It is unnecessary for me to put on paper the many arguments which I could use to convince you of the importance of having schools for these children. You can figure to your own mind three thousand intelligent boys and girls with no one to teach them to read or write. Here is a field for those who are philanthropic, which is ample enough to engage their attention, and be the object of their charities for many years. Without money to build school-houses and to buy books my hands are tied. The bishop of New Mexico has promised help in the way of teachers; but, in my opinion, this important subject should receive the fostering care of the government. These children properly belong to your department, and now, as well as when they have become men and women, are and will be objects which must engage your solicitude. I trust, therefore, that my appeal to you in their behalf will not be in vain.

There is another point to which I beg to call your immediate attention. Last year I requested of you that the surveyor general of New Mexico should cause to be surveyed the Indian reservation. This should be done at once. Not only should the exterior lines be run and be marked by durable mounds, but the irrigable lands should be laid off in ten-acre lots for assignment to different families. Perhaps even lots of a smaller size may be necessary. No permanent organization of the tribes into bands, nor identity of bands with particular fields, can be made fairly and justly until this survey is made. You are aware that there are no public surveys making either in this Territory or in Arizona which would interfere with this work. Not one rood of land has been surveyed in New Mexico since September, 1862, to my knowledge; the reason was, perhaps, on account of Indian difficulties. But there exists no reason why this important reservation may not at once be surveyed, and be cut up into lots. I pray that this may be done at an early day.

Very respectfully, your obedient servant,

JAMES H. CARLETON,
Brigadier General, Commanding.

HON. SECRETARY OF THE INTERIOR, *Washington, D. C.*

HEADQUARTERS DEPARTMENT OF NEW MEXICO,
Santa Fé, N. M., April 24, 1865.

GENERAL: I returned yesterday from the Bosque Redondo. It will be impossible to organize into bands and systematically direct the labors of the nine thousand Indians we have at that point, unless the lands are properly surveyed. I have written two letters to the Secretary of the Interior on the subject. The last one is herewith enclosed. The surveyor general of New Mexico is now in Arizona, and it is uncertain when he will return. Even if he were here, there are no practical surveyors here who could do the work. So I beg respectfully to recommend that the War Department—unless the Department of the Interior will do it—will employ and send out at once some practical surveyors to divide this land, so that particular lots can be given to particular bands and families. To do this by guess is going to lead to endless quarrels. Once I can divide up the land so as to let a given quantity be set apart for a certain number of Indians, and have it defined by a wall which they can make, once the lines are drawn, the great step towards organization will at once commence. Now, I have but a mass of Indians, with no acknowledged head and no subdivisions.

The question about the schools for the three thousand children I have written much about, but can do nothing without authority from Washington to erect the school-houses.

Very respectfully, your obedient servant,

JAMES H. CARLETON,
Brigadier General, Commanding.

ADJUTANT GENERAL UNITED STATES ARMY, *Washington, D. C.*

DEPARTMENT OF NEW MEXICO, ASSISTANT ADJUTANT GENERAL'S OFFICE,
Santa Fé, N. M., July 5, 1865.

Official:

BEN. C. CUTLER,
Assistant Adjutant General.

FORT SUMNER, N. M., *July* 14, 1865.

DEAR GENERAL: I regret to find from your last official letter that the report of insects having made their appearance here weighs heavily upon you. I also sincerely regret to have to tell you that all the corn in the most advanced state is being devoured by worms. I have never witnessed the like. It is truly discouraging. The appearance of the corn in the field is excellent, but the cursed insects seem to devour all the grain in the ear. To add to our misfortune, the continual rainy weather has very much interfered with the harvesting of the wheat. To save that which has been heretofore cut, I have given Captain Rynerson permission to feed it in lieu of an equal amount of quartermaster grain, the amount to be determined by board of survey. Among the wheat the ground is now so wet that reapers cannot stand upon it.

Lest there should be any misunderstanding between Captains Bristol and Rynerson, in regard to the harvesting, I relieved the former from all duty on the farm.

Though to-day is fair, there is no indication that the rain is all gone.

Bean-planting will stop to-day, consequently ploughing will cease until the harvest is secured.

I find that the decision in Sergeant Lagrand's case will let out of service at this post about one-half the regular troops.

The scarcity of troops and severity of duty caused me to bring in the detachment from the Rio Salado. When the Indians heard of their friends' defeat they appeared to dislike it very much. However, they were told that any who left the reservation without permission would be hunted down and killed. They remarked that they never supposed soldiers from this post would kill them. In reply, they were told that soldiers would always obey orders; that it was orders to kill them if they went off without leave.

Trusting you are quite well, I am, general, respectfully yours,

WILLIAM McCLEAVE.

General J. H. CARLETON, *Santa Fé, N. M.*

DEPARTMENT OF NEW MEXICO,
Santa Fé, N. M., July 21, 1865.

Official:

BEN. C. CUTLER,
Assistant Adjutant General.

OFFICE COMMISSARY GENERAL OF SUBSISTENCE,
Washington City, December 28, 1865.

SIR: I have the honor to acknowledge the receipt of your communication of the 23d instant, and in reply respectfully inform you that the expense of subsisting the Navajoes and Apaches at Bosque Redondo reservation from March 1, 1864, to October 1, 1865, (eighteen months,) was about $1,114,981 70.

I have the honor to be, very respectfully, your obedient servant,

A. E. SHIRAS,
Assistant Commissary General Subsistence.

Hon. J. R. DOOLITTLE.
Chairman of Joint Committee to Investigate Indian Affairs, U. S. Senate.

Indorsement on communication from Hon. Charles T. Poston, delegate from Arizona, to the War Department, Washington, D. C., January 12, 1865. *Recommends the establishment of a military post at Amboy; also, an Indian reservation in that vicinity, which requires protection, &c., &c.*

[Referred by General Halleck to headquarters department of New Mexico, January 17, 1865.]

"FEBRUARY 18, 1865.

"Respectfully returned. I do not think there is any military necessity for the establishment of a post at the mouth of Bill Williams's Fork on the Colorado of the West; nor do I agree with the Hon. Mr. Poston about having an Indian reservation on the Colorado.

"There are very grave objections to going to the expense of such an establishment in such an inaccessible country, surrounded as it is by deserts; besides, the Mojave Indians are at peace, and could not with propriety or profit be moved from their part of the valley of that river to another part further down.

"The other Indians, living upon the various slopes of the elevated country from which rise the San Francisco mountains, are not a warlike race, and can easily be managed, if treated with moderation, judgment, and firmness, until the country is filled with white settlers; then, as in California, they can be gathered together at some point, to be chosen with care, where they can be fed and protected until the destiny, which has so unrelentingly followed their race, blots them in their turn from the face of the earth. The Apaches of Arizona, living upon the affluents to the Gila, should, in my judgment, be placed upon a reservation upon the Gila; say somewhere upon the mouth of the Rio de Sauz, where there is an extensive valley, once densely populated, it is supposed, by Aztecs as they journeyed southward in the eleventh century.

"The remains of ancient *acequias* and of villages indicate that this land once sustained a great many people. It can do so again.

"All of which is respectfully submitted:

JAMES H. CARLETON,
Brigadier General, Commanding.

Official:
BEN. C. CUTLER,
Assistant Adjutant General.

DEPARTMENT OF NEW MEXICO, ASSISTANT ADJUTANT GENERAL'S OFFICE,
Santa Fé, N. M., July 26, 1865.

CAPTAIN: It is understood that you were at Fort Fauntleroy several years since when some Navajoes were fired upon by order of a Lieutenant Colonel Chaves.

If you were present on the occasion referred to above, the general commanding desires that you make by return mail a detailed account of the whole affair as you remember it. Great care should be taken to have it exact, as it is to be laid before the congressional Committee on Indian Affairs.

Respectfully, your obedient servant,

BEN. C. CUTLER,
Assistant Adjutant General.

Captain NICHOLAS HODT,
1st New Mexico Cav., Fort Wingate, N. M.

Official:
CYRUS H. DE FORREST, *Aide-de-Camp.*

FORT WINGATE, NEW MEXICO, *September* 7, 1865.

MAJOR: In compliance with instructions received from headquarters department of New Mexico, assistant adjutant general's office, Santa Fé, New Mexico, dated July 26, 1865, I have the honor to make the following statement:

Some time during the month of September, 1861, as near as I can recollect, horse-racing was frequent at Fort Fauntleroy, New Mexico, and high bets made by officers and Navajo Indians at the post. Government stock was staked by the officers as if it were their own. If lost, all right; and if won, so much gained by them by means of government property. I was not an eye-witness of the staking of government property, but proof can be furnished.

The Navajo Indians appeared to be at that time very friendly to the government; they visited the post by hundreds every day, and were rationed on meat and flour. This friendly feeling of the Navajoes was kept up until the time of the horse-races. There were three different races, the third race in order to give the Indians satisfaction. Large bets, larger than on either of the other races, were made on both sides. The Indians flocked in by hundreds, women and children; some of them mounted on fine ponies, richly dressed, and all appeared to be there to see the race, and not with any hostile intentions.

The troops in the post had orders to be under arms, but that they might go to the gate to see the race. About noon the race came off. Lieutenant Ortiz rode Dr. Kavanaugh's horse. The Indian's horse did not run a hundred yards before it ran off the track. I being at the upper end of the track, could not see the cause of it, but the report was that the Indian's bridle broke. The Indians then said the race was not fair, and that the bets should be drawn; the opposite party, not satisfied with the proposition, would not give up what they had won, and consequently the commanding officer gave orders to the officer of the day not to allow the Navajoes inside of the post. The horse was taken inside the post, followed by the whole winning party, the drums beating, fifes and fiddles screeching, &c., &c. So the procession went whooping and hallooing to receive the part they had won. Finally, whilst thus occupied a shot was fired at or near the post. Every man then ran to arm himself. Companies did not regularly form, but every man ran wherever he thought fit. The shot was fired on account of Private Morales, sentinel No. 2, whilst opposing an Indian's entrance to the post. It was said that the Indian was intoxicated and tried to force his entrance past the sentinel. At that instant the shot was fired and the Indian fell. Who fired is not known. As soon as this was ascertained, the Navajoes, squaws and children, ran in all directions and were shot and bayoneted. I tried my best to form the company I was first sergeant of, and succeeded in forming about twenty men—it being very hard work. I then marched out to the east side of the post; there I saw a soldier murdering two little children and a woman. I hallooed immediately to the soldier to stop. He looked up, but did not obey my order. I ran up as quick as I could, but could not get there soon enough to prevent him from killing the two innocent children and wounding severely the squaw. I ordered his belts to be taken off and taken prisoner to the post. On my arrival in the post I met Lieutenant Ortiz with a pistol at full cock, saying, "Give back this soldier his arms, or else I'll shoot you, God damn you," which circumstances I reported to my company commander, he reporting the same to the colonel commanding, and the answer he received from the colonel was, "that Lieutenant Ortiz did perfectly right, and that he gave credit to the soldier who murdered the children and wounded the squaw." Meantime the colonel had given orders to the officer of the day to have the artillery (mountain howitzers) brought out and to open upon the Indians. The sergeant in charge of the mountain howitzers pretended not to understand the order given, for he considered it as an unlawful order; but being cursed by the officer of the day, and threatened, he had to execute the order or else get himself in trouble. The Indians scattered all over the valley below the post, attacked the post-herd, wounded the Mexican herder, but did not succeed in getting any stock; also attacked the expressman some ten miles from the post, took his horse and mail-bag and wounded him in the arm. After the massacre there were no more Indians to be seen about the post with the exception of a few squaws, favorites of the officers. The commanding officer endeavored to make peace again with the Navajoes by sending some of the favorite squaws to talk with the chiefs; but the only satisfaction the squaws received was a good flogging. An expressman was sent shortly after the affairs above mentioned happened, but private letters were not allowed to be sent, and letters that reached the post office at Fauntleroy were found opened but not forwarded. To the best of my knowledge the number of Navajoes killed was twelve or fifteen; the number wounded could not be ascertained. There were only two wounded bucks and one wounded squaw in the hospital. The rest wounded must have been taken away by the tribe.

I am, sir, very respectfully, your obedient servant,

NICHOLAS HODT,
Captain 1st Cavalry, New Mexico Volunteers.

Major BEN. C. CUTLER, A. A. G.,
Department of New Mexico, Santa Fé, N. M.

Official: CYRUS H. DE FORREST, *Aide-de-Camp.*

Report of the cost of feeding Indians at Fort Sumner, New Mexico, in the following months, viz:

March, 1865.—Average number of Indians, 9,160	$70,578 30
April, 1865.—Average number of Indians, 8,893	72,704 97
May, 1865.—Average number of Indians, 8,038	70,861 15
June, 1865.—Average number of Indians, 7,658	53,519 04
July, 1865.—Average number of Indians, 8,244	60,610 94
August, 1865.—Average number of Indians, 7,374	65,773 68
September, 1865.—Average number of Indians, 7,555	58,308 90
	452,356 98

H. B. BRISTOL,
Captain 5th Infantry, U. S. A., A. C. S, I. D.

DISTRICT OF NEW MEXICO, *October* 16, 1865.

Official: CYRUS H. DE FORREST, *Aide-de-Camp.*

Return of Indian captives held in custody at Fort Sumner, New Mexico, for the month of May, 1865.

Number.	Designation of tribes.	PRESENT.					Total absent.	Total present and absent.	Total last return.	ALTERATIONS SINCE LAST RETURN.							
										Gain.				Loss.			
		Men.	Women.	Children.	Infants.	Total.				Births.	Captures.	From other causes.	Total.	Deaths.	Desertions.	From other causes.	Total.
1	Mescalero Apaches	130	175	149	1	455	8	463	463								
2	Gila Apaches	11	5	14		30	1	31	31								
3	Navajoes	2,326	2,712	3,164	275	8,477	1,308	8,477	8,510					33			33
	Total	2,467	2,892	3,327	276	8,962	1,317	8,971	9,004					33			33

REMARKS.—8 male Mescalero Apaches absent with leave since March 25, 1865. 1 Coyotero chief (Miguel) absent with leave since May 12, 1865. Of Navajoes, 12 males and 6 females died, disease unknown; 2 males were drowned in the Pecos; 3 males reported killed by Comanches on the Llano Estacado, on the 13th. An actual account of the tribe shows present, 7,169, leaving absent without leave 1,308.

WILLIAM McCLEAVE,
Major 1st California Cavalry, Commanding.

HEAQUARTERS FORT SUMNER, NEW MEXICO, *May* 31, 1865.

DEPARTMENT OF NEW MEXICO, *Santa Fé, N. M., July* 6, 1865.

Official:

BEN. C. CUTLER, *Assistant Adjutant General.*

Return of Indian captives held in custody at Fort Sumner, New Mexico, for the month of July, 1865.

Number.	Designation of tribes.	PRESENT.					Total absent.	Total present and absent.	Total last return.	ALTERATIONS SINCE LAST RETURN.							
										Gain.				Loss.			
		Men.	Women.	Children.	Infants.	Total.				Births.	Captures.	From other causes.	Total.	Deaths.	Desertions.	From other causes.	Total.
1 2	Mescalero Apaches ...... Gila Apaches .... }	101	184	121	11	417	52	469	507	......	......	......	......	9	29	......	*38
3	Navajoes	1,829	2,314	2,777	233	7,173	......	7,173	8,491	......	......	......	......	......	......	1,318	†1,318
	Total	1,930	2,498	2,918	244	7,590	52	7,642	8,998	......	......	......	......	9	29	1,318	1,356

* Actual count by Captain Murphy on the 28th ultimo, which leaves a balance of thirty-eight to be accounted for since last return; of this number nine have died; the others are absent without leave, or have deserted.

† Actual count by Captain Bristol on the 31st ultimo, being a discrepancy of 1,318 since last return; but there were reported, on last return, 1,002 absent without leave. No doubt many have died, but it is impossible to ascertain the number.

WM. McCLEAVE, *Major 1st California Cavalry, Commanding.*

HEADQUARTERS FORT SUMNER, N. M., *August* 2, 1865.

DEPARTMENT NEW MEXICO, *Santa Fé, N. M*, *August* 10, 1865.

Official:

BEN. C. CUTLER, *Assistant Adjutant General.*

Return of Indian captives held in custody at Fort Sumner, New Mexico, for the month of August, 1865.

Number.	Designation of tribe.	PRESENT.					ABSENT.			Total present and absent.	Total last return.	ALTERATIONS SINCE LAST RETURN.									
												Gain.					Loss.				
		Men.	Women.	Children.	Infants.	Total.	With leave.	Without leave.	Total.			Men.	Women.	Children.	Infants.	Total.	Men.	Women.	Children.	Infants.	Total.
1	Apaches	98	169	112	14	393	25	53	78	471	469	----	----	----	3	3	----	1	----	----	*1
2	Navajoes	2,004	2,156	2,751	240	7,151	----	----	----	7,151	7,173	----	----	----	----	----	----	2	----	----	†22
	Total	2,102	2,325	2,863	254	7,544	25	53	78	7,622	7,642	----	----	----	3	3	----	3	----	----	23

* Actual count made by Captain G. G. Murphy, 1st New Mexico cavalry, on the 31st day of August, 1865, which shows three births and one death during the month.

† Actual count made by Captain H. B. Bristol, 5th United States infantry, on the 31st day of August, 1865, which gives a deficiency of twenty-two from last report; of these, three are known to have died, and it is probable more have died, which were never reported.

WM. McCLEAVE, *Major 1st California Cavalry, Commanding.*

HEADQUARTERS FORT SUMNER, N. M., *August* 31, 1865.

Return of Indian captives held in custody at Fort Sumner, New Mexico, for the month of September, 1865.

Number.	Designation of tribe.	PRESENT.					ABSENT.			Total present and absent.	Total last return.	ALTERATIONS SINCE LAST RETURN.									
												Gain.					Loss.				
		Men.	Women.	Children.	Infants.	Total.	With leave.	Without leave.	Total.			Men.	Women.	Children.	Infants.	Total.	Men.	Women.	Children.	Infants.	Total.
1	Apaches	97	171	120	14	402	----	----	----	402	471	----	----	----	----	----	23	23	23	----	*69
2	Navajoes	2,059	2,210	2,809	240	7,318	----	----	----	7,318	7,151	72	62	60	----	194	9	10	8	----	†27
	Total	2,156	2,381	2,929	254	7,720	----	----	----	7,720	7,622	72	62	60	----	194	32	33	31	----	96

* Actual count made by Captain Murphy on the 29th ultimo, which leaves a balance of sixty-nine to be accounted for since last return; of those, sixty-seven are absent without leave or have deserted; two died from disease.

† Actual count made by First Lieutenant E. C. Baldwin on the 29th ultimo, which shows a gain of one hundred and sixty-seven returned from absent without leave. Died from disease or other causes, twenty-seven.

WM. McCLEAVE, *Major 1st California Cavalry, Commanding.*

HEADQUARTERS FORT SUMNER, N. M., *September* 30, 1865.

FORT SUMNER, NEW MEXICO, *July* 28, 1865.

SIR: In obedience to indorsement on letter from the general commanding, herewith enclosed, I have the honor to report that on the 28th ultimo I counted the Apaches, with the following result:

	Men.	Women.	Boys.	Girls.	Infants.	Total.
Present	101	184	62	59	11	417
Absent with leave	3					3
Absent without leave	16	33				49
Died	2	7				9
						478

Shortly after taking charge of the Apaches I directed the interpreter to make a count, the result of which, as reported by him, showed the total number, present and absent, to be four hundred and seventy-eight belonging to this reservation. Those then reported "absent without leave" are still absent, and since that time the number is somewhat increased. I found great difficulty in making them understand the necessity of their having written passes when they wished to be absent, but they now appreciate its importance and cannot again offend through ignorance.

Twenty-eight of those now absent without leave—seven men among them—took advantage of the temporary absence of Cadetta to leave the reservation, and when the man who was then employed as interpreter was questioned on the subject he denied that any had left. This man has since been discharged. Cadetta assures me that this party are only temporarily absent for the purpose of collecting mescal and fruit, which they believe, and no doubt is, necessary to their health, and that they will shortly return.

On the evening of the 30th ultimo a man and child returned to the reservation after an absence of over five months. The man states that during his absence he has been living with a party of Mascalero Apaches, who reside south of the Guadalupe mountains, somewhere in the vicinity of Fort Quitman, and who equal in numbers those now on the reservation. Three other men left with him for the purpose, he says, of getting their wives, who are living with the band they visited. I have selected two Apaches, (Estrella and Tomas,) in whom I have great confidence, to visit this band and explain to them that if they come it must be with the determination of forever remaining, as they will not be permitted to go back. I have also instructed them to send in any Indians belonging to this reservation whom they may meet. They will leave here this afternoon and be gone about twenty days.

At the request of some of the chiefs I also purpose sending to-day two other Apaches to visit José Maria and others, absent from the reservation, advising them all to come in, to avoid probable collision with the troops.

I have hopes that both parties will be successful. At any rate they will ascertain the exact locality of those they seek; important, if it is determined to send troops against them.

In future, I will, personally, make a count of the Apaches at the end of each month.

Very respectfully, your obedient servant

LAWRENCE G. MURPHY,
Captain 1st Cav, N. M. Vols., Superintendent of Apaches.

Lieutenant B. TAYLOR,
5th U. S. Inf., Post Adjutant, Fort Sumner, N. M.

DEPARTMENT OF NEW MEXICO,
Santa Fé, N. M., August 10, 1865.

Official:

BEN. C. CUTLER,
Assistant Adjutant General.

Hon. J. R. DOOLITTLE, *United States Senate.*

FORT SUMNER, NEW MEXICO, *May* 1, 1865.

SIR: In compliance with instructions, dated "Headquarters Fort Sumner, New Mexico, December 7, 1864," relative to transplanting trees on this reservation, I have the honor to make a full report of the number of trees which were transplanted from the 7th day of December, 1864, to the 30th of April, 1865, and the amount of labor expended, viz:

From the 8th day of December, 1864, to the 10th day of March, 1865, my laboring party consisted of one sergeant, three privates, and five Indians, setting out trees, during which time I transplanted five thousand and forty-eight (5,048) trees, as follows:

1864.	
December 8	70
December 9	70
December 10	70
December 11, (Sunday.)	
December 12	70
December 13	70
December 14	70
December 15	70
December 16	75
December 17	50
December 18, (Sunday.)	
December 19, (stormy.)	
December 20, (stormy.)	
December 21, (snow and frost.)	
December 22, (snow and frost.)	
December 23, (snow and frost.)	
December 24, (snow and frost.)	
December 25, (Sunday.)	
December 26, (snow and frost.)	
December 27, (snow and frost.)	
December 28	46
December 29	46
December 30	46
December 31	47
Total number in December, 1864	800

1865.	
January 1, (Sunday.)	
January 2	54
January 3	54
January 4	54
January 5	54
January 6	54
January 7	54
January 8, (Sunday.)	
January 9	60
January 10	65
January 11	65
January 12	65
January 13	65
January 14	65
January 15, (Sunday.)	
January 16	55
January 17	55
January 18	55
January 19	55
January 20	55
January 21	60
January 22, (Sunday.)	
January 23	55
January 24	53
January 25	53
January 26	53
January 27	53
January 28	53
January 29, (Sunday.)	
January 30	53
January 31	53
	1,470

1865.	
February 1	82
February 2	82
February 3	82
February 4	82
February 5, (Sunday.)	
February 6	82
February 7	82
February 8	82
February 9	82
February 10	82
February 11	82
February 12, (Sunday.)	
February 13	82
February 14	82
February 15	82
February 16	82
February 17	82
February 18	82
February 19, (Sunday.)	
February 20	82
February 21	82
February 22	82
February 23	104
February 24	104
February 25	104
February 26, (Sunday.)	
February 27	104
February 28	104
	2,078

1865.		1865.	
March 1	84	March 6	77
March 2	77	March 7	77
March 3	77	March 8	77
March 4	77	March 9	77
March 5, (Sunday.)		March 10	77
			700

From the 10th of March, 1865, to the 30th day of April my party mustered one corporal and ten Indians and one team to transport. During this time I set out seven thousand and twenty (7,020) branches, viz:

1865.		1865.	
March 11	163	April 6	163
March 12, (Sunday.)		April 7	163
March 13	163	April 8	163
March 14	163	April 9, (Sunday.)	
March 15	163	April 10	163
March 16	163	April 11	163
March 17	163	April 12	163
March 18	163	April 13	163
March 19, (Sunday.)		April 14	163
March 20	163	April 15	163
March 21	163	April 16, (Sunday.)	
March 22	163	April 17	174
March 23	163	April 18	163
March 24	163	April 19	163
March 25	163	April 20	163
March 26, (Sunday.)		April 21	163
March 27	163	April 22	163
March 28	163	April 23, (Sunday)	
March 29	163	April 24	163
March 30	163	April 25	163
March 31	163	April 26	163
April 1	163	April 27	163
April 2, (Sunday.)		April 28	163
April 3	163	April 29	163
April 4	163	April 30, (Sunday.)	
April 5	163		

Total number in December, 1864	800 trees.
Total number in January, 1865	1,470 trees
Total number in February, 1865	2,078 trees.
Total number to March 10, 1865	700 trees.
Total number from March 10 to 31, 1865	1,630 branches.
Total number in April, 1865	5,390 branches.
Total number from December 7, 1864, to April 30, 1865	12,068

These trees were planted in place of those that died, &c., and extending the avenue five miles and on the *acequia madre*. No extra expense has been incurred, excepting rations for the Indians who have worked.

Respectfully submitted:

S. A. GORHAM,
Captain 1st Cal. Cav., in charge of party.

The branches were set out to form a grove in the low lands.

I would respectfully recommend that in another season there would be several branches set out in the same manner, as they can be easily procured.

S. A. GORHAM,
Captain 1st Cal. Cav., Com'dg Co. G.

Lieutenant B. TAYLOR,
Post Adjutant, Fort Sumner, N. M.

DEPARTMENT OF NEW MEXICO,
Santa Fé, N. M., July 5, 1865.

Official:

BEN. C. CUTLER,
Assistant Adjutant General.

SANTA FÉ, NEW MEXICO, *July* 3, 1865.

Present: Hon. J. R Doolittle, chairman; Hon. L. F. S. Foster, Hon. L W. Ross.

Brigadier General James H. Carleton:

I am brigadier general of volunteers and major in the 6th regiment United States cavalry. I have been in the service twenty-five years. I first came to this Territory with General Sumner in 1851, and left in the fall of 1856. I returned again in the summer of 1862, and have been here ever since. I have been in command of this department since the 18th of September, 1862 My principal duties have been in connexion with Indian affairs. According to the best of my information, the facts stated in my printed pamphlet, dated December 16, 1864, are correct, and express my present opinion; and I offer that letter as part of my present statement. The Navajo country is a country of elevated *mesas*, destitute of water, and has some few ranges of mountains. Between these *mesas* are some low lands, whereon some springs and streams are found. These springs or streams are at great distance from each other, as compared with the frequency of water found elsewhere. These waters are of a limited extent and volume; and the best of them sink in the earth at a short distance from their source. There are two exceptions to this general remark. One is the San Juan, a tributary of the Colorado of the West. Along this river are intervals of some extent, but separated from each other by ranges of mountains and *mesas* that abut upon the river. No one of these intervals is large enough for a reservation for one quarter of these Navajoes. Formidable ranges of mountains are near by, in which they could hide, and no force of troops could keep them together. This is on the supposition that a reservation were selected on the San Juan river. Now, the cost of transporting supplies from the Rio Grande to that point to subsist the Indians and to provide for the troops necessary to guard them in that locality would be immense, because the country to be traversed is difficult for the passage of wagons, and has long stretches through sage plains, without water in one or two instances of from forty to sixty miles.

The San Juan runs through a country bearing gold, which will soon attract miners to that region; and even if the Indians were placed there they would soon come into conflicts with that kind of men, and great difficulties and complications would result therefrom. The other exception to which I alluded is that of the Colorado Chiquito or Flax river. This is affluent to the Colorado of the West further down than the San Juan. It is subject to very great floods from the melting of snows on the Mogollon mountains at its source. When these floods have passed by the river is very low, and its valleys become gradually covered with saline efflorescence, fatal to the growth of corn or wheat and the most of vegetables Although this river runs through the old Navajo country, and that people have lived in its vicinity for ages, they themselves have never planted a field of corn along its banks, which may be considered as some evidence that it would not be a good place for a reservation. The distance to the Colorado Chiquito is nearly as great as to the San Juan, and the cost of transportation as much.

There is no unoccupied place in the Territory as large as the Bosque fit for cultivation and capable of irrigation. I should say there is at least ten thousand, and perhaps fifteen thousand acres of land that could be put under water at the Bosque. The Pueblo Indians compare favorably with the lower classes of the other inhabitants of the country. I think the Navajo Indians are naturally as intelligent as any Indians I know of, including the Pueblos. The Pueblo Indians are better informed than the other Indians, from their long contact with the influences of civilization and Christianity. The Pueblos are Catholics. The Navajoes are all pagans with the exception of the Civollettanos. In Castenadas's narrative of the first expedition made into New Mexico under Vasques de Coronada, in say 1543, '44, and '45, it is set forth that Indians were found in pueblos as at the present day. Among these Pueblos doubtless Catholic missionaries established churches and schools, and the Indians of those pueblos became christianized and partially civilized. This has raised them very much above the nomadic Indians of the country in point of intelligence and gentleness. With the exception of one or two intervals of a few years each, there has been a constant state of hostility between the people of New Mexico and the Navajo Indians. Even in these intervals occasional forays were made into the settlements to capture sheep and cattle The Mexicans would follow them into their country to recapture the stolen stock, and would kill some of the Indians and capture some of the women and children and make slaves of them. But in times when open hostilities existed these efforts were increased on each side to capture stock and women and children, so that the country was kept in a continual state of commotion. This was the state of things when we acquired the territory from the republic of Mexico. To the best of my recollection Colonel Doniphan (who came here with General Kearney) made the first expedition into the Navajo country in 1846. Colonel Washington made an expedition into their country in the year 1849; General Sumner in 1851. From 1851 until 1859 there was a period of comparative quiet, interrupted, as I have stated, by occasional forays, particularly on the part of the Navajoes. In 1859 war again broke out, and in 1860 the Navajoes attacked Fort Defiance. About this time Colonel Miles made an expedition into their country, and also Colonel Bonneville; and finally General Canby made a long campaign against them, leading his troops in person. When the Texan invasion of this country occurred, after General Canby's campaign against the Navajoes, and when every soldier was employed to repel that invasion, then the Navajoes, as well as the Apaches, rode over the country rough-shod. This was in the winter of 1861 and in the spring and summer of 1862. I relieved General Canby in command of the department; and this was the condition of the Navajoes and Apaches at that time. The Indian difficulties in New Mexico, since the treaty with Mexico, have obliged the United States to keep in that Territory a force whose average strength has been at least three thousand men, employés and all reckoned in. This covers a period of eighteen years. A large proportion of these troops have been cavalry, the most expensive arm in the military service, especially in New Mexico, where forage is very expensive. The horses required as remounts for this cavalry have to be brought across the plains from the States at great risk and expense. Sometimes large numbers have been stampeded *en route* and have never been heard from since. Many die before they reach this country. Those which arrive here it takes at least a year to acclimate; and after this the loss of horses by death, by being broken down, and lost on scouts, and killed in action, and stolen by Indians, is enormous, compared with losses of cavalry horses in any other country. The same holds true of the mules, more numerous necessarily than the cavalry horses, by reason of the extent of country over which supplies have to be hauled to subsist and clothe the troops. In my opinion the entire expense of maintaining a mounted regiment here amounts to what follows. With the exception of the troops employed to repel the Texan invasion, there has been but little necessity for troops in this country since we acquired it in 1848, unless to fight Indians. And if it should so happen that the nomadic Indians can be placed on reservations and kept there until they become sufficiently domesticated to be contented in that condition of life, I cannot see any reason why troops would be more necessary in New Mexico than in Illinois, except, perhaps, a small police force kept along the boundary line of Mexico. While it is difficult to say exactly, my opinion is, that about one-half of the forces employed have been necessary by the difficulties with the Navajoes. I should say that four hundred cavalry and two hundred infantry would be amply sufficient to keep the Navajoes and Apaches on the reservation at the Bosque Redondo. The Apaches of the bands of Jicarilla, Mescalero and Mimbres not yet captured, number, say, thirteen hundred souls, more or less. These are all of the Apaches that properly belong in New Mexicò; but there are other Apaches in Texas, Chihuahua, Sonora and Arizona, who make inroads into New Mexico, and against whom a military force is necessary here. There are also bands of Ute Indians in New Mexico which need military surveillance. They occupy the northern part of New Mexico, but are mainly located in Utah. If the Apaches who properly belong to New Mexico were settled with the other Apaches at the Bosque Redondo, nine hundred additional troops of the proper proportion of the different arms of the service would be sufficient for police purposes along the boundary line and to prevent inroads from exterior Apaches, provided the troops in Arizona are sufficiently numerous and do their duty. In my opinion, if the nomadic Indians of Arizona and New Mexico were settled on reservations, no more force would be required in this country than sufficient to guard them and to act as a police along the boundary, as before stated. In this connexion I feel constrained to say that much of the hostility manifested by many of the people of New Mexico against the reservation system grows out of the fact that when this system goes into successful operation there will be no more tribes from which they can capture servants, and the military force being reduced to a very small number, the millions of dollars annually expended here on account of the military establishment will, in a great measure, cease. I believe that the Indians upon the reservation at the Bosque Redondo will soon be able to raise sufficient breadstuffs for their support, and I have thought they would be enabled to produce, besides this, enough corn and fodder to sustain a cavalry force in the winter time at that point, should it be necessary to have one there to operate against the Indians of the plains in the summer. Some complaints have been made that there is not sufficient fuel at or near the Bosque Redondo to supply the Indians. In answer to these complaints I will state, that what with the extensive fields of mesquite in that neighborhood, the timber along the southern side of the Staked Plain near by and the cedar and piñon up the river, which can be floated down, there is enough fuel to last a great many years; during which time trees should be cultivated along all the *acequias* and in other suitable places upon the reservation to supply the demand when all the other fuel referred to has become exhausted. The mesquite is a species of acacia, which produces the gum-arabic. In New Mexico the tree becomes dwindled to a dwarf shrub; in Texas it attains its full height of from fifteen to thirty feet, and is there a fine tree. This shrub in New Mexico has very large roots proportionate to what grows above ground, and these roots are dug for fuel. Mesquite roots make a very hot and excellent fire, and but little is wanted in any one lodge.

Whilst the old Navajo country does not possess, in my opinion, any one place large enough for a reservation for that tribe, it is singularly well adapted to pastoral pursuits. The lands of the lower as well as the upper levels are clothed with very nutritious grasses. The places where flocks and herds could come to get water are sufficiently numerous for that purpose, and near them are arable lands enough to raise bread for the shepherds and herdsmen. There is no doubt but that the northern portion of that country is very rich in the precious metals, particularly in gold.

The Mescalero Apaches are, like the Navajoes, nomadic. They are also a patriarchal people, the band being divided into small communities. They are very fierce, brave, daring and perfidious, and experience had shown that treaties or bargains with them had no effect to restrain them from hostilities and depredations. So that when once they were gotten in hand by war, I, as commander of this department, felt that it was due to the people and the government not to trust them any more, and so I sent all those who were captured, or who voluntarily surrendered themselves, to the reservation.

The number of Indians, men, women and children, who have been captured or bought from the Utes, and who live in the families in the Territory, may be safely set down as at least three thousand. So far as my observation has gone the Mexicans treat these Indians with great kindness. After awhile they become conversant with the language, become attached to the families they live in, and very seldom care to run away. If they should attempt to run away I believe they would be captured by their owners. They are held as servants; as "hewers of wood and drawers of water." In my judgment, three out of four of these servants are Navajoes. These servants do not intermarry much with the Mexicans, but the women bear children from illicit intercourse. The offspring of this intercourse are considered as *peons*. The Indians upon the reservation, if properly cared for by the military commander, run no risk of being stolen or attacked.

An Indian named Pino Baca, now at the Bosque Redondo, was captured at Cibolleta, and on the road to the reservation escaped from the guard and ran back to his own country. He was ordered to be recaptured or killed. He was recaptured, taken to Fort Wingate and placed in irons, with a view of sending him to the reservation should an opportunity occur. He again broke loose, was again captured, sent to the Bosque, where he was kept in irons three or four months. He was charged, among other things, with having sold two Navajo children, and was considered a very great scoundrel. Since his release on the 16th of last April, it is said he has behaved himself very well. This selling of children by Navajoes, especially of orphan children, is said to be of not unfrequent occurrence.

SANTA FE, *July* 4, 1865.

Chief Justice Kirby Benedict sworn, and upon inquiries deposeth as follows:

In August next I will have resided twelve years in New Mexio. I came here with the commission of judge, and have been a member of the supreme court and judge of a district up to the present time; since in the summer of 1858 I have been chief justice. During the earlier part of this time the tribe of Navajo Indians kept peaceable relations with the United States government in this Territory and with the inhabitants. This condition of things was manifested a few days after my arrival, when a large deputation of the chiefs and principal men of the tribe came to Santa Fé and made a friendly visit to the governor, who was then also superintendent of Indian affairs in the Territory. A general friendship prevailed until an irritation occurred at Fort Defiance, from a negro having been killed at that place in a quarrel with an Indian who had come to the post The negro is said to have been claimed as the slave of the commanding officer; satisfaction was required of the Navajoes for the killing of the negro. I understand they offered to pay a sum, but the military exacted the delivery up of the Indian who had done the killing. Excuses were alleged, among others, that the Indian had fled beyond the tribe and their reach. The military remaining unsatisfied, hostile feelings grew stronger and stronger on the part of the Navajoes, and the former standing by their exactions, the Navajoes did acts of hostility directed firstly against the military, but which finally extended to and included the inhabitants of the Territory. Stealing, robberies and barbaraties ensued, and the Indians, as a tribe, became involved, until the depredations upon life, security and property were so frequent and ruinous, a campaign was made against them under the command of Colonel Kit Carson, which was successful in bringing them to subjection, and causing a surrender as captives the principal portions of the tribe, men, women and children.

The Navajoes were in the habit of making forays upon the ranches and settlements, stealing, robbing and killing and carrying away captives; the finding of herds and driving off sheep and other animals was carried on to a very ruinous extent; the killing of persons did not seem so much the object of their warfare as an incidental means of succeeding in other depredations. Sometimes, however, barbarous vengeance was exhibited and a thirst for blood. They carried away captives, but I cannot now give any accurate idea of the number. There are in the Territory a large number of Indians, principally females, (women and children,) who have been taken by force, or stealth, or purchased; who have been among the various wild tribes of New Mexico or those adjoining. Of these a large proportion are Navajoes. It is notorious that natives of this country have sometimes made captives of Navajo women and children when opportunities presented themselves; the custom has long existed here of buying Indian persons, especially women and children; the tribes themselves have carried on this kind of traffic. Destitute orphans are sometimes sold by their remote relations; poor parents also make traffic of their children. The Indian persons obtained in any of the modes mentioned are treated by those who claim to own them as their servants and slaves. They are bought and sold by and between the inhabitants at a price as much as is a horse or an ox. Those who buy, detain and use them seem to confide in the long-established custom and practice which prevails, and did prevail before this country was a portion of the United States. Those who hold them are exceedingly sensitive of their supposed interest in them, and easily alarmed at any movements in the civil courts or otherwise to dispossess them of their imagined property. The rich, and those who have some quantities of property, are those chiefly who possess the persons I have mentioned; those usually have much popular influence in the country, and the exertion of this influence is one of the means by which they hope to retain their grasp upon their Indian slaves. The prices have lately ranged very high. A likely girl of not more than eight years old, healthy and intelligent, would be held at a value of four hundred dollars, or more. When they grow to womanhood they sometimes become mothers from the natives of the land, with or without marriage. Their children, however, by the custom of the country, are not regarded as property which may be bought and sold as has been their mothers. They grow up and are treated as having the rights of citizens. They marry and blend with the general population. From my own observations I am not able to form an opinion satisfactory to my own mind of the number of Indians held as slaves or fixed domestic servants without their being the recipients of wages. Persons of high respectability for intelligence, who have made some calculations on the subject, estimate the number at various figures, from fifteen hundred to three thousand, and even exceeding the last number. The more prevalent opinion seems to be they considerably exceed two thousand. As to federal officers holding this description of persons or trafficking in them, I can only say I see them attending the family of Governor Connelly, but whether claimed by his wife, himself, or both, I know not. I am informed the superintendent of Indian affairs has one in his family, but I cannot state by what claim she is retained. From the social position occupied by the Indian agents, I presume all of them, except one, have the presence and assistance of the kind of persons mentioned; I cannot, however, state positively. In the spring of 1862, when Associate Justice Hubbell and myself conveyed our families to the States, he informed me at Las Vegas that he sold one Indian woman to a resident of that place preparatory to crossing the plains. I know of no law in this Territory by which property in a Navajo or other Indian can be recognized in any person whatever, any more than property can be recognized in the freest white man or black man. In 1855, while holding district court in the county of Valencia, a proceeding in *habeas corpus* was had before me on the part of a wealthy woman as petitioner, who claimed the possession and services of a Navajo girl then twelve years old, and who had been held by the petitioner near seven years. On the trial I held the girl to be a free person, and adjudged accordingly. In 1862 a proceeding in *habeas corpus* was instituted before me by an aged man who had held in service many years an Indian woman who had been, when a small child, bought from the Payweha Indians. The right of the master to the possession and services of the woman on the one side, and the right of the woman to her personal freedom, were put distinctly at issue. Upon the hearing I adjudged the woman to be a free woman; I held the claim of the master to be without foundation in law and against natural rights. In each of the cases the party adjudged against acquiesced in the decision, and no appeal was ever taken. In the examination of the cases it appeared that before the United States obtained New Mexico captive and purchased Indians were held here by custom in the same manner as they have been since held. The courts are open to them, but they are so influenced by the circumstances which surround them they do not seem to think of seeking the aid of the law to establish the enjoyment of their right to freedom.

So far as I have learned from history, whether by tradition or otherwise, the Navajo Indians for ages have been at alternate war and peace with the inhabitants who have resided here. They are reputed to have made themselves quite wealthy by robbing through long years the flocks of the people of New Mexico. The Spanish and Mexican governments administered here had frequent troubles with the tribe, and sometimes brought them to continue for a time at peace.

I am unhesitatingly of opinion that the most practicable and effectual mode of securing the peace and progress of the inhabitants against the Indians, especially those upon the northern and western portions of the Territory, and also to promote the economy and other interests of the government and the ultimate welfare of the Indians, would be the confining and restraining the tribes within prescribed limits or reservations, and that these should be selected and maintained as remote as practicable from the settlements of the citizens; that the Indians should be restrained within the limits assigned them by a suitable military force, and aided by the government in adopting the modes of sustaining themselves without depredations upon the lives and property of others.

I have never travelled over the country so long inhabited by the Navajoes, nor have I visited the Bosque Redondo, where the large portion of them are now maintained. My knowledge of those places is derived from various persons, both Americans and Mexicans, with whom I have conversed. Were the Indians not now at the Bosque, and the question was now as to the policy of permanently locating them there, my judgment would be decidedly against the policy.

When New Mexico and her people became included within the United States, there were within the new limits of the Territory about nineteen Indian pueblos or towns and tracts of lands reserved to and occupied by Indians in a kind of semi-civilized state of progress. Some of these were then and still are fully inhabited; others have diminished. They are chiefly scattered up and down upon the Rio Grande, and upon the streams which run not from long distances into that river. They have been located upon places most highly favored with land, water, wood and pastures.

The government, I understand, in confirming to the Pueblos their towns and lands, confirmed to each six miles square. This is, as of course in right should be, irrevocably vested in them. Although these people have some industrious habits, they are not regarded and treated as citizens. They are little governments within the government. These people have the merit of committing but few offences against the laws upon the citizens outside of the pueblos. During my judicial administration at times throughout every county in the Territory, I have as yet seen only one Pueblo Indian arraigned upon an indictment for larceny; still, their progress is little in arts or knowledge. I think intelligent citizens would be an element of more strength than *they* are in the advancement of New Mexico to the rights, power, and dignity of a State. With so much of the best soil and advantages set apart to the Pueblos, I cannot think the policy of bringing Indians from wild tribes, and some of them without the Territory, and locating them upon forty miles square of the Sound river, in magnitude and value, to be a good policy for the future interests of New Mexico. The soil adapted to agriculture here bears but a very small proportion to the immense wastes that cannot be cultivated for the want of water.

As matters now stand, I am not now prepared to express a fixed opinion as to whether it is better to keep the Navajoes upon the Bosque, or remove them to some good place where they long lived. This depends greatly upon the general policy which shall be adopted by the government. If it shall be adopted that the wild tribes around be colonized where lands and waters will admit, near to or in connexion with the citizen's settlements upon these lands, it doubtless would have a "crushing out" effect upon the citizen, and in that event it might be better the Navajoes should remain where others would be colonized. If, on the other hand, New Mexico shall not be adopted as the general reservation for wild tribes, but that they shall be located upon suitable grounds known and suitable to the Indian, far from settlements, then I should think the Navajoes should go with this last suggested policy. I am informed there are sections in the old Navajo country supplied with land and water upon which Indians can be made, with a little aid and just care from government, to subsist and sustain themselves.

I have supposed the similar military force and skill which will keep a tribe of Indians confined and orderly upon a reserve contiguous to settlements, would accomplish the like end upon a reserve selected in a country long adapted to the Indian.

Had the military force and skill supplied by the government have been sufficient to keep the inhabitants from Indian robberies and murders, I think it would have been far better the Indians should have been kept upon their own place of habitation, and I am of opinion it would have been much more favorable to the government.

When the Navajoes have been at hostilities with the Mexican people, the latter have sometimes, in small parties, made campaigns into the Navajo country, and taken, where they could, captives and stock.

Testimony taken at Sante Fé.

Major Griner sworn:

I came first to this Territory in 1851, staid until 1854, and then, again, in 1862, where I have remained since, with the exception of the time of the Texan invasion. I came here first as Indian agent, and was at first assigned to duty at Taos, as agent for the Apaches and Utes, but afterwards acted as general superintendent under Governor Calhoun, and travelled over pretty much all the Territory. I was Indian agent from 1851 until 1853, being then appointed secretary. The great difficulty in our Indian policy is in the selection of Indian agents, who are generally appointed for political services. Mr. Wingfield came here as an agent, because he was the friend of Mr. Dawson, of Georgia; Mr Wolley, an old man of seventy years of age, because he was the friend of Mr. Clay; Mr. Weightman, because he wished to be returned as delegate; and myself, because I could sing a good political song. Neither of us was by habit or education better fitted to be Indian agent than to follow any other business. The general policy of selecting men as agents for political services, rather than fitness for the position, and frequently changing them, is a great cause of all our Indian difficulties, in my opinion. I was changed just as I was about to be of service, and had become acquainted with the Indians, and had acquired their confidence, and could get them to do as I desired. When I left here I went away with a high opinion of the system adopted by the Spaniards—I mean the pueblos, which are reservations. I look upon them as models, and their government as models for Indians Their governments are entirely democratic; they select their own officers and administer their own laws. At first they had no farms, and depended on their own industry for subsistence, and none have ever been found guilty of a criminal offence. The only difficulty in our government doing as the Spaniards did is on account of religion. The Spaniards planted a church in the centre of each pueblo, the priest naming the babies and baptising them; and the priest was in fact the agent of the Spanish government, and had charge of the temporal as well as spiritual affairs. This would of course be impracticable under our government. Mr. Ward, an agent here, has written a paper on the subject, which is published in the commissioner's report of Indian affairs, which is correct. In my experience I have never known a serious difficulty in the Territory between the Indians and citizens which did not originate mainly with the latter. One of the first exciting difficulties in the Territory arose from the capture of Mrs. White, a very beautiful woman, and her little daughter, by the Jicarilla Apaches. I was appointed to investigate it. I found that at Las Vegas the troops had, without any sufficient cause or provocation, fired upon the Indians, and they in revenge joined with some Utes and attacked the next train coming from the States, killing Mr. White and others, and capturing his wife and child; and also the stage, with ten passengers, was taken, and all killed. A war was the consequence. Another instance on the part of Maugus Colorado, the chief of the Apaches: During my administration as acting superintendent of Indian affairs I was present with General Sumner to make a treaty of peace. He was an Indian of remarkable intelligence and great character. I asked him the cause of the difficulties with the people in Chihuahua and Sonora, for at that time, under the treaty with Mexico, we were bound to protect its people from the attacks of the Indians residing in New Mexico. He said: "I will tell you. Some time ago my people were invited to a feast; aguardiente or whiskey was there; my people drank and became intoxicated, and were lying asleep, when a party of Mexicans came in and beat out their brains with clubs. At another a trader was sent among us from Chihuahua. While innocently engaged in trading, often leading to words of anger, a cannon concealed behind the goods was fired upon my people and quite a number were killed. Since that Chihuahua has offered a reward for our scalps, $150 each, and we have been hunted down ever since;" and, with great emphasis and in the most impressive manner, he added, "How can we make peace with such people?" I also have since learned from the agent of the tribe, Dr. Steck, that sixty Indians of the same tribe were poisoned by strychnine. The whole country of Sonora and Chihuahua has been devastated by these Indians. This same chief was afterwards taken prisoner by our own troops and confined in the guard-house, and was killed while so confined by the sentinel. The Navajoes, while Mr. Dodge was their agent and Major Kindrick and Major Backus was in command of the posts in their country, were friendly and peaceable, owing to the prudence and wisdom with which those officers discharged the duties of their stations, and, in my opinion, had they remained, or persons of equal prudence, there would not have been any hostilities on the part of the Navajoes. There was a change of agents and military commanders in their country, and a war broke out in consequence of the killing of a negro boy of Major Brooks's, as I am informed. Another cause of trouble has been in consequence of the capture of their flock and herds, and their women and children for servants. So in relation to the war with the Comanches, who had been at peace with the Mexican people for a great many years. The cause or occasion of that was this: A party of teamsters were killed by the Kiowas and Cheyennes in consequence of the Sand creek massacre. There may have been Comanches among them, but the tribe was not involved, and the campaign under Kit Carson, was made against them last year. About a year ago a Navajo travelling with his wife and two or three children was shot down by a company of Mexican troops. He defended himself bravely to the last, but he was killed and scalped—one of the party giving me an account of it, saying his bravery won their admiration. He brought me the scalp, which I now present to the committee. I am not personally acquainted with the reservation at the Bosque, nor by personal observation am I acquainted with the Navajo country. I think it very unwise and injudicious to place them upon that reservation. First. That was really Comanche country and had never been ceded, and was a cause of complaint by the Comanches, for the Navajoes were their hereditary enemies, and it was abridging their hunting grounds by putting their enemies upon it, the Bosque being to them a choice hunting ground. Second. Taking the Navajoes from their own mountain country and placing them upon the plains at the Bosque is one cause of the mortality said to have existed among them. Third. There is not sufficient extent of country to subsist so large a population as a permanent location. Fourth. Placing the Navajoes and Apaches, two distinct tribes, with different habits and customs, upon the same reservation, the Navajoes being a working and thinking people; the Apaches lacking all those qualifications. Fifth. The immense cost to the government, which has been increased and must continue to be. The Navajoes are a Pueblo Indian, as ruined buildings and acequias show in their country that in former times it has been occupied by Pueblos. Their habits, manners, dress, customs, and manufactures are similar to Pueblos. They were rich Indians, and if let alone would have been so at this time, in my opinion. I have seen the customs of the Mexican government, after their crops were in, to make campaigns against the Navajoes to get their stock, women and children. The Mexicans paid no taxes, and their forays upon the Navajoes were to obtain the means to carry on the government of the department of New Mexico. This was especially the case under Governor Armigo, who had been governor and administered affairs much like a dictator for the eleven years preceding the taking possession by the forces of the United States under General Kearney in 1846. My opinion is that the Navajoes should be restored to their own country and established in pueblos of say one thousand men, with their families, in each pueblo, under the charge of one good agent to each pueblo, holding him responsible for the good behavior of the people. Following as near as possible the Spanish mode of establishing pueblos upon the model of those now existing among us, I think in a few years they could be made self-sustaining, of no cost to the government, and a happy and prosperous people. Their country is peculiarly adapted for that purpose, there being no mines in that country to tempt the cupidity of our people, as I am informed. Their country is very remote and isolated from the settlements. I think a small military force would prevent incursions into or excursions from it. As to the Apaches, I would place them under the care of good agents and keep them in position until they gained the confidence of the Indian people; then show them the necessity and benefit of relying upon themselves and their own exertions to support themselves and their families. Selecting the best places in their own country for small reservations, not exceeding a thousand families in any one reservation or pueblo, I think they could be made self-sustaining in a few years. The Indian department was once under the War Department. Some fifteen years since it was taken away and placed in the Interior Department. From that time, from the Indian department at Washington down to the sub-agents in New Mexico, there has been a constant struggle by the military department to get the control of Indian affairs, and that struggle has been one cause of the difficulties.

Colonel Willis sworn:

I am lieutenant colonel in the 1st regiment New Mexico infantry. I came here as major with the 1st California regiment of infantry. I have been in New Mexico since August, 1862; have been in the military service ever since; have been in service in the Navajo country; I have seen almost all the southern portion of it—all south of Fort Canby; have not visited the northern part of it. I have been also a good deal in the Territory of Arizona. The present condition of Indian affairs in that Territory is not good. All the Indians are hostile except a few of the tribes on the Colorado river. The Coyotéro Apaches, of perhaps one thousand warriors, near the eastern line of Arizona, ranging from the headwaters of the Gila north; the Pinal Apaches, of perhaps fifteen hundred warriors, on the north of the Gila and west of the former; the Tontos, of six or seven hundred warriors, also north of the Gila; the Chiricahuis, of probably not more than five hundred warriors, in the southeast part of Arizona; the Gilanos, a small band of one to two hundred warriors, are all openly hostile.

The Hualpis are not openly hostile, but are accused of making depredations and killing some citizens; but I did not have satisfactory proof of it. They live in the northwest part of Arizona; they have probably one thousand warriors. The Mohaves are friendly; they live near Fort Mohave, on the Colorado river. There are also a few small bands near them who are friendly also. The Pinos and Maricopas, who are in pueblos on the Gila, are friendly; they have about two thousand warriors. They are an industrious people, living by agriculture and stock-raising. The year I was there we obtained of them one million pounds of wheat. They also raise cotton and manufacture their own clothing and blankets; they have always been friendly, and are among the tribes most advanced in civilization; they also assisted us, and sent out parties two or three times against the Apaches. This hostility was existing when I came into the Territory. I was sent out with three companies to establish a post at Prescott, the capital of Arizona. They have, according to my best information, been hostile for a number of years. I am not informed of the cause or occasion of the hostilities. Arizona is capable of settlement by a white population to a considerable extent. The northern portion is one of the finest grazing countries I ever saw, and finely timbered, also. There are not very extensive tracts capable of cultivation; it is only the valleys on the small streams which could be cultivated. I think in that portion of the Territory not more than one acre in a thousand could be cultivated, and in the other portion of the Territory much less. In the north portion there is rain enough to raise crops without irrigation; in the southern portion there is not rain sufficient. It is very rich in minerals. I state this on my own personal observation. In the portion of country near Prescott there are a great number of quartz leads of gold, silver and other metals. I was in California from 1849 till I came here, and was familiar with the California mines, living in them most of the time. But these quartz leads of Arizona far exceed the mines of California. Over a space of territory seventy-five miles square which had been explored, it was completely filled with the finest gold and silver leads I ever saw; also, with copper and other metals. This country is well timbered with fine pine trees for lumber. There is some considerable arable land in the vicinity, but not enough to support a large population in the mines. It is very good grazing country. The Apaches make frequent raids into this mining region to run off flocks and murder and steal. I think a force of two thousand five hundred could subdue these hostile bands, and secure the settlements. There are about fifteen hundred men in this mining district engaged in mining and making explorations. There are also two other mining districts where men are at work—one near Fort Mohave and the other south of the Tucson—of which I speak only from information. I estimate, in the district near Mohaves there are from eight hundred to one thousand miners. From the other district the miners were driven away by the Indians, when the troops were withdrawn to put down the rebellion, and then everybody was obliged to leave that country; but a good many returned. There are probably from five to six hundred in those mines. The mines have been very productive so far as they could work. In consequence of the Indians and the want of machines, they have not been able to work the leads much. The mining regions of Arizona are not as extensive as in California; but in proportion to their extent they can produce as much or more than in California. The census was taken in three districts: in one there were two thousand three hundred, in another one thousand eight hundred, and in another one thousand five hundred people; these included Americans and Mexicans. About one-fifth of these were Mexicans. There were in that Territory five military posts; there is the same number now, manned by eight to nine hundred men. I understand there are more now, some having been sent there from California. The Indians live on game and the mescal or century plant. They eat up the horses and mules they steal, almost as soon as they get them. Their country is so rough that horses are of little use to them. They keep no herds of sheep or cattle; they have no permanent abodes, moving from one place to another. They told us they would never give up fighting as long as there was any mescal in the mountains. If they are subdued, I would advise placing them on reservations, not in their own country, for they could not be kept upon one in it without an immense force. I do not know of any frauds or peculations committed upon the government or the Indians by the civil or military authorities in the Territories of New Mexico and Arizona.

Supplies are carried from California by sea and the Colorado river to within about one hundred miles of Prescott, then by land. The Colorado is navigable for steamboats, which run regularly to Fort Mohave. Boats have been up near five hundred miles.

Colonel Collins sworn:

I came to the Territory first in 1827; I came as a merchant and trader. I traded back and forth from 1827 to 1843, making a trip once in three years. In 1843 I came and went into Old Mexico, and since then I have resided most of the time in Old and New Mexico; and since the war with Mexico I have resided in New Mexico all the time. I was superintendent of Indian affairs from 1857 until 1863, when I turned over the office to Dr. Steck. There has been a state of hostility between the Mexicans and Navajoes ever since I have been here. I took charge of the office in 1857, and at the end of the year the conduct of the Indians was better than it had been previous to that time. This pacific disposition of the Indians was occasioned by the large amount of presents they received that fall. Previous to that time the amount of presents had been small; I issued the goods to them myself. That disposition on the part of the Indians continued until June the next year. Although all depredations on their part had not ceased, still it was the most peaceful time had with the Indians since I had been in the Territory. About the commencement of June a difficulty occurred between the Indians and the troops at Fort Defiance. That difficulty was occasioned by the Indians allowing their animals to run on lands which had been set apart by an arrangement with them as meadow lands for cutting hay for the post. Major Brooks was then in command of the post. The Indians were notified to keep their animals off. Finally, after they had been on the ground several times, a company of mounted men, under Captain McLane, of the rifles, was sent out, who ordered about seventy of the animals shot within the limits of the meadow. The result was, a very short time after this, a black boy, servant of Major Brooks, was killed by the Indians. The killing of the boy led to the war, which has continued up to this time. After the killing of the boy a demand was made by Major Brooks on the principal men of the tribe for the delivery of the murderer, and were finally told that, unless he was given up, in thirty days war would be made on the tribe. At this state of the case the facts were reported to General Garland, who was then in command of the department. General Garland, though not approving of the course which had been pursued, still thought proper not to recede from the demand which had been made, but thought proper to exact it. The result was an expedition against the Indians, under Colonel Miles. My opinion was consulted, and I advised more specific means, and not to commence hostilities until every effort had been made to secure the murderer. An agent was sent out, in co-operation with the troops, to try and get the murderer and preserve the peace. He failed, the Indians refusing to deliver the murderer. The agent went with Captain McLane, with instructions to prevent hostilities until a council could be held with the chiefs, but on the way Captain McLane met some Indians and attacked them, getting wounded himself. Notwithstanding this attack, the Indians were collected and a council held, but it resulted in nothing, the Indians stating that they had no authority to deliver up the murderer, but offered to pay any price for the negro killed. The offer was refused, the troops insisting upon the delivery of the murderer. The consequence was open hostilities. The troops moved against the Indians in every direction, but they were not sufficiently damaged to bring them to terms. After hostilities commenced, I insisted, with General Garland, that, as the war had been commenced, it should be prosecuted until the Indians sued for terms. General Garland concurred in this opinion, but was relieved about this time by Colonel Bonneville. This war continued until some time in November, when an armistice was concluded for thirty days, reporting the circumstances to Colonel Bonneville. Colonel Bonneville and myself concluded to go out and see the Indians at the expiration of the armistice, which would be about the 25th of December, at which time we concluded a peace with the Indians. My opinion was, that the war had been improperly commenced, and was improperly concluded by not making the Indians comply with the demand made upon them. The substance of the treaty was, that all stock taken during hostilities should, as far as practicable, be given up; and Colonel Bonneville agreed to enforce the condition on his part. The treaty was never carried into effect, and in the summer of 1859 another expedition was sent against the Indians, under Major Simonson. He went out with instructions to enforce that condition of the treaty to surrender the captured stock. He failed to do so. That expedition was as great a failure as the other. Hostilities continued. The Indians continued their depredations, committing robberies and murders to a considerable extent, until 1860, when General Canby took command and made an expedition against them. During this time the Mexicans turned loose upon them, captured a good many of their women and children. General Canby made an expedition in 1860. He was not very successful. He went into their country; they asked for peace, and he made a treaty with them and withdrew the troops. They, however, continued their hostile depredations just about as before. About that time the rebellion broke out, and the Texans made their invasion. All the troops were withdrawn from the Navajo country. The Navajoes continued their depredations as usual, until General Carleton came into the country, when he organized his expedition, under Kit Carson, against them. During the hostilities a band of friendly Indians of about three hundred, increased by the addition of those disposed to be friendly to about six hundred, were greatly wronged, in my opinion, at Fort Wingate. There was some difficulty about a horse-race. The Indians, I think, won the race, and the Mexican troops in the service refused to give up stakes, when a quarrel arose, and the troops fired into them; some were killed, and some were wounded. I cannot say that I could, but I was encouraged to think, but for the difficulty about the meadow lands and the killing of the negro boy of Major Brooks, I would have been able to maintain the peace with the Indians. The impression was they were becoming more pacific. The Indians told me in council that they had agreed to surrender the meadow lands to the post. That year there was a drought. The Indians told me that they did not intend to violate the arrangement about the grass. I was with the expedition in 1849, under Colonel Washington, and passed over a good deal of the country. We passed into the country at the head of the Arollo Chaco; went through the valleys; and in one, the valley of Chella, there were perhaps 400 or 500 acres of cultivation, the crops that year looking well. It was a rainy season, and grain and crops looked well, Indian corn, pumpkins, and peaches. The valley of Chella has no running water; it sinks into the sand, and crops there will grow without irrigation; think the whole amount of cultivation in all the valleys would reach 1,500 to 2,000 acres. Such is the character of the country that some years there is rain, say once in four or five years; there is a good crop, and other years a failure. There is plenty of timber—pine, some scrub oak, such as you see in the mountains here. The water that year was plenty. Some of the water brackish, some good. Water in the valley of Chella is good. Water at Fort Defiance is very good. I regard the establishment of Indians on reservations as the only way they can be controlled or kept from hostilities. In regard to the Navajoes, the condition became such they could not have been controlled in their own country. If they had lived in peace they could have lived in that country. It is very large, and the whole of it would have sustained them, and I do not think the government would have thought of removing them, if they had remained at peace. I was at the Bosque Redondo in the spring of 1863; again the other day. I visited it in 1863, as superintendent of Indian affairs, to see if it was sufficient. I became satisfied it was, and my late visit has confirmed and strengthened my opinion. My opinion is, that it is necessary for Indians themselves they should be there. Our population is different from the most of the population of the States, and they are continually liable to get into difficulty with the Indians. It is difficult to prevent it, and it is a matter of security to the Indians themselves, and the women and children, to be placed under the protection of the United States upon a reservation. I intend to apply that remark only to a portion of the population. I think the Navajo country exceeds, in size, the State of Ohio, but it has been somewhat curtailed. A very small proportion of the land can be cultivated by irrigation. I don't think it will ever be settled by any considerable population. The Mexicans have been in the habit of making forays into the Navajo country, bringing out stock and captives; and, I think, some two thousand captives are held in the Territory now. They are held and treated as slaves, but become amalgamated with the Mexicans and lose their identity.

Henry Connelly sworn:

Is present governor of New Mexico. I have resided in this country as a transient and permanent resident over forty years; have been a permanent resident the past eighteen years, during the twenty years preceding residing in Chihuahua; am a native of Virginia. While in Chihuahua the first twelve years, my communications through New Mexico were not frequent; but the latter part of my residence there, since 1843, my communications had been nearly annually through New Mexico before I became a resident of it. I became acquainted, by conversations with citizens, with the relations between the Navajoes and Apaches and Mexicans. Since 1848 I have been intimately acquainted with them. These relations have been generally hostile, a continued warfare. There have been some two years, while Mr. Dodge was agent, of comparative peace and security for stock. The Navajoes made forays to take sheep and stock, killing all who made resistance, their object seeming rather to plunder, especially flocks and herds, than a desire to take life, by attacking towns and villages. The Mexicans generally have been on the defensive. But sometimes they go after them to make reprisals, to get back their own, and to get what more they could. They mutually also captured and held as slaves the women and children of each other. I believe the Mexicans captured the most children, the Indians the most herds. I found that state of things when I came here in 1824. I presume this state of things had existed from time immemorial. It has existed since we acquired the territory from Mexico. I think four years would cover the entire period in which we considered ourselves at peace with the Indians. I think there was no account taken of murders committed, or stock stolen by the Indians, subsequent to 1846; until within a few years it has been made the duty of the prefects to make such account. I think our greatest losses occurred during the Texan invasion of 1862. Without giving an opinion in regard to the present reservation, I think that the system is indispensable to our security. It is founded upon experience; for one hundred years of war has shown that some system has to be adopted to prevent them from destroying one another; and I think the reservation system, by which they are compelled to abandon their nomadic life, and be compelled to attend to agriculture, promises the only change for the better. I would say, further, that the experiment was tried by the Jesuit fathers; and the situation of the Pueblo Indians shows what can be done. I am of opinion that nothing but military surveillance can keep them on the reservations. I am of the opinion there are about fifteen hundred or two thousand Navajoes held as slaves in the Territory. There is no law in regard to buying captives; only proclamations or military orders controlled it. I issued my proclamation advising the people to quit the practice. I never saw any sold, but I know of its being done. Those I have heard of being sold were among those Navajoes who refused to come in, captured by the Utes and Mexicans. This is since my proclamation. Of those who have been scattered about, some have been sent to the reservation. The Mexicans, I have no doubt, unite with the Utes in their capture. Since the establishment of the Indians upon the reservation, all expeditions for the capture of those remaining have been prohibited until lately; since last March some have been captured. Those remaining in their country have committed depredations by stealing sheep and killing shepherds. In the case of Perea, two shepherds were killed, and 500 or 1,000 sheep taken; and the murders committed on the Rio Perquo, where three men were killed and their stock taken. The case of Roman Raca, living in San Matua, near the entire stock of himself and that of some other persons living there was stolen. These are cases which occur to me at this time; there may be others. I am in favor of keeping the Indians at the Bosque until the government finds a a better place for them; and I want the government to be the judge. A copy of the proclamation above referred to I now present to the committee.

PROCLAMATION.

Whereas a suspension of arms, in the prosecution of the war against the Navajo tribe of Indians, exists, as the more hostile part of that tribe is now reduced to and located upon the reservation at the Bosque Redondo, and the remainder of the tribe coming in and surrendering themselves to the military authorities; and

Whereas any hostile demonstration upon the part of our citizens towards the said Indians during this suspension of hostilities would frustrate the intentions and efforts of the government in the peaceable removal of the remainder of this tribe, now collecting around Forts Canby and Wingate, to whom has been granted safety to life and property while there and *in transitu* to the reservation: Therefore,

I, Henry Connelly, governor of New Mexico, do issue this my proclamation, and ordain:

First. That hostilities on the part of the citizens with the remainder of the Navajo tribe of Indians, who have or have not presented themselves at the military posts for removal to the reservation, shall cease.

Second. That all forays by our citizens of a hostile character into the country heretofore or now occupied by any part of the said Navajo tribe of Indians, are hereby positively prohibited under the severest penalties.

Third. That any parties of armed men, with hostile intentions, hereafter found in the Navajo country, will be immediately arrested by the United States troops and sent to the headquarters of the department of New Mexico, there to be dealt with according to law.

Fourth. It is proper in this connexion to warn the people against further traffic in captive Indians. The laws of the country as well as those of justice and humanity positively forbid such a traffic. Measures are now being taken by the Department of the Interior to have all Indians surrendered who have been sold into slavery, and the people therefore have this timely warning to refrain at once from any such traffic in Indian captives as has heretofore been practiced among them.

Done at Santa Fé, this 4th day of May, 1864.

HENRY CONNELLY,
Governor and Commander-in-Chief of the Militia.

By the Governor:

JOHN WATTS, *Private Secretary, in absence of the Secretary of the Territory.*

The Secretary of the Territory is absent. By the assistance of his son, who is left in charge of the office, I have the records of murders and robberies committed in the year 1863 by the Navajo Indians in five of the counties of the Territory, to wit: Socorro, Rio Arriba, Valencia, Santa Fé and Doña Ana. Horses, 224; cattle, 4,178; sheep, 55,040; goats, 5,901. The number of citizens killed in these counties during the year was sixteen. This I think may be taken as a fair estimate of the losses in the above-mentioned counties for several years previous to the year 1863. Other counties not included in this estimate, to wit, Bernalillo, San Miguel, Soas, Mora, and Santa Anna, have also lost largely—perhaps in an equal amount. In answer to the inquiry, I know of no frauds or peculations perpetrated on the government or the Indians by the civil or military authorities.

Louis Kennon sworn:

Am a resident of New Mexico; have been for twelve years last past; am a native of Georgia; am a physician by profession. I am tolerably well acquainted with what is called the Navajo country. I think the Navajoes have been the most abused people on the continent, and that in all hostilities the Mexicans have always taken the initiative with but one exception that I know of. When I first came here the Navajoes were at peace, and had been a long time. There was a pressure brought to bear upon the commander of the department by the Mexicans, and all Americans who pandered to that influence to make war upon the Navajoes. General Garland was commander of the department at that time, and if you asked the Mexicans any reason for making war, they would give no other reason, but that the Navajoes had a great many sheep and horses and a great many children. General Garland resisted their pressure until the unfortunate killing of a negro belonging to an officer at the post. The circumstances as I heard them are these: among the Navajoes there is a great equality between the men and women; women own their own property independent of their husbands, and having property, are entitled to vote in the councils. They also are at liberty, if dissatisfied with their husbands, to leave them at will; but when they do so the husband asks to wipe out the disgrace by killing some one. A case of this kind occurred. An Indian of a wealthy and influential family, had been deserted by his wife in this way, and he having had some real or imagined ill-treatment from this negro slave belonging to Major Brooks, of the 3d infantry, killed him. A demand was made for the surrender of the murderer, or war would follow. He was secreted by his family. The Indians killed some other Indian and brought in his body, insisting that it was the body of the murderer, killed while escaping from arrest. But the soldiers knew the murderer well, and they knew the folly of this pretence, so the demand was still insisted upon. Meanwhile some Navajoes near Albuquerque were murdered and robbed by the Mexicans, and the Navajoes made demand for the surrender of the murderers by General Garland This was refused, and the surrender still insisted upon of the Indian who murdered the negro. The Indians offered to pay for the negro, but failed to surrender the murderer War ensued, and there has been no permanent peace since. There have been intervals of quiet, but no substantial peace. Previous to the killing of the negro, the post had been under the command of two very able and philanthropic gentlemen, Majors Kendricks and Backus, who kept the Navajoes at peace by keeping the Mexicans away from them. I was in the service of the United States as acting assistant surgeon, and was stationed at Fort Defiance in 1858, and was on a campaign against the Indians under Colonel Canby, and was in active service two months. scouting over the country, and therefore I know something about the country. It is ample for the Navajoes. I could not make an approximation as to the amount of arable land. If the Navajoes are ever colonized there they will have to be in five or six pueblos. I don't think I saw a foot of it fit for white settlement, because of its remoteness, and I saw no evidences of mineral wealth in the country. There would be no difficulty in selecting points where a thousand or two thousand souls could live; but no point where five or six thousand could be subsisted together. There is plenty of wood and water at these places. In the old Navajo country, the grazing facilities are inexhaustible. I saw no evidences of minerals; it is a red sandstone country, in which minerals do not exist. I think the number of Navajo captives held as slaves to be underestimated. I think there are from five to six thousand. I know of no family which can raise one hundred and fifty dollars but what purchases a Navajo slave, and many families own four or five—the trade in them being as regular as the trade in pigs or sheep. Previous to the war their price was from seventy-five to a hundred dollars; but now they are worth about four hundred dollars. But the other day some Mexican Indians from Chihuahua were for sale in Santa Fé. I have been conversant with the institution of slavery in Georgia, but the system is worse here, there being no obligation resting on the owner to care for the slave when he becomes old or worthless. Fortunately for the Navajoes, they generally got the better of the Mexicans in their warfares until the Americans came to their rescue. It is my opinion that the Navajoes and other wild Indians should be settled on reservations somewhere Touching the Navajoes, I think they should be settled in their own country in five or six pueblos. If they were divided into bands and so situated, I should want an agent to each pueblo. I would have a large military post in the country, to which the agent of any pueblo could go for assistance if his people did not behave themselves. And I would endeavor to form them on the model of the pueblo towns as being the best kind of Indian reservations. Under the Spanish rule, the church was the centre, around which the pueblo system was gathered—the priest standing in all things as *loco parentis;* and if practicable, I would have the same system now; if not, I would substitute the agent in place of the priest. I was over the Bosque twice before the Indians were placed there; not since. I think it is a bad place to put the Navajoes, and they have a better place in their own country. I think it would be a good place to put the Indians of the plains, if they could be gathered together, and sustained there, as it belongs to them. In 1854 or '55 I passed through that country in company with Major (now General) Carleton, who reported to General Garland that it would be a suitable place for a four-company post. There was nothing decided upon in regard to it, and one or two years after I passed through the Bosque with Captain Ewell, late a general in the Confederate States army, an officer of great experience and judgment, who reported that there was not wood enough there for a four-company post for four or five years. I think there are no serious objections to the water. I think some assistance would have to be given the Navajoes, if put into pueblos, before they became self-sustaining. I would have them under charge of civilians. I think the system of Indian slavery is the origin of all the difficulties. Let the Indians once understand that the government will, and wants to take care of them, and it would not require more than one company to keep the whole nation together.

Major Samuel Allison sworn :

I have been in the Territory since 1848 ; am a Kentuckian by birth ; came here from Coahuila, in Old Mexico ; resided there from 1842 until 1848 ; am acting as clerk of the supreme court and of the first judicial district. With the exception of very short intervals, the Navajoes and Mexicans have been at war with each other. At the time Major Kendricks was in command of Fort Defiance, the Navajoes were quiet. I know this, because I accompanied Governor Merryweather on his trip to Fort Defiance, when presents were distributed to the Indians. There is no question but what the Indians should be placed on a reservation. I have been in the Navajo country, but have never been at the Bosque Redondo. I was sent to the Navajo country in 1852 by Governor Lane to demand the delivery of captives and stock taken by the Indians. I was near the Tunacha mountain five days, in the midst of the planting grounds ; it was near the latter part of April I was there. The northern slope of the Tunacha mountain I found well watered with streams, well timbered, and fine grazing country, and, I should think, susceptible of sustaining a population of at least ten thousand. There was a large number of Indians planting there at the time ; I was there at the time with the acting governor, Mr. Vigil. I think the slope I have described would be the proper place for a reservation for the Navajoes. I think the Navajoes, settled on a reservation in their old country, would require little or no aid from the government for their support. They appeared to have plenty of corn and mutton when I was there. They did not cultivate that land by irrigation. The north and northeast of the Tunacha mountain is an open country ; on the west and south are mountains well covered with timber. I doubt whether a force of six or eight companies could keep them on a reservation in their own country. It is my opinion, and the general opinion, that the Navajoes have taken more stock from the Mexicans than the latter have taken from them. I suppose the old Navajo country was as large in extent as the State of Ohio. I would take the northern slope of the Tunacha mountain, from its southern to its northern spur, as a reservation for the Navajoes. The width of this tract would be very great, and its length from twenty-five to thirty miles. This would comprise what is called Ojo Caliente, Peña Blanca, Ciena, and the streams from the Tunacha mountain. The Navajoes were not all on this tract, but scattered, about one-third on the tract, and the remainder on other sections of the Territory. Much more land on the Tunacha slope could have been put in cultivation than was. They were not cultivating by irrigation at that time, but *acequias* could have been made. The Tunacha mountain, and the great divide between the Pacific and Atlantic waters, would prevent encroachments upon them by the whites.

Percy Ayers sworn :

I have resided in this Territory about thirteen years ; am slightly acquainted with the Bosque Redondo ; I was stationed there about two months in the winter of 1863 ; I took about 163 Apache Indians there from Fort Stanton. In the vicinity of Fort Sumner, the water is wretched ; my whole company and the horses suffered from it. At the time I was there, there was very little water, and of very bad quality ; it operated on man and beast like salts The effect differed with different individuals ; some were affected for a few days with looseness of the bowels ; with others, it was permanent during their stay. This was between the months of January and March. Surgeon Gyther was there in charge of the post I lost several horses, from the badness of the water, I judged. At that time the water ran in a very small stream, but was principally in holes Aside from the question of water, I do not think the Bosque a suitable place for a reservation. There is a great scarcity of wood. The only facilities the Indians had for obtaining wood was by digging the mesquite roots. I have been in a number of scouts through the Navajo country, but do not know of any large tract of land there, on which could be colonized a large number of Indians ; but it could be done in small bodies. In the whole range of their country, I do not think they could support themselves without assistance. I don't think there is a man in New Mexico who could say what was best to be done with the Navajo Indians. It has been a great bone of contention in the Territory. I consider the water at Fort Sumner as unhealthy, a salt stream running into the Pecos north of the fort. Some one hundred and fifty miles below Fort Sumner, in 1856, I saw the Pecos very dry. I have been out of the service about a year and a half, and am now engaged in business in Santa Fé.

John A. Clark sworn :

Am surveyor general of New Mexico and Arizona. I came first to this Territory and entered upon the discharge of my duties as surveyor general in October, 1861, and have continued to discharge the duties of that office up to this time. I have approved the policy of placing the Indians upon reservations as being the only provision to secure peace to our borders. I visited the Bosque Redondo, on the Pecos river, in the spring of 1863, and since then have travelled over the southern portion of the Navajo country and other portions of this Territory and Arizona, but have seen no place within the Territory claimed as the Navajo country west of the Rio Grande, nor any place east of that river unoccupied, so well adapted for the settlement of the Navajoes and New Mexico Apaches as the reservation at the Bosque Redondo. During an extensive official tour through this Territory and Arizona, which I completed in May last, I learned that the Apache and other kindred tribes inhabiting the country east of the Great Colorado river and south of the Colorado Chiquito are at war with us, and of course preventing the settlement of the country and the working and development of the rich mines of that Territory.

Miguel Piño sworn :

Am a native of New Mexico; have resided in Santa Fé forty-four years; am mayor of the city; am a farmer by occupation. During all my lifetime the relations have been almost all the time hostile between the Navajoes and the people of New Mexico. My opinion the way to have a permanent peace is, to have the Indians placed on a reservation; I am not acquainted with the country around the Bosque Redondo, nor with the country formerly occupied by the Navajoes. I think the Indians are well off at the Bosque Redondo if there are troops enough to restrain them.

E. W. Eaton sworn :

I was in command at Fort Wingate, in the Navajo country, from February 1, 1864 until March 1865. I was there when the Navajoes surrendered themselves and came into the fort. The first large party that came in there were about twelve hundred. While on their way in they were pursued by a party of Mexicans, who ran after them to take their flocks and herds, and I had to send out troops to protect them. The Mexicans killed some of the Navajoes and captured some captives and stock. They were not troops, but a party of New Mexican citizens. The Indians were in sufficient force to have resisted them, but were coming in to surrender themselves, and made no resistance for fear the troops would attack them. There were not over fifty or sixty in the party. Some of the chiefs came in ahead and informed me of the facts, and I sent out troops to protect the Indians. Several parties of Navajoes came in afterwards. I sent, in all, some four or five thousand from that post. I became pretty well acquainted with that portion of the Navajo country lying on the Colorado Chiquito, lying on the west side of the Chusca mountain. I am not acquainted with any portion of the Navajo country where a single reservation could be located sufficient to support the Indians on, where they could be guarded. This is my opinion from my own knowledge and the best information I receive. I know of no place capable of sustaining over two thousand. If disposed to settle on reservations, few troops would be required to guard them; but if not disposed to settle, from their knowledge of their country, it would require from two to five thousand men to guard them. I do not think one post could guard them if settled on different reservations; there would have to be a body of troops stationed near or upon each reservation. I was lieutenant colonel of the 1st New Mexico volunteers, but am not now in the service. I have resided in New Mexico since 1849. There has been an almost constant state of hostility existing between the Navajoes and Mexicans. I think the Navajoes succeeded in stealing more stock than the Mexicans, the latter taking more captives. I consider the Mexicans justified in taking the Indian children by way of retaliation for stock stolen during the existence of hostilities. During the existence of hostilities the Mexicans have been in the habit of making unorganized expeditions into the Navajo country to bring out stock and captives. I have not visited the Cañon de Chelle; I have not visited the slope of the Tunacha mountain or the valley of the San Juan; I know nothing of my own knowledge of the capacity of those sections of that country for reservations. I speak from my own knowledge.

James Conklin sworn :

I was born in Canada; raised in St. Louis; am sixty-five years of age; and have resided in this Territory since 1825. I think about half the time there has been war, and the other half peace, between the Navajoes and Mexicans, ever since I have been here, both under the Mexican republic and the United States. The occasion of hostilities has been, the Navajoes have been inclined to steal from the Mexicans, and when they do not, the Mexicans steal from them. During their forays, on both sides, they kill and rob, taking flocks and herds, mules and horses, and cattle and prisoners, and keep them as servants. They take Mexicans for servants, and the Mexicans take Navajoes and make servants of them. This has been a hereditary thing from generation to generation. I have been out into the Navajo country frequently—sometimes in war, sometimes to trade with them, and other times I have been sent out among them, and am well acquainted with all their country and their principal men. I liked them for their industry and disliked them for their stealing. It is a fine country for raising stock, and there are places where they can raise considerable grain. These are scattered about in different places. They generally raise crops without irrigation; in some places they irrigate. It is seldom they fail to raise crops. My opinion is, that it was a bad policy taking them from their own country, because at different times, when sent there by General Carleton and others, I would talk with the principal chiefs after there had been war—and they come in at Junez to make peace—to induce them to make pueblos like pueblos in their own country. They objected, because if one died they always burned up the lodge and left it and went to another place. I tried to impress them that that was a wrong idea, and to show them how much more comfortable they would be in the pueblos. They appeared sometimes to yield assent so far that I thought, if insisted upon, they would yield that point. I had frequent and long talks upon that subject. Sometimes from sunrise to second rise I have smoked and talked with them upon it. I think the best policy would have been to insist upon that. I think with very little assistance and expense they could have been made to do it. My judgment is now that it would be best to return them to their own country and establish them in pueblos containing from one thousand to one thousand five hundred persons in a pueblo; and there are places sufficient to establish them all. There is one place, the mouth of the valley of Chella, where enough could be raised to support three thousand persons. That is the largest spot capable of cultivation, and has other great advantages. There are in the cañon orchards of peaches—as many as a thousand or twelve hundred trees in one place; no other fruit but peaches. I am also acquainted with the Tunacha mountain. On the eastern slope enough could be raised to support about one thousand Navajoes on the different spots of land capable of cultivation without irrigation. There is not water enough for irrigation. They plant corn very deep with a stake and raise very good crops. There is also the Little Chella, near the larger one of that name. Also in the San Juan, where another band generally cultivate lands. If established in different pueblos, I think all the Navajoes could be fixed upon six different pueblos not very far apart, and with proper agents and some aid they would soon become self-sustaining. I think that a small force would have to be kept there to keep them within the limits, and if any were caught to chastise them. I do not think there would be any need of military, except to keep them on their pueblos and prevent them from encroachments too. I do not think the Mexicans have made as many aggressions upon the Navajoes as the Navajoes have upon them.

Anastitius Sandaval sworn:

Am a native of Santa Fé; have always lived in Santa Fé, except a short time in the county of San Miguel; am forty-nine years of age; am a merchant and farmer, and have a mill. Most of the time war has existed between the Navajoes and Mexicans; but little of the time in peace. The object of the Navajoes was to plunder the flocks and kill the people. The Mexicans in turn made expeditions against them and took their flocks and herds. Under General Biscarra there was a treaty of peace which lasted a short time, when the Navajoes broke the treaty and commenced stealing flocks and killing people. A year ago I was on the Bosque reservation. My judgment is that it is better to leave the Navajoes where they now are, than to send them back to their old country.

Filipe Delgado sworn:

Am a native of New Mexico; aged thirty-five; have always resided in the Territory, at Santa Fé, or within fifteen miles of it. My recollection is, that the Navajoes have always been hostile; am at present superintendent of Indian affairs. It is my opinion that putting Indians on reservations is the only way to keep them under control.

[See Smithsonian report for 1855, page 283.]

Surgeon O. M. Bryan sworn:

Am medical director of the department of New Mexico; have acted as such over two years. Weekly reports of the deaths, wounded, and sick are made to me from all the posts. I am of the opinion that the post of Fort Sumner is as healthy as any other post. I receive also reports of the health of the Indians, captives. Within the last two months there has been an average of over eight thousand five hundred Indians on this reservation. On an examination of the weekly returns of the health of the Indians for the months of

May and June, I find an average of ninety-one unfit for duty, sick. Deaths reported in that time, two. The weekly reports do not show the nature of the diseases, but the monthly report which is sent to the Surgeon General does. From my recollection they are suffering mostly from venereal disease, catarrh, and rheumatism. I do not think the character of the disease can be attributed to the water. My attention has been called to this question from some complaints made. I can have some water taken from the Pecos at a low stage, at Fort Sumner, sent to the Surgeon General's office.

SANTA FÉ, *New Mexico.*

Captain W. H. Bell sworn :

Am chief commissary of this department; have acted as such since June, 1864. Some little time before I took charge of affairs the Indians had become a charge to the government; can give an abstract of expenses in my department for the support of the captive Indians until the present time, which will show the monthly expenditures for the Indians, the cost of all supplies. That exhibit I make part of my statement. I was on an exploring expedition under Major Simonson, charged with exploring the whole Navajo country. Hostilities commenced before we left the country, and I went on one scout against the Indians. I made a map of the country and sent it to the War Department. The country consists of valleys, with little water and mesas. There is very little water for irrigable purposes. The greater proportion of the Navajo country lies in what is now Arizona. I have been in the army since 1858. I left the Military Academy at that time. I came out here in 1858 and '59, and staid until August, 1861; then went to Texas. I saw no place for a reservation in the Navajo country capable of sustaining the whole nation. I think the Bosque Redondo is the only place where the Indians could be placed capable of supporting them. The San Juan valley is the only place which approaches a place suitable for a reservation, but if placed there they would have to be strung along a distance of a hundred miles, the valley being in no place more than a mile wide, and in some places not more than three hundred yards—the average of both sides, water and all, being about half a mile; outside of this nothing grows, not even a cactus bush. There is some cottonwood timber in the San Juan valley.

FORT SUMNER, *June* 26, 1865.

George Guyther sworn:

Is surgeon of the 1st New Mexican cavalry; has been medical officer since December 1, 1862, with an interval of about four months, during which time I was at Fort Wingate, New Mexico. From my knowledge of the health of this post, as my experience has enabled me to acquire, I consider it the healthiest place I ever lived in. It is peculiarly healthy because of its locality upon an open plain. Its freedom from stagnant waters, the ability to prevent liquor at the post, and the power to enforce hygienic laws, are the forces which combine to produce the healthy condition of this locality. The altitude is about five thousand feet above the sea. There are, at all seasons of the year, strong winds blowing from various quarters, and these winds prevent the accumulation of mephitic vapors. The water, I have no hesitation in saying, has never proved detrimental at this post. It is quite a common occurrence for newcomers to find a temporary relaxation of the bowels. This is owing, probably, to some mineral constituents of the water. This is only temporary, and in all cases parties find themselves benefited by its use. Dozens of men, who, at other posts, found a cure of various diseases impossible, have been here permanently benefited. I regard the post as a "*Santarium.*" I have made a rough analysis of the waters of the Pecos river, which is the drinking-water of all at the post. When the water is low and clear it is largely impregnated with salts, which, with my limited amount of tests, I found to consist mainly of the sulphate of lime and soda. This condition of the river, its lowness and clearness, exists about four months in the year, these months being variable, as the river rises in the upper country. During the remaining eight months the water is supplied from the melting snows and rains of the upper country, which makes it of the finest character. I have never known any person of any complexion, white man, Indian, or Mexican, seriously affected by the use of the water. The temporary relaxation of the bowels that newcomers experience in the low state of the water has never produced any weakness of the bowels, diarrhœa, of a permanent character. I am cognizant of soldiers coming to this post, who, to my certain knowledge, have been under medical treatment unsuccessfully for chronic diarrhœa for months, and even years, becoming perfectly cured at this post; and, incidentally, I will mention the case of private Skinne, of Lieutenant Porter's company. This man was under my care for chronic diarrhœa at every post from California here, and I did not cure him until he came here. Syphilitic cases, which have defied all treatment, including courses of mineral waters, have been here apparently cured. The medical statistics of tht post are made and kept by me in my own handwriting. These statistics fully bear me oue in the opinion I have given. The number taken sick each month, and the number returned to duty, prove conclusively that it is a most salubrious locality. Furthermore, the deaths at the post have been from diseases brought here, none of which may be attributed to disease originating here. The first of these was from pneumonia in a broken-down syphilitic constitution, brought on from outpost duty; the second, a case of mania; the third was a case of ulceration of the intestines in a confirmed drunkard. These were the only deaths from disease among the troops at this post during a period of over two years and a half. During that time there were always four, and sometimes six, companies stationed at this post. I have had also the medical treatment of all the civilians, and have never known the death of but one, and he was quite an old man. As to the health of the Indians, I have found a large quantity of syphilis and many cases of pneumonia; also, in the fall of the year, some bilious fevers. There is considerable difficulty in curing Indians of either sex of syphilis. I will here state that this syphilis is, in a majority of cases, of long standing, little of it, I think, being the result of recent communication. The difficulty of which I just spoke arises from the dislike of Indians to stay under medical treatment for the time indispensable to a cure. I have had no difficulty in curing pneumonia among them, as, in that disease, they are unable to leave the hospital. It has occasionally happened that the relations of the sick person have carried the patient off clandestinely, to get such benefits as may accrue from the practice of their native medicine-men. The cases of bilious fever yielded readily to treatment. The fevers arose, I think, from the indiscriminate irrigation of crops, by the Indians, at a time when the ground was already thoroughly saturated by rains, which had fallen to the average depth of ten inches in the season; thus producing malaria from the standing water upon the lands. From my knowledge of cultivation by irrigation, there is nothing in a proper system of irrigation to render the locality unhealthy, since a proper amount placed on the land is no more unhealthy than rain or the watering of a garden. I wish here to state that the better education of the Indians in these matters will tend to mitigate the evil. There is nothing in the quality of the water drank at this post calculated to aggravate or produce either of the diseases above mentioned, or any other disease to which they are liable. There is a feeling of superstition among them against being or going into any building where any person has died, and, knowing that, I have never allowed any person to die in a ward of the hospital. I have given an order, and personally seen that it was carried into effect, that all persons who were near dissolution should be carried into an out-house, and I acted thus from a fear, or rather actually that I could not get a sick Indian into the hospital if any one should die in it. While I was in charge of the Indian hospital it was thought all the time the number of out-door patients among the Indians averaged seventy; the in-door patients often as high as twenty-five. The hospital was reserved for the worst cases of sickness among the Indians. Of the hospital cases there were not more than two deaths per month; of the out-door cases, which were light cases, I do not recollect any deaths while I was in charge. I was in charge of the Indian hospital from the 1st of January, 1863, until November, 1863, and from May 1, 1864, to December 31, 1864. An acting assistant surgeon has been in charge the other part of the time to the present time. During June and July of last year varioloid prevailed to considerable extent. I vaccinated near six hundred, many of whom had been vaccinated before. I heard of no deaths, however. I think the general health of the Indians has not been good from the opposition to our medical treatment through the influence of their medicine-men, as well as from their exceedingly dirty and imprudent habits of eating and allowing filth of every character to remain near their huts and lodges. They defecate promiscuously near their huts; they leave offal of every character, dead animals and dead skins, close in the vicinity of their huts, and even their own dead they will leave unburied. If one dies they pull down the hut around the dead body and leave it. There are so many Indians that it would require a large police force to compel them to use greater care and cleanliness. There is nothing in the locality tending to produce disease. It is wholly owing to their own habits The soldiers and citizens have generally enjoyed perfect health. There has been considerable venereal disease among the soldiers at this post, mostly in syphilitic form. I found, when I took charge of the Indians, a large amount of syphilitic disease among them, both male and female. My impression is, that although there has been a mutual communication of disease, yet by far the greatest quantity existed among the Indians, and was imparted by them to the troops. In speaking upon the subject I refer to the Navajoes, and not to the Apaches. Among the Apaches it hardly exists at all. The Navajo women are very loose, and do not look upon fornication as a crime. Within the last few months the most rigid discipline has been adopted, and a provost guard established around the post to prevent all communication between the troops and the Navajo women; and there has been much less disease among them since that order was established. I will further state, that a large portion of the syphilis I find to exist in the Navajo nation is constitutional and hereditary. indicating its existence in the tribe for many years past, and the same is true of the population surrounding them. This hereditary syphilis is not communicated by sexual intercourse. I think the average width of the valley capable of irrigation and cultivation down to the "Point of Rooks," one and one-half mile; the length some sixteen miles, or twenty-four sections, something over 15,000 acres.

Major H. M. Enos sworn:

I have been in New Mexico since November, 1856; am captain in the regular army; I was an officer of the line until 1861, but am now in the quartermaster's department; I have been acting in this department almost all the time I have been in the Territory. The principal military operations, indeed all of them except when invaded by the Texans in 1861 and 1862, have been connected with Indian affairs, and mainly with the Navajoes, since I have been in the department. Upon an average, from two to three regiments of troops have been constantly required, since I have been in the Territory, to carry on military operations against the Navajoes or to protect the inhabitants against their depredations. From earliest history they have been at war with the Mexicans. I have conversed with people eighty years of age, who state that when they were boys they had been at war with the Navajoes; and since our acquisition of the territory from Mexico, that same state of hostilities, in the main, has continued between them and the people of New Mexico. I have never ascertained the annual expense of these regiments. I think, in the quartermaster's department the expense of an infantry regiment would be, annually, from $250,000 to $300,000, and a cavalry regiment $500,000 to $600.000 per annum. This would not include the purchase of horses, nor the payment of troops, but simply the expense of the quartermaster's department to keep the regiment in serviceable condition and transportation. Since I have been in this department there have been twelve to fifteen mounted companies. In the fall of 1858 there was an expedition against the Navajoes, under Colonel Miles; that expedition resulted in a treaty about December, 1858, by which the Indians were not to pass east of a certain line, and they were not to resist the passage of our troops to explore the country. In the summer of 1859 an expedition, under Major Simondson, was sent into their country. This was not hostile; there were no hostilities while they were in the country; as soon as withdrawn, depredations were committed by the Indians in September or October. In the summer of 1860 an expedition was sent against them, under Colonel Canby; portions of four regiments, some 1,500 troops, perhaps 2,000, employed directly or indirectly. This war continued into the winter; operations carried on until into March; considerable stock taken; many killed; Indians reduced, so that they came in and begged for peace and provisions. Hostilities were suspended and the troops withdrawn by the July following from the Territory; only two companies of New Mexico volunteers were kept in the country, at Faunt le Ray. I do not remember of any depredations in the summer of 1861 by the Navajoes; they commenced again in January or February of 1862, and continued them until another expedition was organized in 1863, under General Carleton, commanding the department, and Kit Carson, commanding the expedition. He entered their country in July, 1863, and continued through the winter of 1863-'64, and until several thousand surrendered themselves to the military authorities at Forts Canby and Wingate. The estimates of the Navajoes are from five to ten thousand, and some as high as fifteen thousand. From my best information there are eight or nine thousand, judging from those surrendered and estimates of those who remain in their country. On 31st of December, 1864, there were on the reservation at the Bosque Redondo, 8,354; this is based on the census made by General Carleton From my best information I think not over 500 remain in their old country. There are but two of the chiefs or headmen who have not surrendered or come in yet. The grounds upon which the military authorities have thought fit to remove the Navajoes and place them on a reservation upon the Pecos are: 1st. There is not in their own country a sufficient body of land situate together to make a sufficient reservation for them and to produce grain for their subsistence. 2d. It is less expensive to feed them than to fight them. 3d. That by removing them to their present reservation they are brought nearer the grain-producing districts of New Mexico and the States, and can be supported cheaper than on any reservation in their own country. 4th. That one of the most favorable routes to Arizona leads through the heart of the Navajo country. 5th. Where they now are they are on the extreme frontier settlements of New Mexico, and removed from any thoroughfare or travelled route through the country. 6th. By their removal a large grazing country is thrown open to settlement. I think 600 to 800 men would be sufficient to guard them on the reservation—half cavalry and half infantry. In a few years the number could be greatly reduced. With the Navajoes in their own country, two or three regiments of troops could not prevent them from committing depredations. Where they are now located six or eight hundred men are sufficient. I have been personally on the reservation on the Pecos. I think for farming by irrigation there is no better country in New Mexico or Arizona. I think ten thousand acres or more is capable of irrigation ; the soil and the water sufficient for irrigable purposes. The Navajoes, in their own country, cultivate small patches by irrigation, apparently with as much skill and care as the Mexican population generally. They manufacture blankets in looms of their own construction, some very celebrated for the beautiful arrangement of colors and for durability. I have stated the reasons upon which the military administration of the Territory have based their action in relation to the Navajoes. My own opinion coincides fully. It is the only practical way, in my judgment, for the general government to take care of the Indians. Last October the Indians appeared generally satisfied with the place and the treatment there. I cannot now speak from personal knowledge ; all communication is through interpreters ; I do not understand the Navajo language ; I judged from their appearance and from conversation with the officers. I saw a large number there at work upon *acequias* and farms. There was a surgeon there for the Indians, and a hospital. The health of the Indians last fall was good ; there were but three in the hospital. The water there is rather alkaline ; our officers and men use it ; I have never heard them complain of the water ; troops and officers looked as healthy as at any post I visited ; I have not heard of the water affecting the health of the Indians unfavorably. In their own country I do not think the Navajoes could support themselves without robbing and stealing from the Mexicans around them. The property captured from the Indians is generally sold ; sometimes it is given to the troops The property brought by the Indians when they surrendered they have been allowed to keep. The property found among them belonging to the people was returned to its owners. The Navajoes are very suspicious as to what is to be done with them ; they feared they were to be killed there, and for that cause some wanted to leave the reservation ; that was the only cause experienced. While I was there they tried to get them to enter a large corral for the purpose of counting them ; the Indians objected ; afraid they were going to be murdered ; since then they have consented to go in to have rations issued to them. A lot of them at Faunt le Ray, at a horse-race, on some difficulty about the race, were fired on with mountain howitzers by the New Mexican troops ; some twenty or thirty were killed ; since then they have been more suspicious of our troops ; this was in 1861. I am not able to give the number of warriors of the Comanches, Kiowas and Indians of the Plains My opinion is that an efficient campaign could not be carried on against these Indians without at least 10,000 men in the field ; two-thirds or three-quarters ought to be mounted. To supply the troops and horses, all provisions and transportation would have to come from the States. The price of transportation, per hundred, to this point from Leavenworth is $15 37 ; this would defeat our troops operating from New Mexico ; other defeats along the Arkansas. To keep a regiment of mounted men in the field, besides their pay and original cost of horses and arms, it would cost $1,500,000 per annum. I do not think an expedition of 10,000 men could be put into the field and kept in service for a year for less than $30,000,000 or $35,000,000. I think one year's campaign, with that number of men, could reduce them to submission. They have always had large quantities, and recent reports say that they have captured large quantities, of cattle from the Texans. They are generally well armed ; many have rifles and six-shooters—pistols. They are the most formidable Indians we have to contend with. Our men on horseback are not equal to them on horseback. They will use the bow and arrow on horseback with almost the same precision as on foot. The only way our men can fight them is to ride up to them and dismount. They will never fight unless surprised, unless they are in a position to have a decided advantage. I calculate with 10,000 men they could be surrounded and compelled to fight under such circumstances as to be subjugated in one year's campaign. There have been no hostile acts committed on the settlements of New Mexico ; their depredations have been committed on the routes ; depredations last summer were laid to the Cheyennes ; but it is now believed they are all engaged—Comanches, Kiowas, Arapahoes, and Cheyennes. Since I have been here, until the expedition of the fall of 1859, those Indians have been at peace until last year. My opinion is, that those Indians could come to some amicable treaty of peace unless they are urged on to acts of hostility by white men. Whether such would be the best policy in the long run I have my doubts. I think, sooner or later, they must be punished.

FORT SUMNER, *June* 27, 1865.

Charles L. Warner sworn :

Am physician and surgeon by profession, and now in charge of the Indian hospital. This hospital is built of adobes, one story high, and walls thirty inches in thickness. It is a very cool building ; it is about one hundred and seventy feet long and twenty-five feet wide, with portico along the whole length—wings running back from each end, and surrounded by a wall in rear enclosing a yard or court. From the 12th of January last I have been in charge of this hospital and of the medical treatment of the Indians, and during that time have kept records of all cases and all deaths occurring. I keep a record also of cases out of the hospital. The diseases prevailing among them are venereal, inflammation of the lungs, inflammation of the pleurä, remittent and typhomalarial fevers and rheumatism. The venereal disease existing among them, from all indications, is of long standing; some of it appears to be hereditary and constitutional. We have been successful in the treatment of this disease; none have died from it treated in hospital, nor do I know of any case of death from it treated outside. A great many who have the disease do not come to the hospital for treatment but are treated outside, and quite successfully. The medicine men among them sometimes interfere to prevent the sick from taking our medicines. This disease is found most prevalent among the poorer Indians. I have never found but one or two cases in the families of the chiefs or headmen; the persons afflicted by the disease are looked upon by the tribes as objects of contempt. I regard this post as a very healthy locality. In consequence of the river overflowing a piece of bottom land near some of the lodges of the Indians, there were some malarial fevers among those located there, and I had their lodges moved on to higher ground, and all these symptoms soon disappeared. The water drank at this post by all persons is from the Pecos river. It is most of the time roiled, like the waters of the Missouri, but is good water. When the river is high it comes down principally from the mountains, from rains and melting snows, but when low it partakes more of the nature of the waters of the Aqua Negra and similar springs. As to its constituent qualities, I am quite sure there is some iron among them; it contains also salts of some kinds, but in what proportions I cannot state, as I have not the means at hand to make an accurate analysis, but I think it a very healthy drinking water; when roily it ought to be settled or filtered. The qualities introduced by these Aqua Negra springs tend to make the water healthy. The statistics of this post prove that the drinking water is healthy. I hold in my hand an abstract of the report of sickness, death, and medical treatment at this hospital, including also the outside cases, for the months of January, February and March, 1865. During the month of January there were one hundred and sixty-six cases, and only one death of inflammation of the lungs. During the month of March there were one hundred and fifteen cases and no deaths, and during the month of February there were one hundred and twenty-two cases, and one death from inflammation of the bowels. I have also the monthly report for April. There were one hundred and thirty-three cases and one death from inflammation of the lungs. In the month of May there were one hundred and eighty-eight cases and two deaths one from inflammation of the lungs and one from inflammation of the bowels. The report for the present is not made up yet, but up to this time no death has occurred. The above contains an abstract of all the cases treated in hospital and outside among the lodges of the Indians Of these, the hospital patients would average about twenty per month. From the influence of their medicine men and from their great superstitions in regard to medical treatment, many of them sick will not come to the hospital or be treated by us, and there has been some mortality among them which has not come under my observation, and I am unable to state the entire number of deaths. Considering their numbers, I consider them, on the whole, as healthy. I attribute most of their sickness to irregularity and constipation of the bowels, owing in part, perhaps, to the fact that, drawing their rations once in two days, they eat too much the first day, and in part to their irregularity of habits. From my intercourse among them, while among the older ones there is a desire to go back to their old country, they are, upon the whole, a contented people, and generally of a cheerful and happy disposition. This is especially true of the Navajo population.

FORT SUMNER, *June* 26, 1865.

James M. Giddings sworn:

My age is fifty-three; my native State is Kentucky; first came here in 1835, returned in 1836, came back again in 1840, and have remained here ever since. I have lived on the Pecos, some three or four miles from here, since 1853. I have kept a ranch, cattle and sheep, and have been farming; raise my crops by irrigation by the waters of the Aqua Negra, a branch of the Pecos. In dry times the waters of the Aqua Negra give character to the waters of the Pecos. My stock drink of the Aqua Negra; it is undoubtedly healthy. I have had from eight to thirty-three families in my house or fortification, and have never had any death from disease. Some of them used Pecos and some the Aqua Negra. The water of the Aqua Negra is the same as that from the springs below running into the Pecos. That is a healthy water; it is somewhat diuretic when taken unmixed with the other waters of the Pecos. It runs over some beds of gypsum and is charged with soda and sulphate of lime. I have looked over the lands upon the reservation capable of irrigation.

I once examined the place, contemplating opening a ranch, before it was selected for an Indian reservation. I think the average width of the land capable of irrigation from a mile to a mile and a half. These level lands in this country are very deceptive as to distance, and are more than they appear to the eye ; without measurement one cannot judge correctly. The land is of good quality, decidedly good ; there is plenty of water to irrigate it. It will produce, on an average, thirty bushels of wheat or corn to the acre, of beans twenty-five bushels, and vegetables of all kinds except the Irish potato. Sweet potatoes do well with me. Cabbage, onions, and all garden vegetables grow in great abundance. The grasses on the reservation outside of the lands capable of irrigation are very fine and nutritious, much better than the grasses of the latter. Cattle, sheep, horses and mules keep in good condition all winter without hay, from the natural pasturage. On the lands of the reservation, each section of land one mile square would sustain, summer and winter, one hundred head of cattle. This reservation has been very little used as pasturage grounds by the Mexicans on account of its proximity to the Comanches and other Indians. The establishment of the reservation here does not in any respect abridge the pasturage grounds used by the Mexicans. On the other hand, the opening of the country heretofore occupied by the Navajoes, which is about as large as the State of Ohio, will greatly extend the lands of New Mexico for settlement, while the establishment of the Apaches here has secured for peaceable settlement thirteen thousand seven hundred square miles between the Red river and the Rio Bonito. This reservation would maintain one sheep to the acre, winter and summer, more than one million sheep in all. There is mesquite all over the reservation ; it is the very best kind of fuel. If the mesquite should be exhausted there is any quantity of wood up the Pecos river, between the Gusana and Pecos, and they could get millions of cords of red cedar and piñon, by simply cutting, throwing into the river, and floating it down. The expense of putting it in and taking it out of the river would be small. There are some bottoms here on the river subject to overflow, when if once ploughed and stock kept out, will spring up to cottonwood very thick ; such has been my experience. So all along the acequias. The peach trees would grow finely and produce a great deal of fruit. Peaches, grapes, and apricots do very finely here. I am clearly of opinion this reservation is one of the best for the Indians possibly to be found. It is decidedly best for New Mexico, as it opens a chance to be the greatest wool-producing country in the United States, while the reservation settled by the Navajoes is the best possible protection to New Mexico against the Indians of the plains, the Comanches and others.

FORT SUMNER, *June* 27, 1865.

William R. McCormick sworn :

Am a practical farmer ; have resided in New Mexico three years ; I have looked over the cultivated land on the reservation, the land planted to wheat and corn ; I have given attention to the crops to see the prospects within the last few days ; I estimate the wheat at five or six hundred acres, in four different places. The No. 1 piece of wheat of one hundred and fifty to one hundred and seventy-five acres will, I think, yield twenty bushels per acre ; the No. 2 of one hundred and seventy-five to two hundred acres, fifteen to eighteen bushels ; No. 3 is connected with this--will not exceed from seven to ten bushels per acre ; it is not even on the ground. The corn looks promising, but at this stage of its growth it is impossible to estimate the crop. The crop now upon the ground is no criterion of what might be produced when the system is perfected.

Henry B. Bristol sworn :

Am captain in the 5th United States infantry, and stationed at this post ; I have been here since the 22d of May, 1863 ; I have been part of the time commanding officer of the post, and acting military superintendent of the Navajo Indians. When I came here there was but one Navajo Indian here. He was taken from a Mexican who offered him for sale for ten dollars ; so that all of them have been brought here since I came here. They came at different times. Total number brought here, 8,474 ; of these there were men, 2,325 ; of women, 2,710 ; of children, 3,164 ; infants at the breast, 275. At the last count, on the 30th of April last, there were present 7,169. The difference in numbers is accounted for by deaths not reported, and absence of those who were hunting. Some others reside on the reservation, some twenty to twenty-five miles from the post, and were not present at the count, herding their stock. Some of them are owners of considerable herds of horses and sheep, and a few mules and goats. The number of deaths reported among the Navajoes from all causes, so far as it has come to our knowledge, is two hundred and sixteen since the 1st of February, 1864. The Indian people reside along the valley for nearly twenty-five miles, and some deaths occur without being reported. I have, since my connexion with them, learned the organization, habits, customs and superstitions of the Indians. They are as follows : I have looked over the lands on this reservation capable of irrigation ;

there is in my opinion sufficient to sustain all the Indians on the reservation. I have under cultivation by irrigation about two thousand five hundred acres. Most of the digging of the acequias or ditches has been performed by the Indians, soldiers superintending them in the work; also, much of the ploughing and dropping of corn and the hoeing. Many of the Indians know how to cultivate by irrigation. The young men and boys seem very anxious to learn, and show much aptitude for the work. They have some blacksmiths among them who make good bits; one presented, made by a Navajo, is in the Spanish style. I think they would be apt to learn to be carpenters, tailors and shoemakers. They all handle the awl well in making their necessaries, leggings, &c. The men knit their leggings—some are very good. The women are very industrious, spinning the wool and weaving blankets and girdles. If they had sufficient wool, they could make clothing for the whole tribe; they show themselves contented and happy at work. I have seen sometimes from four to five hundred men at work on the acequias, singing, laughing and happy. I have become well acquainted with their feelings; while many, if asked whether they would prefer to go back to their old country, would say they would, the great mass of them feel that they are well treated and that the present location is a good one for them. There is a good deal of mesquite about the place, upon all the lands around us, for fuel; there are cedar and piñon in large quantities up the river, which can be cut and floated down here. Last spring some Indians, with a few soldiers up the river, cut and floated down with very little trouble and expense some two hundred cords of wood to this post. Up the river the wood is very extensive As to the health of the post, I can say with confidence that it is very healthy. There is as little sickness as at any post I was ever stationed at. The water has never affected me nor any other person I know of, except two new-comers, who said that it slightly relaxed their bowels for a day or two. The Indians have generally been healthy; there has been some sickness among them; I think there has been no more mortality among them or their children than among any equal number of people. As to their diseases, I cannot tell as much as a surgeon; some are said to be affected with venereal, pneumonia and rheumatism. If nothing interferes to prevent the present crops from maturing, as they now promise well, I think we shall raise nearly enough to feed the Indians until next season. There has been made mainly by the Indians nearly thirty miles of acequias, and we contemplate opening other large acequias and feeders, to bring another large tract under cultivation. For this purpose some surveys are necessary, as it would have to be opened fifteen to eighteen miles long, to put the water upon a higher plateau of ground by hugging the base of the hill. The Indians can do the labor with some superintendence, and with that tract under cultivation I am confident, from my experience here, they can raise more than enough for themselves, and to feed the government animals needed at this post, and very nearly if not quite supply the troops at this post with breadstuffs. For peaches, apricots, and grapes the soil is excellent; the river banks are covered with wild grapes. Upon the balance of the reservation there are many springs, besides the river; there are six springs. The pasturage is good, supporting cattle, horses, mules and sheep in large numbers. Hay could be produced to feed during the winter storms. If Congress should appropriate a sum of money sufficient to give a few sheep to each family, I am confident they would keep them and not kill them. From the wool the women would make their clothing, and from the milk feed the children to a considerable extent. The money could be better expended here for that purpose than to attempt to drive them from the States. There ought to be an appropriation for hats and shoes, and some domestics, cotton cloth and calico and a few dyes; and there should also be some farming implements, a blacksmith's and carpenter's shop; there ought to be a grist mill. When the Indians came here, as a general thing, they were very much impoverished and in tatters. I never saw anything like it. Now, they are much better clothed, because the pelts of the sheep slaughtered by the government were given to the poorer classes of the Indians, and their women have made the wool into blankets, and they are now much better clothed. The hides also have been used by them in their lodges, and the green beef-hides have been used by them to make soles for their moccasins. Those who came bringing their flocks and herds with them have increased in the number of their sheep and goats. There is a strong sense of individual property among Navajoes, and sheep are prized by them as the highest species of property. They regard each other's rights of property, and punish with great severity any one who infringes upon it. In one case a Navajo was found stealing a horse; they held a council and put him to death. As an evidence of how they prize sheep, I would state that sixty-one Navajoes raised and gathered 259,000 pounds of corn fodder which they sold to the government at $15 per ton, for which they received sheep at the rate of about $4 per head, and these persons receiving these sheep have little flocks now, which they prize very highly; very few of them have been killed; they are herded with great care, and the wool preserved and manufactured into clothing. I have caused to be sowed upon the Navajo farm, of wheat, 15,000 pounds; of beans, 1,677 pounds; shall probably put in, of beans, 7,000 pounds more; of corn, I have planted 11,387 pounds.

FORT UNION, *June* 20, 1865.

Asa B. Cary sworn :

Is native of Connecticut; twenty-nine years of age; captain in the 13th United States infantry; have been in New Mexico since August, 1860; from August, 1860, to December, 1860, was engaged in the Navajo campaign under Colonel Canby; I was in command of a company; for about a year I was on duty at Albuquerque, as post quartermaster and commissary; was depot commissary here until June, 1863; was in command of troops during the invasion of New Mexico by the Texans in 1862; from that time to July, 1864, was in the campaign against the Navajoes, under Colonel Carson, a part of the time in command of the expedition myself: from June, 1864, to this time, have been on duty in quartermaster's department a portion of the time as chief quartermaster of the department at Santa Fé. From my best information, I think there are about twelve thousand Navajoes; about nine thousand have been captured, or have surrendered and been taken to the reservation on the Pecos. I think there are about three thousand still remaining in their old country. They constitute, with their families, the rich portion of the tribe; they are far removed from their country. I think they have a large amount of stock, sheep, cattle and horses; I think they are rich, because they have not come in to go to the Bosque. When I was in command in 1864, I used every endeavor to learn from the Indians their exact numbers; their ideas of numbers are very indefinite; have not had any communication with those remaining since the nine thousand surrendered; I think they are over on the San Juan and Big Colorado rivers, in the northern part of Arizona. I have seen one chief of the Navajoes, who in answer to my inquiries stated that he was well satisfied at the Bosque, and all his people were satisfied. He spoke to me through an interpreter, very few of them speaking Spanish. In the campaign of 1860, it was estimated that two hundred Indians were killed; their sheep and cattle were also captured; the sheep were issued to the troops as provisions, the horses sold and proceeds turned over to the company, making a company fund; some were used for cavalry purposes, some used up, and some died. In the last campaign, probably not over two hundred and fifty were killed and wounded. All the property they had was captured or surrendered; the captured sheep issued to the troops as part of the meat ration; the horses were bought of the captors by the quartermaster, at twenty dollars per head, and unserviceable horses left in the hands of the captives. The stock surrendered by them was kept by them and taken to the Bosque with them; cannot give the account, but there was a large amount of sheep and horses. The grounds for their removal from their own country were, there had been several campaigns resulting in a treaty—they staying in their own country. Every treaty thus made had been violated, either by Indians themselves or by Mexicans causing Navajoes to retaliate. In their own country, there is no section where they can live together and have sufficient grazing for stock and raise enough for their own support. They were scattered over a great extent of country, many of them very poor, and compelled to depredate to get food. By placing them on a reservation, they could be kept together, and there would be no necessity to depredate or violate treaties. I think it impossible for them to remain in their own country and be at peace with the Mexicans. In a country as rudely cultivated as the Navajo country is, I believe it costs more to keep troops in the country to prevent their depredations, than to guard and feed the Indians on a reservation. These are my views. Many were taken to the reservation by force. Those that were first taken there, as soon as they were made to understand the benefits, remained willingly. About five hundred were taken there in small squads by force. The remainder went voluntarily. It required a great deal of talk to convince them that the Bosque was the best place for them. The distance was about three hundred and fifty miles. At one time I had about three thousand at Fort Canby who were just ready to go when there came in a Mexican and a Zuñi Indian who told them that the purpose was to get them down there and kill or poison them. I had considerable difficulty in disabusing their minds and persuading them to go. This report was made to them more than once, and caused a great deal of dissatisfaction among them. During this time considerable mortality attended them; some one hundred and fifty died, and they attributed their deaths to me, and believed some means had been used to dispose of them. They are very superstitious and were about to leave Fort Canby, but by talking to them, and showing them that those sent to the Bosque were well cared for and comfortable, I succeeded in doing away with that impression, and they said they would go and see for themselves, and did go voluntarily, but would constantly inquire what we wanted them to go for if they were going to be put to death when they got there, showing that they were still suspicious of our intentions towards them. They all went. Some Navajoes who had been to the Bosque previously came up to Fort Canby and informed them how they had been treated. That seemed to satisfy them. Nearly all the chiefs are now at the Bosque. None of the chiefs were captured. All of them but one, who still remains in the Navajo country, came in voluntarily and surrendered themselves, to go to the Bosque with their families, flocks, and herds; some came in before they brought their families, flocks, and horses, to satisfy themselves they were to be well treated The chief who told me he was well satisfied I had seen a good deal of at Fort Canby. He had a good deal of confidence in me. His people were never so well off before. He found everything just as I had told him it would be.

Examination of Captain Cary resumed at Santa Fé July 4, 1865:

I can give an account of the expenses incurred in the quartermaster's department at Fort Canby, but can find no account in the chief quartermaster's office here of the expenses incurred in their transportation to the Bosque. I have been in charge of the quartermaster's department but about a month. While this is a proper office to make reports to, if required, still upon examination I find none. They can be obtained from the chief quartermaster at Washington. I can obtain them and will forward them by mail to the committee. The expenses of the expedition at Fort Canby, from July, 1863, in the quartermaster's department, to the time the expedition was withdrawn from the country, which was in October, were $41,705 33. This includes the purchase of all hay fed to public animals, and the pay of all citizen employés in the quartermaster's department, the purchase of all stores other than those furnished on estimates, and the general and incidental expenses of so large a post as Fort Canby. There was no necessity of the report of the expenses incurred in removing the Indians being made to this office.

FORT SUMNER, *June* 27, 1865.

Laurence G. Murphy sworn:

Am captain in the 1st regiment of cavalry, New Mexican volunteers, and am stationed at this post, and have been here since July, 1864; am military superintendent of the Mescalero and Coyotero Apaches upon the reservation. There are very few of the latter. I have four hundred and seventy-eight, including men, women, and children. It may vary a little, from deaths and births not reported. I had a count about one month ago. There were of

Men	139
Women	178
Children	154
Infants	7
	478

The general health has been very good. It is reported there have been some cases of measles among them, from which four children died; no grown persons. I have no difficulty in getting them the assistance of the surgeon at the hospital. They do not always apply when sick, and try their own remedies of their own medicine-men, and some die under that treatment. Since I have been in charge no Apache under the medical treatment of the surgeon of the Indian hospital, or receiving medicine from him, has died, nor do I know of any Apache having died under these circumstances since I came to the post. The drinking water here has not to my knowledge produced any deleterious effects. It is as healthy as any water I ever drank on the frontiers the last fifteen years. It is almost a general complaint among strangers, that after arriving here it causes a relaxation of the bowels, but experience shows that they get quickly over it without recourse to medicine, and that it contributes to their health instead of being an injury. I think the lands capable of irrigation in the valley from the head of the acequia to the point of rocks, a distance of over sixteen or seventeen miles, and over a half mile wide. I have under cultivation for the Apaches four hundred and fifty acres of corn planted, and I have planted about forty acres of beans, and am still planting beans—the black bean, the common bean of the country. I expect to plant one hundred acres of beans in all. This is about the proper season to plant beans. Besides this, the Apaches have grounds where they plant melons, pumpkins, and chili. These are to be disposed of by the Indians as they think proper. The farm proper is also to be applied to their actual wants, and turned into the government for that purpose. In this work the ploughing and planting has been done principally by some of the soldiers of my company detailed for that purpose. The Indians have made all the acequias for irrigation, about four miles in length. They will also do all the hoeing and the work in their own gardens. The Indians only work four hours in the day, and it requires a good deal of talking to get some to work at all. I have to threaten to stop their rations. They are very apt to make excuses to attend religious rites, feasts, and ceremonies. They are very much disinclined to manual labor. Neither the women nor the aged are required to work. They tell me if I would divide off the farm into lots they would cultivate it without any pressing on my part at all. The objection to that would be, they would use up all the produce of their lots in making an intoxicating drink which they manufacture called ' teeswin," made by boiling the corn and fermenting it, on which they get very drunk. In consequence of that inclination no corn is issued to them. It is all issued in flour. The Navajoes don't make that drink, and corn is issued to them unground. I had to stop the issue of whole corn to the Apaches, for every time it was issued they would get drunk. Of beans, I calculate about twenty-five bushels to the acre, and of corn about thirty bushels. In all, I estimate of beans, in pounds 112,500

Of corn, in pounds 756,000

Total 868,500

Five hundred Indians, for 365 days, at one and one-half pound per day each, 273,750, leaving 594,750 of surplus. I calculate this is worth five cents per pound, or, in round numbers, $29,737 50. I think there will be a ton of fodder per acre, worth $20 per ton, equal to $9,000. I think there will be a surplus in money, or its value, over supporting the Apaches, of $38,737 50. To give each Indian one and one-half pound of beef would cost $30,512. We still have a surplus of $8,225, to be expended in clothes or otherwise. These estimates are, of course, based upon the present prospects. The Apache women work in the gardens, but do not weave or spin. They tan hides, and make coverings for their tents and soles for their moccasins. Outside of the manual labor I prevail on the Indians to do, they do nothing but hunt. The women do all the other work, and the little boys herd the horses, of which they have about three hundred. They prize their horses as their principal wealth. They never keep sheep, but always kill them to eat. In this respect they differ altogether from the Navajoes; they are nomadic, the Ishmaelites of the continent. The head chief, Cadetta, has more influence than any other; but he is not supreme. They trust him to distribute their rations, which are delivered to him in bulk for his tribe once in five days I have never had but one complaint of any partiality or injustice in the distribution of rations, although all know they have a right to complain to me. I am, therefore, satisfied that he deals justly with the members of his tribe. He labors very faithfully, and those immediately under him. I regard him as one of the most reliable Indians on the reservation. In the Navajo country, there are very few places capable of irrigation. I travelled all over it. I saw but one deer and three or four antelopes. The Navajoes being there, could not support themselves except from stealing stock from the Mexicans. There is a good country on the San Juan, but the Utes occupy it, and the Navajoes cannot live there; for the Utes are a powerful and warlike people—would overrun them. I have a printed copy of a letter upon that country and its resources, which I now hand to the committee. There was a board appointed to examine the amount of Indian goods delivered to the Navajoes under the appropriation of 1864 of $100,000. I have a copy of the proceeding, and will furnish the committee with one. The printed letter I believe to be true in all its statements.

[For the Santa Fé Gazette.]

FORT SUMNER, NEW MEXICO, *November* 18, 1864.

MR. EDITOR: I have been for some time past an astonished observer of the efforts made by interested parties in New Mexico, through their organ, the New Mexican, to cause discontent among the people with the establishment of the reservation at the Bosque Redondo. But believing that this opposition would soon cease from convictions of the wisdom of the selection made, I have heretofore refrained from attempting to give my views on this matter; nor would I do so now, but that in the issue of the New Mexican of the 21st ultimo I find that its editors and correspondents have adopted the last resort of all demagogues, who, when their arguments are defective and fail to convince, adopt the very questionable course of supplying their places with low sarcasms and personalities; and as it is evident that as these people commenced their opposition from motives of interest, backed by jealousy, they will *not* be convinced of their errors or swayed from their object by motives of patriotism. It becomes the bounden duty of every citizen of New Mexico who loves its well-being and prosperity to raise his warning voice against the sophisms of those who, regardless alike of their duties as citizens and editors, and of the best interests of the Territory, endeavor by all possible means to renew the Indian atrocities of the past two hundred years. The sending them back to their own country would unquestionably have this effect, and none other. Nor must it be understood that I entertain any fear that the intelligent people of New Mexico can be so influenced against their interests as ever to be brought to countenance such a measure. But people abroad, who know comparatively nothing of our affairs, may in time begin to think that "where there is so much smoke there must be some fire," and, acting on opinions wrongly conceived, use their influence at the seat of government to destroy the only chance of peace which has been vouchsafed this country since 1684.

The most elaborate attempt yet made to advance their views is contained in the issue before referred to, and this, with your permission, I propose to answer. He says: "It is the policy of the general commanding and others (principally contractors, &c.) to urge upon the government the establishing of this reservation." Only one citizen of respectability has as yet appeared in public as the opposer of this reservation, (Don Miguel Romero y Baca,) and it is questionable whether this was his voluntary act. Be this as it may, on the appearance of his protest in the name of the people of San Miguel county, it was indignantly contradicted by most of the intelligent and responsible citizens of the very county which he so misrepresented. But "there were contractors." It is rather improbable that so many contractors are inhabitants of San Miguel; it is well known that such is not the case But, supposing that some of these gentlemen were engaged in supplying the necessary wants of the government, they have more interest in the well-being of San Miguel county and the Territory at large than the editor and his associates can ever hope to acquire; and they were citizens of New Mexico before the said editor had discovered that such a place graced the map of North America. These being the facts, we are bound to believe them when they assert that the present location of the reservation works no injury to the interests of their county, but on the contrary tends materially to promote the well-being of the whole Territory. But there is one whose testimony I propose to offer, whose evidence not even the editor of the New Mexican will dare to deny, being entirely disinterested. Colonel Carson, in his report of the 7th of May last, says: "And here let me observe that the department commander has shown no less wisdom in his policy [meaning that of reservation] than judiciousness in the selection he has made of a reservation. In my campaigns against the Mescalero Apaches and Navajo Indians I have traversed nearly the *whole Territory*, and, in my opinion, a more judicious selection could not have been made; besides, removing these Indians from their former haunts and fastnesses and from old assotions, where they would be continually reminded of the comparative impunity with which they formerly made the citizens to contribute to their support, and rendering it much harder, if not altogether impossible to teach them to depend on their honest industry to supply their wants." Here is the testimony of as loyal a gentleman and as truthful a citizen as ever honored any country or age. And as he says he travelled over the *whole* of the Navajo country, not excepting the Rio Chiquito, with the capabilities of which he is perfectly familiar, can as much be said of those who vaunt its applicability as a site for a reservation? I venture to say not. From the source to the mouth of the Little Colorado there cannot be found a space, sufficient at any one place, where over fifty families could be located. Not more than five such places could be found, and these many miles apart. Here there might be provision for about 1,250 persons, were there not some serious drawbacks. At certain seasons of the year the stream of water is so small as to be wholly insufficient for irrigation, and at others the bottoms overflow, abundant evidence of which can be seen by any one who examines the country. It is possible that in the whole extent of the Navajo country places might be found, at each of which from ten to fifty families might be located, and thus provide for the whole tribe. But this I very much doubt; and they would have to be settled many miles apart; and to think of making them sulf-sustaining thus situated is simply preposterous, a dream which could never be realized; nor can I clearly see how, under such circumstances, the system of a reservation could be carried out. To adopt the plan would be nothing more or less than making another treaty; and we who are not *New* Mexicans know, to our cost, what this means as applied to these Indians. Their history conclusively proves that it was only while force was being applied that they remained well disposed, and that as soon as this force was removed they relapsed into their former habits of lawlessness. Perhaps our sapient friend imagines that they are already so weaned from old associations that with impunity they might be permitted to go back to their former haunts and fastnesses; or does he think, in his ignorance, that when scattered over so vast an extent of country, as would necessarily be the case, this force could be employed? Those who know the Indians and their former country know that in both he is wrong.

He complains of removing them "from a country where it is well known that with a little assistance they can support themselves from the natural resources of the country, into one where their only resource is the product of their own labor." Now I would ask where and in what consist these resources? In game? There is not enough wild game in the Navajo country to subsist the tribe for one day. This is a fact well known to every one who has campaigned through it. There is an old saying that "the Devil is not as bad as he is painted." This is certainly true of the Navajo, and it was the absolute *lack of all resources* which necessitated his raids on the flocks and herds of the people. Perhaps this is the resource of which he writes; and if so, the people of New Mexico, particularly the stock owners, must feel greatly indebted to those who advocate a measure which will remove those Indians from their present location, "where their only resource is the product of this labor," back to their former haunts and fastnesses, where, as Colonel Carson says, "they would be continually reminded of the comparative impunity with which they formerly made the citizens to contribute to their support." Self-preservation—about the only law which controls an Indian—would immediately force them into their former habits, and again would robberies and murders become matters of common occurrence. Better by far that they should occupy twice the quantity of land they now do, accompanied by the certainty that never again will the people be called upon to maintain them as heretofore.

It is true, as he says, that this year's crop was a failure; but for this, nature alone is responsible. It could not be foreseen or prevented. Had it not been for the influx of the "cutting or army worm," they would have raised about seventy-two thousand fanegas of corn—an amount more than sufficient to support them for one year. But it was not alone the reservation which suffered in this manner. The crops throughout many portions of the Territory failed likewise.

I am informed that Mr. L. B. Maxwell, who, in former years, used to dispose of about two thousand fanegas of corn as the surplus produce of his farm, has this year raised scarcely sufficient to feed his animals, notwithstanding that the usual planting was made. Next year, no doubt, he will have better success, and so, also, will the reservation, and when five thousand additional acres will be cultivated, as is intended, we have every reason to feel convinced that next fall will see these Indians self-sustaining. When we consider that, notwithstanding the many difficulties which, last summer, they had to contend against, they cultivated *three thousand acres*, we have every reason to believe in their ability and willingness to support themselves by their industry; and the cheerfulness with which they bore the misfortune attending their labors, only goes to prove that where persons assert that they are contented and happy, they but bear testimony to the naked truth, no matter whether such persons have been here for weeks, months or years.

In estimating the cost of each Indian per diem, your contemporary is mistaken, as usual. Instead of its being forty cents, as he states, it is exactly $15\frac{3}{4}$; and as there will be planted this fall and winter about three thousand acres of wheat, this amount will soon be reduced, if not entirely done away with. So much for his calculations. But supposing that it cost all he says it does; how does he propose to reduce it by removing them, and thus trebling the cost of transportation? Nor would the expense attending this measure be inconsiderable of itself. Let him understand that since 1849 the government has expended about $30,000,000 in their subjugation, and let him add to this amount the losses sustained by the people during the same period, and, if he can comprehend anything, he will understand that it is a measure of economy, the expending on them, even for a longer period than will be necessary, the amount needed for their support, thereby securing peace and safety to the Territory.

Your contemporary expends a great deal of unnecessary sympathy over the hardships of the poor Indian at the Bosque, and it delights me to be able to comfort his philanthropic soul with the assurance that their hardships are purely the offspring of his own too fertile imagination. The Indians on the reservation *do not* "carry wood for fuel on their backs eight or ten miles." On the contrary, the only trouble experienced by those interested in their farms is, that they cannot get them to clear ground of the mesquite fast enough for the ploughs; I need say no more than that the Indians live on these farms. His statement that there was a scarcity of water here last summer is equally incorrect. The fact is, *we had too much*. The rains which fell last summer were more than sufficient to irrigate the farms, and the river was so swollen as to overflow its banks in many places. It is now the middle of November, and the river is as low as it usually is, and yet we have sufficient water to overflow the five thousand acres which is being broken up, besides abundant to supply the domestic wants of the reservation. So much for the "reliable men at Fort Sumner." If all his correspondents are equally *reliable*, his numerous errors are not to be wondered at.

I fear I have already engrossed too much of your space by this article, and, in sooth, I do not see that much remains to be answered. The remainder of his paper is made up of an appeal to the people to beware of the savage instincts and barbarous nature of the Indian, which, according to him, will here receive nurture until it finally rushes forth to slay and destroy; but send them back to their former country and they at once become changed beings—as mild as the sheep now in the possession of their owners, but which they would very quickly appropriate. A little too illogical this to need comment.

I have studiously refrained from taking notice of his personalities, well knowing that the parties referred to are above such attacks; *their* acts speak for them; nor is there anything which I could say which would add to their well-earned claims on the gratitude of this people, and when, as is not unlikely, the owner and editors of the "New Mexican," like their predecessors, will have to seek in other portions of the Union some more congenial society in which for a brief while to figure, and obtain unenviable notoriety, the originators of this reservation will remain beloved and honored citizens of New Mexico, if living; and if dead, mourned as its best benefactors. When the future history of this Territory will be written, the name of General James H. Carleton will stand proudly forth as the only department commander who made its interests his own, and who adopted and carried out the only successful measure ever introduced by which its permanent peace and prosperity were secured.

JUSTICE.

FORT SUMNER.

William L. Rynerson sworn:

Am captain and assistant quartermaster of volunteers, and am now post quartermaster at this post, and acting commissary of subsistence for the Indians on this reservation; have acted as such since 1st of March, 1865. Captain Prince G. D. Morton was my predecessor; he was from Kansas—captain and assistant quartermaster of volunteers. I can furnish to the committee an abstract statement of the costs of issues to the Indians at this post, on account of subsistence. The expense of cultivating their lands is also a matter of account in my department, except the lands cultivated by the Indians themselves, where the only expense to the department is the expense of seed. I can also furnish an approximate statement of the expense of cultivation; the latter consists mainly in teams, utensils, seeds, and the like, and some employés; and the employés of the post sometimes work upon work pertaining to the cultivation of the lands, such as repairing ploughs, &c. The actual employés on the farm are very few—one chief farmer and not more than three assistants; the labor is performed by the Indians, under the superintendency of the troops. The general health of the post is good; I have experienced no difficulty from the water, and have heard of none; some persons speak of the taste, but I regard it healthy. I have no knowledge of anything showing fraud or misappropriation of the funds of the government. There was a charge of that kind made against Captain Morton, and he was tried by court-martial; a copy of the minutes of testimony on the trial is in the hands of Captain Murphy; although he was not convicted upon this charge, he was dismissed the service for disobedience of orders. There is still another investigation pending as to his operations in the quartermaster's department. I estimate the land capable of irrigation upon the reservation from 20,000 to 30,000 acres; the best land lies along the river; if the channel of the river were straightened, that would be good for cultivation. The accompanying paper, marked A, is a true statement of one month's issues to the Indians on the reservation. The paper marked B is a true statement of the amount issued for the months of March, April, and May last past. The paper marked C is an approximate estimate of the expenses incurred by the quartermaster's department in carrying on the farming operations on the reservation.

A.—*Abstract of provisions issued to Indians at Fort Sumner, New Mexico, from May 1 to 31, 1865, by Captain W. L. Rynerson, assistant quartermaster, United States volunteers, and assistant commissary of subsistence.*

Number of return.	Number of Indians.	Number of days.	Number of rations.	Commencing.	Ending.	Bacon.	Price.	Amount.	Beef.	Price.	Amount.	Beef-pluck.	Flour.	Price.	Amount.	Wheat-meal.	Price.	Amount.	Beans.	Price.	Amount.	Corn.	Price.	Amount.
						Lb. oz.	Cts.		Lbs. oz.	Cts.		Lbs.	Lbs. oz.	Cts.		Lbs. oz.	Cts.		Lb. oz.	Cts.		Lbs.	Cts.	
1	3	46	138	Apr. 16	May 31	29 4	30¼	$8 99	123 12	18	$22 27		155 4	10	$15 52									
2	10	10	100	May 1	May 10				75		13 50		100		10 00									
3	8,421	2	16,842	May 2	May 3				12,137 8		2,184 75	494				16,842	17.95	$3,023 14						
4	481	5	2,405	May 2	May 6				1,803 12		324 68					2,000		359 00				405	11	$44 55
5	1	8	8	May 3	May 10				6		1 08		8		80									
6	7,510	2	15,020	May 4	May 5				10,823		1,948 14	442				15,020		2,696 09						
7	7,737	2	15,474	May 6	May 7				11,150 8		2,007 09	455				15,474		2,777 58						
8	481	5	2,405	May 7	May 11				1,803 12		324 67											448		49 28
9	7,737	2	15,474	May 8	May 9				11,163 8		2,009 43	442				6,164 10 9,309 6	17.85	1,106 54 1,661 74						
10	7,737	2	15,474	May 10	May 11				11,176 8		2,011 77	429				15,474		2,762 11						
11	11	10	110	May 11	May 20				82 8		14 85		110		11 00									
12	22	10	220	May 11	May 20	47 4		14 52	196 4		35 33		217 8		24 75				33	8	$2 64			
13	7,737	2	15,474	May 12	May 13				11,176 8		2,011 77	429				9,800		1,749 30						
14	465	5	2,325	May 12	May 16				1,743 12		313 87													
15	1	10	10	May 12	May 21	7 8		2 31					10		1 00									
16	7,734	2	15,468	May 14	May 15				11,172		2,010 96	429				15,468		2,761 04						
17	7,729	2	15,458	May 16	May 17				11,203 8		2,016 63	390				15,458		2,759 25						
18	465	5	2,325	May 17	May 21				1,743 12		313 88					2,000		357 00				325		35 75
19	7,726	2	15,452	May 18	May 19				11,199		2,015 82	390				15,452		2,758 18						
20	19	25	475	Apr. 26	May 20	102		31 36	423 12		76 27		534 6		53 44				71 4		5 70			
21	7,725	2	15,450	May 20	May 21				11,197 8		2,015 55	390				15,450		2,757 83						
22	25	20	500	May 21	June 9	107 4		32 97	446 4		80 33		562 8		56 25				75		6 00			
23	25	11	275	May 21	May 31	58 8		18 00	246 4		44 32		309 6		30 94				41 4		3 30			
24	6	11	66	May 21	May 31				49 8		8 91		66		6 60									
25	1	5	5	May 22	May 26	3 12		1 15					5 10		56				12		6			
26	5	14	70	May 22	June 4	52 8		16 14					78 12		7 88				10 8		84			
27	460	5	2,300	May 22	May 26				1,725		310 50					1,880		335 58				420		46 20
28	7,725	2	15,450	May 22	May 23				11,236 8		2,022 57	351				15,450		2,757 82						
29	7,727	2	15,454	May 24	May 25				11,226 8		2,020 77	364										15,454		1,699 94
30	7,776	2	15,552	May 26	May 27				11,261		2,026 98	403										15,552		1,710 72
31	460	5	2,300	May 27	May 31				1,725		310 50					1,800		321 30				500		55 00
32	7,776	2	15,552	May 28	May 29				11,235		2,022 30	429										15,552		1,710 72
33	7,773	2	15,546	May 30	May 31	9		2 78	11,247 8		2,024 55	403										15,546		1,710 06
Quantity in bulk and amount						417		128 23	180,800 4		32,544 04	6,240	2,187 6		218 74	173,042		30,943 48	231 12		18 54	64,202		7,062 22

Abstract of provisions issued to Indians at Fort Sumner, New Mexico, &c.—Continued.

Number of return.	Number of Indians.	Number of days.	Number of rations.	Commencing.	Ending.	Coffee, green.	Price.	Amount.	Coffee, roasted.	Price.	Amount.	Sugar, brown.	Price.	Amount.	Salt.	Price.	Amount.	Corn-meal.	Price.	Amount.	Total amount.	Remarks.*
						Lbs. oz.	*Cts.*		*Lbs. oz.*	*Cts.*		*Lbs. oz.*	*Cts.*		*Lbs. oz.*	*Cts.*		*Lbs.*	*Cts.*			
1	3	46	138	Apr. 16	May 31				11	55¼	$6 08	20 11	36¼	$7 61							$60 47	Nav'o orp. child'n.
2	10	10	100	May 1	May 10																23 50	In confinement.
3	8,421	2	16,842	May 2	May 3				9 14		5 46	18 9		6 82	250	5¼	$13 12				5,233 99	Navajoes.
4	481	5	2,405	May 2	May 6				4		2 21	7 8		2 75	50		2 63				735 82	Apaches.
5	1	8	8	May 3	May 10																1 88	In confinement.
6	7,510	2	15,020	May 4	May 5				9 12		5 38	18 4		6 71							4,656 32	Navajoes.
7	7,737	2	15,474	May 6	May 7				9 12		5 39	18 4		6 70	250		13 12				4,809 88	Do.
8	481	5	2,405	May 7	May 11				4		2 21	7 8		2 76				1,957	15	$293 55	672 47	Apaches.
9	7,737	2	15,474	May 8	May 9				9 12		5 38	18 4		6 71							4,789 80	Navajoes.
10	7,737	2	15,474	May 10	May 11				7 3		3 97	13 8		4 96							4,782 81	Do.
11	11	10	110	May 11	May 20																25 85	In confinement.
12	22	10	220	May 11	May 20				17 9		9 70	33		12 13	8 4		44				99 52	Working party.
13	7,737	2	15,474	May 12	May 13				7 3		3 97	13 8		4 96				5,674		851 10	4,621 10	Navajoes.
14	465	5	2,325	May 12	May 16				4		2 21	7 8		2 75	50		2 62	2,325		348 75	670 20	Apaches.
15	1	10	10	May 12	May 21																3 31	Guide.
16	7,734	2	15,468	May 14	May 15				7 3		3 97	13 8		4 96	250		13 13				4,794 06	Navajoes.
17	7,729	2	15,458	May 16	May 17	12	53¼	$0 40	6 8		3 60	13 8		4 96							4,784 84	Do.
18	465	5	2,325	May 17	May 21	5		2 66				7 8		2 76							712 05	Apaches.
19	7,726	2	15,452	May 18	May 19	9		4 79				13 8		4 96	250		13 12				4,796 87	Navajoes.
20	19	25	475	Apr. 26	May 20	47 8		25 29				71 4		26 18	17 13		93				219 17	Working party.
21	7,725	2	15,450	May 20	May 21	9		4 79				13 8		4 96							4,783 14	Navajoes.
22	25	20	500	May 21	June 9	50		26 64				75		27 56	18 12		99				230 73	Working party.
23	25	11	275	May 21	May 31	27 8		14 64				41 4		15 16	10 5		54				126 90	Do.
24	6	11	66	May 21	May 31																15 51	In confinement.
25	1	5	5	May 22	May 26	8		27				12		28							2 32	Guide.
26	5	14	70	May 22	June 4	7		3 73				10 8		3 86	2 10		14				32 58	Scouting party.
27	460	5	2,300	May 22	May 26	5		2 66				7 8		2 76	50		2 62				700 32	Apaches.
28	7,725	2	15,450	May 22	May 23	9		4 79				13 8		4 96	250		13 13				4,803 27	Navajoes.
29	7,727	2	15,454	May 24	May 25	9		4 79				13 8		4 96							3,730 46	Do.
30	7,776	2	15,552	May 26	May 27	9		4 79				13 8		4 96	250		13 13				3,760 57	Do.
31	460	5	2,300	May 27	May 31	5		2 66				7 8		2 76							692 22	Apaches.
32	7,776	2	15,552	May 28	May 29	9		4 79				13 8		4 96							3,742 77	Navajoes.
33	7,773	2	15,546	May 30	May 31	9		4 80				13 8		4 96							3,747 15	Do.
Quantity in bulk and amount						211 4		112 49	107 12		59 53	519 4		190 82	1,707 12		89 66	9,956		1,493 40	72,861 15	

*Captive Indians receive three-fourths pound meat and one pound breadstuff to the ration; working parties, full rations.

I certify that I have carefully compared the above abstract with the original ration returns now in my possession, and find that they amount to 417 pounds of bacon, 108,800¼ pounds of beef, 6,240 pounds of beef-pluck, 2,187¾ pounds of flour, 173,042 pounds of wheat-meal, 231¼ pounds of beans, 64,202 pounds of corn, 211¼ pounds of green coffee, 107¾ pounds of roasted coffee, 519¼ pounds of brown sugar, 1,707¾ pounds of salt, and 9,956 pounds of corn-meal.

WM. McCLEAVE, *Major 1st California Cavalry, Commanding.*

B.—Statement of the cost of subsisting the Navajo and Apache Indians at Fort Sumner, New Mexico for three months, commencing on the 1st day of March, and ending on the 31st day of May, 1865.

Subsistence stores issued in March	$70,578 30	
Do .... do ...... April	72,704 97	
Do .... do ...... May	72,861 15	
		$216,144 42
Amount expended for herding beef-cattle and sheep in March	1,800 00	
Do .... do .... do .... April	1,500 00	
Do .... do .... do .... May	1,500 00	
		4,800 00
		220,944 42
Amount paid to chief farmer, $150 per month, three months	450 00	
Do ...... one assistant, as cook, &c., $30 per mo., 3 mos.	90 00	
		540 00
		221,484 42

The foregoing statement is correct.

W. L. RYNERSON,
Captain and A. Q. M. U. S. Vols.

FORT SUMNER, NEW MEXICO, *June* 27, 1865.

C.—*Estimated cost of articles supplied by the quartermaster's department to the Indian farms at Fort Sumner, New Mexico, for three months, March, April, and May, 1865.*

Grain forage for 52 mules and 16 horses, 90 days, 7 pounds each, 42,840 pounds, cost per pound 10 cents	$4,284
10 tons of hay, (fed during same period,) cost $40 per ton	400
Labor of mechanics, 1 carpenter and 1 blacksmith, 2 men, 3 months, at $65 per month	390
2,000 feet hard lumber, at 30 cents per foot	600
500 pounds assorted iron, at 9 cents	45
1,000 pounds assorted steel, at 26 cents	260
200 bushels charcoal, at 25 cents	50
Screws, nails, and damage to tools	75
100 pounds harness leather, for repairs of harness, &c	50
Borax and other small articles	25
100 pounds rope, used in lariats, plough-lines, &c	25
25 per cent. damage to 20 wall tents, 20 common tents, and 6 hospital tents, total cost $3,320	830
10 per cent. damage to 70 sets lead harness, total cost $910	91
	7,125
Service of 68 animals, at 50 cents per day, for 90 days	306
	7,431

The foregoing is as nearly correct as I am able to estimate or approximate.

W. L. RYNERSON,
Captain and A. Q. M., U. S. Vols.

ASSISTANT QUARTERMASTER'S OFFICE,
Fort Sumner, New Mexico, June 27, 1865.

APACHE CHIEFS AND HEADMEN.

Cadette:

Is the head chief of the Mescalaro Apaches. All of the Apaches on the reservation. We can cultivate the land by irrigation. The land down on the river is enough for his tribe; thinks there is water enough to irrigate all their land. There is no grass or wood either. The good grass is too far off, some fifteen or twenty miles. Have used all the mesquite near by, and have to go a good ways to get it now; go out in the morning and return the next morning; it is all gone near us. If we had teams we could get the wood, but at a long distance. If they had burros they could get wood, but it is too far to go. Cadette draws the rations in bulk for all his tribe and distributes them. They do not get flour enough to last five days; it only lasts two days. Have lost a good many, and a good many of my people are now sick, two very sick. They did report to the hospital, but, seeing that all died, they do not report to the hospital now. They call on the physician, but with his assistance they all die. Do not know the physician now in charge; the other one died. There are ten sick now in the tribe. The soldiers do not allow them to come into the fort, but otherwise treat them well. Don't know of any bad women in the tribe; if they did, the punishment would be severe. The tribe is free from any venereal diseases; never had any. They do not like to live here, as they hear of their relations away from here dying, and it makes them feel sad. They have to work to make a living; otherwise, they would not work. All that any one owns he owns by himself, without interference from any one else. They never had any sheep. Do not know how to make blankets like the Navajoes, but think they could learn how. They have always lived by hunting. Before he came here he had no war with the Indians or Mexicans, but lived in peace.

Question by Mr. Ross. Do you know of any other country where you could get along any better than here?

Thinks he could live better in his old country than in this. The water is better, and better grass.

Question Is it the unanimous wish of all the chiefs to go back to their old country?

They would rather go back to their old country. Should they be sent back, they could work there, near Fort Stanton.

Question. Why would you rather work there than here?

My horses have all died but one of starvation.

Question. How is the water?

It is not good, too much alkali, and is the cause of the sickness in the tribe and losing our animals. Thinks they are doing very well here, but still would like to go back. Would like to have schools established in his own country, but not here. Would not have my boys go to school here, but would in my own country. Tell the President that though we live well here, still we would prefer to go back to our old country. Would like to go through some of our performances every day, but cannot, because the people are dying; but are content the way we are now. About six days ago four died, an old man, middle-aged man, a boy, and a girl. Did not call on the physician; died of the measles. The measles have not been among them long. Some died before the measles made their appearance.

Pino Baco, chief of the Cibillobatano:

Draws rations for 194; they all enjoy good health. While he was here to distribute the rations there was enough for all; but when he went to Fort Bascom they did not hold out. The men, women and children in the tribe are industrious and try to raise crops; but the Indians of another tribe cross their fields and tramp down the crop; they would grow very well if not trampled down; have sowed no wheat, but planted corn, beans, melons, pumpkins, and red peppers. There is plenty of water, and my people understand how to irrigate; they raised crops in that way in their old country; they are all considered Catholics; there are a good many children; some 25 or 30 born on the reservation; was brought here a prisoner, and kept in the guard-house in double irons until a month since; was kept in irons at Fort Wingate four months; was captured by the soldiers, and ran away, and for that reason was put in irons at Fort Wingate; have been treated very well since I have been here; and the people are contented and doing well, as well as in their old country; it is better for my people and myself to be here than in my old country; am married, but have no children living; the soldiers here treat us very well.

Antonio Maria:

Have lived with the Navajoes a long time; was captured from the Mexicans, when young, by the Utes, and sold to the Navajoes; was captured with the Navajoes and brought here; like it very much; have a wife and two children; knows how to cultivate by irrigation; thinks this is a good place to raise grain; plenty of water, and good water; the soldiers treat us all well; the Navajoes work very well; they live in as good houses now as they did in their own country; there is plenty of grazing for the stock, which is not interfered with; an old chief told them if they staid here they would all die; so some have left Héréra Viejo.

Epifano Vigil, interpreter, sworn: (explained to the chiefs the object of the committee:)

Herrero and Armigo are the two principal chiefs of the Navajo nation. Herrero has been chief for a good many years. Armigo is here, but unwell. Herrero has not numbered his people ; does not know how many are present on the reservation ; does not know how many are in their old country, but there are three bands, under chiefs Manuelito, Herrero, and Yutachiquito. One chief says Yutachiquito has sixty-four men. Herrero is a cousin of the head chief present. The people are all very well, and working every day. Am married, and have ten sons, all of them here, and seven daughters, all here; all well ; all are married and have families; only one little child is sick. The lodges we have here are about the same we had in our old country. The women have just as good a chance to weave blankets here as in their old country if they had the wool. This is a good grazing country here; plenty of water, but we have not got the stock. If we had the wool we could make our own clothing for the whole tribe. The whole tribe know how to cultivate by irrigation. There is plenty of good land and water; plenty to raise crops for the whole tribe. The men are working here like mules. Mr. Doolittle said to the Indians that "work is civilization ; work makes the white man great."

Question. Is there plenty of wood on the reservation for fuel ?

Answer. There is plenty below here, but we have to go too far for it. Don't know whether fuel could be floated down the river or not ; knows of some floating down ; could pack the wood if we had the burros. The water has alkali in it, and they are afraid it will make them sick ; a good many have been sick and died ; when they drank the water they took sick and died ; and others have got sick by carrying mesquite so far. Those that were attended by the doctor all died ; do not know his name ; he was physician at the hospital. There is a hospital here for us ; but all who go in never come out. We have physicians among ourselves, but they can't cure all ; some must die. They commenced to get sick about last October, and since then every day some of them have died ; so many of them dying they are getting frightened ; a good many of his children and grandchildren have died ; three sons and two daughters have died ; they are dying as though they were shooting at them with a rifle ; they would rather live on the west side of the river, as they do not die there so much ; they are permitted to build houses on that side if they wish to. The people work very well making the ditches, carrying wood, &c., and are pretty contented. Don't know whether the young men could repair the ploughs or not ; is a blacksmith, and from him some of the young men have learned. Herrero Delgadito works in iron—makes bridle bits. Herrero is the name for blacksmith. If we had the tools some of the young men could learn to make things ; could learn very quick to make horse and mule shoes ; can make hatchets and hoes myself, but do not know whether the young men could learn or not. We have hatchets and hoes ; if we had them not, could probably learn to make them. Some living on the east side of the river went away ; none from the west side. Have missed twenty-two rancheros; three have come back. Ganado Mucho knows those who went away very well ; don't know the number that went away ; but fourteen are missing, (mentioning the rancheros ;) fourteen headmen ; don't know how many they took with them ; families and rancheros means the same.

To all the chiefs:

Question. Are the Navajo people on the reservation working pretty well?

Yes, they are, and want to work.

Question. Do the young men like to work and want to work ?

Yes ; the young men work well ; love to work ; even the women.

Question. Are your women and children all pretty well now ?

All are not well ; some of them are sick ; all agree to what Herrero says.

Question. If your people had plenty of wool could they make all the clothes?

Yes ; if we had the wool we could make all the clothes for the tribe. All of them know how to cultivate by irrigation ; thinks there is plenty of land ; but some how the crops do not come out well. Last year the worms destroyed their crops. There is plenty of land, and when the ditches are all cut out there will be land enough ; there is plenty of water ; there is plenty of pasture for all their stock ; some have but 25, 30, or 40, but more have none ; none have a hundred. They try and keep their sheep for their milk, and only kill them when necessary, when the rations are short or smell bad ; they depend on the milk of the sheep to live and to give to the little children ; they are honest and do not kill each other's sheep ; they own their animals themselves, and not in common ; they would like each man to have his own piece of land and work it for himself and his family ; they have not grain, stock, and other things enough ; when they have enough they would like to have their children go to school ; they would not like to have their children go to school until they had learned all kinds of trades, so they could make a living. Some officers at Fort Canby told them when they got here the government would give them herds of horses, sheep, and cattle, and other things they needed, but they have not received them ; they had to lose a good deal of their property on account of the war, and the Utahs stole the rest from them ; have been at war with the Utahs nine years, and about the same number of years with the Mexicans. Before the war with the Utahs and Mexicans, had everything we wanted; but now have lost everything. Herrero was quite young when the war commenced with the Mexicans. In the war everything was stolen on both sides—women and children, flocks When children were taken we kept them, sold them, or gave them back. The Mexicans got the most children; we have only two, and they don't want to go back; have not been in the habit of selling our own children; don't know of an instance. They don't expect to be rich again; but if they had plenty of stock, and wagons to haul their wood, they would prosper again. Some of the soldiers do not treat us well; when at work, if we stop a little they kick us or do something else; but generally they treat us well. We do not mind if an officer punishes us, but do not like to be treated badly by the soldiers. They say their women sometimes come to the tents outside the fort and make contracts with the soldiers to stay with them for a night, and give them five dollars or something else; but in the morning take away what they gave them and kick them off; this happens most every day; in the night they leave the fort and go to the Indian camps; the women are not forced, but consent willingly; a good many of the women have the venereal disease; it has existed among them a good many years in their own country, but was not so common there as it is here; there are remedies to cure the disease, but they cannot get them here; they have no confidence in the medicines given them at the hospital; think it would do them no good; most of the old men know how to cure the disease; they use the root of wild weeds that do not grow here; some of the people are dying here of the disease; some were taken to the hospital, but were not cured; when they find out a person has that disease they report it to the hospital; this they have done for some time; but all they have reported there have died; the custom of the tribe is never to enter a house where a person has died, but abandon it; that is the reason they don't want to go to the hospital; they would prefer a tent out by their camps for a hospital.

By Mr. Ross to Herrero:

Question. Were you made a chief by your own people or by the whites?

By my own people.

To the chiefs:

Question. Would you all like to go back to your old country or remain here?

They would rather prefer to be in their own country, although they have most everything they want here; they are all of this opinion, and would like to have you send them back; and if you have any presents to give them they will distribute them among them. If they were sent back they would promise never to commit an act of hostility.

Question. If you are sent back could you make your own living?

Yes; we could support ourselves; and you could send some troops to see that we kept our promise.

Question. Were many of your people killed when they were brought here?

Not any.

Question. Was any of your stock killed?

No; they took nothing from us.

Question. Do you want us, when we go back, to tell the Great Father and the great council that you would like to be sent back to your old country?

Yes; we would all like to go, and if sent back would go straight back the way we came.

Question. Are the soldiers treating you badly? and if so, let us know.

The soldiers about here treat us very bad—whipping and kicking us.

Question. Do you get enough to eat here?

We do not get enough to eat.

Question How much do you get as a ration?

Question. Is there any game in your own country?

Yes; there is plenty of rabbits, antelope, deer, and wild potatoes. Herrero says they would like to have you send them back to their own country. They think you are the greatest men and can send them back, and they would like to have it done soon.

Mr Ross said, they only wanted to report to Washington their wishes.

They say they will try and work and do all they can to support themselves until they learn what disposition is to be made of them.

Juan Baptiste Laney:

He is a Roman Catholic bishop of New Mexico, Arizona and Colorado. He has resided here fourteen years; has become acquainted with the Pueblo Indians of New Mexico; has visited them all once, and some of them many times. As a people they are good and industrious, of gentle, mild manners, and are Christians. Some among them practice their religion. They are taking care of themselves; their habits do not change; they are docile, honest and law-abiding. They are a moral people, have marriages for life, and are generally virtuous and exemplary. There are nineteen Pueblo villages, containing a population of not less than nine thousand. Some few of the villages are decreasing in size, so that three or four of them are almost without people; others are increasing and flourishing. The pueblos of Santo Domingo, San Felipe, and La Isletta are the most flourishing of all. Some boys from the village of La Isletta have attended our school and are equal to he best Castilians. My opinion is that, if the Navajoes are properly managed upon a reservation, they may be converted into model Pueblos, for they are superior as an Indian race. This system of establishing reservations is the best mode of dealing with the Indians—the only practicable way, in my opinion.

There are a good many Navajo captives among the Mexican families; they make the best of servants. Some families abuse them, while others treat them like their own children. Most of the Mexican families have them; there are more than a thousand of them, perhaps two or three thousand. Part of these captives have been taken in war by the Mexicans, and part have been purchased from the Indians, such as the Utes, who are constantly at war with the Navajoes. These slaves have been bought and sold in this manner for years, but of late the traffic has been greatly diminished through the agency of General Carleton, and also in a certain degree through that of other persons.

I think, upon the whole, that the Indians are decreasing. The Pueblos fall under this remark In my opinion, it is the best policy to place the wild Indians on reservations; no one at a distance can form any idea of the extent of the depredations committed by the wild bands of hostile Indians; hundreds of persons have been killed by them every year during the fourteen years I have lived here.

In relation to the reservation of the Bosque Redondo, I came to present a plan for the erection of school buildings at the Bosque Redondo. The expense of erecting the buildings will be about $13,000. I will say in behalf of the church I represent, that in case government lends some proper aid, I will do all in my power to assist in the civilization and Christianizing of these Indians. I will further say that under my charge there are at present some young men engaged establishing a school among the Navajoes with some show of success. But some buildings are required before the school can be successfully founded. I have already advanced two thousand dollars for their erection.

The following remarks are most respectfully submitted to the honorable congressional Committee on Indian Affairs, relative to the habits and customs of the Navajo Indians now on the Bosque Redondo reservation. My information is principally derived from Jesus, a Mexican interpreter, who is a captive and has been among them fifteen years; as also from my own personal observations during the last two years, and lately as their military superintendent. Jesus informs me that there are eight tribes, and that they are known as follows: 1. Chusco; 2. T'sa-hah-hi; 3. Teish-en-desh-keis; 4. Say-al-chee-nil-kia; 5. Lo-co-cha-ki-a; 6. Cha-Chill-il-t'so; 7 and 8. Cañon Chelle.

The Navajoes have no recognized head or chief. When one or more are successful in battle or fortunate in their raids to the settlements on the Rio Grande, he is endowed with the title of captain or chief. This honor or office only lasts for such a time as it suits his associates and companions to confer the honor upon him or them. All act in all things independently of each other. The captains or chiefs have little, if any, authority, and are without force.

There is no marriage ceremony among them except bargain and sale; a young man wishing a woman for his wife ascertains who her father is; he goes and states the cause of his visit and offers from one to fifteen horses for the daughter. The consent of the father is absolute, and the one so purchased assents or is taken away by force. All the marriageable women or squaws in a family can be taken in a similar manner by the same individual; *i. e.*, he can purchase wives as long as his property holds out. Their separations are by mutual consent, when either are at liberty to go in search of other wives and husbands. A woman or man from one village can marry a man or woman from another, or *vice versa.* They have from one to six wives, frequently more. Incest is not known. When a quarrel arises among them or in a family on account of the plurality of wives, the difficulty is usually settled by the man sending the woman he thinks the least of away from his lodge. The children belong to the mother, and receive one name when small, which they take from her; another name is given when they grow up. They are usually called after bodies of water, salt lakes, rivers, &c., &c. When the father dies, what things belonging to him that are not deposited with the corpse are given to the male relatives. A fair division is not made; the strongest usually get the bulk of the effects. The dead are laid or buried in ravines or crevices of rocks; the body is covered with brush and stone; (on the reservation they destroy their hoes, spades and shovels, and throw them on the grave or abandon them at the house of the deceased;) deposit a few things in the grave and carry the body to its resting-place on one of his finest horses; the animal is then led some four or five hundred yards from the grave, where he is killed, and the saddle, bridle and equipments are broken and thrown upon him. After the death of any one no infant is permitted to be at the breast of its mother, nor do the old or young eat or drink until after the burial service is performed. This is only among the relatives of the deceased. A house is never used after a person has died in it; they vacate the premises at once. Immediately after a death occurs a vessel containing water is placed near the dwelling of the deceased, where it remains over night; in the morning two naked Indians come to get the body for burial, with their hair falling over and upon their face and shoulders. When the ceremony is completed they retire to the water, wash, dress, do up their hair, and go about their usual avocations

It is believed by the Navajoes that all the spirits of the departed souls go to a marsh, where they remain in an unsettled state for four days, when they discover a ladder leading them to a world below the one they now inhabit. Some of their people never reach this place, but are lost forever; this they cannot explain. They worship two great spirits, father and mother. They reside where the sun rises and sets. After reaching the foot of the ladder that takes them to their new world, they there behold their father and mother combing their hair; this performance they look on in silence for a few suns, when they return or climb the ladder back into the swamp to become clean and purified, when they again go to where they first saw their two spirits combing their hair. Here they remain for eternity in peace, happiness and plenty. All the cereals, seeds and pits of fruits that are lost, drop down into this future world and grow more luxuriantly than with us.

In their own country, I am informed that little if any venereal disease exists. Their Indian doctors gather herbs high up in the mountains, which is said to be a sure and permanent cure for both syphilis and gonorrhœa. The former is called aiz-za—the latter be-kel-clod; one is used as a tea—the other dried in the sun, pulverized and applied to the parts affected. For all the common diseases they use feathers, stones, charms, roots, leaves, antelope toes, cranes' bills, etc., etc. Sometimes they paint themselves with charred wood. They also use sweat-houses built of poles covered with grass and dirt, or small excavations in the earth, having been previously filled with red-hot stones. Witchcraft is practiced among them to an alarming extent. The interpreter informs me that he has seen an Indian apparently in perfect health drop dead. The witches at one time put the evil spirit in his wife; she was about to die, when some other witches administered a little bear's gall, dried in the sun, when she immediately recovered. This is the only medicine known to cure a person so affected; they prize it very highly and carry it about their persons in very small buckskin bags. It is believed that a witch can pierce the heart of one of her enemies at almost any distance with the quill of a porcupine, or that she can extract one in some manner from between or through the ribs so as to not affect or hurt the person. Charms for everything, in almost countless numbers, are used. For rain a long round stone is used; these they think fall from the clouds when it thunders. That for snow is only known to a very few, and is used when they run off stock, and is intended to obliterate the tracks and baffle pursuit of its owners. Their ceremonies and manœuvres with this, their great charm, are done in secret and by a select few.

In conclusion, I would state that, as a class, the Navajoes are more industrious and better laborers than any other Indians; many of them understand irrigation and their mode of farming sufficiently well, with proper management, to become in a few years a self-sustaining people. The women weave their blankets and dresses, or pail cloddy, as they term them; the men knit, and a few of them can make a fair specimen of a Mexican bit; and, without doubt, they will make good mechanics, if properly encouraged, in a short time,

All of which is respectfully submitted.

I am, gentlemen, very respectfully, your obedient servant,

H. B BRISTOL,
Captain 5th United States Infantry, M. S. Navajoes.

Statement made by the priest Antonio José Martinez, curate of Taos, New Mexico, sent to the government of his excellency General Don Antonio Lopez de Santa Anna, relating to the civilization of the wild tribes which dwell in the vicinity of the department of New Mexico. Taos, 1843.

Your Excellency: The priest, Antonio José Martinez, curate of Taos, department of New Mexico, having studied for some time, aided by certain estimates derived from observations, the affairs of this department, which relate to the miserable condition of the Indian tribes around and in this most interesting part of our republic, and, on that account, ought to be well cared for, with a solicitude until now dispensed with, has made a plan which he places before your excellency, with the hope that the necessity of the case will urge its immediate execution. It is as follows: Although the vast uncultivated fields are deserted, they were once occupied by these wild nations, and it was formerly observed that, at a time anterior to the Mexican empire, they were inhabited by an intelligent, numerous, and industrious people, the aborigines of our republic. It is well known that, from time immemorial, these tribes subsisted and maintained themselves by hunting the buffalo, the deer, and other animals, in the same manner now followed by the Indians of the north and east; also by pillage, committing depredations sometimes against each other, and often uniting against us. But these first natural resources are decreasing so much, that perhaps these means of subsistence will soon fail them, and they will be compelled to end, as they have done heretofore, by pillage. Hence, it is evident that their ability of obtaining means of support in this way is very doubtful, without resulting in serious consequences to our republic; therefore, to prevent such occurrences this suggestion is made: Let some lands or homestead be granted to them, in some fixed territories, to cultivate, enabling them to follow some honest callings or useful industries, thereby receiving the advantages of being all under the influence and system of civilization of our government. Though some difficulties may arise, it will eventually bring some good results, and tend greatly to the welfare of our republic. This is the reason that prompts me, as a patriot, interested in the prosperity of my country, to suggest a plan which, owing to the emergency, requires its immediate realization by measures adopted by our government, and under the most advantageous laws in order to promote the success of this important object.

It is a true and notorious fact that the wild tribes dwelling in the vicinity, as well as in different parts of this department of New Mexico, live by the produce of the chase and robberies, since they neither cultivate the lands nor raise cattle, which is done only by the Navajo tribe, unfortunately the most ferocious and the most faithless in their treaties of peace, whenever they happen to make any, (No. 1.) This tribe is the only laborious one in raising stock, in agriculture, and in various other industries. Regularly, however, they wander to make invasions in the country and wage war against our people. The time employed in these raids is necessarily lost to labor; the fields left uncultivated do not produce enough for their maintenance; and the result is, that, unable to live on the production of the soil alone, they have recourse to pillage also. But what shall we say of the others, which must be in greater number than the inhabitants of this department?

At first it is not noticed, that when there was a greater abundance of game and wild animals than at present, (they have nearly disappeared now,) no necessity existed for robbery and pillage. How much more there is to-day.

It is a fact that the various species of deer and other game which formerly roamed the plains in great quantity, throughout the country north, crossing the east to the south, have diminished to some extent. In different parts of the semicircle which runs across the south, passing through the west, the buffalo seems to have almost disappeared in those localities where, at first, they were thought to be inexhaustible, and multiplying under the special dispensation of the Almighty. But the experience of the present state of things shows the above statement to be true, and is corroborated by travellers, and also by Indians, who are compelled to go further than heretofore, and remain sometimes two months without bringing any dry meat, which formerly was obtained in large quantities. Now they encounter the same difficulties, but stay away from four to five months, and not only return exhausted, after travelling over a vast extent of ground, but even without their horses, and frequently without anything at all. This is further affirmed by the settlers residing in the different points at the north, who bring with them a great quantity of all sorts of articles to exchange for buffaloes, and thus form a traffic very beneficial in various ways to the Indians, (2) obliging them to extend the hunt of the above animals for a greater return, in order to sustain themselves, and obtain the articles sold by the traders. Urged by this necessity, there is no such limitation to the destruction of buffaloes as is observed by the economy of different nations, which at certain periods forbid and limit the hunting season; in this manner protecting these animals, and the most precious, which are breeding in the spring, though the latter are not even spared, and thus causes the loss of millions of calves. It is easily imagined that an attack made upon a herd of buffalo cows amounting to three or four thousand, the most part of them with calves, running away to a distance of fifty or sixty leagues, must naturally cause a great loss, if not of the totality, at least of the greatest part of the young ones, as it is proved by experience. What would, then, be the destruction if these attacks were now renewed every day in different localities, either by the Indians or by us?

It is certain, and the fact is undeniable, that the buffaloes must greatly diminish in consequence, and that this constant slaughter will finally result in the extinction of the species in a very short time. Therefore, if at present the decrease of their principal resource is so much felt by the Indians, and proves insufficient to their maintenance, they are all the more obliged to resort to pillage and robbery, thus doing great injuries not only to our department, but to others of the Mexican republic, already unable to tolerate them, since such damages end in the ruin of the farms, and place the lives of our fellow-citizens in jeopardy. How much more will be the havoc, in a few years, if this necessary resource disappears, (and the buffalo is considered the principal one,) since these people do not cultivate the soil for a subsistence? Such is the case, even among those who are at peace with them ; not committing acts of open hostility, but stealthily, and taking refuge among the people of their own nation, each one taking whatever animals they may have stolen ; and should our forces overtake them, they will never deliver their booty, but will also ask indemnity, more especially the Apaches and Utes. Not only that, but it is their custom every year, in the autumn, to place their huts near the corn-fields, and steal maize and other productions, thus causing an important loss to the farmers. They also do the same when the flocks of sheep and horned cattle are in the fields, killing a large number openly, and even assault the shepherds. All this tends to prove that they require for their subsistence other means than those which nature has provided for them, since these are insufficient already.

It must also be noticed that the flesh of the buffalo, as well as that of other animals, does not constitute the principal nourishment of the above-named nations ; they have besides, in quantity, bread, corn, vegetables, and many other things bought by them with the skins, and even the grease, of the animals obtained in hunting. With these same skins they dressed themselves, made shoes, and covered their tents ; in a word, their only industry and mode of living is the product of the chase, which to them is everything. But in a certain time this will fail entirely and leave these wild tribes without means of support. Therefore, in order to promote the welfare of our people, these Indians ought to be brought up to a military career, since it cannot be done otherwise ; also, to the cultivation of the soil, to the raising of cattle, and other industrial pursuits.

But will they adopt the above? Very likely not. Should this step be taken by our government, perhaps the evils will fall back on us ; for these tribes would seize the opportunity to unite together, enter into a conspiracy similar to the one which has already taken place against us—would then become powerful by their large number and warlike tactics, and carry their depredations and invasions even into our villages, as often occurs in different localities, and thus result in great losses inflicted on our people, who have become intimidated. What has been the success of the raids made by the Indians in the various villages or settlements during the present year, in this department? The Navajoes have killed men and women, brought some of the two sexes into captivity, as they did in the valleys of Lobato, Rio Colorado, and in other vicinities of Santa Fé, the capital, and on the outskirts and parts of Rio Abajo. The same thing was done by the Comanches in different departments from Paso del Norte, Carussal, and the intermediate places, Chihuahua, along the coast as far as the boundaries of Durango, and even passing there, turning round Texas, and in Texas itself. Did not the Apaches attack, rob, and destroy some villages near Sonora, and commit depredations among the people in the interior of Chihuahua? The inhabitants were so frightened, that they brought a proportion of the payment of certain annual pensions to obtain peace. Ah! there our arms have lost their honor, and our valiant fellow-citizens have been degraded ; our worthy citizens of Chihuahua, who so often desired to gather laurels in New Mexico, and perhaps retake those that fell from the hands of the defenders of its streets and houses, killed by that most vile mob, the Apaches. Then how can it be otherwise than not to feel a certain fear, should the barbarous nations unite and conspire to exact their means of support at the cost of our own misfortune? It is to be dreaded, your excellency, that here is the evil that threatens the destruction of our great Mexican republic, if the remedy already spoken of is not used. Therefore there is no other, except that of inducing them to live in civilized society, to cultivate lands, to exercise various arts or industries, to raise cattle, and adhere to the rest of the institutions belonging to the system of government adopted by our republic for this multitude of barbarous nations. In doing this, it will tend to their civilization and welfare, thus strengthening the foundation of our republic, now impaired and in danger from them, and for whose happiness and regeneration so much anxiety is felt by the supreme powers pledged for their greater aggrandizement and prosperity. Now is the proper time, the most opportune, and the most acceptable, which will pass away with the opportunity, if any more delays take place before adopting important measures.

The fact must also be acknowledged that this plan will increase the encouragements for this enterprise, and offer great inducements ; inasmuch that the great inhabited territories occupied by these wandering and unsettled nations are mountainous, and have a numerous population usefully engaged in cutting timber, in working the mineral wealth contained in the interior of these mountains, and which formerly, and even now, supplied the abundance of their metals to enrich our republic. Then, also, the vast quantity of pastures would maintain and tend to increase the stock of cattle ; and in the principal localities there is a great number of well-distributed rivers, many of them in great proportion, with plenty of water, regulated by the wisdom of the Creator. In other parts of this republic, with all these advantages, the lands are well adapted for the purpose of agriculture, and would give a great abundance of produce. The climate is temperate, and the severity of cold weather is rarely felt, except in certain mountainous districts, where the shepherds in these latitudes bring their cattle down the valleys, and thus avoid the severity of the winter. In a word, if all these plans referred to are realized they will result towards peace, security, and advantages for our government, and for this vast number of inhabitants formed by the barbarous nations.

Perhaps what has been stated in the foregoing paragraph will appear hyperbolical. No, sir. Your excellency, with his high penetration, will perceive the correctness of the results which will bring greater advantages to the enterprise, and greater difficulties. Still, it is necessary to take the initiative against the adverse circumstances which are contrary to the welfare of our republic. What is related or stated in the foregoing paragraph forms all the encouragements which ought to induce the active and efficient provision of the supreme powers of the high government, represented in the worthy person of your excellency, to deliberate, resolve, and finally bring the enterprise to an end, which will realize great advantages to the Mexican republic, in doubling the number of civilized inhabitants, and the rest of other prosperities in proportion, and with them the cessation of hostilities from the barbarous tribes, which actually destroy life, properties, degrades and turns her into ridicule before the other cultivated nations, when they contemplate the injuries caused by these vile mobs, which are left and remain without being severely punished by us. It is evident that it is in their nature, though belonging to the same human species, but with all the want of education, dragging a vagrant and uncertain life ; therefore, to avoid this, it is urgent to create among them a feeling of self-respect, a love of order, and to govern their actions by other ideas than that of cruelty, since they have neither honor, decency, nor conscience, and only consider as superior those that are the bravest and most skilful to kill—their enemies as well as others. Hence is the only fear they have, and which prevents them from committing evils ; but being gifted with reason, they are capable of discipline, as it has been observed by many who are converted, and who remain with us. It is remarked that they have a certain docility, good temper, religious tendency, and respect for the authority and the law. They all give the best hope that, with culture and civilization, they will end by adhering to their duties and by acknowledging their duties to the government ; and then this republic, which at the time of her conquest obtained the name of New World, will take a greater ascendant, and attract the attention of the civilized universe, raise her glories to the same level as those of the great nations, and in reality will succeed in being her own mistress, since the neighboring nations only predominate because they are independent and aggressive.

Though, in accordance with the subject and its importance, I could detail this statement more to the point, yet it is already explained sufficiently to the sagacious penetration of your excellency. I do not desire to intrude, but simply to propose the idea with the deference and gratitude due to the high privilege which directs free speech, and as it becomes a country-loving citizen, who thus desires all the attainable welfare possible ; and if he has erred in this present matter he will submit cheerfully to a refusal ; but considering his earnest intentions, he will be excused on account of his good faith, and appear, therefore, worthy of attention.

I conclude in proposing for the enterprise, that each principal nation be impressed with the fact that the quantity of game is already insufficient for their maintenance; that they must follow the example of all men in cultivating the lands given by mother Nature, sow and reap the fruits of agricultural pursuits, and thus provide themselves with the means of living by their labor ; devote themselves to industries and other callings of civilization ; fix their residence in permanent localities, settle, erect buildings, and raise cattle ; all under the protection of the government, which will be granted to those that are acknowledged as subjects—such protection as has already been offered in the above.

I conclude in praying your excellency to be pleased to give attention to the above statement, and to the present crisis. Awaiting the convenience of its being acted upon,

I remain, &c.,

ANTONIO JOSÉ MARTINEZ.

TAOS, *New Mexico, November* 28, 1843.

NOTE 1. It has always been observed that when the Navajo tribes were at peace with our government, they always promised fidelity to the treaty, but complied with it one, two, or three years only, and the peace seldom lasted longer.

NOTE 2. At the time of the Spanish rule the foreigners from North America were not allowed to erect forts and establish commercial relations with the North American Indians, as the Spaniards were jealous that, under this pretext, they might cause some troubles with the Indians; but the liberality of our government allowed them to build such forts since the year 1832, near the shores of the Rio del Naposte, del Rio Chato, and near other intermediate places between the plains inhabited by the above nations. But, besides the useful and necessary articles, the traders sold them also liquors and ardent spirits, which were prohibited. The result was that these nations became extremely demoralized, and were prompted to a greater destruction of buffaloes, in order to satisfy their appetite for strong drinks, which they obtained in exchange. They also made raids in our department in order to steal cattle which were bought of them by the proprietors of these forts, thus encouraging and inducing the idle and ill-intentioned ones among us to follow their example, and become cattle-robbers; selling their booty to the inhabitants or proprietors of the forts, as above said.

SUB-REPORT OF MR. HUBBARD.

WASHINGTON, D. C., *January* 8, 1866.

SIR: The field assigned to myself and Mr. Windom was so extensive that upon consultation we concluded to divide the territory, he taking Minnesota, and myself Nebraska and Dakota.

Pursuant to this arrangement I visited the Omahas, Yankton Sioux, Ponca, and Crow Creek agencies. I also visited Fort Sully in company with the commission composed of General Edmunds, General Sibley, Colonel Taylor, General Curtis, and Mr. Guernsey to make treaties with the Sioux of the upper Missouri, and called upon the Winnebagoes at the Omaha agency. At the time I visited the Omaha agency I found the chiefs absent upon a hunt, consequently I did not have a conference with them. This agency is in a very good condition. Many of the Indians have comfortable houses and are surrounded with many of the conveniences of civilized life. Their crops were abundant, and from all I could see and learn I should think the business of the agency was very well managed. The mission school, under the charge of Rev. Mr. Birt, is not as well attended as it should be, but yet good results seem to have attended the labors of those engaged in the work.

WINNEBAGOES.

I found a large portion of this band living upon the Omaha reservation. These Indians are entitled to the protection and liberal assistance of the government. For years past they have at all times been the faithful and fast friends of the whites. Located upon a fine reservation in Minnesota, with good houses and farms, they had made considerable advancement toward civilization. Many of them had learned to read and write and had acquired habits of industry and economy. The fearful massacre of 1862 at and near the Sioux agency justly created in the minds of the people of Minnesota a feeling of distrust and hostility towards all Indians, and they very naturally demanded not only the removal of those engaged in the massacre, but also the Winnebagoes. At the third session of the thirty-seventh Congress an act was passed providing for the peaceful and quiet removal of these Indians. In the spring of 1863 arrangements were made for their removal. Transportation was provided; and, as they allege without previous warning, they were informed that they must remove. They remonstrated against the injustice of such a course, but their remonstrances were without avail. Those having charge of their removal were deaf to all of their entreaties. They either could not or would not grant relief. They were taken from their reservation and crowded upon boats and conveyed to what was then intended should be their future reservation at Crow creek. All were much dissatisfied with the location. It was in the vicinity of their enemies the Sioux, and the whole country was parched and dried up from the effects of the long and severe drought of that and the preceding season. Some attempts were made to raise crops that season, but they were total failures, and even the grass was dried up as early as June. To add to their sufferings and discouragements, many of their members became sick and died of diseases induced by the changes and exposure connected with their removal. They resolved not to remain upon this reservation, and between the months of June and December large numbers made their way down the Missouri in canoes. Of these many landed at different points on the river and managed to live through the winter of 1863-'64, and a great many reached the Omaha reservation. Their sufferings during the winter were terrible. Destitute of suitable clothing to protect them from the severity of that climate, destitute of suitable lodges to live in, and suitable food, many died from want, starvation, and exposure. Those who remained at Crow creek, as will be seen from the testimony relating to that agency, suffered nearly if not quite as much as those who left. In the spring and summer of 1864 nearly all of this band were concentrated upon the Omaha reservation, where they now remain. Last March a treaty was made with the Omahas for the purchase of a portion of their reservation for this band, and it now awaits the action of the Senate. They complain of their treatment, and it is certainly indefensible. If it became necessary to remove them from Minnesota the removal should have been effected under circumstances less humiliating and with more consideration for their welfare and comfort and the preservation of their property, and to a location better adapted to the pursuits of agriculture. I am informed that they were well supplied with grain, stock, and implements of husbandry at the time of their removal, most of which was wasted and destroyed, as but little of their property could be taken with them. It is substantially true that their removal caused the loss of all their personal effects, and they are now, without any cause or provocation on their part, reduced to a condition of destitution.

I do not undertake, nor is it my province in this report, to locate the responsibility of the outrages and wrongs which have been inflicted upon this friendly and loyal band of Indians.

Of one thing we may be assured—that no government can permit such injuries to go unredressed without incurring the penalty of treaties broken and justice violated.

These Indians are now without any reservation or home, and must thus remain until their treaty with the Omahas has been acted upon.

I cannot but feel that the government should deal liberally with them, and in some way, in part at least, indemnify them for the losses and damages they have sustained.

YANKTON AGENCY.

The general appearance of this agency at the time I visited it was not favorable. The buildings, imperfectly constructed by Agent Redfield some years ago with poor lumber, has become old and somewhat dilapidated. Many fields heretofore cultivated had been abandoned. Those fields which the agent and Indians had attempted to cultivate this season, from causes in part disclosed by the evidence, were producing a much better crop of weeds than corn.

The severe drought of 1863 and '64 prevented them from raising crops, though efforts were made by the agent and Indians to do so. This failure left them in a measure destitute of food, and a large portion of their annuities was necessarily expended in the purchase of provisions, which should, under other circumstances, have been expended in improvement, upon the agency and in laying the foundation for their advancement in civilization. The drought of 1864 extended through the spring and into the summer of 1865. This added to the destruction caused by the presence of millions of grasshoppers, so far interfered with the efforts of the agent and Indians that but a small crop has been raised this season. They are now in a state of much destitution and want, and quite a large amount of their annuities must be expended in the purchase of provisions for the coming winter. All of the chiefs, with one or two exceptions, met me at Yancton, and my conference was had with them at that place. None made speeches but Pa-la-me-opa-pi, The Man that was Struck by the Ree, and White Medicine Cow. Pa-la-me-opa-pi is the head chief and a man of mark and distinction among his people. His speech, aside from exaggeration peculiar to his race and the circumstances by which he is surrounded, contains a great deal of good sense and practical wisdom. Some of his points are most forcibly presented. The whole speech is worthy of a careful reading. He is very desirous that his band should become civilized and self-sustaining; and, with much earnestness of manner, he urged that some of the most important provisions of the treaty, and especially the one relating to a school-house, &c., had been disregarded. I am compelled to admit that upon some of these points his statements, as will appear from the evidence, are too nearly true to be contradicted. The old chief laments their present condition, and expresses the conviction that the treaty has done them more harm than good. He seems to have lost confidence in the government and in all white men. His suggestions in relation to traders are especially worthy of attention. He sees that white men in their dealings with each other are largely benefited by fair and legitimate competition in business; that the monopoly their single trader enjoys of the trade of the entire band, while enriching the trader, deprives the Indians of many advantages which a better competition would secure to them.

The present agent of this band entered upon his duties about the first of last May. The season has been so unfavorable, owing to the circumstances named and others appearing in the testimony, (to which I refer for particulars,) that his earnest efforts to improve the condition of his Indians have been but partially successful.

For particulars relating to this agency I refer to the testimony.

PONCA AGENCY.

At this agency I found the Indians comfortable and reasonably contented. They had raised a fine crop of corn, sufficient, if carefully used, to take them through the winter. The principal chiefs visited Washington last March, and entered into a supplemental treaty by which their old reservation is to be extended to the Missouri river. All are now very anxious that this treaty should be confirmed, for reasons stated in the speeches of the chiefs, and they also desire that their agency buildings may be removed to the bottom lands of the Missouri. I think their wishes in these respects should be gratified. I visited the site to which it is proposed to remove these buildings and found it very desirable; the soil is good; timber in abundance surrounds and adjoins the prairie at the point where the agency buildings should be located. The business of this agency appears to be well managed.

I think the former agent made some injudicious expenditures in the erection of an unnecessarily large and expensive school-house, but I have not been able to ascertain that he was guilty of any fraud in his expenditures. I took but little evidence at this agency.

CROW CREEK AGENCY.

The Sissiton, Wahpaton, and Medawakanton band of the Sioux is the only band of Indians now residing upon this agency. There are about one thousand of them, of which only one hundred and twenty-eight are men. A part of this band were the originators of, and the principal actors in, the Minnesota massacre, but that portion now located at this agency did not actively participate in it. In consequence of this outbreak, at the 3d session of the 37th Congress the annuities of the entire band were forfeited to the government; and since that date the Indians now at Crow creek have been subsisted and maintained by the government.

I was very agreeably disappointed in the appearance of these Indians. They are the most intelligent and cultivated of any that I have visited. Many of them can read and write in their own language. They have schools, under the control of Rev. Mr. Williamson, with a daily average attendance, as he informed me, of over one hundred, and a church with over two hundred members. They are perfectly submissive and resigned, ready to do anything that the government may require, but ask that they may be relocated upon a reservation with soil and climate better adapted to agricultural pursuits. They say they are willing to work and raise crops, if located where the soil will yield them. They do not think their present reservation suitable for such a purpose. Their efforts to raise crops have so often failed that they are discouraged and disheartened. Since leaving Minnesota the sufferings of this band have at times been severe. I will not recite the evidence, but, in my judgment, it shows that their treatment, to speak of it in the mildest term, has not been humane.

For the facts connected with this point, and the management of the affairs of the agency, I refer you to the testimony of Messrs. Williamson, Pond, Haynes, Lamore, and others, who testify upon this subject.

The records of the Indian department show that a very large amount of supplies was purchased for the Indians at this agency during the year commencing June, 1863, and ending June, 1864. During the year the government paid for not less than 1,788,488 pounds of beef, gross weight; 433,121 pounds of flour; 143,560 pounds of pork, (mess;) and 319,576 pounds of shelled corn, all purchased for the Indians of this agency, though it is probable that the number staying at the agency during the year did not average, per week, more than two thousand five hundred. In addition to the above, there was furnished to the Winnebagoes, who had left Crow creek, at the Omaha agency, in April, May, and June, 1864, 91,377 pounds of beef, net, and 91,377 pounds of flour, yet the Indians suffered for the want of food. The prices paid for these supplies were liberal, and in most instances high, though the quality was certainly most inferior.

It is due to Major Balcomb to state that while he acted for these Indians, during the winter of 1863 and 1864, he acted under the orders of his superintendent, and all the supplies for these Indians and the Winnebagoes were purchased and delivered at the agency by the superintendent.

The present agent did not enter upon his duties until late in the spring. By good management he has this season succeeded in raising some good corn, but the quantity was so limited that it was soon exhausted. He appears to be laboring faithfully to discharge his duties and to improve the condition of his Indians, and I think his efforts will be attended with satisfactory results.

Should crops upon the reservation fail another season, the good of the Indians and the interests of the government will imperatively demand their removal to some other location.

DACOTAH SUPERINTENDENCY.

Heretofore but a very small portion of the business of this Territory has been transacted through this office. The Indian agents of the Territory have generally reported directly to the Indian commissioner. Governor Edmonds, ex officio Indian superintendent, has of late devoted a good deal of attention to Indian matters, and appears to be faithfully laboring to introduce order and system into the affairs of his superintendency.

I took no evidence in relation to this superintendency, as its operations cover but a short space of time, and embraces but a very limited number of transactions outside of the regular office business.

On my way to Fort Sully, and during my stay there, I met and conferred with a large number of the chiefs of the different bands of the Sioux. Nearly all complained of the violation of their treaties, and the bad faith, dishonesty, and misconduct of the agents and traders. They say the goods designed for them under their treaties with the government do not reach them; that they are taken by their agents, traders, &c.

These statements must be received with a great deal of allowance; many of them are undoubtedly exaggerated, but it would be remarkable if all of their complaints, made so generally, were entirely destitute of truth. After making due allowance for all exaggerations, I am forced to the conclusion that in some instances wrongs must have been committed; but with the great uncertainty and doubt which now surrounds the transactions of agents and traders in this frontier region, together with the difficulty of obtaining correct information on the subject, the honest may be confounded with the dishonest. The innocent may suffer with the guilty unless great care is exercised in coming to conclusions in relation to the past, but every reasonable effort should be made to prevent wrongs and abuses in the future. The careful selection of men as agents and traders will do much to bring about this result. If none but honest men could be selected to deal with the Indians, none of these troubles would be met with. If such men only could be sent into the Indian country they would, in a short time, correct these abuses, restore confidence among the Indians, and redeem the Indian department from the suspicions which have sometimes attached to it.

The efforts of the treaty commission at Fort Sully were attended with gratifying success. Treaties were made, as will appear from their report, with several bands of the Sioux, and I think good results may be anticipated from them. Too much space would be occupied if I was to attempt a more extended notice of their labors.

The testimony taken by me, and papers connected with the same, are herewith submitted. To investigate fully the affairs of all these agencies would require much more time than I have been allowed to devote to it. Heretofore copies of the papers and records connected with the business of the agencies have not been preserved at the agencies, and the evidence was taken in the absence of such papers and records, and, consequently, is very general, and not altogether satisfactory to myself.*

Very respectfully,

A. W. HUBBARD.

Hon. J. R. DOOLITTLE, *Chairman, &c.*

Examination of the Yankton chiefs before the Hon. A. W. Hubbard, commissioner.

YANKTON, DAKOTA TERRITORY, *August* —.

Pa-la-ne-apo-pe, or The Man that was Struck by the Ree, spoke as follows:

My friend, you sent a letter to our agency requesting our (chiefs) presence here. My friend, I have a good leg; it is sound; there are no sores upon it, and I want to go to Washington to see my Great Father. The reason I want to see my Great Father is, I desire to make my report to him in person, but the agents say if I go he will not pay any attention to me; that he is full of business with the whites. My belly is full of what I want to say to him. My friend, you are sent by my grandfather. I think you will do just as all the rest—make money. I should think if my grandfather would want to see me to make my report in person.

I cannot say much. The Great Spirit knows that I speak the truth; knows what I say. When I went to see my grandfather, he told me I should have my reserve; that I should have fifty miles up and down the Missouri river for fifty years, and I might become rich and high up; but I am like one on a high snow bank; the sun shines and continually melts it away, and it keeps going down and down until there is nothing left. When I went to make my treaty, my grandfather agreed, if I would put three young men to work, he would put one white laborer with them to learn them; that I should put three young men to learn ploughing, and he would put one white man to learn them; also, three to sow, three to learn the carpenter's trade, three to learn the blacksmith's trade, and such other trades as we should want; and my great grandfather was to furnish one white man for each trade to learn the young men. My grandfather also said that a school should be established for the nation to learn them to read and write; that the young boys and girls should go to school, and that the young men who worked should have the same pay as the whites. My grandfather told me if my young men would go to work that the money going to those who would not work should be given to those who would work. None of these things have been fulfilled. If my grandfather had told me that I must split rails, I could have tried it, and then perhaps my young men would have tried; but they would say, how could I learn them when I did not know how myself. If I try to get my young men to plough, they would say, if you cannot plough how can we; there is no one to learn them, and the same thing would be true if I should try to get the young men to run the

* The testimony taken speaks for itself. I have not thought it my duty in this report to comment upon the same, either to criminate or exculpate particular persons.

saw-mill or work at any other trade; if I do not know myself, how can I learn the young men; and the same thing would be the case if I try to get the young men to build a house; if I don't know myself, how can I learn them. If I should get all the young men, half-breeds and Indians, and put them in a room, and pick out those who have big arms and hands, and take a big bar of iron and tell them to work it, they would not know how. If I were to take all the young men and girls, half-breeds and Indians, and tell them that we will go in that house and take pen and ink and write, how could I make letters as they ought to be made; I never learned myself.

My friend, I think if my young men knew how to sow, farm, carpenter, and do everything else, I could send the white men away; we ourselves should have the money paid the white men, and we should have plenty of money. If we had been learned all these things we could support ourselves, have plenty of money, have schools, and I could have written my great grandfather, and have got a letter from him; I could have written him myself what I wanted.

My grandfather sent me two agents, and I understood the governor was over them. I came down here (Yankton) and the governor was gone to Washington. I staid three days, and then went back home.

I think I gave my land to my grandfather. When I signed the treaty I told them I never would sign for the pipestone quarry. I wanted to keep it myself; but I understand white men are going there and getting and breaking up the stone.

I would have to tell my grandfather that I made a treaty with him, and I would have to ask him how many goods he is going to give me; and I would tell him that I want him to give me the invoices of my goods, that I may know what I am entitled to. I do not want corn thrown to me the same as to hogs. If I could get my invoices I should always know what belongs to me. Every time our goods come I have asked the agent for the invoices, but they never show me the invoices; they can write what they please, and they go and show it to my grandfather, and he thinks it all right. I think, my friend, my grandfather tells me lies. My friend, what I give a man I don't try to take back. I think, my friend, there is a great pile of money belonging to us which we never yet have received.

I think the Great Spirit hears what I say. When they bring the goods to the agency, my goods are all mixed up with the agent's goods; I can't tell my goods from the trader's goods. I think if you go to all the nations, you will not find any who has been used as I have been. My grandfather told me I should have a warehouse separate from the agents; he told me I should take one hundred and sixty acres of land for my own use, and that I should have plenty of land to raise hay for the stock. All the hay on my bottom land is cut by the white man to sell. I asked for hay, but I can get none—white man cut it; I can't tell who gets the money for the hay, but I think Redfield got some money for hay; my ponies can have no hay. I think, my friend, if you go up to my agency you will have a bad feeling; you will feel bad for me to see the situation I am in, and to see my buildings, after what my grandfather told me.

The first agent was Redfield; and when he came there he borrowed blankets from me to sleep upon, and agreed to return them, but never did, though I asked for them. Goods have been stored up stairs in the warehouse, and have all disappeared; perhaps the rats eat them; I don't know what became of them. If they bring any goods for the Indians to eat and put them in the warehouse, the agents live out of them, and the mess-house where travellers stop has been supplied from the Indians' goods, and pay has been taken by the agents, and they have put the money in their pockets and taken it away with them. I have seen them take the goods from the storehouse of the Indians and take them to the mess-house, and I have had to pay for a meal for myself at the mess-house, and so have others of our Indians had to pay for meals at the mess-house, prepared from their own goods.

I understand that the agents are allowed fifteen hundred dollars per year for salary. I think fifteen hundred dollars is not much—not more than enough to last a month, the way they live; they bring all their families there, and friends also. When the agents have been there one, two and three years, their property increases—the goods in their house and their household furniture increase. When Redfield left the agency, a steamboat came in the night and took away fifteen boxes of goods, so that the Indians would not know it; but the Indians were too sharp for him. When Redfield came up he brought his nephew to be trader for the Indians, and one night he took a load of flour out of the shed where the Indians' flour was, and carried it to his store to sell out to the Indians. My friend, what I say about his taking the flour I did not see with my own eyes, but my young men came and told me so. Because I wanted the blankets that I loaned Redfield, he got mad and never answered me, and never gave me the blankets.

My friend, a great many things have been going on, but they do them in the night, so as to blind me. What I say I see myself. After Redfield took away the fifteen boxes he sent back and took away more. I think all these young chiefs have eyes, the same as I, and that they have seen these things. I went down to Washington twice to see my grandfather, and the third time I went I came back by the Missouri. When I went down I saw many stores full of goods; the suttlers come to our agency and make money and then go off. I think if we had two stores it would be better for us. If I had understood from what my grandfather told me, that I was to be treated as I have been, I would never have done as I have done; I never would have signed the treaty. Mr. Redfield said to me, "when I am gone you will meet with a great many agents; but you will never meet one like me." I think I never want to see one like him.

When I made my treaty these young men (chiefs) were there, and my grandfather told me that the half-breeds should have some portion of the money. When I was making the treaty the half breeds were all about me, my body was sweet, and my grandfather told me that I could give the money to any I pleased. These white men had Indian women for wives; and they came with their accounts against the Indians and gave them to Redfield. They told me if I would help them get the money I should always have plenty of money myself; they would always assist me. I told them I did not believe what they said; that if I should give them the money and should come into their house they would tell me to go out of their house. After I gave them the money they all scattered, and I cannot see them. After what I have done for them, given them the money, these white men have gone away and left their half-breed children for me to support and take care of. But when the agents come with money, the white men come from every direction and get the money, and then go away and spend the money at groceries. I think, after I have paid them so much, they ought to treat me better. I do not want any more of the half-breed money paid Joseph Lionais, Eli Bedard, Charles Ruleoux, August Trovercier, John B. La Plant, Bruno Coneyer, Theophile Bruginer, and Joseph Preoux. The half-breeds that live with the Indians are poor, and I want the money that has been paid the above-named half-breeds retained hereafter and paid over to the tribe towards supporting the poor half-breeds with the Indians. According to the treaty, there is $20,000 belonging to the poor orphan children, but I don't know what has become of it. If the white men should get their money again they would spend it for whiskey, and I want their shares of the money stopped. The reason I am saying this is, the white men and half-breeds, whom we did not provide for by treaty, are displeased with us because we did not give them a share of the money.

Among our nations there are a great many tribes come every year. The Tetons and others come down, and sometimes steal horses, and then the white men lay it to the Yanktons, and come to us to get pay for the stolen horses because we have got a treaty. They came last fall with their claim for stolen horses to the agent, and the agent showed it to the interpreter, and he told the agent that the Indians who stole the horses did not belong to the Yanktons; and the whites said if we had another interpreter they could collect their claims. Our grandfather has given this young man, Charles Pecout, a medal and made him a chief.

I am now done with the management of Agent Redfield and the half-breeds, and now commence upon other matters.

Strike the Ree continues as follows:

August 26.—My friend, yesterday we had a talk, and to-day we will commence with Mr. Agent Burleigh's agency. My grandfather, Mr. Redfield, the first agent, did not tell me the same things that my grandfather told me, neither did Agent Burleigh, but both of them told me lies; they filled my belly with lies. Everybody has got a copy of the treaty I made with my grandfather, I suppose. I suppose you are sent by my grandfather to represent the great council. I am here to represent my great council. The money my grandfather sent me has been thrown away. You know who threw it away. The guns, ammunition, wagons, horses, and everything have been thrown away. I can tell who threw them away. The reason the whites have trouble with the Indians is on account of the agents. When the goods come they are not according to the treaty; they never fulfil the treaty. When the agent goes away he says he is going to leave these things to be done by his successor. When Agent Burleigh came he made fine promises of what he would do. I asked for my invoice, but he would not let me have it; and I told him what my grandfather told me. I think the agents are all alike. The agent puts his foot on me as though I were a skunk. And the agents are all getting rich and we are getting poor.

My friend, what I am telling you is the truth, and what I have seen. What the agents have done in the night, I cannot tell. That is the reason I am telling you this; I want you to report it to my grandfather. I want to go to Washington; and I wish you to do all you can with my grandfather to induce him to let me come there next winter. I want to see my grandfather to ascertain how much money and goods have been sent me, and that I may know how much has been stolen and who stole it. I would like to have the agents there with my grandfather when I talk to him, that they may hear what I have to say. If there was a bible there for them to swear upon, they could not swear that they had not stolen the goods.

My friend, I feel glad to see you; and if I could see my grandfather I should feel better. When Burleigh brought the goods the first time he put the goods on the bank of the river; and there was one bale of fine goods with them, and Burleigh said the goods belonged to the Indians; and one of my young men come and told me about the fine bale of goods, and I went and examined it, and it was fine goods, and would have made nice breech-clouts; but we received none of it, and don't know what become of it. This was the second year Burleigh was there. The first year Burleigh was there, Redfield brought and distributed the goods. The first goods Burleigh undertook to bring there was the first fall of his agency, but the goods were sunk. For my part, I don't wish to hide anything. My friend, if you had come to see me, I could have gone into a council-house with you, and could have said what I wanted to say to you without any one being round to fill my ears. My friend, I know what matters you want to inquire about. I think you are the man to try and do some good to my nation, and my heart feels good. I do not speak a lie. They have got my head so turned that I cannot say what I want to say now, and I will stop now and come and talk more this afternoon.

A steamboat arrived with our goods, and the goods were put out; Burleigh said they were our goods, and they were marked for us; there were five boxes. There were some officers and soldiers there. The boxes remained there on the bank until the next day. At night somebody scratched the marks off and put on other marks (This statement was witnessed by Medicine Cow and Walking Elk.) They saw it done. The soldiers told the Indians that the goods belonged to the Indians. At another time, Doctor Burleigh had some calico for us, and said he would take it to his house, so that the Indian girls could learn to sew. My daughter went and made one dress, which was given her for making it. Five or six Indian girls went and sewed there, and all got dresses. They were two days there. After the young girls sewed two days apiece and got a dress apiece, they never saw anything more of the calico, and never got any more. Another time, Doctor Burleigh told us he had some ploughs for us. After that I saw one of them at Booge's store. We never had any of them. I told Charles Lamont's wife to take good care of that plough; that the whites might come round and, seeing it, take it. That is the way our property goes.

Doctor Burleigh one time came to me and asked me to grant him a favor, and wanted me to agree that he should give a plough away, and I told him to do so; I did not want to disagree with him; and then immediately he came and wanted me to give away another, and I told him to do so; I did not want to disagree with him.

Medicine Cow spoke as follows:

I shall speak of Agent Burleigh At one time Doctor Burleigh told me he was going to put some goods away for the poor; some calico, scarlet cloth, &c. In the fall, La Frambois, who has an Indian wife and lives with the Two-Kettle band, came down to get some goods; but the trader had none that he wanted, and La Frambois then said he would go below and get some goods to trade with the Indians; but Doctor Burleigh told him not to go, and that he could have the blankets, calico, scarlet cloth, and all kinds of cloth that had been kept for fall and for the old and the poor. I told him if he paid for them I could say nothing, and he took them and carried them away. The next spring he came back and I asked him for the pay for the goods; there were $1,700 worth; but he said he could not pay for them, as he had paid Doctor Burleigh for them. Then I took the chiefs to Doctor Burleigh and told him to pay us the money he received from La Frambois for our goods; but he said he had got no money. There were plenty of whites and soldiers about at the time.

I am glad you are here. You know the cause of the murders in Minnesota; if you do not, I do; the agents were the cause. Our agents never give us what our grandfather sends us. I think when the whites make an agreement with each other they do as they agree with each other. If the whites did as they agree with the Indians, there would not be so much difficulty. The agents bring goods, but do not give them to us. When the agent brought us money we asked him to let us see it; but more than half was carried back to the house and we never received it. One time he got and told us that he would keep it until winter, but he never let us have it. The blacksmith won't work for the common Indians, but works for the chiefs and all white men. If the common Indians go to him he will tell them to go away.

I think all the work Doctor Burleigh had done was done for himself. He purchased lots of cattle and things. When he came there he only had a trunk, but now he is high up—rich. Once in a while I went and asked Doctor Burleigh about the money, and he said he saved it for all the Indians, and we did not get it.

When Agent Conger came there he and Doctor Burleigh were together, and we felt bad to see him with the new agent. We went and told Doctor Burleigh that we wanted him to give us the money which he had taken from us; but he would not. I told him if he did not I would tell my grandfather when I went to see him.

I think a great many of our tribe have frozen to death, and a great many have died of starvation. When I was talking that way to Doctor Burleigh he said he did not care what I said to him; that all up and down the Missouri river all the big men and generals were on his side. The reason I talk this way, the governor said I must not talk so hard against a young man. The doctor told me I was against him. I answered, "Yes; you are always against the Indians; you never try to do anything for us."

Another time Doctor Burleigh came and brought us money, and gave us two dollars in paper money and some three and some one dollar, and we don't know what he did with the gold money, but we want to know, and we want to know if that is the way our grandfather does with us. I think if they had asked the young men to learn at school they would have done so; they would willingly attend the school and learn, but they have never had an opportunity. For my part I think the agents have been an injury to us. When we moved here we had to dig the ground with our fingers. We have done as the whites told us. When Burleigh told us to be soldiers we became soldiers; we burnt the dirt lodges, as he told us; but we were not paid for being soldiers. We tried hard to please the whites. We have often told the same things to the big men before, but it made no difference; but we are glad to see you and hope you will do us some good. One time the doctor (Burleigh) came up and said he had got plenty of goods to keep us all winter; that he had 4,000 sacks of flour, and plenty of blankets; but we found out that he was not telling the truth; he put it into the store and we had to buy it. One time he told us he was going to keep seven large boxes of goods (one containing traps) for another time, to be distributed to us; but we never received any of these goods, excepting three of our young men got three guns and three suits of clothes as a reward for killing a Santee, and that was all we got. I asked Burleigh to do right; but Burleigh's interpreter would not tell him right. I told him to get another interpreter. Things are no better now. The new agent has come, but he is like a man in the middle of the prairie. Burleigh cleaned the agency of everything, and the new agent has nothing to go on with; no cattle, no wagons, no ploughs, in fact nothing; everything has melted away like a snow bank in the summer's sun. I think our grandfather don't know what is done with the money, from what you say to us to-day. I think everything on the agency is gone, and one saw-mill does us no good; there is no one to attend to it It is the business of the agent to attend to it. It would take a month to start it We have no lumber. There is no one to attend to our blacksmith shop, nor the carpenter shop; all the tools are gone. Sometimes the blacksmith does some things for the Indians, but works mostly for whites. Since the new agent came, there is a good blacksmith. When Burleigh came to the agency there were two mules there, and they are there now; and there were also two horses, but Burleigh went away and swapped them away for two bob-tailed horses, and the Indians have never since seen their horses or the bob-tails.

Medicine Cow closed here, and The Man that was Struck by the Ree continued as follows:

My friend, we are now done with the agent, and we will now commence with the soldiers. The first year they came up in this country, I think my grandfather must have told them to commence on me, and that is the reason I commence thus with them. I would like to know if my grandfather told them to commence against me first; I should think so, the way they treated us. The first time they came up our young men had nothing to eat, and had gone over the Missouri river to hunt, and the soldiers killed seven of them. The Two-Kettle band and the Low Yanktonais were friendly, and were then on my reservation at the time, and some of them went out with my young men to hunt, and were among the seven that were killed; they were all friendly to the whites. When General Sully returned from his expedition, and was crossing my reserve, there were some of the Indian women married to half-breeds, and they had houses, and the soldiers went in and drove all the persons in them out, and robbed the houses of all there was in them. I would like to know if my grandfather told them to do so. I do not think he did. (All the chiefs present assent to this.) One of my chiefs, Little Swan, now here, had a house, and the soldiers broke in and destroyed all his goods, furniture, utensils and tools, and all the property of his band, the same being stored there. I would like to know if my grandfather told the soldiers when they returned from the expedition with their horses worn out, lost or stolen, to take horses from the Yanktons, in place of those they had lost or had worn out and broken down; I don't believe he did, but that is the way the soldiers did. I think the way the white men treated us is worse than the wolves do. We have a way in the winter of putting our dead up on scaffolds up from the ground, but the soldiers cut down the scaffolds and cut off the hair of the dead, and if they had good teeth they pulled them out, and some of them cut off the heads of the dead and carried them away. One time one of my young men and two squaws went over the river to Fort Randall, and a soldier wanted one of the squaws to do something with; he wanted to sleep with her, and she refused to sleep with him; one of the Indians asked the other squaw if she would sleep with the soldier, and she said she would; but the soldier would not have her, but wanted the other squaw, and claimed that the Indian was trying to prevent him from sleeping with his (the Indian's) squaw, his wife, and the Indian, fearing trouble, started for the ferry, and the soldier shot the Indian, though the Indian got over it. Another time when General Sully came up he passed through the middle of our field, turned all his cattle and stock into our corn and destroyed the whole of it. The ears of some were then a foot long; the corn was opposite Fort Randall, and they not only destroyed the corn but burnt up the fence. I think no other white man would do so; I do not think my grandfather told them to do so. The soldiers set fire to the prairie and burnt up four of our lodges and all there was in them, and three horses. When my corn is good to eat they cross the river from Fort Randall and eat it, and when it is not good they throw it in the river. I think my reserve is very small; the soldiers cut all my wood and grass, and I think this is bad treatment. The above in regard to the soldiers applies to my three chiefs on the reserve opposite Fort Randall, and I will now speak of things at my agency when the soldiers came down from the expedition last fall. At that time myself and others were out on a hunt, and had put our goods under the floors; but when the expedition came down the soldiers broke open the houses, destroyed our pans and kettles, and fired into the stoves and kettles. The soldiers are very drunken and come to our place—they have arms and guns; they run after our women and fire into our houses and lodges; one soldier came along and wanted one of our young men to drink, but he would not, and turned to go away, and the soldier shot at him. Before the soldiers came along we had good health; but once the soldiers come along they go to my squaws and want to sleep with them, and the squaws being hungry will sleep with them in order to get something to eat, and will get a bad disease, and then the squaws turn to their husbands and give them the bad disease.

I would like to know if my grandfather tells the soldiers to get all my hay. Every year great contracts are made for cutting hay for Fort Randall, and they cut the hay all off our land, and I would like to know if my grandfather gave them permission to cut all the hay and take the money. I never see any of the money myself They take all my mowing machines, bought with my money, to cut hay to sell to the soldiers, and I cannot get the mowing machines to cut anything for ourselves, and I have no use of them. I think the agents are in partnership with these men cutting hay to sell to the soldiers. The reason I think the agent had a hand in cutting hay for the soldiers is, because one year Burleigh gave all of us chiefs fifty dollars each for the hay cut upon the contract. Last spring I asked him for the money for the hay he cut last year, and he told me he could not give it to me, because he had spent it last winter to get us something to eat; but I do not know whether he did or not. I hope you will report these things to my grandfather, and have him stop those men from cutting the hay right off. I think if they would return me my mowing machines I could cut part of the hay on the contract, and I must have some for my ponies; I wish you would attend to it. When I started to come down here they were getting ready to cut hay on another contract for the soldiers at Fort Randall. If they would return our mowing machines we could take the contract ourselves; we have some white men and half-breeds who could assist us, but they want it all themselves. The reason I talk thus is, I think all is wrong. I know the young man who has the contract; I think he has had it two years before. When he breaks any part of the mowing machine he goes to my blacksmith shop and carpenter shop to repair it; it is all paid for out of my annuity fund. It is Hedges who has the contract. Thompson, our blacksmith, has had charge of cutting the hay on the contracts for the past two years, and is getting ready to cut it this year.

Worse than that is the treatment I have received. For the past two winters soldiers have been quartered in my houses, and they go in my blacksmith and carpenter shops and work and repair whatever they have that needs it, and they burn my wood, and I have received no pay for all this. I think, my friend, when you come to see us, you will find a bad smell, and will want to put your coat to your mouth, and will want to get away. I don't know what the soldiers were sent there for, they do us no good. They did their private jobs in and around our houses, and they smell bad. I don't think my grandfather has but very little money; he only sends us about five dollars apiece, and all the white men round come and want to get what we do receive, for horses that some other Indians have stolen, but laid to the Yanktons, because they receive annuities. When the two men were shot the other day at Brulé creek, the governor sent me word to take the Indians away from that place, but none of those Indians belonged to me. Some of the white men come and lay round my place and get out of money, and go and kill their own cattle, and go and lay the killing to the Yanktons, and then go and get pay for them out of our money.

Since I made the treaty I am an American. My new agent told me the other day that the old Commissioner of Indian Affairs had been stealing part of the annuities, and that a better man had been put in his place. At this I felt good, and I put on my hat, I felt so good, my heart so big. My new agent is an entirely different man; he shows me the invoices, and I think he is a good man for us. He hired a blacksmith right off. My friend, what I am going to tell you is the truth. We only get five dollars apiece; we have only had one trader; he often makes us feel bad; he sells us goods so high it makes us cry; I think there ought to be two traders; I want two traders. I think if you come up to our agency you will laugh in the first place, and then be mad to see our storehouse in the same building with the trader's store. I want the store moved away a mile, so that it won't be so handy to our goods; I want you to have this changed. I hope my grandfather will see that the store is moved away from my warehouse, because the trader's store is under the floor where my goods are stored. I sometimes have bad dreams; I feel that there may be cracks that my goods may fall through.

I am done. Again I say, my friend, I am glad you have come to see us, and I hope will report all I have said to the Great Father, and that you will do us good. The Great Spirit knows that I have spoken the truth.

Strike the Ree here ends his spoech.

The foregoing speeches were made in the presence of the chiefs Crazy Bull, Jumping Thunder, Walking Elk, White Medicine Cow, Little White Swan and Pretty Boy, and one Indian warrior, who all assented thereto.

YANKTON INDIAN AGENCY, *August* 28, 1865.

Colin Campbell, being duly sworn, deposes as follows:

First question. How long have you resided at this agency?

First answer. Ever since Redfield came here as agent.

Second question. Did Redfield erect a school-house at this agency?

Second answer. No; he did not. Knew nothing wrong in his management.

Third question. How did Burleigh manage the affairs of the agency?

Third answer. I have no personal knowledge. The Indians complained a good deal. I am entitled to receive annuities every year, as one of the half-breeds under the treaty and agreement of the chiefs, but Mr. Burleigh never paid me the whole of it. I made a contract with him, by which I sold him one-half of my annuity. The following is a copy of the contract, to wit:

"In consideration of Colin Campbell, of Greenwood, Dakota Territory, having assigned and set over to me one-half of his claim against the United States under the Yankton treaty, and guaranteed the same to me, I agree to do and perform the following for the said Campbell:

"1st. To erect and finish a good and comfortable timber [house] upon a quarter section of government land below Bonhomme, and give him a warrant to pay for the same when the said land comes into market.

"2d. To put into said house one hundred and fifty dollars' worth of furniture, among which shall be one good cook stove.

"3d. To place thereon, as the property of said Campbell, and pay for the same, 3 yoke of oxen, 3 yokes, 4 chains, 25 cows, 25 2-year old heifers, 25 1-year old heifers, 1 bull, 6 stock hogs, 2 ploughs, 1 harrow, 1 corn plough, 4 hoes, 5 shovels, 5 axes, 3 hay forks, 1 grindstone, 2 scythes and snaths—all of which is to be accomplished within one year and six months from this date.

"In witness whereof, I hereunto set my hand and seal this 12th day of January, 1862.

"W. A. BURLEIGH. [L. S.]

"In presence of—

"A. J. FOULK."

YANKTON INDIAN AGENCY, *August* 29, 1865.

John J. Thompson, of lawful age, being duly sworn, deposes and says as follows:

First question. What is your name and occupation, and where do you reside?

First answer. My name is John J. Thompson, and am now residing at the Yankton agency and have been residing here three years the first of last December. While Mr. Burleigh was here I was acting as blacksmith.

Second question. While you were blacksmith, what efforts did you make to learn any Indians blacksmithing?

Second answer. Three years this season Doctor Burleigh wanted me to take an Indian boy to learn the trade; and he hired an Indian man at the rate of twelve dollars per [month] to work in the blacksmith shop and to learn the trade, and he remained there about three months, and learned to do some of the common things to be learned in a shop, and then some of the other Indians told him he was foolish for working, that the white men were made to work for the Indians, and so he left, and that was the last that was done to learn an Indian to work in the blacksmith shop. The Indians are indolent, and deem it disgraceful to work. I left the employment of the agency last October, the first of the month.

Third question. What do you know about school being kept for the education of the Indian children?

Third answer. I think, for a while, Doctor Burleigh's sister taught some kind of a school; but I don't know what kind of a one. There is no school-house, and has not been here.

Fourth question. Who was employed as a physician here?

Fourth answer. Doctor Barrett was employed when I came here, and remained some eighteen months after I came here, and had been here some four or five months before I came.

Fifth question. What do you know about the employés of the agency working for Doctor Burleigh on his farm near Bonhomme?

Fifth answer. Henry Clairmore and Louis Mallett, who had been employés at the agency, worked at Burleigh's farm; but, whether they were paid at the time as employés of the agency or not, [I do not know.]

Sixth question. What do you know about the management of the affairs of the agency by Doctor Burleigh?

Sixth answer. I know of no wrong or mismanagement of the affairs of the agency by Doctor Burleigh.

Seventh question. Do you know anything about the goods of the Indians and trader being mixed together?

Seventh answer. I know nothing of the kind. Sometimes they have sold in the trader's store goods of the same pattern of the Indian goods, and the Indians have concluded from that they were the goods of the Indians.

Eighth question. Do you know of any of the Indians' flour being sold by the trader?

Eighth answer. I do not; nor do I know of Doctor Burleigh using any for his own private use. The flour for the Indians is generally marked "Yankton Sioux," and I have never seen any of that mark in the store.

Ninth question. What do you know about Hedges using the Indians' mowing machines, teams, &c.?

Ninth answer. Last year I cut the hay myself for Hedges to fill the contract at Fort Randall. We took up one of the Yankton mowing machines to use in case we should break one of the other machines, but did not use it, but returned it to the warehouse. We used one yoke of the Indians' oxen and one wagon; at least, the oxen had always been used about the agency, and I supposed they belonged to the Indians, but know nothing about it. Doctor Burleigh and Hedges told me they paid the Indians for the hay.

Tenth question. What do you know of Hedges' having Indians freight for him?

Tenth answer. I have been in Hedges's store and know of his having the Indians to take freight up to his store near Fort Randall, and know he always paid them liberally.

Eleventh question. The Indians complain that they could not always get blacksmithing done for themselves, for the reason that the blacksmith was working for whites?

Eleventh answer. I never refused to work for them; I always did all the work they needed; I always tried to accommodate them; but sometimes, when they were about going out on a hunt, many of them would come at the same time and want guns, tins, and everything mended all at once, and because I could not work for all at the same time they would complain.

Twelfth question. Have been employed in Hedges's store?

Twelfth answer. I have been in the employ of Hedges, the trader, since last October, but have not been in the store all the time; sometimes I was away, employed elsewhere for him.

Thirteenth question. What has been the general course of his dealing with the Indians at his store?

Thirteenth answer. It has been honorable He has paid them a good price for their robes; from seven to fifteen dollars apiece. When the Indians pay money for goods, he sells just as cheap to them as to white men. Sometimes, when the robe is poor, he sells the goods higher, for the reason that they want as much for a poor robe as a good one, unless it is a very poor robe.

Fourteenth question. Have you been present when the goods have been distributed to the Indians?

Fourteenth answer. I have, and have sometimes assisted in carrying the goods out of the warehouse. Before distributing goods he would generally separate the goods going to the different bands, and carry them down separately. Sometimes some of the goods would be kept until fall for future distribution, and I know of no instance of the Indian goods being given to white men except when we were raising the mill. When we were raising the mill, help was scarce, and Doctor Burleigh told some soldiers that if they would assist in raising the mill he would give them a check shirt apiece; they did so, and he gave them a check shirt each, saying that it was Indian work and it ought to be paid for out of their goods.

JOHN J. THOMPSON.

Frederick Carmon, of lawful age, being duly sworn, deposes as follows:

First question. What is your name and residence?

First answer. My name is Frederick Carmon. I reside at the Yankton agency, and have resided here since the fall of 1861, with the exception of an absence of a little over a year, from the spring of 1864 until July, 1865.

Second question. What has been your occupation at the Yankton agency?

Second answer. Carpenter.

Third question. What has been your compensation?

Third answer. Fifty dollars per month.

Fourth question. Where were you during your absence?

Fourth answer. I was travelling about; went to the Nemaha reservation and to Des Moines and other places; did not remain at any place any length of time.

Fifth question. Who acted as carpenter at this agency while you were gone?

Fifth answer. I do not know.

Sixth question. Who has been blacksmith since you came here?

Sixth answer. Thompson; the first six months a man by the name of Smith was also blacksmith at the time.

Seventh question. Has a school been taught here in which Indians have been taught?

Seventh answer. Doctor Banett taught school awhile, and I believe Mr. Faulks's daughter also kept school some. The school was not kept up the year round, but part of the time.

Eighth question. Was any school being taught when you left for Nemaha?

Eighth answer. No, sir.

Ninth question. How were you paid?

Ninth answer. In money generally. I used to receipt on three or four different papers, and don't know whether fifty dollars per month was inserted; but supposed it was.

Tenth question. Do you know how Burleigh transacted his business?

Tenth answer. I do not know personally.

Eleventh question. Does Hedges use the Indians' mowing machine?

Eleventh answer. No, sir.

Twelfth question. What do you know about efforts being made to learn the Indians the different trades?

Twelfth answer. Efforts have been made at different times, but without much success. The other Indians would laugh at them and call them squaws, and then the Indians who were trying to learn would become ashamed and quit.

Thirteenth question. Has any school-house been erected at this agency?

Thirteenth answer. I do not know of any. I do not know of a building which was calculated for a school-house.

Fourteenth question. Is the trader's store under the Indian warehouse?

Fourteenth answer. It is.

Fifteenth question. Who was the farmer, engineer, and miller while you have been here; also tinner?

Fifteenth answer. John Burleigh was farmer as long as Doctor Burleigh was agent. He was here most of the time, but absent occasionally; I do not know how much. He was a brother of Doctor Burleigh. D. P. Bradford was the engineer most of the time. Penrose was engineer when I came here, and remained three or four months after I came here. Bradford was here most of the time. Aleck Keeler, a hand here, acted as miller in what milling was done. A Mr. Macklin acted as tinner. Mr. Bradford, the engineer, was here off and on when the mill was run, but was not engaged all the time.

F. CARMON.

PONCA AGENCY, DAKOTA TERRITORY, *September* 1, 1865.

Testimony taken before Hon. A. W. HUBBARD, member of congressional Indian commission.

Frank Roy, being duly sworn, deposed as follows :

That he resides at the Ponca agency, and has resided there ever since the agency was established ; that he acted as interpreter for Agent Hoffman.

First question. State how many of the payments to the Indians by Hoffman were made in gold.

First answer. The first payment made by him was made in gold, and the second payment but little gold was paid—I think not more than one-third of the amount ; all the other payments have been made in currency.

YANKTON INDIAN AGENCY, *August* 29, 1865.

Louis Mallett, of lawful age, being duly sworn, deposes as follows :

First question. What is your name and occupation, and where do you reside?

First answer. My name is Louis Mallett, and I am a laborer, and now reside at the Yankton agency.

Second question. Have you worked for Doctor Burleigh?

Second answer. Last autumn I worked at Bonhomme, on Burleigh's farm, and the year before I worked about three or four months. Last summer I was there through planting and remained until after haying. Burleigh paid me, but I do not know whether he paid me as an employé of the agency or not. I also worked at the agency some while Burleigh was agent.

YANKTON INDIAN AGENCY, *August* 28, 1865.

Examination before Hon. A. W. HUBBARD, member of congressional Indian commission.

Zephir Rencounter, being duly sworn, deposes as follows :

First question. Where do you now reside?

First answer. I reside at Crow Creek agency.

Second question. Where have you resided for the past five or six years?

Second answer. I resided here, at the Yankton agency, three years of that time, and the remainder of that time I have resided at Bonhomme.

Third question. State whether you were at this agency while Mr. Redfield was agent here.

Third answer. I was here one year, and about two years while Mr. Burleigh was agent, and was interpreter part of the time.

Fourth question. State what you know about a school-house being erected at this agency by Mr. Redfield.

Fourth answer. None was erected by him, though I understood he was to erect one ; and no school-house has been erected by subsequent agents.

Fifth question. State whether any school has been kept at the Yankton agency?

Fifth answer. None was kept while Mr. Redfield was here. During Mr. Burleigh's agency a Mr. Banett taught Mr. Burleigh's children for a time. In the first place he tried to get some of the Indian children into his school, but did not succeed very well, and abandoned the enterprise.

Sixth question. Do you know of any one else being employed to teach the Indians here?

Sixth answer. No, sir.

Seventh question. If there had been any teacher here teaching the Indians would you probably have known it?

Seventh answer. I think I would, because I have been here frequently even when I did not reside here. I am a relation of the Yankton Indians.

Eighth question. Were there any mechanic shops erected by Redfield while here?

Eighth answer. A blacksmith shop and a carpenter shop.

Ninth question. Was any dwelling-house erected by Redfield for the interpreter, and one for the miller?

Ninth answer. He erected a double house ; part of it to be occupied by the miller and part by the interpreter.

Tenth question. Was any house erected for the engineer and farmer?

Tenth answer. Yes, sir ; a sort of double house.

Eleventh question. What do you know as to the manner in which Redfield transacted the business of the agency?

Eleventh answer. I have no knowledge in that respect.

Twelfth question. What do you know about the manner in which Burleigh transacted the business of the agency?

Twelfth answer. I have no personal knowledge, but I heard some complaint.

Thirteenth question. What efforts have been made to learn the Indians the blacksmith trade, the carpenter trade, and other mechanical pursuits, and also agricultural pursuits?

Thirteenth answer. Some efforts were made to learn Indians to work in the blacksmith shop, but were not very successful; also some tried to learn to farm, but the Indians abandoned it.

Fourteenth question. What amount of annuity are you entitled to yearly as a Yankton half-breed, under the treaty and the agreement of the Yankton chiefs?

Fourteenth answer. I do not know. When Redfield was here I needed goods for my family and he gave me a thousand dollars' worth out of the warehouse of the agency, with the agreement that the amount should be deducted out of my annuity, and the matter remained unadjusted until Burleigh came, and he then receipted for my annuity for three years for the thousand dollars of goods got of Redfield. After this Burleigh told me that my annuity amounted to fifteen hundred dollars a year, and I then entered into a contract with Burleigh by which I sold him one-half of my annuity so long as it should last, for which he was to give me twenty head of cows, one hundred chickens, build me a house a story and a half high, with two rooms in it, each nineteen feet long by sixteen feet wide, and he was to furnish the house with a table for each room, bureau, one dozen chairs, looking-glass, one cooking stove, one parlor stove.

Fifteenth question. Did you get the twenty cows?

Fifteenth answer. He delivered seventeen of the cows to me; they were worth twenty-five dollars a head.

Sixteenth question. Did he build the house; and if so, what kind of a house?

Sixteenth answer. Built a log house.

Seventeenth question. Did he pay you the balance?

Seventeenth answer. He paid me twenty-five chickens, one cooking stove, and six chairs, and that is all I have received from him.

Eighteenth question. What receipts have you signed for the annuity?

Eighteenth answer. I have signed receipts each year for the full amount.

Nineteenth question. Did you give Burleigh a power of attorney to draw your annuity?

Nineteenth answer. I did.

YANKTON INDIAN AGENCY, *August* 29, 1865.

F. B. Chardon, of lawful age, being duly sworn, did depose and say:

First question. What is your name and residence?

First answer. F. B. Chardon, and reside at the Yankton agency, and have resided here five or six years.

Second question Who acted as carpenter while Mr Burleigh was agent?

Second answer. Fred. Carmon. Mr. Bradford, the engineer, sometimes did rough work about the mill

Third question. Who acted as blacksmith?

Third answer. John Thompson was blacksmith.

Fourth question. Who acted as tinner, and who was miller?

Fourth answer. Mr. Ruhe was miller when any grinding was done. But little milling was done, and most any one could do it. Mr. Macklin was tinner.

Fifth question Was there any teacher here?

Fifth answer. Doctor Banett was employed as teacher, and taught Doctor Burleigh's children and some of Mr. Faulk's children, (one of them,) and part of the time some of Mr. Owen's children, but the Indians did not go to his school. I think Doctor Banett was here as teacher and doctor nearly two years. After Doctor Banett left they had no regular teacher or doctor. John Burleigh acted as doctor some and gave out medicine when the Indians wanted it.

Sixth question. Was a Miss Faulk employed as teacher while Doctor Burleigh was agent here?

Sixth answer. I heard she was, but I never saw any one go to school to her, nor do I know where she taught.

Seventh question. Were any efforts made while Burleigh was here to learn any of the Indians to read and write or any trades?

Seventh answer. No efforts were made to learn them to read and write. They tried to learn one Indian the tinner's trade, but he disagreed with the tinner and left. There was one in the mill, but I think he worked for wages. Those who have attempted to learn the Indians trades have expected too much of them; they are not like white folks; and those who have tried to learn them have not succeeded. They must be humored and learned gradually.

Eighth question. Have you been present at payments made to the Indians and half-breeds made by Doctor Burleigh?

Eighth answer. I was present at two payments of the half-breeds. The first payment by him was made in paper money. I think this payment was made the first fall after the doctor came here. The half-breeds were absent, and were sent for and came to the agency. He told us he had our money for us, and assembled us in the council-room, but did not tell us how much was coming to us. He then asked us to sign the receipts before he showed us any money. Some refused to sign the receipts until they knew how much money they were going to get. I did not sign for two days. I do not draw any money myself, but my children do, and I was to sign myself for them. That time they were to draw for three years, and I drew for them sixty-five dollars and some cents for the three years. Since then I have drawn fifty dollars a year for them, and have receipted each year for that amount to Doctor Burleigh.

Ninth question. What do you know about Mr. Burleigh having purchased some of the half-breeds' claims for annuity?

Ninth answer. I know he entered into a written agreement with Colin Campbell for the purchase of half of his annuity. He also purchased one-half of Zephir Rencounter's annuity. He built a house for Mr. Campbell at Bonhomme, I understand, and also let him have one yoke of oxen, three cows, one heifer, three calves. That is all he has paid Mr. Campbell. Mr. Campbell has never been down at Bonhomme to live in the house, and was not willing to go there and live unless Burleigh would give him a deed for the land, and some difficulties have occurred about the delivery of the property Burleigh was to give him, and he would not go there to live, and those difficulties remain unadjusted between them.

Tenth question. Do you know how much money has been paid Mr. Campbell?

Tenth answer. I do not know. He has received some things out of the trader's store at various times, and also received some things from Doctor Burleigh himself from the warehouse, and when the time for payment came Doctor Burleigh would make out Mr. Campbell's account and pay what he said was the balance due. He never gave Campbell his account, but would tell him how much he owed him and how much money was coming to him, and then Campbell would sign the receipts, and Campbell never knew how much he did get. Burleigh always kept the one-half under the agreement. Mr. Campbell is very old and deaf, and for the past year or two has been almost incompetent to do business, and it is very difficult to make him understand or comprehend anything. The goods that Burleigh gave Campbell out of the warehouse were marked Walter A. Burleigh, agent of the Yankton Indians, but I do not know whether they belonged to the Indians or Doctor Burleigh.

Eleventh question. Do you know of Doctor Burleigh using the Indian goods at any time?

Eleventh answer. He fitted out La Frambois with an outfit for the upper country, consisting of tobacco, sugar, coffee, blankets, white cotton cloth, and a good many other things which I cannot enumerate. I cannot state the quantity of each. I saw the goods all in a pile together, and saw them loaded in a wagon and start off. The load was drawn by two mules, and there was a full load. These goods were Indian goods. They had been laid away to be distributed in the fall, and were selected out of the annuity brought here in the spring or summer. The Indians complained to Doctor Burleigh about it, and there was a great fuss, and all the Indians gathered to fight Burleigh and frightened him, and he then issued to them what goods were left. All the goods which came here to Doctor Burleigh were marked alike, and the Indians could not distinguish their goods from Burleigh's. Doctor took such as he claimed as his, and left the balance for the Indians.

Twelfth question. Do you know of any of the employés employed at the agency by Doctor Burleigh working on Doctor Burleigh's farm at Bonhomme.

Twelfth answer. Some of them worked there. Mr. Bradford, the engineer, worked down on Burleigh's farm. Jerry Brottion worked there; John Burleigh also worked there; also Mr. Owens and Mr. Ruffner; but I do not know how they were paid. Frank Jondreau also worked down there. They were working at the agency part of the time and part of the time they worked on Burleigh's farm at Bonhomme. His farm is about thirty-five or forty miles from the agency. Some of the employés of the agency hauled goods for Mr. Hedges, the trader, with the Indians' teams.

Thirteenth question. How have the payments been made to the half-breeds?

Thirteenth answer. When I have been here the payments have always been made in paper money.

Fourteenth question. How have the payments of money to the Indians been made?

Fourteenth answer. I witnessed the payment in 1862, and the payment to them at that time was made principally in paper money. He would give them four dollars in paper money and one in gold, and to some of them he paid four dollars in gold and one in paper money. Where there was a large family he would pay four dollars in gold and the balance in paper money. Payments were made at the rate of five dollars per head and were made to the heads of the family.

Fifteenth question. Have you been present at any payments made since 1862?

Fifteenth answer. I have been at all the payments since but one.

Sixteenth question. How have the payments been made since then?

Sixteenth answer. Have been paid in paper money.

Seventeeth question. What do you know about the chief Strike the Ree demanding the invoices at the time the goods have been distributed to the Indians?

Seventeenth answer. I have often heard him demand to see the invoices, but Burleigh always refused to let him see the invoices.

Eighteenth question. What do you know about the quality of the flour that has been delivered here this year?

Eighteenth answer. It has been of very inferior quality and black; that is what I have received and all that I have seen, and I suppose it has all been of the same quality.

Nineteenth question. State what inducement or means have heretofore been made to induce or compel the Indians to buy the goods of the trader.

Nineteenth answer. The store of the trader is the only place the Indians can buy goods on orders. The agent gives orders on the trader and the Indians have to pay whatever price he asks. Flour is now $9 per sack. Heretofore at times they have had to pay as high as $10 per sack. They now get two and a half pounds of sugar for a dollar. Coffee is fifty cents per pound.

Twentieth question. What do you know about the Indians being satisfied with the management of the agency affairs while Burleigh and Redfield were here?

Twentieth answer. They were very much dissatisfied. I married Campbell's niece, and have been with the Yankton Indians ten years.

Twenty-first question. What do you know about Hedges, the contractor for furnishing hay at Fort Randall, using the Indians' mowing machines, oxen, and wagons, &c.?

Twenty-first answer. He has hitherto used them in cutting hay on his contracts, and has repaired them at the blacksmith and carpenter shops belonging to the agency. I have no knowledge of the Indians being paid anything for the use of them or for repairing them.

F. B. CHARDON.

YANKTON INDIAN AGENCY, *August* 29, 1865.

Alexis C. Young, being duly sworn, deposes as follows:

First question. What is your name, and how long have you resided at this (Yankton) agency?

First answer. My name is Alexis Young, and I have resided here five years.

Second question. In what capacity have you been employed here?

Second answer. The first three years I was employed as laborer by Dr. Burleigh, and I have been acting as interpreter about one year and a half under Doctor Burleigh, and I am now interpreter under Agent Conger.

Third question. Do you know of Doctor Burleigh using any of the Indian goods for his own use?

Third answer. I do not. If he did so, I did not see it.

Fourth question. What do you know about schools being kept here, and efforts made to learn the Indians to read and write and to learn trades?

Fourth answer. No efforts have been made to teach the Indians; Dr. Banett taught school one winter, and I saw Burleigh's family—sisters and sisters-in-law, and his brothers—at Doctor Banett's school; I have never seen any school open for the Indians; I do not know of any other teacher being employed, though I heard that they were going to employ one. I have wanted to send my two daughters to school for the past five years, but I have had no opportunity There are at least twenty-five half-breed children that want to go to school now, and have wanted to go to school; there are plenty of half-breeds and Indian children that would go to school if there was an opportunity; there has been no school-house here, and no place fit for a school.

Fifth question. Has there been a physician employed here?

Fifth answer. Doctor Banett was here about two years, and there has been no other physician here until Agent Conger came. John Burleigh, who acted as boss farmer, tried to be doctor, too, and gave the Indians medicine; Mrs. Burleigh, the mother of Agent

Burleigh, gave the Indians medicine when John Burleigh was away ; I did not understand that either of them were educated physicians.

Sixth question. What do you know about the quality of the flour distributed to the Indians this spring?

Sixth answer. It was very poor and black ; the flour makes very poor bread ; I had a barrel.

Seventh question. What do you know about the condition of the agency when Doctor Burleigh turned it over to Major Conger, the new agent?

Seventh answer. It was in a very bad condition ; Major Conger found himself like a man in the middle of a prairie, with nothing to do with. There was no blacksmith, nor carpenter. For the last six months prior to Doctor Burleigh's leaving there was no blacksmith and no engineer; we had had no engineer since last August. There had been no carpenter for over a year.

Eighth question. Do you draw annuities under the treaty and agreement of the chiefs?

Eighth answer. Burleigh has always paid me $200 a year, and my two daughters $100 apiece each year.

Ninth question. What do you know about the Indian goods and Burleigh's goods being mixed up together?

Ninth answer. Doctor Burleigh's goods—I can't say whether his goods were marked different from the Indians' goods or not. The traders' goods were marked differently. When the goods were landed here Doctor Burleigh would say that certain boxes belonged to him, and they would be set apart for him.

A. C. YOUNG.

YANKTON INDIAN AGENCY, *August* 29, 1865.

H. M. Conger, of lawful age, being duly sworn, deposed as follows :

First question. What is your name, residence, and occupation?

First answer. H. M. Conger ; resides at the Yankton agency, and have resided here since the first of May, the present year ; I am acting in the capacity of farmer for the agency ; I came here with Mr. Conger, the present agent, who arrived here about the first day of May, 1865.

Second question. State the condition of affairs here when your brother took possession.

Second answer. The affairs of the agency were in a bad condition ; they had been two or three days, and had ploughed fifteen or twenty acres. Found the agency destitute of teams, with the exception of one span of mules and two yokes of oxen ; there were plenty of ploughs and harrows ; there were two wagons and one truck used at the mill ; there was also an ambulance for light purposes. In order to get in crops we hired teams to plough ; we ploughed and put in about one hundred and fifty acres ; found some seed corn here, but it was poor ; we planted it, but it did not come up, except on the very wet land. Doctor Burleigh had sent for seed, but it did not arrive here in season. I think there are about fifty acres of the corn come up ; it has come up in several different patches.

Third question. How does it happen that Charles E. Hedges is trader here? State what you know about it.

Third answer. Mr. Mobley came here with the intention of acting as trader. After he arrived here Mr. Hedges made an arrangement with him by which Mr. Hedges became the trader, and Mr Mobley went back home. Hedges paid Mobley six thousand dollars, but I do not know personally whether it was paid in consideration of Mobley relinquishing the tradership, or for something else.

Fourth question. Did Mobley have any goods or property here to dispose of which Hedges got of him?

Fourth answer. Not that I know of; he may have had.

Fifth question. Do you know the prices at which Mr. Hedges sells the goods to the Indians?

Fifth answer. The prices are as stated by Mr. Chardon in his affidavit, which I heard ; he has been selling them common prints at about three yards for the dollar ; blue drilling and check gingham at fifty cents per yard.

Sixth question What do you know about Hedges, the hay contractor, using the Indians' mowing machines to cut hay for Fort Randall?

Sixth answer. Hedges uses his own machines this year, and his own teams. I don't know what he has hitherto done : there is an understanding between Mr. Conger and the Indians that they shall have pay for the hay cut by Mr. Hedges this year.

H. M. CONGER.

FORT RANDALL, *Sptember* 2, 1865.

TERRITORY OF DAKOTA, *County of Todd:*

William Cox, of lawful age, being duly sworn, doth depose and say as follows:

First question. What is your name, residence, and occupation?

First answer. William Cox; reside at Fort Randall.

Second question. State what knowledge you have of the injuries sustained by the Yankton Indians at the hands of the soldiers under General Sully.

Second answer. A few rails were probably taken from the fence of Little Swan, above this post, by the soldiers, but not to my knowledge; but the Indians took off more than the soldiers At the agency the soldiers camped about four miles from the houses they said were injured; I was there the next day, and saw no damage done, except some few windows that were out; don't know whether they had glass windows or not, but they generally board up their windows. I often travel by the agency, and did at that time; I have seen no other damage there. For the past six years I often have passed over the reservation; during the past six years, part of the time, have carried the mail over that part of the reservation above here; I have carried the mail over the reservation above here for the past two years.

Third question. Do you know that the damage done down at the agency, that you saw, was done by the soldiers?

Third answer. I do not.

Fourth question. State whether, if the Indians had sustained any serious damage at the hands of the soldiers, you would likely have known of it.

Fourth answer. I think I would. I can talk some with the Yankton Indians, and can understand them, and have frequently had conversations with them during the past two or three years, and never heard of their complaint for damages until since Congress allowed them $10,000 for damages done by soldiers. I was at the agency this last spring, and Little Swan wanted to find some person to make out papers for him for his share of the damages; he did not know what his damages were, but wanted his papers made out by some white man, so that he could get his share; he was afraid some of the other chiefs would get more than their share.

Fifth question. What amount, if any, of damages have been committed against the property of the Indians (Yanktons) by the soldiers?

Fifth answer. All the damages sustained by them at the hands of the soldiers did not exceed five hundred dollars, and I doubt whether or not one hundred dollars would not cover all.

WILLIAM COX.

FORT RANDALL, DAKOTA, *September* 2, 1865.

Examination before Hon. A. W. Hubbard, commissioner.

Samuel M. Pollock, colonel of the 6th regiment Iowa volunteer cavalry, being duly sworn, deposed as follows:

First question. State your name, occupation for the past three years, and your residence.

First answer. My name is Samuel M. Pollock, and reside at Dubuque, Iowa. I am colonel of the 6th regiment Iowa volunteer cavalry, and have been serving in Dakota Territory for some over two years.

Second question. State what you know about injuries committed against the Yankton Sioux Indians by soldiers belonging to the command of General Sully.

Second answer. Some time in December, 1864, I received a communication from General Sully, wherein he stated that Mr. Burleigh, the agent of the Yankton Indians, complaining of some depredations and damages done to the property and houses of Smutty Bear below the agency, by the last company of the 6th regiment Iowa cavalry that passed down that fall, and directing me to go to the agency and investigate the facts in relation to such damages and depredations and report the same to him. In accordance with these directions of General Sully, I went to the Yankton Indian agency to investigate and report the facts in relation to such depredations and injuries On arriving at the agency, I found that Mr. Burleigh was not at home at the agency I was of the opinion that the damages done, as represented by Mr. Burleigh, had been very much exaggerated, and that there was no certainty as to the persons who had committed the depredations complained of. I came to that conclusion as the result of the inquiries I made after I arrived at the agency. In order that the investigation might be made more satisfactory, I returned to my post at Fort Randall, and await the return of Mr. Burleigh, and return again to the agency and take the testimony of Mr. Burleigh and any witnesses he might produce who knew anything of the alleged depredations. Learning that Mr. Burleigh had returned, I again went to the agency, saw Mr. Burleigh and informed him of the object of my visit, and desired his testimony and that of any witnesses he might produce, who knew anything in relation to the depredations. Mr. Burleigh informed me that he was away from the agency at the time of the alleged depredations, and knew nothing about the depredations except what the Indians had told him ; that he had no personal knowledge of the matter. I asked him then to produce his witnesses. He referred me to some men belonging to company B, Dakota cavalry ; but upon inquiry of them they knew nothing about who did it. I then asked him to send for the Indians who knew something about it, if there were such. He then sent for an Indian whom he called his principal chief, by the name of Strike the Ree. Upon inquiry of him, Strike the Ree said to me, through the interpreter, that some damages had been done to some of the houses and property taken away at Smutty Bear's camp ; that the Indians had been absent from these houses on a hunt for about two months ; that neither he nor they (the Indians) knew who done the damages, and that the only reason he thought soldiers might have done the damage was, that shots had been fired through the windows ; that the houses had been opened, and some log chains and nails had been taken away ; and also spoke of some other article or articles that had been taken away, but I do not now remember what article or articles, but the chains and nails were the principal articles he complained of being taken. He also said that there were a great many trains and teams passing these houses. He seemed to know nothing more about it. Unable to obtain any evidence as to who committed the depredations, I took no evidence as to the amount of damage ; but from the statements of Strike the Ree and other persons as to the amount of damage, I did not estimate the amount of damage done to exceed fifty dollars ; and from the character of the articles taken, I did not suppose that the damage done was committed by soldiers, as they would not likely take log chains and nails when marching through the country, but think those articles were taken by citizens teaming through the country, as they would more likely need such articles.

Third question. Have you any personal knowledge of the soldiers under General Sully committing any damage against the property of the Yankton Sioux Indians?

Third answer. I have not, aside from the horses eating grass upon the reservation, and the soldiers cutting wood to cook with while encamped upon the reservation.

Fourth question. State whether the prairie on the reservation passed over by the command, and upon which the horses fed, was enclosed with fences, and whether the horses were turned into any enclosure?

Fourth answer. The prairie was not enclosed ; I have never seen any enclosed meadows on the Yankton reservation ; the grass eaten was the unfenced wild grass of the open prairie ; the horses were not turned into any enclosure ; the fuel taken was the fuel necessary to cook with while the command was passing over the reservation, and while encamped upon it ; no unnecessary damage was done so far as I know ; my connexion with the military here for the past two years has been such, that if any unnecessary damage had been done I would have been likely to know it.

Fifth question. Do you know of any damage being done to the cornfields of the Yanktons by the soldiers ; and if so, what damage?

Fifth answer. Of my own personal knowledge, I do not ; I have heard that some damages were done to their corn, but it was done in connexion with the military in the fall of 1862, before I came into the country, as I understood it ; if any damage has been done since I know nothing of it.

Sixth question. State what, if anything, you know about the Yankton graves on the reservation being interfered with by soldiers.

Sixth answer. I have no knowledge of any such interference ; I marched through the Yankton reservation in May, 1865, with four companies under my command, and stopped at the agency to water the animals belonging to the command, and I know that at that time there was no interference with the Yankton graves ; but what may have been done by other soldiers marching across the reservation, I have no knowledge.

Seventh question. State whether you have taken timber from the reservation for the use of this post ; and if so, the circumstances under which the same was taken.

Seventh answer. There is a great scarcity of timber suitable for saw-logs that can be sawed with such small saws as there are at this post upon the military reservation. There was no lumber to repair the quarters at the post, nor plank to make coffins for deceased soldiers, which was absolutely necessary for the comfort of the men and for making coffins, and I applied to Mr. Burleigh for the privilege of obtaining timber for that purpose from the Indian reservation ; he said he had no objections to my taking it, but it would be better to ask the permission of his Indian chiefs ; they would feel better about it. Strike the Ree, his principal chief, gave his consent, and Mr. Burleigh told me I could take what I wanted ; and accordingly, I took a number of saw-logs for the purpose above stated. Strike the Ree said that some of his Indians would want some plank to make coffins for their dead, and they have had plank from this post for that purpose, and some coffins have been made for them by the hands attached to the quartermaster's office.

Eighth question. State the circumstances under which an Indian was shot by a soldier in April or May, 1864, near this post.

Eighth answer. The circumstances as shown by an investigation had by me at the time—I cannot speak of my own personal knowledge—were as follows: I was in command of this post at the time. The officer of the day was instructed to close the bar upon all steamboats stopping at the post, so that soldiers could not procure liquor. A steamboat came up the Missouri river, and the bar was closed by the officer of the day and no liquor was sold. The boat for some purpose, after passing the post, landed again a short distance above the post. Private Gaffney, of company G, 6th Iowa cavalry, procured whiskey from the boat and became intoxicated. On his return to the post he met one Indian man and two squaws. Gaffney and this party got into a difficulty about a bottle of whiskey which Gaffney had. In the melee Gaffney shot the Indian man in the back with one of Smith and Wesson's No. 1 revolvers. The soldier was placed in confinement, charges preferred against him and forwarded to district headquarters. The Indian was cared for by the surgeon at the post, and in a short time recovered from his wounds. Gaffney was kept under arrest until the following fall, when he was discharged from service under a surgeon's certificate of disability. The reason he was not tried I suppose was as follows: General Sully soon after arrived on his expedition, and took Gaffney along with him to Fort Sully, and after the expedition left there, there were not enough officers left to constitute a court to try him at Fort Sully and, in addition, the witnesses necessary to establish the charges against him were on the expedition above that place. The reason Gaffney was left there, he was so badly ruptured that he could not well accompany the expedition.

Ninth question. Have you any knowledge of the Indians being driven out of their tepees by soldiers?

Ninth answer. I have not of my own personal knowledge, and no complaints of that character were made to me by Mr. Burleigh at the time of alleged offence of that character; but long after the alleged time he complained to me. I understood that in the winter of 1863 and 1864, Charles De Gray, the interpreter at that time at Fort Randall, ran the Indians out of their houses or tepees with a revolver. De Gray was represented to me as intoxicated at the time. He is a half-breed Yankton Indian, and I immediately discharged him from his position as interpreter. He was not a soldier. I know of no other instance of Indians being run out of their houses or tepees. In respect to Captain Moreland having killed some Indians on Ponca creek, a full investigation has been had and reported.

S. M. POLLOCK, *Colonel 6th Iowa Cavalry.*

DAKOTA TERRITORY, CROW CREEK AGENCY, *September* 6, 1865.

Examination as to affairs of Yankton Indians before Hon. A. W. HUBBARD, member Indian commission.

Daniel P. Bradford, of lawful age, being duly sworn, deposed as follows:

First question. State your name and residence.

First answer. Daniel P. Bradford; reside at Bonhomme, in this Territory.

Second question. State whether, for the past three or four years, you have been employed on the Yankton agency; and if so, in what capacity?

Second answer. For the past three years I have been employed there during the summer as engineer.

Third question. State what you know about the tinner at the agency making tin for the trader.

Third answer. A year ago last summer, though I am not positive, I was sitting in company with Burleigh, the agent, near the council, and Hedges, the trader, wanted to buy some camp kettles of Burleigh. There was some conversation between Burleigh and Hedges about the price, and Burleigh told him he might have them at a certain price, which witness does [not] now recollect, and then Hedges's assistant went and got them. The tinner was in the shop and delivered them according to the order of Agent Burleigh. There were between two and three dozen of the camp kettles of the large size.

Fourth question. State what you know of Agent Burleigh slaughtering the beef cattle belonging to the Indians and selling the beef.

Fourth answer. Personally, I do not. He used to kill beef at the agency and sell the beef. I used to buy beef about every time he killed, but don't know that the beef belonged to the agency. When I moved there two years ago last spring, I took with me a fat cow. Burleigh wanted to buy her for beef, as he said. I replied that I could not sell her, as it was the only cow I had; and then he said he would give any cow he had upon the agency in exchange for her, and directed Silas Strader to make the exchange, which was done, and the cow was killed and disposed of; that is, sold out as usual to those about the agency, used in the mess-house, and Burleigh's family. I don't know whether the cow belonged to the Indians, or was Indian property, or whether it was private property. I never knew the difference between the stock belonging to the Indians or to Burleigh.

Fifth question. State what you may know of Burleigh using for his own purposes lumber cut at the agency?

Fifth answer. Burleigh took some lumber from the agency saw-mill to his place at Bonhomme I don't know how much ; think there was at least two loads.

Sixth question. Do you know of his using any of the property of the agency at his farm at Bonhomme?

Sixth answer. I have known of his using some of the wagons of the Indians down there.

Seventh question. Do you know of any of the employés of the agency working on Burleigh's Bonhomme farm? If so, state the particulars.

Seventh answer. I do. John Thompson worked there a year ago the past spring at least a month, I should think. Micklin, (James, I think,) the tinner at the agency, also worked there at the same time ; I think he worked there a good deal longer than Thompson. Mallet and Protean also worked there at that time. Also, Henry Claymore, another employé of the agency, worked there ; but, whether they were employés of the agency at the time, I cannot say.

Eighth question. While you were at work on the agency, how could you distinguish the property belonging to the agency and that belonging to Burleigh, individually?

Eighth answer. I could not distinguish them. I frequently bought flour and meat of Burleigh at the agency. I sometimes had as high as seven hands, and have quite a family. Don't know who it belonged to.

Ninth question. Do you know of John Thompson, the blacksmith, doing blacksmith work for outside parties and taking pay for it?

Ninth answer. I know of his doing a good deal of work for parties other than the Indians and those connected wtth the agency, and I think he took pay for it ; at least, I have frequently heard him say how much he had made during the day for doing outside work, and have heard him dun parties for pay for work he had done.

D. P. BRADFORD.

DAKOTA TERRITORY, YANKTON, *September* 11, 1865.

Examination before Hon. A. W. HUBBARD, member of congressional Indian commission.

Patrick H. Conger, being duly sworn, deposed as follows:

First answer. My name is Patrick H. Conger. My present residence is the Yankton agency, Dakota, at which place I am acting as the agent of the Yankton Indians, and have been acting as such agent since about the first of May last.

Second question. State generally the condition of the agency at the time you took possession.

Second answer. I have reported the condition of the agency at that time to Governor Edmonds, of Dakota Territory, and that report contains the facts in relation to the agency.

Third question. State whether Agent Burleigh left with you any records and papers showing the manner in which the business of his agency had been conducted.

Third answer. He did not, except he left a copy of the regulations of the department; and on or about the first of July he gave me, at his farm at Bonhomme, a few letters of instructions, which he tore out of a scrap-book.

Fourth question. State in what condition you found the wagons and farming implements belonging to the agency.

Fourth answer. I found two or three old wagons, which were unfit for use, two of which I have had prepared. The ploughs were in good condition, so far as I have found them. There were also two old mowers, though I do not know whether they belonged to the agency or not. The ploughs were scattered about in different places.

Fifth question. State under what circumstances Charles E. Hedges became trader at the Yankton agency.

Fifth answer. I took a man by the name of Mobley to the Yankton agency, expecting to make him the trader, and he, with that understanding, purchased the stock of goods of Charles E. Hedges, the old trader, amounting, I believe, to between twelve and thirteen thousand dollars There being some difficulty about the payment for the goods, there was a proposition to either sell or buy back—I don't know which made the proposition—and I consented that if Hedges could satisfy Mobley, I would recommend

Hedges for trader. I understood that an arrangement was made by which Hedges gave Mobley six thousand dollars more than Mobley was to give for the goods, and took the goods back, and I agreed to recommend Hedges for trader. I have no knowledge of Hedges agreeing to pay any further sum for the right to the tradership; but I have understood that he agreed to give my brother Hiram M. Conger six thousand dollars, by reason of his waiving his prospective operations with Mobley, as he came out with Mobley expecting to have some interest with Mobley in the trade. The trade now belongs exclusively to Hedges, no other party being in interest with him to my knowledge.

Sixth question. Please state the manner in which the mess-house at the Yankton agency managed.

Sixth answer. Temporarily, I have hired Mr. Wood and wife and his furniture for seventy-five dollars per month to manage and conduct the mess-house, and I furnish the provisions and receive the receipts; but intend, as soon as possible, to procure some person to manage and conduct it on their own account.

Seventh question. Was there any school in operation upon the agency, or school-house fit for a school, at the time you took possession?

Seventh answer. There was neither school nor school-house.

Eighth question. State the number of Indians belonging to your agency.

Eighth answer. I have no means of knowing, as I have never enumerated them; but have been informed by Mr. Burleigh that there are between twenty-three and twenty-four hundred. I expect to enumerate them this fall.

Ninth question. State whether they have any means of subsistence for the coming winter excepting a resort to the chase.

Ninth answer. They have no means of subsistence except to a limited extent, and will have to depend principally upon the chase for their subsistence.

P. H. CONGER.

St. Joseph, Missouri, *October* 20, 1865.

Dear Sir: I have just received your application for my views upon Indian matters, and especially for facts in the management of Mr. Burleigh, late agent of the Yanktons.

As to Mr. Burleigh, my knowledge of his general administration is not sufficiently personal to make it of value to you, and you have probably heard as much of his operations as I. But the general fact that the Yankton Indians are growing more and more degraded, that instead of acquiring knowledge and property they are poorer than ever, while agents and other whites among them have grown rich; and also the general fact that from firm friends before the treaty they have become latent enemies, are patent to us all. These things could not be without something radically wrong. There was a time when the life of every settler in Dakota, if not in northwestern Iowa, seemed to depend upon his ability to fly. Strong efforts were made to induce the Yanktons to join their Minnesota brethren in the war. It is now known they were restrained only by a minority of their chiefs, sustained by a military force among them. In a council held by the secretary while acting governor, old Strike the Ree, after many and long complaints, was reminded of the duty of being peaceable and not doing like his friends in Minnesota. The old man started, almost jumped from his seat, seized the secretary by the shoulder, and with a slow but almost convulsive earnestness, exclaimed: "You blame the Minnesota Indians They did wrong, but you do not know the cause. We know it! we know it! You do not. For long winters and summers they had been cheated and robbed by the agents and traders. They complained, but the Great Father would not make it right. Their hearts became bad; they thirsted for blood; they got plenty. We have the same cause to kill as our friends in Minnesota. But this (pointing to a cross suspended from his neck) keeps my heart right. I would not let my young men fight. The Yanktons have never killed a white man." The interpreter, who is generally bungling enough, seemed to catch the spirit of the orator, and the whole so startled the secretary that he was able a few days after to give me almost every word. We have other and far more convincing evidence that the Yanktons were with difficulty restrained. If they enjoy the full benefits of their treaty, why this hostility? Lewis and Clark, more than sixty years ago, were treated by them as honored guests. French traders and trappers, before and ever since, have lived among them in perfect security. The first settlers of northwestern Iowa and upper Nebraska found them friends. Why the change, as we are showering upon them the gifts of a munificent treaty?

But there is one clause, and a most important one, in their treaty, to which I wish to call your attention. I refer to the fourth section of article 4 of the treaty of April 19, 1858, which provides for the education of the savage. I had hardly come into the Territory when there was developed a marked difference of opinion and sympathy between myself and most of the other officials upon our Indian relations. I saw that no attempt had been made by Mr. Burleigh's predecessor to execute the above section, and believing it to be the only provision of any value to the Indian, I expressed a strong desire to see the work of civilization begin. I did not doubt but in this I should have the sympathy of Mr. Burleigh and his superintendent, the governor, and fully appreciated the difficulties of the enterprise. But I soon found that there was no design to do anything in this direction, though I will do Mr. Burleigh the justice to say that he disclaimed any responsibility himself; that he threw the blame partly upon his predecessor who had used up the fund for building a school-house, partly upon the Almighty, who had decreed the extinction of the Indian race, and partly upon the Indian bureau, which would not permit him to try any vain experiments upon them. The subject not being within my official duties, I could do nothing, but I could not, without deep emotion, view this fine band, comparatively flourishing, till in an evil day they were wheeled into making a treaty, going the downward road of all treaty-making Indians. For the general fund of the tribe I care little. If faithfully used to feed and clothe, it would be little better than a curse, and it had better be thrown into the Missouri than used to stimulate indolence or become an endless source of fraud and strife.

"4th. To expend ten thousand dollars to build a school-house or school-houses, and to establish and maintain one or more normal schools (so far as said sum will go) for the education, training of said Indians in letters, agriculture, the mechanic arts and housewifery, which school or schools shall be managed and conducted in such manner as the Secretary of the Interior shall direct; the said Indians hereby stipulating to keep constantly thereat, during at least nine months in the year, all their children between the ages of seven and eighteen years; and if any of the parents, or others having the care of children, shall refuse or neglect to send them to school, such parts of their annuities as the Secretary of the Interior may direct shall be withheld from them, and may be applied as he may deem just and proper; and such further sum, in addition to said ten thousand dollars, as shall be deemed necessary and proper by the President of the United States, shall be reserved and taken from their said annuities, and applied annually, during the pleasure of the President, to the support of said schools, and to furnish said Indians with assistance and aid and instruction in agriculture and mechanical pursuits, including the working of the mills, hereafter mentioned, as the Secretary of the Interior may consider necessary and advantageous for said Indians; and all instruction in reading shall be in the English language. And the said Indians hereby stipulate to furnish from among themthemselves the number of young men that may be required as apprentices or assistants in the mills and mechanics' shops, and at least three persons to work constantly with each white laborer employed for them in agriculture and mechanical pursuits, it being understood that such white laborers and assistants as may be so employed *are* thus employed more for the instruction of said Indians than merely to work for their benefit; and that the laborers so to be furnished by the Indians may be allowed a fair and just compensation for their services, to be fixed by the Secretary of the Interior, and to be paid out of the shares of annuity of such Indians as are able to work but refuse or neglect to do so. And whenever the President of the United States shall be satisfied of a failure on the part of said Indians to fulfil the aforesaid stipulations, he may, at his discretion, discontinue the allowance and expenditure of the sums so provided and set apart for said school or schools, and assistance and instruction."

I know not how the well-known desires of Strike the Ree, Mad Bull, and the other more intelligent Indians could have been more clearly expressed than by this section. Its subject-matter was their chief inducement to make the treaty. They are wise and good men, black though they be, and well know that in the constant encroachments of the white man their long existence depends upon their becoming civilized, and their influence has always been in the direction of industry and the white man's wisdom. For the benefits of this section principally they gave up the best part of their country, and often and bitterly do they complain that their Great Father has forgotten his promises. You are aware as well as I that this section of the treaty has been wholly disregarded. When I left the Territory last year, not a single Yankton had been taught the English language or any habits of industry whatever. No serious attempt had been made in that direction. More than seven years of the first ten, during which they were to receive their largest annuities, have already passed. Over four hundred and fifty thousand dollars in all have been paid over for this tribe, and what is there to show for it? Certainly the ten thousand dollars and the additional sums provided in this section have been squandered or misappropriated.

I hope, my dear sir, you will call the attention of Congress and the country to this treaty and this its so gross violation. It cannot be that the heart of our people is dead; that we have lost all faith; that they will tolerate so gross a wrong, even though committed upon only a band of savages. To do right in this thing involves no expense, but may save many millions It is only to place the education fund of the Indians in the hands of some independent religious body or board, who can have no interests but in favor of the Indian and require the agents to act in harmony with them. The schools should not be, they cannot be, under the management of the agent. Let him be the best of men, and he can give them no adequate attention. I know of no existing competent educating agency except the missionary societies or boards, and if the money were placed in their hands the treaty, at least, might be observed, and as much good done the Indian as the present miserable Indian system will permit.

But perhaps Indian elevation is no part of the American idea. Perhaps our people as well as their government will the degradation and final extinction of the race. If so, the means employed are entirely adequate. You know as well as I, that the Yanktons have been sinking lower and lower ever since they were gathered upon their reserve. And this is not owing to the progress of white settlements; there are none near, and no white man comes among the tribe not brought there by the agent. The intercourse laws are well observed; and yet, while everything seems to be brought to bear to sink the savage, there is nothing whatever to elevate him. There was no Sabbath, no worship, no lecture, no school, no regular industry, nothing whatever to check the downward drag, while the dance, with its brutalizing and crime-exciting harangues, was encouraged and often purchased for the entertainment of visitors, and the traffic in their young women was greatly stimulated by the white men and soldiers brought to their village. The very largesses of government, which should be only used for the advancement of industry and knowledge, are but bounties to indolence as well as the source of jealousies and strife. This "wiping out" a race may be sport to us, at least to such of us as may figure in the Department of the Interior, but it is no sport to the frontier settler or the peaceful traveller across the plains. Neither is it sport to those excellent old chiefs who are doomed to see their people sink away into the earth, crowded out of sight by the very means they had employed to give them a firm tread.

Strike the Ree is bowed to the earth, as well with age as sorrow for his people. He had regarded this treaty provision for their elevation as the crowning act of a life devoted to their welfare. How great is his disappointment every speech shows. In June, 1863, the old man opened a council by describing his interview with the Great Father in Washington, at the time they gave up their country. He set forth some of the things he promised them, of which the most prominent was the education of their young men and women. He stated that they were very careful to write all things down upon paper, and that he and the Great Father each kept a copy of the writing. But he perceived that the Great Father had long ago lost his copy of the writing and forgotten all there was in it; but he had kept his copy very careful and well remembered what it said, and he would inform the agent, that he might do as the Great Father had promised, &c., &c. This was the council in which the agent and Strike the Ree had their long controversy about the inventory of the goods that were sent them, the chief insisting that the paper should be shown him, to be submitted to a friendly half-breed for comparison with the goods delivered, and the agent steadily refusing to grant his request. I was not present at the opening of the council, and was informed by others of this opening speech. Many times have I heard of the utterance of the same complaint, and with all the eloquence and sometimes bitterness of a paternal head of a wronged people. Only a day or two since I noticed in the Missouri Democrat a report of a council held by General Curtis at Fort Randall, in which is given part of the speech of Strike the Ree. It is well reported, with the single exception that "grandfather" is not, but "Great Father" is, the Indian name for the President. The rich full voice, the slow, emphatic utterance and earnest manner of the old chief is alone wanting to give it its proper force. Says the reporter:

Pa-la-ne-opa-pe, (The Man that was struck by the Ree,) chief of the Yankton Sioux, replied in substance as follows: "Friends, my people are friendly to the white man. Our grandfather promised us (referring to the treaty of 1858) money, a school-house and blacksmith shop. I have seen neither, but I believe that it is no fault of our grandfather; he has done all in his power to keep his promise. I believe our money is being kept for us, and when it is paid we shall receive the interest with it; you should pay it. My young men, squaws and children are starving; the black spots you see on the hills before you are the graves of many of my people. When we receive anything from the white man it is given as you would throw it to a hog. The Indian stands as upon a snow-bank; the sun of prosperity shines brightly for others, but it is gradually melting away his support, and by and by all will be gone. Our grandfather at Washington promised that we should be raised up, but his young men put their feet on us and keep us down; that is the way the white man treats us."

To those who have been familiar with our intercourse with the Yanktons every line is a volume, and in proof of the truth of this eloquent complaint, I need only cite our gross breach of the provisions of the before cited section of the treaty. That clause is the only one possessing any value whatever to the Indian. Carried out in its spirit, with some essential changes in our Indian policy, it would gradually make the tribe a self-supporting, orderly community. As it is, he is simply going to destruction, where, I fear, our people and their government desire to send him. But to my mind our whole Indian policy, as tending to the civilization of the Indian, seems as stupid as its execution is rotten. If honestly executed it might preserve peace upon the border and save our hearthstones from the horrors of Minnesota; but to civilize, it can hardly be supposed to have been intended.

The essentials of civilized society are *laws and institutions*, which imply, 1st. The magistracy or public force for protection and restraint. 2d. Homes and family and security in their enjoyment. 3d. Property, and stimulus to its acquirement. 4th. Knowledge, with its inducements and opportunities. 5th. Religion, and its subordination to the moral sentiments. 6th. Industry, as the basis of everything.

Civilization will not tolerate the absence of either, and yet, in our blind if not hypocritical essays in that direction, we ignore every one. We flatter the Indian by so far respecting his independence, and so far only, as to leave him without law. Savage and lawless society are synonyms. To impose laws and provide for their execution would involve care and responsibility, a change in our system, a very different and less expensive administration. But conquest can in no other way be compensated or even excused Rome atoned for her tyranny by her laws, and Spain might teach us a lesson that should humble us. The Indian has no law; it is his chief characteristic. The chiefs are leaders in war, and their very slight power in peace is greatly diminished by their treaty relations with us. The Indian has no home. He may squat for a time and raise a crop or two, but acquires no title to anything but the crop. He knows nothing of property in land, and we are very careful that he shall never learn it The numerous instances I have heard of, where, under the influences of missionaries and other friendly white men, half civilized and friendly Sioux and Winnebagoes have created homes with the hope of holding them for themselves and children, and when they have been driven from them by our own government, must thoroughly satisfy the Indian that, so far as we can prevent it, he shall never in this regard be less a savage than now. One of the hardest things to teach him is to value his own property or respect that of another. The instinct of property is as clear in him as in the rest of the human race, but his habits and notions render respectable accumulations impossible. Our policy of denying him a permanent home does not greatly tend to overcome those habits. In regard to the education of the savage, to giving him knowledge, industry and religion, I have shown our gross disregard of our contract in relation to one tribe. History records no grosser breach of faith. *Ex uno disce omnes.*

The missionaries are the Indians best friends, and have done all yet done for them. Yet many of them seem strangely destitute of common sense. A theological seminary is not the best of schools for an Indian tutor. 'Tis no wonder the great Dr. Edmonds became weary of his Indian congregation in old Berkshire. His subtle metaphysics were worse than thrown away, and his rigid observances must have made the savage long for the woods. Not long since a good missionary, not far from the Missouri, became anxious his people should observe the Sabbath. He told them that if they worked or hunted on Sunday God would be angry with them, that the crops would not grow and they would get no game. One of the chiefs, whose faith was not the firmest, resolved to test the matter. So he planted his corn on Sunday and gave it extra culture, being careful to do all his work on the Sabbath. The experiment was watched with interest by the tribe, and the chief had an unusually fine crop. All the people pronounced the missionary a liar, and the chief took an additional wife. A visiting preacher afterwards talked to the same people upon the same subject, and told them how the Lord made all things in six days and rested on the seventh. They listened respectfully, but the story, not at all spiritualized by the interpreter, was the next day made sport of in the village. They thought the white man's God could not be so powerful as represented, or a week's work would not have made him so tired. I refer to this not to disparage the work of the missionaries, the Indian would be poor indeed without them, but to account in part for their ill success.

I have thus indicated some of my views. I can now readily understand what was so mysterious to me once, the Indian problem; how the Delawares, for instance, who have been steadily pushed back ever since their first treaty with Penn, should be dwindled in numbers and still but half civilized. An agent for this tribe once cited me their slow progress as a demonstration of the Indians' incapacity. But to suppose that a wild people, who meet civilization on its meanest side, without laws, without ambition, except that which makes him more a savage, with no rational stimulus to industry, driven from Dan to Beersheba with no possibility of permanent home or property, subjugated, but instead of being subjected to the conqueror's laws, pushed off beyond their reach, will readily adopt the manners and ideas of the conquerer, would be to suppose a miracle.

Many, perhaps a majority in Congress, would prefer honesty and good faith in an Indian administration, but I have little hope in your action. There are too many hungry politicians to feed, there is too profound an ignorance in your body, and there is too great an indifference among the people. Upon the subject of Indian rights we are as thoroughly corrupt as in reference to those of the slave, until driven to consider them in order to save ourselves. I sometimes think we are without a moral sense, without any practical regard to what is just and right. It would seem that we had been smitten enough to begin to consider, but perhaps not. We may have to spend a few more hundred millions to suppress Indian hostilities, enough perhaps to break down our already strained credit, before we begin to inquire why we and not our neighbors are ever involved in Indian war.

I am, very respectfully, your obedient servant,

P. BLISS.

Hon. A. W. HUBBARD.

Charles E. Hedges, being examined, makes the following statement:

First question. Where do you now reside, and where have you resided the past three years, and what has been your business?

First answer. Since March 9, 1862, have resided at the Yankton Indian agency, and have been the licensed trader there during that time.

Second question. Do you know how the mess-house at that agency has been carried on during the past three years, and whether the provisions were taken from the Indian goods?

Second answer. During the year 1862, and until about July, 1863, S. B. Shroder and wife were hired by Doctor Burleigh to take charge of it, and at the same time Shroder worked at anything that needed to be done about the agency, such as choring, ploughing, hauling, &c. The provisions were mostly purchased at St. Louis by Doctor Burleigh. He used to purchase his family supplies and provisions for the mess-house at St. Louis. I do not know that any provisions were furnished the mess-house out of the Indian goods. After Shroder left Foster T. Wheeler had charge of it, and I think continued in charge of it until about June, 1864, and it was managed about the way as when Shroder had charge of it. Wheeler himself done the cooking while he managed it, and also done some cooking while Shroder managed it. After Wheeler left, Jacob Rufner and wife had the management of the mess-house on their own account. They sometimes purchased supplies of me for the mess-house.

Third question. Can you explain why it is that Shroder, Wheeler, and Rufner, and others who were paid as laborers upon the agency, gave vouchers and received pay for boarding hands at the mess-house? and if so, please explain.

Third answer. Sometimes hands employed by the agent to work on the agency were paid so much per quarter and their board, and were boarded at the mess-house, and in order to cover the price of the board, whoever happened to be in charge of the mess-house gave vouchers for their board.

Fourth question. Please state whether any of the supplies purchased of you for the Indians, such as bacon, beef, sugar, coffee, &c., were used in the mess-house.

Fourth answer. Not that I know of. Most of the goods purchased of me for the Indians were issued directly to the Indians from my store.

Fifth question. Who received the profits arising from the mess-house?

Fifth answer. It was always represented to me that there were no profits but a continual loss.

Sixth question. Where did you board, and whom did you pay for your board?

Sixth answer. I boarded at the mess-house. Up to the time Jacob Rufner took charge of the mess-house I had my board for making out Doctor Burleigh's quarterly accounts. After that I paid Jacob Rufner for my board.

Seventh question. State whether you sold large quantities of goods and provisions to Burleigh, the agent; and state whether large profits were made on your sales to him, and whether Burleigh shared such profits with you.

Seventh answer. I did sell Agent Burleigh large quantities of supplies. Sometimes I made large profits and sometimes I did not, but on the average I made fair profits. Doctor Burleigh had no interest in my profits, directly or indirectly. I never shared the profits with him. I sold goods to Burleigh at the same price that I sold to others—at the market price.

Eighth question. What do you know about Elias Wall, F. Cannon, F. D. Pease, W. A Dempsey, John W. Owens, and W. A. Burleigh being allowed large amounts for property destroyed or stolen by the Indians? and also state particulars in relation to the allowance of $400 for horses stolen by the Yankton Indians from you.

Eighth answer. Colonel Falk undertook the collection of Wall, Pease, Cannon, and Dempsey's claims, and collected the testimony, which testimony was forwarded by Doctor Burleigh to the Commissioner of Indian Affairs, who ordered the claims paid, and directed how it should be done. I made out the vouchers for the claims as ordered to be paid by the Commissioner. My claim, and the claim of W. A. Burleigh and John W. Owens, and the testimony in support of each claim, were submitted by Doctor Burleigh to the Commissioner of Indian Affairs, and by the latter ordered to be paid. I made out the vouchers in accordance with the claims that they had been sworn to and which had been ordered paid. All I know about the claims is what is contained in the testimony offered in support of them. I know nothing personally about it. As to my own horses, they were stolen from a farm about thirty-five miles below the Yankton agency. I was not at the farm at the time they were stolen, but I procured the testimony of witnesses who were there at the time as to their being stolen by the Indians, and that evidence was submitted by Doctor Burleigh to the Commissioner of Indian Affairs, and it was ordered paid by the Commissioner. The horses were worth the four hundred dollars. I was offered that for them. I received the four hundred dollars, paying no part thereof to either Doctor Burleigh, the Commissioner of Indian Affairs, or any other parties.

Ninth question. Had Agent Burleigh any interest with you in your store at the Yankton agency, or the profits thereof?

Ninth answer. On the 9th of March, 1862, I purchased the stock of goods at the Yankton agency of A. J. Faulk, for which I paid him $6,000, and Doctor Burleigh and Faulk both stated to me that Doctor Burleigh had no interest in the store and goods whatever. I conducted the business on my own account.

Tenth question. What do you know about a soldier being employed in the blacksmith shop in the winter of 1864 and 1865, and how paid?

Tenth answer. I know that Timothy Prindle worked in the shop at that time while Thompson, the regular blacksmith, was east, and he was paid the same as any other blacksmith.

Eleventh question. State what, if anything, you know about Burleigh selling the Indian goods to traders and others; and if to any one, state to whom, and when, and the quantity.

Eleventh answer. I never knew of his doing anything of the kind.

Twelfth question. Did Burleigh ever sell or put into your store Indian goods to be sold?

Twelfth answer. In a few instances he exchanged dry goods (in small quantities) for provisions which they needed more than the dry goods; and when Doctor Burleigh stated that he had no provisions for the Indians and no money to buy provisions, such exchanges were made just as I would make exchanges with any other parties.

Thirteenth question. State by what authority you cut hay on the reservation and sold to the United States.

Thirteenth answer. I have at all times when I have cut hay on the agency obtained permission from the agent, and always cut on ground that was never used or required for the agency or the Indians, and I always have paid them one dollar per ton for all that I cut. The money I paid to the agent, and he paid it to the chiefs. I bought the grass standing and cut it at my own expense. If I had not cut it it would have been burned off.

Fourteenth question. State how long you resided at the Yankton agency, and what you know about schools being kept for the Indian children.

Fourteenth answer. I first went to the Yankton agency, Dakota Territory, in the spring of 1862, and remained there most of my time up to the close of Agent Burleigh's term of office as agent for the Yankton Sioux Indians. I am and have been familiar with the management of the affairs of that agency. In reference to the schools which have been in operation there, I know that Agent Burleigh employed two female teachers at the agency from time to time. That at one time he purchased some three hundred dollars' worth of different kinds of prints, linseys, flannels, needles, thread, &c., for the purpose of having the Indian girls instructed in sewing and learning them to make their own clothing, &c. Also, that had the Indian children been disposed to attend school, they could have done so. The difficulty in teaching or keeping school at the Yankton agency is to induce Indian children to attend the school. They will not submit to the necessary confinement and have no application, and their parents have always discouraged them from doing so. The Indians generally expressed themselves satisfied with Agent Burleigh's management of affairs with the exception of individual cases.

CHARLES E. HEDGES.

Pay-roll of employés.

We, the undersigned, employés of the Yankton Indian agency, acknowledge to have received from W. A. Burleigh, United States Yankton agent, the sums set opposite our respective names, in full of our services for the fourth quarter of 1864, ending with the 31st day of December, 1864.

No.	Names.	Employment	Commenced service.	Quarterly pay.	Annual pay.	Date of discharge.	Total paid.	Signatures.	Witness.
1	John H. Burleigh	Farmer and physician	Oct. 1, 1864	$200 00	$800 00	Dec. 31	$200 00	John H. Burleigh.	
2	Timothy Prindle	Blacksmith	do	215 00	860 00	do	215 00	T. H. Prindle.	
3	John Mechling	Tin and coppersmith	do	215 00	860 00		215 00	John Mechling.	
4	Prescott Follansbee	Carpenter	do	215 00	860 00	do	215 00	P. Follansbee.	
5	Jer'h Protean	Laborer	do	*40 00			120 00	Jer'h his × mark Protean	Chas. E. Hedges.
6	T. B. Burleigh	do	do	*40 00			120 00	T. B. Burleigh.	
7	John Ponca	do	do	*40 00			120 00	John his × mark Ponca	Chas. E. Hedges.
							1,205 00		

* Per month.

I certify, on honor, that the above account is correct and just, and that I have actually, this 31st day of December, 1864, paid the amount thereof.

W. A. BURLEIGH, *United States Yankton Agent.*

EXECUTIVE OFFICE, *Yankton, D. T.*, *May* 19, 1865.

SIR: In compliance with instructions contained in a letter of the honorable Commissioner of Indian Affairs, under date of March 24, last. copy of extract of which is as follows, viz: "and give him (you) the necessary instructions in regard to the duties of his office," &c., I have the honor, herewith, to present you with such instructions as are deemed necessary for your guidance at the present time, reserving the right to alter or change them from time to time, as the exigencies of the case may require, or the interest of the government or Indians may seem to indicate.

1. You will obtain from Major Burleigh as thorough a knowledge of the condition and management at the agency, and disposition and habits of the Indians under your charge, as possible.

2. You will hold all employés to strict accountability as to the employment of their time, and the work accomplished by them, and keep a full and accurate account of the time of each, and see that no persons are needlessly employed, but only such as are absolutely necessary to carry on the current business of the agency.

3. In all cases when possible to do so, you will encourage the employment of Indians in agricultural pursuits, allowing them in each case a reasonable compensation therefor in proportion to the amount of time they are thus employed, their usefulness, &c., calling ten hours a day's work.

4. You will, upon perfecting the reorganization at the agency under your charge, report to this office the names of all persons employed by you, in what capacity, their compensation, and the time of their entering upon the discharge of their duties; also such changes in your working force, from time to time, as you may see fit to make.

5. Leave of absence will not be granted to employés, except for the most urgent and satisfactory reasons, and in all such cases deductions of salary will be made for such absence.

6. You will not allow disorderly or dissolute persons to stay at the agency, as it is deemed far better to send such persons away at once, than to allow them to stay only to create dissensions and trouble among the Indians.

7. You will permit no intoxicating liquor to be brought, kept, sold, or given away on the reservation. It will be your duty, and you are clothed with ample authority, to destroy all such liquor at once

8. You will advise fully with this office at all times on the subject of the current business at the agency, and make requisitions for such funds as you deem necessary to carry on the business, giving reasons or stating the necessity for such application.

I am, sir, very respectfully, your obedient servant,

NEWTON EDMUNDS,

Governor and ex officio Supt. Indian Affairs.

Major P. H. CONGER,

U. S. Indian Agent, Yankton Agency.

DAKOTA TERRITORY, EXECUTIVE OFFICE,

Yankton, May 2, 1865.

SIR: Since writing you on the 17th ultimo on the subject of seeds for the Yankton Indians, I have visited that agency, and found that no preparation had been made towards preparing the ground on that reservation for spring crops. I was there ten days ago; went up with Agent Burleigh, who had just returned from Washington.

I requested Dr. Burleigh at once to set some teams at work ploughing the ground and preparing it for the Indians to crop.

I found no teams at the agency in condition for business; indeed, the Indians (with the exception of their head chief) have no teams fit for work. Under these circumstances, I requested Doctor Burleigh to put his own teams at work for them until some other arrangement could be made, which I suppose he has done.

The past winter has been very severe when the Yanktons were on their winter hunt, and the result is, they lost (as I am credibly informed) one hundred and sixty-five head of horses and several yokes of oxen. In consequence of this loss I deem it absolutely necessary that some purchases of working oxen should be at once made for them.

Agent Conger seems powerless under these circumstances to place affairs at that agency in a condition satisfactory to the Indians, or even himself, and must of necessity find himself embarrassed until relieved by a remittance of funds to cover his current expenditures, which must be quite heavy for the next month or two. The Indians, also, have very little upon which to subsist while their crops are growing.

I beg leave, therefore, to request that a remittance be made to the undersigned to relieve him from present embarrassment, and enable him to transact the current business of the agency for the next three months; and I cannot see how he can get along short of twelve or fifteen thousand dollars, to be used in the purchase of provisions for the Indians, teams, (oxen,) beef, corn, and payment of employés, say, for the next three months.

I would at the same time feel greatly obliged for such suggestions as may occur to you in relation to the expenditure of the funds asked for.

I am, sir, very respectfully, your obedient servant,

NEWTON EDMUNDS,
Governor and ex officio Supt Indian Affairs.

Hon WM. P. DOLE,
Commissioner Indian Affairs, Washington, D. C.

YANKTON SIOUX AGENCY, DAKOTA TERRITORY,
Greenwood, July 15, 1865.

SIR: In compliance with your instructions under date of July 11, 1865, to make a full report of the condition of my agency at the time I entered upon the duties of my office, I have the honor to report: That I arrived here on the first of May, and found Mr. Burleigh (the late agent) awaiting my arrival and ready to surrender to me, as his successor, the charge of the Indians, which he did on the day of my arrival. Some days, however, elapsed before he delivered to me the papers, &c., belonging to the office, he requiring some time to arrange and close his accounts.

I regret, sir, that I am compelled to state that I found the condition of things not very satisfactory. The buildings are miserable, and in a dilapidated condition, the fences badly out of repair, and little or no preparation made to raise a crop the coming season. I found no teams, (except one span of old and very small mules, which were worthless,) and no cattle or stock of any kind that belonged to the agency; and in the various mechanical shops belonging to the agency the same condition of things existed; the tools that had belonged to the same, the most of them, had been broken or lost, so that, sir, I found myself in rather a poor condition to commence operations.

However, I set to work, hired some ploughing done, (by paying what seemed to me an enormous price,) and succeeded in getting some two hundred acres of corn planted in tolerable season; but most of the seed proved bad, and we had to replant; so, with bad seed and the grasshoppers together, we have succeeded in raising only a few scattering acres of tolerable corn; I should judge in all from twenty to twenty-five acres.

I find the Indians docile and friendly, but from what observations I have made, my opinion is that they are the most indolent and improvident race of people on the earth; indeed, it is counted a disgrace with them to labor, and none of them seldom do, except the squaws or a few of the old men. The young men spend their time (when not out on a hunt) in lounging about in the most comfortable places they can find, telling stories and smoking their pipes, and without one day's provisions for themselves and families in advance. They are as happy and as contented as lords, provided always they have for the *present* their own bellies filled.

As to schools for the Indians, I find none in operation, and I am assured by them that there never has been any school organized or kept for them on this reservation. There is no building here for that purpose, and none that is in any way suitable, or that could be spared, for that use; and, sir, while upon this subject, I beg leave to call your attention, and also the attention of the department at Washington. to article four and section four of the treaty between the United States and the Yankton tribe of Sioux or Dacotah Indians, in which the United States stipulate and agree to expend the sum of ten thousand dollars, (over and beside the regular annuities,) in erecting a suitable building or buildings to establish and maintain one or more normal labor schools for the instruction and benefit of the said Indians.

The head chief of this nation and one of the parties to the treaty has repeatedly complained to me since my arrival, and says his Great Father has not kept his word with him, for he promised him when he signed the treaty and sold his lands to the United States, that he should have a school-house, and teachers to learn his children to read and write and to do all kinds of business like the white man. I would suggest that the *present* is a most auspicious time to commence in this matter, and with your permission I will ask leave to submit a plan and estimate (at an early day) for a school-house to be built next summer.

I am requested also to report the number of missionaries or religious instructors among these Indians. As with the schools, I have to report, none; and I understand that there never has been any that made a permanent stay among them. I have had conversation with a number of the chiefs and headmen on the subject, and they all express a desire to have a priest come and live with them. They are strongly prejudiced in favor of the Catholic religion, and I think it very doubtful whether they would consent to receive any other; I am certain a good Catholic would be capable of exercising more influence over them than any other could hope to do for a long time. I have promised the chiefs that I will ask Bishop Smythe, of Dubuque, to send them a priest.

I am also invited to make any suggestion I may deem proper in reference to the government and management of the Indians, with a view to their advancement in the arts of civilization. My brief experience hardly qualifies me to offer advice; yet were I to do so it would be, to strictly observe all treaty obligations, and teach by example, as well as precept, that it is the desire of the government to benefit and not to oppress the Indians. I am of the opinion that the present Indian system, if properly administered, is as good as can be devised; at least, the Indians say that, let their agent be as bad as he may, they would still prefer him to the military.

It is not possible for me at this time to furnish you with the census of the tribe, as nearly all of them are now on the plains hunting buffalo, and will not return to the reservation before about the first of October, when I expect the most of them will be present to receive their fall supplies; when I propose to make an accurate enumeration, as required in your instructions.

Trusting, sir, that you may receive this hasty and imperfect report, and excuse me for this time. I have the honor to subscribe myself,

Very respectfully, your obedient servant,

P. H. CONGER, *United States Yankton Agent.*

Hon. NEWTON EDMUNDS,
Governor and ex officio Supt. Indian Affairs.

DAKOTA TERRITORY, EXECUTIVE OFFICE,
Yankton, August 7, 1865.

SIR: I have the honor to enclose, herewith, special report of P. H. Conger, esq., United States Indian agent of the Yankton Sioux Indians, together with his letter of transmittal to this office. It has been a subject of much regret that greater effort was not made to get into the ground a much larger crop for these Indians, as the season has been most auspicious, for corn especially. Their neighbors, the Poncás, (only ten miles distant,) will, I think, have from six to eight thousand bushels of corn, several hundred bushels potatoes, and a large quantity of squashes, pumpkins, turnips, &c.

The Yankton agency never having been under my charge until Major Conger's appointment, I felt great delicacy in urging upon their former agent the necessity of prompt and vigorous action in farming operations, by way of making ample provision for the subsistence of this tribe the coming season. I however requested him to make every effort to prepare the land under cultivation for cropping, and he told me he would do so; and I supposed the work was going on until after Major Conger's arrival, who informed me that no ground had yet been prepared.

I cannot fully agree with Major Conger in reference to all these Indians. Some of them are willing and ready to work, and with proper encouragement the number may, in my opinion, be vastly increased, greatly to the advantage of individuals, and the general welfare of the whole, as a nation. With this object in view, I instructed Major Conger on entering upon his duties, to encourage the employment of Indians in agricultural pursuits, allowing them compensation therefor, &c.; indeed, this has been done at other agencies with marked results favorable to a continuance of the policy.

Whether this course has been pursued by him or not I am unable to state, as he has not as yet seen fit to report the names of his employés to this office. I trust, however, that every effort will be made to advance not only these, but all Indians who are settled upon reservations, in agricultural and mechanical pursuits, with the view of placing them, at no distant day, in a condition to support themselves.

The chiefs profess, in my interviews with them, to desire this, and I doubt not, if met with a proper spirit on the part of agents, it will prove most advantageous to the various tribes. In adopting this policy of encouraging Indians to work, I find more or less opposition to encounter, as it is thought to prejudice the interests of some white persons who might otherwise find employment at the various agencies; but if the plan meets your approval, I shall continue it, hoping that good may be the result.

I am, sir, very respectfully, your obedient servant,

NEWTON EDMUNDS,
Governor and ex officio Supt. Indian Affairs

Hon. D. N. COOLEY,
Commissioner of Indian Affairs, Washington, D. C.

[Muster-roll omitted.]

USHER'S LANDING, *June* 8, 1863.

I do hereby certify that the Winnebago Indians included in the foregoing muster-roll were started from their tale reservation on the 6th day of May, 1863; that they were accompanied thence to their reservation near Fort Randall, on the Missouri river, by me; and that they were provided with sufficient food of a good quality, and otherwise suitably cared for by the contractors while *en route*.

J. R CLEVELAND,
Special Agent to accompany Winnebagoes.

USHER'S LANDING, *June* 8, 1863.

I certify, on honor, that the foregoing muster-roll of first party of Winnebago Indians removed by P. Chouteau, jr., & Co., under their contract dated St Louis, Missouri, April 16, 1863, is correct, and that the said Indians were delivered to me on their reservation near Fort Randall, on the Missouri river, on the 8th day of June, 1863; that they were accompanied by —— Cleveland, special agent, and twenty-one United States soldiers, and that the above-named contractors are entitled to compensation, for transporting and subsisting —— hundred —— Indians, and for transporting twenty-one soldiers, as stipulated in contract above referred to.

CLARK W. THOMPSON,
Superintendent Indian Affairs.

USHER'S LANDING, *June* 8, 1863.

I do hereby certify that the Winnebago Indians included in the foregoing muster-roll were started from their late reservation on the 8th day of May, 1863; that they were accompanied thence to their reservation near Fort Randall, on the Missouri river, by me; and that they were provided with sufficient food of a good quality, and otherwise suitably cared for by the contractors, *en route*. I also certify, that said contractors transported, exclusive of one hundred pounds to each Indian, nineteen thousand six hundred and seventy-one (19,671) pounds of freight from the late reservation near Mankato to reservation near Fort Randall, on the Missouri river.

J. C. RAMSEY,
Special Agent to accompany Winnebagoes.

USHER'S LANDING, *June* 8, 1863.

I certify, on honor, that the foregoing muster-roll of second party of Winnebago Indians removed by P. Chouteau, jr., & Co., under their contract dated St. Louis, Missouri, April 16, 1863, is correct, and that the said Indians and freight were delivered to me on their reservation near Fort Randall, on the Missouri river, on the 8th day of June, 1863; that they were accompanied by J. C. Ramsey, special agent, and twenty United States soldiers, and that the above-named contractors are entitled to compensation for transporting nineteen thousand six hundred and seventy-one (19,671) pounds of freight and twenty United States soldiers, and for transporting and subsisting four hundred and —— Indians, according to terms of contract above referred to.

CLARK W. THOMPSON,
Superintendent Indian Affairs.

[Muster-roll omitted.]

USHER'S LANDING, *June* 24, 1863.

I do hereby certify that the Winnebago Indians included in the foregoing muster-roll were started from their late reservation on the 11th day of May, 1863; that they were accompanied thence to their reservation near Fort Randall, on the Missouri river, by me; and that they were furnished with sufficient food of a good quality, and otherwise suitably cared for by the contractors while *en route*. I also certify, that said contractors transported, exclusive of one hundred pounds to each Indian, twenty-eight thousand four hundred and eighty (28,480) pounds of freight from the late reservation near Mankato to present reservation near Fort Randall, on the Missouri river.

CHARLES K. WINNE,
Special Agent to accompany Winnebagoes.

USHER'S LANDING, *June* 24, 1863.

I certify, on honor, that the foregoing muster-roll of third party of Winnebago Indians removed by P. Chouteau, jr., & Co., under their contract dated St. Louis, Missouri, April 16, 1863, is correct, and that the said Indians and freight were delivered to me on their reservation near Fort Randall, on the Missouri river, on the 24th day of June, 1863; that they were accompanied by C. K. Winne, special agent, one officer and thirty-nine soldiers; and that the above-named contractors are entitled to compensation for transporting twenty-eight thousand four hundred and eighty (28,480) pounds of freight, one officer and thirty-nine soldiers; and for transporting and subsisting eight hundred and —— Indians, according to terms of contract above referred to.

CLARK W. THOMPSON,
Superintendent Indian Affairs.

The UNITED STATES to P. CHOUTEAU, Jr., & Co., DR.

1863.	For transportation of guard accompanying Winnebago and Sioux Indians from St. Paul to Usher's Landing, viz: 4 commissioned officers, 135 soldiers and 1 laundress; 140 persons at $25	$3,500

Received, at Chicago, August 31, 1863, of Clark W. Thompson, superintendent of Indian affairs, three thousand five hundred dollars in full of this account.
$3,500.

P. CHOUTEAU, JR., & CO.

[Triplicates.]

I certify, on honor, that the above account is correct and just, and that I have actually, this 31st day of August, 1863, paid the amount thereof.

CLARK W. THOMPSON,
Superintendent Indian Affairs.

The UNITED STATES to P. CHOUTEAU, Jr., & Co., DR.

1863.	For transporting for the Winnebago Indians extra freight from Mankato to Usher's Landing, 48,151 pounds extra freight, at $3 26	$1,569 72
	For transporting sixty-two horses from Winnebago agency to Usher's Landing, at $15 per head	930 00
		2,499 72

Received, at Chicago, August 31, 1863, of Clark W. Thompson, superintendent Indian affairs, twenty-four hundred and ninety-nine and $\frac{72}{100}$ dollars, in full of this account.
$2,499 72.

P. CHOUTEAU, JR., & CO.

[Triplicates.]

I certify, on honor, that the above account is correct and just, and that I have actually, this 31st day of August, 1863, paid the amount thereof.

CLARK W. THOMPSON,
Superintendent Indian Affairs.

THE UNITED STATES to P. CHOUTEAU, Jr., & Co., DR.

1863.	For removing and subsisting Sioux Indians as per contract dated 16th of April, 1863, 1,318 Sioux Indians, at $25 per head	$32,950 00
	771 Indians subsisted 26 days, at 10 cents per day	2,004 60
	547 Indians subsisted 25 days, at 10 cents per day	1,367 50
		36,322 10

Received, at Chicago, August 31, 1863, of Clark W. Thompson, superintendent Indian affairs, thirty-six thousand three hundred and twenty-two and $\frac{10}{100}$ dollars, in full of this account.
$36,322 10.

P. CHOUTEAU, JR., & CO.

[Triplicates.]

I certify, on honor, that the above account is correct and just, and that I have actually, this 31st day of August, 1863, paid the amount thereof.

CLARK W. THOMPSON,
Superintendent Indian Affairs.

The UNITED STATES to P. CHOUTEAU, Jr., & Co., DR.

1863.	For removing and subsisting Winnebago Indians as per contract dated 16th day of April, 1863, 1,945 Winnebago Indians, at $25 per head	$48,625 00
	703 Indians subsisted 34 days, at 10 cents per day	2,390 20
	432 Indians subsisted 32 days, at 10 cents per day	1,382 40
	810 Indians subsisted 45 days, at 10 cents per day	3,645 00
		56,042 60

Received, at Chicago, August 31, 1863, of Clark W. Thompson, superintendent of Indian affairs, fifty six thousand and forty-two $\frac{60}{100}$ dollars, in full of this account.
$56,042 60.

P. CHOUTEAU, JR., & CO.

[Triplicates.]

I certify, on honor, that the above account is correct and just, and that I have actually, this 31st day of August, 1863, paid the amount thereof.

CLARK W. THOMPSON,
Superintendent Indian Affairs.

The UNITED STATES to F. D. PEASE, DR.

1864.		
Sept. 30.	To my claim against the Yankton Sioux Indians, for depredations committed upon my property, as per claim submitted and allowed by the Commissioner of Indian Affairs	$2,571 00

Received, at Yankton agency, September 30, 1864, of W. A. Burleigh, United States Yankton agent, twenty-five hundred and seventy-one dollars, in full of the above account.
$2,571 00.

J. D. PEASE.

[Triplicates.]

I certify, on honor, that the above account is correct and just, and that I have actually, this 30th day of September, 1864, paid the amount thereof.

W. A. BURLEIGH,
U. S. Yankton Agent.

The UNITED STATES to W. A. DEMPSEY, DR.

1864.		
Sept. 30.	To my claim against the Yankton Sioux Indians for depredations committed upon my property, as per claim submitted and allowed by the Commissioner of Indian Affairs	$611 00

Received, at Yankton agency, September 30, 1864, of W. A. Burleigh, United States Yankton agent, six hundred and eleven dollars, in full of the above account.
$611 00.

W. A. DEMPSEY.

[Triplicates.]

I certify, on honor, that the above account is correct and just, and that I have actually, this 30th day of September, 1864, paid the amount thereof.

W. A. BURLEIGH,
U. S. Yankton Agent.

The UNITED STATES to FREDERICK CARMAN, DR.

1864.		
Sept. 30.	To my claim against the Yankton Sioux Indians for depredations committed upon my property, as per claim submitted and allowed by the Commissioner of Indian Affairs	$550 00

Received, at Yankton agency, September 30, 1864, of W. A. Burleigh, United States Yankton agent, five hundred and fifty dollars, in full of the above account.
$550.

F. CARMAN.

[Triplicates.]

I certify, on honor, that the above account is correct and just, and that I have actually, this 30th day of September, 1864, paid the amount thereof.

W. A. BURLEIGH,
U. S. Yankton Agent.

The UNITED STATES to JOHN W. OWENS, DR.

1864.		
Sept. 30.	To my claim against the Yankton Sioux Indians for depredations committed upon my property, as per claim submitted and allowed by the Commissioner of Indian Affairs	$750 00

Received, at Yankton agency, September 30, 1864, of W. A. Burleigh, United States Yankton agent, seven hundred and fifty dollars, in full of the above account.

JOHN W. OWENS.

[Triplicates.]

I certify, on honor, that the above account is correct and just, and that I have actually, this 30th day of September, 1864, paid the amount thereof.

W. A. BURLEIGH,
U. S. Yankton Agent.

The UNITED STATES to CHARLES E. HEDGES, DR.

1864.		
June 10.	For 11,500 pounds bacon, at 15 cents	$1,725 00

Received, at Yankton agency, June 10, 1864, of W. A. Burleigh, United States Yankton agent, seventeen hundred and twenty-five dollars, in full of the above account.
$1,725.

CHARLES E. HEDGES

[Triplicates.]

I certify, on honor, that the above account is correct and just, and that I have actually, this 10th day of June, 1864, paid the amount thereof.

W. A. BURLEIGH,
U. S. Yankton Agent.

The UNITED STATES to CHARLES E. HEDGES, DR.

1864.		
Nov. 30.	For 80 yards linsey, at 80 cents	$64 00
	For 75 yards red flannel, at 85 cents	63 75
	For 60 yards cassimere, at $1 75	105 00
	For 151 boys' coats, at $6	90 00
	For 30 2½-point white Mackinac blankets, at $9	270 00
	For 30 2-point white Mackinac blankets, at $8	240 00
	For 20 sacks flour, at $10	200 00
	For 500 pounds bacon, at 20 cents	100 00
		1,132 75

Received, at Yankton agency, November 30, 1864, of W. A. Burleigh, United States Yankton agent, eleven hundred and thirty-two and $\frac{75}{100}$ dollars, in full of the above account.

CHARLES E. HEDGES.

[Triplicates]

I certify, on honor, that the above account is correct and just, and that I have actually, this 30th day of November, 1864, paid the amount thereof.

W. A. BURLEIGH,
U. S. Yankton Agent.

The UNITED STATES to D. T. HEDGES, DR.

1864.		
March 19.	400 bushels corn, at $2	$800 00
	200 bushels seed corn, at $2 50	500 00
		1,300 00

Received, at Yankton agency, March 18, 1864, of W. A. Burleigh, United States Yankton agent, thirteen hundred dollars, in full of the above account.

D. T. HEDGES.

[Triplicates.]

I certify, on honor, that the above account is correct and just, and that I have actually, this 18th day of March, 1864, paid the amount thereof.

W. A. BURLEIGH,
U. S. Yankton Agent.

The UNITED STATES to ELLIS W. WALL, DR.

1864.		
Sept. 30.	To my claim against the Yankton Sioux Indians for depredations committed upon my property, as per claim submitted and allowed by the Commissioner of Indian Affairs	$1,313 75

Received, at Yankton agency, September 30, 1864, of W. A. Burleigh, United States Yankton agent, thirteen hundred and thirteen $\frac{75}{100}$ dollars, in full of the above account.
$1,313 75.

E. W. WALL.

[Triplicates]

I certify, on honor, that the above account is correct and just, and that I have actually, this 30th day of September, 1864, paid the amount thereof.

W. A. BURLEIGH,
U. S. Yankton Agent.

The UNITED STATES to W. A. BURLEIGH, DR.

1865.		
April 30.	For 1 gray horse	$200 00
	For 1 gray horse	125 00
	For 1 roan horse	125 00
	For 2 bay horses	200 00
		650 00

The above horses were stolen by the Yankton Indians on the 13th day of September, 1864. Ordered to be paid by Commissioner of Indian Affairs.

Received, at Yankton agency, April 30, 1865, of W. A. Burleigh, United States Yankton agent, six hundred and fifty dollars, in full of the above account.
$650.

W. A. BURLEIGH.

[Triplicates.]

I certify, on honor, that the above account is correct and just, and that I have actually, this 30th day of April, 1865, paid the amount thereof.

W. A. BURLEIGH,
U. S. Yankton Agent.

TERRITORY OF DAKOTA, *Charles Mix County, ss:*

Before the subscriber, a notary public in and for said county, personally came John W. Owens, who, having been duly sworn according to law, deposeth and saith, that he resides on the farm of W. A Burleigh, in Bonhomme county, Territory aforesaid; that on the 14th day of September last three Indians of the Yanktonais bands, believed to be from the district lodges on the James river, came to the premises aforementioned and stole away therefrom the following property, viz:

Two gray horses, belonging to C. E. Hedges, of the value of four hundred dollars. Five horses belonging to W. A. Burleigh, viz: One gray horse of the value of two hundred dollars; one grey horse of the value of one hundred and twenty-five dollars; one roan horse of the value of one hundred and twenty-five dollars; two bay horses of the value of two hundred dollars.

Deponent further saith, that he knows that said Indians belong to a band of Yanktonais residing in the district lodges on the James river. Deponent further saith, that the above-mentioned horses were of the actual value named, to wit, one thousand and fifty dollars, and that none of them have been returned to said farm or to their owners to the best of his knowledge or belief.

JOHN W. OWENS.

[SEAL] Sworn and subscribed at my office, in the county aforesaid, this 21st day of November, 1863.

JOHN MECHLING.

Testimony of George D. Hill.

Question. State whether you are acquainted with Major Burleigh and with his manner of dealing with his Indians at the Yankton agency while acting as agent of said Indians. Also, generally, what you know about schools being kept at such agency, and the general management of the affairs of said agency.

Answer. I have acted as surveyor general of Dakota Territory since 1861; that my office is located at Yankton, about sixty miles below the said Yankton Indian agency; that I have known Major Burleigh since the summer of 1861, and have frequently visited the said agency; that I once visited said agency with Governor Jayne, then Governor of Dakota Territory, for the purpose of examining into the management of the said Burleigh as agent, Governor Jayne being superintendent of Indian affairs for that Territory at the time; that we stayed several days and examined thoroughly into the condition of the Indians and the management of the said Burleigh, Indian agent, and became satisfied that the affairs of the said agency were conducted with unusual discretion and judgment, under very many difficulties, interposed by men who had formerly been connected with said agency. I have been present at the payment of said Indians, know several of the chiefs personally, and have always, when at the said agency, been impressed with the general good order, regularity, and satisfaction which seemed to prevail among the Indians. These Indians, during the administration of Dr. Burleigh and during the panic prevailing upon the frontier subsequent to the Minnesota massacre, for a long time, have always been friendly and have acted as protection to the settlers below from the hostile Indians above, and the people of Dakota are largely indebted to the said Agent Burleigh for the energy and ability he displayed in organizing such protection and keeping his Indians quiet and friendly to the whites during this period, notwithstanding the war then prevailing which disturbed greatly the relations of the government with the Indians, and the loss of the crops upon said agency in consequence of the great drought and influx of grasshoppers and locusts which entirely destroyed all the crops in that country for two seasons.

In regard to the existence of schools upon said agency, I would state that I conversed with the teachers while at the agency, who informed me they were teaching all who would attend school, and that upon one occasion I visited the school with Dr. Barrett, then acting as teacher; that the teachers expressed great regret at the indifference manifested by the parents in regard to the education of the children. I would further state that, in my opinion and to my knowledge, the general management of said agency by Major Burleigh has been good, vigorous, and faithful, and that I have heard the leading Indians admit this since he left the agency; and further say not.

GEORGE D. HILL.

PONCA INDIANS.

PONCA INDIAN AGENCY, *August* 31, 1865.

Iron Whip spoke as follows:

I think my Great Father sent you to see my condition. I will tell you all about it. When I first went to Washington my Great Father told me I must work; I should have houses. I have never been able to raise anything here until this season. Last winter he gave us our old place where we used to be, and we like it better. This place you see is a pretty place, but wood is scarce. In the winter it kills our women to get wood. We have no horses, and we want to go to our old place We don't like to lose our houses here. They are good; but we think if we had teams we could move them. The houses here are of no use to us. We rather be on the bank of the river, where we can fish and we can see the boats, and our goods can come there and we can see them. Some of the boxes of goods may be opened before we see them, and if we are at our old place we can see the boxes. Sometimes there is not calico enough to give us a yard apiece. Our Great Father gave us a mill, but there is no one to run it and none of us have been learned to work in it, and there is no one to learn us. I have got a blacksmith shop and carpenter's shop, but there is no one to learn us to work and none of us have been learned. Here is this house; it is of but little use to us. We were to have a school-house here and be learned to read and write, but there has been no one to teach us. We can count money pretty well, and we rather have our annuities paid to us in money rather than in goods. If we have money we can buy our own goods. Last year our annuities—our money—were expended in provisions. This year we have raised a crop, and it will not be necessary to spend our annuity for provisions, and we would like to have it in money. I think our Father spends a great deal of money to build these houses and for workmen; spends a great deal of money to support this country. Father, I don't see any other way to make a living than to do as white folks do. I would like to be white folks. I see white folks have teams, and they haul everything they want to and do whatever they want to, and I would like to do so. This is a very good place, but it is very much better on the Ponca bottom; plenty of wood there; and if the agency cannot put as much buildings there as there are here, still we rather go there if they cannot put half as much. Father, there is another thing I want to speak of to you. Two men on the Ponca bottom have claims there and two on the point, and they have been making much money there cutting wood. Since the government has given them that land we have offered them four hundred dollars apiece for their claims, but they want a thousand dollars We cannot give that, but we can have the balance, and those white men may stay there on their claims; they may stay if they can. Father, this building—it makes me feel bad; it hurts my feelings to leave it; but if we move down on the bottom we might get some one to protect it for us so that hostile Indians can't burn it up. Indians sometimes come in and kill our old people, and if we left it unprotected those Indians might come in and destroy it. You see our field here; it is right close here. When our women take the hoe and go to the field the hostile Indians lay in wait and kill them right before our eyes. Many Indians in the field, but we had no guns. They killed two this spring. But I wait and see what my Great Father will do. He said he would protect me. Father, about ten days ago we were hungry and wanted something to eat, and we send out our young men to hunt and get us something to eat, and when they got out about one hundred miles the Indians kill two of our young men right off, and they come back without anything. We cannot go out without being killed. I went down to Washington again last winter. All the tribes around me whip me, kill my people, and also kill whites about me. I went down last winter. My Great Father tell me he fix me and give me fifteen thousand dollars to fix me up if the Indians kill me, and wait patiently to see what my Great Father do for me. I don't war, but take my Great Father's advice and keep peaceable. Here is my first neighbor here. When I went down to Washington my Great Father made me shake hands with them and be neighbors and keep peace, but they steal five of our horses; don't know whether they will pay or not, but I still keep peace with them as my Father told me. The Pawnees keep peace with us. All the Indians have a bad name, doing bad, but I believe we have not a bad name. I try to keep my young men in and keep them from going to war and keep them peaceable. If you want to hear everything, I will tell you that my Great Father told me last winter to keep the peace, and I have lost four people since, having been killed by the hostile Indians, and have had six horses stolen by the Indians. Another thing: you know every place where the people stay we have a trader, and we think they have our interpreter to trade for them. We wish they would let our interpreter alone. As soon as we gather up our corn we would like to have some soldiers go out with us to hunt, and we would like to have some soldiers to protect us while we harvest the upper end of our field of corn. All our agents have treated us well. Our present agent is a new one and we don't know what he will do.

Hard Walker spoke as follows:

All what the chief (Whip) told you is true. I hope and wish you to assist me all you can, when you get to Washington, about these things. When I was down there I left some things there. I want to know what word the Great Father has sent us. What the old chief said about all our Indians wanting to move to Ponca bottom is true. We want to go there. I wish you would say something to our trader. He sells very high. It almost makes me cry. I wish you to advise him to sell cheaper.

FORT RANDALL, DAKOTA, *September* 2, 1865.

DAKOTA TERRITORY, *County of Todd:*

Samuel C. Haynes, of lawful age, being duly sworn, deposed as follows:

First question. What is your name, residence, and occupation?

First answer. My name is Samuel C. Haynes, and I reside at Bradford, Chickasaw county, Iowa. I am assistant surgeon of the 6th regiment Iowa volunteer cavalry.

Second question. State whether, in the winter of 1863 and 1864, you were stationed at the Crow Creek Indian agency, Dakota Territory.

Second answer. I was.

Third question. State the manner in which the Winnebago and Santee Indians were fed at that agency at that time.

Third answer. When I first went there rations of beef and flour were issued to them once a week, and I think some few beans were issued to them, but no sugar and coffee; the rations were not issued in sufficient quantities to subsist them. Some time about the middle of the winter a large vat was constructed, of cottonwood lumber, about six feet square and six feet deep, in connexion with the steam saw-mill, with a pipe leading from the boiler into the vat. Into the vat was thrown beef, beef heads, entrails of the beeves, some beans, flour, and pork. I think there was put into the vat two barrels of flour each time, which was not oftener than once in twenty-four hours. This mass was then cooked by the steam from the boiler passing through the pipe into the vat. When that was done, all the Indians were ordered to come there with their pails and get it. It was dipped out to the Indians with a long-handled dipper made for the purpose. I cannot say the quantity given to each. It was of about the consistency of very thin gruel. The Indians would pour off the thinner portion and eat that which settled at the bottom. As it was dipped out of the vat some of the Indians would get the thinner portions and some would get some meat. I passed there frequently when it was cooking, and was often there when it was being issued, and it had a very offensive odor; it had the odor of the contents of the entrails of the beeves. I have seen the settlings of the vat after they were through issuing it to the Indians, when they were cleaning it out, and the settlings smelt like carrion—like decomposed meat. The Santees and Winnebagoes were fed from this vat; some of the Indians refused to eat it, saying they could not eat it, it made them sick The Winnebagoes protested against such filthy cooking, and said they could not eat it; they told the agent that it was only fit for hogs, and they were not hogs they said. They were fed in this way about a month. From an estimate I made from information derived from the persons who issued the food through the winter to the Indians there, the quantity of food issued to them per day did not exceed eight ounces per head for man, woman, and child. The great part of the cattle slaughtered for the Indians were very poor; occasionally one would be tolerable beef; a large number of them were cattle that came through from Mankato, Minnesota, and hauled goods, some portion of them for the agency and some for the traders, Hawley & Hubbell; they arrived at the agency in November or December, and some of the cattle were worked at the agency before being slaughtered, and became so poor that they reeled as they walked, and were then slaughtered for the Indians. I understood that corn, belonging to the Winnebagoes, left at their old agency in Minnesota, was started with the train and fed out upon the way to the cattle and horses of the train; after the train arrived at Crow Creek agency I saw some traces of the corn in the wagons. My knowledge in regard to the quality of the bacon brought from Minnesota in that train is not very good, but I saw some of it, and it was poor, and some of it I know was not fit to eat. It was piled up in the warehouse in bulk. The flour was very inferior and coarse. The entrails of the beeves thrown into the vat the Indians said were not washed, and I should think by the smell that they were not.

Fourth question. State what you know about Indians being employed to cut wood at the Crow Creek agency, and how they were paid.

Fourth answer. Indians, mostly Winnebagoes, were employed to cut wood for the saw-mill and for fires in the buildings of the agency, and they were paid with provisions taken out of the Indian warehouse.

Fifth question. State whether there was much sickness among the Indians there.

Fifth answer. There was some sickness and a number of deaths. The Indians reported several deaths from starvation; they were constantly begging for something to eat, and I visited the lodges frequently while they were sick and found them destitute of food. The issue of food was generally made on Saturdays, which would generally be all consumed by Monday or Tuesday, and the rest of the week they would be entirely destitute. From what I saw and know, I am satisfied that the representations of Indians as to some of the Indians dying of starvation were true. Towards spring they issued twice a week, but there was no increase of the quantity of the rations or allowance.

Sixth question. State who was at Crow Creek in charge of the Indians when you were there.

Sixth answer. They were principally under the charge of Balcombe.

Seventh question. How long were you there, and in what capacity?

Seventh answer. I was there from October, 1863, until June, 1864, and I was acting as surgeon of the military post there.

Eighth question. What do you know about fresh beef being brought there on the train which came there from Minnesota, as above stated?

Eighth answer. Fresh beef was brought in on the train, and the men with the train told me that some of the oxen gave out and could not travel, and they killed them and brought them in for beef for the Indians. This beef was very poor, bloody, and badly dressed.

Ninth question. What do you know about beef being slaughtered in the winter and piled away in snow in the warehouse?

Ninth answer. Quite a large number of cattle were slaughtered during the winter and put away in the warehouse in snow; and what beef was left until spring spoiled, and the Indians ate it as long as it was possible to eat it, and I think they had to throw away some of it.

Tenth question. State what shifts the Indians resorted to to get something to eat.

Tenth answer. They were destitute of corn, but they would steal from the horses when they could while the horses were being fed by the soldiers; they would pick up the corn left by the horses when fed; they would eat wolves poisoned by the soldiers; they would skin the wolf for the sake of the carcass to eat; they also ate the horses that died through the winter. I mean the horses belonging to the soldiers.

Eleventh question. When rations of soup were issued from the vat were any other rations issued, and how often was soup issued from the vat?

Eleventh answer. No other rations were issued during that time. Soup from the vat was all they had, and I think it was only issued every other day.

S. C. HAYNES,
Assistant Surgeon 6th Iowa Cavalry.

FORT RANDALL, DAKOTA, *September* 2, 1865

TERRITORY OF DAKOTA, *County of Todd:*

Joseph A. Hansell, of lawful age, being duly sworn, deposed as follows :

First question. What is your name, residence, and occupation, and where have you been stationed?

First answer. My name is Joseph A. Hansell; reside at Marion, Linn county, Iowa. My occupation for the past two or three years has been that of a soldier in company K, 6th Iowa cavalry ; am now stationed at Fort Randall. From some time in October, 1863, until in May, 1864, I was stationed at Crow Creek agency.

Second question. State whether, during that time, you had opportunities of seeing the kind and quality of food issued to the Santees and Winnebagoes.

Second answer. I had good opportunities of seeing and knowing about the food issued to them.

Third question. Have you heard the deposition of Doctor Haynes read ; and if so, how does your knowledge and recollection agree with the statements he therein makes in relation to the quantity and quality of the food issued to the Indians at the Crow Creek agency, and the manner of cooking and issuing the same to them?

Third answer. From my knowledge I believe the statements he therein makes are true. From my own personal knowledge I know them to be true.

Fourth question. What do you know about fresh beef being brought there in the train?

Fourth answer. Fresh beef was brought in that train. The men with the train told me it was cattle that gave out and they had to slaughter them, and they had brought them over to feed the Indians, and they put them in the warehouse with the other provisions of the Indians.

Fifth question. What do you know about the cattle slaughtered there for the Indians?

Fifth answer. The cattle slaughtered for the Indians were a hard lot of cattle, poor, and not fit for beef; they were too poor for work cattle. They killed a large number and put them in ricks outside the warehouse until it commenced thawing and smelling, and then they stacked them up in snow in the warehouse.

Sixth question. What provision was made for keeping the cattle through the winter?

Sixth answer. I think no provision was made for that purpose. I saw none, and should have known it if there had been any. After the cattle came there they killed them about as fast as they could, and piled them up in the warehouse in snow. I think there was some over two hundred head of cattle came in in that train.

Seventh question. Do you know of any suffering among the Indians on account of insufficient quantities of food?

Seventh answer. I do; at least I am satisfied that was the case. I know of the Indians eating wolves that had been poisoned by the soldiers, and horses that had died. I also know of their eating mules that died with the glanders; and they picked up and ate the corn scattered about where we fed our horses. I smelt the odor arising from the vat, as described by Doctor Haynes in his deposition. The entrails, head, and feet were thrown into the vat. The flour was third-rate and very poor at that. I think they had no sugar or coffee, and no vegetables excepting a few beans.

Eighth question. What do you know about the Indians being employed and paid?

Eighth answer. They worked about the agency cutting wood, and were paid with provisions out of the warehouse of the Indians.

Ninth question. State what you know about the cattle slaughtered for the Indians being the cattle brought from Minnesota in the train.

Ninth answer. I know they came in with the train from Minnesota, and were hauling the wagons and goods. They were the train.

Tenth question. Please state what you know about there being game in that section of the country?

Tenth answer. I don't think there is any game there of any account. Our boys went out frequently, but never found any of any consequence. The Winnebagoes went out hunting as far as they dared to, but were not successful. It is generally understood not to be a game country.

JOSEPH A. HANSELL.

FORT RANDALL, *September* 2, 1865.

DAKOTA TERRITORY, *Todd county:*

Samuel C. Haynes, of lawful age, being duly sworn, deposed as follows:

First question. What is your name, residence, and occupation?

First answer. Samuel C. Haynes; reside at Bradford, Chickasaw county, Iowa; am a surgeon (assistant) of the 6th regiment Iowa volunteer cavalry.

Second question. Where have you been stationed for the past year?

Second answer. From September, 1864, until the middle of July, 1865, I was stationed as the surgeon at the post at Berthold, Dakota.

Third question. State whether Arickarees, Mandans, and Grovons, (Gros Ventres,) are located there at Berthold?

Third answer. They are. Their village comes up to the fort.

Fourth question. How many of them are there?

Fourth answer. The warriors of the three nations number from five hundred to seven hundred.

Fifth question. How do they subsist?

Fifth answer. On the corn they raise and the buffalo they catch, of which they have an abundant supply. They are weak in strength, compared with the Sioux. They are friendly to the whites. The Sioux are constantly committing depredations upon them; and they are not of sufficient strength to protect themselves from the Sioux, and need the protection of the whites.

Sixth question. What do you think of one company of soldiers being sufficient to protect them?

Sixth answer. I do not think one company, of the usual numbers of our companies, is sufficient. That post is in the heart of the Sioux nation.

Seventh question. What do you think they most need?

Seventh answer. Clothing, and tools to work with; also guns.

Eighth question. When you left this summer, had they received any annuities?

Eighth answer. They had not. There was a small amount of hard bread and flour in store for them at the time I left. They were making considerable complaint because they had not received their annuities, and were becoming considerably uneasy.

S. C. HAYNES,
Assistant Surgeon 6th Iowa Cavalry.

FORT RANDALL, *September* 2, 1865.

TERRITORY OF DAKOTA, *Todd county:*

Asa G. White, being duly sworn, deposed as follows:

First question. What is your name, residence, and occupation, and where have you been stationed?

First answer. My name is Asa G. White; reside at Linn county, Iowa; am a soldier in company K, 6th Iowa cavalry, stationed now at Fort Randall. From October, 1863, until May, 1864, I was stationed at Crow Creek agency, Dakota.

Second question. Have you heard the depositions of Doctor Haynes and Joseph Hansell, and how do you coincide or agree with their statements?

Second answer. From my own knowledge, I am satisfied that their statements are true. The cattle were brought through from Minnesota, hauling goods for the agency and traders, and, after being slaughtered, were first put up in ricks outside the warehouse, where they remained until they became stale and began to thaw, when they were put in the warehouse and packed in snow.

Third question. When the Indians were fed out of the vat, did they receive any other rations?

Third answer. During that time they received no other rations. The Indians complained bitterly of the insufficiency of food; and if they had anything to trade, they preferred food in payment in preference to money. I think the soup was issued as often as every other day; and it may have been issued every day some of the time.

ASA G. WHITE.

CROW CREEK AGENCY, *September* 5, 1865.

TERRITORY OF DAKOTA:

David Faribault, of lawful age, being duly sworn, deposed as follows:

First question. State your name and residence.

First answer. David Faribault; have resided at this (Crow Creek) agency since July, 1863.

Second question. State the condition of the Indians at this agency, as to clothing and provisions, since you have been here.

Second answer. They have suffered much for both clothing and provisions. I am a half-breed myself, and when I first came here I was unknown, and had to live as the Indians did, as I was out of employment. I have a Santee wife. At times they have been two days without anything to eat, especially the women who had no men to provide for them; and most of them were in that condition at first, as less than a hundred men came here with them. In the fall or winter of the same year I came a half-breed woman by the name of Moore starved to death.

Third question. State the kind of flour you got in the winter of 1863 and 1864.

Third answer. It was very coarse, black, and sticky, and so poor that it was almost impossible to make bread of it. I do not mean that all of it was so poor, but a portion of it. The Indians received about a pound per week for each person.

Fourth question. What kind of beef did the Indians get?

Fourth answer. Very poor beef; not much fat about it. They would always select the poorest to give the Indians. If there was a good piece, they would take it and give it to the boarding-house here; and when Balcombe's family were here he selected the best also for them. Some issues the Indians would get nothing but heads, and sometimes nothing but entrails and feet; and if they would not take that, they could not get anything.

Fifth question. Did the Indians receive any pork?

Fifth answer. No pork was issued to the Indians, generally; but sometimes pork was issued to the Indians that worked, in payment for their work, at the rate of three pounds for the dollar.

Sixth question. State whether the condition of the Indians was such that they could go and hunt for a living.

Sixth answer. It was not. They had no guns nor horses, and but few men, and they were unacquainted with the country. When they got guns along in that winter, about 50 in number, they started on a hunt to James river. There were about 500 of them, and but one pony, and that belonged to Mr. Williamson, the missionary. This was about the first of February. They were compelled to pack their wood on their backs as far as the James river, about 60 miles. The reason they went on this hunt was because they were so near starved. One aged woman became exhausted, and they had to leave her about forty miles out. They had no provisions to leave with her, and she has never been seen since. They succeeded in finding some buffalo, and were partially successful in supplying themselves with food. They got out of provisions before they found any buffalo.

Seventh question. Were you here at the time the Indians were supplied with soup? and if so, state the particulars.

Seventh answer. I was; but did not go near it much. I saw some of it, and tried to eat some of it, but could not; the smell was offensive.

Eighth question. State what you know of the supplies of beef and flour last winter.

Eighth answer. The supply was about the same as the year before, in kind and quality.

Ninth question. Do you know of Santee women being pressed so hard with hunger that they prostituted themselves in order to get something to eat?

Ninth answer. I know of many such cases—women who were virtuous before they came here. Others, who had daughters, would sell them for something to eat. I have known the Indians here during the winter eating dead mules and horses and poisoned wolves. Numbers of the women have left the agency and gone to Forts Sully, Randall, Wadsworth, the Yankton agency, and other points, to obtain their living. I think, if they had plenty to subsist on here, they would not leave the agency. They have never raised any crops here until this season, it has been so dry. They have tried to raise crops each season.

Tenth question. How many Santee men are there here now?

Tenth answer. I suppose there are about one hundred men that are able to work, and about nine hundred women and children.

DAVID FARIBAULT.

CROW CREEK AGENCY, TERRITORY OF DAKOTA, *September* 5, 1865.

Examination of F. J. De Witt, Indian trader, as to affairs.

F. J. De Witt, being duly sworn, deposed as follows:

First question. State your name, residence, and occupation.

First answer. F. J. De Witt; reside at Crow Creek agency; am trader at this agency.

Second question. Were you here in the fall of 1863, when Hubbell & Hawley's train came in from Minnesota, and in what condition were the cattle?

Second answer. I was; some of them, probably three-fourths, were in a very good condition.

Third question. State how long they were kept here before they were slaughtered, and the condition in which they were then.

Third answer. About three weeks when they commenced. A part of the cattle from Minnesota went to Sioux City and hauled up a train of wheat before being slaughtered. I think all the cattle that had not been worked were in a good condition; those having been worked were very thin. Some of the cattle that went in the train to Sioux City for wheat, becoming worn down and unable to travel, were slaughtered and brought back for the Indians; that is my impression. I did not see them slaughtered, but have no doubt but that it was so.

Fourth question. What kind of freight was brought from Minnesota in Hubbell & Hawley's train in the fall of 1865?

Fourth answer. Flour and supplies for the agency, and goods for the traders, Hubbell & Hawley.

Fifth question. Do you know who furnished the cattle brought over in that train?

Fifth answer. I understand it was Mr. Hubbell.

Sixth question. Do you know where they were weighed or estimated?

Sixth answer. No; they were not weighed here, to the best of my knowledge. Do not know whether their estimate was made here or not.

Seventh question. State what you know of the condition of the Indians at this agency during the winter of 1863 and 1864.

Seventh answer. They were not comfortably clothed, and I am satisfied that they were not well fed, and that there was some suffering for the want of clothing and food.

Eighth question. Did you see the cattle that were slaughtered here for the winter of 1864 and 1865, and their condition?

Eighth answer. I did; saw the train that came in with the cattle; think I saw them all about the time they were slaughtered. Their condition was very good when they came here, but were kept here so long before they were slaughtered that they became very poor. The reason they were kept so long was, they had to keep them until cold weather in order to keep them; there was no salt to salt them with. Balcombe was very anxious for cold weather to come, in order that he could kill them; the season had been very dry and feed was very scarce; there was no hay here belonging to the agency, but other parties had hay here, which could have been had at a very high price, I think.

Ninth question. How well did the beef keep the past winter?

Ninth answer. It kept very well through the winter, but in May it became so poor that it was not fit to eat.

Tenth question. What was the condition of the Indians at this agency the past winter?

Tenth answer. They had not a sufficiency of clothing, and I am satisfied that they did not have a sufficient amount of food to eat.

Eleventh question. At what prices do you sell goods?

Eleventh answer. Sugar sixty cents per pound when I sell in quantities of ten to twenty-five cents' worth at the time; but at fifty cents per pound when sold by the pound. Flour at twelve dollars per sack by the single sack; ten dollars by the quantity. Coffee at sixty cents per pound when sold by the pound; but when sold by ten or fifteen cents' worth, we sell at the rate of one dollar. Calico fifty cents per yard. Tobacco —.

F. J. DE WITT.

CROW CREEK AGENCY, *September* 5, 1865.

Statements of the chiefs of the Santees before Hon. A. W. HUBBARD, member of congressional Indian commission.

Chief Passing-Hail—Wasuhiya-ye-dom—says:

It has been a long time since I have heard such talk, and I am very glad. Myself and three of these chiefs with him here were at Washington, and heard what the grandfather told them, and we know we live by what the government gives them, and we abide by what the government does for us. At Redwood they took all the young and smart men and put them in prison, and they took all the chiefs and women and children and put them in Fort Snelling. They done with us as they would grain, shaking it to get out the best, and then brought our bodies over here; that is, took everything from us and brought us over here with nothing. Colonel Thompson stood by us and told us that we would get no more money as annuities, but would get more goods and more to eat. Colonel Thompson told us these things, and then he went to Washington and then came back in the winter. Colonel Thompson, when he got back, told us our goods had been bought and were on the way here; but the goods did not arrive here until the next spring, and when they did come we thought there were not as many as ought to have come; there were not enough to go round. When the provisions were brought here the agent told us the food was to be divided between us and the Winnebagoes, and only five sacks of flour were given us per week through the winter; they were issued to us each Saturday. They brought beef and piled it up here; they built a box and put the beef in it and steamed it and made soup; they put salt and pepper in it, and that is the reason these hills about here are filled with children's graves; it seemed as though they wanted to kill us. We have grown up among white folks, and we know the ways of white folks. White folks do not eat animals that die themselves; but the animals that died here were piled up with the beef here and were fed out to us; and when the women and children, on account of their great hunger, tried to get the heads, blood, and entrails, when the butchering was being done, they were whipped and put in the guard-house. It is not right for me to omit anything. The heads, entrails, and liver were piled about here in the stockade, and the agent would keep watch of them, and when he wanted some work done he would pay for the work with the most rotten part of it. He employed the Indians to work, and paid them with the most rotten part, as above stated. Last fall the agent told us to go out on a hunt, and while they were out on the hunt the goods came, and we suppose the reason he wanted us to go on the hunt was, that he did not want us to see what was done with the goods. Last fall the agent called the chiefs and said he would give us the goods. The next day we came up, and the agent, from the top window of the warehouse, threw out the goods; he threw out a dress for each woman and a blanket for each family. I think there were over one hundred blankets given out at that time. They brought us here to a windy country, and we supposed the wind had blown the goods away; but we heard afterwards that there were some round in the houses in the stockade. We heard that the agent traded some of our goods away, and we suppose he traded them for robes and furs. We think if he had not have traded them away there would have been plenty to go round, and the women would not have been crying with cold. You told me that you wanted me to tell all that the agent did. The agent would send us out hunting, and while out hunting the young men would be killed—that is, some of them; were killed by the Winnebagoes, as I suppose. What I have stated were some of the actions of the Winnebagoes; but when we came here, certain laws were given us by the grandfather; but we are not going to take the matter into our hands, but await the action of the grandfather. I will tell you one thing more: you are a straightforward man, and told me to talk.

The President gave us some laws, and we have changed ourselves to white men, put on white man's clothes and adopted the white man's ways, and we supposed we would have a piece of ground somewhere where we could live; but no one can live here and live like a white man. I have changed my body to a white man's body. I have not told any lie. You told me to tell the truth, and I have done so. I forgot one thing. We wanted the agent to get David Faribault for interpreter, but he would not do so, and we did not have an interpreter of our own, and so we were like men in the night, in the dark. When the agent wanted any work done, instead of calling upon us he would employ the Winnebagoes, and then pay them out of the provisions that were common to both Santees and Winnebagoes.

CROW CREEK AGENCY, TERRITORY OF DAKOTA, *September* 5, 1865.

Examination before Hon. A. W. HUBBARD, member of congressional Indian commission.

Edward R. Pond, being duly sworn, deposed as follows:

First question. State your name, occupation, and residence.

First answer. My name is Edward R. Pond; have resided at Crow Creek agency since September, 1863; occupation mission teacher of the Santee Indians.

Second question. State whether you were here through the winter of 1863 and 1864.

Second answer. I was, with the exception that I made one trip to Sioux City and one to Yankton in November.

Third question. State generally the condition of the Santees through that winter as to provisions and clothing.

Third answer. They had very little to eat, and what they did have was of very poor quality. They had but little clothing, not enough to protect them from the cold. There had been no clothing issued to them for more than a year. They suffered severely from exposure and want of clothing.

Fourth question. State the quantity of provisions issued to them per week.

Fourth answer. I think, through the month of January they had soup; from the 1st of February to the 1st of April, nine sacks of flour were issued per week to them, I think. There were five hundred bushels of wheat ground here at this agency and issued to the Santees and Winnebagoes, unbolted. The flour issued to them was of very poor quality, next thing to shorts.

Fifth question. State the quality and quantity of the beef issued to them during that winter.

Fifth answer. I do not recollect the quantity; but the beef was very poor. The cattle were brought here from Minnesota in November, 1863, and about half of them worked on the trip over. Some of these cattle, after making the trip from Minnesota, went to Sioux city and brought up 500 bushels of wheat before being slaughtered.

Sixth question. State what you know of fresh beef being brought in on the train that came in from Minnesota in November, 1863.

Sixth answer. Some was brought in. I understood it was beef from cattle that gave out on the trip. It was destitute of fat, bloody, poor, and in a filthy condition.

Seventh question. Was any beef brought in on the train that went to Sioux City and brought up wheat, as above stated?

Seventh answer. There was. I understood it was beef from cattle that had given out on the trip; it was very poor, destitute of fat, and no white man would eat it, I think, unless in a starving condition. It had lain on the wagons until it was pretty much dried out. In the winter of 1863 and 1864 the cattle brought from Minnesota and Sioux City were slaughtered by the Indians and spread out in the stockade to freeze; and after being frozen, as much as the warehouse would contain was piled up in the warehouse, and the residue was piled up outside the warehouse. They put snow with it and covered it with sawdust. Towards spring some of the beef became spoiled and tainted and produced an offensive odor in the neighborhood of the warehouse, but they continued to issue it as long as it lasted, which was near the 1st of June. When the cattle were slaughtered they were little more than skin and bones; many of them were too poor to work.

Eighth question. Was any pork or bacon brought over in the train from Minnesota in November, 1863? and if so, state the condition of it, and quantity.

Eighth answer. Some was brought over in that train. I understood that it was pork that belonged to the Winnebago agency in Minnesota, and that it was taken out of the barrels and piled in the wagon boxes in bulk. It was poor pork.

Ninth question. State the particulars as to the manner soup was made that winter; describe it.

Ninth answer. A large cottonwood box, about eight feet square and eight feet deep, was made, and a pipe led from the steam-engine of the saw-mill into the bottom of this box. They filled the box about half-full of water and put in beef, pork, and flour, and steamed it until it was all reduced to a pulp. It was then given out to such of the Indians as came after it. I did not go round the box much, but I think the odor about it became offensive. The box, I think, was made by direction of Superintendent Thompson, and he was here when the first mess was prepared. I tasted the first mess, and it tasted of the cottonwood, and it was poor soup.

Tenth question. State whether there was a great deal of suffering here that winter from the want of sufficient clothing and food?

Tenth answer. There was; there was one woman that died of starvation, the Indians said, and I heard of several who were sick on account of starvation. The women and children, in order to get something to eat, cut and carried about three hundred cords of wood, three feet long, an average of half a mile; they carried the wood on their backs. They were paid, I think, for cutting and carrying the wood two dollars per cord in flour, at the rate of twelve and a half cents per pound. The wood was used principally by the agents and employés and for the saw-mill, and was paid for out of the Indians' flour. Young children, as young as ten years, and very old women, were engaged in cutting and carrying the wood; one old woman so old and used up that she could not hunt round and find where her pile was, so as to put her wood with it. Government mules, so poor that they died of exposure, were eaten by the Indians. One or two horses died in the course of the winter, which the Indians ate; also they ate wolves; the wolves had been poisoned with strychnine by the soldiers and Indians in order to catch them. They will not eat either mules, horses, or wolves except to save them from starvation. The Winnebagoes also ate of the dead mules, horses, and wolves that winter. On the 1st of February the Santees were in so much need of something to eat that five hundred men, women and children started out on foot hunting buffalo; they had no ponies at the time, and there were but about seventy or eighty of the five hundred that could be called men; they expected to go out from sixty to seventy miles before they could find any buffalo, and one hundred miles before they could find a plenty.

Eleventh question. Who made the contract for furnishing the beef that winter?

Eleventh answer. I think Superintendent Thompson. Hubbell & Hawley were the contractors who furnished the beef. Hubbell came across with the train and brought some goods for the Indians and some for himself in that train. The cattle were not weighed here, and I don't think they were estimated here.

Twelfth question. Were you present at the distribution of the goods to the Indians in the spring of 1864?

Twelfth answer. I was not present when the goods were divided among the chiefs.

Thirteenth question. Do you know how the goods have been generally distributed here since they have been here? and if so, state.

Thirteenth answer. The agent generally divides them out in piles in the warehouse, the chiefs not being present, and the chiefs sign the vouchers before they get the goods. They divide or separate one pile for each.

Fourteenth question. How do they know when they get all their goods?

Fourteenth answer. They do not know. I have heard them say a good many times that they did not know more than if they were blind.

Fifteenth question. How were the Indians provided for during the fall of 1864 and the winter of 1864 and 1865 in provision and clothing?

Fifteenth answer. A train came here from Minnesota in August loaded with flour; 1,000 sacks, I understood, but I was not present, but afterwards saw the flour. I had a couple of sacks of that flour; it was so poor that I could not use it; one of the sacks I got was picked out for the best flour, but the sack weighed ten pounds after the flour was emptied; it had been wet. The flour was wet coming from Minnesota, and was of such poor quality that it was unfit for ordinary cooking purposes. Another train arrived here from Minnesota in October, with 1,000 sacks flour; that flour had not been wet. The flour brought in these two trains belonged to the Winnebagoes and Santees jointly. The flour by the last train was about of the same quality as the first. This flour was issued to the Indians last fall and winter. The beef cattle came from Minnesota and hauled the flour above mentioned, and also goods for Hubbell & Hawley, the traders, and I understood they were furnished by Hubbell & Hawley. They were in a little better order than the year before, but still they were very poor. The cattle were herded close to the agency until the first of November; after that they were herded about nine miles and upwards up the Missouri river until about the second week in December, when they were slaughtered. I understood from one of the employés that there were about five hundred of the beef cattle. A very hard storm drove the cattle down here. They were scattered from one or two miles above the agency down three or four miles below. Three or four of them perished in the storm; one lay down by the river, and was so weak and feeble that it could not get up, but died; another got down near the saw-mill, and they cut its throat to save it; another was dead and frozen up above, and was found several days after; it was brought down and cut up in quarters, with the hide on, and put in with the other beef; the other two were skinned and put in with the other beef. The next day they commenced to slaughter the beef. The cattle were very poor and thin in flesh. Major Balcombe gave me the privilege of picking out of the whole two or three hundred cattle two of the best quarters, and it was with great difficulty that I could pick them out; there was no fat on that that I picked out; this was after they were killed and brought into the stockade. After the cattle were slaughtered they were brought into the stockade and spread round so as to freeze solid; after which they were packed in the warehouse in snow and covered with sawdust; and some of it was in the warehouse when Major Stone took possession, the 5th of June. At that time there was considerable beef in the warehouse, and much of it was alive with worms, and the stench about it was intolerable. About the 1st of October, 1864, the agent sent them on a hunt, promising them that, in about two months, he would issue them clothing. This was Balcombe. At the end of two months (December 1) he issued them some goods, but I do not know whether he issued them all or not. They were a good deal better off in clothing, and some better off in food, than the winter before. There were not more than about half as many Indians here as the winter before; if there had been they would have been no better off. Some of the Indians did not dare to live here last winter, fearing they would starve. The issue from the 1st January until warm weather was twelve or fourteen quarters per week, and when it commenced to spoil they gave them more. After Agent Stone came here, in June, beef, to the amount of ten or fifteen beeves, that was full of worms, was thrown out.

Sixteenth question. Who employs you as teacher here among the Indians?

Sixteenth answer. The American Board of Commissioners for Foreign Missions. The government has no teacher here to teach the Indians.

Seventeenth question. Do you know of any instances of harsh treatment of the Indians by Major Balcombe?

Seventeenth answer. One year ago last winter several women and a boy, being very hungry, killed one of the cattle to eat, and Major Balcombe put them in a very cold house in very cold weather and kept them there nearly a week without fire, and day times he took them and had them work round and fed them on bread and water. On another occasion, while they were slaughtering the cattle, Balcombe ordered them not to let the women come near where they were butchering, but some disobeyed and went near to get the blood, when he seized them there in numbers and put them in a cold house and kept them over night without fire. One of the women had a baby one week old, which she had left at her house, and some woman brought it up to be nursed, but Balcombe refused to let it be nursed, but finally relented and let it go in, and the woman that brought it up gave her one of her blankets.

EDWARD R. POND.

TERRITORY OF DAKOTA, CROW CREEK AGENCY, *September* 6, 1865.

Examination as to management of Indian affairs at Crow Creek agency, before Hon. A. W. Hubbard, commissioner.

Judson Lamoure, of lawful age, being duly sworn, deposed as follows:

First question. State your name and residence.

First answer. Judson Lamoure; now reside at Crow Creek agency.

Second question. State what you know of the sale or disposition of cattle belonging to this agency by Thompson (superintendent) and others.

Second answer. In the first place, Thompson let a contract to Choteau to furnish cattle for this agency, and the contract was sub-let to Booze, and I brought the cattle up to this agency for Booze; there were ninety-three head—mostly oxen for beef and work, and some cows; they were weighed at Sioux City; they received the cattle here, and I returned to Sioux City, but immediately left there; on my return here with goods for Superintendent Thompson, and on reaching Choteau creek, I met sixty-seven head of the same cattle I brought to the agency, as above stated, they having strayed from the agency. I drove them back as far as Fort Randall, where I met Thomas Powers and a Frenchman whom Thompson had sent after the cattle. We stopped at Fort Randall two days; and while there a train belonging to Thomas Powers and F. D. Pease came along. The cattle in this train were small and young and pretty well worn out; I turned the sixty-seven head over to Powers; Powers & Pease then turned their oxen in the train in among the sixty-seven head, and picked the same number out of the sixty-seven head; the ones they picked out were the largest and best, and were fat and nice cattle; fifteen yoke were thus exchanged. We then came on up to the agency together, and when we arrived here I made a statement of how I had found the cattle and turned them over to Powers, and how Powers & Pease had exchanged cattle, and also made some statement to Thompson's assistant (Adams.) I offered to show Thompson the cattle exchanged, and he said he had not time to attend to it. Pease & Powers then sold the fifteen yoke of oxen they had picked out of the sixty-seven head to Thompson, the superintendent, and they also sold the fifteen yoke they put into among the sixty-seven head. I do not know what number Powers reported to Thompson that he had found. I told Thompson the number I found and turned over to Powers. The cattle were all marked with tar on the hip, and the mark was there plain to be seen. Afterwards eleven yoke of cattle were sent up by Booze. I brought them up and turned them over to Thompson. Afterwards I was at Sioux City, and Thomas Powers came there with two yoke of the same cattle, and went on to Council Bluffs with the same cattle. Powers was hauling goods for himself. I know that Powers & Pease, while freighting for government that summer between Forts Randall and Sully, came along here frequently with their cattle worn out and broken down, and Adams, assistant superintendent, would exchange with them, and take their broken-down cattle and let them have good cattle; and when Powers & Pease got through freighting that fall, and had worked them down, they sold the whole train to Adams for the agency. This was done in my presence. When Powers & Pease turned over and sold their whole train to Adams, as above stated, the cattle were worked down thin and poor and not fit for beef, and probably would not have lived through the winter. They were slaughtered for the Indians. During the first transaction above stated, Superintendent Thompson was here, but when Powers & Pease turned the train over, as above stated, Thompson was not here. At one time I had charge of a train for Booze, freighting from Sioux City to Sully, and while passing this agency some of my cattle got foot-sore and poor, and knowing that Adams had exchanged with others, I went to him and requested him to exchange with me, and he said he would do so, and I went and examined his herd, and not finding any that were better than mine I did not exchange. One time, on my return from Fort Sully with a train, I had got out of provisions when I got here, and went to Adams and bought some crackers, some fresh beef, and also got a spade and two chains and four or five ox-yokes, and five pairs of ox-bows, and in payment for all these I gave him a buffalo robe. These things I bought belonged to this agency.

Third question. State anything you know about the condition and suffering of the Indians at this agency.

Third answer. I know that whenever I passed here with a train the Indian women of both the Santees and Winnebagoes would come to the train and beg, and offer to prostitute themselves in order to get something to eat; and I have seen the same thing done at all other points where I have seen them. They left the agency and went to Fort Randall and Fort Sully and prostituted themselves for something to eat. They said they had to do so in order to get something to eat. I mean, this has been the case heretofore. For the past three months since I have been in the employ of the agency they have had enough to enable them to get along, though the allowance has been rather short. When they have come and said they had not enough to eat, I have taken the pains to go to their lodges and ascertain for myself, and when I found that they were destitute, I took measures to relieve them; when sick I have visited them to see what could be done for them. I have been in charge of the issuing most of the time since I have been here.

Fourth question. State whether the fifteen yoke of cattle that strayed from the agency, and that were put into the train of Pease & Powers at Fort Randall, and the fifteen yoke they turned out of their train and put in their places, were afterwards sold to Thompson for the use of the agency.

Fourth answer. They were; we got here on the third of July, and they were sold to Thompson in a few days afterwards. Pease told me he sold the cattle to Thompson, and I saw them there frequently among the agency stock and working about the agency.

Fifth question. What do you know about Pease selling some cows and young cattle to Thompson?

Fifth answer. He sold him in the neighborhood of thirty head—I think it was twenty-nine head—when Thompson was on his way here to establish this agency.

Sixth question. Do you know how many cattle there were in the train that Powers & Pease sold and turned over to Adams, as above stated?

Sixth answer. I don't know certainly, but think there were from thirty to forty yoke; I was present when it was done.

Seventh question. Were you engaged in putting up hay for Agent Burleigh, of the Yankton agency, in 1864?

Seventh answer. I was employed putting up hay for him at Bonhomme.

Eighth question. State the place where and for what purpose the hay was put up.

Eighth answer. The hay was put up at Emanuel creek, a short distance above Bonhomme, and was put up for the purpose of feeding Burleigh's individual stock.

Ninth question. State who assisted you in putting it up.

Ninth answer. Had some six hands; two of them, Louis Mallett and ——— Proteau, had been in the employ of the Yankton agency. John Thompson, the blacksmith at the agency, came down there and repaired the mowing machine and helped us start the machine. Thompson took us to the hay-field and showed us where to work. While cutting hay we broke two or three sickles and took them to the agency blacksmith shop to be repaired. Provisions were brought from the agency, but I do not know whether the provisions belonged to the agency or Burleigh, individually. I asked Burleigh how it happened that the machine we were using was the same kind of a machine they had at the agency; he said he bought the one we were using and the one at the agency for the Indians, and he thought one was enough for the Indians, and took the one we had down to his own place. He afterwards traded the machine we were using for another one, which I saw on his Bonhomme farm last June. We were three weeks putting up this hay. Emanuel creek is about twenty-six or eight miles from the Yankton agency.

Tenth question. State what conversation, if any, you had with Burleigh last season in respect to his method of making money at the agency.

Tenth answer. In a conversation with me, he stated that the best way of making money out of the appropriations was in buying cattle for the Indians; and I asked him if that accounted for the large number of cattle he had on his farm, and he replied that it did.

Eleventh question. State what number, if you know, of cattle he had on his farm.

Eleventh answer. He had about two hundred and fifty head in September, 1864.

JUDSON LAMOURE.

FORT RANDALL, *September* 8, 1865.

TERRITORY OF DAKOTA, *County of Todd:*

Monroe Creighton, of lawful age, being duly sworn, deposed as follows:

First question. State your name, occupation, and where you have resided the past year.

First answer. My name is Monroe Creighton; am a member of company H, 6th Iowa cavalry, and from the 7th day of October, 1864, until July 2, 1865, I was stationed at Fort Sully, Dakota.

Second question. Who were the traders at that point during the time you were stationed there?

Second answer. Burguin, Graumey, Galpin & Co, Powers & Pease, Pierre Choteau & Co, and Charles Pruneau.

Third question. State whether you were about their stores much, and whether you knew their course of trade.

Third answer. I was in the stores frequently, in fact nearly every day; there was no day passed but that I was in some of the stores. This was the case through the entire winter and spring, and I became very well acquainted with their course of dealing.

Fourth question. Please state the manner of dealing by Burguin, Graumey & Co.; state the particulars.

Fourth answer. I have known Lieutenant Hesselberger, of company H, to buy government blankets of soldiers and sell them to Burguin & Co., and they would give one of these blankets for two buffalo robes; government blankets cost three dollars and fifty cents, and robes were worth then from twelve to fifteen dollars. I have seen them trade three or four cups of very poor sugar for a robe worth from ten to twelve dollars. They usually gave two or three cups of coffee for a robe; the cups used for measuring sugar or coffee were pint cups. I often saw them give ten Iroquois shells and one California for a robe. The traders told me that the Iroquois shells were worth one dollar and a half per dozen, and the California shell is not worth over a dollar, I think. The prices I have named are about the usual price of robes paid the Indians by the traders. The price of three-point black Indian blankets was three robes, worth as above stated. I have seen them trade a butcher-knife and a little vermilion (paint) for a robe; have also seen them trade from four to seven plugs of the commonest copperas tobacco for a robe, and also give about a fifty-pound sack of flour for three robes. All the traders there traded at about the same rates. I have often seen them trade in all the stores, and there was little or no difference in the price paid by the traders to the Indians for robes, though some of the boys used to say that they thought that Powers was sometimes a little more liberal in the prices paid for robes, but I never could see much difference. Burguin & Co. often gave Major House, the commander of the post, fine robes, and also gave one or more robes to all the officers there.

M. CREIGHTON.

YANKTON AGENCY, *September* 9, 1865.

TERRITORY OF DAKOTA:

B. E. Wood, of lawful age, being duly sworn, deposed as follows:

First question. State your name and occupation and residence, and where you were in the summer of 1863.

First answer. B. E. Wood; reside at the Yankton agency, and from July 7, 1863, to November of that year, I was stopping at the Crow Creek agency.

Second question. State what you know about Mr. Adams, assistant superintendent, exchanging oxen belonging to the Crow Creek agency, with parties passing there with trains.

Second answer. I know that in the summer of 1863, while I was there, he exchanged an ox that would work for an ox in Burguin's train, that was broken down and worn out, and that he received either ten or fifteen dollars to boot. I do not now recollect the exact amount, though Adams told me at the time.

B. E. WOOD.

FORT RANDALL, *September* 8, 1865.

DAKOTA TERRITORY, *County of Todd:*

James Havens, of lawful age, being duly sworn, deposed as follows:

First question. State your name, occupation, and where you have been stationed for the past year.

First answer. My name is James Havens; am a member of company L, 6th Iowa cavalry, and from July, 1864, to the spring of 1865, I was stationed at Fort Sully, Dakota.

Second question. State what you know, if anything, about loads of goods being taken from the trading post of Choteau & Co., at Fort Sully, and traded to Indians outside of the post.

Second answer. I heard that loads of goods were being taken outside of the post in the night and traded to Indians, and one night I watched and saw a load of goods taken from Choteau & Co.'s store—one night outside the garrison, and the wagon containing the goods was gone until the next night, when it returned without the goods.

Third question. State what prices did the traders at that post usually pay for robes?

Third answer. For a robe they would give from one cup to a cup and a half of sugar and a cup of coffee. They would give sometimes one of the large California shells for a fifteen-dollar robe. I bought a California shell at the same store for one dollar. The prices named above were the prices paid by the traders at Fort Sully to the Indians.

JAMES HAVENS.

YANKTON AGENCY, *September* 9, 1865.

TERRITORY OF DAKOTA, *County of* ——— *:*

John P. Williamson, of lawful age, being first duly sworn, deposed as follows:

First question. State your name, occupation, and place of residence.

First answer. John P. Williamson; I am a missionary among the Santee Indians under the American Board of Commissioners for Foreign Missions, and have been for five years. I have always made my home among the Santee Indians, my father having been a missionary before me. I have been absent from them at times; now reside at Crow Creek agency, Dakota, and have resided there since the agency has been established.

Second question. Please state the condition of the Santee Indians and what their condition has been since they have been at Crow Creek, and state the particulars as to the manner they have been clothed and subsisted, and also state their treatment during their removal from Minnesota to their present agency.

Second answer. There were thirteen hundred and twenty-four of the Santee Indians that left Fort Snelling for Crow Creek agency. They were taken down the Mississippi river on two steamboats; one of the boats stopped at Hannibal, Missouri, and the Indians on that boat crossed to St. Joseph on the railroad; the other boat continued round by river to St. Joseph, and there all the Indians were put upon one boat. On the route there were sixteen deaths. The Indians were very much crowded on the boat from St. Joseph up the river; it was in the month of May. It was suffocating to go on the lower deck; they were entirely excluded from the cabin and confined entirely to the lower and upper decks. They were so crowded that there was not room enough for all of them to lie down at the same time. I came round with them. They were fed on hard bread and mess pork not cooked; there was poor opportunity to cook the pork except at night when the boat stopped. The quantity of provisions was short, not more than about one-half of soldier's rations. They had neither sugar nor coffee, and no vegetables. They had nothing to eat but hard bread and the mess pork above mentioned, on the trip up from St. Joseph, except two beeves bought at Sioux City We were about ten or twelve days making the trip from St. Joseph to Crow Creek agency, and were without medical attention or supplies of any kind on the trip. There was a great deal of sickness occasioned from want of proper food, and confinement on the boat. The diseases consisted mostly of diarrhœa and fevers. For six weeks after they arrived at Crow Creek they died at the average rate of three or four a day. In that time one hundred and fifty died, and during the first six months two hundred of them died, and I think that at least one hundred and fifty of them died on account of the bad treatment they received after they left Fort Snelling. We arrived at Crow Creek on the first day of June, 1863. When we arrived there the season was very dry, and what vegetation there had been was dried up and no crop of any kind was raised; some corn was planted, but it wilted up before it was four inches high; most of it, however, did not come up at all. The Indians, during the summer, were fed upon flour and pork; I do not recollect the quantity given them, but there was not a great deal of complaint as to quantity; they wanted beef, but none was given them until fall. They suffered somewhat for want of vegetables and fresh meat during the summer, and also suffered for the want of medical supplies. During the fall the supply began gradually to fail; they gradually issued less, and the Indians made great complaint. About the first of December their supplies arrived from Minnesota; I think there were over a hundred wagons in the train, loaded with goods and supplies for the Santees and Winnebagoes, and goods for the traders, Hubbell and Hawley. The supplies hauled in that train for the Santees consisted of flour. I understood, when the train started from Minnesota it contained corn for the Santees, but none came to Crow Creek agency; some pork was brought, but none of it was issued to the Santee Indians; some of it was given out to Indians in payment for work. After the arrival of that train the rations issued to the Indians at that agency then consisted of flour and beef. The quantity issued was very short, but I cannot now recollect how much it was. The beef furnished was from the cattle that hauled the supplies from Minnesota as above stated. They had hauled the train over three hundred miles in the month of November, with nothing to eat but the dry prairie grass; there were no settlements on the route the train came. These cattle were very poor; some of the cattle in the train died or gave out and were killed on the trip, and they brought the meat in on the train for the Indians, and it was issued to the Indians. About New Year's about four hundred head of the cattle were slaughtered; there was no hay or anything for them to eat at that time, and there had not been any since they had been there, except the dry prairie grass which the frost had killed. The beef after being slaughtered was piled up in the warehouse in snow—that is, what they could get into the warehouse, and the remainder was piled up out doors about the warehouse. They said this beef was to keep the Indians until the coming June; a large part of it was little more than skin and bones—it was black and poor. It was stated that Hubbell and Hawley had the contract for supplying the agency with flour, and soon after the arrival of that train from Minnesota, over one hundred head of the best of the oxen were picked out by Hubbell and Hawley and yoked up and sent in a train to Sioux City, a distance of two hundred and forty miles, to haul up flour. They returned from the trip some time in February with the flour, and the oxen were then slaughtered and issued to the Indians. Some time in January they commenced issuing soup to the Indians; it was made in a large cottonwood vat, being cooked by steam carried from the boiler of the saw-mill, in a pipe, to the vat. The ingredients were: the vat was partially filled with water, and then they threw in several quarters of beef, being first chopped, and a sack or two of flour. The first time they put in beans, but not afterwards; they also put in the heart and lights. I heard the entrails were put in, but did not see it done; I did not go there after the first time when it was filled. The Indians often showed me the soup. I tasted it, but could not eat it; that is, it was very unpalatable, though I suppose I could eat it rather than starve. The soup was issued every other day; it was made every day, but issued one day to the Santees, and the next day to the Winnebagoes, and while soup was issued to the Indians no other food was issued to them. The Indians were very much dissatisfied, and said they could not live on soup. Colonel Thompson told them if they could live elsewhere they had better go, but he did not want them to go to the white settlements. After this a great many of them left the agency and scattered up and down the river; some went to Fort Sully, and some to Fort Randall, to get something to eat. No clothing had been issued to them since the fall of 1862, and consequently they suffered a great deal for the want of sufficient clothing. Their condition was such that I encouraged them to go on a buffalo hunt, and I went with them, but I considered it very hazardous for them to go on account of their liability to perish on account of the storms and cold, in their unprotected condition. It was about the first of February, but I considered it necessary to go in order to save them from starvation; about three hundred went on the hunt. I believe if all the Santees and Winnebagoes had stayed at the agency, that winter many of them would have starved to death. On this hunt they had about fifty guns, furnished by Colonel Thompson, and had no ponies, except mine, which I took. We were absent about six weeks, and cannot speak of their treatment during my absence. When I got back they had quit issuing soup, and they were issuing flour and the beef above spoken of. They issued about one-fourth of a pound of flour per head and three-fourths of a pound of beef per head during the spring and summer, though sometimes more or less, depending upon how many Indians were absent. Sometimes flour and meat were issued to the Indians that worked, in payment for their work; they were always willing to work. During the summer of 1864, Hubbell and Hawley brought in another train from Minnesota, loaded with flour, I think about a thousand sacks; the wagons were not covered, and they came over three hundred miles in that way, and there had been a great deal of rain upon the flour. I have seen sacks of that flour weighed after knocking out all the loose flour, and the sack would weigh nearly thirty pounds. This flour was issued to the Indians by the sack, ninety-eight pounds to the sack, but when the Indians emptied the sacks they would often have to turn the sacks wrong-side out and knock off the flour with clubs or axes. The flour was second-rate.

The beef for the winter of 1864 and 1865 was killed and packed up the same as the winter before, and was of a little better quality, but still a great deal of it was very poor beef. More than half the Indians were gone during the entire winter, that is, more than half the Santees; their issues during that winter were about three-eighths of a pound of flour and nearly a pound of beef per head per day; the flour was second-rate flour. Many of them left last fall and went over towards the settlements in Minnesota, and did not return until spring, and did not receive their clothing. During the fall, winter and spring of 1863 and 1864 the Indians went as far as thirty miles up and down the Missouri river from the agency, to the different camps of the military expeditions, to pick up the scattered corn that had been left by the horses and mules when fed, for the purpose of eating it, and also to pick up dead mules and horses to eat. There was a great deal of suffering from want of food and clothing, and I am satisfied that one woman actually died of starvation. The influence upon the Indians, occasioned by the want of sufficient food and clothing, has been very bad, and has had a demoralizing effect upon the Indians, many of the women being compelled to prostitute their daughters in order to obtain food and clothing, and many women were compelled to prostitute themselves in order to enable themselves to get something to eat. I am satisfied that there were a great many such cases occasioned by actual suffering and starvation.

Third question. State whether you have a church at the Crow Creek agency, the number of communicants, and the religious condition of the Indians?

Third answer. We have a church there of the Presbyterian denomination, with about two hundred communicants, who mostly joined the church about the time of removal and along at times since. Their attendance upon the religious services is quite good; the church is always filled; it will seat about two hundred.

Fourth question. State the condition of the school.

Fourth answer. The school is very encouraging; the average attendance is a little over one hundred; the whole number of pupils during the year has been about three hundred. There is a great desire on the part of the Indians to learn, and this has greatly increased since their removal to Crow Creek agency. The progress of the pupils has often been retarded on account of their being compelled to go off and hunt food.

Fifth question. Do you know of Chester Adams, assistant superintendent, exchanging oxen with parties passing the agency with trains? State particulars.

Fifth answer. I do remember of two or three cases where he exchanged oxen belonging to the agency for lame oxen or broken-down oxen.

Sixth question. Has there been any physician at the agency?

Sixth answer. For a short time the Winnebago physician supplied the Santees with medicines, but for a year past no provision has been made for medicine or medical attention. They very much need and are very desirous to have a physician; it would be an act of mercy on the part of the government to furnish them with one.

JOHN P. WILLIAMSON.

DAKOTA TERRITORY, VERMILLION, *September* 12, 1865.

Examination of Mahlon Wilkinson, Indian agent, as to affairs of Upper Missouri Indians.

Mahlon Wilkinson, being duly sworn, deposed:

First question. State your name and residence.

First answer. My name is Mahlon Wilkinson, and reside at Vermillion, Dakota, and am Indian agent for the Crows, Assinneboines, Arickarees, Gros Ventres, and Mandans.

Second question. State the location, number, and general condition of the Crows.

Second answer. Their number is four thousand, as near as I have been able to ascertain. Their country is the entire valley of the Yellowstone, above Brazos houses, running north to the Missouri river, at or near the mouth of the Milk river. They are north of the Missouri river now, having been driven from their own country by the hostile Sioux. Parties on boats going up the Missouri river estimated a party of Sioux on the south side of the Missouri river, who were after the Crow Indians, at fifteen hundred warriors; and they were the Indians that fired into the boats the present season. The Crows are too weak to fight the Sioux, and go north of the Missouri river for safety. They are very friendly, and are the best Indians on the Missouri river, I think. They are in good condition, have a plenty of horses, and subsist by the chase. They are anxious (all that I have seen) to make a treaty, and their children to learn to read and write, and have a permanent place of abode, where they can raise corn, and be like the white people.

Third question. State the number, location, and condition of the Assinneboines.

Third answer. Their number is about four thousand, and their country is that part of the Yellowstone valley below the Crows, and north to the British possessions, though I do not know the exact boundaries of their country; but they traverse the whole of that part of the country north of the Missouri river, and most of them are now in the British possessions. They are perfectly friendly with not only the whites but with all their neighboring tribes; and they are poor. They are willing to make treaties, or do most anything that government may ask of them. I think a treaty should be made with them, in order to extinguish their title to a large portion of their country, to accommodate the travel to Montano and Idaho, and for the purpose of making room for other Indians that may be sent there.

Fourth question. State the number of the Arickarees, Gros Ventres, and Mandans; also, location and number.

Fourth answer. These three tribes live together, and number about two thousand. They are at Fort Berthold during the summer, and in winter go into winter quarters away from the fort. They are perfectly friendly to the whites, and want to make a treaty. They say they have been promised a treaty. They want protection, and say that they are hemmed in by the Sioux. But they want a treaty, so that they can have protection; and want to unite with the Crows, and the Crows want to unite with them. They cultivate and raise a good deal of corn. I think last year they raised about twenty thousand bushels of corn and cultivated at least six hundred acres of corn.

Fifth question. What amount of goods do you annually distribute to all these Indians?

Fifth answer. Last year I distributed to all of these tribes a little less than eleven thousand dollars' worth, and this year there is a little less than eight thousand dollars' worth for distribution. The treaty, under which goods to these Indians are distributed, has now expired.

Sixth question. State your opinion as to the necessity of further treaties being made with these Indians.

Sixth answer. If we wish to preserve friendly relations with these Indians, it is absolutely necessary that treaties be made with them.

Seventh question. State what you know as to the manner in which the trade with the Indians is conducted by the licensed traders.

Seventh answer. All the trade is now being done by the Northwestern Fur Company, and I am very well satisfied with their way of conducting the trade; and think, under the regulations they have adopted, many of the abuses of the old fur company will be corrected. I was dissatisfied with the manner in which the American Fur Company conducted their business.

Eighth question. Have you made a distribution of goods to the Indians under your care this season?

Eighth answer. I have not. I could not distribute to the Crows and Assinneboines; only about eight of the Crows and twenty of the Assinneboines came in. The goods are all stored at Fort Union. I was expecting a second shipment of goods for the Arickarees, Gros Ventres, and Mandans, and am awaiting the arrival of such shipment before distributing to them.

MAHLON WILKINSON.

DAKOTA CITY, NEBRASKA TERRITORY, *October* 3, 1865.

Examination of Little Hill, chief, as to treatment of the Winnebago Indians.

Chief Little Hill spoke as follows:

You are one of our friends, as it appears. We are very glad to meet you here. Here are some of our old chiefs with me, but not all. And we will tell you something about how we have lived for the four years past. Now, you see me here to-day. Formerly I did not live as I do now. We used to live in Minnesota. While we lived in Minnesota we used to live in good houses, and always take our Great Father's advice, and do whatever he told us to do. We used to farm and raise a crop of all we wanted every year. While we lived there we had teams of our own. Each family had a span of horses or oxen to work, and had plenty of ponies; now, we have nothing. While we lived in Minnesota another tribe of Indians committed depredations against the whites, and then we were compelled to leave Minnesota. We did not think we would be removed from Minnesota; never expected to leave; and we were compelled to leave so suddenly that we were not prepared; not many could sell their ponies and things they had. The superintendent of the farm for the Winnebagoes was to take care of the ponies we left there and bring them on to us wherever we went; but he only brought to Crow Creek about fifty, and the rest we do not know what became of them. Most all of us had put in our crops that spring before we left, and we had to go and leave everything but our clothes and household things; we had but four days' notice. Some left their houses just as they were, with their stoves and household things in them. They promised us that they would bring all our ponies, but they only brought fifty, and the hostile Sioux came one night and stole all of them away. In the first place, before we started from Minnesota, they told us that they had got a good country for us, where they were going to put us. The interpreter here with me now (Bradford L. Porter) was appointed interpreter, on the first boat that came round, to see to things for the Indians on the trip round. After we got on the boat we were as though in a prison. We were fed on dry stuff all the time.. We started down the Mississippi river, and then up the Missouri to Dakota Territory, and there we found our superintendent, and stopped there, (at, Crow Creek.) Before we left Minnesota they told us that the superintendent had started on ahead of us, and would be there before us, and that he had plenty of Indians, and would have thirty houses built for us before we got there. After we got there they sometimes give us rations, but not enough to go round most of the time. Some would have to go without eating two or three days. It was not a good country; it was all dust. Whenever we cooked anything it would be full of dust. We found out after a while we could not live there. Sometimes the women and children were sick, and some of them died; and we think many of them died because they could not get enough to eat while they were sick. We don't know who was to blame for our bad treatment—whether it was our superintendent, Thompson, or whether it was our agent. We don't blame our agent, Balcombe. He used to treat us very well while we were in Minnesota, and we cannot say who was to blame at Crow Creek. For the past three years we suppose our Great Father has sent us enough goods, provisions, and money, but we do not think we have got half of it. Sometimes some of the women and children don't get much of what they ought to have, only a piece of calico, or something like that. After we had remained at Crow Creek awhile we discovered, or found out, that the whole tribe could not stay there. There was not enough to eat. The first winter one party (Minnesheik's gang) started down the Missouri river as far as Fort Randall, where they wintered. Before Clark Thompson, the superintendent, left us, (the first fall after we went there,) he had a cottonwood trough made and put beef in it, and sometimes a whole barrel of flour and a piece of pork, and let it stand a whole night, and the next morning, after cooking it, would give us some of it to eat. We tried to use it, but many of us got sick on it and died. I am telling nothing but the truth now. They also put in the unwashed intestines of the beeves and the liver and lights, and, after dipping out the soup, the bottom would be very nasty and offensive. Some of the old women and children got sick on it and died.

Now, I will speak about our annuity goods. I think some of our goods—I know pretty near where they have gone to. One time Major Balcombe told me to take some goods in the store. Major B. went into our storehouse and got the goods and gave them to me, and told me to take them in the store and leave them, and I did. There were six pieces of calico that I carried into the store. One time I went in the store, and the storekeeper told me they would have goods to-morrow. Next morning I went in again and saw some goods there, and I think the goods belonged to the Winnebagoes, because no teams came there that night from no way. What I have told you, not only I know, but some of these chiefs know also. I know one thing certain, that the pork and flour we left in Minnesota, that belonged to us, was brought over to Crow Creek and sold to us by Hawley & Hubbell, our storekeepers at Crow Creek. I will pass and not say more about the provision, and say of things since we left Crow Creek. For myself, in the first place, I thought I could stay there for a while and see the country. But I found out it wasn't a good country. I lost six of my children, and so I came down the Missouri river. When I got ready to start, some soldiers came there and told me if I started they would fire at me. I had thirty canoes ready to start. No one interceded with the soldiers to permit me to go; but the next night I got away and started down the river, and when I got down as far as the town of Yankton I found a man there and got some provisions; then came on down further and got more provisions of the military authorities, and then went on to the Omahas. After we got to the Omahas, somebody gave me a sack of flour; and some one told us to go to the other side of the Missouri and camp, and we did so. We thought we would keep on down the river, but some one came and told us to stay, and we have been there ever since. Since that time Mr. Graff has been finding rations for us; and I have been chief thirty years, and have never seen such a man. He is a good man. He has been feeding us good beef, flour, and sometimes corn, ever since we have been down there. There is another good man close by us, and that is Colonel Furnas. We the chiefs have no particular complaint to make against our present agent. It is some of our young men that speak against him. We are very glad that Mr. Graff feeds us, and hope he will keep on. We don't know how long he will feed us. You see us here now. We are most all naked; the whole tribe. Some of the tribe are more destitute of clothing than we are. We got some goods here now which the Great Father sent us. They are lying in the Omaha warehouse, and we don't know but that the rats have eat them. There are a good many women and children that are naked and cannot come out of their tents. Some of the young men work out and get something for some of them to wear. The time I went to Washington last winter I asked the commissioner about my goods, and he said the goods had already been sent, and when I got back the agent would give them to us. But when we ask our agent for them he will not give them to us. The reason, I suppose, he will not give us our goods, he is mad with us, because our young men have been talking that the major would be removed and a new agent appointed; and we suppose he was mad about it, and when we went and asked for the goods he told us to go to our new agent. That is the last word I have heard from the agent. Would like you to see about it. We left a good country in Minnesota. We like our present place on the Omaha reservation very well, and, if our treaty is ratified, we shall be well satisfied.

DAKOTA CITY, *October* 3, 1865.

TERRITORY OF NEBRASKA, *County of Dakota:*

Examination of Winnebago chiefs in relation to treatment of their tribe.

Chief Big Bear spoke as follows:

I am very glad to see you here, and that the Great Father has sent you here to examine into our affairs. What Little Hill, our chief, has said is all true. I have never seen the Winnebagoes so poor as they are now. I know there is an annuity of twenty thousand dollars per year coming to us; sometimes we get part of it, sometimes eight dollars per year, and I don't know what becomes of the balance. I know since I have been in chief's place I always have tried to see that the Indians get their money and goods. Many years ago we used to get lots of goods; when we were in the State of Iowa the men used to get two pairs of blankets and the women got five blankets apiece, but I don't know what becomes of the goods now. One time last winter I went to our agent and wanted to see the invoice of our goods, but he would not let me see it. We are to have twenty thousand dollars in goods each year, but I don't think the goods we get are worth that amount. During the three years past we have not received goods enough; some of the men did not get a blanket, and some of the women did not get blankets; some of the women only got two or three yards of calico. I think the twenty thousand dollars ought to buy goods enough to go round. Before we left Minnesota we used to have an abundance of provisions. What I have said to you is true. Little Hill told you about the soup made in the cottonwood trough at Crow Creek; it is all true; I tasted it; it was bad. One time my wife went and got some and I tasted it, but could not swallow it, and told her to go and throw it out—the dogs might eat it. I would not eat that soup; I had to go two or three days without anything to eat. I was very sick, and had hard time to get any one to work for me so that my family could get along. I can stand it two or three days without anything to eat now, but it was very hard then. All I have said is true, and I have nothing further to say now.

NEBRASKA TERRITORY, *Dakota City*, *October* 3, 1865.

Examination of Little Chief in relation to treatment of Winnebago Indians.

Whirling Thunder, chief, spoke as follows:

What these two chiefs, Little Hill and Big Bear, have said before me is very true, and now I will have to say a few words. Some years ago we used to get lots of goods and money, and the agent would get them and show them to us that we might see that all was going on right. At that time Mr. Fletcher was agent for us. At that time we always got our money in gold and silver; now, since Major Balcombe has been our agent, he has mostly given us orders on the store. Major Balcombe, when he first came as our agent at Minnesota, bought berries of our women and paid them out of the Indian flour. What I have said, with what Little Hill and Big Bear have said, is all. We shall not forget Dr. Graff.

DAKOTA CITY, *October* 3, 1865.

TERRITORY OF NEBRASKA, *County of Dakota:*

Examination of Chief Decorah as to treatment of Winnebago Indians.

Chief Decorah stated as follows:

I am very glad to see you here, and that the Great Father has sent you to see us. I suppose he sent you to see how we are getting along and how we are treated now. What these three chiefs, Little Hill, Big Bear, and Whirling Thunder, have said to you before me, is very true. Hitherto we have received twenty thousand dollars per year, and last year we got but fifteen thousand dollars, and I want to know what has become of the other five thousand. I hope you will get our goods this fall, and I hope our friend Docter Graff will help us to get our goods this fall. I hope our agent, Major Balcombe, will not pay any attention to the complaints of our young men, but listen to the chiefs. I hope hereafter we will live well, get a good country and live in it. This is all I have to say. We don't blame Major Balcombe for all these things; some one else may be to blame; we don't know.

DAKOTA CITY, NEBRASKA, *October* 3, 1865.

Examination of Bradford L. Porter as to treatment of Winnebagoes.

Bradford L. Porter, of lawful age, being duly sworn, doth depose and say :

I am a member of the Winnebago tribe of Indians, and am thirty-nine years of age, and have been acting as a teacher in the Winnebago schools, and have always been with the tribe. Have been teaching school seven years. On the 4th day of May, 1863, I went on a steamboat at Mankato, Minnesota, to go to Crow Creek ; there were about eleven hundred of the Winnebagoes on the boat, and we went to Hannibal, Missouri, and there crossed by railroad to St. Joseph, and there got on the West Wind and went up the Missouri river to Crow Creek, where we arrived June 10. I acted as an interpreter for the Indians with me on that trip, a part of my duty being to see the sick ; the rations were principally hard bread and bacon, sometimes a little baker's bread ; we had no tea nor coffee. I issued the rations to the Indians generally. A Mr. Cleaveland furnished the rations and sometimes issued ; sometimes he issued flour, but not much, because we could not cook it on the boat. We boiled some of our meat at Fort Snelling, which lasted awhile. Our rations were insufficient in quantity ; we were crowded on the boat ; there was considerable sickness on the boat. In the fall after we got to Crow Creek, our beef was mostly very poor, nothing but skin and bones some of it. The first year we were at Crow Creek about one hundred barrels of pork and some flour were issued to the Indians who worked, in payment for their work. I was at Crow Creek when the soup was made in the cottonwood kettle, under the direction of Superintendent Thompson. I have seen them put in unwashed intestines into the soup, also lights and liver of the beeves ; they also put in mess pork just as it was taken out of the brine. The soup was very bad ; it would make some of the Indians vomit to eat it. Some portion of the time we were at Crow Creek we were well fed, and at other times nearly starved. Thompson was there most of the time the first season until some time in December, and controlled the affairs of the agency, and Major Balcombe had but little to do while Thompson was there.

BRADFORD L. PORTER.

NEW YORK, *April* 15, 1865.

The UNITED STATES, for Upper Missouri Sioux, bought of CRONIN, HURXTHAL & SEARS,

10 pairs 2½ pt. white Mac. blankets, at $17	$170 00
20 pairs 3 pt. scarlet Mac. blankets, at $24	480 00
15 pairs 3 pt. indigo Mac. blankets, at $24	360 00
15 pairs 2½ pt. indigo Mac. blankets, at $20	300 00
15 pairs 2½ pt. gentian Mac. blankets, at $16	240 00
68 yards saved list blue cloth, at $4 50	306 00
6 pounds cotton thread, at $2	12 00
601¾ yards calico, at 45 cents	270 79
403 yards checks, stripes and plaids, at 60 cents	241 80
4 gross worsted gartering, at $5	20 00
97 yards plaid linseys, at 65 cents	63 05
92¾ yards brown drilling, at 60 cents	55 65
135½ yards ticking, at 75 cents	101 62
4 dozen linen shirts, at $17	68 00
4 pairs wrappers, at $5	20 00
Case and strapping	3 29
	2,712 20

FORT SULLY, DAKOTA TERRITORY, *October* 23, 1865.

Edward T. Latta, being duly sworn, is examined by Hon. A. W. HUBBARD, and testifies as follows :

Question. State your name, residence, and your occupation at the present time.

Answer. Edward T. Latta ; my residence is Leavenworth city, Kansas ; I am in the trading post here ; that is about all my occupation ; I have no trade at home.

Question. State the capacity in which you are acting at this place.

Answer. I am acting as clerk for T. Brenguier & Co. ; I came up here for J. A. Coffey & Co.

Question. Have you taken charge of Indian matters here—distributing Indian goods?

Answer. I have—a very small portion.

Question. Under whose direction were those distributions made?

Answer. Under the directions of S. M. Latta, the agent.

Question. State where S. M. Latta resides.

Answer. At Leavenworth city, Kansas.

Question. State how long it has been since he was here.

Answer. What time he went from here I could not say; he was here on or about the 1st of May last.

Question. How long did he remain here?

Answer. I could not say, as I was in Iowa when he came up here; I went to Iowa the last of November.

Question. Has he been here at this post for the last three months?

Answer. He has not.

Question. What amount of goods have you distributed here?

Answer. Three thousand one hundred and thirty-one dollars, value.

Question. Where had those goods been stored since their arrival here up to the time of distribution?

Answer. In T. Brenguier & Co.'s warehouse.

Question. Were those goods distributed by you for the agent?

Answer. Yes, under his instructions.

Question. What became of the vouchers?

Answer. The receipts? I forwarded them to him.

Question. Has there been any other person here acting as Indian agent within the last three or four months besides yourself?

Answer. No, sir.

Question. Has the Indian agent any interest with the traders at this point, in the trade?

Answer. No, sir.

Question. Have you any knowledge of when the agent will be here again?

Answer. He would have been here at the time this commission came up, (and he wrote me to that effect,) but he lost his youngest child, and his wife was so unwell he could not leave. I think he will be here in a week or two.

Question. What do you know about the manner in which trade is conducted with the Indians by the traders at this post? Do you know anything about the manner in which it is conducted?

Answer. I do not. I have not been in the trading room, but in an adjoining room, and I do not know. I do not do any trading whatever.

Question. Is there anybody doing any trading here under license from Mr. Latta, as agent?

Answer. I think not—indeed, I may say, there is not. All the license he has given is to Coffee & Co., and they are not here.

Question. Do you know where the agent for the upper part of the river, Wilkinson, is?

Answer. I do not; I am not acquainted with him.

Question. Do you know how the business of his agency is conducted?

Answer. I do not.

Question. Does that cover all you know about these subjects?

Answer. Yes, sir.

Question. Do you know of anything else that would be of interest or importance to us in connexion with matters here?

Answer. I do not believe I do.

I, William Tripp, make the following affidavit:

That I visited the Yankton agency, in Dakota Territory, while Colonel Redfield was the agent for the Yankton Indians, and saw the condition of that tribe at that time. That while the Hon. W. A. Burleigh was their agent I often visited said agency, and during the winter of 1865 was stationed at said agency with troops, and had a good opportunity of knowing how the business of that agency was conducted by Agent Burleigh. The condition of the Indians, their habits and general appearance, were much improved during Agent Burleigh's administration. Their chiefs and leading men expressed themselves entirely satisfied with Agent Burleigh, and regretted that he was to leave them and a new man was to take his place.

WILLIAM TRIPP.

Testimony of John Mechling, of Kittanning, Pennsylvania.

Deponent, after being duly sworn, makes the following affidavit:

Question. Were you at the Yankton agency, in Dakota Territory, while W. A. Burleigh was agent for the Yankton Indians; and if so, how long?

Answer. I reached said agency May 22, 1861, in company with W. A. Burleigh, when he entered upon the discharge of his duties at the agency, and remained there as employé upon said agency until the 5th day of July, 1865, when I left said agency for my home in Pennsylvania.

Question. What was your employment at said agency?

Answer. I was employed at said agency by W. A. Burleigh, as a tin and coppersmith, and required in his absence to manage the affairs of said agency.

Question. What do you know about his distribution of the Indian annuity goods during his administration at said agency?

Answer. I was present at the distribution of the goods to the Yankton Indians, to all bands, and I know that all the goods received by said Burleigh were received by the chiefs of their respective bands; and I know that all of the goods that were received by the said Burleigh for the said Indians were delivered by the said Burleigh to the same band for which they were intended.

Question. Were you present at the last payment to said Indians by the said Burleigh?

Answer. I was; and saw the amount paid to each Indian during the four years that the said Burleigh acted as agent, and know that each Indian received all that the pay-roll showed to be their due, and know that they represented themselves fully satisfied with the payments.

Question. What do you know about the flour that was purchased for said Indians last spring by Agent Burleigh?

Answer. I was present when a steamboat reached the agency last spring with a large lot of flour for the Yankton Indians. It was all delivered to the Indians by the said Burleigh from said boat, after the use of which the Indians expressed themselves fully satisfied.

Question. What was the condition of the Yankton agency in 1865, when Agent Burleigh left there, compared with what it was when he took charge of it?

Answer. Its condition was permanently improved, to wit: The erection of many useful and valuable buildings for mills, work-shops, &c., in addition to a large number of comfortable houses for Indians for residences, and a thousand acres ploughed and fenced for the use of said Indians.

Question. How were Agent Burleigh's private family supplies kept—by themselves or separate and apart from those of the Indians?

Answer. They were all kept separate, and marked in a manner to distinguish each from the other.

Question. What became of the stock purchased by Agent Burleigh for the use of the Indians?

Answer. They were killed and consumed by the Indians upon said agency, as the Indians told me, to keep them from starvation.

Question. State whether or not said Burleigh made any effort, and if so, what, to instruct the Indian boys in the mechanic arts?

Answer. I know that Agent Burleigh made his best efforts to instruct the Indian boys in the arts of agriculture and mechanics, and their parents would not allow it to be done. All Indians regard labor as disgraceful.

Question. State what you know, if anything, about a school for Indians during the first two years of the administration of Doctor Burleigh as agent of said Indians.

Answer. The doctor, during the two first years of his administration, had two female schools established and continued for the education of the young Indians. But it proved a failure, for the reason that the Indians could not be prevailed upon to attend sufficiently regular to accomplish any practical purpose.

Question. Were you usually present at the half-breed payments, and do you know how the payments were made by Agent Burleigh?

Answer. I was always present at the half-breed payments, and know that they were paid the amounts in cash, as stated on their pay-rolls

Question. What do you know about goods purchased by Frank La Frambois at the Yankton agency, A. D. 1861?

Answer. I know that Mr. Burleigh let Mr. Frambois have about four hundred dollars worth of goods belonging to Mr. Falk, the Indian trader at the agency, upon the order of C. E. Galpin, Mr. Falk being absent at the time.

Question. Were you present at the distribution of the annuity goods to the Yankton Indians by Agent Redfield in the spring of 1861; and if so, what proportion were distributed?

Answer. I was present, and the goods were all distributed at the time.

Question. During the time while you were employed at the Yankton agency by Agent Burleigh, did you work for said Burleigh upon his farm or anywhere else, except at said agency for the Indians?

Answer. I never did.

Question. During the time of Doctor Burleigh's holding the office of agent of the Yankton Indians, did you know of any of the agency employés working for Doctor Burleigh upon his farm or elsewhere, except upon the agency?

Answer. I did not; and such could not have been the case without my knowledge.

Question. Do you know whether or not the Indians called upon Agent Burleigh to see the invoices of the annuity goods at any time; and if so, were they allowed to see them?

Answer. I do; and Agent Burleigh caused them to be read in their presence and hearing by a person of their own selection, and that person uniformly went with the agent and the chiefs and saw that they were all distributed to them.

Question. What do you know, if anything, about timber and other material for a school-house which Agent Burleigh cut and hauled during the first year that he was at the agency?

Answer. Doctor Burleigh cut and hauled timber, and furnished other material to build a school-house, and then at the request of Struck by the Ree, head chief of the Yankton Indians, when the Indian troubles commenced, used it in constructing a block-house for the protection of the whites and Indians at the Yankton agency.

Question. What was done with the farming tools purchased by Agent Burleigh while in charge at the Yankton agency?

Answer. They were all either delivered to the Indians or left by said Burleigh in the warehouse upon the agency when Doctor Burleigh left said agency last June.

Question. When the Indians' goods were landed at the agency, how were they guarded until they were delivered to the Indians?

Answer. The Indians requested the privilege of guarding their own goods until they were distributed to them, and were provided with arms and ammunition by Agent Burleigh for that purpose, and always guarded their goods night and day until they were distributed *per capita*.

Question. What was the condition of the Yankton Indians when Agent Burleigh left them, compared with their condition when he became their agent?

Answer. Very much improved in all respects.

Question. How did the Indians regard Agent Burleigh?

Answer. They were fully satisfied with Doctor Burleigh as agent, and all trouble was occasioned by a few French and half-breeds, who could not be permitted by said Burleigh to mingle with and demoralize the Indians.

JOHN MECHLING.

Testimony of Charles E. Galpin:

Question. State what you know of the purchase of goods from Doctor Burleigh by F. La Frambois, and of the general management of the affairs of the Yankton agency under said Burleigh's charge.

Answer. Charles E. Galpin, being duly sworn, depose and says, that he is a resident of Dakota Territory; am acquainted with Hon. W. A. Burleigh, late agent of the Yankton Indians; that during the autumn of 1861 I caused to be purchased of A. J. Faulk, at that time trader at the Yankton agency, for the use of F. La Frambois and his family, goods and merchandise to the amount of ($418 68) four hundred and eighteen and $\frac{68}{100}$ dollars, as per bill hereunto attached, and that I paid Mr. A. J. Faulk for the same on the 16th day of November, 1862. Mr. F. La Frambois has been in my employ for the past eighteen years, and these are the only goods which he has ever received from Mr. Faulk or any other person at the said Yankton agency.

I further state that I have been familiar with the Yankton Indians for the past twenty years, and have traded with them each and every year during said time. I speak and understand perfectly their language, and during the administration of Mr. Burleigh, as their agent, have had frequent conversations with their principal men, in regard to the said Burleigh and their intercourse with the United States, and I always found them more disposed to the general government, somewhat to my surprise under the peculiar circumstances under which Mr. Burleigh assumed the said agency, and I am happy to say that the condition of the Indians was greatly improved, both morally and physically, under his administration, and the Indians always expressed themselves satisfied with the same.

The goods referred to in this affidavit were delivered to Mr. La Frambois by Mr. W. A. Burleigh in the absence of Mr. Faulk, but I paid Mr. Faulk for the same at the time above stated.

This deponent further states, that during the years 1861 and '62 I was at the said Yankton agency with my wife, who is a Sioux woman, and learned from her and others of the Yankton tribe that a school was in operation at the said agency.

I further state that the transactions between the said Burleigh and Charles F. Picotti and Colvin Campbell, in relation to their half-breed money and lands, were entered into by said Burleigh at my request, and at the earnest solicitation of the said Picotti and Campbell, and I know the said transactions to be fair, honest, and legitimate on the part of said Burleigh.

Sworn and subscribed to before me this 22d day of February, 1866.

C. E. GALPIN.

1861.			
Oct. 26.	To cash	$10 00	
	300 pounds sugar, at 15 cents	45 00	
	50 pounds coffee, at 25 cents	12 50	
	6 pounds tea, at 70 cents	4 20	
	100 pounds tobacco, at 28 cents	28 00	
	4 bushels corn, at $1 25	5 00	
	4 sacks flour, at $5	20 00	
	12½ yards gray list cloth, at $1 50	18 75	
	20½ yards scarlet, at $2	41 00	
	63 yards ticking, at 20 cents	12 60	
	43 yards blue drilling, at 20 cents	8 60	
	230 yards print, at 15 cents	34 50	
	12 red wool shirts, at $1 25	15 00	
	2 knit jackets, at $1 50	3 00	
	2 dozen coarse combs	1 50	
	1 dozen fine combs	75	
	2 papers pins	25	
	12 spools thread	75	
	8 pounds beads	10 00	
	35 bushels small cut	3 50	
	1 sack shot	3 00	
	30 yards bleached cotton, at 20 cents	6 00	
	16 yards striped shirting	3 00	
	40 yards plaid	14 00	
	16 yards check, at 20 cents	3 20	
	1 drab cap	50	
	12 assorted butcher knives	4 00	
	6 pairs woollen socks	2 40	
	6 sets ear-rings	75	
	1 broadcloth overcoat	12 00	
	6½ yards satinet	5 00	
	By 1 double wagon and set harness		$100 00
	To 24½ yards blue list cloth, at 62 cents	64 19	
	145 yards shirting, at 15 cents	21 75	
	1 set dominoes	1 50	
	1 frying pan, 1 coffee mill	2 25	
	4 thimbles	24	
		418 68	100 00
	Settled by Charles E. Galpin. Note, November 16, 1862, for		318 68
			418 68

Deposition of Thomas C. Powers.

Said Thomas C. Powers being duly sworn, states as follows:

First question. State your place of residence and occupation.

First answer. I am residing at Fort Sully at this time, but two years ago I lived at Yankton, Dakota Territory.

Second question. State the business in which you were engaged in the summer and fall of 1863.

Second answer. I was then acting as surveyor at the Crow Creek Indian agency; this was the case until some time in August, and the remainder of the season I worked for and n company with Pease, having some interest with him.

Third question. State what you know about some cattle straying away from the agency, and about Judd Lamore being sent for them.

Third answer. Some cattle strayed away from the agency, and Colonel Thompson, the superintendent, came to me and requested me to go and hunt them up. I went. I met Judd Lamore at Randall. He had stopped them, and told me it was worth twenty-five dollars. He wanted to know if I would pay him; that he had had a good deal of trouble in running after them, &c. I told him I would speak favorably of it to Colonel Thompson. The cattle, numbering some seventy or eighty head, were taken back to the agency, in charge of Mr. Cooper, along with Lamore. I did not go back with the cattle, but went along up to the agency two or three days afterwards. The cattle had arrived at the agency before I got there. Colonel Thompson paid Lamore the twenty-five dollars on my recommendation.

Fourth question. State whether you sold to Colonel Thompson any of these cattle or any other cattle which had strayed away from the agency.

Fourth answer. I did not; I never made any such sales either directly or indirectly, and know nothing of any such sales being made.

Fifth question. How long were you in the employ of Colonel Thompson in connexion with the cattle-hunting-up, &c.?

Fifth answer. About six or seven days.

Sixth question. State what you know about Adams, who acted as farmer or assistant superintendent, exchanging the cattle of the agency for other cattle belonging to freighters,

Sixth answer. I know of his exchanging cattle with parties in one instance, but I am certain that Adams got the best of the bargain. He got that which was fit for beef, in exchange for work cattle. I do not know of Colonel Thompson making any such ex changes, and Colonel Thompson was not present at the time the exchange named wa made; the colonel was then absent from the agency, and did not know of it.

Seventh question. State the manner generally in which Colonel Thompson managed the affairs of the agency while controlling the same as superintendent.

Seventh answer. I am satisfied the business was well managed by him. I think no favoritism was shown, either in the purchase of supplies or the employment of laborers.

THOMAS C. POWERS.

[CIRCULAR.]

RACINE, *Wisconsin*, *May* 10, 1865.

SIR: As you have had considerable experience in the administration of Indian affairs, o other means of observation, I am instructed by the Joint Committee of Congress charged to make inquiry into the condition of the Indian tribes, and their treatment by the civil and military authorities, to submit for your consideration the following questions, and to ask an answer in writing, viz:

1st. During how long a period, and in what capacity, in the civil or military service, have you had experience in Indian affairs; or, what other means of observation have you had, and with what tribe or tribes?

2d. Are they increasing or decreasing in numbers, and from what causes?

3d. What diseases are most common and most fatal among them, and from what causes?

4th. To what extent does intoxication prevail among them, and what legislation, or practical regulation by the department, do you suggest to prevent or mitigate the evil?

5th. From your best information and belief, to what extent does prostitution prevail among them, and the diseases consequent upon it; and to what extent does it diminish their numbers and enfeeble their offspring?

6th. State any other fact bearing upon the causes of their decay, and what, if any, is the best practical remedy?

7th. Which, in your opinion, is the best policy, as white settlements advance and surround Indian reservations—to maintain the Indians upon them and endeavor to resist encroachments, or to remove them to new reserves, remote from settlements?

8th. Is it best that their lands should be held in common, or in severalty?

9th. If held in severalty, is it safe to confer the power of alienation of real estate upon Indians; if so, upon what classes, and under what limitations?

10th. What proportion of them, upon their reservations, give attention to agriculture, or stock-raising; and which are they, males or females, half-breeds or full-bloods?

11th. What has been the effect of schools among them, and what kind of schools do you recommend as most advantageous for them, and what is your opinion of manual-labor schools?

12th. What has been the effect of Christian missions among them, and what do you recommend upon that subject?

13th. As to the country called the Indian territory, what do you recommend in relation to that, after its pacification? Should it be held by the tribes, under former treaty stipulations, or under new treaty arrangements; or be organized into a territorial government for the civilized tribes; and if the latter, upon what conditions and limitations as to residence, suffrage, eligibility to office, and powers of the separate tribes therein?

14th. Ought money annuities to Indians to be discontinued, as far as consistent with treaty obligations?

15th. What proportion actually reaches the hands of the Indians?

16th. What proportion is received by the trader for goods and supplies already advanced?

17th. What proportion is squandered for intoxicating drinks, or in gambling?

18th. What can be practically done to secure the Indian against the two latter evils when payments in money, or in supplies of goods and clothing, are made?

19th. What is the practical operation of the "*order system*" adopted by the licensed traders among them? State your opinion of the merits of the same.

20th. Under what department of the government, the War Department or the Interior, should the Bureau of Indian Affairs be placed, to secure the best and most economical administration of it? State your opinion and reasons.

21st. In setting apart reserves, is it advisable to do so by treaty with the tribes, or to do so by law, or by regulation of the department, enforcing the same by arms?

22d. What proportion of the children are orphans, and to what extent would it be practicable for the Indian Bureau to place orphan children in the families of Christian white men, to be trained and educated in the English language and in the habits of civilized life?

23d. State any other matter of fact which, in your opinion, would improve the present system of Indian affairs in principle, or in administration, and prevent frauds upon the Indian and upon the government.

You will please forward your answer by mail, directed to me at Racine, Wisconsin, on or before the first day of September next.

Respectfully, yours,

J. R. DOOLITTLE, *Chairman, &c.*

Reply of General Pope.

HEADQUARTERS DEPARTMENT OF THE MISSOURI,
St. Louis, Missouri, ———, 1865.

SIR: Your letter enclosing a list of printed questions concerning Indian affairs, &c., has been received, and the following replies submitted:

To question 1st. As captain of topographical engineers, United States army, I spent a great portion of the time from May, 1849, to September, 1859, on the plains and in the mountains, on military and exploration duty, and in that period have had more or less acquaintance with almost all the Indian tribes between the great lakes and the Colorado of the West, and between the Gulf of Mexico and the northern boundary of the United States.

My opportunities for observation have been good, as I have been brought into direct contact with most of the tribes, and have been in several instances called upon by the government for reports concerning them, and concerning military dispositions for protection of overland routes to California and frontier settlements in Texas, Arkansas, Kansas, Iowa, Minnesota, and the Territories west of these States.

From 1862 to February, 1865, I have been commanding the department of the northwest, which included the States of Wisconsin, Minnesota and Iowa, and the Territories of Dakota and Montana. Since February 4, 1865, I have had added to this command the States of Kansas and Missouri, and the Territories of Colorado, Nebraska and Utah. The tribes of Indians with which I have had more or less acquaintance are the Chippewas of the Great Lakes, Winnebagoes, Sioux, Arapahoes, Cheyennes, Pawnees, Comanches, Kiowas, Apaches of the Plains, Lipans, Apaches of New Mexico and Arizona, Jicarilla Apaches, Navajoes, and Utes.

To question 2d. They are rapidly decreasing in numbers from various causes: By disease; by wars; by cruel treatment on the part of the whites—both by irresponsible persons and by government officials; by unwise policy of the government, or by inhumane and dishonest administration of that policy; and by steady and resistless encroachments of the white emigration toward the west, which is every day confining the Indians to narrower limits, and driving off or killing the game, their only means of subsistence.

To question 3d. I think venereal diseases, particularly secondary syphilis, the most common and destructive. It is to be doubted whether one Indian, man or woman, in five, is free from this disease or its effects.

To question 4th. The Indian has a natural and wholly uncontrollable passion for ardent spirits, and will get drunk when he can; a fact well known to Indian traders, who minister to this propensity for their pecuniary profit.

To question 5th. It is difficult to answer this question, unless the fact of the universal prevalence of venereal diseases is sufficient evidence of prostitution.

To question 7th. This question is fully answered in the printed copies of my letters and reports to the War Department on the subject, which are hereto appended, and to which I ask the special attention of your committee.

To question 8th. Same answer as above.

To question 9th. Same answer as above.

To question 11th. Same answer as above.

Question 12th. The effect has not, in my opinion, been so perceptible or so good as it ought to have been, or as was fairly to be expected; arising mainly from the fact that the Christian missionaries and instructors have never had a fair opportunity, for reasons fully set forth in the printed letters and reports referred to in my answer to question 7th. The reason, for this want of success in christianizing and civilizing the Indians, (as far as such a thing can be done,) and the means to obviate the difficulties so far insuperable, are fully set forth in these printed documents.

To questions 14th, 15th, 16th, 17th, and 18th. Reference is made to the same printed documents, above referred to, in which my opinions of all these matters are fully given.

To question 19th. I am utterly opposed to the whole system of trade with Indians, as it exists at present. The printed documents heretofore mentioned contain a code of trade regulations which, in my opinion, would obviate many of the evils and frauds upon the Indians of the present system of trading. They were carefully drawn up by me, and submitted to the government for approval; but have not yet been approved, as they are believed to be, in some respects, not in accordance with the laws of Congress on the subject. The attention of your committee is respectfully invited to them.

Question 20th. Aside from any question whether the Indian agents appointed from civil life, and for small political services, or the officers of the army, commanding on the frontier, are most likely to administer honestly and faithfully a public trust, involving heavy disbursements of money and goods, and opportunities for land speculations and other species of fraud, it seems to me very clear that the present divided jurisdiction of Indian affairs is the worst possible arrangement. When the Indians are at war with the whites, the duty of controlling them falls upon the army. The moment the Indians exhibit, or are supposed to exhibit, a desire for peace, the civil agents step in to make it.

Of course there is, and must always be, debatable ground between a condition of war and a condition of peace, upon which the military and civil officers are rarely agreed. Conflicts of authority and of jurisdiction and differences of opinion are constantly arising which have no result, except to render the whole management of Indian relations inefficient, to say no worse. The Indian agents, influenced by contractors, by traders, and by the merchants from whom Indian supplies are bought, are constantly anxious to make treaties of peace with Indians. Every such treaty involves the expenditure of much money, and the oftener treaties are made the larger are the profits to everybody, except the Indian and the government. Officers of the army, who have spent their whole lives on the frontier, and who are held responsible for every murder, every robbery, and every irregularity committed by Indians, and whom long experience has made familiar with Indian character and habits, are better qualified, perhaps, to judge of the proper time and the proper circumstances to make a treaty with Indians, and of the most judicious terms of such a treaty, in view of future quiet, than a civil agent, recently appointed, who has no experience, whatever, of frontier life, and no practical knowledge whatever of the business with which he is intrusted, nor of the people with whom he is to deal. Whether this is so or not, it is quite certain that a business thus divided between two departments, acting independently of each other—except so far as they may choose to act in concert—must be done in an inefficient and unsatisfactory manner. It is my opinion, as, I doubt not, it is the opinion of every man who has ever considered the matter, that the whole management of the Indians should be confided to one branch of the government, and not confused and distracted by the operations of two sets of officials, differing in opinion and embarrassing each other by conflicting action.

Whether the whole subject should be committed to the Interior Department or the War Department seems easy to answer.

The necessity of using soldiers to protect emigration and frontier settlements, and to enforce the observance of treaties with Indians, demands that the War Department should have very much to do with our Indian relations and the management of Indian affairs. There is no such necessity for any action of the Interior Department, and the Indian Bureau is merely an excrescence upon that department. Army officers on the frontier can now, as they did in former times, perform all the duties of Indian agents and superintendents, without any increase of army pay. They can make such treaties with Indians as are thought judicious by the government, and they have the military power to enforce any treaties they do make. The Indian, when he makes an agreement with a commander of military forces, understands very well that he is dealing with a man who can force him to observe his agreement, and he respects both the man and his own promises accordingly.

That army officers would disburse money and goods to the Indians with as much honesty and prudence as the Indian agent is not to be questioned. Aside, therefore, from other reasons why the whole care of the Indians should be committed to the War Department, it is very certain that by doing so the entire army of Indian agents can be mustered out of the service, and their pay and expenses saved to the government.

My main reason, however, for saying that the War Department should have exclusive control of Indian affairs is based upon the absolute conviction that those affairs would be better and more honestly administered, and that our Indian relations would at once be placed upon a footing far more satisfactory, both to the government and to the Indian.

To question 21st. It is better to set apart reserves by the action of the proper department, to be subsequently confirmed by law, and to enforce their occupation by the Indians.

It is needless, as it seems to me, to give reasons for this opinion The government knows the situation, the progress and direction of emigration and of frontier settlement, and its own power to protect Indians upon the reservations assigned them, better than the Indians can possibly know such things. It is certain that the government is not now able to assign or to assure to the Indians reservations sufficiently extensive to enable them to subsist themselves by hunting. They must, therefore, be partially subsisted by the government, and, of course, such places must be selected for reservations as are easy of access by steamer or railroad, otherwise the expense to the government will be extremely great.

To question 22d. I cannot answer this question.

To question 23d. My views and opinions concerning Indian affairs are the result of more than ten years of constant service on the frontier among Indians. They are fully set forth in the printed letters and reports made by me at various times to the War Department, and hereto appended.

I respectfully refer your committee to these documents for details, and for the reasons upon which I base my answers to many of the foregoing questions.

As I have been influenced in these views and my action upon them solely by a purpose to serve the public interests, by endeavoring to point out and, as far as I could, correct abuses in the present administration of Indian affairs, protect the Indian as well as the government against fraud and wrong, and at least remove the reproach of inhumanity to the Indian tribes, now justly chargeable upon the government through the conduct of many of its agents, I trust your committee will examine with what attention they fairly merit the letters and reports in question.

I am, sir, respectfully, your obedient servant,

JOHN POPE,
Major General U. S. A.

Hon. J. R. Doolittle,
Chairman of Joint Committee to examine into Indian Affairs.

Reply of John T. Sprague, colonel 7th regiment U. S. infantry.

St. Louis, Mo., *August* 12, 1865.

Sir: In answer to the interrogatories contained in your printed letter of May 10, 1865, I have the honor to give the result of my experience among the various Indian tribes in as brief and in as concise a manner as possible.

It is a subject upon which it is almost impracticable to be brief, involving as it does the amelioration of a neglected race as well as the honor of our country.

Question 1. "During how long a period and in what capacity in the civil or military service have you had experience in Indian affairs, or what other means of observation have you had, and with what tribe or tribes?"

Answer. In the years of 1831 and 1832 I was an assistant Indian agent in paying annuities to the Chippewa, Winnebago, and Ottawa tribes of Indians, located in Michigan, Illinois, and Wisconsin. In the year of 1836, upon the conclusion of the Creek war, I had placed under my charge, (then a lieutenant U. S. A.,) by Major General Jesup, commanding the armies in the field, 3,140 Creek, Seminole, and Tallahassee Indians, located in Georgia and Alabama, which I emigrated to the vicinity of Fort Gibson, Arkansas, and placed them on the reservation assigned them, on the Verdigris and Neosho rivers. I was six months on the road, and crossed the Mississippi at Memphis, Tennessee. In January, 1837, I proceeded to the Choctaw nation, and paid the annuity at Fort Towson, Arkansas. In April, 1837, I was ordered by the Secretary of War to report to the Commissioner of Indian Affairs for duty, and was instructed to remove from Michigan, Illinois, and Wisconsin all the Indians I could find roaming through those States. I assembled in camps near Chicago fifteen hundred, and emigrated them to Council Bluffs, on the Missouri river.

From 1839 to 1848 I participated in the Florida war, and was in constant intercourse with Creek, Tallahassee, and Seminole Indians, at peace and in active hostilities.

I emigrated to Arkansas 1,200 hostile Indians. During the years of 1849, '50, '51, '55, '57, and '58, I was actively in and out of the field with and against the various tribes of Indians occupying Texas and New Mexico.

My association with Indians has been intimate and extensive, and I have always felt a deep interest in their welfare.

Question 2. "Are they increasing or decreasing in numbers, and from what causes?"

Answer. The Indians are decreasing in numbers, caused by their proximity to the white man. So soon as Indians adopt the habits of white men they begin to decrease, aggravated by imbibing all the vices and none of their virtues. Other causes exist, too numerous to be detailed in this paper.

Question 3. "What diseases are most common and most fatal among them, and from what causes?"

Answer. The children die rapidly and suddenly from dysentery and measles, and from neglect and exposure to the weather. The adults die from fevers, small-pox, drunkenness, and disease engendered from sexual intercourse. These diseases are among the men and women in the most malignant form, as the Indian doctors are unable to manage them. Indulgence in liquor, exposure, and the absence of remedies aggravate the disease. In this, striking at the very basis of procreation, is to be found the active cause of the destruction of the Indian race.

Question 4. "To what extent does intoxication prevail among them, and what legislation or practical regulation by the department do you suggest to prevent or mitigate the evil?"

Answer. Intoxication among Indians is excessive and unlimited. When liquor can be obtained, men, women, and children will indulge in it, and will sell all they possess to procure it. In New Mexico the Indians have quite a trade among themselves in making and selling whiskey.

Congress should pass the most stringent laws to prevent the sale of liquor; let them be brief and to the point, that the offender may be brought to immediate punishment. The department should issue regulations and instructions, based upon law and call upon the nearest military commander to aid in executing them. It is utterly futile to rely upon juries and the support of neighboring communities. Stern, prompt and efficient action is necessary, and reliable men as agents to execute laws and instructions are indispensable.

Question 5. "From your best information and belief, to what extent does prostitution prevail among them, and the diseases consequent upon it, and to what extent does it diminish their numbers and enfeeble their offspring?"

Answer. Prostitution is unlimited; a free, full indulgence commences in youth among both sexes. I cannot say to what extent this indulgence diminishes their numbers, not having statistics before me, but I know it is fast destroying the race, and will continue to until a high moral sense of right and wrong is inculcated. To limit, or to stop it, at the present time, the attempt might as well be made among the buffaloes and the deer. They fight among themselves upon the subject like animals, and fear of summary punishment is the only cause of restraint. It is a common thing to see women going about with their ears and hair cut off for infidelity. Jealousy exists among the Indians to a great extent. Prostitution destroys their offspring by planting disease early in life.

Question 6. "State any other fact bearing upon the causes of their decay, and what, if any, is the best practical remedy?"

Answer. This question admits of a wide range. The decrees of a wise Providence, the encroachments of the white man, civilization in all its forms, inefficient and unfaithful agents, injustice and abuse, want of proper and judicious attention—all these cause the rapid extinction of the Indian race. The remedy is in improving their condition through the enacting of wise laws, which should be executed by wise, honest, and judicious men—those who have patience and sagacity enough to break up the stubbornness of the Indian's prejudices, not by harsh punishments, false promises and neglect, but by kind and appropriate advice, and by careful attention to habits, vices, and wants, at the same time cultivating their thoughts, habits, and feelings.

Question 7. "Which, in your opinion, is the best policy, as white settlements advance and surround Indian reservations—to maintain the Indians upon them, and endeavor to resist encroachments, or to remove them to new reserves, remote from settlements?"

Answer. I should remove the Indian to new reserves remote from settlements. I am satisfied the Indian cannot improve in the vicinity of white settlements.

Question 8. "Is it best that their lands should be held in common or in severalty?"

Answer. It is best that the Indian lands should be held in common, provided they are managed by judicious laws and regulations, and executed by honest and competent agents. The Indian cannot long possess land in person, as no law or regulation can reach the swindling movements and sagacity of the white man.

Question 9. "If held in severalty, is it safe to confer the power of alienation of real estate upon Indians? If so, upon what classes and under what limitation?"

Answer. Should not be held in severalty.

Question 10. "What proportion of them upon their reservations give attention to agriculture or stock-raising, and which are they—males or females, half-breeds or full-bloods?"

Answer. A small proportion give attention to agriculture upon reservations, or to stock-raising. Most of those who do are women. The half-breeds give some attention to stock-raising, being interested in fast horses, &c.

A full-blooded Indian is always idle: necessity alone causes him to be employed. With proper management much can be done for the Indian race upon reservations. They can be induced to labor, not constantly, but at certain hours.

The raising of stock of all kinds, as well as grains, might be carried to a great extent if the Indian was convinced that, at a certain time, he would have money in exchange. To work for what they are to eat or to wear is absurd to an Indian; but let him be satisfied that money is to be the result, he can be induced to work more than under any other circumstances. The women are always industrous. Half-breeds are troublesome. They have all the vices of the whites, bad tempers, and are discontented, set bad examples, and cause complaints against the government, and make combinations to the prejudice of their agents. Military authority and advice have a beneficial control over them. They fear the commissioned officer. From their knowledge of the English language, and familiarity with the white man, they consider their agents as inferior to themselves—mere servants.

Question 11th. "What has been the effect of schools among them, and what kind of schools do you recommend as most advantageous for them; and what is your opinion of manual labor schools?"

Answer. The success of schools among them has been a failure; I speak generally.

There are a few instances where a school has succeeded; but, when compared with the effort made and money expended, schools have failed. This has been owing mainly to the want of good, practical, honest and judicious teachers. The mere schoolmaster effects but little: he should be a man of matured mind, good practical common sense, with patience and kindness, and, above all, having at heart the improvement of the race, and willing to make sacrifices to attain it. A school with such a teacher, introducing work at proper intervals, mingled with sports and agreeable occupations, with the prospect of obtaining some money on New Year's or some festival day, will do much towards the instruction of Indian children, at the same time excite a high degree of interest among the parents.

In teaching the Indian, restraints and privations must be avoided; confinement, and a sense of limitation to his head, feet, and hands, make him uncomfortable.

With some ingenuity and tact an Indian can be improved mentally and physically, without his being made conscious that he is restricted in his liberty.

Instead of teaching an Indian boy his letters within the limits of a school house, confined for hours, I would take him to the woods, and with a bow and arrow, or a rifle, instruct him to shoot at A, B, or C, at fifty or a hundred yards, and gather around him parents and sisters to see it done. In this manner, instruction can be enlarged by experience and tact, until the Indian almost unconsciously learns to read and write.

Manual labor schools are of the most troublesome as well as the most unsuccessful character. The prospect of money for their toil is the only inducement for the Indian to work. These schools, like all others, depend upon the capacity of the head man. Such men are difficult to obtain, particularly when small salaries are given. Honest and capable men will not exile themselves to the Indian country unless well paid.

Question 12th. "What has been the effect of Christian missions among them, and what do you recommend upon that subject?"

Answer. Christian missions have done good, but the results have not corresponded with the means employed. These missions have the same fault as other schools—too much confinement, nothing practical.

To have successful missions, a first class of men should be employed, with a salary corresponding with their ability and zeal. They should take their families with them, and by teachings and example impress upon the Indian, male and female, the necessity of marriage, and the impropriety of the beastly intercourse existing among them. Make the marriage ceremony a holy one by mingling with it the customs of the Indian and the sacredness of the white man.

Indolent and inefficient men will take these positions with a small income, (when the place should be filled by the first men in the country,) thus defeating the wise and benevolent purposes of the government. It leads to peculation, speculation and deception, which the Indian soon discovers, and thereby defeats entirely the teacher's admonitions and instructions.

Question 13th. "As to the country called the Indian territory, what do you recommend in relation to that, after its pacification; should it be held by the tribes under former treaty stipulations, or under new treaty arrangements; or be organized into a territorial government for the civilized tribes; and if the latter, upon what conditions and limitations as to residence, suffrage, eligibility to office, and powers of the separate tribes therein?"

Answer. I have not the space, nor have I had sufficient time, nor am I possessed of the necessary information to answer this inquiry satisfactorily to myself.

The country known as the Indian country should be carefully looked into. It is now in a very unsettled state. I would have it surveyed and examined, then have a meeting at desirable points of all the Indian tribes, abrogate old treaties as far as practicable, set apart certain portions of lands for certain tribes. In fact, reorganize the whole Indian country, form new treaties, and make new arrangements, endeavor to satisfy all tribes, and then cause military posts to be erected at commanding points, and commence anew to inform the Indian what he was to do, and what he was to expect from the general government; at the same time, have such laws passed and regulations made as will prevent the encroachments and impositions of the white man.

Question 14th. "Ought money annuities to Indians to be discontinued as far as consistent with treaty obligations?"

Answer. Money annuities should be discontinued to the Indians.

Question 15th. "What proportion actually reaches the Indians?"

Answer. Very little, if any.

Question 16th. "What proportion is received by the trader for goods and supplies already advanced?"

Answer. The whole, if he can wrest it from the Indian. During the period previous to paying the annuity, liquor is often sold to Indians and entered upon his account as calico, shirts, blankets, strouding, beads, &c.

Question 17th. "What proportion is squandered for intoxicating drinks or in gambling?"

Answer. Very near the whole.

Question 18th. "What can be practically done to secure the Indian against the latter evils when payments in money or in supplies of goods and clothing are made?"

Answer. The War Department should require the military commander nearest to the point of payment to organize a board, of not less nor more than three commissioned officers of his command, to examine the agent's accounts before the day of payment, and report the same to him in a full and formal written statement, which is to be approved by him, and at the proper time forwarded to the department, together with such remarks as he sees fit to make. In regard to the payment of money, this board should be present on the day of payment, and see that the proportion due each is placed in his or her hands; then the trader, upon presenting his account approved, should be paid the amount due him. This is the only method I can suggest; even this is doubtful.

I have seen the trader present to an Indian woman a mere scrap of paper with a few figures upon it as evidence of her indebtedness, and when she hesitated she was seized and the money wrested from her clenched hand, while her children were crying around her. If a white man or an Indian interposed he did it at the hazard of his life. General Cass, then governor of Michigan in 1830 and 1831, required the Indian agent to put the money into the hand of the Indian, and let him pay the trader, instead of the agent paying it from his table, thus recognizing the account of the trader without the Indian having anything to say in the matter. I have known instances where the agent had a percentage upon all the money that he would pay into the hands of the trader. However stringent the orders were in the payment of annuities or in making treaties, my experience has taught me that money, enough of it, and paid at the right time in a secret manner, generally abrogated all laws and regulations.

Question 19th. "What is the practical operation of the order system adopted by the licensed traders among them? State your opinion of the merits of the same."

Answer. I have no knowledge of the order system referred to.

Question 20th. "Under what department of the government, the War Department or the Interior, should the Bureau of Indian Affairs be placed to secure the best and most economical administration of it? State your opinion and reasons."

Answer. Under the War Department, for this reason: In dealing with the Indians they like to see the evidence of power and authority. The officer's uniform, the presence and prompt obedience of soldiers, the general authority exercised by officers of the army under their observation from day to day, their ability and means of punishment—all these create in the Indian's mind respect and reverence, as well as obedience, and he looks upon the military officer, with his sword and uniform and soldiers about him, as the direct representative of his Great Father in Washington. A military officer has his commission at stake. He is bound to execute orders derived from an experienced source; his speculations and opinions are not regarded, but he must follow the instructions derived from a department, the policy of which must be respected and adhered to. He is subject to prompt punishment. His position is one for life. He feels independent in the execution of orders from a department which will give him protection, encouragement, as well as reward. He is surrounded by a class of men who have a professional pride in the discharge of duties intrusted to them. The commanding officer, as well as the soldier, have a generous and kindly feeling for the Indian, and have deep sympathy in his condition.

Question 21st. "In setting apart reserves, is it advisable to do so by treaty with the tribes, or to do so by law, or by regulation of the department, enforcing the same by arms?"

Answer. The War Department should set apart reserves and maintain them by stringent orders and instructions applicable to the necessities of the case. Laws cannot be enacted to reach the changes, incidents, and encroachments in an Indian country and upon reservations.

Question 22d. "What proportion of the children are orphans, and to what extent would it be practicable for the Indian Bureau to place orphan children in the families of Christian white men, to be trained and educated in the English language and in the habits of civilized life?"

Answer. I am unable to answer this question, there being so many contingencies connected with it. It can only be answered when the occasion arises, and then upon consultation with the chief of the tribe. I cannot say, having no data before me, what proportion of children are orphans. This would depend much upon the location of the tribe and the diseases of the climate.

Question 23d. "State any other matter of fact which, in your opinion, would improve the present system of Indian affairs, in principle or in administration, and prevent frauds upon the Indians and the government."

Answer. The Indian affairs of our country should be, as I have briefly stated, under the control of the War Department. Experience upon the frontier has shown me the necessity of this. There can be no division of authority in those delicate and responsible duties. In times of difficulty the War Department is compelled to exert its authority to restore order and punish offenders; and unless this can be exercised without being embarrassed by acts of agents acting under instructions from another department, the efforts of the military will prove unavailing, and result in causing the Indian to doubt the fidelity as well as the power of our government. I am satisfied the Indian can be made a valuable auxiliary force in protecting the frontier. The policy of our government has been generous and kind, but, from numerous causes, it has been perverted.

Twenty years of my service in the United States army, out of thirty, have been spent upon the Indian frontier. The United States flag, the Catholic church, and the Indians have been my companions. I have conducted upwards of six thousand Indians—men, women, and children—from their homes on the east side of the Mississippi to the west, and located them upon reservations granted by the government. I have been in daily intercourse with them in their camps and villages. I have met them in battle, and have counselled with them in peace, and have ate and slept for days and weeks in their camps and wigwams, and am satisfied that, with a generous and protective policy, the Indian can be successfully brought under the beneficial influences of civilization, and be made to protect the frontier instead of being its terror. Treat them kindly, generously, and honestly; fulfil all treaties and promises with the most scrupulous fidelity, when it will be found that they will yield to laws, advice, and regulations with much more alacrity than the men or citizens by whom they are surrounded. To control the Indian you must have his unlimited confidence. They are good judges of human nature, and can detect insincerity or dishonesty with wonderful accuracy. The age in which we live calls for a Christian policy towards this race, and a faithful administration; utter extermination is their destiny, unless the strong arm of government is interposed to stay the current now sweeping them to destruction. It can be done by wise councils, judicious laws and regulations, and through the instrumentality of competent and honest men. Liberal salaries should be paid to agents of every class, securing good men, thus avoiding the seductive influences of presents, rewards, and speculations. Indian agents should become Christian missionaries, and unless they embark in the undertaking with a determination to serve their God and their country, all efforts of the civil or military authorities will prove unavailing in improving the condition of the Indian.

JOHN T. SPRAGUE,
Colonel 7th Regiment U. S. Infantry,
Chief of Staff to Brevet Major General John Pope, Comm'dg Dep't of Missouri.

Hon. JAMES R. DOOLITTLE,
Chairman, &c., &c., Racine, Wisconsin.

Reply of Brigadier General James H. Carleton.

HEADQUARTERS DEPARTMENT OF NEW MEXICO,
Santa Fé, N. M., July 25, 1865.

SIR: I have had the honor to receive your printed letter dated at Racine, Wisconsin, May 10, 1865, and which propounds in regular sequence twenty-three questions, with reference to Indian affairs, to which you ask my answers in writing.

Question 1st. "During how long a period, and in what capacity, in the civil or military service, have you had experience in Indian affairs; or what other means of observation have you had, and with what tribe or tribes?"

Answer. I was appointed a 2d lieutenant in the United States first dragoons, October 18, 1839. In the spring of 1841 I was sent to Fort Gibson, in the Cherokee nation. Saw more or less of the Cherokees, Creeks, and Seminoles from that time until the spring of 1842. Then I went to Council Bluffs, now in Iowa, where I became acquainted with the Pottawatomies, In the fall of 1843 I went to Fort Leavenworth, then near the Delawares, Kickapoos, and Shawnees. In 1844 I was one of an armed expedition to visit the four bands of Pawnees on Platte river. These were the Grand Pawnees, the Republican Pawnees, the Pawnees Tepage, and the Loup Pawnees. With these we held councils. Then they were supposed to number—all told—about 12,000 souls. Thence we visited and held councils with the Ottoes and Missourias, at Belleview; and thence visited and held councils with the Iowas and the Sacs and Foxes, then living on the west bank of the Missouri river, a little south of Jeffrey's Point. In the spring and summer of 1845 I went with General Kearney in his expedition to the Rocky mountains. We held councils with the Ogallalla and Brulé bands of Sioux, at Scott's Bluffs, and at Fort Laramie; with the Arapaho and some Gros Ventres between Fort Laramie and Lodge Pole creek; with the Cheyennes between that point and where Denver City now stands; and with a band of the Comanches below Bent's fort, on the Arkansas.

After the Mexican war, I was stationed at Fort Leavenworth again, from the fall of 1848 until the spring of 1851, except six months which I spent at Fort Kearney, above the Pawnee villages, and at Fort Laramie. In the spring of 1851 I went to New Mexico, when there were opportunities, to see something of the Apaches, Utahs, Navajoes, and Pueblo Indians. In 1857 I left New Mexico, and in 1858 went to California, where I was stationed at Fort Tejon, within twelve miles of an Indian reservation. In 1859 I went across the desert to the Mountain Meadows in Utah. In this long march I saw a good many Pah-Utes—(Water Utes.) In 1860, made a campaign against them, having my headquarters on the Mojave river. In 1862, came to the Maricopa and Pimo villages, on the Gila, and to the Papago village at San Xavier du Bac, in Arizona. Thence I came to New Mexico again, where I have had some experience with Indian affairs, as you will see by my General Orders No. 3, series for 1863, and No. 4, series for 1864, copies of which I have had the honor to send you. All the experience I have had of Indian affairs has been afforded by what I have been able to observe of them in the service named; during much of which, I only occupied the position of a subaltern, and was not called upon by official obligation or duty to be more than a casual observer of their character, habits, numbers, &c., &c.

Question 2d. "Are they increasing or decreasing in numbers, and from what causes?"

Answer. As a general rule, the Indians alluded to are decreasing very rapidly in numbers, in my opinion. The causes for this have been many, and may be summed up as follows:

1st. Wars with our pioneers and our armed forces; change of climate and country among those who have been moved from east of the Mississippi to the far west.

2d. Intemperance, and the exposure consequent thereupon.

3d. Venereal diseases, which they are unable, from lack of medicines and skill, to eradicate from their systems, and which, among Indians who live nearest the whites, is generally diffused either in scrofula or some other form of its taint.

4th. Small-pox, measles, and cholera—diseases unknown to them in the early days of the country.

5th. The causes which the Almighty originates, when in their appointed time He wills that one race of men—as in races of lower animals—shall disappear off the face of the earth and give place to another race, and so on, in the great cycle traced out by Himself, which may be seen, but has reasons too deep to be fathomed by us. The races of the mammoths and mastodons, and the great sloths, came and passed away: the red man of America is passing away!

Question 3d. "What diseases are most common and most fatal among them; and from what causes?"

Answer. Inflammation of the lungs, or pneumonia; fevers; and, as before stated, venereal, small-pox, measles, and cholera. The last three diseases as epidemics, not in sporadic cases.

Question 4th. "To what extent does intoxication prevail among them, and what legislation, or practical regulation by the department, do you suggest to prevent or mitigate the evil?"

Answer. Among Indians living near the settlements, intoxication prevails very generally. If it does not, it is because from poverty on the part of the Indian, or scarçity of liquor on the part of the whites, there is nothing to get drunk upon. Very stringent laws, faithfully executed, might mitigate, but can never stop the evil. Your whiskey-seller will be found on the top of the Wind River mountains, if your troops go there and have money, or your Indian goes there with his beaver-skin, his buffalo robe, his buckskin, his pony, or his squaw. Some one of these articles of trade will be sure to draw the liquor forward, in spite of your laws to hold it back. This is true, and should be looked squarely in the face.

Question 5th. "From your best information and belief, to what extent does prostitution prevail among them, and the diseases consequent upon it; and to what extent does it diminish their numbers and enfeeble their offspring?"

Answer. Prostitution prevails to a great extent among the Navajoes, the Maricopas, and the Yuma Indians; and its attendant diseases, as before stated, have more or less tainted the blood of the adults; and by inheritance of the children, who, from diseased parents, become possessed of but feeble energies, feeble vitality—in short, become emasculated in body and mind. The Pimos, Apaches, Delawares, Kickapoos, Shawnees, Creeks, and Comanches, are really virtuous—as a rule—so far as promiscuous commerce between the sexes may go. This cannot be said of the Cherokees, Seminoles, Pottawatomies, Pawnees, the Sioux, Arapahoes, Cheyennes, or Kiowas. They are all more or less erotic in their temperaments and habits, and in proportion as they are so, their offspring are more or less enfeebled.

Question 6th. "State any other fact bearing upon the causes of their decay; and what, if any, is the best practical remedy?"

Answer. This question seems to be answered, so far as I know, by what I have already stated. The best practical remedy must lie in teaching the people the evils to which their course of life tends, and in educating them up to that point where, from moral principles that can be taught them, they will of themselves do right. Now, they do many acts of wrong from sheer ignorance of the moral and physical consequences. The natural decay incident to their race must find its remedy in a power above that of mortals.

Question 7th. "Which, in your opinion, is the best policy, as white settlements advance and surround Indian reservations—to maintain the Indians upon them, and endeavor to resist encroachments, or to remove them to new reserves, remote from settlements?"

Answer. Maintain the Indians upon such reservations, and resist the encroachments of the whites. It must come to this sooner or later; because, from the rapid spread over the unoccupied lands of the tidal wave or "*bore*" of the great and advancing ocean of pale-faces, you will soon have no places suited by climate and extent to which to remove them, so that they can be remote from the settlements. Therefore, place them upon reservations *now*, and hold those reservations inviolate. In the great and rising sea here prefigured, those reservations will be islands; and, as time elapses and the race dies out, these islands may become less and less, until, finally, the great sea will ingulf them one after another, until they become known only in history, and at length are blotted out of even that, forever.

Question 8th. "Is it best that their lands should be held in common, or in severalty?"

Answer. In my opinion, the lands should be held in severalty. Surveys should be carefully made, and each family or head of family should have a part allotted to him. The human being, white or red or black, who plants a tree or a vine, or builds a house, or makes a field or garden, identifies himself with it—loves it; his children are born there, and the associations connected with all these things constitute and give birth to what we call *home* love and *home* feeling. We have taken quite enough from the Indian. Let them

28

have and keep really a home. If they have rights at all upon the earth, that is one of the dearest. Let us not rob them of that.

Question 9th. "If held in severalty, is it safe to confer the power of alienation of real estate upon Indians; if so, upon what classes, and under what limitations?"

Answer. It would not be safe to confer the power of alienation of lands held thus in severalty by the Indians. They are too easily duped by the designing, or tempted by the wicked, to be intrusted with such a power. They should have only the powers in this regard which a ward holds under a guardian.

Question 10th. "What proportion of them, upon their reservations, give attention to agriculture, or stock-raising; and which are they, males or females, half-breeds or full bloods?"

Answer. The young Indians upon the Navajo reservation, which is just starting in New Mexico, are the most docile and industrious. The full-grown ones are lazy, and can hardly be reclaimed from their savage desire to roam about and lead a life of idleness. They must die off, and the young ones grow up to take their places, before any marked improvement in this people will be observed. I am not familiar enough with other Indians upon reservations to answer this question fully.

Question 11th. "What has been the effect of schools among them, and what kind of schools do you recommend as most advantageous for them; and what is your opinion of manual-labor schools?"

Answer. I cannot answer this question, from lack of knowledge of the progress made or not made by schools among the Indians. Manual-labor schools, in my opinion, are the best schools for the Indian children.

Question 12th. "What has been the effect of Christian missions among them, and what do you recommend upon that subject?"

Answer. So far as my observation has gone, the Roman Catholic missionaries are the ones who the soonest teach the Indian the truth of Christianity. The solemn pomp and attractive ceremonial of that church seem to catch soonest and hold most enduringly the attention and thoughts and, finally, the belief of the Indian. I pass no judgment on this creed or that; I simply state a fact; and were it left with me, I would have all teachers, male and female, and all clergy for wild or nomadic Indians, of that church. After the Indian becomes civilized, and commences to think for himself on articles of faith, or on the points which divide our Christian churches, then let all denominations, which desire to do so, establish schools and churches among them. If you let them all have access to the Indians at *first*, and before the latter have become at all civilized, I think the teacher of future rewards and punishments, and the teacher of universal salvation, &c., &c., would be apt to raise puzzles and marvels in their unsophisticated minds, of so serious a character as to make them prefer the good old, steady-going, unchangeable pagan creed of their fathers, to the many trails to happiness which they would thus be placed upon. And when those trails diverge to all points of the compass, would it not be hard to convince them that each one *surely* led to the Christian's heaven? To use one of their own forcible expressions, (but with no irreverence,) such diverse teachings they would certainly call "bad medicine."

Question 13th. "As to the country called the Indian territory, what do you recommend in relation to that, after its pacification? Should it be held by the tribes, under former treaty stipulations, or under new treaty arrangements, or be organized into a territorial government for the civilized tribes; and if the latter, upon what conditions and limitations as to residence, suffrage, eligibility to office, and powers of the separate tribes therein?"

Answer. Let the Cherokees, Creeks, Choctaws, Chickasaws, and Seminoles have their separate lands defined, if you please, but let their country be erected into a Territory. To do this, make new treaty stipulations, if necessary. The rights of suffrage, I think, should be uniform, and such as Congress in its wisdom may devise. This is a matter upon which any opinion of mine would be of but little value. The tribes thus united would sooner become homogeneous. Their territorial governor, judges, &c., at first, and until those Indians became educated to this new step towards civilization, and towards taking their place in the family of States, should be appointed from Americans. An Indian governor or judge, taken from any one of these tribes, at first would be an object of dislike on the part of the Indians belonging to other tribes than his own. The delegate could be elected, and, at first, taken from the tribes in rotation. Equality of powers and rights of the separate tribes in such a Territory should be a *sine qua non*. Northward, by and by, you can doubtless place the Delawares, Shawnees, Kickapoos, Pottawatomies, Sacs and Foxes, Senecas, Wyandotts, Caddoes, and the scattering Mohawks, contiguous to each other, and erect them into a Territory. They are all more or less of the old Algonquin stock. They would not be apt to fraternize readily with the Indians who came from North and South Carolina, Georgia, Florida, Alabama and Mississippi. Perhaps, in after years, you could get the Sioux and Chippewas to come into such an arrangement. There your territorial government for Indians would end. The remaining Indians should be gotten upon reservations, there to fulfil their destinies as before set forth.

Question 14th. "Ought money annuities to Indians to be discontinued, as far as consistent with treaty obligations?"

Answer. Money annuities should be discontinued as far as practicable.

Question 15th. "What proportion actually reaches the hands of the Indians?"

Answer. A very small proportion.

Question 16th. "What proportion is received by the trader for goods and supplies already advanced?"

Answer. A very large proportion.

Question 17th. "What proportion is squandered for intoxicating drinks or in gambling?"

Answer. Nearly or quite all that the Indian gets over and above what he owes, and what is literally grabbed from him, at "*the payment*," by the trader.

Question 18th. "What can be practically done to secure the Indian against the two latter evils, when payments in money or in supplies of goods and clothing are made?"

Answer. Keep all the traders away from "the payment."

Question 19th. "What is the practical operation of the 'order system' adopted by the licensed traders among them? State your opinion of the merits of the same."

Answer. It operates very badly to the Indian, and inures greatly to the interest of those who give the orders. If I understand the question rightly, Major General Hitchcock can give much information on all these abuses. He has been engaged in inquiries into them. This was in 1841 and in 1842.

Question 20th. "Under what department of the government, the War Department or the Interior, should the Bureau of Indian Affairs be placed, to secure the best and most economical administration of it? State your opinion and reasons."

Answer. In my opinion, the Indian Bureau should be placed under the War Department, as it was before the Department of the Interior was created and organized. My reasons for this are: When under the War Department, which also controls the forces operating in Indian countries, there would be no conflicts of opinion about what should be done in a given case; for, as the fountain whence might emanate instructions, whether to commanders, superintendents, or agents, would be one, so the different streams of authority and regulations, descending through these subordinates, would be of the same character. In my opinion, the office of Commissioner of Indian Affairs should be abolished, if it be incompatible with the law to have an officer of the army to fill it *ex officio*. Contemplating the placing of the Indian Bureau under the direction of the War Department, and organizing it systematically, so that its operations should harmonize with those of the troops, and the two run together as parts of the same machine, with no cogs mismatching, no jarrings, no belts loose, &c., it would be next to impossible to find a citizen who would understand Indian affairs, Indians, Indian countries, Indian wants, &c., and at the same time understand military affairs. But it is easy to find many an officer in the United States army who, from long service in Indian countries, understands all these matters. If it be more an object to have the business between the government and Indians managed by fixed rules, and without uncertainty and confusion and delay, than to have the place and patronage of the Indian Bureau exist, irrespective of these considerations, the plan here suggested seems in my mind to meet that object. For I would have not only the head of the Indian Bureau an officer of the army, but each commander of a military department should be *ex officio* superintendent of Indian affairs for all the Indians in that department; and the commander of one post nearest any one tribe of Indians in that department should be the agent, *ex officio*, for that tribe.

The money appropriated by Congress for any one tribe should pass into the hands of the quartermaster's department, and should be disbursed *per se*, if the law so require, or expended for goods to be bought in the market as army supplies are bought. These goods should be issued in presence of witnesses, and accounted for as army clothing is accounted for; and the returns of property and money accounts should be made by the same system as that of other property and money accounts of the army. I could go into all the details of this matter to show that by the plan proposed the Indians would be sure to get their rights, and the treasury of the United States have evidence that its money had gone out and been expended legitimately for a *quid pro quo*. The chief quartermaster of a department would disburse money and distribute effects for Indians under the direction and superintendence of the department commander, who would have neither interest nor responsibility in the matter, except to see the duty done properly. The same chain of responsibility and of direction and supervision would be held by the quartermaster and commander of a post. By this system it is difficult to see how the Indians could fail to get their just dues, and all without a cent of expense additional to that at present paid to the army. Your whole Indian department, as at present organized, could then be entirely abolished. How much would be saved to the United States by this it is not for me to say.

I desired to give you the opinion of Lieutenant Colonel Nelson H. Davis, U. S. A., inspector general of this department, on some of the points raised by your interrogatories, and I accordingly addressed to him a letter on the subject. He has had many years' experience with Indians, and his is a valuable opinion. His reply to my letter is as follows:

INSPECTOR GENERAL'S OFFICE, DEPARTMENT OF NEW MEXICO,
Santa Fé, N. M., July 29, 1865.

GENERAL: I have the honor to acknowledge the receipt of your communication of this date, asking for my written opinion in answer to the following questions propounded by the Hon. J. R. Doolittle, U. S. Senate, chairman of the congressional committee, now making inquiries into the condition of the Indian tribes.

Question. "Under what department of the government, the War Department or the Interior, should the Bureau of Indian Affairs be placed, to secure the best and most economical administration of it? State your opinion and reasons."

Question. "What proportion of the children are orphans; and to what extent would it be practicable for the Indian Bureau to place orphan children in the families of Christian white men, to be trained and educated in the English language, and in the habits of civilized life?"

Question. "State any other matter or fact which, in your opinion, would improve the present system of Indian affairs, in principle or in administration, to prevent frauds upon the Indians and upon the government."

In answer to the first question, I would state that a large portion of my military service has been upon the Indian frontier, and from a personal knowledge and experience of the operation of the present system for the management of our Indians, as practiced, it has long been a settled conviction in my mind that the Bureau of Indian Affairs should be under the control of the War Department.

My reasons for the above expressed opinion are based upon the conviction that a knowledge of and experience with Indians demonstrates that the true policy of the government for their control and management, with a view to their good, and to the economy and good of the United States, should be of rigorous firmness, but a just, honest, and consistent one; and one that protects them in their rights against the aggressions of the white man, while punishing them for their thefts and hostilities committed upon the latter, and one which should faithfully fulfil all promises made to them by authorized government agents, and which has a sufficient military force to cause it to be rigidly executed, to command due respect from them, and inspire fear of punishment for wrongs done by them. A weak, lenient and persuasive policy towards Indians but excites for it their contempt, and is considered by them as the result of cowardice and fear. That the true policy as demonstrated has not been pursued by the Indian department, through its agents, for the government of our wild Indian tribes, is too apparent, and susceptible of ample proof. In the first place, an adequate military force is necessary to carry out this policy, which the Indian department has not; and when it calls upon the War Department for the necessary means of protection, and enforcing its orders, it not unfrequently happens that the two departments do not co-operate harmoniously. The misapplication of money, goods, &c., appropriated by Congress for our Indians, much of which has gone to enrich appointees of the Indian Bureau and their friends; the deceptions often practiced to secure their annuities, and induce them to cede away their lands, as was the case in Minnesota, where certain bands were persuaded and coerced to cede away lands belonging to the Yanktonais, which was one of the principal causes of the late Indian war there, and the massacre of over two thousand (2,000) people, with the destruction of much valuable property; the interference in their social relations by the not unfrequent taking and prostitution of their squaws, forcibly, or without their consent; and the introduction of illicit trade among them by lawless frontiersmen, particularly in intoxicating liquor, destroying their domestic peace and happiness, and inciting them to acts of hostility upon the white inhabitants; the unauthorized and make-shift promises, too often made them to gratify the cupidity and desires of the appointees of the Indian department and others, or to shield them temporarily from anticipated violence or attacks from the Indians; and the variable course pursued by different Indian superintendents and agents for the management of our Indian tribes, due to their ignorance of the character and wants of the Indians, or a desire to promote selfish interests, sufficiently prove, I think, that the present system for their government is not a just, honest, and consistent one.

To the above causes, and aggressions of white men upon our Indians, many of our Indian wars had their inception, and in illustration of which may be cited those in California and Oregon in 1850 and 1851; the massacres in Minnesota and of Spirit Lake, as well as much of the Indian trouble and hostilities which for years have occurred west of the Missouri river, on the plains, and elsewhere. Tribes that were friendly in the early emigration to California in 1849 and 1850 were excited to hostility by the unprovoked and outrageous shooting of their people by emigrants. Some tribes have, no doubt, ever been treacherous and hostile to the white race. It may be laid down as an axiom, that the true policy for the government of Indians should embrace a sufficient military power for its faithful execution with regard to their protection and punishment, as also of the white inhabitants, and for the accomplishment of those objects of the government that may have in view their improvement and civilization, and the development of our country's vast resources and the general prosperity of our people. The War Department alone can furnish this power, and its officers and agents, with but little additional aid and expense to what would otherwise be required, can *ex officio* discharge the duties of Indian superintendents, agents, &c., with, I think, much better success and results, and, certainly, with greater economy to the general government, than results from the present system; but this change of policy would destroy considerable political patronage, and, therefore, it may prove an insurmountable object to its accomplishment

That the War Department has possessed the confidence of our Indians more than any other department of our government may be inferred from the fact that Indian tribes, from the Pacific to the Mississippi river, have generally expressed their confidence in the regular army, through its officers, stating that by them they had not been deceived, cheated, and abused, and asking that they might be their agents, and manage for them their affairs with the government.

Such was the feeling more recently manifested in this department by the Navajo nation of Indians, when over eight thousand (8,000) surrendered to the military authorities, and consented to go upon a reservation, referring to Major (now Professor) Kendrick, who commanded Fort Defiance, and Captain Carey, since commanding the same post in their country. It seems reasonable to suppose that the policy which should command the respect and confidence of the Indians, while exercising a wholesome fear over them, would be better for their government than one which did not.

In answer to the second question, I am unable to state what proportion of Indian children are orphans; many that really are not, are to all intents and purposes such, from the absence of parental care, and because of living at large, or, I might say, about loose, in their tribes.

I think it would be not only practicable, but beneficial to them, and to the interest of the government, to place, while young, orphans and those circumstanced as above stated in good white families, to be civilized, educated, and learned such trades as they should manifest an aptness for; the girls make excellent house servants.

In answer to the third and last question, I would suggest that, so far as practicable, all Indians be placed on reservations, and, where necessary, a military post be established thereon, with sufficient force to control them and enforce the orders of the government with respect to them; and that they should be exclusively under the control and authority of said military force. That, so far as practicable, they should be instructed and made to cultivate the soil, raise stock, learn trades, for which many evince great aptness, and thus acquire the habits of peace and civilization, and, like the Puebla Indians, become self-supporting. Until which time, agricultural implements, wearing apparel, and a certain amount of goods and trinkets to gratify their wants, uncivilized tastes and vanity, should be furnished them, and agents and overseers employed to teach and direct them in their work.

Where it is not practicable to get Indians upon a reservation, and they are hostile, I would suggest the establishment of a strong military post in the heart of their country, and make war upon them, with the utmost vigor, until they accepted the offer of peace upon conditions of settling on a reservation designated by the government, and ceasing their hostilities.

Until established on a reservation, they should be located, as fast as they consented to peace, within striking and controlling distance of the post, and all trade with them should be at the post, and under the direction of the military authorities.

The law with respect to illicit trade with them, and particularly in the articles of intoxicating liquor, arms and ammunition, should be most rigidly and scrupulously enforced.

The commanding officers of military departments and districts in the Indian country should be *ex officio* superintendents of Indians in their respective commands; and the commanding officers of military posts in the Indian country should be *ex officio* Indian agents, and act under the authority of the commanding officers of the departments or districts in which they are situated.

I think the entire control of the Indians should be exercised by the War Department. Such seems to be the rule of action of the English government, and their success in the government of Indians, seems to contrast most favorably as compared with ours. In conclusion, I would state, as of vital importance to our government and people, (to my mind,) the necessity of the government fixing upon some policy for the administration of our Indian affairs which shall be unchangeable, and faithfully carried out.

I am, very respectfully, your obedient servant,

N. H. DAVIS,
Assistant Inspector General U. S. A.

I beg to indorse all that Colonel Davis says, as expressing my own views.

Question 21st. "In setting apart reserves, is it advisable to do so by treaty with the tribes, or to do so by law, or by regulation of the department, enforcing the same by arms?"

Answer. As a rule, I would, especially for all wild tribes, have reservations set apart by law, and enforce the same by arms. I would not make treaties at all with such Indians. To go through the forms of making a treaty with a party, when the government is determined to have matters its own way anyhow, is a mockery beneath the dignity of the United States. We can do right without resorting to any theatricals simply for effect.

I have been obliged, from the press of other business, to catch up my pen at odd times, to answer your questions, and have had no opportunity to elaborate my replies, so that they would take up less room.

The subject of your inquiry is one of vast importance to the Indians, to the people, and to the government; and the country feels confident, that from the ability, justice, and humanity (justice and humanity to the white man as well as to the red man) of the committee, much good will be sure to result from its labors in so vast a field.

Very respectfully, your obedient servant,

JAMES H. CARLETON,
Brigadier General, Commanding Department.

Hon. J. R. DOOLITTLE, *U. S. Senate,*
Chairman of Congressional Committee, Racine, Wisconsin.

Reply of Colonel C. Carson.

FORT LYONS, COLORADO TERRITORY,
August 19, 1865.

CAPTAIN: I have the honor to report, for the information of the department commander, that on leaving Taos for Fort Union, New Mexico, I mislaid a letter from him, containing certain interrogatories propounded by the Hon. J. R. Doolittle, U. S. Senate, (chairman of congressional committee now making inquiries into Indian affairs,) and requesting answers to the same. On arriving at Fort Union, my time was necessarily occupied in making preparations for special service on the plains, which it was important should not be delayed; no time was therefore left me to answer them from that post.

I now take the earliest opportunity to reply in a general manner to those points impressed upon my memory as the most important, from a careful perusal of the letter in question.

From a long-continued residence among, or in the immediate vicinity of Indians, and from a personal observation of their manners, habits, and customs, acquired both in private life and the transaction of official business as an agent of the federal government, I have been long convinced that the only rule that can be successfully applied for their governance is one firm, yet just, consistent and unchangeable; for the Indian, judging only by the effect of that which appeals to his senses, as brought directly before his observation, regards with contempt a weak and indecisive policy as the result of hesitation, fear, and cowardice, whilst a changeable and capricious one excites his apprehension and distrust. Both of these courses should be cautiously avoided.

The rule for the government of Indians should be strong enough to inspire their respect and fear, yet protecting them from both internal dissension and external aggression. This can only be effected by a military rule, and I am therefore of opinion that the sole control of the Indians should be vested with the War Department. As at present managed, jealousies among the employés of the different departments naturally exist, and they are too often actuated by feelings of prejudice, which result in a want of that harmonious co-operation of action in the execution of official duties, so necessary to effect successful results. Indian agents, appointed solely by political influence, are often swayed by feelings of personal gain in the transaction of their business, making the government appear to act in bad faith towards the savages; then making promises, impossible to fulfil, to shield themselves from attack, they excite feelings of hostility that can only be quenched in blood. To this cause, and that of repeated acts of aggression on the part of the numerous reckless frontiersmen that swarm upon the borders of the Indian territory, may be attributed many, if not most, of our recent Indian wars, massacres, and murders, extending from Minnesota to California.

The peculiarity of the Indians' position now calls for prompt, decisive, and energetic action. The old idea of forcing them westward is exploded by the discovery of the California gold-fields and rich mines of mineral on the eastern slope of the Sierra Nevada, alluring thither in constantly increasing numbers swarms of hardy adventurers. Instead of forcing them backwards before its steady advance, civilization now encircles them with its chain of progress, and each year, as it passes away, sees the chain drawing rapidly closer around the hunting grounds of the red men of the prairie. A short-sighted policy might infer from, and leave to, this cause their extermination. That it would be accomplished is certain, but humanity shudders at the picture of the extermination of thousands of human beings until every means is tried and found useless for their redemption, whilst high motives of right impel us, out of respect to ourselves and duty to the Indians, to protect our citizens, assist in the settlement of the almost unknown interior of our country, and relieve and assist whilst controlling the red men of the west, as their hunting grounds vanish before the sturdy energy of the pioneer and backwoodsman.

If placed on reservations, with wise rules enforced by military power, the settlers will be protected from their predatory raids, and they themselves be safe against the reckless injustice of those outlaws of society thronging upon the border, whose criminality has too often been the means of rousing the Indians to thoughts of vengeance, and carrying fire and desolation to many a homestead in the west.

Allow me to suggest the necessity of extreme caution and circumspection in locating Indians, to prevent internal dissensions, upon reservations. Different tribes, besides being of different degrees of advancement in civilization, have feuds of long standing to excite them, ambition of chiefs to satisfy, and long-cherished traditions of delayed revenge to gratify.

There is nothing inimical in the bold, courageous, marauding Comanche—the wild, treacherous, nomadic Apache—the hardy, industrious, agricultural Navajo, or the lazy, degraded, almost brutalized Digger. These tribes are types of the different North American Indians, and from these, or a more extensive list carefully prepared, classifications should be made to govern officers intrusted with their removal, for it is not probable that reservations can be set apart for each tribe; and where several are located together, the nearer their characters assimilate the greater will be the success, whilst the danger will decrease in the same proportion, for one wild tribe looks down on another with a contemptuous pride—strange to us, but perfectly natural to their untutored minds, as they possess a less degree of skill in the barbaric virtues of murder, violence, and theft.

The causes to which may be attributed the present rapid decrease of the Indians are continued cruel wars among themselves, prevalence of venereal diseases, and the inordinate use of intoxicating liquors. The first of these can alone be stopped by force, and, in order to pave the way for the success of any Indian policy, should be so stopped at once. The latter of these causes being due in a great measure to their intercourse with the white men, humanity and justice demand that prompt measures be taken to arrest their fatal progress.

The beneficial results derived from placing the Navajoes upon a reservation is a successful vindication of the policy, an example of the propriety of military rule, and appears to be actuated by feelings of humanity, charity, and sound political economy. A consideration of the latter question might seem more the province of the statesman than the soldier; but in deciding a policy that has at heart the welfare of hundreds of thousands of human beings, that seeks to convert them from fierce and reckless murderers to peaceful tillers of the soil, from a source of continued expense to one of actual benefit—to remove far from the white settler, and inspire confidence and respect in the savage, I am satisfied the teachings of experience will not be overlooked or even lightly regarded. Time must elapse ere really practical results can be derived from any Indian policy; but if the one so favorably commenced in New Mexico be carried into effect with other tribes, I am indulging in no chimerical or utopian idea in believing that in the next generation civilization can advance undisturbed into the vast interior of our country, whilst from the reservations the hum of busy, productive industry will resound, and the prayers of Christianity be heard from every tribe, and America stand proudly foremost among nations as the exemplar of mercy, humanity, and philanthropy, as she now does of civilization and progress.

Commanding officers of posts on Indian reservations should be de facto Indian agents; then representing the power of the government, by inflicting punishment for misdeeds, and being also dispenser of its benefits, they will be looked up to with increased respect and fear, whilst the benefit in a point of economy is undoubted. This system would seem to afford greater checks to the accomplishment of frauds, and greater facilities for their detection when perpetrated.

I am, captain, very respectfully, your obedient servant,

C. CARSON,
Col. 1st N. M. Cavalry.

Captain B. C. CUTLER,
Ass't Adj't Gen'l Dep't of N. M., Santa Fé, N. M.

Reply of Brigadier General G. Wright.

BRIGADE HEADQUARTERS DISTRICT OF CALIFORNIA,
Sacramento, June 30, 1865.

SIR: I have had the honor to receive from the Hon. Mr. Nesmith, the United States senator from the State of Oregon, and member of your committee, a copy of your circular, dated at Racine, Wisconsin, May 10, 1865; and inasmuch as I have had considerable experience in the administration of Indian affairs, as well as other means of observation, during a long period of service in the army, mostly in the Indian countries or on the frontier of civilization, I take great pleasure in replying *seriatim* to the questions you have done me the honor to propound for my consideration.

I. For more than forty years I have been an officer in the army of the United States, serving on the borders of the great northwestern lakes, the Upper Mississippi and Missouri rivers, in Florida during the war in that country, and for the last thirteen years in the department of the Pacific; from 1852 to 1855 in the northern district of California and southern portion of Oregon, and for the next five and a half years in command of Oregon and the Territory of Washington; and then for three years in command of the department of the Pacific, embracing the whole of our country west of the Rocky mountains.

During this long period I have been in command of many military expeditions against the hostile Indians, especially in Oregon and the Territory of Washington, in 1856, and lastly in 1858, when a great combination was formed by many warlike tribes in that country, threatening destruction to all the settlements east of the Cascades. I met the enemy in two hard-fought battles, in both of which they were thoroughly defeated, and finally sued for peace; and accepting the terms I granted them, they have remained perfectly quiet and peaceable ever since. The history of that campaign was published in general orders, by the lieutenant general commanding the army, in November, 1858, and noticed by the honorable Secretary of War in his report of the same year to the President.

II. The Indian tribes are rapidly decreasing in numbers, especially west of the Rocky mountains, caused in some measure by the wars waged against them, and more particularly by the encroachments of the whites upon their hunting grounds and fisheries and other means of subsistence, and by the readiness with which they adopt the vices of the whites rather than their virtues; hence their numbers are rapidly diminished by disease and death.

III. Syphilis and pulmonary diseases, arising from vicious conduct, intemperance, and exposure.

IV. It is only among those Indians who reside near the white settlements that intoxication prevails to any extent. The only practical course to prevent or mitigate the evil is to collect the Indians on reservations under military control, and exclusively under military jurisdiction.

V. Prostitution, and the diseases consequent upon it, do not prevail to any extent except among those Indians living with or in the neighborhood of the white people.

VI. The only practical remedy to prevent the total extinction of the Indian tribes, is to separate them entirely from the white race.

VII. Remove the Indians to new reservations remote from settlements.

VIII. On the reservation let every family have a piece of land and cultivate for itself, and a portion of the reservation set apart to be cultivated in common, all under the direction of the supervisor.

IX. Confer no power of alienation of real estate upon Indians; they are naturally great gamblers.

X. This question can better be answered by the supervisor.

XI. Schools have a good effect. Provide for a Protestant minister on every reservation, having under him assistants to teach schools.

XII. The effect of Christian missions among Indians is good, and it is recommended that they be maintained.

XIII. After the pacification of the Indian territory, let a section of country be set apart for their permanent residence, and known as "Indian territory," from which exclude all whites, and place the territory under the control of the War Department, under such regulations as the Congress may make or approve.

XIV. Yes. Indians have no need of money—whiskey-sellers will get it all. Government will furnish Indians what is absolutely necessary.

XV. Very little, I imagine, from what I have heard.

XVI. Cannot say.

XVII. Most of it, I have no doubt.

XVIII. Give the Indians no money and exclude the whites from their country.

XIX. Cannot say anything on this subject.

XX. The War Department, unquestionably; I have seen the working of the Indian Bureau under both, and unhesitatingly give the preference to the War Department. So long as peace and quiet prevail among the Indians, and they are well furnished with supplies by the Indian agent, everything goes on smoothly; but when wars come and difficulties arise among the different tribes or with the white people, they always resort to the military commander to settle their affairs. I have had much to do in this way.

XXI. Let it be done by law and enforced by arms; make it a military colony.

XXII. It will be a good plan to place orphan children in the families of Christian white men to be trained and educated.

XXIII. Collect the Indians on great reservations, and protect the interests of the Indians and of the government by the strong arm of the military.

With great respect, I have the honor to be your obedient servant,

G. WRIGHT,
Brig. Gen'l U. S. A., Commanding.

Hon. J. R. DOOLITTLE,
Chairman of the Joint Committee of Congress,
Charged to make inquiry into the condition of the Indian tribes, &c., &c.

Reply of J. Harlan, United States Indian agent.

CHEROKEE AGENCY, CHEROKEE NATION,
August 1, 1865.

SIR: I have the honor to send you my answer to the several questions propounded by the congressional committee, through you as chairman, &c.

Question 1. During how long a period, and in what capacity, in the civil or military service, have you had experience in Indian affairs; or, what other means of observation have you had, and with what tribe or tribes?

Answer. I was appointed United States Indian agent for the Cherokee Indians, September 19, 1862, and on the sixth day of October following I entered on the duties of my office. Since that time, nearly three years, I have been almost constantly with the Cherokees. I have had, however, at different and for considerable periods of time, refugee Indians, Kickapoos, Creeks, Uches, Seminoles, Chickasaws, and Choctaws under my charge. I have, of course, had more experience with the Cherokees than with any other tribe. But living most of the time at Fort Gibson, guarded by three regiments of Indians, and in the Indian country, where the loyal refugee Indians came for protection, I had many opportunities of seeing and more of hearing what their wants were. Previous to my appointment I had had no experience in Indian affairs.

Question 2. Are they increasing or decreasing in numbers, and from what causes?

Answer. If there ever was any census of the Cherokee Indians taken, I cannot find it, and suppose it was lost in the general destruction which was made of the books and papers in the office of the former agents. From information derived from well-informed persons in the nation, I suppose the Cherokees remained with but little change from original numbers. From the same source, I learn that their number was about 22,000 at the commencement of the late rebellion; of these about 8,500 joined the rebellion and went south; and about 13,500 remained in the nation. Many of these were disloyal. Many of the men who joined the rebellion left their families in the nation. Against the wives and children of the rebels left in the nation no word or act of disloyalty could be proved, and they had to be treated as loyal, and possibly were. The children, certainly, were not disloyal. What became of those who went south I have no information; but of those who remained I can speak with some general knowledge. Early in the year 1861, rebel emissaries came into the Indian country, for the purpose of making the Indians dissatisfied with us, and to induce them to join the south and take up arms in the war then raging. The Cherokees, generally, under the influence of their chief, John Ross, assumed a kind of "Kentucky neutrality" Later in that year that neutrality was thrown off, and two rebel regiments were raised in the Cherokee nation, and became a part of the rebel army. Many Cherokees refused to join the rebel army, and some who did, finding themselves deceived, voluntarily returned and joined the Union army. Some made their way out of the nation. Some removed to places more secure from molestation from their brethren, and from the rebel army then in the nation. And many joined with Opotheholo, a loyal Creek, who crossed the Arkansas river with a part of his people, out of his own reservation, and into that of the Cherokees. He was pursued by a much larger force than his own; a battle was fought, and Opotheholo was victor. The rebel force was largely re-enforced; another battle was fought, and that brave, loyal and able commander and chief was defeated, with great loss in the battle, and still greater in the pursuit. The night after the battle, snow fell to the depth of one foot or more, and the weather became terribly cold. In the battle and the pursuit, which was long and fierce and bloody, his party had lost most of their beds and bedding, wearing apparel, horses, and provisions. In such weather and such a snow, stripped of almost all they had, they had to find their way into Kansas. Horses and Indians froze to death. Hundreds were frozen in their extremities. Some recovered, and many died. In the Cherokee nation, the rebel Indians were let loose on the loyal Cherokees by the rebel army, and protected by them, in murdering, robbing, and capturing the loyal Cherokees, and stealing their horses, cattle, wagons, hogs, farming utensils, beds, bedding and clothing, and burning their houses, barns and fencing, and everything else which they could find, and could not carry away. Some fled into the mountains, abandoning everything they had, glad to escape with their lives. And these remained for months in the winter season, exposed, in their destitute condition, to all the inclemencies of the season, and many died of exposure. In the spring of 1863 the small-pox broke out among them. No amount of persuasion could induce a large majority of them to be vaccinated. They took it in the natural way, and great numbers died. Most of the Cherokee men who remained in the nation, or who returned to it from the south, enlisted in the Union army as "home guard." In April, 1863, three Indian regiments, with sometimes some white or colored regiments, were stationed at Fort Gibson, to protect the property and persons of the Cherokee people. Just how the Cherokees were protected, the present condition of their country shows. The military held Fort Gibson, and all that large tract of country, as far as the guns in Fort Gibson would reach, and no more. When a bushwhacking party crossed the Arkansas river into the Cherokee nation, the Indians, all that were out, were called in to protect Fort Gibson. They knew Fort Gibson was in no danger, but their families were. They were, against their will, as it were, tied head and foot in the fort, while their families in the country were insulted, outraged, plundered, sometimes murdered or carried in captivity out of the country. True, generally, when a band of bushwhackers were in the country, if they were discovered as well mounted, a force of infantry, about one-half their ascertained numbers, was sent out to capture them. The bushwhackers loaded themselves with plunder and left the nation. The pursuing force did the same, only they did not leave the nation. They returned to Fort Gibson, loaded with plunder, and crowned with glory, reported great success in driving the enemy from the country, and rested from their labors. This is no fancy sketch, nor the ludicrous history of a single campaign. It is the veritable history of the war on this frontier. The Cherokee nation have been robbed by their enemies, of one-fourth of all they had, and by their friends and protectors of the balance, until they are literally destitute. In their destitute condition, deprived of everything except the insufficient supply of clothing, blankets, and provisions furnished by the government, (and frequently within five miles of the fort.) Deprived of that, and the clothing they wore, and the pony they rode, if they had one, it is not strange that many died. From all these causes combined, and others to be named under their appropriate questions, I am satisfied their number has decreased in three years, of those who remained in the nation, not much (if any) less than two thousand five hundred, over the natural increase by birth. These causes removed, I can give no more than a mere conjecture as to increase or decrease. My conjecture, however, is that an increase is not the most probable. I think the Cherokees, like all other tribes of Indians, will decrease not so rapidly as other tribes less civilized; but surely decrease, and by all the causes which have decreased other tribes.

Question 3. What diseases are most common and most fatal among them, and from what causes?

Answer. I think this country, generally, is a healthy one; but few local causes of disease. There are some cases of autumnal complaints. Bilious fever and fever and ague are the most common. There are more of such on the larger rivers than on the high lands. Of these diseases few die. But they are too frequently imperfectly cured. An Indian is careless of exposure. In their weak condition, poorly doctored, and worse nursed, the wet, cold and changeable weather of the winter and spring finds them, and some inflammatory disease carries them off.

Question 4. To what extent does intoxication prevail among them, and what legislation, or practical regulation by the department, do you suggest to prevent or mitigate the evil?

Answer. I am satisfied, from all I have seen, that intoxication generally prevails among Indians, and that the Cherokees are not exceptions. Since I have been in the Cherokee nation, whiskey has not been plenty. In the commissary, sick certificates to officers were necessary to obtain it. The great numbers of sick officers, when the commissary had it, or when it was smuggled in by others, was astonishing. From what I could see, I supposed that white and Indian officers got most of the whiskey; but that the white officers drank what they got, and the Indian officers, more liberal, divided theirs with the soldiers. The consequence was, that more white than Indian officers were seen reeling on the streets, and more Indian than white common soldiers following the unworthy example. Some Indians are wholly temperate; some take a dram, and no more, and are never drunk; some get drunk occasionally, and some get drunk at all times when they can get it. My experience, owing to the scarcity of whiskey, since I have been among the Cherokees, is not worth much; but I believe that it is true that the first two classes above mentioned are smaller than among an equal number of white men; and the two last, vastly larger. All that legislation can do to prevent or mitigate the evil has been done already. The Cherokees have a law now in force, almost the "Maine law," which, I am told, they executed with vigor, before the late rebellion, and may do so again. The Indian agents, subagents, the Indians and the military, by act of Congress, can search for and destroy whiskey found in the nation contrary to law, and anybody can prosecute the offending party in the courts. This seems to me sufficient. I can suggest nothing more.

Question 5. From your best information and belief, to what extent does prostitution prevail among them, and the diseases consequent upon it; and to what extent does it diminish their numbers and enfeeble their offspring?

Answer. That prostitution, to a lamentable extent, does prevail, and the diseases consequent upon it, all admit and none deny. Such is my information and belief. Aside from any information derived from physicians and others, I can see—no one can help seeing—every day, evidence of both. Their laws on the subject of marriage and marital rights are most crude. They provide for a license to marry, and certain officers and ministers of the Gospel are authorized to solemnize the marriage under the license. Children of such a marriage are legitimate, and inherit their father's property. They have what is called "blanket marriages." They just live together as husband and wife, and children of such marriages are legitimate, if there was no previous marriage. Polygamy, to any extent, is not punished by their laws, but they have no law allowing it. A man may, at any time after his marriage, abandon his wife and children. They have no law compelling a man, however able, to support either his wife or children. They are frequently left very poor, to be raised by the mother. Not taught by their mother to labor, nature teaches them to live; and not unfrequently they learn to get that living in the most irregular way.

To what extent venereal diseases diminish their numbers and enfeeble their offspring, with me can only be conjecture. But that it does both is very certain. A frequent recurrence of such diseases with both sexes causes impotence, and prevents natural increase, undermines their constitutions, and shortens their lives. When the disease has not occurred with such malignity, or has not recurred so often as to cause impotence, it greatly enfeebles the powers of procreation. This enfeebled constitution is inherited by their children, and their lives are shortened. From all this I infer their numbers are diminished, their increase is prevented, and their offspring enfeebled; but to what extent I cannot say.

Question 6. State any other fact bearing upon the causes of their decay, and what is the best practical remedy.

Answer. In addition to the causes above stated there are other causes; two may be mentioned: their quarrels are very bitter; their hatred and love of revenge are not momentary; they endure during the life of the parties. When an opportunity offers, the death of one or both parties alone settles the matter. Sometimes the quarrel is inherited by friends and relations, and many lives are lost every year from this cause. One other cause may be stated: they are very superstitious; they believe in demons, witches, ghosts, good and evil spirits, and many other kindred beliefs. They too frequently believe those, or some of them, to be the cause of their diseases, and doctor the patient more to appease the demon and drive him away, than otherwise to cure the disease. When medicine is left by a physician, it is rarely taken as directed. Some old woman or old man, the uglier, more deformed, and more ignorant the better, comes in, and by charms and incantations drives off the physician, if not the demon and the disease. Intelligent Indians have discarded such a belief, but the unintelligent adhere to it; and this costs the nation many lives every year.

Question 7. Which, in your opinion, is the best policy as white settlements advance and surround Indian reservations—to maintain the Indians upon them, and endeavor to resist encroachments, or to remove them to new reserves remote from settlements?

Answer. It is best, in my opinion, to maintain the Cherokees and all other civilized and partly civilized tribes on their present reservations.. The great object of the government is, or ought to be, to educate, civilize, and Christianize the Indians as fast as possible. When that is accomplished, to admit them as citizens of the United States. The Cherokees have had churches, school-houses, schools and seminaries, all pretty well supported, and will have them again in a few years. The best plan, in my opinion, is to bring them in contact with those who speak the English language, from whom the children will learn it. When that is learned, the great difficulty is overcome of giving them an English education. A great evil befell the Cherokee nation when Sequoyah invented the Cherokee alphabet. The sooner the Cherokee alphabet and the Cherokee language cease to be used, the better. Their business, trading, laws, must be carried on in English. Arts and sciences must be taught them in English, and not in Cherokee, for in that language they have no terms or names for these. Educate them first, christianity and civilization will certainly follow. Civilization and Christianity travel slowly when they precede education, as every Christian effort to civilize and Christianize the uneducated heathen proves. Before the rebellion the Cherokees had salt-works, mills, farms, houses—many fine ones, and hope to have them again. Their country is a fine country for stock, and they had vast herds, and were proud of it. They are greatly attached to their homes and country. If they are removed, it must be by force. We never will get their consent to be removed. To deprive them of their country and all these improvements by force, would be national folly, sin, and everlasting disgrace. The reason why it will be done, if it is ever done, makes the matter worse if possible, just because white men want the country. The whole Indian country is one of the finest on this continent. For that reason the white man wants to get it. And for the same reason, among others, the Indians want to retain it. They bought it—they paid for it; they have title to it—they own it; it is theirs. Just what excuse we can have or feign, I cannot at present see. When white men want it bad enough, reason enough, such as it is, will be given to have it done.

In their last treaty, still in force, they even promised protection as part of the consideration for their homes in Georgia. The Indians do not believe that the government cared whether they were protected or not. I find it somewhat difficult to convince an Indian that it did. If I were to judge alone by the qualities of the friends and protectors employed, I should find it diffiuclt to keep myself convinced that it did. That they were shamefully neglected admits of no dispute. Unprotected, they were driven about from place to place; robbed and plundered; their property ruthlessly destroyed, when it could not be carried off; their friends and relations butchered or carried into captivity. Almost all the Indians in the army were held in Fort Gibson to protect it, while their property and families were left a prey to the enemy, and far worse than that, left a prey to their friends and protectors. They have lost nearly all they had but their homes. Now to deprive them of that, by any means, and find new homes where they would not be molested by white settlements, would send them among the wild tribes of the west, professional thieves, robbers and murderers—the Bedouins of America—when they would be plundered and murdered by these wild surrounding tribes; or they might be compelled to join with them, and from their superior intelligence and knowledge of fire-arms, they might become able instructors of these professional plunderers and murderers. One thing to me seems certain, their advance in civilization will receive a back-set not to be recovered in fifty years, if ever. Even if they consent to an exchange of homes, which I think they never will do, and we give them homes as good as they now have, they will never think so, and be dissatisfied, and think themselves cheated by design by us, and be far more likely to follow the bad example of their new neighbors than to set them better. It is astonishing how fast they have retrograded in four years. The best and most intelligent portion of the Cherokee people often remark, with regret, the rapid strides which vice and immorality have made during the four years of war and neglect. I hope for our sake, as professing Christians, that they may not be removed from their present homes. I hope for their sake it may not be done. I hope the good which education, Christianity, and civilization have already done them may not be lost. They have to live somewhere. My decided opinion is, they should be fully protected in their present homes, and encouraged by every means in our power to regain what they have lost.

Question 8. Is it best that their lands should be held in common, or in severalty?

Answer. For very many years to come, and after many changes all for the better, and after the males have gone to work, as farmers should do, and the females assume household duties, it will be the only safe way for the Indians to hold their lands in common. As it now is, and ought to continue, if an Indian gets tired of the place where he lives, he can sell it and go on to any other common land, make an improvement, and build a cabin and call it his home. This would not be so if lands were held in severalty. This would cease as soon as their lands are severed. When, as it now is, they wish to change location, they sell or abandon their improvements and have to work into another—a benefit rather than an injury; but if they had to buy, they would soon have nothing to buy with. This remark does not apply to the rich or to the energetic, but it does apply to a vast number of Indians who are comparatively poor and indolent; too numerous a class to overlook. I think until intelligence, industry and energy are much more generally diffused among Cherokees, it will be too soon to sever their lands.

Question 9. If held in severalty, is it safe to confer the power of alienation of real estate upon Indians; if so, upon what classes, and under what limitations?

Answer. When the time comes for severing their lands, and it is done, withhold the power of alienation until the system has been fairly tested and distinctly understood by them. This will take many years—not less than twenty-five—and then it will do to allow the power of alienation. It would, even then, be a wise provision to allow one person to hold only two at most of family rights, rendering all other purchases void. When his children become of age he might, in the name of his adult son or daughter, purchase a like home for them, absolutely as they severally become of age. I would allow any to sell, but limit purchases even to an Indian; and never to a white man until the Indians are admitted citizens of the United States, and then only after the Indians by their proper authority ask it.

Question 10. What proportion of them, upon their reservations, give attention to agriculture, or stock-raising; and which are they, males or females, half-breeds or full-bloods?

Answer. Nearly all the Cherokees, in a small way, cultivate their lands. Only a very small number cultivate largely. Generally, with those who raise grain, a small field of corn—with a very few of those—a small field of wheat, and a vegetable garden, constitute their farm products. A few cultivate more largely, but too many, one-fourth perhaps, raise less than will make their bread. The Indian men are generally indolent and careless. The women are generally slow at their work, but steady and industrious, and will do a considerable amount of labor. In too many cases the women have to do most of the work that is done.

The cultivation by the best farmers among the Cherokees, I think, has always been defective, and with the poorer farmers abominable. This country is subject to drought. Their lands are very rich. They plough for all crops too shallow; and corn, when growing, they cultivate too little. Their shallow ploughing on their rich land of a wet season produces a good crop. Of a dry season their crops are poor. Their dry seasons are as common as their wet ones If their grounds were broken deeply, and their corn kept clear of weeds, but few of their seasons are so dry as to prevent a large yield. Their grounds properly cultivated of a wet season produce as fine crops of grain as I ever saw.

Horses, mules, cattle, sheep and hogs are reared with so little trouble and expense that at the beginning of the late rebellion almost all the Cherokees had some stock. Many had large stocks, and a few had them of their own raising by thousands. They have not, heretofore, had to feed their stock of any kind in winter, except a few for use; but their herds of all kinds lived, and the grown ones, not too old, kept fat all winter. Young stock, generally, got lean, but few, if any, died of starvation. In a country where all stock winters itself, natural increase even from a small beginning soon swells into vast herds.

The half-breeds generally attended to their farms and stock, and many grew wealthy. The full-bloods generally did not so well, it seems, attend to their stock, and too frequently left cultivation to the women and children, who could only raise a scanty subsistence, and but few grew wealthy. Among the full-bloods I think most of them have discarded the notion that labor is disgraceful to a man. But I think but few of them are covetous of any honors conferred by industry.

Their laws allow husband and wife to own separate property. It is not uncommon among full-bloods for the women to own most of the stock, and generally as much as their husbands. Among half-breeds the women generally own separate property, but not to so great an extent. The half-bloods were greatly more wealthy than full-bloods, and owned, I believe, all the great herds. The half-bloods had the greater portion of the wealth and energy of the nation. These generally joined the rebels and went south, and left almost all their wealth in the nation. A very general determination now exists among the Cherokees who remained loyal that the rebel Cerokees shall not be allowed to return and form a part of the nation unless they submit to conditions not now likely to be accepted.

Question 11. What has been the effect of schools among them, and what kind of schools do you recommend as most advantageous for them, and what is your opinion of manual-labor schools?

Answer. The effect of schools has been just the same among the Indians that it would have been in a white community. The Cherokees, as a people, do not lack capacity. Their indolence is their drawback.

Hereafter, when treaties are made with the Cherokees, by which money is their due, we ought to insist on a large part or all of it to be funded, and the interest only paid to the nation for educational purposes. The common school system, as nearly as practicable of the eastern States, is, I think, the best for them. English schools only should be supported. Schools to teach the Cherokee language should receive no encouragement whatever. The sooner they are abandoned the better. Even the full-bloods, when they find the English schools free, will support them in time. They have many of their own people now, and soon would have more, who speak both languages, able to teach in their common schools. This is a great advantage in teaching the children who speak the English language imperfectly.

Manual-labor schools, I am satisfied, would do a vast amount of good, and are well worth an experiment if we could get them attended. The patient industry and perseverance necessary in a pupil in a manual-labor school is certainly not common in a young Indian, but there are exceptions As many of their orphans as could be got into these schools should be placed there. In them they would learn the English language, receive some education, and be taught how to work : all very necessary in their reformation. It is estimated that there are twelve hundred orphans in the nation ; of this number enough could be got in the schools to test the matter as an experiment. I am by no means, however, sanguine that manual-labor schools will be successful. If fully tried they would be, but I fear they will not receive a full and fair trial.

Question 12. What has been the effect of Christian missions among them, and what do you recommend upon that subject?

Answer. I am satisfied that Christian missions among the Cherokees have had nothing but a salutary influence, and ought to be aided and encouraged by every means in our power. Educate them, and then teach them by precept and example that our ways are better than their ways, and our faith is better than their faith, and civilization follows as a consequence.

I would recommend that no bad man, or man of doubtful reputation, should be sent among them. A competent salary, sufficient to command talents, industry and zeal in his great work, should be provided. The means of bestowing alms and rendering aid in proper cases to a limited amount, it is also well to provide. Manual-labor schools and other schools should be connected with the missionary establishment, and be a part of it. No young single man should be employed. The danger of setting an evil example is too great. "Lead us not into temptation" was, and is, a wise precaution as well for missionaries as others.

Question 13. As to the country called the Indian territory, what do you recommend in relation to that, after its pacification ; should it be held by the tribes under former treaty stipulations, or under new treaty arrangements ; or be organized into a territorial government for the civilized tribes ; and if the latter, upon what conditions and limitations as to residence, suffrage, eligibility to office, and the powers of the separate tribes therein?

Answer. My opinion is that the country called the Indian territory, which is now held by the more civilized tribes, should continue to be held by them. Whether under former treaty stipulations or new ones, I am, for want of sufficient information, unable at present to say. Circumstances may have arisen, or may arise, which have or will render new ones necessary. At present I see none. We have granted to the Cherokees by patent, as I am informed, their present reservation. If that is so, our duty is very plain. We have but to comply with our treaty stipulations. Protect them on their present reservation as we are bound by treaty, or with their free consent buy their lands. It is not an open question what we think would be the best for us or for them, but what we and they think, and what they will agree shall be done. We have so long and so often recognized in them a sort of sovereignty, the treaty-making power, and the obligatory force of these treaties on us, that it would be unjust in us and unjust to them now to deny them any of the rights heretofore conceded or implied.

Your question seems to imply but one territory for all the civilized tribes, which, I suppose, includes the Cherokees, Creeks, Uches, Seminoles, Choctaws and Chickasaws, and perhaps some others. Two-fifths of the Cherokees, one-half or more of the Creeks, Uches, and Seminoles, nine-tenths of the Choctaws and Chickasaws, were rebels and joined the south in the late rebellion. They are rebels still, and will so continue a long time, if not forever. Now all these in one territory, the rebels will unite and vote for rebels, and the consequence is certain—a rebel will be elected to Congress. This circumstance alone will embitter the feud, and keep this rebel feeling awake and active ; and having the majority at the start, the power perpetuates itself and will grow stronger. In this generation none but a rebel will be elected.

The Creeks, Seminoles, and Uches are but different bands of the Creeks, and united are the most numerous of these tribes. The Choctaws and Chickasaws are of one origin, and are but Choctaws. These united are the next to the strongest of these tribes. The Cherokees, the most intelligent, are the smallest of these tribes. The rebel Creeks, Seminoles, and Uches will return to the nation when they choose. They are as numerous, or more so than the loyal portion, and must be allowed to return, but they cannot force the Union portion to love them. The rebel Choctaws and Chickasaws are nearly the whole of these nations, and can come home when they please, and impose just such conditions on the Union men as they choose ; and hate will make these conditions hard enough. The question among them may be, will they have a rebel Creek or a rebel Choctaw ; but it never can or will be, shall they have a Union man or a Cherokee. The Union Cherokees are as certainly disfranchised as they can be. Make but one territory for their nation of people, speaking as they do their languages, no one understanding the other, no feeling in common, no interest in common, each jealous of the other, and each one unwilling, if in his power, to do anything which would be a benefit to the other. These three powers your question seems to suppose may be formed into one territory. Our governor and judges might be appointed for the Indian territory and do well enough ; but if a territory is formed, each nation ought to have its own delegate, or else there should be none at all.

If a territorial government is formed, I think as few conditions and limitations as to suffrage, residence, or eligibility to office, as is compatible with their change of government, should be made. Their separate tribal organizations should, without doubt, remain just as they are ; they must not be touched.

I believe, however, that better than any of these, and best of all, is, for the present and for a long time to come, to leave them just as they are.

Question 14. Ought money annuities to Indians to be discontinued as far as consistent with treaty obligations?

Answer. When we get clear of our present treaty obligations for the payment of money annuities to all Indians, I would make no more. I would, in all treaties with them or in any way by which we become indebted to them, hold the principal in trust and pay them the interest only, and that payment for the benevolent purposes of establishing missionary institutions, their education, their civilization, their Christianization, and for the useful purposes of procuring seeds, farming implements, and domestic animals. Indians are not very self-relying. When they have money annuities falling due, their general indolent habits easily pursuade them that their coming annuities will supply them, and they neglect to make the proper exertion to supply their wants.

The time has come with many, and soon will with all the tribes in the United States, when they will be unable to support themselves by the chase, and must either support themselves by their labor or starve. And the sooner they begin to labor the better for all concerned. And we ought to make the office to aid them ; and aid them to engage in agricultural pursuits as fast as we can induce them to receive it, instead of money annuities now due or to become due. The Cherokees before the late rebellion had what they wanted, but now, in their present destitute condition, such aid would be vastly more advantageous than money annuities.

Of the amount paid to the Indians nominally by the government, I think it would be safe to say more than ninety-nine per cent. was actually paid to the traders, and less than one per cent. to the Indians. I only saw seven dollars paid to an Indian. When an Indian's name was called a trader stated his claim ; the Indian said "Uh!" Whether that was yes or no I could not say, but the money was paid to the trader.

Question 16. What proportion is received by the traders for goods and supplies already advanced?

Answer. In the only payment I ever saw made, the proportion was as I stated in the preceding answer. It was all claimed, and nobody disputed it, for goods and supplies already advanced.

Question 17. What proportion is squandered for intoxicating drinks or in gambling?

Answer. I have no knowledge whatever. In the only payment I ever saw made, so little was received by the Indians (that little was all paid to one Indian, and he was a temperate man) that I could form no opinion. As a general rule, Indians love stimulating drinks, and are inveterate gamblers. Never having made a money payment, I can only judge from payments made by the United States paymasters for military services. Whiskey was sometimes not to be had, and generally only by a few. Gambling was general at these payments, but, as well as I could judge, only for small amounts.

I have issued goods and clothing frequently to the Cherokees, and sometimes to the Creeks, Seminoles, and Uches. I never saw any disposition by any to sell either. All Indians are fond of dress, and the tribes last named have adopted the fashion of the white people. When they have the means they generally dress themselves neatly, tastefully, and even elegantly. They manifest both taste and judgment in their selection of goods. The dresses of the women are well and neatly fitted and well made.

Question 18. What can be practically done to secure the Indian against the two latter evils, when payments in money or goods and clothing are made?

Answer. My answer to question 4th answers this question, to which I refer. I am satisfied that all that legislation can do has been already done.

Question 19. What is the practical operation of the "order system" adopted by the licensed traders among them? State your opinion of the merits of the same.

Answer. I have seen just enough of the "order system" to know what it is, but not enough to form any decided opinion about it. I had a suspicion that all was not right. I can hardly believe that if its practical operation was favorable to the Indians that the traders would have adopted it. If favorable to the trader, it ought not to be tolerated. The Indians, the least civilized the worse, are unable to protect themselves against white men. They ought to be protected by every means in our power. Close watching is no inconvenience to an honest trader, and does the Indian some good if any trader is disposed to be dishonest. I do not see any great good the "order system" can do a trader, or any great harm it can do the Indians; it may do both. "Caution is the parent of safety."

Question 15. What proportion actually reaches the hands of the Indians?

Answer. I never saw but one payment of Indian annuities in money made. Then between thirty-one and thirty-two dollars was due each one. Twenty-five dollars was paid. Nobody told me what became of the six or seven dollars not paid. I was not quite Paul Pry enough to inquire. I guess it went to the support of the ministry, as a preacher was engaged in the payment.

Question 21. In setting apart reserves, is it advisable to do so by treaty with the tribes, or to do so by law, or by regulation of the department, enforcing the same by arms?

Answer. I think the best and only way for us now to set apart Indian reserves is to do so by treaty with the tribes. The next best way to do it is by law. The very worst way is by regulation of a department enforcing it by arms. We have made treaties with the Indian tribes, and in so many other ways acknowledged that they have rights; we ought not now to be allowed to say they have none. This regulating Indians out of one Territory into another, enforcing it by arms, is always oppressive, and can only be justified as a necessary war measure in time of actual hostility. To do so in time of peace would show that we were willing to be oppressors without the necessity. All our transactions with the Indian tribes should be done by treaty, and only by treaty. If the Indians have a country which we want, and they will sell, we may buy it. If they refuse to sell, it is their right so to do, and there is no remedy. If my neighbor has land which I want worse than he does, and have more use for it than he has, yet if he refuses to sell I must be contented. And very common honesty and morality forbids me to harass his enjoyment so as to make him willing to sell. An individual who would violate this rule would be considered a scoundrel. It is just as well for a nation to be honest and moral as it is for an individual.

Question 20. Under what department of the government, the War Department or the Interior, should the Indian Bureau be placed, to secure the best and most economical administration of it? State your opinion and reasons.

Answer. I know, from three years' experience, that an Indian agent has constant employment; if ever idle, he is neglecting or postponing some duty which ought to be performed. These duties are sometimes important in the eyes of the agent, sometimes of but little and sometimes of no importance whatever. They all seem important to the person wishing them attended to, and he is dissatisfied if they are not. Some reside a long way from the agency, and it is of some importance to have his business done, or even refused, if need be, at his first visit to save a second. An agency ought always to be established as nearly central as possible in the Territory; justice requires this. Let who will be or act as Indian agent, he ought always to be at his agency ready to discharge his duty. If the Bureau of Indian Affairs should be transferred to the War Department, still an Indian agent has to be appointed, or the duty be done by some military officer designated for that purpose. If he attends well to his duties of Indian agent, he will have no time to attend to his military duty. If some officer be designated who has no military duty to perform, or so few as to leave him time to attend to the duties of agent, would it not be well to abolish such an office, and, if desirable, appoint him an Indian agent. If an army officer could attend to his military duty and the duty of Indian agent for his army pay, the agent's salary would be saved; but that is all. In most cases it is most probable that the military post of the officer will be a long way from the tribe for which he is to do the duties of agent. In such a case, when he is at one, he will be away and neglecting the other, and one or the other or both will be imperfectly done. If the pay is increased, corresponding to the increased amount of labor required, as it should be, then nothing is saved in money, and nothing gained in any way, but this much lost. What ought to be well done must and will be but imperfectly performed. The work has to be done by men, some of whom will do their duty if they can, and some will not; and whether they are in or out of the army makes no difference. But when you assign a man more duty than he can perform, some of it must remain undone.

I can see no more connexion or affinity between military affairs and the Indian Bureau than there is between military affairs and any other bureau in any of the departments.

I believe the War Department already in this country has as much power and influence as it is entirely safe for it to possess. I also think the change wholly unnecessary. We may some day have to regret this conferring unnecessary power and influence on the War Department. Where it now is it can do no harm—the change might.

I see, or I think I see, a wish manifested by officers of the army to maintain the army hereafter on too grand a scale to meet my approbation. Transfer the Indian bureau to the War Department, and army officers and army contractors furnish the supplies; this, of itself, creates the necessity for retaining enough army officers over and above what is required for the military service to perform the civil duty of the Indian department. The pay of the army officers is higher than equal grades in civil employment. On the score of honesty, faithfulness, and ability, I suppose there is no difference. There are capable, honest, and faithful men in the army and out of it, and still some that are not. I see nothing to gain by the change. I never would confer any power on the War Department of our government except the power to regulate and manage the army, and keep that as small in times of peace as is consistent with safety.

Question 22. What proportion of the children are orphans, and to what extent would it be practical for the Indian bureau to place orphan children in the families of Christian white men, to be trained and educated in the English language and in the habits of civilized life?

Answer. From the best information I can get, and from all I can see and know, I am of opinion there are not less than twelve, and perhaps fifteen hundred orphans in the nation. The proportion not far from one-third of all the children. There are many of these—say one-third, or four or five hundred—whose fathers and mothers have separated and taken other husbands and wives, and both abandoned the offspring of the previous marriage. The Cherokees have no law compelling parents to support their children, and no law prohibiting as many subsequent marriages as may suit the taste of parties. Their laws do bastardize the children of all marriages but the first, the first husband or wife being alive. And all these are orphans as well as those whose parents are dead. Some instances of bad faith on the part of the government officers, and many more suspected by them, will make the Indians very slow to agree to any such arrangement, and slow to encourage a beginning. Any one must be well acquainted with Indian character before he can be made to believe how proud and jealous they are. If either their pride or jealousy should be aroused, but little or nothing could be done. Confidence with an Indian is of slow growth, and must receive no back-set whatever during an experiment, or all is lost. What their fathers did successfully they will do; what their fathers never tried and proved they are very slow to try or prove. I am of opinion that among the Cherokees many half-bloods, and some—a few—full-bloods, would set an example with their orphan relations. If tried, it must be successful, and the Indians will see it. There is no want of the keenest sagacity among the Indian tribes and among the Cherokees; their natural sagacity is considerably improved by education and association with intelligent and educated persons; and the intelligent ones will not fail to see the advantage this will be to their people. The measure commends itself to my mind with great force, and promises great good to the Cherokees, without any pecuniary benefit to the white race. In too many of our transactions with the Indian tribes they think we have the advantage. Our interest in the transaction was certain; theirs in prospect only. Our interest was pressed early and late; theirs attended to when we had nothing else to do. This judgment seems too severe. They have some acts committed, and omitted whatever was intended, which show part of which they complain. A part of the considerations for the lands in Georgia, North Carolina, Tennessee, and Alabama, was promised protection. When they wanted protection, their men in our army, we suffered their people to be robbed and murdered for more than two years, until their property was destroyed or carried off, until they had nothing left worth coming after, when their poverty—not our arms—protected them. This they know, for they felt it and feel it still. This and other acts makes them distrustful of everything proposed by white men.

This is a sort of missionary measure, and must meet with a hearty response from that quarter. Our missionary societies, with very little effort, can be enlisted in this cause. It would give an opportunity to put in practice their benevolent inclinations. Let each one who is a fit person to have the care of an Indian child have one, and train him up in the way he should go, and great good will be the result. No one measure for the reformation and improvement of the Indian tribes promises more good, if they would generally adopt it. If they will try it as an experiment, which I think they will do, at least their prejudice will be overcome in time, and much good will be done. I think the Cherokees will be more easily induced to adopt the measure than any of the surrounding tribes.

In all treaties hereafter made I would try to insert a clause, and insist on it, for all or as many of their orphans as they will consent to being given up and trained and educated in Christian families by white men in the English language and in the habits of civilized life.

29

As I suggested in a former answer, I repeat it: I would insert a clause in every treaty hereafter made with any and all tribes setting apart a missionary fund to aid this and other missionary objects.

Respectfully submitted.

J. HARLAN,
United States Indian Agent.

Hon. J. R. DOOLITTLE, *Chairman, &c.*

Reply of H. W. Martin, United States Indian agent.

SAC AND FOX AGENCY, KANSAS,
September 12, 1865.

SIR: I have the honor to acknowledge the receipt of your circular letter of May 10, 1865, embracing twenty-three questions, in relation to Indian affairs. In reply, I will try to answer them in their order.

1. I have had some acquaintance with the Shawnees, Pottawatomies, Kansas and Delawares, for the past nine years. In 1862 I spent six months as special Indian agent, accompanying the Indian brigade part of the time, in the Indian territory, where I came in contact with the Cherokees, Creeks, Chickasaws, Choctaws, Osages, and various other tribes, and for the last two and a half years I have been agent for the Sacs and Foxes, and Chippewa and Christian Indians, residing in the Sac and Fox reserve.

2. This tribe are steadily decreasing in number, from various causes—their manner of living, exposure to cold and wet, and especially to drunkenness. Nine out of ten of them will get drunk if they can get the liquor. When drunk they abuse one another, and by exposure contract disease, and death follows.

3. The diseases most fatal are consumption, aided, I think, by all the diseases that follow prostitution—syphilis, scrofula, &c.

4. Intoxication prevails to an alarming extent among all the western tribes of which I have any knowledge. I do not know that I can make any suggestion that would be worth anything to you or the committee. In my opinion the laws and regulations are sufficient, if promptly and faithfully executed. In order that offenders may be promptly punished, give United States commissioners the power to fine and imprison for selling liquor and stealing timber and ponies from the Indians, and for other depredations in the Indian country, for the reason that we have no trouble in getting witnesses before a United States commissioner on the *reserve*; but it is almost impossible to get Indian witnesses before the court, for when court sits, nine chances to one the witnesses will be out on the buffalo hunt, and cannot be brought before the court. The result is the offender is discharged. This applies especially to Blanket Indians, who have great aversion to going to or before our courts.

5 and 6. I respectfully refer to the statement of Dr. A. Wiley, who has been the physician to this tribe for the past four years.

7. In my opinion it will be impossible to maintain Blanket Indians on reserves, surrounded by white settlers in the State of Kansas, or any other State. Indians who have adopted the customs of the whites may possibly remain within the State. But Blanket Indians should be removed as early as possible to the Indian territory.

8. Blanket Indians will hold their lands in common, and a large number of them change or move three or four times in one year, living in one part of the reserve to-day, and in another part to-morrow.

9. I do not think it safe to confer the power of alienation upon any full-blood Indian in the United States; and if conferred on the half-breeds except in special cases, in nine cases out of ten they would soon squander it, and become a dead weight on their own or some other tribe.

10. Most of the labor on this reserve is performed by the women. Among the full-bloods, the men consider it a disgrace to work. The half-breeds to some extent naturally follow their example, while a few adopt the customs of the whites, and live like them. Almost every family in this tribe raises corn, beans, and pumpkins enough to do them. Almost their entire wealth is in ponies, but three or four raising any cattle or hogs.

11. I would recommend manual-labor schools, under the control of Protestant teachers, for the reason that Catholics educate rather than elevate the Indian.

12. Among Blanket Indians, I think all missionaries ought to be practical teachers; the more civilized should be supplied with missionaries.

13. I do not feel competent to answer the question, but will give my opinion. What is now called the Indian territory ought to be held under new treaty stipulations, with pro-

visions for locating all the tribes in the western States, south of a given line, and to be kept exclusively for the Indians. I would consider it unwise to establish a territorial government over the Indians at the present time.

14. I think money annuities ought to be discontinued altogether.

15. I cannot answer this question, as my experience has been confined to the order system.

16. At this agency, none.

17. A large portion of the balances paid in money, together with sale of ponies, furs, &c., is squandered in drinking and gambling.

18. A United States commissioner with power to fine and imprison.

19. I consider the order system the best ever adopted for the Indians. Orders are issued to each head of the families and single persons, which is placed to their credit. They supply their wants from time to time until the order is taken up in flour, bacon, sugar, coffee, blankets, &c., &c.—such as make up the clothing of a Blanket Indian; the women and children getting their share of clothing and provisions. Many of them trade on the order from payment to payment, having a balance due them after paying their account, ranging from one to twenty dollars; the result is that the Sac and Fox Indians are the best fed and clothed tribe that I have seen in the State; while I am very certain, that if the annuity were paid in money, a large number of women and children would not receive one cent.

20. In my opinion the Bureau of Indian Affairs should be placed under the control of the Interior Department, and removed as far as possible from the military, with a view of keeping down the war spirit among the Indians.

21. In my opinion all reserves should be set apart, by treaty with the tribe or tribes, and faithfully adhered to by the government, holding the tribe accountable to the treaty stipulations, whch is the peaceable way of dealing with Indians.

22. I am unable to state the proportion of orphan children in this tribe, but believe it to be very large. In relation to placing them in the families of Christians, I give it as my opinion, that while there is so large a number of orphan white children totally neglected by *Christian white men*, I have but little faith in their doing anything for orphan Indian children, and especially as the former can be educated and made useful citizens with one-tenth part the trouble that will be required to make a good citizen of the latter.

23. I would recommend manual-labor schools, the children to reside at the mission as their home, and to be entirely under the control of the teachers and agent. Parents should have no control over them whatever.

Very respectfully, your obedient servant,

H. W. MARTIN,
United States Indian Agent.

Hon. J. R. DOOLITTLE,
Chairman, &c., Racine, Wisconsin.

SAC AND FOX AGENCY, KANSAS,
August 18, 1865.

SIR: To the questions put by you concerning the social condition of the Sac and Fox nation of Indians, in answer to question No. 5, will say, without doubt, prostitution has and does exist to a fearful extent in this nation. The facts upon which I predicate this statement are:

1. The constitutional degeneracy of a large majority of the nation; almost every patient that presents himself or herself, "bears the marks of the beast." In a large majority of cases, every excoriation, every sore, and every wound, takes upon itself that indolent and sluggish disposition characteristic of syphilis, and the remedies administered in genuine syphilis are indicated in their cases.

2. Their domestic relations are calculated to create and foster prostitution. A man takes a woman as his wife; then puts her away upon the most simple pretext, takes another, and she leaves because he takes a second; or perhaps she may remain, and the man has two or more wives if he wishes. In fact their domestic relations are nothing but a system of prostitution, (at least would be among whites, its effects being the same as like causes would produce among whites.)

6. Drunkenness has been another cause which has tended to waste this nation; but the rigid measures you have instituted, and the energetic manner in which you have enforced those measures, have caused whiskey to become quite a stranger among this people. The Indian has possessed himself of all the vices of civilization, and nothing but the virtues of

civilization can place him in a savable condition. He must be treated as a wayward child, placing him as far from vicious influences as possible, and then educate him above them.

Respectfully, your obedient servant,

ALBERT WILEY, M. D.,
Physician to the Sac and Fox Nation.

H. W. MARTIN,
United States Indian Agent.

Reply of W. H. Waterman, Superintendent of Indian affairs.

OFFICE SUPERINTENDENT INDIAN AFFAIRS,
Olympia, Washington Territory, August 31, 1865.

SIR: I have the honor to acknowledge the receipt of your circular, dated May 10, containing a list of inquiries relative to Indian affairs.

Below please notice my answer to those inquiries in the order of their numbers.

1. My experience in Indian affairs has been acquired in the capacity of superintendent Indian affairs in Washington Territory, upon the duties of which office I entered about one year ago.

2. I think the Indian tribes are generally decreasing in numbers. The higher their attainments in the habits of civilization, the less their decrease in number, and in some of the tribes the population is holding its own, and possibly in a few on the increase. This is true, however, of but few tribes who have adopted the habits of civilization, in regard to their dwellings, food, clothing and employment.

3. The most prevalent and most fatal diseases among Indians are diseases of the lungs and scrofula; marks of the latter being visible upon the persons of multitudes of them at an early age, and fastening itself upon the lungs, hurries them to premature death. These diseases are induced upon them by the necessary exposure of their mode of life, and the demoralization growing out of their contact with debased and unprincipled white men.

4. Indians located in the vicinity of towns, where the temptation is before them, are much addicted to intemperance; and although the legislation is very strict on the subject of furnishing intoxicating liquors to them, yet under our present system, and with the present state of public feeling on the subject, it is found very difficult, and in many cases quite impossible to inflict upon the offender the penalty of the law. There is a manifest disposition on the part of the people to screen this class of offenders from justice. When tried by a jury it is found practically impossible to obtain a verdict against them, however clear and unequivocal the evidence. If the form of trial could be more arbitrary and independent of the people, I think the ends of justice would be much more likely to be subserved, and the Indians would be better protected against the most serious impediment in the way of their elevation. If the trial could be before a United States commissioner, and proper care be taken in the selection of the man to perform the duties of that office, I think the interdiction of the evil could be made very effective.

5. I have no doubt that prostitution is very general among most of the tribes. This is one of the concomitant evils of intemperance, and its prevalence is greater or less in proportion to the facilities they have for obtaining liquor. Both of these sources of demoralization become less in proportion to the degree of moral and Christian influence brought to bear upon them. And in those agencies which are remote from business centres, and which are under the control of earnest, devoted Christian men, there is very little complaint of either of these evils; but where vigilance on the part of agents is wanting, and where the low state of the public morals is such that the people connive at and encourage these immoralities, habits of prostitution are very general, and the effect is very marked upon the health both of the parents and their offspring. The diseases immediately consequent upon this habit result more remotely in the scrofulous and pulmonary complaints, so very prevalent among them, and which are rapidly wasting the health and life of the race. Very few infants born of diseased parents live to pass the period of infancy, and multitudes of those who have attained the age of manhood and womanhood fall by consumption before reaching the age of 30—a necessary result of the immorality of intemperance and licentiousness, hastened, of course, to its termination, by the exposure of their savage mode of life. I have no doubt that three-fourths of the mortality among those tribes whose numbers are rapidly decreasing is the result, remotely or directly, of licentious intercourse with debased white men, who induce them to the practice by furnishing them with intoxicating drinks; and I cannot forbear expressing my strong desire that some form of legal proceedings be instituted by which men of this class may be brought to condign punishment; and that, in my

opinion, can only be done by the admission of Indian testimony, before some officer appointed by the general government.

The heresy is so common in the minds of the people, that "*the Indian has no rights that the white men are bound to respect*"—*that he is doomed to extermination and the faster he disappears the better*—that it is impossible to obtain justice in our ordinary courts.

6 and 12. I choose to connect the 6th and 12th questions together, and in reply to say, that in my judgment there is no power given under heaven among men, whereby either the souls or the bodies of a barbarous race can be saved, except the power of the Christian religion; and that this power can be brought to bear upon them only through the agency of men inspired by a true missionary spirit.

The principle holds good everywhere and always, that when a weak race comes in contact with a stronger race, the contact will be at one of the two extremes of social life. The savage has nothing in him by nature to affiliate him with civilization in its better manifestation, and civilization, in the absence of Christian love, has nothing in it to prompt it to go out after the savage, to make sacrifices for his improvement, or to seek to bring him on to its own level.

Hence, when two races are thus brought in contact, the savage will naturally affiliate with the lowest forms of social life in the stronger race; the lower and the more degraded the social manifestations on the part of the latter, the more natural and the more intimate will be the contact. Hence it is in all cases where attempts are made by government or by individuals to bring civilization to the Indians without the aid of religion, that the Indians take on the vices instead of the virtues of civilization, and are made worse instead of better by their contact with the white race. This is seen everywhere: the lowest, the meanest, the most licentious and morally corrupt of the white race are the intimate associates of the Indians, so far as the two races are brought at all into social contact. And you can only bring civilization to the weaker race by presenting its highest manifestation as seen in the love, the charity, the patience, and self-sacrificing benevolence of Christianity. If you will bring these two extremes of humanity into contact in the spirit of the true missionary, and, after the example of Jesus, our great pattern, who continually brought himself into contact with the worst and weakest, the most ignorant and degraded of the race, that he might win them to come on to his moral level, that he might assimilate them to his type of humanity, and thus redeem them from their degradation, then the contact will be salutary to the Indians, and Christianity will work out the same results on them as on other men. This statement is abundantly borne out by facts, not only in America, but everywhere. To whatever heathen race the missionary has gone with the torch of Christianity in his hand and in the spirit of his master, he has attained success in communicating not only the lessons of religion, but by conferring in a greater or less degree the blessings of civilization. Among our own tribes the following declaration will be found to hold good. In proportion as Indian agencies are conducted and managed in a true Christian spirit, making the religion of the New Testament the basis of all intercourse with the Indians, in that proportion do the immoralities and the diseases of the race become less. Sin and sickness are closely allied, and in proportion as you banish the one do you cure the other. We have in this Territory one agency that is truly a missionary station. It is true there are local and physical advantages in its favor which some other reservations do not enjoy. It is remote from business centres, the land is arable and fertile, and the climate is congenial. There are fewer influences and temptations to evil in its surroundings than in those of other agencies, and while all due credit should be given to these favorable circumstances, yet there is another fact which distinguishes it from all the others. The agent himself is a Christian missionary, and all the employés under him are Christian men. The business of the agency is being done in a Christian spirit, and the result is there is less of immorality, less of disease, less of decay, more industry, more agriculture, more mechanical art, better habitations, and in every respect more of the comforts of civilized life in connexion with that agency than any other in the Territory. I most devoutly wish that all our Indian agencies were organized in the same manner and conducted in the same spirit.

7. In regard to the question of removing Indians from their reservations, I desire to say that while the interests of both white men and Indians seem sometimes to be embarrassed by the reservations being situated in the midst of white settlements, yet it is very difficult to remove Indians from localities where their home has been for a long time without dissatisfaction and injustice. Indians are attached to their local habitation, near which are the graves of their fathers and friends and the associations of their childhood. They dislike to be dispossessed of them, and though they may be tempted for a consideration to surrender their possessions, and retreat before the aggressions of white settlements, yet it is very difficult to suit them with a new location; they are apt to be discontented, dissatisfied, and unhappy, by reason of the removal, however much may be done for them in a pecuniary way to atone for what they regard as a sacrifice. As a general principle, there-

fore, to which there may be exceptions in particular cases, I think the Indians should be maintained on their reservations and protected there in all their rights.

8 and 9. I think it would induce more of settled permanence with them if they could hold small tracts of land in severalty, which they could call their own, and on which they could be encouraged to establish their homes and make improvements for their comfort. Especially would this be true of such as are inclined to abandon their wild mode of life and imitate the domestic habits of the whites. But in no case should Indians be intrusted with power to alienate title, except by treaty with the general government.

10. The answer to this inquiry must be different with different reservations, depending upon the situation and quality of the land reserved to them, and the policy of the men appointed to administer their affairs. When the reservations are located on good agricultural land, and where proper efforts are made on the part of agents and employers to encourage them and aid and instruct them, they turn their hands to agriculture with commendable success. But where the reservations are heavily timbered, difficult to clear, and rather sterile when cleared, it is impossible to make much progress in the cultivation of crops, and the Indians continue to subsist by fishing and hunting. By reference to the reports from different agents, showing the amount of crops raised and the amount of stock owned by the Indians, it will be easy to compare the different reservations in regard to the progress made in farming. On those reservations where farming is done to any considerable extent the Indians generally interest themselves in it, both males and females, the latter doing frequently the greater part of the labor.

11. There are but two schools in practical operation among Indians in the Territory. One on the Yakama reservation, under Agent Wilber, and the other a Catholic school, on the Tulalip reservation, under the superintendence of Father Chirouse. These are both manual-labor schools, and for their results reference must be had to the reports of those having them in charge, which reports will be transmitted, together with my annual report to the Commissioner of Indian Affairs, in a few days. There is no doubt that every school for the education of Indians should be established on the manual-labor system. The art of living, and of doing the work which a living implies, are among the most important lessons to be learned in their schools, and these lessons can only be learned by actual practice.

13. In reply to the 13th question, I have to say that my knowledge of the Indian territory is too limited to give value to my judgment on the subject here propounded. If a territorial government could be organized in a region where soil, climate, and other physical characteristics were congenial to the welfare of the Indians, and there could be placed over them and among them good men, who would make their abode pleasant and inviting by introducing among them the blessings of a true Christian civilization, there might be hope that in due time other Indians could be induced to evacuate their present possessions and emigrate hither, and that the change would inure to the benefit of the white settlements without harm or injustice to the Indians. It must be borne in mind, however, that jealousy is a leading trait of the Indian character, and that the task of harmonizing strange tribes in proximate localities would be very difficult, and the experiment one of doubtful success.

14. In reply to the 14th question, I have no hesitation in answering yes; for I firmly believe that money given directly to Indians is in nearly every instance a positive injury.

15. Annuities under my administration are not distributed in the form of money, but of other valuables. In making the disbursements of these funds, my policy is to subserve the best interests of the Indians. In some of the agencies the greater proportion of the annuity money is invested in stocks, tools, and improvements, and where goods are preferred, I purchase only necessary articles, and those of the most serviceable quality, all of which are, so far as I know, delivered to the Indians in good faith.

16. No debts due traders are ever recognized here in the distribution of annuities

17. Nor do I think the Indians are in the habit of trading off their annuities for intoxicating drinks. They sometimes gamble among themselves, often winning or losing their most needed articles of apparel.

18. The practice of gambling is no doubt a crime, and should be treated as such in the administration of the affairs of the department. Too much pains to discourage and prevent the practice cannot be taken.

19. The order system is not known within my superintendency.

20. Most emphatically do I say that the Indian Bureau should remain as it is, under the Department of the Interior, and my reasons are—

1st. That Bibles, and not bayonets, are the proper instruments by which to reclaim savages and confer the blessings of civilization; and

2d. That the influence of the soldiery, when brought in contact with Indians, is invariably demoralizing and corrupting. If it be the policy of the government to so administer Indian affairs as to secure the extermination of the Indian race in the shortest time possible, then I would say place them under the military; but if the policy be that which becomes a Christian government, to bestow upon them the blessings of a true Christian civilization, then I say keep the soldiery as far as possible from them, and send in their stead the missionary of the cross, with the Bible in one hand and the plough in the other, and through that instrumentality make them know that the government is their best and truest friend, and not a treacherous enemy.

21. In setting apart reserves, it should be done by treaty with the tribes in an amicable, just, and satisfactory manner, and never by coercion. This is their right, and unless we respect all their rights in a matter so vital to their interests, we cannot hope they will be satisfied or peaceful.

22. I cannot say what proportion of Indian children in this Territory are orphans—I think not a large proportion; but whether orphans or not, it would be an incalculable benefit if they could be taken entirely away from their parents and placed in charity schools to be educated. I would not recommend that this be done arbitrarily, in violation of the parent's will, but I would recommend that every possible inducement be offered to the parents to thus dispose of their children, and in the case of orphans it should be done without respect to the will of the Indians at all.

23. In reply to the last inquiry, I have simply to say, let good men, and none but good men, be put into the Indian service—men of Christian sympathies, men of pure character, men whose highest ambition is not to obtain spoils, but to confer benefits and blessings on a poor, despised, and perishing race. If this rule be carefully adhered to, the Indian race may be greatly improved physically, morally, and socially, and in proportion as this is done will the safety and the welfare of the white people, who are in contact with them, be secured.

All which is respectfully submitted by your humble and obedient servant,

WM. H. WATERMAN,
Sup't Indian Affairs, W. T.

Hon. James R. Doolittle,
Chairman Senate Committee on Indian Affairs.

Reply of J. Ward, Indian agent.

Pueblo Agency, Peña Blanca, New Mexico,
August 24, 1865.

Sir: Upon my return from some of the pueblos south from the agency, where I had been on business connected with my duties, I had the honor, through Major John Greiner, United States depositary, at Santa Fé, New Mexico, to receive the "circular" left by you, and which I will now endeavor to answer to the best of my knowledge and belief.

Your honor will please bear in mind that my experience in Indian affairs is mostly confined to this Territory, having had but little to do with Indians in any other portion of the country.

As I presume that the "circular" will be used in connexion with this, I will simply make my answers agreeable to the numbers of the several inquiries therein contained.

1. Previous to my entering the Indian service here, I served as interpreter of the Spanish language in the quartermasters' department with the army in Mexico, during the war. After peace was made, in 1848, I still continued in the same department until August, 1851, having served during this period in different capacities at Jefferson Barracks, Missouri, Fort Leavenworth, Missouri, and in the department of Texas and Mew Mexico.

On the first day of September, 1851, I entered the service of the Indian department in this Territory, as interpreter, and in May, 1852, I was placed in the office of the superintendent of Indian affairs, as clerk, which situation I held until June, 1861, when I had the honor to receive my present appointment from our late lamented President. The entire period of my services in this department being now fourteen years.

2. The Indians within this superintendency are beyond the least doubt decreasing in numbers. The opinion of late Superintendent Steck, and that of many other gentlemen on this subject, is, that the main cause of their decreasing results from marrying relatives, as they seldom, if ever, marry out of the tribe.

3. I am not aware of the particular "causes of the diseases," but many of them, particularly the wild tribes, suffer much from rheumatism, gonorrhœa, fevers and small-pox; the last usually proves to be their most fatal enemy. The Utahs, Apaches and Navajoes, a few years ago, lost a great many of their people from this malady.

4. Most of the Indians here are addicted to this habit, "intoxication;" many of the

Pueblos form an exception. It is very difficult to make any useful suggestions on this point, at least so far as our Indians are concerned, from the fact of their approximation to the settlements and daily intercourse with the inhabitants thereof, many of whom will neither respect magistrates nor the laws of the country, and will sell or barter liquor to Indians wherever and whenever an opportunity offers, regardless of all considerations and consequences. The "rules and regulations" of the Indian Bureau having never been put in force in this or any other particular case, they having become a "dead letter," there is no restriction whatever, and the agents of this branch of the service are absolutely powerless.

Again, the provisions made in sections 20 and 21 of the "intercourse act" seem to be intended exclusively for the Indian country. They should be made so as to embrace *all* cases, whether *in* or *out* of the Indian country, and under all circumstances imposing heavier penalties, which should be strictly enforced. The officers of this branch of the service should be vested with all the power necessary to execute and carry them out, even by force of arms. Few examples of this kind would be apt to have a salutary effect. This is about the only remedy to prevent or mitigate the evil.

5. From my best information and belief, prostitution prevails among them to a considerable extent, and the diseases consequent upon it have the same tendency to diminish their numbers, and to enfeeble their offspring, as the same kind of disease has with other people, and perhaps more, in consequence of their treatment of the same, and the want of proper means and care. Strange as it may appear to your honor, "prostitution" increases among them as fast as they intermingle with the whites, and the effects of the diseases consequent upon it become more perceivable. In the support of this statement, I need go no further than trading establishments, military posts, and such other places where they are in frequent intercourse with the whites.

6. The particular cause of their decay beyond what has already been stated, in our opinion, must be attributed to their mode of living, and the circumstances surrounding them. Situated as most of the Indians are, they must necessarily undergo much suffering and privations. An Indian will go without eating for two or three days without scarcely showing to be the worse for it; but as soon as opportunity offers he will eat without measure or precaution, and without being over-nice as to the quality of the viands. In many instances they will resort to mule and horse meat, prairie dogs, and the like. The former is frequently eaten by them in a state of putridity; indeed it would be hard to say what Indians would not eat at times. Besides, they contract vices that weaken and vitiate the system, rendering it more liable to attacks from disease, and less able to resist its influences when attacked. Hence many of them die from diseases that ordinarily seldom prove fatal.

I can think of no "practical remedy" to prevent their decay; in fact there can be none, so long as they are permitted or compelled to roam at large over mountains and valleys, deprived of all benefits, and even of the care of their agents. And until they are placed in suitable localities and proper care taken of them, we may look for no alteration for the better in their condition, and consequently their decay is bound to continue.

7. The policy of the government, if I understand it properly, is—if not, it *should* be—to place the Indians on reserves, and to aid them until they are able to take care of themselves. This being the case, it is obvious that the Indian as well as the white man necessarily requires and must have suitable tracts of land upon which to make his home and that of his future generations. Hence the reservations should be carefully selected; they should be well supplied with good land, for cultivation and pasturage, with sufficient good water for drinking, irrigation and all other necessary purposes, timber for building and for fuel, with as many other advantages as possible; all of which requisites it must be admitted are absolutely necessary to make a *permanent reserve* what it should be.

Now it must be borne in mind that such tracts of land as above described are precisely such as are sought after by the white settlers; and if the government is to remove the Indians as fast as the settlers "advance," and take a fancy to those localities, probably to be abandoned by them in few years, after having taken possession of the same, which is not unfrequently the case, there would be *no end* to the removal of reserves, saying nothing of the enormous expense which would naturally be incurred, and the trouble and vexation incident to the prosecution of a work of this kind. Again, one of the principal things to be borne in mind is, that whenever the Indians proposed to be placed upon any reserve should become sufficiently advanced and reconciled, so as to induce them to remain of their own accord, and to take care of themselves, the effect which would be produced by removing them to *new* localities could not but bring about a bad state of feeling. Besides, a system of this kind would not only excite the prejudice of the Indians, but would also discourage them, and would naturally diminish their confidence and faith in the justice, ability and power of the government, all of which should by all possible means be avoided.

Were the policy of removing reserves, as before alluded to, to be continued, after several years it would, no doubt, task the goverment to find suitable localities upon which to place the Indians. This would certainly be the case in this Territory, where the proportion of arable land is so small to that which, for the want of water, has never been nor ever will be cultivated. Indian reservations, as before stated, must have all or as many requisites as possible; and once such localities are found and Indians placed thereon, the government should endeavor, by all means, to keep them within the same, and "resist encroachments" at all hazards. Of course the selection of the proposed reserves should, from the commencement, be made as remote from the settlements as possible and as circumstances would admit.

It is no use to dodge the question any longer. Too much time has already been lost. The fact is, we have the Indians on our lands, and the government is in duty bound to take care of and protect them regardless of all newspaper scribblers and bombast about "wiping them out," and the like and all other outside pressure, which has no other effect than to keep up bad feelings and to prejudice the minds of many against the Indian service and every one connected therewith. There should be strong barriers between the citizens and the Indians, and both should be made to know their place.

It behooves the government to take strong measures in regard to its Indian policy, and the sooner this is done the better it will be for all concerned. Otherwise, we may expect nothing else but the continuance of trouble and confusion in the mangement of our Indian affairs on the frontiers, particularly in this portion, where so much enmity exists between the two races.

8. The lands of the reserves, should by all means, be held by the tribe or band in "common;" after which it should be allotted in severalty, so that each family might have sufficient land out of which to support themselves. This would give them a better encouragement to work the lands, and would make them feel more independent, and at the same time would with proper care prevent the lands from falling into the hands of "outsiders," after the same were turned over to the Indians. Laws should also be enacted to prevent the Indians from selling or otherwise disposing of any portion thereof, which should also prohibit citizens of all kinds from purchasing, renting, or in any manner getting possession of any part of the same. They should not be allowed to get the least foothold within any reserve.

The main and principal cause of most of the troubles and difficulties between the Mexican citizens and our Pueblo Indians results from the "encroachments" of the former, who will manage, "by hook or by crook," to get some foothold within the grants of the latter. This, however, results from the want of proper power and authority on the part of the officers of the department. Otherwise these Indians live happily and contented, and prove themselves in no way to be such hideous and disgusting neighbors as some people would be led to believe.

9. I do not believe it would be proper or "safe" to confer the power of alienation of real estate upon Indians, were their lands to be held by them in severalty, at least for many years after having been placed in possession of the same, and until they proved themselves to be sufficiently advanced in civilization to know how to appreciate the benefit of a home, and even then I doubt its propriety. Indeed I would not even now recommend such power being conferred upon any of the Pueblo Indians of this Territory, notwithstanding their advanced condition.

10. The reserve system not having been sufficiently tested in this country, I cannot well give a positive answer.

Among the Utahs and Apaches, however, the females usually do the most, if not all, the work. I have seen them even saddle their husbands' horses, whilst the lazy scamps would be standing or lying about. This is not the case with the Navajoes; they have more respect for their females, and as a general rule treat them kindly. In their own country I have seen them work both in the fields and out of them Next to the Pueblos, I can safely say that they are the most industrious Indian women that I have ever seen. When they are at peace and quietly at home in their country, the same can be said of the men; I have frequently seen them making saddles, bridles, and many other necessary articles, as well as working in the fields. I would venture the assertion, that the Navajo Indians can be safely put down as being the most advanced, in every sense of the word, of any wild tribe under the jurisdiction of our government. And had it not been for the almost constant wars of retaliation between them and the Mexican citizens, and the want of proper management toward them on the part of our authorities, both civil and military, they would have long since proved this fact.

The Pueblos also treat their females well, and the labor performed by them is mostly confined to household affairs About the time of gathering their crops the females usually assist, outside of this, in making pottery, which they do to a great extent. They are by no means overburdened with work. All other work is performed by the men.

11. No regular schools have ever been established by the government for the benefit of the Indians in this country. Hence the effect which they might have produced, strictly speaking, is not known. If I except the school which was kept for some time at the pueblo

of Laguna, by the Rev. Samuel Gorman, which was confined to few children of the pueblo, nothing of the kind has existed among our Indians during my experience. But there can be no doubt that proper schools under the management of the right kind of persons, such as would take sufficient interest in the welfare and advancement of the children in their charge, and who would be willing to undergo the privations and annoyances incident to a task of this kind among Indians, could not but have a good effect, and prove a blessing to them. It should be borne in mind, that in order to educate and place Indian children on the path of civilization, they must be taken away from under the influence and control of their people. This, of course, should not entirely prohibit the parents and relatives from an opportunity of seeing them at certain specified periods, so as to satisfy them that their children are doing well.

At first the children should be treated with the utmost kindness in order to reconcile them to the sudden change, and make them become attached to those by whom they might be surrounded. Very light punishment should be inflicted for their childish offences; they should not be overburdened with study, neither with long confinement in the school-room at any time. The entire education of the young Indian should be confined to the most simple and useful rudiments, thus making his progress as easy and smooth as possible. Of course all this could be altered by degrees, keeping time, as it were, with their growth and advancement. Moderation in all things should be strictly observed with them by the persons in charge, who should also possess a sufficient share of *patience*, this being one if not the main requisite in dealing and managing with Indians; indeed it frequently requires all the "patience of Job."

The children to be selected for the school should not be too young; they should be at least from ten to twelve years of age, at which age they are more apt to learn and take notice of things. These I consider to be some of the leading points necessary to be observed for a successful management of schools for the benefit of Indian children.

As to the *exact* working of the "manual-labor schools," I have no experience.

12. "Christian missions" among the Indians can certainly do no harm, but I doubt the propriety of preaching the gospel to wild Indians before they are sufficiently advanced to comprehend and know how to appreciate what is told to them on the subject. In my opinion religion is one of the last things that should be introduced to the Indian unless it goes hand in hand with education and other advancements in civilization; and this must, as a matter of course, commence with the rising generation.

It is next to an impossibility to convert an adult wild Indian into a civilized man, and it is out of the question to think, even for a moment, that he will give up all his notions, superstitions, and prejudices upon mere appeals to his reason. The civilization of the Indian, at best, cannot but be slow work. It is hopeless to expect the old Indian to reform. The middle aged, with his roving disposition and habits of life, will take hold of the work, if ever he does, cautiously and suspiciously, and the only hope of success is centred in their children.

Please see report of the Hon. ——— ———, Indian affairs, for 1864, page 192, for my remarks therein contained, in regard to the effect of religion among the Pueblo Indians of this country.

13. My experience is so limited in regard to the so-called "Indian Territory," and the true condition and circumstances surrounding the Indians thereof, and of the effects produced by former treaty stipulations, as not to warrant me in expressing an opinion.

14. "Money annuities" to Indians should be discontinued, and instead thereof good and substantial articles should be furnished to them.

15. In my belief the proportion of money which actually reaches the hands of the Indians, if any, must be very limited, or perhaps enough to allow them to get intoxicated and sufficiently infuriated to do some mischief, or to lose their horses, guns, or some other article, all of which usually lead to trouble.

16. In my opinion, the proportion of money received by the trader for goods and supplies, "already advanced," must be nearly the whole, as the Indians, like the majority of their more civilized neighbors, will get things on credit just so long as they find any one to trust them. Whilst, on the other hand, the trader being satisfied that his money is secured, will be very apt to let them have credit to the full amount of their annuities; of course there may be some exceptions, but I believe they are very few.

17. The proportion of money squandered for intoxicating drinks, or in gambling, I will venture to say is the entire balance, if any, as before stated, is left to him after the traders and others are paid. Most Indians will both drink and gamble whenever they have the means to do so, and on such occasions, particularly when near the settlements or among white men, they unavoidably fall among "sharks," alias civilized men, who usually take good care to strip them, not only out of what little money they have, but also out of every thing else they can.

18. It is rather difficult to suggest any practical plan to secure the Indians against the

evils of "drinking and gambling" so long as they are allowed to roam at large and be entirely away from under the care and supervision of their agents, particularly just after receiving their annuities or presents, at which time many of the goods received may be of little or no use to them. As I have already stated, "money annuities" should not be paid to them, and, when it could be conveniently done, no goods nor any other articles, except such as they actually stood in need of, should be turned over to them at the time of the payment or distribution—nothing more than their actual wants should demand. The remainder ought to be retained by their agents, to be issued as times and circumstances should require it, with a careful discrimination on the part of the agents in the distribution of the same between the industrious and the idle, the orderly and the thriftless. Besides this, the "rules and regulations" of the Indian Bureau should be strictly enforced, whenever an opportunity offered, without fear or favoritism.

19. I can express no opinion as to the merits of the "order system," having had no opportunity to ascertain its effects.

20. I am certainly in favor that the Indian bureau should be under the department which would insure the most beneficial results to the service. But I do not think that any material benefit would be derived from the removing of the Indian Bureau from the Interior Department and placing it under the War Department, neither do I think that by doing so would secure any better or a more economical administration of its affairs. Besides, this bureau has already been under the War Department, and the fact of its having been transferred to that of the Interior, by an act of Congress, evidently shows that its practical workings under that department could not have given entire satisfaction. I look upon the Indian service as being one of the *most* important branches of the government, and is certainly one that is bound to exist for many years to come; and, in my humble opinion, instead of its being under any particular department, if it could possibly be done, it should be organized into a perfect system, with a complete code for its guidance. For just so long at it remains subservient to any department, as it now is, just so long it will be considered as a secondary affair, and its officers, its rules and regulations, and everything else connected therewith, will be looked upon and treated accordingly.

When we take into consideration that there are about *three hundred and fifty thousand* souls (Indians) under the jurisdiction of the government, scattered as it were all over creation, and that this multitude is in charge of about *seventy-five* persons, in the shape of superintendents and agents, and to this mere handful of men the entire population of the nation look to for the good management of the affairs under their respective charge, as well as for the good behavior and the civilization of the Indians; and that upon these few individuals are heaped the curses and abuses of at least one-half of the enlightened community, simply because they do not prevent the Indians from stealing something to eat when they are hungry, or from committing depredations, many of which are brought about by the indiscretion of the whites themselves; and when we reflect that this handful of officers are, strictly speaking, without power or authority, having to beg their way through, upon the most important occasions, either from the military or some other department, and not unfrequently even from the very citizens, the necessity of making the Indian service what it should be becomes more apparent every day.

A radical change is absolutely needed, and until the bureau is placed in its true and legitimate position the officers thereof will struggle in vain; *time* has already sufficiently proved this fact.

21. "In setting apart reserves," in my opinion, should be done by regulations, even by force of arms should it be necessary. Treaty stipulations would be apt to be violated, and whenever this would be the case recourse to arms would be inevitable, which would bring about the same trouble and expense incident to such movements, all of which might be avoided by taking firm and decided measures from the commencement.

22. The proportion of orphan children among our Indians is not easily arrived at, but I am satisfied that there are a great many. Whenever children are thus left their relatives usually take charge of them and will claim them as their own, and, as far as my experience goes, they seem to do well by them.

As to the policy of placing orphan children in the families of Christian white men, we are decidedly in favor; but much care should be taken in the selection of such families; they should be held under some kind of agreement so far as the care and education of the children are concerned, otherwise many of them would avail themselves of the services of the poor creatures without any care as to their welfare or education, on which event it would be far better to leave the children with their relatives, unless the bureau itself should take care of them. Indian boys, in fact all young Indians, when brought into contact with the whites, unless much care is taken with them, are more apt to take up with the vices of the whites than with their good morals, after which they invariably make the worst kind of characters.

23. One of the great, if not the greatest, drawbacks in the management of our Indian

affairs is, beyond any doubt, the constant and frequent changes of the officers of this service, particularly of Indian agents. In my opinion every officer of this branch of the government should be appointed during good behavior, instead of four years or during the pleasure of the President, whilst a policy of this kind could not but bring about a great reform in the management of the affairs, and would secure a more economical administration in many ways; at the same time it would not in the least lessen the power of the government over superintendents, Indian agents, or any other person thus appointed.

It must be obvious to your honor that the effect produced by changing superintendents and Indian agents, particularly the latter, as often as it is usually done, cannot but prove detrimental, both to the interest of the government and that of the Indians in general. Under the present policy an Indian agent is not safe in his position, and he cannot feel otherwise; in fact, he is a temporary "machine," subject not only to political influences, but also to the malice of any one of his enemies who might think proper to get up something against him, and have him removed from office, with a view either to secure the same for himself or some one of his favorites, or even to gratify his malice, without giving the agent a chance to defend himself, as it is now the case; which, under the policy recommended, could not well be done without a proper investigation, which would give the agent a chance to prove whether he was innocent of the charges or otherwise. This, as a matter of course, would make an agent feel more secure in his position, and would make him act more independently in the management of his affairs, and would, at the same time, make him take more interest in the affairs of the government, knowing, as he would, that so long as he acted honestly and faithfully toward the government and the Indians under his charge, that not only his office was secured, but also that he had nothing to fear from *politics* nor any other outside pressure.

Under the present system an Indian agent, as well as others, is compelled in most cases to meddle in politics, either to obtain his office in the first place, or afterwards to retain the same; and he cannot but make both enemies and friends. Thus, while the former are arrayed against him, many of the latter invariably expect him to bestow upon them his public favors, which the agent cannot well avoid, and it is not unfrequently that favors thus bestowed operate against the interests both of the government and the Indians.

Thus, comparatively speaking, the agent, for the most part, is politically fostered, which cannot but have a bad effect. Besides, it is not to be expected that an agent who knows not what moment he is going to be "turned out" of his office, whether he performs his duties honestly and properly or otherwise, can take the same interest that a man would who would know that the holding of his office was entirely dependent upon a proper and faithful discharge of his duties.

There are other considerations of equally vast importance, which, in my opinion, should suggest themselves in favor of my remarks. An Indian agent, in order to be able to perform his duties properly, should be well acquainted with the routine of his office. He should have as much experience as possible of the Indian character. He should be well acquainted with the tribe or band under his charge, their disposition, habits, and customs, and should be well acquainted with the country inhabited by them, as well as with its resources. To gain these necessary advantages, your honor will perceive that it must require time and a great deal of labor. Besides, it is out of the question to think of gaining the good will and confidence of the Indians upon a short acquaintance. Time and good management must do the work. The Indian is naturally haughty, reserved, incredulous, and suspicious—all of which must be worked upon and be overcome before an agent can wield anything like a due proportion of influence over them, and be able to manage them with any degree of success. The worst feature of the policy of removing and changing agents so often is, that the Indian lose faith in the statements of the same, and frequently not without good cause, as the following remarks will clearly prove.

Since the organization of the Indian department in this Territory, now about fourteen years, the office of superintendent has been in the charge of eleven different persons—six regularly appointed and five acting or *pro tem.* superintendents—whilst the four agencies properly within this superintendency have been during the same period under the management of no less than *thirty-eight* different individuals—thirty regularly appointed Indian agents and eight special agents—all of whom, as it is to be expected, had their different plans, notions, and views in regard to the management of Indian affairs, and, as a matter of course, their advices to the Indians were in perfect accordance. Besides, as I have frequently seen it, during the intervals between the changing of some of these officers the Indians would be for months at a time without any agent whatever.

Again: it is to be regretted that so little care is apparently taken by the government in the relations of persons to fill the places of superintendents and Indian agents. It seems that *politics* have more to do with it than any regard for the interest of the service or the welfare of the Indian. These remarks are made with all due respect; I make them from personal observation and experience. It can be safely said that one-half, at least, of the persons thus appointed have no qualifications whatever to fill those stations; in some instances we will venture to say that some of them never saw a live Indian outside of a museum or some other place of exhibition previous to receiving their appointments, and perhaps never been away from home in their lives.

Perhaps there is no branch of the government in which a more careful selection of men is required than in this very service. It requires a combination of qualifications and experience, which, without them, a person can never become a good and efficient agent.

At this very moment the entire department here, with one exception, is in the hands of men who can neither understand, read, nor write a word of English—the very language in which all their accounts, reports, &c., must be made out. I simply make mention of these facts for the purpose of illustrating and supporting my remarks in regard to the effect which politics seem to have in the appointment of officers to this service, and not from any desire to cast reflection upon the gentlemen alluded to.

In conclusion, sir, I would further remark, with the utmost respect, that such has been the management, or rather the want of management of our Indian affairs in this Territory, by the combined effects of the changes already alluded to, the want of proper co-operation on the part of the heads of the several departments, the enmity existing between the Mexican citizens and the Indians, the want of proper power and authority on the part of the officers of this service—*politics* on one side and *speculation* on the other—that it can be safely said, without fear of successful contradiction, the condition of the Indians of this Territory is no better to-day than on that day when the government took possession of the same in 1846. This state of affairs is certainly discouraging; nevertheless, it is a stubborn reality, and I would consider myself criminally guilty, and would be lacking in the faithful discharge of my duties, were I to attempt to disguise or to give the subject any other color. And, furthermore, it is evident that there is no hope for better results, unless your honor, and those to whom this immense task is confided, will devise some plan to remedy the evils. Otherwise, millions upon millions will continue to be expended, lives will be sacrificed, but all to no purpose.

I very much regret my inability to do justice to so great a subject as the one treated upon. And your honor can rest assured that my remarks have been made free from *bias*, my only desire being to comply with your request to the best of my understanding, with the hope, also, that they may prove of some use in promoting the interest of the government and the condition and elevation of the Indians.

All of which is respectfully submitted by your obedient servant,

JOHN WARD, *Indian Agent.*

Hon. JAMES R. DOOLITTLE,
Chairman, &c., Racine, Wisconsin.

Reply of M. M. Davis, United States Indian agent.

UNITED STATES INDIAN AGENCY,
Appleton, Wisconsin, August 31, 1865.

SIR: In compliance with your request in a letter dated May 10, 1865, I submit the following reply to your several interrogatories:

1. I have served as United States Indian agent for the Green Bay agency since the 16th of June, 1861. I have had no experience in the military service in connexion with any of the organized tribes of Indians. The Menomonees, Oneidas, Stockbridges, and Munsees comprise the tribes of this agency, the two latter being united in one organization. With one exception, I have had nothing to do with any Indians beyond the limits of this agency. In the summer of 1863, when some depredations were committed by the roving Winnebagoes, in the western part of this State, at the solicitation of gentlemen of my acquaintance in that portion of the State, I repaired to the locality of the most serious trouble, and from New Lisbon, in Juneau county, submitted a report to the Commissioner of Indian Affairs on the 4th of August, 1863. This report will be found on page 366, report from Commissioner of Indian Affairs for 1863.

2. The Menomonee Indians have decreased about 100 in four years. In 1861 they numbered about 1,900. Now they number about 1,800. The cause of this decrease is attributable to epidemics of dysentery and erysipelas, to the small-pox and loss of soldiers in the military service. You are aware that this tribe is in a transition state. But very few can speak English at all. Four years ago one-half of them were Blanket Indians, now less than one-fourth retain their original dress. A large proportion of them have more faith in their own "medicine men," and a "medicine dance," than in a white physician. Hence a physician is seldom called, and a large per cent. of the sick die.

The Oneidas, Stockbridges, and Munsees are civilized Indians. Although they have lost a great proportion of their enlisted men in the military service, and both tribes have suffered from the small-pox during the past year, there is no material decrease in numbers. Their habits of civilized life keep their numbers good. They are remote from physicians, and seldom employ them, but they use ordinary precautions common to civilized life against the introduction and spread of epidemic and contagious diseases.

3. The most common disease among the tribes of this agency is pneumonia. As a matter of course, with inflammation of the lungs, we get inflammation of the pleura or pleurisy. The Indians call all lung diseases consumption, but there is very little tubercular disease among them. Inflammation of the lungs and pleura is caused by great exposure to heat and cold. Hepatic diseases, or derangement of the liver, are frequently met. I do not think this class of diseases is more common than among the white population. The causes are the same as among the whites. All the eruptive diseases, as small-pox, measles, scarlatina, and erysipelas, prove very fatal, because the course of the disease is rapid, and the sick get but little care ; and if a physician is called, it is generally at a period too late to render any assistance. For the same reasons inflammation of the lungs proves very fatal.

4. Intoxication prevails to a very great extent among the Oneidas. On the east of their settlement, and but a few miles distant, are Depere, Fort Howard, and Green Bay. These towns afford any amount of facilities for liquor traffic with Indians.

There is considerable intoxication among the Menomonees, Stockbridges, and Munsees. The facilities for obtaining spirituous liquor do not exist to such an extent as with the Oneidas. I do not know that I have any data which will enable me to give you the per cent. among the several tribes of adult Indians who drink spirituous liquor whenever they can get it. I think, however, that one-half of the Oneidas are addicted to this practice, and perhaps one-fourth of the adults of the other tribes. In this agency there is scarcely a crime committed by an Indian, either in or out of the Indian country, which is not directly attributable to the use of intoxicating liquor. No matter how kind and good a disposition an Indian may have when sober, under the influence of intoxicating drink he becomes a savage, who does violence to his best friend as readily as to his worst enemy. With a few amendments to the present United States statutes, I believe it practicable to substantially stop this traffic with the Indians. I would have the present law of Congress amended so as to make it the duty of all persons holding office under, or in the employment of, the United States, in the military service, and all persons employed in the Indian service, including United States marshals and their deputies, to arrest without warrant any Indian found intoxicated, and commit such Indian to jail or other safe place of keeping until he or she should become sufficiently sober to testify in court. I would then have them brought before a United States court commissioner, and ask them to disclose the name of the person and place where the liquor was obtained that produced the drunkenness. When the name of the party was disclosed, it should be the duty of the commissioner to issue his warrant for the arrest of the party furnishing the liquor ; and on the testimony of the Indian bind him over to the next term of the United States court. If the Indian would not disclose the name of the party, or place where the liquor was obtained, I would have the commissioner remand the Indian to jail, and there keep him until he would disclose, or until the commissioner was satisfied that he could not do so. If the Indian should swear falsely, I would have him punished by the same law that punishes a white man for doing the same thing. I think a good practical regulation of the department would be to authorize agents to strike the name of any Indian from the pay-roll who should be found intoxicated during payment, also to suspend from office any chief or headman who is in the habit of getting intoxicated. I have spoken confidently of the practicability of suppressing the liquor traffic with the Indians. Permit me to tell you why I have faith. After the act of February, 1862, two men were indicted for selling liquor to Menomonee Indians near Shawano. These indictments were in the United States district court at the July term. The cases went over until the next January, and during this time, from July to January, the liquor traffic about the Menomonee reservation was absolutely stopped. At the January term when the cases were called, the district judge, A. G. Miller, in the presence of the indicted parties, and from the bench, censured those who were responsible for bringing such cases into court. He said it was no use to try to stop the traffic ; that it would be carried on as long as there were Indians and white men ; that it was a great hardship for these poor men (the prisoners) to come from Shawano, to Milwaukie, on such business, &c., &c. The cases were not tried at that time, but one of them was tried in April thereafter. At this trial every essential fact was proved on the part of the prosecution. The district attorney was sure of his case, but when the court charged the jury they were told that the prosecution had not proved that the defendant knew these persons were Indians when he, the defendant, sold them the liquor. The jury were befogged, and the criminal went home to dabble again in the whiskey traffic, being satisfied that no man could prove before Judge Miller that he could even tell an Indian from a white man. I am satisfied that a few convictions in a United States court would essentially stop the traffic in this State.

5. "From my best information and belief," I think that from 25 to 30 per cent. of the adult females, under fifty years of age, in the Oneida tribe are unchaste. The per cent. of prostitutes in the other tribes of this agency is much less. This is the result of location of the respective reservations. The diseases consequent upon prostitution are not so prevalent as might be expected. I have known but few cases of syphilis. The persons contracting this disease have but few children, and these are generally short-lived.

6. A large proportion of the Indian children die quite young. This is in consequence of great exposures and want of proper care in sickness. I apprehend that in proportion as the habits of civilization are adopted by the Indian tribes the per cent. of their mortality will decrease.

7. I do not believe it to be the best policy to remove Indians *merely* because white settlements surround them.

8. I think Indian lands should be held in severalty.

9. I would not confer the power of alienation of real estate upon Indians.

10. I should say that three fourths of the Oneida, Stockbridge, and Munsee tribes give their attention to agriculture. Many of them are good farmers. The women generally work in the fields. The Stockbridge women, however, are an exception to this rule. These tribes pay but little attention to stock-raising; I mean by this that but little effort is made to improve their breeds of animals. I do not think that half-bloods have more enterprise than full-bloods.

11. The effect of schools among the tribes of this agency is good. The children taught by females make the best progress. I have a favorable opinion of manual-labor schools.

12. "Christian missions" have had a varied effect in this agency. I have no doubt that the Protestant Episcopal and Methodist Episcopal missions have had a favorable influence in the Oneida tribe, but I am confident that the Roman Catholic priests who have served as missionaries among the Menomonees have had a bad influence in that tribe. The only real missionary that this tribe have had is Mrs. Rosalia Dousman, a Catholic and a good Christian woman. She has been a teacher in this tribe for more than thirty years. By her precept, her example, and constant effort to instruct and elevate these Indians, she has raised them from mere savages to the position they now occupy.

I think superintendents and agents should be instructed to remove from the Indian country all persons interfering with official instructions or with employés.

13. I do not feel competent to make any recommendation in regard to the country called the Indian territory; I have thought, however, that the condition of the civilized tribes of this agency would be much improved if new homes could be found for them in this Indian territory. I believe our civilized tribes ought to live under a territorial government; they ought to have laws for the protection of property and punishment of crime. I would give all civilized Indians in the Indian territory the right to vote in the election of all territorial officers not appointed by the executive authority. Electors should also be eligible to office. By creating offices for Indians to fill in exclusively Indian territory, we should do very much towards weaning them from old habits, customs, and systems.

14. I would discontinue money annuities to Indians as far as consistent with treaty obligations. They would be better served if their annuities were paid in the actual necessaries of life.

15. In this agency every dollar of the annuities is paid directly to the Indians.

16. I think three-fourths of the annuities go to the traders at the time of payment. The Indian takes his money and goes to the trader and settles his account. The licensed traders in this agency are not permitted to charge an Indian any more for goods than citizens have to pay for the same article.

17. I do not think that more than a tenth of the annuities is squandered for intoxicating drinks and gambling. Their sugars and furs buy more whiskey than their annuities.

18. I have given my views at length in regard to suppressing the liquor traffic. If possible I would have some indellible mark on goods and clothing furnished Indians, and make such goods contraband in the hands of all persons except Indians.

19. There is no "order system" adopted by the licensed traders of this agency.

20. I know of no reason why the Bureau of Indian Affairs may not be administered in a satisfactory manner under the department of the Interior. If the western or southwestern tribes are to continue in a hostile attitude, it is quite possible that the War Department would manage the affairs of the bureau better, for the time being, than the Interior Department.

21. I think it would be quite as well to have reserves set apart by regulation of the department. The Indians would be apt to get better farming lands.

22. A very small proportion of the children in this agency are orphans. The relations

of orphan children generally appear very much attached to them. It would undoubtedly be better for the children to be placed in the families of Christian white men than to remain with their own people. There might be some difficulty in obtaining the consent of the relations of orphan children to this change, but the change would certainly be better for the children.

23. I do not know as I can offer any suggestions in the way of improvement in the present system of Indian affairs, except such as I have alluded to above. I think it would be a great improvement to gather the civilized tribes in one territory with an organized territorial government, under which the experiment of self-government among themselves might safely be tried. The adoption of such a course would be good economy for the federal government. A much less number of officials would be required in the service, and I apprehend that the frauds upon the Indians and upon the government would be largely diminished.

I have the honor to be your obedient servant,

M. M. DAVIS,
U. S. Indian Agent.

Hon. J. R. Doolittle,
Chairman, &c., Racine, Wisconsin.

Reply of General Hoffman.

Washington, D. C., *June* 27, 1865.

Sir: I have the honor to acknowledge the receipt of your letter of the 10th of May, 1865, submitting certain questions in reference to the administration of Indian affairs, and respectfully beg leave to offer the following replies, viz:

1st. I have been in the army since 1829, during most of which time I have served in the Indian country at Fort Leavenworth, Fort Laramie, Fort Smith, on the Arkansas river, in Florida, and in California. At Fort Leavenworth I met some of the civilized Indians of that frontier, Wyandotts, Kickapoos, Delawares, Shawnees; and at Fort Smith the Choctaws, Creeks, Chickasaws, and other tribes. On the plains I met the Pawnees, Sioux, Cheyennes, Arrapahoes, Kansas, (or Kaws,) Osages, Kiowas, Comanches, Apaches, and Eutes; and in California the Root-diggers, Pi-Eutes, Mohaves, Yumas, and other tribes.

2d. Generally they are decreasing in numbers; the civilized from drunkenness and vices and diseases introduced among them by white men; the wild Indians from wars among themselves and with the whites, and from scarcity of food and exposure.

3d. Pulmonary and venereal diseases are most common among them, but they suffer frequently with small-pox carried among them by white people.

4th. Intoxication prevails among them everywhere whenever they can get the liquor. They know the evil attending its use, and generally desire that it may not be brought among them; but if it is within their reach, they cannot resist the temptation to indulge in its use, and they seldom finish a debauch without its being attended by fatal consequences to some of them. Much legislation has been had to provide a mode of putting a stop to this evil, and while there was an Indian territory with a boundary beyond which white people could not pass without a permit, it was possible to very much limit the trade in whiskey; but even then the laws were evaded by the fur companies, and much alcohol was introduced into the Indian country and sold to employés and Indians at enormous prices. At this time, when there are roads running in various directions through the Indian country, it would be almost impossible to put a stop to this infernal traffic in any other way than by putting great powers, without appeal, in the hands of military commanders near the Indians, and even then there would be no positive assurance that the laws would be faithfully executed. At the present time, I presume it would be impossible under any circumstances to convict and punish a white man for selling liquor to an Indian, and nothing better can be expected, so long as the matter is dependent on a trial before a justice or a jury. Along the frontier, particularly the Pacific coast, it is a very common impression that the Indians should be exterminated, and the impression has been acted on more than once, and until a new system is adopted the efforts of the government to protect the Indians must result in little better than a total sacrifice of the whole investment so far as the Indians are concerned.

5th. Among the semi-civilized Indians on the borders of the western States, from Lake Superior to Texas, prostitution is a common thing, with a prevalence of the diseases consequent upon it, which must necessarily diminish their numbers and enfeeble their offspring, but I am unable to say to what extent. Among the Indians on the plains a certain latitude is given to married women with the approbation of the husband; but beyond this, any violation of the marriage tie or illicit intercourse of unmarried women is severely punished, and it is rarely indulged in; and while they are protected from contact with whites the natural increase of their numbers is not retarded, but the presence of white people among them shows itself by the vices they introduce and the sure consequence follows. In California and Oregon the most virulent diseases have been everywhere spread among the Indians, and those who are not otherwise destroyed are fast being carried off by this terrible scourge.

6th. I am unable to state any other specific cause of decay, unless it is the natural improvidence, recklessness, and idleness of Indians, which leads them to make any sacrifice of health or property to gratify their immediate desires.

7th. The further Indians are removed from white settlements the better for them; and since there are large tracts of country between the Missouri river and the settlements of California, unfit for occupation by a white population but suitable to Indians, I would recommend that the wild Indians be collected on reservations assigned to them in this region. The semi-civilized Indians on the borders of Missouri and Arkansas understand the value of their country too well to be willing to exchange it for the desert prairies which lie west of them, and the government will scarcely be able to do more for them than protect them as far as possible from being cheated out of their property by the unprincipled white people who live about and among them.

8th. Their lands should be held in common.

9th. Answer to question 8.

10th. Of the civilized Indians, a large part of them, including the females, give attention to agriculture and stock-raising—both half-breed and full-blood. Among the wild Indians little attention is given to either, and only by the females.

11th. The effect of schools held among the Indians has been very good, but where young men have been educated at schools in the States—as at Johnson's school in Kentucky years ago—the effect has been pernicious. They carried with them to these people all the vices they had learned among the white people, and little that was good. In my opinion, manual-labor schools would be productive of the best results.

12th. I am unable to say what has been the effect of Christian missions among the Indians; but they should produce much good, and I would recommend that worthy ministers of good practical sense be encouraged to labor among them.

13th. I would recommend that the country called the Indian territory, after the pacification, be held by the tribes under former treaty stipulations, with only such modifications as may be absolutely necessary; that it be organized into a territorial government for the tribes occupying it, under a military governor, and an executive council to be elected from each tribe in proportion to its population by the votes of the members of the tribe, suffrage being given only to males over 21 years of age. A councilman should be able to write his name, and should be born a member of the tribe. The Cherokees and Choctaws, and possibly other tribes, would perhaps best be under a military governor by themselves.

14th. Money annuities to Indians should be discontinued as far as possible, and, instead, expenditures for their common good, under the direction of the War Department, by an officer of the regular army, should be made.

15th. I am unable to say what proportion of annuities actually reaches the hands of the Indians, but I have no doubt that they have little or no benefit from it.

16th. A large part of it is owed to traders for supplies sold at exorbitant prices.

17th. Except in rare cases, all that is not consumed in paying debts to traders.

18th. Appoint an officer to be the guardian of the tribe and reside with them, permit no debts to be contracted without his authority, and authorize him to distribute money and clothing at his discretion. He to be held accountable to the War Department for the honest and faithful performance of his duties.

19th. If the "order system" means the privilege of Indians to make purchases of licensed traders on orders upon the agent in anticipation of annuities, I consider it as open to great abuses, which are no doubt taken advantage of, and it should not be tolerated. Instead of licensed traders, I would recommend that government stores be established with each tribe, where, under the direction of the officer in charge, Indians could be permitted to purchase on credit.

20th. In my opinion, the Bureau of Indian Affairs should be placed under the control of the War Department. I have seen much abuse in the management of Indian affairs by Indian agents, who are under little or no tangible responsibility. The responsibility of an officer of the army is direct and immediate, having other eyes upon him than the simple Indians, and the chances of honesty and integrity to the government and to the Indians is almost insured. A storekeeper and treasurer might be appointed from civil life, to be under the control of, and responsible to the officer in charge. An Indian agent has no influence with Indians beyond what he obtains by having in his hands the distribution of annuities or presents, and if they behave well it is in the hope of reward—not through the fear of punishment. If the authority over them is in the hands of an officer of the army, his authority is enforced by the troops he commands, and their presence exercises a much greater influence over them than promise of reward or any threat of punishment at a future day.

21st. Reserves should be set apart by regulations of the department; the Indians should be placed upon it and told what the government will do for them—a promise which should never be broken—and what they must do. Treaties are of little value, except to purchase their lands; an Indian observes a treaty only when his interest or his fears compel him to do so. All reserves should be under military rule, to keep the Indians in order, and to protect them against the vicious whites who will force themselves among them.

22d. I am unable to answer, but I doubt if it would be possible to induce Indian women, who have orphan children in charge, to consent to their being taken away from them.

23d. I have nothing further to suggest in regard to the administration of Indian affairs. The details and the execution must be put in the hands of competent men of incorruptible integrity.

I have the honor to be, very respectfully, your obedient servant,

W. HOFFMAN,
Brevet Brigadier General U. S. A.

Hon. J. R. DOOLITTLE,
Chairman Joint Committee of Congress, Racine, Wisconsin.

Reply of General Sully.

HEADQUARTERS NORTHWEST INDIAN EXPEDITION,
Sioux City, Iowa, June 10, 1865.

SIR: Your communication of May 10 I received a few days ago, and in replying to it I will answer your questions as they are numbered in the letter.

1. Since I entered the army in 1841, with the exception of the time during the Mexican war and the first two years of the rebellion, when I was south, I have, I may say, been constantly stationed in the Indian country. I have been with the Seminoles of Florida, with the various tribes of Indians in southern California, Oregon, and in the eastern part of California, with all the bands of the Minnesota Sioux, with the Winnebagoes, Chippewas, with all the bands of the western or Teton Sioux, with the Omahas, Poncas, Pawnees, Cheyennes, Rees, Mandan, Gros Ventres, and Crows.

2. The tribes that come in close contact with the whites and civilization are fast decreasing. Change in their mode of life, and in the fact of their learning all the vices and few of the virtues of the whites, is, in my opinion, the cause of their decrease.

3. Venereal diseases among those who have been living near settlements, also whiskey, are the diseases most common. Small-pox is often introduced among different tribes by accident, and is very fatal.

4. Intoxication prevails to some extent among tribes that live near settlements, but as a general rule, with the exception of very old men and old squaws, I do not think the Indians can be considered addicted to intoxication. Among some of the wild tribes, I have known them utterly refuse to have anything to do with whiskey. This I am told by traders who have tried to sell it to them. But the Indian, like the white man, if he lives where whiskey is plentiful, will acquire a taste for it, and when he does he becomes as debased as the lowest white drunkard. It is already against the law to introduce whiskey into the Indian country, but it is evaded. Large quantities are brought from the British line, by English half-breeds, to trade, and this it is impossible for us to prevent, without our troops can get permission to cross the frontier. I think we have laws enough on the subject, if they were only enforced; perhaps it would be well to add a law making it an offence for any one who sells or even gives a drop of ardent spirits to an Indian in any of the territories of the United States.

5. There is a very wide and remarkable difference in different tribes in regard to prostitution. While some tribes are disgustingly loose in their habits, there are other tribes living in the same country who are remarkable for their virtue. The Ree Indians, for example, carry this vice to a very great extent, and decrease in a fearful state, in fact destroying the nation. On the contrary, the females of most of the *wild* bands of Sioux, called the Teton Sioux, set an example of virtue worthy of being copied by any white civilized nation. I believe the contact with depraved specimens of the white population, a taste for luxuries, only to be procured by money, are the principal causes of the females falling into this vice; where they do fall, they soon become very much depraved, and disease naturally follows.

6. I know of no other facts that are the cause of their decay. A total change in the system now adopted towards the Indians will in the end effect a remedy. I have given

much of my attention to this subject, and feel sure that with a proper system in our Indian affairs, the Indians who are now a curse and a nuisance to the country can be made a peaceful part of our community, if not a beneficial part. I can state this more fully in answer to your questions that follow.

7. As regards the system of making reservations, and pushing the Indians from the east, from the west, from the north, and from the south, and concentrating them into one section of the country, it has, in my opinion, been a very bad policy. It should cease, and should have ceased years ago. At a great expense the government have taken away trouble from one section of country, to concentrate it on the borders of another. I do not altogether disapprove of the system of Indian reservations, but I do of the constant changes of reservations. The Indians once on their reservation, should be protected there by our laws, and in every respect made amenable to our laws; when they transgress them they should be punished, and if the civil authorities are not able to enforce the laws, then the military should be called on. I believe in separating bands of Indians as widely apart as possible, thus destroying their individuality, their nationality. So far from concentrating them and treating them as we do a foreign nation, it would be better when people wished the land the Indians occupy, instead of pushing them into the wilderness, to even purchase a tract of land in some of our densely populated eastern States, and place them there; for there, in a few years, they would be forced to adopt the habits of civilized life, or they would soon become extinct. I will take as an example of this case the Minnesota Sioux. Not many years ago the different bands of this nation were settled on the Mississippi, Wabasha's band at the town of Wabasha, Red Wing's band at Red Wing, &c. When it became necessary to settle that country, instead of sending them on a reservation up the St. Peter's or Minnesota river, it would have been better to say to them, "We must have your lands; each family will seek his locality or farm." Settlers would then be allowed to settle around each separate band; of course, in consideration of the land taken from them, the government would assist them with cattle, agricultural implements, and establish schools for the instruction of their children, letting them know they were protected in all their rights the same as white men, and in regard to the reservations now in existence I would adopt the same rule.

There are only two rules to follow: one is to drive them off further, starve them and drive them to desperation, till we have to adopt some mode of ridding ourselves of an encumbrance, or to reclaim them from their savage life, and by kindness and education make them peaceable if you cannot make them useful members of our community; but above all things, don't send Indian agents and traders among them to rob them of what the government appropriates for their improvement.

8. It is best the lands should be held in severalty, as I have already stated.

9. I would not propose to confer the power of alienation of real estate upon Indians, for this generation, at least, but their children who might fall heir, after they have been civilized and educated, should have full right, when they arrived at the proper age, to do what they pleased with their property.

10. There is a very great difference in regard to the amount of agriculture the different tribes of Indians attend to. Among those nomadic tribes who live in a country abounding with game, in wild fruits and roots that can be eaten, it is hard to bring them down to cultivate the soil. Their instinct teaches them to wander out on the prairie to hunt, and the sections of country they inhabit are ill-fitted for agricultural purposes.

In the children of such tribes I would inculcate a taste to raise stock, as the Jesuit priests did in California at their missions. All who have lived in California before it was settled can testify to their success, and the immense herds belonging to these Indian missions. With other tribes, such as the Rees, Mandans, Gros Ventres, and several tribes in Arizona, (whose names I cannot recollect,) cultivation of the soil is carried on with great success. I would mention as an example the Pimas Indians on the Gila river. Most of the work, however, is done always by the squaws. The *he* Indian is too proud to work. His duties are war and the chase. As regards half-breeds, I regard them a very bad mixture As a general thing they retain too many of the bad qualities of the Indians, and too few of the good qualities of the whites.

11. Schools and education have not been attended to as much as they should be. Congress appropriates money for this purpose, but little of it generally is expended in schools. I recommend that the children of the Indians, male and female, be *made* to go to school, that the boys be taught to work at different trades and farming, the girls to sew, wash, and cook, and above all teach them habits of cleanliness. Do this, and you do all required to reclaim the savage and make him a useful being.

12. Christian missions as a general thing have not been a success. Persons should be sent as missionaries with good *practical common sense*. I think that comparatively little good can be done the present generation by education or religion; but by the establishment of missionary schools, the missionary establishments protected by troops, in order to protect

those who join the establishment against the attacks of their hostile brethren, an immense amount of good might be done.

13. In regard to the country called Indian territory, as I said before, the Indians should hold their lands, but they should as far as possible be separated, to destroy the feelings they have of their being a separate nation, of which they are very proud. By degrees, as they become educated and civilized, they will consider themselves citizens of the United States and be proud of that.

14. Money annuities should be entirely discontinued. It is the principal source of all the trouble at our Indian agencies.

15. It is my opinion that very little of it reaches the hands of the Indians.

16. As a general thing the greater part of the annuities is already pledged to the traders at the agency for goods furnished before it is paid, and the Indians rarely see any of the money.

17. I don't think much of the Indian annuities are squandered for intoxicating drink and gambling, for the simple reason that the trader (for there is only one allowed) pockets most of the money.

18. Don't make any money payments to the Indians; issue them clothing and supplies when they are in need of them, but let this be done in the way I shall hereafter mention.

19. The operation of the order system is bad. Very frequently I have seen during an annual Indian payment, nearly all the Indians of the nation collected together from a distance, waiting weeks and months for their goods to arrive, and every day being told that their supplies would reach soon. They would wait more patiently than any body of white men would, till all of their small stock of provisions would become exhausted, and their families almost starving. Then the agent would give the Indians orders on the trader at the place, by which the trader pockets all the money due the Indians—half starved, not knowing what he pays, or the value of what he buys. As a general rule but one trader is allowed at an agency; his prices he and the agent regulate. At last the goods are near at hand, and the payment must take place; the agent then persuades a number of Indians to go on a hunt, and while this number is away the goods are distributed to those who remain.

20. The Indian department unquestionably should be under the War Department. It is to the troops the friendly Indian looks for protection against hostile bands, and from the troops the agent or trader calls for protection, when his Indians, exasperated at repeated impositions, threaten to take his life. The Secretary of the Interior may believe one policy the best to adopt towards certain bands, and the Secretary of War may think it necessary to act quite differently. Thus different orders are issued to the agents and to the troops. Frequently Indians become so troublesome it is necessary to turn them over to the hands of the military entirely, and in the midst of the war, before peace and quiet is established, the agent or some other official is empowered to make a treaty and pay the Indians large sums to behave themselves, thus greatly interfering with military success. It is a common saying among Indians, that when they are in want of more annuities, all they have to do is to kill a few white men and steal a few horses.

21. In setting apart reservations it should be done by the department, acting justly towards the Indians. It could be done by treaty, but it amounts to the same thing, for the Indians can neither read nor write nor understand our language, and are at our mercy. The services of an interpreter have to be used to make a treaty, frequently some unprincipled half-breed, whom speculators can bribe to interpret just as they like. What is to prevent these Indians from signing a treaty, the purport of which they know nothing whatever about? Many of our Indian treaties are made in this way, and then we say the Indian refuses to live up to his treaty.

22. I approve very much of the placing of orphan children in the families of Christians for education and civilization.

23. In conclusion, I would state, in order to better the condition of the Indian and protect him from fraud, I would have the Indian agencies stationed at military posts, the commanding officer being the superintendent; at each post there should be an agent, also there should be established missionary schools. The annuity goods should be purchased by some one directed for that purpose, and the goods sent to the post. On its arrival the commanding officer should order a council of three senior officers of the army to examine the goods, compare them with the invoices and with the price current of the city where these goods were purchased, and then to hand in their report, under oath that the amount expended for the goods is correct, to the commanding officer, to be forwarded by him. The goods should be distributed in the presence of officers and under the orders of the commanding officer. If this plan was adopted I doubt if you would find so many persons in the country seeking after the position of Indian agent, for then there would be no chance of their making a fortune on a salary of $1,500 a year.

To show what good can be done in the way of improving the Indian race and making them useful, I would call your attention to the various missions in New Mexico and California. If you travel over that country you will be surprised at the magnificent buildings you will occasionally meet with in the midst of a perfectly desert and deserted country. They are called missions of some saints or other. These buildings and all the improvements, flourishing fields, mills, herds of cattle, &c., are the work of a few priests and the wild Indians. Now, I am not a Catholic, nor do I wish to advocate any particular sect of religion, but this I must say, the priests are actuated by a desire to promote the interests of their church. You may call this fanaticism if you will, but it is sincere, and there is no selfish, personal feeling in it. The wild savage soon sees this and appreciates it. Then, again, in their forms of religious ceremonies there is a mystery, a solemnity, that strikes the ignorant Indian with awe, or as they term it "big medicine." We all know that the Catholic religion has the most strength in a community where the people are most ignorant. Pure religion, of course, comes from the heart, but it is the forms and ceremonies of the Catholic church, like dress parades and grand reviews in armies, that effect the discipline of the church as in the army. On this account I think that the missions I recommended above should be placed in the hands of the Catholic clergy in preference to any other sect. Another thing I would recommend at these military and religious stations in the Indian country, and that is the organizing by degrees of a military force of Indians. I would begin with a few at first; I would issue to them arms, rations, and clothing fitted to their tastes and habits. I would use this force as a police force in the village and as pickets and scouts. By degrees I would increase this force and enforce discipline more strictly; and if hostile Indians attack the Indians, I would make *Indian war* on them by offering a reward for the scalps of any warlike Indian. I would send parties and capture their women and children, make the women work at the mission and educate the children by force. This may appear unchristianlike, but with the savages a woman is treated as bad as any negro laborer formerly was in our country, and it would be a mercy to her to be under the control of a Christian mission. After the war was over I would allow the husbands and fathers to visit their squaws and children, and if, after they had been a year in charge of the mission as prisoners, they wished to rejoin their husbands, or the husbands to come and live at the mission, I would let them do so. By locating these missions in portions of the country under the protection of troops, in a few years they would be flourishing settlements, strong enough to protect themselves. And as soon as they became sufficiently strong and civilized I would withdraw the troops and let them have all the benefits of the laws of the country like any white man. They certainly have an equal right to the land we occupy; and as soon as they are fitted for it, they have the right to be citizens of the United States.

With much respect, your obedient servant,

ALF. SULLY,
Brevet Major General.

Hon. J. R. DOOLITTLE,
Chairman Congressional Committee.

Reply of Inspector General R. B. Marcy.

ST. LOUIS, MO., *August* 8, 1865.

SIR: General Pope has just handed me your circular of May 10, 1865, with a request that I would give my views regarding the interrogatories therein contained.

It affords me great pleasure to comply with the general's request, as I believe that important modifications can be made in our Indian policy, which will produce results highly beneficial to the interests of both the United States and the Indians.

I have served as a commissioned officer in the United States army thirty-three years, the greater part of the time upon the western frontier among the following tribes of Indians, viz:

Chippeways, Menomonees, Winnebagoes, Choctaws, Chickasaws, Cherokees, Creeks, Seminoles, Delawares, Shawnees, Sioux, Comanches, Kiowas, Pawnees, Witchetaws, and Apaches.

It is a well-established fact that the wild tribes of the plains and the partially civilized tribes near the settlements have been rapidly diminishing in numbers for many years—the former from the effects of exposure and fatigue upon long expeditions in pursuit of game and in war, and from the effects of hunger, which causes have produced great mortality, especially among the very old, young, and infirm.

The Indian as soon as he comes in contact with the white man at once imbibes all his vices and very few of his virtues. The men become addicted to drunkenness and the women to prostitution, and these vices are propagated and fostered by the influence and example of unscrupulous white traders and others who come most directly in contact with them.

Many die from the effects of colds, rheumatism, and other kindred diseases, brought on by intemperance and exposure, and large numbers die from venereal diseases, which spread rapidly among them, and for which they have no effectual remedies.

While encamped with the southern Comanches in 1854, a great many of them who were suffering from the most virulent form of this terrible disease crowded around my surgeon and entreated him to give them medicine which would afford relief. There is no doubt that the disease must exercise a powerful influence in enfeebling and degenerating the race.

To obviate these evils is a question somewhat difficult of solution, but the remedy which occurs to me as the most efficacious and permanent is to place them upon reservations, furnish them with farmers, school teachers, and physicians, and instruct them in the arts of civilization, and until they become accustomed to their new sphere of existence and abandon their predatory habits, it would be necessary to establish military posts near them to guard them against the demoralizing influences of unprincipled white men, and at the same time to confine them to the limits of their reservations.

The prairie Indians and their ancestors from time immemorial have been hunters, and lived upon the products of the chase. They have never planted a seed nor raised a crop, and are perfectly ignorant of the first rudiments of agriculture. The buffalo and other wild animals of the plains are rapidly disappearing, and it will only be a very few years before game will no longer furnish these people a subsistence. They must then either be subsisted by the government, taught to provide their own subsistence by agriculture, or starve.

As a measure of economy and enlightened humanity, I think the plan I have recommended is the wisest. In carrying this into operation, I think it probable that the adult males, who have a great antipathy to manual labor, will not willingly adopt such novel habits of life, but the women and children will work, and I believe they may gradually become civilized.

The experiment has been tested with the Choctaws, Chickasaws, Cherokees, Creeks, Delawares, and other Indians, and has been successful. Those Indians, as a general rule, are better farmers and live more comfortably than the poor white people of the southwestern States. They till the soil successfully and raise large numbers of cattle, hogs, &c., but during the past four years the Cherokees and Creeks have been robbed of large numbers of their cattle by people from Kansas. Indeed, so flagrant had been these outrages, that during the last summer I found the entire country along Grand river for one hundred and fifty miles totally depopulated, when at the commencement of the rebellion it was well settled with Cherokee farmers. They were obliged to abandon their farms to save what few cattle remained to them.

The Choctaws, Chickasaws, Creeks, and Cherokees have schools and churches among them; their children are being educated, and many of the adults are able to read and write. This has all been brought about by the labors of Christian missionaries, who have exercised a very beneficial influence over them; indeed, it may safely be said that their civilization is altogether due to the efforts of those worthy people.

In answer to question No. 13, I would locate the Indians upon reservations adapted to the culture of grain, and not upon barren wastes such as were assigned to the Winnebagoes on the Upper Missouri river, where the government was obliged to issue rations to them from day to day. I would not convey any lands to them by treaty stipulations, but regard the Indians as tenants, who could be removed at the pleasure of the government; this would enable the United States, without any breach of faith, to remove them to other localities whenever the lands they occupied were required for more important purposes.

The advantages of this policy over that now existing will be seen from the following remarks:

In 1831 the United States entered into a treaty with the Choctaws, whereby the government ceded to them that large tract of country lying between the Canadian and Red rivers, and extending from the western boundary of Arkansas to the 100th meridian of west longitude, embracing four times as much land as they and their neighbors—the Chickasaws—have ever been able to occupy or use, so that three-fourths of this beautiful farming country now lies unoccupied.

As I was very familiar with this particular section, having been stationed here for several years, and traversed it in several different directions, I in 1863 addressed a letter to the honorable Secretary of War, in which I took the liberty to suggest that, as the Choctaws and Chickasaws had taken up arms against the United States, and had been fighting in the rebel ranks ever since the war began, whether it would not be a proper punishment for their treason to take from them all that portion of their reservation which they do not occupy, and convert it into a new territory, which would be far preferable for agricultural purposes to any of the other Territories.

In that communication I entered into an estimate of the amount of land embraced within the reservation, and enclosed a map showing the limits of the settled portion.

I am of opinion, from all I have learned of men who have had good opportunities of judging, and from my own observations, that a great portion of the money which has been sent out for payment to the northwestern Indians during the past ten years has never reached them. I would, therefore, discontinue all money annuities, as they only serve to fill the pockets of agents and traders, and furnish whiskey to the Indians; but if these annuities are to be continued, I would restore the functions of disbursing agents to the commanding officers of military posts, and require the payments to be made in presence of the subordinate commissioned officers. This will insure a perfectly just and equitable distribution of the money among the Indians.

I would not allow a trader to go among them, but place such articles as are necessary and useful in the hands of commanding officers of military posts, to be distributed from time to time as the Indians need them.

If any one objects to the system I have recommended, I would ask him if he has ever heard of a single instance where the Indians were ever defrauded of a dollar of their annuities during the time they were disbursed through military channels. I would also ask him if he has not heard of many instances where poor men were appointed Indian agents, and who, after four years' service upon a salary of $1,800 a year, retired to private life with large fortunes. If he answers the last question in the negative, I am forced to acknowledge that I have heard of many instances.

I am, very respectfully, your obedient servant,

R. B. MARCY,
Inspector General U. S. A.

Hon. J. R. DOOLITTLE,
United States Senator, Racine, Wisconsin.

Reply of M. Gookins, United States Indian agent.

WICHITA INDIAN AGENCY,
Butler County, Kansas, August 20, 1865.

SIR: In reply to your inquiries of May 10, last, I will say, in answer to the 1st question: I entered the public service in August, 1863, in the capacity of a special Indian agent, and remained one year—spending my time with the Cherokee, Creek, Seminole, and Euchee Indians, in the vicinity of Fort Gibson, C. N. Since August, 1864, I have acted as agent of the affiliated tribes of Indians of the Wichita agency, comprising the Wichitas, Caddoes, a portion of the Shawnees, Wacos, and several other small tribes, who are refugees from their former homes. And I will here remark that whatever statement I may make, or opinions express, may be understood as applying to the tribes above mentioned, unless some particular tribe is specially mentioned.

2. Are they increasing in numbers or decreasing, and from what causes?

Answer. They are rapidly decreasing, and have been more especially since the commencement of the late war; the causes are many and various. Many might answer the question by saying it is the fatal destiny to which the race is doomed; that they must become extinct to give place to a higher civilization. When we so often hear the expression, "We never shall have peace until the whole race is exterminated"—knowing this feeling of antagonism is so prevalent in the west, entertained by the race having the power—it is not difficult to understand one of the causes of their decrease; when in eight cases in every ten, the interruptions of peace is first caused by the aggressions of white men on the rights of the Indians. To elucidate the historical fact, that they are decreasing, and to give an opinion as to the primary and secondary causes, would require more space than can well be given to this paper.

3. What diseases are most common and most fatal among them, &c.?

Answer. My experience has mostly been confined to those who have been made refugees by the exigencies of the war, and diseases among them have been many and fatal; exposure to hunger, cold, want of clothing, and destitution generally, has promoted and engendered many diseases among them; the most fatal, however, is the small-pox; they adhere tenaciously to their superstitious modes of treating it, and reject all others—hence its fatal results.

4 To what extent does intoxication prevail, &c.?

Answer. The North American Indians have always manifested as strong an inherent liking for intoxicating drinks as any race we know of, and the extent of intoxication is just as great as it is possible for them to obtain the means of gratifying their appetites. Unprincipled men will, and do smuggle liquors into the Indian country; and unfortunately there are too many whose duty it is to suppress it, who, either from love of gain or a love of whiskey, encourage it. One violation of the law often creates widespread difficulties. The intercourse laws, if rigidly enforced, are sufficient; and I cannot suggest any better "practical regulation" than to place men of integrity in responsible positions, and promptly displace every one who fails in the discharge of his known duty, or wilfully violates the law.

5. In answer to your 5th question, I will say that, in most of the tribes with which I have had intercourse, there is a great laxity in morals, and on the particular point embraced in your inquiry it is carried to extremes. The evil has greatly increased during the war. The Indians, as refugees from their homes, have been massed together, permitting promiscuous intercourse; their contact with licentious white men stimulates their animal passions to a great extent, while with some of the tribes their females are made merchandise of by their husbands and acquaintances; forced to it, they sometimes say, by actual suffering for life sustenance. It is easy then to imagine, under such circumstances, the degree and increase of this evil. To what extent it "diminishes their numbers and enfeebles their offspring," I cannot speak understandingly, but the effects are doubtless very deleterious.

6. State any other facts bearing upon the causes of their decay, and what, if any, is the best practicable remedy?

Answer. The answer to this has in part been anticipated in replying to the second. The history of the race for 150 years shows their constant decrease. The immediate causes which come under our own observation are their wars among themselves; their hostilities with the whites, in the aggregate of which they are great losers; their licentious and intemperate habits, which increase rather than diminish, as they come in contact with what we are pleased to call civilization; the fatal diseases which prevail among them, which they know not how to treat. While from causes named, and for want of sufficient food, clothing, and shelter, and great exposure, their natural increase falls far short of their losses. More than this, the deep-settled hostility of the stronger against the weaker race, in all localities where there are Indians, is of itself a sufficient cause of their rapid decrease. I have just witnessed a case in point: two days were spent in trying to impanel a jury, in Chase county, Kansas, who would accord the same rights of legal protection to an Indian that they would to a white man. I have no doubt but the proof would have shown a case of wilful and deliberate murder of an Indian by a soldier; yet when men were examined touching their qualifications as jurors they would say to the court they would not find a man guilty in such a case, and under the same state of facts, when they would if the victim had been a white man; and some of them said they only blamed the soldier for not killing more of them. No jury could be had; the case was dismissed, and the murderer discharged. You ask the general question, "what, if any, is the best practicable remedy?" There is none.

In answer to the 7th I would say that, if it were practicable "to remove them to new reserves, remote from settlements, where they would not be encroached upon," it would be the best policy; but experience and the progressive character of our people teach us that it is not. In every view of the case which I have been able to take, the conclusions are all against the Indians. I believe that nothing better can be done than to try to protect them in their present homes.

8. Is it best that their lands should be held in common or in severalty?

Answer. My experience would say in severalty.

9. Alienation, &c.?

Answer. To confer the power of alienation upon the full-blood Indians would be equivalent in eight cases out of ten to divesting them of their lands; with the mixed race it would be different; many of them would retain their property, and might safely be trusted with the power.

10. Agriculture, &c.?

Answer. My experience on this head is quite limited. In passing through the Cherokee, Creek, and Seminole countries, however, I see evidences of thrift and prosperity, which existed before the rebellion, to a greater extent than I expected to find; better houses and other improvements; and I think would be likely to again after pacification. The Caddoes and Shawnees of my agency give considerable attention to farming; the other tribes but little. The first named tribes had large herds of cattle. Among the full-bloods the females perform nearly all the labor. The mixed-bloods assimilate towards the habits of the whites, about in regular gradation of degree of blood.

11 and 12. I have no experience derived from personal observation in the operations of schools and missions, they having all been suspended since the war. Although some encouraging progress has been made in schools, it is generally conceded that the expectations of their managers have not been fully realized: progress is very slow; and there seems to

be very little adaptation among them of transmitting their acquirements one to another. Manual-labor schools, I suppose, prosper somewhat, as does farming, according to blood-mixture. A disinclination to work among the full-bloods is seen in schools as elsewhere. The schools have not generally answered the expectations of their foster parents. Christian missions have effected, in the aggregate, much good, and should be encouraged.

13. The several points embraced in the 13th question I have reflected much upon, but I have not really an opinion satisfactory to myself. The Cherokee, Creek, Choctaw, and Chickasaw nations, as they are called, embrace a section of as good, perhaps the best, country lying west of the Mississippi river. This progressive age seems to require that their resources should be developed and improved, either by purchasing them, throwing them open to the white population, or encouraging the present owners by advancing them in the manner your question implies. The manner of doing this is a question for legislation, and one, as I have said, I have not formed a very definite opinion upon.

14. Ought money annuities to Indians to be discontinued, as far as consistent with treaty obligations?

Answer. Yes.

15. What proportion actually reaches their hands?

Answer. Probably one-fourth.

16. What proportion is received by traders for goods and supplies already advanced?

Answer. One-half, I think.

17. What proportion is squandered in intoxicating drinks, or in gambling?

Answer. The "proportion" is just all they have, when the means to gratify their propensities are within their reach.

18. What can practically be done to secure the Indians against the two latter evils when payments in money, or supplies in goods and clothing, are made?

Answer. All that is required is for you to keep honest and faithful men in office; men who are willing to serve the government, for what they agreed to, by accepting their appointments. But if you find them making two or three thousand dollars a year over their salaries, you may know they are not men of integrity, however plausible may be their explanations.

19. The "order system" is sometimes abused, but if the orders are controlled by agents and men who look to the interest of the Indians and the saving of their means, I think the system a good one, and often a matter of much convenience.

20. I am not sufficiently acquainted with the difference, if there be a material one, in the practical operations of the two systems, and should think it of but little consequence under what department these things were managed at Washington. But as to the practical operations of carrying into effect the laws and regulations of Congress, I deem it of great importance that the details of the operations should be carried out by men whose time, interests, and attentions would be undivided, and made the first consideration.

21. "In setting apart reserves," I should deem it advisable to do so by treaty, as they would be better understood by the Indians, and less liable to change.

22. What proportion of children are orphans?

Answer. I cannot say what proportion, but there are a great many orphans among them. The headmen, however, very generally adopt them, and they seem, especially the full-bloods, very reluctant to part with them, they having no appreciation of the advantages that might result to their race; this, with their general distrust of the whites, would deter them from consenting to any such arrangement as your question proposes. I should have but little faith in its success if attempted.

To the last question, I don't know that I can add anything more than has already been expressed or implied in my answers to the preceding questions.

Although considerable time has elapsed since the receipt of your circular letter, absence from my agency, and pressing engagements when here, having had until very recently no assistant, I have not been able to give the subject as much attention as I could wish, and not having time to revise it, I must submit this my first and very imperfect draught.

I am, very respectfully, your obedient servant,

MILO GOOKINS, *United States Indian Agent.*

Hon. J. R. DOOLITTLE, *Chairman Congressional Committee.*

Reply of Governor Evans, Superintendent of Indian Affairs.

COLORADO SUPERINTENDENCY INDIAN AFFAIRS,
Denver, September 1, 1865.

SIR: In reply to your questions in regard to "the condition of the Indian tribes, and their treatment by the civil and military authorities," I have the honor to answer as follows:

Question 1. "During how long a period, and in what capacity, in the civil or military service, have you had experience in Indian affairs, or what other means of observation have you had, and with what tribe or tribes?"

Answer. I have been ex officio superintendent of Indian affairs in Colorado Territory for three years and four months, and have had no other means of personal observation of the administration of Indian affairs. My intercourse has been confined to the Arapahoes, Cheyennes, Kiowas, Comanche, Apache, and Ute tribes.

Your second, third, fourth, fifth, and sixth questions will be more satisfactorily answered by agents, my intercourse as superintendent not bringing me into such intimate acquaintance with them as the agents possess, and not enabling me to answer from personal observation.

Question 7. "Which, in your opinion, is the best policy, as white settlements advance and surround Indian reservations, to maintain the Indians upon them, and endeavor to resist encroachments, or to remove them to new reserves remote from settlements?"

Answer. My experience has been entirely with wild Indians, and it would seem to be the better policy with them to keep them remote from settlements, and to try to bring the influences of civilization to bear upon them, so as to teach them submission to authority, and to bring them under some sort of control before they are brought into contact with the settlements.

Question 8. "Is it best that their lands should be held in common or severalty?"

Answer. I should think in severalty, as they generally have their personal interests recognized even among the wildest tribes.

Question 9. "If held in severalty, is it safe to confer the power of alienation of real estate upon Indians? If so, upon what classes, and under what limitations?"

Answer. I should not think it safe to confer the power of alienation of real estate upon them, at least until they are thoroughly civilized and prepared for citizenship.

Questions 10th, 11th, 12th, 13th, 14th, 15th, 16th, 17th, 18th and 19th.

Answer. I have no experience from which to answer these questions.

Question 20. "Under what department of the government, the War Department or the Interior, should the Bureau of Indian Affairs be placed, to secure the best and most economical administration of it?"

Answer. My judgment can only be given from actual observation as to the wild or nomadic tribes. I have little doubt that they can be more successfully and economically managed by the War Department. The necessity of a force to keep them quiet is too palpable to be denied; and if the entire management is committed to the military, it would harmonize the influences and authority of their management, and prevent misunderstandings and conflicts which confuse the untutored Indian and create distress.

To control the wild Indian by giving him presents and by the presence of troops should be one object, and under one head or directing power.

Question 21. "In setting apart reserves, is it advisable to do so by treaty with the tribes, or to do so by law, or by the regulation of the department, enforcing the same by arms?"

Answer. I have little doubt it would have been better to have controlled the whole matter by law, instead of treaty, had the plan been inaugurated; whether it can be so changed now without more difficulty than benefit is doubtful.

Question. 22. "What proportion of the children are orphans, and to what extent would it be practicable for the Indian bureau to place orphan children in the families of Christian white men, to be trained and educated in the English language, and in the habits of civilized life?"

Answer. I have no information as to the number of orphans. My opinion is, that the distribution of the Indian children among white families might be secured by consent of their parents, to a large extent, if taken while young, as children are often a great burden to their parents among poor and suffering tribes. This, however, will necessarily be a work of time, and assurance to the Indians of good care of their children.

Question 23. "State any other matter or fact which, in your opinion, would improve the present system of Indian affairs, in principle or in administration, and prevent frauds upon the Indian and upon the government."

Answer. More promptness, system, and certainty in complying with treaty stipulations, and a selection of presents better calculated to minister to the wants instead of the fancy of the Indians is important. These should certainly be secured, so far as the tribes on the plains and in the Rocky mountains are concerned. Without a great change in these respects, it will be folly to talk of maintaining peace except by large military forces.

Perhaps the distribution through the War Department might meet some of these wants and check fraud.

I have the honor to be, very respectfully, your obedient servant,

JNO. EVANS,

Governor and ex officio Superintendent Indian Affairs.

Hon. J. R. Doolittle, *U. S. Senator, Racine, Wisconsin.*

Reply of Abram Bennett, Kickapoo land agent.

TROY, DONIPHAN COUNTY, KANSAS,
August 15, 1865.

SIR: In answer to your request to give in writing my opinion and answers to certain questions propounded in a printed circular in regard to the Indian treatment and department, I shall answer in detail.

1. I have served near one year as agent of the Kickapoo tribe of Indians, during which time I closely observed the Indian character, endeavoring to acquaint myself with his wants and necessities.

2. All history as well as observation alike teaches us the rapid decline of the Indians in numbers. The causes producing this result are various.

1st. The various tribes, especially of the mountain regions, are continually at war with each other, thereby destroying each other.

2d. The females marry too early in life in consequence of their numbers being much less than the men, which cause produces alike the early demise of the mother, having had but few children, and they quite feeble and short-lived.

3d. The females being but the slaves of their lords, the husbands, have but little time to take care of their offspring, hence many of them die in infancy for want of proper care. Intemperance and indolent lives of the men are also sources of early death. Among other prominent causes of disease among them are their habits in sleeping and eating; generally they sleep with head covered, summer or winter, from twelve to fourteen hours per day, and eat but one full meal, greatly overloading the stomach to the detriment of health.

3. Diseases among the Indians vary much, according to climate and habits of the Indians. In western countries the Indians mostly settle along the streams, where they are subject to fevers of various kinds, and perhaps more die with these diseases than any other. Such diseases as are contagious, viz: small-pox, measles, mumps, and whooping-cough take off many, as they have not the means to take care of them as those diseases demand.

4. Intoxication prevails to a great extent among them, especially along our thoroughfares. The only means to prevent it, in my opinion, would be to make it a penitentiary offence to sell or give them liquor, and the duty of all civil and military officers to enforce the law under severe penalties.

5. Prostitution prevails to an alarming extent among the tribes that are in close proximity to the whites, whom I consider the principal cause of their prostitution, and as a consequence posterity is enfeebled and life thus shortened.

6. I have no facts to state in regard to their decay that will not be embraced under some other head.

7. In regard to the close proximity of the white settlements, I have but one opinion, and that is to keep the Indians and whites as far apart as possible for the good of the Indian, not that I think the white race would deteriorate the Indian if an average class of the white race would first approach them, but it is a truth that the majority of the first settlers of a country are far below that standard; hence the vices of the whites are learned and but few of their virtues.

8. My opinion is that their lands should be held in common.

9. It is unsafe to confer the right of alienation upon the Indian except in a few isolated cases, and in regard to those few it would not be best, in my opinion, to confer this right upon him.

10. A considerable proportion of those tribes in close proximity to the whites give their attention to agriculture as the only means of support, as with white emigration game recedes, but the manual labor is generally performed by the females. Considerable stock is raised by them, mostly hogs and ponies; cattle are mostly consumed for beef, keeping this kind of stock quite low.

11. Schools have quite a beneficial effect. The manual-labor schools, in my opinion, would be greatly preferable. Whilst going to school the children should be kept constantly under the supervision and control of their teachers.

12. Christian missions in connexion with schools are quite beneficial; outside of these, but labor lost.

13. In regard to the Indian territory, if that is the most suitable place for the Indians, I would recommend its being organized into a territorial government, and, as far as practicable, the various tribes collected and placed thereon, with equal privileges and representation according to numbers, keeping the representation small, having the separate tribes to make and control their own domestic relations and regulations, but all to conform with the laws and regulations of the general government.

14. Money annuities, under a proper trade system, may be given or continued to the Indians. The regulations in regard to trade and traders with Indians should be

very strict, and under the supervision of some one that could not have any interest in the trade, and then such trade would be of decided advantage to the Indian, for by these means he can secure the means of sustenance from year to year, and not himself have any of the money after paying his creditors, as money itself would, in the great majority of cases, be more injury than advantage to him.

15 and 16. Is already answered under other heads.

17. Most of the money received is squandered for drink or is gambled away,

18. First, I do not consider it any evil to pay the trader for goods received; secondly, if a proper system of trade was established among them the latter evil would be removed, as their money would be taken up in necessary articles for sustenance and clothing.

19. I have had no experience and no chance for observation in regard to the order system, and hence cannot give opinion.

20. The War Department would certainly be the most economical department under which to place the Indian bureau, and I see no good reason why it would not be as good for the interest of the Indian.

21. In setting apart reserves, my opinion is it should be done by law, and, if necessary, enforce obedience. My reasons are: Treaties generally engender hard feelings in the tribes, by which the chiefs lose their control over the members of the tribe, whilst respect to chiefs is essential to the proper government of the tribe, and not unfrequently have the Indians to be compelled to comply by force of arms with their own treaty stipulations.

22. I do not think, as a general rule, it would be of any special advantage to the tribe of Indians in general to have their children raised by white Christians, as they have a great aversion to any Indian that departs from their rules and usages; and I am opposed to the mixture of the races, and hence, as the educated Indian child is not to remain among the whites, he would be the object of jealousy and contempt among his brethren when he returned.

23. My opinion is, to collect the various tribes of Indians and place them under a territorial government, granting them as many privileges as consistent with good government, controlling them with the military when necessary; establishing a suitable number of manual-labor schools among them, and compelling the attendance of the children, as will secure a common English education; keeping the whites from among them as much as possible, is the best thing, in my opinion, that can be done for the Indian race.

Yours, truly,

ABRAM BENNETT,
Late Agent of the Kickapoos.

Hon. J. R. DOOLITTLE, *Chairman, &c.*

Reply of P. P. Elder.

BALDWIN CITY, KANSAS,
August 12, 1865.

SIR: I have the honor to acknowledge the receipt of your circular, containing twenty-three questions, relative to Indian affairs. Hoping to aid you in so important and laudable a purpose as a reform in the administration of the affairs of the Indian bureau, I cheerfully state my conclusions, reasons not being called for.

I would call your attention to my annual reports of 1862, '63, and '64 for some of my reasons and conclusions.

1. I was United States Indian agent for Neosho agency from May 1, 1861, to March 31, 1865, and resigned from choice and disgust of the management of the affairs in the southern superintendency and commission of Indian affairs—the Osages, Senecas, Quapaws, and Senecas and Shawnees—and have been a close observer of the management of Indian affairs for nine years in this State.

2. The Quapaws, Senecas, and Senecas and Shawnees, are fast passing away. Whiskey, want of vegetable living, scrofula affection, exposure to the malarias incident to timber and water localities.

More than all others, attempted civilization. The Osages are not decreasing so much; live in their natural way—on the hunt; not so much connected with whites, and only a few make pretensions to civilized habits; among which are the most deaths.

4. Just the extent that they can get anything that will intoxicate; they love it as babes do milk, and ducks water. It only wants a good, efficient, and honest agent to enforce the present statutes and exercise vigilance; no additional legislation will effect anything without more zeal on the part of agents.

5. Not to a very great extent in the Neosho agency, especially among those who recognize the marriage relation.

6. Requires much space to give any intelligible answer; you only ask conclusions, not reasons. Their connexions with the habits, customs, and vices of civilized life. In a word, it is the aboriginal race giving way to the forward and inevitable progress of the white race. It is the gradual and sure enforcement of the law of rise and progress—decay, &c. There can be no remedy suggested by any living person.

7. Without any bias of feeling from my locality, but from a deep sense of feeling for the unfortunate Indians, I do most emphatically say remove the Indians. 1st. Because the Indian universally prefers to remove; dislikes white settlements contiguous. White settlements, with their attendant evils to Indians, carry death to their doors, worse than the malaria or the Arabian simoom.

8 and 9. In common, most certainly, if your object is to benefit and preserve the Indian race. Any other title is to allow them to be swindled by unprincipled whites. To hold lands in severalty, with power to alienate, is to place that unfortunate people at the mercy of all unprincipled juntos of merciless knaves which infest an Indian country for private gain from either private or public plunder, and nine out of ten of the government officials in the Indian bureau, from the late Secretary of the Interior down, will aid them in their nefarious schemes. Such injustice and want of good faith on the part of those who (mis) represent the government, is the cause of all the hostile feelings now extant. Titles in severalty, with power to alienate, is to ultimately make them paupers.

10. Nearly all the small tribes which have laid aside the hunt, and now cultivate the soil and raise stock, horses, &c., are confined mostly to first bloods—Quapaws, Senecas, and Shawnees. In these tribes men as well as women work. The Osages raise only a limited amount of corn and horses; live by hunting buffaloes. In this tribe women are comparatively slaves. Agricultural pursuits are confined to half-bloods and those who have attended the school.

11 and 12. Schools have had a most decided influence, among all the tribes under my observation, for the better. Schools and churches among the Indian tribes, however wild, have a more perceivable impression than any other influence. "Ignorance breeds superstition;" that, to a great extent, comprises their religious faith. Much that is called religion among red or white is superstition based on error; hence the Catholic religion more readily commends itself to their benighted minds, embracing as it does a definite idea of morality and a Supreme Being, and when connected with schools has a most controlling influence. I believe in turning the education and religious teachings of the Indian tribes over to the devotedness and tender mercies of the Catholics.

13. Under new treaties, by all means. These Indian tribes have been as much disturbed and disorganized as the whites in any disloyal State. The Indians expect it, look for it, and demand it. They want "reconstructing." You organize that country into a civil government, with franchise, representation, &c., and the educated and half-breeds only would remain any length of time; all others would, in time, remove on to the Rio Grande and headwaters of the Colorado and Red rivers. Each tribe would be tenacious to retain their several tribal organizations under whatever organization you place them. This question requires a long essay or Congress speech.

14. I refer you to my annual report of 1862. Most certainly.

15. Possibly twenty-five per cent.; generally not one-tenth.

16. Three-fourths, and in some instances the whole, is charged up to them, whether they have the goods or not.

17. The women that draw as heads of families generally purchase the necessaries of life; young men go where they can get whiskey. Gambling is not practiced very extensively among the Indians of my acquaintance.

18. The influence and vigilance of agents properly exercised over traders and Indians. The schools and priests will do much.

19. The real object of the "order system" is, 1st, to confine the entire Indian trade to the licensed trader, in which trade the agent has an interest, direct or indirect. 2d. To prevent Indians from going to white villages with their money. 3d. To get rid of trusting them; all competition is prevented, and they can sell for 100 to 125 per cent profit, and the only real good to the Indian is, it may prevent his spending his money at white villages for whiskey, and hence no money should be paid them.

20. Under the war, if even by regular officers instead of volunteers, for under the latter I have no hope to prevent cheating and stealing. In time of peace the Indian Bureau is the most corrupt of any branch of the government. If the War Department has the power to try and punish by military commission such men, then let the War Department have it.

21. By treaty, always; a treaty is the Indian's Bible—a sacred stipulation; every generation is made familiar with all its provisions by councils in their wigwams. Indians

never violate treaty stipulations unless provoked by improper conduct on the part of whites.

22. I would judge about one-fifth of the children are orphans. Better place the children to the schools, under the care of the priests and agents.

23. This is the most extensive and difficult of all habits of civilization, and agricultural pursuits must be the prominent feature of the policy of the federal government towards the several tribes of Indians in the future. A few of all tribes will incline thereto, and partially adopt the same from necessity, not choice. Thus inroads will be secured upon the minds so benighted, and ultimately the most benefit and comfort can be extended to them on their passage to annihilation as a race. Humanity and Christianity should prompt those in power to some such course. In a word, they want, and should have in the next half century, the treatment of a sick child whom the doctors have given up to die.

To prevent frauds on the Indians and the government. I hardly had an idea there was any one connected with the Indian bureau who desired to prevent, on the other hand aided to open wide the avenues of plunder, so the dividends would be the larger. The eight per cent. would be increased to ten, and peradventure fifteen. Combinations, well and fully organized and confidentially carried on for the last few years and now, that no Indian agent dare raise his voice against to expose, for fear of removal through the paid services and influence of one who worked with him. That combination has cost the government and Indians more than one-half of a million in the last year. The old American Fur Company never had as much power in the Indian bureau. The only character they ever had has been acquired by the countless thousands of ill-gotten gains. "Is there no hand on high to save?"

Already their conduct has brought disgrace upon an administration I have labored for over twenty years to bring into power; and in many instances Buchanan's administration is shaded. Nor have they ceased since your advent into and through Kansas; your visit and investigation has no terror to them. The place to investigate Indian frauds is Leavenworth, Lawrence, and Fort Gibson; I know nothing of further west.

The combination runs through all the ramifications of commissioners, superintendents, agents, contractors, and traders.

You ask my opinion as to the remedy. "Eternal vigilance is the price of blood." Let there be, as I now believe there is, an honest and faithful Secretary of the Interior, who will resist all bribery, however big the claims, and nerve enough to hear and investigate complaints and charges down through all the grades of offices.

Let the Commissioner of Indian Affairs and superintendents be investigated and exposed as the lowest agent, contractor, or trader. Contractors can do no harm only when aided by officers of the government. Let there be a show, a determination on the part of the heads of departments to watch, scrutinize, and hold responsible every grade of office and every person connected with and responsible to the government.

While there is such a manifest looseness on the part of the higher officers, what can you expect of the lower? The only inquiry that has been for the last few years has been, "How much can be made out of it?" "How can you cover the money with vouchers?" Men who were distinguished office-holders under Buchanan, only for their shrewdness for public plunder, and "knowing how it was done," were the first to be taken into the confidence of the officers of the Indian bureau, and have to this day been continued there, a stench in the nostrils of all honest men.

Make the criminal code more stringent; make cheating, stealing, aiding, accessories, &c., criminal, and then punish, and the whole body politic will say "amen."

Contracts are now actually let to the highest bidder. We all know how it is done—easily explained.

In closing, sir, permit me to say that I have not written under the sting of removal from office, for I repeat that I resigned from choice and disgust, and Senator Pomeroy knows it. I have not recommended the Catholic religion from any exalted opinion I have of it, being a Protestant. I have written hastily and with feeling, and had this been anything but a private document I should have written smoother and used less hard names. I mean what I say, and say what I mean.

Nothing would give me more pleasure than to aid in bringing to justice those who have and will continue to plunder a crippled country.

Very respectfully, your obedient servant,

P. P. ELDER.

Hon. J. R. Doolittle,
Chairman, &c., Racine, Wisconsin.

Reply of L. J. Keithly, late Indian agent.

CIMARRON AGENCY, NEW MEXICO,
August 8, 1865.

SIR: In compliance with your circular of May 10, 1865, I have the honor to reply as follows:

1. I have been Indian agent nearly three years at the Cimarron agency, New Mexico, during which time I have had the Mohuacheuta and Jicarilla Apache Indians under my charge.

2. I believe both these bands are increasing a little.

3. I am unable to state what diseases are most common among them; they have generally been healthy.

4. Intoxication prevails to a fearful extent among them, and the only remedy I can suggest is to put them on reservations, where such laws and police regulations can be established and enforced as shall prevent the introduction of liquor among them, either by the whites or themselves.

5. I believe that prostitution does not prevail among them to such an extent as to diminish their numbers or to enfeeble their offspring.

7. In my opinion reservations should not be selected and set apart hastily by the government; but when once selected and set apart, under due consideration as to the country, locality, and surrounding circumstances, and the Indians put upon them, they should be maintained there, and such laws and regulations enacted and enforced as would effectually secure them in their rights, and prevent the encroachments of white settlements.

8. In my opinion, it would be best for the Indians to hold their land in severalty, because, if held in common, it would tend to retard their advancement, as a tribe, in the arts of civilization, and more or less discourage the industrious ones among them, and operate as an encouragement to the idle and vicious; while, on the other hand, if held in severalty, it would afford to the industrious the benefits and comforts resulting from their labor and enterprise, and, no doubt, would in a short time be the means of inducing the balance to adopt like habits of industry.

9. I believe it would be better not to confer upon the Indians the power to alienate their real estate.

10. These Indians raise no stock except a few horses. The Mohuaches have never, to my knowledge, planted any grain or vegetables, but the Jicarillas have planted small patches of land, from time to time, in corn, wheat and pumpkins, which was cultivated by both men and women.

11. There have been no schools among the wild tribes of this Territory since it came under the jurisdiction of the United States. I believe that manual-labor schools would be most advantageous for them.

12. As soon as the Indians are put upon reservations, I would recommend that Christian missions be permitted to go and establish manual-labor schools among them; but until then any attempt to establish missions or schools among the Indians would only be money and labor lost.

17. I am unable to state what proportion of their presents is squandered for intoxicating drinks, but I am confident they squander a large part of their presents and clothing for liquor and in gambling.

18. There can nothing be practically done to secure the Indians against these two evils of drinking and gambling so long as they are permitted to roam at large through the settlements.

19. There are no licensed traders among these Indians.

20. I am not prepared to give an opinion in regard to which of the departments of the government the Bureau of Indian Affairs should be placed.

21. I believe it would be better to set apart reservations for the Indians by law or regulations, as the government, in its wisdom, shall deem most proper and expedient, without the intervention of treaty stipulations with the different tribes; for, as a general thing, the Indians will sign almost any treaty that may be prepared for them, having no intention to comply therewith at the time they sign it. They will ultimately have to be forced to go upon the reservations set apart for them, and compelled to remain there by force of arms. This is my firm belief as regards the Indians of New Mexico.

22. I am unable to state how many orphan children there are among them; and as to placing them in families of Christian white men, I believe it would be impracticable, as there are, comparatively speaking, but few families living in the Territory who speak the English language.

The answers to the questions propounded are predicated upon the characteristics of the Indians of New Mexico.

All of which is respectfully submitted.

LEVI J. KEITHLY,
Late Indian Agent.

Hon. J. R. DOOLITTLE, *Chairman, &c.*

Reply of Captain Charles Kerber, 1st Colorado cavalry.

HEADQUARTERS, FORT GARLAND, C. T.,
August 8, 1865.

SIR: The questions laid before me by you, as chairman of the joint committee of Congress, charged to make inquiry into the condition of the Indian tribes, I have the honor to answer as follows, viz:

1. From 1855 to 1860 I was stationed as an enlisted man in New Mexico; since 1861, as an officer in 1st regiment of Colorado volunteers in the Territory of Colorado. I am acquainted with Gila Apaches and Navajoes; more, though, with the Ute Indians.

2. They are decreasing in numbers in consequence of diseases and fighting.

3. Small-pox and sexual diseases.

4. To a very small extent among the Ute Indians of this region.

6. Sufficient; decay of the Indians is undoubtedly caused through need of food. The hunting grounds are decreasing daily in consequence of the advance of white settlements; game is getting scarce, and the natural consequence is that the Indians suffer much.

7. Indian reservations should be protected against encroachments.

8. In common.

10. Five per cent. of the Ute Indians are farming. They all raise horses, though without paying particular attention to it. The women have to do all the work; the warrior considers work a disgrace to manhood.

11. Have not seen any schools among them, and they will not visit them frequently, so long as the Indians are not living in permanent villages. Manual-labor schools, to teach them to make baskets, weave blankets, &c., will undoubtedly do a great deal of good among any Indians. The scholars must be encouraged by giving them small gifts. Manual-work schools I consider a preparation for other schools. Not too much patience can be recommended to teachers; all have to be taught at first in a playing way, and a teacher who would hold those Indians right down to work would spoil all, and make work still more disgusting to them.

12. Christian missions I indorse very much; and to begin with, Catholic missions will have more success than others, in consequence of their showy ceremonies.

14. Money annuities should be discontinued, so fas as consistent with treaty obligations. Too much chance for swindle.

17. Ute Indians squander a great deal of their annuities in gambling with the Mexican population.

18. Heavy punishment to anybody who is found guilty of gambling with Indians or furnishing to them intoxicating liquors. In this part of the country there is hardly any notice taken by civil authorities concerning the sale of liquors to Indians.

19. I do not consider it good; too much chance for smuggling whiskey and swindling the Indians after being intoxicated.

20. Under the War Department, because the latter has already sufficient officers on the frontiers to attend to Indian affairs, alongside their military duties; further, officers on the frontiers have more experience in such matters than political men sent from the States to the Territories. Undoubtedly not every officer is fit to meddle in Indian affairs. All such officers should have experience in Indian character, be kind but determined; look at the Indians as human beings, but not as brutes.

It is my opinion that an officer in Indian affairs can do more good through kindness than through brutal treatment; and the satisfaction to have assisted in the civilization of poor human beings should be of more worth to him than to be trumpeted out in newspapers as a great fighting man.

21. By treaty; and the latter should be enforced at present with arms until the Indians have sufficient civilization to understand the good and meaning of the laws.

22. This will not be indorsed by the Indians themselves; they would sooner sell the orphans. I do not consider it a good idea for this part of the country, because it would turn into the well-known Mexican peonage.

23. The distribution of annuities should never take place without the presence of some

officer, who should take care that the goods presented are the same which were sent by the Indian bureau; that the Indian agents do not retain some of the goods under false excuses. The Indian bureau cannot be too careful in the selection of Indian agents; it is not an office which is well paid, considering the great responsibilities and duties of an agent; but still so many seek this office. Is it philanthropy? Oh! no; it is that fine chance there is to make so many fine dollars by swindling the government, and, what is still more despisable, the Indians. I am not an Indian lover, sir, but I consider it the duty of any Christian to give those Indians a fair treatment, and make somewhat allowance for their uncivilization. In consequence of the great prejudice existing on the frontiers against the Indians most of our troubles with the latter arise, and a military officer cannot be too cautious in investigating all the complaints brought before him by the population against the Indians before he resolves to fight them. I could introduce facts here which would only too well prove the truth of the above statement, but it may look as if I wish to praise myself and offer myself as an example in such matters to my brother officers; therefore I withhold them.

What I have said, sir, alludes mostly to the Ute Indians, among whom I was stationed since October, 1863.

Most respectfully, I am, sir, and offer myself your very obedient servant,

CHARLES KERBER,
Capt. Detachment, Battalion 1st Colorado Cavl'y, Com'dg Post.

Reply of J. B. Maxfield, missionary to Pawnees.

PAWNEE SCHOOL, *August*, 1865.

In reply to inquiries contained in your circular of May 10, I make the following answers *seriatim*:

1. During the last two years I have served as teacher to the Pawnee manual-labor school. Prior to that time I lived in close proximity to the Otoe tribe, during a portion of which time I was employed at their mission

2. Both of these tribes are decreasing rapidly. The causes will appear in the following answer to third question:

3. As far as my observation reaches, the whole mass, or at least a majority of both tribes, is pervaded with a scrofulous taint. They are likewise very liable to attacks of the endemic diseases of this western country.

4. At the time of my residence in the vicinity of the Otoes intoxication prevailed among them to an alarming extent. Among the Pawnees none of the effects of whiskey are to be perceived to any extent. No liquors of any kind would be found here unless they were brought by the whites.

5. Prostitution prevails universally among the Pawnees. I am not aware of any exceptions. As might be expected, venereal diseases engendered and diffused by this vice exist in the same ratio. Its effects are perceivable everywhere in this tribe. It is, in my opinion, the grand cause which is destroying them, and will ultimately result in their entire annihilation as a race, unless checked by civilizing them. Its deadly virus permeates the entire nation. I am confident that there is not an entire family in the tribe completely free from its presence. I believe that two-thirds of the deaths are caused by this disease.

6. Their irregular mode of life likewise tends to their decay; being frequently without an adequate supply of food, and eating inordinate quantities upon obtaining a supply.

7. I am opposed to Indian reservations, either adjacent to or remote from the settlements, as a permanent govermental policy. Any system that looks to a recognition and perpetuation of their tribal organization under the system of chieftaincies is radically defective, and will have no other result than the swift and sure destruction of the remnant of the race. The chieftaincy should be abolished, and if they are permitted to retain a government distinct from the United States authority, should be permitted to choose their own rulers for a limited length of time only. Under the present system, if a chief stands in the way of a dishonest agent he unchiefs him, and appoints a more pliable one in his stead.

8. Their lands, so far as practicable, should be held most certainly in severalty. There are but few tribes where this is impracticable, and these are the pastoral ones further west.

9. It is not safe to confer the right of alienating real estate indiscriminately upon these Indians; it should be limited to a very few, if any, and then under the supervision and sanction of a government officer.

10. The females of these tribes perform all the labor in the fields, raising corn, squashes, beans, &c. Men do not labor, but hunt, smoke, and idle.

11. Well-conducted schools among these Indians have undoubtedly accomplished much good Manual-labor schools, where the children are maintained in the institution, are greatly preferable, involving no greater outlay, all things considered, than those of other classes.

12. Christian missions being more permanent than government schools, and not affected by the constant political changes, which neutralize to a great degree their otherwise good effects, are, from these considerations, to be preferred. Their tendency has been good, saving no doubt much money to the government, apart from the moral results attained. I would recommend that all such schools be placed under the control of some one of the various religious denominations of the country, always limiting them to those of Protestant character. Those churches, nearly all of them, have missionary boards incorporated by law making them responsible for the proper disposition of all funds intrusted to their care.

13. As to the Indian territory after its pacification, I have not the opportunity to acquaint myself with the matter sufficient to form an opinion.

14. In regard to paying money annuities, I have no hesitancy in saying that by all means they should be discontinued. Let the amounts due them be paid in goods that will be of some service to them—farming implements, culinary utensils, clothing, &c. No blankets, but coats and pants, &c. Government should prohibit blankets from being introduced among them. It would be a god-send to the Indians if there never was another blanket made in the world. Their abandonment will be the first step in civilization. Beeds, bells, ear-rings, broaches, fish-hooks, sashes, and all such articles, are worse than useless. The system of licensed traders, placing the whole tribe at the mercy of an avaricious and often dishonest person, who enjoys an exclusive monopoly of the trade, should be abolished entirely. Instead of this, I would recommend the appointment of government officers to superintend this matter, government furnishing the goods, adding a sufficient per cent. to the original cost to cover expenses, including appointees' salaries, and at these rates allow each one to trade during the course of the year, the whole amount coming to each one as his share of the annuity. Under the present arrangement, a few of the leading men in the tribe receive the goods distributed, while those who need them most receive none.

15. About one-fifth. I make this statement thus high, so that it may not be too little. It is considerably larger than has been received here during the last two years. I can give no clearer idea of the amounts they receive of their annuity money than giving an instance—a usual occurrence, not an isolated case: in April of this year the Commissioner of Indian Affairs wrote the trader here (who is his son-in-law) that the Indians would draw ten thousand dollars in advance of the usual payment for 1865 and 1866, their fiscal year ending June 30, and telling him to get ready for that amount of trade; subsequently, the agent telegraphed here from Baltimore, Maryland, to have the census taken, a dividend struck, and orders issued to them on the trader for that amount. This was done—a dividend being struck; but as much dissatisfaction existed against the trader, the chiefs forbid the tribe to draw any orders. At this time many of the tribe were actually starving. Things remained in this state for some days, when a council was called, at which I was present Three other whites were there, including the trader and his clerk. There was much ill-feeling manifested by the Indians, and there was doubtless much danger of an outbreak. They alleged that the trader charged extortionate prices, gave short weight and measure, &c.; and failing to obtain any reduction of prices, resolved not to trade any on credit—to wait until the agent came with the money, and then trade where they pleased. I mingled freely with them, and knowing that there would be no payment until they traded, and knowing also that the sick and poor would perish in great numbers, I advised them to trade. After holding off for a few days, they concluded to trade, and orders were issued to them. They had traded but a few days when a telegram was received from the agent, only one hundred and seventy miles away, of which this is the import: "Tell chiefs and head men I am coming with money and goods; will be up in a few days." Upon hearing this I was grieved to think that I had advised the Indians to trade. As it was, they almost ceased to trade until the arrival of the agent; after a few days he arrived, and in council with them next day told them that he had a few goods for them, but no money. They resumed trading, and continued until nine thousand dollars was credited them by the trader. The Indians never saw the money; it was never here; it remained in the bank at Omaha. The agent and trader went down there and settled; the money never coming on the reservation. This, as I stated before, is not a solitary example—the invariable practice to hold back the payment until the Indians are forced to buy of the trader until the payment is absorbed. These Indians paid eight dollars a sack for flour while trading on credit, while in sight of their village a much better quality of flour could be bought for six and a half dollars per sack, in cash.

16. The above statement will answer this question.

17. The answer to 4th question.

18. The answer to 4th question.

19. The practical working of the money-order system is simply to furnish the trader with greater facilities to plunder the Indians than they heretofore possessed. For an instance a family consists of seven persons entitled to three dollars per head, total twenty-one dollars; this dividend may be struck in August, and he with his ticket in his possession may wait until December for the payment; then, under the pressure of approaching winter and want, may trade a few dollars the next day after the payment may be made; but his order for the whole amount has gone into the hands of the trader and he can get no money, but is forced to trade it out. There is no perceivable good resulting from it, but much harm.

20. I am not acquainted with this country and those tribes, and hence not sufficiently posted to give an opinion.

21. In the present state of Indian affairs it would be unwise to designate Indian reservations, except by treaty with the tribes.

22. From the best information I am able to obtain, fully one-fourth of the children are orphans. Orphans are invariably adopted by their relatives; nothing but force would take them from the tribes and place them in Christian families. The scheme is impracticable.

My opinion is, in regard to Indian affairs and the present system, that they are miserable failures. Millions of money have been spent, thousands of lives sacrificed, and yet that the government has signally failed either to civilize the Indians or secure the safety of the frontiers is patent to all; it can never be done under the present system. No wholesome fear of the government has been impressed on their minds. Deal with them as with other men, and we have nothing to fear. As long as the government continues to buy their friendship, so long will it be held in contempt. Give him his rights and make him amenable to the laws of the land as other men, and protect him in the enjoyment of his rights, and most of the embarrassments inseparable from the present system will disappear. Let them not be made the prey and sport of political favoritism to be plundered by every dishonest and broken-down politician who voted for a member of Congress. If such persons must have place for services received, let them not be placed where their peculations, by inflaming the passions of savages, will endanger the lives of innocent women and children. It is susceptible of the clearest proof that the present hostilities of our western Indians were precipitated if not caused by the mal-practices of government officers. The cause of the war declared by the Brulé Sioux was the result of a wanton and unprovoked attack upon them by the instrumentality of the old agent of this tribe. At the very time of this attack their camp was on the hill above Cottonwood, and they held unrestrained intercourse with the garrison there until some time after the attack upon them near here by the United States troops. I know that any sentiment that does not throw the entire blame upon the Indian is extremely unpopular here; but as I am not a newly imported man from the east, my convictions are the results of long years of experience and personal observation; therefore are they held with the greater tenacity by me, and I think that they are likewise entitled from these considerations to the greater weight. Hoping that some scheme may be evolved that will secure the much-desired results of enlightening and civilizing these tribes and secure the permanent tranquillity of the frontier settlements, and that these results may be speedily attained, I have the honor to be, your obedient servant,

JNO B. MAXFIELD,
Missionary to Pawnees.

Hon. J. R. DOOLITTLE, *Chairman, &c.*

Reply of John G. Pratt, United States Indian agent.

OFFICE OF THE U. S. AGENCY FOR THE DELAWARE INDIANS,
Leavenworth City, Kansas, September 15, 1865.

SIR: The following is respectfully submitted to you, in answer to the circular addressed to Indian agents and others under date of May 10, 1865, respecting the condition of Indian tribes and their treatment by the civil and military authorities of the United States, and is presented in the order in which such inquiry is made, to wit:

1. For the past thirty years, principally as a minister of the gospel among the Shawnee, Wyandott, Delaware, Munsee, Pottawatomie, and Ottawa tribes of Indians in the State of Kansas, but more recently as United States Indian agent for the Delaware tribe.

2. There has been no remarkable increase or decrease in the population of the respective tribes, but the Indian blood, from intermarriage, has been lessened; the Delaware tribe, however, have increased in numbers some three hundred.

3. Pneumonia and scrofula, from exposure and want of proper attention on their part.

4. To a very great extent; remove them from contact with the whites.

5. It is general among all Indians of full-blood; syphilis and scrofula to a great extent.

6. General exposure during infancy, and a want of proper medical treatment of females and offspring; their gross and irregular mode of life; bad habits.

7. Remove them to new reservations.

8. It is more satisfactory to Indians to hold their lands in common, but to their interest to hold them in severalty, thereby obviating the abandonment of personal effects consequent upon removal from place to place over the reservation.

9. Upon recommendation of the United States Indian agent to the Commissioner of Indian Affairs of the persons capable of managing their affairs.

10. About one-fifth, mostly females; much, however, is done by compensated labor.

11. Has been very advantageous, so long as they can be kept from contact with their associates; manual-labor schools, in all cases, best adapted for their mental as well as physical improvement.

12. It has been attended with beneficial results in very many instances, especially among the Ottawa Indians, and merits encouragement.

13. Under new treaty stipulations, by which they might have a territorial form of government, simplified as much as possible, every nation retaining its nationality and controled by regulations of their own adoption, as will best subserve the interest of their respective tribes.

14. Should not be discontinued; if they make bad use of money, they do so with any other article that could be supplied.

15. About forty per cent. in money under the order system.

16. About sixty per cent.

17. Unable to determine.

18. Very little, as they would squander it at some future time; it should be understood that not all of them make such improper use of annuities; there are fair exceptions in every tribe.

19. It enables the trader to secure his money at the semi-annual payments, and their families can procure supplies through the season, as is necessary for a support, when they could not obtain such articles from merchants without money.

20. The management and conduct of Indian affairs are of sufficient magnitude and importance to constitute that office, more independent of the Department of War and Interior than has heretofore been the case.

21. Treaty.

22. The number is quite considerable; the suggestion is good; chief difficulty would be in obtaining consent of relatives.

23. Indicated above. See 20.

I am, very respectfully,

JOHN G. PRATT,
United States Indian Agent.

Hon. J. R. DOOLITTLE,
Racine, Wisconsin.

Reply of Mahlon Stubbs, superintendent of manual-labor school.

FRIENDS' KANSAS MANUAL-LABOR MISSION SCHOOL,
7th Month 25, 1865.

FRIEND J. R. DOOLITTLE: I received thy circular of 5th month 10th, in due time, and will endeavor to answer the questions therein propounded to the best of my ability.

1st answer. I have been among the Kaw or Kansas Indians two years and four months, and have been acting as superintendent of a manual-labor school for said tribe. I have had some acquaintance with Pottawatomies, Osages, Otoes, Kickapoos, Kiowas, and have visited Delawares and Shawnees, but the Kaws are all I shall attempt to speak for from actual knowledge, except in regard to schools.

2d answer. They are decreasing from several causes: over indulgence in their animal propensities, exposure, intoxicating liquors, irregular and filthy habits, &c.

3d answer. The diseases most common are pneumonia, scrofula, consumption, liver complaints, chills and fevers, &c., &c., from causes stated in 2d answer.

4th answer. Intoxication prevails at times to an alarming extent. The most practical regulation I can suggest to mitigate the evil is for the Indian department to authorize each agent to erect a small substantial jail, invest said agent with power to arrest all Indians found intoxicated, and confine them until they will inform where and of whom they obtained the liquor, and the evidence so obtained shall be a sufficient warrant for the arrest and trial of said offender; if found guilty, fined just enough to pay all costs; and for the punishment, be confined in said jail for such length of time as the Indian department may determine; and that there be a shrewd detective officer appointed (one will answer for two or three tribes) to search out and detect such offenders. My reasons for such summary punishment are, that most, if not all, the Indian troubles are caused by this nefarious traffic. The government, and those wishing and working for the good of the Indians, may spend thousands of money and years of privation and toil, while some unprincipled wretch, for a few paltry dollars, will undo, and, if possible, sink them lower in degradation and misery; and the fining process, among these Indians at least, amounts to a mere farce.

5th answer. On this subject I cannot speak positively, but believe it prevails to an injurious extent, from the fact that they marry the girls quite young, as young as nine years, and their children are puny and scrofulous, and numbers of them die in infancy.

6th answer. I believe the foregoing are the main causes of decay among them; and the remedy I would suggest is, in making treaties, have one article stipulating that each man shall have but one wife, and she shall be of marriageable size, and that they shall keep as many children in school as their funds will educate—an equal number of males and females; the agent to have power to enforce this rule. I believe that all Indians should be treated by the government as a judicious parent treats his own children.

7th answer. If Indians are to be civilized, (which they will have to be, or become extinct,) it will not be done so speedily when they are separated from the whites, as it will be to allow them to mingle with respectable white people. In my opinion it will be decidedly preferable to maintain them on small reservations, (all reservations, as far as I know, are too large,) say one square mile to one hundred Indians is amply sufficient; sell the balance, and assist them in improving their homes so they can maintain themselves.

8th answer. Their lands should be held in severalty.

9th answer. Not confer the power of alienation until they are citizenized.

10th answer. Most of this tribe give some attention to agriculture, both full-bloods, half-breeds, males, and females. The half-breeds raise cattle and horses, full-bloods none, except ponies.

11th answer. The effect of schools has been good, and I would recommend manual-labor schools exclusively, as all male Indians are more or less averse to labor.

12th answer. The effect has been good so far as my observation extends, and I would recommend it in connexion with manual-labor schools.

13th answer. As to this I cannot speak advisedly, except I disapprove of concentrating Indians in any special territory; give them small reservations, with the understanding they are to provide for themselves.

14th answer. Money annuities should by all means be discontinued as soon as practicable. Unprincipled white men would not desire to settle in and around reservations if it was not for the Indian's money; and perhaps a large portion of the American people would make little effort to be self-supporting, if they had an indulgent parent or government to lean upon for the necessaries and luxuries of life.

15th answer. They get the full amount in goods, but at large per cent. The trader having to wait one year charges such high per cent. they do not get near the amount they would if the goods were bought and delivered by a trusty agent.

16th answer. The trader gets nine-tenths.

17thn aswer. Very little that is obtained by other means.

18th answer. In regard to this, I would suggest that there be an honorable and responsible agent employed, to give bond and security for the faithful performance of his duty, at a stipulated salary; to take their funds and lay it out for such goods as are really useful and necessary, (not for beads, paints, ear-bobs, &c., this surely should be prohibited,) and let the Indians have the goods at cost, or, if thought best, let the department specify such per cent. as will pay his salary, but not allow him to trade on his own account. And here the detective officer might be of advantage. In this way they might get their dues, which they cannot under the present system.

19th answer. I believe this system is better than for them to have the money paid them, but not as just as the plan proposed in 18th answer, owing to the high per cent.

20th answer. By all means, under the department of the Interior. My reasons are, that soldiers have a bad influence over Indians when they come in contact with them. I fully believe they furnish them liquor, and learn them to play cards, swear, and other vices.

21st answer. I think it better to do so by treaty with the tribes; if they have strict justice done them there will seldom be any need of using force. The motto in dealing with Indians should be justice and firmness.

22d answer. Near one-half the children in this tribe are orphans—that is, one or the other of the parents is deceased. They could not be taken from them only to a limited extent except by force.

23d answer. I wish to state, in conclusion, that one great improvement in the management of Indian affairs, both morally and financially, would be to intrust Indian agencies to none but honest, temperate, and reliable men, and then not remove them except for sufficient cause shown, and not merely at the suggestion of some member of Congress. And here again the detective officer would be valuable.

I am aware this is very imperfect, but my deep interest in the welfare of the government and Indians must be my excuse.

Respectfully,

MAHLON STUBBS,
Superintendent, &c.

Replies to circular letter of Hon. J. R. Doolittle, chairman of the Indian committee, of 16th May, 1865.

1. Agent for the Iowa and Sac and Foxes of Missouri Indians since April 15, 1861.

2. The births are about equal to the deaths.

3. Scrofula and consumption.

4. Intemperance prevails to a great extent. Have tried almost everything I could think of to prevent it. Have succeeded better by prevailing on the Indians to pass a law that no spirituous liquor should be brought on the reservation, and to appoint ten of their braves as a police to enforce the law, and to give each one found drunk ten lashes for the first offence, and twenty for the next.

5 and 6. Prostitution prevails to a great extent, and the disease consequent upon it. Were it not for this and whiskey, these tribes would increase about ten per cent. per annum.

7. Maintain the Indians on small reservation and resist encroachments.

8 and 9. I consider it best to hold their lands in severalty. And to those who are far enough advanced in civilization to manage their own affairs, confer the power of alienation, and divide their portion of all annuity due the tribe, on condition that they or their children never be permitted to settle on any reservation, or in any way share the benefit of a treaty with any tribe.

10. All the male portion of the Iowas give attention to agriculture, the women doing but a small portion of the outdoor labor. About one-eighth raise stock. About one-third of the outdoor labor of the Sac and Foxes of Missouri is performed by the men, the women doing the majority of the labor. They raise but little stock, except ponies.

11. The Iowas have had a school for about six years. It has been a great benefit to them in learning our language, but cannot be considered an entire success.

12. The mission near Highland, Kansas, has been a great advantage to the Iowas, and laid the groundwork of their civilization. I cannot see but little if any benefit they have been to the Sac and Foxes of Missouri.

13. Should the partially civilized Indians be moved to the Indian territory, in all cases would recommend new treaty, and that they be permitted to send an Indian as a delegate to Congress.

14, 15, 16, and 17. Under the present system about one-half of their annuities is paid in money; about one-half of this amount goes into the hands of the Indians, and the balance to the trader. A few will spend all the money they receive for whiskey and gambling, while the majority make the proper use of it. The balance of the annuity due them is expended for agriculture, &c., &c.

18. The best mode to secure to those who squander their money is to furnish them with useful and beneficial articles.

19. Have no experience with the order system; believe it would be an advantage here, as those who are disposed to squander their money would receive beneficial articles for it.

20. Cannot see any reason why there should be a change.

21. In setting apart reservations, would do so by treaty.

22. About one-twelfth part of the children are orphans. They are always taken care of by their relatives or friends. Think it advisable to place orphans in a Christian family.

Reply of Antonio José Martinez.

TAOS, NEW MEXICO, *July* 26, 1865.

SIR: The pamphlet made in Racine, Wisconsin, dated May 10th of the present year, and received at Taos on July the 11th, was sent to me for the purpose of answering the list of questions contained therein on the subject of Indian affairs. These inquiries number 23, and I proceed to submit the required information, to the best of my knowledge and belief, as follows:

To the first question, upon what I know relating to the Indians, and in what manner they are treated, I have to state, that from the first year of this century, since I was nine years old, I have remarked that the Navajoes, who inhabit the villages west of New Mexico, situated on the Rio Abajo, sometimes were at peace, and at other times at war. They always observed this alternative, though the first periods were longer, say from four to five years, but seldom more than the second, which were from two, three, and even five years.

Then New Mexico was under the authority of the Spanish government, which maintained one hundred soldiers of the line, with their respective officers, in the city of Santa Fé, the capital. The governor was always the colonel, being the first officer of the troops sent from the State of Chihuahua and others; but never from New Mexico, though the soldiers and officers were from here, and when Mexico became independent of Spain, sometimes the highest officer was governor; sometimes, also, a native citizen of the country would hold the superintendence of Indian affairs when the soldiers took the field in times of war. By the orders of the governor, the inhabitants were drafted, in order to place the army on a good footing so as to enforce respect, even to conquering the Indians, and thus obtain peace; so it occurred with the Navajoes. The men who were to make the campaign amounted from five to six hundred, perhaps one thousand. As said above, only a small number of the soldiers went; the largest number stopped in the pasture lands to protect the cattle that remained, and thus maintained themselves during the summer and winter without need of buying any provisions. As for the rest of them, until they had completed the number, they made a requisition on the inhabitants in the vicinity in certain proportions. Some furnished provisions at their own expense; others offered riding animals, tents, equipments, subsistence for themselves, arms, powder, shot, and arrows as well as bows; and when they were assembled to start on their enterprise they were all passed in review; those who were not mounted were made to purchase their equipments and ammunition, and though the government forces took a great quantity with them, none was distributed until what the others carried was entirely exhausted, and for this were exempt from contributions. When the Mexican government resolved upon levying some taxes on New Mexico, an insurrection was progressing in the passes and in other points north, during which a man called Perez was killed, with other employés. Perez was governor in 1837. Another war took place in 1838, in which the insurgents were promptly defeated.

Towards the west of the Territory lies the land inhabited by the Yutas; opposite Santa Fé, Abiquiu and other populations, even to that of the Conejos, which are further north. The former leave and take their nomadic dwellings in different localities in search of game, upon which they live, though this has decreased a great deal. The Yuta nation own but few miles of territory; the exact number is not ascertained—certainly less than the Navajoes, who possibly own as many as twenty miles, since they form the most numerous nation contiguous to the lands west of the lower villages inhabited by the Yutas, as said above.

The Yutas, since I have acquired the use of reason, were always at peace with New Mexico; notwithstanding which they stole and killed some cattle, such as cows and ewes, whenever these happened to be grazing in the pasture lands. Sometimes these Indians would camp at certain periods near the villages and farms, assaulting the shepherds, stealing corn, and committing other depredations; they would also reside near the country-seats for the same purpose, as it has happened, but in the meanwhile always at peace, and when accused of the above would say for their defence that the children had done it, yet they would pay whenever the theft was well proven against them. But after the year 1843, I am not certain which, some chiefs arrived at the city of Santa Fé to hold an interview with the governor, whose name was Martinez, from the State of Chihuahua, behaving insolently towards him; the troops fired and killed one of them. This, to my knowledge, was the first insurrection of the Yutas; but after this there was another one in New Mexico against the United States government. At that time, also, there was a revolt of the Apaches, called Jicarillas, who always lived between the villages and the intermediate mountains, working and selling earthenwares to our people. They trespassed upon the lands of the Yutas, in the eastern part of the Territory, in search of buffaloes and other game, although they had some in great quantity in their own section of the country. But in this insurrection they were severely punished, and soon after they concluded a peace with the Yutas, which exists to the present day.

The north of the Territory is occupied by the multitude of Caiguas, Ases, Cuampes, and other tribes of Indians, nearly touching the Comanches, who inhabit the east of New Mexico, and near the Apaches, who are called Colloteros, and of various other tribes living south.

The Caiguas and the Indians from the north never were at war with New Mexico, but only with travellers, who at different times were badly robbed of their droves of horses, and some of them were killed, but in these excursions they regularly disguised themselves to prevent detection; still, when they were in their cabins, they would always receive well those who came to trade with them. The Comanches in the olden times and previous to this century were at war, but since they met with a severe disaster, where a great many of them were killed in a campaign, they abandoned the idea of fighting against New Mexico until that which occurred the year before, but since they were always faithful in keeping peace with us; still if they made raids in the States of Mexico to steal and to wage war, they were not robbers like the Apaches, the Yutas, and others from the north, as it happened, and has been said before. Yet the southern Apaches were generally at war with New Mexico, and with few intervals of peace. Concerning the present state of things I do not know how they are; at different times they made several raids and treaties of peace, but never kept their promises.

The Spanish government had appropriated certain sums of money to be used in giving clothing and ornaments only to the peaceful Indians; not to all, but to the chiefs and other important persons who came with them to ratify the treaty of peace. This appropriation was called a fund or alloyed treasure. The above relates to the first question.

To the second inquiry, upon the increase or decrease of the Indians, I have to say that they diminish more than they increase; the cause is owing to the fact of their being always at war with each other—the Yutas constantly against the nations of the north, and also with the Comanches, against whom they made already several campaigns. The two latter retaliated on them by passing across their lands or pursuing them when hunting the buffalo. These frequent skirmishes always caused the death of a great number on both sides, alternately victorious, carrying the children and some of the females captive, selling some in New Mexico, killing others, and ill-treating the rest so much that many of them died.

The Apaches Jicarillas and those from the south always were at war with the Comanches: this, with our own troubles with them, appears to be the cause of their decreasing so much instead of remaining in a state of equal proportion.

I will now proceed to answer the third question, relating to the diseases the most common and the most fatal among the Indians. I am of opinion that hunger, of which they often suffer since the produce of the chase and profits of robberies are growing less, added also to the delays in travelling, which retards the supplies of provisions sent from New Mexico, exposure to the severe winters, their insufficient and movable habitations, badly constructed and unfit to resist the rigorous cold, and other disadvantages, tend greatly to cause sickness and death among them. When the measles and small-pox first appeared the mortality was immense, and though those that were seized by these diseases were abandoned, and a great many fled to avoid the contagion, the loss among the Indians was excessive. This, I think, will give an adequate idea and the cause of their decreasing so much.

To the fourth, fifth, and sixth inquiries, on the extent of their relations with each other; on the intemperance, and what practical regulation could be enforced to prevent the prevailing prostitution and the diseases arising therefrom; the cause of their decadence, and what are the remedies, practicable or otherwise, if there are any, I am of opinion that the result of the preceding remarks will answer these questions. I suppose that the humors or fluid of the Indians, according to their quantity, and the flesh and blood being stronger than those of others of the human race, must render them more susceptible to the corruption engendered by diseases; brought upon them also by excesses in vices of physical abuse, thus breaking the laws of nature, who punishes her violators. The drinking of spirituous liquors, which is used lately by the Indians, proves very injurious to their health, and causes a great many diseases. I think that the remedy would be to induce them to temperance, to live in healthy and permanent places, to build good houses, till the land, plant corn, raise cattle, and adapt themselves to other industries; and now and then the men will go hunting, using the game for food, and the skins to make shoes—always owning a place to live in with their families; prohibit the sale of ardent spirits, encourage them to peace and good will towards other nations with which they were at war; give them the idea that there is a God, Author, Creator, and Preserver of us all, and whom we acknowledge, worship, and thank; who desires that all men be in good relations with each other, and to whom He has given the ideas of the immortality of the soul, of the end of all earthly joys after our life, and the punishment of wicked deeds, by Him, the Supreme Judge of all.

To the seventh question, upon the police (policy?) of the populations for the Indians; to the eighth, upon whether their lands were preserved in common or separately; and to the ninth, relating to the faculty or privilege granted to them of transferring their original properties, I am inclined to suggest that the Indian populations ought to be kept in the fields or localities far from the villages of the whites, in places adapted for corn-growing, sufficiently provided with water for irrigation and timber; but not all in one locality, but in several others suitable and convenient to their means and capacities of cultivating them. Some villagers accquainted with the lands, and the way these are disposed by the Indians, have informed me that the properties are kept in common, so as to prevent some families from ruining themselves, by transferring them to others, and thus be left in poverty to wander and to rob. I would propose that they should be allowed to come to the villages of the white only to traffic under certain legal measures not to mess together as heretofore, as this is the cause of their planning thefts, promoting rebellion and other injurious projects, prompted by revenge to rise in arms.

In regard to the tenth question, upon the agricultural reservations, and the raising of cattle, I believe, as said in the previous answer, that, for the purpose of cultivating lands, it requires intelligent persons to till and render the soil productive, so as to derive the benefits resulting therefrom, and to produce and gather such grains as are sown here in New Mexico. Then, after two or three years at the most, of their own accord they will adapt themselves to that change of life, and will feel a pleasure and interest in working—seeing the advantages of being maintained in abundance. As to raising cattle, it is the easiest. There are already some who are tending flocks of ewes, goats, cows, and horses, principally those from the Navajo tribe, which is acknowledged among the others as the most industrious, and set as an example to the rest of them.

As to the eleventh question, relating to schools, and what system of education could be recommended for them, I think there are none of any kind. The teaching of agriculture the building of dwellings, carpentry and smithery, the weaving of cloth and wool for cloaks and other parts of dress, all of which being the most necessary to the community, ought to be taught at first, enabling the Indians to live quietly in good order, and thus apply themselves to these different pursuits

Concerning the twelfth question, upon the Christian missions among them, there has been no others since the old ones. When the Spaniards conquered New Mexico, they brought Franciscan missionaries, at the same time with civilization. The cultivation of lands, the building of houses, were the means with which the Indians expressed their gratitude to the government and to the Christian religion, and to the white populations among which they lived.

This means would have been a great deal more advantageous to the wild tribes than what is expected now from them; to begin first by the measures suggested in the resolutions on the fourth, fifth, and sixth questions, although the principles did have the desired effect relatively to spirituality, it will succeed in time, and the good results in promoting the temporal affairs, which are the primary objects of the government, will be realized

Referring to the thirteenth question, upon which an opinion is requested—how are the Indians to be governed after peace is concluded in the Territory?—I think that until the additions to the stipulations are contracted, it will be proper to give them special laws in view of the present circumstances, and other means sufficient to operate in the experiment, until the governor can certify that the Indians are completely civilized. Schools and other industries will enable them to know the laws and the most important means to preserve public order; then it will be possible to impose upon them a territorial government, and give them the right of electing their officers.

On the fourteenth question, relating to annuities, I am of the opinion that sufficient ones have been appropriated to provide them with farming implements, tools for building, salaries of overseers, who direct them in their different labors, enough to furnish them with seeds for planting, but none for provisions or clothing; for this they had to rely upon the animals killed in hunting and the produce of corn-fields. In the mean time they can obtain the rest by their work and industries.

The fifteenth question, upon the actual proportion of Indians. I do not understand the meaning of this inquiry, but the tenth question states in what proportion the trader receives the goods and supplies; yet I have to say that those who go among them to trade bring with them maize, bread, and other articles of food, cloaks and cloth, receiving, in exchange, hides, cattle, and other chattels they may have—as these Indians cannot be trusted—first giving a small present without charge, before beginning the bargain or purchase. It cannot be ascertained in advance what quantity will be sold, but a great many loads are sent there at a venture.

In regard to the seventeenth question, concerning the dissipation of the Indians, such as drunkenness and gambling, prompted by the use of alcoholic liquors, which they drink in great quantity, buying them at exorbitant price, and for this reason ought to be forbidden, under some severe penalities on the villagers who bring them. Concerning gambling, I cannot say that they do it to any extent; I have heard that they often bet in the horse and foot races, but I am not acquainted with their other games.

The eighteenth question, relating to the payment in supply, silver or clothing, which is made: I know that the Indians of New Mexico cannot be trusted, all sales being on the cash principle; and if the traders make any other arrangements with those who own habitations around the Indian rancheros, I know nothing.

Nineteenth question. In answer to the sixteenth inquiry, I have said what I knew of the practice and system with which the villages of these populations were regulated in New Mexico.

To the twentieth question, as to where the Commission on Indian Affairs ought to be located, whether in the War or Interior Department, I think it ought to be in the former, owing to their good informations in matters relating to the Indian insurrections, treaties of peace, and everything pertaining to them, besides being more connected and in accordance with the labors of the War Department.

To the twenty-first question, on the arrangement of the separate reservations, either by treaties with the Indians, by laws or regulations enforced by arms, I think that at the beginning it ought not to be with all the tribes at once, but one after the other, negotiating with the chiefs whose authorities they acknowledge, or through such other individuals who consider themselves as principals; then give them to understand that already the buffalo cannot support all the nations; that this principal resource, with all the different species of game and poultry which formerly were their means of subsistence, are disappearing very fast; that the idea of war by a nation with another, that living upon pillage and robbery, are all wrong, and in time will bring them to complete ruin and destruction. That they ought to acknowledge all men as brothers—sons of a common Father, who is God, Creator, Author and Preserver of all existence.

Concerning the twenty-second question, upon the education of the Indian orphans, and those although not orphans: I think it would be proper and convenient to place them in the families of the whites, obliging them to go to school to learn English or Spanish, and thus obtain the faculty to read, write, and be acquainted with other branches of education—receiving instructions in manners, morals, religion, and other acquirements of civilization, and in time they will be able to serve their own nations, by enlightening with the knowledge received as above.

To conclude, I answer the twenty-third and last question, on which I give the following opinion:

1st. The part of the tribe of the Navajoes, which is at war, is more numerous than that which resides in the Bosque Redondo as a reserve. This war is the cause of a great many robberies, murders, and injuries to the inhabitants of New Mexico. Many of them who fled from the reserve brought arms, powder, shot, and a quantity of other things, as well as a great number of cattle stolen in their flight. I am of opinion to hold and keep the Navajo reserve as an example to the others, and subsequently the reservations of other tribes which cannot support themselves, except at the cost or expense of the government, only in the manner and with the economy as suggested by me in the 7th, 8th, 9th, 10th, and 14th answers, which contain various and important details; if these cannot be acted upon, the necessity of the case will require the force of arms, since without civilization they cannot be maintained.

2d. The Indians must be impressed with the fact that the help given to them in the shape of food and raiment, as well as other things, is not in fear of them, as they suppose, but because our government has pity for their poverty and precarious life, relying upon the chase, pillage, and war against each other, or against civilized nations, for their subsistence.

3d. That the employés appointed for the work of establishing Indian populations must be honest, intelligent, and worthy of their position, regardless of political parties, differing from those who intend to defraud and not fulfil the duties of their office.

4th. That there is an idea that the Indians captive and bought from their fathers, similar to the Yutas, who sell their sons and daughters in exchange for horses and other objects, are held as slaves. No, they are servants, and are well treated; if they marry, they are free to live in their master's house and pass their life as they please, the same as with the sons of Indians, who, if not married when attaining their majority, become free after their marriage.

The above is in answer to all the questions you have put to me.

I am, with much respect, your obedient servant,

ANTONIO JOSÉ MARTINEZ.

Hon. J. R. Doolittle,
Chairman of the Committee on Indian Affairs.

Pithole City, Pennsylvania,
September, 1865.

Senator: Your letter of the 7th of July, written from Santa Fé, New Mexico, was received some weeks ago. I have delayed answering until I could refresh my memory by an examination of such papers as I could find at my home in Wisconsin. You ask for a concise statement of the facts in regard to "the breaking out of hostilities with the Navajo Indians, while I was in command of Fort Defiance, the circumstances preceding it, the killing of my negro servant," &c., which has been the subject of an inquiry.

I took command of Fort Defiance in the latter part of November, 1857. Perfectly peaceful relations existed with the Indians, who were in the habit of visiting the post daily. By treaty and general understanding there were four distinct places given to the fort as grass or hay lands—Los Trigos; Ewell's camp, upper and lower; Amarillo, and the cañon adjoining the fort. In the summer of 1857, before my assuming command, the force at the post was reduced, by withdrawing all the companies but one, for an expedition against the Indians on the Gila. The Navajoes, taking advantage of this, and on the plea of an unusual dry season, put their animals on these grass or hay grounds, and used all the grass, save on the grounds in the immediate vicinity of the garrison. A small force was sent out to drive them off, but the command was largely outnumbered, and it required much discretion on the part of the officer in command to avoid a repetition of the affair at Fort Kearney the year before, known as the "Grattan affair." A large force was sent to the post as soon as it could be got there, to punish the Indians; but when they arrived it was found that all the grass was gone, and the officer in command, Colonel Loring, had a kind of talk or council with the Indians, in which their offence was overlooked, and they again renewed their promises to respect our rights to the hay. Thus I found things. In the spring of 1858 parties were occasionally sent out to look after the meadow lands; one of these parties, consisting of only two men, was sent in May to Ewell's Camp, found a quantity of stock on the meadow, which they drove off; but the Indians, being in large numbers there, drove the animals back again, and one of them, Manuelito, recognized as head man of the nation, came into the garrison with the two men, who reported what had occurred. On questioning Manuelito, he acknowledged he had put the animals on the meadow, claimed the meadows were his, and that he intended to keep them there—he became, in fact, perfectly defiant: He was notified that force would be sent to kill everything found depredating. That night, or the next, a force was sent out under Captain McLane, since killed, who found a number of horned cattle on the ground, that were fired upon and killed. I regretted to learn that cattle instead of horses were found and had been destroyed, as I had tried to encourage the Indians to engage in raising cattle in place of horses. For some days the Indians were very shy about coming into the garrison, when Zarcellos Largos, one of their most influential and crafty men, came to make inquiries about the cattle. The matter was explained to him, and he said if we were satisfied the Indians were, and they resumed their usual visits to the garrison, and respected faithfully our meadows. Now, an effort was made to connect this affair with the killing of the negro boy, entirely by persons remote from the garrison. I think, and I believe it was the opinion of every body at the garrison, there was not a particle of connexion in the two affairs; certainly the Indians themselves never intimated any such thing. The cattle were killed in last part of May or fore part of June; the servant was shot about the 12th of July. One morning an Indian came into the garrison and offered a blanket for sale. It was remembered afterwards that he seemed to hang around the bake-houses and other places that soldiers would be like to resort to singly. He finally sold his blanket to a camp woman, whose quarters were not far from my own, between my quarters and the well at which we got our water. As the Indian got on his horse, the servant happened to come along, and as he passed, the Indian drew out his bow and arrow, shooting the boy in the back, between the shoulders, mortally wounding him. He died in three days after. The Indian put spurs to his horse, and got away before any alarm could be given.

These facts were communicated to the headmen of the different bands as soon as possible, and a demand made for the surrender of the murderer. It is proper to say that the servant died with the assertion that he had never seen or spoken to the Indian before, and that he had not said a word, nor done any manner of act to give cause of offence. In fact, the murder was most wilful and causeless. The Indians said—and there never appeared to be any reason to doubt the story—that this Indian had been at a dance the night before, and had a quarrel with his wife; that he left the dance, and set out to appease his offended feelings and pride by killing the first "outsider" he would meet. The Indians asserted this was a customary way of acting under such circumstances. The same reason was assigned on two former occurrences of the same kind, at the same post, on one of which occasions they gave up the murderer, who was executed. When a demand was made for the surrender of the murderer of the servant, the chiefs said such was not their custom; they were referred to the case above alluded to; they said that was a poor man without friends, but they would not give up any more. They were willing to compromise, as they were in the habit of doing with Mexicans and Pueblo Indians, by paying any agreed upon amount in horses and sheep. This plan was not listened to for a moment. The delivery of the murderer or war was the alternative offered. The Indians then contended that the murderer had fled beyond the limits of the nation. They pretended they would send for him, and began to ask for time, &c. Everything was done that was possible to bring them to a sense of the enormity of the crime. They finally brought in word they were after and in close pursuit of the murderer, and would bring him in, dead or alive; and sure enough the next day they brought in the body of a man that they had killed, which on examination proved to be that of one of their captives—in reality a Mexican; when this was made known to them, they admitted the fact, and said they had done all they could or would do. Before this, however, I was superseded in command by the late Colonel Miles, who conducted the campaign to its close.

Very respectfully,

W. T. H. BROOK.

Hon. J. R. DOOLITTLE,
United States Senator, Racine, Wisconsin.

SUB-REPORT OF MR. HIGBY.

Mr. CHAIRMAN: I herewith submit to the committee the information I gathered during the months of July, August, and September last. In accordance with the plan of the committee, dividing up the labor among its several members, I arrived in California the last of June, and in a few days after my arrival, in company with Mr. Maltby, the superintendent of Indian affairs for the State, I left San Francisco to visit the different Indian reservations, and by the last of August had been upon all the reservations in the State, and during the tour I made such observations and obtained such facts as time and circumstances would allow.

At Crescent City, in the northern part of the State, I parted with Mr. Maltby. He returned to San Francisco, re-visiting the Hoopa Valley reservation on his return, to re-appraise with the agent there and the United States surveyor the property of the settlers in that valley, that, with their approval, the government might purchase it for reservation purposes. I continued my journey north to the city of Portland, in the State of Oregon, for the purpose of meeting and conferring with Senator Nesmith, with whose labors mine were intimately associated on the Pacific coast; but I found, on my arrival in Portland, he had left for the eastern part of his State and the Territory of Idaho to examine into the condition of reservations there. I had yet to go into the State of Nevada, before returning to the city of Washington; so I did not remain in Portland, but went by first steamer to San Francisco. From San Francisco, by steamer, railroad, stage and riding horseback, I made my way to Fort Churchill, in the State of Nevada. This is a central point midway between the only two reservations in the State. Here I found some of our volunteers stationed, under the command of Lieutenant Colonel A. E. Hooker, who kindly offered his services to aid me in my labors. He sent men to each of the two reservations, distant from five to seven hours' ride, to notify agents and Indians to come to the fort and confer with me. The soldier sent out to the northern reservation reported on his return that he could not find the agent nor any prominent Indian. All he could learn of the agent was, that he left the reservation some weeks before, and had not been seen upon it since. From the Southern or Walker River reservation, the agent, Franklin Campbell, placed there temporarily by the superintendent, and about twenty Indians came to the fort. The information obtained there, and at Carson City, and herewith submitted, shows but little advance made in Indian affairs in the State of Nevada as yet. The statement of Mr. Warren Wassen, who kindly offered any aid he could give, was taken at Carson City, on my return from Fort Churchill. The superintendent of Indian affairs for the State, Mr. Lockhart, was absent in the city of Washington, as I was informed. I did not see him, and have no doubt the information was correct.

Large sums of money have been appropriated by the government during the last ten or more years, to be expended in the State of California for the purpose of buying the friendship of the Indians and to better their condition. I regret much that such liberal appropriations do not exhibit more fruit and a much better condition of things. The benevolence of the government has far exceeded its beneficence While the government has been liberal in its appropriations, it has not properly guarded the avenues by which these appropriations must go in order to reach the Indians, nor sufficiently provided for their impartial distribution.

While I am clear in the opinion that there should be some changes in the system of conducting our Indian affairs, and in which changes, I have no doubt, all the members of the committee will agree, it gives me pleasure to be able to speak favorably of the administration of Indian affairs in the State of California at the present time. Mr. Maltby, the superintendent, is a man of strict integrity, is very attentive to his business, and exhibits great interest in the welfare and improvement of the Indians. Whatever he receives from the government for the use and benefit of the Indians he will faithfully disburse among them. The agents are careful, considerate men, and appear to have the confidence of the Indians. While the Indians complained of the articles they received from government, on account of their very poor quality, they had no complaints to make against the agents.

Mr. Franklin Campbell, the acting agent on the Walker River reservation, in Nevada, of whom I have made mention already, was highly spoken of by all, both white men and Indians. I believe he has since been duly appointed agent of that reservation. I saw no one else in Nevada connected with the Indian department except Mr. Parker, at Carson City, who had just been appointed superintendent of the State, but had not yet entered upon the duties of his office. I am not informed beyond the statements herewith submitted what should be done in that State in reference to Indian affairs.

There are now in the State of California four reservations. The government is paying rent for Tule River farm, used for Indian reservation, and also for lands on which Indians are kept at Smith river, called the Smith River reservation; the latter is the most northern in the State, and the former is the most southern. Nome Cult or Round Valley reservation is central in its location in comparison with the others, and at present furnishes facilities for sustaining more Indians with less expense than any other reservation in the State. The government has there several thousand acres of land free of rent charge. There have been some intrusions by way of locations of claims that will doubtless be disposed of without much trouble. This valley is singular in its formation; it is about six miles in length by about four miles in width, and is surrounded by a mountain barrier twenty to thirty miles in extent, and has but a narrow outlet for drainage. The valley is estimated to contain from fourteen to sixteen thousand acres, the larger part of which is fine agricultural land. Under proper culture the valley is capable of sustaining several thousand Indians. I am inclined to the opinion that the government should have the entire control of the whole valley, and that it should be used entirely for reservation purposes; this would require the removal of several settlers now occupying portions of the valley, but by what tenure they hold the lands I am not able to say, or whether they have any title other than possession. The statements I obtained at the reservation gave but little light upon the subject.

Mendocino station is treated as a part of the Nome Cult reservation, having only an employé there. The report of the superintendent shows that the Indians will soon be removed, if not already, to Round Valley, and the station be entirely abandoned. Hoopa Valley reservation is yet in an unsettled condition. If the settlers in the valley accept the appraisement recently made, of which I have spoken, the whole valley unencumbered will belong to the government. The necessity that called for this step is to be deplored. It is quite inaccessible; is surrounded by high mountain barriers, and contains only about fifteen hundred acres of land. The great merit in the movement in making the valley a reservation is to appease a band of several hundred Indians, whose home is in the valley and mountains adjacent, and who have been very troublesome by their frequent depredations made upon the white settlements. If those Indians could have been removed to some reservation already provided, it would have been far better, but it was contended that they could not be successfully removed. Smith River reservation lies upon the coast in the extreme northern part of the State; it is within a few miles of Oregon line. Government pays rent for the lands that make this reservation. The location is a very good one; it is eligible, and the land fertile. Reports herewith submitted explain the condition of things there very fully, together with the statements taken during my visit there. I think, however, that very soon the government can provide for all the Indians in the State on three reservations—one in the north, one central, and one in the south. Tule River farm now used as a reservation, with some lands adjacent, would make a good reservation. The lands are fertile and the location eligible. I have no doubt, however, but there are other locations equally as good in every respect.

Changes can easily be made, and the system of providing for and managing the Indians greatly improved by the observance of good faith towards them. Mental, moral, and religious instruction would be a blessing to them, and appropriations now made and properly expended by the government for this purpose, in my judgment, would be not only just to them, but in time would be a saving financially to the government.

Statement taken at San Francisco, California, July 8, 1865.

STATE OF CALIFORNIA, *County of San Francisco:*

H. F. W. Hoffman, being duly sworn, deposeth and says, that he is a resident of the city of San Francisco, California, having resided there about twelve years, and in the State fifteen years; that he has been acting as clerk for the superintendent of Indian affairs for nearly four years past—about three years under John P. H. Wentworth, one year under Austin Wiley, and about two months under Charles Maltby; during which time John P. H. Wentworth was superintendent of Indian affairs for the southern district of California, and George M. Hanson and Elijah Steele were superintendents for the northern districts of California; Messrs. Wentworth and Steele being legislated out of office by the consolidation of the departments during the thirty-eighth Congress, and Austin Wiley appointed as superintendent for the whole State, and subsequently Charles Maltby, the present superintendent. During a portion of the time above specified there had been two reserves or farms in the southern district, viz: the Tejon reserve, located in Los Angeles county, and the Tule River farm, in Tulare county, the latter rented by the department. The Tejon reserve was abandoned the latter part of the year 1863, the late Surveyor General E. F. Beale claiming the same under a United States patent. The average number of Indians on the Tejon reserve has been about nine hundred; sometimes as many as eighteen hundred have been fed by the department. At Tule River the average has been about six hundred. The office of the agency for the southern district has always been located at San Francisco, and at the commencement of Mr. Hanson's administration he removed the office of the northern district from Yuba City to the same place, to be again removed (when Elijah Steele relieved Mr. Hanson) to Yreka, Siskiyou county. Previous to the consolidation of the two departments the reserves, both north and south, were placed in charge of supervisors, appointed by the respective superintendents, and the Indians in the southern district received their subsistence either by purchase made through the superintendent or the crops raised upon the reserves by their own labor, the Indians appearing always ready and willing to work provided they could be assured that the fruits of that labor would be appropriated only to their own use, having from experience heretofore frequently suffered by the dishonesty of agents in selling the crops raised upon the farms; at least such have been the current reports, causing the removal of several of the agents. The Indians living on these reserves have always appeared contented and happy, apparently well satisfied with their condition, during the cold and wet weather living in adobe houses, constructed of mud, and in the summer-time in brush and tule tents, made from brush and tule grass. No trading posts have ever been allowed upon the reserves, all provisions and necessary articles for carrying on the same being purchased abroad, either at San Francisco or the nearest convenient town. The males have been taught to farm, while the females have received more or less instruction in sewing, who have rendered very efficient service in making up garments for the men and children. These Indians are mostly mission Indians or their descendants, many having received religious instruction from the padres connected with the old missions. No schools have been established, or religious instruction ever been imparted to these Indians at any time, to my knowledge, since the occupation of California by our government, but they have always evinced a disposition to be peaceable and quiet.

In the northern district during the past four years there have been the following reservations, viz: the Nome Cult or Round Valley reservation, and the Mendocino reservation, both situated in Mendocino county; the Klamath reserve, in Klamath county, abandoned, and the Indians removed to Smith river, in Del Norte county, now known as the Smith River farm, and rented, and the Hoopa reservation; at present rented, but not yet accepted by the department.

H. F. W. HOFFMAN.

Statements taken at Tule Farm Indian reservation, California, July 14 *and* 15, 1865.

STATE OF CALIFORNIA, *County of Tulare:*

George L. Hoffman, being duly sworn, deposeth and says, that he resides upon the Tule River farm, at Tule river, which farm is used as an Indian reserve; that he is employed by the United States government upon the said farm as special agent, and has also been acting as employé and supervisor in the service of the Indian department since July, 1862; was employed at Tejon reserve about seven months, at which time there were about seven hundred Indians. While at Tejon between eight and nine hundred Indians arrived from Owen's River valley. The Tejon was abandoned the latter part of the year 1863, the reserve being claimed by E. F. Beale, (late surveyor general, and formerly superintendent of Indian affairs for California,) under a United States patent. At this time some of the Tejon Indians left there with a portion of those brought from Owen's river to Tule River farm. When I was ordered to Tule river there were probably fifteen hundred Indians remaining on the Tejon; about five hundred of these left for Tule river, including four hundred Owens River and one hundred Tejon, which increased the number at Tule river to about eight hundred, there being three hundred living there at the time. Probably fifty Indians have come in from Owen's river since I have been in charge; the balance of those brought from there, say four or five hundred, have returned to their old haunts at Owen's river, and there has been a wastage of fifty, probably, since the removal from Tejon.

The Indians have always appeared well contented with their condition. It requires some exertion to obtain the requisite amount of work, but it is performed faithfully and well under proper training. These Indians are good teamsters and plough-boys, and can perform all the labor of raising a crop. There has never been any system of education among them, if you except the knowledge of the use of farming implements; no religious instruction has ever been imparted; the government of the children is left entirely with the mothers.

During my labors on the Tejon reserve Theodore Boschulte was supervisor and John P. H. Wentworth superintendent of Indian affairs for the southern district of California. The Indians were well supplied with clothing and food, there being usually about one distribution of the former every year. Crops of wheat and barley were raised upon the Tejon while I was there, which were issued to the Indians; there was also some stock belonging to this reserve, consisting of mules, horses, and cattle, the latter being killed and issued to the Indians. Wheat, barley, corn, beans, pumpkins, sweet potatoes, and all vegetables which grow to good advantage are raised upon the Tule River farm, which farm is leased from Thomas P. Madden, of San Francisco, who holds the same under a United States patent.

I visited the Owen's River Indians about the middle of November, 1864; was there about ten days. There is no reservation in the Owen's River valley, but the few Indians I saw appeared as well contented, apparently, as those at Tule. I was sent there by Superintendent Austin Wiley, to supply food to these Indians, and thereby prevent threatened hostilities; found but twenty-five Indians, and ascertained they had been stampeded by the threats of the settlers in the valley. The Indians were raising grass-nuts, (which is a prominent article of their food,) by irrigation.

At the time the Tejon was abandoned, Alexander Godey was acting as the agent of E. F. Beale, a former superintendent of Indian affairs. Godey was camped on the reserve herding Beale's sheep; he was openly acting as the agent of Beale for the six months previous, serving notices in Beale's name, &c. I was at the time he was acting as such agent employed at the Tejon and Tule River reserves, J. P. H. Wentworth being superintendent at that time. For at least three months of the six above mentioned, Godey was acting also as agent of the Tejon reserve. Theodore Boschulte was in charge at the time of tht abandonment of the Tejon reserve. I came to Tule river in November, 1862; there was no fencing at this time upon the farm; has since been temporarily fenced by government, with willows; no substantial improvements are being made upon the farm, as the farm is leased. The Indians here are living in brush and tule huts. About one thousand acres are enclosed by fence; a portion of that has been appropriated by John D. Tyler, say about seventy acres; he was formerly an employé on the reserve, and had assisted in the making of a portion of this fencing. Tyler entered this seventy acres in January, 1864, being at the time in government employ. The land at the time he entered it was planted to a crop, and he had been in the employ of government three months before he entered it. One crop had been harvested since it was fenced; he has cut a crop of wheat and barley from this ground, not of his own planting, but a volunteer crop, from a crop planted by government. Tyler is now upon these premises, and holds it on the ground of its being government land, and not on the Madden farm. No consent was ever given to Tyler from the Indian department to go upon this land, or to harvest this crop, heretofore spoken of. He has now a house upon this land, and is living there with his family; was living there in December of 1864.

When Mr. Wentworth came up on his way from Tejon to San Francisco, about the first of October, 1863, he left a letter with me to take back to Boschulte, the supervisor, advising him to lease the house on the Tejon and remove to another, as the Indians were to be removed to Fort Tejon, but when I arrived at the reserve the Indians had been removed, and Boschulte had left for the fort. Fort Tejon is situated in Los Angeles county, about one hundred and twenty miles from Tule River farm, and is in the State of California. Owen's River valley, before mentioned, is in the county of Tulare, State of California.

GEO. L. HOFFMAN.

TULE RIVER FARM, *July* 14, 1865.

October 1, 1863, to April 1, 1864, 2 employés	$50	per month.
April 1, 1863, to May 25, 1864, 1 employé	50	"
May 25, 1863, to Sept. 1, 1864, 3 employés	50	"
Dec. 1, 1863, to July 15, 1865, 2 employés	50	"
Special agent	150	"

The above is a statement of the number of employés and the amount paid to them, as above specified, on Tule River farm, (Indian,) Tulare county, California.

GEO. L. HOFFMAN,
Special Indian Agent.

STATE OF CALIFORNIA, *County of Tulare:*

O. A. Wilcox, being duly sworn, deposes and says, that he has been employed at the Tule River farm since December, 1864; has lived in the vicinity since December, 1856, within about three miles of the reserve, which he had frequently visited. The Indians were first brought here in 1857; Ridley had then charge of the place, and it was occupied as a reserve at the time Madden located and took possession of the farm. The Indians were taken away to the Tejon some time in 1857, I think, in the fall of that year, and brought back in government teams in 1858. Vineyard had charge of the Tejon at this time, and Thomas J. Henley was superintendent of Indian affairs, and Madden was clerk for Henley. Ridley notified settlers not to settle here, stating that it was a government reserve, which notice was given before Madden located. Dorsey, the agent on the farm, planted about one hundred peach-trees and about five hundred grape-vines, and there are now at this time about one-half that number bearing fruit. The only permanent building on the farm was built by government.

O. A. WILCOX.

STATE OF CALIFORNIA *County of Tulare:*

T. P. Johnson, being duly sworn, deposes and says, that he resides at Tule river, about two miles from the reserve; has resided there about seven years; came there in 1857. Mr. Ridley had charge when I first came here, and told me he was acting as special agent for the government; at that time there were about three hundred Indians living on the farm. Dorsey succeeded Ridley as agent, either of which was in charge at the time Madden located on this land, which was then occupied by government as a reserve, and Indians were then cared for by the government upon it. At this time Colonel Vineyard, Thomas P. Madden, Dr. Hayes, and Colonel Mormon, were all employed in the Indian department, and they all aided in locating the farm for Madden.

T. P. JOHNSON.

STATE OF CALIFORNIA, *County of Tulare:*

Robert Daley, being duly sworn, says, that he resides at Tule river, Tulare county, California; resided there about three months, keeping a public house. He was in the military service of the United States from 1861 to 1864; about three and a half years as first lieutenant in the 2d cavalry, California volunteers. He was, during that service, on the Tejon reservation and at Owen's river, both in California; at Tejon nearly two months in 1863, and at Owen's river from the 1st of April to April 8, 1863.

Theodore Boschulte was supervisor in charge of the Tejon reservation. He (Daley) went to the Tejon about the 20th of July, with seven hundred and fifty Owen's River or Monache Indians, who had been brought from Owen's river. After remaining at Tejon a few days he picked out camps for the Indians on the reserve. The Indians were forbidden by Alexander Godey (who was agent for Mr. Beale) to cut brush with which to make their houses. He (Daley) waited upon Godey and forbid his disturbing or interfering with the Indians, as he was left in command with orders to keep the Indians upon the reservation. The next day Godey drove his stock of cattle in among the Indians and herded them in their camps; he then forced him (Godey) to remove his stock off the reservation.

Theodore Boschulte, supervisor on the Tejon reserve, was removed by John P. H. Wentworth, superintendent of Indian affairs, and Alexander Godey was appointed in his place while agent for Beale; and a telegram was sent to Boschulte by superintendent Wentworth to turn over the government property to Godey, the new appointee as supervisor; but deponent having possession of the property, would not turn it over, Boschulte being absent at that time. Godey came to deponent and told him if he would give him (Godey) possession of the property, he, deponent, could make $2,000 or $3,000 as well as not. Deponent declined having further conversation with him, and refused his offer. Deponent aided in bringing from Owen's river the seven hundred and fifty Indians that were taken to the Tejon reservation. The party in charge of the Indians left Owen's river with one thousand Indians; two hundred and fifty escaped en route to the Tejon. The attempt was made afterwards to remove the seven hundred and fifty Indians (Owen's River) to Fort Tejon, a distance of twenty miles, and at least two hundred and fifty of the seven hundred and fifty escaped. They were removed by Captain M. A. McLaughlin, then in the military service and in command of Fort Tejon.

R. DALEY.

STATE OF CALIFORNIA, *County of Tulare:*

Wm. B. Poer, being duly sworn, deposes and says, that he resides at Visalia, Tulare county, California; has resided in said county since August, 1856. He is acquainted with the Tule River Indian farm, and knows its location, and has known the tract of land ever since he has lived in the county. In the fall of 1856 this farm was used by the government as an Indian reservation. Alonzo Ridley was the first agent to his knowledge who had charge of this reservation under the government in the fall of 1856. Ridley brought the first Indians together on this reservation. Deponent's attention was called to the farm and what was done about it, from the fact that he and Thomas P. Johnson at one time attempted to pre-empt the land, and supposed they had done so, but one Thomas P. Madden got the start of them by covering the same with school warrants in advance of them. Mr. Madden was reputed to be employed in the Indian department of the government at the time he so located this land. Mr. Ridley, the agent, posted a written notice upon the premises that the tract was claimed as an Indian reservation. It was the general understanding among the people here in the vicinity of the reservation at the time Mr. Ridley posted this written notice, that it was claimed and held as an Indian reservation. This notice was given by Mr. Ridley, the agent, before Mr. Madden located the land or claimed it.

WM. B. POER.

Statement taken at San Francisco, California.

STATE OF CALIFORNIA, *County of San Francisco:*

Austin Wiley, late superintendent of Indian affairs for California, being duly sworn, deposeth and saith as follows:

The Indians along the border of the northern coast were peaceable, and inclined to be friendly to the whites, when settlements were first established among them. Along the Klamath and its tributaries as well as on the Trinity, Mad river, Eel river, and lining the entire coast from Point St. George to below Mendocino, they were very numerous.

A marked distinction existed between the Indians living on the coast and those inhabiting the mountains; the former being more indolent and improvident, while the latter possessed more of the bravery, cunning, and superstition peculiar to the savage of the northwest.

The mountain Indians subsisted largely on game, which of every variety was very abundant, and was killed with their bows and arrows, in the use of which they were very expert. In addition to this, they semi-annually built fish-dams across the various rivers and mountain streams, and caught immense quantities of salmon, which they smoked or dried and laid away for winter use. They also gathered acorns, roots, and certain grass-seed in large quantities, and in respect of food, as well as deerskins for clothing, and comfortable houses for shelter, were well provided for.

The Indians living on the coast, at the mouth of the rivers, and around Humboldt bay, subsisted principally upon muscles and fish, which they caught on the beach and in the rivers, as well as stranded whales, or whatever else in the shape of food presented itself, and required the least expenditure of labor in securing. They, too, gathered roots, seeds, and berries in considerable quantities, had comparatively comfortable houses, and in their lazy way evidently enjoyed life.

The burden of the labor among both mountain and coast Indans fell upon the squaws; they were depended upon to gather the firewood, to pound the acorns or seed, to provide a good supply of berries in their season, and to perform all the drudgery, while their lords and masters basked in the sun, or indulged in the favorite pastime of gambling.

The mountain Indians associate but little with those on the coast, and seldom, if ever, intermarry, seeming to consider themselves a superior class.

It is extremely difficult to convey an idea of the social divisions that exist among these strange beings. Unlike the tribes of the east, they are divided into small bands, who build rude houses on the banks of some river or mountain creek, and seem to live within themselves almost a separate people. In some instances these rancherias consist of only a few families, and in others several hundred souls are congregated. In the early days these different rancherias had chiefs, or heads, known as Mow-wee-mas, their influence being principally derived from their age, number of relatives and wealth, which consisted chiefly of white deerskins, canoes, the scalp of the red-headed woodpecker, and aliqua-chiek, (a hollow shell which is still known as Indian money.) Latterly, however, the young Indians, those that have grown up among the whites, have been the leaders, and still possess the power for good or harm.

Their associations have been as a general thing with the worst class of whites, and with their disposition to learn all that is bad, and their savage instincts to guide them in practicing what they have been taught, they have become a dangerous enemy.

The Indians living on the banks of a river generally take the name of the stream. When the Klamath, Trinity, Redwood or Mad River Indians are spoken of, the Indians living on the rivers of that name are designated, and not any particular tribe, for though united in a certain sense, they do not form a distinct tribe, each rancheria having its head and often being arrayed against another in quarrels and open fights. It is a remarkable fact that a separate and distinct language is spoken by the Indians on these different rivers, or on nearly all of them. The Indians on the Klamath river speak a different language from those on the Trinity, one of its tributaries. The Indians on Redwood creek, some twenty miles south, speak another; and those on Mad river yet another; so that but few of them are able to converse with one another, and at present they frequently make use of the English that each has picked up in communication among themselves.

The fact of this complete division and of there being no recognized head, either to the northern coast Indians as a body, or to the semi-united tribes on a river, renders it exceedingly difficult to treat with them, or to successfully colonize them on reservations.

When placed together they do not harmonize—retaining their petty divisions and being distrustful of one another.

They are naturally indolent and degraded in their minds and habits, though not devoid of a certain kind of intelligence. They are superstitious in the extreme, seeming to derive more of the little moral restraint they exhibit from this than any other source.

In 1851 and 1852, about two years after white men had first penetrated their country, signs of mistrust and discontent began to be made manifest among the mountain Indians. At this time they had no fire-arms and were unskilled in their use. As to the cause of the unfriendly feeling that now sprung up, it is difficult to speak positively, but doubtless to their association with the whites as packers and herdsmen, and the co-habitation of their squaws with unprincipled white men, may be traced the principal causes of the threatened hostilities.

In 1851 a man and boy were murdered between Trinidad and the Klamath river, and shortly after the family of a Mr. Blackburn, at Young's ferry, on the Klamath river, met with a like fate. These hostilities were confined to one rancheria, and were discountenanced by the other Indians along the river. The whites from these acts became satisfied that the Klamath Indians were not to be treated as though they were powerless for harm or void of Indian nature. Peace, however, was established, and with the exception of numerous personal collisions between individual white men and Indians, generally concerning squaws, and resulting in the killing of an Indian occasionally, no further trouble occurred until the winter of 1855.

By this time the Klamath and adjacent Indians had made considerable advancement in learning the use of fire-arms, and had procured a considerable number, as well as ammunition, principally in exchange for squaws. In December, 1855, they raised at several points along the Klamath simultaneously, and murdered seven men in one day.

Captain (now General) Judah was then stationed at Fort Humboldt, and repaired at once with his command to the scene of trouble. In the mean time two companies of volunteers had been raised for the occasion, and had severely chastised the Indians in several engagements. Some difficulty having occurred between the commanding officer of the regular troops and the volunteers, it was finally settled by both withdrawing from the field. S. G. Whipple was sent there as an agent by Superintendent Henley, and through his good judgment and discretion further bloodshed was avoided, and peace in that section restored He established a reservation on the Klamath river, which was carried on under various agents, until in the winter of 1861-'62 the improvements were washed away and most of the arable land destroyed by the severe freshet, which necessitated a removal. Smith river was then selected by Superintendent Hanson, and the government property, together with the Indians on the reservation, (except the Klamaths,) were removed to that point.

Since the outbreak in 1855 the Indians on the Klamath river have remained peaceable. A few individuals may have been engaged in the late war, but the majority have been quiet. They are the most numerous and powerful band in the northwestern portion of the State, and deserve more attention from the government than they have heretofore received They subsist themselves entirely, and do not lack for food. An annual distribution of clothing and a little tobacco (of which they are passionately fond) would give them much encouragement, and would be but an act of tardy justice on the part of the government.

In 1856 the Indians on Redwood creek, Upper Mad river, Grouse creek, and headwaters of Eel river, began to express bitter hostility, and now commenced a war that ere its close resulted in the loss of many valuable lives, the destruction of an immense amount of property, and the killing of a large number of Indians.

The trails leading from Humboldt bay to the various trading posts on the Trinity, Klamath, and Salmon rivers were waylaid, and many travellers and packers murdered. Train were robbed, and depredations were committed on every hand. Parties of citizens were raised occasionally when a fresh murder had been committed, and many of the offending Indians met with a summary punishment. The fiendish Diggers excited the ungovernable passions of the whites by the horrible mutilation of the bodies of their victims, and they retaliated on the Indians by the commission of acts that disgraced humanity—murdering women and children in some instances, and killing Indians wherever found, guilty or not. During this time a force of United States troops, under command of Major Raines, was stationed at Fort Humboldt, but for want of concert of action between the troops and settlers nothing was done by the military authorities toward the suppression of these hostilities. Matters went on from bad to worse, until in 1858, in response to frequent petitions from the people, Governor Weller called out a company of volunteers to serve for three months. This company was commanded by Captain Messic, and labored hard while in service; they, however, gained but little advantage over the Indians, as the natives resorted to their usual mode of warfare—waylay, shoot and run.

Before the close of his campaign Captain Messic succeeded in taking quite a number of prisoners, and finally induced a large number of Indians to come in. These numbered in all some nine hundred, and were taken to the Mendocino reservation, by water, by order of the superintendent, and against the earnest protest of the people of Humboldt, who were well aware that by such a course the fruits of the campaign would be entirely lost. These Indians remained to enjoy the care and protection of the government but a very short time. Nearly all of them found their way back to their old homes more embittered and hostile than ever before. But fifty of these prisoners now remain on the reservation; a small portion of the remainder are among those now at Hoopa reservation, but the majority of them have passed away during the sanguinary war lately brought to a close.

The peace that succeeded the removal of the prisoners taken in the Messic campaign was of short duration, and when war again commenced, it was waged with revengeful desperation on the part of the Indians, all of the tribes of the north participating excepting the Klamaths and the Indians on Lower Mad and Eel rivers.

The Hoopas, second in number and strength to the Klamaths, and the shrewdest and bravest as well as best armed of any of the tribes, pretended to be friendly to the whites, but evidently furnished ammunition and harbored the Indians who were at war. Many white men were killed, the Indians seeming bent on the extermination of all the settlers, killing their best friends as soon as their worst enemies. The stock of the settlers was shot down in malicious mischief, their houses burned, and the country laid waste. The deeds of the whites in retaliation were scarcely less inhuman—a war of extermination being openly talked of, which, although it was opposed by all the more respectable and influential citizens, culminated on the 3d of April, 1859, in the disgraceful massacre on Indian island of about 150 Indians, principally women and children. This barbarous proceeding so incensed the authorities that the settlers of that section were left almost to the mercy of the Indians, being principally dependent on their own exertions for protection.

The Indians at the mouth of Mad river were about this time removed to the Klamath reservation by Sub-Agent D. E. Buell; this course being taken more for their protection than from any fear entertained of their committing any depredations, as they had always remained peaceful and shown themselves the friends of the whites. The most of them are yet on the Smith River reservation, being comparatively comfortably provided for.

From 1859 to 1861 disturbances were continually occurring, depredations being committed by the Indians, and mountain Indians being killed by the whites wherever found. Two companies of volunteers at different times made short campaigns against the Indians, but gained no material advantage over them. In 1861 General Wright sent a full regiment of troops (the 2d infantry, California volunteers) to the Humboldt military district, and the citizens were led to hope that the war would be brought to a close.

The campaign inaugurated by Colonel Lippitt proved, generally speaking, a failure. Quite a number of prisoners were taken in the Eel river country, and in all a considerable number of Indians were killed, but the extent and daring of hostilities increased rather than diminished. Men were murdered and houses burned under the very eyes of the troops, and the citizens of such towns as Arcata were shot down in daylight while pursuing their customary avocations.

After more than a year of unsuccessful and expensive operations this regiment was relieved by a battalion of mountaineers, consisting of six companies of infantry, raised principally in the counties suffering from the war, and commanded by Lieutenant Colonel S. G. Whipple. The Hoopa Indians about this time openly took the field, and were the leading spirits among the savages in the bloody hostilities that ensued. All the settlers from the mountains were driven in and their improvements burned. The vast herds of stock that ranged on the fine grazing land back from the coast were swept away. Their depredations extended to the Salmon river and into the adjoining county of Trinity. The mail-carrier on the route to Weaverville was killed, and also the postmaster at Albeville. Travel was entirely stopped, except at night, or under guard of a heavy escort. The business interests of the country were well-nigh destroyed, and gloom supplanted the peace and prosperity that had previously rendered that district among the most attractive in the State.

The war was carried on with varying success for nearly two years, many Indians falling before the well-directed blows of the troops, while they in turn suffered not a little. A large number of prisoners were taken in the southern portion of Humboldt and in Mendocino county, and the hostile Indians in that region effectually suppressed. The Hoopa, Redwood, South Fork, and Grouse Creek bands were the remaining foe, and it was found impossible to take them prisoners. Skilled in the use of arms, naturally intelligent, and perfectly at home in the rough country they roamed over, it would have been the work of years to have thoroughly subdued them by the force of arms alone—even by the unmerciful policy of extermination, which it would have been necessary to resort to. They suffered much during the winter of 1863, and were finally induced to come into Hoopa valley and be fed by the military authorities as a condition of peace, but persistently refused to surrender their arms, and would not consent to be removed to any reservation then established. In this condition I found them in August, 1864, and through the co-operation of the military authorities arranged the terms of a permanent peace, the main conditions of which were a surrender of their arms and a return to peace on their part, and the establishment of the Hoopa reservation on the part of the government.

Since terms were entered into with these Indians, so far as I know, the Indians have kept their portion of the agreement in good faith, and I feel confident that if the promise which has been made them (that they shall be subsisted from their own labor in Hoopa valley) is kept, no further trouble with them need be apprehended. They should be made to feel that the valley belongs to them, and that the government feels an interest in their welfare, and will protect them in their rights. I would recommend that no other Indians be placed on that reservation, and that all surplus produce that can be raised be disposed of for their benefit or given to the Klamaths. By this means they will be satisfied and able to make their own living in their own way, which is what they want. They are inclined to be peaceable, and there is no danger of trouble with them, unles it be inaugurated by bad white men, which can be best prevented by retaining them in their present isolated position, and managing them with reason and firmness.

There are still remaining on the peninsula at Humboldt Point several hundred Indian prisoners, taken during the late war, who are subsisted principally by the military authorities. They have not been removed to any of the northern reservations on account of the strong feeling against such a course among the people of that section, who fear they will return to their old homes and renew disturbances, a feeling which to a great extent I shared in. It had been my intention, in case I was obliged to make some disposition of them, and was refused permission to take them south, to remove them late in the fall—a few to Smith river, and the remainder to Round valley.

The few Indians remaining in the mountains at the headwaters of Eel river, I believe, can be induced to come into Round valley, upon being satisfied of protection and subsistence. This done, and the arrangements commenced strictly carried out, I firmly believe Indian troubles in the Humboldt military district will be heard of no more.

The Indians of the north have been greatly decimated by the various wars, and are comparatively powerless. They have been a wronged and suffering race, and humanity and justice demand that the government do all in its power to ameliorate their condition and protect them in their declining days.

AUSTIN WILEY.

Statements taken at Mendocino station, California, 24th and 25th July, 1865.

STATE OF CALIFORNIA, *County of Mendocino:*

E. J. Whipple, being duly sworn, says, he resides at the Mendocino station of the Nome Cult reservation, and is in charge of the stations under the Indian department of the government of the United States, and has been in the employ of the government in the Indian department since January, 1857—the first six months at Noyo, which was then the headquarters of the Mendocino reservation, about ten miles from this station. This station is on what was once the Mendocino reservation, upon the northern or northwestern part of it. The remainder of the time at this point. This place is also called and familiarly known as the Bedahto station. There are about five hundred Indians at this station, or that belong here; some of this number are temporarily absent now. There are from 1,200 to 1,500 acres here under enclosure, a portion of which is cultivated wholly by the Indians. The principal products are barley, oats, peas, potatoes, turnips, carrots, and beets. Some cows, horses, and oxen, are also kept. The Indians appear willing to labor. Last year, about six months, a Catholic priest was on this reservation, his time being divided between this station and Round valley, giving instructions to the Indians; he was under government employ. With this exception there has been no instruction, either religious or moral, or of any kind, except to labor, to my knowledge, since I have been in government employ. There have been no schools for the children; all care of them has been left to their parents. For the last three or four years, except the last year, there have been four employés beside the agent. Previous to that, probably there were three times as many employes for four or five years, to my knowledge. Formerly there were physician, clerk, blacksmith, carpenter, and fisherman employed regularly, who, for the last three or four years, have not been employed only at intervals; besides there were more laborers employed formerly. I have reference to the employés on the Mendocino reservation, which in the last year was reduced to the Mendocino station, and made a part of the Nome-Cult reservation, which is principally at Round valley, in this county. S. J. Henley was superintendent when I was first employed; J. Y. McDuffie succeeded Henley; John A. Driebelbis succeeded McDuffie; George M. Hanson succeeded Driebelbis; E. Steele succeeded Hanson; Austin Wiley succeeded Steele, and Charles Maltby succeeded Wiley, and is now the superintendent. I should think the number of Indians up to 1860 on the Mendocino reservation would average 1,500. Since then there have not been more than there are now, except a few months—during Mr. Hanson's superintendency—there were four or five hundred more Indians than now.

I know the tract of land called the Cully-Bool, situate upon the south bank of the Noyo river at its mouth. There were enclosed by government from two hundred to two hundred and fifty acres of land. I superintended the hauling of the rails to fence it. There was a house and some fence on the land when the government entered upon it. Government put from 5,000 to 7,000 rails and 1,500 posts, about that number, into the fence built upon Cully-Bool station. It was built in the spring of 1857. A crop on the ground, and improvements on the place, were purchased in the fall of 1856 of one William Davis by Henley, the superintendent of Indian affairs, for the government, so it was generally understood. It was occupied as government property under Henley's administration. John Simpson had charge of the station when I first came on to the reservation. I know William H. Ray; he was for a time employed on the reservation; a part of the time fisherman at the Noyo, and part of the time was in charge of Cully-Bool station; I should think in charge of the station about two years, cultivating the ground and farming. While in charge of the station he was discharged from government service, and, without removing, held possession of Cully-Bool station and claimed the premises, with the improvements, but offered to government the privilege to remove the improvements, fences, &c., if so desired. Cully-Bool station was much better land than the land occupied north of the Noyo for reservation purposes. Government built a barn, a frame barn, and log potato-house upon this station, beside the fence spoken of. I should think the improvements, fences, and buildings put upon the Cully-Bool station by government cost, say, eight hundred dollars, and were worth that sum. Mr. Ray left the station for a time, and Robert Burns took possession, or was placed in possession by the agent for the government. Ray commenced suit against Burns and recovered the possession, and afterwards sold the premises to Joseph Hardy, who still has the possession.

The Mendocino reservation includes twenty-five thousand acres of land, extending from the south bank of the Noyo river to one mile north of the mouth of Ten Mile river. The first lands occupied by the government were on the north side of the Noyo, between it and Ten Mile river, which is to the north of the Noyo, and about ten miles from it. I should think fifteen hundred acres were enclosed at first, extending from the Noyo north along the coast, and running back from the ocean, with post-and-rail fence; and on the ground enclosed were erected fine dwelling-houses, two barns, a carpenter and blacksmith shop, both under one roof. I think, on reflection, that but three dwellings were erected by government; that two of them were upon the ground when located as a reservation. That portion of the reservation was occupied up to 1864. There are no Indians living upon those premises, neither is any one occupying them for the government now. The ground is not cultivated, and the buildings are vacant. I should think the improvements there in fences and buildings named, cost from $5,000 to $6,000.

The Bedahto station, where we now are, is on the northern portion of the Mendocino reservation, between Ten Mile river and the northern boundary of the reservation, and includes all on the north side of the south fork of Ten Mile river, and has enclosed from 1,200 to 1,500 acres of land—much of it natural fence; probably 10,000 rails and posts on the premises in fence, to enclose the amount of land named. The buildings are a dwelling, barn, and smoke-house—frame buildings. The improvements at this station, fences and buildings named, cost, say $25,000. The estimates made are in gold coin. There are about twenty head of horses and cattle belonging to government at this station, and some farming utensils to cultivate the premises enclosed. Clothing and other supplies, to a limited extent, have been brought to the reservation to be distributed to the Indians annually. I think, for the year 1860, three-fourths of the indebtedness that accrued in carrying on the Mendocino reservation is still due from the government to the employés, and those who furnished supplies. I know the government is indebted yet for a large amount, but the precise amount I cannot say. The failure of government to pay in 1860 was through the death of H. L Ford, the disbursing agent of the reservation. The money had been paid to him for disbursement, but he died before the money was disbursed, and government stopped its disbursement and took possession of it. Under Driebelbis, I think, in 1861, a large amount of indebtedness accrued against government that has never been paid. Driebelbis received money from the government to liquidate the indebtedness; what he did with the money I do not know, but he did not pay the debts. I think during Driebelbis's administration of Indian affairs there were no supplies, neither clothing nor anything else, brought to the Mendocino reservation. There were a few purchases made by the supervisor for supplies, and the debts made for such purchases are still unpaid. The employés were only partially paid in 1861; a large portion of their pay is still due. Under Hanson, superintendent, there is one quarter's pay due employés, and a large amount of indebtedness for supplies. E. Steele, during his administration of Indian affairs, paid everything promptly upon the Mendocino reservation. I am the only employé now at this station, and am under the agent of the Nome-Cult reservation; my pay is $50 per month.

I think government paid about eight hundred dollars for the improvements and crop on Cully-Bool station, and Davis gave possession to government. This amount was paid to Davis, who held it previous to government going into possession.

E. J. WHIPPLE.

STATE OF CALIFORNIA, *County of Mendocino:*

W. H. Ray, being duly sworn, deposes and says: I reside in Humboldt county, State of California, and was once in the employ of the Indian department of the government on the Mendocino reservation; time, from fall of 1856 till some time in 1861. I was employed most of the time at Noyo river, southern part of the reservation, and had charge of the fishing station. I was employed by Capt. H. L. Ford, who was acting as sub-agent under Col. Henley, the then superintendent of Indian affairs.

On the south bank of the Noyo river there was enclosed a field of about two hundred and forty acres, by direction of Capt. Ford, the sub-agent. I think said field was enclosed in the year 1857, and crops raised on it by the department for three or four years. In the year 1859, Capt. Ford told me that this enclosure did not belong to the reservation; that the southern boundary of the reservation only came to the southern bank of the Noyo river. The two hundred and forty acres was high land—never overflowed by the river or the ocean. In 1861, I think, I filed a possessory claim to, or pre-empted and took possession of, this tract as government land. I had possession about six months, then left it for a while, and during my absence Capt. Smith, supervisor under Mr. Hanson, the then superintendent, placed a Mr. Burns, one of the employés of the Indian department, in possession. I then commenced suit against Mr. Burns, the employé, in the district court of the State, and regained possession, and the Indian department has not had possession since. During the time I was in the employ of the Indian department there were three different superintendents, Col. Henley, J. Y. McDuffie, and J. A. Driebelbis. McDuffie and Driebelbis did not pay me for the services I rendered the department within about nine hundred dollars of the amount due me. The money due me under McDuffie was $666 66. This indebtedness had all accrued before I took the land in possession. For the indebtedness which accrued under McDuffie I forwarded proper vouchers to the department at Washington. I have never received any pay from the department on those vouchers forwarded. At the time I took possession of this tract of land I should think there was about three-fourths of a mile of redwood fence upon it, with house and barn, all placed there by the government. There had been a crop raised on the place the year I pre-empted the land, but no employé was residing upon the premises at the time I filed my pre-emption claim. I am not in possession of the place now; I held possession about three years, and then sold out to Capt. Joseph Hardee. I received $2,000 for it. I did not put on any new buildings during my possession; I added to the fence on the place about 2,100 rails. There was no understanding between myself and the sub-agent concerning my taking possession of the premises. I was not an employé of the government at the time I filed my pre-emption claim to the above-mentioned land. There was one other time, previous to the time of my pre-emption, in which there was no employé of the government residing on the premises.

W. H. RAY.

STATE OF CALIFORNIA, *County of Mendocino:*

James Townsend, being duly sworn, deposes and says: I reside at Noyo River, Big River township, county of Mendocino; I have resided there since October, 1861, I think. I am agent of the Noyo mill; I have never been in the employ of the government. The mill, I think, was built in the year 1858; it was built by A. W. McPherson. The dwellings there were also erected by him. McPherson and Wetherbee are now the owners of the property. Col. Henley was in charge of the Indian department at the time the mill was built. The mill and buildings are erected on the north side and north bank of the Noyo river. The mill is used for manufacturing lumber. McPherson was not in the employ of the government. I understand that McPherson and Henley arranged in reference to the building of the mill, Henley giving permission to erect the mill and other buildings there. I do not know that any consideration was given to any one for the privilege to build the mill there.

JAMES TOWNSEND.

STATE OF CALIFORNIA, *County of Mendocino:*

F. E. Warren, being sworn, says: I reside at the Noyo, Big River township, Mendocino county. I was in the employ of the Indian department of the government about three years at the Nome-Lackee, Tejon, and Mendocino reservations; part of the time as teamster and part as overseer in charge of a station. I was engaged about three months at Nome-Lackee, about nine at Tejon, and the balance of the time at Mendocino. I was at Nome-Lackee during the winter of 1854-'55. Capt. H. L. Ford was in charge at the time. I went directly from there to the Tejon reservation, which was under charge of Alonzo Ridley. Capt. Ford had also charge of Mendocino reservation. There were between five and six hundred Indians at Tejon, and at one time, during the winter of 1856, about two thousand at the Mendocino reservation. At Nome-Lackee they had just put in a large crop; I did not remain till it was harvested. At Tejon there was a large quantity of wheat on hand of the previous year's crop. I helped to harvest the crop of the year that I was there; it was a light one. The wheat they had on hand they issued to the Indians. They put in crops on the Mendocino reservation, near Fort Bragg, while I was there. I believe there were raised three crops; they were not very good ones. The crops raised on the Cully-Bool station were good. Cully-Bool station was on the south side of the Noyo river, bounded west and north by the ocean and river. It was fenced by the government. I had charge there at the time part of the fence was built. I should think about ten thousand rails were put into fence on the Cully-Bool station. I built the barn while there in employ of the government, and the house and a crop on the ground were bought together. A man by the name of Davis was on the land, and claimed it; government bought the house and crop of Davis and he gave up the possession to the government, and several crops were raised there after the above purchase. I should think there were about two hundred acres in the premises given up to the government on the Cully-Bool station. A man by the name of Wm. Ray was in charge of this station under the government, being an employé. He continued in possession, and held it against the government. Ray sold the land to a Capt. Hardy, who still has the land in possession. Col. Henley made the purchase of Davis, and obtained possession of the premises. I think that all the title Ray had was a possessory title.

F. E. WARREN.

Statements taken at Nome Cult or Round Valley reservation, July 27, 28, *and* 29, 1865.

STATE OF CALIFORNIA, *County of Mendocino, ss:*

Capt. B. L. Fairfield, being sworn, says: I am agent on the Nome-Cult reservation, in Round valley, Mendocino county, State of California, and have been about two months. I have been in the employ of the Indian department of the government here since June, 1864, except about one month. W. P. Melendy was agent here at the time I came. E. Steele was superintendent of Indian affairs of the northern district of the State. Austen Wiley succeeded Mr. Steele, and became superintendent for the whole the 18th of June, 1864. Charles Maltby succeeded Mr. Wiley, as I am informed, about the 5th of May, 1865. I was discharged the 5th day of April, 1865, and came back and became agent soon after Mr. Maltby took charge or became superintendent.

The reservation has under enclosure about twenty-seven hundred (2,700) acres of land. The fence is known as Virginia, or rail, fence, and is an excellent fence. This year we have over three hundred acres of wheat on the reservation; one hundred acres of barley, yielding one thousand seventeen (1,017) bushels; seventy-five acres of oats; one hundred and eighty acres of corn, which, from present appearances, will yield at least three thousand (3,000) bushels; and ninety acres of garden vegetables. We have about four thousand bushels of last year's wheat on hand, and three hundred bushels of corn of last year's crop. The wheat raised upon the reservation this year will amount to at least five thousand (5,000) bushels, which, with last year's wheat, amounts to nine thousand (9,000) bushels. We have cut on the reservation at least one hundred and seventy-five tons of hay. We have under control here three hundred and seventy head of cattle of all grades, besides others at large; how many of the latter I cannot tell. We have two hundred and seventy hogs of all sizes, eighteen mules, and twenty horses.

Mr. Wiley hired the Hotaling farm, so-called, which has been occupied by the Indian department the last year, or part of it. The year will not be up until the first day of November next. On this farm we will cut, probably, about one hundred acres of grain of all kinds. We have cut some hay, I should say about fifty tons, on the Hotaling farm. This is all we get from this farm except the pasturing.

I should think there are from nine hundred to one thousand (900 to 1,000) Indians on the reservation, of all ages and sexes. They go and come. They will go out among the farmers and work for awhile and return; they will go out and wander among the mountains for a season and return, and often more will return than go away; new ones come in with those that go out.

Of the twenty-seven hundred acres of land enclosed on the reservation, at least nine hundred acres in addition to what has been cultivated the last year could have been cultivated as well and as easily as what has been cultivated, and would have been as productive. It might have required a little more labor of teams and tools to have cultivated it. The rent paid for the Hotaling farm, and labor bestowed in its cultivation, have been a total loss. The same labor put upon the reservation, upon land unoccupied there, would have been far more productive, besides the improvement it would have been to the reservation. The land upon the farm rented is not near as good as land unimproved upon the reservation and under enclosure. The crops raised upon the farm rented are not near as good as the crops raised upon the reservation.

J. W. B. Yocom was the agent next before me; he resided in a house on the Hotaling farm, or the farm rented. I reside in a house on the reservation. Mr. Yocom left the valley and went into Humboldt county, this State, soon after I became agent. From the house on the Hotaling farm to the house at the station on the reservation, where I reside, is a little over two miles. J. G. Short, one of the employés in the Indian department, is living in the Hotaling house with his family. I sent him there, under instructions from Mr. Maltby, superintendent, from a house on the reservation, where he was living, to keep possession until the lease should expire, first of November next.

During Mr. Wiley's superintendency clothing was furnished sufficient to clothe twenty-five to thirty Indians, and about two hundred pairs of shoddy blankets, a very miserable article. There is some military clothing—a few pairs of pants, a few coats, and some capes—turned over by General McDowell. We have not near enough clothing to clothe all the Indians. Many of the Indians labor without any clothing at all. Some of the Indians manage to get clothing independent of the Indian department. The Indians are industrious, and work readily and willingly. During the time of seeding and harvesting the Indians work more hours each day than white people, as a general rule. With proper care, attention, and management this reservation could be made self-sustaining in a short time.

There are parts of several tribes of Indians now upon this reservation. The Ukie Indians, natives of this valley, between three hundred and four hundred in number; the Wilakies are the mountain Indians, from the mountains surrounding the valley; the Sacramento Valley Indians, and the Pitt River Indians. No two tribes speak the same language. One tribe has no quarrel or difficulty with another, but live peaceably together.

No attention has been given by the department to instructing the Indians, except in common labor. There has been no school for the Indian children, nor any religious instruction. The children have been left entirely with their parents, and subject to their management and control. The Indians live in houses made of slabs split from oak logs. There have been no substantial buildings erected for the Indians to live in. There are two stations upon the reservation, and at the two stations some thirteen log buildings, which, with certain repairs, can nearly all be made suitable for the purposes intended.

After the Hotaling farm was rented by the Indian department, great improvement in building fences and making gates, &c., was made upon that farm under Yocom's agency. No improvements in fences were made on the reservation after the Hotaling farm was rented. There were many rails split out on the reservation after the Hotaling farm was rented, but they were most of them hauled to the Hotaling farm, and laid into fences there, or taken to Captain Douglas, at Fort Wright, situated in the valley.

The land occupied by settlers in the valley is generally by possession only; no other title is pretended to be had by most of them.

There is a piece of land on the reservation, about fifteen hundred (1,500) acres, that was once enclosed, but is not now, the fence having gone to decay. We wish to enclose it for pasturage and other uses, but several parties, Eberle and others, have taken up claims upon it. It is some of the best lands on the reservation.

B. L. FAIRFIELD.

STATE OF CALIFORNIA, *County of Mendocino, ss:*

W. H. Johnston, being sworn, says: I reside in Round valley, Mendocino county, State of California; I have resided here permanently since 1861; I have been here often from the time the first settlement was made, which was in 1856.

I am farming; my farm joins the reservation on the south. I purchased my improvements of Mr. Witt. Mr. Witt is one of the oldest settlers.

I have been employed on the reservation about one and a half year; commenced in March, 1863, and continued until May, 1864, then from September last to first January following. My business was farming, building fence, blacksmithing—all kinds of work I was put to. I was overseeing the Indians, showing them how to work, and what to do. The Indians worked as readily and willingly as white people generally.

It will be two years next month since the Indians have had any clothing of consequence issued to them by the department. Mr. Hanson issued the last clothing of any amount. Most of the Indians that have clothing get it independent of the department. It is said they get clothing by prostitution of their females with the whites. Many of the Indians work on the reservation nearly or quite naked.

Mr. Wiley has been in the valley twice while superintendent: first, when he received the property; second, when he rented the Hotaling farm. Mr. Wiley's excuse for hiring the farm was, that he thought the reservation would be too wet to raise a crop. The truth is, the reservation (most of it) will raise a better crop in wet or dry weather than the Hotaling farm. There was, in my opinion, no honest excuse for hiring the Hotaling farm. The reservation would raise an abundance for all the Indians there were on it last year, and all that are on it this year.

G. W. B. Yocom was agent under Mr. Wiley, superintendent. Yocom had hogs belonging to the reservation on the Hotaling farm, and marked them differently from the reservation mark; and reservation hogs under Yocom's management disappeared mysteriously. Wiley told Yocom to mark the hogs differently from reservation mark. Yocom moved into a house on the Hotaling farm soon after it was rented. From house on Hotaling farm to station on reservation is about two miles. I think there is under enclosure in the Hotaling farm at least two sections or twelve hundred and eighty acres of land.

W. H. JOHNSTON.

STATE OF CALIFORNIA, *County of Mendocino, ss:*

Martin Corbett, being sworn, says: I reside in Round valley, Mendocino county, State of California, and have resided here since July, 1857; T. J. Henley was superintendent of Indian affairs, and S. P. Storms was agent. When I came into the valley Mr. Storms, the agent, was living at the station on the reservation, about two miles from the house on the Hotaling farm. Storms was agent a year or more after I came into the valley. The reservation was located in 1856. Storms built the house on the Hotaling farm. Henley and Storms were reputed to be the owners of that farm at that time. I should think there were over one thousand acres of land under enclosure on the Hotaling farm.

I have land in the valley under enclosure—three hundred and twenty acres of land. My land is adjoining the reservation on the south side. I am on section 36, south half. The north half is enclosed in the reservation. I have been on this land ever since I came into the valley in 1857. Some fence was built and some houses on the reservation in the fall of 1857. I never entered the land I occupy; I simply went upon it and fenced, and have continued to occupy and cultivate the land.

I never saw a notice from Henley, as superintendent, reserving lands for reservation purposes. I saw a notice that J. Y. McDuffie, the superintendent that succeeded Henley, posted. I saw the notice immediately after McDuffie became superintendent.

MARTIN CORBETT.

STATE OF CALIFORNIA, *County of Mendocino, ss:*

Captain C. D. Douglas, being sworn, says: I am a captain in the second infantry, California volunteers, and have under my command a company stationed in Round valley,

Mendocino county and State of California. I have been stationed in the valley since December, 1862.

While travelling in company with Lawrence Batail, between Round valley and Ukiah city, in May, 1863, in conversation about Indian matters in Round valley, he stated that he was an employé on the reservation under Colonel Henley as superintendent, and S. P. Storms as agent, and that the house and barn and all the improvements upon the Storms place were made by the white employés and the Indians from the reservation, and that material, such as windows, nails, locks, &c., for the house, nails for barn, &c., were taken from the reservation; that he understood the lumber used in building the barn and house was reservation lumber, procured for the purpose of building granaries on the reservation, and that the cost of the house and barn were understood to be about five thousand ($5,000) dollars.

Some two or three weeks after the above conversation, I met, in San Francisco, S. P. Storms, who had been agent of Indian affairs at Nome-Cult or Round Valley reservation, and repeated to him the above conversation, which I had had with Lawrence Batail, which he neither denied nor acknowledged; I then asked him if the place had actually cost him five thousand ($5,000) dollars; he answered that it did not cost him five thousand ($5,000) dollars, but it did cost five thousand ($5,000) dollars; I then asked him who paid for the building of the barn, house, and other improvements on the place; he answered that the party who did pay for it was able to stand it; I asked him if Colonel Henley had any share in or claim on the place; he answered that it was so understood.

The house, barn, and improvements spoken of above are the same, situated on the Hotaling farm, so called, near the reservation, and is under rent this year by the Indian department, I am informed. J. G. Short, one of the employés on the reservation, is living in the house with his family.

C. D. DOUGLAS,
Captain 2d Infantry, California Volunteers.

STATE OF CALIFORNIA, *County of Mendocino, ss:*

Charles H. Eberle, being sworn, says: I reside in Round valley, Mendocino county, State of California, and have resided here since the summer of 1857; Thomas J. Henley was superintendent of Indian affairs then, Vincent E. Geiger was agent of the Nome-Lackee reservation, and the Nome-Cult reservation was then a detached farm or post of the Nome-Lackee reservation. S. P. Storms had charge of the Nome-Cult farm or post at that time. At the time I came here I should think there were less than one hundred Indians on the reservation of the Nevada tribe. The Indian department commenced in 1856 in the valley. Charles H. Bourne and S. P. Storms together located what is now familiarly known as the Hotaling place or farm in 1856. There were some buildings on the reservation when I came in 1857. The present house on the Hotaling farm was partly built when I came, but was not finished and occupied until 1858. Bourne and Storms occupied another house, now vacant on the farm, until the present one was finished. They and some twenty employés occupied together. Bourne and Storms were ranching or stock-raising. The barn on the Hotaling farm was built after I came here, in 1858 or 1859; the lumber for the barn was whip-sawed out in the hills. Mr. Squires had charge of building the barn. I think Mr. Devinney and Mr. Former helped to whip-saw the lumber for the barn. Storms employed Squires to come in from outside to build the barn. When I came in the employés were living in the mess-house on the reservation. It was difficult to tell who were employés, for everybody nearly ate there; it was the same at the Hotaling farm. I was in the employ of the Indian department about six months in 1858. I had charge of the pack train, and was going to and fro between this valley and Nome-Lackee. After I had been packing awhile with government mules, Storms put in some of their mules with the government mules, and ordered me to bring all freight, whether government freight, their freight, or freight of others. At Nome-Lackee the mules were all fed from government produce, and all the men had government provisions, and we drew double rations to provide for outsiders that fed upon us. I went to Tehama once with government mules, and brought in freight for Storms & Co. When Mr. Geiger found out how it was, he stopped me from carrying freight for Storms & Co. Henley, the superintendent, was a partner with Storms and Bourne. Whatever I receipted for to Geiger at Nome Lackee, I delivered at Nome-Cult reservation. Things were very much mixed; it was difficult to tell government property from property Storms, Bourne, and Henley claimed as their property. At the time of the Fraser river excitement one of the employés took away one of the government mules. There was but little fencing, and government and Storms & Co.'s cattle all run together.

Storms, Henley, and Bourne had a brand, "S. H. B.," as early as 1858. There was another brand, a big "G," and I have heard Storms claim all cattle that had the "G" brand on. I have seen cattle with "S. H. B." brand on. I have seen Storms & Co. mark cattle at rodeos with the "G." brand, and no other. Mr. Storms was gone from the valley much of the time; he was back and forward, and most of the time, when in the valley, stayed on the reservation. Bourne looked more particularly after Hotaling farm or stock there. I helped Bourne to drive in some cattle at one time, and after they got them here they put on the "G" brand. We drove them from Chard's, near Tehama, about sixty-five miles from here.

I am farming and stock-raising; I am occupying a place at the upper or north end of the valley. I have about one hundred and forty acres enclosed. I claim five hundred and sixty acres. I hold four hundred and forty acres by certificate from the State as swamp and overflowed land; I think it was surveyed in 1860; it was surveyed by the deputy of the county surveyor of Mendocino county. The four hundred and forty acres are on section 30, government survey. Eighty acres of the one hundred and twenty are on section 30, and the balance, or forty acres, on section 19, government survey. I hold the one hundred and twenty acres simply by occupancy. I have never cultivated any of the swamp and overflowed land, except some six to eight acres. There is a good deal of the land boggy and wet; there is very little of it wet now. I do not think a crop of wheat or other grain could be raised in the ordinary seasons. I do not know but a corn crop could be raised by putting it in late on portions of it. There was none of the land I have taken ever enclosed by government for reservation purposes. I purchased of a locater in 1858; he located in 1857; I went on to it to live in 1858; it is the land where I now live. Mr. Henley was superintendent when I went on to it.

C. H. EBERLE.

STATE OF CALIFORNIA, *County of Mendocino, ss:*

J. G. Short, being sworn, says: I reside in Round valley, in Mendocino county, State of California. I came here in 1861, and have resided here since then, except about one year I have been absent. I have been in the employ of the government in the Indian department while residing here. George M. Hanson was superintendent when I came here. There have been five different agents at this reservation since I came here—James Short, my father, W. P. Melendy, S. M. Farren, G. W. B. Yocom, and Captain B. L. Fairfield. I think there were some fifteen hundred Indians on the reservation when I came here; there were more than are now on the reservation. There was not near as much land enclosed on the reservation then as now. There were not as many buildings then as now. Some buildings have been erected since; I should think about one-fifth have been added. Many Indians have gone away—stole away; some have died. I think they are wasting away; more die than are born. We have no difficulty in keeping them to labor; they are industrious and do nearly all of the farm labor. White men are employed only as overseers, to show the Indians what to do and how to do it. I lived in a house on the reservation until about first June last; I then, under instructions from Captain Fairfield, moved into the house on the Hotaling farm near the reservation. The farm was hired by Mr. Wiley, superintendent, last year, and Mr. Yocom, the agent, lived in the house until a few days after I moved into it in June last. Mr. Wiley said he hired the Hotaling farm because he did not want to depend on the reservation in case of a wet season. My opinion is, that the Hotaling farm will not stand as much moisture, and produce a crop, as the land on the reservation. The reservation has generally produced better in wet seasons than the Hotaling farm. There is far more land on the reservation under enclosure, that has not been cultivated, than all the land cultivated on the Hotaling farm the past year by the Indian department, and better and more productive land. In my opinion, the department has lost much by occupying and cultivating the Hotaling farm, instead of cultivating the land on the reservation that has been idle. There is far more produce raised on the reservation on hand of old crop, and raised this year, than will be needed to sustain the Indians through the year, or until another crop is produced. Of grain raised on the reservation alone, I should think there was twice as much as would be needed to sustain the Indians we have now through the year. We have raised on the Hotaling farm nothing but grain and some hay that we have cut, and a few vegetables in the garden for family use. There has been considerable fence made and a great deal rebuilt by the Indian department on the Hotaling farm since we have occupied it; several new gates have been made. The farm was in no condition for use until a great deal of work was done in repairing and building fences. The rails used in building new fence and repairing of the old were made on the reservation by reservation hands, and drawn to the Hotaling farm by reservation teams. There has been little or nothing done on the fences upon the reservation the last year. Great attention seemed to be given by Wiley and Yocom to the Hotaling farm, and little or none to the reservation. There is a piece of land, from twelve hundred to fifteen hundred acres, belonging to the reservation, once under enclosure, a part of which is now claimed by Eberle and Bourne and Owen, and have some of it under enclosure. Mr. Yocom, while agent, told me they forbid his fencing the ground. The reservation fence once around this ground has been in part carried away, and part has decayed and fallen down. The land is open to common, except what Eberle and Owen and Bourne have enclosed. It is all excellent land, and nearly all is good land for cultivation.

J. G. SHORT.

STATE OF CALIFORNIA, *County of Mendocino, ss:*

Sanders Hornbrook, being sworn, says: I reside in Round valley, Mendocino county, State of California. I have resided here off and on ever since 1856. I drove stock here in 1856, and took up land in the valley that year. I put in crops here in 1857. I did not bring my family to reside permanently till 1859 or 1860, but have been here nearly all the time myself since I came first in 1856. My business has been stock-raising and farming. T. J. Henley was superintendent of Indian affairs, and S. P. Storms had charge of the reservation in this valley. In and around the valley were camped and lived in their wild way at least five thousand (5,000) Indians when I first came here; but few of them were on the reservation, probably from one hundred to two hundred. How many they fed I cannot say; they had but few provisions to feed them on. This reservation was then called the Nome-Cult or Round Valley farm or post. It was a part of the Nome-Lackee reservation, which reservation I think is fifty to fifty-five miles from here. Vincent E. Geiger was agent at Nome-Lackee reservation, and was seldom here. Storms lived on the reservation here while he was agent; after that he lived at the Hotaling place, which was known as the Storms, Henley, and Bourne ranch or farm. Bourne lived at the Hotaling place, and had charge while Storms was agent and lived on the reservation. The house and barn on the Hotaling place were built by Storms & Co.; they commenced building it in 1857, and it was two or three years before they finished it; the barn, I think, was built in 1858 or 1859.

I am occupying one hundred and sixty acres of land; my title is merely possession; the land is all enclosed and on section 7, township 22, range 12. The place I took up in 1857 I traded for the one I now occupy. My land is enclosed with rail and board fence. I have a little dwelling and shed, granary, corn-crib, and smoke-house on the premises; they are not extensive buildings, but answer the purpose.

I took up a claim in 1856, abandoned it, and took up another claim in 1857, which latter claim was the one I traded for the one I now occupy. Charles Bourne, the Bourne spoken of above, lived at the Hotaling place; had charge of it three years, more or less, and assisted in building the house and barn on the place spoken of. I saw a notice posted by J. Y. McDuffie, when he was superintendent, notifying people in the valley of the lands reserved here for Indian reservation; I think the notice was put up in 1859.

S. HORNBROOK.

STATE OF CALIFORNIA, *County of Mendocino, ss:*

D. M. Dorman, being sworn, says: I have resided for the most part since the spring of 1857 in Round valley, Mendocino county, State of California. My business has been stock-raising, farming, and lumber and flouring business. The mills are in the northwest part of the valley, in the edge of the valley, situate on a stream that comes into the valley, the mills being water-mills. My brother and myself are occupying a ranch in the valley besides the mill property. The mill property is on section 23, township 23, range 13. Myself and brother have three hundred and twenty acres of land on sections 1 and 12, lying in a body and all enclosed. We have had the place since 1859. We purchased merely the possession. It was not enclosed when we purchased. There was a house on each of the two claims. We have lived on, occupied, and cultivated this land since the spring of 1860. I have never been a regular employé on the reservation. I have known all the superintendents and agents of the Indian department that have had charge of the Nome-Cult reservation in this valley. I know Indians belonging to the reservation were employed on the Hotaling farm, so called, while Storms was agent. They were sometimes on the reservation and sometimes on the Hotaling farm. I mean by the Hotaling place or farm the place occupied by Storms, Henley, and Bourne, and is the place now occupied under rent by the Indian department. I think the house was built under the superintendence of Bourne, and the barn built under the superintendence of Storms after he left the reservation as agent. Storms claimed about twelve hundred acres at the Hotaling place; I have heard him say so. My judgment is that the distance from the Hotaling house to station on reservation is about two and one-half miles.

D. M. DORMAN.

STATE OF CALIFORNIA, *County of Mendocino ss:*

James H. Thomas, being sworn, says: I reside in Round valley, Mendocino county, State of California, and have resided here since 1856. My business has been ranching and farming. I have three hundred and twenty acres of land; about two hundred and eighty acres of it is enclosed. I took it up in 1858; I hold it by possession only; it lies in sections 11 and 12, all in one body. I was well acquainted with S. P. Storms, agent at one time of the Nome Cult-reservation in this valley, and knew T. J. Henley, the superintendent, but I knew very little of their business in connexion with the reservation—not enough to know whether well or badly conducted.

JAMES H. THOMAS.

STATE OF CALIFORNIA, *County of Mendocino, ss:*

Charles Kendrick, being sworn, says: I reside on the Nome-Cult reservation, in Round valley, Mendocino county, State of California, and have resided there about two years. I have been in the valley since the fall of 1860 or 1861; the balance of the time, which was the first part of the time, I lived and worked on the Hotaling farm, so called, and worked for S. P Storms, who had been agent on the reservation, and A. P. Hotaling. When I first went to work on the reservation, Dr. W. P. Melendy had charge; George M. Hanson was superintendent. The Indians were far better clothed while Hanson and Steele were superintendents than they have been since. Under Austin Wiley they had little or no clothing. The Hotaling farm was rented by Wiley for the Indian department. The agent, G. W. B. Yocom, lived there while he was agent, and one employé lived with him, and another employé resided with him a few weeks; I mean employés on the reservation. A great deal of fencing was done by Yocom on the Hotaling farm; a good many Indians were employed in putting up the fence; the carpenter was employed in making gates. A good many rails were split upon the reservation and hauled on to the Hotaling farm and put into fence by Yocom, and the Indians and teams from the reservation were used to haul hay to the military post in the valley, from the Hotaling place, in winter and spring of 1865. At least six new gates with posts were built by employés from the reservation on the Hotaling farm, after the department went into possession. All the time the Indian department has had possession of the Hotaling farm, a dozen head of horses and mules, and, I should think, fifteen head of cattle, belonging to Hotaling, have been on the place. I hauled from the reservation to Hotaling farm about one thousand bushels of corn—that amount when shelled—under orders from Mr. Wiley, superintendent, the larger part of which corn was fed out there to a large drove of hogs called Hotaling hogs; they were not reservation hogs. Twelve tons of hay—about that amount—were sold off from the reservation to quartermaster at Fort Wright, while Mr. Wiley was superintendent and Yocom agent. Eighty-five hogs were pastured on the stubble of the grain lands of reservation from September, 1864, to March, 1865, and fed in addition with grain amounting to one hundred and fourteen dollars and eighty cents ($114 80.) A Mr. Barnum had charge of the hogs here; they were not reservation hogs. Barnum resided on the reservation all winter, boarded and had horse kept, and was not employed on reservation. Ten thousand pounds of corn were sold to Chandler, a hog merchant, while Wiley was superintendent. About three hundred bushels of potatoes were sold from the reservation in fall of 1864 and winter of 1864-'65. A band of cattle belonging to Bourne and Owen were fed on the reservation in fall of 1864. They paid Yocom for their feed over one hundred and ten ($110) dollars.

CHARLES KENDRICK.

Statements taken at Hoopa Valley reservation, California, August 5, 1865.

STATE OF CALIFORNIA, *County of Klamath, ss:*

Robert L. Stockton, being sworn, says: I reside on Hoopa reservation, Klamath county, State of California, and have resided here since the 28th of November, 1864. Since that time I have been agent on this reservation for the Indian department.

There are about six hundred and fifty (650) Indians on this reservation. I have found no difficulty in getting the Indians to labor. They do all the labor on the reservation except the white employés, who are employed to show the Indians what to do and instruct them how to do. Some are apt to learn how to do farm work; others do not learn so readily. The males do the most of the farm labor; a few of the females work on the farm, but most of the time they are gathering wild seeds and acorns in the season of them.

With few exceptions, the Indians on this reservation have not been on any reservation under control of the Indian department until this valley was made such in 1864. Most of the Indians here are natives of this valley, and have always lived here and on the lands now being used for reservation purposes.

There are no schools for the children, and there has been no religious instruction imparted to the Indians up to this time. The children are subject to the control of their parents. There are from one hundred and seventy-five (175) to one hundred and ninety (190) children. The men and women are mostly clothed, the children are mostly naked. There was a distribution of clothing last winter. The following is the invoice of the goods sent to this reservation last January, while Mr. Wiley was superintendent, viz:

15 pairs 3-point blankets.
15 " 2½ " "
12 gross buttons.
50 pairs men's brogans.
688 yards Tunic calico.
231½ " turkey red calico.
24 Canadian belts.
5 dozen spool cotton.
7 pounds cotton thread.
24 cotton handkerchiefs.
24 " " extra.
12 " shawls.
5 coats, beaver.
6 " cassimere.
5 " melton.
5 " black cloth.
123½ yards drills, brown.
102¼ " flannel, red.
3 dozen hats.
12 " knitting pins.
112½ yards linseys, plaid.
2 M needles.
5 pairs pants, beaver.
6 " " cassimere.
5 " " melton.
5 " " black cloth.
6 dozen hickory shirts.
488 yards stripes.
129 " satinett.
12 pairs women's shoes.
5 dozen pairs shears.
12 woollen shawls.
4 dozen thimbles.
2 pounds thread, linen.
149 yards ticking.
1 pair wrappers.

We have under cultivation four hundred and fifty-nine (459) acres; three hundred and twenty acres into wheat, eighty-two into oats, thirty-six into corn, twenty-one into potatoes. The crop is about one-third average or ordinary crop. I do not think we will have sufficient to support the Indians until harvest next year.

Of the lands appraised for reservation purposes I should judge about one thousand (1,000) acres are enclosed. I should think about all is enclosed that is available. The balance over and above the four hundred and fifty-nine (459) acres under cultivation is lying idle for want of teams and seed to cultivate. We have horses and cattle—about thirty-six (36) head of cattle, three (3) horses, and one (1) colt. These we can pasture upon the hills outside of the reservation. One farm has been left out of the appraisement, Mr. Campbell's, which lies in the upper end of the valley proper. I should think about two hundred (200) acres of it, more or less, lies in the valley; the land in quality about the same as balance of the valley or the lands appraised. Mr. Wiley, superintendent, thought there was sufficient without it.

Forty thousand (40,000) pounds of wheat were purchased of Mr. Norton, one of the residents of the valley, in February last, by Mr. Wiley; I do not know what price was paid for the wheat, and all I know about the price I saw a copy of the contract that Mr. Norton had, which specified four ($4) dollars per bushel.

The farms of J. Violett, Brock Pollard, J. Latham, and the enclosure of W. M. Scott and Asa Pratt were included in the appraisement, made by the appraisers appointed by Superintendent Wiley, for reservation purposes. They are all situated on the mountains, and are very much higher than Hoopa valley, and some distance from it. I should say the nearest farm or place appraised is one and one-half mile from Hoopa Valley, and the one most remote is about five miles from Hoopa valley.

There have been no more Indians on this reservation at any time since I came here than there are now.

ROBERT L. STOCKTON.

STATE OF CALIFORNIA, *County of Klamath*, *ss:*

William M. Scott, being sworn, says: I reside in Hoopa valley, Klamath county, State of California. I have been an employé on the reservation in the Indian department since 21st of February last. I have resided in this valley since fall of 1854. One of the farms appraised for the reservation purposes was mine, or I put the improvements upon it.

Austin Wiley, superintendent, first applied to me or notified me of intention to make an Indian reservation in this valley in August, 1864.

Our most accessible point to get merchandise or other articles from market is Arcata, Humboldt county, about forty (40) miles from this valley ; the route is over mountainous country, and the only way to get freight over it is by mules. All other points are far more distant and more difficult and expensive to get freight from. Merchandise, during the year 1864, cost four (4) cents per pound freight from Arcata to this valley. Latter part of the year 1864, after the valley was used for reservation purposes, flour was worth about six (6) cents per pound ; that was the market price here. I sold wheat last fall for seed for three and a half ($3 50) dollars per bushel ; that was about the market price. I don't know what was the price in the winter. There was none sold to my knowledge except a lot Mr. Wiley, superintendent, purchased, and what he gave I don't know.

The farm of Mr. Thomas G. Campbell, at the upper end of the valley, is considered as part of Hoopa valley. His farm was not appraised with the other farms for reservation purposes. The farms of J. Violett, Brock Pollard, J. Latham, and the farm of William Scott and Asa Pratt, were included in the appraisement, made under the instructions of Superintendent Wiley, for reservation purposes. They are all situate in the mountains ; the nearest one is one and one-half mile from the valley proper or Hoopa valley.

In speaking of prices of various articles and freight, I mean in coin.

WM. M. SCOTT.

STATE OF CALIFORNIA, *County of Klamath, ss :*

John L. Southmayd, being sworn, says : I reside at Eureka, Humboldt county, State of California. My business is stock-raising and furnishing stock for beef.

From 1st September, 1864, till 1st June, 1865, market price of beef in Hoopa Valley was from seven and one-half ($7\frac{1}{2}$) to eight (8) cents per pound.

A part of that time I supplied the military post in the valley with beef.

The prices I named are in coin.

JOHN L. SOUTHMAYD.

Statements taken at Smith River reservation, California, August 11 *and* 12, 1865.

STATE OF CALIFORNIA, *County of Del Norte, ss :*

Wm. Bryson, being sworn, says : I reside on Smith River reservation, Del Norte county, State of California, and have resided here since January, 1862, and during that time to the present, except about six months, have been in government employ in the Indian department on this reservation. Since the first of last January I have been agent. I was clerk from first July, 1861, three months in office of superintendent at Yuba City, this State, and then, till 20th January following, I was supervisor on Klamath reservation, this State.

I think there are about six hundred (600) Indians now on this reservation ; I have no means of telling the precise number. The males and females both labor in the field. They labor quite willingly. We cultivate, that is we plough, plant, and sow this season about three hundred and seventy-five (375) acres of land. Crops are wheat, oats, and peas, some beans and corn, and vegetables, such as potatoes, turnips, &c. We have never bought anything of provision kind for the Indians on this reservation since the first year. The first year we bought provisions for them until the first crop came in, which was about first of September, 1862.

There has been no instruction, religious or moral, given or imparted to the Indians on this reservation since I have been here, except about two months, in summer of 1863, a lady taught a school here and the Indian children attended. They made considerable improvement under her instruction. The Indian children are under control of their parents, all the control there is over them. The females cut and make clothing for both male and female ; so much they have been instructed. Those who labor on the land have white overseers, in some instances Indian overseers, to show them what to do and how to do it. We never have had half enough clothing for all of them. Some of the laborers would be entirely naked was it not for old clothes and rags they pick up. There are Indians living near the reservation who live and provide for themselves. Their outward appearance is much better than that of the reservation Indians ; they are better clothed and appear more healthy, and have better houses to live in. They select their own ground for their houses, and seem to take more pains in building. The outside Indians seem to have a horror of the reservation ; they look upon it as a punishment to be taken to a reservation to live. I attribute it to bad management of reservations. I think as a general rule on the reservations they have not been provided with houses, provisions, and clothing as they should have been. They have had promises in reference to houses, provisions, and clothing that have not been fulfilled. My opinion is that the Indians are generally in worse condition on the reservations than off of them, and it arises from the fact that the Indian department in this State has been very badly managed. I believe the reservation system properly conducted is a very good one, if not the best, both for the Indians and the government. A reservation properly conducted can be made nearly, if not quite, self-sustaining. The Indians want the products of the reservation to be used for their benefit. I believe they would be encouraged to labor, and produce enough surplus to purchase their clothing, if they could be assured that the surplus would be so used.

There was a surplus of oats sent off from the reservation, the product of 1864, of sixty-three thousand six hundred (63,600) pounds, worth here two and one-half ($2\frac{1}{2}$) cents per pound, amounting to fifteen hundred and ninety ($1,590) dollars. They were shipped to San Francisco by order of Superintendent Wiley. Also sixteen and one-half ($16\frac{1}{2}$) tons of hay, worth here at least eight ($8) dollars per ton, or one hundred and thirty-two ($132) dollars were taken away to Crescent City, fifteen miles distant in this county, and sold there by order of same superintendent. I don't know that the avails of oats or hay have come back to the reservation.

The employés upon the reservation have received nothing since March, 1864, except Mr. Haight, one of the employés, received one hundred and fifty ($150) dollars since. There is considerable due employés for services previous to 1864.

There were twenty thousand (20,000) feet of lumber purchased, at eighteen ($18) dollars per thousand, amounting to three hundred and sixty ($360) dollars, and used on the reservation for Indian houses same year. One hundred pairs of blankets were sent to the reservation in 1864 by Mr. Wiley. Such blankets can be purchased at Crescent City for two and one-half ($2 50) dollars per pair, retail price. Two dozen camp kettles came same time blankets came, probably worth no more than from fifteen to eighteen ($15 to $18) dollars per dozen. We received a lot of merchandise this spring or latter part of winter, purchased by the Indian department at Washington, and forwarded, consisting of blankets, cloths, and clothing. Mr. Wiley, a short time before he went out of office, I think in March or April last, sent to the reservation one thousand gunny bags, which he said in a letter cost thirty five ($35) dollars per hundred. They are of very inferior quality, evidently second-hand bags, many of them being patched and darned.

The first five months of Mr. Wiley's administration I was not in charge, and do not know what he may have sent to the reservation.

The reason I was not longer on the Klamath reservation was, the flood of December, 1861, destroyed that reservation, and a part of the Indians were taken to Smith River valley, to what is now called the Smith River reservation. The Indians that were on the Klamath reservation, known as the Klamath Indians, remained along the banks of the Klamath river, and were never removed to any reservation. The Klamath Indians at that time were estimated at twenty-two hundred (2,200.) They lived on the Klamath river, below the mouth of the Trinity river. This estimate is made from the opinion of other men better informed than I. We estimate the number of Indians brought from the Klamath reservation in 1862, at from three hundred to four hundred (300 to 400) These three hundred to four hundred Indians were Humboldt Indians. Nearly all have remained on the reservation since they were brought here ; a few have run away. I should say the first Indians brought to this reservation were from ninety to one hundred, (90 to 100,) brought from Humboldt Bay in December, 1861. I do not include them in the three hundred to four hundred just spoken of as brought from the Klamath reservation. In the fall of 1862 eight hundred and thirty (830) Humboldt Indians were brought here. I think about two hundred of them ran away, and the balance have died here, except those named, say six hundred.

The reservation is leased land. We have had from four hundred to six hundred acres under lease ever since we came here in 1862, and there has been nothing paid for rent of land except two hundred ($200) dollars paid in December, 1862, and excepting eighty acres of land, the grain rent of which has been paid two years of the time. All the balance of the rent, far as I know, has never been paid. I have received nothing for services during the last year, and a large amount is due me from the government for services previous to that year. The rent to be paid for the land is to be four and five dollars ($4 and $5) dollars per acre. There is more land under lease this year than named above, but it is not all cultivated ; it is pasture and common.

I think outside of the reservation and in the vicinity of it, say between reservation and Crescent City, there are five hundred Indians living in their usually wild way, by hunting and fishing. They do not look to government for support. From this reservation to Hoopa Valley reservation is about one hundred and fifty miles, over very mountainous country—no wheel road, nothing but trails—or go by sea about eighty miles and then forty miles by mountain trail. To Round valley it is two hundred and fifty miles, I should think ; two hundred miles by water and fifty miles by rough mountain trail. Under Mr. Hanson's superintendency it cost the government two and one-half ($2 50) dollars per head by steamer to transport Indians from Humboldt bay to Crescent City, a distance of eighty miles. I do not think it can be done now. The land transportation would cost far more than the transportation by water.

WM. BRYSON.

STATE OF CALIFORNIA, *County of Del Norte, ss:*

Ithamar Davison, being sworn, says: I reside on the Smith River reservation, Del Norte county. State of California; I am an employé on the reservation. I came here first of March, 1864. I was an employé on the Klamath reservation, Klamath county, State of California, from 15th August, 1858, until August, 1861. T. J. Henley was superintendent when I was first employed. D. E. Buel was agent on the Klamath reservation when I went there. McDuffie succeeded Henley as superintendent, and Driebelbis succeeded McDuffie. The Klamath reservation was destroyed in December, 1861. The Humboldt Indians that were on that reservation were taken to Smith River valley, to what is now called the Smith River reservation. A portion of the Klamath reservation was cultivated; the Indians were employed in its cultivation. With the fish they caught the Indians were supplied with food from the products of the reservation, except at one time Mr. Buel bought about five tons of flour. I do not remember of any other provisions being purchased. Both males and females worked on the land in its cultivation; they work here the same.

There has been no school for Indian children on any reservation where I have been employed. During the time I was employed, and no instructions were imparted to the older ones, except to learn them how to farm, and how to make their own clothes. The children have been under control of their parents.

I have not received anything for services since I came here, 1st of March, 1864, except the first month I received pay from Mr. Steele, the superintendent. I am to receive fifty ($50) dollars per month. Austin Wiley was superintendent from fore part of May, 1864, until latter part of May, 1865. He took possession here first of July, 1864. He took from the reservation sixty-three thousand six hundred (63,600) pounds of oats to San Francisco in October, 1864. Oats sold here immediately after for two and one-half ($2\frac{1}{2}$) cents per pound. He took away sixteen and one-half ($16\frac{1}{2}$) tons of hay, worth at least eight ($8) dollars per ton, and also forty (40) beef hides. He sent one hundred pairs of blankets, one thousand sacks, second hand, many of them patched and mended, and two dozen camp kettles. Some clothing came, but that was forwarded from the east by the Indian department. He bought a lot of lumber, I believe twenty thousand (20,000) feet, at eighteen ($18) dollars per thousand, to build houses for the Indians. Some horseshoes and horse nails and iron came also.

ITHAMAR DAVISON.

Report obtained at Fort Churchill, Nevada, September 11, 1865.

HEADQUARTERS SUB-DISTRICT OF NEVADA,
Fort Churchill, May 9, 1865.

LIEUTENANT: I have the honor to report, for the information of the general commanding, that settlers at Carson lake, and also on Truckee river, requested me to send troops to those localities, informing me that they anticipated trouble with the Indians.

On the morning of the 3d of May I left this post for the Carson lake, taking with me 1st Lieutenant D. Vanderhoof, company C, Nevada infantry, 2d Lieutenant D. H. Pine, Nevada infantry, and detachment company E, Nevada cavalry, consisting of fifteen men, withsix days' supplies. Arrived in camp at Cottonwood station, on the overland road, at three o'clock p. m., having marched twenty-six miles.

4th. Left camp at 4.40 a. m.; arrived at Taylor's ranch, on the Carson river, near the lake, at 9.30 a. m., that being the place previously designated by me to meet the whites and Indians.

5th. A large number of Indians and some twenty settlers met me at Mr. Taylor's house. In conversation with the Indians I soon learned that the excitement was caused by the peaceable Indians from the Humboldt coming to the Carson lake to avoid trouble, and the Indians living in the vicinity, not knowing the cause of so many coming in, supposed that a general war of extermination was about to commence, and to confirm them in this belief some reckless white man had told them that I was coming with soldiers to kill them all. They had commenced sending away their squaws and children and burning their wigwams. The white settlers seeing these movements on the part of the Indians, in turn became alarmed, and despatched a messenger to me in great haste, but through my interpreter, Richard Washington, I soon learned the facts in the case, and they assured me of their great desire for peace with the whites. I talked with the whites and Indians about three hours, assuring them that I would protect the good and punish the bad of either party. At five o'clock p. m. I left with the command for St. Clair's station; arrived there at 6.15 p. m, where we camped during the night, having marched five miles.

6th. Took up line of march direct for Truckee river at five o'clock a. m. Having procured an affidavit that a citizen named Cook had been exulting over the death of President Lincoln, I despatched Lieutenant Pine with one enlisted man to arrest Cook, and deliver him over to the commanding officer at Fort Churchill, which was done. Arrived at reservation house on Truckee river at 1.15 p. m., distance twenty-eight miles.

7th. Had talk with the Indians, who informed me that the agent had told them lies, and otherwise treated them badly, having hired the reservation to white men to keep their stock on it, receiving the money for the same, and appropriating it to their own use; and when the Indians would ask the agent for something to help them to procure subsistence or clothing, he would tell them that all the money he received had to be turned over to the Indian department, and if they gave any trouble he would send to Fort Churchill for troops, and clean them out. Upon an investigation of the treatment of the Indians by the agent, I am really surprised to know that they have borne all these impositions so patiently. Last year twenty-five thousand ($25,000) dollars were appropriated for the purpose of cultivating the Truckee and Walker River reserves. The money has disappeared, and not one pound of anything is being raised on either reserve for the Indians, and the agents are determined to continue their impositions further by herding stock on the reserves, and consuming the grass, the seed of which, if permitted to mature, would afford them a great part of their subsistence. I told the Indians to remain peaceable, and injure no white man; and now, since the war is over, our Great Father at Washington would do something for them, and in the mean time, if any of the whites abused them, not to resent it but come to me and make their complaints, and I would investigate the matter and punish the guilty party. I also requested the whites to take all their stock off of the reserve. I talked to the Indians about four hours, and they appeared much pleased with all I told them.

8th. I left camp on Truckee river at 4.30 a. m., arrived at Fort Churchill at 12.45 p. m., having travelled thirty miles.

Very respectfully, your obedient servant,

C. McDERMOTT,
Lieut. Colonel 2d California Cavalry, Comd'g Sub-District, Nevada.

Lieut. E. D. WAITE,
Acting Assistant Adjutant General, Sacramento, Cal.

Official:

E. D. WAITE, *A. A. A. G.*

Official:

R. C. DRUM, *A. A. G.*

(The foregoing report indorsed "Report of expedition to Sink of Carson and Truckee reservations.")

BRIGADE HEADQUARTERS, SACRAMENTO, *May* 17, 1865.

Respectfully forwarded to department headquarters, with recommendation that copy be furnished to congressional committee appointed to inquire into Indian affairs on the coast.

G. WRIGHT,
Brigadier General, Commanding.

Statement taken at Fort Churchill, Nevada, September 11, 1865.

STATE OF NEVADA, *Lyon county, Fort Churchill, ss:*

Franklin Campbell, being sworn, says: I reside at Walker River reservation, and have resided there off and on since 1st of April, 1862, first from 1st April, 1862, until first October, 1863; then from first October, 1864, up to the present time; was absent from first October, 1863, to first October, 1864. I have been acting as agent most of the time that I have been on the reservation. The Walker River reservation is about sixty miles long by twelve miles wide, including the Walker lake, which takes up probably one-third of the reservation. I should think on the reservation there are about four thousand (4,000) acres of arable land, river bottom, fine loam soil; will produce well, or has produced well whenever cultivated. There is one board house on the reservation, say twenty-five by fifteen feet, one story high; no finish inside, only cloth lining and paper. Should think at present prices such a house could be built for $250 to $300. This house was built, I think in spring of 1860, also an adobe stable. It could not have cost much, for it was built by the Indians under the superintendence of Warren Wasson, who was then the acting agent; so I have been informed. Those two are the only buildings on the reservation. There is no fencing, only corrals, small and insignificant. There has been no cultivation on the reservation. At present there are about 500 to 600 Indians on the reservation, living in their usual wild way by hunting, fishing, and gathering seeds. At certain seasons of the year from 1,500 to 2,000 Indians gather on to the reservation to fish, and they naturally belong to the reservation. They resort to Walker river and lake every year to catch fish for food. I think the Indians at Walker river and lake, and the Indians at Upper Sink of Carson, can be domesticated together upon the Walker River reservation, and the Indians at Lower Sink of Carson, the Humboldt Indians and the Indians upon the Truckee and around Pyramid lake, can be domesticated together on the northern reservation on Truckee and Round Pyramid lake. A large number of Indians at Upper Sink of Carson are included in the 1,500 to 2,000 Indians that gather annually for fishing in Walker river and lake. These Indians are known as the Pah-Ute Indians, though among themselves they have their clare names. There have been distributed, to my personal knowledge, to certain Indians, or Indians in certain localities, clothing, cloths, blankets, &c. I distributed for Mr. Lockhart, the agent, to Indians at Lower Sink of Carson, in fall of 1863, I believe about Christmas, about sixty single blankets, some white Mackinaw three-point blankets, and some red blankets, and some gray blankets marked U. S., about one thousand (1,000) yards of white drilling, twelve hundred (1,200) yards of calico, certainly one bale of hickory shirting, and I am not certain but two bales, one bale of blue drilling, between 500 and 700 yards, one bale of plaids, and I am not certain but two bales, and one bale of double-width woollen blue cloth. The Indians present to whom these goods were distributed would number between 300 and 400. About the Lower Sink of Carson, and to a part of whom these goods were distributed, live some eight hundred (800) Indians, or that locality is the centre of about that number. I know personally of no other distributions, except of some hats and overalls distributed to the boys in haying under Mr. Lockhart. At a time, though, while Mr. Lockhart was east, other clothing was distributed, in the fall of 1862—about 150 shirts, about same number of overalls, and about 600 yards of calico. These latter were distributed at reservation house on Walker river.

The reservation house on Walker River reservation is from this post by trail about twenty-five miles distant, and can be rode in four or five hours; by wagon road the distance is about thirty miles, and can be rode in from six to eight hours. I learned from Mr. Lockhart, the whites present, and from the Indians, that a distribution of clothing was made by Mr. Lockhart to the Indians at Walker river the same fall (in November) that I distributed in December to the Indians at Lower Sink of Carson. I have heard of no distribution of clothing since of consequence. The Indians at Walker river and lake have been peaceable and quiet ever since I have known them, except two that are now prisoners at the post on a charge of murder, and a half a dozen friends of theirs that have been disarmed. The Indians to whom I distributed goods at Lower Sink of Carson in 1863 had just previous taken money from the white inhabitants. They returned nearly all of the money at my request at the time I distributed the goods. Their excuse for taking the money was that the lands the whites were occupying were theirs, and the occupants ought to pay them something for the lands. The reservation house at Walker river is about fifteen miles this side of the lake. From here to Upper Sink of Carson is twenty-six miles, and the Indians there, included with the Indians on Walker river and lake, will amount to two thousand (2,000) at least. There are now a few miners (white) working on the Walker river reservation. A toll-road runs across the reservation, called the Wellington toll-road, a continuation of the Big Tree road in California, on towards Austin, in this State. Two mules are the only live stock on the reservation belonging to the government.

I should speak of provisions distributed in winter of 1861–'62; I should think about one ton of flour was distributed to the Indians on the Walker River reservation, and some seven beeves killed and distributed, but I think the beeves were not purchased by government money. In winter of 1862–'63 five beeves were received from rancheros in pay for allowing their stock to graze on the reservation, which were killed and distributed to the Indians. From the best information I can get, there are about six hundred (600) Indians living around Pyramid lake. There is a reservation around that lake, I believe it is called Pyramid Lake reservation. A man by the name of Gibson has been acting agent there. Lockhart told Gibson he better leave there, as he had no means of paying or supporting him. Lockhart told me he said this to Gibson last spring. Lockhart went east in April last, I think, and has not been back since, as I have heard. I was on the Pyramid Lake reservation in February, 1864. There was no land fenced or cultivated on the reserve at that time that I saw, and from all information there was no fencing nor cultivation, and at that time there was no saw-mill built on the reserve, although I had heard talk of building one. There is a house built on the reserve, or one was at that time built by Lockhart or his order; simply a board house; very small; I should say cost from $175 to $200. There was no other building at that time on the reserve. I should say the house on that reserve is about thirty-four miles from this post. From this post to that house on the reserve there is a good wagon road. The country is such that you can drive a buggy there in five or six hours. The house on reserve is thirteen or fourteen miles this side of Pyramid lake. There were thirty (30) head of cattle killed on the Walker River reservation and distributed to the Indians. I understood that they were procured from whites, who herded their stock on the reservation, in payment for herding their stock there. This was last winter. The Indians catch, in Walker lake and river, annually from 150 to 200 tons of fish, I should think, and they gather seed from the bunch-grass. The natural resources or products of the reservation are not sufficient to support the Indians. Land must be cultivated and planted. I think there would be no difficulty in inducing the Indians to labor, and I believe in a short time a reservation could be made self-sustaining with proper management. There have been purchased for the Walker River reservation, or brought on to it for use, a spade, a hoe, a few scythes, rakes, and forks, the latter for haying purposes in cutting and gathering the grasses that grow spontaneous and wild upon the reserve. I have cut and put up seventy (70) tons of hay on the reserve, but have done it at my own expense; had to hire money to get along with the work. No means had been furnished to do anything on the reserve last year. I had provisions for myself and interpreter, Richard Washington, an Indian, from Mr. Lockhart to July last; since then have taken care of ourselves. There has been no instruction to Indians, either adult or child. Most of them are clothed. They work and buy clothing. My opinion is that these Indians are not only susceptible of improvement, but would readily yield to teachers, and make great progress with proper tuition.

FRANKLIN CAMPBELL.

Deposition of Second Lieutenant Justin Edwards.

STATE OF NEVADA, *Fort Churchill:*

Lieutenant Justin Edwards, being sworn, says: I am 2d lieutenant in company F, first battalion Nevada cavalry volunteers; I have been in the United States service since April 4, 1864. I have been stationed during the time from May 24, 1865, to August 15, following, at Walker River Indian reservation, State of Nevada. A man by the name of Franklin Campbell has been acting as agent on that reservation under Mr. Lockhart. I know very nearly the boundaries of the reservation. I do not know the number of Indians on the reservation, but I should judge from observation there were 300 to 400 of them. They are scattered much over the reservations in different parts. I should judge the reservation, by travelling over it, was fifty miles long by about twelve miles wide on an average. The Indians are scattered all along the reservation in length—that is, along the river and lake of the same name. The Indians are cultivating no ground; no white men are cultivating ground for them. There is nothing being raised by cultivation for the Indians there; they are living in their usually wild way; their huts are made principally of willow, and they fish, hunt, and gather grass-seeds, &c. All the government buildings on the reservation are a small house and small stable. The house is built of plain, rough boards; I should judge about ten to twelve feet wide to eighteen feet long, one-story, not finished inside; cost $150, more or less. Stable is built of adobe or sundried brick, in size about ten by eighteen feet. I should think it did not cost over $150, or could have been built for that money. There is no fencing except two small corrals, one each side of the stable, enclosed by a willow fence, each including about one-eighth of an acre of ground. The agent has not cultivated any ground to my knowledge. I do not think he has received any government supplies from the Indian department, for he and the interpreter, an Indian named Richard Washington, lived at my camp two months while I was stationed there. The agent was doing nothing, but was there in suspense waiting for instructions from Mr. Lockhart or his successor, as it was talked that Mr. Lockhart was going to resign, and he has since resigned, I understand. I had twenty-five men with me under my command there. The Indians were quiet. While I was stationed there I was sent out to arrest two Indians for the murder of two white men at Walker lake. I had some difficulty in finding the two Indians, but found them, and arrested them without any resistance. Richard Washington, the interpreter, and two other Indians assisted in finding the murderers. Other Indians were anxious that they be arrested, but were afraid to assist for fear the relatives of the murderers would kill them. These Indians are those known as the Pah-Utes. I am ordered to

Fort Independence, Owen's river, State of California, with a detachment of twenty-three men, and to report for duty. I leave Tuesday, the 12th instant. I know nothing whatever except by report in relation to the Pyramid Lake reservation in this State.

JUSTIN EDWARDS,
2d Lieut. Company F, 1st Bat. Nevada Cavalry Vols.

Statement and suggestions relating to Indian affairs in Nevada from 1858 *to* 1865.

CARSON CITY, NEVADA, *September* 18, 1865.

DEAR SIR: Being at Virginia City on the 16th instant I met J. R. Lovejoy, esq., and in a casual conversation with him he informed me that he had just discovered that the timber reservation on the Truckee river was actually and permenantly located for a government reservation, and said, further, that he had been engaged in taking care of that property for the government; that he had kept intruders off of it, &c.

Mr. Lovejoy informed me that his business then in Virginia City was to meet some gentlemen with whom he had arranged to advance the money to pay for "half-breed Indian land scrip" to cover 5,000 acres of said timber reservation; that he had just engaged the scrip at Carson City, but having learned since his arrival in Virginia City that the said timber reservation was to be continued as a government reserve, he did not intend to locate said scrip, as it would be useless to do so. I then saw him in conversation with Mr. Leet, the gentleman whom it was said purchased the aforesaid timber lot and saw-mill of Clark Thompson, esq. Senator Nye and one or two other gentlemen, with whom I had not the honor of an acquaintance, were engaged in the conversation last mentioned.

This half-breed scrip, as you know, was issued to half-breed Indians by the government in lieu of some reservations which were abolished. It is not transferable, the intention of Congress being to secure the land for the use of the half-breed Indians in whose favor it was issued.

This scrip has been extensively used in this State by settlers and others to secure title to lands where they claimed more than one hundred and sixty acres, or for some other reason were unable to pre-empt. It sells for about five dollars per acre, and is located in the name of the Indian by an agent acting under the authority of a power of attorney from him. When the location is confirmed at Washington, the agent conveys by deed the title from the Indian to the settler or purchaser of the scrip.

I drop you this hasty letter not knowing whether the information will be of any use to you. My only motive is a desire to assist in protecting the interest of the government, which I fear has been, and is still likely to be further abused in connexion with this timber reservation.

You are at liberty to make any use you please of this letter. However, if the information is of no consequence to you, please destroy it, as I do not desire the animosity of those parties unnecessarily.

Very respectfully,

WARREN WASSON.

Hon. WILLIAM HIGBY,
San Francisco, California.

CARSON CITY, NEVADA, *September* 11, 1865.

DEAR SIR: Your communication of the 7th instant, requesting such information as I possess in regard to Indian affairs, past and present, in this State, together with suggestions as to the best policy to be pursued towards these Indians in the future, is before me. In compliance therewith, I respectfully submit the following statement of facts and suggestions:

In the summer of A. D. 1858 Frederick Dodge, esq., Indian agent for the Carson Valley agency, comprising the western portion of Utah Territory, now the State of Nevada, arrived and entered upon the discharge of his duties. I made his acquaintance early in the spring of 1859 at my ranch in Long valley, a tributary of Honey lake. My nearest white neighbor at that time on this side of the Sierras was forty (40) miles distant. Both the Washoe and Pah-Ute tribes made my place a sort of council rendezvous, it being near the line of their respective Territories, and my acquaintance and standing among them enabled me to be of great service to Mr. Dodge.

In the summer of 1859 the whites in considerable numbers moved into Long valley; I sold my improvements to them and moved to Carson valley, settling upon the land now owned by me.

The first year of Mr. Dodge's administration was spent in visiting the various Indian camps within his agency, issuing hickory shirts, overalls, tobacco, &c., to them as presents, and in viewing the country for the purpose of recommending proper situations for two reservations in accordance with instructions from the department. From various localities described by Mr. Dodge the department selected and caused to be set apart two reservations described as follows: one on the Truckee river, commencing at a point one (1) mile above the Tower crossing or great bend of the Truckee, and extending down the river to and including the lake of the same, (Pyramid lake,) and embracing the lands contiguous on each side of the river and lake; the other on Walker river, commencing at the great bend, about twenty-five (25) miles above the lake (Walker) and running down to and including the same, and embracing the contiguous land on both sides of the river and lake. The external boundaries of these reservations have since been established by official survey, under the authority of the department. In my estimation, the amount of arable land embraced within both reservations will not, in the aggregate, exceed ten thousand (10,000) acres, the most of which is within the one on the Truckee. The Truckee reservation contains an abundance of good timber, sufficient for all its necessities. The Walker reservation has very little timber, and but little land suitable for cultivation.

During the year above mentioned Dodge expended out of his own private funds about five thousand dollars ($5,000) for an outfit, consisting of four mules, harness for same, carriage, or ambulance as he termed it, pack-saddles, presents for the Indians, provisions, and pay of employés. Dodge made requisition for that amount on Jacob Forney, esq., the then superintendent of Indian affairs for Utah Territory, but who put him off from time to time with promises to send the amount soon, but which he did not do. Dodge's private funds being exhausted, never having had any public ones, he could do no good by remaining; he therefore went to Salt Lake to see Forney, who refused him an interview, but wrote him a note instructing him to return to his agency, and funds would be furnished him at the earliest convenience of Mr. Forney. Dodge being indignant, forced his way into Forney's private apartment and gave him a sound thrashing, compelling him to furnish a draft on St. Louis for the amount, but which, when sent there, was protested, Forney having overdrawn that year's appropriation for the Indian service in Utah. In the mean time Dodge returned to his agency, expecting in due time the funds from St. Louis, but which did not come. He then visited Washington and tendered his resignation, which was not accepted; the Commissioner, A. B. Greenwood, though, reimbursed him, and relieved his agency from the supervision of the superintendent of Utah, authorizing him to report direct to Washington.

In June, 1860, Dodge returned to Carson valley and found a bloody war in full blast between the whites and his Indians, inaugurated by some villanous whites who stole some ponies of the Pah-Utes, and who tied up and whipped one or two Indians, (so the Indians said,) who retaliated by murdering four white men found at the place where these outrages had been committed.

About the tenth (10th) of May, 1860, some hundred or more settlers, hastily armed and organized, proceeded to the Truckee reservation for the purpose of chastising the Indians, which resulted in a shameful defeat of the whites, who left sixty or eighty (60 or 80) of their number upon the field slain, and their horses, arms, and effects in the hands of the Indians, greatly encouraging them. Two hundred United States soldiers were then sent from California, who, being joined by citizens of this then Territory, and of the adjoining counties of California, formed an expedition numbering about eight hundred (800) men, proceeded against the Indians about the first of June. The Indians made but a feeble resistance on the open field, losing about seven or eight of their number, and killing about the same number of the whites, when they fled to their strongholds in the mountains, pursued by about two hundred (200) mounted volunteers, without effect, who lost one man and then returned to the main force. The citizens then disbanded and returned to their homes, leaving the soldiers in the field, who did not again engage the Indians, but proceeded to the Carson river and established Fort Churchill.

Michael Bushey, a mountaineer of much experience, was engaged as guide and scout for the expedition, but was killed by the Indians the first time he left the command; I was employed in his place, and was thus engaged when Dodge arrived. I suggested to Dodge the importance of an immediate interview with the hostile Indians, and volunteered to go into the mountains and bring them to the Truckee reservation, and which I did by his authority, and he then and there concluded a settlement of the existing difficulties upon the basis of forgetting the past and doing right in the future. The Indians complained of many outrages, doubtless committed by lawless vagabond whites, and in turn acknowledged doing many things themselves not consistent with our ideas of right.

Under the impression that my services were indispensable to the success of this arrangement, on account of my experience among the Indians and my personal acquaintance with and influence over the principal chiefs of the Pah-Utes, Mr. Dodge induced me to engage in his service, at a compensation of $125 per month and my expenses paid, until peace and quiet was restored among them.

The Pah-Utes inhabiting the country south of the Carson river, including those on the Walker reservation, did not participate in or approve of the war, except a few of the restless and ambitious young men; and for this reason Dodge built the first house on the Walker reservation, intending at the time to build more extensively upon the Truckee as soon as he should be satisfied that the Truckee Indians would not renew the war. From the time of his arrival in June, up to September 1, 1860, Mr. Dodge expended about five thousand dollars ($5,000) in the erection of the outside part of a house on the Walker reservation, provisions, presents for Indians, pay of employés, &c., which exhausted the funds furnished him by the Commissioner.

In order to set forth to the department the condition and necessities of his agency more fully than could be done by writing, he left for Washington about the first of September, 1860, taking my receipt for the government property, and leaving me in full charge of the agency.

No outbreak of any serious character occurred among the Indians while I had charge of the agency, although on several occasions it required my utmost exertions to prevent them from resenting the almost daily outrages committed upon them by white men—several of their men being shot down in cold blood for no cause except that they were Pah-Utes. Many of their horses were stolen, and other outrages too revolting to commit to paper were perpetrated upon them.

About the middle of April, 1861, some two-thirds of the fighting strength of the Pah-Utes assembled at Walker lake, headed by W-ahee, (Fox,) second war chief of the tribe, instigated by some disloyal white men, and entered into a conspiracy to begin a general onslaught by killing me and all connected with the agency. Their plot was kept a profound secret, but relatives of my interpreter (an Indian) informing him, he fled without warning me; his flight, however, alarmed me, and by intimidation I compelled a young Indian to divulge the secret. My teamster being absent for provisions, I could not leave the reservation to inform the officers at Fort Churchill without jeopardizing the safety of the property; therefore, prompt action on my part was necessary. I succeeded in frightening Wa-hee so that he fled to Oregon, and induced the other Indians to abandon their bloodthirsty project, and return the interpreter and the government horse and saddle he had taken with him. Wa-hee returned in April, 1862, and was killed by his own people, about the first of May, for the horrible outrages committed by him.

Settlers settled upon the upper end of the Truckee reservation in the fall of 1860, built log cabins, fenced and ploughed some ground. I warned them to leave, which they did immediately, but returned again in the summer of 1861, and were not removed, but are, I believe, still occupying the land.

I had great difficulty during my administration of affairs to prevent whites from settling upon the reservations, and stock men from herding stock on them, to the destruction of the grass seeds one of the principal sources of subsistence of the Indians; also to prevent traders and fishermen from depriving them of their winter's supply of fish by cheating them out of it entirely.

From September 1, 1860, to March 31, 1861, I expended about three thousand (3,000) dollars, improving the Walker reservation, for presents to the Indians, provisions, pay of an interpreter, and one teamster, and my own compensation. I erected a valuable and permanent adobe building, 14 by 30 feet, finished off the house commenced by Dodge, made a small garden mainly for the purpose of testing the soil and climate for future farming purposes, a corral, &c. The presents to the Indians consisted of hickory shirts, overalls, and calico, costing on the average $1 50 to clothe each Indian in a manner of which they were proud, and was really useful to them. Tobacco was dealt out to the chiefs in small quantities on all occasions.

Mr. Dodge furnished the means to settle up to the above date, but did not return in the spring of 1861, as he intended doing when he left, but resigning the office of Indian agent, was appointed to a lieutenancy in the regular army, and was killed on the Mississippi river during the war.

I may here as well state that, from actual personal knowledge of Mr. Dodge, I know he was scrupulously honest and zealous in the discharge of his duties, but unacquainted with Indian character, and, therefore, unfit for the position of Indian agent.

From the establishment of the agency up to March 31, 1861, the expenses as above stated were about thirteen thousand dollars, ($13,000,) while the property, including the improvements upon the reservations, was worth about four thousand (4,000) dollars.

No appropriation by Congress had ever been made for this agency, and the above amount was paid by the Commissioner of Indian Affairs out of the contingent fund, as I was informed.

During the quarter ending June 30, 1861, the expenses, exclusive of the pay of the interpreter, teamster, and myself, amounted to nearly $350, mostly for presents necessarily used in the settlement of the Wa-hee difficulty above referred to; our pay for that time amounting to six hundred dollars, ($600,) making a total of nine hundred and fifty dollars, all of which I paid out of my private funds.

Upon the 13th day of July, 1861, I submitted this matter to Governor J. W. Nye, superintendent, &c., who had then arrived and taken charge of affairs, when he promised to see that I was paid at a very early day. Nothing, however, was done in the matter until after I had left the service. Late in 1862 I took the matter into my own hands and sent a statement to the department, together with my account properly made out. The department disallowed $41 66⅔ per month on my pay, and the amount paid by me for a small quantity of provisions that I had on hand at the Walker reservation when Governor Nye took charge. The Commissioner of Indian Affairs sent me a draft for the remainder of my account, and upon which I received legal tender notes, worth at that time only fifty cents on the dollar in gold, which was what I had paid out.

At the request of the superintendent, I remained in his employ up to August 31, 1862, during which time the services I performed consisted entirely in visiting the various Indian tribes within the superintendency, and twice I was sent to Owen's river, California. Whenever a difficulty broke out, or was anticipated, I was sent to adjust it—being so employed most of the time, and kept the entire time travelling in the service. Partial accounts of some of these trips and of my doings will be found in my reports to the superintendent under dates as follows: January 12, 1862, January 28, 1862, April 20, 1862, and May 10, 1862, embodied in the reports of the superintendent under dates February 3, 1862, and June 17, 1862, addressed to the Commissioner of Indian Affairs, Washington, D. C., and published in his annual report for A. D. 1862—reports Nos. 46 and 47. Accounts of other trips taken by me were not published, and being of about the same character of proceedings as those above referred to, I deem their detail here unimportant. I will state, however, that after I had quit the Indian service in Nevada, at the request of Brigadier General Wright, honorable L. Stanford, then governor of California, and John P. H. Wentworth, superintending agent for the southern district of that State, I went three hundred miles south, to Owen's river, California, and collected the hostile Indians of that region to enable Mr. Wentworth to meet them in council and settle that war.

In May, 1862, I received a commission dated March 6, 1862, appointing me United States marshal for Nevada Territory, but owing to the peculiar judicial arrangement of our courts at that time, the duties of that office did not interfere with my engagements with the superintendent of Indian affairs On the 27th day of October, 1862, I received a commission dated August 29, 1862, appointing me assessor of internal revenue for the district of Nevada, and I am now engaged in the discharge of the duties of that office, and have been almost constantly since the receipt of the above-named commission.

There are now within this State two distinct tribes of Indians, viz: the Pah-Utes and the Washoes; the Pah-Utes number about three thousand five hundred (3,500) souls, the Washoes about three hundred, (300,) both tribes having diminished over one-half within the past six years, the result of small-pox and other diseases, together with war and famine. Part of the Shoshones tribe roam over and inhabit the eastern part of the State, and a part of the Modock and the Bannack tribes inhabit the northern portion. I am not acquainted with the numbers of these tribes belonging within this State.

The Pah-Utes and Washoe Indians are peaceably disposed, and would, with proper management, soon acquire many of the arts of civilized life, and support themselves by honest industry.

I would recommend most earnestly the same course to be pursued towards them, so far as altered times and circumstances will permit, with the few exceptions hereinafter named, that I had the honor to suggest in my reports to Governor Nye, dated July 13, 1861, and August 13, 1861, as published in the annual report of the honorable the Commissioner of Indian Affairs for the year 1861, pages 113, 114, 115, and 116.

The exceptions which I would suggest to my report of August, 1861, above referred to, are as follows: "And in April of each year to the Pah-Utes, in fancy articles, $1,500; and in April of each year to the Washoe, in fancy articles, $150;" these items being no longer necessary.

This recommendation was made on account of my observations, that in the spring of the year the Indians were more inclined to be troublesome, their horses being fat, and themselves able to subsist in large bands at almost any point, giving them a temporary feeling of independence, while a few such presents from the government at such times would keep them quiet.

In my report to Governor Nye, dated April 12, 1862, before referred to, I called his attention to this matter, and asked that the sums named for "fancy articles" be issued in hickory shirts and overalls. The Indians were at that time much dissatisfied, and I thought the recommendation necessary; it was not, however, acted upon. I would not now recommend the issue of anything but useful articles to them.

The Truckee reserve possesses superior advantages in respect to soil, climate, and timber, and with proper cultivation would produce abundant crops, which would encourage the Indians to additional exertions.

Crops on the Walker reservation would not be as certain, and would cost more to produce. These two reservations, properly managed, are sufficient to sustain all the Indians in this State; but unless they are so managed, the sooner they are abolished the better.

The first appropriation for the Indian service in Nevada was made July 5, 1862, (U. S. Stat, vol. 1861–'62, page 529,) $20,000, for the purpose of making a treaty with the Shoshones or Snakes. The next was made July 17, 1862, (U. S. Stat, vol. 1861–'62, page 629,) "for pay of interpreter, $500; for presents of goods and clothing to the Indians, to be expended by the superintendent of Indian affairs, $5,000; for incidental expenses in Nevada Territory, including office and travelling expenses, $2,000; making the total $7,500." The next was made March 3, 1863, (U. S. Stat., vol. 1862–'63, page 791,) "for general incidental expenses of the Indian service in Nevada Territory, presents of goods, agricultural implements, and other useful articles, and to assist them to locate in permanent abodes, and sustain themselves by the pursuits of civilized life, to be expended under the direction of the Secretary of the Interior, $25,000." The next was made June 25, 1864, (U. S. Stat, vol. 1863–'64, page 179,) for the same purposes and of the same amount, $25,000. The appropriations made by the last Congress for Indian service in Nevada was the same purpose and amount as the two last foregoing, to wit, $25,000. Making the aggregate appropriated for the Indian service in Nevada, since the organization of the Territory, (no appropriation having been made before,) exclusive of the appropriation of twenty thousand dollars for treaty with the Shoshones or Snakes, and the last twenty-five thousand dollars named above, the sum of fifty-seven thousand five hundred dollars, ($57,500.) I am not in possession of the facts necessary to enable me to answer your questions as to how these appropriations have been expended. In my judgment they have not been judiciously expended.

No improvements of any amount or nature have been made on the Walker reservation since I left there in June, 1861.

I have not been to the Truckee reservation since 1862; there were no improvements there at that time, and all that I now know about improvements on that reservation is hearsay. I am credibly informed that all the improvements now on the Truckee reservation belonging to the government consis tof a small house worth about $600, about five acres of ploughed ground, upon which nothing has yet been raised, and an attempt to build a saw-mill; an insufficient dam was put across the river, but was washed away by the currents, and a considerable race or canal has been dug, but is wrong end up, or, at least, has not fall enough to conduct the water. The labor expended on this saw-mill enterprise at the reservation, I am informed, would cost about $1,500 or $2,000. There are several settlers or intruders having some improvements now on the Truckee reservation. There is a timber lot reserved for the use of the proposed saw-mill, located on the Truckee river about forty miles above the Truckee Indian reservation; think it was located in the fall of 1862; do not remember the exact number, but believe it contains about 28,000 acres; is heavily timbered, of a good quality, and would be cheap at five dollars per acre for the privilege of taking off the timber only. I regard the timber lot as being worth over one hundred thousand dollars, ($100,000,) and think it could be readily sold for that amount. A large number of logs have been cut upon this timber lot, which were to have been run down the river to the saw-mill, but it is said they have been mostly destroyed by fire. I have thus described about all the improvements on the reservations.

There is or was a man by the name of Gibson employed on the Truckee reserve, in the capacity of what they call "local agent," and another on the Walker reservation, Franklin Campbell by name, whom I know to be a good, honest, and reliable man, much esteemed by the Indians. The reservations are not cultivated, nor either moral, educational, or religious instruction imparted to the Indians upon either of them. There are probably not more than a hundred Indians on either reservation at this season of the year—during the fishing season—and in the winter they come into the reservations. I have always felt a deep interest in the welfare of the Pah-Ute Indians, believing that they are better disposed, more industrious, temperate, and virtuous, and more susceptible of civilization than any other tribe upon the continent.

For the above reasons, please excuse me for making the following suggestions with a view to their advancement:

First. That there be but one superintendent, or agent, having entire charge of the whole affair, there being no good reason why the duties cannot be performed by one, while, otherwise, there is always a conflict of jurisdiction between the superintendents and the agents, causing mutual disagreements, injurious to both the government and the Indians, while, as a matter of economy, one is to be preferred. The necessary employés can be hired cheaper without commissioning them, which inflates their ideas of compensation.

Second. That the department prevent traders and intruders from going upon the reservation

Third That the Hon. the Secretary of the Interior require the last appropriation to be expended for specific purposes, and not left to the discretion of any superintendent or agent.

I would respectfully suggest the following as a proper apportionment:

For school-house on the Truckee reservation, 16 by 30 feet in size	$1.000
For dwelling-house, 16 by 40 feet	1,250
For stable for animals, 15 by 40 feet	300
For two large breaking ploughs, to cut, 20 inches each	150
For three small ploughs	150
For eight yoke of oxen, yokes and chains	1,600
For four team mules	800
For one set of harness for four mules	150
For one four-mule wagon	300
For one ox wagon	250
For fifty harrow teeth	50
For one hay press	250
For rakes, pitchforks, scythes, axes, hoes, shovels, &c	300
For blacksmith shop and tools, with tools for wood-work	800
For school-books, stationery, lights, &c	300
For medicines	50
For salary of teacher, blacksmith, and farmer, at $1,800 each per annum, with board	5,400
For provisions for employés	2,500
For garden seeds, grains, &c	2,000
For feed for teams	400
For provisions and clothing for the Indians	3,000
For ten milch cows	300
For travelling expenses of agent and of interpreter	2,200
For contingent expenses, unforeseen	1,500
Total	25,000

All the above items could be purchased of the best quality for the prices set opposite them.

I would not recommend any improvements on the Walker reservation next year, for reasons before given in this statement. With twenty-five thousand dollars judiciously expended as above apportioned, a crop could be produced next summer, including the wild hay that could be harvested, that would bring in this market over thirty thousand dollars, ($30,000,) if sold. The surplus, over what would be required to feed the Indians, teams, and employés, would furnish seeds for both reservations for the next year, and part could be sold, which, with an appropriation of twenty thousand dollars, ($20,000,) would put the reservations in a condition soon to be self-sustaining. Many of the Indians now understand all kinds of work necessary to carry on this arrangement, except teaching school and blacksmithing.

Richard A. Washington, a Pah-Ute by birth, now about nineteen (19) years of age, who was educated by Agent Dodge, and is now employed as interpreter at the Walker reserve, is a very correct reader, excellent penman, and good mathematician, would be of great service as assistant teacher, and could soon manage a school himself, and would take great pride in doing so.

I have the honor to be, very respectfully, your obedient servant,

WARREN WASSON.

Hon. W. Higby.

Report of the Superintendent of Indian Affairs in California.

Office of Indian Affairs, California,
San Francisco, November 8, 1865.

Sir: I have the honor to forward to you the enclosed statement of the present condition of the several Indian reservations, and the Indian service within my superintendency.

Your late visit to the different reservations in this State, as a member of the Committee on Indian Affairs, renders a lengthy report unnecessary.

The Round Valley reservation, in charge of B. L. Fairfield, agent, is in a prosperous and satisfactory condition. The number of Indians on the reservation September 30th ultimo was nine hundred and forty. Since arrived from Humboldt bay three hundred and fifty, who have been held at that place several months as prisoners of war by the military authorities. They are well pleased with their change of location, and will no doubt remain on the reservation satisfied and contented.

The removal of the Indians from Mendocino station to Round valley has been ordered, and will be effected as soon as possible. The public property is being removed from that station to Round valley, and no crops will be raised or Indians subsisted there after the present season.

The Indians of Mendocino and Lake counties have applied, through a large delegation, for permission to locate upon the Round Valley reservation. They number some eighteen hundred. They were informed that provision would be made for their reception early in the spring. From these several sources the number of Indians on the reservation will be largely increased; probably three thousand will be in charge of the agent next season.

We have now at Round valley a large amount of subsistence—some fifteen thousand bushels of grain besides vegetables, and the agent is preparing for a large increase of crops the ensuing season. Three thousand additional acres of land are being enclosed this winter for cultivation and pasturage. The future prospects of this reservation for raising and providing subsistence for the Indians are all that could be desired.

It is only necessary for the future and entire prosperity of this reservation that provision be made by Congress for the full possession of the valley by the government for Indian purposes. This being obtained, and an appropriation made sufficient to furnish the reservation with some additional stock-cattle and hogs, and to purchase the saw and grist mills on private lands adjoining the valley, the reservation should no longer be a charge upon the government, but should, and I believe could, be made self-sustaining.

The reservations of Nome-Lackee and Mendocino having been abandoned, and of no further use to the Indian service, the lands and improvements should be disposed of, and the proceeds thereof applied to the payment for the improvements of those settlers on the Round Valley reservation who are entitled to compensation. I think, to make these lands more available, a board of commissioners should be appointed to classify and value the lands on said reservations according to their location and fertility, and that they also be authorized to make a valuation of the improvements of those settlers in Round valley, who should receive a compensation for the same; and further, that they be empowered to exchange those lands before mentioned for improvements in Round valley, when it can be done with advantage to the government and satisfaction to the settlers.

It is very important that this question of the entire occupancy of Round valley for reservation purposes should be settled during the present session of Congress. Justice to the settlers demands it, and steps should be taken to ascertain how far they are entitled to compensation, and then provision should be made for their payment.

The improvements of the settlers in Hoopa valley have been reassessed by the board of appraisers appointed by the act of Congress of March 3, 1865, under instructions of the Commissioner of Indian Affairs, and the report forwarded to him for the approval of the Secretary of the Interior. If the report is approved the money, I presume, will be paid, and the question of the permanent location of that reservation settled.

The prospect, present and future, of this reservation is not so flattering as that of Round valley. The crops of grain are very light, only twenty-two hundred bushels of wheat being raised on three hundred and twenty acres sown; crops of peas and oats a failure; corn and potatoes about half a crop. The small amount raised is owing in part to the late planting and unusual drought. The failure of the crops leaves the reservation without sufficient subsistence for the Indians the present season after replacing twenty-three thousand pounds of flour borrowed of the military department.

The agent is preparing to plant a large crop this winter, and if the season should be favorable I think a considerable surplus will be raised, which can be sold at good prices, and the proceeds applied to the purchase of cattle and clothing for the Indians on the reservation.

This reservation being only partially supplied with working-stock necessary for the cultivation of the lands, a considerable amount of money will be required to purchase additional teams and stock-cattle, and some additional subsistence for the Indians the present season.

At Smith River reservation the crops are good, and subsistence for the Indians is abundant. Large quantities of salmon and other fish are being caught, and for the support of the reservation but little money is required, except for the payment of the employés and rents for lands leased for the use of the reservation. I would recommend that the lands now occupied and some adjoining, sufficient for a reservation, be purchased, or the place be abandoned next season, and the Indians removed to Round valley. Twenty thousand dollars would be required to purchase for reservation purposes lands sufficient to provide for and subsist all the Indians now upon the reservation and those within Del Norte county, numbering thirteen hundred, not at present provided for, the most of whom at no distant day will have to be cared for. If funds cannot be provided for the purchase of these lands, I would recommend the removal of the Indians, and so much of the public property as cannot be disposed of to an advantage, to Round valley next season. This could be done, I think, at an expense not exceeding five thousand dollars.

With the facilities for subsisting Indians at Round valley, I cannot see the necessity of three reservations in northern California; and I can, with propriety, recommend that measures be taken having in view the ultimate colonizing of all the Indians in the northern part of the State at Round valley. The rapid decrease of the Indians in numbers, and the great change that is taking place in their habits and customs by contact with the whites, together with the fact that they are gradually acquiring the disposition to be provided for on reservations, will, I think, enable the Indian department to effect this desirable object within a few years; and if the reservation policy is to be continued, which I think is the proper one for the Indians in this State, the natural advantages of Round valley for a reservation point it out as the most appropriate location for the Indians of northern California that could be selected.

At Tule river the Indians are being subsisted upon lands claimed by Thomas P. Madden. Twelve hundred and eighty acres are at present leased of him, at a yearly rental of one thousand ($1,000) dollars.

The Indian service here is laboring under the disadvantage of occupying rented lands. While this is the case, little can be done in making permanent improvements or improving the condition of the Indians. The number of Indians in the southern portion of the State makes it necessary that at an early day a large and permanent reservation should be established, and I think that the present location is as desirable as any that could be selected. But to be valuable and advantageous to the service the title to the land should be in the government. The land now occupied, with adjoining public lands, is sufficient for the wants and subsistence of all the Indians that will need to be colonized in the southern portion of the State. The advantages of irrigation on the present location and adjoining lands, which is so necessary in the south, makes it very desirable, and as this can be done by the labor of the Indians, good crops are insured every year.

The lands at present leased of Thomas P. Madden comprise the south half of section 33, the south half of section 34, south half of section 32, south half of northeast quarter of section 32, south half of northwest quarter of section 33, south half of northeast quarter of section 33, and south half of northwest quarter of section 34, all in township 21 south, range 28 east, Mount Diablo meridian, containing twelve hundred and eighty acres. These lands were located by him as school lands, in the land office at Visalia, in the years 1857–'58, under the laws of the State of California.

I am gratified in being able to report that the condition of the Indians on the different reservations, except those at Hoopa valley, so far as subsistence is concerned, is satisfactory. The arrival of the Indian goods from New York, and their distribution to the several agencies, is having a happy effect on the Indians, and is relieving to a great extent their suffering for the want of clothing, of which a very limited supply has been furnished for several years.

In this connexion I desire to state my belief that blankets and other goods can be purchased in San Francisco, such as are required for the Indian service, at less cost than goods of the same kind can be delivered here purchased in New York. Mission Mills blankets, of an excellent quality, suitable for Indians, and as good as should be purchased, are being sold to the Indian department on this coast at five ($5) dollars per pair, coin. Blankets for this superintendency cost in New York from fifteen to twenty-one and one-half dollars in currency, and transportation to be added. I think when goods can be obtained here as cheaply as they can be delivered from New York, they should be purchased here. The kind wanted can be more readily secured, the danger and delay of transportation avoided, and the merchants and manufacturers of this coast benefited.

But little has been done in this State by the Indian department to improve the intellectual or moral condition of the Indians. I think there should be a change in this respect. From observation made during my recent visits to the different reservations, I am satisfied that by the establishment of schools on them and the employment of proper and competent female teachers, much good can be accomplished in instructing the youth of both sexes, teaching them in the English language to read, and the females to sew and make the garments necessary for family use, and training them to habits of cleanliness and morality, in which they are sadly deficient. I propose as far as possible in the spring to establish schools, and would respectfully recommend that an appropriation of two thousand dollars be made for the payment of teachers, to be employed in this laudable effort to improve their condition.

I enclose estimate of funds necessary for the Indian service in the California superintendency for the fiscal year ending June 30, 1867. The amount estimated for the purchase of cattle, clothing, &c , is ten thousand dollars less than was appropriated for the present fiscal year, and I think the service necessarily demands the amount as estimated. A considerable amount is wanted for the purchase of stock, cattle, and hogs for the reservation, which will place them in a condition to be self-sustaining. This is more particularly necessary at Round valley, as it is expected that a large surplus of grain will be raised on that reservation the incoming season, and to dispose of it to advantage to the Indian service it should be converted into pork and beef, to do which it will be necessary to purchase stock, cattle, and hogs.

It is expected that at Round valley next spring a large number of Indians will be added to the number already there, and as they will be destitute of clothing, and those on the reservations are but partially supplied this season, I think the amount to be expended for clothing next season should not be less than the amount purchased this season, which was twenty-seven thousand ($27,000) dollars.

The amount estimated for the purchase of the saw and grist mills in Round valley is a necessity for the reservation, and would be money well expended. The saw-mill would furnish lumber for all the buildings needed on the reservation, with no expense to the government, and would save the price of the mills in two years. The grist-mill for the reservation is equally needed.

All of which is respectfully submitted.

CHARLES MALTBY,
Superintendent of Indian Affairs, California.

Hon. William Higby,
Member of Committee on Indian Affairs, Washington, D. C.

Estimate of funds necessary for the Indian service in the California superintendency for the fiscal year ending June 30, 1867.

For cattle, clothing, teams, and farming implements	$45,000 00
incidental expenses, including travelling expenses of superintendent and agents	6,000 00
pay of superintendent of Indian affairs	3,600 00
clerk for superintendent	1,800 00
four Indian agents	7,200 00
four physicians, four blacksmiths, four assistant blacksmiths, four carpenters, and four farmers	12,000 00
four teachers	2,000 00
purchase of saw-mill and grist-mill at Round valley	5,000 00
Total	82,600 00

CHARLES MALTBY,
Superintendent of Indian Affairs, California.

Report of W. Bryson, agent at Smith River reservation, California.

Smith River Indian Agency,
Crescent City, California, November 22, 1865.

Sir: I have the honor to transmit herewith, as per your request when you and Superintendent Maltby were here last summer, a tabular statement showing the number of farms, number of acres, improvements, and value thereof, located in Smith River valley, Del Norte county, California, on the west side of the creek running through the valley, embracing the farms now occupied by the government for Indian purposes, known as Smith River Indian reservation, including also 2,000 acres of land located on the south side of Smith river, known as the Scott ranch, which is very desirable property for the government to include in this purchase, it being valuable as a stock farm, and much of it rich fertile land, and highly susceptible of cultivation, if needed for that purpose. There are also some 300 or 400 Smith river Indians living on this land in comfortable houses, subsisting themselves without any expense to the government. Nothing but the river separates this land from the present reservation.

The accompanying statement embraces all the land which, in my opinion, is needed for Indian purposes in this valley for the present, which will cost $56,500 in coin. or in legal-tender notes at their current value in San Francisco at the time payment is made, the prices being fixed by the parties themselves. A portion of this land is rented for the coming season at four and five dollars per acre, and the sooner bought the sooner rents will stop. This property, in my opinion, is very cheap, and well adapted to all the purposes of an Indian reserve, the soil being fertile of itself, and the outside facilities for Indian subsistence almost unsurpassed—there being wild fruits, fish, acorns, and cereals or wild roots in abundance at almost all seasons of the year, which costs nothing, and constitutes an important part of the Indians' living. And surely it is cheaper and more humane for the government to buy this property, and give the Indians a permanent and comfortable home, than to incur a greater expense by continuing their former policy of driving them from place to place without the assurance of a home and comfort anywhere.

You will confer a great favor on me if you will step into the Department of the Interior, and look up my accounts against the Indian department, as well as all other accounts due from this agency. Much of this indebtedness is for rent of land cultivated to subsist the Indians two, three, and four years ago ; some for subsistence furnished about that time, and some for salaries of employés. These accounts were all duly forwarded by late Superintendent E. Steele to the department at Washington, and I presume you will find them all there on file with all the certificates and explanations necessary to secure examination and payment; but if on examination any further evidence of their justness is needed, you will please advise me of the same.

I have just received and issued the Indian goods sent here from Washington. They were very deficient in quantity and some in quality. I think if the whole lot had been sold at auction on their arrival at Crescent City they would not have brought money enough to pay the cost of transportation. I feel confident I could take the money they cost, and buy nearly or quite twice the amount in California, at such times, and in such quantities and qualities as are needed. Then why not send the money out, and let the agents make their own purchases, since they can do it so much cheaper and better?

Respectfully, your obedient servant,

WILLIAM BRYSON, *Indian Agent.*

Hon. Wm. Higby, M. C., *Washington City.*

	No. of acres of land.	No. of acres under fence.	No. of acres under cultivation.	No. of dwelling-houses.	No. of outhouses, stables, &c.	No. of barns.	No. of rods of rail fence.	No. of rods of board fence.	No. of fruit trees.	No. of Indian houses.	Average value per acre.	Total valuation.	
Saville & Darby	1,000	223	223	1	10	1	1,000	240	1,000	108	------	$12,000	Known on the chart as the bevel land.
David Haight	280	280	42	1	3	1	700	------	300	------	------	3,000	
Henry Smith	240	165	133	----	2	1	240	120	------	------	------	3,000	Thompson and Simonfield.
L. W. Jones	160	160	94	1	2	1	900	------	310	------	------	4,000	Michael Smith.
Henry Wesbrook	160	100	60	1	2	1	900	------	600	------	------	4,000	
B. W. McCormick	80	80	64	1	3	1	530	------	100	------	------	2,500	40 acres as L. W. Jones.
Wesley Mitchell	480	400	95	2	2	----	1,440	------	150	------	------	8,000	Hays and M. Smith.
Felix Scott	2,000	2,000	250	2	----	1	2,880	------	------	50	------	20,000	Not on the chart.
Total	4,400	3,408	961	9	34	7	8,590	360	2,460	158	$12 84	56,500	In gold coin.

The above statement shows the number of acres under actual cultivation at the present time, with their improvements, &c. In addition to this, there could be at least 1,000 acres more put under cultivation within the same limits when needed, which is now used for grazing purposes, which is equally as fertile as that now under cultivation. An estimate of the cost of the entire valley I sent to Superintendent Maltby, which he will forward to you, but I think the land above stated is just what should be purchased for the present.

WILLIAM BRYSON, *Indian Agent.*

INDEX.

www.ingramcontent.com/pod-product-compliance
Lightning Source LLC
LaVergne TN
LVHW010740120826
845150LV00009B/440

* 9 7 8 1 4 2 5 5 6 0 1 2 6 *